THE COMPLETE
TALES AND POEMS
OF
EDGAR ALLAN POE

The Complete
TALES AND POEMS
OF
Edgar Allan Poe

WITH SELECTIONS

FROM HIS CRITICAL WRITINGS

WITH AN INTRODUCTION AND EXPLANATORY NOTES
BY
ARTHUR HOBSON QUINN,

TEXTS ESTABLISHED, WITH BIBLIOGRAPHICAL NOTES,
BY
EDWARD H. O'NEILL

BARNES
&NOBLE
BOOKS
NEW YORK

1992 Barnes & Noble Books

ISBN 0-88029-366-7 *casebound*
ISBN 1-56619-603-5 *leatherbound*

Printed and bound in the United States of America

02 03 04 05 MC 25 24 23 22 21 20 19 18
02 03 ML 10

QF

*Printed on a stock made especially for
Barnes & Noble in the USA by Lyons Falls Pulp & Paper.
It is milled acid-free for archival durability and manufactured without chlorine
in a process that avoids the discharge of toxic by-products into the environment.*

PREFACE

This volume is intended primarily for the general reader, but it is hoped that it will also be of interest to the student of Poe who wishes the correct text and certain biographical and bibliographical information. Poe revised his works so often that it has been necessary to obtain, not only the last known publication that Poe could have supervised, but also to determine, if possible, whether he actually did so. The bibliographical notes indicate the different appearances of the poem, short story, or criticism during Poe's lifetime, and also that one which has been chosen as the standard text. Where autograph manuscripts are available, they have naturally been preferred.

The thanks of the editors are due to Dr. Clarence S. Brigham of the American Antiquarian Society, Dr. Luther Evans of the Library of Congress, Mr. Henry M. Lydenberg, Lieutenant Colonel Richard Gimbel and Mr. Anthony Frayne of the Gimbel Collection, and the Library Staff of the University of Pennsylvania for invaluable assistance in securing for collating purposes the original editions of books and periodicals. They are indebted also to the Faculty Research Committee of the University of Pennsylvania for providing funds for travel and research.

The editors are indebted to the courtesy of Miss Belle da Costa Greene, Director of the Morgan Library, in granting permission to use certain manuscripts of Poe; and of the Century Association of New York for making available Poe's alterations in the Lorimer Graham Copy of The Raven and Other Poems.

The editors also appreciate the cordial permission of certain publishers to collate this text with those under their control: Ginn &

Company for the Killis Campbell edition of Poe's poems, Harcourt, Brace & Company for Campbell's edition of the short stories, and T. Y. Crowell & Company for the Virginia edition of Poe's works.

A. H. Q.

E. H. O'N.

CONTENTS

Contents

III. TALES

Contents

THE COMPLETE
TALES AND POEMS
OF
EDGAR ALLAN POE

I

INTRODUCTION

Edgar Poe was born in Boston, January 19, 1809. His parents, David Poe, Jr., and Elizabeth Arnold Poe, were members of the stock company at the Boston Theatre. There was, however, nothing of New England in his ancestry. His father was the son of David Poe, born in Ireland, who had served as Deputy Quartermaster General in Baltimore, during the Revolution. David Poe, Jr., was born in Baltimore, July 18, 1784, and made his debut on the stage of the Charleston Theatre in 1803. He was a handsome, erratic, and irascible young man, who probably drank too much and was only a fair actor.

Elizabeth Arnold, on the other hand, has left a tradition of charm and unremitting industry. Coming from England in 1796 with her mother, an actress of some ability, Elizabeth Arnold spent her life in the American theatre, at a time when that profession was still under the shadow of the disapproval of the respectable element in society, especially in New England, where she began her career. She became a popular figure from

Boston to Charleston, and after her first husband, Charles Hopkins, died in 1805, she married David Poe, Jr. They had three children, William Henry, Edgar, and Rosalie, all born under the unfavorable circumstances attending the life of actors of that period. When Elizabeth Poe died in Richmond in 1811, she had separated from her husband, whose known history ends in New York City in 1809. She had made a brave struggle to care for her three little children, and to her son Edgar she left a heritage of courage, dramatic ability, and personal charm. William Henry was taken by his grandparents in Baltimore, while two young matrons of Richmond, Mrs. John Allan and Mrs. William Mackenzie, assumed charge of Edgar and of Rosalie.

This adoption of Edgar Poe by Mrs. John Allan, who, childless herself, had been attracted by the little boy, colored his entire life. John Allan was a prosperous Scottish merchant, well established in Richmond. Edgar was brought up in comfortable surroundings, was sent to good schools, and, though not legally adopted, was regarded generally in Richmond as the son of the house. When Allan's business took them to England in 1815, Edgar saw Scotland, where Allan's people lived, and, after a brief visit there, spent five years in England, where he was sent to two schools, the first being kept by the Misses Dubourg, whose name appears in "The Murders in the Rue Morgue." The second, the Manor House School, presided over by Dr. John Bransby, is pictured vividly in "William Wilson." Here he was taught Latin, French, history, and literature and was known as "Edgar Allan."

Financial reverses forced Allan's return to Richmond in 1820, but he continued to send Edgar Poe to school. Years later the headmaster, Joseph H. Clarke, testified that his pupil was not conspicuously studious but always stood well in his class, was "remarkable for self-respect," and had "imaginative powers" of a high order. Poe studied Horace, Cicero, and Homer at Clarke's school and continued classical and mathematical studies at the academy of William Burke, which he entered in 1823. In his school days in Richmond he seems to have suffered from the fact that his parents had been actors, but his athletic successes, especially in swimming, won him some local fame. Through one of his school friends, Robert Stanard, he met Mrs. Jane Craig Stanard, a young matron whose kindness to Poe made her his first ideal passion. For her he wrote the first "To Helen," one of his finest lyrics.

John Allan, through the death of his uncle, became in 1825 a comparatively rich man. He seems, however, to have begun to lose interest in Edgar Poe. He certainly interfered with Poe's first love episode, his engagement to Sarah Elmira Royster, in which opposition he was joined by her father. It is not necessary to take this love story too seriously; it was a boy and girl affair, but together with other reasons to be given later, it may have caused Allan to send Poe to the University of Virginia, at Charlottesville, to keep him away from Richmond.

When Poe registered at the university in February 1826, the college was beginning its second year. Founded by Thomas Jefferson on the model of a German university, it provided little guidance or discipline. But the instruction in the Schools of Ancient and Modern Languages, which Poe entered, was of high quality. John Allan provided him at his entrance with only $110 to pay the annual charges of $350, and Poe fell into debt at once, for board and other necessary expenses. In consequence, he gambled and unfortunately lost about $2,000, which John Allan declined to pay. Allan also refused to settle Poe's legitimate expenses for clothing, and at the end of the term, in December 1826, Poe's formal education was ended. He had taken honors in Latin and French, had studied Italian and Spanish, and had read some history, including Marshall's *Life of Washington*. He had learned to drink more than was good for him, however, and he had been a witness of brutal fights among the students and had been part of a life that was unrestrained and at times dissipated. Yet the Faculty Minutes, which are filled with cases of discipline, do not contain his name as an offender.

On Poe's return to Richmond the differences between him and Allan became acute. Perhaps Allan's infidelities became known to Poe, who would naturally resent them on Mrs. Allan's behalf, or perhaps his slurs upon the Poe family, to which Edgar Poe refers later, in a letter from West Point, were the cause. In any event, Poe ran away to Boston in March 1827. He was now upon his own resources, untrained for any occupation, and with a deep sense of resentment against the man who had cast him off. In Boston he persuaded an obscure printer to issue a volume of poems, *Tamerlane and Other Poems, by a Bostonian*, which brought him no money and attracted no critical attention, but which brings now about $15,000 as a collector's item. Desperate, apparently, he enlisted in the United States Army as a private soldier on May 26, 1827, giving his name as Edgar A. Perry.

Poe was first assigned to Battery H of the First Artillery at Fort Independence, Boston Harbor, and was transferred in November to Fort Moultrie, on Sullivan's Island, in Charleston Harbor. In December 1828 his battery was sent to Fortress Monroe, in Virginia. Poe never included his army experience in his autobiographical accounts, evidently being ashamed of his enlistment, but he filled up the two years with accounts of a fictitious European trip. Yet his record in the Army was a good one. He rose to the rank of sergeant major, and when after considerable delay Allan agreed to recommend his release, Poe carried with him several testimonials from the officers of the regiment as to his ability and his sobriety. Mrs. Allan died on February 28, 1829, and Poe obtained a furlough, too late to see her alive, but in time to attend her funeral in Richmond. Some reconciliation took place, for Allan joined in seconding Poe's application of admission to West Point.

While waiting for his appointment as a cadet, Poe lived mainly in

Baltimore, learning to know his grandmother, his aunt, Mrs. Clemm, his brother Henry, and his little cousin Virginia. His principal efforts were spent in obtaining a publisher for his second volume of verse, *Al Aaraaf, Tamerlane and Minor Poems*, which appeared in Baltimore in December 1829. The poems in this volume received some favorable notice in advance of publication in John Neal's *Yankee*, in Boston, and the letter from Poe that Neal included in his review shows that he was conscious that, in spite of discouragements, poetry was the main purpose of his life. Allan refused to help him in the publication of *Al Aaraaf*, but occasionally sent him some money. Unfortunately Poe still owed Sergeant Graves, who had acted as his substitute in the military formalities attendant upon his release from the Army, and he wrote to Graves, in May 1830, telling him he could not obtain the money, since "Mr. A. is not very often sober." Graves sent this letter to John Allan and the consequences can be imagined. According to John Allan's will, two illegitimate sons were born to him in July 1830, and he was courting his second wife, whom he married in October 1830. The boy he had brought up as one of his family became therefore more and more a liability to him, which he was not anxious to discharge. Poe took the entrance examinations for West Point in June 1830 and entered upon his duties as a cadet in July. His stay was brief, however, and it is difficult to see why he entered the Military Academy, for he must have known the discipline would be strict and the drill a repetition of his Army training. A long letter that he sent to Allan on January 3, 1831, written evidently in reply to one upbraiding him for the Graves episode, reviews their entire relationship, and states that Allan had refused the allowance that cadets usually were given by their relatives. Unable to resign without Allan's consent, Poe deliberately provoked his dismissal from the Academy by neglecting his duties and breaking the rules. Leaving the Point in February 1831, he went to New York City, where he secured the publication of the *Poems* of 1831, containing first drafts of some of his greatest poems, like "To Helen," "Israfel," and "The City in the Sea." Poe had secured subscriptions from some of his comrades at West Point.

How Poe lived during the next two years is a mystery. Joining the household of Mrs. Clemm in Baltimore, he made an unsuccessful effort to obtain a position as a teacher, and his letters to Allan speak of the utmost poverty. He was not idle, however, for when a prize was offered by the *Philadelphia Saturday Courier*, in June, 1831, he submitted five stories, none of which won the prize. They were printed anonymously, however, in the *Courier* during 1832, but it is doubtful if he received any payment for them. He went through the harrowing experience of offering his stories to magazines and having them rejected, and after a long silence he appealed in April 1833 to Allan in a letter that is truly a cry from the depths. He concluded it:

"Without friends, without any means, consequently, of obtaining employment, I am perishing — absolutely perishing for want of aid. And yet I am not idle — nor addicted to any vice — nor have I committed any offence against society which would render me deserving of so hard a fate. For God's sake, pity me and save me from destruction."

It was his last appeal to John Allan, who died on March 27, 1834, not mentioning Poe in his will. A ray of good fortune came, however, in 1833. Poe won a prize of fifty dollars offered by the *Baltimore Saturday Visiter* in a short-story contest, with "The Manuscript Found in a Bottle." One of the judges, John Pendleton Kennedy, a lawyer and a novelist, helped Poe financially, aided him in placing his stories, and secured for him the position of editor of the *Southern Literary Messenger* in Richmond.

Poe began his editorial connection with the *Messenger* in the summer of 1835 and as soon as he could arrange for a residence, brought Mrs. Clemm and Virginia to Richmond in October. His letter to them, written on August 29, reveals how passionately he loved his young cousin and how desperately lonely he was without her. A marriage license was issued on September 22, but notwithstanding all that has been written about a "secret marriage," no actual ceremony took place until May 16, 1836.

Notwithstanding the attitude of T. W. White, the proprietor of the *Messenger*, who did not announce Poe's editorship until October, the magazine soon felt the effect of his skillful management. His reviews soon established the paper as the leading critical journal in the South, and his stories attracted national attention. While Poe was not our first critic, he was our first great critic. He was independent both of British criticism and of publishing connections in this country, and his keen analysis relentlessly held up to ridicule the pretentious and the absurd. He was quick, however, to recognize new talent, and such reviews as those on the poetry of Joseph Rodman Drake and Fitz-Greene Halleck were the occasion of a discussion of the nature of poetry which is still valid. Poe built up the circulation of the *Messenger* from five hundred to thirty-five hundred copies, but in January 1836 he ceased to be editor. Some time later he gave the reason, that "the drudgery was excessive, the salary contemptible." His salary was ten dollars weekly, but there were apparently extra payments, and it was probably his desire to work in a larger field that took him, in February 1837, to New York. His usual ill luck brought this venture into the hard times of 1837. He completed his *Narrative of Arthur Gordon Pym*, but publication was postponed by Harper's until 1838. So realistic were the descriptions of the voyage to the Antarctic Ocean that it was treated in England as a true story. Yet the best portion of the tale begins when Poe trusts to his own imagination for the terrors of the savages' attack and the destruction of Pym's canoe by the mysterious figure, whiter than snow.

Disappointed in New York, he began in 1838 his most productive period, in Philadelphia. He was attracted by its pre-eminence at that time as a publishing center. Here he published his *Conchologist's First Book,* a piece of hack-work in which his knowledge of shells was reflected. One of his greatest short stories, "Ligeia," and one of his most striking poems, "The Haunted Palace," appeared in 1838, and in July 1839 he became associated with William E. Burton in the editing of the *Gentleman's Magazine.* Burton was an actor and manager, who needed assistance in the conduct of the periodical, and Poe also contributed short stories and verse, among the former "The Fall of the House of Usher." He fell out with Burton, however, and in June 1840 gave up his position, partly because of his great desire to have a journal of his own, to be called *The Penn Magazine.* This was to be of higher grade than "Burton's" or "Godey's," the popular magazines of the day.

His other great desire was achieved in the publication, late in 1839, of his *Tales of the Grotesque and Arabesque,* his first volume of short stories, twenty-five in number. He received from Lea & Blanchard, the publishers, the copyright and twenty copies of the book, but no financial return. Poe believed that this publication would help him in selling his stories to periodicals, for his support depended entirely upon them. His anxiety about Virginia led him to move in 1839 or 1840 to a house near Fairmount Park, and for a time the fresh air resulted in some improvement in her health. His constant struggle to make a living made him welcome an offer from George R. Graham, who had purchased Burton's magazine and combined it with *The Casket,* under the name of *Graham's Magazine.* Poe and Graham made it the leading periodical of its kind in the United States by the policy, which apparently no one had yet discovered, of paying good prices to its contributors. They secured in this way the foremost American writers, and before Poe left the editorial chair, the circulation had risen from five thousand to thirty-five thousand copies. In April 1841 Poe published in *Graham's* "The Murders in the Rue Morgue," the first of his stories of ratiocination, as he called them, or, in the popular phrase, detective stories. His central character, Monsieur Dupin, solved his puzzles, not by mechanical means, but by reasoning, based upon analysis of the characters and situations, and Poe's detective stories, in consequence, remain unsurpassed today. His talent for analysis resulted also in his challenge to readers of *Graham's* to send in cryptograms for solution, which he invariably solved. Poe joined Graham partly because he believed the latter would in turn join him in publishing *The Penn Magazine.* Poe as usual was ahead of his time. His idea of issuing two magazines, one for the mass of the public and one for a more select audience, has been successfully carried out today.

Poe's reviews in *Graham's Magazine* were notable. In his criticism of Longfellow's *Ballads,* he defined Poetry as the "Rhythmical Creation of

Beauty," while in his review of Hawthorne's *Twice-Told Tales* he established a standard definition for the short story that has remained undisturbed through all later discussion of the topic.

Poe left *Graham's* in May 1842, because he still had hopes for the *Penn Magazine* and because his editorial salary of eight hundred dollars was too small, he naturally felt, for his services. He was hopeful, too, of obtaining a clerical position in Washington, but here again he was unlucky. He was a Whig in politics, and his party was in power only twice during his lifetime. His visit to Washington in 1843, when he yielded to the temptation of taking too much drink, ended his hope of political office.

To his other anxieties was added the fluctuation in Virginia's health. In January 1842, while singing at her piano, in the house at Fairmount, she broke a blood-vessel. The constant fear, with recurrent hopes for her recovery, was, as Poe wrote to his young correspondent Eveleth, six years later, an ever present torment. But she gave him also the happiness that comes to anyone who devotes himself to a wife who rewards his self-sacrifice by her own worship. One of the most persistent errors in biographies of Poe lies in the references to Virginia as a permanent "child wife," although contemporary evidence, when masculine, constantly refers to her grace and her talent, especially in music.

In the spring of 1843 the family moved to a cottage on North Seventh Street, in the district called Spring Garden. It still remains the most comfortable of all their residences now standing. But the specter of want was over it. Poe was without regular employment, and the new magazine venture, *The Stylus*, for which he had such high hopes, came to nothing. He won a hundred dollars for "The Gold Bug" in a prize contest, and sold stories occasionally to annuals or a magazine, but it needed all Mrs. Clemm's economy to keep the family going. He published in 1843 the first of what he hoped would be a series of booklets containing reprints of his tales. But the first number of *The Prose Romances of Edgar A. Poe*, consisting of "The Murders in the Rue Morgue" and "The Man That was Used Up," was also the last. It sold for twelve and one half cents, and, ironically, the Library of Congress has insured one of the very few copies now existing for fifty thousand dollars!

In April 1844 Poe moved to New York City, tempted perhaps by its growing importance. His first publication, "The Balloon Hoax," which appeared in the *New York Sun* of April 13, 1844, described an imaginary trip of a balloon across the Atlantic Ocean in three days, so realistically that thousands were deceived. At first he made some money by letters to the *Columbia Spy* describing New York City. Poe was always interested in the localities in which he lived and he "roamed far and wide over this island of Manhattan" just as he had floated down the Wissahickon Creek in Philadelphia before he wrote "Morning on the Wissa-

hiccon." Poe lived in several houses in New York City, soon taking Virginia out of the neighborhood of the Hudson River, near Eighty-fourth Street, where the air was more bracing than in the city.

Notwithstanding his growing fame as a writer of short stories, "The Gold Bug" having a circulation of 300,000 copies, he still had difficulty in making a living. He prepared a new edition of his *Tales of the Grotesque and Arabesque*, under the title of *Phantasy Pieces*, carefully revising his texts, but Harper's declined to publish the new edition. Lowell had been asked to write a biography of Poe for *Graham's Magazine*, and at his request Poe sent him a very interesting analysis of his feelings and his work at this time. He rightly chose his new story, "The Purloined Letter," as the best of his tales of ratiocination, and his epigram: "Man is now only more active, not more happy — nor more wise — than he was 6000 years ago," is still, perhaps, as valid as it was in 1844. Lowell spoke of Poe in this article as "the most discriminating, philosophical and fearless critic upon imaginative works who has written in America."

Necessity made him accept a post on the staff of the *New York Mirror*, edited by Nathaniel Parker Willis. Here "The Raven" appeared on January 29, 1845, copied in advance of publication from the February issue of the *American Review*. This poem probably attracted more attention than any American poem before its day. Its lasting fame is due not only to the magnificent phrasing, but also to the picture of the devotion of a lover, "dreaming dreams no mortal ever dared to dream before." It was begun undoubtedly in one of those moments of despair when Virginia's death seemed to be approaching.

In March 1845 Poe left the *Mirror* and became one of the editors of the *Broadway Journal*, and a sharer in the profits, if there were any. He was working at this time about fourteen hours a day, writing, and delivering a lecture on "The Poets and Poetry of America," yet was not making a living. An edition of his *Tales* appeared in 1845, but it contained only twelve stories. He was to receive a royalty of eight cents a copy on a book that sold for fifty cents. It was the first and only time he derived any revenue from a volume of his short stories. His best criticisms in the *Broadway Journal* dealt with the drama and theatre, in which he made a plea for more natural acting.

Poe was never unsocial, and while the accounts of his attendance at the gatherings of writers at the homes of Anne Lynch and others are usually overstressed, he and sometimes Virginia attended these parties, and he was generous in his response to requests to recite his poetry. Probably most of the guests were women. Poe at all times kindled to feminine sympathy. Early in 1845 he met Frances Sargent Osgood, a poetess of some ability, who was to remain the warm friend of both Poe and Virginia and who, when she was herself dying in 1850, paid a glowing tribute to his character and to his devotion to his wife. Yet their relations were made by some busybodies the occasion of unpleasant notoriety.

The Raven and Other Poems, the last collected edition of his poetry to appear under his own editorial care, was published in November 1845. Thirty poems, beginning with "The Raven" and ending, curiously, with the first "To Helen," make up the volume, which was dedicated to Mrs. Browning. In the Preface, Poe said:

"Events not to be controlled have prevented me from making, at any time, any serious effort in what, under happier circumstances, would have been the field of my choice. With me, poetry has been not a purpose but a passion."

In October, Poe had gone to Boston, to read an original poem, on the invitation of the Boston Lyceum. He could not write occasional poetry, so he read "Al Aaraaf," and unfortunately, later in the evening, made some remarks about Boston that raised a new crop of enemies for him.

In the same month he obtained complete control of the *Broadway Journal.* Now, at last, he had what he had been longing for, a magazine of his own. But despite valiant efforts he could not keep the *Journal* alive and it expired in January 1846. He had no capital, and while he was one of the most competent editors of his day, he could not understand that a magazine must lose money at the start. In any event, the *Broadway Journal* was a weekly, not the monthly of a high type in which he was really interested.

Poe was active in criticism during 1846. In April appeared his essay "The Philosophy of Composition," in which he analyzed the process by which he created "The Raven." Few believe he wrote the poem in this artificial way, but it contained some very interesting general reflections of his poetic creed.

In May he began in *Godey's Lady's Book* of Philadelphia a series of articles on the writers in and near New York City, entitled "The Literati." These created a great deal of excitement and led to one libel suit. Poe's judgments were usually accurate, but occasionally he let his talent for satire run away with him, and his criticism of Dr. Thomas Dunn English caused a reply that accused Poe of forgery and of being "an assassin in morals." English's attack was printed in the *Evening Mirror,* no longer under Willis's charge, so Poe sued this paper for libel, and was awarded damages in the amount of $225.

In 1846 Poe secured a home in a small cottage at Fordham, at that time thirteen miles out of the city, near what is now East 192nd Street. In this modest house, of one story and an attic, which is now a Poe memorial, Poe watched Virginia slowly fading away. The strain was evidently making even the work necessary to their support very difficult for him, and if it had not been for Willis's appeal for financial help, and the friendly efforts of Mrs. Marie Louise Shew, a widow with some medical training, it is hard to see how the family could have survived. Yet Poe kept up a brave struggle, cheered a bit by his growing recognition in France, where his stories were being translated, and by an extended and

favorable critique that appeared in the *Revue des Deux Mondes*. Testimony given later by the friends he made in the faculty of St. John's College at Fordham is definitely against his drinking to excess at this time.

Virginia died on January 30, 1847. Poe collapsed after the long strain, and Mrs. Shew's diagnosis was probably correct. She believed that he had a lesion of the brain which made it dangerous to give him stimulants and yet he needed them to bring him up from the fever caused, as she wrote later, "by actual want and hunger and cold, having been borne by this heroic husband in order to supply food, medicine and comforts to his dying wife." What Poe thought of Mrs. Shew is shown in the two poems he addressed to her.

He gradually returned to health, at least mentally, for one of his finest poems, "Ulalume," was published in December 1847, and in 1848 he read his prose poem *Eureka* before the Society Library in New York City. It was Poe's attempt at a solution of the creation and ultimate destiny of the universe, and it was published by Putnam, who made what he considered a generous advance of fourteen dollars! *Eureka* has usually been avoided by Poe's critics, but it by no means deserves this neglect. Of course Poe did not solve the riddle of the universe, but then, no one else has done so, and his theories bear, in some respects, sufficient similarity to the more scientific findings of modern astronomical physicists, like the late Sir Arthur Eddington, to prove that Poe's mind was in no sense deteriorating but was capable of clear and consistent thinking upon a difficult subject.

After Virginia's death, Poe became involved in several episodes with his women friends that have been either overstressed or misinterpreted. Three of them, however, have attracted so much attention that the correct facts must be given, stripped of the sentimentalities that have clouded them. The second "To Helen" was written for Mrs. Sarah Helen Power Whitman, an attractive widow and poetess of Providence, Rhode Island, whom Poe had seen in 1845 but whom he did not meet until 1848. They became engaged to be married, but the brief engagement was broken by Mrs. Whitman, largely because of the opposition of her mother. There is an artificial note in Poe's many letters to her, yet there was a sincere affection between them. In 1860 Mrs. Whitman published an able defense of Poe's character and a brilliant analysis of his writings, under the title of *Edgar Poe and His Critics*.

The courtship of Mrs. Whitman was partly a literary adventure, but Poe's devotion to Mrs. Richmond bore more resemblance to a love affair. Mrs. Charles Richmond (Nancy Locke Heywood), whom Poe always called "Annie," lived in Lowell, Massachusetts, where Poe met her when he lectured there in June 1848. He loved her passionately and urged her to come and live near him (and Mrs. Clemm), but she acted with self-respect through the episode and evidently had no intention of leaving her husband. Yet she remained, even after Poe's death, one of his

staunchest defenders. Poe describes her in his story of "Landor's Cottage." To her he wrote his poem "For Annie." Poe tells in his letters to "Annie" how one magazine after another was postponing payment to him. He wrote his best critical essay on poetry, "The Poetic Principle," late in 1848, as a lecture, taking it with him on his last trip to Richmond.

On June 30, 1849 he left New York City, stopping at Philadelphia, where he went to the home of John Sartain, editor of the *Union Magazine*, in a distracted condition, believing he was being pursued. Sartain, C. C. Burr, and George Lippard, the novelist, took care of him and he left Philadelphia on July 13. In Richmond he seemed to take on a new lease of life. He lived at the Swan Tavern, a respectable hotel, near the residence of his old friends, the Mackenzies, with whom Rosalie was still living. He renewed his boyhood love affair with Sarah Elmira Royster Shelton, now a widow, and lectured with some success on "The Poetic Principle." Poe made a brave effort to avoid drinking, a difficult matter in a hospitable Southern city, even joining the "Sons of Temperance." He wrote for the *Richmond Examiner* and was busily engaged in projects for the *Stylus*, his pet illusion.

The marriage between Mrs. Shelton and Poe was fixed for October 17, and Poe left Richmond for New York City to bring Mrs. Clemm to the wedding. He spent the evening of September 26 with Mrs. Shelton, and, after stopping at the office of Dr. John Carter, took supper with some friends and apparently boarded the boat for Baltimore, about four o'clock on the morning of September 27, in good condition. From this point on, until October 3, the events of the last days of Edgar Poe are uncertain. He apparently arrived in Baltimore on the morning of September 28, tried to call on his friend Dr. N. C. Brooks, but found him out. He was well known in Baltimore and it seems unlikely that he would have remained unnoticed there for six days. The most creditable account, given originally by Thomas H. Lane, who had helped him in the last days of the *Broadway Journal*, is to the effect that he came to Philadelphia, spent the night at the residence of James P. Moss, a friend of Poe, and left in rather poor condition, probably on September 30, intending to go to New York. Instead by mistake he took the train to Baltimore.

According to Poe's letter of September 18 to Mrs. Clemm, he expected to stop in Philadelphia to call on a poetess whose verses he was to edit, and he asked his aunt to write to him in that city. Disregarding other and less tangible accounts, the next certainty lies in a letter received by his friend Dr. J. E. Snodgrass, in Baltimore, on October 3, from a printer named Walker who wrote:

"Dear Sir:
"There is a gentleman, rather worse for wear, at Ryan's 4th Ward Polls, who goes under the cognomen of Edgar A. Poe, and who appears in great distress, and he says he is acquainted with you, and I assure you he is in need of immediate assistance."

Dr. Snodgrass found Poe at Gunner's Hall, a public house at 44 East Lombard Street, and he and Henry Herring, the husband of Poe's aunt, Elizabeth Poe, took him to the Washington College Hospital on the afternoon of October 3. He did not regain consciousness sufficiently to tell Dr. Moran, the attending physician, how he arrived at this condition. Poe died at five o'clock on Sunday morning, October 7, and was buried on October 9 in the Presbyterian Cemetery at Fayette and Green Streets, in the lot that had belonged to his grandfather, David Poe. In 1875 his coffin was removed to the southeastern corner of the cemetery, where his monument now stands.

The mystery so often associated with Poe's life and nature is unjustified. Based, in the beginning, upon Griswold's *Memoir*, full of falsehoods and half-truths, it has been augmented by conjectures and assumptions of biographers more interested in turning a phrase than in ascertaining facts. He was in reality a hard-working man of letters whose poems and stories were above the level of the periodicals of his day, upon which he depended for support. His editorial labors, successful as they were, were ill-paid, and his lack of powerful friends kept him from political office. His volumes of verse or prose paid him little or nothing, and his fearless and at times ill-natured criticisms made him enemies. Handicapped by Virginia's illness and by an inherited tendency to drink, in which he found temporary relief from his troubles, he made a brave struggle to succeed and finally succumbed to conditions that he could not overcome. He was human and when he was attacked he struck back, not always wisely and in a few cases, unfairly. But his work has grown steadily in the estimation of the best critical judgments, here and abroad. Without the aid of any cult of admirers who build upon his achievements a reputation for discrimination, or without any strong popular appeal to a democratic audience, he has won his position by the power of an imagination and by the beauty of a style that have baffled the many imitators who have tried in vain to reach the shining level where he remains secure.

ARTHUR HOBSON QUINN

II

POEMS

Tamerlane

Kind solace in a dying hour!
 Such, father, is not (now) my theme —
I will not madly deem that power
 Of Earth may shrive me of the sin
 Unearthly pride hath revell'd in —
I have no time to dote or dream:
You call it hope — that fire of fire!
It is but agony of desire:
If I *can* hope — Oh God! I can —
 Its fount is holier — more divine —
I would not call thee fool, old man,
 But such is not a gift of thine.

Know thou the secret of a spirit
 Bow'd from its wild pride into shame.
O yearning heart! I did inherit
 Thy withering portion with the fame,
The searing glory which hath shone
Amid the jewels of my throne,
Halo of Hell! and with a pain
Not Hell shall make me fear again —
O craving heart, for the lost flowers
And sunshine of my summer hours!
The undying voice of that dead time,
With its interminable chime,
Rings, in the spirit of a spell,
Upon thy emptiness — a knell.

I have not always been as now:
The fever'd diadem on my brow
 I claim'd and won usurpingly --
Hath not the same fierce heirdom given
 Rome to the Cæsar — this to me?
 The heritage of a kingly mind,
And a proud spirit which hath striven
 Triumphantly with human kind.

On mountain soil I first drew life:
 The mists of the Taglay have shed
 Nightly their dews upon my head,
And, I believe, the winged strife
And tumult of the headlong air
Have nestled in my very hair.

So late from Heaven — that dew — it fell
 ('Mid dreams of an unholy night)
Upon me with the touch of Hell,
 While the red flashing of the light
From clouds that hung, like banners, o'er,
 Appeared to my half-closing eye
 The pageantry of monarchy,
And the deep trumpet-thunder's roar
 Came hurriedly upon me, telling
 Of human battle, where my voice,
 My own voice, silly child! was swelling
 (O! how my spirit would rejoice,
And leap within me at the cry)
The battle-cry of Victory!

The rain came down upon my head
 Unshelter'd — and the heavy wind
 Rendered me mad and deaf and blind.
It was but man, I thought, who shed
Laurels upon me: and the rush,
 The torrent of the chilly air
Gurgled within my ear the crush
 Of empires — with the captive's prayer —
The hum of suitors — and the tone
Of flattery round a sovereign's throne.

My passions, from that hapless hour,
 Usurp'd a tyranny which men
Have deem'd, since I have reach'd to power,
 My innate nature — be it so:
 But, father, there liv'd one who, then,
Then — in my boyhood — when their fire
 Burn'd with a still intenser glow
(For passion must, with youth, expire)
 E'en *then* who knew this iron heart
 In woman's weakness had a part.

I have no words — alas! — to tell
The loveliness of loving well!
Nor would I now attempt to trace
The more than beauty of a face
Whose lineaments, upon my mind,
Are — shadows on th' unstable wind:
Thus I remember having dwelt
 Some page of early lore upon,
With loitering eye, till I have felt
The letters — with their meaning — melt
 To fantasies — with none.

O, she was worthy of all love!
 Love — as in infancy was mine —
'Twas such as angel minds above
 Might envy; her young heart the shrine
On which my every hope and thought
 Were incense — then a goodly gift,
 For they were childish and upright —
Pure — as her young example taught:
 Why did I leave it, and, adrift,
 Trust to the fire within, for light?

We grew in age — and love — together —
 Roaming the forest, and the wild;
My breast her shield in wintry weather —
 And, when the friendly sunshine smil'd,
And she would mark the opening skies,
I saw no Heaven — but in her eyes.

Young Love's first lesson is — the heart:
 For 'mid that sunshine, and those smiles,
When, from our little cares apart,
 And laughing at her girlish wiles,
I'd throw me on her throbbing breast,
 And pour my spirit out in tears —
There was no need to speak the rest —
 No need to quiet any fears
Of her — who ask'd no reason why,
But turned on me her quiet eye!

Yet *more* than worthy of the love
My spirit struggled with, and strove,
When, on the mountain peak, alone,
Ambition lent it a new tone —
I had no being — but in thee:
 The world, and all it did contain
In the earth — the air — the sea —
 Its joy — its little lot of pain
That was new pleasure — the ideal,
 Dim, vanities of dreams by night —
And dimmer nothings which were real —
 (Shadows — and a more shadowy light!)
Parted upon their misty wings,
 And, so, confusedly, became
 Thine image and — a name — a name!
Two separate — yet most intimate things.

I was ambitious — have you known
 The passion, father? You have not:
A cottager, I mark'd a throne
Of half the world as all my own,
 And murmur'd at such lowly lot —
But, just like any other dream,
 Upon the vapor of the dew
My own had past, did not the beam
 Of beauty which did while it thro'
The minute — the hour — the day — oppress
My mind with double loveliness.

We walk'd together on the crown
Of a high mountain which look'd down
Afar from its proud natural towers
 Of rock and forest, on the hills —
The dwindled hills! begirt with bowers
 And shouting with a thousand rills.

I spoke to her of power and pride,
 But mystically — in such guise
That she might deem it nought beside
 The moment's converse; in her eyes
I read, perhaps too carelessly,
 A mingled feeling with my own —
The flush on her bright cheek, to me
 Seem'd to become a queenly throne
Too well that I should let it be
 Light in the wilderness alone.

I wrapp'd myself in grandeur then
 And donn'd a visionary crown —
 Yet it was not that Fantasy
 Had thrown her mantle over me —
But that, among the rabble — men,
 Lion ambition is chain'd down —
And crouches to a keeper's hand —
Not so in deserts where the grand —
The wild — the terrible conspire
With their own breath to fan his fire.

Look 'round thee now on Samarcand! —
 Is she not queen of Earth? her pride
Above all cities? in her hand
 Their destinies? in all beside
Of glory which the world hath known
Stands she not nobly and alone?
Falling — her veriest stepping-stone
Shall form the pedestal of a throne —
And who her sovereign? Timour — he
 Whom the astonished people saw
Striding o'er empires haughtily
 A diadem'd outlaw!

O, human love! thou spirit given,
On Earth, of all we hope in Heaven!
Which fall'st into the soul like rain

Upon the Siroc-wither'd plain,
And, failing in thy power to bless,
But leav'st the heart a wilderness!
Idea! which bindest life around
With music of so strange a sound
And beauty of so wild a birth —
Farewell! for I have won the Earth.

When Hope, the eagle that tower'd, could see
 No cliff beyond him in the sky,
His pinions were bent droopingly —
 And homeward turn'd his soften'd eye.
'T was sunset: when the sun will part
There comes a sullenness of heart
To him who still would look upon
The glory of the summer sun.
That soul will hate the ev'ning mist
So often lovely, and will list
To the sound of the coming darkness (known
To those whose spirits harken) as one
Who, in a dream of night, *would* fly
But *cannot* from a danger nigh.

What tho' the moon — the white moon —
Shed all the splendor of her noon,
Her smile is chilly — and *her* beam,
In that time of dreariness, will seem
(So like you gather in your breath)
A portrait taken after death.
And boyhood is a summer sun
Whose waning is the dreariest one.
For all we live to know is known,
And all we seek to keep hath flown.
Let life, then, as the day-flower, fall
With the noon-day beauty — which is all.

I reach'd my home — my home no more —
 For all had flown who made it so.
I pass'd from out its mossy door,
 And, tho' my tread was soft and low,
A voice came from the threshold stone
Of one whom I had earlier known —
 O, I defy thee, Hell, to show
 On beds of fire that burn below,
 An humbler heart — a deeper wo.

Song

Father, I firmly do believe —
 I *know* — for Death who comes for me
 From regions of the blest afar,
Where there is nothing to deceive,
 Hath left his iron gate ajar,
 And rays of truth you cannot see
 Are flashing thro' Eternity —
I do believe that Eblis hath
A snare in every human path —
Else how, when in the holy grove
I wandered of the idol, Love,
Who daily scents his snowy wings
With incense of burnt offerings

From the most unpolluted things,
Whose pleasant bowers are yet so riven
Above with trellis'd rays from Heaven
No mote may shun — no tiniest fly —
The light'ning of his eagle eye —
How was it that Ambition crept,
 Unseen, amid the revels there,
Till growing bold, he laughed and leapt
 In the tangles of Love's very hair?

(1827)

Song

I saw thee on thy bridal day —
 When a burning blush came o'er thee,
Though happiness around thee lay,
 The world all love before thee:

And in thine eye a kindling light
 (Whatever it might be)
Was all on Earth my aching sight
 Of Loveliness could see.

That blush, perhaps, was maiden shame —
 As such it well may pass —
Though its glow hath raised a fiercer flame
 In the breast of him, alas!

Who saw thee on that bridal day,
 When that deep blush *would* come o'er thee,
Though happiness around thee lay,
 The world all love before thee.

 (1827)

Dreams

Oh! that my young life were a lasting dream!
My spirit not awak'ning till the beam
Of an Eternity should bring the morrow.
Yes! tho' that long dream were of hopeless sorrow,
'T were better than the cold reality
Of waking life, to him whose heart must be,
And hath been still, upon the lovely earth,
A chaos of deep passion, from his birth.
But should it be — that dream eternally
Continuing — as dreams have been to me
In my young boyhood — should it thus be giv'n,
'T were folly still to hope for higher Heav'n.
For I have revell'd, when the sun was bright
I' the summer sky, in dreams of living light
And loveliness, — have left my very heart
In climes of mine imagining, apart
From mine own home, with beings that have been
Of mine own thought — what more could I have seen?
'T was once — and only once — and the wild hour
From my remembrance shall not pass — some pow'r
Or spell had bound me — 't was the chilly wind
Came o'er me in the night, and left behind
Its image on my spirit — or the moon
Shone on my slumbers in her lofty noon
Too coldly — or the stars — howe'er it was,
That dream was as that night-wind — let it pass.

I *have been* happy, tho' [but] in a dream.
I have been happy — and I love the theme:
Dreams! in their vivid coloring of life,
As in that fleeting, shadowy, misty strife
Of semblance with reality which brings
To the delirious eye, more lovely things
Of Paradise and Love — and all our own!
Than young Hope in his sunniest hour hath known.

 (1827)

Spirits of the Dead

I

Thy soul shall find itself alone
'Mid dark thoughts of the gray tombstone —
Not one, of all the crowd, to pry
Into thine hour of secrecy.

II

Be silent in that solitude,
 Which is not loneliness — for then
The spirits of the dead who stood
 In life before thee are again
In death around thee — and their will
Shall overshadow thee: be still.

III

The night, tho' clear, shall frown —
And the stars shall look not down
From their high thrones in the heaven,
With light like Hope to mortals given —
But their red orbs, without beam,
To thy weariness shall seem
As a burning and a fever
Which would cling to thee for ever.

IV

Now are thoughts thou shalt not banish,
Now are visions ne'er to vanish;
From thy spirit shall they pass
No more — like dew-drop from the grass.

V

The breeze — the breath of God — is still —
And the mist upon the hill,
Shadowy — shadowy — yet unbroken,
Is a symbol and a token —
How it hangs upon the trees,
A mystery of mysteries!

(1827)

Evening Star

'T was noontide of summer,
 And mid-time of night;
And stars, in their orbits,
 Shone pale, thro' the light
Of the brighter, cold moon,
 'Mid planets her slaves,
Herself in the Heavens,
 Her beam on the waves.
 I gaz'd a while
 On her cold smile;
Too cold — too cold for me.
 There pass'd, as a shroud,
 A fleecy cloud,
And I turn'd away to thee,
 Proud Evening Star,
 In thy glory afar,
And dearer thy beam shall be;
 For joy to my heart
 Is the proud part
Thou bearest in Heav'n at night,
 And more I admire
Thy distant fire
Than that colder, lowly light.

(1827)

A Dream within a Dream

Take this kiss upon the brow!
And, in parting from you now,
Thus much let me avow —
You are not wrong, who deem
That my days have been a dream;
Yet if Hope has flown away
In a night, or in a day,
In a vision, or in none,
Is it therefore the less *gone?*
All that we see or seem
Is but a dream within a dream.

I stand amid the roar
Of a surf-tormented shore,
And I hold within my hand
Grains of the golden sand —
How few! yet how they creep
Through my fingers to the deep,
While I weep — while I weep!
O God! can I not grasp
Them with a tighter clasp?
O God! can I not save
One from the pitiless wave?
Is *all* that we see or seem
But a dream within a dream?

(1827)

Stanzas

How often we forget all time, when lone
Admiring Nature's universal throne;
Her woods — her wilds — her mountains — the intense
Reply of HERS *to* OUR *intelligence!*

I

In youth have I known one with whom the Earth,
In secret, communing held — as he with it,
In daylight, and in beauty from his birth:
Whose fervid, flick'ring torch of life was lit
From the sun and stars, whence he had drawn forth
A passionate light — such for his spirit was fit —
And yet that spirit knew not — in the hour
Of its own fervor — what had o'er it power.

II

Perhaps it may be that my mind is wrought
To a fever by the moonbeam that hangs o'er,
But I will half believe that wild light fraught
With more of sov'reignty than ancient lore
Hath ever told — or is it of a thought
The unembodied essence, and no more,
That with a quick'ning spell doth o'er us pass
As dew of the night-time, o'er the summer grass?

III

Doth o'er us pass, when, as th' expanding eye
To the lov'd object — so the tear to the lid
Will start, which lately slept in apathy?
And yet it need not be — (that object) hid
From us in life — but common — which doth lie
Each hour before us — but *then* only, bid
With a strange sound, as of a harp-string broken,
T' awake us — 'T is a symbol and a token

IV

Of what in other worlds shall be — and giv'n
In beauty by our God, to those alone
Who otherwise would fall from life and Heav'n,
Drawn by their heart's passion, and that tone,
That high tone of the spirit which hath striv'n,
Tho' not with Faith — with godliness — whose throne
With desp'rate energy 't hath beaten down;
Wearing its own deep feeling as a crown.

(1827)

A Dream

In visions of the dark night
 I have dreamed of joy departed,
But a waking dream of life and light
 Hath left me broken-hearted.

Ah! what is not a dream by day
 To him whose eyes are cast
On things around him with a ray
 Turned back upon the past?

That holy dream — that holy dream,
 While all the world were chiding,
Hath cheered me as a lovely beam
 A lonely spirit guiding.

What though that light, thro' storm and night,
 So trembled from afar,
What could there be more purely bright
 In Truth's day-star?

(1827)

"The Happiest Day—the Happiest Hour"

The happiest day — the happiest hour
 My sear'd and blighted heart hath known,
The highest hope of pride and power,
 I feel hath flown.

Of power! said I? Yes! such I ween;
 But they have vanish'd long, alas!
The visions of my youth have been —
 But let them pass.

And, pride, what have I now with thee?
 Another brow may ev'n inherit
The venom thou hast pour'd on me —
 Be still, my spirit.

The happiest day — the happiest hour
 Mine eyes shall see — have ever seen,
The brightest glance of pride and power
 I feel — have been:

But were that hope of pride and power
 Now offer'd, with the pain
Ev'n *then* I felt — that brightest hour
 I would not live again:

For on its wing was dark alloy,
 And as it flutter'd — fell
An essence — powerful to destroy
 A soul that knew it well.

 (1827)

The Lake: To _____

In spring of youth it was my lot
To haunt of the wide world a spot
The which I could not love the less —
So lovely was the loneliness
Of a wild lake, with black rock bound,
And the tall pines that towered around.

But when the Night had thrown her pall
Upon that spot, as upon all,
And the mystic wind went by
Murmuring in melody,
Then — ah, then — I would awake
To the terror of the lone lake.

Yet that terror was not fright,
But a tremulous delight —
A feeling not the jewelled mine
Could teach or bribe me to define —
Nor Love — although the Love were thine.

Death was in that poisonous wave,
And in its gulf a fitting grave
For him who thence could solace bring
To his lone imagining,
Whose solitary soul could make
An Eden of that dim lake.

(1827)

Sonnet — To Science

Science! true daughter of Old Time thou art!
 Who alterest all things with thy peering eyes.
Why preyest thou thus upon the poet's heart,
 Vulture, whose wings are dull realities?
How should he love thee? or how deem thee wise,
 Who wouldst not leave him in his wandering
To seek for treasure in the jewelled skies,
 Albeit he soared with an undaunted wing?
Hast thou not dragged Diana from her car,
 And driven the Hamadryad from the wood
To seek a shelter in some happier star?
 Hast thou not torn the Naiad from her flood,
The Elfin from the green grass, and from me
The summer dream beneath the tamarind tree?

(1829)

Al Aaraaf

PART I

O! NOTHING earthly save the ray
(Thrown back from flowers) of Beauty's eye,
As in those gardens where the day
Springs from the gems of Circassy —
O! nothing earthly save the thrill
Of melody in woodland rill —
Or (music of the passion-hearted)
Joy's voice so peacefully departed
That, like the murmur in the shell,
Its echo dwelleth and will dwell —
Oh, nothing of the dross of ours —
Yet all the beauty — all the flowers
That list our Love, and deck our bowers —
Adorn yon world afar, afar —
The wandering star.

'T was a sweet time for Nesace — for there
Her world lay lolling on the golden air,
Near four bright suns — a temporary rest —
An oasis in desert of the blest.
Away — away — 'mid seas of rays that roll
Empyrean splendor o'er th' unchained soul —
The soul that scarce (the billows are so dense)
Can struggle to its destin'd eminence —
To distant spheres, from time to time, she rode,
And late to ours, the favor'd one of God —
But, now, the ruler of an anchor'd realm,
She throws aside the sceptre — leaves the helm,
And, amid incense and high spiritual hymns,
Laves in quadruple light her angel limbs.

Now happiest, loveliest in yon lovely Earth,
Whence sprang the "Idea of Beauty" into birth
(Falling in wreaths thro' many a startled star,
Like woman's hair 'mid pearls, until, afar,
It lit on hills Achaian, and there dwelt),
She look'd into Infinity — and knelt.
Rich clouds, for canopies, about her curled —
Fit emblems of the model of her world —

Seen but in beauty — not impeding sight
Of other beauty glittering thro' the light —
A wreath that twined each starry form around,
And all the opal'd air in color bound.

All hurriedly she knelt upon a bed
Of flowers: of lilies such as rear'd the head
On the fair Capo Deucato, and sprang
So eagerly around about to hang
Upon the flying footsteps of — deep pride —
Of her who lov'd a mortal — and so died.
The Sephalica, budding with young bees,
Uprear'd its purple stem around her knees:
And gemmy flower, of Trebizond misnam'd —
Inmate of highest stars, where erst it sham'd
All other loveliness: its honied dew
(The fabled nectar that the heathen knew)
Deliriously sweet, was dropp'd from Heaven,
And fell on gardens of the unforgiven
In Trebizond — and on a sunny flower
So like its own above, that, to this hour,
It still remaineth, torturing the bee
With madness, and unwonted reverie:
In Heaven, and all its environs, the leaf
And blossom of the fairy plant, in grief
Disconsolate linger — grief that hangs her head,
Repenting follies that full long have fled,
Heaving her white breast to the balmy air,
Like guilty beauty, chasten'd, and more fair:
Nyctanthes, too, as sacred as the light
She fears to perfume, perfuming the night:
And Clytia pondering between many a sun,
While pettish tears adown her petals run:
And that aspiring flower that sprang on Earth —
And died, ere scarce exalted into birth,
Bursting its odorous heart in spirit to wing
Its way to Heaven, from garden of a king:
And Valisnerian lotus thither flown
From struggling with the waters of the Rhone:
And thy most lovely purple perfume, Zante!
Isola d'oro! — Fior di Levante!
And the Nelumbo bud that floats for ever
With Indian Cupid down the holy river —
Fair flowers, and fairy! to whose care is given
To bear the Goddess' song, in odours, up to Heaven:

" Spirit! that dwellest where,
 In the deep sky,
The terrible and fair,
 In beauty vie!
Beyond the line of blue —
 The boundary of the star
Which turneth at the view
 Of thy barrier and thy bar —
Of the barrier overgone
 By the comets who were cast
From their pride, and from their throne,
 To be drudges till the last —
To be carriers of fire
 (The red fire of their heart)
With speed that may not tire
 And with pain that shall not part —
Who livest — *that* we know —
 In Eternity — we feel —
But the shadow of whose brow
 What spirit shall reveal?
Tho' the beings whom thy Nesace,
 Thy messenger, hath known,
Have dream'd for thy Infinity
 A model of their own —
Thy will is done, Oh, God!
 The star hath ridden high
Thro' many a tempest, but she rode
 Beneath thy burning eye;
And here, in thought, to thee —
 In thought that can alone
Ascend thy empire and so be
 A partner of thy throne —
By winged Fantasy,
 My embassy is given,
Till secrecy shall knowledge be
 In the environs of Heaven."

She ceas'd — and buried then her burning cheek
Abash'd, amid the lilies there, to seek
A shelter from the fervour of His eye;
For the stars trembled at the Deity.
She stirr'd not — breath'd not — for a voice was there
How solemnly pervading the calm air!
A sound of silence on the startled ear
Which dreamy poets name "the music of the sphere."

Ours is a world of words: Quiet we call
"Silence" — which is the merest word of all.
All Nature speaks, and ev'n ideal things
Flap shadowy sounds from visionary wings —
But ah! not so when, thus, in realms on high
The eternal voice of God is passing by;
And the red winds are withering in the sky!

 "What tho' in worlds which sightless cycles run,
Link'd to a little system and one sun —
Where all my love is folly, and the crowd
Still think my terrors but the thunder cloud,
The storm, the earthquake, and the ocean wrath
(Ah! will they cross me in my angrier path?) —
What tho' in worlds which own a single sun
The sands of Time grow dimmer as they run,
Yet thine is my resplendency, so given
To bear my secrets thro' the upper Heaven.
Leave tenantless thy crystal home, and fly,
With all thy train, athwart the moony sky —
Apart — life fire-flies in Sicilian night,
And wing to other worlds another light!
Divulge the secrets of thy embassy
To the proud orbs that twinkle — and so be
To ev'ry heart a barrier and a ban
Lest the stars totter in the guilt of man!"

 Up rose the maiden in the yellow night,
The single-mooned eve! — on Earth we plight
Our faith to one love — and one moon adore —
The birth-place of young Beauty had no more.
As sprang that yellow star from downy hours
Up rose the maiden from her shrine of flowers,
And bent o'er sheeny mountain and dim plain
Her way — but left not yet her Therasæan reign.

PART II

High on a mountain of enamell'd head —
Such as the drowsy shepherd on his bed
Of giant pasturage lying at his ease,
Raising his heavy eyelid, starts and sees
With many a mutter'd "hope to be forgiven,"
What time the moon is quadrated in Heaven —
Of rosy head, that towering far away

Into the sunlit ether, caught the ray
Of sunken suns at eve — at noon of night,
While the moon danc'd with the fair stranger light —
Uprear'd upon such height arose a pile
Of gorgeous columns on th' unburthen'd air,
Flashing from Parian marble that twin smile
Far down upon the wave that sparkled there,
And nursled the young mountain in its lair.
Of molten stars their pavement, such as fall
Thro' the ebon air, besilvering the pall
Of their own dissolution, while they die —
Adorning then the dwellings of the sky.
A dome, by linked light from Heaven let down,
Sat gently on these columns as a crown —
A window of one circular diamond, there,
Look'd out above into the purple air,
And rays from God shot down that meteor chain
And hallow'd all the beauty twice again,
Save when, between th' Empyrean and that ring,
Some eager spirit flapp'd his dusky wing.
But on the pillars Seraph eyes have seen
The dimness of this world: that greyish green
That Nature loves the best for Beauty's grave
Lurk'd in each cornice, round each architrave —
And every sculptur'd cherub thereabout
That from his marble dwelling peeréd out,
Seem'd earthly in the shadow of his niche —
Achaian statues in a world so rich!
Friezes from Tadmor and Persepolis,
From Balbec, and the stilly, clear abyss
Of beautiful Gomorrah! O, the wave
Is now upon thee — but too late to save!

Sound loves to revel in a summer night:
Witness the murmur of the grey twilight
That stole upon the ear, in Eyraco,
Of many a wild star gazer long ago —
That stealeth ever on the ear of him
Who, musing, gazeth on the distance dim,
And sees the darkness coming as a cloud —
Is not its form — its voice — most palpable and loud?

But what is this? — it cometh — and it brings
A music with it — 't is the rush of wings —
A pause — and then a sweeping, falling strain,

And Nesace is in her halls again.
From the wild energy of wanton haste
 Her cheeks were flushing, and her lips apart;
And zone that clung around her gentle waist
 Had burst beneath the heaving of her heart.
Within the centre of that hall to breathe
She paus'd and panted, Zanthe! all beneath,
The fairy light that kiss'd her golden hair
And long'd to rest, yet could but sparkle there!

 Young flowers were whispering in melody
To happy flowers that night — and tree to tree;
Fountains were gushing music as they fell
In many a star-lit grove, or moon-lit dell;
Yet silence came upon material things —
Fair flowers, bright waterfalls, and angel wings —
And sound alone, that from the spirit sprang,
Bore burthen to the charm the maiden sang:

 " 'Neath blue-bell or streamer —
 Or tufted wild spray
 That keeps from the dreamer
 The moonbeam away —
 Bright beings! that ponder,
 With half closing eyes,
 On the stars which your wonder
 Hath drawn from the skies,
 Till they glance thro' the shade, and
 Come down to your brow
 Like — eyes of the maiden
 Who calls on you now —
 Arise! from your dreaming
 In violet bowers,
 To duty beseeming
 These star-litten hours —
 And shake from your tresses,
 Encumber'd with dew,
 The breath of those kisses
 That cumber them too
 (O, how, without you, Love!
 Could angels be blest?) —
 Those kisses of true love
 That lull'd ye to rest!
 Up! — shake from your wing
 Each hindering thing:

The dew of the night —
 It would weigh down your flight;
And true love caresses —
 O! leave them apart:
They are light on the tresses,
 But lead on the heart.

"Ligeia! Ligeia!
 My beautiful one!
Whose harshest idea
 Will to melody run,
O! is it thy will
 On the breezes to toss?
Or, capriciously still,
 Like the lone Albatross,
Incumbent on night
 (As she on the air)
To keep watch with delight
 On the harmony there?

"Ligeia! wherever
 Thy image may be,
No image shall sever
 Thy music from thee.
Thou hast bound many eyes
 In a dreamy sleep —
But the strains still arise
 Which *thy* vigilance keep —
The sound of the rain
 Which leaps down to the flower,
And dances again
 In the rhythm of the shower —
The murmur that springs
 From the growing of grass
Are the music of things —
 But are modell'd, alas! —
Away, then, my dearest,
 O! hie thee away
To springs that lie clearest
 Beneath the moon-ray —
To lone lake that smiles,
 In its dream of deep rest,
At the many star-isles
 That enjewel its breast —
Where wild flowers, creeping,

Have mingled their shade,
On its margin is sleeping
 Full many a maid —
Some have left the cool glade, and
 Have slept with the bee —
Arouse them, my maiden,
 On moorland and lea —
Go! breathe on their slumber,
 All softly in ear,
The musical number
 They slumber'd to hear —
For what can awaken
 An angel so soon,
Whose sleep hath been taken
 Beneath the cold moon,
As the spell which no slumber
 Of witchery may test,
The rhythmical number
 Which lull'd him to rest? "

 Spirits in wing, and angels to the view,
A thousand seraphs burst th' Empyrean thro',
Young dreams still hovering on their drowsy flight —
Seraphs in all but "Knowledge," the keen light
That fell, refracted, thro' thy bounds, afar,
O Death! from eye of God upon that star:
Sweet was that error — sweeter still that death —
Sweet was that error — ev'n with *us* the breath
Of Science dims the mirror of our joy —
To them 't were the Simoom, and would destroy —
For what (to them) availeth it to know
That Truth is Falsehood — or that Bliss is Woe?
Sweet was their death — with them to die was rife
With the last ecstasy of satiate life —
Beyond that death no immortality —
But sleep that pondereth and is not "to be" —
And there — oh! may my weary spirit dwell —
Apart from Heaven's Eternity — and yet how far from Hell!

 What guilty spirit, in what shrubbery dim,
Heard not the stirring summons of that hymn?
But two: they fell: for Heaven no grace imparts
To those who hear not for their beating hearts.
A maiden-angel and her seraph-lover —
O! where (and ye may seek the wide skies over)

Al Aaraaf 37

Was Love, the blind, near sober Duty known?
Unguided Love hath fallen — 'mid "tears of perfect moan."

He was a goodly spirit — he who fell:
A wanderer by moss-y-mantled well —
A gazer on the lights that shine above —
A dreamer in the moonbeam by his love:
What wonder? for each star is eye-like there,
And looks so sweetly down on Beauty's hair;
And they, and ev'ry mossy spring were holy
To his love-haunted heart and melancholy.
The night had found (to him a night of wo)
Upon a mountain crag, young Angelo —
Beetling it bends athwart the solemn sky,
And scowls on starry worlds that down beneath it lie.
Here sate he with his love — his dark eye bent
With eagle gaze along the firmament:
Now turn'd it upon her — but ever then
It trembled to the orb of EARTH again.

"Ianthe, dearest, see! how dim that ray!
How lovely 't is to look so far away!
She seemed not thus upon that autumn eve
I left her gorgeous halls — nor mourn'd to leave.
That eve — that eve — I should remember well —
The sun-ray dropp'd, in Lemnos, with a spell
On th' Arabesque carving of a gilded hall
Wherein I sate, and on the draperied wall —
And on my eyelids — O the heavy light!
How drowsily it weigh'd them into night!
On flowers, before, and mist, and love they ran
With Persian Saadi in his Gulistan:
But O that light! — I slumber'd — Death, the while,
Stole o'er my senses in that lovely isle
So softly that no single silken hair
Awoke that slept — or knew that he was there.

"The last spot of Earth's orb I trod upon
Was a proud temple call'd the Parthenon.
More beauty clung around her column'd wall
Than ev'n thy glowing bosom beats withal,
And when old Time my wing did disenthral —
Thence sprang I — as the eagle from his tower,
And years I left behind me in an hour.
What time upon her airy bounds I hung,
One half the garden of her globe was flung,

Unrolling as a chart unto my view —
Tenantless cities of the desert too!
Ianthe, beauty crowded on me then,
And half I wish'd to be again of men."

"My Angelo! and why of them to be?
A brighter dwelling-place is here for thee —
And greener fields than in yon world above,
And woman's loveliness — and passionate love."

"But, list, Ianthe! when the air so soft
Fail'd, as my pennon'd spirit leapt aloft,
Perhaps my brain grew dizzy — but the world
I left so late was into chaos hurl'd —
Sprang from her station, on the winds apart,
And roll'd, a flame, the fiery Heaven athwart.
Methought, my sweet one, then I ceased to soar,
And fell — not swiftly as I rose before,
But with a downward, tremulous motion thro'
Light, brazen rays, this golden star unto!
Nor long the measure of my falling hours,
For nearest of all stars was thine to ours —
Dread star! that came, amid a night of mirth,
A red Dædalion on the timid Earth."

"We came — and to thy Earth — but not to us
Be given our lady's bidding to discuss:
We came, my love; around, above, below,
Gay fire-fly of the night we come and go,
Nor ask a reason save the angel-nod
She grants to us, as granted by her God —
But, Angelo, than thine grey Time unfurl'd
Never his fairy wing o'er fairier world!
Dim was its little disk, and angel eyes
Alone could see the phantom in the skies,
When first Al Aaraaf knew her course to be
Headlong thitherward o'er the starry sea —
But when its glory swell'd upon the sky,
As glowing Beauty's bust beneath man's eye,
We paus'd before the heritage of men,
And thy star trembled — as doth Beauty then!"

Thus, in discourse, the lovers whiled away
The night that waned and waned and brought no day.
They fell: for Heaven to them no hope imparts
Who hear not for the beating of their hearts.

(1829)

Romance

Romance, who loves to nod and sing,
With drowsy head and folded wing,
Among the green leaves as they shake
Far down within some shadowy lake,
To me a painted paroquet
Hath been — a most familiar bird —
Taught me my alphabet to say —
To lisp my very earliest word
While in the wild wood I did lie,
A child — with a most knowing eye.
Of late, eternal Condor years
So shake the very Heaven on high
With tumult as they thunder by,
I have no time for idle cares
Through gazing on the unquiet sky.
And when an hour with calmer wings
Its down upon my spirit flings —
That little time with lyre and rhyme
To while away — forbidden things!
My heart would feel to be a crime
Unless it trembled with the strings.

(1829)

To _____

The bowers whereat, in dreams, I see
 The wantonest singing birds,
Are lips — and all thy melody
 Of lip-begotten words.

Thine eyes, in Heaven of heart enshrined,
 Then desolately fall,
O God! on my funereal mind
 Like starlight on a pall.

Thy heart — *thy* heart! — I wake and sigh,
 And sleep to dream till day
Of the truth that gold can never buy —
 Of the baubles that it may.

(1829)

To the River _____

Fair river! in thy bright, clear flow
 Of crystal, wandering water,
Thou art an emblem of the glow
 Of beauty — the unhidden heart —
 The playful maziness of art
In old Alberto's daughter;
But when within thy wave she looks —
 Which glistens then, and trembles —
Why, then, the prettiest of brooks
 Her worshipper resembles;
For in his heart, as in thy stream,
 Her image deeply lies —
His heart which trembles at the beam
 Of her soul-searching eyes.

 (1829)

To _____

I heed not that my earthly lot
 Hath — little of Earth in it —
That years of love have been forgot
 In the hatred of a minute: —
I mourn not that the desolate
 Are happier, sweet, than I,
But that *you* sorrow for *my* fate
 Who am a passer by.

 (1829)

Fairy-Land

Dim vales — and shadowy floods —
And cloudy-looking woods,
Whose forms we can't discover
For the tears that drip all over:
Huge moons there wax and wane —

Again — again — again —
Every moment of the night —
Forever changing places —
And they put out the star-light
With the breath from their pale faces.
About twelve by the moon-dial,
One more filmy than the rest
(A kind which, upon trial,
They have found to be the best)
Comes down — still down — and down
With its centre on the crown
Of a mountain's eminence,
While its wide circumference
In easy drapery falls
Over hamlets, over halls,
Wherever they may be —
O'er the strange woods — o'er the sea —
Over spirits on the wing —
Over every drowsy thing —
And buries them up quite
In a labyrinth of light —
And then, how deep! — O, deep,
Is the passion of their sleep.
In the morning they arise,
And their moony covering
Is soaring in the skies,
With the tempests as they toss,
Like — almost any thing —
Or a yellow Albatross.
They use that moon no more
For the same end as before,
Videlicet, a tent —
Which I think extravagant:
Its atomies, however,
Into a shower dissever,
Of which those butterflies
Of Earth, who seek the skies,
And so come down again
(Never-contented things!)
Have brought a specimen
Upon their quivering wings.

(1829)

To Helen

Helen, thy beauty is to me
 Like those Nicéan barks of yore,
That gently, o'er a perfumed sea,
 The weary, way-worn wanderer bore
 To his own native shore.

On desperate seas long wont to roam,
 Thy hyacinth hair, thy classic face,
Thy Naiad airs have brought me home
 To the glory that was Greece,
 And the grandeur that was Rome.

Lo! in yon brilliant window-niche
 How statue-like I see thee stand,
 The agate lamp within thy hand!
Ah, Psyche, from the regions which
 Are Holy Land!

 (1831)

Israfel

And the angel Israfel, whose heart-strings are a lute, and who has the sweetest voice of all God's creatures. — KORAN

In Heaven a spirit doth dwell
 "Whose heart-strings are a lute";
None sing so wildly well
As the angel Israfel,
And the giddy stars (so legends tell),
Ceasing their hymns, attend the spell
 Of his voice, all mute.

Tottering above
 In her highest noon,
 The enamoured moon
Blushes with love,
 While, to listen, the red levin
 (With the rapid Pleiads, even,
 Which were seven,)
 Pauses in Heaven.

Israfel

And they say (the starry choir
 And the other listening things)
That Israfeli's fire
Is owing to that lyre
 By which he sits and sings —
The trembling living wire
 Of those unusual strings.

But the skies that angel trod,
 Where deep thoughts are a duty,
Where Love's a grown-up God,
 Where the Houri glances are
Imbued with all the beauty
 Which we worship in a star.

Therefore, thou art not wrong,
 Israfeli, who despisest
An unimpassioned song;
To thee the laurels belong,
 Best bard, because the wisest!
Merrily live, and long!

The ecstasies above
 With thy burning measures suit —
Thy grief, thy joy, thy hate, thy love,
 With the fervour of thy lute —
 Well may the stars be mute!

Yes, Heaven is thine; but this
 Is a world of sweets and sours;
 Our flowers are merely — flowers,
And the shadow of thy perfect bliss
 Is the sunshine of ours.

If I could dwell
Where Israfel
 Hath dwelt, and he where I,
He might not sing so wildly well
 A mortal melody,
While a bolder note than this might swell
 From my lyre within the sky.

(1831)

The City in the Sea

Lo! Death has reared himself a throne
In a strange city lying alone
Far down within the dim West,
Where the good and the bad and the worst and the best
Have gone to their eternal rest.
There shrines and palaces and towers
(Time-eaten towers that tremble not!)
Resemble nothing that is ours.
Around, by lifting winds forgot,
Resignedly beneath the sky
The melancholy waters lie.

No rays from the holy heaven come down
On the long night-time of that town;
But light from out the lurid sea
Streams up the turrets silently —
Gleams up the pinnacles far and free —
Up domes — up spires — up kingly halls —
Up fanes — up Babylon-like walls —
Up shadowy long-forgotten bowers
Of sculptured ivy and stone flowers —
Up many and many a marvellous shrine
Whose wreathéd friezes intertwine
The viol, the violet, and the vine.

Resignedly beneath the sky
The melancholy waters lie.
So blend the turrets and shadows there
That all seem pendulous in air,
While from a proud tower in the town
Death looks gigantically down.

There open fanes and gaping graves
Yawn level with the luminous waves;
But not the riches there that lie
In each idol's diamond eye —
Not the gaily-jewelled dead
Tempt the waters from their bed;
For no ripples curl, alas!
Along that wilderness of glass —

No swellings tell that winds may be
Upon some far-off happier sea —
No heavings hint that winds have been
On seas less hideously serene.

But lo, a stir is in the air!
The wave — there is a movement there!
As if the towers had thrust aside,
In slightly sinking, the dull tide —
As is their tops had feebly given
A void within the filmy Heaven.
The waves have now a redder glow —
The hours are breathing faint and low —
And when, amid no earthly moans,
Down, down that town shall settle hence,
Hell, rising from a thousand thrones,
Shall do it reverence.

(1831)

The Sleeper

At midnight, in the month of June,
I stand beneath the mystic moon.
An opiate vapor, dewy, dim,
Exhales from out her golden rim,
And softly dripping, drop by drop,
Upon the quiet mountain top,
Steals drowsily and musically
Into the universal valley.
The rosemary nods upon the grave;
The lily lolls upon the wave;
Wrapping the fog about its breast,
The ruin moulders into rest;
Looking like Lethe, see! the lake
A conscious slumber seems to take,
And would not, for the world, awake.
All Beauty sleeps! — and lo! where lies
Irene, with her Destinies!

Oh, lady bright! can it be right —
This window open to the night?
The wanton airs, from the tree-top,
Laughingly through the lattice drop —

The bodiless airs, a wizard rout,
Flit through thy chamber in and out,
And wave the curtain canopy
So fitfully — so fearfully —
Above the closed and fringéd lid
'Neath which thy slumb'ring soul lies hid,
That, o'er the floor and down the wall,
Like ghosts the shadows rise and fall!
Oh, lady dear, hast thou no fear?
Why and what art thou dreaming here?
Sure thou art come o'er far-off seas,
A wonder to these garden trees!
Strange is thy pallor! strange thy dress!
Strange, above all, thy length of tress,
And this all solemn silentness!

The lady sleeps! Oh, may her sleep,
Which is enduring, so be deep!
Heaven have her in its sacred keep!
This chamber changed for one more holy,
This bed for one more melancholy,
I pray to God that she may lie
Forever with unopened eye,
While the pale sheeted ghosts go by!

My love, she sleeps! Oh, may her sleep,
As it is lasting, so be deep!
Soft may the worms about her creep!
Far in the forest, dim and old,
For her may some tall vault unfold —
Some vault that oft hath flung its black
And wingéd pannels fluttering back,
Triumphant, o'er the crested palls
Of her grand family funerals —

Some sepulchre, remote, alone,
Against whose portals she hath thrown,
In childhood, many an idle stone —
Some tomb from out whose sounding door
She ne'er shall force an echo more,
Thrilling to think, poor child of sin!
It was the dead who groaned within.

(1831)

Lenore

Ah, broken is the golden bowl! — the spirit flown forever!
Let the bell toll! — a saintly soul floats on the Stygian river;
And, Guy De Vere, hast *thou* no tear? — weep now or never more!
See! on yon drear and rigid bier low lies thy love, Lenore!
Come, let the burial rite be read — the funeral song be sung! —
An anthem for the queenliest dead that ever died so young —
A dirge for her the doubly dead in that she died so young.

"Wretches! ye loved her for her wealth and ye hated her for her pride,
And, when she fell in feeble health, ye blessed her — that she died: —
How *shall* the ritual, then, be read? — the requiem how be sung
By you — by yours, the evil eye, — by yours, the slanderous tongue
That did to death the innocence that died, and died so young?"

Peccavimus; yet rave not thus! but let a Sabbath song
Go up to God so solemnly the dead may feel no wrong!
The sweet Lenore "hath gone before," with Hope that flew beside,
Leaving thee wild for the dear child that should have been thy bride —
For her, the fair and *debonair,* that now so lowly lies,
The life upon her yellow hair, but not within her eyes —
The life still there upon her hair — the death upon her eyes.

"Avaunt! — avaunt! from fiends below the indignant ghost is riven —
From Hell unto a high estate far up within the Heaven —
From grief and groan to a golden throne beside the King of Heaven! —
Let *no* bell toll, then! — lest her soul, amid its hallowed mirth,
Should catch the note as it doth float up from the damnéd Earth!
And I! — to-night my heart is light! — no dirge will I upraise,
But waft the angel on her flight with a Pæan of old days!"

(1831)

The Valley of Unrest

Once it smiled a silent dell
Where the people did not dwell;
They had gone unto the wars,
Trusting to the mild-eyed stars,
Nightly, from their azure towers,
To keep watch above the flowers,

In the midst of which all day
The red sun-light lazily lay.
Now each visitor shall confess
The sad valley's restlessness.
Nothing there is motionless —
Nothing save the airs that brood
Over the magic solitude.
Ah, by no wind are stirred those trees
That palpitate like the chill seas
Around the misty Hebrides!
Ah, by no wind those clouds are driven
That rustle through the unquiet Heaven
Uneasily, from morn till even,
Over the violets there that lie
In myriad types of the human eye —
Over the lilies there that wave
And weep above a nameless grave!
They wave: — from out their fragrant tops
External dews come down in drops.
They weep: — from off their delicate stems
Perennial tears descend in gems.

(1831)

The Coliseum

Type of the antique Rome! Rich reliquary
Of lofty contemplation left to Time
By buried centuries of pomp and power!
At length — at length — after so many days
Of weary pilgrimage and burning thirst
(Thirst for the springs of lore that in thee lie),
I kneel, an altered and an humble man,
Amid thy shadows, and so drink within
My very soul thy grandeur, gloom, and glory!

Vastness! and Age! and Memories of Eld!
Silence! and Desolation! and dim Night!
I feel ye now — I feel ye in your strength —
O spells more sure than e'er Judæan king
Taught in the garden of Gethsemane!
O charms more potent than the rapt Chaldee
Ever drew down from out the quiet stars!

Here, where a hero fell, a column falls!
Here, where the mimic eagle glared in gold,
A midnight vigil holds the swarthy bat!
Here, where the dames of Rome their gilded hair
Waved to the wind, now wave the reed and thistle!
Here, where on golden throne the monarch lolled,
Glides, spectre-like, unto his marble home,
Lit by the wan light of the hornéd moon,
The swift and silent lizard of the stones!

But stay! these walls — these ivy-clad arcades —
These mouldering plinths — these sad and blackened shafts —
These vague entablatures — this crumbling frieze —
These shattered cornices — this wreck — this ruin —
These stones — alas! these gray stones — are they all —
All of the famed and the colossal left
By the corrosive Hours to Fate and me?

"Not all" — the Echoes answer me — "not all!
Prophetic sounds and loud, arise forever
From us, and from all Ruin, unto the wise,
As melody from Memnon to the Sun.
We rule the hearts of mightiest men — we rule
With a despotic sway all giant minds.
We are not impotent — we pallid stones.
Not all our power is gone — not all our fame —
Not all the magic of our high renown —
Not all the wonder that encircles us —
Not all the mysteries that in us lie —
Not all the memories that hang upon
And cling around about us as a garment,
Clothing us in a robe of more than glory."

(1833)

To One in Paradise

Thou wast that all to me, love,
 For which my soul did pine —
A green isle in the sea, love,
 A fountain and a shrine,
All wreathed with fairy fruits and flowers,
 And all the flowers were mine.

Ah, dream too bright to last!
 Ah, starry Hope! that didst arise
But to be overcast!
 A voice from out the Future cries,
"On! on!" — but o'er the Past
 (Dim gulf!) my spirit hovering lies
Mute, motionless, aghast!

For, alas! alas! with me
 The light of Life is o'er!
No more — no more — no more —
 (Such language holds the solemn sea
To the sands upon the shore)
 Shall bloom the thunder-blasted tree,
Or the stricken eagle soar!

And all my days are trances,
 And all my nightly dreams
Are where thy grey eye glances,
 And where thy footstep gleams —
In what ethereal dances,
 By what eternal streams.

(1834)

Hymn

At morn — at noon — at twilight dim —
Maria! thou hast heard my hymn!
In joy and wo — in good and ill —
Mother of God, be with me still!
When the Hours flew brightly by,
And not a cloud obscured the sky,
My soul, lest it should truant be,
Thy grace did guide to thine and thee;
Now, when storms of Fate o'ercast
Darkly my Present and my Past,
Let my Future radiant shine
With sweet hopes of thee and thine!

(1835)

To F_____

Beloved! amid the earnest woes
 That crowd around my earthly path —
(Drear path, alas! where grows
Not even one lonely rose) —
 My soul at least a solace hath
In dreams of thee, and therein knows
An Eden of bland repose.

And thus thy memory is to me
 Like some enchanted far-off isle
In some tumultuous sea —
Some ocean throbbing far and free
 With storms — but where meanwhile
Serenest skies continually
Just o'er that one bright island smile.

(1835)

To F_____s S. O_____d

Thou wouldst be loved? — then let thy heart
 From its present pathway part not!
Being everything which now thou art,
 Be nothing which thou art not.
So with the world thy gentle ways,
 Thy grace, thy more than beauty,
Shall be an endless theme of praise,
 And love — a simple duty.

(1835)

Scenes from "Politian"

AN UNPUBLISHED DRAMA

I

ROME. *A hall in a palace.* ALESSANDRA *and* CASTIGLIONE

ALESSANDRA. Thou art sad, Castiglione.
CASTIGLIONE. Sad! — not I.
Oh, I'm the happiest man in Rome!

A few days more, thou knowest, my Alessandra,
Will make thee mine. Oh, I am very happy!

 ALESSANDRA. Methinks thou hast a singular way of showing
Thy happiness! — what ails thee, cousin of mine?
Why didst thou sigh so deeply?

 CASTIGLIONE. Did I sigh?
I was not conscious of it. It is a fashion,
A silly — a most silly fashion I have
When I am *very* happy. Did I sigh? [*sighing*]

 ALESSANDRA. Thou didst. Thou art not well. Thou hast indulged
Too much of late, and I am vexed to see it.
Late hours and wine, Castiglione, — these
Will ruin thee! thou art already altered —
Thy looks are haggard — nothing so wears away
The constitution as late hours and wine.

 CASTIGLIONE. [*musing*] Nothing, fair cousin, nothing — not even
 deep sorrow —
Wears it away like evil hours and wine.
I will amend.

 ALESSANDRA. Do it! I would have thee drop
Thy riotous company, too — fellows low-born —
Ill suit the like with old Di Broglio's heir
And Alessandra's husband.

 CASTIGLIONE. I will drop them.

 ALESSANDRA. Thou wilt — thou must. Attend thou also more
To thy dress and equipage — they are over plain
For thy lofty rank and fashion — much depends
Upon appearances

 CASTIGLIONE. I'll see to it.

 ALESSANDRA. Then see to it! — pay more attention, sir,
To a becoming carriage — much thou wantest
In dignity.

 CASTIGLIONE. Much, much, oh much I want
In proper dignity.

 ALESSANDRA. [*haughtily*] Thou mockest me, sir!

 CASTIGLIONE. [*abstractedly*] Sweet, gentle Lalage!

 ALESSANDRA. Heard I aright?
I speak to him — he speaks of Lalage!
Sir Count! [*places her hand on his shoulder*] what art thou dreaming?
 he's not well!
What ails thee, sir?

 CASTIGLIONE. [*starting*] Cousin! fair cousin! — madam!
I crave thy pardon — indeed I am not well.
Your hand from off my shoulder, if you please —
This air is most oppressive! — Madam — the Duke!

ENTER DI BROGLIO

DI BROGLIO. My son, I've news for thee! — hey? — what's the mat-
ter? [*observing* ALESSANDRA]
I' the pouts? Kiss her, Castiglione! kiss her,
You dog, make it up, I say, this minute!
I've news for you both. Politian is expected
Hourly in Rome — Politian, Earl of Leicester!
We'll have him at the wedding. 'T is his first visit
To the imperial city.
 ALESSANDRA. What! Politian
Of Britain, Earl of Leicester?
 DI BROGLIO. The same, my love.
We'll have him at the wedding. A man quite young
In years, but grey in fame. I have not seen him,
But Rumor speaks of him as of a prodigy
Pre-eminent in arts and arms, and wealth,
And high descent. We'll have him at the wedding.
 ALESSANDRA. I have heard much of this Politian.
Gay, volatile, and giddy — is he not?
And little given to thinking.
 DI BROGLIO. Far from it, love.
No branch, they say, of all philosophy
So deep abstruse he has not mastered it.
Learned as few are learned.
 ALESSANDRA. 'T is very strange!
I have known men have seen Politian
And sought his company. They speak of him
As of one who entered madly into life,
Drinking the cup of pleasure to the dregs.
 CASTIGLIONE. Ridiculous! Now I have seen Politian
And know him well — nor learned nor mirthful he.
He is a dreamer and a man shut out
From common passions.
 DI BROGLIO. Children, we disagree.
Let us go forth and taste the fragrant air
Of the garden. Did I dream, or did I hear
Politian was a *melancholy* man?

 EXEUNT

II

A lady's apartment, with a window open and looking into a garden.
LALAGE, *in deep mourning, reading at a table on which lie some books and
a hand mirror. In the background,* JACINTA (*a servant maid*) *leans care-
lessly upon a chair.*

LALAGE. Jacinta! is it thou?
JACINTA. [*pertly*] Yes, Ma'am, I'm here.
LALAGE. I did not know, Jacinta, you were in waiting.
Sit down! — let not my presence trouble you —
Sit down! — for I am humble, most humble.
JACINTA. [*aside*] 'T is time.

> [JACINTA *seats herself in a sidelong manner upon the chair, resting her elbows upon the back, and regarding her mistress with a contemptuous look.* LALAGE *continues to read.*]

LALAGE. "It in another climate," so he said,
"Bore a bright golden flower, but not i' this soil!"

> [*pauses — turns over some leaves, and resumes.*]

"No lingering winters there, nor snow, nor shower —
But Ocean ever to refresh mankind
Breathes the shrill spirit of the western wind."
Oh, beautiful! — most beautiful! — how like
To what my fevered soul doth dream of Heaven!
O happy land! [*pauses*] She died! — the maiden died!
O still more happy maiden who couldst die!
Jacinta!

> [JACINTA *returns no answer, and* LALAGE *presently resumes.*]

Again! — a similar tale
Told of a beauteous dame beyond the sea!
Thus speaketh one Ferdinand in the words of the play —
"She died full young" — one Bossola answers him —
"I think not so — her infelicity
Seemed to have years too many" — Ah, luckless lady!
Jacinta! [*Still no answer*]

Here's a far sterner story
But like — oh, very like in its despair
Of that Egyptian queen, winning so easily
A thousand hearts — losing at length her own.
She died. Thus endeth the history — and her maids
Lean over her and weep — two gentle maids
With gentle names — Eiros and Charmion!
Rainbow and Dove! — Jacinta!
JACINTA. [*pettishly*] Madam, what *is* it?
LALAGE. Wilt thou, my good Jacinta, be so kind
As go down in the library and bring me
The Holy Evangelists.
JACINTA. Pshaw! [*Exit*]
LALAGE. If there be balm
For the wounded spirit in Gilead it is there!

Dew in the night-time of my bitter trouble
Will there be found — "dew sweeter far than that
Which hangs like chains of pearl on Hermon hill."

> [*Re-enter* JACINTA, *and throws a volume on the table.*]

JACINTA. There, ma'am, 's the book. Indeed she is very troublesome.

> [*aside*]

LALAGE. [*astonished*] What didst thou say, Jacinta? Have I done aught
To grieve thee or to vex thee? — I am sorry.
For thou hast served me long and ever been
Trustworthy and respectful. [*resumes her reading*]

JACINTA. I can't believe
She has any more jewels — no — no — she gave me all. [*aside*]

LALAGE. What didst thou say, Jacinta? Now I bethink me
Thou hast not spoken lately of thy wedding.
How fares good Ugo? — and when is it to be?
Can I do aught? — is there no farther aid
Thou needest, Jacinta?

JACINTA. "Is there no *farther* aid!"
That's meant for me. [*aside*] I'm sure, Madam, you need not
Be always throwing those jewels in my teeth.

LALAGE. Jewels! Jacinta, — now indeed, Jacinta,
I thought not of the jewels.

JACINTA. Oh! perhaps not!
But then I might have sworn it. After all,
There's Ugo says the ring is only paste,
For he's sure the Count Castiglione never
Would have given a real diamond to such as you;
And at the best I'm certain, Madam, you cannot
Have use for jewels *now*. But I might have sworn it. [*Exit*]

> [LALAGE *bursts into tears and leans her head upon the table — after a short pause raises it.*]

LALAGE. Poor Lalage! — and is it come to this?
Thy servant maid! — but courage! — 't is but a viper
Whom thou hast cherished to sting thee to the soul!

> [*Taking up the mirror.*]

Ha! here at least's a friend — too much a friend
In earlier days — a friend will not deceive thee.
Fair mirror and true! now tell me (for thou canst)
A tale — a pretty tale — and heed thou not
Though it be rife with woe. It answers me.
It speaks of sunken eyes, and wasted cheeks,
And Beauty long deceased — remembers me
Of Joy departed — Hope, the Seraph Hope,

Inurned and entombed! — now, in a tone
Low, sad, and solemn, but most audible,
Whispers of early grave untimely yawning
For ruined maid. Fair mirror and true! thou liest not!
Thou hast no end to gain — no heart to break —
Castiglione lied who said he loved —
Thou true — he false! — false! — false!

> [*While she speaks, a* MONK *enters her apartment,
> and approaches unobserved.*]

MONK. Refuge thou hast,
Sweet daughter! in Heaven. Think of external things!
Give up thy soul to penitence, and pray!

LALAGE. [*arising hurriedly*] I *cannot* pray! — My soul is at war with
 God!
The frightful sounds of merriment below
Disturb my senses — go! I cannot pray —
The sweet airs from the garden worry me!
Thy presence grieves me — go! — thy priestly raiment
Fills me with dread — thy ebony crucifix
With horror and awe!

MONK. Think of thy precious soul!

LALAGE. Think of my early days! — think of my father
And mother in Heaven! think of our quiet home,
And the rivulet that ran before the door!
Think of my little sisters! — think of them!
And think of me! — think of my trusting love
And confidence — his vows — my ruin — think — think
Of my unspeakable misery! — begone!
Yet stay! yet stay! — what was it thou saidst of prayer
And penitence? Didst thou not speak of faith
And vows before the throne?

MONK. I did.

LALAGE. 'T is well.
There *is* a vow were fitting should be made —
A sacred vow, imperative, and urgent,
A solemn vow!

MONK. Daughter, this zeal is well!

LALAGE. Father, this zeal is anything but well!
Hast thou a crucifix fit for this thing?
A crucifix whereon to register
 This sacred vow? [*He hands her his own*]
 [*shuddering*]
Not that — Oh! no! — no! — no — !
Not that! Not that — I tell thee, holy man,
Thy raiments and thy ebony cross affright me!
Stand back! I have a crucifix myself, —

I have a crucifix! Methinks 't were fitting.
The deed — the vow — the symbol of the deed —
And the deed's register should tally, father!

> [*Draws a cross-handled dagger and raises it on high.*]

Behold the cross wherewith a vow like mine
Is written in Heaven!

 MONK. Thy words are madness, daughter,
And speak a purpose unholy — thy lips are livid —
Thine eyes are wild — tempt not the wrath divine!
Pause ere too late! — oh, be not — be not rash!
Swear not the oath — oh, swear it not!

 LALAGE. 'T is sworn!

III

An apartment in a palace. POLITIAN *and* BALDAZZAR

 BALDAZZAR. —— Arouse thee now, Politian!
Thou must not — nay indeed, indeed, thou shalt not —
Give way unto these humors. Be thyself!
Shake off the idle fancies that beset thee,
And live, for now thou diest!

 POLITIAN. Not so, Baldazzar!
Surely I live.

 BALDAZZAR. Politian, it doth grieve me
To see thee thus.

 POLITIAN. Baldazzar, it doth grieve me
To give thee cause for grief, my honored friend.
Command me, sir! what wouldst thou have me do?
At thy behest I will shake off that nature
Which from my forefathers I did inherit,
Which with my mother's milk I did imbibe,
And be no more Politian, but some other.
Command me, sir!

 BALDAZZAR. To the field then — to the field —
To the senate or the field.

 POLITIAN. Alas! alas!
There is an imp would follow me even there!
There is an imp *hath* followed me even there!
There is — what voice was that?

 BALDAZZAR. I heard it not.
I heard not any voice except thine own,
And the echo of thine own.

 POLITIAN. Then I but dreamed.

 BALDAZZAR. Give not thy soul to dreams: the camp — the court

Befit thee — Fame awaits thee — Glory calls —
And her, the trumpet-tongued, thou wilt not hear
In hearkening to imaginary sounds
And phantom voices.
 POLITIAN. It *is* a phantom voice!
Didst thou not hear it *then?*
 BALDAZZAR. I heard it not.
 POLITIAN. Thou heardst it not! — Baldazzar speak no more
To me, Politian, of thy camps and courts.
Oh! I am sick, sick, sick, even unto death,
Of the hollow and high-sounding vanities
Of the populous Earth! Bear with me yet awhile!
We have been boys together — school-fellows —
And now are friends — yet shall not be so long —
For in the eternal city thou shall do me
A kind and gentle office, and a Power —
A Power august, benignant and supreme —
Shall then absolve thee of all farther duties
Unto thy friend.
 BALDAZZAR. Thou speakest a fearful riddle
I *will* not understand.
 POLITIAN. Yet now as Fate
Approaches, and the Hours are breathing low,
The sands of Time are changed to golden grains,
And dazzle me, Baldazzar. Alas! alas!
I *cannot* die, having within my heart
So keen a relish for the beautiful
As hath been kindled within it. Methinks the air
Is calmer now than it was wont to be —
Rich melodies are floating in the winds —
A rarer loveliness bedecks the earth —
And with a holier lustre the quiet moon
Sitteth in heaven. — Hist! hist! thou canst not say
Thou hearest not *now*, Baldazzar?
 BALDAZZAR. Indeed I hear not.
 POLITIAN. Not hear it! — listen now! listen! — the faintest sound
And yet the sweetest that ear ever heard!
A lady's voice! — and sorrow in the tone!
Baldazzar, it oppresses me like a spell!
Again! — again! — how solemnly it falls
Into my heart of hearts! that eloquent voice
Surely I never heard — yet it were well
Had I *but* heard it with its thrilling tones
In earlier days!
 BALDAZZAR. I myself hear it now.

Be still! — the voice, if I mistake not greatly,
Proceeds from yonder lattice — which you may see
Very plainly through the window — it belongs,
Does it not? unto this palace of the Duke.
The singer is undoubtedly beneath
The roof of his Excellency — and perhaps
Is even that Alessandra of whom he spoke
As the betrothed of Castiglione,
His son and heir.

 POLITIAN. Be still! — it comes again!

 VOICE. [*very faintly*]

 "And is thy heart so strong
 As for to leave me thus
 Who hath loved thee so long
 In wealth and wo among?
 And is thy heart so strong
 As for to leave me thus?
 Say nay — say nay!"

 BALDAZZAR. The song is English, and I oft have heard it
In merry England — never so plaintively —
Hist! hist! it comes again!

 VOICE. [*more loudly*]

 "Is it so strong
 As for to leave me thus
 Who hath loved thee so long
 In wealth and wo among?
 And is thy heart so strong
 As for to leave me thus?
 Say nay — say nay!"

 BALDAZZAR. 'T is hushed and all is still!

 POLITIAN. All *is not* still.

 BALDAZZAR. Let us go down.

 POLITIAN. Go down, Baldazzar, go!

 BALDAZZAR. The hour is growing late — the Duke awaits us, —
Thy presence is expected in the hall
Below. What ails thee, Earl Politian?

 VOICE. [*distinctly*]

 "Who hath loved thee so long,
 In wealth and wo among,
 And is thy heart so strong?
 Say nay — say nay!"

 BALDAZZAR. Let us descend! — 't is time. Politian, give
These fancies to the wind. Remember, pray,
Your bearing lately savored much of rudeness
Unto the Duke. Arouse thee! and remember!

POLITIAN. Remember? I do. Lead on! I *do* remember. [*going*]
Let us descend. Believe me, I would give,
Freely would give the broad lands of my earldom
To look upon the face hidden by yon lattice —
"To gaze upon that veiled face, and hear
Once more that silent tongue."
 BALDAZZAR. Let me beg you, sir,
Descend with me — the Duke may be offended.
Let us go down, I pray you.
 VOICE. [*loudly*] "Say nay — say nay!"
 POLITIAN. [*aside*] 'T is strange! — 't is very strange — methought
 the voice
Chimed in with my desires and bade me stay! [*approaching the window*]
Sweet voice! I heed thee, and will surely stay.
Now be this Fancy, by Heaven, or be it Fate,
Still will I not descend. Baldazzar, make
Apology unto the Duke for me;
I go not down to-night.
 BALDAZZAR. Your lordship's pleasure
Shall be attended to. Good-night, Politian.
 POLITIAN. Good-night, my friend, good-night.

IV

The gardens of a palace — Moonlight. LALAGE *and* POLITIAN

 LALAGE. And dost thou speak of love
To *me*, Politian? — dost thou speak of love
To Lalage? — ah, wo — ah, wo is me!
This mockery is most cruel — most cruel indeed!
 POLITIAN. Weep not! oh, sob not thus! — thy bitter tears
Will madden me. Oh, mourn not, Lalage —
Be comforted! I know — I know it all,
And *still* I speak of love. Look at me, brightest
And beautiful Lalage! — turn here thine eyes!
Thou askest me if I could speak of love,
Knowing what I know, and seeing what I have seen.
Thou askest me that — and thus I answer thee —
Thus on my bended knee I answer thee. [*kneeling*]
Sweet Lalage, *I love thee — love thee — love thee*;
Thro' good and ill — thro' weal and woe I *love thee*;
Not mother, with her first-born on her knee,
Thrills with intenser love than I for thee.
Not on God's altar, in any time or clime,
Burned there a holier fire than burneth now

Within my spirit for *thee*. And do I love?
Even for thy woes I love thee — even for thy woes —
Thy beauty and thy woes.
 LALAGE. Alas, proud Earl,
Thou dost forget thyself, remembering me!
How, in thy father's halls, among the maidens
Pure and reproachless, of thy princely line,
Could the dishonored Lalage abide?
Thy wife, and with a tainted memory —
My seared and blighted name, how would it tally
With the ancestral honors of thy house,
And with thy glory?
 POLITIAN. Speak not to me of glory!
I hate — I loathe the name; I do abhor
The unsatisfactory and ideal thing.
Art thou not Lalage and I Politian?
Do I not love — art thou not beautiful —
What need we more? Ha! glory! — now speak not of it:
But all I hold most sacred and most solemn —
By all my wishes now — my fears hereafter —
By all I scorn on earth and hope in heaven —
There is no deed I would more glory in,
Than in thy cause to scoff at this same glory
And trample it under foot. What matters it —
What matters it, my fairest, and my best,
That we go down unhonored and forgotten
Into the dust — so we descend together.
Descend together — and then — and then perchance —
 LALAGE. Why dost thou pause, Politian?
 POLITIAN. And then perchance
Arise together, Lalage, and roam
The starry and quiet dwellings of the blest,
And still —
 LALAGE. Why dost thou pause, Politian?
 POLITIAN. And still *together — together.*
 LALAGE. Now, Earl of Leicester!
Thou *lovest* me, and in my heart of hearts
I feel thou lovest me truly.
 POLITIAN. Oh, Lalage! [*throwing himself upon his knee*]
And thou lovest *me*?
 LALAGE. Hist! hush! within the gloom
Of yonder trees methought a figure past —
A spectral figure, solemn, and slow, and noiseless —
Like the grim shadow Conscience, solemn and noiseless.
 [*Walks across and returns.*]

I was mistaken — 't was but a giant bough
Stirred by the autumn wind. Politian!

 POLITIAN. My Lalage — my love! why art thou moved?
Why dost thou turn so pale? Not Conscience' self,
Far less a shadow which thou likenest to it,
Should shake the firm spirit thus. But the night wind
Is chilly — and these melancholy boughs
Throw over all things a gloom.

 LALAGE. Politian!
Thou speakest to me of love. Knowest thou the land
With which all tongues are busy — a land new found —
Miraculously found by one of Genoa —
A thousand leagues within the golden west?
A fairy land of flowers, and fruit, and sunshine,
And crystal lakes, and over-arching forests,
And mountains, around whose towering summits the winds
Of Heaven untrammelled flow — which air to breathe
Is Happiness now, and will be Freedom hereafter
In days that are to come?

 POLITIAN. O, wilt thou — wilt thou
Fly to that Paradise — my Lalage, wilt thou
Fly thither with me? There Care shall be forgotten,
And Sorrow shall be no more, and Eros be all.
And life shall then be mine, for I will live
For thee, and in thine eyes — and thou snalt be
No more a mourner — but the radiant Joys
Shall wait upon thee, and the angel Hope
Attend thee ever; and I will kneel to thee
And worship thee, and call thee my beloved,
My own, my beautiful, my love, my wife,
My all; — oh, wilt thou — wilt thou, Lalage,
Fly thither with me?

 LALAGE. A deed is to be done —
Castiglione lives!

 POLITIAN. And he shall die! [Exit]

 LALAGE. [after a pause] and — he — shall — die! — alas!
Castiglione die? Who spoke the words?
Where I am? — what was it he said? — Politian!
Thou *art* not gone — thou art not *gone*, Politian.
I *feel* thou art not gone — yet dare not look,
Lest I behold thee not; thou *couldst* not go
With those words upon thy lips — O, speak to me!
And let me hear thy voice — one word — one word,
To say thou art not gone, — one little sentence,
To say how thou dost scorn — how thou dost hate

My womanly weakness. Ha! ha! thou *art* not gone —
O speak to me! I *knew* thou wouldst not go!
I knew thou wouldst not, couldst not, *durst* not go.
Villain, thou *art* not gone — thou mockest me!
And thus I clutch thee — thus! —— He is gone, he is gone —
Gone — gone. Where am I? —— 't is well — 't is very well!
So that the blade be keen — the blow be sure,
'T is well, 't is *very* well — alas! alas! [*Exit*]

V

The suburbs. POLITIAN *alone*

POLITIAN. This weakness grows upon me. I am faint,
And much I fear me ill — it will not do
To die ere I have lived! — Stay — stay thy hand,
O Azrael, yet awhile! — Prince of the Powers
Of Darkness and the Tomb, O pity me!
O pity me! let me not perish now,
In the budding of my Paradisal Hope!
Give me to live yet — yet a little while:
'T is I who pray for life — I who so late
Demanded but to die! — what sayeth the Count?

ENTER BALDAZZAR

BALDAZZAR. That knowing no cause of quarrel or of feud
Between the Earl Politian and himself,
He doth decline your cartel.
POLITIAN. *What* didst thou say?
What answer was it you brought me, good Baldazzar?
With what excessive fragrance the zephyr comes
Laden from yonder bowers! — a fairer day,
Or one more worthy Italy, methinks
No mortal eyes have seen! — *what* said the Count?
BALDAZZAR. That he, Castiglione, not being aware
Of any feud existing, or any cause
Of quarrel between your lordship and himself
Cannot accept the challenge.
POLITIAN. It is most true —
All this is very true. When saw you, sir,
When saw you now, Baldazzar, in the frigid
Ungenial Britain which we left so lately,
A heaven so calm as this — so utterly free
From the evil taint of clouds? — and he did *say*?

BALDAZZAR. No more, my lord, than I have told you, sir:
The Count Castiglione will not fight,
Having no cause for quarrel.
 POLITIAN. Now this is true —
All very true. Thou art my friend, Baldazzar,
And I have not forgotten it — thou 'lt do me
A piece of service; wilt thou go back and say
Unto this man, that I, the Earl of Leicester,
Hold him a villain? — thus much, I prithee, say
Unto the Count — it is exceeding just
He should have cause for quarrel.
 BALDAZZAR. My lord! — my friend! —
 POLITIAN. [aside] 'T is he — he comes himself! [aloud] Thou rea-
sonest well.
I know what thou wouldst say — not send the message —
Well! — I will think of it — I will not send it.
Now prythee, leave me — hither doth come a person
With whom affairs of a most private nature
I would adjust.
 BALDAZZAR. I go — to-morrow we meet,
Do we not? — at the Vatican.
 POLITIAN. At the Vatican. [Exit BALDAZZAR]

ENTER CASTIGLIONE

 CASTIGLIONE. The Earl of Leicester here!
 POLITIAN. I *am* the Earl of Leicester, and thou seest,
Dost thou not? that I am here.
 CASTIGLIONE. My lord, some strange,
Some singular mistake — misunderstanding —
Hath without doubt arisen: thou hast been urged
Thereby, in heat of anger, to address
Some words most unaccountable, in writing,
To me, Castiglione; the bearer being
Baldazzar, Duke of Surrey. I am aware
Of nothing which might warrant thee in this thing,
Having given thee no offence. Ha! — am I right?
'T was a mistake? — undoubtedly — we all
Do err at times.
 POLITIAN. Draw, villain, and prate no more!
 CASTIGLIONE. Ha! — draw? — and villain? have at thee then at once,
Proud Earl! [draws]
 POLITIAN. [drawing] Thus to the expiatory tomb,
Untimely sepulchre, I do devote thee
In the name of Lalage!

CASTIGLIONE. [*letting fall his sword and recoiling to the extremity of the stage*]

of Lalage!
Hold off — thy sacred hand — avaunt I say!
Avaunt — I will not fight thee — indeed I dare not.

POLITIAN. Thou wilt not fight with me didst say, Sir Count?
Shall I be baffled thus? — now this is well.
Didst say thou *darest* not? Ha!

CASTIGLIONE. I dare not — dare not —
Hold off thy hand — with that beloved name
So fresh upon thy lips I will not fight thee —
I cannot — dare not.

POLITIAN. Now by my halidom
I do believe thee! — coward, I do believe thee!

CASTIGLIONE. Ha! — coward! — this may not be!

[*Clutches his sword and staggers towards* POLITIAN,
*but his purpose is changed before reaching him,
and he falls upon his knee at the feet of the Earl.*]

 Alas! my lord,
It is — it is — most true. In such a cause
I am the veriest coward. O pity me!

POLITIAN. [*greatly softened*] Alas! — I do — indeed I pity thee.

CASTIGLIONE. And Lalage —

POLITIAN. Scoundrel! — *arise and die!*

CASTIGLIONE. It needeth not be — thus — thus — O let me die
Thus on my bended knee. It were most fitting
That in this deep humiliation I perish.
For in the fight I will not raise a hand
Against thee, Earl of Leicester. Strike thou home — [*baring his bosom*]
Here is no let or hindrance to thy weapon —
Strike home. I *will not* fight thee.

POLITIAN. Now's Death and Hell!
Am I not — am I not sorely — grievously tempted
To take thee at thy word? But mark me, sir!
Think not to fly me thus. Do thou prepare
For public insult in the streets — before
The eyes of the citizens. I'll follow thee —
Like an avenging spirit I'll follow thee,
Even unto death. Before those whom thou lovest —
Before all Rome, I'll taunt thee, villain — I'll taunt thee,
Dost hear? with *cowardice* — thou *wilt not* fight me?
Thou liest! thou *shalt!*
 [*Exit*]

CASTIGLIONE. Now this indeed is just!
Most righteous, and most just, avenging Heaven!

(1835–1836)

Bridal Ballad

The ring is on my hand,
 And the wreath is on my brow;
Satins and jewels grand
Are all at my command,
 And I am happy now.

And my lord he loves me well;
 But, when first he breathed his vow,
I felt my bosom swell —
For the words rang as a knell,
And the voice seemed *his* who fell
In the battle down the dell,
 And who is happy now.

But he spoke to re-assure me,
 And he kissed my pallid brow,
While a reverie came o'er me,
And to the church-yard bore me,
And I sighed to him before me
(Thinking him dead D'Elormie),
 "Oh, I am happy now!"

And thus the words were spoken,
 And this the plighted vow;
And, though my faith be broken,
And, though my heart be broken,
Here is a ring, as token
 That I am happy now! —
Behold the golden token
 That *proves* me happy now!

Would God I could awaken!
 For I dream I know not how,
And my soul is sorely shaken
Lest an evil step be taken, —
Lest the dead who is forsaken
 May not be happy now.

(1837)

Sonnet — To Zante

Fair isle, that from the fairest of all flowers
 Thy gentlest of all gentle names dost take,
How many memories of what radiant hours
 At sight of thee and thine at once awake!
How many scenes of what departed bliss!
 How many thoughts of what entombéd hopes!
How many visions of a maiden that is
 No more — no more upon thy verdant slopes!
No more! alas, that magical sad sound
 Transforming all! Thy charms shall please *no more,* —
Thy memory *no more!* Accurséd ground
 Henceforth I hold thy flower-enamelled shore,
O hyacinthine isle! O purple Zante!
"Isola d'oro! Fior di Levante!"

 (1837)

The Haunted Palace

In the greenest of our valleys
 By good angels tenanted,
Once a fair and stately palace —
 Radiant palace — reared its head.
In the monarch Thought's dominion,
 It stood there!
Never seraph spread a pinion
 Over fabric half so fair!

Banners yellow, glorious, golden,
 On its roof did float and flow
(This — all this — was in the olden
 Time long ago),
And every gentle air that dallied,
 In that sweet day,
Along the ramparts plumed and pallid,
 A wingéd odor went away.

Wanderers in that happy valley,
 Through two luminous windows, saw
Spirits moving musically,
 To a lute's well-tunéd law,
Round about a throne where, sitting,
 Porphyrogene,
In state his glory well befitting,
 The ruler of the realm was seen.

And all with pearl and ruby glowing
 Was the fair palace door,
Through which came flowing, flowing, flowing,
 And sparkling evermore,
A troop of Echoes, whose sweet duty
 Was but to sing,
In voices of surpassing beauty,
 The wit and wisdom of their king.

But evil things, in robes of sorrow,
 Assailed the monarch's high estate.
(Ah, let us mourn! — for never morrow
 Shall dawn upon him, desolate!)
And round about his home the glory
 That blushed and bloomed,
Is but a dim-remembered story
 Of the old time entombed.

And travellers, now, within that valley,
 Through the red-litten windows see
Vast forms that move fantastically
 To a discordant melody,
While, like a ghastly rapid river,
 Through the pale door
A hideous throng rush out forever,
 And laugh — but smile no more.

 (1839)

Sonnet — Silence

There are some qualities — some incorporate things,
 That have a double life, which thus is made
A type of that twin entity which springs
 From matter and light, evinced in solid and shade.

There is a two-fold *Silence* — sea and shore —
 Body and soul. One dwells in lonely places,
 Newly with grass o'ergrown; some solemn graces,
Some human memories and tearful lore,
Render him terrorless: his name's "No More."
He is the corporate Silence: dread him not!
 No power hath he of evil in himself;
But should some urgent fate (untimely lot!)
 Bring thee to meet his shadow (nameless elf,
That haunteth the lone regions where hath trod
No foot of man), commend thyself to God!

(1840)

The Conqueror Worm

Lo! 't is a gala night
 Within the lonesome latter years!
An angel throng, bewinged, bedight
 in veils, and drowned in tears,
Sit in a theatre, to see
 A play of hopes and fears,
While the orchestra breathes fitfully
 The music of the spheres.

Mimes, in the form of God on high,
 Mutter and mumble low,
And hither and thither fly —
 Mere puppets they, who come and go
At bidding of vast formless things
 That shift the scenery to and fro,
Flapping from out their Condor wings
 Invisible Wo!

That motley drama — oh, be sure
 It shall not be forgot!
With its Phantom chased for evermore
 By a crowd that seize it not,
Through a circle that ever returneth in
 To the self-same spot,
And much of Madness, and more of Sin,
 And Horror the soul of the plot.

But see, amid the mimic rout,
 A crawling shape intrude!
A blood-red thing that writhes from out
 The scenic solitude!
It writhes! — it writhes! — with mortal pangs
The mimes become its food,
And seraphs sob at vermin fangs
 In human gore imbued.

Out — out are the lights — out all!
 And, over each quivering form,
The curtain, a funeral pall,
 Comes down with the rush of a storm,
While the angels, all pallid and wan,
 Uprising, unveiling, affirm
That the play is the tragedy, "Man,"
 And its hero, the Conqueror Worm.

 (1843)

Dream-Land

By a route obscure and lonely,
Haunted by ill angels only,
Where an Eidolon, named NIGHT,
On a black throne reigns upright,
I have reached these lands but newly
From an ultimate dim Thule —
From a wild weird clime that lieth, sublime,
 Out of SPACE — out of TIME.

Bottomless vales and boundless floods,
And chasms, and caves, and Titan woods,
With forms that no man can discover
For the tears that drip all over;
Mountains toppling evermore
Into seas without a shore;
Seas that restlessly aspire,
Surging, unto skies of fire;
Lakes that endlessly outspread
Their lone waters — lone and dead, —
Their still waters — still and chilly
With the snows of the lolling lily.

By the lakes that thus outspread
Their lone waters, lone and dead, —
Their sad waters, sad and chilly
With the snows of the lolling lily, —
By the mountains — near the river
Murmuring lowly, murmuring ever, —
By the grey woods, — by the swamp
Where the toad and the newt encamp, —
By the dismal tarns and pools
 Where dwell the Ghouls, —
By each spot the most unholy —
In each nook most melancholy, —
There the traveller meets, aghast,
Sheeted Memories of the Past —
Shrouded forms that start and sigh
As they pass the wanderer by —
White-robed forms of friends long given,
In agony, to the Earth — and Heaven.

For the heart whose woes are legion
'T is a peaceful, soothing region —
For the spirit that walks in shadow
'T is — oh, 't is an Eldorado!
But the traveller, travelling through it,
May not — dare not openly view it;
Never its mysteries are exposed
To the weak human eye unclosed;
So wills its King, who hath forbid
The uplifting of the fringéd lid;
And thus the sad Soul that here passes
Beholds it but through darkened glasses.

By a route obscure and lonely,
Haunted by ill angels only,
Where an Eidolon, named NIGHT,
On a black throne reigns upright,
I have wandered home but newly
From this ultimate dim Thule.

(1844)

Edgar Allan Poe

The Raven

Once upon a midnight dreary, while I pondered, weak and weary,
Over many a quaint and curious volume of forgotten lore —
While I nodded, nearly napping, suddenly there came a tapping,
As of some one gently rapping, rapping at my chamber door.
" 'T is some visitor," I muttered, "tapping at my chamber door —
 Only this and nothing more."

Ah, distinctly I remember it was in the bleak December;
And each separate dying ember wrought its ghost upon the floor.
Eagerly I wished the morrow; — vainly I had sought to borrow
From my books surcease of sorrow — sorrow for the lost Lenore —
For the rare and radiant maiden whom the angels name Lenore —
 Nameless *here* for evermore.

And the silken, sad, uncertain rustling of each purple curtain
Thrilled me — filled me with fantastic terrors never felt before;
So that now, to still the beating of my heart, I stood repeating,
" 'T is some visitor entreating entrance at my chamber door —
Some late visitor entreating entrance at my chamber door; —
 This it is and nothing more."

Presently my soul grew stronger; hesitating then no longer,
"Sir," said I, "or Madam, truly your forgiveness I implore;
But the fact is I was napping, and so gently you came rapping,
And so faintly you came tapping, tapping at my chamber door,
That I scarce was sure I heard you" — here I opened the door; —
 Darkness there and nothing more.

Deep into that darkness peering, long I stood there wondering, fearing,
Doubting, dreaming dreams no mortal ever dared to dream before;
But the silence was unbroken, and the stillness gave no token,
And the only word there spoken was the whispered word, "Lenore?"
This I whispered, and an echo murmured back the word "Lenore!"
 Merely this and nothing more.

Back into the chamber turning, all my soul within me burning,
Soon again I heard a tapping somewhat louder than before.
"Surely," said I, "surely that is something at my window lattice;
Let me see, then, what thereat is, and this mystery explore —
Let my heart be still a moment and this mystery explore; —
 'T is the wind and nothing more!"

Open here I flung the shutter, when, with many a flirt and flutter,
In there stepped a stately Raven of the saintly days of yore;
Not the least obeisance made he; not a minute stopped or stayed he;
But, with mien of lord or lady, perched above my chamber door —
Perched upon a bust of Pallas just above my chamber door —
　　　　　Perched, and sat, and nothing more.

Then this ebony bird beguiling my sad fancy into smiling,
By the grave and stern decorum of the countenance it wore,
"Though thy crest be shorn and shaven, thou," I said, "art sure no craven,
Ghastly grim and ancient Raven wandering from the Nightly shore —
Tell me what thy lordly name is on the Night's Plutonian shore!"
　　　　　Quoth the Raven, "Nevermore."

Much I marvelled this ungainly fowl to hear discourse so plainly,
Though its answer little meaning — little relevancy bore;
For we cannot help agreeing that no living human being
Ever yet was blessed with seeing bird above his chamber door —
Bird or beast upon the sculptured bust above his chamber door,
　　　　　With such name as "Nevermore."

But the Raven, sitting lonely on the placid bust, spoke only
That one word, as if his soul in that one word he did outpour.
Nothing farther then he uttered — not a feather then he fluttered —
Till I scarcely more than muttered, "Other friends have flown before —
On the morrow *he* will leave me, as my Hopes have flown before."
　　　　　Then the bird said, "Nevermore."

Startled at the stillness broken by reply so aptly spoken,
"Doubtless," said I, "what it utters is its only stock and store
Caught from some unhappy master whom unmerciful Disaster
Followed fast and followed faster till his songs one burden bore —
Till the dirges of his Hope that melancholy burden bore
　　　　　Of 'Never — nevermore.'"

But the Raven still beguiling my sad fancy into smiling,
Straight I wheeled a cushioned seat in front of bird and bust and door;
Then, upon the velvet sinking, I betook myself to linking
Fancy unto fancy, thinking what this ominous bird of yore —
What this grim, ungainly, ghastly, gaunt, and ominous bird of yore
　　　　　Meant in croaking "Nevermore."

This I sat engaged in guessing, but no syllable expressing
To the fowl whose fiery eyes now burned into my bosom's core;
This and more I sat divining, with my head at ease reclining

On the cushion's velvet lining that the lamp-light gloated o'er,
But whose velvet-violet lining with the lamp-light gloating o'er,
 She shall press, ah, nevermore!

Then, methought, the air grew denser, perfumed from an unseen censer
Swung by seraphim whose foot-falls tinkled on the tufted floor.
"Wretch," I cried, "thy God hath lent thee — by these angels he hath
 sent thee
Respite — respite and nepenthe from thy memories of Lenore;
Quaff, oh, quaff this kind nepenthe and forget this lost Lenore!"
 Quoth the Raven, "Nevermore."

"Prophet!" said I, "thing of evil! — prophet still, if bird or devil! —
Whether Tempter sent, or whether tempest tossed thee here ashore,
Desolate yet all undaunted, on this desert land enchanted —
On this home by Horror haunted — tell me truly, I implore —
Is there — *is* there balm in Gilead? — tell me — tell me, I implore!"
 Quoth the Raven, "Nevermore."

"Prophet!" said I, "thing of evil! — prophet still, if bird or devil!
By that Heaven that bends above us — by that God we both adore —
Tell this soul with sorrow laden if, within the distant Aidenn,
It shall clasp a sainted maiden whom the angels name Lenore —
Clasp a rare and radiant maiden whom the angels name Lenore."
 Quoth the Raven, "Nevermore."

"Be that word our sign of parting, bird or fiend!" I shrieked, upstarting —
"Get thee back into the tempest and the Night's Plutonian shore!
Leave no black plume as a token of that lie thy soul hath spoken!
Leave my loneliness unbroken! — quit the bust above my door!
Take thy beak from out my heart, and take thy form from off my door!"
 Quoth the Raven, "Nevermore."

And the Raven, never flitting, still is sitting, *still* is sitting
On the pallid bust of Pallas just above my chamber door;
And his eyes have all the seeming of a demon's that is dreaming,
And the lamp-light o'er him streaming throws his shadow on the floor;
And my soul from out that shadow that lies floating on the floor
 Shall be lifted — nevermore!
 (1845)

Eulalie — A Song

I dwelt alone
In a world of moan,
And my soul was a stagnant tide,
Till the fair and gentle Eulalie became my blushing bride —
Till the yellow-haired young Eulalie became my smiling bride.

Ah, less — less bright
The stars of the night
Than the eyes of the radiant girl!
And never a flake
That the vapor can make
With the moon-tints of purple and pearl,
Can vie with the modest Eulalie's most unregarded curl —
Can compare with the bright-eyed Eulalie's most humble and careless
curl.

Now Doubt — now Pain
Come never again,
For her soul gives me sigh for sigh,
And all day long
Shines, bright and strong,
Astarte within the sky,
While ever to her dear Eulalie upturns her matron eye —
While ever to her young Eulalie upturns her violet eye.

(1845)

A Valentine

For her these lines are penned, whose luminous eyes,
 Brightly expressive as the twins of Lœda,
Shall find her own sweet name that, nestling, lies
 Upon this page, enwrapped from every reader.
Search narrowly this rhyme, which holds a treasure
 Divine — a talisman — an amulet
That must be worn at heart. Search well the measure;
 The words — the letters themselves. Do not forget
The trivialest point, or you may lose your labor.
 And yet there is in this no Gordian knot

Which one might not undo without a sabre,
 If one could merely understand the plot.
Enwritten upon this page whereon are peering
 Such eager eyes, there lies, I say, *perdu*,
A well-known name, oft uttered in the hearing
 Of poets, by poets; as the name is a poet's, too.
Its letters, although naturally lying —
 Like the knight Pinto (Mendez Ferdinando) —
Still form a synonym for truth. Cease trying!
 You will not read the riddle though you do the best you *can* do.

(1846)

To M. L. S_____

Of all who hail thy presence as the morning —
Of all to whom thine absence is the night —
The blotting utterly from out high heaven
The sacred sun — of all who, weeping, bless thee
Hourly for hope — for life — ah! above all,
For the resurrection of deep-buried faith
In Truth, in Virtue, in Humanity —
Of all who, on Despair's unhallowed bed
Lying down to die, have suddenly arisen
At thy soft-murmured words, "Let there be light!"
At the soft-murmured words that were fulfilled
In the seraphic glancing of thine eyes —
Of all who owe thee most — whose gratitude
Nearest resembles worship — oh, remember
The truest — the most fervently devoted,
And think that these weak lines are written by him —
By him who, as he pens them, thrills to think
His spirit is communing with an angel's.

(1847)

Ulalume — A Ballad

The skies they were ashen and sober;
 The leaves they were crispéd and sere —
 The leaves they were withering and sere:
It was night, in the lonesome October
 Of my most immemorial year:

It was hard by the dim lake of Auber,
 In the misty mid region of Weir —
It was down by the dank tarn of Auber,
 In the ghoul-haunted woodland of Weir.

Here once, through an alley Titanic,
 Of cypress, I roamed with my Soul —
 Of cypress, with Psyche, my Soul.
These were days when my heart was volcanic
 As the scoriac rivers that roll —
 As the lavas that restlessly roll
Their sulphurous currents down Yaanek
 In the ultimate climes of the Pole —
That groan as they roll down Mount Yaanek
 In the realms of the Boreal Pole.

Our talk had been serious and sober,
 But our thoughts they were palsied and sere —
 Our memories were treacherous and sere;
For we knew not the month was October,
 And we marked not the night of the year
 (Ah, night of all nights in the year!) —
We noted not the dim lake of Auber
 (Though once we had journeyed down here) —
We remembered not the dank tarn of Auber,
 Nor the ghoul-haunted woodland of Weir.

And now, as the night was senescent
 And star-dials pointed to morn —
 As the star-dials hinted of morn —
At the end of our path a liquescent
 And nebulous lustre was born,
Out of which a miraculous crescent
 Arose with a duplicate horn —
Astarte's bediamonded crescent
 Distinct with its duplicate horn.

And I said: "She is warmer than Dian;
 She rolls through an ether of sighs —
 She revels in a region of sighs.
She has seen that the tears are not dry on
 These cheeks, where the worm never dies,
And has come past the stars of the Lion,
 To point us the path to the skies —
 To the Lethean peace of the skies —

Come up, in despite of the Lion,
 To shine on us with her bright eyes —
Come up through the lair of the Lion,
 With love in her luminous eyes."

But Psyche, uplifting her finger,
 Said: "Sadly this star I mistrust —
 Her pallor I strangely mistrust:
Ah, hasten! — ah, let us not linger!
 Ah, fly! — let us fly! —for we must."
In terror she spoke, letting sink her
 Wings till they trailed in the dust —
In agony sobbed, letting sink her
 Plumes till they trailed in the dust —
 Till they sorrowfully trailed in the dust.

I replied: "This is nothing but dreaming:
 Let us on by this tremulous light!
 Let us bathe in this crystalline light!
Its Sibyllic splendor is beaming
 With Hope and in Beauty to-night: —
 See! — it flickers up the sky through the night!
Ah, we safely may trust to its gleaming,
 And be sure it will lead us aright —
We surely may trust to a gleaming,
 That cannot but guide us aright,
 Since it flickers up to Heaven through the night."

Thus I pacified Psyche and kissed her,
 And tempted her out of her gloom —
 And conquered her scruples and gloom;
And we passed to the end of the vista,
 But were stopped by the door of a tomb —
 By the door of a legended tomb;
And I said: "What is written, sweet sister,
 On the door of this legended tomb?"
 She replied: "Ulalume — Ulalume! —
 'T is the vault of thy lost Ulalume!"

Then my heart it grew ashen and sober
 As the leaves that were crispéd and sere —
 As the leaves that were withering and sere;
And I cried: "It was surely October
 On *this* very night of last year
 That I journeyed — I journeyed down here! —

That I brought a dread burden down here —
On this night of all nights in the year,
Ah, what demon hath tempted me here?
Well I know, now, this dim lake of Auber —
This misty mid region of Weir —
Well I know, now, this dank tarn of Auber,
This ghoul-haunted woodland of Weir."

Said we, then — the two, then: "Ah, can it
Have been that the woodlandish ghouls —
The pitiful, the merciful ghouls —
To bar up our way and to ban it
From the secret that lies in these wolds —
From the thing that lies hidden in these wolds —
Have drawn up the spectre of a planet
From the limbo of lunary souls —
This sinfully scintillant planet
From the Hell of the planetary souls?"

(1847)

An Enigma

"Seldom we find," says Solomon Don Dunce,
"Half an idea in the profoundest sonnet.
Through all the flimsy things we see at once
As easily as through a Naples bonnet —
Trash of all trash! — how *can* a lady don it?
Yet heavier far than your Petrarchan stuff —
Owl-downy nonsense that the faintest puff
Twirls into trunk-paper the while you con it."
And, veritably, Sol is right enough.
The general tuckermanities are arrant
Bubbles — ephemeral and *so* transparent —
But *this* is, now, — you may depend upon it —
Stable, opaque, immortal — all by dint
Of the dear names that lie concealed within 't.

(1848)

To _____ _____ _____

Not long ago, the writer of these lines,
In the mad pride of intellectuality,
Maintained "the power of words" — denied that ever
A thought arose within the human brain
Beyond the utterance of the human tongue;
And now, as if in mockery of that boast,
Two words — two foreign soft dissyllables —
Italian tones made only to be murmured
By angels dreaming in the moonlit "dew
That hangs like chains of pearl on Hermon hill" —
Have stirred from out the abysses of his heart,
Unthought-like thoughts that are the souls of thought,
Richer, far wilder, far diviner visions
Than even the seraph harper, Israfel,
Who has "the sweetest voice of all God's creatures,"
Could hope to utter. And I! my spells are broken.
The pen falls powerless from my shivering hand.
With thy dear name as text, though bidden by thee,
I cannot write — I cannot speak or think,
Alas, I cannot feel; for 't is not feeling,
This standing motionless upon the golden
Threshold of the wide-open gate of dreams,
Gazing, entranced, adown the gorgeous vista,
And thrilling as I see upon the right,
Upon the left, and all the way along
Amid empurpled vapors, far away
To where the prospect terminates — *thee only.*

 (1848)

To Helen

I saw thee once — once only — years ago:
I must not say *how* many — but *not* many.
It was a July midnight; and from out
A full-orbed moon, that, like thine own soul, soaring,
Sought a precipitate pathway up through heaven,
There fell a silvery-silken veil of light,
With quietude, and sultriness, and slumber,

Upon the upturn'd faces of a thousand
Roses that grew in an enchanted garden,
Where no wind dared to stir, unless on tiptoe —
Fell on the upturn'd faces of these roses
That gave out, in return for the love-light,
Their odorous souls in an ecstatic death —
Fell on the upturn'd faces of these roses
That smiled and died in this parterre, enchanted
By thee, and by the poetry of thy presence.

Clad all in white, upon a violet bank
I saw thee half reclining; while the moon
Fell on the upturn'd faces of the roses,
And on thine own, upturn'd — alas, in sorrow!

Was it not Fate that, on this July midnight —
Was it not Fate (whose name is also Sorrow)
That bade me pause before that garden-gate,
To breathe the incense of those slumbering roses?
No footstep stirred: the hated world all slept,
Save only thee and me. (Oh, Heaven! — oh, God!
How my heart beats in coupling those two words!
Save only thee and me). I paused — I looked —
And in an instant all things disappeared.
(Ah, bear in mind this garden was enchanted!)
The pearly lustre of the moon went out:
The mossy banks and the meandering paths,
The happy flowers and the repining trees,
Were seen no more: the very roses' odors
Died in the arms of the adoring airs.
All — all expired save thee — save less than thou:
Save only the divine light in thine eyes —
Save but the soul in thine uplifted eyes.
I saw but them — they were the world to me.
I saw but them — saw only them for hours —
Saw only them until the moon went down.
What wild heart-histories seemed to lie enwritten
Upon those crystalline, celestial spheres!
How dark a wo! yet how sublime a hope!
How silently serene a sea of pride!
How daring an ambition! yet how deep —
How fathomless a capacity for love!

But now, at length, dear Dian sank from sight,
Into a western couch of thunder-cloud;

And thou, a ghost, amid the entombing trees
Didst glide away. *Only thine eyes remained*.
They *would not* go — they never yet have gone.
Lighting my lonely pathway home that night,
They have not left me (as my hopes have) since.
They follow me — they lead me through the years.
They are my ministers — yet I their slave.
Their office is to illumine and enkindle —
My duty, *to be saved* by their bright light,
And purified in their electric fire,
And sanctified in their elysian fire.
They fill my soul with Beauty (which is Hope),
And are far up in Heaven — the stars I kneel to
In the sad, silent watches of my night;
While even in the meridian glare of day
I see them still — two sweetly scintillant
Venuses, unextinguished by the sun!

(1848)

Eldorado

Gaily bedight,
A gallant knight,
In sunshine and in shadow,
Had journeyed long,
Singing a song,
In search of Eldorado.

But he grew old —
This knight so bold —
And o'er his heart a shadow
Fell as he found
No spot of ground
That looked like Eldorado.

And, as his strength
Failed him at length,
He met a pilgrim shadow —
'Shadow,' said he,
'Where can it be —
This land of Eldorado?'

'Over the Mountains
Of the Moon,
Down the Valley of the Shadow,
Ride, boldly ride,'
The shade replied, —
'If you seek for Eldorado!'

(1849)

For Annie

Thank Heaven! the crisis,
The danger, is past,
And the lingering illness
Is over at last —
And the fever called "Living"
Is conquered at last.

Sadly, I know
I am shorn of my strength,
And no muscle I move
As I lie at full length —
But no matter! — I feel
I am better at length.

And I rest so composedly,
Now, in my bed,
That any beholder
Might fancy me dead —
Might start at beholding me,
Thinking me dead.

The moaning and groaning,
The sighing and sobbing,
Are quieted now,
With that horrible throbbing
At heart: — ah, that horrible,
Horrible throbbing!

The sickness — the nausea —
The pitiless pain —
Have ceased, with the fever
That maddened my brain —
With fever called "Living"
That burned in my brain.

And oh! of all tortures
 That torture the worst
Has abated — the terrible
 Torture of thirst
For the naphthaline river
 Of Passion accurst: —
I have drank of a water
 That quenches all thirst: —

Of a water that flows,
 With a lullaby sound,
From a spring but a very few
 Feet under ground —
From a cavern not very far
 Down under ground.

And ah! let it never
 Be foolishly said
That my room it is gloomy
 And narrow my bed;
For man never slept
 In a different bed —
And, to *sleep*, you must slumber
 In just such a bed.

My tantalized spirit
 Here blandly reposes,
Forgetting, or never
 Regretting, its roses —
Its old agitations
 Of myrtles and roses:

For now, while so quietly
 Lying, it fancies
A holier odor
 About it, of pansies —
A rosemary odor,
 Commingled with pansies —
With rue and the beautiful
 Puritan pansies.

And so it lies happily,
 Bathing in many
A dream of the truth
 And the beauty of Annie —
Drowned in a bath
 Of the tresses of Annie.

She tenderly kissed me,
 She fondly caressed,
And then I fell gently
 To sleep on her breast —
Deeply to sleep
 From the heaven of her breast.

When the light was extinguished,
 She covered me warm,
And she prayed to the angels
 To keep me from harm —
To the queen of the angels
 To shield me from harm.

And I lie so composedly,
 Now, in my bed
(Knowing her love),
 That you fancy me dead —
And I rest so contentedly,
 Now, in my bed
(With her love at my breast),
 That you fancy me dead —
That you shudder to look at me,
 Thinking me dead: —

But my heart it is brighter
 Than all of the many
Stars of the heaven,
 For it sparkles with Annie —
It glows with the fire
 Of the love of my Annie —
With the thought of the light
 Of the eyes of my Annie.

 (1849)

Sonnet — To My Mother

Because I feel that, in the Heavens above,
 The angels, whispering to one another,
Can find, among their burning terms of love,
 None so devotional as that of "Mother,"
Therefore by that sweet name I long have called you —
 You who are more than mother unto me,

And fill my heart of hearts, where Death installed you
 In setting my Virginia's spirit free.
My mother — my own mother, who died early,
 Was but the mother of myself; but you
Are mother to the one I loved so dearly,
 And thus are dearer than the mother I knew
By that infinity with which my wife
 Was dearer to my soul than its soul-life.

(1849)

Annabel Lee

It was many and many a year ago,
 In a kingdom by the sea,
That a maiden there lived whom you may know
 By the name of Annabel Lee; —
And this maiden she lived with no other thought
 Than to love and be loved by me.

She was a child and *I* was a child,
 In this kingdom by the sea,
But we loved with a love that was more than love —
 I and my Annabel Lee —
With a love that the wingéd seraphs of Heaven
 Coveted her and me.

And this was the reason that, long ago,
 In this kingdom by the sea,
A wind blew out of a cloud by night
 Chilling my Annabel Lee;
So that her highborn kinsmen came
 And bore her away from me,
To shut her up in a sepulchre
 In this kingdom by the sea.

The angels, not half so happy in Heaven,
 Went envying her and me: —
Yes! that was the reason (as all men know,
 In this kingdom by the sea)
That the wind came out of a cloud, chilling
 And killing my Annabel Lee.

But our love it was stronger by far than the love
　　Of those who were older than we —
　　Of many far wiser than we —
And neither the angels in Heaven above
　　Nor the demons down under the sea,
Can ever dissever my soul from the soul
　　Of the beautiful Annabel Lee: —

For the moon never beams without bringing me dreams
　　Of the beautiful Annabel Lee;
And the stars never rise but I see the bright eyes
　　Of the beautiful Annabel Lee;
And so, all the night-tide, I lie down by the side
Of my darling, my darling, my life and my bride,
　　In her sepulchre there by the sea —
　　In her tomb by the side of the sea.

　　　　　　　　　　　　　　　　　　　　(1849)

The Bells

I

　　Hear the sledges with the bells —
　　　　Silver bells!
What a world of merriment their melody foretells!
　　How they tinkle, tinkle, tinkle,
　　　　In the icy air of night!
　　While the stars that oversprinkle
　　All the heavens, seem to twinkle
　　　　With a crystalline delight;
　　　　Keeping time, time, time,
　　　　In a sort of Runic rhyme,
To the tintinnabulation that so musically wells
　　From the bells, bells, bells, bells,
　　　　Bells, bells, bells —
　　From the jingling and the tinkling of the bells.

II

　　Hear the mellow wedding bells —
　　　　Golden bells!
What a world of happiness their harmony foretells!
　　　Through the balmy air of night
　　　How they ring out their delight! —

From the molten-golden notes,
And all in tune,
What a liquid ditty floats
To the turtle-dove that listens, while she gloats
On the moon!
Oh, from out the sounding cells,
What a gush of euphony voluminously wells!
How it swells!
How it dwells
On the Future! — how it tells
Of the rapture that impels
To the swinging and the ringing
Of the bells, bells, bells —
Of the bells, bells, bells, bells,
Bells, bells, bells —
To the rhyming and the chiming of the bells!

III

Hear the loud alarum bells —
Brazen bells!
What a tale of terror, now, their turbulency tells!
In the startled ear of night
How they scream out their affright!
Too much horrified to speak,
They can only shriek, shriek,
Out of tune,
In a clamorous appealing to the mercy of the fire,
In a mad expostulation with the deaf and frantic fire,
Leaping higher, higher, higher,
With a desperate desire,
And a resolute endeavor
Now — now to sit, or never,
By the side of the pale-faced moon.
Oh, the bells, bells, bells!
What a tale their terror tells
Of Despair!
How they clang, and clash, and roar!
What a horror they outpour
On the bosom of the palpitating air!
Yet the ear, it fully knows,
By the twanging
And the clanging,
How the danger ebbs and flows;
Yet the ear distinctly tells,

In the jangling
And the wrangling,
How the danger sinks and swells,
By the sinking or the swelling in the anger of the bells —
Of the bells, —
Of the bells, bells, bells, bells,
Bells, bells, bells —
In the clamor and the clangor of the bells!

IV

Hear the tolling of the bells —
Iron bells!
What a world of solemn thought their monody compels!
In the silence of the night,
How we shiver with affright
At the melancholy menace of their tone!
For every sound that floats
From the rust within their throats
Is a groan.
And the people — ah, the people —
They that dwell up in the steeple,
All alone,
And who tolling, tolling, tolling,
In that muffled monotone,
Feel a glory in so rolling
On the human heart a stone —
They are neither man nor woman —
They are neither brute nor human —
They are Ghouls: —
And their king it is who tolls: —
And he rolls, rolls, rolls,
Rolls
A pæan from the bells!
And his merry bosom swells
With the pæan of the bells!
And he dances, and he yells;
Keeping time, time, time,
In a sort of Runic rhyme,
To the pæan of the bells —
Of the bells: —
Keeping time, time, time,
In a sort of Runic rhyme,
To the throbbing of the bells —
Of the bells, bells, bells —
To the sobbing of the bells;

Keeping time, time, time,
 As he knells, knells, knells,
In a happy Runic rhyme,
 To the rolling of the bells —
Of the bells, bells, bells: —
 To the tolling of the bells —
Of the bells, bells, bells, bells,
 Bells, bells, bells —
To the moaning and the groaning of the bells.

(1849)

UNCOLLECTED VERSES

Elizabeth

Elizabeth, it surely is most fit
[Logic and common usage so commanding]
In thy own book that *first* thy name be writ,
Zeno and other sages notwithstanding;
And *I* have other reasons for so doing
Besides my innate love of contradiction;
Each poet — *if* a poet — in pursuing
The muses thro' their bowers of Truth or Fiction,
Has studied very little of his part,
Read nothing, written less — in short's a fool
Endued with neither soul, nor sense, nor art,
Being ignorant of one important rule,
Employed in even the theses of the school —
Called — I forget the heathenish Greek name —
[Called anything, its meaning is the same]
"Always write *first* things uppermost in the heart."

Serenade

So sweet the hour, so calm the time,
I feel it more than half a crime,
When Nature sleeps and stars are mute,
To mar the silence ev'n with lute.
At rest on ocean's brilliant dyes
An image of Elysium lies:

Serenade

Seven Pleiades entranced in Heaven,
Form in the deep another seven:
Endymion nodding from above
Sees in the sea a second love.
Within the valleys dim and brown,
And on the spectral mountain's crown,
The wearied light is dying down,
And earth, and stars, and sea, and sky
Are redolent of sleep, as I
Am redolent of thee and thine
Enthralling love, my Adeline.
But list, O list, — so soft and low
Thy lover's voice tonight shall flow,
That, scarce awake, thy soul shall deem
My words the music of a dream.
Thus, while no single sound too rude
Upon thy slumber shall intrude,
Our thoughts, our souls — O God above!
In every deed shall mingle, love.

III

TALES

Metzengerstein

Pestis eram vivus — moriens tua mors ero. MARTIN LUTHER

HORROR and fatality have been stalking abroad in all ages. Why then give a date to this story I have to tell? Let it suffice to say, that at the period of which I speak, there existed, in the interior of Hungary, a settled although hidden belief in the doctrines of the Metempsychosis. Of the doctrines themselves — that is, of their falsity, or of their probability — I say nothing. I assert, however, that much of our incredulity — as La Bruyere says of all our unhappiness — *"vient de ne pouvoir etre seuls."*

But there are some points in the Hungarian superstition which were fast verging to absurdity. They — the Hungarians — differed very essentially from their Eastern authorities. For example, *"The soul,"* said the

former — I give the words of an acute and intelligent Parisian — *"ne demeure qu'un seul fois dans un corps sensible: au reste — un cheval, un chien, un homme même, n'est que la ressemblance peu tangible de ces animaux."*

The families of Berlifitzing and Metzengerstein had been at variance for centuries. Never before were two houses so illustrious, mutually embittered by hostility so deadly. Indeed at the era of this history, it was observed by an old crone of haggard and sinister appearance, that "fire and water might sooner mingle than a Berlifitzing clasp the hand of a Metzengerstein." The origin of this enmity seems to be found in the words of an ancient prophecy — "A lofty name shall have a fearful fall when, as the rider over his horse, the mortality of Metzengerstein shall triumph over the immortality of Berlifitzing."

To be sure the words themselves had little or no meaning. But more trivial causes have given rise — and that no long while ago — to consequences equally eventful. Besides, the estates, which were contiguous, had long exercised a rival influence in the affairs of a busy government. Moreover, near neighbors are seldom friends; and the inhabitants of the Castle Berlifitzing might look, from their lofty buttresses, into the very windows of the palace Metzengerstein. Least of all had the more than feudal magnificence, thus discovered, a tendency to allay the irritable feelings of the less ancient and less wealthy Berlifitzings. What wonder then, that the words, however silly, of that prediction, should have succeeded in setting and keeping at variance two families already predisposed to quarrel by every instigation of hereditary jealousy? The prophecy seemed to imply — if it implied anything — a final triumph on the part of the already more powerful house; and was of course remembered with the more bitter animosity by the weaker and less influential.

Wilhelm, Count Berlifitzing, although loftily descended, was, at the epoch of this narrative, an infirm and doting old man, remarkable for nothing but an inordinate and inveterate personal antipathy to the family of his rival, and so passionate a love of horses, and of hunting, that neither bodily infirmity, great age, nor mental incapacity, prevented his daily participation in the dangers of the chase.

Frederick, Baron Metzengerstein, was, on the other hand, not yet of age. His father, the Minister G——, died young. His mother, the Lady Mary, followed him quickly after. Frederick was, at that time, in his fifteenth year. In a city, fifteen years are no long period — a child may be still a child in his third lustrum: but in a wilderness — in so magnificent a wilderness as that old principality, fifteen years have a far deeper meaning.

The beautiful Lady Mary! How *could* she die? — and of consumption! But it is a path I have prayed to follow. I would wish all I love to perish of that gentle disease. How glorious — to depart in the heyday of the young blood — the heart of all passion — the imagination all fire — amid

the remembrances of happier days — in the fall of the year — and so be buried up forever in the gorgeous autumnal leaves!

Thus died the Lady Mary. The young Baron Frederick stood without a living relative by the coffin of his dead mother. He placed his hand upon her placid forehead. No shudder came over his delicate frame — no sigh from his flinty bosom. Heartless, self-willed and impetuous from his childhood, he had reached the age of which I speak through a career of unfeeling, wanton, and reckless dissipation; and a barrier had long since arisen in the channel of all holy thoughts and gentle recollections.

From some peculiar circumstances attending the administration of his father, the young Baron, at the decease of the former, entered immediately upon his vast possessions. Such estates were seldom held before by a nobleman of Hungary. His castles were without number. The chief in point of splendor and extent. was the "Chateau Metzengerstein." The boundary line of his dominions was never clearly defined; but his principal park embraced a circuit of fifty miles.

Upon the succession of a proprietor so young, with a character so well known, to a fortune so unparalleled, little speculation was afloat in regard to his probable course of conduct. And, indeed, for the space of three days, the behavior of the heir out-heroded Herod, and fairly surpassed the expectations of his most enthusiastic admirers. Shameful debaucheries — flagrant treacheries — unheard-of atrocities — gave his trembling vassals quickly to understand that no servile submission on their part — no punctilios of conscience on his own — were thenceforward to prove any security against the remorseless fangs of a petty Caligula. On the night of the fourth day, the stables of the castle Berlifitzing were discovered to be on fire; and the unanimous opinion of the neighborhood added the crime of the incendiary to the already hideous list of the Baron's misdemeanors and enormities.

But during the tumult occasioned by this occurrence, the young nobleman himself sat apparently buried in meditation, in a vast and desolate upper apartment of the family palace of Metzengerstein. The rich although faded tapestry hangings which swung gloomily upon the walls, represented the shadowy and majestic forms of a thousand illustrious ancestors. *Here,* rich-ermined priests, and pontifical dignitaries, familiarly seated with the autocrat and the sovereign, put a veto on the wishes of a temporal king, or restrained with the fiat of papal supremacy the rebellious sceptre of the Arch-enemy. *There,* the dark, tall statures of the Princes Metzengerstein — their muscular war-coursers plunging over the carcasses of fallen foes — startled the steadiest nerves with their vigorous expression; and *here,* again, the voluptuous and swan-like figures of the dames of days gone by, floated away in the mazes of an unreal dance to the strains of imaginary melody.

But as the Baron listened, or affected to listen, to the gradually increasing uproar in the stables of Berlifitzing — or perhaps pondered upon

some more novel, some more decided act of audacity — his eyes became unwittingly rivetted to the figure of an enormous, and unnaturally colored horse, represented in the tapestry as belonging to a Saracen ancestor of the family of his rival. The horse itself, in the foreground of the design, stood motionless and statue-like — while farther back, its discomfited rider perished by the dagger of a Metzengerstein.

On Frederick's lip arose a fiendish expression, as he became aware of the direction which his glance had, without his consciousness, assumed. Yet he did not remove it. On the contrary, he could by no means account for the overwhelming anxiety which appeared falling like a pall upon his senses. It was with difficulty that he reconciled his dreamy and incoherent feelings with the certainty of being awake. The longer he gazed the more absorbing became the spell — the more impossible did it appear that he could ever withdraw his glance from the fascination of that tapestry. But the tumult without becoming suddenly more violent, with a compulsory exertion he diverted his attention to the glare of ruddy light thrown full by the flaming stables upon the windows of the apartment.

The action, however, was but momentary; his gaze returned mechanically to the wall. To his extreme horror and astonishment, the head of the gigantic steed had, in the meantime, altered its position. The neck of the animal, before arched, as if in compassion, over the prostrate body of its lord, was now extended, at full length, in the direction of the Baron. The eyes, before invisible, now wore an energetic and human expression, while they gleamed with a fiery and unusual red; and the distended lips of the apparently enraged horse left in full view his gigantic and disgusting teeth.

Stupefied with terror, the young nobleman tottered to the door. As he threw it open, a flash of red light, streaming far into the chamber, flung his shadow with a clear outline against the quivering tapestry; and he shuddered to perceive that shadow — as he staggered awhile upon the threshold — assuming the exact position, and precisely filling up the contour, of the relentless and triumphant murderer of the Saracen Berlifitzing.

To lighten the depression of his spirits, the Baron hurried into the open air. At the principal gate of the palace he encountered three equerries. With much difficulty, and at the imminent peril of their lives, they were restraining the convulsive plunges of a gigantic and fiery-colored horse.

"Whose horse? Where did you get him?" demanded the youth, in a querulous and husky tone of voice, as he became instantly aware that the mysterious steed in the tapestried chamber was the very counterpart of the furious animal before his eyes.

"He is your own property, sire," replied one of the equerries, "at least

he is claimed by no other owner. We caught him flying, all smoking and foaming with rage, from the burning stables of the Castle Berlifitzing. Supposing him to have belonged to the old Count's stud of foreign horses, we led him back as an estray. But the grooms there disclaim any title to the creature; which is strange, since he bears evident marks of having made a narrow escape from the flames.

"The letters W. V. B. are also branded very distinctly on his forehead," interrupted a second equerry; "I supposed them, of course, to be the initials of Wilhelm Von Berlifitzing — but all at the castle are positive in denying any knowledge of the horse."

"Extremely singular!" said the young Baron, with a musing air, and apparently unconscious of the meaning of his words. "He is, as you say, a remarkable horse — a prodigious horse! although, as you very justly observe, of a suspicious and untractable character; let him be mine, however," he added, after a pause, "perhaps a rider like Frederick of Metzengerstein, may tame even the devil from the stables of Berlifitzing."

"You are mistaken, my lord; the horse, as I think we mentioned, is *not* from the stables of the Count. If such had been the case, we know our duty better than to bring him into the presence of a noble of your family."

"True!" observed the Baron, dryly; and at that instant a page of the bedchamber came from the palace with a heightened color, and a precipitate step. He whispered into his master's ear an account of the sudden disappearance of a small portion of the tapestry, in an apartment which he designated; entering, at the same time, into particulars of a minute and circumstantial character; but from the low tone of voice in which these latter were communicated, nothing escaped to gratify the excited curiosity of the equerries.

The young Frederick, during the conference, seemed agitated by a variety of emotions. He soon, however, recovered his composure, and an expression of determined malignancy settled upon his countenance, as he gave peremptory orders that a certain chamber should be immediately locked up, and the key placed in his own possession.

"Have you heard of the unhappy death of the old hunter Berlifitzing?" said one of his vassals to the Baron, as, after the departure of the page, the huge steed which that nobleman had adopted as his own, plunged and curvetted, with redoubled fury, down the long avenue which extended from the chateau to the stables of Metzengerstein.

"No!" said the Baron, turning abruptly toward the speaker, "dead! say you?"

"It is indeed true, my lord; and, to a noble of your name, will be, I imagine, no unwelcome intelligence."

A rapid smile shot over the countenance of the listener. "How died he?"

"In his rash exertions to rescue a favorite portion of his hunting stud, he has himself perished miserably in the flames."

"I—n—d—e—e—d—!" ejaculated the Baron, as if slowly and deliberately impressed with the truth of some exciting idea.

"Indeed;" repeated the vassal.

"Shocking!" said the youth, calmly, and turned quietly into the chateau.

From this date a marked alteration took place in the outward demeanor of the dissolute young Baron Frederick Von Metzengerstein. Indeed, his behavior disappointed every expectation, and proved little in accordance with the views of many a manœuvering mamma; while his habits and manner, still less than formerly, offered any thing congenial with those of the neighboring aristocracy. He was never to be seen beyond the limits of his own domain, and, in this wide and social world, was utterly companionless — unless, indeed, that unnatural, impetuous, and fiery-colored horse, which he henceforward continually bestrode, had any mysterious right to the title of his friend.

Numerous invitations on the part of the neighborhood for a long time, however, periodically came in. "Will the Baron honor our festivals with his presence?" "Will the Baron join us in a hunting of the boar?" — "Metzengerstein does not hunt;" "Metzengerstein will not attend," were the haughty and laconic answers.

These repeated insults were not to be endured by an imperious nobility. Such invitations became less cordial — less frequent — in time they ceased altogether. The widow of the unfortunate Count Berlifitzing was even heard to express a hope "that the Baron might be at home when he did not wish to be at home, since he disdained the company of his equals; and ride when he did not wish to ride, since he preferred the society of a horse." This to be sure was a very silly explosion of hereditary pique; and merely proved how singularly unmeaning our sayings are apt to become, when we desire to be unusually energetic.

The charitable, nevertheless, attributed the alteration in the conduct of the young nobleman to the natural sorrow of a son for the untimely loss of his parents — forgetting, however, his atrocious and reckless behavior during the short period immediately succeeding that bereavement. Some there were, indeed, who suggested a too haughty idea of self-consequence and dignity. Others again (among them may be mentioned the family physician) did not hesitate in speaking of morbid melancholy, and hereditary ill-health; while dark hints, of a more equivocal nature, were current among the multitude.

Indeed, the Baron's perverse attachment to his lately-acquired charger — an attachment which seemed to attain new strength from every fresh example of the animal's ferocious and demon-like propensities — at length became, in the eyes of all reasonable men, a hideous and unnatural fervor. In the glare of noon — at the dead hour of night — in sickness or

in health — in calm or in tempest — the young Metzengerstein seemed rivetted to the saddle of that colossal horse, whose intractable audacities so well accorded with his own spirit.

There were circumstances, moreover, which coupled with late events, gave an unearthly and portentous character to the mania of the rider, and to the capabilities of the steed. The space passed over in a single leap had been accurately measured, and was found to exceed, by an astounding difference, the wildest expectations of the most imaginative. The Baron, besides, had no particular *name* for the animal, although all the rest in his collection were distinguished by characteristic appellations. His stable, too, was appointed at a distance from the rest; and with regard to grooming and other necessary offices, none but the owner in person had ventured to officiate, or even to enter the enclosure of that particular stall. It was also to be observed, that although the three grooms, who had caught the steed as he fled from the conflagration at Berlifitzing, had succeeded in arresting his course, by means of a chain-bridle and noose — yet no one of the three could with any certainty affirm that he had, during that dangerous struggle, or at any period thereafter, actually placed his hand upon the body of the beast. Instances of peculiar intelligence in the demeanor of a noble and high-spirited horse are not to be supposed capable of exciting unreasonable attention — especially among men who, daily trained to the labors of the chase, might appear well acquainted with the sagacity of a horse — but there were certain circumstances which intruded themselves per force upon the most skeptical and phlegmatic; and it is said there were times when the animal caused the gaping crowd who stood around to recoil in horror from the deep and impressive meaning of his terrible stamp — times when the young Metzengerstein turned pale and shrunk away from the rapid and searching expression of his earnest and human-looking eye.

Among all the retinue of the Baron, however, none were found to doubt the ardor of that extraordinary affection which existed on the part of the young nobleman for the fiery qualities of his horse; at least, none but an insignificant and misshapen little page, whose deformities were in everybody's way, and whose opinions were of the least possible importance. He — if his ideas are worth mentioning at all — had the effrontery to assert that his master never vaulted into the saddle without an unaccountable and almost imperceptible shudder; and that, upon his return from every long-continued and habitual ride, an expression of triumphant malignity distorted every muscle in his countenance.

One tempestuous night, Metzengerstein, awaking from a heavy slumber, descended like a maniac from his chamber, and, mounting in hot haste, bounded away into the mazes of the forest. An occurrence so common attracted no particular attention, but his return was looked for with intense anxiety on the part of his domestics, when, after some hours' absence. the stupendous and magnificent battlements of the Chateau

Metzengerstein, were discovered crackling and rocking to their very foundation, under the influence of a dense and livid mass of ungovernable fire.

As the flames, when first seen, had already made so terrible a progress that all efforts to save any portion of the building were evidently futile, the astonished neighborhood stood idly around in silent and pathetic wonder. But a new and fearful object soon rivetted the attention of the multitude, and proved how much more intense is the excitement wrought in the feelings of a crowd by the contemplation of human agony, than that brought about by the most appalling spectacles of inanimate matter.

Up the long avenue of aged oaks which led from the forest to the main entrance of the Chateau Metzengerstein, a steed, bearing an unbonneted and disordered rider, was seen leaping with an impetuosity which outstripped the very Demon of the Tempest, and extorted from every stupefied beholder the ejaculation — "horrible."

The career of the horseman was indisputably, on his own part, uncontrollable. The agony of his countenance, the convulsive struggle of his frame, gave evidence of superhuman exertion: but no sound, save a solitary shriek, escaped from his lacerated lips, which were bitten through and through in the intensity of terror. One instant, and the clattering of hoofs resounded sharply and shrilly above the roaring of the flames and the shrieking of the winds — another, and, clearing at a single plunge the gate-way and the moat, the steed bounded far up the tottering staircases of the palace, and, with its rider, disappeared amid the whirlwind of chaotic fire.

The fury of the tempest immediately died away, and a dead calm sullenly succeeded. A white flame still enveloped the building like a shroud, and, streaming far away into the quiet atmosphere, shot forth a glare of preternatural light; while a cloud of smoke settled heavily over the battlements in the distinct colossal figure of — a horse.

The Duc De L'Omelette

And stepped at once into a cooler clime. COWPER

K EATS fell by a criticism. Who was it died of *"The Andromache"*? *
Ignoble souls! — De L'Omelette perished of an ortolan. *L'histoire en est brève*. Assist me, Spirit of Apicius!

* Montfleury. The author of the *Parnasse Réformé* makes him thus speak in Hades: — "*L'homme donc qui voudrait savoir ce dont Je suis mort, qu'il ne de-mande pas si'l fût de fievre ou de podagre ou d'autre chose, mais qui'l entende que ce fut de 'L'Andromache.'*"

A golden cage bore the little winged wanderer, enamored, melting, indolent, to the *Chaussée D'Antin*, from its home in far Peru. From its queenly possessor La Bellissima, to the Duc De L'Omelette, six peers of the empire conveyed the happy bird.

That night the Duc was to sup alone. In the privacy of his bureau he reclined languidly on that ottoman for which he sacrificed his loyalty in outbidding his king — the notorious ottoman of Cadêt.

He buries his face in the pillow. The clock strikes! Unable to restrain his feelings, his Grace swallows an olive. At this moment the door gently opens to the sound of soft music, and lo! the most delicate of birds is before the most enamored of men! But what inexpressible dismay now overshadows the countenance of the Duc? — "Horreur! — chien! — Baptiste! — l'oiseau! ah, bon Dieu! cet oiseau modeste que tu as deshabillé de ses plumes, et que tu as servi sans papier!" It is superfluous to say more: — the Duc expired in a paroxysm of disgust.* * *

"Ha! ha! ha!" said his Grace on the third day after his decease.

"He! he! he!" replied the Devil faintly, drawing himself up with an air of *hauteur*.

"Why, surely you are not serious," retorted De L'Omelette. "I have sinned — *c'est vrai* — but, my good sir, consider! — you have no actual intention of putting such — such barbarous threats into execution."

"No *what?*" said his majesty — "come, sir, strip!"

"Strip, indeed! very pretty i' faith! no, sir, I shall *not* strip. Who are you, pray, that I, Duc De L'Omelette, Prince de Foie-Gras, just come of age, author of the 'Mazurkiad,' and Member of the Academy, should divest myself at your bidding of the sweetest pantaloons ever made by Bourdon, the daintiest *robe-de-chambre* ever put together by Rombert — to say nothing of the taking my hair out of paper — not to mention the trouble I should have in drawing off my gloves?"

"Who am I? — ah, true! I am Baal-Zebub, Prince of the Fly. I took thee, just now, from a rose-wood coffin inlaid with ivory. Thou wast curiously scented, and labelled as per invoice. Belial sent thee, — my Inspector of Cemeteries. The pantaloons, which thou sayest were made by Bourdon, are an excellent pair of linen drawers, and thy *robe-de-chambre* is a shroud of no scanty dimensions."

"Sir!" replied the Duc, "I am not to be insulted with impunity! — Sir! I shall take the earliest opportunity of avenging this insult! — Sir! you shall hear from me! In the meantime *au revoir!*" — and the Duc was bowing himself out of the Satanic presence, when he was interrupted and brought back by a gentleman in waiting. Hereupon his Grace rubbed his eyes, yawned, shrugged his shoulders, reflected. Having become satisfied of his identity, he took a bird's eye view of his whereabouts.

The apartment was superb. Even De L'Omelette pronounced it *bien comme il faut*. It was not its length nor its breadth, — but its height — ah, that was appalling! — There was no ceiling — certainly none — but a

dense whirling mass of fiery-colored clouds. His Grace's brain reeled as he glanced upward. From above, hung a chain of an unknown blood-red metal — its upper end lost, like the city of Boston, *parmi les nues*. From its nether extremity swung a large cresset. The Duc knew it to be a ruby; but from it there poured a light so intense, so still, so terrible, Persia never worshipped such — Gheber never imagined such — Mussulman never dreamed of such when, drugged with opium, he has tottered to a bed of poppies, his back to the flowers, and his face to the God Apollo. The Duc muttered a slight oath, decidedly approbatory.

The corners of the room were rounded into niches. Three of these were filled with statues of gigantic proportions. Their beauty was Grecian, their deformity Egyptian, their *tout ensemble* French. In the fourth niche the statue was veiled; it was *not* colossal. But then there was a taper ankle, a sandalled foot. De L'Omelette pressed his hand upon his heart, closed his eyes, raised them, and caught his Satanic Majesty — in a blush.

But the paintings! — Kupris! Astarte! Astoreth! — a thousand and the same! And Rafaelle has beheld them! Yes, Rafaelle has been here; for did he not paint the——? and was he not consequently damned? The paintings — the paintings! O luxury! O love! — who, gazing on those forbidden beauties, shall have eyes for the dainty devices of the golden frames that besprinkled, like stars, the hyacinth and the porphyry walls?

But the Duc's heart is fainting within him. He is not, however, as you suppose, dizzy with magnificence, nor drunk with the ecstatic breath of those innumerable censers. *C'est vrai que de toutes ces choses il a pensé beaucoup — mais!* The Duc De L'Omelette is terror-stricken; for, through the lurid vista which a single uncurtained window is affording, lo! gleams the most ghastly of all fires!

Le pauvre Duc! He could not help imagining that the glorious, the voluptuous, the never-dying melodies which pervaded that hall, as they passed filtered and transmuted through the alchemy of the enchanted window-panes, were the wailings and the howlings of the hopeless and the damned! And there, too! — there! — upon the ottoman! — who could *he* be? — he, the *petitmaître* — no, the Deity — who sat as if carved in marble, *et qui sourit*, with his pale countenance, *si amérement?*

Mais il faut agir — that is to say, a Frenchman never faints outright. Besides, his Grace hated a scene — De L'Omelette is himself again. There were some foils upon a table — some points also. The Duc had studied under B——; *il avait tué ses six hommes*. Now, then, *il peut s'échapper*. He measures two points, and, with a grace inimitable, offers his Majesty the choice. *Horreur!* his Majesty does not fence!

Mais il joue! — how happy a thought! — but his Grace had always an excellent memory. He had dipped in the "*Diable*" of Abbé Gualtier. Therein it is said "*que le Diable n'ose pas refuser un jeu d'écarté.*"

But the chances — the chances! True — desperate: but scarcely more desperate than the Duc. Besides, was he not in the secret? — had he not

skimmed over Père Le Brun? — was he not a member of the Club Vingt-un? *"Si je perds,"* said he, *"je serai deux fois perdu* — I shall be doubly dammed — *voilà tout!* (Here his Grace shrugged his shoulders.) *Si je gagne, je reviendrai à mes ortolans — que les cartes soient préparées!"*

His Grace was all care, all attention — his Majesty all confidence. A spectator would have thought of Francis and Charles. His Grace thought of his game. His Majesty did not think; he shuffled. The Duc cut.

The cards were dealt. The trump is turned — it is — it is — the king! No — it was the queen. His Majesty cursed her masculine habiliments. De L'Omelette placed his hand upon his heart.

They play. The Duc counts. The hand is out. His Majesty counts heavily, smiles, and is taking wine. The Duc slips a card.

"C'est à vous à faire," said his Majesty, cutting. His Grace bowed, dealt, and arose from the table *en presentant le Roi.*

His Majesty looked chagrined.

Had Alexander not been Alexander, he would have been Diogenes; and the Duc assured his antagonist in taking leave, *"que s'il n'eût été De L'Omelette il n'aurait point d'objection d'être le Diable."*

A Tale of Jerusalem

Intensos rigidam in frontem ascendere canos
Passus erat

LUCAN

—— *a bristly* bore.

TRANSLATION

Let us hurry to the walls," said Abel-Phittim to Buzi-Ben-Levi and Simeon the Pharisee, on the tenth day of the month Thammuz, in the year of the world three thousand nine hundred and forty-one — "let us hasten to the ramparts adjoining the gate of Benjamin, which is in the city of David, and overlooking the camp of the uncircumcised; for it is the last hour of the fourth watch, being sunrise; and the idolaters, in fulfilment of the promise of Pompey, should be awaiting us with the lambs for the sacrifices."

Simeon, Abel-Phittim, and Buzi-Ben-Levi, were the Gizbarim, or sub-collectors of the offering, in the holy city of Jerusalem.

"Verily," replied the Pharisee, "let us hasten: for this generosity in the heathen is unwonted; and fickle-mindedness has ever been an attribute of the worshippers of Baal."

"That they are fickle-minded and treacherous is as true as the Penta-teuch," said Buzi-Ben-Levi, "but that is only towards the people of Adonai. When was it ever known that the Ammonites proved wanting to their own interests? Methinks it is no great stretch of generosity to allow us lambs for the altar of the Lord, receiving in lieu thereof thirty silver shekels per head!"

"Thou forgettest, however, Ben-Levi," replied Abel-Phittim, "that the Roman Pompey, who is now impiously besieging the city of the Most High, has no assurity that we apply not the lambs thus purchased for the altar, to the sustenance of the body, rather than of the spirit."

"Now, by the five corners of my beard!" shouted the Pharisee, who be-longed to the sect called The Dashers (that little knot of saints whose manner of *dashing* and lacerating the feet against the pavement was long a thorn and a reproach to less zealous devotees — a stumbling-block to less gifted perambulators) — "by the five corners of that beard which, as a priest, I am forbidden to shave! — have we lived to see the day when a blaspheming and idolatrous upstart of Rome shall accuse us of appro-priating to the appetites of the flesh the most holy and consecrated ele-ments? Have we lived to see the day when — "

"Let us not question the motives of the Philistine," interrupted Abel-Phittim, "for to-day we profit for the first time by his avarice or by his generosity; but rather let us hurry to the ramparts, lest offerings should be wanting for that altar whose fire the rains of heaven cannot extin-guish, and whose pillars of smoke no tempest can turn aside."

That part of the city to which our worthy Gizbarin now hastened, and which bore the name of its architect, King David, was esteemed the most strongly fortified district of Jerusalem; being situated upon the steep and lofty hill of Zion. Here, a broad, deep, circumvallatory trench, hewn from the solid rock, was defended by a wall of great strength erected upon its inner edge. This wall was adorned, at regular interspaces, by square towers of white marble; the lowest sixty, and the highest one hundred and twenty cubits in height. But, in the vicinity of the gate of Benjamin, the wall arose by no means from the margin of the fosse. On the contrary, be-tween the level of the ditch and the basement of the rampart, sprang up a perpendicular cliff of two hundred and fifty cubits, forming part of the precipitous Mount Moriah. So that when Simeon and his associates ar-rived on the summit of the tower called Adoni-Bezek — the loftiest of all the turrets around about Jerusalem, and the usual place of conference with the besieging army — they looked down upon the camp of the enemy from an eminence excelling by many feet that of the Pyramid of Cheops, and, by several, that of the temple of Belus.

"Verily," sighed the Pharisee, as he peered dizzly over the precipice, "the uncircumcised are as the sands by the seashore — as the locusts in the wilderness! The valley of The King hath become the valley of Adommin."

"And yet," added Ben-Levi, "thou canst not point me out a Philistine — no, not one — from Aleph to Tau — from the wilderness to the battlements — who seemeth any bigger than the letter Jod!"

"Lower away the basket with the shekels of silver!" here shouted a Roman soldier in a hoarse, rough voice, which appeared to issue from the regions of Pluto — "lower away the basket with the accursed coin which it has broken the jaw of a noble Roman to pronounce! Is it thus you evince your gratitude to our master Pompeius, who, in his condescension, has thought fit to listen to your idolatrous importunities? The god Phœbus, who is a true god, has been charioted for an hour — and were you not to be on the ramparts by sunrise? Ædepol! do you think that we, the conquerors of the world, have nothing better to do than stand waiting by the walls of every kennel, to traffic with the dogs of the earth? Lower away! I say — and see that your trumpery be bright in color and just in weight!"

"El Elohim!" ejaculated the Pharisee, as the discordant tones of the centurion rattled up the crags of the precipice, and fainted away against the temple — "El Elohim! — who is the God Phœbus? — whom doth the blasphemer invoke? Thou, Buzi-Ben-Levi! who art read in the laws of the Gentiles, and hast sojourned among them who dabble with the Teraphim! — is it Nergal of whom the idolater speaketh? — or Ashimah? — or — Nibhaz? — or Tartak? — or Adramalech? — or Anamalech? — or Succoth-Benith? — or Dragon? — or Belial? — or Baal-Perith? — or Baal-Peor? — or Baal-Zebub?"

"Verily it is neither — but beware how thou lettest the rope slip too rapidly through thy fingers; for should the wicker-work chance to hang on the projection of yonder crag, there will be a woful outpouring of the holy things of the sanctuary."

By the assistance of some rudely constructed machinery, the heavily laden basket was now carefully lowered down among the multitude; and, from the giddy pinnacle, the Romans were seen gathering confusedly round it; but owing to the vast height and the prevalence of a fog, no distinct view of their operations could be obtained.

Half an hour had already elapsed.

"We shall be too late!" sighed the Pharisee, as at the expiration of this period, he looked over into the abyss — "we shall be too late! we shall be turned out of office by the Katholim."

"No more," responded Abel-Phittim, — "no more shall we feast upon the fat of the land — no longer shall our beards be odorous with frankincense — our loins girded up with fine linen from the Temple."

"Raca!" swore Ben-Levi, "Raca! do they mean to defraud us of the purchase money? or, Holy Moses! are they weighing the shekels of the tabernacle?

"They have given the signal at last!" cried the Pharisee — "they have given the signal at last! — pull away, Abel-Phittim! — and thou, Buzi-

Ben-Levi, pull away! — for verily the Philistines have either still hold upon the basket, or the Lord hath softened their hearts to place therein a beast of good weight!" And the Gizbarim pulled away, while their burthen swung heavily upwards through the still increasing mist.

"Booshoh he!" — as, at the conclusion of an hour, some object at the extremity of the rope became indistinctly visible — "Booshoh he!" was the exclamation which burst from the lips of Ben-Levi.

"Booshoh he! — for shame! — it is a ram from the thickets of Engedi, and as rugged as the valley of Jehosaphat!"

"It is a firstling of the flock," said Abel-Phittim, "I know him by the bleating of his lips, and the innocent folding of his limbs. His eyes are more beautiful than the jewels of the Pectoral, and his flesh is like the honey of Hebron."

"It is a fatted calf from the pastures of Bashan," said the Pharisee, "the heathen have dealt wonderfully with us! — let us raise up our voices in a psalm! — let us give thanks on the shawm and on the psaltery — on the harp and on the huggab — on the cythern and on the sackbut!"

It was not until the basket had arrived within a few feet of the Gizbarium, that a low grunt betrayed to their perception a *hog* of no common size.

"Now El Emanu!" slowly, and with upturned eyes ejaculated the trio, as, letting go their hold, the emancipated porker tumbled headlong among the Philistines, "El Emanu! — God be with us — *it is the unutterable flesh!*"

Loss of Breath

A TALE NEITHER IN NOR OUT OF "BLACKWOOD"

O breathe not, etc. Moore's Melodies

THE MOST notorious ill-fortune must in the end yield to the untiring courage of philosophy — as the most stubborn city to the ceaseless vigilance of an enemy. Shalmanezer, as we have it in holy writings, lay three years before Samaria; yet it fell. Sardanapalus — see Diodorus — maintained himself seven in Nineveh; but to no purpose. Troy expired at the close of the second lustrum; and Azoth, as Aristæus declares upon his honour as a gentleman, opened at last her gates to Psammetichus, after having barred them for the fifth part of a century. . . .

"Thou wretch! — thou vixen! — thou shrew!" said I to my wife on the morning after our wedding; "thou witch! — thou hag! — thou whipper-snapper — thou sink of iniquity! — thou fiery-faced quintessence of all

that is abominable! — thou — thou — " here standing upon tiptoe, seizing her by the throat, and placing my mouth close to her ear, I was preparing to launch forth a new and more decided epithet of opprobrium, which should not fail, if ejaculated, to convince her of her insignificance, when to my extreme horror and astonishment I discovered that *I had lost my breath.*

The phrases "I am out of breath," "I have lost my breath," etc., are often enough repeated in common conversation; but it had never occurred to me that the terrible accident of which I speak could *bona fide* and actually happen! Imagine — that is if you have a fanciful turn — imagine, I say, my wonder — my consternation — my despair!

There is a good genius, however, which has never entirely deserted me. In my most ungovernable moods I still retain a sense of propriety, *et le chemin des passions me conduit* — as Lord Edouard in the "Julie" says it did him — *à la philosophie véritable.*

Although I could not at first precisely ascertain to what degree the occurence had affected me, I determined at all events to conceal the matter from my wife, until further experience should discover to me the extent of this my unheard of calamity. Altering my countenance, therefore, in a moment, from its bepuffed and distorted appearance, to an expression of arch and coquettish benignity, I gave my lady a pat on the one cheek, and a kiss on the other, and without saying one syllable (Furies! I could not), left her astonished at my drollery, as I pirouetted out of the room in a *Pas de Zephyr.*

Behold me then safely ensconced in my private *boudoir,* a fearful instance of the ill consequences attending upon irascibility — alive, with the qualifications of the dead — dead, with the propensities of the living — an anomaly on the face of the earth — being very calm, yet breathless.

Yes! breathless. I am serious in asserting that my breath was entirely gone. I could not have stirred with it a feather if my life had been at issue, or sullied even the delicacy of a mirror. Hard fate! — yet there was some alleviation to the first overwhelming paroxysm of my sorrow. I found, upon trial, that the powers of utterance which, upon my inability to proceed in the conversation with my wife, I then concluded to be totally destroyed, were in fact only partially impeded, and I discovered that had I, at that interesting crisis, dropped my voice to a singularly deep guttural, I might still have continued to her the communication of my sentiments; this pitch of voice (the guttural) depending, I find, not upon the current of the breath, but upon a certain spasmodic action of the muscles of the throat.

Throwing myself upon a chair, I remained for some time absorbed in meditation. My reflections, be sure, were of no consolatory kind. A thousand vague and lachrymatory fancies took possesion of my soul — and even the idea of suicide flitted across my brain; but it is a trait in the perversity of human nature to reject the obvious and the ready, for

the far-distant and equivocal. Thus I shuddered at self-murder as the most decided of atrocities while the tabby cat purred strenuously upon the rug, and the very water dog wheezed assiduously under the table; each taking to itself much merit for the strength of its lungs, and all obviously done in derision of my own pulmonary incapacity.

Oppressed with a tumult of vague hopes and fears, I at length heard the footsteps of my wife descending the staircase. Being now assured of her absence, I returned with a palpitating heart to the scene of my disaster.

Carefully locking the door on the inside, I commenced a vigorous search. It was possible, I thought, that, concealed in some obscure corner, or lurking in some closet or drawer, might be found the lost object of my inquiry. It might have a vapory — it might even have a tangible form. Most philosophers, upon many points of philosophy, are still very unphilosophical. William Godwin, however, says in his "Mandeville," that "invisible things are the only realities," and this, all will allow, is a case in point. I would have the judicious reader pause before accusing such asseverations of an undue quantum of absurdity. Anaxagoras, it will be remembered, maintained that snow is black, and this I have since found to be the case.

Long and earnestly did I continue the investigation: but the contemptible reward of my industry and perseverance proved to be only a set of false teeth, two pair of hips, an eye, and a bundle of *billets-doux* from Mr. Windenough to my wife. I might as well here observe that this confirmation of my lady's partiality for Mr. W. occasioned me little uneasiness. That Mrs. Lackobreath should admire anything so dissimilar to myself was a natural and necessary evil. I am, it is well known, of a robust and corpulent appearance, and at the same time somewhat diminutive in stature. What wonder, then, that the lath-like tenuity of my acquaintance, and his altitude, which has grown into a proverb, should have met with all due estimation in the eyes of Mrs. Lackobreath. But to return.

My exertions, as I have before said, proved fruitless. Closet after closet — drawer after drawer — corner after corner — were scrutinized to no purpose. At one time, however, I thought myself sure of my prize, having, in rummaging a dressing-case, accidentally demolished a bottle of Grandjean's Oil of Archangels — which, as an agreeable perfume, I here take the liberty of recommending.

With a heavy heart I returned to my *boudoir* — there to ponder upon some method of eluding my wife's penetration, until I could make arrangements prior to my leaving the country, for to this I had already made up my mind. In a foreign climate, being unknown, I might, with some probability of success, endeavor to conceal my unhappy calamity — a calamity calculated, even more than beggary, to estrange the affections of the multitude, and to draw down upon the wretch the well-merited

indignation of the virtuous and the happy. I was not long in hesitation. Being naturally quick, I committed to memory the entire tragedy of "Metamora." I had the good fortune to recollect that in the accentuation of this drama, or at least of such portion of it as is allotted to the hero, the tones of voice in which I found myself deficient were altogether unnecessary, and the deep guttural was expected to reign monotonously throughout.

I practised for some time by the borders of a well frequented marsh; — herein, however, having no reference to a similar proceeding of Demosthenes, but from a design peculiarly and conscientiously my own. Thus armed at all points, I determined to make my wife believe that I was suddenly smitten with a passion for the stage. In this, I succeeded to a miracle; and to every question or suggestion found myself at liberty to reply in my most frog-like and sepulchral tones with some passage from the tragedy — any portion of which, as I soon took great pleasure in observing, would apply equally well to any particular subject. It is not to be supposed, however, that in the delivery of such passages I was found at all deficient in the looking asquint — the showing my teeth — the working my knees — the shuffling my feet — or in any of those unmentionable graces which are now justly considered the characteristics of a popular performer. To be sure they spoke of confining me in a straitjacket — but, good God! they never suspected me of having lost my breath.

Having at length put my affairs in order, I took my seat very early one morning in the mail stage for ——, giving it to be understood, among my acquaintances, that business of the last importance required my immediate personal attendance in that city.

The coach was crammed to repletion; but in the uncertain twilight the features of my companions could not be distinguished. Without making any effectual resistance, I suffered myself to be placed between two gentlemen of colossal dimensions; while a third, of a size larger, requesting pardon for the liberty he was about to take, threw himself upon my body at full length, and falling asleep in an instant, drowned all my guttural ejaculations for relief, in a snore which would have put to blush the roarings of the bull of Phalaris. Happily the state of my respiratory faculties rendered suffocation an accident entirely out of the question.

As, however, the day broke more distinctly in our approach to the outskirts of the city, my tormentor, arising and adjusting his shirt-collar, thanked me in a very friendly manner for my civility. Seeing that I remained motionless (all my limbs were dislocated and my head twisted on one side), his apprehensions began to be excited; and arousing the rest of the passengers, he communicated, in a very decided manner, his opinion that a dead man had been palmed upon them during the night for a living and responsible fellow-traveller; here giving me a thump on the right eye, by way of demonstrating the truth of his suggestion.

Hereupon all, one after another (there were nine in company), be-
lieved it their duty to pull me by the ear. A young practising physician,
too, having applied a pocket-mirror to my mouth, and found me without
breath, the assertion of my persecutor was pronounced a true bill; and
the whole party expressed a determination to endure tamely no such im-
positions for the future, and to proceed no farther with any such carcasses
for the present.

I was here, accordingly, thrown out at the sign of the "Crow" (by
which tavern the coach happened to be passing), without meeting with
any farther accident than the breaking of both my arms, under the left
hind wheel of the vehicle. I must besides do the driver the justice to
state that he did not forget to throw after me the largest of my trunks,
which, unfortunately falling on my head, fractured my skull in a manner
at once interesting and extraordinary.

The landlord of the "Crow," who is a hospitable man, finding that my
trunk contained sufficient to indemnify him for any little trouble he
might take in my behalf, sent forthwith for a surgeon of his acquaintance,
and delivered me to his care with a bill and receipt for ten dollars.

The purchaser took me to his apartments and commenced operations
immediately. Having cut off my ears, however, he discovered signs of
animation. He now rang the bell, and sent for a neighboring apothecary
with whom to consult in the emergency. In case of his suspicions with
regard to my existence proving ultimately correct, he, in the meantime,
made an incision in my stomach, and removed several of my viscera for
private dissection.

The apothecary had an idea that I was actually dead. This idea I en-
deavored to confute, kicking and plunging with all my might, and mak-
ing the most furious contortions — for the operations of the surgeon had,
in a measure, restored me to the possession of my faculties. All, however,
was attributed to the effects of a new galvanic battery, wherewith the
apothecary, who is really a man of information, performed several curi-
ous experiments, in which, from my personal share in their fulfillment,
I could not help feeling deeply interested. It was a course of mortification
to me, nevertheless, that although I made several attempts at conversa-
tion, my powers of speech were so entirely in abeyance, that I could not
even open my mouth; much less, then, make reply to some ingenious but
fanciful theories of which, under other circumstances, my minute ac-
quaintance with the Hippocratian pathology would have afforded me a
ready confutation.

Not being able to arrive at a conclusion, the practitioners remanded
me for farther examination. I was taken up into a garret; and the surgeon's
lady having accommodated me with drawers and stockings, the surgeon
himself fastened my hands, and tied up my jaws with a pocket-handker-
chief — then bolted the door on the outside as he hurried to his dinner,
leaving me alone to silence and to meditation.

I now discovered to my extreme delight that I could have spoken had not my mouth been tied up with the pocket-handkerchief. Consoling myself with this reflection, I was mentally repeating some passages of the "Omnipresence of the Deity," as is my custom before resigning myself to sleep, when two cats, of a greedy and vituperative turn, entering at a hole in the wall, leaped up with a flourish *à la Catalani*, and alighting opposite one another on my visage, betook themselves to indecorous contention for the paltry consideration of my nose.

But, as the loss of his ears proved the means of elevating to the throne of Cyrus, the Magian or Mige-Gush of Persia, and as the cutting off his nose gave Zopyrus possession of Babylon, so the loss of a few ounces of my countenance proved the salvation of my body. Aroused by the pain, and burning with indignation, I burst, at a single effort, the fastenings and the bandage. Stalking across the room I cast a glance of contempt at the belligerents, and throwing open the sash to their extreme horror and disappointment, precipitated myself, very dexterously, from the window.

The mail-robber W——, to whom I bore a singular resemblance, was at this moment passing from the city jail to the scaffold erected for his execution in the suburbs. His extreme infirmity and long continued ill health had obtained him the privilege of remaining unmanacled; and habited in his gallows costume — one very similar to my own, — he lay at full length in the bottom of the hangman's cart (which happened to be under the windows of the surgeon at the moment of my precipitation) without any other guard than the driver, who was asleep, and two recruits of the sixth infantry, who were drunk.

As ill-luck would have it, I alit upon my feet within the vehicle. W——, who was an acute fellow, perceived his opportunity. Leaping up immediately, he bolted out behind, and turning down an alley, was out of sight in the twinkling of an eye. The recruits, aroused by the bustle, could not exactly comprehend the merits of the transaction. Seeing, however, a man, the precise counterpart of the felon, standing upright in the cart before their eyes, they were of the opinion that the rascal (meaning W——) was after making his escape, (so they expressed themselves,) and, having communicated this opinion to one another, they took each a dram, and then knocked me down with the butt-ends of their muskets.

It was not long ere we arrived at the place of destination. Of course nothing could be said in my defence. Hanging was my inevitable fate. I resigned myself thereto with a feeling half stupid, half acrimonious. Being little of a cynic, I had all the sentiments of a dog. The hangman, however, adjusted the noose about my neck. The drop fell.

I forbear to depict my sensations upon the gallows; although here, undoubtedly, I could speak to the point, and it is a topic upon which nothing has been well said. In fact, to write upon such a theme it is neces-

sary to have been hanged. Every author should confine himself to matters of experience. Thus Mark Antony composed a treatise upon getting drunk.

I may just mention, however, that die I did not. My body *was*, but I had no breath *to be*, suspended; and but for the knot under my left ear (which had the feel of a military stock) I dare say that I should have experienced very little inconvenience. As for the jerk given to my neck upon the falling of the drop, it merely proved a corrective to the twist afforded me by the fat gentleman in the coach.

For good reasons, however, I did my best to give the crowd the worth of their trouble. My convulsions were said to be extraordinary. My spasms it would have been difficult to beat. The populace *encored*. Several gentlemen swooned; and a multitude of ladies were carried home in hysterics. Pinxit availed himself of the opportunity to retouch, from a sketch taken upon the spot, his admirable painting of the "Marsyas flayed alive."

When I had afforded sufficient amusement, it was thought proper to remove my body from the gallows; — this the more especially as the real culprit had in the meantime been retaken and recognized, a fact which I was so unlucky as not to know.

Much sympathy was, of course, exercised in my behalf, and as no one made claim to my corpse, it was ordered that I should be interred in a public vault.

Here, after due interval, I was deposited. The sexton departed, and I was left alone. A line of Marston's "Malcontent" —

Death's a good fellow and keeps open house —

struck me at that moment as a palpable lie.

I knocked off, however, the lid of my coffin, and stepped out. The place was dreadfully dreary and damp, and I became troubled with *ennui*. By way of amusement, I felt my way among the numerous coffins ranged in order around. I lifted them down, one by one, and breaking open their lids, busied myself in speculations about the mortality within.

"This," I soliloquized, tumbling over a carcass, puffy, bloated, and rotund — "this has been, no doubt, in every sense of the word, an unhappy — an unfortunate man. It has been his terrible lot not to walk but to waddle — to pass through life not like a human being, but like an elephant — not like a man, but like a rhinoceros.

"His attempts at getting on have been mere abortions, and his circumgyratory proceedings a palpable failure. Taking a step forward, it has been his misfortune to take two toward the right, and three toward the left. His studies have been confined to the poetry of Crabbe. He can have no idea of the wonder of a *pirouette*. To him a *pas de papillon* has been an abstract conception. He has never ascended the summit of a hill. He has never viewed from any steeple the glories of a metropolis. Heat has been his mortal enemy. In the dog-days his days have been the

days of a dog. Therein, he has dreamed of flames and suffocation — of mountains upon mountains — of Pelion upon Ossa. He was short of breath — to say all in a word, he was short of breath. He thought it extravagant to play upon wind instruments. He was the inventor of self-moving fans, wind-sails, and ventilators. He patronized Du Pont the bellows-maker, and he died miserably in attempting to smoke a cigar. His was a case in which I feel a deep interest — a lot in which I sincerely sympathize.

"But here," — said I — "here" — and I dragged spitefully from its receptacle a gaunt, tall and peculiar-looking form, whose remarkable appearance struck me with a sense of unwelcome familiarity — "here is a wretch entitled to no earthly commiseration." Thus saying, in order to obtain a more distinct view of my subject, I applied my thumb and forefinger to its nose, and causing it to assume a sitting position upon the ground, held it thus, at the length of my arm, while I continued my soliloquy.

— "Entitled," I repeated, "to no earthly commiseration. Who indeed would think of compassioning a shadow? Besides, has he not had his full share of the blessings of mortality? He was the originator of tall monuments — shot-towers — lightning-rods — Lombardy poplars. His treatise upon "Shades and Shadows" has immortalized him. He edited with distinguished ability the last edition of "South on the Bones." He went early to college and studied pneumatics. He then came home, talked eternally, and played upon the French-horn. He patronized the bagpipes. Captain Barclay, who walked against Time, would not walk against *him*. Windham and Allbreath were his favorite writers, — his favorite artist, Phiz. He died gloriously while inhaling gas — *levique flatu corrupitur*, like the *fama pudicitæ* in Hieronymus.* He was indubitably a" —

"How *can* you? — how — *can* — you?" — interrupted the object of my animadversions, gasping for breath, and tearing off, with a desperate exertion, the bandage around its jaws — "how *can* you, Mr. Lackobreath, be so infernally cruel as to pinch me in that manner by the nose? Did you not see how they had fastened up my mouth — and you *must* know — if you know any thing — how vast a superfluity of breath I have to dispose of! If you do *not* know, however, sit down and you shall see. In my situation it is really a great relief to be able to open one's mouth — to be able to expatiate — to be able to communicate with a person like yourself, who do not think yourself called upon at every period to interrupt the thread of a gentleman's discourse. Interruptions are annoying and should undoubtedly be abolished — don't you think so? — no reply, I beg you, — one person is enough to be speaking at a time. — I shall be done by and by, and then you may begin. — How the devil, sir, did you get into

* Tenera res in feminis fama pudicitiae, et quasi flos pulcherrimus, cito ad levem marcessit auram, levique flatu corrumpitur, maxime, &c. — Hieronymus ad Salvinam.

this place? — not a word I beseech you — been here some time myself
— terrible accident! — heard of it, I suppose? — awful calamity! — walk-
ing under your windows — some short while ago — about the time you
were stage-struck — horrible occurrence! — heard of "catching one's
breath," eh? — hold your tongue I tell you! — I caught somebody else's!
— had always too much of my own — met Blab at the corner of the street
— wouldn't give me a chance for a word — couldn't get in a syllable edge-
ways — attacked, consequently, with epilepsis — Blab made his escape
— damn all fools! — they took me up for dead, and put me in this place —
pretty doings all of them! — heard all you said about me — every word
a lie — horrible! — wonderful — outrageous! — hideous! — incomprehen-
sible! — et cetera — et cetera — et cetera — et cetera —— "

It is impossible to conceive my astonishment at so unexpected a dis-
course; or the joy with which I became gradually convinced that the
breath so fortunately caught by the gentleman (whom I soon recognized
as my neighbor Windenough) was, in fact, the identical expiration mis-
laid by myself in the conversation with my wife. Time, place, and cir-
cumstances rendered it a matter beyond question. I did not, however,
immediately release my hold upon Mr. W.'s proboscis — not at least
during the long period in which the inventor of Lombardy poplars con-
tinued to favor me with his explanations.

In this respect I was actuated by that habitual prudence which has
ever been my predominating trait. I reflected that many difficulties might
still lie in the path of my preservation which only extreme exertion on
my part would be able to surmount. Many persons, I considered, are
prone to estimate commodities in their possession — however valueless
to the then proprietor — however troublesome, or distressing — in direct
ratio with the advantages to be derived by others from their attainment,
or by themselves from their abandonment. Might not this be the case
with Mr. Windenough? In displaying anxiety for the breath of which
he was at present so willing to get rid, might I not lay myself open to the
exactions of his avarice? There are scoundrels in this world, I remem-
bered with a sigh, who will not scruple to take unfair opportunities with
even a next door neighbor, and (this remark is from Epictetus) it is pre-
cisely at that time when men are most anxious to throw off the burden
of their own calamities that they feel the least desirous of relieving them
in others.

Upon considerations similar to these, and still retaining my grasp upon
the nose of Mr. W., I accordingly thought proper to model my reply.

"Monster!" I began in a tone of the deepest indignation — "monster
and double-winded idiot! — dost *thou*, whom for thine iniquities it has
pleased heaven to accurse with a two-fold respiration — dost *thou*, I say,
presume to address me in the familiar language of an old acquaintance?
— 'I lie,' forsooth! and 'hold my tongue,' to be sure! — pretty conversa-
tion indeed, to a gentleman with a single breath! — all this, too, when

I have it in my power to relieve the calamity under which thou dost so justly suffer — to curtail the superfluities of thine unhappy respiration."

Like Brutus, I paused for a reply — with which, like a tornado, Mr. Windenough immediately overwhelmed me. Protestation followed upon protestation, and apology upon apology. There were no terms with which he was unwilling to comply, and there were none of which I failed to take the fullest advantage.

Preliminaries being at length arranged, my acquaintance delivered me the respiration; for which (having carefully examined it) I gave him afterward a receipt.

I am aware that by many I shall be held to blame for speaking in a manner so cursory, of a transaction so impalpable. It will be thought that I should have entered more minutely, into the details of an occurrence by which — and this is very true — much new light might be thrown upon a highly interesting branch of physical philosophy.

To all this I am sorry that I cannot reply. A hint is the only answer which I am permitted to make. There were *circumstances* — but I think it much safer upon consideration to say as little as possible about an affair so delicate — *so delicate*, I repeat, and at the time involving the interests of a third party whose sulphurous resentment I have not the least desire, at this moment, of incurring.

We were not long after this necessary arrangement in effecting an escape from the dungeons of the sepulchre. The united strength of our resuscitated voices was soon sufficiently apparent. Scissors, the Whig editor, republished a treatise upon "the nature and origin of subterranean noises." A reply — rejoinder — confutation — and justification — followed in the columns of a Democratic Gazette. It was not until the opening of the vault to decide the controversy, that the appearance of Mr. Windenough and myself proved both parties to have been decidedly in the wrong.

I cannot conclude these details of some very singular passages in a life at all times sufficiently eventful, without again recalling to the attention of the reader the merits of that indiscriminate philosophy which is a sure and ready shield against those shafts of calamity which can neither be seen, felt, nor fully understood. It was in the spirit of this wisdom that, among the ancient Hebrews, it was believed the gates of Heaven would be inevitably opened to that sinner, or saint, who, with good lungs and implicit confidence, should vociferate the word "*Amen!*" It was in the spirit of this wisdom that, when a great plague raged at Athens, and every means had been in vain attempted for its removal, Epimenides, as Laertius relates, in his second book, of that philosopher, advised the erection of a shrine and temple "to the proper God."

LYTTLETON BARRY.

Bon-Bon

Quand un bon vin meuble mon estomac
Je suis plus savant que Balzac —
Plus sage que Pibrac;
Mon bras seul faisant l'attaque
De la nation Cossaque,
La mettroit au sac;
De Charon je passerois le lac
En dormant dans son bac;
J'irois au fier Eac,
Sans que mon coeur fît tic ni tac,
Presenter du tabac.

French Vaudeville

T HAT Pierre Bon-Bon was a *restaurateur* of uncommon qualifications, no man who during the reign of ——, frequented the little Café in the cul-de-sac Le Febvre at Rouen, will, I imagine, feel himself at liberty to dispute. That Pierre Bon-Bon was, in an equal degree, skilled in the philosophy of that period is, I presume still more especially undeniable. His *pâtés à la fois* were beyond doubt immaculate; but what pen can do justice to his essays *sur la Nature* — his thoughts *sur l'Ame* — his observations *sur l'Esprit?* If his *omelettes* — if his *fricandeaux* were inestimable, what *littérateur* of that day would not have given twice as much for an "*Idée de Bon-Bon*" as for all the trash of "*Idées*" of all the rest of the *savants?* Bon-Bon had ransacked libraries which no other man had ransacked — had read more than any other would have entertained a notion of reading — had understood more than any other would have conceived the possibility of understanding; and although, while he flourished, there were not wanting some authors at Rouen to assert "that his *dicta* evinced neither the purity of the Academy, nor the depth of the Lyceum" — although, mark me, his doctrines were by no means very generally comprehended, still it did not follow that they were difficult of comprehension. It was, I think, on account of their self-evidency that many persons were led to consider them abstruse. It is to Bon-Bon — but let this go no farther — it is to Bon-Bon that Kant himself is mainly indebted for his metaphysics. The former was indeed not a Platonist, nor strictly speaking an Aristotelian — nor did he, like the modern Leibnitz, waste those precious hours which might be employed in the invention of a *fricasée* or, *facili gradu*, the analysis of a sensation, in frivolous attempts at reconciling the obstinate oils and waters of ethical discussion. Not at all. Bon-Bon was

Ionic — Bon-Bon was equally Italic. He reasoned à *priori* — He reasoned also à *posteriori*. His ideas were innate — or otherwise. He believed in George of Trebizonde — He believed in Bossarion. Bon-Bon was emphatically a — Bon-Bonist.

I have spoken of the philosopher in his capacity of *restaurateur*. I would not, however, have any friend of mine imagine that, in fulfilling his hereditary duties in that line, our hero wanted a proper estimation of their dignity and importance. Far from it. It was impossible to say in which branch of his profession he took the greater pride. In his opinion the powers of the intellect held intimate connection with the capabilities of the stomach. I am not sure, indeed, that he greatly disagreed with the Chinese, who held that the soul lies in the abdomen. The Greeks at all events were right, he thought, who employed the same words for the mind and the diaphragm.* By this I do not mean to insinuate a charge of gluttony, or indeed any other serious charge to the prejudice of the metaphysician. If Pierre Bon-Bon had his failings — and what great man has not a thousand? — if Pierre Bon-Bon, I say, had his failings, they were failings of very little importance — faults indeed which, in other tempers, have often been looked upon rather in the light of virtues. As regards one of these foibles, I should not even have mentioned it in this history but for the remarkable prominency — the extreme *alto relievo* — in which it jutted out from the plane of his general disposition. He could never let slip an opportunity of making a bargain.

Not that he was avaricious — no. It was by no means necessary to the satisfaction of the philosopher, that the bargain should be to his own proper advantage. Provided a trade could be effected — a trade of any kind, upon any terms, or under any circumstances — a triumphant smile was seen for many days thereafter to enlighten his countenance, and a knowing wink of the eye to give evidence of his sagacity.

At any epoch it would not be very wonderful if a humor so peculiar as the one I have just mentioned, should elicit attention and remark. At the epoch of our narrative, had this peculiarity *not* attracted observation, there would have been room for wonder indeed. It was soon reported that, upon all occasions of the kind, the smile of Bon-Bon was wont to differ widely from the downright grin with which he would laugh at his own jokes, or welcome an acquaintance. Hints were thrown out of an exciting nature; stories were told of perilous bargains made in a hurry and repented of at leisure; and instances were adduced of unaccountable capacities, vague longings, and unnatural inclinations implanted by the author of all evil for wise purposes of his own.

The philosopher had other weaknesses — but they are scarcely worthy our serious examination. For example, there are few men of extraordinary profundity who are found wanting in an inclination for the bottle.

* φρεϝες

Whether this inclination be an exciting cause, or rather a valid proof of
such profundity, it is a nice thing to say. Bon-Bon, as far as I can learn,
did not think the subject adapted to minute investigation; — nor do I.
Yet in the indulgence of a propensity so truly classical, it is not to be
supposed that the *restaurateur* would lose sight of that intuitive dis-
crimination which was wont to characterize, at one and the same time,
his *essais* and his *omelettes*. In his seclusions the Vin de Bourgogne had
its allotted hour, and there were appropriate moments for the Côtes du
Rhone. With him Sauterne was to Medoc what Catullus was to Homer.
He would sport with a syllogism in sipping St. Peray, but unravel an
argument over Clos de Vougeot, and upset a theory in a torrent of
Chambertin. Well had it been if the same quick sense of propriety had
attended him in the peddling propensity to which I have formerly alluded
— but this was by no means the case. Indeed to say the truth, *that* trait
of mind in the philosophic Bon-Bon *did* begin at length to assume a
character of strange intensity and mysticism, and appeared deeply tinc-
tured with the *diablerie* of his favorite German studies.

To enter the little Café in the cul-de-sac Le Febvre was, at the period
of our tale, to enter the *sanctum* of a man of genius. Bon-Bon was a man
of genius. There was not a *sous-cusinier* in Rouen, who could not have
told you that Bon-Bon was a man of genius. His very cat knew it, and
forebore to whisk her tail in the presence of the man of genius. His large
water-dog was acquainted with the fact, and upon the approach of his
master, betrayed his sense of inferiority by a sanctity of deportment, a
debasement of the ears, and a dropping of the lower jaw not altogether
unworthy of a dog. It is, however, true that much of this habitual respect
might have been attributed to the personal appearance of the meta-
physician. A distinguished exterior will, I am constrained to say, have its
way even with a beast; and I am willing to allow much in the outward
man of the *restaurateur* calculated to impress the imagination of the
quadruped. There is a peculiar majesty about the atmosphere of the little
great — if I may be permitted so equivocal an expression — which mere
physical bulk alone will be found at all times inefficient in creating. If,
however, Bon-Bon was barely three feet in height, and if his head was
diminutively small, still it was impossible to behold the rotundity of
his stomach without a sense of magnificence nearly bordering upon the
sublime. In its size both dogs and men must have seen a type of his
acquirements — in its immensity a fitting habitation for his immortal
soul.

I might here — if it so pleased me — dilate upon the matter of habili-
ment, and other mere circumstances of the external metaphysician. I
might hint that the hair of our hero was worn short, combed smoothly
over his forehead, and surmounted by a conical-shaped white flannel
cap and tassels — that his pea-green jerkin was not after the fashion of
those worn by the common class of *restaurateurs* at that day — that the

sleeves were something fuller than the reigning costume permitted — that the cuffs were turned up, not as usual in that barbarous period, with cloth of the same quality and color as the garment, but faced in a more fanciful manner with the particolored velvet of Genoa — that his slippers were of a bright purple, curiously filigreed, and might have been manufactured in Japan, but for the exquisite pointing of the toes, and the brilliant tints of the binding and embroidery — that his breeches were of the yellow satin-like material called *aimable* — that his sky-blue cloak, resembling in form a dressing-wrapper, and richly bestudded all over with crimson devices, floated cavalierly upon his shoulders like a mist of the morning — and that his *tout ensemble* gave rise to the remarkable words of Benevenuta, the Improvisatrice of Florence, "that it was difficult to say whether Pierre Bon-Bon was indeed a bird of Paradise, or rather a very Paradise of perfection." I might, I say, expatiate upon all these points if I pleased, — but I forbear; merely personal details may be left to historical novelists, — they are beneath the moral dignity of matter-of-fact.

I have said that "to enter the Café in the cul-de-sac Le Febvre was to enter the *sanctum* of a man of genius" — but then it was only the man of genius who could duly estimate the merits of the *sanctum.* A sign, consisting of a vast folio, swung before the entrance. On one side of the volume was painted a bottle; on the reverse a *pâté.* On the back were visible in large letters *Œuvres de Bon-Bon.* Thus was delicately shadowed forth the two-fold occupation of the proprietor.

Upon stepping over the threshold, the whole interior of the building presented itself to view. A long, low-pitched room, of antique construction, was indeed all the accommodation afforded by the Café. In a corner of the apartment stood the bed of the metaphysician. An array of curtains, together with a canopy *à la Grecque,* gave it an air at once classic and comfortable. In the corner diagonally opposite, appeared, in direct family communion, the properties of the kitchen and the *bibliothèque.* A dish of polemics stood peacefully upon the dresser. Here lay an ovenful of the latest ethics — there a kettle of dudecimo *mélanges.* Volumes of German morality were hand and glove with the gridiron — a toasting-fork might be discovered by the side of Eusebius — Plato reclined at his ease in the frying-pan — and contemporary manuscripts were filed away upon the spit.

In other respects the *Café de Bon-Bon* might be said to differ little from the usual *restaurants* of the period. A fireplace yawned opposite the door. On the right of the fireplace an open cupboard displayed a formidable array of labelled bottles.

It was here, about twelve o'clock one night during the severe winter of ——, that Pierre Bon-Bon, after having listened for some time to the comments of his neighbours upon his singular propensity — that Pierre Bon-Bon, I say, having turned them all out of his house, locked the door

upon them with an oath, and betook himself in no very pacific mood to the comforts of a leather-bottomed arm-chair, and a fire of blazing fagots.

It was one of those terrific nights which are only met with once or twice during a century. It snowed fiercely, and the house tottered to its centre with the floods of wind that, rushing through the crannies in the wall, and pouring impetuously down the chimney, shook awfully the curtains of the philosopher's bed, and disorganized the economy of his *pâté*-pans and papers. The huge folio sign that swung without, exposed to the fury of the tempest, creaked ominously, and gave out a moaning sound from its stanchions of solid oak.

It was in no placid temper, I say, that the metaphysician drew up his chair to its customary station by the hearth. Many circumstances of a perplexing nature had occurred during the day, to disturb the serenity of his meditations. In attempting *des œufs à la Princesse*, he had unfortunately perpetrated an *omelette à la Reine*; the discovery of a principle in ethics had been frustrated by the overturning of a stew; and last, not least, he had been thwarted in one of those admirable bargains which he at all times took such especial delight in bringing to a successful termination. But in the chafing of his mind at these unaccountable vicissitudes, there did not fail to be mingled some degree of that nervous anxiety which the fury of a boisterous night is so well calculated to produce. Whistling to his more immediate vicinity the large black water-dog we have spoken of before, and settling himself uneasily in his chair, he could not help casting a wary and unquiet eye toward those distant recesses of the apartment whose inexorable shadows not even the red firelight itself could more than partially succeed in overcoming. Having completed a scrutiny whose exact purpose was perhaps unintelligible to himself, he drew close to his seat a small table covered with books and papers, and soon became absorbed in the task of retouching a voluminous manuscript, intended for publication on the morrow.

He had been thus occupied for some minutes when "I am in no hurry, Monsieur Bon-Bon," suddenly whispered a whining voice in the apartment.

"The devil!" ejaculated our hero, starting to his feet, overturning the table at his side, and staring around him in astonishment.

"Very true," calmly replied the voice.

"Very true! — what is very true? — how came you here?" vociferated the metaphysician, as his eye fell upon something which lay stretched at full length upon the bed.

"I was saying," said the intruder, without attending to the interrogatives, — "I was saying that I am not at all pushed for time — that the business upon which I took the liberty of calling, is of no pressing importance — in short, that I can very well wait until you have finished your Exposition."

"My Exposition! — there now! — how do *you* know? — how came *you* to understand that I was writing an Exposition? — good God!"

"Hush!" replied the figure, in a shrill undertone; and, arising quickly from the bed, he made a single step toward our hero, while an iron lamp that depended over-head swung convulsively back from his approach.

The philosopher's amazement did not prevent a narrow scrutiny of the stranger's dress and appearance. The outlines of his figure, exceedingly lean, but much above the common height, were rendered minutely distinct, by means of a faded suit of black cloth which fitted tight to the skin, but was otherwise cut very much in the style of a century ago. These garments had evidently been intended for a much shorter person than their present owner. His ankles and wrists were left naked for several inches. In his shoes, however, a pair of very brilliant buckles gave the lie to the extreme poverty implied by the other portions of his dress. His head was bare, and entirely bald, with the exception of a hinder part, from which depended a *queue* of considerable length. A pair of green spectacles, with side glasses, protected his eyes from the influence of the light, and at the same time prevented our hero from ascertaining either their color or their conformation. About the entire person there was no evidence of a shirt; but a white cravat, of filthy appearance, was tied with extreme precision around the throat, and the ends hanging down formally side by side gave (although I dare say unintentionally) the idea of an ecclesiastic. Indeed, many other points both in his appearance and demeanor might have very well sustained a conception of that nature. Over his left ear, he carried, after the fashion of a modern clerk, an instrument resembling the *stylus* of the ancients. In a breast-pocket of his coat appeared conspicuously a small black volume fastened with clasps of steel. This book, whether accidentally or not, was so turned outwardly from the person as to discover the words *"Rituel Catholique"* in white letters upon the back. His entire physiognomy was interestingly saturnine — even cadaverously pale. The forehead was lofty, and deeply furrowed with the ridges of contemplation. The corners of the mouth were drawn down into an expression of the most submissive humility. There was also a clasping of the hands, as he stepped toward our hero — a deep sigh — and altogether a look of such utter sanctity as could not have failed to be unequivocally prepossessing. Every shadow of anger faded from the countenance of the metaphysician, as, having completed a satisfactory survey of his visiter's person, he shook him cordially by the hand, and conducted him to a seat.

There would however be a radical error in attributing this instantaneous transition of feeling in the philosopher, to any one of those causes which might naturally be supposed to have had an influence. Indeed, Pierre Bon-Bon, from what I have been able to understand of his disposition, was of all men the least likely to be imposed upon by any speciousness of exterior deportment. It was impossible that so accurate an observer

of men and things should have failed to discover, upon the moment, the real character of the personage who had thus intruded upon his hospitality. To say no more, the conformation of his visiter's feet was sufficiently remarkable — he maintained lightly upon his head an inordinately tall hat — there was a tremulous swelling about the hinder part of his breeches — and the vibration of his coat tail was a palpable fact. Judge, then, with what feelings of satisfaction our hero found himself thrown thus at once into the society of a person for whom he had at all times entertained the most unqualified respect. He was, however, too much of the diplomatist to let escape him any intimation of his suspicions in regard to the true state of affairs. It was not his cue to appear at all conscious of the high honor he thus unexpectedly enjoyed; but, by leading his guest into the conversation, to elicit some important ethical ideas, which might, in obtaining a place in his contemplated publication, enlighten the human race, and at the same time immortalize himself — ideas which, I should have added, his visiter's great age, and well-known proficiency in the science of morals, might very well have enabled him to afford.

Actuated by these enlightened views, our hero bade the gentleman sit down, while he himself took occasion to throw some fagots upon the fire, and place upon the now re-established table some bottles of *Mousseux.* Having quickly completed these operations, he drew his chair *vis-à-vis* to his companion's, and waited until the latter should open the conversation. But plans even the most skilfully matured are often thwarted in the outset of their application — and the *restaurateur* found himself *nonplussed* by the very first words of his visiter's speech.

"I see you know me, Bon-Bon," said he; "ha! ha! ha! — he! he! he! — hi! hi! hi! — ho! ho! ho! — hu! hu! hu!" — and the devil, dropping at once the sanctity of his demeanor, opened to its fullest extent a mouth from ear to ear, so as to display a set of jagged and fang-like teeth, and, throwing back his head, laughed long, loudly, wickedly, and uproariously, while the black dog, crouching down upon his haunches, joined lustily in the chorus, and the tabby cat, flying off at a tangent, stood up on end, and shrieked in the farthest corner of the apartment.

Not so the philosopher; he was too much a man of the world either to laugh like the dog, or by shrieks to betray the indecorous trepidation of the cat. It must be confessed, he felt a little astonishment to see the white letters which formed the words "*Rituel Catholique*" on the book in his guest's pocket, momently changing both their color and their import, and in a few seconds, in place of the original title the words *Régitre des Condamnés* blazed forth in characters of red. This startling circumstance, when Bon-Bon replied to his visiter's remark, imparted to his manner an air of embarrassment which probably might not otherwise have been observed.

"Why sir," said the philosopher, "why sir, to speak sincerely — I be-

lieve you are — upon my word — the d——dest — that is to say, I think — I imagine — I *have* some faint — some *very* faint idea — of the remarkable honor —— "

"Oh! — ah! — yes! — very well!" interrupted his Majesty; "say no more — I see how it is." And hereupon, taking off his green spectacles, he wiped the glasses carefully with the sleeve of his coat, and deposited them in his pocket.

If Bon-Bon had been astonished at the incident of the book, his amazement was now much increased by the spectacle which here presented itself to view. In raising his eyes, with a strong feeling of curiosity to ascertain the color of his guest's, he found them by no means black, as he had anticipated — nor gray, as might have been imagined — nor yet hazel nor blue — nor indeed yellow nor red — nor purple — nor white — nor green — nor any other color in the heavens above, or in the earth beneath, or in the waters under the earth. In short, Pierre Bon-Bon not only saw plainly that his Majesty had no eyes whatsoever, but could discover no indications of their having existed at any previous period — for the space where eyes should naturally have been was, I am constrained to say, simply a dead level of flesh.

It was not in the nature of the metaphysician to forbear making some inquiry into the sources of so strange a phenomenon, and the reply of his Majesty was at once prompt, dignified, and satisfactory.

"Eyes! my dear Bon-Bon — eyes! did you say? — oh! — ah! — I perceive! The ridiculous prints, eh, which are in circulation, have given you a false idea of my personal appearance? Eyes! — true. Eyes, Pierre Bon-Bon, are very well in their proper place — *that*, you would say, is the head? — right — the head of a worm. To *you*, likewise, these optics are indispensable — yet I will convince you that my vision is more penetrating than your own. There is a cat I see in the corner — a pretty cat — look at her — observe her well. Now, Bon-Bon, do you behold the thoughts — the thoughts, I say, — the ideas — the reflections — which are being engendered in her pericranium? There it is, now — you do not! She is thinking we admire the length of her tail and the profundity of her mind. She has just concluded that I am the most distinguished of ecclesiastics, and that you are the most superficial of metaphysicians. Thus you see I am not altogether blind; but to one of my profession, the eyes you speak of would be merely an incumbrance, liable at any time to be put out by a toasting-iron, or a pitchfork. To you, I allow, these optical affairs are indispensable. Endeavor, Bon-Bon, to use them well; — *my* vision is the soul."

Hereupon the guest helped himself to the wine upon the table, and pouring out a bumper for Bon-Bon, requested him to drink it without scruple, and make himself perfectly at home.

"A clever book that of yours, Pierre," resumed his Majesty, tapping our friend knowingly upon the shoulder, as the latter put down his glass

after a thorough compliance with his visiter's injunction. "A clever book that of yours, upon my honor. It's a work after my own heart. Your arrangement of the matter, I think, however, might be improved, and many of your notions remind me of Aristotle. That philosopher was one of my most intimate acquaintances. I liked him as much for his terrible ill temper, as for his happy knack at making a blunder. There is only one solid truth in all that he has written, and for that I gave him the hint out of pure compassion for his absurdity. I suppose, Pierre Bon-Bon, you very well know to what divine moral truth I am alluding?"

"Cannot say that I —— "

"Indeed! — why it was I who told Aristotle that by sneezing, men expelled superfluous ideas through the proboscis."

"Which is — hiccup! — undoubtedly the case," said the metaphysician, while he poured out for himself another bumper of Mousseux, and offered his snuff-box to the fingers of his visiter.

"There was Plato, too," continued his Majesty, modestly declining the snuff-box and the compliment it implied — "there was Plato, too, for whom I, at one time, felt all the affection of a friend. You knew Plato, Bon-Bon? — ah, no, I beg a thousand pardons. He met me at Athens, one day, in the Parthenon, and told me he was distressed for an idea. I bade him write, down that $o \ \nu o \upsilon s \ \epsilon \sigma \tau \iota \nu \ \alpha \upsilon \lambda o s$. He said that he would do so, and went home, while I stepped over to the pyramids. But my conscience smote me for having uttered a truth, even to aid a friend, and hastening back to Athens, I arrived behind the philosopher's chair as he was inditing the '$\alpha \upsilon \lambda o s$'."

"Giving the lambda a fillip with my finger, I turned it upside down. So the sentence now read '$o \ \nu o \upsilon s \ \epsilon \sigma \tau \iota \nu \ \alpha \upsilon \gamma o s$', and is, you perceive, the fundamental doctrines in his metaphysics."

"Were you ever at Rome?" asked the *restaurateur*, as he finished his second bottle of Mousseux, and drew from the closet a larger supply of Chambertin.

But once, Monsieur Bon-Bon, but once. There was a time," said the devil, as if reciting some passage from a book — "there was a time when occurred an anarchy of five years, during which the republic, bereft of all its officers, had no magistracy besides the tribunes of the people, and these were not legally vested with any degree of executive power — at that time, Monsieur Bon-Bon — at that time *only* I was in Rome, and I have no earthly acquaintance, consequently, with any of its philosophy." *

"What do you think of — what do you think of — hiccup! — Epicurus?"

"What do I think of *whom*?" said the devil, in astonishment, "you cannot surely mean to find any fault with Epicurus! What do I think of

* Ils écrivaient sur la Philosophie (*Cicero, Lucretius, Seneca*) mais c'était la Philosophie Grecque. — *Condorcet.*

Epicurus! Do you mean me, sir? — I am Epicurus! I am the same philosopher who wrote each of the three hundred treatises commemorated by Diogenes Laertes."

"That's a lie!" said the metaphysician, for the wine had gotten a little into his head.

"Very well! — very well, sir! — very well, indeed, sir!" said his Majesty, apparently much flattered.

"That's a lie!" repeated the *restaurateur*, dogmatically; "that's a — hiccup! — a lie!"

"Well, well, have it your own way!" said the devil, pacifically, and Bon-Bon, having beaten his Majesty at an argument, thought it his duty to conclude a second bottle of Chambertin.

"As I was saying," resumed the visiter — "as I was observing a little while ago, there are some very *outré* notions in that book of yours Monsieur Bon-Bon. What, for instance, do you mean by all that humbug about the soul? Pray, sir, what *is* the soul?"

"The — hiccup! — soul," replied the metaphysician, referring to his MS., "is undoubtedly —— "

"No, sir!"

"Indubitably —— "

"No, sir!"

"Indisputably —— "

"No, sir!"

"Evidently —— "

"No, sir!"

"Incontrovertibly —— "

"No, sir!"

"Hiccup! —— "

"No, sir!"

"And beyond all question, a —— "

"No sir, the soul is no such thing!" (Here the philosopher, looking daggers, took occasion to make an end, upon the spot, of his third bottle of Chambertin.)

"Then — hic-cup! — pray, sir — what — what is it?"

"That is neither here nor there, Monsieur Bon-Bon," replied his Majesty, musingly. "I have tasted — that is to say, I have known some very bad souls, and some too — pretty good ones." Here he smacked his lips, and, having unconsciously let fall his hand upon the volume in his pocket, was seized with a violent fit of sneezing.

He continued.

"There was the soul of Cratinus — passable: Aristophanes — racy: Plato — exquisite — not your Plato, but Plato the comic poet; your Plato would have turned the stomach of Cerberus — faugh! Then let me see! there were Naevius, and Andronicus, and Plautus, and Terentius. Then there were Lucilius, and Catullus, and Naso, and Quintus Flaccus, —

dear Quinty! as I called him when he sung a *seculare* for my amusement, while I toasted him, in pure good humor, on a fork. But they want *flavor*, these Romans. One fat Greek is worth a dozen of them, and besides will *keep*, which cannot be said of a Quirite. — Let us taste your Sauterne."

Bon-Bon had by this time made up his mind to *nil admirari*, and endeavored to hand down the bottles in question. He was, however, conscious of a strange sound in the room like the wagging of a tail. Of this, although extremely indecent in his Majesty, the philosopher took no notice: — simply kicking the dog, and requesting him to be quiet. The visiter continued:

"I found that Horace tasted very much like Aristotle; — you know I am fond of variety. Terentius I could not have told from Menander. Naso, to my astonishment, was Nicander in disguise. Virgilius had a strong twang of Theocritus. Martial put me much in mind of Archilochus — and Titus Livius was positively Polybius and none other."

"Hic-cup!" here replied Bon-Bon, and his Majesty proceeded:

"But if I *have a penchant*, Monsieur Bon-Bon — if I *have a penchant*, it is for a philosopher. Yet, let me tell you, sir, it is not every dev — I mean it is not every gentleman who knows how to *choose* a philosopher. Long ones are *not* good; and the best, if not carfeully shelled, are apt to be a little rancid on account of the gall."

"Shelled!"

"I mean taken out of the carcass."

"What do you think of a — hic-cup! — physician?"

"*Don't* mention them! — ugh! ugh!" (Here his Majesty retched violently.) "I never tasted but one — that rascal Hippocrates! — smelt of asafoetida — ugh! ugh! ugh! — caught a wretched cold washing him in the Styx — and after all he gave me the cholera morbus."

"The — hiccup — wretch!" ejaculated Bon-Bon, "the — hic-cup! — absorption of a pill-box!" — and the philosopher dropped a tear.

"After all," continued the visiter, "after all, if a dev — if a gentleman wishes to *live*, he must have more talents than one or two; and with us a fat face is an evidence of diplomacy."

"How so?"

"Why, we are sometimes exceedingly pushed for provisions. You must know that, in a climate so sultry as mine, it is frequently impossible to keep a spirit alive for more than two or three hours; and after death, unless pickled immediately (and a pickled spirit is *not* good), they will — smell — you understand, eh? Putrefaction is always to be apprehended when the souls are consigned to us in the usual way."

"Hiccup! — hiccup! — good God! how *do* you manage?"

Here the iron lamp commenced swinging with redoubled violence, and the devil half started from his seat; — however, with a slight sigh, he recovered his composure, merely saying to our hero in a low tone: "I tell you what, Pierre Bon-Bon, we *must* have no more swearing."

The host swallowed another bumper, by way of denoting thorough comprehension and acquiescence, and the visitor continued.

"Why, there are *several* ways of managing. The most of us starve: some put up with the pickle: for my part I purchase my spirits *vivente corpore*, in which case I find they keep very well."

"But the body! — hiccup! — the body!"

"The body, the body — well, what of the body? — oh! ah! I perceive. Why, sir, the body is not *at all* affected by the transaction. I have made innumerable purchases of the kind in my day, and the parties never experienced any inconvenience. There were Cain and Nimrod, and Nero, and Caligula, and Dionysius, and Pisistratus, and — and a thousand others, who never knew what it was to have a soul during the latter part of their lives; yet, sir, these men adorned society. Why isn't there A——, now, whom you know as well as I? Is *he* not in possession of his faculties, mental and corporeal? Who writes a keener epigram? Who reasons more wittily? Who — but stay! I have his agreement in my pocket-book."

Thus saying, he produced a red leather wallet, and took from it a number of papers. Upon some of these Bon-Bon caught a glimpse of the letters *Machi — Maza — Robesp* — with the words *Caligula, George, Elizabeth*. His Majesty selected a narrow slip of parchment, and from it read aloud the following words:

"In consideration of certain mental endowments which it is unnecessary to specify, and in further consideration of one thousand louis d'or, I being aged one year and one month, do hereby make over to the bearer of this agreement all my right, title, and appurtenance in the shadow called my soul. (Signed) A" * (Here His Majesty repeated a name which I did not feel justified in indicating more unequivocally.)

"A clever fellow that," resumed he; "but like you, Monsieur Bon-Bon, he was mistaken about the soul. The soul a shadow, truly! The soul a shadow; Ha! ha! ha! — he! he! he! — hu! hu! hu! Only think of a fricasseed shadow!"

"*Only* think — hiccup! — of a fricasseed shadow!" exclaimed our hero, whose faculties were becoming much illuminated by the profundity of his Majesty's discourse.

"Only think of a hiccup! — fricasseed shadow!! Now, damme! — hiccup! — humph! If *I* would have been such a — hiccup! — nincompoop! *My* soul, Mr. — humph!"

"*Your* soul, Monsieur Bon-Bon?"

"Yes, sir — hiccup! — *my* soul is —— "

"What, sir?"

"No shadow, damme!"

"Did you mean to say —— "

"Yes, sir, *my* soul is — hiccup! — humph! — yes, sir."

* *Quere*-Arouet?

"Did you not intend to assert ——— "

"My soul is — hiccup! — peculiarly qualified for — hiccup! — a ——— "

"What, sir?"

"Stew."

"Ha!"

"Soufflée."

"Eh!"

"Fricassée."

"Indeed!"

"Ragout and fricandeau — and see here, my good fellow! I'll let you have it — hiccup! — a bargain." Here the philosopher slapped his Majesty upon the back.

"Couldn't think of such a thing," said the latter calmly, at the same time rising from his seat. The metaphysician stared.

"Am supplied at present," said his Majesty.

"Hiccup — e-h?" said the philosopher.

"Have no funds on hand."

"What?"

"Besides, very unhandsome in me — "

"Sir!"

"To take advantage of ——— "

"Hiccup!"

"Your present disgusting and ungentlemanly situation."

Here the visiter bowed and withdrew — in what manner could not precisely be ascertained — but in a well-concerted effort to discharge a bottle at "the villain," the slender chain was severed that depended from the ceiling, and the metaphysician prostrated by the downfall of the lamp.

Ms. Found in a Bottle

Qui n'a plus qu'un moment à vivre
N'a plus rien à dissimuler.

Quinault — Atys

OF my country and of my family I have little to say. Ill-usage and length of years have driven me from the one, and estranged me from the other. Hereditary wealth afforded me an education of no common order, and a contemplative turn of mind enabled me to methodise the stores which early study very diligently garnered up. Beyond all things, the works of the German moralists gave me great delight; not from any ill-advised admiration of their eloquent madness, but from the ease with

which my habits of rigid thought enabled me to detect their falsities. I have often been reproached with the aridity of my genius; a deficiency of imagination has been imputed to me as a crime; and the Pyrrhonism of my opinions has at all times rendered me notorious. Indeed, a strong relish for physical philosophy has, I fear, tinctured my mind with a very common error of this age — I mean the habit of referring occurrences, even the least susceptible of such reference, to the principles of that science. Upon the whole, no person could be less liable than myself to be led away from the severe precincts of truth by the *ignes fatui* of superstition. I have thought proper to premise thus much, lest the incredible tale I have to tell should be considered rather the raving of a crude imagination, than the positive experience of a mind to which the reveries of fancy have been a dead letter and a nullity.

After many years spent in foreign travel, I sailed in the year 18—, from the port of Batavia, in the rich and populous island of Java, on a voyage to the Archipelago of the Sunda Islands. I went as passenger — having no other inducement than a kind of nervous restlessness which haunted me as a fiend.

Our vessel was a beautiful ship of about four hundred tons, copper-fastened, and built at Bombay of Malabar teak. She was freighted with cotton-wool and oil, from the Lachadive Islands. We had also on board coir, jaggeree, ghee, cocoanuts, and a few cases of opium. The stowage was clumsily done, and the vessel consequently crank.

We got under way with a mere breath of wind, and for many days stood along the eastern coast of Java, without any other incident to beguile the monotony of our course than the occasional meeting with some of the small grabs of the Archipelago to which we were bound.

One evening, leaning over the taffrail, I observed a very singular isolated cloud, to the N. W. It was remarkable, as well for its color as from its being the first we had seen since our departure from Batavia. I watched it attentively until sunset, when it spread all at once to the eastward and westward, girding in the horizon with a narrow strip of vapor, and looking like a long line of low beach. My notice was soon afterward attracted by the dusky-red appearance of the moon, and the peculiar character of the sea. The latter was undergoing a rapid change, and the water seemed more than usually transparent. Although I could distinctly see the bottom, yet, heaving the lead, I found the ship in fifteen fathoms. The air now became intolerably hot, and was loaded with spiral exhalations similar to those arising from heated iron. As night came on, every breath of wind died away, and a more entire calm it is impossible to conceive. The flame of a candle burned upon the poop without the least perceptible motion, and a long hair, held between the finger and thumb, hung without the possibility of detecting a vibration. However, as the captain said he could perceive no indication of danger, and as we were drifting in bodily to shore, he ordered the sails to be furled, and the anchor let

go. No watch was set, and the crew, consisting principally of Malays, stretched themselves deliberately upon deck. I went below — not without a full presentiment of evil. Indeed, every appearance warranted me in apprehending a Simoom. I told the captain of my fears; but he paid no attention to what I said, and left me without deigning to give a reply. My uneasiness, however, prevented me from sleeping, and about midnight I went upon deck. As I placed my foot upon the upper step of the companion-ladder, I was startled by a loud, humming noise, like that occasioned by the rapid revolution of a mill-wheel, and before I could ascertain its meaning, I found the ship quivering to its center. In the next instant a wilderness of foam hurled us upon our beam-ends, and, rushing over us fore and aft, swept the entire decks from stem to stern.

The extreme fury of the blast proved, in a great measure, the salvation of the ship. Although completely water-logged, yet, as her masts had gone by the board, she rose, after a minute, heavily from the sea, and, staggering awhile beneath the immense pressure of the tempest, finally righted.

By what miracle I escaped destruction, it is impossible to say. Stunned by the shock of the water, I found myself, upon recovery, jammed in between the stern-post and rudder. With great difficulty I gained my feet, and looking dizzily around, was at first struck with the idea of our being among breakers; so terrific, beyond the widest imagination, was the whirlpool of mountainous and foaming ocean within which we were engulfed. After a while I heard the voice of an old Swede, who had shipped with us at the moment of our leaving port. I hallooed to him with all my strength, and presently he came reeling aft. We soon discovered that we were the sole survivors of the accident. All on deck, with the exception of ourselves, had been swept overboard; the captain and mates must have perished as they slept, for the cabins were deluged with water. Without assistance we could expect to do little for the security of the ship, and our exertions were at first paralyzed by the momentary expectation of going down. Our cable had, of course, parted like pack-thread, at the first breath of the hurricane, or we should have been instantaneously overwhelmed. We scudded with frightful velocity before the sea, and the water made clear breaches over us. The frame-work of our stern was shattered excessively, and, in almost every respect, we had received considerable injury; but to our extreme joy we found the pumps unchoked, and that we had made no great shifting of our ballast. The main fury of the blast had already blown over, and we apprehended little danger from the violence of the wind; but we looked forward to its total cessation with dismay; well believing, that in our shattered condition, we should inevitably perish in the tremendous swell which would ensue. But this very just apprehension seemed by no means likely to be soon verified. For five entire days and nights — during which our only subsistence was a small quantity of jaggeree, procured with great difficulty from the forecastle

— the hulk flew at a rate defying computation, before rapidly succeeding flaws of wind, which, without equalling the first violence of the Simoom, were still more terrific than any tempest I had before encountered. Our course for the first four days was, with trifling variations, S. E. and by S.; and we must have run down the coast of New Holland. On the fifth day the cold became extreme, although the wind had hauled round a point more to the northward. The sun arose with a sickly yellow lustre, and clambered a very few degrees above the horizon — emitting no decisive light. There were no clouds apparent, yet the wind was upon the increase, and blew with a fitful and unsteady fury. About noon, as nearly as we could guess, our attention was again arrested by the appearance of the sun. It gave out no light, properly so called, but a dull and sullen glow without reflection, as if all its rays were polarized. Just before sinking within the turgid sea, its central fires suddenly went out, as if hurriedly extinguished by some unaccountable power. It was a dim, silver-like rim, alone, as it rushed down the unfathomable ocean.

We waited in vain for the arrival of the sixth day — that day to me has not arrived — to the Swede never did arrive. Thenceforward we were enshrouded in pitchy darkness, so that we could not have seen an object at twenty paces from the ship. Eternal night continued to envelope us, all unrelieved by the phosphoric sea-brilliancy to which we had been accustomed in the tropics. We observed, too, that, although the tempest continued to rage with unabated violence, there was no longer to be discovered the usual appearance of surf, or foam, which had hitherto attended us. All around were horror, and thick gloom, and a black sweltering desert of ebony. Superstitious terror crept by degrees into the spirit of the old Swede, and my own soul was wrapt in silent wonder. We neglected all care of the ship, as worse than useless, and securing ourselves as well as possible, to the stump of the mizen-mast, looked out bitterly into the world of ocean. We had no means of calculating time, nor could we form any guess of our situation. We were, however, well aware of having made farther to the southward than any previous navigators, and felt great amazement at not meeting with the usual impediments of ice. In the meantime every moment threatened to be our last — every mountainous billow hurried to overwhelm us. The swell surpassed anything I had imagined possible, and that we were not instantly buried is a miracle. My companion spoke of the lightness of our cargo, and reminded me of the excellent qualities of our ship; but I could not help feeling the utter hopelessness of hope itself, and prepared myself gloomily for that death which I thought nothing could defer beyond an hour, as, with every knot of way the ship made, the swelling of the black stupendous seas became more dismally appalling. At times we gasped for breath at an elevation beyond the albatross — at times became dizzy with the velocity of our descent into some watery hell, where the air grew stagnant, and no sound disturbed the slumbers of the kraken.

We were at the bottom of one of these abysses, when a quick scream from my companion broke fearfully upon the night. "See! see!" cried he, shrieking in my ears, "Almighty God! see! see!" As he spoke I became aware of a dull sullen glare of red light which streamed down the sides of the vast chasm where we lay, and threw a fitful brilliancy upon our deck. Casting my eyes upwards, I beheld a spectacle which froze the current of my blood. At a terrific height directly above us, and upon the very verge of the precipitous descent, hovered a gigantic ship of perhaps four thousand tons. Although upreared upon the summit of a wave more than a hundred times her own altitude, her apparent size still exceeded that of any ship of the line or East Indiaman in existence. Her huge hull was of a deep dingy black, unrelieved by any of the customary carvings of a ship. A single row of brass cannon protruded from her open ports, and dashed from the polished surfaces the fires of innumerable battle-lanterns which swung to and fro about her rigging. But what mainly inspired us with horror and astonishment, was that she bore up under a press of sail in the very teeth of that supernatural sea, and of that ungovernable hurricane. When we first discovered her, her bows were alone to be seen, as she rose slowly from the dim and horrible gulf beyond her. For a moment of intense terror she paused upon the giddy pinnacle as if in contemplation of her own sublimity, then trembled, and tottered, and — came down.

At this instant, I know not what sudden self-possession came over my spirit. Staggering as far aft as I could, I awaited fearlessly the ruin that was to overwhelm. Our own vessel was at length ceasing from her struggles, and sinking with her head to the sea. The shock of the descending mass struck her, consequently, in that portion of her frame which was already under water, and in the inevitable result was to hurl me, with irresistible violence, upon the rigging of the stranger.

As I fell, the ship hove in stays, and went about; and to the confusion ensuing I attributed my escape from the notice of the crew. With little difficulty I made my way, unperceived, to the main hatchway, which was partially open, and soon found an opportunity of secreting myself in the hold. Why I did so I can hardly tell. An indefinite sense of awe, which at first sight of the navigators of the ship had taken hold of my mind, was perhaps the principle of my concealment. I was unwilling to trust myself with a race of people who had offered, to the cursory glance I had taken, so many points of vague novelty, doubt, and apprehension. I therefore thought proper to contrive a hiding-place in the hold. This I did by removing a small portion of the shifting-boards, in such a manner as to afford me a convenient retreat between the huge timbers of the ship.

I had scarcely completed my work, when a footstep in the hold forced me to make use of it. A man passed by my place of concealment with a feeble and unsteady gait. I could not see his face, but had an opportunity of observing his general appearance. There was about it an evidence of

great age and infirmity. His knees tottered beneath a load of years, and his entire frame quivered under the burthen. He muttered to himself, in a low broken tone, some words of a language which I could not understand, and groped in a corner among a pile of singular-looking instruments, and decayed charts of navigation. His manner was a wild mixture of the peevishness of second childhood, and the solemn dignity of a God. He at length went on deck, and I saw him no more.

A feeling, for which I have no name, has taken possession of my soul — a sensation which will admit of no analysis, to which the lessons of by-gone time are inadequate, and for which I fear futurity itself will offer me no key. To a mind constituted like my own, the latter consideration is an evil. I shall never — I know that I shall never — be satisfied with regard to the nature of my conceptions. Yet it is not wonderful that these conceptions are indefinite, since they have their origin in sources so utterly novel. A new sense — a new entity is added to my soul.

It is long since I first trod the deck of this terrible ship, and the rays of my destiny are, I think, gathering to a focus. Incomprehensible men! Wrapped up in meditations of a kind which I cannot divine, they pass me by unnoticed. Concealment is utter folly on my part, for the people *will not* see. It is but just now that I passed directly before the eyes of the mate; it was no long while ago that I ventured into the captain's own private cabin, and took thence the materials with which I write, and have written. I shall from time to time continue this journal. It is true that I may not find an opportunity of transmitting it to the world, but I will not fail to make the endeavor. At the last moment I will enclose the MS. in a bottle, and cast it within the sea.

An incident has occurred which has given me new room for meditation. Are such things the operation of ungoverned chance? I had ventured upon deck and thrown myself down, without attracting any notice, among a pile of ratlin-stuff and old sails, in the bottom of the yawl. While musing upon the singularity of my fate, I unwittingly daubed with a tar-brush the edges of a neatly folded studding-sail which lay near me on a barrel. The studding-sail is now bent upon the ship, and the thoughtless touches of the brush are spread out in the word DISCOVERY.

I have made my observations lately upon the structure of the vessel. Although well armed, she is not, I think, a ship of war. Her rigging, build, and general equipment, all negative a supposition of this kind. What she *is not*, I can easily perceive; what she *is*, I fear it is impossible to say. I know not how it is, but in scrutinizing her strange model and singular cast of spars, her huge size and overgrown suits of canvas, her severely simple bow and antiquated stern, there will occasionally flash across my mind a sensation of familiar things, and there is always mixed up with

such indistinct shadows of recollection, an unaccountable memory of old foreign chronciles and ages long ago. . . .

I have been looking at the timbers of the ship. She is built of a material to which I am a stranger. There is a peculiar character about the wood which strikes me as rendering it unfit for the purpose to which it has been applied. I mean its extreme *porousness*, considered independently of the worm-eaten condition which is a consequence of navigation in these seas, and apart from the rottenness attendant upon age. It will appear perhaps an observation somewhat over-curious, but this would have every characteristic of Spanish oak, if Spanish oak were distended by any natural means.

In reading the above sentence, a curious apothegm of an old weather-beaten Dutch navigator comes full upon my recollection. "It is as sure," he was wont to say, when any doubt was entered of his veracity, "as sure as there is a sea where the ship itself will grow in bulk like the living body of the seaman." . . .

About an hour ago, I made bold to trust myself among a group of the crew. They paid me no manner of attention, and, although I stood in the very midst of them all, seemed utterly unconscious of my presence. Like the one I had at first seen in the hold, they all bore about them the marks of a hoary old age. Their knees trembled with infirmity; their shoulders were bent double with decrepitude; their shrivelled skins rattled in the wind; their voices were low, tremulous, and broken; their eyes glistened with the rheum of years; and their gray hairs streamed terribly in the tempest. Around them, on every part of the deck, lay scattered mathematical instruments of the most quaint and obsolete construction. . . .

I mentioned, some time ago, the bending of a studding-sail. From that period, the ship, being thrown dead off the wind, has continued her terrific course due south, with every rag of canvas packed upon her, from her truck to her lower studding-sail booms, and rolling every moment her top-gallant yard-arms into the most appalling hell of water which it can enter into the mind of man to imagine. I have just left the deck, where I find it impossible to maintain a footing, although the crew seem to experience little inconvenience. It appears to me a miracle of miracles that our enormous bulk is not swallowed up at once and forever. We are surely doomed to hover continually upon the brink of eternity, without taking a final plunge into the abyss. From billows a thousand times more stupendous than any I have ever seen, we glide away with the facility of the arrowy sea-gull; and the colossal waters rear their heads above us like demons of the deep, but like demons confined to simple threats, and forbidden to destroy. I am led to attribute these frequent escapes to the only natural cause which can account for such effect. I must suppose the ship to be within the influence of some strong current, or impetuous under-tow. . . .

I have seen the captain face to face, and in his own cabin — but, as I expected, he paid me no attention. Although in his appearance there is, to a casual observer, nothing which might bespeak him more or less than man, still a feeling of irrepressible reverence and awe mingled with the sensation of wonder with which I regarded him. In stature, he is nearly my own height; that is, about five feet eight inches. He is of a well-knit and compact frame of body, neither robust nor remarkable otherwise. But it is the singularity of the expression which reigns upon the face — it is the intense, the wonderful, the thrilling evidence of old age so utter, so extreme, which excites within my spirit a sense — a sentiment ineffable. His forehead, although little wrinkled, seems to bear upon it the stamp of a myriad of years. His gray hairs are records of the past, and his grayer eyes are sybils of the future. The cabin floor was thickly strewn with strange, iron-clasped folios and mouldering instruments of science, and obsolete, long-forgotten charts. His head was bowed down upon his hands, and he pored, with a fiery, unquiet eye, over a paper which I took to be a commission, and which, at all events, bore the signature of a monarch. He muttered to himself — as did the first seaman whom I saw in the hold — some low peevish syllables of a foreign tongue; and although the speaker was close to my elbow, his voice seemed to reach my ears from the distance of a mile. . . .

The ship and all in it are imbued with the spirit of Eld. The crew glide to and fro like the ghosts of buried centuries; their eyes have an eager and uneasy meaning; and when their fingers fall athwart my path in the wild glare of the battle-lanterns, I feel as I have never felt before, although I have been all my life a dealer in antiquities, and have imbibed the shadows of fallen columns at Balbec, and Tadmor, and Persepolis, until my very soul has become a ruin. . . .

When I look around me, I feel ashamed of my former apprehension. If I trembled at the blast which has hitherto attended us, shall I not stand aghast at a warring of wind and ocean, to convey any idea of which, the words tornado and simoon are trivial and ineffective? All in the immediate vicinity of the ship, is the blackness of eternal night, and a chaos of foamless water; but, about a league on either side of us, may be seen, indistinctly and at intervals, stupendous ramparts of ice, towering away into the desolate sky, and looking like the walls of the universe. . . .

As I imagined, the ship proves to be in a current — if that appellation can properly be given to a tide which, howling and shrieking by the white ice, thunders on to the southward with a velocity like the headlong dashing of a cataract. . . .

To conceive the horror of my sensations, is, I presume, utterly impossible; yet a curiosity to penetrate the mysteries of these awful regions, predominates even over my despair, and will reconcile me to the most hideous aspect of death. It is evident that we are hurrying onward to some exciting knowledge — some never-to-be-imparted secret, whose at-

tainment is destruction. Perhaps this current leads us to the southern pole itself. It must be confessed that a supposition apparently so wild has every probability in its favor. . . .

The crew pace the deck with unquiet and tremulous step; but there is upon their countenance and expression more of the eagerness of hope than of the apathy of despair.

In the meantime the wind is still in our poop, and, we carry a crowd of canvass, the ship is at times lifted bodily from out the sea! Oh, horror upon horror! — the ice opens suddenly to the right, and to the left, and we are whirling dizzily, in immense concentric circles, round and round the borders of a gigantic amphitheatre, the summit of whose walls is lost in the darkness and the distance. But little time will be left me to ponder upon my destiny! The circles rapidly grow small — we are plunging madly within the grasp of the whirlpool — and amid a roaring, and bellowing, and thundering of ocean and tempest, the ship is quivering — oh God! and — going down!

The "MS. Found in a Bottle," was originally published in 1831, and it was not until many years afterward that I became acquainted with the maps of Mercator, in which the ocean is represented as rushing, by four mouths, into the (northern) Polar Gulf, to be absorbed into the bowels of the earth; the Pole itself being represented by a black rock, towering to a prodigious height. — E. A. P.

The Assignation

Stay for me there! I will not fail
To meet thee in that hollow vale
[Exequy on the death of his wife, by Henry King, Bishop of Chichester.]

ILL-FATED and mysterious man! — bewildered in the brilliancy of thine own imagination, and fallen in the flames of thine own youth! Again in fancy I behold thee! Once more thy form hath risen before me! — not — oh! as thou art — in the cold valley and shadow — but as thou *shouldst be* — squandering away a life of magnificent meditation in that city of dim visions, thine own Venice — which is a star-beloved Elysium of the sea, and the wide windows of whose Palladian palaces look down with a deep and bitter meaning upon the secrets of her silent waters. Yes! I repeat it — as thou *shouldst be.* There are surely other worlds than this — other thoughts than the thoughts of the multitude — other speculations than the speculation of the sophist. Who then shall call thy con-

duct into question? who blame thee for thy visionary hours, or denounce those occupations as a wasting away of life, which were but the overflowings of thine everlasting energies?

It was at Venice, beneath the covered archway there called the *Ponte di Sospiri*, that I met, for the third or fourth time the person of whom I speak. It is with a confused recollection that I bring to mind the circumstances of that meeting. Yet I remember — ah! how should I forget? — the deep midnight, the Bridge of Sighs, the beauty of woman, and the Genius of Romance that stalked up and down the narrow canal.

It was a night of unusual gloom. The great clock of the Piazza had sounded the fifth hour of the Italian evening. The square of the Campanile lay silent and deserted, and the lights in the old Ducal Palace were dying fast away. I was returning home from the Piazetta, by way of the Grand Canal. But as my gondola arrived opposite the mouth of the canal San Marco, a female voice from its recesses broke suddenly upon the night, in one wild, hysterical, and long-continued shriek. Startled at the sound, I sprang upon my feet; while the gondolier, letting slip his single oar, lost it in the pitchy darkness beyond a chance of recovery, and we were consequently left to the guidance of the current which here sets from the greater into the smaller channel. Like some huge and sable-feathered condor, we were slowly drifting down toward the Bridge of Sighs, when a thousand flambeaux flashing from the windows, and down the staircases of the Ducal Palace, turned all at once that deep gloom into a livid and praeternatural day.

A child, slipping from the arms of its own mother, had fallen from an upper window of the lofty structure into the deep and dim canal. The quiet waters had closed placidly over their victim; and, although my own gondola was the only one in sight, many a stout swimmer, already in the stream, was seeking in vain upon the surface, the treasure which was to be found, alas! only within the abyss. Upon the broad black marble flagstones at the entrance of the palace, and a few steps above the water, stood a figure which none who then saw can have ever since forgotten. It was the Marchesa Aphrodite — the adoration of all Venice — the gayest of the gay — the most lovely where all were beautiful — but still the young wife of the old and intriguing Mentoni, and the mother of that fair child, her first and only one, who now, deep beneath the murky water, was thinking in bitterness of heart upon her sweet caresses, and exhausting its little life in struggles to call upon her name.

She stood alone. Her small, bare and silvery feet gleamed in the black mirror of marble beneath her. Her hair, not as yet more than half loosened for the night from its ball-room array, clustered, amid a shower of diamonds, round and round her classical head, in curls like those of the young hyacinth. A snowy-white and gauze-like drapery seemed to be nearly the sole covering to her delicate form; but the mid-summer and midnight air was hot, sullen, and still, and no motion in the statue-like

form itself, stirred even the folds of that raiment of very vapor which hung around it as the heavy marble hangs around the Niobe. Yet — strange to say! — her large lustrous eyes were not turned downward upon that grave wherein her brightest hope lay buried — but riveted in a widely different direction! The prison of the Old Republic is, I think, the stateliest building in all Venice — but how could that lady gaze so fixedly upon it, when beneath her lay stifling her only child? Yon dark, gloomy niche, too, yawns right opposite her chamber window — what, then *could* there be in its shadows — in its architecture — in its ivy-wreathed and solemn cornices — that the Marchesa di Mentoni had not wondered at a thousand times before? Nonsense — Who does not remember that, at such a time as this, the eye, like a shattered mirror, multiplies the images of its sorrow, and sees in innumerable far-off places, the wo which is close at hand?

Many steps above the Marchesa, and within the arch of the water-gate, stood, in full dress, the Satyr-like figure of Mentoni himself. He was occasionally occupied in thrumming a guitar, and seemed *ennuyé* to the very death, as at intervals he gave directions for the recovery of his child. Stupefied and aghast, I had myself no power to move from the upright position I had assumed upon first hearing the shriek, and must have presented to the eyes of the agitated group a spectral and ominous appearance, as with pale countenance and rigid limbs, I floated down among them in that funereal gondola.

All efforts proved in vain. Many of the most energetic in the search were relaxing their exertions, and yielding to a gloomy sorrow. There seemed but little hope for the child; (how much less than for the mother!) but now, from the interior of that dark niche which has been already mentioned as forming a part of the Old Republican prison, and as fronting the lattice of the Marchesa, a figure muffled in a cloak, stepped out within reach of the light, and, pausing a moment upon the verge of the giddy descent, plunged headlong into the canal. As, in an instant afterward, he stood with the still living and breathing child within his grasp, upon the marble flagstones by the side of the Marchesa, his cloak, heavy with the drenching water, became unfastened, and, falling in folds about his feet, discovered to the wonder-stricken spectators the graceful person of a very young man, with the sound of whose name the greater part of Europe was then ringing.

No word spoke the deliverer. But the Marchesa! She will now receive her child— she will press it to her heart — she will cling to its little form, and smother it with her caresses. Alas! *another's* arms have taken it from the stranger — *another's* arms have taken it away, and borne it afar off, unnoticed, into the palace! And the Marchesa! Her lip — her beautiful lip trembles; tears are gathering in her eyes — those eyes which, like Pliny's acanthus, are "soft and almost liquid." Yes! tears are gathering in those eyes — and see! the entire woman thrills throughout the soul,

and the statue has started into life! The pallor of the marble countenance, the swelling of the marble bosom, the very purity of the marble feet, we behold suddenly flushed over with a tide of ungovernable crimson; and a slight shudder quivers about her delicate frame, as a gentle air at Napoli about the rich silver lilies in the grass.

Why *should* that lady blush! To this demand there is no answer — except that, having left, in the eager haste and terror of a mother's heart, the privacy of her own *boudoir*, she has neglected to enthral her tiny feet in their slippers, and utterly forgotten to throw over her Venetian shoulders that drapery which is their due. What other possible reason could there have been for her so blushing? — for the glance of those wild appealing eyes? — for the unusual tumult of that throbbing bosom? — for the convulsive pressure of that trembling hand? — that hand which fell, as Mentoni turned into the palace, accidentally, upon the hand of the stranger. What reason could there have been for the low — the singularly low tone of those unmeaning words which the lady uttered hurriedly in bidding him adieu? "Thou hast conquered," she said, or the murmurs of the water deceived me; "thou hast conquered — one hour after sunrise — we shall meet — so let it be!"

The tumult had subsided, the lights had died away within the palace, and the stranger, whom I now recognized, stood alone upon the flags. He shook with inconceivable agitation, and his eyes glanced around in search of a gondola. I could not do less than offer him the service of my own; and he accepted the civility. Having obtained an oar at the water-gate, we proceeded together to his residence, while he rapidly recovered his self-possession, and spoke of our former slight acquaintance in terms of great apparent cordiality.

There are some subjects upon which I take pleasure in being minute. The person of the stranger — let me call him by this title, who to all the world was still a stranger — the person of the stranger is one of these subjects. In height he might have been below rather than above the medium size: although there were moments of intense passion when his frame actually *expanded* and belied the assertion. The light, almost slender symmetry of his figure promised more of that ready activity which he evinced at the Bridge of Sighs, than of that Herculean strength which he has been known to wield without an effort, upon occasions of more dangerous emergency. With the mouth and chin of a deity — singular, wild, full, liquid eyes, whose shadows varied from pure hazel to intense and briliant jet — and a profusion of curling, black hair, from which a forehead of unusual breadth gleamed forth at intervals all light and ivory — his were features than which I have seen none more classically regular, except, perhaps, the marble ones of the Emperor Commodus. Yet his countenance was, nevertheless, one of those which all men have seen at some period of their lives, and have never afterward seen again. It had

no peculiar, it had no settled predominant expression to be fastened upon the memory; a countenance seen and instantly forgotten, but forgotten with a vague and never-ceasing desire of recalling it to mind. Not that the spirit of each rapid passion failed, at any time, to throw its own distinct image upon the mirror of that face — but that the mirror, mirror-like, retained no vestige of the passion, when the passion had departed.

Upon leaving him on the night of our adventure, he solicited me, in what I thought an urgent manner, to call upon him *very* early the next morning. Shortly after sunrise, I found myself accordingly at his Palazzo, one of those huge structures of gloomy yet fantastic pomp, which tower above the waters of the Grand Canal in the vicinity of the Rialto. I was shown up a broad winding staircase of mosaics, into an apartment whose unparalleled splendor burst through the opening door with an actual glare, making me blind and dizzy with luxuriousness.

I knew my acquaintance to be wealthy. Report had spoken of his possessions in terms which I had even ventured to call terms of ridiculous exaggeration. But as I gazed about me, I could not bring myself to believe that the wealth of any subject in Europe could have supplied the princely magnificence which burned and blazed around.

Although, as I say, the sun had arisen, yet the room was still brilliantly lighted up. I judge from this circumstance, as well as from an air of exhaustion in the countenance of my friend, that he had not retired to bed during the whole of the preceding night. In the architecture and embellishments of the chamber, the evident design had been to dazzle and astound. Little attention had been paid to the *decora* of what is technically called *keeping*, or to the proprieties of nationality. The eye wandered from object to object, and rested upon none — neither the *grotesques* of the Greek painters, nor the sculptures of the best Italian days, nor the huge carvings of untutored Egypt. Rich draperies in every part of the room trembled to the vibration of low, melancholy music, whose origin was not to be discovered. The senses were oppressed by mingled and conflicting perfumes, reeking up from strange convolute censers, together with multitudinous flaring and flickering tongues of emerald and violet fire. The rays of the newly risen sun poured in upon the whole, through windows, formed each of a single pane of crimson-tinted glass. Glancing to and fro, in a thousand reflections, from curtains which rolled from their cornices like cataracts of molten silver, the beams of natural glory mingled at length fitfully with the artificial light, and lay weltering in subdued masses upon a carpet of rich, liquid-looking cloth of Chili gold.

"Ha! ha! ha! — ha! ha! ha!" — laughed the proprietor, motioning me to a seat as I entered the room, and throwing himself back at full-length upon an ottoman. "I see," said he, perceiving that I could not immediately reconcile myself to the *bienseance* of so singular a welcome, — "I see you are astonished at my apartment — at my statues — my pictures

— my originality of conception in architecture and upholstery! absolutely drunk, eh, with my magnificence? But pardon me, my dear sir; (here his tone of voice dropped to the very spirit of cordiality,) pardon me for my uncharitable laughter. You appeared so *utterly* astonished. Besides, some things are so completely ludicrous, that a man *must* laugh, or die. To die laughing must be the most glorious of all glorious deaths! Sir Thomas More — a very fine man was Sir Thomas More — Sir Thomas More died laughing, you remember. Also in the *Absurdities* of Ravisius Textor, there is a long list of characters who came to the same magnificent end. Do you know, however," continued he, musingly, "that at Sparta (which is now Palæochori), at Sparta, I say, to the west of the citadel, among a chaos of scarcely visible ruins, is a kind of *socle*, upon which are still legible the letters ΛΑΞΜ. They are undoubtedly part of ΓΕΛΑΞΜΑ. Now, at Sparta were a thousand temples and shrines to a thousand different divinities. How exceedingly strange that the altar of Laughter should have survived all the others! But in the present instance," he resumed, with a singular alteration of voice and manner, "I have no right to be merry at your expense. You might well have been amazed. Europe cannot produce any thing so fine as his, my little legal cabinet. My other apartments are by no means of the same order — mere *ultras* of fashionable insipidity. This is better than fashion — is it not? Yet this has but to be seen to become the rage — that is, with those who could afford it at the cost of their entire patrimony. I have guarded, however, against any such profanation. With one exception, you are the only human being, besides myself and my *valet*, who has been admitted within the mysteries of the imperial precincts, since they have been bedizzened as you see!"

I bowed in acknowledgment — for the overpowering sense of splendor and perfume and music, together with the unexpected eccentricity of his address and manner, prevented me from expressing in words, my appreciation of what I might have construed into a compliment.

"Here," he resumed, arising and leaning on my arm as he sauntered around the apartment, "here are paintings from the Greeks to Cimabue, and from Cimabue to the present hour. Many are chosen, as you see, with little deference to the opinions of Virtu. They are all, however, fitting tapestry for a chamber such as this. Here, too, are some *chef-d'œuvres* of the unknown great; and here, unfinished designs by men, celebrated in their day, whose very names the perspicacity of the academies has left to silence and to me. What think you," said he, turning abruptly as he spoke, — "what think you of this Madonna della Pieta?"

"It is Guido's own!" I said, with all the enthusiasm of my nature, for I had been poring intently over its surpassing loveliness. "It is Guido's own! — how *could* you have obtained it? she is undoubtedly in painting what Venus is in sculpture."

"Ha!" said he, thoughtfully, "the Venus? — the beautiful Venus? — the Venus of the Medici? — she of the diminutive head and the gilded

hair? Part of the left arm [here his voice dropped so as to be heard with difficulty], and all the right, are restorations, and in the coquetry of that right arm lies, I think, the quintessence of all affectation. Give *me* the Canova! The Apollo, too, is a copy — there can be no doubt of it — blind fool that I am, who cannot behold the boasted inspiration of the Apollo! I cannot help — pity me! — I cannot help preferring the Antinous. Was it not Socrates who said that the statuary found his statue in the block of marble? Then Michæl Angelo was by no means original in his couplet —

> 'Non ha l'ottimo artista alcun concetto
> Chè un marmo solo in se non circunscriva.' "

It has been, or should be remarked, that, in the manner of the true gentleman, we are always aware of a difference from the bearing of the vulgar, without being at once precisely able to determine in what such difference consists. Allowing the remark to have applied in its full force to the outward demeanor of my acquaintance, I felt it, on that eventful morning, still more fully applicable to his moral temperament and character. Nor can I better define that peculiarity of spirit which seemed to place him so essentially apart from all other human beings, than by calling it a *habit* of intense and continual thought, pervading even his most trivial actions — intruding upon his moments of dalliance — and interweaving itself with his very flashes of merriment — like adders which writhe from out the eyes of the grinning masks in the cornices around the temples of Persepolis.

I could not help, however, repeatedly observing, through the mingled tone of levity and solemnity with which he rapidly descanted upon matters of little importance, a certain air of trepidation — a degree of nervous *unction* in action and in speech — an unquiet excitability of manner which appeared to me at all times unaccountable, and upon some occasions even filled me with alarm. Frequently, too, pausing in the middle of a sentence whose commencement he had apparently forgotten, he seemed to be listening in the deepest attention, as if either in momentary expectation of a visitor, or to sounds which must have had existence in his imagination alone.

It was during one of these reveries or pauses of apparent abstraction, that, in turning over a page of the poet and scholar Politian's beautiful tragedy, "The Orfeo" (the first native Italian tragedy), which lay near me upon an ottoman, I discovered a passage underlined in pencil. It was a passage towards the end of the third act — a passage of the most heart-stirring excitement — a passage which, although tainted with impurity, no man shall read without a thrill of novel emotion — no woman without a sigh. The whole page was blotted with fresh tears; and, upon the opposite interleaf, were the following English lines, written in a hand so very different from the peculiar characters of my acquaintance, that I had some difficulty in recognizing it as his own.

Thou wast that all to me, love,
 For which my soul did pine —
A green isle in the sea, love,
 A fountain and a shrine,
All wreathed with fairy fruits and flowers;
 And all the flowers were mine.

Ah, dream too bright to last!
 Ah, starry Hope, that didst arise
But to be overcast!
 A voice from out the Future cries,
"Onward!" — but o'er the Past
 (Dim gulf!) my spirit hovering lies,
Mute — motionless — aghast!

For alas! alas! with me
 The light of life is o'er.
"No more — no more — no more,"
 (Such language holds the solemn sea
To the sands upon the shore,)
 Shall bloom the thunder-blasted tree,
Or the stricken eagle soar!

Now all my hours are trances;
 And all my nightly dreams
Are where thy dark eye glances,
 And where thy footstep gleams,
In what ethereal dances,
 By what Italian streams.

Alas! for that accursed time
 They bore thee o'er the billow,
From Love to titled age and crime,
 And an unholy pillow! —
From me, and from our misty clime,
 Where weeps the silver willow!

That these lines were written in English — a language with which I had not believed their author acquainted — afforded me little matter for surprise. I was too well aware of the extent of his acquirements, and of the singular pleasure he took in concealing them from observation, to be astonished at any similar discovery; but the place of date, I must confess, occasioned me no little amazement. It had been originally written *London*, and afterward carefully overscored — not, however, so effectually as to conceal the word from a scrutinizing eye. I say, this occasioned me no little amazement; for I well remember that, in a former conversation with my friend, I particularly inquired if he had at any time met

in London the Marchesa di Mentoni (who for some years previous to
her marriage had resided in that city), when his answer, if I mistake not,
gave me to understand that he had never visited the metropolis of Great
Britain. I might as well here mention, that I have more than once heard,
(without, of course, giving credit to a report involving so many improb-
abilities,) that the person of whom I speak, was not only by birth, but
in education, an *Englishman*.

"There is one painting," said he, without being aware of my notice
of the tragedy, — "there is still one painting which you have not seen."
And throwing aside a drapery, he discovered a full-length portrait of the
Marchesa Aphrodite.

Human art could have done no more in the delineation of her super-
human beauty. The same ethereal figure which stood before me the pre-
ceding night upon the steps of the Ducal Palace, stood before me once
again. But in the expression of the countenance, which was beaming all
over with smiles, there still lurked (incomprehensible anomaly!) that
fitful stain of melancholy which will ever be found inseparable from the
perfection of the beautiful. Her right arm lay folded over her bosom.
With her left she pointed downward to a curiously fashioned vase. One
small, fairy foot, alone visible, barely touched the earth; and, scarcely
discernible in the brilliant atmosphere which seemed to encircle and
enshrine her loveliness, floated a pair of the most delicately imagined
wings. My glance fell from the painting to the figure of my friend, and
the vigorous words of Chapman's *Bussy D'Ambois*, quivered instinc-
tively upon my lips:

> He is up
> There like a Roman statue! He will stand
> Till Death hath made him marble!

"Come," he said at length, turning toward a table of richly enamelled
and massive silver, upon which were a few goblets fantastically stained,
together with two large Etruscan vases, fashioned in the same extraor-
dinary model as that in the foreground of the portrait, and filled with
what I supposed to be Johannisberger. "Come," he said, abruptly, "let
us drink! It is early — but let us drink. It is *indeed* early," he continued,
musingly, as a cherub with a heavy golden hammer made the apartment
ring with the first hour after sunrise: "it is *indeed* early — but what mat-
ters it? let us drink! Let us pour out an offering to yon solemn sun which
these gaudy lamps and censers are so eager to subdue!" And having made
me pledge him in a bumper, he swallowed in rapid succession several
goblets of the wine.

"To dream," he continued, resuming the tone of his desultory con-
versation, as he held up to the rich light of a censer one of the magnifi-
cent vases — "to dream has been the business of my life. I have therefore

framed for myself, as you see, a bower of dreams. In the heart of Venice could I have erected a better? You behold around you, it is true, a medley of architectural embellishments. The chastity of Ionia is offended by antediluvian devices, and the sphynxes of Egypt are outstretched upon carpets of gold. Yet the effect is incongruous to the timid alone. Proprieties of place, and especially of time, are the bugbears which terrify mankind from the contemplation of the magnificent. Once I was myself a decorist; but that sublimation of folly has palled upon my soul. All this is now the fitter for my purpose. Like these arabesque censers, my spirit is writhing in fire, and the delirium of this scene is fashoning me for the wilder visons of that land of real dreams whther I am now rapidly departing." He here paused abruptly, bent his head to his bosom, and seemed to listen to a sound which I could not hear. At length, erecting his frame, he looked upwards, and ejaculated the lines of the Bishop of Chichester:

> Stay for me there! I will not fail,
> To meet thee in that hollow vale.

In the next instant, confessing the power of the wine, he threw himself at full length upon an ottoman.

A quick step was now heard upon the staircase, and a loud knock at the door rapidly succeeded. I was hastening to anticipate a second disturbance, when a page of Mentoni's household burst into the room, and faltered out, in a voice choking with emotion, the incoherent words, "My mistress! — my mistress! — Poisoned! — poisoned! Oh, beautiful Aphrodite!"

Bewildered, I flew to the ottoman, and endeavored to arouse the sleeper to a sense of the startling intelligence. But his limbs were rigid — his lips were livid — his lately beaming eyes were riveted in *death*. I staggered back toward the table — my hand fell upon a cracked and blackened goblet — and a consciousness of the entire and terrible truth flashed suddenly over my soul.

Berenice

DICEBANT *mihi sodales, si sepulchrum amicæ visitarem, curas meas aliquantulum fore levatas.* — EBN ZAIAT

MISERY is manifold. The wretchedness of earth is multiform. Overreaching the wide horizon as the rainbow, its hues are as various as the hues of the arch, as distinct too, yet as intimately blended. Overreaching

the wide horizon as the rainbow! How is it that from beauty I have derived a type of unloveliness? from the covenant of peace a simile of sorrow? But as in ethics, evil is a consequence of good, so in fact, out of joy is sorrow born. Either the memory of past bliss is the anguish of to-day, or the agonies which *are* have their origin in the ecstasies which *might have been.*

My baptismal name is Egæus, that of my family I will not mention. Yet there are no towers in the land more time-honoured than my gloomy, grey, hereditary halls. Our line has been called a race of visionaries; and in many striking particulars — in the character of the family mansion, in the frescoes of the chief saloon, in the tapestries of the dormitories, in the chiselling of some buttresses in the armoury, but more especially in the gallery of antique paintings, in the fashion of the library chamber, and lastly, in the very peculiar nature of the library's contents — there is more than sufficient evidence to warrant the belief.

The recollections of my earliest years are connected with that chamber, and with its volumes — of which latter I will say no more. Here died my mother. Herein was I born. But it is mere idleness to say that I had not lived before — that the soul has no previous existence. You deny it — let us not argue the matter. Convinced myself, I seek not to convince. There is, however, a remembrance of aerial forms — of spiritual and meaning eyes — of sounds, musical yet sad; a remembrance which will not be excluded; a memory like a shadow — vague, variable, indefinite, unsteady; and like a shadow, too, in the impossibility of my getting rid of it while the sunlight of my reason shall exist.

In that chamber was I born. Thus awaking from the long night of what seemed, but was not, nonentity, at once into the very regions of fairy land — into a palace of imagination — into the wild dominions of monastic thought and erudition — it is not singular that I gazed around me with a startled and ardent eye — that I loitered away my boyhood in books, and dissipated my youth in revery; but it *is* singular, that as years rolled away, and the noon of manhood found me still in the mansion of my fathers — it *is* wonderful what stagnation there fell upon the springs of my life — wonderful how total an inversion took place in the character of my commonest thought. The realities of the world affected me as visions, and as visions only, while the wild ideas of the land of dreams became, in turn, not the material of my every-day existence, but in very deed that existence utterly and solely in itself.

Berenice and I were cousins, and we grew up together in my paternal halls. Yet differently we grew — I, ill of health, and buried in gloom — she, agile, graceful, and overflowing with energy; hers the ramble on the hill-side — mine, the studies of the cloister; I, living within my own heart, and addicted, body and soul, to the most intense and painful meditation — she, roaming carelessly through life, with no thought of

the shadows in her path, or the silent flight of the raven-winged hours. Berenice! — I call upon her name — Berenice! — and from the gray ruins of memory a thousand tumultuous recollections are startled at the sound! Ah, vividly is her image before me now, as in the early days of her light-heartedness and joy! Oh, gorgeous yet fantastic beauty! Oh, sylph amid the shrubberies of Arnheim! Oh, naiad among its fountains! And then — then all is mystery and terror, and a tale which should not be told. Disease — a fatal disease, fell like the simoom upon her frame; and even, while I gazed upon her, the spirit of change swept over her, pervading her mind, her habits and her character, and, in a manner the most subtle and terrible, disturbing even the identity of her person! Alas! the destroyer came and went! — and the victim — where was she? I knew her not — or knew her no longer as Berenice!

Among the numerous train of maladies superinduced by that fatal and primary one which effected a revolution of so horrible a kind in the moral and physical being of my cousin, may be mentioned as the most distressing and obstinate in its nature, a species of epilepsy not unfrequently terminating in *trance* itself — trance very nearly resembling positive dissolution, and from which her manner of recovery was, in most instances, startlingly abrupt. In the meantime, my own disease — for I have been told that I should call it by no other appellation — my own disease, then, grew rapidly upon me, and assumed finally a monomaniac character of a novel and extraordinary form — hourly and momently gaining vigor — and at length obtaining over me the most incomprehensible ascendency. This monomania, if I must so term it, consisted in a morbid irritability of those properties of the mind in metaphysical science termed the *attentive*. It is more than probable that I am not understood; but I fear, indeed, that it is in no manner possible to convey to the mind of the merely general reader, an adequate idea of that nervous *intensity of interest* with which, in my case, the powers of meditation (not to speak technically) busied and buried themselves, in the contemplation of even the most ordinary objects of the universe.

To muse for long unwearied hours, with my attention riveted to some frivolous device on the margin or in the typography of a book; to become absorbed, for the better part of a summer's day, in a quaint shadow falling aslant upon the tapestry or upon the floor; to lose myself, for an entire night, in watching the steady flame of a lamp, or the embers of a fire, to dream away whole days over the perfume of a flower; to repeat, monotonously, some common word, until the sound, by dint of frequent repetition, ceased to convey any idea whatever to the mind; to lose all sense of motion or physical existence, by means of absolute bodily quiescence long and obstinately persevered in: such were a few of the most common and least pernicious vagaries induced by a condition of the mental faculties, not, indeed, altogether unparalleled, but certainly bidding defiance to any thing like analysis or explanation.

Yet let me not be misapprehended. The undue, earnest, and morbid attention thus excited by objects in their own nature frivolous, must not be confounded in character with that ruminating propensity common to all mankind, and more especially indulged in by persons of ardent imagination. It was not even, as might be at first supposed, an extreme condition, or exaggeration of such propensity, but primarily and essentially distinct and different. In the one instance, the dreamer, or enthusiast, being interested by an object usually *not* frivolous, imperceptibly loses sight of this object in a wilderness of deductions and suggestions issuing therefrom, until, at the conclusion of a day-dream *often replete with luxury*, he finds the *incitamentum*, or first cause of his musings, entirely vanished and forgotten. In my case, the primary object was *invariably frivolous*, although assuming, through the medium of my distempered vision, a refracted and unreal importance. Few deductions, if any, were made; and those few pertinaciously returning in upon the original object as a centre. The meditations were *never* pleasureable; and, at the termination of the revery, the first cause, so far from being out of sight, had attained that supernaturally exaggerated interest which was the prevailing feature of the disease. In a word, the powers of mind more particularly exercised were, with me, as I have said before, the *attentive*, and are, with the day-dreamer, the *speculative*.

My books, at this epoch, if they did not actually serve to irritate the disorder, partook, it will be perceived, largely, in their imaginative and inconsequential nature, of the characteristic qualities of the disorder itself. I well remember, among others, the treatise of the noble Italian, Cœlius Secundus Curio, "*De Amplitudine Beati Regni Dei*"; St. Austin's great work, "The City of God"; and Tertullian's "*De Carne Christi*," in which the paradoxical sentence, "*Mortuus est Dei filius; credibile est quia ineptum est; et sepultus resurrexit; certum est quia impossible est*," occupied my undivided time, for many weeks of laborious and fruitless investigation.

Thus it will appear that, shaken from its balance only by trivial things, my reason bore resemblance to that ocean-crag spoken of by Ptolemy Hephestion, which steadily resisting the attacks of human violence, and the fiercer fury of the waters and the winds, trembled only to the touch of the flower called Asphodel. And although, to a careless thinker, it might appear a matter beyond doubt, that the alteration produced by her unhappy malady, in the *moral* condition of Berenice, would afford me many objects for the exercise of that intense and abnormal meditation whose nature I have been at some trouble in explaining, yet such was not in any degree the case. In the lucid intervals of my infirmity, her calamity, indeed, gave me pain, and, taking deeply to heart that total wreck of her fair and gentle life, I did not fail to ponder, frequently and bitterly, upon the wonder-working means by which so strange a revolution had been so suddenly brought to pass. But these reflections partook

not of the idiosyncrasy of my disease, and were such as would have occurred, under similar circumstances, to the ordinary mass of mankind. True to its own character, my disorder revelled in the less important but more startling changes wrought in the *physical* frame of Berenice — in the singular and most appalling distortion of her personal identity.

During the brightest days of her unparalleled beauty, most surely I had never loved her. In the strange anomaly of my existence, feelings with me, *had never been* of the heart, and my passions *always were* of the mind. Through the gray of the early morning — among the trellised shadows of the forest at noonday — and in the silence of my library at night — she had flitted by my eyes, and I had seen her — not as the living and breathing Berenice, but at the Berenice of a dream; not as a being of the earth, earthly, but as the abstraction of such a being; not as a thing to admire, but to analyze; not as an object of love, but as the theme of the most abstruse although desultory speculation. And *now* — now I shuddered in her presence, and grew pale at her approach; yet, bitterly lamenting her fallen and desolate condition, I called to mind that she had loved me long, and, in an evil moment, I spoke to her of marriage.

And at length the period of our nuptials was approaching, when, upon an afternoon in the winter of the year — one of those unseasonably warm, calm, and misty days which are the nurse of the beautiful Halcyon,* — I sat (and sat, as I thought, alone) in the inner apartment of the library. But uplifting my eyes, I saw that Berenice stood before me.

Was it my own excited imagination — or the misty influence of the atmosphere — or the uncertain twilight of the chamber — or the gray draperies which fell around her figure — that caused in it so vacillating and indistinct an outline? I could not tell. She spoke no word; and I — not for words could I have uttered a syllable. An icy chill ran through my frame; a sense of insufferable anxiety oppressed me; a consuming curiosity pervaded my soul; and, sinking back upon the chair, I remained for some time breathless and motionless, with my eyes riveted upon her person. Alas! its emaciation was excessive, and not one vestige of the former being lurked in any single line of the contour. My burning glances at length fell upon the face.

The forehead was high, and very pale, and singularly placid; and the once jetty hair fell partially over it, and overshadowed the hollow temples with innumerable ringlets, now of a vivid yellow, and jarring discordantly, in their fantastic character, with the reigning melancholy of the countenance. The eyes were lifeless, and lustreless, and seemingly pupilless, and I shrank involuntarily from their glassy stare to the contemplation of the thin and shrunken lips. They parted; and in a smile of pe-

* For as Jove, during the winter season, gives twice seven days of warmth, men have called this clement and temperate time the nurse of the beautiful Halcyon. — *Simonides.*

culiar meaning, *the teeth* of the changed Berenice disclosed themselves slowly to my view. Would to God that I had never beheld them, or that, having done so, I had died!

The shutting of a door disturbed me, and looking up, I found that my cousin had departed from the chamber. But from the disordered chamber of my brain, had not, alas! departed, and would not be driven away, the white and ghastly *spectrum* of the teeth. Not a speck on their surface — not a shade on their enamel — not an indenture in their edges — but what the brief period of her smile had sufficed to brand in upon my memory. I saw them *now* even more unequivocally than I beheld them *then*. The teeth! — the teeth! — they were here, and there, and everywhere, and visibly and palpably before me; long, narrow, and excessively white, with the pale lips writhing about them, as in the very moment of their first terrible development. Then came the full fury of my *monomania*, and I struggled in vain against its strange and irresistible influence. In the multiplied objects of the external world I had no thoughts but for the teeth. For these I longed with a frenzied desire. All other matters and all different interests became absorbed in their single contemplation. They — they alone were present to the mental eye, and they, in their sole individuality, became the essence of my mental life. I held them in every light. I turned them in every attitude. I surveyed their characteristics. I dwelt upon their peculiarities. I pondered upon their conformation. I mused upon the alteration in their nature. I shuddered as I assigned to them, in imagination, a sensitive and sentient power, and even when unassisted by the lips, a capability of moral expression. Of Mad'-selle Sallé it has been well said: *"Que tous ses pas etaient des sentiments,"* and of Berenice I more seriously believed *que tous ses dents etaient des idées. Des idées!* — ah, here was the idiotic thought that destroyed me! *Des idées!* — ah, *therefore* it was that I coveted them so madly! I felt that their possession could alone ever restore me to peace, in giving me back to reason.

And the evening closed in upon me thus — and then the darkness came, and tarried, and went — and the day again dawned — and the mists of a second night were now gathering around — and still I sat motionless in that solitary room — and still I sat buried in meditation — and still the *phantasma* of the teeth maintained its terrible ascendancy, as, with the most vivid and hideous distinctness, it floated about amid the changing lights and shadows of the chamber. At length there broke in upon my dreams a cry as of horror and dismay; and thereunto, after a pause, succeeded the sound of troubled voices, intermingled with many low moanings of sorrow or of pain. I arose from my seat, and throwing open one of the doors of the library, saw standing out in the antechamber a servant maiden, all in tears, who told me that Berenice was — no more! She had been seized with epilepsy in the early morning, and now, at the

closing in of the night the grave was ready for its tenant, and all the preparations for the burial were completed.

I found myself sitting in the library and again sitting there alone. It seemed to me that I had newly awakened from a confused and exciting dream. I knew that it was now midnight, and I was well aware, that since the setting of the sun, Berenice had been interred. But of that dreary period which intervened I had no positive, at least no definite, comprehension. Yet its memory was replete with horror — horror more horrible from being vague, and terror more terrible from ambiguity. It was a fearful page in the record of my existence, written all over with dim, and hideous, and unintelligible recollections. I strived to decypher them, but in vain; while ever and anon, like the spirit of a departed sound, the shrill and piercing shriek of a female voice seemed to be ringing in my ears. I had done a deed — what was it? I asked myself the question aloud, and the whispering echoes of the chamber answered me — *"what was it?"*

On the table beside me burned a lamp, and near it lay a little box. It was of no remarkable character, and I had seen it frequently before, for it was the property of the family physician; but how came it *there*, upon my table, and why did I shudder in regarding it? These things were in no manner to be accounted for, and my eyes at length dropped to the open pages of a book, and to a sentence underscored therein. The words were the singular but simple ones of the poet Ebn Zaiat: — *"Dicebant mihi sodales si sepulchrum amicæ visitarem, curas meas aliquantulum fore levatas."* Why, then, as I perused them, did the hairs of my head erect themselves on end, and the blood of my body become congealed within my veins?

There came a light tap at the library door — and, pale as the tenant of a tomb, a menial entered upon tiptoe. His looks were wild with terror, and he spoke to me in a voice tremulous, husky and very low. What said he? — some broken sentences I heard. He told of a wild cry disturbing the silence of the night — of the gathering together of the household — of a search in the direction of the sound; and then his tones grew thrillingly distinct as he whispered me of a violated grave — of a disfigured body enshrouded, yet still breathing — still palpitating — *still alive!*

He pointed to my garments; they were muddy and clotted with gore. I spoke not, and he took me gently by the hand: it was indented with the impress of human nails. He directed my attention to some object against the wall. I looked at it for some minutes: it was a spade. With a shriek I bounded to the table, and grasped the box that lay upon it. But I could not force it open; and, in my tremor, it slipped from my hands, and fell heavily, and burst into pieces; and from it, with a rattling sound, there rolled out some instruments of dental surgery, intermingled with thirty-two small, white, and ivory-looking substances that were scattered to and fro about the floor.

Morella

Αυτο καθ αυτο μεθ αυτου μονοειδες αιει ον

ITSELF, *by itslf, solely,* ONE *everlastingly, and single.*

PLATO: Sympos.

WITH a feeling of deep yet most singular affection I regarded my friend Morella. Thrown by accident into her society many years ago, my soul from our first meeting, burned with fires it had never before known; but the fires were not of Eros, and bitter and tormenting to my spirit was the gradual conviction that I could in no manner define their unusual meaning or regulate their vague intensity. Yet we met; and fate bound us together at the altar; and I never spoke of passion nor thought of love. She, however, shunned society, and, attaching herself to me alone rendered me happy. It is a happiness to wonder; it is a happiness to dream.

Morella's erudition was profound. As I hope to live, her talents were of no common order — her powers of mind were gigantic. I felt this, and, in many matters, became her pupil. I soon, however, found that, perhaps on account of her Presburg education, she placed before me a number of those mystical writings which are usually considered the mere dross of the early German literature. These, for what reason I could not imagine, were her favourite and constant study — and that in process of time they became my own, should be attributed to the simple but effectual influence of habit and example.

In all this, if I err not, my reason had little to do. My convictions, or I forget myself, were in no manner acted upon by the ideal, nor was any tincture of the mysticism which I read to be discovered, unless I am greatly mistaken, either in my deeds or in my thoughts. Persuaded of this, I abandoned myself implicitly to the guidance of my wife, and entered with an unflinching heart into the intricacies of her studies. And then — then, when poring over forbidden pages, I felt a forbidden spirit enkindling within me — would Morella place her cold hand upon my own, and rake up from the ashes of a dead philosophy some low, singular words, whose strange meaning burned themselves in upon my memory. And then, hour after hour, would I linger by her side, and dwell upon the music of her voice, until at length its melody was tainted with terror, and there fell a shadow upon my soul, and I grew pale, and shuddered inwardly at those too unearthly tones. And thus, joy suddenly faded into horror, and the most beautiful became the most hideous, as Hinnon became Ge-Henna.

It is unnecessary to state the exact character of those disquisitions which, growing out of the volumes I have mentioned, formed, for so long a time, almost the sole conversation of Morella and myself. By the learned in what might be termed theological morality they will be readily conceived, and by the unlearned they would, at all events, be little understood. The wild Pantheism of Fichte; the modified Παλιγγενεδια of the Pythagoreans; and, above all, the doctrines of *Identity* as urged by Schelling, were generally the points of discussion presenting the most of beauty to the imaginative Morella. That identity which is termed personal, Mr. Locke, I think, truly defines to consist in the saneness of rational being. And since by person we understand an intelligent essence having reason, and since there is a consciousness which always accompanies thinking, it is this which makes us all to be that which we call *ourselves*, thereby distinguishing us from other beings that think, and giving us our personal identity. But the *principium indivduationis*, the notion of that identity *which at death is or is not lost for ever*, was to me, at all times, a consideration of intense interest; not more from the perplexing and exciting nature of its consequences, than from the marked and agitated manner in which Morella mentioned them.

But, indeed, the time had now arrived when the mystery of my wife's manner oppressed me as a spell. I could no longer bear the touch of her wan fingers, nor the low tone of her musical language, nor the lustre of her melancholy eyes. And she knew all this, but did not upbraid; she seemed conscious of my weakness or my folly, and, smiling, called it fate. She seemed also conscious of a cause, to me unknown, for the gradual alienation of my regard; but she gave me no hint or token of its nature. Yet was she woman, and pined away daily. In time the crimson spot settled steadily upon the check, and the blue veins upon the pale forehead became prominent; and one instant my nature melted into pity, but in the next I met the glance of her meaning eyes, and then my soul sickened and became giddy with the giddiness of one who gazes downward into some dreary and unfathomable abyss.

Shall I then say that I longed with an earnest and consuming desire for the moment of Morella's decease? I did; but the fragile spirit clung to its tenement of clay for many days, for many weeks and irksome months, until my tortured nerves obtained the mastery over my mind, and I grew furious through delay, and, with the heart of a fiend, cursed the days and the hours and the bitter moments, which seemed to lengthen and lengthen as her gentle life declined, like shadows in the dying of the day.

But one autumnal evening, when the winds lay still in heaven, Morella called me to her bedside. There was a dim mist over all the earth, and a warm glow upon the waters, and amid the rich October leaves of the forest, a rainbow from the firmament had surely fallen.

"It is a day of days," she said, as I approached; "a day of all days either

to live or die. It is a fair day for the sons of earth and life — ah, more fair for the daughters of heaven and death!"

I kissed her forehead, and she continued:

"I am dying, yet shall I live."

"Morella!"

"The days have never been when thou couldst love me — but her whom in life thou didst abhor, in death thou shalt adore."

"Morella!"

"I repeat I am dying. But within me is a pledge of that affection — ah, how little! — which thou didst feel for me, Morella. And when my spirit departs shall the child live — thy child and mine, Morella's. But thy days shall be days of sorrow — that sorrow which is the most lasting of impressions, as the cypress is the most enduring of trees. For the hours of thy happiness are over and joy is not gathered twice in a life, as the roses of Pæstum twice in a year. Thou shalt no longer, then, play the Teian with time, but, being ignorant of the myrtle and the vine, thou shalt bear about with thee thy shroud on the earth, as do the Moslemin at Mecca."

"Morella!" I cried, "Morella! how knowest thou this?" but she turned away her face upon the pillow and a slight tremor coming over her limbs, she thus died, and I heard her voice no more.

Yet, as she had foretold, her child, to which in dying she had given birth, which breathed not until the mother breathed no more, her child, a daughter, lived. And she grew strangely in stature and intellect, and was the perfect resemblance of her who had departed, and I loved her with a love more fervent than I had believed it possible to feel for any denizen of earth.

But, ere long the heaven of this pure affection became darkened, and gloom, and horror, and grief swept over it in clouds. I said the child grew strangely in stature and intelligence. Strange, indeed, was her rapid increase in bodily size, but terrible, oh! terrible were the tumultuous thoughts which crowded upon me while watching the development of her mental being. Could it be otherwise, when I daily discovered in the conceptions of the child the adult powers and faculties of the woman? when the lessons of experience fell from the lips of infancy? and when the wisdom or the passions of maturity I found hourly gleaming from its full and speculative eye? When, I say, all this became evident to my appalled senses, when I could no longer hide it from my soul, nor throw it off from those perceptions which trembled to receive it, is it to be wondered at that suspicions, of a nature fearful and exciting, crept in upon my spirit, or that my thoughts fell back aghast upon the wild tales and thrilling theories of the entombed Morella? I snatched from the scrutiny of the world a being whom destiny compelled me to adore, and in the rigorous seclusion of my home, watched with an agonizing anxiety over all which concerned the beloved.

And as years rolled away, and I gazed day after day upon her holy, and

mild, and eloquent face, and poured over her maturing form, day after day did I discover new points of resemblance in the child to her mother, the melancholy and the dead. And hourly grew darker these shadows of similitude, and more full, and more definite, and more perplexing, and more hideously terrible in their aspect. For that her smile was like her mother's I could bear; but then I shuddered at its too perfect *identity*, that her eyes were like Morella's I could endure; but then they, too, often looked down into the depths of my soul with Morella's own intense and bewildering meaning. And in the contour of the high forehead, and in the ringlets of the silken hair, and in the wan fingers which buried themselves therein, and in the sad musical tones of her speech, and above all — oh, above all, in the phrases and expressions of the dead on the lips of the loved and the living, I found food for consuming thought and horror, for a worm that *would* not die.

Thus passed away two lustra of her life, and as yet my daughter remained nameless upon the earth. "My child," and "my love," were the designations usually prompted by a father's affection, and the rigid seclusion of her days precluded all other intercourse. Morella's name died with her at her death. Of the mother I had never spoken to the daughter; it was impossible to speak. Indeed, during the brief period of her existence, the latter had received no impressions from the outward world, save such as might have been afforded by the narrow limits of her privacy. But at length the ceremony of baptism presented to my mind, in its unnerved and agitated condition, a present deliverance from the terrors of my destiny. And at the baptismal font I hesitated for a name. And many titles of the wise and beautiful, of old and modern times, of my own and foreign lands, came thronging to my lips, with many, many fair titles of the gentle, and the happy, and the good. What prompted me then to disturb the memory of the buried dead? What demon urged me to breathe that sound, which in its very recollection was wont to make ebb the purple blood in torrents from the temples to the heart? What fiend spoke from the recesses of my soul, when amid those dim aisles, and in the silence of the night, I whispered within the ears of the holy man the syllables — Morella? What more than fiend convulsed the features of my child, and overspread them with hues of death, as starting at that scarcely audible sound, she turned her glassy eyes from the earth to heaven, and falling prostrate on the black slabs of our ancestral vault, responded — "I am here!"

Distinct, coldly, calmly distinct, fell those few simple sounds within my ear, and thence like molten lead rolled hissingly into my brain. Years — years may pass away, but the memory of that epoch never. Nor was I indeed ignorant of the flowers and the vine — but the hemlock and the cypress overshadowed me night and day. And I kept no reckoning of time or place, and the stars of my fate faded from heaven, and therefore the earth grew dark, and its figures passed by me like flitting shadows, and

among them all I beheld only — Morella. The winds of the firmament breathed but one sound within my ears, and the ripples upon the sea murmured evermore — Morella. But she died; and with my own hands I bore her to the tomb; and I laughed with a long and bitter laugh as I found no traces of the first in the charnel where I laid the second. — Morella.

Lionizing

—— all people went
Upon their ten toes in wild wonderment.
Bishop Hall's Satires.

I AM, that is to say I *was*, a great man, but I am neither the author of Junius nor the man in the mask, for my name, I believe, is Robert Jones, and I was born somewhere in the city of Fum-Fudge.

The first action of my life was the taking hold of my nose with both hands. My mother saw this and called me a genius: — my father wept for joy and presented me with a treatise on Nosology. This I mastered before I was breeched.

I now began to feel my way in the science, and soon came to understand that, provided a man had a nose sufficiently conspicuous, he might, by merely following it, arrive at a Lionship. But my attention was not confined to theories alone. Every morning I gave my proboscis a couple of pulls and swallowed a half-dozen of drams.

When I came of age my father asked me, one day, if I would step with him into his study.

"My son," he said, when we were seated, "what is the chief end of your existence?"

"My father," I answered, "it is the study of Nosology."

"And what, Robert," he inquired, "is Nosology?"

"Sir," I said, "it is the science of Noses."

"And can you tell me," he demanded, "what is the meaning of a nose?"

"A nose, my father," I replied, greatly softened, "has been variously defined by about a thousand different authors." [Here I pulled out my watch.] "It is now noon, or thereabouts — We shall have time enough to get through with them all before midnight. To commence then: — The nose, according to Bartholinus, is that protuberance — that bump — that excresence — that —— "

"Will do, Robert," interrupted the good old gentleman. "I am thunderstruck at the extent of your information — I am positively — upon

my soul." [Here he closed his eyes and placed his hand upon his heart.] "Come here!" [Here he took me by the arm.] "Your education may now be considered as finished — it is high time you should scuffle for yourself — and you cannot do a better thing than merely follow your nose — so — so — so — " [Here he kicked me down stairs and out of the door.] — "So get out of my house, and God bless you!"

As I felt within me the divine *afflatus,* I considered this accident rather fortunate than otherwise. I resolved to be guided by the paternal advice. I determined to follow my nose. I gave it a pull or two upon the spot, and wrote a pamphlet on Nosology forthwith.

All Fum-Fudge was in an uproar.

"Wonderful genius!" said the Quarterly.

"Superb physiologist!" said the Westminster.

"Clever fellow!" said the Foreign.

"Fine writer!" said the Edinburgh.

"Profound thinker!" said the Dublin.

"Great man!" said Bentley.

"Divine soul!" said Fraser.

"One of us!" said Blackwood.

"Who can he be?" said Mrs. Bas-Bleu.

"What can he be?" said big Miss Bas-Bleu.

"Where can he be?" said little Miss Bas-Bleu. — But I paid these people no attention whatever — I just stepped into the shop of an artist.

The Duchess of Bless-my-Soul was sitting for her portrait; the Marquis of So-and-So was holding the Duchess' poodle; the Earl of This-and-That was flirting with her salts; and his Royal Highness of Touch-me-Not was leaning upon the back of her chair.

I approached the artist and turned up my nose.

"Oh, beautiful!" sighed her Grace.

"Oh, my!" lisped the Marquis.

"Oh, shocking!" groaned the Earl.

"Oh, abominable!" growled his Royal Highness.

"What will you take for it?" asked the artist.

"For his *nose!*" shouted her Grace.

"A thousand pounds," said I, sitting down.

"A thousand pounds?" inquired the artist, musingly.

"A thousand pounds," said I.

"Beautiful!" said he, entranced.

"A thousand pounds," said I.

"Do you warrant it?" he asked, turning the nose to the light.

"I do," said I, blowing it well.

"Is it *quite* original?" he inquired, touching it with reverence.

"Humph!" said I, twisting it to one side.

"Has *no* copy been taken?" he demanded, surveying it through a microscope.

"None," said I, turning it up.

"*Admirable!*" he ejaculated, thrown quite off his guard by the beauty of the manœuvre.

"A thousand pounds," said I.

"A *thousand* pounds?" said he.

"Precisely," said I.

"A thousand *pounds?*" said he.

"Just so," said I.

"You shall have them," said he. "What a piece of *virtu!*" So he drew me a check upon the spot, and took a sketch of my nose. I engaged rooms in Jermyn street, and sent her Majesty the ninety-ninth edition of the "Nosology," with a portrait of the proboscis. That sad little rake, the Prince of Wales, invited me to dinner.

We are all lions and *recherchés*.

There was a modern Platonist. He quoted Porphyry, Iamblicus, Plotinus, Proclus, Hierocles, Maximus Tyrius, and Syrianus.

There was a human-perfectibility man. He quoted Turgot, Price, Priestly, Condorcet, De Stäel, and the "Ambitious Student in Ill-Health."

There was Sir Positive Paradox. He observed that all fools were philosophers, and that all philosophers were fools.

There was Æstheticus Ethix. He spoke of fire, unity, and atoms; bipart and pre-existent soul; affinity and discord; primitive intelligence and homoömeria.

There was Theologos Theology. He talked of Eusebius and Arianus; heresy and the Council of Nice; Puseyism and consubstantialism; Homousios and Homouioisios.

There was Fricassée from the Rocher de Cancale. He mentioned Muriton of red tongue; cauliflowers with *velouté* sauce; veal *à la* St. Menehoult; marinade *à la* St. Florentin; and orange jellies *en mosäiques*.

There was Bibulus O'Bumper. He touched upon Latour and Markbrünnen; upon Mosseux and Chambertin; upon Richbourg and St. George; upon Haubrion, Leonville, and Medoc; upon Barac and Preignac; upon Grâve, upon Sauterne, upon Lafitte, and upon St. Peray. He shook his head at Clos de Vougeot, and told with his eyes shut, the difference between Sherry and Amontillado.

There was Signor Tintontintino from Florence. He discoursed of Cimabué, Arpino, Carpaccio, and Argostino — of the gloom of Caravaggio, of the amenity of Albano, of the colors of Titian, of the frows of Rubens, and of the waggeries of Jan Steen.

There was the President of the Fum-Fudge University. He was of the opinion that the moon was called Bendis in Thrace, Bubastis in Egypt, Dian in Rome, and Artemis in Greece.

There was a Grand Turk from Stamboul. He could not help thinking that the angels were horses, cocks, and bulls; that somebody in the sixth

heaven had seventy thousand heads; and that the earth was supported by a sky-blue cow with an incalculable number of green horns.

There was Delphinus Polyglott. He told us what had become of the eighty-three lost tragedies of Æschylus; of the fifty-four orations of Isæus; of the three hundred and ninety-one speeches of Lysias; of the hundred and eighty treatises of Theophrastus; of the eighth book of the conic sections of Apollonius; of Pindar's hymns and dithyrambics; and of the five and forty tragedies of Homer Junior.

There was Ferdinand Fitz-Fossillus Feltspar. He informed us all about internal fires and tertiary formations; about aeriforms, fluidiforms, and solidforms; about quartz and marl; about schist and schorl; about gypsum and trap; about talc and calc; about blende and horn-blende; about mica-slate and pudding-stone; about cyanite and lepidolite; about hæmatite and tremolite; about antimony and calcedony; about manganese and whatever you please.

There was myself. I spoke of myself; — of myself, of myself, of my-self; — of Nosology, of my pamphlet, and of myself. I turned up my nose, and I spoke of myself.

"Marvellous clever man!" said the Prince.

"Superb!" said his guests; — and next morning her Grace of Bless-my-soul paid me a visit.

"Will you go to Almack's, pretty creature?" she said, tapping me under the chin.

"Upon honor," said I.

"Nose and all?" she asked.

"As I live," I replied.

"Here then is a card, my life. Shall I say you *will* be there?"

"Dear Duchess, with all my heart."

"Pshaw, no! — but with all your nose?"

"Every bit of it, my love," said I: — so I gave it a twist or two, and found myself at Almack's.

The rooms were crowded to suffocation.

"He is coming!" said somebody on the staircase.

"He is coming!" said somebody farther up.

"He is coming!" said somebody farther still.

"He is come!" exclaimed the Duchess, "He is come, the little love!" — and, seizing me firmly by both hands, she kissed me thrice upon the nose.

A marked sensation immediately ensued.

"*Diavolo!*" cried Count Capricornutti.

"*Dios guarda!*" muttered Don Stiletto.

"*Mille tonnerres!*" ejaculated the Prince de Grenouille.

"*Tousand teufel!*" growled the Elector of Bluddennuff.

It was not to be borne. I grew angry. I turned short upon Bludden-nuff.

"Sir!" said I to him, "you are a baboon."

"Sir," he replied, after a pause, "*Donner und Blitzen!*"

This was all that could be desired. We exchanged cards. At Chalk-Farm, the next morning, I shot off his nose — and then called upon my friends.

"*Bête!*" said the first.

"Fool!" said the second.

"Dolt!" said the third.

"Ass!" said the fourth.

"Ninny!" said the fifth.

"Noodle!" said the sixth.

"Be off!" said the seventh.

At all this I felt mortified, and so called upon my father.

"Father," I asked, "what is the chief end of my existence?"

"My son," he replied, "it is still the study of Nosology; but in hitting the Elector upon the nose you have overshot your mark. You have a fine nose, it is true; but then Bluddennuff has none. You are damned, and he has become the hero of the day. I grant you that in Fum-Fudge the greatness of a lion is in proportion to the size of his proboscis — but, good heavens! there is no competing with a lion who has no proboscis at all."

Hans Phaall*

By late accounts from Rotterdam, that city seems to be in a high state of philosophical excitement. Indeed, phenomena have there occurred of a nature so completely unexpected — so entirely novel — so utterly at variance with preconceived opinions — as to leave no doubt on my mind that long ere this all Europe is in an uproar, all physics in a ferment, all reason and astronomy together by the ears.

It appears that on the —— day of ——, (I am not positive about the date), a vast crowd of people, for purposes not specifically mentioned, were assembled in the great square of the Exchange in the well-conditioned city of Rotterdam. The day was warm — unusually so for the season — there was hardly a breath of air stirring; and the multitude were

* There is, strictly speaking, but little similarity between this sketchy trifle and the very celebrated and very beautiful "Moon-story" of Mr. Locke — but as both have the character of *hoaxes*, (although one is in the tone of banter, the other of downright earnest) and as both *hoaxes* are on the same subject, the moon — the author of "Hans Phaall" thinks it necessary to say, *in self-defence*, that his own jeu-d'esprit was published, in the Southern Literary Messenger, about three weeks previously to the appearance of Mr. L's in the New York "Sun." Fancying a similarity which does not really exist, some of the New York papers copied "Hans Phaall," and collated it with the Hoax — with the view of detecting the writer of the one in the writer of the other.

in no bad humor at being now and then besprinkled with friendly show-
ers of momentary duration, that fell from large white masses of cloud
which chequered in a fitful manner the blue vault of the firmament.
Nevertheless, about noon, a slight but remarkable agitation became ap-
parent in the assembly: the clattering of ten thousand tongues succeeded;
and, in an instant afterward, ten thousand faces were upturned toward
the heavens, ten thousand pipes descended simultaneously from the
corners of ten thousand mouths, and a shout, which could be compared
to nothing but the roaring of Niagara, resounded long, loudly, and furi-
ously, through all the environs of Rotterdam.

The origin of this hubbub soon became sufficiently evident. From be-
hind the huge bulk of one of those sharply-defined masses of cloud already
mentioned, was seen slowly to emerge into an open area of blue space,
a queer, heterogeneous, but apparently solid substance, so oddly shaped,
so whimsically put together, as not to be in any manner comprehended,
and never to be sufficiently admired, by the host of sturdy burghers who
stood open-mouthed below. What could it be? In the name of all the
vrows and devils in Rotterdam, what could it possibly portend? No one
knew; no one could imagine; no one — not even the burgomaster Myn-
heer Superbus Von Underduk — had the slightest clew by which to un-
ravel the mystery; so, as nothing more reasonable could be done, every
one to a man replaced his pipe carefully in the corner of his mouth, and
cocking up his right eye towards the phenomenon, puffed, paused, wad-
dled about, and grunted significantly — then waddled back, grunted,
paused, and finally — puffed again.

In the meantime, however, lower and still lower toward the goodly
city, came the object of so much curiosity, and the cause of so much
smoke. In a very few minutes it arrived near enough to be accurately
discerned. It appeared to be — yes! it *was* undoubtedly a species of
balloon; but surely no *such* balloon had ever been seen in Rotterdam
before. For who, let me ask, ever heard of a balloon manufactured en-
tirely of dirty newspapers? No man in Holland certainly; yet here, under
the very noses of the people, or rather at some distance *above* their
noses was the identical thing in question, and composed, I have it on
the best authority, of the precise material which no one had ever be-
fore known to be used for a similar purpose. It was an egregious in-
sult to the good sense of the burghers of Rotterdam. As to the shape
of the phenomenon, it was even still more reprehensible. Being little
or nothing better than a huge foolscap turned upside down. And this
similitude was regarded as by no means lessened when, upon nearer
inspection, there was perceived a large tassel depending from its apex,
and, around the upper rim or base of the cone, a circle of little instru-
ments, resembling sheep-bells, which kept up a continual tinkling to the
tune of Betty Martin. But still worse. Suspended by blue ribbons to the
end of this fantastic machine, there hung, by way of car, an enormous

drab beaver hat, with a brim superlatively broad, and a hemispherical crown with a black band and a silver buckle. It is, however, somewhat remarkable that many citizens of Rotterdam swore to having seen the same hat repeatedly before; and indeed the whole assembly seemed to regard it with eyes of familiarity; while the vrow Grettel Phaall, upon sight of it, uttered an exclamation of joyful surprise, and declared it to be the identical hat of her good man himself. Now this was a circumstance the more to be observed, as Phaall, with three companions, had actually disappeared from Rotterdam about five years before, in a very sudden and unaccountable manner, and up to the date of this narrative all attempts had failed of obtaining any intelligence concerning them whatsoever. To be sure, some bones which were thought to be human, mixed up with a quantity of odd-looking rubbish, had been lately discovered in a retired situation to the east of Rotterdam, and some people went so far as to imagine that in this spot a foul murder had been committed, and that the sufferers were in all probability Hans Phaall and his associates. But to return.

The balloon (for such no doubt it was) had now descended to within a hundred feet of the earth, allowing the crowd below a sufficiently distinct view of the person of its occupant. This was in truth a very droll little somebody. He could not have been more than two feet in height; but this altitude, little as it was, would have been sufficient to destroy his equilibrium, and tilt him over the edge of his tiny car, but for the intervention of a circular rim reaching as high as the breast, and rigged on to the cords of the balloon. The body of the little man was more than proportionately broad, giving to his entire figure a rotundity highly absurd. His feet, of course, could not be seen at all, although a horny substance of suspicious nature was occasionally protruded through a rent in the bottom of the car, or to speak more properly, in the top of the hat. His hands were enormously large. His hair was extremely gray, and collected in a cue behind. His nose was prodigiously long, crooked, and inflammatory; his eyes full, brilliant, and acute; his chin and cheeks, although wrinkled with age, were broad, puffy, and double; but of ears of any kind or character there was not a semblance to be discovered upon any portion of his head. This odd little gentleman was dressed in a loose surtout of sky-blue satin, with tight breeches to match, fastened with silver buckles at the knees. His vest was of some bright yellow material; a white taffety cap was set jauntily on one side of his head; and, to complete his equipment, a blood-red silk handkerchief enveloped his throat, and fell down, in a dainty manner, upon his bosom, in a fantastic bow-knot of super-eminent dimensions.

Having descended, as I said before, to about one hundred feet from the surface of the earth, the little old gentleman was suddenly seized with a fit of trepidation, and appeared disinclined to make any nearer approach to *terra firma*. Throwing out, therefore, a quantity of sand from a canvas

bag, which he lifted with great difficulty, he became stationary in an instant. He then proceeded, in a hurried and agitated manner, to extract from a side-pocket in his surtout a large morocco pocket-book. This he poised suspiciously in his hand, then eyed it with an air of extreme surprise, and was evidently astonished at its weight. He at length opened it, and drawing therefrom a huge letter sealed with red sealing-wax and tied carefully with red tape, let it fall precisely at the feet of the burgomaster, Superbus Von Underduk. His Excellency stooped to take it up. But the aeronaut, still greatly discomposed, and having apparently no farther business to detain him in Rotterdam, began at this moment to make busy preparations for departure; and it being necessary to discharge a portion of ballast to enable him to reascend, the half dozen bags which he threw out, one after another, without taking the trouble to empty their contents, tumbled, every one of them, most unfortunately upon the back of the burgomaster, and rolled him over and over no less than one-and-twenty times, in the face of every man in Rotterdam. It is not to be supposed, however, that the great Underduk suffered this impertinence on the part of the little old man to pass off with impunity. It is said, on the contrary, that during each and every one of his one-and-twenty circumvolutions he emitted no less than one-and-twenty distinct and furious whiffs from his pipe, to which he held fast the whole time with all his might, and to which he intends holding fast until the day of his death.

In the meantime the balloon arose like a lark, and, soaring far away above the city, at length drifted quietly behind a cloud similar to that from which it had so oddly emerged, and was thus lost forever to the wondering eyes of the good citiezns of Rotterdam. All attention was now directed to the letter, the descent of which, and the consequences attending thereupon, had proved so fatally subversive of both person and personal dignity to his Excellency, the illustrious Burgomaster Mynheer Superbus Von Underduk. That functionary, however, had not failed, during his circumgyratory movements, to bestow a thought upon the important subject of securing the packet in question, which was seen, upon inspection, to have fallen into the most proper hands, being actually addressed to himself and Professor Rub-a-dub, in their official capacities of President and Vice-President of the Rotterdam College of Astronomy. It was accordingly opened by those dignitaries upon the spot, and found to contain the following extraordinary, and indeed very serious, communications.

To their Excellencies Von Underduk and Rub-a-dub, President and Vice-President of the States' College of Astronomers, in the city of Rotterdam.

Your Excellencies may perhaps be able to remember an humble artizan, by name Hans Phaall, and by occupation a mender of bellows, who,

with three others, disappeared from Rotterdam, about five years ago, in a manner which must have been considered by all parties at once sudden, and extremely unaccountable. If, however, it so please your Excellencies, I, the writer of this communication, am the identical Hans Phaall himself. It is well known to most of my fellow citizens, that for the period of forty years I continued to occupy the little square brick building, at the head of the alley called Sauerkraut, in which I resided at the time of my disappearance. My ancestors have also resided therein time out of mind — they, as well as myself, steadily following the respectable and indeed lucrative profession of mending of bellows. For, to speak the truth, until of late years, that the heads of all the people have been set agog with politics, no better business than my own could an honest citizen of Rotterdam either desire or deserve. Credit was good, employment was never wanting, and on all hands there was no lack of either money or good-will. But, as I was saying, we soon began to feel the effects of liberty and long speeches, and radicalism, and all that sort of thing. People who were formerly the very best customers in the world, had now not a moment of time to think of us at all. They had, so they said, as much as they could do to read about the revolutions, and keep up with the march of intellect and the spirit of the age. If a fire wanted fanning, it could readily be fanned with a newspaper; and as the government grew weaker, I have no doubt that leather and iron acquired durability in proportion, for, in a very short time, there was not a pair of bellows in all Rotterdam that ever stood in need of a stitch or required the assistance of a hammer. This was a state of things not to be endured. I soon grew as poor as a rat, and, having a wife and children to provide for, my burdens at length became intolerable, and I spent hour after hour in reflecting upon the most convenient method of putting an end to my life. Duns, in the meantime, left me little leisure for contemplation. My house was literally besieged from morning till night, so that I began to rave, and foam, and fret like a caged tiger against the bars of his enclosure. There were three fellows in particular who worried me beyond endurance, keeping watch continually about my door, and threatening me with the law. Upon these three I internally vowed the bitterest revenge, if ever I should be so happy as to get them within my clutches; and I believe nothing in the world but the pleasure of this anticipation prevented me from putting my plan of suicide into immediate execution, by blowing my brains out with a blunderbuss. I thought it best, however, to dissemble my wrath, and to treat them with promises and fair words, until, by some good turn of fate, an opportunity of vengeance should be afforded me.

One day, having given my creditors the slip, and feeling more than usually dejected, I continued for a long time to wander about the most obscure streets without object whatever, until at length I chanced to stumble against the corner of a bookseller's stall. Seeing a chair close

at hand, for the use of customers, I threw myself doggedly into it, and, hardly knowing why, opened the pages of the first volume which came within my reach. It proved to be a small pamphlet treatise on Speculative Astronomy, written either by Professor Encke of Berlin or by a Frenchman of somewhat similar name. I had some little tincture of information on matters of this nature, and soon became more and more absorbed in the contents of the book, reading it actually through twice before I awoke to a recollection of what was passing around me. By this time it began to grow dark, and I directed my steps toward home. But the treatise had made an indelible impression on my mind, and, as I sauntered along the dusky streets, I revolved carefully over in my memory the wild and sometimes unintelligible reasonings of the writer. There are some particular passages which affected my imagination in a powerful and extraordinary manner. The longer I meditated upon these the more intense grew the interest which had been excited within me. The limited nature of my education in general, and more especially my ignorance on subjects connected with natural philosophy, so far from rendering me diffident of my own ability to comprehend what I had read, or inducing me to mistrust the many vague notions which had arisen in consequence, merely served as a farther stimulus to imagination; and I was vain enough, or perhaps reasonable enough, to doubt whether those crude ideas which, arising in ill-regulated minds, have all the appearance, may not often in effect possess all the force, the reality, and other inherent properties, of instinct or intuition; and whether, to proceed a step farther, profundity itself might not, in matters of a purely speculative nature, be detected as a legitimate source of falsity and error. In other words, I believed, and still do believe, that truth, is frequently of its own essence, superficial, and that, in many cases, the depth lies more in the abysses where we seek her, than in the actual situations wherein she may be found. Nature herself seemed to afford me corroboration of these ideas. In the contemplation of the heavenly bodies it struck me forcibly that I could not distinguish a star with nearly as much precision, when I gazed on it with earnest, direct and undeviating attention, as when I suffered my eye only to glance in its vicinity alone. I was not, of course, at that time aware that this apparent paradox was occasioned by the center of the visual area being less susceptible of feeble impressions of light than the exterior portions of the retina. This knowledge, and some of another kind, came afterwards in the course of an eventful five years, during which I have dropped the prejudices of my former humble situation in life, and forgotten the bellows-mender in far different occupations. But at the epoch of which I speak, the analogy which a casual observation of a star offered to the conclusions I had already drawn, struck me with the force of positive conformation, and I then finally made up my mind to the course which I afterwards pursued.

It was late when I reached home, and I went immediately to bed.

My mind, however, was too much occupied to sleep, and I lay the whole
night buried in meditation. Arising early in the morning, and contriv-
ing again to escape the vigilance of my creditors, I repaired eagerly to
the bookseller's stall, and laid out what little ready money I possessed,
in the purchase of some volumes of Mechanics and Practical Astronomy.
Having arrived at home safely with these, I devoted every spare moment
to their perusal, and soon made such proficiency in studies of this nature
as I thought sufficient for the execution of my plan. In the intervals of
this period, I made every endeavor to conciliate the three creditors who
had given me so much annoyance. In this I finally succeeded — partly
by selling enough of my household furniture to satisfy a moiety of their
claim, and partly by a promise of paying the balance upon completion
of a little project which I told them I had in view, and for assistance in
which I solicited their services. By these means — for they were ignorant
men — I found little difficulty in gaining them over to my purpose.

Matters being thus arranged, I contrived, by the aid of my wife and
with the greatest secrecy and caution, to dispose of what property I had
remaining, and to borrow, in small sums, under various pretences, and
without paying any attention to my future means of repayment, no in-
considerable quantity of ready money. With the means thus accruing
I proceeded to procure at intervals, cambric muslin, very fine, in pieces
of twelve yards each; twine; a lot of the varnish of caoutchouc; a large
and deep basket of wicker-work, made to order; and several other articles
necessary in the construction and equipment of a balloon of extraordi-
nary dimensions. This I directed my wife to make up as soon as possible,
and gave her all requisite information as to the particular method of
proceeding. In the meantime I worked up the twine into a net-work of
sufficient dimensions; rigged it with a hoop and the necessary cords;
bought a quadrant, a compass, a spy-glass, a common barometer with
some important modifications, and two astronomical instruments not so
generally known. I then took opportunities of conveying by night, to a
retired situation east of Rotterdam, five iron-bound casks, to contain
about fifty gallons each, and one of a larger size; six tinned ware tubes,
three inches in diameter, properly shaped, and ten feet in length; a
quantity of a *particular metallic substance, or semi-metal*, which I shall
not name, and a dozen demijohns of *a very common acid*. The gas to be
formed from these latter materials is a gas never yet generated by any
other person than myself — or at least never applied to any similar pur-
pose. The secret I would make no difficulty in disclosing, but that
it of right belongs to a citizen of Nantz, in France, by whom it was
conditionally communicated to myself. The same individual submitted
to me, without being at all aware of my intentions, a method of con-
structing balloons from the membrane of a certain animal, through
which substance any escape of gas was nearly an impossibility. I found
it, however, altogether too expensive, and was not sure, upon the whole,

whether cambric muslin with a coating of gum caoutchouc, was not equally as good. I mention this circumstance, because I think it probable that hereafter the individual in question may attempt a balloon ascension with the novel gas and material I have spoken of, and I do not wish to deprive him of the honor of a very singular invention.

On the spot which I intended each of the smaller casks to occupy respectively during the inflation of the balloon, I privately dug a hole two feet deep; the holes forming in this manner a circle twenty-five feet in diameter. In the centre of this circle, being the station designed for the large cask, I also dug a hole three feet in depth. In each of the five smaller holes, I deposited a canister containing fifty pounds, and in the larger one a keg holding one hundred and fifty pounds, of cannon powder. These — the keg and canisters — I connected in a proper manner with covered trains; and having let into one of the canisters the end of about four feet of slow match, I covered up the hole, and placed the cask over it, leaving the other end of the match protruding about an inch, and barely visible beyond the cask. I then filled up the remaining holes, and placed the barrels over them in their destined situation.

Besides the articles above enumerated, I conveyed to the depôt, and there secreted, one of M. Grimm's improvements upon the apparatus for condensation of the atmospheric air. I found this machine, however, to require considerable alteration before it could be adapted to the purposes to which I intended making it applicable. But, with severe labor and unremitting perseverance, I at length met with entire success in all my preparations. My balloon was soon completed. It would contain more than forty thousand cubic feet of gas; would take me up easily, I calculated, with all my implements, and, if I managed rightly, with one hundred and seventy-five pounds of ballast into the bargain. It had received three coats of varnish, and I found the cambric muslin to answer all the purposes of silk itself, quite as strong and a good deal less expensive.

Everything being now ready, I exacted from my wife an oath of secrecy in relation to all my actions from the day of my first visit to the bookseller's stall; and promising, on my part, to return as soon as circumstances would permit, I gave her what little money I had left, and bade her farewell. Indeed I had no fear on her account. She was what people call a notable woman, and could manage matters in the world without my assistance. I believe, to tell the truth, she always looked upon me as an idle boy, a mere make-weight, good for nothing but building castles in the air, and was rather glad to get rid of me. It was a dark night when I bade her good-bye, and taking with me, as *aides-de-camp,* the three creditors who had given me so much trouble, we carried the balloon, with the car and accoutrements, by a roundabout way, to the station where the other articles were deposited. We there found them all unmolested, and I proceeded immediately to business.

It was the first of April. The night, as I said before, was dark; there was not a star to be seen; and a drizzling rain, falling at intervals, rendered us very uncomfortable. But my chief anxiety was concerning the balloon, which, in spite of the varnish with which it was defended, began to grow rather heavy with the moisture; the powder also was liable to damage. I therefore kept my three duns working with great diligence, pounding down ice around the central cask, and stirring the acid in the others. They did not cease, however, importuning me with questions as to what I intended to do with all this apparatus, and expressed much dissatisfaction at the terrible labor I made them undergo. They could not perceive, so they said, what good was likely to result from their getting wet to the skin, merely to take a part in such horrible incantations. I began to get uneasy, and worked away with all my might, for I verily believe the idiots supposed that I had entered into a compact with the devil, and that, in short, what I was now doing was nothing better than it should be. I was, therefore, in great fear of their leaving me altogether. I contrived, however, to pacify them by promises of payment of all scores in full, as soon as I could bring the present business to a termination. To these speeches they gave, of course, their own interpretation; fancying, no doubt, that at all events I should come into possession of vast quantities of ready money; and provided I paid them all I owed, and a trifle more, in consideration of their services, I dare say they cared very little what became of either my soul or my carcass.

In about four hours and a half I found the balloon sufficiently inflated. I attached the car, therefore, and put all my implements in it — not forgetting the condensing apparatus, a copious supply of water, and a large quantity of provisions, such as pemmican, in which much nutriment is contained in comparatively little bulk. I also secured in the car a pair of pigeons and a cat. It was now nearly daybreak, and I thought it high time to take my departure. Dropping a lighted cigar on the ground, as if by accident, I took the opportunity, in stooping to pick it up, of igniting privately the piece of slow match, whose end, as I said before, protruded a very little beyond the lower rim of one of the smaller casks. This manœuvre was totally unperceived on the part of the three duns; and, jumping into the car, I immediately cut the single cord which held me to the earth, and was pleased to find that I shot upward, carrying with all ease one hundred and seventy-five pounds of leaden ballast, and able to have carried up as many more.

Scarcely, however, had I attained the height of fifty yards, when, roaring and rumbling up after me in the most horrible and tumultuous manner, came so dense a hurricane of fire, and smoke, and sulphur, and legs and arms, and gravel, and burning wood, and blazing metal, that my very heart sunk within me, and I fell down in the bottom of the car, trembling with unmitigated terror. Indeed, I now perceived that I had entirely overdone the business, and that the main consequences of

the shock were yet to be experienced. Accordingly, in less than a second, I felt all the blood in my body rushing to my temples, and immediately thereupon, a concussion, which I shall never forget, burst abruptly through the night, and seemed to rip the very firmament asunder. When I afterward had time for reflection, I did not fail to attribute the extreme violence of the explosion, as regarded myself, to its proper cause — my situation directly above it, and in the line of its greatest power. But at the time, I thought only of preserving my life. The balloon at first collapsed, then furiously expanded, then whirled round and round with horrible velocity, and finally, reeling and staggering like a drunken man, hurled me with great force over the rim of the car, and left me dangling, at a terrific height, with my head downward, and my face outwards, by a piece of slender cord about three feet in length, which hung accidentally through a crevice near the bottom of the wicker-work, and in which, as I fell, my left foot became most providentially entangled. It is impossible — utterly impossible — to form any adequate idea of the horror of my situation. I gasped convulsively for breath — a shudder resembling a fit of the ague agitated every nerve and muscle of my frame — I felt my eyes starting from their sockets — a horrible nausea overwhelmed me — and at length I fainted away.

How long I remained in this state it is impossible to say. It must, however, have been no inconsiderable time, for when I partially recovered the sense of existence, I found the day breaking, the balloon at a prodigious height over a wilderness of ocean, and not a trace of land to be discovered far and wide within the limits of the vast horizon. My sensations, however, upon thus recovering, were by no means so rife with agony as might have been anticipated. Indeed, there was much of incipient madness in the calm survey which I began to take of my situation. I drew up to my eyes each of my hands, one after the other, and wondered what occurrence could have given rise to the swelling of the veins, and the horrible blackness of the fingernails. I afterward carefully examined my head, shaking it repeatedly, and feeling it with minute attention, until I succeeded in satisfying myself that it was not, as I had more than half suspected, larger than my balloon. Then, in a knowing manner, I felt in both my breeches pockets, and, missing therefrom a set of tablets and a toothpick case, endeavored to account for their disappearance, and not being able to do so, felt inexpressibly chagrined. It now occurred to me that I suffered great uneasiness in the joint of my left ankle, and a dim consciousness of my situation began to glimmer through my mind. But, strange to say! I was neither astonished nor horror-stricken. If I felt any emotion at all, it was a kind of chuckling satisfaction at the cleverness I was about to display in extricating myself from this dilemma; and I never, for a moment, looked upon my ultimate safety as a question susceptible of doubt. For a few minutes I remained wrapped in the profoundest meditation. I have a distinct recollection of frequently

compressing my lips, putting my forefinger to the side of my nose, and making use of other gesticulations and grimaces common to men who, at ease in their arm-chairs, meditate upon matters of intricacy or importance. Having, as I thought, sufficiently collected my ideas, I now, with great caution and deliberation, put my hands behind my back, and unfastened the large iron buckle which belonged to the waistband of my inexpressibles. This buckle had three teeth, which, being somewhat rusty, turned with great difficulty on their axis. I brought them, however, after some trouble, at right angles to the body of the buckle, and was glad to find them remain firm in that position. Holding the instrument thus obtained within my teeth, I now proceeded to untie the knot of my cravat. I had to rest several times before I could accomplish this manœuvre; but it was at length accomplished. To one end of the cravat I then made fast the buckle, and the other end I tied, for greater security, tightly around my wrist. Drawing now my body upwards, with a prodigious exertion of muscular force, I succeeded, at the very first trial, in throwing the buckle over the car, and entangling it, as I had anticipated, in the circular rim of the wicker-work.

My body was now inclined towards the side of the car, at an angle of about forty-five degrees; but it must not be understood that I was therefore only forty-five degrees below the perpendicular. So far from it, I still lay nearly level with the plane of the horizon; for the change of situation which I had acquired, had forced the bottom of the car considerably outwards from my position, which was accordingly one of the most imminent and deadly peril. It should be remembered, however, that when I fell, in the first instance, from the car, if I had fallen with my face turned toward the balloon, instead of turned outwardly from it, as it actually was; or if, in the second place, the cord by which I was suspended had chanced to hang over the upper edge, instead of through a crevice near the bottom of the car, — I say it may be readily conceived that, in either of these supposed cases, I should have been unable to accomplish even as much as I had now accomplished, and the wonderful adventures of Hans Phaall would have been utterly lost to posterity. I had therefore every reason to be grateful; although, in point of fact, I was still too stupid to be anything at all, and hung for, perhaps, a quarter of an hour in that extraordinary manner, without making the slightest farther exertion whatsoever, and in a singularly tranquil state of idiotic enjoyment. But this feeling did not fail to die rapidly away, and thereunto succeeded horror, and dismay, and a chilling sense of utter helplessness and ruin. In fact, the blood so long accumulating in the vessels of my head and throat, and which had hitherto buoyed up my spirits with madness and delirium, had now begun to retire within their proper channels, and the distinctness which was thus added to my perception of the danger, merely served to deprive me of the self-possession and courage to encounter it. But this weakness was, luckily for me, of no very

long duration. In good time came to my rescue the spirit of despair, and, with frantic cries and struggles, I jerked my way bodily upwards, till at length, clutching with a vise-like grip the long-desired rim, I writhed my person over it, and fell headlong and shuddering within the car.

It was not until some time afterward that I recovered myself sufficiently to attend to the ordinary cares of the balloon. I then, however, examined it with attention, and found it, to my great relief, uninjured. My implements were all safe, and, fortunately, I had lost neither ballast nor provisions. Indeed, I had so well secured them in their places, that such an accident was entirely out of the question. Looking at my watch, I found it six o'clock. I was still rapidly ascending, and my barometer gave a present altitude of three and three-quarter miles. Immediately beneath me in the ocean, lay a small black object, slightly oblong in shape, seemingly about the size, and in every way bearing a great resemblance to one of those childish toys called a domino. Bringing my telescope to bear upon it, I plainly discerned it to be a British ninety-four-gun ship, close-hauled, and pitching heavily in the sea with her head to the W. S. W. Besides this ship, I saw nothing but the ocean and the sky, and the sun, which had long arisen.

It is now high time that I should explain to your Excellencies the object of my perilous voyage. Your Excellencies will bear in mind that distressed circumstances in Rotterdam had at length driven me to the resolution of committing suicide. It was not, however, that to life itself I had any positive disgust, but that I was harassed beyond endurance by the adventitious miseries attending my situation. In this state of mind, wishing to live, yet wearied with life, the treatise at the stall of the bookseller opened a resource to my imagination. I then finally made up my mind. I determined to depart, yet live — to leave the world, yet continue to exist — in short, to drop enigmas, I resolved, let what would ensue, to force a passage, if I could, to the moon. Now, lest I should be supposed more of a madman than I actually am, I will detail, as well as I am able, the considerations which led me to believe that an achievement of this nature, although without doubt difficult, and incontestably full of danger, was not absolutely, to a bold spirit, beyond the confines of the possible.

The moon's actual distance from the earth was the first thing to be attended to. Now, the mean or average interval between the *centres* of the two planets is 59.9643 of the earth's equatorial radii, or only about 237,000 miles. I say the mean or average interval. But it must be borne in mind that the form of the moon's orbit being an ellipse of eccentricity amounting to no less than 0.05484 of the major semi-axis of the ellipse itself, and the earth's centre being situated in its focus, if I could, in any manner, contrive to meet the moon, as it were, in its perigee, the above mentioned distance would be materially diminished. But, to say nothing at present of this possibility, it was very certain that, at all events, from

the 237,000 miles I would have to deduct the radius of the earth, say 4,000, and the radius of the moon, say 1,080, in all 5,080, leaving an actual interval to be traversed, under average circumstances, of 231,920 miles. Now this, I reflected, was no very extraordinary distance. Travelling on land has been repeatedly accomplished at the rate of thirty miles per hour, and indeed a much greater speed may be anticipated. But even at this velocity, it would take me no more than 322 days to reach the surface of the moon. There were, however, many particulars inducing me to believe that my average rate of travelling might possibly very much exceed that of thirty miles per hour, and, as these considerations did not fail to make a deep impression upon my mind, I will mention them more fully hereafter.

The next point to be regarded was a matter of far greater importance. From indications afforded by the barometer, we find that, in ascensions from the surface of the earth we have, at the height of 1,000 feet, left below us about one-thirtieth of the entire mass of atmospheric air; that at 10,600 we have ascended through nearly one-third; and that at 18,000, which is not far from the elevation of Cotopaxi, we have surmounted one-half the material, or, at all events, one-half the *ponderable*, body of air incumbent upon our globe. It is also calculated that at an altitude not exceeding the hundredth part of the earth's diameter — that is, not exceeding eighty miles — the rarefaction would be so excessive that animal life could in no manner be sustained, and, moreover, that the most delicate means we possess of ascertaining the presence of the atmosphere would be inadequate to assure us of its existence. But I did not fail to perceive that these latter calculations are founded altogether on our experimental knowledge of the properties of air, and the mechanical laws regulating its dilation and compression, in what may be called, comparatively speaking, *the immediate vicinity* of the earth itself; and, at the same time, it is taken for granted that animal life is and must be essentially *incapable of modification* at any given unattainable distance from the surface. Now, all such reasoning and from such data must, of course, be simply analogical. The greatest height ever reached by man was that of 25,000 feet, attained in the aeronautic expedition of Messieurs Gay-Lussac and Biot. This is a moderate altitude, even when compared with the eighty miles in question; and I could not help thinking that the subject admitted room for doubt and great latitude for speculation.

But, in point of fact, an ascension being made to any given altitude, the ponderable quantity of air surmounted in any *farther* ascension is by no means in proportion to the additional height ascended (as may be plainly seen from what has been stated before), but in a ratio constantly decreasing. It is therefore evident that, ascend as high as we may, we cannot, literally speaking, arrive at a limit beyond which no atmosphere is to be found. It *must exist*, I argued; although it *may* exist in a state of infinite rarefaction.

On the other hand, I was aware that arguments have not been wanting to prove the existence of a real and definite limit to the atmosphere, beyond which there is absolutely no air whatsoever. But a circumstance which has been left out of view by those who contend for such a limit, seemed to me, although no positive refutation of their creed, still a point worthy very serious investigation. On comparing the intervals between the successive arrivals of Encke's comet at its perihelion, after giving credit, in the most exact manner, for all the disturbances due to the attractions of the planets, it appears that the periods are gradually diminishing; that is to say, the major axis of the comet's ellipse is growing shorter, in a slow but perfectly regular decrease. Now, this is precisely what ought to be the case, if we suppose a resistance experienced from the comet from an extremely *rare ethereal medium* pervading the regions of its orbit. For it is evident that such a medium must, in retarding the comet's velocity, increase its centripetal, by weakening its centrifugal, force. In other words, the sun's attraction would be constantly attaining greater power, and the comet would be drawn nearer at every revolution. Indeed, there is no other way of accounting for the variation in question. But again. The real diameter of the same comet's nebulosity is observed to contract rapidly as it approaches the sun, and dilate with equal rapidity in its departure towards its aphelion. Was I not justifiable in supposing, with M. Valz, that this apparent condensation of volume has its origin in the compression of the same ethereal medium I have spoken of before, and which is only denser in proportion to its solar vicinity? The lenticular-shaped phenomenon, also called the zodiacal light, was a matter worthy of attention. This radiance, so apparent in the tropics, and which cannot be mistaken for any meteoric lustre, extends from the horizon obliquely upward, and follows generally the direction of the sun's equator. It appeared to me evidently in the nature of a rare atmosphere extending from the sun outward, beyond the orbit of Venus at least, and I believed indefinitely farther.* Indeed, this medium I could not suppose confined to the path of the comet's ellipse, or to the immediate neighborhood of the sun. It was easy, on the contrary, to imagine it pervading the entire regions of our planetary system, condensed into what we call atmosphere at the planets themselves, and perhaps at some of them modified by considerations, so to speak, purely geological.

Having adopted this view of the subject, I had little further hesitation. Granting that on my passage I should meet with atmosphere *essentially* the same as at the surface of the earth, I conceived that, by means of the very ingenious apparatus of M. Grimm, I should readily be enabled to condense it in sufficient quantity for the purposes of respiration. This would remove the chief obstacle in a journey to the moon. I had

* The zodiacal light is probably what the ancients called *Trabes. Emicant Trabes quos docos vocant.* — Pliny, lib. 2, p. 26.

indeed spent some money and great labor in adapting the apparatus to the object intended, and confidently looked forward to its successful application, if I could manage to complete the voyage within any reasonable period. This brings me back to the *rate* at which it might be possible to travel.

It is true that balloons, in the first stage of their ascensions from the earth, are known to rise with a velocity comparatively moderate. Now, the power of elevation lies altogether in the superior lightness of the gas in the balloon compared with the atmospheric air; and, at first sight, it does not appear probable that, as the balloon acquires altitude, and consequently arrives successively in atmospheric strata of densities rapidly diminishing — I say, it does not appear at all reasonable that, in this its progress upwards, the original velocity should be accelerated. On the other hand, I was not aware that, in any recorded ascension, a diminution was apparent in the absolute rate of ascent; although such should have been the case, if on account of nothing else, on account of the escape of gas through balloons ill-constructed, and varnished with no better material than the ordinary varnish. It seemed, therefore, that the effect of such escape was only sufficient to counterbalance the effect of some accelerating power. I now considered that, provided in my passage I found the medium I had imagined, and provided that it should prove to be actually and *essentially* what we denominate atmospheric air, it could make comparatively little difference at what extreme state of rarefaction I should discover it — that is to say, in regard to my power of ascending — for the gas in the balloon would not only be itself subject to rarefaction partially similar (in proportion to the occurrence of which, I could suffer an escape of so much as would be requisite to prevent explosion), but, *being what it was,* would, at all events, continue specifically lighter than any compound whatever of mere nitrogen and oxygen. In the meantime, the force of gravitation would be constantly diminishing, in proportion to the squares of the distances, and thus, with a velocity prodigiously accelerating, I should at length arrive in those distant regions where the force of the earth's attraction would be superseded by that of the moon. In accordance with these ideas, I did not think it worth while to encumber myself with more provisions than would be sufficient for a period of forty days.

There was still, however, another difficulty, which occasioned me some little disquietude. It has been observed, that, in balloon ascensions to any considerable height, besides the pain attending respiration, great uneasiness is experienced about the head and body, often accompanied with bleeding at the nose, and other symptoms of an alarming kind, and growing more and more inconvenient in proportion to the altitude attained.* This was a reflection of a nature somewhat startling. Was it not

* Since the original publication of Hans Phaall, I find that Mr. Green, of Nassau-balloon notoriety, and other late aeronauts, deny the assertions of Humboldt, in this

probable that these symptoms would increase indefinitely, or at least until terminated by death itself? I finally thought not. Their origin was to be looked for in the progressive removal of the *customary* atmospheric pressure upon the surface of the body, and consequent distention of the superficial blood-vessels — not in any positive disorganization of the animal system, as in the case of difficulty in breathing, where the atmospheric density is *chemically insufficient* for the due renovation of blood in a ventricle of the heart. Unless for default of this renovation, I could see no reason, therefore, why life could not be sustained even in a *vacuum*; for the expansion and compression of chest, commonly called breathing, is action purely muscular, and the *cause*, not the *effect*, of respiration. In a word, I conceived that, as the body should become habituated to the want of atmospheric pressure, the sensations of pain would gradually diminish — and to endure them while they continued, I relied with confidence upon the iron hardihood of my constitution.

Thus, may it please your Excellencies, I have detailed some, though by no means all, the considerations which led me to form the project of a lunar voyage. I shall now proceed to lay before you the result of an attempt so apparently audacious in conception, and, at all events, so utterly unparalleled in the annals of mankind.

Having attained the altitude before mentioned, that is to say three miles and three-quarters, I threw out from the car a quantity of feathers, and found that I still ascended with sufficient rapidity; there was, therefore, no necessity for discharging any ballast. I was glad of this, for I wisted to retain with me as much weight as I could carry, for reasons which will be explained in the sequel. I as yet suffered no bodily inconvenience, breathing with great freedom, and feeling no pain whatever in the head. The cat was lying very demurely upon my coat, which I had taken off, and eyeing the pigeons with an air of *nonchalance*. These latter being tied by the leg, to prevent their escape, were busily employed in picking up some grains of rice scattered for them in the bottom of the car.

At twenty minutes past six o'clock, the barometer showed an elevation of 26,400 feet, or five miles to a fraction. The prospect seemed unbounded. Indeed, it is very easily calculated by means of spherical geometry, what a great extent of the earth's area I beheld. The convex surface of any segment of a sphere is, to the entire surface of the sphere itself, as the versed sine of the segment to the diameter of the sphere. Now, in my case, the versed sine — that is to say, the *thickness* of the segment beneath me — was about equal to my elevation, or the elevation of the point of sight above the surface. "As five miles, then, to eight thousand," would express the proportion of the earth's area seen by me. In other words, I beheld as much as a sixteen-hundredth part of the

respect, and speak of a *decreasing* inconvenience, — precisely in accordance with the theory here urged in a mere spirit of banter.

whole surface of the globe. The sea appeared unruffled as a mirror, al-
though, by means of the spy-glass, I could perceive it to be in a state of
violent agitation. The ship was no longer visible, having drifted away,
apparently to the eastward. I now began to experience, at intervals, se-
vere pain in the head, especially about the ears — still, however, breath-
ing with tolerable freedom. The cat and pigeons seemed to suffer no
inconvenience whatsoever.

At twenty minutes before seven, the balloon entered a long series of
dense cloud, which put me to great trouble, by damaging my condens-
ing apparatus and wetting me to the skin. This was, to be sure, a singular
recontre, for I had not believed it possible that a cloud of this nature
could be sustained at so great an elevation. I thought it best, however,
to throw out two five-pound pieces of ballast, reserving still a weight of
one hundred and sixty-five pounds. Upon so doing, I soon rose above the
difficulty, and perceived immediately, that I had obtained a great in-
crease in my rate of ascent. In a few seconds after my leaving the cloud,
a flash of vivid lightning shot from one end of it to the other, and caused
it to kindle up, throughout its vast extent, like a mass of ignited and glow-
ing charcoal. This, it must be remembered, was in the broad light of day.
No fancy may picture the sublimity which might have been exhibited by
a similar phenomenon taking place amid the darkness of the night. Hell
itself might have been found a fitting image. Even as it was, my hair stood
on end, while I gazed afar down within the yawning abysses, letting imag-
ination descend, as it were, and stalk about in the strange vaulted halls,
and ruddy gulfs, and red ghastly chasms of the hideous and unfathomable
fire. I had indeed made a narrow escape. Had the balloon remained a very
short while longer within the cloud — that is to say — had not the incon-
venience of getting wet, determined me to discharge the ballast, inevi-
table ruin would have been the consequence. Such perils, although little
considered, are perhaps the greatest which must be encountered in bal-
loons. I had by this time, however, attained too great an elevation to be
any longer uneasy on this head.

I was now rising rapidly, and by seven o'clock the barometer indicated
an altitude of no less than nine miles and a half. I began to find great
difficulty in drawing my breath. My head, too, was excessively painful;
and, having felt for some time a moisture about my cheeks, I at length
discovered it to be blood, which was oozing quite fast from the drums of
my ears. My eyes, also, gave me great uneasiness. Upon passing the hand
over them they seemed to have protruded from their sockets in no incon-
siderable degree; and all objects in the car, and even the balloon itself,
appeared distorted to my vision. These symptoms were more than I had
expected, and occasioned me some alarm. At this juncture, very impru-
dently, and without consideration, I threw out from the car three five-
pound pieces of ballast. The accelerated rate of ascent thus obtained,
carried me too rapidly, and without sufficient gradation, into a highly

rarefied stratum of the atmosphere, and the result had nearly proved fatal to my expedition and to myself. I was suddenly seized with a spasm which lasted for more than five minutes, and even when this, in a measure, ceased, I could catch my breath only at long intervals, and in a gasping manner — bleeding all the while copiously at the nose and ears, and even slightly at the eyes. The pigeons appeared distressed in the extreme, and struggled to escape; while the cat mewed piteously, and, with her tongue hanging out of her mouth, staggered to and fro in the car as if under the influence of poison. I now too late discovered the great rashness of which I had been guilty in discharging the ballast, and my agitation was excessive. I anticipated nothing less than death, and death in a few minutes. The physical suffering I underwent contributed also to render me nearly incapable of making any exertion for the preservation of my life. I had, indeed, little power of reflection left, and the violence of the pain in my head seemed to be greatly on the increase. Thus I found that my senses would shortly give way altogether, and I had already clutched one of the valve ropes with the view of attempting a descent, when the recollection of the trick I had played the three creditors, and the possible consequences to myself, should I return, operated to deter me for the moment. I lay down in the bottom of the car, and endeavored to collect my faculties. In this I so far succeeded as to determine upon the experiment of losing blood. Having no lancet, however, I was constrained to perform the operation in the best manner I was able, and finally succeeded in opening a vein in my right arm, with the blade of my penknife. The blood had hardly commenced flowing when I experienced a sensible relief, and by the time I had lost about half a moderate basin full, most of the worst symptoms had abandoned me entirely. I nevertheless did not think it expedient to attempt getting on my feet immediately; but, having tied up my arm as well as I could, I lay still for about a quarter of an hour. At the end of this time I arose, and found myself freer from absolute *pain* of any kind than I had been during the last hour and a quarter of my ascension. The difficulty of breathing, however, was diminished in a very slight degree, and I found that it would soon be positively necessary to make use of my condenser. In the meantime, looking toward the cat, who was again snugly stowed away upon my coat, I discovered to my infinite surprise, that she had taken the opportunity of my indisposition to bring into light a litter of three little kittens. This was an addition to the number of passengers on my part altogether unexpected; but I was pleased at the occurrence. It would afford me a chance of bringing to a kind of test the truth of a surmise, which, more than anything else, had influenced me in attempting this ascension. I had imagined that the *habitual* endurance of the atmospheric pressure at the surface of the earth was the cause, or nearly so, of the pain attending animal existence at a distance above the surface. Should the kittens be found to suffer uneasiness *in an equal degree with*

their mother, I must consider my theory in fault, but a failure to do so I should look upon as a strong confirmation of my idea.

By eight o'clock I had actually attained an elevation of seventeen miles above the surface of the earth. Thus it seemed to me evident that my rate of ascent was not only on the increase, but that the progression would have been apparent in a slight degree even had I not discharged the ballast which I did. The pains in my head and ears returned, at intervals, with violence, and I still continued to bleed occasionally at the nose; but, upon the whole, I suffered much less than might have been expected. I breathed, however, at every moment, with more and more difficulty, and each inhalation was attended with a troublesome spasmodic action of the chest. I now unpacked the condensing apparatus, and got it ready for immediate use.

The view of the earth, at this period of my ascension, was beautiful indeed. To the westward, the northward, and the southward, as far as I could see, lay a boundless sheet of apparently unruffled ocean, which every moment gained a deeper and a deeper tint of blue and began already to assume a slight appearance of convexity. At a vast distance to the eastward, although perfectly discernible, extended the islands of Great Britain, the entire Atlantic coasts of France and Spain, with a small portion of the northern part of the continent of Africa. Of individual edifices not a trace could be discovered, and the proudest cities of mankind had utterly faded away from the face of the earth. From the rock of Gibraltar, now dwindled into a dim speck, the dark Mediterranean sea, dotted with shining islands as the heaven is dotted with stars, spread itself out to the eastward as far as my vision extended, until its entire mass of waters seemed at length to tumble headlong over the abyss of the horizon, and I found myself listening on tiptoe for the echoes of the mighty cataract. Overhead, the sky was of a jetty black, and the stars were brilliantly visible.

The pigeons about this time seeming to undergo much suffering, I determined upon giving them their liberty. I first untied one of them, a beautiful gray-mottled pigeon, and placed him upon the rim of the wicker-work. He appeared extremely uneasy, looking anxiously around him, fluttering his wings, and making a loud cooing noise, but could not be persuaded to trust himself from off the car. I took him up at last, and threw him to about half a dozen yards from the balloon. He made, however, no attempt to descend as I had expected, but struggled with great vehemence to get back, uttering at the same time very shrill and piercing cries. He at length succeeded in regaining his former station on the rim, but had hardly done so when his head dropped upon his breast, and he fell dead within the car. The other one did not prove so unfortunate. To prevent his following the example of his companion, and accomplishing a return, I threw him downward with all my force, and was pleased to find him continue his descent, with great velocity,

making use of his wings with ease, and in a perfectly natural manner. In a very short time he was out of sight, and I have no doubt he reached home in safety. Puss, who seemed in a great measure recovered from her illness, now made a hearty meal of the dead bird, and then went to sleep with much apparent satisfaction. Her kittens were quite lively, and so far evinced not the slightest sign of any uneasiness whatever.

At a quarter-past eight, being no longer able to draw breath without the most intolerable pain, I proceeded forthwith to adjust around the car the apparatus belonging to the condenser. This apparatus will require some little explanation, and your Excellencies will please to bear in mind that my object, in the first place, was to surround myself and car entirely with a barricade against the highly rarefied atmosphere in which I was existing, with the intention of introducing within this barricade, by means of my condenser, a quantity of this same atmosphere sufficiently condensed for the purposes of respiration. With this object in view I had prepared a very strong perfectly air-tight, but flexible gum-elastic bag. In this bag, which was of sufficient dimensions, the entire car was in a manner placed. That is to say, it (the bag) was drawn over the whole bottom of the car, up its sides, and so on, along the outside of the ropes, to the upper rim or hoop where the net-work is attached. Having pulled the bag up in this way, and formed a complete enclosure on all sides, and at botttom, it was now necessary to fasten up its top or mouth, by passing its material over the hoop of the net-work — in other words, between the net-work and the hoop. But if the net-work were separated from the hoop to admit this passage, what was to sustain the car in the meantime? Now the net-work was not permanently fastened to the hoop, but attached by a series of running loops or nooses. I therefore undid only a few of these loops at one time, leaving the car suspended by the remainder. Having thus inserted a portion of the cloth forming the upper part of the bag, I refastened the loops — not to the hoop, for that would have been impossible, since the cloth now intervened — but to a series of large buttons, affixed to the cloth itself, about three feet below the mouth of the bag; the intervals between the buttons having been made to correspond to the intervals between the loops. This done, a few more of the loops were unfastened from the rim, a farther portion of the cloth introduced, and the disengaged loops then connected with their proper buttons. In this way it was possible to insert the whole upper part of the bag between the net-work and the hoop. It is evident that the hoop would now drop down within the car, while the whole weight of the car itself, with all its contents, would be held up merely by the strength of the buttons. This, at first sight, would seem an inadequate dependence; but it was by no means so, for the buttons were not only very strong in themselves, but so close together that a very slight portion of the whole weight was supported by any one of them. Indeed, had the car and contents been three times heavier than they

were, I should not have been at all uneasy. I now raised up the hoop again within the covering of gum-elastic, and propped it at nearly its former height by means of three light poles prepared for the occasion. This was done, of course, to keep the bag distended at the top, and to preserve the lower part of the net-work in its proper situation. All that now remained was to fasten up the mouth of the enclosure; and this was readily accomplished by gathering the folds of the material together, and twisting them up very tightly on the inside by means of a kind of stationary tourniquet.

In the sides of the covering thus adjusted round the car, had been inserted three circular panes of thick but clear glass, through which I could see without difficulty around me in every horizontal direction. In that portion of the cloth forming the bottom, was likewise, a fourth window, of the same kind, and corresponding with a small aperture in the floor of the car itself. This enabled me to see perpendicularly down, but having found it impossible to place any similar contrivance overhead, on account of the peculiar manner of closing up the opening there, and the consequent wrinkles in the cloth, I could expect to see no objects situated directly in my zenith. This, of course, was a matter of little consequence; for had I even been able to place a window at top, the balloon itself would have prevented my making any use of it.

About a foot below one of the side windows was a circular opening, eight inches in diameter, and fitted with a brass rim adapted in its inner edge to the windings of a screw. In this rim was screwed the large tube of the condenser, the body of the machine being, of course, within the chamber of gum-elastic. Through this tube a quantity of the rare atmosphere circumjacent being drawn by means of a *vacuum* created in the body of the machine, was thence discharged, in a state of condensation, to mingle with the thin air already in the chamber. This operation being repeated several times, at length filled the chamber with atmosphere proper for all the purposes of respiration. But in so confined a space it would, in a short time, necessarily become foul, and unfit for use from frequent contact with the lungs. It was then ejected by a small valve at the bottom of the car — the dense air readily sinking into the thinner atmosphere below. To avoid the inconvenience of making a total *vacuum* at any moment within the chamber, this purification was never accomplished all at once, but in a gradual manner — the valve being opened only for a few seconds, then closed again, until one or two strokes from the pump of the condenser had supplied the place of the atmosphere ejected. For the sake of experiment I had put the cat and kittens in a small basket, and suspended it outside the car to a button at the bottom, close by the valve, through which I could feed them at any moment when necessary. I did this at some little risk, and before closing the mouth of the chamber, by reaching under the car with one of the poles before mentioned to which a hook had been attached.

By the time I had fully completed these arrangements and filled the chamber as explained, it wanted only ten minutes of nine o'clock. During the whole period of my being thus employed, I endured the most terrible distress from difficulty of respiration, and bitterly did I repent the negligence or rather fool-hardiness, of which I had been guilty, of putting off to the last moment a matter of so much importance. But having at length accomplished it, I soon began to reap the benefit of my invention. Once again I breathed with perfect freedom and ease — and indeed why should I not? I was also agreeably surprised to find myself, in a great measure, relieved from the violent pains which had hitherto tormented me. A slight headache, accompanied with a sensation of fulness or distention about the wrists, the ankles, and the throat, was nearly all of which I had now to complain. Thus it seemed evident that a greater part of the uneasiness attending the removal of atmospheric pressure had actually *worn off*, as I had expected, and that much of the pain endured for the last two hours should have been attributed altogether to the effects of a deficient respiration.

At twenty minutes before nine o'clock — that is to say, a short time prior to my closing up the mouth of the chamber, the mercury attained its limit, or ran down, in the barometer, which, as I mentioned before, was one of an extended construction. It then indicated an altitude on my part of 132,000 feet, or five-and-twenty miles, and I consequently surveyed at that time an extent of the earth's area amounting to no less than the three hundred-and-twentieth part of its entire superficies. At nine o'clock I had again lost sight of land to the eastward, but not before I became aware that the balloon was drifting rapidly to the N. N. W. The convexity of the ocean beneath me was very evident indeed, although my view was often interrupted by the masses of cloud which floated to and fro. I observed now that even the lightest vapors never rose to more than ten miles above the level of the sea.

At half past nine I tried the experiment of throwing out a handful of feathers through the valve. They did not float as I had expected; but dropped down perpendicularly, like a bullet, *en masse*, and with the greatest velocity — being out of sight in a very few seconds. I did not at first know what to make of this extraordinary phenomenon; not being able to believe that my rate of ascent had, of a sudden, met with so prodigious an acceleration. But it soon occurred to me that the atmosphere was now far too rare to sustain even the feathers; that they actually fell, as they appeared to do, with great rapidity; and that I had been surprised by the united velocities of their descent and my own elevation.

By ten o'clock I found that I had very little to occupy my immediate attention. Affairs went swimmingly, and I believed the balloon to be going upward with a speed increasing momently although I had no longer any means of ascertaining the progression of the increase. I suf-

fered no pain or uneasiness of any kind, and enjoyed better spirits than
I had at any period since my departure from Rotterdam, busying my-
self now in examining the state of my various apparatus, and now in
regenerating the atmosphere within the chamber. This latter point I
determined to attend to at regular intervals of forty minutes, more on
account of the preservation of my health, than from so frequent a reno-
vation being absolutely necessary. In the meanwhile I could not help
making anticipations. Fancy revelled in the wild and dreamy regions of
the moon. Imagination, feeling herself for once unshackled, roamed at
will among the ever-changing wonders of a shadowy and unstable land.
Now there were hoary and time-honored forests, and craggy precipices,
and waterfalls tumbling with a loud noise into abysses without a bot-
tom. Then I came suddenly into still noonday solitudes, where no wind
of heaven ever intruded, and where vast meadows of poppies, and
slender, lily-looking flowers spread themselves out a weary distance, all
silent and motionless forever. Then again I journeyed far down away
into another country where it was all one dim and vague lake, with a
boundary line of clouds. And out of this melancholy water arose a forest
of tall eastern trees, like a wilderness of dreams. And I have in mind
that the shadows of the trees which fell upon the lake remained not
on the surface where they fell, but sunk slowly and steadily down, and
commingled with the waves, while from the trunks of the trees other
shadows were continually coming out, and taking the place of their
brothers thus entombed. "This then," I said thoughtfully, "is the very
reason why the waters of this lake grow blacker with age, and more
melancholy as the hours run on." But fancies such as these were not
the sole possessors of my brain. Horrors of a nature most stern and most
appalling would too frequently obtrude themselves upon my mind,
and shake the innermost depths of my soul with the bare supposition of
their possibility. Yet I would not suffer my thoughts for any length of
time to dwell upon these latter speculations, rightly judging the real
and palpable dangers of the voyage sufficient for my undivided attention.

At five o'clock, p. m., being engaged in regenerating the atmosphere
within the chamber, I took that opportunity of observing the cat and
kittens through the valve. The cat herself appeared to suffer again very
much, and I had no hesitation in attributing her uneasiness chiefly to a
difficulty in breathing; but my experiment with the kittens had resulted
very strangely. I had expected, of course, to see them betray a sense of
pain, although in a less degree than their mother; and this would have
been sufficient to confirm my opinion concerning the habitual endurance
of atmospheric pressure. But I was not prepared to find them, upon close
examination, evidently enjoying a high degree of health, breathing with
the greatest ease and perfect regularity, and evincing not the slightest
sign of any uneasiness whatever. I could only account for all this by ex-
tending my theory, and supposing that the highly rarefied atmosphere

around might perhaps not be, as I had taken for granted, chemically insufficient for the purposes of life, and that a person born in such a medium might, possibly, be unaware of any inconvenience attending its inhalation, while, upon removal to the denser strata near the earth, he might endure tortures of a similar nature to those I had so lately experienced. It has since been to me a matter of deep regret that an awkward accident, at this time, occasioned me the loss of my little family of cats, and deprived me of the insight into this matter which a continued experiment might have afforded. In passing my hand through the valve, with a cup of water for the old puss, the sleeves of my shirt became entangled in the loop which sustained the basket, and thus, in a moment, loosened it from the bottom. Had the whole actually vanished into air, it could not have shot from my sight in a more abrupt and instantaneous manner. Positively, there could not have intervened the tenth part of a second between the disengagement of the basket and its absolute and total disappearance with all that it contained. My good wishes followed it to the earth, but of course, I had no hope that either cat or kittens would ever live to tell the tale of their misfortune.

At six o'clock, I perceived a great portion of the earth's visible area to the eastward involved in thick shadow, which continued to advance with great rapidity, until, at five minutes before seven, the whole surface in view was enveloped in the darkness of night. It was not, however, until long after this time that the rays of the setting sun ceased to illumine the balloon; and this circumstance, although of course fully anticipated, did not fail to give me an infinite deal of pleasure. It was evident that, in the morning, I should behold the rising luminary many hours at least before the citizens of Rotterdam, in spite of their situation so much farther to the eastward, and thus, day after day, in proportion to the height ascended, would I enjoy the light of the sun for a longer and a longer period. I now determined to keep a journal of my passage, reckoning the days from one to twenty-four hours continuously, without taking into consideration the intervals of darkness.

At ten o'clock, feeling sleepy, I determined to lie down for the rest of the night; but here a difficulty presented itself, which, obvious as it may appear, had escaped my attention up to the very moment of which I am now speaking. If I went to sleep as I proposed, how could the atmosphere in the chamber be regenerated in the interim? To breathe it for more than an hour, at the farthest, would be a matter of impossibility; or, if even this term could be extended to an hour and a quarter, the most ruinous consequences might ensue. The consideration of this dilemma gave me no little disquietude; and it will hardly be believed, that, after the dangers I had undergone, I should look upon this business in so serious a light, as to give up all hope of accomplishing my ultimate design, and finally make up my mind to the necessity of a descent. But this hesitation was only momentary. I reflected that man is

the veriest slave of custom, and that many points in the routine of his
existence are deemed *essentially* important, which are only so *at all* by
his having rendered them habitual. It was very certain that I could not
do without sleep; but I might easily bring myself to feel no inconven-
ience from being awakened at intervals of an hour during the whole
period of my repose. It would require but five minutes at most to regen-
erate the atmosphere in the fullest manner, and the only real difficulty
was to contrive a method of arousing myself at the proper mo-
ment for so doing. But this was a question which, I am willing to con-
fess, occasioned me no little trouble in its solution. To be sure, I had
heard of the student who, to prevent his falling asleep over his books,
held in one hand a ball of copper, the din of whose descent into a basin
of the same metal on the floor beside his chair, served effectually to
startle him up, if, at any moment, he should be overcome with drowsi-
ness. My own case, however, was very different indeed, and left me no
room for any similar idea; for I did not wish to keep awake, but to be
aroused from slumber at regular intervals of time. I at length hit upon
the following expedient, which, simple as it may seem, was hailed by
me, at the moment of discovery, as an invention fully equal to that of
the telescope, the steam-engine, or the art of printing itself.

It is necessary to premise, that the balloon, at the elevation now at-
tained, continued its course upward with an even and undeviating
ascent, and the car consequently followed with a steadiness so perfect
that it would have been impossible to detect in it the slightest vacilla-
tion whatever. This circumstance favored me greatly in the project I
now determined to adopt. My supply of water had been put on board in
kegs containing five gallons each, and ranged very securely around the
interior of the car. I unfastened one of these, and taking two ropes tied
them tightly across the rim of the wicker-work from one side to the
other; placing them about a foot apart and parallel, so as to form a
kind of shelf, upon which I placed the keg, and steadied it in a hori-
zontal position. About eight inches immediately below these ropes,
and four feet from the bottom of the car I fastened another shelf —
but made of thin plank, being the only similar piece of wood I had.
Upon this latter shelf, and exactly beneath one of the rims of the keg,
a small earthern pitcher was deposited. I now bored a hole in the end of
the keg over the pitcher, and fitted in a plug of soft wood, cut in a taper-
ing or conical shape. This plug I pushed in or pulled out, as might hap-
pen, until, after a few experiments, it arrived at that exact degree of
tightness, at which the water, oozing from the hole, and falling into the
pitcher below, would fill the latter to the brim in the period of sixty
minutes. This, of course, was a matter briefly and easily ascertained, by
noticing the proportion of the pitcher filled in any given time. Having
arranged all this, the rest of the plan is obvious. My bed was so con-
trived upon the floor of the car, as to bring my head, in lying down,

immediately below the mouth of the pitcher. It was evident, that, at the expiration of an hour, the pitcher, getting full, would be forced to run over, and to run over at the mouth, which was somewhat lower than the rim. It was also evident, that the water thus falling from a height of more than four feet, could not do otherwise than fall upon my face, and that the sure consequences would be, to waken me up instantaneously, even from the soundest slumber in the world.

It was fully eleven by the time I had completed these arrangements, and I immediately betook myself to bed, with full confidence in the efficiency of my invention. Nor in this matter was I disappointed. Punctually every sixty minutes was I aroused by my trusty chronometer, when, having emptied the pitcher into the bung-hole of the keg, and performed the duties of the condenser, I retired again to bed. These regular interruptions to my slumber caused me even less discomfort than I had anticipated; and when I finally arose for the day, it was seven o'clock, and the sun had attained many degrees above the line of my horizon.

April 3d. I found the balloon at an immense height indeed, and the earth's apparent convexity increased in a material degree. Below me in the ocean lay a cluster of black specks, which undoubtedly were islands. Far away to the northward I perceived a thin, white, and exceedingly brilliant line, or streak, on the edge of the horizon, and I had no hesitation in supposing it to be the southern disk of the ices of the Polar Sea. My curiosity was greatly excited, for I had hopes of passing on much farther to the north, and might possibly, at some period, find myself placed directly above the Pole itself. I now lamented that my great elevation would, in this case, prevent my taking as accurate a survey as I could wish. Much, however, might be ascertained. Nothing else of an extraordinary nature occurred during the day. My apparatus all continued in good order, and the balloon still ascended without any perceptible vacillation. The cold was intense, and obliged me to wrap up closely in an overcoat. When darkness came over the earth, I betook myself to bed, although it was for many hours afterward broad daylight all around my immediate situation. The water-clock was punctual in its duty, and I slept until next morning soundly, with the exception of the periodical interruption.

April 4th. Arose in good health and spirits, and was astonished at the singular change which had taken place in the appearance of the sea. It had lost, in a great measure, the deep tint of blue it had hitherto worn, being now of a grayish-white, and of a lustre dazzling to the eye. The islands were no longer visible; whether they had passed down the horizon to the southeast, or whether my increasing elevation had left them out of sight, it is impossible to say. I was inclined, however, to the latter opinion. The rim of ice to the northward was growing more and more apparent. Cold by no means so intense. Nothing of importance occurred,

and I passed the day in reading, having taken care to supply myself with books.

April 5th. Beheld the singular phenomenon of the sun rising while nearly the whole visible surface of the earth continued to be involved in darkness. In time, however, the light spread itself over all, and I again saw the line of ice to the northward. It was now very distinct, and appeared of a much darker hue than the waters of the ocean. I was evidently approaching it, and with great rapidity. Fancied I could again distinguish a strip of land to the eastward, and one also to the westward, but could not be certain. Weather moderate. Nothing of any consequence happened during the day. Went early to bed.

April 6th. Was surprised at finding the rim of ice at a very moderate distance, and an immense field of the same material stretching away off to the horizon in the north. It was evident that if the balloon held its present course, it would soon arrive above the Frozen Ocean, and I had now little doubt of ultimately seeing the Pole. During the whole of the day I continued to near the ice. Toward night the limits of my horizon very suddenly and materially increased, owing undoubtedly to the earth's form being that of an oblate spheroid, and my arriving above the flattened regions in the vicinity of the Arctic circle. When darkness at length overtook me, I went to bed in great anxiety, fearing to pass over the object of so much curiosity when I should have no opportunity of observing it.

April 7th. Arose early, and, to my great joy, at length beheld what there could be no hesitation in supposing the northern Pole itself. It was there, beyond a doubt, and immediately beneath my feet; but, alas! I had now ascended to so vast a distance, that nothing could with accuracy be discerned. Indeed, to judge from the progression of the numbers indicating my various altitudes, respectively, at different periods, between six A.M. on the second of April, and twenty minutes before nine A.M. of the same day (at which time the barometer ran down), it might be fairly inferred that the balloon had now, at four o'clock in the morning of April the seventh, reached a height of *not less*, certainly, than 7,254 miles above the surface of the sea. This elevation may appear immense, but the estimate upon which it is calculated gave a result in all probability far inferior to the truth. At all events I undoubtedly beheld the whole of the earth's major diameter; the entire northern hemisphere lay beneath me like a chart orthographically projected: and the great circle of the equator itself formed the boundary line of my horizon. Your Excellencies may, however, readily imagine that the confined regions hitherto unexplored within the limits of the Arctic circle, although situated directly beneath me, and therefore seen without any appearance of being foreshortened, were still, in themselves, comparatively too diminutive, and at too great a distance from the point of sight, to admit of any very accurate examination. Nevertheless, what could be

seen was of a nature singular and exciting. Northwardly from that huge
rim before mentioned, and which, with slight qualification, may be
called the limit of human discovery in these regions, one unbroken, or
nearly unbroken, sheet of ice continues to extend. In the first few de-
grees of this its progress, its surface is very sensibly flattened, farther
on depressed into a plane, and finally, becoming *not a little concave*, it
terminates, at the Pole itself, in a circular centre, sharply defined, whose
apparent diameter subtended at the balloon an angle of about sixty-five
seconds, and whose dusky hue, varying in intensity, was, at all times,
darker than any other spot upon the visible hemisphere, and occasionally
deepened into the most absolute and impenetrable blackness. Farther
than this, little could be ascertained. By twelve o'clock the circular
centre had materially decreased in circumference, and by seven P.M
I lost sight of it entirely; the balloon passing over the western limb of
the ice, and floating away rapidly in the direction of the equator.

April 8th. Found a sensible diminution in the earth's apparent di-
ameter, besides a material alteration in its general color and appearance.
The whole visible area partook in different degrees of a tint of pale
yellow, and in some portions had acquired a brilliancy even painful to
the eye. My view downward was also considerably impeded by the
dense atmosphere in the vicinity of the surface being loaded with clouds,
between whose masses I could only now and then obtain a glimpse of the
earth itself. This difficulty of direct vision had troubled me more or less for
the last forty-eight hours; but my present enormous elevation brought
closer together, as it were, the floating bodies of vapor, and the incon-
venience became, of course, more and more palpable in proportion to my
ascent. Nevertheless, I could easily perceive that the balloon now hovered
above the range of great lakes in the continent of North America, and
was holding a course, due south, which would bring me to the tropics.
This circumstance did not fail to give me the most heartful satisfaction,
and I hailed it as a happy omen of ultimate success. Indeed, the direction
I had hitherto taken, had filled me with uneasiness; for it was evident
that, had I continued it much longer, there would have been no possi-
bility of my arriving at the moon at all, whose orbit is inclined to the
ecliptic at only the small angle of 5° 8′ 48″.

April 9th. To-day the earth's diameter was greatly diminished, and
the color of the surface assumed hourly a deeper tint of yellow. The
balloon kept steadily on her course to the southward, and arrived, at
nine P.M., over the northern edge of the Mexican Gulf.

April 10th. I was suddenly aroused from slumber, about five o'clock
this morning, by a loud, crackling, and terrific sound, for which I could
in no manner account. It was of very brief duration, but, while it lasted,
resembled nothing in the world of which I had any previous experience.
It is needless to say that I became excessively alarmed, having, in the
first instance, attributed the noise to the bursting of the balloon. I exam-

ined all my apparatus, however, with great attention, and could dis-
cover nothing out of order. Spent a great part of the day in meditating
upon an occurrence so extraordinary, but could find no means what-
ever of accounting for it. Went to bed dissatisfied, and in a state of
great anxiety and agitation.

April 11th. Found a startling diminution in the apparent diameter
of the earth, and a considerable increase, now observable for the first
time, in that of the moon itself, which wanted only a few days of being
full. It now required long and excessive labor to condense within the
chamber sufficient atmospheric air for the sustenance of life.

April 12th. A singular alteration took place in regard to the direction
of the balloon, and although fully anticipated, afforded me the most
unequivocal delight. Having reached, in its former course, about the
twentieth parallel of southern latitude, it turned off suddenly, at an
acute angle, to the eastward, and thus proceeded throughout the day,
keeping nearly, if not altogether, *in the exact plane of the lunar elipse.*
What was worthy of remark, a very perceptible vacillation in the car
was a consequence of this change of route — a vacillation which pre-
vailed, in a more or less degree, for a period of many hours.

April 13th. Was again very much alarmed by a repetition of the loud,
crackling noise which terrified me on the tenth. Thought long upon
the subject, but was unable to form any satisfactory conclusion. Great
decrease in the earth's apparent diameter, which now subtended from
the balloon an angle of very little more than twenty-five degrees. The
moon could not be seen at all, being nearly in my zenith. I still continued
in the plane of the elipse, but made little progress to the eastward.

April 14th. Extremely rapid decrease in the diameter of the earth.
To-day I became strongly impressed with the idea, that the balloon
was now actually running up the line of apsides to the point of perigee
— in other words, holding the direct course which would bring it im-
mediately to the moon in that part of its orbit the nearest to the earth.
The moon iself was directly overhead, and consequently hidden from
my view. Great and long-continued labor necessary for the condensa-
tion of the atmosphere.

April 15th. Not even the outlines of continents and seas could now
be traced upon the earth with anything approaching distinctness. About
twelve o'clock I became aware, for the third time, of that appalling
sound which had so astonished me before. It now, however, continued
for some moments, and gathered intensity as it continued. At length,
while, stupefied and terror-stricken, I stood in expectation of I knew not
what hideous destruction, the car vibrated with excessive violence, and a
gigantic and flaming mass of some material which I could not distinguish,
came with a voice of a thousand thunders, roaring and booming by the
balloon. When my fears and astonishment had in some degree subsided,
I had little difficulty in supposing it to be some mighty volcanic frag-

ment ejected from that world to which I was so rapidly approaching, and, in all probability, one of that singular class of substances occasionally picked up on the earth, and termed meteoric stones for want of a better appellation.

April 16th. To-day, looking upward as well as I could, through each of the side windows alternately, I beheld, to my great delight, a very small portion of the moon's disk protruding, as it were, on all sides beyond the huge circumference of the balloon. My agitation was extreme; for I had now little doubt of soon reaching the end of my perilous voyage. Indeed, the labor now required by the condenser had increased to a most oppressive degree, and allowed me scarcely any respite from exertion. Sleep was a matter nearly out of the question. I became quite ill, and my frame trembled with exhaustion. It was impossible that human nature could endure this state of intense suffering much longer. During the now brief interval of darkness a meteoric stone again passed in my vicinity, and the frequency of these phenomena began to occasion me much apprehension.

April 17th. This morning proved an epoch in my voyage. It will be remembered that, on the thirteenth, the earth subtended an angular breadth of twenty-five degrees. On the fourteenth this had greatly diminished; on the fifteenth a still more remarkable decrease was observable; and, on retiring on the night of the sixteenth, I had noticed an angle of no more than about seven degrees and fifteen minutes. What, therefore, must have been my amazement, on awakening from a brief and disturbed slumber, on the morning of this day, the seventeenth, at finding the surface beneath me so suddenly and wonderfully *augmented* in volume, as to subtend no less than thirty-nine degrees in apparent angular diameter! I was thunderstruck! No words can give any adequate idea of the extreme, the absolute horror and astonishment, with which I was seized possessed, and altogether overwhelmed. My knees tottered beneath me — my teeth chattered — my hair started up on end. "The balloon, then, had actually burst!" These were the first tumultuous ideas that hurried through my mind: "The balloon had positively burst! — I

falling — falling with the most impetuous, the most unparalleled velocity! To judge by the immense distance already so quickly passed over, it could not be more than ten minutes, at the farthest, before I should meet the surface of the earth, and be hurled into annihilation!" But at length reflection came to my relief. I paused; I considered; and I began to doubt. The matter was impossible. I could not in any reason have so rapidly come down. Besides, although I was evidently approaching the surface below me, it was with a speed by no means commensurate with the velocity I had at first so horribly conceived. This consideration served to calm the perturbation of my mind, and I finally succeeded in regarding the phenomenon in its proper point of view. In fact, amazement must have fairly deprived me of my senses, when I could not see the

vast difference, in appearance, between the surface below me, and the surface of my mother earth. The latter was indeed over my head, and completely hidden by the balloon, while the moon — the moon itself in all its glory — lay beneath me, and at my feet.

The stupor and surprise produced in my mind by this extraordinary change in the posture of affairs was perhaps, after all, that part of the adventure least susceptible of explanation. For the *bouleversement* in itself was not only natural and inevitable, but had been long actually anticipated as a circumstance to be expected whenever I should arrive at that exact point of my voyage where the attraction of the planet should be superseded by the attraction of the satellite — or, more precisely, where the gravitation of the balloon toward the earth should be less powerful than its gravitation toward the moon. To be sure I arose from a sound slumber, with all my senses in confusion, to the contemplation of a very startling phenomenon, and one which, although expected, was not expected at the moment. The revolution itself must, of course, have taken place in an easy and gradual manner, and it is by no means clear that, had I even been awake at the time of the occurrence, I should have been made aware of it by any *internal* evidence of an inversion — that is to say, by any inconvenience or disarrangement, either about my person or about my apparatus.

It is almost needless to say that, upon coming to a due sense of my situation, and emerging from the terror which had absorbed every faculty of my soul, my attention was, in the first place, wholly directed to the contemplation of the general physical appearance of the moon. It lay beneath me like a chart — and although I judged it to be still at no inconsiderable distance, the indentures of its surface were defined to my vision with a most striking and altogether unaccountable distinctness. The entire absence of ocean or sea, and indeed of any lake or river, or body of water whatsoever, struck me, at first glance, as the most extraordinary feature in its geological condition. Yet, strange to say, I beheld vast level regions of a character decidedly alluvial, although by far the greater portion of the hemisphere in sight was covered with innumerable volcanic mountains, conical in shape, and having more the appearance of artificial than of natural protuberance. The highest among them does not exceed three and three-quarter miles in perpendicular elevation; but a map of the volcanic districts of the Campi Phlegræi would afford to your Excellencies a better idea of their general surface than any unworthy description I might think proper to attempt. The greater part of them were in a state of evident eruption, and gave me fearfully to understand their fury and their power, by the repeated thunders of the miscalled meteoric stones, which now rushed upward by the balloon with a frequency more and more appalling.

April 18th. To-day I found an enormous increase in the moon's apparent bulk — and the evidently accelerated velocity of my descent be-

gan to fill me with alarm. It will be remembered, that, in the earliest stage of my speculations upon the possibility of a passage to the moon, the existence, in its vicinity, of an atmosphere, dense in proportion to the bulk of the planet, had entered largely into my calculations; this too in spite of many theories to the contrary, and, it may be added, in spite of a general disbelief in the existence of any lunar atmosphere at all. But, in addition to what I have already urged in regard to Encke's comet and the zodiacal light, I had been strengthened in my opinion by certain observations of Mr. Schroeter, of Lilienthal. He observed the moon when two days and a half old, in the evening soon after sunset, before the dark part was visible, and continued to watch it until it became visible. The two cusps appeared tapering in a very sharp faint prolongation, each exhibiting its farthest extremity faintly illuminated by the solar rays, before any part of the dark hemisphere was visible. Soon afterward, the whole dark limb became illuminated. This prolongation of the cusps beyond the semicircle, I thought, must have arisen from the refraction of the sun's rays by the moon's atmosphere. I computed, also, the height of the atmosphere (which could refract light enough into its dark hemisphere to produce a twilight more luminous than the light reflected from the earth when the moon is about $32°$ from the new) to be 1,356 Paris feet; in this view, I supposed the greatest height capable of refracting the solar ray, to be 5,376 feet. My ideas on this topic had also received confirmation by a passage in the eighty-second volume of the Philosophical Transactions, in which it is stated that at an occultation of Jupiter's satellites, the third disappeared after having been about $1''$ or $2''$ of time indistinct, and the fourth became indiscernible near the limb.*

Upon the resistance or, more properly, upon the support of an atmosphere, existing in the state of density imagined, I had, of course, entirely depended for the safety of my ultimate descent. Should I then, after all, prove to have been mistaken, I had in consequence nothing better to expect, as a *finale* to my adventure, than being dashed into atoms against the rugged surface of the satellite. And, indeed, I had now every reason to be terrified. My distance from the moon was comparatively

* Havelius writes that he has several times found, in skies perfectly clear, when even stars of the sixth and seventh magnitude were conspicuous, that, at the same altitude of the moon, at the same elongation from the earth, and with one and the same excellent telescope, the moon and its maculæ did not appear equally lucid at all times. From the circumstances of the observation, it is evident that the cause of this phenomenon is not either in our air, in the tube, in the moon, or in the eye of the spectator, but must be looked for in something (an atmosphere?) existing about the moon.

Cassini frequently observed Saturn, Jupiter, and the fixed stars, when approaching the moon to occultation, to have their circular figure changed into an oval one; and, in other occultations, he found no alteration of figure at all. Hence it might be supposed, that *at some times* and not at others, there is a dense matter encompassing the moon wherein the rays of the stars are refracted.

trifling, while the labor required by the condenser was diminished not
at all, and I could discover no indication whatever of a decreasing rarity
in the air.

April 19th. This morning, to my great joy, about nine o'clock, the
surface of the moon being frightfully near, and my apprehensions ex-
cited to the utmost, the pump of my condenser at length gave evident
tokens of an alteration in the atmosphere. By ten, I had reason to believe
its density considerably increased. By eleven, very little labor was neces-
sary at the apparatus; and at twelve o'clock, with some hesitation, I
ventured to unscrew the tourniquet, when, finding no inconvenience
from having done so, I finally threw open the gum-elastic chamber, and
unrigged it from around the car. As might have been expected, spasms
and violent headache were the immediate consequences of an experi-
ment so precipitate and full of danger. But these and other difficulties
attending respiration, as they were by no means so great as to put me in
peril of my life, I determined to endure as I best could, in consideration
of my leaving them behind me momently in my approach to the denser
strata near the moon. This approach, however, was still impetuous in
the extreme; and it soon became alarmingly certain that, although I had
probably not been deceived in the expectation of an atmosphere dense in
proportion to the mass of the satellite, still I had been wrong in supposing
this density, even at the surface, at all adequate to the support of the great
weight contained in the car of my balloon. Yet this *should* have been the
case, and in an equal degree as at the surface of the earth, the actual gravity
of bodies at either planet supposed in the ratio of the atmospheric con-
densation. That it *was not* the case, however, my precipitous downfall
gave testimony enough; why it was not so, can only be explained by a
reference to those possible geological disturbances to which I have for-
merly alluded. At all events I was now close upon the planet, and com-
ing down with the most terrible impetuosity. I lost not a moment,
accordingly, in throwing overboard first my ballast, then my water-kegs,
then my condensing apparatus and gum-elastic chamber, and finally
every article within the car. But it was all to no purpose. I still fell with
horrible rapidity, and was now not more than half a mile from the sur-
face. As a last resource, therefore, having got rid of my coat, hat, and
boots, I cut loose from the balloon *the car itself*, which was of no incon-
siderable weight, and thus, clinging with both hands to the net-work,
I had barely time to observe that the whole country, as far as the eye
could reach, was thickly interspersed with diminutive habitations, ere
I tumbled headlong into the very heart of a fantastical-looking city, and
into the middle of a vast crowd of ugly little people, who none of them
uttered a single syllable, or gave themselves the least trouble to render
me assistance, but stood, like a parcel of idiots, grinning in a ludicrous
manner, and eyeing me and my balloon askant, with their arms set
a-kimbo. I turned from them in contempt, and, gazing upward at the

earth so lately left, and left perhaps for ever, beheld it like a huge, dull, copper shield, about two degrees in diameter, fixed immovably in the heavens overhead, and tipped on one of its edges with a crescent border of the most brilliant gold. No traces of land or water could be discovered, and the whole was clouded with variable spots, and belted with tropical and equatorial zones.

Thus, may it please your Excellencies, after a series of great anxieties, unheard of dangers, and unparalleled escapes, I had, at length, on the nineteenth day of my departure from Rotterdam, arrived in safety at the conclusion of a voyage undoubtedly the most extraordinary, and the most momentous, ever accomplished, undertaken, or conceived by any denizen of earth. But my adventures yet remain to be related. And indeed your Excellencies may well imagine that, after a residence of five years upon a planet not only deeply interesting in its own peculiar character, but rendered doubly so by its intimate connection, in capacity of satellite, with the world inhabited by man, I may have intelligence for the private ear of the States' College of Astronomers of far more importance than the details, however wonderful, of the mere *voyage* which so happily concluded. This is, in fact, the case. I have much — very much which it would give me the greatest pleasure to communicate. I have much to say of the climate of the planet; of its wonderful alternations of heat and cold; of unmitigated and burning sunshine for one fortnight, and more than polar frigidity for the next; of a constant transfer of moisture, by distillation like that *in vacuo*, from the point beneath the sun to the point the farthest from it; of a variable zone of running water; of the people themselves; of their manners, customs, and political institutions; of their peculiar physical construction; of their ugliness; of their want of ears, those useless appendages in an atmosphere so peculiarly modified; of their consequent ignorance of the use and properties of speech; of their substitute for speech in a singular method of inter-communication; of the incomprehensible connection between each particular individual in the moon with some particular individual on the earth — a connection analogous with, and depending upon, that of the orbs of the planet and the satellites, and by means of which the lives and destinies of the inhabitants of the one are interwoven with the lives and destinies of the inhabitants of the other; and above all, if it so please your Excellencies — above all, of those dark and hideous mysteries which lie in the outer regions of the moon — regions which, owing to the almost miraculous accordance of the satellite's rotation on its own axis with its sidereal revolution about the earth, have never yet been turned, and, by God's mercy, never shall be turned, to the scrutiny of the telescopes of man. All this, and more — much more — would I most willingly detail. But, to be brief, I must have my reward. I am pining for a return to my family and to my home; and as the price of any farther communication on my part — in consideration of the light

which I have it in my power to throw upon many very important branches of physical and metaphysical science — I must solicit, through the influence of your honorable body, a pardon for the crime of which I have been guilty in the death of the creditors upon my departure from Rotterdam. This, then, is the object of the present paper. Its bearer, an inhabitant of the moon, whom I have prevailed upon, and properly instructed, to be my messenger to the earth, will await your Excellencies' pleasure, and return to me with the pardon in question, if it can, in any manner, be obtained.

I have the honor to be, etc., your Excellencies' very humble servant,

HANS PHAALL.

Upon finishing the perusal of this very extraordinary document, Professor Rub-a-dub, it is said, dropped his pipe upon the ground in the extremity of his surprise, and Mynheer Superbus Von Underduk having taken off his spectacles, wiped them, and deposited them in his pocket, so far forgot both himself and his dignity, as to turn round three times upon his heel in the quintessence of astonishment and admiration. There was no doubt about the matter — the pardon should be obtained. So at least swore, with a round oath, Professor Rub-a-dub, and so finally thought the illustrious Von Underduk, as he took the arm of his brother in science, and without saying a word, began to make the best of his way home to deliberate upon the measures to be adopted. Having reached the door, however, of the burgomaster's dwelling, the professor ventured to suggest that as the messenger had thought proper to disappear — no doubt frightened to death by the savage appearance of the burghers of Rotterdam — the pardon would be of little use, as no one but a man of the moon would undertake a voyage to so vast a distance. To the truth of this observation the burgomaster assented, and the matter was therefore at an end. Not so, however, rumors and speculations. The letter, having been published, gave rise to a variety of gossip and opinion. Some of the over-wise even made themselves ridiculous by decrying the whole business as nothing better than a hoax. But hoax, with these sort of people, is, I believe, a general term for all matters above their comprehension. For my part, I cannot conceive upon what data they have founded such an accusation. Let us see what they say:

Imprimus. That certain wags in Rotterdam have certain especial antipathies to certain burgomasters and astronomers.

Don't understand at all.

Secondly. That an odd little dwarf and bottle conjurer, both of whose ears, for some misdemeanor, have been cut off close to his head, has been missing for several days from the neighboring city of Bruges.

Well — what of that?

Thirdly. That the newspapers which were stuck all over the little balloon were newspapers of Holland, and therefore could not have been

made in the moon. They were dirty papers — very dirty — and Gluck, the printer, would take his Bible oath to their having been printed in Rotterdam.

He was mistaken — undoubtedly — mistaken.

Fourthly, That Hans Phaall himself, the drunken villain, and the three very idle gentlemen styled his creditors, were all seen, no longer than two or three days ago, in a tippling house in the suburbs, having just returned, with money in their pockets, from a trip beyond the sea.

Don't believe it — don't believe a word of it.

Lastly. That it is an opinion very generally received, or which ought to be generally received, that the College of Astronomers in the city of Rotterdam, as well as all other colleges in all other parts of the world, — not to mention colleges and astronomers in general, — are, to say the least of the matter, not a whit better, nor greater, nor wiser than they ought to be.

King Pest

A TALE CONTAINING AN ALLEGORY

The gods do bear and will allow in kings
The things which they abhor in rascal routes.
 B U C K H U R S T's *Tragedy of Ferrex and Porrex.*

ABOUT twelve o'clock one night in the month of October, and during the chivalrous reign of the third Edward, two seamen belonging to the crew of the "Free and Easy," a trading schooner plying between Sluys and the Thames, and then at anchor in that river, were much astonished to find themselves seated in the tap-room of an ale-house in the parish of St. Andrews, London — which ale-house bore for sign the portraiture of a "Jolly Tar."

The room, although ill-contrived, smoke-blackened, low-pitched, and in every other respect agreeing with the general character of such places at the period — was nevertheless, in the opinion of the grotesque groups scattered here and there within it, sufficiently well adapted to its purpose.

Of these groups our two seamen formed, I think, the most interesting, if not the most conspicuous.

The one who appeared to be the elder, and whom his companion addressed by the characteristic appellation of "Legs," was at the same time much the taller of the two. He might have measured six feet and a half, and an habitual stoop in the shoulders seemed to have been the necessary consequence of an altitude so enormous. Superfluities in height

were, however, more than accounted for by deficiencies in other respects. He was exceedingly thin; and might, as his associates asserted, have answered, when drunk, for a pennant at the mast-head, or, when sober, have served for a jib-boom. But these jests, and others of a similar nature, had evidently produced, at no time, any effect upon the cachinnatory muscles of the tar. With high cheek-bones, a large hawk-nose, retreating chin, fallen under-jaw, and huge protruding white eyes, the expression of his countenance, although tinged with a species of dogged indifference to matters and things in general, was not the less utterly solemn and serious beyond all attempts at imitation or description.

The younger seaman was, in all outward appearance, the converse of his companion. His stature could not have exceeded four feet. A pair of stumpy bow-legs supported his squat, unwieldy figure, while his unusually short and thick arms, with no ordinary fists at their extremities, swung off dangling from his sides like the fins of a sea-turtle. Small eyes, of no particular color, twinkled far back in his head. His nose remained buried in the mass of flesh which enveloped his round, full, and purple face: and his thick upper-lip rested upon the still thicker one beneath with an air of complacent self-satisfaction, much heightened by the owner's habit of licking them at intervals. He evidently regarded his tall shipmate with a feeling half-wondrous, half-quizzical; and stared up occasionally in his face as the red setting sun stares up at the crags of Ben Nevis.

Various and eventful, however, had been the peregrinations of the worthy couple in and about the different tap-houses of the neighborhood during the earlier hours of the night. Funds even the most ample, are not always everlasting: and it was with empty pockets our friends had ventured upon the present hostelrie.

At the precise period, then, when this history properly commences, Legs and his fellow, Hugh Tarpaulin, sat, each with both elbows resting upon the large oaken table in the middle of the floor, and with a hand upon either cheek. They were eying, from behind a huge flagon of unpaid-for "humming-stuff," the portentous words, "No Chalk," which to their indignation and astonishment were scored over the doorway by means of that very mineral whose presence they purported to deny. Not that the gift of deciphering written characters — a gift among the commonalty of that day considered little less cabalistical than the art of inditing — could, in strict justice, have been laid to the charge of either disciple of the sea; but there was, to say the truth, a certain twist in the formation of the letters — an indescribable lee-lurch about the whole — which foreboded, in the opinion of both seamen, a long run of dirty weather; and determined them at once, in the allegorical words of Legs himself, to "pump ship, clew up all sail, and scud before the wind."

Having accordingly disposed of what remained of the ale, and looped up the points of their short doublets, they finally made a bolt for the

street. Although Tarpaulin rolled twice into the fireplace, mistaking it for the door, yet their escape was at length happily effected — and half after twelve o'clock found our heroes ripe for mischief, and running for life down a dark alley in the direction of St. Andrew's Stair, hotly pursued by the landlady of the "Jolly Tar."

At the epoch of this eventful tale, and periodically, for many years before and after, all England, but more especially the metropolis, resounded with the fearful cry of "Plague!" The city was in a great measure depopulated — and in those horrible regions, in the vicinity of the Thames, where, amid the dark, narrow, and filthy lanes and alleys, the Demon of Disease was supposed to have had his nativity, Awe, Terror, and Superstition were alone to be found stalking abroad.

By authority of the king such districts were placed *under ban*, and all persons forbidden, under pain of death, to intrude upon their dismal solitude. Yet neither the mandate of the monarch, nor the huge barriers erected at the entrance of the streets, nor the prospect of that loathsome death which, with almost absolute certainty, overwhelmed the wretch whom no peril could deter from the adventure, prevented the unfurnished and untenanted dwellings from being stripped, by the hand of nightly rapine, of every article, such as iron, brass, or lead-work, which could in any manner be turned to a profitable account.

Above all, it was usually found, upon the annual winter opening of the barriers, that locks, bolts, and secret cellars had proved but slender protection to those rich stores of wines and liquors which, in consideration of the risk and trouble of removal, many of the numerous dealers having shops in the neighborhood had consented to trust, during the period of exile, to so insufficient a security.

But there were very few of the terror-stricken people who attributed these doings to the agency of human hands. Pest-spirits, plague-goblins, and fever-demons were the popular imps of mischief; and tales so blood-chilling were hourly told, that the whole mass of forbidden buildings was, at length, enveloped in terror as in a shroud, and the plunderer himself was often scared away by the horrors his own depredations had created; leaving the entire vast circuit of prohibited district to gloom, silence, pestilence, and death.

It was by one of the terrific barriers already mentioned, and which indicated the region beyond to be under the Pest-ban, that, in scrambling down an alley, Legs and the worthy Hugh Tarpaulin found their progress suddenly impeded. To return was out of the question, and no time was to be lost, as their pursuers were close upon their heels. With thoroughbred seamen to clamber up the roughly fashioned plank-work was a trifle; and, maddened with the twofold excitement of exercise and liquor, they leaped unhesitatingly down within the enclosure, and holding on their drunken course with shouts and yellings, were soon bewildered in its noisome and intricate recesses.

Had they not, indeed, been intoxicated beyond moral sense, their reeling footsteps must have been palsied by the horrors of their situation. The air was cold and misty. The paving-stones, loosened from their beds, lay in wild disorder amid the tall rank grass, which sprang up around the feet and ankles. Fallen houses choked up the streets. The most fetid and poisonous smells everywhere prevailed — and by the aid of that ghastly light which, even at midnight, never fails to emanate from a vapory and pestilential atmosphere, might be discerned lying in the by-paths and alleys, or rotting in the windowless habitations, the carcass of many a nocturnal plunderer arrested by the hand of the plague in the very perpetration of his robbery.

But it lay not in the power of images, or sensations, or impediments such as these, to stay the course of men who, naturally brave, and at that time especially, brimful of courage and of "humming-stuff," would have reeled, as straight as their condition might have permitted, undauntedly into the very jaws of Death. Onward — still onward stalked the grim Legs, making the desolate solemnity echo and re-echo with yells like the terrific war-whoop of the Indian; and onward, still onward rolled the dumpy Tarpaulin, hanging on to the doublet of his more active companion, and far surpassing the latter's most strenuous exertions in the way of vocal music, by bull-roarings *in basso*, from the profundity of his stentorian lungs.

They had now evidently reached the stronghold of the pestilence. Their way at every step or plunge grew more noisome and more horrible — the paths more narrow and more intricate. Huge stones and beams falling momently from the decaying roofs above them, gave evidence, by their sullen and heavy descent, of the vast height of the surrounding houses; and while actual exertion became necessary to force a passage through frequent heaps of rubbish, it was by no means seldom that the hand fell upon a skeleton or rested upon a more fleshy corpse.

Suddenly, as the seamen stumbled against the entrance of a tall and ghastly-looking building, a yell more than usually shrill from the throat of the excited Legs, was replied to from within, in a rapid succession of wild, laughter-like, and fiendish shrieks. Nothing daunted at sounds, which, of such a nature, at such a time, and in such a place, might have curdled the very blood in hearts less irrevocably on fire, the drunken couple rushed headlong against the door, burst it open, and staggered into the midst of things with a volley of curses.

The room within which they found themselves proved to be the shop of an undertaker, but an open trap-door, in a corner of the floor near the entrance, looked down upon a long range of wine-cellars, whose depths the occasional sound of bursting bottles proclaimed to be well-stored with their appropriate contents.

In the middle of the room stood a table — in the centre of which again arose a huge tub of what appeared to be punch. Bottles of various wines

and cordials, together with jugs, pitchers, and flagons of every shape and quality, were scattered profusely upon the board. Around it, upon coffin-tressels, was seated a company of six. This company I will endeavor to delineate one by one.

Fronting the entrance, and elevated a little above his companions, sat a personage who appeared to be the president of the table. His stature was gaunt and tall, and Legs was confounded to behold in him a figure more emaciated than himself. His face was as yellow as saffron — but no feature excepting one alone, was sufficiently marked to merit a particular description. This one consisted in a forehead so unusually and hideously lofty, as to have the appearance of a bonnet or crown of flesh superadded upon the natural head. His mouth was puckered and dimpled into an expression of ghastly affability, and his eyes, as indeed the eyes of all at table, were glazed over with the fumes of intoxication. This gentleman was clothed from head to foot in a richly-embroidered black silk-velvet pall, wrapped negligently around his form after the fashion of a Spanish cloak.— His head was stuck full of sable hearse-plumes, which he nodded to and fro with a jaunty and knowing air; and, in his right hand, he held a huge human thigh-bone, with which he appeared to have been just knocking down some member of the company for a song.

Opposite him, and with her back to the door, was a lady of no whit the less extraordinary character. Although quite as tall as the person just described, she had no right to complain of his unnatural emaciation. She was evidently in the last stages of a dropsy; and her figure resembled nearly that of the huge puncheon of October beer which stood, with the head driven in, close by her side, in a corner of the chamber. Her face was exceedingly round, red, and full; and the same peculiarity, or rather want of peculiarity, attached itself to her countenance, which I before mentioned in the case of the president — that is to say, only one feature of her face was sufficiently distinguished to need a separate characterization: indeed the acute Tarpaulin immediately observed that the same remark might have applied to each individual person in the party; every one of whom seemed to possess a monopoly of some particular portion of physiognomy. With the lady in question this portion proved to be the mouth. Commencing at the right ear, it swept with a terrific chasm to the left — the short pendants which she wore in either auricle continually bobbing into the aperture. She made, however, every exertion to keep her mouth closed and look dignified, in a dress consisting of a newly-starched and ironed shroud coming up close under her chin, with a crimpled ruffle of cambric muslin.

At her right hand sat a diminutive young lady whom she appeared to patronize. This delicate little creature, in the trembling of her wasted fingers, in the livid hue of her lips, and in the slight hectic spot which tinged her otherwise leaden complexion, gave evident indications of a

galloping consumption. An air of extreme *haut ton,* however, pervaded her whole appearance; she wore in a graceful and *dedage* manner, a large and beautiful winding-sheet of the finest India lawn; her hair hung in ringlets over her neck; a soft smile played about her mouth; but her nose, extremely long, thin, sinuous, flexible, and pimpled, hung down far below her under-lip, and, in spite of the delicate manner in which she now and then moved it to one side or the other with her tongue, gave to her countenance a somewhat equivocal expression.

Over against her, and upon the left of the dropsical lady, was seated a little puffy, wheezing, and gouty old man, whose cheeks reposed upon the shoulders of their owner, like two huge bladders of Oporto wine. With his arms folded, and with one bandaged leg deposited upon the table, he seemed to think himself entitled to some consideration. He evidently prided himself much upon every inch of his personal appearance, but took more especial delight in calling attention to his gaudy-colored surtout. This, to say the truth, must have cost him no little money, and was made to fit him exceedingly well — being fashioned from one of the curiously embroidered silken covers appertaining to those glorious escutcheons which, in England and elsewhere, are customarily hung up, in some conspicuous place, upon the dwellings of departed aristocracy.

Next to him, and at the right hand of the president, was a gentleman in long white hose and cotton drawers. His frame shook, in a ridiculous manner, with a fit of what Tarpaulin called "the horrors." His jaws, which had been newly shaved, were tightly tied up by a bandage of muslin; and his arms being fastened in a similar way at the wrists, prevented him from helping himself too freely to the liquors upon the table; a precaution rendered necessary, in the opinion of Legs, by the peculiarly sottish and wine-bibbing cast of his visage. A pair of prodigious ears, nevertheless, which it was no doubt found impossible to confine, towered away into the atmosphere of the apartment, and were occasionally pricked up in a spasm, at the sound of the drawing of a cork.

Fronting him, sixthly and lastly, was situated a singularly stiff-looking personage, who being afflicted with paralysis, must, to speak seriously, have felt very ill at ease in his unaccommodating habiliments. He was habited, somewhat uniquely, in a new and handsome mahogany coffin. Its top or head-piece pressed upon the skull of the wearer, and extended over it in the fashion of a hood, giving to the entire face an air of indescribable interest. Armholes had been cut in the sides for the sake not more of elegance than of convenience; but the dress, nevertheless, prevented its proprietor from sitting as erect as his associates; and as he lay reclining against his tressel, at an angle of forty-five degrees, a pair of huge goggle eyes rolled up their awful whites toward the ceiling in absolute amazement at their own enormity.

Before each of the party lay a portion of a skull, which was used as

a drinking-cup. Overhead was suspended a human skeleton, by means of a rope tied round one of the legs and fastened to a ring in the ceiling. The other limb, confined by no such fetter, stuck off from the body at right angles, causing the whole loose and rattling frame to dangle and twirl about at the caprice of every occasional puff of wind which found its way into the apartment. In the cranium of this hideous thing lay a quantity of ignited charcoal, which threw a fitful but vivid light over the entire scene; while coffins, and other wares appertaining to the shop of an undertaker, were piled high up around the room, and against the windows, preventing any ray from escaping into the street.

At sight of this extraordinary assembly, and of their still more extraordinary paraphernalia, our two seamen did not conduct themselves with that degree of decorum which might have been expected. Legs, leaning against the wall near which he happened to be standing, dropped his lower jaw still lower than usual, and spread open his eyes to their fullest extent; while Hugh Tarpaulin, stooping down so as to bring his nose upon a level with the table, and spreading out a palm upon either knee, burst into a long, loud, and obstreperous roar of very ill-timed and immoderate laughter.

Without, however, taking offence at behavior so excessively rude, the tall president smiled very graciously upon the intruders — nodded to them in a dignified manner with his head of sable plumes — and, arising, took each by an arm, and led him to a seat which some others of the company had placed in the meantime for his accommodation. Legs to all this offered not the slightest resistance, but sat down as he was directed; while the gallant Hugh, removing his coffin-tressel from its station near the head of the table, to the vicinity of the little consumptive lady in the winding sheet, plumped down by her side in high glee, and pouring out a skull of red wine, quaffed it to their better acquaintance. But at this presumption the stiff gentleman in the coffin seemed exceedingly nettled; and serious consequences might have ensued, had not the president, rapping upon the table with his truncheon, diverted the attention of all present to the following speech:

"It becomes our duty upon the present happy occasion —— "

"Avast there!" interrupted Legs, looking very serious, "avast there a bit, I say, and tell us who the devil ye all are, and what business ye have here, rigged off like the foul fiends, and swilling the 'snug blue ruin' stowed away for the winter by my honest ship-mate, Will Wimble, the undertaker!"

At this unpardonable piece of ill-breeding, all the original company half-started to their feet, and uttered the same rapid succession of wild fiendish shrieks which had before caught the attention of the seamen. The president, however, was the first to recover his composure, and at length, turning to Legs with great dignity, recommenced:

"Most willingly will we gratify any reasonable curiosity on the part of

guests so illustrious, unbidden though they be. Know then that in these dominions I am monarch, and here rule with undivided empire under the title of 'King Pest the First.'

"This apartment, which you no doubt profanely suppose to be the shop of Will Wimble the undertaker — a man whom we know not, and whose plebeian appellation has never before this night thwarted our royal ears — this apartment, I say, is the Dais-Chamber of our Palace, devoted to the councils of our kingdom, and to other sacred and lofty purposes.

"The noble lady who sits opposite is Queen Pest, our Serene Consort. The other exalted personages whom you behold are all of our family, and wear the insignia of the blood royal under the respective titles of 'His Grace the Arch Duke Pest-Iferous' — 'His Grace the Duke Pest-Ilential' — 'His Grace the Duke Tem-Pest' — and 'Her Serene Highness the Arch Duchess Ana-Pest.'

"As regards," continued he, "your demand of the business upon which we sit here in council, we might be pardoned for replying that it concerns, and concerns *alone*, our own private and regal interest, and is in no manner important to any other than ourself. But in consideration of those rights to which as guests and strangers you may feel yourselves entitled, we will furthermore explain that we are here this night, prepared by deep research and accurate investigation, to examine, analyze, and thoroughly determine the indefinable spirit — the incomprehensible qualities and nare — of those inestimable treasures of the palate, the wines, ales, and liquors of this goodly metropolis: by so doing to advance not more our own designs than the true welfare of that unearthly sovereign whose reign is over us all, whose dominions are unlimited, and whose name is 'Death.' "

"Whose name is Davy Jones!" ejaculated Tarpaulin, helping the lady by his side to a skull of liqueur, and pouring out a second for himself.

"Profane varlet!" said the president, now turning his attention to the worthy Hugh, "profane and execrable wretch! — we have said, that in consideration of those rights which, even in thy filthy person, we feel no inclination to violate, we have condescended to make reply to thy rude and unseasonable inquiries. We nevertheless, for your unhallowed intrusion upon our councils, believe it our duty to mulct thee and thy companion in each a gallon of Black Strap — having imbibed which to the prosperity of our kingdom — at a single draught — and upon your bended knees — ye shall be forthwith free either to proceed upon your way, or remain and be admitted to the privileges of our table, according to your respective and individual pleasures."

"It would be a matter of utter unpossibility," replied Legs, whom the assumption and dignity of King Pest the First had evidently inspired with some feelings of respect, and who arose and steadied himself by the table as he spoke — "it would, please your majesty, be a matter of utter unpossibility to stow away in my hold even one fourth part of that same

liquor which your majesty has just mentioned. To say nothing of the stuffs placed on board in the forenoon by way of ballast, and not to mention the various ales and liqueurs shipped this evening at different seaports, I have, at present, a full cargo of 'humming-stuff' taken in and duly paid for at the sign of the 'Jolly Tar.' You will therefore, please your majesty, be so good as to take the will for the deed — for by no manner of means either can I or will I swallow another drop — least of all a drop of that villainous bilge-water that answers to the hail of 'Black Strap.'"

"Belay that!" interrupted Tarpaulin, astonished not more at the length of his companion's speech than at the nature of his refusal — "Belay that, you lubber! — and I say, Legs, none of your palaver. My hull is still light, although I confess you yourself seem to be a little top-heavy; and as far as the matter of your share of the cargo, why rather than raise a squall I would find stowage-room for it myself, but —— "

"This proceeding," interposed the president, "is by no means in accordance with the terms of the mulct or sentence, which is in its nature Median, and not to be altered or recalled. The conditions we have imposed must be fulfilled to the letter, and that without a moment's hesitation — in failure of which fulfillment we decree that you do here be tied neck and heels together, and duly drowned as rebels in yon hogshead of October beer!"

"A sentence! — a sentence! — a righteous and just sentence! — a glorious decree! — a most worthy and upright, and holy condemnation!" shouted the Pest family altogether. The king elevated his forehead into innumerable wrinkles; the gouty little old man puffed like a pair of bellows; the lady of the winding-sheet waved her nose to and for; the gentleman in the cotton drawers pricked up his ears; she of the shroud gasped like a dying fish; and he of the coffin looked stiff and rolled up his eyes. "Ugh! ugh! ugh!" chuckled Tarpaulin, without heeding the general excitation, "ugh! ugh! ugh! — ugh! ugh! ugh! ugh! — ugh! ugh! ugh! — I was saying," said he — "I was saying when Mr. King Pest poked in his marlinspike, that as for the matter of two or three gallons more or less of Black Strap, it was a trifle to a tight sea-boat like myself not overstowed — but when it comes to drinking the health of the Devil (whom God assoilzie) and going down upon my marrow bones to his ill-favored majesty there, whom I know, as well as I know myself to be a sinner, to be nobody in the whole world but Tim Hurlygurly the stage-player! — why! it's quite another guess sort of thing, and utterly and altogether past my comprehension."

He was not allowed to finish this speech in tranquillity. At the name of Tim Hurlygurly the whole assembly leaped from their seats.

"Treason!" shouted his Majesty King Pest the First.

"Treason!" said the little man with the gout.

"Treason!" screamed the Arch Duchess Ana-Pest.

"Treason!" muttered the gentleman with his jaws tied up.

"Treason!" growled he of the coffin.

"Treason! treason!" shrieked her majesty of the mouth; and seizing by the hinder part of his breeches the unfortunate Tarpaulin, who had just commenced pouring out for himself a skull of liqueur, she lifted him high into the air, and let him fall without ceremony into the huge open puncheon of his beloved ale. Bobbing up and down, for a few seconds, like an apple in a bowl of toddy, he, at length, finally disappeared amid the whirlpool of foam which, in the already effervescent liquor, his struggles easily succeeded in creating.

Not tamely, however, did the tall seaman behold the discomfiture of his companion. Jostling King Pest through the open trap, the valiant Legs slammed the door down upon him with an oath, and strode toward the centre of the room. Here tearing down the skeleton which swung over the table, he laid it about him with so much energy and good-will that, as the last glimpses of light died away within the apartment, he succeeded in knocking out the brains of the little gentleman with the gout. Rushing then with all his force against the fatal hogshead full of October ale and Hugh Tarpaulin, he rolled it over and over in an instant. Out poured a deluge of liquor so fierce — so impetuous — so overwhelming — that the room was flooded from wall to wall — the loaded table was overturned — the tressels were thrown upon their backs — the tub of punch into the fire-place — and the ladies into hysterics. Piles of death-furniture floundered about. Jugs, pitchers, and carboys mingled promiscuously in the *melée*, and wicker flagons encountered desperately with bottles of junk. The man with the horrors was drowned upon the spot — the little stiff gentleman floated off in his coffin — and the victorious Legs, seizing by the waist the fat lady in the shroud, rushed out with her into the street, and made a bee-line for the "Free and Easy," followed under easy sail by the redoubtable Hugh Tarpaulin, who, having sneezed three or four times, panted and puffed after him with the Arch Duchess Ana-Pest.

Shadow — A Parable

Yea, though I walk through the valley of the Shadow:

Psalm of David.

YE who read are still among the living; but I who write shall have long since gone my way into the region of shadows. For indeed strange things shall happen, and secret things be known, and many centuries shall pass

away, ere these memorials be seen of men. And, when seen, there will be
some to disbelieve, and some to doubt, and yet a few who will find much
to ponder upon in the characters here graven with a stylus of iron.

The year had been a year of terror, and of feelings more intense than
terror for which there is no name upon the earth. For many prodigies
and signs had taken place, and far and wide, over sea and land, the black
wings of the Pestilence were spread abroad. To those, nevertheless, cun-
ning in the stars, it was not unknown that the heavens wore an aspect of
ill; and to me, the Greek Oinos, among others, it was evident that now
had arrived the alternation of that seven hundred and ninety-fourth year
when, at the entrance of Aries, the planet Jupiter is conjoined with the
red ring of the terrible Saturnus. The peculiar spirit of the skies, if I mis-
take not greatly, made itself manifest, not only in the physical orb of
the earth, but in the souls, imaginations, and meditations of mankind.

Over some flasks of the red Chian wine, within the walls of a noble
hall, in a dim city called Ptolemais, we sat, at night, a company of seven.
And to our chamber there was no entrance save by a lofty door of brass:
and the door was fashioned by the artisan Corinnos, and, being of rare
workmanship, was fastened from within. Black draperies, likewise, in the
gloomy room, shut out from our view the moon, the lurid stars, and the
peopleless streets — but the boding and the memory of Evil they would
not be so excluded. There were things around us and about of which I
can render no distinct account — things material and spiritual — heavi-
ness in the atmosphere — a sense of suffocation — anxiety — and, above
all, that terrible state of existence which the nervous experience when
the senses are keenly living and awake, and meanwhile the powers of
thought lie dormant. A dead weight hung upon us. It hung upon our
limbs — upon the household furniture — upon the goblets from which
we drank; and all things were depressed, and borne down thereby — all
things save only the flames of the seven lamps which illumined our revel.
Uprearing themselves in tall slender lines of light, they thus remained
burning all pallid and motionless; and in the mirror which their lustre
formed upon the round table of ebony at which we sat, each of us there
assembled beheld the pallor of his own countenance, and the unquiet
glare in the downcast eyes of his companions. Yet we laughed and were
merry in our proper way — which was hysterical; and sang the songs of
Anacreon — which are madness; and drank deeply — although the purple
wine reminded us of blood. For there was yet another tenant of our
chamber in the person of young Zoilus. Dead, and at full length he lay,
enshrouded; the genius and the demon of the scene. Alas! he bore no
portion in our mirth, save that his countenance, distorted with the
plague, and his eyes, in which Death had but half extinguished the fire
of the pestilence, seemed to take such interest in our merriment as the
dead may haply take in the merriment of those who are to die. But al-
though I, Oinos, felt that the eyes of the departed were upon me, still I

forced myself not to perceive the bitterness of their expression, and gazing down steadily into the depths of the ebony mirror, sang with a loud and sonorous voice the songs of the son of Teios. But gradually my songs they ceased, and their echoes, rolling afar off among the sable draperies of the chamber, became weak, and undistinguishable, and so faded away. And lo! from among those sable draperies where the sounds of the song departed, there came forth a dark and undefined shadow — a shadow such as the moon, when low in heaven, might fashion from the figure of a man: but it was the shadow neither of man nor of God, nor of any familiar thing. And quivering awhile among the draperies of the room, it at length rested in full view upon the surface of the door of brass. But the shadow was vague, and formless, and indefinite, and was the shadow neither of man nor of God — neither God of Greece, nor God of Chaldæa, nor any Egyptian God. And the shadow rested upon the brazen doorway, and under the arch of the entablature of the door, and moved not, nor spoke any word, but there became stationary and remained. And the door whereupon the shadow rested was, if I remember aright, over against the feet of the young Zoilus enshrouded. But we, the seven there assembled, having seen the shadow as it came out from among the draperies, dared not steadily behold it, but cast down our eyes, and gazed continually into the depths of the mirror of ebony. And at length I, Oinos, speaking some low words, demanded of the shadow its dwelling and its appellation. And the shadow answered, "I am SHADOW, and my dwelling is near to the Catacombs of Ptolemais, and hard by those dim plains of Helusion which border upon the foul Charonian canal." And then did we, the seven, start from our seats in horror, and stand trembling, and shuddering, and aghast, for the tones in the voice of the shadow were not the tones of any one being, but of a multitude of beings, and, varying in their cadences from syllable to syllable fell duskly upon our ears in the well-remembered and familiar accents of many thousand departed friends.

Four Beasts in One — The Homo-Cameleopard

Chacun a ses vertus.

CRÉBILLON's Xerxes.

ANTIOCHUS EPIPHANES is very generally looked upon as the Gog of the prophet Ezekiel. This honor is, however, more properly attributable to Cambyses, the son of Cyrus. And, indeed, the character of the Syrian

monarch does by no means stand in need of any adventitious embellish-
ment. His accession to the throne, or rather his usurpation of the sov-
ereignty, a hundred and seventy-one years before the coming of Christ;
his attempt to plunder the temple of Diana at Ephesus; his implacable
hostility to the Jews; his pollution of the Holy of Holies; and his miser-
able death at Taba, after a tumultuous reign of eleven years, are circum-
stances of a prominent kind, and therefore more generally noticed by
the historians of his time than the impious, dastardly, cruel, silly, and
whimsical achievements which make up the sum total of his private life
and reputation.

Let us suppose, gentle reader, that it is now the year of the world three
thousand eight hundred and thirty, and let us, for a few minutes, imagine
ourselves at that most grotesque habitation of man, the remarkable
city of Antioch. To be sure there were, in Syria and other countries, sixteen
citie of that appellation, besides the one to which I more particularly
allude. But *ours* is that which went by the name of Antiochia Epi-
daphne, from its vicinity to the little village of Daphne, where stood a
temple to that divinity. It was built (although about this matter there
is some dispute) by Seleucus Nicanor, the first king of the country after
Alexander the Great, in memory of his father Antiochus, and became
immediately the residence of the Syrian monarchy. In the flourishing
times of the Roman Empire, it was the ordinary station of the prefect
of the eastern provinces; and many of the emperors of the queen city
(among whom may be mentioned, especially, Verus and Valens) spent
here the greater part of their time. But I perceive we have arrived at the
city itself. Let us ascend this battlement, and throw our eyes upon the
town and neighboring country.

"What broad and rapid river is that which forces its way, with innu-
merable falls, through the mountainous wilderness, and finally through
the wilderness of buildings?"

That is the Orontes, and it is the only water in sight, with the excep-
tion of the Mediterranean, which stretches, like a broad mirror, about
twelve miles off to the southward. Every one has seen the Mediterranean;
but let me tell you, there are few who have had a peep at Antioch. By
few, I mean, few who, like you and me, have had, at the same time, the
advantages of a modern education. Therefore cease to regard that sea,
and give your whole attention to the mass of houses that lie beneath us.
You will remember that it is now the year of the world three thousand
eight hundred and thirty. Were it later— for example, were it the year
of our Lord eighteen hundred and forty-five, we should be deprived of
this extraordinary spectacle. In the nineteenth century Antioch is — that
is to say, Antioch *will be* — in a lamentable state of decay. It will have
been, by that time, totally destroyed, at three different periods, by three
successive earthquakes. Indeed, to say the truth, what little of its former

self may then remain, will be found in so desolate and ruinous a state that the patriarch shall have removed his residence to Damascus. This is well. I see you profit by my advice, and are making the most of your time in inspecting the premises — in

> — satisfying your eyes
> With the memorials and the things of fame
> That most renown this city. —

I beg pardon; I had forgotten that Shakespeare will not flourish for seventeen hundred and fifty years to come. But does not the appearance of Epidaphne justify me in calling it *grotesque*?

"It is well fortified; and in this respect is as much indebted to nature as to art."

Very true.

"There are a prodigious number of stately palaces."

There are.

"And the numerous temples, sumptuous and magnificent, may bear comparison with the most lauded of antiquity."

All this I must acknowledge. Still there is an infinity of mud huts, and abominable hovels. We cannot help perceiving abundance of filth in every kennel, and, were it not for the over-powering fumes of idolatrous incense, I have no doubt we should find a most intolerable stench. Did you ever behold streets so insufferably narrow, or houses so miraculously tall? What a gloom their shadows cast upon the ground! It is well the swinging lamps in those endless colonnades are kept burning throughout the day; we should otherwise have the darkness of Egypt in the time of her desolation.

"It is certainly a strange place! What is the meaning of yonder singular building? See! it towers above all others, and lies to the eastward of what I take to be the royal palace."

That is the new Temple of the Sun, who is adored in Syria under the title of Elah Gabalah. Hereafter a very notorious Roman Emperor will institute this worship in Rome, and thence derive a cognomen, Heliogabalus. I dare say you would like to take a peep at the divinity of the temple. You need not look up at the heavens; his Sunship is not there — at least not the Sunship adored by the Syrians. *That* deity will be found in the interior of yonder building. He is worshipped under the figure of a large stone pillar terminating at the summit in a cone or *pyramid*, whereby is denoted Fire.

"Hark — behold! — who *can* those ridiculous beings be, half naked, with their faces painted, shouting and gesticulating to the rabble?"

Some few are mountebanks. Others more particularly belong to the race of philosophers. The greatest portion, however — those especially who belabor the populace with clubs — are the principal courtiers of the

palace, executing, as in duty bound, some laudable comicality of the king's.

"But what have we here? Heavens! the town is swarming with wild beasts! How terrible a spectacle! — how dangerous a peculiarity!"

Terrible, if you please; but not in the least degree dangerous. Each animal, if you will take the pains to observe, is following, very quietly, in the wake of its master. Some few, to be sure, are led with a rope about the neck, but these are chiefly the lesser or timid species. The lion, the tiger, and the leopard are entirely without restraint. They have been trained without difficulty to their present profession, and attend upon their respective owners in the capacity of *valets-de-chambre*. It is true, there are occasions when Nature asserts her violated dominions; — but then the devouring of a man-at-arms, or the throttling of a consecrated bull, is a circumstance of too little moment to be more than hinted at in Epidaphne.

"But what extraordinary tumult do I hear? Surely this is a loud noise even for Antioch! It argues some commotion of unusual interest."

Yes — undoubtedly. The king has ordered some novel spectacle — some gladiatorial exhibition at the hippodrome — or perhaps the massacre of the Scythian prisoners — or the conflagration of his new palace — or the tearing down of a handsome temple — or, indeed, a bonfire of a few Jews. The uproar increases. Shouts of laughter ascend the skies. The air becomes dissonant with wind instruments, and horrible with clamor of a million throats. Let us descend, for the love of fun, and see what is going on! This way — be careful! Here we are in the principal street, which is called the street of Timarchus. The sea of people is coming this way, and we shall find a difficulty in stemming the tide. They are pouring through the alley of Heraclides, which leads directly from the palace; — therefore the king is most probably among the rioters. Yes; — I hear the shouts of the herald proclaiming his approach in the pompous phraseology of the East. We shall have a glimpse of his person as he passes by the temple of Ashimah. Let us ensconce ourselves in the vestibule of the sanctuary; he will be here anon. In the meantime let us survey this image. What is it? Oh! it is the god Ashimah in proper person. You perceive, however, that he is neither a lamb, nor a goat, nor a satyr; neither has he much resemblance to the Pan of the Arcadians. Yet all these appearances have been given — I beg pardon — *will* be given — by the learned of future ages, to the Ashimah of the Syrians. Put on your spectacles, and tell me what it is. What is it?

"Bless me! it is an ape!"

True — a baboon; but by no means the less a deity. His name is a derivation of the Greek *Simia* — what great fools are antiquarians! But see! — see! — yonder scampers a ragged little urchin. Where is he going? What is he bawling about? What does he say? Oh! he says the king is coming in triumph; that he is dressed in state; that he has just finished putting to

death, with his own hand, a thousand chained Israelitish prisoners! For
this exploit the ragamuffin is lauding him to the skies. Hark! here comes
a troop of a similar description. They have made a Latin hymn upon the
valor of the king, and are singing it as they go:

> Mille, mille, mille,
> Mille, mille, mille,
> Decollavimus, unus homo!
> Mille, mille, mille, mille, decollavimus!
> Mille, mille, mille,
> Vivat qui mille mille occidit!
> Tantum vini habet nemo
> Quantum sanguinis effudit!*

Which may be thus paraphrased:

> A thousand, a thousand, a thousand,
> A thousand, a thousand, a thousand,
> We, with one warrior, have slain!
> A thousand, a thousand, a thousand, a thousand.
> Sing a thousand over again!
> Soho! — let us sing
> Long life to our king,
> Who knocked over a thousand so fine!
> Soho! — let us roar,
> He has given us more
> Than all Syria can furnish of wine!

"Do you hear that flourish of trumpets?"

Yes: the king is coming! See! the people are aghast with admiration,
and lift up their eyes to the heavens in reverence. He comes; — he is
coming; — there he is!

"Who? — where? — the king? — do not behold him — cannot say that
I perceive him."

Then you must be blind.

"Very possible. Still I see nothing but a tumultuous mob of idiots and
madmen, who are busy in prostrating themselves before a gigantic came-
leopard, and endeavoring to obtain a kiss of the animal's hoofs. See! the
beast has very justly kicked one of the rabble over — and another — and
another — and another. Indeed, I cannot help admiring the animal for
the excellent use he is making of his feet."

Rabble, indeed! — why these are the noble and free citizens of Epi-
daphne! Beasts, did you say? — take care that you are not overheard. Do

* Flavius Vospicus says, that the hymn here introduced was sung by the rabble
upon the occasion of Aurelian, in the Sarmatic war, having slain, with his own hand,
nine hundred and fifty of the enemy.

you not perceive that the animal has the visage of a man? Why, my dear
sir, that cameleopard is no other than Antiochus Epiphanes, Antiochus
the Illustrious, King of Syria, and the most potent of all the autocrats of
the East! It is true, that he is entitled, at times, Antiochus Epimanes —
Antiochus the madman — but that is because all people have not the
capacity to appreciate his merits. It is also certain that he is at present
ensconced in the hide of a beast, and is doing his best to play the part of
a cameleopard; but this is done for the better sustaining his dignity as
king. Besides, the monarch is of gigantic stature, and the dress is there-
fore neither unbecoming nor over large. We may, however, presume he
would not have adopted it but for some occasion of especial state. Such,
you will allow, is the massacre of a thousand Jews. With how superior a
dignity the monarch perambulates on all fours! His tail, you perceive, is
held aloft by his two principal concubines, Elline and Argelais; and his
whole appearance would be infinitely prepossessing, were it not for the
protuberance of his eyes, which will certainly start out of his head, and
the queer color of his face, which has become nondescript from the
quantity of wine he has swallowed. Let us follow him to the hippodrome,
whither he is proceeding, and listen to the song of triumph which he is
commencing:

> Who is king but Epiphanes?
> Say — do you know?
> Who is king but Epiphanes?
> Bravo! — bravo!
> There is none but Epiphanes,
> No — there is none:
> So tear down the temples,
> And put out the sun!

Well and strenuously sung! The populace are hailing him 'Prince of
Poets,' as well as 'Glory of the East,' 'Delight of the Universe,' and 'Most
Remarkable of Cameleopards.' They have *encored* his effusion, and —
do you hear? — he is singing it over again. When he arrives at the hippo-
drome, he will be crowned with the poetic wreath, in anticipation of his
victory at the approaching Olympics.

"But, good Jupiter! what is the matter in the crowd behind us?"

Behind us, did you say? — oh! ah! — I perceive. My friend, it is well
that you spoke in time. Let us get into a place of safety as soon as pos-
sible. Here! — let us conceal ourselves in the arch of this aqueduct, and
I will inform you presently of the origin of the commotion. It has turned
out as I have been anticipating. The singular appearance of the cameleop-
ard with the head of a man, has, it seems, given offence to the notions
of propriety entertained, in general, by the wild animals domesticated in
the city. A mutiny has been the result; and, as is usual upon such occa-
sions, all human efforts will be of no avail in quelling the mob. Several

of the Syrians have already been devoured; but the general voice of the four-footed patriots seems to be for eating up the cameleopard. 'The Prince of Poets,' therefore, is upon his hinder legs, running for his life. His courtiers have left him in the lurch, and his concubines have followed so excellent an example. 'Delight of the Universe,' thou art in a sad predicament! 'Glory of the East,' thou art in danger of mastication! Therefore never regard so piteously thy tail; it will undoubtedly be draggled in the mud, and for this there is no help. Look not behind thee, then, at its unavoidable degradation; but take courage, ply thy legs with vigor, and scud for the hippodrome! Remember that thou art Antiochus Epiphanes. Antiochus the Illustrious! — also 'Prince of Poets,' 'Glory of the East,' 'Delight of the Universe,' and 'Most Remarkable of Cameleopards!' Heavens! what a power of speed thou art displaying! What a capacity for leg-bail thou art developing! Run, Prince! — Bravo, Epiphanes! — Well done, Cameleopard! — Glorious Antiochus! — He runs! — he leaps! — he flies! Like an arrow from a catapult he approaches the hippodrome! He leaps! — he shrieks! — he is there! This is well; for hadst thou, 'Glory of the East,' been half a second longer in reaching the gates of the Amphitheatre, there is not a bear's cub in Epidaphne that would not have had a nibble at thy carcase. Let us be off — let us take our departure! — for we shall find our delicate modern ears unable to endure the vast uproar which is about to commence in celebration of the king's escape! Listen! it has already commenced. See! — the whole town is topsy-turvy.

"Surely this is the most populous city of the East! What a wilderness of people! what a jumble of all ranks and ages! what a multiplicity of sects and nations! what a variety of costumes! what a Babel of languages! what a screaming of beasts! what a tinkling of instruments! what a parcel of philosophers!"

Come let us be off.

"Stay a moment! I see a vast hubbub in the hippodrome; what is the meaning of it, I beseech you?"

That? — oh, nothing! The noble and free citizens of Epidaphne being, as they declare, well satisfied of the faith, valor, wisdom, and divinity of their king, and having, moreover, been eye-witnesses of his late superhuman agility, do think it no more than their duty to invest his brows (in addition to the poetic crown) with the wreath of victory in the footrace — a wreath which it is evident he *must* obtain at the celebration of the next Olympiad, and which, therefore, they now give him in advance.

Mystification

Slid, if these be your "passados" and "montantes," I'll have none o' them.

NED KNOWLES.

THE BARON RITZNER VON JUNG was a noble Hungarian family, every member of which (at least as far back into antiquity as any certain records extend) was more or less remarkable for talent of some description — the majority for that species of *grotesquerie* in conception of which Tieck, a scion of the house, has given a vivid, although by no means the most vivid exemplifications. My acquaintance with Ritzner commenced at the magnificent Chateau Jung, into which a train of droll adventures, not to be made public, threw me during the summer months of the year 18—. Here it was I obtained a place in his regard, and here, with somewhat more difficulty, a partial insight into his mental conformation. In later days this insight grew more clear, as the intimacy which had at first permitted it became more close; and when, after three years separation, we met at G——n, I knew all that it was necessary to know of the character of the Baron Ritzner von Jung.

I remember the buzz of curiosity which his advent excited within the college precincts on the night of the twenty-fifth of June. I remember still more distinctly, that while he was pronounced by all parties at first sight "the most remarkable man in the world," no person made any attempt at accounting for his opinion. That he was *unique* appeared so undeniable, that it was deemed impertinent to inquire wherein the uniquity consisted. But, letting this matter pass for the present, I will merely observe that, from the first moment of his setting foot within the limits of the university, he began to exercise over the habits, manners, persons, purses, and propensities of the whole community which surrounded him, an influence the most extensive and despotic, yet at the same time the most indefinite and altogether unaccountable. Thus the brief period of his residence at the university forms an era in its annals, and is characterized by all classes of people appertaining to it or its dependencies as "that very extraordinary epoch forming the domination of the Baron Ritzner von Jung."

Upon his advent to G——n, he sought me out in my apartments. He was then of no particular age, by which I mean that it was impossible to form a guess respecting his age by any data personally afforded. He might have been fifteen or fifty, and *was* twenty-one years and seven months. He was by no means a handsome man — perhaps the reverse. The contour of his face was somewhat angular and harsh. His forehead was lofty and very fair; his nose a snub; his eyes large, heavy, glassy, and meaningless.

About the mouth there was more to be observed. The lips were gently protruded, and rested the one upon the other, after such a fashion that it is impossible to conceive any, even the most complex, combination of human features, conveying so entirely, and so singly, the idea of unmitigated gravity, solemnity and repose.

It will be perceived, no doubt, from what I have already said, that the Baron was one of those human anomalies now and then to be found, who make the science of *mystification* the study and the business of their lives. For this science a peculiar turn of mind gave him instinctively the cue, while his physical appearance afforded him unusual facilities for carrying his prospects into effect. I firmly believe that no student at G——n, during that renowned epoch so quaintly termed the domination of the Baron Ritzner von Jung, ever rightly entered into the mystery which overshadowed his character. I truly think that no person at the university, with the exception of myself, ever suspected him to be capable of a joke, verbal or practical: — the old bull-dog at the garden-gate would sooner have been accused, — the ghost of Heraclitus, — or the wig of the Emeritus Professor of Theology. This, too, when it was evident that the most egregious and unpardonable of all conceivable tricks, whimsicalities and buffooneries were brought about, if not directly by him, at least plainly through his intermediate agency or connivance. The beauty, if I may so call it, of his art *mystifique*, lay in that consummate ability (resulting from an almost intuitive knowledge of human nature, and a most wonderful self-possession,) by means of which he never failed to make it appear that the drolleries he was occupied in bringing to a point, arose partly in spite, and partly in consequence of the laudable efforts he was making for their prevention, and for the preservation of the good order and dignity of Alma Mater. The deep, the poignant, the overwhelming mortification, which upon each such failure of his praiseworthy endeavors, would suffuse every lineament of his countenance, left not the slightest room for doubt of his sincerity in the bosoms of even his most skeptical companions. The adroitness, too, was no less worthy of observation by which he contrived to shift the sense of the grotesque from the creator to the created — from his own person to the absurdities to which he had given rise. In no instance before that of which I speak, have I known the habitual mystific escape the natural consequence of his manœuvres — an attachment of the ludicrous to his own character and person. Continually enveloped in an atmosphere of whim, my friend appeared to live only for the severities of society; and not even his own household have for a moment associated other ideas than those of the rigid and august with the memory of the Baron Ritzner von Jung.

During the epoch of his residence at G——n it really appeared that the demon of the *dolce far niente* lay like an incubus upon the university. Nothing, at least, was done beyond eating and drinking and making merry. The apartments of the students were converted into so many

pot-houses, and there was no pot-house of them all more famous or more frequented than that of the Baron. Our carousals here were many, and boisterous, and long, and never unfruitful of events.

Upon one occasion we had protracted our sitting until nearly daybreak, and an unusual quantity of wine had been drunk. The company consisted of seven or eight individuals besides the Baron and myself. Most of these were young men of wealth, of high connection, of great family pride, and all alive with an exaggerated sense of honor. They abounded in the most ultra German opinions respecting the *duello*. To these Quixotic notions some recent Parisian publications, backed by three or four desperate and fatal recounters at G——n, had given new vigor and impulse; and thus the conversation, during the greater part of the night, had run wild upon the all-engrossing topic of the times. The Baron, who had been unusually silent and abstracted in the earlier portion of the evening, at length seemed to be aroused from his apathy, took a leading part in the discourse, and dwelt upon the benefits, and more especially upon the beauties, of the received code of etiquette in passages of arms with an ardor, an eloquence, an impressiveness, and an affectionateness of manner, which elicited the warmest enthusiasm from his hearers in general, and absolutely staggered even myself, who well knew him to be at heart a ridiculer of those very points for which he contended, and especially to hold the entire *fanfaronade* of duelling etiquette in the sovereign contempt which it deserves.

Looking around me during a pause in the Baron's discourse (of which my readers may gather some faint idea when I say that it bore resemblance to the fervid, chanting, monotonous, yet musical sermonic manner of Coleridge), I perceived symptoms of even more than the general interest in the countenance of one of the party. This gentleman, whom I shall call Hermann, was an original in every respect — except, perhaps, in the single particular that he was a very great fool. He contrived to bear, however, among a particular set at the university, a reputation for deep metaphysical thinking, and, I believe, for some logical talent. As a duellist he had acquired great renown, even at G——n. I forget the precise number of victims who had fallen at his hands; but they were many. He was a man of courage undoubtedly. But it was upon his minute acquaintance with the etiquette of the *duello*, and the *nicety* of his sense of honor, that he most especially prided himself. These things were a hobby which he rode to the death. To Ritzner, ever upon the lookout for the grotesque, his peculiarities had for a long time past afforded food for mystification. Of this, however, I was not aware; although, in the present instance, I saw clearly that something of a whimsical nature was upon the *tapis* with my friend, and that Hermann was its especial object.

As the former proceeded in his discourse, or rather monologue I perceived the excitement of the latter momently increasing. At length he spoke; offering some objection to a point insisted upon by R., and giving

his reasons in detail. To these the Baron replied at length (still maintaining his exaggerated tone of sentiment) and concluding, in what I thought very bad taste, with a sarcasm and a sneer. The hobby of Hermann now took the bit in his teeth. This I could discern by the studied hair-splitting *farrago* of his rejoinder. His last words I distinctly remember. "Your opinions, allow me to say, Baron von Jung, although in the main correct, are, in many nice points, discreditable to yourself and to the university of which you are a member. In a few respects they are even unworthy of serious refutation. I would say more than this, sir, were it not for the fear of giving you offence (here the speaker smiled blandly), I would say, sir, that your opinions are not the opinions to be expected from a gentleman."

As Hermann completed this equivocal sentence, all eyes were turned upon the Baron. He became pale, then excessively red; then, dropping his pocket-handkerchief, stooped to recover it, when I caught a glimpse of his countenance, while it could be seen by no one else at the table. It was radiant with the quizzical expression which was its natural character, but which I had never seen it assume except when we were alone together, and when he unbent himself freely. In an instant afterward he stood erect, confronting Hermann; and so total an alteration of countenance in so short a period I certainly never saw before. For a moment I even fancied that I had misconceived him, and that he was in sober earnest. He appeared to be stifling with passion, and his face was cadaverously white. For a short time he remained silent, apparently striving to master his emotion. Having at length seemingly succeeded, he reached a decanter which stood near him, saying as he held it firmly clenched — "The language you have thought proper to employ, Mynheer Hermann, in addressing yourself to me, is objectionable in so many particulars, that I have neither temper nor time for specification. That my opinions, however, are not the opinions to be expected from a gentleman, is an observation so directly offensive as to allow me but one line of conduct. Some courtesy, nevertheless, is due to the presence of this company, and to yourself, at this moment, as my guest. You will pardon me, therefore, if, upon this consideration, I deviate slightly from the general usage among gentlemen in similar cases of personal affront. You will forgive me for the moderate tax I shall make upon your imagination, and endeavor to consider, for an instant, the reflection of your person in yonder mirror as the living Mynheer Hermann himself. This being done, there will be no difficulty whatever. I shall discharge this decanter of wine at your image in yonder mirror, and thus fulfil all the spirit, if not the exact letter, of resentment for your insult, while the necessity of physical violence to your real person will be obviated."

With these words he hurled the decanter, full of wine, against the mirror which hung directly opposite Hermann; striking the reflection of his person with great precision, and of course shattering the glass into fragments. The whole company at once started to their feet, and, with

the exception of myself and Ritzner, took their departure. As Hermann went out, the Baron whispered me that I should follow him and make an offer of my services. To this I agreed; not knowing precisely what to make of so ridiculous a piece of business.

The duellist accepted my aid with his stiff and *ultra recherché* air, and, taking my arm, led me to his apartment. I could hardly forbear laughing in his face while he proceeded to discuss, with the profoundest gravity, what he termed "the refinedly peculiar character" of the insult he had received. After a tiresome harangue in his ordinary style, he took down from his book shelves a number of musty volumes on the subject of the *duello*, and entertained me for a long time with their contents; reading aloud, and commenting earnestly as he read. I can just remember the titles of some of the works. There were the "Ordonnance of Philip le Bel on Single Combat"; the "Theatre of Honor," by Favyn, and a treatise "On the Permission of Duels," by Andiguier. He displayed, also, with much pomposity, Brantôme's "Memoirs of Duels," published at Cologne, 1666, in the types of Elzevir — a precious and unique vellum-paper volume, with a fine margin, and bound by Derôme. But he requested my attention particularly, and with an air of mysterious sagacity, to a thick octavo, written in barbarous Latin by one Hédelin, a Frenchman, and having the quaint title, "*Duelli Lex Scripta, et non; aliterque.*" From this he read me one of the drollest chapters in the world concerning "*Injuriæ per applicationem, per constructionem, et per se,*" about half of which, he averred, was strictly applicable to his own "refinedly peculiar" case, although not one syllable of the whole matter could I understand for the life of me. Having finished the chapter, he closed the book, and demanded what I thought necessary to be done. I replied that I had entire confidence in his superior delicacy of feeling, and would abide by what he proposed. With this answer he seemed flattered, and sat down to write a note to the Baron. It ran thus:

SIR, — My friend, M. P.——, will hand you this note. I find it incumbent upon me to request, at your earliest convenience, an explanation of this evening's occurrences at your chambers. In the event of your declining this request, Mr. P. will be happy to arrange, with any friend whom you may appoint, the steps preliminary to a meeting.

With sentiments of perfect respect,

Your most humble servant,
JOHANN HERMANN.

To the Baron Ritzner von Jung,
August 18th, 18—.

Not knowing what better to do, I called upon Ritzner with this epistle. He bowed as I presented it; then, with a grave countenance, motioned me to a seat. Having perused the cartel, he wrote the following reply, which I carried to Hermann.

SIR, — Through our common friend, Mr. P., I have received your note of this evening. Upon due reflection I frankly admit the propriety of the explanation you suggest. This being admitted, I still find great difficulty, (owing to the *refinedly peculiar* nature of our disagreement, and of the personal affront offered on my part,) in so wording what I have to say by way of apology, as to meet all the minute exigencies, and all the variable shadows, of the case. I have great reliance, however, on that extreme delicacy of discrimination, in matters appertaining to the rules of etiquette, for which you have been so long and so pre-eminently distinguished. With perfect certainty, therefore, of being comprehended, I beg leave, in lieu of offering any sentiments of my own, to refer you to the opinions of Sieur Hédelin, as set forth in the ninth paragraph of the chapter of "*Injuriæ per applicationem, per constructionem, et per se,*" in his "*Duelli Lex scripta, et non; aliterque.*" The nicety of your discernment in all the matters here treated, will be sufficient, I am assured, to convince you *that the mere circumstance of me referring you* to this admirable passage, ought to satisfy your request, as a man of honor, for explanation.

With sentiments of profound respect,

Your most obedient servant,

VON JUNG.

The Herr Johann Hermann,
August 18th, 18—.

Hermann commenced the perusal of this epistle with a scowl, which, however, was converted into a smile of the most ludicrous self-complacency as he came to the rigmarole about *Injuriæ per applicationem, per constructionem, et per se.* Having finished reading, he begged me, with the blandest of all possible smiles, to be seated, while he made reference to the treatise in question. Turning to the passage specified, he read it with great care to himself, then closed the book, and desired me, in my character of confidential acquaintance, to express to the Baron von Jung his exalted sense of his chivalrous behavior, and, in that of second, to assure him that the explanation offered was of the fullest, the most honorable, and the most unequivocally satisfactory nature.

Somewhat amazed at all this, I made my retreat to the Baron. He seemed to receive Hermann's amicable letter as a matter of course, and after a few words of general conversation, went to an inner room and brought out the everlasting treatise "*Duelli Lex scripta, et non; aliterque.*" He handed me the volume and asked me to look over some portion of it. I did so, but to little purpose, not being able to gather the least particle of meaning. He then took the book himself, and read me a chapter aloud. To my surprise, what he read proved to be a most horribly absurd account of a duel between two baboons. He now explained the mystery; showing that the volume, as it appeared *prima facie,* was written upon

the plan of the nonsense verses of Du Bartas; that is to say, the language was ingeniously framed so as to present to the ear all the outward signs of intelligibility, and even of profundity, while in fact not a shadow of meaning existed. The key to the whole was found in leaving out every second and third word alternately, when there appeared a series of ludicrous quizzes upon a single combat as practised in modern times.

The Baron afterwards informed me that he had purposely thrown the treatise in Hermann's way two or three weeks before the adventure, and that he was satisfied, from the general tenor of his conversation, that he had studied it with the deepest attention, and firmly believed it to be a work of unusual merit. Upon this hint he proceeded. Hermann would have died a thousand deaths rather than acknowledge his inability to understand anything and everything in the universe that had ever been written about the *duello*.

<div align="right">LITTLETON BARRY.</div>

Silence — A Fable

<div align="center">
Ευδουσιν δ'ορεοων χορυφαι τε και φαραγγες

Πρωνες τε και χαραδραι

ALCMAN.

The mountain pinnacles slumber, valleys, crags and caves are silent.
</div>

LISTEN to *me*," said the Demon, as he placed his hand upon my head. "The region of which I speak is a dreary region in Libya, by the borders of the river Zaire, and there is no quiet there, nor silence.

"The waters of the river have a saffron and sickly hue; and they flow not onward to the sea, but palpitate forever and forever beneath the red eye of the sun with a tumultuous and convulsive motion. For many miles on either side of the river's oozy bed is a pale desert of gigantic water-lilies. They sigh one unto the other in that solitude, and stretch toward the heavens their long and ghastly necks, and nod to and fro their everlasting heads. And there is an indistinct murmur which cometh out from among them like the rushing of subterrene water. And they sigh one unto the other.

"But there is a boundary to their realm — the boundary of the dark, horrible, lofty forest. There, like the waves about the Hebrides, the low underwood is agitated continually. But there is no wind throughout the heaven. And the tall primeval trees rock eternally hither and thither with a crashing and mighty sound. And from their high summits, one by one, drop everlasting dews. And at the roots strange poisonous flowers lie writhing in perturbed slumber. And overhead, with a rustling and loud noise, the gray clouds rush westwardly forever, until they roll, a

cataract, over the fiery wall of the horizon. But there is no wind through-
out the heaven. And by the shores of the river Zaire there is neither quiet
nor silence.

"It was night, and the rain fell; and, falling, it was rain, but, having
fallen, it was blood. And I stood in the morass among the tall lilies, and
the rain fell upon my head — and the lilies sighed one unto the other in
solemnity of their desolation.

"And, all at once, the moon arose through the thin ghastly mist, and
was crimson in color. And mine eyes fell upon a huge gray rock which
stood by the shore of the river, and was lighted by the light of the moon.
And the rock was gray, and ghastly, and tall, — and the rock was gray.
Upon its front were characters engraven in the stone; and I walked
through the morass of water-lilies, until I came close unto the shore,
that I might read the characters upon the stone. But I could not de-
cypher them. And I was going back into the morass, when the moon
shone with a fuller red, and I turned and looked again upon the rock,
and upon the characters, and the characters were DESOLATION.

"And I looked upward, and there stood a man upon the summit of
the rock; and I hid myself among the water-lilies that I might discover
the actions of the man. And the man was tall and stately in form, and
was wrapped up from his shoulders to his feet in the toga of old Rome.
And the outlines of his figure were indistinct — but his features were
the features of a deity; for the mantle of the night, and of the mist, and
of the moon, and of the dew, had left uncovered the features of his face.
And his brow was lofty with thought, and his eye wild with care; and,
in the few furrows upon his cheek I read the fables of sorrow, and weari-
ness, and disgust with mankind, and a longing after solitude.

"And the man sat upon the rock, and leaned his head upon his hand,
and looked out upon the desolation. He looked down into the low un-
quiet shrubbery, and up into the tall primeval trees, and up higher at the
'rustling heaven, and into the crimson moon. And I lay close within
shelter of the lilies, and observed the actions of the man. And the man
trembled in the solitude; — but the night waned, and he sat upon the
rock.

"And the man turned his attention from the heaven, and looked out
upon the dreary river Zaire, and upon the yellow ghastly waters, and
upon the pale legions of the water-lilies. And the man listened to the
sighs of the water-lilies, and to the murmur that came up from among
them. And I lay close within my covert and observed the actions of the
man. And the man trembled in the solitude; — but the night waned and
he sat upon the rock.

"Then I went down into the recesses of the morass and waded afar in
among the wilderness of the lilies, and called unto the hippopotami
which dwelt among the fens in the recesses of the morass. And the hip-
popotami heard my call, and came, with the behemoth, unto the foot

of the rock, and roared loudly and fearfully beneath the moon. And I lay close within my covert and observed the actions of the man. And the man trembled in the solitude; — but the night waned and he sat upon the rock.

"Then I cursed the elements with the curse of tumult; and a frightful tempest gathered in the heaven, where, before, there had been no wind. And the heaven became livid with the violence of the tempest — and the rain beat upon the head of the man — and the floods of the river came down — and the river was tormented into foam — and the water-lilies shrieked within their beds — and the forest crumbled before the wind — and the thunder rolled — and the lightning fell — and the rock rocked to its foundation. And I lay close within my covert and observed the actions of the man. And the man trembled in the solitude; — but the night waned and he sat upon the rock.

"Then I grew angry and cursed, with the curse of *silence*, the river, and the lilies, and the wind, and the forest, and the heaven, and the thunder, and the sighs of the water-lilies. And they became accursed, and *were still*. And the moon ceased to totter up its pathway to heaven — and the thunder died away — and the lightning did not flash — and the clouds hung motionless — and the waters sunk to their level and remained — and the trees ceased to rock — and the water-lilies sighed no more — and the murmur was heard no longer from among them, nor any shadow of sound throughout the vast illimitable desert. And I looked upon the characters of the rock, and they were changed; and the characters were SILENCE.

"And mine eyes fell upon the countenance of the man and his countenance was wan with terror. And, hurriedly, he raised his head from his hand, and stood forth upon the rock and listened. But there was no voice throughout the vast illimitable desert, and the characters upon the rock were SILENCE. And the man shuddered, and turned his face away, and fled afar off, in haste, so that I beheld him no more."

Now there are fine tales in the volumes of the Magi — in the iron-bound, melancholy volumes of the Magi. Therein, I say, are glorious histories of the Heaven, and of the Earth, and of the mighty sea — and of the Genii that overruled the sea, and the earth, and the lofty heaven. There was much lore too in the sayings which were said by the Sibyls; and holy, holy things were heard of old by the dim leaves that trembled around Dodona — but, as Allah liveth, that fable which the Demon told me as he sat by my side in the shadow of the tomb, I hold to be the most wonderful of all! And as the Demon made an end of his story, he fell back within the cavity of the tomb and laughed. And I could not laugh with the Demon, and he cursed me because I could not laugh. And the lynx which dwelleth forever in the tomb, came out therefrom, and lay down at the feet of the Demon, and looked at him steadily in the face.

Ligeia

And the will therein lieth, which dieth not. Who knoweth, the mysteries of the will,
with its vigor? For God is but a great will pervading all things by nature of its
intentness. Man doth not yield himself to the angels, nor unto death utterly,
save only through the weakness of his feeble will.

JOSEPH GLANVILL.

I CANNOT, for my soul, remember how, when, or even precisely where,
I first became acquainted with the lady Ligeia. Long years have since
elapsed, and my memory is feeble through much suffering. Or, perhaps,
I cannot *now* bring these points to mind, because, in truth, the character
of my beloved, her rare learning, her singular yet placid cast of beauty,
and the thrilling and enthralling eloquence of her low musical language,
made their way into my heart by paces so steadily and stealthily progres-
sive, that they have been unnoticed and unknown. Yet I believe that I
met her first and most frequently in some large, old, decaying city near
the Rhine. Of her family — I have surely heard her speak. That it is of
a remotely ancient date cannot be doubted. Ligeia! Ligeia! Buried in
studies of a nature more than all else adapted to deaden impressions of
the outward world, it is by that sweet word alone — by Ligeia — that I
bring before mine eyes in fancy the image of her who is no more. And
now, while I write, a recollection flashes upon me that I have *never known*
the paternal name of her who was my friend and my betrothed, and
who became the partner of my studies, and finally the wife of my bosom.
Was it a playful charge on the part of my Ligeia? or was it a test of my
strength of affection, that I should institute no inquiries upon this point?
or was it rather a caprice of my own — a wildly romantic offering on the
shrine of the most passionate devotion? I but indistinctly recall the fact
itself — what wonder that I have utterly forgotten the circumstances
which originated or attended it? And, indeed, if ever that spirit which
is entitled *Romance* — if ever she, the wan and the misty-winged *Ash-
tophet* of idolatrous Egypt, presided, as they tell, over marriages ill-
omened, then most surely she presided over mine.

There is one dear topic, however, on which my memory fails me not.
It is the *person* of Ligeia. In stature she was tall, somewhat slender, and,
in her latter days, even emaciated. I would in vain attempt to portray
the majesty, the quiet ease of her demeanor, or the incomprehensible
lightness and elasticity of her footfall. She came and departed as a
shadow. I was never made aware of her entrance into my closed study,
save by the dear music of her low sweet voice, as she placed her marble
hand upon my shoulder. In beauty of face no maiden ever equalled her.

It was the radiance of an opium-dream— an airy and spirit-lifting vision more wildly divine than the phantasies which hovered about the slumbering souls of the daughters of Delos. Yet her features were not of that regular mold which we have been falsely taught to worship in the classical labors of the heathen. "There is no exquisite beauty," says Bacon, Lord Verulam, speaking truly of all the forms and *genera* of beauty, "without some *strangeness* in the proportion." Yet, although I saw that the features of Ligeia were not of a classic regularity — although I perceived that her loveliness was indeed "exquisite," and felt that there was much of "strangeness" pervading it, yet I have tried in vain to detect the irregularity and to trace home my own perception of "the strange." I examined the contour of the lofty and pale forehead — it was faultless — how cold indeed that word when applied to a majesty so divine! — the skin rivalling the purest ivory, the commanding extent and repose, the gentle prominence of the regions above the temples; and then the raven-black, the glossy, the luxuriant, and naturally-curling tresses, setting forth the full force of the Homeric epithet, "hyacinthine!" I looked at the delicate outlines of the nose — and nowhere but in the graceful medallions of the Hebrews had I beheld a similar perfection. There were the same luxurious smoothness of surface, the same scarcely perceptible tendency to the aquiline, the same harmoniously curved nostrils speaking the free spirit. I regarded the sweet mouth. Here was indeed the triumph of all things heavenly — the magnificent turn of the short upper lip — the soft, voluptuous slumber of the under — the dimples which sported, and the color which spoke — the teeth glancing back, with a brilliancy almost startling, every ray of the holy light which fell upon them in her serene and placid yet most exultingly radiant of all smiles. I scrutinized the formation of the chin — and, here too, I found the gentleness of breadth, the softness and the majesty, the fulness and the spirituality, of the Greek — the contour which the god Apollo revealed but in a dream, to Cleomenes, the son of the Athenian. And then I peered into the large eyes of Ligeia.

For eyes we have no models in the remotely antique. It might have been, too, that in these eyes of my beloved lay the secret to which Lord Verulam alludes. They were, I must believe, far larger than the ordinary eyes of our own race. They were even fuller than the fullest of the gazelle eyes of the tribe of the valley of Nourjahad. Yet it was only at intervals — in moments of intense excitement — that this peculiarity became more than slightly noticeable in Ligeia. And at such moments was her beauty — in my heated fancy thus it appeared perhaps — the beauty of beings either above or apart from the earth — the beauty of the fabulous Houri of the Turk. The hue of the orbs was the most brilliant of black, and far over them, hung jetty lashes of great length. The brows, slightly irregular in outline, had the same tint. The "strangeness," however, which I found in the eyes was of a nature distinct from the formation, or the color, or

the brilliancy of the features, and must, after all, be referred to the *expression*. Ah, word of no meaning! behind whose vast latitude of mere sound we intrench our ignorance of so much of the spiritual. The expression of the eyes of Ligeia! How for long hours have I pondered upon it! How have I, through the whole of a midsummer night, struggled to fathom it! What was it — that something more profound than the well of Democritus — which lay far within the pupils of my beloved. What *was* it? I was possessed with a passion to discover. Those eyes! those large, those shining, those divine orbs! they became to me twin stars of Leda, and I to them devoutest of astrologers.

There is no point, among the many incomprehensible anomalies of the science of mind, more thrillingly exciting than the fact — never, I believe, noticed in the schools — that in our endeavors to recall to memory something long forgotten, we often find ourselves *upon the very verge* of remembrance, without being able, in the end, to remember. And thus how frequently, in my intense scrutiny of Ligeia's eyes, have I felt approaching the full knowledge of their expression — felt it approaching — yet not quite be mine — and so at length entirely depart! And (strange, oh, strangest mystery of all!) I found, in the commonest objects of the universe, a circle of analogies to that expression. I mean to say that subsequently to the period when Ligeia's beauty passed into my spirit, there dwelling as in a shrine, I derived, from many existences in the material world, a sentiment such as I felt always aroused within me by her large and luminous orbs. Yet not the more could I define that sentiment, or analyze, or even steadily view it. I recognized it, let me repeat, sometimes in the survey of a rapidly-growing vine — in the contemplation of a moth, a butterfly, a chrysalis, a stream of running water. I have felt it in the ocean — in the falling of a meteor. I have felt it in the glances of unusually aged people. And there are one or two stars in heaven (one especially, a star of the sixth magnitude, double and changeable, to be found near the large star in Lyra) in a telescopic scrutiny of which I have been made aware of the feeling. I have been filled with it by certain sounds from stringed instruments, and not unfrequently by passages from books. Among innumerable other instances, I well remember something in a volume of Joseph Glanvill, which (perhaps merely from its quaintness — who shall say?) never failed to inspire me with the sentiment: "And the will therein lieth, which dieth not. Who knoweth the mysteries of the will, with its vigor? For God is but a great will pervading all things by nature of its intentness. Man doth not yield him to the angels, nor unto death utterly, save only through the weakness of his feeble will."

Length of years and subsequent reflection have enabled me to trace, indeed, some remote connection between this passage in the English moralist and a portion of the character of Ligeia. An *intensity* in thought, action, or speech was possibly, in her, a result, or at least an index, of that

gigantic volition which, during our long intercourse, failed to give other and more immediate evidence of its existence. Of all the women whom I have ever known, she, the outwardly calm, the ever-placid Ligeia, was the most violently a prey to the tumultuous vultures of stern passion. And of such passion I could form no estimate, save by the miraculous expansion of those eyes which at once so delighted and appalled me — by the almost magical melody, modulation, distinctness, and placidity of her very low voice — and by the fierce energy (rendered doubly effective by contrast with her manner of utterance) of the wild words which she habitually uttered.

I have spoken of the learning of Ligeia: it was immense — such as I have never known in woman. In the classical tongues was she deeply proficient, and as far as my own acquaintance extended in regard to the modern dialects of Europe, I have never known her at fault. Indeed upon any theme of the most admired because simply the most abstruse of the boasted erudition of the Academy, have I *ever* found Ligeia at fault? How singularly — how thrillingly, this one point in the nature of my wife has forced itself, at this late period only, upon my attention! I said her knowledge was such as I have never known in woman — but where breathes the man who has traversed, and successfully, *all* the wide areas of moral, physical, and mathematical science? I saw not then what I now clearly perceive that the acquisitions of Ligeia were gigantic, were astounding; yet I was sufficiently aware of her infinite supremacy to resign myself, with a child like confidence, to her guidance through the chaotic world of metaphysical investigation at which I was most busily occupied during the earlier years of our marriage. With how vast a triumph — with how vivid a delight — with how much of all that is ethereal in hope did I *feel*, as she bent over me in studies but little sought — but less known — that delicious vista by slow degrees expanding before me, down whose long, gorgeous, and all untrodden path, I might at length pass onward to the goal of a wisdom too divinely precious not to be forbidden.

How poignant, then, must have been the grief with which, after some years, I beheld my well-grounded expectations take wings to themselves and fly away! Without Ligeia I was but as a child groping benighted. Her presence, her readings alone, rendered vividly luminous the many mysteries of the transcendentalism in which we were immersed. Wanting the radiant lustre of her eyes, letters, lambent and golden, grew duller than Saturnian lead. And now those eyes shone less and less frequently upon the pages over which I pored. Ligeia grew ill. The wild eyes blazed with a too — too glorious effulgence; the pale fingers became of the transparent waxen hue of the grave; and the blue veins upon the lofty forehead swelled and sank impetuously with the tides of the most gentle emotion. I saw that she must die — and I struggled desperately in spirit with the grim Azrael. And the struggles of the passionate wife were, to

my astonishment, even more energetic than my own. There has been much in her stern nature to impress me with the belief that, to her, death would have come without its terrors; but not so. Words are impotent to convey any just idea of the fierceness of resistance with which she wrestled with the Shadow. I groaned in anguish at the pitiable spectacle. I would have soothed — I would have reasoned; but in the intensity of her wild desire for life — for life — *but* for life — solace and reason were alike the uttermost of folly. Yet not until the last instance, amid the most convulsive writhings of her fierce spirit, was shaken the external placidity of her demeanor. Her voice grew more gentle — grew more low — yet I would not wish to dwell upon the wild meaning of the quietly uttered words. My brain reeled as I hearkened, entranced to a melody more than mortal — to assumptions and aspirations which mortality had never before known.

That she loved me I should not have doubted; and I might have been easily aware that, in a bosom such as hers, love would have reigned no ordinary passion. But in death only was I fully impressed with the strength of her affection. For long hours, detaining my hand, would she pour out before me the overflowing of a heart whose more than passionate devotion amounted to idolatry. How had I deserved to be so blessed by such confessions? — how had I deserved to be so cursed with the removal of my beloved in the hour of her making them? But upon this subject I cannot bear to dilate. Let me say only, that in Ligeia's more than womanly abandonment to a love, alas! all unmerited, all unworthily bestowed, I at length, recognized the principle of her longing, with so wildly earnest a desire, for the life which was now fleeing so rapidly away. It is this wild longing — it is this eager vehemence of desire for life — *but* for life — that I have no power to portray — no utterance capable of expressing.

At high noon of the night on which she departed, beckoning me, peremptorily, to her side, she bade me repeat certain verses composed by herself not many days before. I obeyed her. They were these: —

> Lo! 'tis a gala night
> Within the lonesome latter years!
> An angel throng, bewinged, bedight
> In veils, and drowned in tears,
> Sit in a theatre, to see
> A play of hopes and fears,
> While the orchestra breathes fitfully
> The music of the spheres.
>
> Mimes, in the form of God on high,
> Mutter and mumble low,
> And hither and thither fly;

Mere puppets they, who come and go
　　At bidding of vast formless things
That shift the scenery to and fro,
　　Flapping from out their Condor wings
　　Invisible Wo!

That motley drama! — oh, be sure
　　It shall not be forgot!
With its Phantom chased for evermore,
　　By a crowd that seize it not.
Through a circle that ever returneth in
　　To the self-same spot;
And much of Madness, and more of Sin
　　And Horror, the soul of the plot!

But see, amid the mimic rout
　　A crawling shape intrude!
A blood-red thing that writhes from out
　　The scenic solitude!
It writhes! — it writhes! — with mortal pangs
　　The mimes become its food,
And the seraphs sob at vermin fangs
　　In human gore imbued.

Out — out are the lights — out all!
　　And over each quivering form,
The curtain, a funeral pall,
　　Comes down with the rush of a storm —
And the angels, all pallid and wan,
　　Uprising, unveiling, affirm
That the play is the tragedy, "Man,"
　　And its hero, the Conqueror Worm.

"O God!" half shrieked Ligeia, leaping to her feet and extending her arms aloft with a spasmodic movement, as I made an end of these lines — "O God! O Divine Father! — shall these things be undeviatingly so? — shall this Conqueror be not once conquered? Are we not part and parcel in Thee? Who — who knoweth the mysteries of the will with its vigor? Man doth not yield him to the angels, *nor unto death utterly*, save only through the weakness of his feeble will."

And now, as if exhausted with emotion, she suffered her white arms to fall, and returned solemnly to her bed of death. And as she breathed her last sighs, there came mingled with them a low murmur from her lips. I bent to them my ear, and distinguished, again, the concluding words of the passage in Glanvill: "*Man doth not yield him to the angels, nor unto death utterly, save only through the weakness of his feeble will.*"

She died: and I, crushed into the very dust with sorrow, could no longer endure the lonely desolation of my dwelling in the dim and decaying city by the Rhine. I had no lack of what the world calls wealth, Ligeia had brought me far more, very far more, than ordinarily falls to the lot of mortals. After a few months, therefore, of weary and aimless wandering, I purchased and put in some repair, an abbey, which I shall not name, in one of the wildest and least frequented portions of fair England. The gloomy and dreary grandeur of the building, the almost savage aspect of the domain, the many melancholy and time-honored memories connected with both, had much in unison with the feelings of utter abandonment which had driven me into that remote and unsocial region of the country. Yet although the external abbey, with its verdant decay hanging about it, suffered but little alteration, I gave way, with a child-like perversity, and perchance with a faint hope of alleviating my sorrows, to a display of more than regal magnificence within. For such follies, even in childhood, I had imbibed a taste, and now they came back to me as if in the dotage of grief. Alas, I feel how much even of incipient madness might have been discovered in the gorgeous and fantastic draperies, in the solemn carvings of Egypt, in the wild cornices and furniture, in the Bedlam patterns of the carpets of tufted gold! I had become a bounden slave in the trammels of opium, and my labors and my orders had taken a coloring from my dreams. But these absurdities I must not pause to detail. Let me speak only of that one chamber, ever accursed, whither, in a moment of mental alienation, I led from the altar as my bride — as the successor of the unforgotten Ligeia — the fair-haired and blue-eyed Lady Rowena Trevanion, of Tremaine.

There is no individual portion of the architecture and decoration of that bridal chamber which is not now visibly before me. Where were the souls of the haughty family of the bride, when, through thirst of gold, they permitted to pass the threshold of an apartment so bedecked, a maiden and a daughter so beloved? I have said, that I minutely remember the details of the chamber — yet I am sadly forgetful on the topics of deep moment; and here there was no system, no keeping, in the fantastic display, to take hold upon the memory. The room lay in a high turret of the castellated abbey, was pentagonal in shape, and of capacious size. Occupying the whole southern face of the pentagon was the sole window — an immense sheet of unbroken glass from Venice — a single pane, and tinted of a leaden hue, so that the rays of either the sun or moon passing through it, fell with a ghastly lustre on the objects within. Over the upper portion of this huge window, extended the trellis-work of an aged vine, which clambered up the massy walls of the turret. The ceiling of gloomy-looking oak, was excessively lofty, vaulted, and elaborately fretted with the wildest and most grotesque specimens of a semi-Gothic, semi-Druidical device. From out the most central recess of this melancholy vaulting, depended, by a single chain of gold with

long links, a huge censer of the same metals, Saracenic in pattern, and
with many perforations so contrived that there writhed in and out of
them, as if endued with a serpent vitality, a continual succession of parti-
colored fires.

Some few ottomans and golden candelabra, of Eastern figure, were
in various stations about; and there was the couch, too — the bridal
couch — of an Indian model, and low, and sculptured of solid ebony,
with a pall-like canopy above. In each of the angles of the chamber
stood on end a gigantic sarcophagus of black granite, from the tombs of
the kings over against Luxor, with their aged lids full of immemorial
sculpture. But in the draping of the apartment lay, alas! the chief phan-
tasy of all. The lofty walls, gigantic in height — even unproportionably
so — were hung from summit to foot, in vast folds, with a heavy and mas-
sive-looking tapestry — tapestry of a material which was found alike as
a carpet on the floor, as a covering for the ottomans and the ebony bed,
as a canopy for the bed and as the gorgeous volutes of the curtains which
partially shaded the window. The material was the richest cloth of gold.
It was spotted all over, at irregular intervals, with arabesque figures,
about a foot in diameter, and wrought upon the cloth in patterns of the
most jetty black. But these figures partook of the true character of the
arabesque only when regarded from a single point of view. By a contriv-
ance now common, and indeed traceable to a very remote period of
antiquity, they were made changeable in aspect. To one entering the
room, they bore the appearance of simple monstrosities; but upon a
farther advance, this appearance gradually departed; and, step by step,
as the visiter moved his station in the chamber, he saw himself sur-
rounded by an endless succession of the ghastly forms which belong to
the superstition of the Norman, or arise in the guilty slumbers of the
monk. The phantasmagoric effect was vastly heightened by the artificial
introduction of a strong continual current of wind behind the draperies
— giving a hideous and uneasy animation to the whole.

In halls such as these — in a bridal chamber such as this — I passed,
with the Lady of Tremaine, the unhallowed hours of the first month of
our marriage — passed them with but little disquietude. That my wife
dreaded the fierce moodiness of my temper — that she shunned me, and
loved me but little — I could not help perceiving; but it gave me rather
pleasure than otherwise. I loathed her with a hatred belonging more to
demon than to man. My memory flew back (oh, with what intensity of
regret!) to Ligeia, the beloved, the august, the beautiful, the entombed.
I revelled in recollections of her purity, of her wisdom, of her lofty —
her ethereal nature, of her passionate, her idolatrous love. Now, then,
did my spirit fully and freely burn with more than all the fires of her
own. In the excitement of my opium dreams (for I was habitually fet-
tered in the shackles of the drug), I would call aloud upon her name, dur-
ing the silence of the night, or among the sheltered recesses of the glens by

day, as if, through the wild eagerness, the solemn passion, the consuming ardor of my longing for the departed, I could restore her to the pathways she had abandoned — ah, *could* it be for ever? — upon the earth.

About the commencement of the second month of the marriage, the Lady Rowena was attacked with sudden illness, from which her recovery was slow. The fever which consumed her rendered her nights uneasy; and in her perturbed state of half-slumber, she spoke of sounds, and of motions, in and about the chamber of the turret, which I concluded had no origin save in the distemper of her fancy, or perhaps in the phantasmagoric influences of the chamber itself. She became at length convalescent — finally, well. Yet but a brief period elapsed, ere a second more violent disorder again threw her upon a bed of suffering; and from this attack her frame, at all times feeble, never altogether recovered. Her illnesses were, after this epoch, of alarming character, and of more alarming recurrence, defying alike the knowledge and the great exertions of her physicians. With the increase of the chronic disease, which had thus, apparently, taken too sure hold upon her constitution to be eradicated by human means, I could not fail to observe a similiar increase in the nervous irritation of her temperament, and in her excitability by trivial causes of fear. She spoke again, and now more frequently and pertinaciously, of the sounds — of the slight sounds — and of the unusual motions among the tapestries, to which she had formerly alluded.

One night, near the closing in of September, she pressed this distressing subject with more than usual emphasis upon my attention. She had just awakened from an unquiet slumber, and I had been watching, with feelings half of anxiety, half of vague terror, the workings of her emaciated countenance. I sat by the side of her ebony bed, upon one of the ottomans of India. She partly arose, and spoke, in an earnest low whisper, of sounds which she *then* heard, but which I could not hear — of motions which she *then* saw, but which I could not perceive. The wind was rushing hurriedly behind the tapestries, and I wished to show her (what, let me confess it, I could not *all* believe) that those almost inarticulate breathings, and those very gentle variations of the figures upon the wall, were but the natural effects of that customary rushing of the wind. But a deadly pallor, over-spreading her face, had proved to me that my exertions to reassure her would be fruitless. She appeared to be fainting, and no attendants were within call. I remembered where was deposited a decanter of light wine which had been ordered by her physicians, and hastened across the chamber to procure it. But, as I stepped beneath the light of the censer, two circumstances of a startling nature attracted my attention. I had felt that some palpable although invisible object had passed lightly by my person; and I saw that there lay upon the golden carpet, in the very middle of the rich lustre thrown from the censer, a shadow — a faint, indefinite shadow of angelic aspect — such as might be fancied for the shadow of a shade. But I was wild with the

excitement of an immoderate dose of opium, and heeded these things but little, nor spoke of them to Rowena. Having found the wine, I recrossed the chamber, and poured out a gobletful, which I held to the lips of the fainting lady. She had now partially recovered, however, and took the vessel herself, while I sank upon an ottoman near me, with my eyes fastened upon her person. It was then that I became distinctly aware of a gentle foot-fall upon the carpet, and near the couch; and in a second thereafter, as Rowena was in the act of raising the wine to her lips, I saw, or may have dreamed that I saw, fall within the goblet, as if from some invisible spring in the atmosphere of the room, three or four large drops of a brilliant and ruby colored fluid. If this I saw — not so Rowena. She swallowed the wine unhesitatingly, and I forebore to speak to her of a circumstance which must, after all, I considered, have been but the suggestion of a vivid imagination, rendered morbidly active by the terror of the lady, by the opium, and by the hour.

Yet I cannot conceal it from my own perception that, immediately subsequent to the fall of the ruby-drops, a rapid change for the worse took place in the disorder of my wife; so that, on the third subsequent night, the hands of her menials prepared her for the tomb, and on the fourth, I sat alone with her shrouded body, in that fantastic chamber which had received her as my bride. Wild visions, opium-engendered, flitted, shadow-like, before me. I gazed with unquiet eye upon the sarcophagi in the angles of the room, upon the varying figures of the drapery, and upon the writhing of the parti-colored fires in the censer overhead. My eyes then fell, as I called to mind the circumstances of a former night, to the spot beneath the glare of the censer where I had seen the faint traces of the shadow. It was there, however, no longer; and breathing with greater freedom, I turned my glances to the pallid and rigid figure upon the bed. Then rushed upon me a thousand memories of Ligeia — and then came back upon my heart, with the turbulent violence of a flood, the whole of that unutterable wo with which I had regarded *her* thus enshrouded. The night waned; and still, with a bosom full of bitter thoughts of the one only and supremely beloved, I remained gazing upon the body of Rowena.

It might have been midnight, or perhaps earlier, or later, for I had taken no note of time, when a sob, low, gentle, but very distinct, startled me from my revery. I *felt* that it came from the bed of ebony — the bed of death. I listened in an agony of superstitious terror — but there was no repetition of the sound. I strained my vision to detect any motion in the corpse — but there was not the slightest perceptible. Yet I could not have been deceived. I *had* heard the noise, however faint, and my soul was awakened within me. I resolutely and perseveringly kept my attention riveted upon the body. Many minutes elapsed before any circumstance occurred tending to throw light upon the mystery. At length it became evident that a slight, a very feeble, and barely noticeable tinge

of color had flushed up within the cheeks, and along the sunken small veins of the eyelids. Through a species of unutterable horror and awe, for which the language of mortality has no sufficiently energetic expression, I felt my heart cease to beat, my limbs grow rigid where I sat. Yet a sense of duty finally operated to restore my self-possession. I could no longer doubt that we had been precipitate in our preparations — that Rowena still lived. It was necessary that some immediate exertion be made; yet the turret was altogether apart from the portion of the abbey tenanted by the servants — there were none within call — I had no means of summoning them to my aid without leaving the room for many minutes — and this I could not venture to do. I therefore struggled alone in my endeavors to call back the spirit still hovering. In a short period it was certain, however, that a relapse had taken place; the color disappeared from both eyelid and cheek, leaving a wanness even more than that of marble; the lips became doubly shrivelled and pinched up in the ghastly expression of death; a repulsive clamminess and coldness overspread rapidly the surface of the body; and all the usual rigorous stiffness immediately supervened. I fell back with a shudder upon the couch from which I had been so startlingly aroused, and again gave myself up to passionate waking visions of Ligeia.

An hour thus elapsed, when (could it be possible?) I was a second time aware of some vague sound issuing from the region of the bed. I listened — in extremity of horror. The sound came again — it was a sigh. Rushing to the corpse, I saw — distinctly saw — a tremor upon the lips. In a minute afterward they relaxed, disclosing a bright line of the pearly teeth. Amazement now struggled in my bosom with the profound awe which had hitherto reigned there alone. I felt that my vision grew dim, that my reason wandered; and it was only by a violent effort that I at length succeeded in nerving myself to the task which duty thus once more had pointed out. There was now a partial glow upon the forehead and upon the cheek and throat; a perceptible warmth pervaded the whole frame; there was even a slight pulsation at the heart. The lady *lived*; and with redoubled ardor I betook myself to the task of restoration. I chafed and bathed the temples and the hands, and used every exertion which experience, and no little medical reading, could suggest. But in vain. Suddenly, the color fled, the pulsation ceased, the lips resumed the expression of the dead, and, in an instant afterward, the whole body took upon itself the icy chilliness, the livid hue, the intense rigidity, the sunken outline, and all the loathsome peculiarities of that which has been, for many days, a tenant of the tomb.

And again I sunk into visions of Ligeia — and again (what marvel that I shudder while I write?) *again* there reached my ears a low sob from the region of the ebony bed. But why shall I minutely detail the unspeakable horrors of that night? Why shall I pause to relate how, time after time, until near the period of the gray dawn, this hideous drama of revivifica-

tion was repeated; how each terrific relapse was only into a sterner and apparently more irredeemable death; how each agony wore the aspect of a struggle with some invisible foe; and how each struggle was succeeded by I know not what of wild change in the personal appearance of the corpse? Let me hurry to a conclusion.

The greater part of the fearful night had worn away, and she who had been dead once again stirred — and now more vigorously than hitherto, although arousing from a dissolution more appalling in its utter hopelessness than any. I had long ceased to struggle or to move, and remained sitting rigidly upon the ottoman, a helpless prey to a whirl of violent emotions, of which extreme awe was perhaps the least terrible, the least consuming. The corpse, I repeat, stirred, and now more vigorously than before. The hues of life flushed up with unwonted energy into the countenance — the limbs relaxed — and, save that the eyelids were yet pressed heavily together, and that the bandages and draperies of the grave still imparted their charnel character to the figure, I might have dreamed that Rowena had indeed shaken off, utterly, the fetters of Death. But if this idea was not, even then, altogether adopted, I could at least doubt no longer, when, arising from the bed, tottering, with feeble steps, with closed eyes, and with the manner of one bewildered in a dream, the thing that was enshrouded advanced boldly and palpably into the middle of the apartment.

I trembled not — I stirred not — for a crowd of unutterable fancies connected with the air, the stature, the demeanor, of the figure, rushing hurriedly through my brain, had paralyzed — had chilled me into stone. I stirred not — but gazed upon the apparition. There was a mad disorder in my thoughts — a tumult unappeasable. Could it, indeed, be the *living* Rowena who confronted me? Could it, indeed, be Rowena *at all* — the fair-haired, the blue-eyed Lady Rowena Trevanion of Tremaine? Why, *why* should I doubt it? The bandage lay heavily about the mouth — but then might it not be the mouth of the breathing Lady of Tremaine? And the cheeks — there were the roses as in her noon of life — yes, these might indeed be the fair cheeks of the living Lady of Tremaine. And the chin, with its dimples, as in health, might it not be hers? — but *had she then grown taller since her malady?* What inexpressible madness seized me with that thought? One bound, and I had reached her feet! Shrinking from my touch, she let fall from her head, unloosened, the ghastly cerements which had confined it, and there streamed forth into the rushing atmosphere of the chamber huge masses of long and dishevelled hair; *it was blacker than the raven wings of the midnight!* And now slowly opened *the eyes* of the figure which stood before me. "Here then, at least," I shrieked aloud, "can I never — can I never be mistaken — these are the full, and the black, and the wild eyes — of my lost love — of the Lady — of the Lady Ligeia."

How to Write a Blackwood Article

"In the name of the prophets — figs!!"

Cry of Turkish fig-peddler.

I PRESUME everybody has heard of me. My name is the Signora Psyche Zenobia. This I know to be a fact. Nobody but my enemies ever calls me Suky Snobbs. I have been assured that Suky is but a vulgar corruption of Psyche, which is good Greek, and means "the soul " (that's me, I'm *all* soul) and sometimes "a butterfly," which latter meaning undoubtedly alludes to my appearance in my new crimson satin dress, with the sky-blue Arabian *mantelet*, and the trimmings of green *agraffas*, and the seven flounces of orange-colored *auriculas*. As for Snobbs — any person who should look at me would be instantly aware that my name wasn't Snobbs. Miss Tabitha Turnip propagated that report through sheer envy. Tabitha Turnip indeed! Oh the little wretch! But what can we expect from a turnip? Wonder if she remembers the old adage about "blood out of a turnip," &c.? [Mem. put her in mind of it the first opportunity.] [Mem. again — pull her nose.] Where was I? Ah! I have been assured that Snobbs is a mere corruption of Zenobia, and that Zenobia was a queen — (So am I. Dr. Moneypenny always calls me the Queen of the Hearts) — and that Zenobia, as well as Psyche, is good Greek, and that my father was "a Greek," and that consequently I have a right to our patronymic, which is Zenobia and not by any means Snobbs. Nobody but Tabitha Turnip calls me Suky Snobbs. I am the Signora Psyche Zenobia.

As I said before, everybody has heard of me. I am that very Signora Psyche Zenobia, so justly celebrated as corresponding secretary to the "*Philadelphia, Regular, Exchange, Tea, Total, Young, Belles, Lettres, Universal, Experimental, Bibliographical, Association, To, Civilize, Humanity.*" Dr. Moneypenny made the title for us, and says he chose it because it sounded big like an empty rum-puncheon. (A vulgar man that sometimes — but he's deep.) We all sign the initials of the society after our names, in the fashion of the R. S. A., Royal Society of Arts — the S. D. U. K., Society for the Diffusion of Useful Knowledge, &c., &c. Dr. Moneypenny says that S. stands for *stale*, and that D. U. K. spells duck, (but it don't,) that S. D. U. K. stands for Stale Duck and not for Lord Brougham's society — but then Dr. Moneypenny is such a queer man that I am never sure when he is telling me the truth. At any rate we always add to our names the initials P. R. E. T. T. Y. B. L. U. E. B. A. T. C. H. — that is to say, Philadelphia, Regular, Exchange, Tea, Total, Young, Belles, Lettres, Universal, Experimental, Bibliographical, Asso-

ciation, To, Civilize, Humanity — one letter for each word, which is a decided improvement upon Lord Brougham. Dr. Moneypenny will have it that our initials give our true character — but for my life I can't see what he means.

Notwithstanding the good offices of the Doctor, and the strenuous exertions of the association to get itself into notice, it met with no very great success until I joined it. The truth is, the members indulged in too flippant a tone of discussion. The papers read every Saturday evening were characterized less by depth than buffoonery. They were all whipped syllabub. There was no investigation of first causes, first principles. There was no investigation of any thing at all. There was no attention paid to that great point, the "fitness of things." In short there was no fine writing like this. It was all low — very! No profundity, no reading, no metaphysics — nothing which the learned call spirituality, and which the unlearned choose to stigmatize as cant. [Dr. M. says I ought to spell "cant" with a capital K — but I know better.]

When I joined the society it was my endeavor to introduce a better style of thinking and writing, and all the world knows how well I have succeeded. We get up as good papers now in the P. R. E. T. T. Y. B. L. U. E. B. A. T. C. H. as any to be found even in Blackwood. I say, Blackwood, because I have been assured that the finest writing, upon every subject, is to be discovered in the pages of that justly celebrated Magazine. We now take it for our model upon all themes, and are getting into rapid notice accordingly. And, after all, it's not so very difficult a matter to compose an article of the genuine Blackwood stamp, if one only goes properly about it. Of course I don't speak of the political articles. Everybody knows how *they* are managed, since Dr. Moneypenny explained it. Mr. Blackwood has a pair of tailor's-shears, and three apprentices who stand by him for orders. One hands him the "Times," another the "Examiner" and a third a "Gulley's New Compendium of Slang-Whang." Mr. B. merely cuts out and intersperses. It is soon done — nothing but "Examiner," "Slang-Whang," and "Times" — then "Times," "Slang-Whang," and "Examiner" — and then "Times," "Examiner," and "Slang-Whang."

But the chief merit of the Magazine lies in its miscellaneous articles; and the best of these come under the head of what Dr. Moneypenny calls the *bizarreries* (whatever that may mean) and what everybody else calls the *intensities*. This is a species of writing which I have long known how to appreciate, although it is only since my late visit to Mr. Blackwood (deputed by the society) that I have been made aware of the exact method of composition. This method is very simple, but not so much so as the politics. Upon my calling at Mr. B.'s, and making known to him the wishes of the society, he received me with great civility, took me into his study, and gave me a clear explanation of the whole process.

"My dear madam," said he, evidently struck with my majestic ap-

pearance, for I had on the crimson satin, with the green *agraffas*, and orange-colored *auriclas*. "My *dear* madam," said he, "sit down. The matter stands thus: In the first place your writer of intensities must have very black ink, and a very big pen, with a very blunt nib. And, mark me, Miss Psyche Zenobia!" he continued, after a pause, with the most expressive energy and solemnity of manner, "mark me! — *that pen — must — never be mended!* Herein, madam, lies the secret, the soul, of intensity. I assume upon myself to say, that no individual, of however great genius ever wrote with a good pen — understand me, — a good article. You may take it for granted, that when manuscript can be read it is never worth reading. This is a leading principle in our faith, to which if you cannot readily assent, our conference is at an end."

He paused. But, of course, as I had no wish to put an end to the conference, I assented to a proposition so very obvious, and one, too, of whose truth I had all along been sufficiently aware. He seemed pleased, and went on with his instructions.

"It may appear invidious in me, Miss Psyche Zenobia, to refer you to any article, or set of articles, in the way of model or study; yet perhaps I may as well call your attention to a few cases. Let me see. There was 'The Dead Alive,' a capital thing! — the record of a gentleman's sensations when entombed before the breath was out of his body — full of tastes, terror, sentiment, metaphysics, and erudition. You would have sworn that the writer had been born and brought up in a coffin. Then we had the 'Confessions of an Opium-eater' — fine, very fine! — glorious imagination — deep philosophy — acute speculation — plenty of fire and fury, and a good spicing of the decidedly unintelligible. That was a nice bit of flummery, and went down the throats of the people delightfully. They would have it that Coleridge wrote the paper — but not so. It was composed by my pet baboon, Juniper, over a rummer of Hollands and water, 'hot, without sugar.' " [This I could scarcely have believed had it been anybody but Mr. Blackwood, who assured me of it.] "Then there was 'The Involuntary Experimentalist,' all about a gentleman who got baked in an oven, and came out alive and well, although certainly done to a turn. And then there was 'The Diary of a Late Physician,' where the merit lay in good rant, and indifferent Greek — both of them taking things with the public. And then there was 'The Man in the Bell,' a paper by-the-by, Miss Zenobia, which I cannot sufficiently recommend to your attention. It is the history of a young person who goes to sleep under the clapper of a church bell, and is awakened by its tolling for a funeral. The sound drives him mad, and, accordingly, pulling out his tablets, he gives a record of his sensations. Sensations are the great things after all. Should you ever be drowned or hung, be sure and make a note of your sensations — they will be worth to you ten guineas a sheet. If you wish to write forcibly, Miss Zenobia, pay minute attention to the sensations."

"That I certainly will, Mr. Blackwood," said I.

"Good!" he replied. "I see you are a pupil after my own heart. But I must put you *au fait* to the details necessary in composing what may be denominated a genuine Blackwood article of the sensation stamp — the kind which you will understand me to say I consider the best for all purposes.

"The first thing requisite is to get yourself into such a scrape as no one ever got into before. The oven, for instance, — that was a good hit. But if you have no oven or big bell, at hand, and if you cannot conveniently tumble out of a balloon, or be swallowed up in an earthquake, or get stuck fast in a chimney, you will have to be contented with simply imagining some similar misadventure. I should prefer, however, that you have the actual fact to bear you out. Nothing so well assists the fancy, as an experimental knowledge of the matter in hand. 'Truth is strange,' you know, 'stranger than fiction' — besides being more to the purpose."

Here I assured him I had an excellent pair of garters, and would go and hang myself forthwith.

"Good!" he replied, "do so; — although hanging is somewhat hacknied. Perhaps you might do better. Take a dose of Brandreth's pills, and then give us your sensations. However, my instructions will apply equally well to any variety of misadventure, and in your way home you may easily get knocked in the head, or run over by an omnibus, or bitten by a mad dog, or drowned in a gutter. But to proceed.

"Having determined upon your subject, you must next consider the tone, or manner, of your narration. There is the tone didactic, the tone enthusiastic, the tone natural — all common-place enough. But then there is the tone laconic, or curt, which has lately come much into use. It consists in short sentences. Somehow thus: Can't be too brief. Can't be too snappish. Always a full stop. And never a paragraph.

"Then there is the tone elevated, diffusive, and interjectional. Some of our best novelists patronize this tone. The words must be all in a whirl, like a humming-top, and make a noise very similar, which answers remarkably well instead of meaning. This is the best of all possible styles where the writer is in too great a hurry to think.

"The tone metaphysical is also a good one. If you know any big words this is your chance for them. Talk of the Ionic and Eleatic schools — of Archytas, Gorgias, and Alcmæon. Say something about objectivity and subjectivity. Be sure and abuse a man named Locke. Turn up your nose at things in general, and when you let slip any thing a little *too* absurd, you need not be at the trouble of scratching it out, but just add a foot-note and say that you are indebted for the above profound observation to the '*Kritik der reinem Vernunft*,' or to the '*Metaphysithe Anfongsgrunde der Noturwissenchaft*.' This would look erudite and — and — and frank.

"There are various other tones of equal celebrity, but I shall mention only two more — the tone transcendental and the tone heterogeneous.

In the former the merit consists in seeing into the nature of affairs a very great deal farther than anybody else. This second sight is very efficient when properly managed. A little reading of the 'Dial' will carry you a great way. Eschew, in this case, big words; get them as small as possible, and write them upside down. Look over Channing's poems and quote what he says about a 'fat little man with a delusive show of Can.' Put in something about the Supernal Oneness. Don't say a syllable about the Infernal Twoness. Above all, study innuendo. Hint everything — assert nothing, If you feel inclined to say 'bread and butter,' do not by any means say it outright. You may say any thing and every thing *approaching* to 'bread and butter.' You may hint at buck-wheat cake, or you may even go so far as to insinuate oat-meal porridge, but if bread and butter be your real meaning, be cautious, my *dear* Miss Psyche, not on any account to say 'bread and butter!' "

I assured him that I should never say it again as long as I lived. He kissed me and continued:

"As for the tone heterogeneous, it is merely a judicious mixture, in equal proportions, of all the other tones in the world, and is consequently made up of every thing deep, great, odd, piquant, pertinent, and pretty.

"Let us suppose now you have determined upon your incidents and tone. The most important portion — in fact, the soul of the whole business, is yet to be attended to — I allude to *the filling up*. It is not to be supposed that a lady, or gentleman either, has been leading the life of a book worm. And yet above all things it is necessary that your article have an air of erudition, or at least afford evidence of extensive general reading. Now I'll put you in the way of accomplishing this point. See here!" (pulling down some three or four ordinary-looking volumes, and opening them at random). "By casting your eye down almost any page of any book in the world, you will be able to perceive at once a host of little scraps of either learning or *bel-espritism*, which are the very thing for the spicing of a Blackwood article. You might as well note down a few while I read them to you. I shall make two divisions: first, *Piquant Facts for the Manufacture of Similes*; and, second, *Piquant Expressions to be introduced as occasion may require*. Write now!" — and I wrote as he dictated.

"PIQUANT FACTS FOR SIMILES. 'There were originally but three Muses — Melete, Mneme, Aœde — meditation, memory, and singing.' You may make a good deal of that little fact if properly worked. You see it is not generally known, and looks *recherche*. You must be careful and give the thing with a downright improviso air.

"Again. 'The river Alpheus passed beneath the sea, and emerged without injury to the purity of its waters.' Rather stale that, to be sure, but, if properly dressed and dished up, will look quite as fresh as ever.

"Here is something better. 'The Persian Iris appears to some persons to possess a sweet and very powerful perfume, while to others it is per-

fectly scentless.' Fine that, and very delicate! Turn it about a little, and it will do wonders. We'll have some thing else in the botanical line. There's nothing goes down so well, especially with the help of a little Latin. Write!

" 'The *Epidendrum Flos Aeris*, of Java, bears a very beautiful flower, and will live when pulled up by the roots. The natives suspend it by a cord from the ceiling, and enjoy its fragrance for years.' That's capital! That will do for the similes. Now for the Piquant Expressions.

"PIQUANT EXPRESSIONS. '*The Venerable Chinese novel Ju-Kiao-Li.*' Good! By introducing these few words with dexterity you will evince your intimate acquaintance with the language and literature of the Chinese. With the aid of this you may possibly get along without either Arabic, or Sanscrit, or Chickasaw. There is no passing muster, however, without Spanish, Italian, German, Latin, and Greek. I must look you out a little specimen of each. Any scrap will answer, because you must depend upon your own ingenuity to make it fit into your article. Now write!

" '*Aussi tendre que Zaire*' — as tender as Zaire — French. Alludes to the frequent repetition of the phrase, *la tendre Zaire*, in the French tragedy of that name. Properly introduced, will show not only your knowledge of the language, but your general reading and wit. You can say, for instance, that the chicken you were eating (write an article about being choked to death by a chicken-bone) was not altogether *aussi tendre que Zaire*. Write!

> '*Van muerte tan escondida,*
> *Que no te sienta venir,*
> *Porque el plazer del morir,*
> *No mestorne a dar la vida.*'

"That's Spanish — from Miguel de Cervantes. 'Come quickly, O death! but be sure and don't let me see you coming, lest the pleasure I shall feel at your appearance should unfortunately bring me back again to life.' This you may slip in quite *a propos* when you are struggling in the last agonies with the chicken-bone. Write!

> '*Il pover 'huomo che non se'n era accorto,*
> *Andava combattendo, e era morto.*'

That's Italian, you perceive — from Ariosto. It means that a great hero, in the heat of combat, not perceiving that he had been fairly killed, continued to fight valiantly, dead as he was. The application of this to your own case is obvious — for I trust, Miss Psyche, that you will not neglect to kick for at least an hour and a half after you have been choked to death by that chicken-bone. Please to write!

> '*Und sterb'ich doch, no sterb'ich denn*
> *Durch sie — durch sie!*'

That's German — from Schiller. 'And if I die, at least I die — for thee — for thee!' Here it is clear that you are apostrophizing the *cause* of your disaster, the chicken. Indeed what gentleman (or lady either) of sense, *wouldn't* die, I should like to know, for a well fattened capon of the right Molucca breed, stuffed with capers and mushrooms, and served up in a salad-bowl, with orange-jellies *en mosaiques*. Write! (You can get them that way at Tortoni's) — Write, if you please!

"Here is a nice little Latin phrase, and rare too, (one can't be too *recherche* or brief in one's Latin, it's getting so common — *ignoratio elenchi*. He has committed an *ignoratio elenchi* — that is to say, he has understood the words of your proposition, but not the idea. The man was *a fool*, you see. Some poor fellow whom you address while choking with that chicken-bone, and who therefore didn't precisely understand what you were talking about. Throw the *ignoratio elenchi* in his teeth, and, at once, you have him annihilated. If he dares to reply, you can tell him from Lucan (here it is) that speeches are mere *anemonæ verborum*, anemone words. The anemone, with great brilliancy, has no smell. Or, if he begins to bluster, you may be down upon him with *insomnia Jovis*, reveries of Jupiter — a phrase which Silius Italicus (see here!) applies to thoughts pompous and inflated. This will be sure and cut him to the heart. He can do nothing but roll over and die. Will you be kind enough to write?

"In Greek we must have some thing pretty — from Demosthenes, for example.

Ανηρ ο φευγοεν και παλιν μακησεται

There is a tolerably good translation of it in Hudibras —

'For he that flies may fight again,
Which he can never do that's slain.'

In a Blackwood article nothing makes so fine a show as your Greek. The very letters have an air of profundity about them. Only observe, madam, the astute look of that Epsilon! That Phi ought certainly to be a bishop! Was ever there a smarter fellow than that Omicron? Just twig that Tau! In short, there is nothing like Greek for a genuine sensation-paper. In the present case your application is the most obvious thing in the world. Rap out the sentence, with a huge oath, and by way of *ultimatum* at the good-for-nothing dunder-headed villain who couldn't understand your plain English in relation to the chicken-bone. He'll take the hint and be off, you may depend upon it."

These were all the instructions Mr. B. could afford me upon the topic in question, but I felt they would be entirely sufficient. I was, at length, able to write a genuine Blackwood article, and determined to do it forthwith. In taking leave of me, Mr. B. made a proposition for the purchase of the paper when written; but as he could offer me only fifty guineas

a sheet, I thought it better to let our society have it, than sacrifice it for so paltry a sum. Notwithstanding this niggardly spirit, however, the gentleman showed his consideration for me in all other respects, and indeed treated me with the greatest civility. His parting words made a deep impression upon my heart, and I hope I shall always remember them with gratitude.

"My dear Miss Zenobia," he said, while the tears stood in his eyes, "is there *anything* else I can do to promote the success of your laudable undertaking? Let me reflect! It is just possible that you may not be able, so soon as convenient, to — to — get yourself drowned, or — choked with a chicken-bone, or — or hung, — or — bitten by a — but stay! Now I think me of it, there are a couple of very excellent bull-dogs in the yard — fine fellows, I assure you — savage, and all that — indeed just the thing for your money — they'll have you eaten up, *auriculas* and all, in less than five minutes (here's my watch!) — and then only think of the sensations! Here! I say — Tom! — Peter! — Dick, you villain! — let out those" — but as I was really in a great hurry, and had not another moment to spare, I was reluctantly forced to expedite my departure, and accordingly took leave *at once* — somewhat more abruptly, I admit, than strict courtesy would have otherwise allowed.

It was my primary object upon quitting Mr. Blackwood, to get into some immediate difficulty, pursuant to his advice, and with this view I spent the greater part of the day in wandering about Edinburgh, seeking for desperate adventures — adventures adequate to the intensity of my feelings, and adapted to the vast character of the article I intended to write. In this excursion I was attended by one negro-servant, Pompey, and my little lap-dog Diana, whom I had brought with me from Philadelphia. It was not, however, until late in the afternoon that I fully succeeded in my arduous undertaking. An important event then happened of which the following Blackwood article, in the tone heterogeneous, is the substance and result.

A Predicament

What chance, good lady, hath bereft you thus?

COMUS.

I T was a quiet and still afternoon when I strolled forth in the goodly city of Edina. The confusion and bustle in the streets were terrible Men were talking. Women were screaming. Children were choking. Pigs were whistling. Carts they rattled. Bulls they bellowed. Cows they lowed.

Horses they neighed. Cats they caterwauled. Dogs they danced. *Danced!*
Could it then be possible? *Danced!* Alas, thought I, *my* dancing days are
over! Thus it is ever. What a host of gloomy recollections will ever and
anon be awakened in the mind of genius and imaginative contemplation,
especially of a genius doomed to the everlasting, and eternal, and con-
tinual, and, as one might say, the — *continued* — yes, the *continued and
continuous*, bitter, harassing, disturbing, and, if I may be allowed the
expression, the *very* disturbing influence of the serene, and godlike, and
heavenly, and exalted, and elevated, and purifying effect of what may
be rightly termed the most enviable, the most *truly* enviable — nay! the
most benignly beautiful, the most deliciously ethereal, and, as it were,
the most *pretty* (if I may use so bold an expression) *thing* (pardon me,
gentle reader!) in the world — but I am always led away by my feelings.
In *such* a mind, I repeat, what a host of recollections are stirred up by a
trifle! The dogs danced! *I* — I *could* not! They frisked — I wept. They
capered — I sobbed aloud. Touching circumstances! which cannot fail
to bring to the recollection of the classical reader that exquisite passage
in relation to the fitness of things, which is to be found in the commence-
ment of the third volume of that admirable and venerable Chinese novel
the *Jo-Go-Slow*.

In my solitary walk through the city I had two humble but faithful
companions. Diana, my poodle! sweetest of creatures! She had a quantity
of hair over her one eye, and a blue ribband tied fashionably around her
neck. Diana was not more than five inches in height, but her head was
somewhat bigger than her body, and her tail being cut off exceedingly
close, gave an air of injured innocence to the interesting animal which
rendered her a favorite with all.

And Pompey, my negro! — sweet Pompey! how shall I ever forget
thee? I had taken Pompey's arm. He was three feet in height (I like to
be particular) and about seventy, or perhaps eighty, years of age. He had
bow-legs and was corpulent. His mouth should not be called small, nor
his ears short. His teeth, however, were like pearl, and his large full eyes
were deliciously white. Nature had endowed him with no neck, and had
placed his ankles (as usual with that race) in the middle of the upper
portion of the feet. He was clad with a striking simplicity. His sole gar-
ments were a stock of nine inches in height, and a nearly-new drab over-
coat which had formerly been in the service of the tall, stately, and
illustrious Dr. Moneypenny. It was a good overcoat. It was well cut. It
was well made. The coat was nearly new. Pompey held it up out of the
dirt with both hands.

There were three persons in our party, and two of them have already
been the subject of remark. There was a third — that person was myself.
I am the Signora Psyche Zenobia. I am *not* Suky Snobbs. My appearance
is commanding. On the memorable occasion of which I speak I was

habited in a crimson satin dress, with a sky-blue Arabian mantelet. And the dress had trimmings of green agraffas, and seven graceful flounces of the orange-colored auricula. I thus formed the third of the party. There was the poodle. There was Pompey. There was myself. We were *three.* Thus it is said there were originally but three Furies — Melty, Nimmy, and Hetty — Meditation, Memory, and Fiddling.

Leaning upon the arm of the gallant Pompey, and attended at a respectable distance by Diana, I proceeded down one of the populous and very pleasant streets of the now deserted Edina. On a sudden, there presented itself to view a church — a Gothic cathedral — vast, venerable, and with a tall steeple, which towered into the sky. What madness now possessed me? Why did I rush upon my fate? I was seized with an uncontrollable desire to ascend the giddy pinnacle, and then survey the immense extent of the city. The door of the cathedral stood invitingly open. My destiny prevailed. I entered the ominous archway. Where then was my guardian angel? — if indeed such angels there be. *If!* Distressing monosyllable! what a world of mystery, and meaning, and doubt, and uncertainty is there involved in thy two letters! I entered the ominous archway! I entered; and, without injury to my orange-colored auriculas, I passed beneath the portal, and emerged within the vestibule. Thus it is said the immense river Alfred passed, unscathed, and unwetted, beneath the sea.

I thought the staircase would never have an end. *Round!* Yes, they went round and up, and round and up and round and up, until I could not help surmising, with the sagacious Pompey, upon whose supporting arm I leaned in all the confidence of early affection — I *could* not help surmising that the upper end of the continuous spiral ladder had been accidentally, or perhaps designedly, removed. I paused for breath; and, in the meantime, an accident occurred of too momentous a nature in a moral, and also in a metaphysical point of view, to be passed over without notice. It appeared to me — indeed I was quite confident of the fact — I could not be mistaken — no! I had, for some moments, carefully and anxiously observed the motions of my Diana — I say that *I could not be* mistaken — Diana *smelt a rat!* At once I called Pompey's attention to the subject, and he — he agreed with me. There was then no longer any reasonable room for doubt. The rat had been smelled — and by Diana. Heavens! shall I ever forget the intense excitement of the moment? Alas! what is the boasted intellect of man? The rat! — it was there — that is to say, it was somewhere. Diana smelled the rat. I — *I could* not! Thus it is said the Prussian Isis has, for some persons, a sweet and very powerful perfume, while to others it is perfectly scentless.

The staircase had been surmounted, and there were now only three or four more upward steps intervening between us and the summit. We still ascended, and now only one step remained. One step! One little, little

step! Upon one such little step in the great staircase of human life how vast a sum of human happiness or misery depends! I thought of myself, then of Pompey, and then of the mysterious and inexplicable destiny which surrounded us. I thought of Pompey! — alas, I thought of love! I thought of my many false *steps* which have been taken, and may be taken again. I resolved to be more cautious, more reserved. I abandoned the arm of Pompey, and, without his assistance, surmounted the one remaining step, and gained the chamber of the belfry. I was followed immediately afterward by my poodle. Pompey alone remained behind. I stood at the head of the staircase, and encouraged him to ascend. He stretched forth to me his hand, and unfortunately in so doing was forced to abandon his firm hold upon the overcoat. Will the gods never cease their persecution? The overcoat is dropped, and, with one of his feet, Pompey stepped upon the long and trailing skirt of the overcoat. He stumbled and fell — this consequence was inevitable. He fell forward, and, with his accursed head, striking me full in the — in the breast, precipitated me headlong, together with himself, upon the hard, filthy, and detestable floor of the belfry. But my revenge was sure, sudden, and complete. Seizing him furiously by the wool with both hands, I tore out a vast quantity of black, and crisp, and curling material, and tossed it from me with every manifestation of disdain. It fell among the ropes of the belfry and remained. Pompey arose, and said no word. But he regarded me piteously with his large eyes and — sighed. Ye Gods — that sigh! It sunk into my heart. And the hair — the wool! Could I have reached that wool I would have bathed it with my tears, in testimony of regret. But alas! it was now far beyond my grasp. As it dangled among the cordage of the bell, I fancied it alive. I fancied that it stood on end with indignation. Thus the *happy-dandy Flos Aeris* of Java bears, it is said, a beautiful flower, which will live when pulled up by the roots. The natives suspend it by a cord from the ceiling and enjoy its fragrance for years.

Our quarrel was now made up, and we looked about the room for an aperture through which to survey the city of Edina. Windows there were none. The sole light admitted into the gloomy chamber proceeded from a square opening, about a foot in diameter, at a height of about seven feet from the floor. Yet what will the energy of true genius not effect? I resolved to clamber up to this hole. A vast quantity of wheels, pinions, and other cabalistic-looking machinery stood opposite the hole, close to it; and through the hole there passed an iron rod from the machinery. Between the wheels and the wall where the hole lay there was barely room for my body — yet I was desperate, and determined to persevere. I called Pompey to my side.

"You perceive that aperture, Pompey. I wish to look through it. You will stand here just beneath the hole — so. Now, hold out one of your hands, Pompey, and let me step upon it — thus. Now, the other hand, Pompey, and with its aid I will get upon your shoulders."

He did every thing I wished, and I found, upon getting up, that I could easily pass my head and neck through the aperture. The prospect was sublime. Nothing could be more magnificent. I merely paused a moment to bid Diana behave herself, and assure Pompey that I would be considerate and bear as lightly as possible upon his shoulders. I told him I would be tender of his feelings — *ossi tender que beefsteak*. Having done this justice to my faithful friend, I gave myself up with great zest and enthusiasm to the enjoyment of the scene which so obligingly spread itself out before my eyes.

Upon this subject, however, I shall forbear to dilate. I will not describe the city of Edinburgh. Every one has been to the city of Edinburgh. Every one has been to Edinburgh — the classic Edina. I will confine myself to the momentous details of my own lamentable adventure. Having, in some measure, satisfied my curiosity in regard to the extent, situation, and general appearance of the city, I had leisure to survey the church in which I was, and the delicate architecture of the steeple. I observed that the aperture through which I had thrust my head was an opening in the dial-plate of a gigantic clock, and must have appeared, from the street, as a large key-hole, such as we see in the face of the French watches. No doubt the true object was to admit the arm of an attendant, to adjust, when necessary, the hands of the clock from within. I observed also, with surprise, the immense size of these hands, the longest of which could not have been less than ten feet in length, and, where broadest, eight or nine inches in breadth. They were of solid steel apparently, and their edges appeared to be sharp. Having noticed these particulars, and some others, I again turned my eyes upon the glorious prospect below, and soon became absorbed in contemplation.

From this, after some minutes, I was aroused by the voice of Pompey, who declared that he could stand it no longer, and requested that I would be so kind as to come down. This was unreasonable, and I told him so in a speech of some length. He replied, but with an evident misunderstanding of my ideas upon the subject. I accordingly grew angry, and told him in plain words, that he was a fool, that he had committed an *ignoramus e-clench-eye*, that his notions were mere *insommary Bovis*, and his words little better than *an ennemywerrybor'em*. With this he appeared satisfied, and I resumed my contemplations.

It might have been half an hour after this altercation when, as I was deeply absorbed in the heavenly scenery beneath me, I was startled by something very cold which pressed with a gentle pressure on the back of my neck. It is needless to say that I felt inexpressibly alarmed. I knew that Pompey was beneath my feet, and that Diana was sitting, according to my explicit directions, upon her hind legs, in the farthest corner of the room. What could it be? Alas! I but too soon discovered. Turning my head gently to one side, I perceived, to my extreme horror, that the huge, glittering, scimetar-like minute-hand of the clock had, in the course

of its hourly revolution, *descended upon my neck*. There was, I knew, not a second to be lost. I pulled back at once — but it was too late. There was no chance of forcing my head through the mouth of that terrible trap in which it was so fairly caught, and which grew narrower and narrower with a rapidity too horrible to be conceived. The agony of that moment is not to be imagined. I threw up my hands and endeavored, with all my strength, to force upward the ponderous iron bar. I might as well have tried to lift the cathedral itself. Down, down, down it came, closer and yet closer. I screamed to Pompey for aid; but he said that I had hurt his feelings by calling him "an ignorant old squint-eye." I yelled to Diana; but she only said "bow-wow-wow," and that I had told her "on no account to stir from the corner." Thus I had no relief to expect from my associates.

Meantime the ponderous and terrific *Scythe of Time* (for I now discovered the literal import of that classical phrase) had not stopped, nor was it likely to stop, in its career. Down and still down, it came. It had already buried its sharp edge a full inch in my flesh, and my sensations grew indistinct and confused. At one time I fancied myself in Philadelphia with the stately Dr. Moneypenny, at another in the back parlor of Mr. Blackwood receiving his invaluable instructions. And then again the sweet recollection of better and earlier times came over me, and I thought of that happy period when the world was not all a desert, and Pompey not altogether cruel.

The ticking of the machinery amused me. *Amused me*, I say, for my sensations now bordered upon perfect happiness, and the most trifling circumstances afforded me pleasure. The eternal *click-clak, click-clak, click-clak* of the clock was the most melodious of music in my ears, and occasionally even put me in mind of the graceful sermonic harangues of Dr. Ollapod. Then there were the great figures upon the dial-plate — how intelligent, how intellectual, they all looked! And presently they took to dancing the Mazurka, and I think it was the figure V. who performed the most to my satisfaction. She was evidently a lady of breeding. None of your swaggerers, and nothing at all indelicate in her motions. She did the pirouette to admiration — whirling round upon her apex. I made an endeavor to hand her a chair, for I saw that she appeared fatigued with her exertions — and it was not until then that I fully perceived my lamentable situation. Lamentable indeed! The bar had buried itself two inches in my neck. I was aroused to a sense of exquisite pain. I prayed for death, and, in the agony of the moment, could not help repeating those exquisite verses of the poet Miguel De Cervantes:

> Vanny Buren, tan escondida
> Query no te senty venny
> Pork and pleasure, delly morry
> Nommy, torny, darry, widdy!

But now a new horror presented itself, and one indeed sufficient to startle the strongest nerves. My eyes, from the cruel pressure of the machine, were absolutely starting from their sockets. While I was thinking how I should possibly manage without them, one actually tumbled out of my head, and, rolling down the steep side of the steeple, lodged in the rain gutter which ran along the eaves of the main building. The loss of the eye was not so much as the insolent air of independence and contempt with which it regarded me after it was out. There it lay in the gutter just under my nose, and the airs it gave itself would have been ridiculous had they not been disgusting. Such a winking and blinking were never before seen. This behavior on the part of my eye in the gutter was not only irritating on account of its manifest insolence and shameful ingratitude, but was also exceedingly inconvenient on account of the sympathy which always exists between two eyes of the same head, however far apart. I was forced, in a manner, to wink and to blink, whether I would or not, in exact concert with the scoundrelly thing that lay just under my nose. I was presently relieved, however, by the dropping out of the other eye. In falling it took the same direction (possibly a concerted plot) as its fellow. Both rolled out of the gutter together, and in truth I was very glad to get rid of them.

The bar was now four inches and a half deep in my neck, and there was only a little bit of skin to cut through. My sensations were those of entire happiness, for I felt that in a few minutes, at farthest, I should be relieved from my disagreeable situation. And in this expectation I was not at all deceived. At twenty-five minutes past five in the afternoon, precisely, the huge minute-hand had proceeded sufficiently far on its terrible revolution to sever the small remainder of my neck. I was not sorry to see the head which had occasioned me so much embarrassment at length make a final separation from my body. It first rolled down the side of the steeple, then lodge, for a few seconds, in the gutter, and then made its way, with a plunge, into the middle of the street.

I will candidly confess that my feelings were now of the most singular — nay, of the most mysterious, the most perplexing and incomprehensible character. My senses were here and there at one and the same moment. With my head I imagined, at one time, that I, the head, was the real Signora Psyche Zenobia — at another I felt convinced that myself, the body, was the proper identity. To clear my ideas on this topic I felt in my pocket for my snuff-box, but, upon getting it, and endeavoring to apply a pinch of its grateful contents in the ordinary manner, I became immediately aware of my peculiar deficiency, and threw the box at once down to my head. It took a pinch with great satisfaction, and smiled me an acknowledgement in return. Shortly afterward it made me a speech, which I could hear but indistinctly without ears. I gathered enough, however, to know that it was astonished at my wishing to remain alive

under such circumstances. In the concluding sentences it quoted the
noble words of Ariosto —

> *Il pover hommy che non sera corty*
> *And have a combat tenty erry morty;*

thus comparing me to the hero who, in the heat of the combat, not per-
ceiving that he was dead, continued to contest the battle with inextin-
guishable valor. There was nothing now to prevent my getting down from
my elevation, and I did so. What it was that Pompey saw so *very* peculiar
in my appearance I have never yet been able to find out. The fellow
opened his mouth from ear to ear, and shut his two eyes as if he were
endeavoring to crack nuts between the lids. Finally, throwing off his
overcoat, he made one spring for the staircase and disappeared. I hurled
after the scoundrel these vehement words of Demosthenes —

> *Andrew O'Phlegethon, you really make haste to fly,*

and then turned to the darling of my heart, to the one-eyed! the shaggy-
haired Diana. Alas! what a horrible vision affronted my eyes? *Was* that a
rat I saw skulking into his hole? *Are* these the picked bones of the little
angel who has been cruelly devoured by the monster? Ye gods! and what
do I behold — *is* that the departed spirit, the shade, the ghost, of my
beloved puppy, which I perceive sitting with a grace so melancholy, in
the corner? Hearken! for she speaks, and, heavens! it is in the German of
Schiller —

> "Unt stubby duk, so stubby dun
> Duk she! duk she!"

Alas! and are not her words too true?

> "And if I died, at least I died
> For thee — for thee."

Sweet creature! she *too* has sacrificed herself in my behalf. Dogless, nig-
gerless, headless, what *now* remains for the unhappy Signora Psyche
Zenobia? Alas — *nothing!* I have done.

The Devil in the Belfry

What o'clock is it? Old Saying.

Everybody knows, in a general way, that the finest place in the world
is — or, alas, *was* — the Dutch borough of Vondervotteimittiss. Yet as
it lies some distance from any of the main roads, being in a somewhat

out-of-the-way situation, there are perhaps very few of my readers who have ever paid it a visit. For the benefit of those who have *not*, therefore, it will be only proper that I should enter into some account of it. And this is indeed the more necessary, as with the hope of enlisting public sympathy in behalf of the inhabitants, I design here to give a history of the calamitous events which have so lately occurred within its limits. No one who knows me will doubt that the duty thus self-imposed will be executed to the best of my ability, with all that rigid impartiality, all that cautious examination into facts, and diligent collation of authorities, which should ever distinguish him who aspires to the title of historian.

By the united aid of medals, manuscripts, and inscriptions, I am enabled to say, positively, that the borough of Vondervotteimittiss has existed, from its origin, in precisely the same condition which it at present preserves. Of the date of this origin, however, I grieve that I can only speak with that species of indefinite definiteness which mathematicians are, at times, forced to put up with in certain algebraic formulæ. The date, I may thus say, in regard to the remoteness of its antiquity, cannot be less than any assignable quantity whatsoever.

Touching the derivation of the name Vondervotteimittiss, I confess myself, with sorrow, equally at fault. Among a multitude of opinions upon this delicate point — some acute, some learned, some sufficiently the reverse — I am able to select nothing which ought to be considered satisfactory. Perhaps the idea of Grogswigg — nearly coincident with that of Kroutaplenttey — is to be cautiously preferred. — It runs: — *Vondervotteimittis — Vonder, lege Donder — Votteimittis, quasi und Bleitziz — Bleitziz obsol: pro Blitzen."* This derivative, to say the truth, is still countenanced by some traces of the electric fluid evident on the summit of the steeple of the House of the Town-Council. I do not choose, however, to commit myself on a theme of such importance, and must refer the reader desirous of information to the *"Oratiunculæ de Rebus Præter-Veteris,"* of Dundergutz. See, also, Blunderbuzzard *"De Derivationibus,"* pp. 27 to 5010, Folio, Gothic edit., Red and Black character, Catch-word and No Cypher; wherein consult, also, marginal notes in the autograph of Stuffundpuff, with the Sub-Commentaries of Gruntundguzzell.

Notwithstanding the obscurity which thus envelops the date of the foundation of Vondervotteimittis, and the derivation of its name, there can be no doubt, as I said before, that it has always existed as we find it at this epoch. The oldest man in the borough can remember not the slightest difference in the appearance of any portion of it; and, indeed, the very suggestion of such a possibility is considered an insult. The site of the village is in a perfectly circular valley, about a quarter of a mile in circumference, and entirely surrounded by gentle hills, over whose summit the people have never yet ventured to pass. For this they assign the very good reason that they do not believe there is anything at all on the other side.

Round the skirts of the valley (which is quite level, and paved throughout with flat tiles), extends a continuous row of sixty little houses. These, having their backs on the hills, must look, of course, to the centre of the plain, which is just sixty yards from the front door of each dwelling. Every house has a small garden before it, with a circular path, a sun-dial, and twenty-four cabbages. The buildings themselves are so precisely alike, that one can in no manner be distinguished from the other. Owing to the vast antiquity, the style of architecture is somewhat odd, but it is not for that reason the less strikingly picturesque. They are fashioned of hard-burned little bricks, red, with black ends, so that the walls look like a chess-board upon a great scale. The gables are turned to the front, and there are cornices, as big as all the rest of the house, over the eaves and over the main doors. The windows are narrow and deep, with very tiny panes and a great deal of sash. On the roof is a vast quantity of tiles with long curly ears. The woodwork, throughout, is of a dark hue and there is much carving about it, with but a trifling variety of pattern for, time out of mind, the carvers of Vondervotteimittiss have never been able to carve more than two objects — a time-piece and a cabbage. But these they do exceedingly well, and intersperse them, with singular ingenuity, wherever they find room for the chisel.

The dwellings are as much alike inside as out, and the furniture is all upon one plan. The floors are of square tiles, the chairs and tables of black-looking wood with thin crooked legs and puppy feet. The mantel-pieces are wide and high, and have not only time-pieces and cabbages sculptured over the front, but a real time-piece, which makes a prodigious ticking, on the top in the middle, with a flower-pot containing a cabbage standing on each extremity by way of outrider. Between each cabbage and the time-piece, again, is a little China man having a large stomach with a great round hole in it, through which is seen the dial-plate of a watch.

The fireplaces are large and deep, with fierce crooked-looking fire-dogs. There is constantly a rousing fire, and a huge pot over it, full of sauer-kraut and pork, to which the good woman of the house is always busy in attending. She is a little fat old lady, with blue eyes and a red face, and wears a huge cap like a sugar-loaf, ornamented with purple and yellow ribbons. Her dress is of orange-colored linsey-woolsey, made very full behind and very short in the waist — and indeed very short in other respects, not reaching below the middle of her leg. This is somewhat thick, and so are her ankles, but she has a fine pair of green stockings to cover them. Her shoes — of pink leather — are fastened each with a bunch of yellow ribbons puckered up in the shape of a cabbage. In her left hand she has a little heavy Dutch watch; in her right she wields a ladle for the sauer-kraut and pork. By her side there stands a fat tabby cat, with a gilt toy-repeater tied to its tail, which "the boys" have there fastened by way of a quiz.

The boys themselves are, all three of them, in the garden attending the pig. They are each two feet in height. They have three-cornered cocked hats, purple waistcoats reaching down to their thighs, buckskin knee-breeches, red woollen stockings, heavy shoes with big silver buckles, and long surtout coats with large buttons of mother-of-pearl. Each, too, has a pipe in his mouth, and a little dumpy watch in his right hand. He takes a puff and a look, and then a look and a puff. The pig — which is corpulent and lazy — is occupied now in picking up the stray leaves that fall from the cabbages, and now in giving a kick behind at the gilt repeater, which the urchins have also tied to his tail, in order to make him look as handsome as the cat.

Right at the front door, in a high-backed leather-bottomed armed chair, with crooked legs and puppy feet like the tables, is seated the old man of the house himself. He is an exceedingly puffy little old gentleman, with big circular eyes and a huge double chin. His dress resembles that of the boys — and I need say nothing farther about it. All the difference is, that his pipe is somewhat bigger than theirs, and he can make a greater smoke. Like them, he has a watch, but he carries his watch in his pocket. To say the truth, he has something of more importance than a watch to attend to — and what that is, I shall presently explain. He sits with his right leg upon his left knee, wears a grave countenance, and always keeps one of his eyes, at least, resolutely bent upon a certain remarkable object in the centre of the plain.

This object is situated in the steeple of the House of the Town Council. The Town Council are all very little, round, oily, intelligent men, with big saucer eyes and fat double chins, and have their coats much longer and their shoe-buckles much bigger than the ordinary inhabitants of Vondervotteimittiss. Since my sojourn in the borough, they have had several special meetings, and have adopted these three important resolutions:

"That it is wrong to alter the good old course of things:"

"That there is nothing tolerable out of Vondervotteimittiss:" and —

"That we will stick by our clocks and our cabbages."

Above the session-room of the Council is the steeple, and in the steeple is the belfry, where exists, and has existed time out of mind, the pride and wonder of the village — the great clock of the borough of Vondervotteimittiss. And this is the object to which the eyes of the old gentlemen are turned who sit in the leather-bottomed arm-chairs.

The great clock has seven faces — one in each of the seven sides of the steeple — so that it can be readily seen from all quarters. Its faces are large and white, and its hands heavy and black. There is a belfry-man whose sole duty is to attend to it; but this duty is the most perfect of sinecures — for the clock of Vondervotteimittis was never yet known to have anything the matter with it. Until lately, the bare supposition of such a thing was considered heretical. From the remotest period of an-

tiquity to which the archives have reference, the hours have been regularly struck by the big bell. And, indeed the case was just the same with all the other clocks and watches in the borough. Never was such a place for keeping the true time. When the large clapper thought proper to say "Twelve o'clock!" all its obedient followers opened their throats simultaneously, and responded like a very echo. In short, the good burghers were fond of their sauer-kraut, but then they were proud of their clocks.

All people who hold sinecure offices are held in more or less respect, and as the belfry-man of Vondervotteimittiss has the most perfect of sinecures, he is the most perfectly respected of any man in the world. He is the chief dignitary of the borough, and the very pigs look up to him with a sentiment of reverence. His coat-tail is *very* far longer — his pipe, his shoe-buckles, his eyes, and his stomach, *very* far bigger — than those of any other old gentleman in the village; and as to his chin, it is not only double, but triple.

I have thus painted the happy estate of Vondervotteimittiss: alas, that so fair a picture should ever experience a reverse!

There has been long a saying among the wisest inhabitants, that "no good can come from over the hills"; and it really seemed that the words had in them something of the spirit of prophecy. It wanted five minutes of noon, on the day before yesterday, when there appeared a very odd-looking object on the summit of the ridge of the eastward. Such an occurrence, of course, attracted universal attention, and every little old gentleman who sat in a leather-bottomed arm-chair turned one of his eyes with a stare of dismay upon the phenomenon, still keeping the other upon the clock in the steeple.

By the time that it wanted only three minutes to noon, the droll object in question was perceived to be a very diminutive foreign-looking young man. He descended the hills at a great rate, so that every body had soon a good look at him. He was really the most finicky little personage that had ever been seen in Vondervotteimittiss. His countenance was of a dark snuff-color, and he had a long hooked nose, pea eyes, a wide mouth, and an excellent set of teeth, which latter he seemed anxious of displaying, as he was grinning from ear to ear. What with mustachios and whiskers, there was none of the rest of his face to be seen. His head was uncovered, and his hair neatly done up in *papillotes*. His dress was a tight-fitting swallow-tailed black coat (from one of whose pockets dangled a vast length of white handkerchief), black kerseymere knee-breeches, black stockings, and stumpy-looking pumps, with huge bunches of black satin ribbon for bows. Under one arm he carried a huge *chapeau-de-bras*, and under the other a fiddle nearly five times as big as himself. In his left hand was a gold snuff-box, from which, as he capered down the hill, cutting all manner of fantastic steps, he took snuff incessantly with an air of the greatest possible self-satisfaction. God bless me! — here was a sight for the honest burghers of Vondervotteimittiss!

To speak plainly, the fellow had, in spite of his grinning, an audacious and sinister kind of face; and as he curvetted right into the village, the old stumpy appearance of his pumps excited no little suspicion; and many a burgher who beheld him that day would have given a trifle for a peep beneath the white cambric handkerchief which hung so obtrusively from the pocket of his swallow-tailed coat. But what mainly occasioned a righteous indignation was, that the scoundrelly popinjay, while he cut a fandango here, and a whirligig there, did not seem to have the remotest idea in the world of such a thing as *keeping time* in his steps.

The good people of the borough had scarcely a chance, however, to get their eyes thoroughly open, when, just as it wanted half a minute of noon, the rascal bounced, as I say, right into the midst of them; gave a *chassez* here, and a *balancez* there; and then, after a *pirouette* and a *pas-de-zephyr*, pigeon-winged himself right up into the belfry of the House of the Town Council, where the wonder-stricken belfry-man sat smoking in a state of dignity and dismay. But the little chap seized him at once by the nose; gave it a swing and a pull; clapped the big *chapeau-de-bras* upon his head; knocked it down over his eyes and mouth; and then, lifting up the big fiddle, beat him with it so long and so soundly, that what with the belfry-man being so fat, and the fiddle being so hollow, you would have sworn that there was a regiment of double-bass drummers all beating the devil's tattoo up in the belfry of the steeple of Vondervotteimittiss.

There is no knowing to what desperate act of vengeance this unprincipled attack might have aroused the inhabitants, but for the important fact that it now wanted only half a second of noon. The bell was about to strike, and it was a matter of absolute and pre-eminent necessity that every body should look well at his watch. It was evident, however, that just at this moment the fellow in the steeple was doing something that he had no business to do with the clock. But as it now began to strike, nobody had any time to attend to his manœuvres, for they had all to count the strokes of the bell as it sounded.

"One!" said the clock.

"Von!" echoed every little old gentleman in every leather-bottomed arm-chair in Vondervotteimittiss. "Von!" said his watch also; "von!" said the watch of his vrow; and "von!" said the watches of the boys, and the little gilt repeaters on the tails of the cat and pig.

"Two!" continued the big bell; and

"Doo!" repeated all the repeaters.

"Three! Four! Five! Six! Seven! Eight! Nine! Ten!" said the bell.

"Dree! Vour! Fibe! Sax! Seben! Aight! Noin! Den!" answered the others.

"Eleven!" said the big one.

"Eleben!" assented the little ones.

"Twelve!" said the bell.

"Dvelf!" they replied perfectly satisfied, and dropping their voices.

"Und dvelf it is!" said all the little old gentlemen, putting up their watches. But the big bell had not done with them yet.

"*Thirteen!*" said he.

"Der Teufel!" gasped the little old gentlemen, turning pale, dropping their pipes, and putting down all their right legs from over their left knees.

"Der Teufel!" groaned they, "Dirteen! Dirteen!! — Mein Gott, it is Dirteen o'clock!!"

Why attempt to describe the terrible scene which ensued? All Vondervotteimittiss flew at once into a lamentable state of uproar.

"Vot is cum'd to mein pelly?" roared all the boys — "I've been ongry for dis hour!"

"Vot is com'd to mein kraut?" screamed all the vrows, "It has been done to rags for this hour!"

"Vot is cum'd to mein pipe?" swore all the little old gentlemen, "Donder and Blitzen; it has been smoked out for dis hour!" — and they filled them up again in a great rage, and sinking back in their arm-chairs, puffed away so fast and so fiercely that the whole valley was immediately filled with impenetrable smoke.

Meantime the cabbages all turned very red in the face, and it seemed as if old Nick himself had taken possession of every thing in the shape of a time-piece. The clocks carved upon the furniture took to dancing as if bewitched, while those upon the mantel-pieces could scarcely contain themselves for fury, and kept such a continual striking of thirteen, and such a frisking and wriggling of their pendulums as was really horrible to see. But, worse than all, neither the cats nor the pigs could put up any longer with the behavior of the little repeaters tied to their tails, and resented it by scampering all over the place, scratching and poking, and squeaking and screeching, and caterwauling and squalling, and flying into the faces, and running under the petticoats of the people, and creating altogether the most abominable din and confusion which it is possible for a reasonable person to conceive. And to make matters still more distressing, the rascally little scape-grace in the steeple was evidently exerting himself to the utmost. Every now and then one might catch a glimpse of the scoundrel through the smoke. There he sat in the belfry upon the belfry-man, who was lying flat upon his back. In his teeth the villain held the bell-rope, which he kept jerking about with his head, raising such a clatter that my ears ring again even to think of it. On his lap lay the big fiddle, at which he was scraping, out of all time and tune, with both hands, making a great show, the nincompoop! of playing "Judy O'Flannagan and Paddy O'Rafferty."

Affairs being thus miserably situated, I left the place in disgust, and now appeal for aid to all lovers of correct time and fine kraut. Let us proceed in a body to the borough, and restore the ancient order of things in Vondervotteimittiss by ejecting that little fellow from the steeple.

The Man That Was Used Up

A TALE

OF THE LATE BUGABOO AND KICKAPOO CAMPAIGN

Pleurez, pleurez, mes yeux, et fondez vous en eau!
La moitie de ma vie a mis l'autre au tombeau.

CORNEILLE.

I CANNOT just now remember when or where I first made the acquaintance of that truly fine-looking fellow, Brevet Brigadier General John A. B. C. Smith. Some one *did* introduce me to the gentleman, I am sure — at some public meeting, I know very well — held about something of great importance, no doubt — at some place or other, I feel convinced, — whose name I have unaccountably forgotten. The truth is — that the introduction was attended, upon my part, with a degree of anxious embarrassment which operated to prevent any definite impressions of either time or place. I am constitutionally nervous — this, with me, is a family failing, and I can't help it. In especial, the slightest appearance of mystery — of any point I cannot exactly comprehend — puts me at once into a pitiable state of agitation.

There was something, as it were, remarkable — yes, *remarkable*, although this is but a feeble term to express my full meaning — about the entire individuality of the personage in question. He was, perhaps, six feet in height, and of a presence singularly commanding. There was an *air distingue* pervading the whole man, which spoke of high breeding, and hinted at high birth. Upon this topic — the topic of Smith's personal appearance — I have a kind of melancholy satisfaction in being minute. His head of hair would have done honor to a Brutus; — nothing could be more richly flowing, or possess a brighter gloss. It was of a jetty black; — which was also the color, or more properly the no-color of his unimaginable whiskers. You perceive I cannot speak of these latter without enthusiasm; it is not too much to say that they were the handsomest pair of whiskers under the sun. At all events, they encircled, and at times partially overshadowed, a mouth utterly unequalled. Here were the most entirely even, and the most brilliantly white of all conceivable teeth. From between them, upon every proper occasion, issued a voice of surpassing clearness, melody, and strength. In the matter of eyes, also, my acquaintance was pre-eminently endowed. Either one of such a pair was worth a couple of the ordinary ocular organs. They were of a deep hazel exceedingly large and lustrous; and there was perceptible about them,

ever and anon, just that amount of interesting obliquity which gives pregnancy to expression.

The bust of the General was unquestionably the finest bust I ever saw. For your life you could not have found a fault with its wonderful proportion. This rare peculiarity set off to great advantage a pair of shoulders which would have called up a blush of conscious inferiority into the countenance of the marble Apollo. I have a passion for fine shoulders, and may say that I never beheld them in perfection before. The arms altogether were admirably modelled. Nor were the lower limbs less superb. These were, indeed, the *ne plus ultra* of good legs. Every connoisseur in such matters admitted the legs to be good. There was neither too much flesh nor too little, — neither rudeness nor fragility. I could not imagine a more graceful curve than that of the *os femoris*, and there was just that due gentle prominence in the rear of the *fibula* which goes to the conformation of a properly proportioned calf. I wish to God my young and talented friend Chiponchipino, the sculptor, had but seen the legs of Brevet Brigadier General John A. B. C. Smith.

But although men so absolutely fine-looking are neither as plenty as reasons or blackberries, still I could not bring myself to believe that *the remarkable* something to which I alluded just now, — that the odd air of *je ne sais quoi* which hung about my new acquaintance, — lay altogether, or indeed at all, in the supreme excellence of his bodily endowments. Perhaps it might be traced to the *manner;* — yet here again I could not pretend to be positive. There *was* a primness, not to say stiffness, in his carriage — a degree of measured and, if I may so express it, of rectangular precision attending his every movement, which, observed in a more diminutive figure, would have had the least little savor in the world of affectation, pomposity, or constraint, but which, noticed in a gentleman of his undoubted dimensions, was readily placed to the account of reserve, *hauteur* — of a commendable sense, in short, of what is due to the dignity of colossal proportion.

The kind friend who presented me to General Smith whispered in my ear some few words of comment upon the man. He was a *remarkable* man — a *very* remarkable man — indeed one of the *most* remarkable men of the age. He was an especial favorite, too, with the ladies — chiefly on account of his high reputation for courage.

"In *that* point he is unrivalled — indeed he is a perfect desperado — a downright fire-eater, and no mistake," said my friend, here dropping his voice excessively low, and thrilling me with the mystery of his tone.

"A downright fire-eater, and *no* mistake. Showed *that*, I should say, to some purpose, in the late tremendous swamp-fight, away down South, with the Bugaboo and Kickapoo Indians." [Here my friend opened his eyes to some extent.] "Bless my soul! — blood and thunder, and all that! — *prodigies* of valor! — heard of him of course? — you know he's the man ——"

"Man alive, how *do* you do? why, how *are* ye? *very* glad to see ye, indeed!" here interrupted the General himself, seizing my companion by the hand as he drew near, and bowing stiffly but profoundly, as I was presented. I then thought (and I think so still) that I never heard a clearer nor a stronger voice, nor beheld a finer set of teeth: but I *must* say that I was sorry for the interruption just at that moment, as, owing to the whispers and insinuations aforesaid, my interest had been greatly excited in the hero of the Bugaboo and Kickapoo campaign.

However, the delightfully luminous conversation of Brevet Brigadier General John A. B. C. Smith soon completely dissipated this chagrin. My friend leaving us immediately, we had quite a long *tête-à-tête*, and I was not only pleased but *really* — instructed. I never heard a more fluent talker, or a man of greater general information. With becoming modesty, he forebore, nevertheless, to touch upon the theme I had just then most at heart — I mean the mysterious circumstances attending the Bugaboo war — and, on my own part, what I conceive to be a proper sense of delicacy forbade me to broach the subject; although, in truth, I was exceedingly tempted to do so. I perceived, too, that the gallant soldier preferred topics of philosophical interest, and that he delighted, especially, in commenting upon the rapid march of mechanical invention. Indeed, lead him where I would, this was a point to which he invariably came back.

"There is nothing at all like it," he would say; "we are a wonderful people, and live in a wonderful age. Parachutes and rail-roads — man-traps and spring-guns! Our steam-boats are upon every sea, and the Nassau balloon packet is about to run regular trips (fare either way only twenty pounds sterling) between London and Timbuctoo. And who shall calculate the immense influence upon social life — upon arts — upon commerce — upon literature — which will be the immediate result of the great principles of electro-magnetics! Nor, is this all, let me assure you! There is really no end to the march of invention. The most wonderful — the most ingenious — and let me add, Mr. — Mr. — Thompson, I believe, is your name — let me add, I say the most *useful* — the most truly *useful* — mechanical contrivances are daily springing up like mushrooms, if I may so express myself, or, more figuratively, like — ah — grasshoppers — like grasshoppers, Mr. Thompson — about us and ah — ah — ah — around us!"

Thompson, to be sure, is not my name; but it is needless to say that I left General Smith with a heightened interest in the man, with an exalted opinion of his conversational powers, and a deep sense of the valuable privileges we enjoy in living in this age of mechanical invention. My curiosity, however, had not been altogether satisfied, and I resolved to prosecute immediate inquiry among my acquaintances, touching the Brevet Brigadier General himself, and particularly respecting the tremendous events *quorum pars magna fuit*, during the Bugaboo and Kickapoo campaign.

The first opportunity which presented itself, and which (*horresco referens*) I did not in the least scruple to seize, occurred at the Church of the Reverend Doctor Drummummupp, where I found myself established, one Sunday, just at sermon time, not only in the pew, but by the side of that worthy and communicative little friend of mine, Miss Tabitha T. Thus seated, I congratulated myself, and with much reason, upon the very flattering state of affairs. If any person knew any thing about Brevet Brigadier General John A. B. C. Smith, that person it was clear to me, was Miss Tabitha T. We telegraphed a few signals and then commenced, *soto voce*, a brisk *tête-à-tête*.

"Smith!" said she in reply to my very earnest inquiry: "Smith! — why, not General John A. B. C.? Bless me, I thought you *knew* all about *him!* This is a wonderfully inventive age! Horrid affair that! — a bloody set of wretches, those Kickapoos! — fought like a hero — prodigies of valor — immortal renown. Smith! — Brevet Brigadier General John A. B. C.! — why, you know he's the man ——"

"Man," here broke in Doctor Drummummupp, at the top of his voice, and with a thump that came near knocking the pulpit about our ears; "man that is born of a woman hath but a short time to live; he cometh up and is cut down like a flower!" I started to the extremity of the pew, and perceived by the animated looks of the divine, that the wrath which had nearly proved fatal to the pulpit had been excited by the whispers of the lady and myself. There was no help for it; so I submitted with a good grace, and listened, in all the martyrdom of dignified silence, to the balance of that very capital discourse.

Next evening found me a somewhat late visitor at the Rantipole Theatre, where I felt sure of satisfying my curiosity at once, by merely stepping into the box of those exquisite specimens of affability and omniscience, the Misses Arabella and Miranda Cognoscenti. That fine tragedian, Climax, was doing Iago to a very crowded house, and I experienced some little difficulty in making my wishes understood; especially as our box was next the slips, and completely overlooked the stage.

"Smith!" said Miss Arabella, as she at length comprehended the purport of my query; "Smith? — why, not General John A. B. C.?"

"Smith!" inquired Miranda, musingly. "God bless me, did you ever behold a finer figure?"

"Never, madam, but *do* tell me ——"

"Or so inimitable grace?"

"Never, upon my word! — But pray, inform me ——"

"Or so just an appreciation of stage effect?"

"Madam!"

"Or a more delicate sense of the true beauties of Shakespeare? Be so good as to look at that leg!"

"The devil!" and I turned again to her sister.

"Smith!" said she, "why, not General John A. B. C.? Horrid affair

that, wasn't it? — great wretches, those Bugaboos — savage and so on — but we live in a wonderfully inventive age! — Smith! — O yes! great man! — perfect desperado — immortal renown — prodigies of valor! *Never heard!*" [This was given in a scream.] "Bless my soul! why, he's the man ——"

> "— mandragora
> Nor all the drowsy syrups of the world
> Shall ever medicine thee to that sweet sleep
> Which thou ow'dst yesterday!"

here roared our Climax just in my ear, and shaking his fist in my face all the time, in a way that I *couldn't* stand, and I *wouldn't*. I left the Misses Cognoscenti immediately, went behind the scenes forthwith, and gave the beggarly scoundrel such a thrashing as I trust he will remember till the day of his death.

At the *soirée* of the lovely widow, Mrs. Kathleen O'Trump, I was confident that I should meet with no similar disappointment. Accordingly, I was no sooner seated at the card-table, with my pretty hostess for a *vis-a-vis*, than I propounded those questions the solution of which had become a matter so essential to my peace.

"Smith!" said my partner, "why, not General John A. B. C.? Horrid affair that, wasn't it? — diamonds did you say? — terrible wretches those Kickapoos! — we are playing *whist*, if you please, Mr. Tattle — however, this is the age of invention, most certainly *the* age, one may say — *the* age *par excellence* — speak French? — oh, quite a hero — perfect desperado! — *no hearts*, Mr. Tattle? I don't believe it! — Immortal renown and all that! — prodigies of valor! *Never heard!!* — why, bless me, he's the man ——"

"Mann? — *Captain* Mann!" here screamed some little feminine interloper from the farthest corner of the room. "Are you talking about Captain Mann and the duel? —oh, I *must* hear — do tell — go on, Mrs. O'Trump! — do now go on!" And go on Mrs. O'Trump did — all about a certain Captain Mann, who was either shot or hung, or should have been both shot and hung. Yes! Mrs. O'Trump, she went on, and I — I went off. There was no chance of hearing any thing farther that evening in regard to Brevet Brigadier General John A. B. C. Smith.

Still I consoled myself with the reflection that the tide of ill-luck would not run against me forever, and so determined to make a bold push for information at the rout of that bewitching little angel, the graceful Mrs. Pirouette.

"Smith!" said Mrs. P., as we twirled about together in a *pas de zephyr*, "Smith? — why, not General John A. B. C.? Dreadful business that of the Bugaboos, wasn't it? — dreadful creatures, those Indians! — *do* turn out your toes! I really am ashamed of you — man of great courage, poor fellow! — but this is a wonderful age for invention — O dear me, I'm

out of breath — quite a desperado — prodigies of valor — *never heard!!* — can't believe it — I shall have to sit down and enlighten you — Smith! why, he's the man ——"

"Man-*Fred*, I tell you!" here bawled out Miss Bas-Bleu, as I led Mrs. Pirouette to a seat. "Did ever anybody hear the like? It's Man-*Fred*, I say, and not at all by any means Man-*Friday*." Here Miss Bas-Bleu beckoned to me in a very peremptory manner; and I was obliged, will I nill I, to leave Mrs. P. for the purpose of deciding a dispute touching the title of a certain poetical drama of Lord Byron's. Although I pronounced, with great promptness, that the true title was Man-*Friday*, and not by any means Man-*Fred* yet when I returned to seek Mrs. Pirouette she was not to be discovered, and I made my retreat from the house in a very bitter spirit of animosity against the whole race of the Bas-Bleus.

Matters had now assumed a really serious aspect, and I resolved to call at once upon my particular friend, Mr. Theodore Sinivate; for I knew that here at least I should get something like definite information.

"Smith!" said he, in his well known peculiar way of drawling out his syllables; "Smith! — why, not General John A. B. C.? Savage affair that with the Kickapo-o-o-os, wasn't it? Say, don't you think so? — perfect despera-a-ado — great pity, 'pon my honor! — wonderfully inventive age! — pro-o-odigies of valor! By the by, did you ever hear about Captain Ma-a-a-n?"

"Captain Mann be d—d!" said I; "please to go on with your story."

"Hem! — oh well! — quite *la méme cho-o-ose*, as we say in France. Smith, eh? Brigadier-General John A. B. C.? I say" — [here Mr. S. thought proper to put his finger to the side of his nose] — "I say, you don't mean to insinuate now, really and truly, and conscientiously, that you don't know all about that affair of Smith's, as well as I do, eh? Smith? John A — B — C.? Why, bless me, he's the ma-a-an ——"

"Mr. Sinivate," said I, imploringly, "*is* he the man in the mask?"

"No-o-o!" said he, looking wise, "nor the man in the mo-o-on."

This reply I considered a pointed and positive insult, and so left the house at once in high dudgeon, with a firm resolve to call my friend, Mr. Sinivate, to a speedy account for his ungentlemanly conduct and ill breeding.

In the meantime, however, I had no notion of being thwarted touching the information I desired. There was one resource left me yet. I would go to the fountain head. I would call forthwith upon the General himself, and demand, in explicit terms, a solution of this abominable piece of mystery. Here, at least, there should be no chance for equivocation. I would be plain, positive, peremptory — as short as pie-crust — as concise as Tacitus or Montesquieu.

It was early when I called, and the General was dressing, but I pleaded urgent business, and was shown at once into his bedroom by an old negro valet, who remained in attendance during my visit. As I entered the

chamber, I looked about, of course, for the occupant, but did not im-
mediately perceive him. There was a large and exceedingly odd looking
bundle of something which lay close by my feet on the floor, and, as I
was not in the best humor in the world, I gave it a kick out of the way.

"Hem! ahem! rather civil that, I should say!" said the bundle, in one
of the smallest, and altogether the funniest little voices, between a squeak
and a whistle, that I ever heard in all the days of my existence.

"Ahem! rather civil that, I should observe."

I fairly shouted with terror, and made off, at a tangent, into the farthest
extremity of the room.

"God bless me, my dear fellow!" here again whistled the bundle, "what
— what — what — why, what *is* the matter? I really believe you don't
know me at all."

What *could* I say to all this — what *could* I? I staggered into an arm-
chair, and, with staring eyes and open mouth, awaited the solution of the
wonder.

"Strange you shouldn't know me though, isn't it?" presently re-
squeaked the nondescript, which I now perceived was performing upon
the floor some inexplicable evolution, very analogous to the drawing on
of a stocking. There was only a single leg, however, apparent.

"Strange you shouldn't know me though, isn't it? Pompey, bring me
that leg!" Here Pompey handed the bundle a very capital cork leg, al-
ready dressed, which it screwed on in a trice; and then it stood upright
before my eyes.

"And a bloody action it *was*," continued the thing, as if in a soliloquy;
"but then one mustn't fight with the Bugaboos and Kickapoos, and think
of coming off with a mere scratch. Pompey, I'll thank you now for that
arm. Thomas" [turning to me] "is decidedly the best hand at a cork leg; but
if you should ever want an arm, my dear fellow, you must really let me
recommend you to Bishop." Here Pompey screwed on an arm.

"We had rather hot work of it, that you may say. Now, you dog, slip
on my shoulders and bosom. Pettit makes the best shoulders, but for a
bosom you will have to go to Ducrow."

"Bosom!" said I.

"Pompey, will you *never* be ready with that wig? Scalping is a rough
process, after all; but then you can procure such a capital scratch at De
L'Orme's."

"Scratch!"

"Now, you nigger, my teeth! For a *good* set of these you had better go
to Parmly's at once; high prices, but excellent work. I swallowed some
very capital articles, though, when the big Bugaboo rammed me down
with the butt end of his rifle."

"Butt end! ram down!! my eye!!!"

"O yes, by the way, my eye — here, Pompey, you scamp, screw it in!
Those Kickapoos are not so very slow at a gouge; but he's a belied man,

that Dr. Williams, after all; you can't imagine how well I see with the eyes of his make."

I now began very clearly to perceive that the object before me was nothing more nor less than my new acquaintance, Brevet Brigadier General John A. B. C. Smith. The manipulations of Pompey had made, I must confess, a very striking difference in the appearance of the personal man. The voice, however, still puzzled me no little; but even this apparent mystery was speedily cleared up.

"Pompey, you black rascal," squeaked the General, "I really do believe you would let me go out without my palate."

Hereupon, the negro, grumbling out an apology, went up to his master, opened his mouth with the knowing air of a horse-jockey, and adjusted therein a somewhat singular-looking machine, in a very dexterous manner, that I could not altogether comprehend. The alteration, however, in the entire expression of the General's countenance was instantaneous and surprising. When he again spoke, his voice had resumed all that rich melody and strength which I had noticed upon our original introduction.

"D—n the vagabonds!" said he, in so clear a tone that I positively started at the change, "D—n the vagabonds! they not only knocked in the roof of my mouth, but took the trouble to cut off at least seven-eighths of my tongue. There isn't Bonfanti's equal, however, in America, for really good articles of this description. I can recommend you to him with confidence," [here the General bowed,] "and assure you that I have the greatest pleasure in so doing."

I acknowledged his kindness in my best manner, and took leave of him at once, with a perfect understanding of the true state of affairs — with a full comprehension of the mystery which had troubled me so long. It was evident. It was a clear case. Brevet Brigadier General John A. B. C. Smith was the man — was *the man that was used up.*

The Fall of the House of Usher

Son cœur est un luth suspendu;
Sitôt qu'on le touche il résonne.

DE BERANGER.

DURING the whole of a dull, dark, and soundless day in the autumn of the year, when the clouds hung oppressively low in the heavens, I had been passing alone, on horseback, through a singularly dreary tract of country, and at length found myself, as the shades of evening drew on,

within view of the melancholy House of Usher. I know not how it was —
but, with the first glimpse of the building, a sense of insufferable gloom
pervaded my spirit. I say insufferable; for the feeling was unrelieved by
any of that half-pleasurable, because poetic, sentiment, with which the
mind usually receives even the sternest natural images of the desolate or
terrible. I looked upon the scene before me — upon the mere house, and
the simple landscape features of the domain — upon the bleak walls —
upon the vacant eye-like windows — upon a few rank sedges — and upon
a few white trunks of decayed trees — with an utter depression of soul,
which I can compare to no earthly sensation more properly than to the
after-dream of the reveller upon opium — the bitter lapse into every-day
life — the hideous dropping off of the veil. There was an iciness, a sink-
ing, a sickening of the heart — an unredeemed dreariness of thought
which no goading of the imagination could torture into aught of the
sublime. What was it — I paused to think — what was it that so unnerved
me in the contemplation of the House of Usher? It was a mystery all
insoluble; nor could I grapple with the shadowy fancies that crowded
upon me as I pondered. I was forced to fall back upon the unsatisfactory
conclusion, that while, beyond doubt, there *are* combinations of very
simple natural objects which have the power of thus affecting us, still
the analysis of this power lies among considerations beyond our depth.
It was possible, I reflected, that a mere different arrangement of the par-
ticulars of the scene, of the details of the picture, would be sufficient to
modify, or perhaps to annihilate its capacity for sorrowful impression;
and, acting upon this idea, I reined my horse to the precipitous brink of
a black and lurid tarn that lay in unruffled lustre by the dwelling, and
gazed down — but with a shudder even more thrilling than before —
upon the remodelled and inverted images of the gray sedge, and the
ghastly tree-stems, and the vacant and eye-like windows.

Nevertheless, in this mansion of gloom I now proposed to myself a
sojourn of some weeks. Its proprietor, Roderick Usher, had been one of
my boon companions in boyhood; but many years had elapsed since our
last meeting. A letter, however, had lately reached me in a distant part
of the country — a letter from him — which, in its wildly importunate
nature, had admitted of no other than a personal reply. The MS. gave
evidence of nervous agitation. The writer spoke of acute bodily illness —
of a mental disorder which oppressed him — and of an earnest desire to
see me, as his best and indeed his only personal friend, with a view of
attempting, by the cheerfulness of my society, some alleviation of his
malady. It was the manner in which all this, and much more, was said —
it was the apparent *heart* that went with his request — which allowed
me no room for hesitation; and I accordingly obeyed forthwith what I
still considered a very singular summons.

Although, as boys, we had been even intimate associates, yet I really
knew little of my friend. His reserve had been always excessive and

habitual. I was aware, however, that his very ancient family had been noted, time out of mind, for a peculiar sensibility of temperament, displaying itself, through long ages, in many works of exalted art, and manifested, of late, in repeated deeds of munificent yet unobtrusive charity, as well as in a passionate devotion to the intricacies, perhaps even more than to the orthodox and easily recognizable beauties, of musical science. I had learned, too, the very remarkable fact, that the stem of the Usher race, all time-honored as it was, had put forth, at no period, any enduring branch; in other words, that the entire family lay in the direct line of descent, and had always, with very trifling and very temporary variations, so lain. It was this deficiency, I considered, while running over in thought the perfect keeping of the character of the premises with the accredited character of the people, and while speculating upon the possible influence which the one, in the long lapse of centuries, might have exercised upon the other — it was this deficiency, perhaps of collateral issue, and the consequent undeviating transmission, from sire to son, of the patrimony with the name, which had, at length, so identified the two as to merge the original title of the estate in the quaint and equivocal appellation of the "House of Usher" — an appellation which seemed to include, in the minds of the peasantry who used it, both the family and the family mansion.

I have said that the sole effect of my somewhat childish experiment — that of looking down within the tarn — had been to deepen the first singular impression. There can be no doubt that the consciousness of the rapid increase of my superstition — for why should I not so term it? — served mainly to accelerate the increase itself. Such, I have long known, is the paradoxical law of all sentiments having terror as a basis. And it might have been for this reason only, that, when I again uplifted my eyes to the house itself, from its image in the pool, there grew in my mind a strange fancy — a fancy so ridiculous, indeed, that I but mention it to show the vivid force of the sensations which oppressed me. I had so worked upon my imagination as really to believe that about the whole mansion and domain there hung an atmosphere peculiar to themselves and their immediate vicinity — an atmosphere which had no affinity with the air of heaven, but which had reeked up from the decayed trees, and the gray wall, and the silent tarn — a pestilent and mystic vapor, dull, sluggish, faintly discernible and leaden-hued.

Shaking off from my spirit what *must* have been a dream, I scanned more narrowly the real aspect of the building. Its principal feature seemed to be that of an excessive antiquity. The discoloration of ages had been great. Minute fungi overspread the whole exterior, hanging in a fine tangled web-work from the eaves. Yet all this was apart from any extraordinary dilapidation. No portion of the masonry had fallen; and there appeared to be a wild inconsistency between its still perfect adaptation of parts, and the crumbling condition of the individual stones. In

this there was much that reminded me of the specious totality of old woodwork which has rotted for long years in some neglected vault, with no disturbance from the breath of the external air. Beyond this indication of extensive decay, however, the fabric gave little token of instability. Perhaps the eye of a scrutinizing observer might have discovered a barely perceptible fissure, which, extending from the roof of the building in front, made its way down the wall in a zig-zag direction, until it became lost in the sullen waters of the tarn.

Noticing these things, I rode over a short cuaseway to the house. A servant in waiting took my horse, and I entered the Gothic archway of the hall. A valet, of stealthy step, then conducted me, in silence, through many dark and intricate passages in my progress to the *studio* of his master. Much that I encountered on the way contributed, I know not how, to heighten the vague sentiments of which I have already spoken. While the objects around me — while the carvings of the ceilings, the sombre tapestries of the walls, the ebon blackness of the floors, and the phantasmagoric armorial trophies which rattled as I strode, were but matters to which, or to such as which, I had been accustomed from my infancy — while I hesitated not to acknowledge how familiar was all this — I still wondered to find how unfamiliar were the fancies which ordinary images were stirring up. On one of the staircases, I met the physician of the family. His countenance, I thought, wore a mingled expression of low cunning and perplexity. He accosted me with trepidation and passed on. The valet now threw open a door and ushered me into the presence of his master.

The room in which I found myself was very large and lofty. The windows were long, narrow, and pointed, and at so vast a distance from the black oaken floor as to be altogether inaccessible from within. Feeble gleams of encrimsoned light made their way through the trellised panes, and served to render sufficiently distinct the more prominent objects around; the eye, however, struggled in vain to reach the remoter angles of the chamber, or the recesses of the vaulted and fretted ceiling. Dark draperies hung upon the walls. The general furniture was profuse, comfortless, antique, and tattered. Many books and musical instruments lay scattered about, but failed to give any vitality to the scene. I felt that I breathed an atmosphere of sorrow. An air of stern, deep, and irredeemable gloom hung over and pervaded all.

Upon my entrance, Usher arose from a sofa on which he had been lying at full length, and greeted me with a vivacious warmth which had much in it, I at first thought, of an overdone cordiality — of the constrained effort of the *ennuyé* man of the world. A glance, however, at his countenance convinced me of his perfect sincerity. We sat down; and for some moments, while he spoke not, I gazed upon him with a feeling half of pity, half of awe. Surely, man had never before so terribly altered, in so brief a period, as had Roderick Usher! It was with difficulty that I

could bring myself to admit the identity of the wan being before me with the companion of my early boyhood. Yet the character of his face had been at all times remarkable. A cadaverousness of complexion; an eye large, liquid, and luminous beyond comparison; lips somewhat thin and very pallid, but of a surpassingly beautiful curve; a nose of a delicate Hebrew model, but with a breadth of nostril unusual in similar formations; a finely moulded chin, speaking, in its want of prominence, of a want of moral energy; hair of a more than web-like softness and tenuity; — these features, with an inordinate expansion above the regions of the temple, made up altogether a countenance not easily to be forgotten. And now in the mere exaggeration of the prevailing character of these features, and of the expression they were wont to convey, lay so much of change that I doubted to whom I spoke. The now ghastly pallor of the skin, and the now miraculous lustre of the eye, above all things startled and even awed me. The silken hair, too, had been suffered to grow all unheeded, and as, in its wild gossamer texture, it floated rather than fell about the face, I could not, even with effort, connect its Arabesque expression with any idea of simple humanity.

In the manner of my friend I was at once struck with an incoherence — an inconsistency; and I soon found this to arise from a series of feeble and futile struggles to overcome an habitual trepidancy — an excessive nervous agitation. For something of this nature I had indeed been prepared, no less by his letter than by reminiscences of certain boyish traits, and by conclusions deduced from his peculiar physical conformation and temperament. His action was alternately vivacious and sullen. His voice varied rapidly from a tremulous indecision (when the animal spirits seemed utterly in abeyance) to that species of energetic concision — that abrupt, weighty, un-hurried, and hollow-sounding enunciation — that leaden, self-balanced, and perfectly modulated guttural utterance, which may be observed in the lost drunkard, or the irreclaimable eater of opium, during the periods of his most intense excitement.

It was thus that he spoke of the object of my visit, of his earnest desire to see me, and of the solace he expected me to afford him. He entered, at some length, into what he conceived to be the nature of his malady. It was, he said, a constitutional and a family evil and one for which he despaired to find a remedy — a mere nervous affection, he immediately added, which would undoubtedly soon pass off. It displayed itself in a host of unnatural sensation. Some of these, as he detailed them, interested and bewildered me; although, perhaps, the terms and the general manner of their narration had their weight. He suffered much from a morbid acuteness of the senses; the most insipid food was alone endurable; he could wear only garments of certain texture; the odors of all flowers were oppressive; his eyes were tortured by even a faint light; and there were but peculiar sounds, and these from stringed instruments, which did not inspire him with horror.

To an anomalous species of terror I found him a bounden slave. "I shall perish," said he, "I *must* perish in this deplorable folly. Thus, thus, and not otherwise, shall I be lost. I dread the events of the future, not in themselves, but in their results. I shudder at the thought of any, even the most trivial, incident, which may operate upon this intolerable agitation of soul. I have, indeed, no abhorrence of danger, except in its absolute effect — in terror. In this unnerved, in this pitiable, condition I feel that the period will sooner or later arrive when I must abandon life and reason together, in some struggle with the grim phantasm, FEAR."

I learned, moreover, at intervals, and through broken and equivocal hints, another singular feature of his mental condition. He was enchained by certain superstitious impressions in regard to the dwelling which he tenanted, and whence, for many years, he had never ventured forth — in regard to an influence whose supposititious force was conveyed in terms too shadowy here to be re-stated — an influence which some peculiarities in the mere form and substance of his family mansion had, by dint of long sufferance, he said, obtained over his spirit — an effect which the *physique* of the gray walls and turrets, and of the dim tarn into which they all looked down, had at length, brought about upon the *morale* of his existence.

He admitted, however, although with hesitation, that much of the peculiar gloom which thus afflicted him could be traced to a more natural and far more palpable origin — to the severe and long-continued illness — indeed to the evidently approaching dissolution — of a tenderly beloved sister, his sole companion for long years, his last and only relative on earth. "Her decease," he said, with a bitterness which I can never forget, "would leave him (him, the hopeless and the frail) the last of the ancient race of the Ushers." While he spoke, the lady Madeline (for so was she called) passed through a remote portion of the apartment, and, without having noticed my presence, disappeared. I regarded her with an utter astonishment not unmingled with dread; and yet I found it impossible to account for such feelings. A sensation of stupor oppressed me as my eyes followed her retreating steps. When a door, at length, closed upon her, my glance sought instinctively and eagerly the countenance of the brother; but he had buried his face in his hands, and I could only perceive that a far more than ordinary wanness had overspread the emaciated fingers through which trickled many passionate tears.

The disease of the lady Madeline had long baffled the skill of her physicians. A settled apathy, a gradual wasting away of the person, and frequent although transient affections of a partially cataleptical character were the unusual diagnosis. Hitherto she had steadily borne up against the pressure of her malady, and had not betaken herself finally to bed; but on the closing in of the evening of my arrival at the house, she succumbed (as her brother told me at night with inexpressible agitation) to the prostrating power of the destroyer; and I learned that the glimpse

I had obtained of her person would thus probably be the last I should obtain — that the lady, at least while living, would be seen by me no more.

For several days ensuing, her name was unmentioned by either Usher or myself; and during this period I was busied in earnest endeavors to alleviate the melancholy of my friend. We painted and read together, or I listened, as if in a dream, to the wild improvisations of his speaking guitar. And thus, as a closer and still closer intimacy admitted me more unreservedly into the recesses of his spirit, the more bitterly did I perceive the futility of all attempt at cheering a mind from which darkness, as if an inherent positive quality, poured forth upon all objects of the moral and physical universe in one unceasing radiation of gloom.

I shall ever bear about me a memory of the many solemn hours I thus spent alone with the master of the House of Usher. Yet I should fail in any attempt to convey an idea of the exact character of the studies, or of the occupations, in which he involved me, or led me the way. An excited and highly distempered ideality threw a sulphureous lustre over all. His long improvised dirges will ring forever in my ears. Among other things, I hold painfully in mind a certain singular perversion and amplification of the wild air of the last waltz of Von Weber. From the paintings over which his elaborate fancy brooded, and which grew, touch by touch, into vaguenesses at which I shuddered the more thrillingly, because I shuddered knowing not why — from these paintings (vivid as their images now are before me) I would in vain endeavor to educe more than a small portion which should lie within the compass of merely written words. By the utter simplicity, by the nakedness of his designs, he arrested and overawed attention. If ever mortal painted an idea, that mortal was Roderick Usher. For me at least, in the circumstances then surrounding me, there arose out of the pure abstractions which the hypochondriac contrived to throw upon his canvass, an intensity of intolerable awe, no shadow of which felt I ever yet in the contemplation of the certainly glowing yet too concrete reveries of Fuseli.

One of the phantasmagoric conceptions of my friend, partaking not so rigidly of the spirit of abstraction, may be shadowed forth, although feebly, in words. A small picture presented the interior of an immensely long and rectangular vault or tunnel, with low walls, smooth, white and without interruption or device. Certain accessory points of the design served well to convey the idea that this excavation lay at an exceeding depth below the surface of the earth. No outlet was observed in any portion of its vast extent, and no torch or other artificial source of light was discernible; yet a flood of intense rays rolled throughout, and bathed the whole in a ghastly and inappropriate splendor.

I have just spoken of that morbid condition of the auditory nerve which rendered all music intolerable to the sufferer, with the exception of certain effects of stringed instruments. It was, perhaps, the narrow

limits to which he thus confined himself upon the guitar which gave birth, in great measure, to the fantastic character of his performances. But the fervid *facility* of his *impromptus* could not be so accounted for. They must have been, and were, in the notes, as well as in the words of his wild fantasias (for he not unfrequently accompanied himself with rhymed verbal improvisations), the result of that intense mental collectedness and concentration to which I have previously alluded as observable only in particular moments of the highest artificial excitement. The words of one of these rhapsodies I have easily remembered. I was, perhaps, the more forcibly impressed with it as he gave it because, in the under or mystic current of its meaning, I fancied that I perceived, and for the first time, a full consciousness on the part of Usher of the tottering of his lofty reason upon her throne. The verses, which were entitled "The Haunted Palace," ran very nearly, if not accurately, thus: —

I

In the greenest of our valleys,
 By good angels tenanted,
Once a fair and stately palace —
 Radiant palace — reared its head.
In the monarch Thought's dominion —
 It stood there!
Never seraph spread a pinion
 Over fabric half so fair.

II

Banners yellow, glorious, golden,
 On its roof did float and flow
(This — all this — was in the olden
 Time long ago)
And every gentle air that dallied,
 In that sweet day,
Along the ramparts plumed and pallid,
 A winged odor went away.

III

Wanderers in that happy valley
 Through two luminous windows saw
Spirits moving musically
 To a lute's well-tunéd law;
Round about a throne, where sitting
 (Porphyrogene!)
In state his glory well befitting,
 The ruler of the realm was seen.

IV

And all with pearl and ruby glowing
 Was the fair palace door,
Through which came flowing, flowing, flowing
 And sparkling evermore,
A troop of Echoes whose sweet duty
 Was but to sing,
In voices of surpassing beauty,
 The wit and wisdom of their king.

V

But evil things, in robes of sorrow,
 Assailed the monarch's high estate;
(Ah, let us mourn, for never morrow
 Shall dawn upon him, desolate!)
And, round about his home, the glory
 That blushed and bloomed
Is but a dim-remembered story
 Of the old time entombed.

VI

And travellers now within that valley,
 Through the red-litten windows see
Vast forms that move fantastically
 To a discordant melody;
While, like a rapid ghastly river,
 Through the pale door,
A hideous throng rush out forever,
 And laugh — but smile no more.

I well remember that suggestions arising from this ballad led us into a train of thought wherein there became manifest an opinion of Usher's which I mention not so much on account of its novelty (for other men * have thought thus), as on account of the pertinacity with which he maintained it. This opinion, in its general form, was that of the sentience of all vegetable things. But, in his disordered fancy the idea had assumed a more daring character, and trespassed, under certain conditions, upon the kingdom of inorganization. I lack words to express the full extent, or the earnest *abandon* of his persuasion. The belief, however, was connected (as I have previously hinted) with the gray stones of the home of his forefathers. The conditions of the sentience had been here, he

* Watson, Dr. Percival, Spallanzani, and especially the Bishop of Landaff. — See "Chemical Essays," vol. 5.

imagined, fulfilled in the method of collocation of these stones — in the order of their arrangement, as well as in that of the many *fungi* which overspread them, and of the decayed trees which stood around — above all, in the long undisturbed endurance of this arrangement, and in its reduplication in the still waters of the tarn. Its evidence — the evidence of the sentience — was to be seen, he said (and I here started as he spoke), in the gradual yet certain condensation of an atmosphere of their own about the waters and the walls. The result was discoverable, he added, in that silent yet importunate and terrbile influence which for centuries had moulded the destinies of his family, and which made *him* what I now saw him — what he was. Such opinions need no comment, and I will make none.

Our books — the books which, for years, had formed no small portion of the mental existence of the invalid — were, as might be supposed, in strict keeping with this character of phantasm. We pored together over such works as the "Ververt et Chartruse" of Gresset; the "Belphegor" of Machiavelli; the "Heaven and Hell" of Swendenborg; the "Subterranean Voyage of Nicholas Klimm" by Holberg; the "Chiromancy" of Robert Flud, of Jean D'Indagine and of De la Chambre; the "Journey into the Blue Distance" of Tieck; and the "City of the Sun" of Campanella. One favorite volume was a small octavo edition of the "Directorium Inquisitorium," by the Dominican Eymeric de Gironne; and there were passages in Pomponius Mela, about the old African Stayrs and Œgipans, over which Usher would sit dreaming for hours. His chief delight, however, was found in the perusal of an exceedingly rare and curious book in quarto Gothic — the manual of a forgotten church — the *Vigiliæ Mortuorum secundum Chorum Ecclesiæ Maguntinæ.*

I could not help thinking of the wild ritual of this work, and of its probable influence upon the hypochondriac, when, one evening, having informed me abruptly that the lady Madeline was no more, he stated his intention of preserving her corpse for a fortnight (previously to its final interment), in one of the numerous vaults within the main walls of the building. The worldly reason, however, assigned for this singular proceeding, was one which I did not feel at liberty to dispute. The brother had been led to his resolution (so he told me) by consideration of the unusual character of the malady of the deceased, of certain obstrusive and eager inquiries on the part of her medical men, and of the remote and exposed situation of the burial-ground of the family. I will not deny that when I called to mind the sinister countenance of the person whom I met upon the staircase, on the day of my arrival at the house, I had no desire to oppose what I regarded as at best but a harmless, and by no means an unnatural precaution.

At the request of Usher, I personally aided him in the arrangements for the temporary entombment. The body having been encoffined, we two alone bore it to its rest. The vault in which we placed it (and which

had been so long unopened that our torches, half smothered in its op-
pressive atmosphere, gave us little opportunity for investigation) was
small, damp, and entirely without means of admission for light; lying, at
great depth, immediately beneath that portion of the building in which
was my own sleeping apartment. It had been used, apparently, in remote
feudal times, for the worst purposes of a don-jon-keep, and, in later days,
as a place of deposit for powder, or some other highly combustible sub-
stance, as a portion of its floor, and the whole interior of a long archway
through which we reached it, were carefully sheathed with copper. The
door, of massive iron, had been, also, similarly protected. Its immense
weight caused an unusually sharp, grating sound, as it moved upon its
hinges.

Having deposited our mournful burden upon tressels within this region
of horror, we partially turned aside the yet unscrewed lid of the coffin,
and looked upon the face of the tenant. A striking similitude between
the brother and sister now first arrested my attention; and Usher, divin-
ing, perhaps, my thoughts, murmured out some few words from which
I learned that the deceased and himself had been twins, and that sym-
pathies of a scarcely intelligible nature had always existed between them.
Our glances, however, rested not long upon the dead — for we could
not regard her unawed. The disease which had thus entombed the lady
in the maturity of youth, had left, as usual in all maladies of a strictly
cataleptical character, the mockery of a faint blush upon the bosom and
the face, and that suspiciously lingering smile upon the lip which is so
terrible in death. We replaced and screwed down the lid, and, having
secured the door of iron, made our way, with toil, into the scarcely less
gloomy apartments of the upper portion of the house.

And now, some days of bitter grief having elapsed, an observable
change came over the features of the mental disorder of my friend. His
ordinary manner had vanished. His ordinary occupations were neglected
or forgotten. He roamed from chamber to chamber with hurried, un-
equal, and objectless step. The pallor of his countenance had assumed, if
possible, a more ghastly hue — but the luminousness of his eye had utterly
gone out. The once occasional huskiness of his tone was heard no more;
and a tremulous quaver, as if of extreme terror, habitually characterized
his utterance. There were times, indeed, when I thought his unceasingly
agitated mind was laboring with some oppressive secret, to divulge which
he struggled for the necessary courage. At times, again, I was obliged to
resolve all into the mere inexplicable vagaries of madness, for I beheld
him gazing upon vacancy for long hours, in an attitude of the profoundest
attention, as if listening to some imaginary sound. It was no wonder that
his condition terrified — that it infected me. I felt creeping upon me,
by slow yet uncertain degrees, the wild influences of his own fantastic yet
impressive superstitions.

It was, especially, upon retiring to bed late in the night of the seventh

or eighth day after the placing of the lady Madeline within the don-jon, that I experienced the full power of such feelings. Sleep came not near my couch — while the hours waned and waned away. I struggled to reason off the nervousness which had dominion over me. I endeavored to believe that much, if not all of what I felt, was due to the bewildering influence of the gloomy furniture of the room — of the dark and tattered draperies, which, tortured into motion by the breath of a rising tempest, swayed fitfully to and fro upon the walls, and rustled uneasily about the decorations of the bed. But my efforts were fruitless. An irrepressible tremor gradually pervaded my frame; and, at length, there sat upon my very heart an incubus of utterly causeless alarm. Shaking this off with a gasp and a struggle, I uplifted myself upon the pillows, and, peering earnestly within the intense darkness of the chamber, hearkened — I know not why, except that an instinctive spirit prompted me — to certain low and indefinite sounds which came, through the pauses of the storm, at long intervals, I knew not whence. Overpowered by an intense sentiment of horror, unaccountable yet unendurable, I threw on my clothes with haste (for I felt that I should sleep no more during the night), and endeavored to arouse myself from the pitiable condition into which I had fallen by pacing rapidly to and fro through the apartment.

I had taken but few turns in this manner, when a light step on an adjoining staircase arrested my attention. I presently recognized it as that of Usher. In an instant afterward he rapped, with a gentle touch, at my door, and entered, bearing a lamp. His countenance was, as usual, cadaverously wan — but, moreover, there was a species of mad hilarity in his eyes — an evidently restrained *hysteria* in his whole demeanor. His air appalled me — but any thing was preferable to the solitude which I had so long endured, and I even welcomed his presence as a relief.

"And you have not seen it?" he said abruptly, after having stared about him for some moments in silence — "you have not then seen it? — but, stay! you shall." Thus speaking, and having carefully shaded his lamp, he hurried to one of the casements, and threw it freely open to the storm.

The impetuous fury of the entering gust nearly lifted us from our feet. It was, indeed, a tempestuous yet sternly beautiful night, and one wildly singular in its terror and its beauty. A whirlwind had apparently collected its force in our vicinity; for there were frequent and violent alterations in the direction of the wind; and the exceeding density of the clouds (which hung so low as to press upon the turrets of the house) did not prevent our perceiving the life-like velocity with which they flew careering from all points against each other, without passing away into the distance. I say that even their exceeding density did not prevent our perceiving this — yet we had no glimpse of the moon or stars, nor was there any flashing forth of the lightning. But the under surfaces of the huge masses of agitated vapor, as well as all terrestrial objects immediately around us, were glowing in the unnatural light of a faintly luminous and

distinctly visible gaseous exhalation which hung about and enshrouded the mansion.

"You must not — you shall not behold this!" said I, shuddering, to Usher, as I led him, with a gentle violence, from the window to a seat. "These appearances, which bewilder you, are merely electrical phenomena not uncommon — or it may be that they have their ghastly origin in the rank miasma of the tarn. Let us close this casement; — the air is chilling and dangerous to your frame. Here is one of your favorite romances. I will read, and you shall listen: — and so we will pass away this terrible night together."

The antique volume which I had taken up was the "Mad Trist" of Sir Launcelot Canning; but I had called it a favorite of Usher's more in sad jest than in earnest; for, in truth, there is little in its uncouth and unimaginative prolixity which could have had interest for the lofty and spiritual ideality of my friend. It was, however, the only book immediately at hand; and I indulged a vague hope that the excitement which now agitated the hypochondriac, might find relief (for the history of mental disorder is full of similar anomalies) even in the extremeness of the folly which I should read. Could I have judged, indeed, by the wild overstrained air of vivacity with which he hearkened, or apparently hearkened, to the words of the tale, I might well have congratulated myself upon the success of my design.

I had arrived at that well-known portion of the story where Ethelred, the hero of the Trist, having sought in vain for peaceable admission into the dwelling of the hermit, proceeds to make good an entrance by force. Here, it will be remembered, the words of the narrative run thus:

"And Ethelred, who was by nature of a doughty heart, and who was now mighty withal, on account of the powerfulness of the wine which he had drunken, waited no longer to hold parley with the hermit, who, in sooth, was of an obstinate and maliceful turn, but feeling the rain upon his shoulders, and fearing the rising of the tempest, uplifted his mace outright, and, with blows, made quickly room in the plankings of the door for his gauntleted hand; and now pulling therewith sturdily, he so cracked, and ripped, and tore all asunder, that the noise of the dry and hollow-sounding wood alarumed and reverberated throughout the forest."

At the termination of this sentence I started and, for a moment, paused; for it appeared to me (although I at once concluded that my excited fancy had deceived me) — it appeared to me that, from some very remote portion of the mansion, there came, indistinctly to my ears, which might have been, in its exact similarity of character, the echo (but a stifled and dull one certainly) of the very cracking and ripping sound which Sir Launcelot had so particularly described. It was, beyond doubt, the coincidence alone which had arrested my attention; for, amid the rattling of the sashes of the casements, and the ordinary commingled noises of the still increasing storm, the sound, itself, had nothing,

surely, which should have interested or disturbed me. I continued the story:

"But the good champion Ethelred, now entering within the door, was sore enraged and amazed to perceive no signal of the maliceful hermit, but, in the stead thereof, a dragon of a scaly and prodigious demeanor, and of a fiery tongue, which sate in guard before a palace of gold, with a floor of silver; and upon the wall there hung a shield of shining brass with this legend enwritten —

> Who entereth herein, a conqueror hath bin;
> Who slayeth the dragon, the shield he shall win.

And Ethelred uplifted his mace, and struck upon the head of the dragon, which fell before him, and gave up his pesty breath, with a shriek so horrid and harsh, and withal so piercing, that Ethelred had fain to close his ears with his hands against the dreadful noise of it, the like whereof was never before heard."

Here again I paused abruptly, and now with a feeling of wild amazement — for there could be no doubt whatever that, in this instance, I did actually hear (although from what direction it proceeded I found it impossible to say) a low and apparently distant, but harsh, protracted, and most unusual screaming or grating sound — the exact counterpart of what my fancy had already conjured up for the dragon's unnatural shriek as described by the romancer.

Oppressed, as I certainly was, upon the extraordinary coincidence, by a thousand conflicting sensations, in which wonder and extreme terror were predominant, I still retained sufficient presence of mind to avoid exciting, by an observation, the sensitive nervousness of my companion. I was by no means certain that he had noticed the sounds in question; although, assuredly, a strange alteration had, during the last few minutes, taken place in his demeanor. From a position fronting my own, he had gradually brought round his chair, so as to sit with his face to the door of the chamber; and thus I could but partially perceive his features, although I saw that his lips trembled as if he were murmuring inaudibly. His head had dropped upon his breast — yet I knew that he was not asleep, from the wide and rigid opening of the eye as I caught a glance of it in profile. The motion of his body, too, was at variance with this idea — for he rocked from side to side with a gentle yet constant and uniform sway. Having rapidly taken notice of all this, I resumed the narrative of Sir Launcelot, which thus proceeded:

"And now, the champion, having escaped from the terrible fury of the dragon, bethinking himself of the brazen shield, and of the breaking up of the enchantment which was upon it, removed the carcass from out of the way before him, and approached valorously over the silver pavement of the castle to where the shield was upon the wall; which in sooth

tarried not for his full coming, but fell down at his feet upon the silver floor, with a mighty great and terrible ringing sound."

No sooner had these syllables passed my lips, than — as if a shield of brass had indeed, at the moment, fallen heavily upon a floor of silver — I became aware of a distinct, hollow, metallic, and clangorous, yet apparently muffled, reverberation. Completely unnerved, I leaped to my feet; but the measured rocking movement of Usher was undisturbed. I rushed to the chair in which he sat. His eyes were bent fixedly before him, and throughout his whole countenance there reigned a stony rigidity. But, as I placed my hand upon his shoulder, there came a strong shudder over his whole person; a sickly smile quivered about his lips; and I saw that he spoke in a low, hurried, and gibbering murmur, as if unconscious of my presence. Bending closely over him I at length drank in the hideous import of his words.

"Not hear it? — yes, I hear it, and have heard it. Long — long — long — many minutes, many hours, many days, have I heard it — yet I dared not — oh, pity me, miserable wretch that I am! — I dared not — I *dared* not speak! *We have put her living in the tomb!* Said I not that my senses were acute? I *now* tell you that I heard her first feeble movement in the hollow coffin. I heard them — many, many days ago — yet I dared not — *I dared not speak!* And now — to-night — Ethelred — ha! ha! — the breaking of the hermit's door, and the death-cry of the dragon, and the clangor of the shield — say, rather, the rending of her coffin, and the grating of the iron hinges of her prison, and her struggles within the coppered archway of the vault! Oh! whither shall I fly? Will she not be here anon? Is she not hurrying to upbraid me for my haste? Have I not heard her footstep on the stair? Do I not distinguish that heavy and horrible beating of her heart? Madman!" — here he sprang furiously to his feet, and shrieked out his syllables, as if in the effort he were giving up his soul — *"Madman! I tell you that she now stands without the door!"*

As if in the superhuman energy of his utterance there had been found the potency of a spell, the huge antique panels to which the speaker pointed threw slowly back, upon the instant, their ponderous and ebony jaws. It was the work of the rushing gust — but then without those doors there *did* stand the lofty and enshrouded figure of the lady Madeline of Usher. There was blood upon her white robes, and the evidence of some bitter struggle upon every portion of her emaciated frame. For a moment she remained trembling and reeling to and fro upon the threshold — then, with a low moaning cry, fell heavily inward upon the person of her brother, and in her violent and now final death-agonies, bore him to the floor a corpse, and a victim to the terrors he had anticipated.

From that chamber, and from that mansion, I fled aghast. The storm was still abroad in all its wrath as I found myself crossing the old causeway. Suddenly there shot along the path a wild light, and I turned to see whence a gleam so unusual could have issued; for the vast house and

its shadows were alone behind me. The radiance was that of the full, setting, and blood-red moon, which now shone vividly through that once barely-discernible fissure, of which I have before spoken as extending from the roof of the building, in a zig-zag direction, to the base. While I gazed, this fissure rapidly widened — there came a fierce breath of the whirlwind — the entire orb of the satellite burst at once upon my sight — my brain reeled as I saw the mighty walls rushing asunder — there was a long tumultuous shouting sound like the voice of a thousand waters — and the deep and dank tarn at my feet closed sullenly and silently over the fragments of the *"House of Usher."*

William Wilson

What say of it? what say CONSCIENCE *grim,*
That spectre in my path?

C H A M B E R L A I N ' s Pharronida.

LET me call myself, for the present, William Wilson. The fair page now lying before me need not be sullied with my real appellation. This has been already too much an object for the scorn — for the horror — for the detestation of my race. To the uttermost regions of the globe have not the indignant winds bruited its unparalleled infamy? Oh, outcast of all outcasts most abandoned! — to the earth art thou not forever dead? to its honors, to its flowers, to its golden aspirations? — and a cloud, dense, dismal, and limitless, does it not hang eternally between thy hopes and heaven?

I would not, if I could, here or today, embody a record of my later years of unspeakable misery and unpardonable crime. This epoch — these later years — took unto themselves a sudden elevation in turpitude, whose origin alone it is my present purpose to assign. Men usually grow base by degrees. From me, in an instant, all virtue dropped bodily as a mantle. From comparatively trivial wickedness I passed, with the stride of a giant, into more than the enormities of an Elah-Gabalus. What chance — what one event brought this evil thing to pass, bear with me while I relate. Death approaches; and the shadow which foreruns him has thrown a softening influence over my spirit. I long, in passing through the dim valley, for the sympathy — I had nearly said for the pity — of my fellow men. I would fain have them believe that I have been, in some measure, the slave of circumstances beyond human control. I would wish them to seek out for me, in the details I am about to give, some little oasis of *fatality* amid a wilderness of error. I would have them allow — what they

cannot refrain from allowing — that, although temptation may have ere-while existed as great, man was never *thus*, at least, tempted before — certainly, never *thus* fell. And is it therefore that he has never thus suffered? Have I not indeed been living in a dream? And am I not now dying a victim to the horror and the mystery of the wildest of all sublunary visions?

I am the descendant of a race whose imaginative and easily excitable temperament has at all times rendered them remarkable; and, in my earliest infancy, I gave evidence of having fully inherited the family character. As I advanced in years it was more strongly developed; becoming, for many reasons, a cause of serious disquietude to my friends, and of positive injury to myself. I grew self-willed, addicted to the wildest caprices, and a prey to the most ungovernable passions. Weak-minded, and beset with constitutional infirmities akin to my own, my parents could do but little to check the evil propensities which distinguished me. Some feeble and ill-directed efforts resulted in complete failure on their part, and, of course, in total triumph on mine. Thenceforward my voice was a household law; and at an age when few children have abandoned their leading-strings, I was left to the guidance of my own will, and became, in all but name, the master of my own actions.

My earliest recollections of a school-life, are connected with a large, rambling, Elizabethan house, in a misty-looking village of England, where were a vast number of gigantic and gnarled trees, and where all the houses were excessively ancient. In truth, it was a dream-like and spirit-soothing place, that venerable old town. At this moment, in fancy, I feel the refreshing chilliness of its deeply-shadowed avenues, inhale the fragrance of its thousand shrubberies, and thrill anew with undefinable delight, at the deep hollow note of the church-bell, breaking, each hour, with sullen and sudden roar, upon the stillness of the dusky atmosphere in which the fretted Gothic steeple lay imbedded and asleep.

It gives me, perhaps, as much of pleasure as I can now in any manner experience, to dwell upon minute recollections of the school and its concerns. Steeped in misery as I am — misery, alas! only too real — I shall be pardoned for seeking relief, however slight and temporary, in the weakness of a few rambling details. These, moreover, utterly trivial, and even ridiculous in themselves, assume, to my fancy, adventitious importance, as connected with a period and a locality when and where I recognize the first ambiguous monitions of the destiny which afterward so fully overshadowed me. Let me then remember.

The house, I have said, was old and irregular. The grounds were extensive, and a high and solid brick wall, topped with a bed of mortar and broken glass, encompassed the whole. This prison-like rampart formed the limit of our domain; beyond it we saw but thrice a week — once every Saturday afternoon, when, attended by two ushers, we were permitted to take brief walks in a body through some of the neighboring

fields — and twice during Sunday, when we were paraded in the same formal manner to the morning and evening service in the one church of the village. Of this church the principal of our school was pastor. With how deep a spirit of wonder and perplexity was I wont to regard him from our remote pew in the gallery, as, with step solemn and slow, he ascended the pulpit! This reverend man, with countenance so demurely benign, with robes so glossy and so clerically flowing, with wig so minutely powdered, so rigid and so vast, — could this be he who, of late, with sour visage, and in snuffy habiliments, administered, ferule in hand, the Draconian Laws of the academy? Oh, gigantic paradox, too utterly monstrous for solution!

At an angle of the ponderous wall frowned a more ponderous gate. It was riveted and studded with iron bolts, and surmounted with jagged iron spikes. What impressions of deep awe did it inspire! It was never opened save for the three periodical egressions and ingressions already mentioned; then, in every creak of its mighty hinges, we found a plenitude of mystery — a world of matter for solemn remark, or for more solemn meditation.

The extensive enclosure was irregular in form, having many capacious recesses. Of these, three or four of the largest constituted the play-ground. It was level, and covered with fine hard gravel. I well remember it had no trees, nor benches, nor any thing similar within it. Of course it was in the rear of the house. In front lay a small parterre, planted with box and other shrubs, but through this sacred division we passed only upon rare occasions indeed — such as a first advent to school or final departure thence, or perhaps, when a parent or friend having called for us, we joyfully took our way home for the Christmas or Midsummer holydays.

But the house! — how quaint an old building was this! — to me how veritable a palace of enchantment! There was really no end to its windings — to its incomprehensible subdivisions. It was difficult, at any given time, to say with certainty upon which of its two stories one happened to be. From each room to every other there were sure to be found three or four steps either in ascent or descent. Then the lateral branches were innumerable — inconceivable — and so returning in upon themselves, that our most exact ideas in regard to the whole mansion were not very far different from those with which we pondered upon infinity. During the five years of my residence here, I was never able to ascertain with precision, in what remote locality lay the little sleeping apartment assigned to myself and some eighteen or twenty other scholars.

The school-room was the largest in the house — I could not help thinking, in the world. It was very long, narrow, and dismally low, with pointed Gothic windows and a ceiling of oak. In a remote and terror-inspiring angle was a square enclosure of eight or ten feet, comprising the *sanctum*, "during hours," of our principal, the Reverend Dr. Bransby. It was a solid structure, with massy door, sooner than open which in the absence of

the "Dominie," we would all have willingly perished by the *peine forte et dure*. In other angles were two other similar boxes, far less reverenced, indeed, but still greatly matters of awe. One of these was the pulpit of the "classical" usher, one of the "English and mathematical." Interspersed about the room, crossing and recrossing in endless irregularity, were innumerable benches and desks, black, ancient, and time-worn, piled desperately with much bethumbed books, and so beseamed with initial letters, names at full length, grotesque figures, and other multiplied efforts of the knife, as to have entirely lost what little of original form might have been their portion in days long departed. A huge bucket with water stood at one extremity of the room, and a clock of stupenduous dimensions at the other.

Encompassed by the massy walls of this venerable academy, I passed, yet not in tedium or disgust, the years of the third lustrum of my life. The teeming brain of childhood requires no external world of incident to occupy or amuse it; and the apparently dismal monotony of a school was replete with more intense excitement than my riper youth has derived from luxury, or my full manhood from crime. Yet I must believe that my first mental development had in it much of the uncommon — even much of the *outré*. Upon mankind at large the events of very early existence rarely leave in mature age any definite impression. All is gray shadow — a weak and irregular remembrance — an indistinct regathering of feeble pleasures and phantasmagoric pains. With me this is not so. In childhood I must have felt with the energy of a man what I now find stamped upon memory in lines as vivid, as deep, and as durable as the *exergues* of the Carthaginian medals.

Yet in fact — in the fact of the world's view — how little was there to remember! The morning's awakening, the nightly summons to bed; the connings, the recitations; the periodical half-holidays, and perambulations; the play-ground, with its broils, its pastimes, its intrigues; — these, by a mental sorcery long forgotten, were made to involve a wilderness of sensation, a world of rich incident, a universe of varied emotion, of excitement, the most passionate and spirit-stirring. *"Oh, le bon temps que se siecle de fer!"*

In truth, the ardor, the enthusiasm, and the imperiousness of my disposition, soon rendered me a marked character among my schoolmates, and by slow, but natural gradations, gave me an ascendancy over all not greatly older than myself; — over all with a single exception. This exception was found in the person of a scholar, who, although no relation, bore the same christian and surname as myself; — a circumstance, in fact, little remarkable; for notwithstanding a noble descent, mine was one of those every-day appellations which seem, by prescriptive right, to have been, time out of mind, the common property of the mob. In this narrative I have therefore designated myself as William Wilson — a fictitious title not very dissimilar to the real. My namesake alone, of those who in

school phraseology constituted "our set," presumed to compete with me in the studies of the class — in the sports and broils of the play-ground — to refuse implicit belief in my assertions, and submission to my will — indeed, to interfere with my arbitrary dictation in any respect whatsoever. If there is on earth a supreme and unqualified depotism, it is the despotism of a master-mind in boyhood over the less energetic spirits of its companions.

Wilson's rebellion was to me a source of the greatest embarrassment; the more so as, in spite of the bravado with which in public I made a point of treating him and his pretensions, I secretly felt that I feared him, and could not help thinking the equality which he maintained so easily with myself, a proof of his true superiority; since not to be overcome cost me a perpetual struggle. Yet this superiority — even this equality — was in truth acknowledged by no one but myself; our associates, by some unaccountable blindness, seemed not even to suspect it. Indeed, his competition, his resistance, and especially his impertinent and dogged interference with my purposes, were not more pointed than private. He appeared to be destitute alike of the ambition which urged, and of the passionate energy of mind which enabled me to excel. In his rivalry he might have been supposed actuated solely by a whimsical desire to thwart, astonish, or mortify myself; although there were times when I could not help observing, with a feeling made up of wonder, abasement, and pique, that he mingled with his injuries, his insults, or his contradictions, a certain most inappropriate, and assuredly most unwelcome *affectionateness* of manner. I could only conceive this singular behavior to arise from a consummate self-conceit assuming the vulgar airs of patronage and protection.

Perhaps it was this latter trait in Wilson's conduct, conjoined with our identity of name, and the mere accident of our having entered the school upon the same day, which set afloat the notion that we were brothers, among the senior classes in the academy. These do not usually inquire with much strictness into the affairs of their juniors. I have before said, or should have said, that Wilson was not, in a most remote degree, connected with my family. But assuredly if we *had* been brothers we must have been twins; for, after leaving Dr. Bransby's, I casually learned that my namesake was born on the nineteenth of January, 1813 — and this is a somewhat remarkable coincidence; for the day is precisely that of my own nativity.

It may seem strange that in spite of the continual anxiety occasioned me by the rivalry of Wilson, and his intolerable spirit of contradiction, I could not bring myself to hate him altogether. We had, to be sure, nearly every day a quarrel in which, yielding me publicly the palm of victory, he, in some manner, contrived to make me feel that it was he who had deserved it; yet a sense of pride on my part, and a veritable dignity on his own, kept us always upon what are called "speaking terms,"

while there were many points of strong congeniality in our tempers, operating to awake in me a sentiment which our position alone, perhaps, prevented from ripening into friendship. It is difficult, indeed, to define, or even to describe, my real feelings toward him. They formed a motley and heterogeneous admixture; — some petulant animosity, which was not yet hatred, some esteem, more respect, much fear, with a world of uneasy curiosity. To the moralist it will be necessary to say, in addition, that Wilson and myself were the most inseparable companions.

It was no doubt the anomalous state of affairs existing between us, which turned all my attacks upon him, (and there were many, either open or covert) into the channel of banter or practical joke (giving pain while assuming the aspect of mere fun) rather than into a more serious and determined hostility. But my endeavors on this head were by no means uniformly successful, even when my plans were the most wittily concocted; for my namesake had much about him, in character, of that unassuming and quiet austerity which, while enjoying the poignancy of its own jokes, has no heel of Achilles in itself, and absolutely refuses to be laughed at. I could find, indeed, but one vulnerable point, and that, lying in a personal peculiarity, arising, perhaps, from constitutional disease, would have been spared by any antagonist less at his wit's end than myself; — my rival had a weakness in the faucial or guttural organs, which precluded him from raising his voice at any time *above a very low whisper*. Of this defect I did not fail to take what poor advantage lay in my power.

Wilson's retaliations in kind were many; and there was one form of his practical wit that disturbed me beyond measure. How his sagacity first discovered at all that so petty a thing would vex me, is a question I never could solve; but having discovered, he habitually practised the annoyance. I had always felt aversion to my uncourtly patronymic, and its very common, if not plebeian prænomen. The words were venom in my ears; and when, upon the day of my arrival, a second William Wilson came also to the academy, I felt angry with him for bearing the name, and doubly disgusted with the name because a stranger bore it, who would be the cause of its two-fold repetition, who would be constantly in my presence, and whose concerns, in the ordinary routine of the school business, must inevitably, on account of the detestable coincidence, be often confounded with my own.

The feeling of vexation thus engendered grew stronger with every circumstance tending to show resemblance, moral or physical, between my rival and myself. I had not then discovered the remarkable fact that we were of the same age; but I saw that we were of the same height, and I perceived that we were even singularly alike in general contour of person and outline of feature. I was galled, too, by the rumor touching a relationship, which had grown current in the upper forms. In a word, nothing could more seriously disturb me, (although I scrupulously concealed such disturbance), than any allusion to a similarity of mind, person, or con-

dition existing between us. But, in truth, I had no reason to believe that (with the exception of the matter of relationship, and in the case of Wilson himself), this similarity had ever been made a subject of comment, or even observed at all by our schoolfellows. That *he* observed it in all its bearings, and as fixedly as I, was apparent; but that he could discover in such circumstances so fruitful a field of annoyance, can only be attributed, as I said before, to his more than ordinary penetration.

His cue, which was to perfect an imitation of myself, lay both in words and in actions; and most admirably did he play his part. My dress it was an easy matter to copy; my gait and general manner were without difficulty, appropriated; in spite of his constitutional defect, even my voice did not escape him. My louder tones were, of course, unattempted, but then the key, — it was identical; *and his singular whisper, it grew the very echo of my own.*

How greatly this most exquisite portraiture harassed me (for it could not justly be termed a caricature), I will not now venture to describe. I had but one consolation — in the fact that the imitation, apparently, was noticed by myself alone, and that I had to endure only the knowing and strangely sarcastic smiles of my namesake himself. Satisfied with having produced in my bosom the intended effect, he seemed to chuckle in secret over the sting he had inflicted, and was characteristically disregardful of the public applause which the success of his witty endeavors might have so easily elicited. That the school, indeed, did not feel his design, perceive its accomplishment, and participate in his sneer, was, for many anxious months, a riddle I could not resolve. Perhaps the *gradation* of his copy rendered it not so readily perceptible; or, more possibly, I owed my security to the masterly air of the copyist, who, disdaining the letter (which in a painting is all the obtuse can see), gave but the full spirit of his original for my individual contemplation and chagrin.

I have already more than once spoken of the disgusting air of patronage which he assumed toward me, and of his frequent officious interference with my will. This interference often took the ungracious character of advice; advice not openly given, but hinted or insinuated. I received it with a repugnance which gained strength as I grew in years. Yet, at this distant day, let me do him the simple justice to acknowledge that I can recall no occasion when the suggestions of my rival were on the side of those errors or follies so usual to his immature age and seeming inexperience; that his moral sense, at least, if not his general talents and worldly wisdom, was far keener than my own; and that I might, to-day, have been a better and thus a happier man, had I less frequently rejected the counsels embodied in those meaning whispers which I then but too cordially hated and too bitterly despised.

As it was I at length grew restive in the extreme under his distasteful supervision, and daily resented more and more openly, what I considered his intolerable arrogance. I have said that, in the first years of our con-

nection as schoolmates, my feelings in regard to him might have been
easily ripened into friendship; but, in the latter months of my residence
at the academy, although the intrusion of his ordinary manner had, be-
yond doubt, in some measure, abated, my sentiments, in nearly similar
proportion, partook very much of positive hatred. Upon one occasion
he saw this, I think, and afterward avoided, or made a show of avoid-
ing me.

It was about the same period, if I remember aright, that, in an alterca-
tion of violence with him, in which he was more than usually thrown
of his guard, and spoke and acted with an openness of demeanor rather
foreign to his nature, I discovered, or fancied I discovered, in his accent,
in his air, and general appearance, a something which first startled, and
then deeply interested me, by bringing to mind dim visions of my earliest
infancy — wild, confused, and thronging memories of a time when
memory herself was yet unborn. I cannot better describe the sensation
which oppressed me, than by saying that I could with difficulty shake
off the belief of my having been acquainted with the being who stood
before me, at some epoch very long ago — some point of the past even
infinitely remote. The delusion, however, faded rapidly as it came; and
I mention it at all but to define the day of the last conversation I there
held with my singular namesake.

The huge old house, with its countless sub-divisions, had several large
chambers communicating with each other, where slept the greater num-
ber of the students. There were, however (as must necessarily happen in
a building so awkwardly planned), many little nooks or recesses, the
odds and ends of the structure; and these the economic ingenuity of
Dr. Bransby had also fitted up as dormitories; although, being the merest
closets, they were capable of accommodating but a single individual.
One of these small apartments was occupied by Wilson.

One night, about the close of my fifth year at the school, and im-
mediately after the altercation just mentioned, finding every one wrapped
in sleep, I arose from bed, and, lamp in hand, stole through a wilderness
of narrow pasages, from my own bedroom to that of my rival. I had long
been plotting one of those ill-natured pieces of practical wit at his ex-
pense in which I had hitherto been so uniformly unsuccessful. It was my
intention, now, to put my scheme in operation and I resolved to make
him feel the whole extent of the malice with which I was imbued. Having
reached his closet, I noiselessly entered, leaving the lamp, with a shade
over it, on the outside. I advanced a step and listened to the sound of
his tranquil breathing. Assured of his being asleep, I returned, took the
light, and with it again approached the bed. Close curtains were around
it, which, in the prosecution of my plan, I slowly and quietly withdrew,
when the bright rays fell vividly upon the sleeper, and my eyes at the
same moment, upon his countenance. I looked; — and a numbness, an

iciness of feeling instantly pervaded my frame. My breast heaved, my knees tottered, my whole spirit became possessed with an abjectless yet intolerable horror. Gasping for breath, I lowered the lamp in still nearer proximity to the face. Were these — *these* the lineaments of William Wilson? I saw, indeed, that they were his, but I shook as if with a fit of ague, in fancying they were not. What *was* there about them to confound me in this manner? I gazed; — while my brain reeled with a multitude of incoherent thoughts. Not thus he appeared — assuredly not *thus* — in the vivacity of his waking hours. The same name! the same contour of person! the same day of arrival at the academy! And then his dogged and meaningless imitation of my gait, my voice, my habits, and my manner! Was it, in truth, within the bounds of human possibility, that *what I now saw* was the result, merely, of the habitual practise of this sarcastic imitation? Awestricken, and with a creeping shudder, I extinguished the lamp, passed silently from the chamber, and left, at once, the halls of that old academy, never to enter them again.

After a lapse of some months, spent at home in mere idleness, I found myself a student at Eton. The brief interval had been sufficient to enfeeble my remembrance of the events at Dr. Bransby's, or at least to effect a material change in the nature of the feelings with which I remembered them. The truth — the tragedy — of the drama was no more. I could now find room to doubt the evidence of my senses; and seldom called up the subject at all but with wonder at the extent of human credulity, and a smile at the vivid force of the imagination which I hereditarily possessed. Neither was this species of skepticism likely to be diminished by the character of the life I led at Eton. The vortex of thoughtless folly into which I there so immediately and so recklessly plunged, washed away all but the froth of my past hours, ingulfed at once every solid or serious impression, and left to memory only the veriest levities of a former existence.

I do not wish, however, to trace the course of my miserable profligacy here — a profligacy which set at defiance the laws, while it eluded the vigilance of the institution. Three years of folly, passed without profit, had but given me rooted habits of vice, and added, in a somewhat unusual degree, to my bodily stature, when, after a week of soulless dissipation, I invited a small party of the most dissolute students to a secret carousal in my chambers. We met at a late hour of the night; for our debaucheries were to be faithfully protracted until morning. The wine flowed freely, and there were not wanting other and perhaps more dangerous seductions; so that the gray dawn had already faintly appeared in the east while our delirious extravagance was at its height. Madly flushed with cards and intoxication, I was in the act of insisting upon a toast of more than wonted profanity, when my attention was suddenly diverted by the violent, although partial, unclosing of the door of the apartment,

and by the eager voice of a servant from without. He said that some person, apparently in great haste, demanded to speak with me in the hall.

Wildly excited with wine, the unexpected interruption rather delighted than surprised me. I staggered forward at once, and a few steps brought me to the vestibule of the building. In this low and small room there hung no lamp; and now no light at all was admitted, save that of the exceedingly feeble dawn which made its way through the semicircular window. As I put my foot over the threshold, I became aware of the figure of a youth about my own height, and habited in a white kerseymere morning frock, cut in the novel fashion of the one I myself wore at the moment. This the faint light enabled me to perceive; but the features of his face I could not distinguish. Upon my entering, he strode hurriedly up to me, and, seizing me by the arm with a gesture of petulant impatience, whispered the words "William Wilson" in my ear.

I grew perfectly sober in an instant.

There was that in the manner of the stranger, and in the tremulous shake of his uplifted finger, as he held it between my eyes and the light, which filled me with unqualified amazement; but it was not this which had so violently moved me. It was the pregnancy of solemn admonition in the singular, low, hissing utterance; and, above all, it was the character, the tone, *the key*, of those few, simple, and familiar, yet *whispered* syllables, which came with a thousand thronging memories of by-gone days, and struck upon my soul with the shock of a galvanic battery. Ere I could recover the use of my senses he was gone.

Although this event failed not of a vivid effect upon my disordered imagination, yet was it evanescent as vivid. For some weeks, indeed, I busied myself in earnest inquiry, or was wrapped in a cloud of morbid speculation. I did not pretend to disguise from my perception the identity of the singular individual who thus perseveringly interfered with my affairs, and harassed me with his insinuated counsel. But who and what was this Wilson? — and whence came he? — and what were his purposes? Upon neither of these points could I be satisfied — merely ascertaining, in regard to him, that a sudden accident in his family had caused his removal from Dr. Bransby's academy on the afternoon of the day in which I myself had eloped. But in a brief period I ceased to think upon the subject, my attention being all absorbed in a contemplated departure for Oxford. Thither I soon went, the uncalculating vanity of my parents furnishing me with an outfit and annual establishment, which would enable me to indulge at will in the luxury already so dear to my heart — to vie in profuseness of expenditure with the haughtiest heirs of the wealthiest earldoms in Great Britain.

Excited by such appliances to vice, my constitutional temperament broke forth with redoubled ardor, and I spurned even the common restraints of decency in the mad infatuation of my revels. But it were absurd to pause in the detail of my extravagance. Let it suffice, that

among spendthrifts I out-Heroded Herod, and that, giving name to a multitude of novel follies, I added no brief appendix to the long catalogue of vices then usual in the most dissolute university of Europe.

It could hardly be credited, however, that I had, even here, so utterly fallen from the gentlemanly estate, as to seek acquaintance with the vilest arts of the gambler by profession, and, having become an adept in his despicable science, to practice it habitually as a means of increasing my already enormous income at the expense of the weak-minded among my fellow-collegians. Such, nevertheless, was the fact. And the very enormity of this offence against all manly and honorable sentiment proved, beyond doubt, the main if not the sole reason of the impunity with which it was committed. Who, indeed, among my most abandoned associates, would not rather have disputed the clearest evidence of his senses, than have suspected of such courses, the gay, the frank, the generous William Wilson — the noblest and most liberal commoner at Oxford — him whose follies (said his parasites) were but the follies of youth and unbridled fancy — whose errors but inimitable whim — whose darkest vice but a careless and dashing extravagance?

I had been now two years successfully busied in this way, when there came to the university a young *parvenu* nobleman, Glendenning — rich, said report, as Herodes Atticus — his riches, too, as easily acquired. I soon found him of weak intellect, and, of course, marked him as a fitting subject for my skill. I frequently engaged him in play, and contrived, with the gambler's usual art, to let him win considerable sums, the more effectually to entangle him in my snares. At length, my schemes being ripe, I met him (with the full-intention that this meeting should be final and decisive) at the chambers of a fellow-commoner (Mr. Preston), equally intimate with both, but who, to do him justice, entertained not even a remote suspicion of my design. To give this a better coloring, I had contrived to have assembled a party of some eight or ten, and was solicitously careful that the introduction of cards should appear accidental, and originate in the proposal of my contemplated dupe himself. To be brief upon a vile topic, none of the low finesse was omitted, so customary upon similar occasions, that it is a just matter for wonder how any are still found so besetted as to fall its victim.

We had protracted our sitting far into the night, and I had at length effected the manœuvre of getting Glendenning as my sole antagonist. The game, too, was my favorite *écarté*. The rest of the company, interested in the extent of our play, had abandoned their own cards, and were standing around us as spectators. The *parvenu*, who had been induced by my artifices in the early part of the evening, to drink deeply, now shuffled, dealt, or played, with a wild nervousness of manner for which his intoxication, I thought, might partially, but could not altogether account. In a very short period he had become my debtor to a large amount, when, having taken a long draught of port, he did precisely what I had

been coolly anticipating — he proposed to double our already extravagant stakes. With a well-feigned show of reluctance, and not until after my repeated refusal had seduced him into some angry words which gave a color of *pique* to my compliance, did I finally comply. The result, of course, did but prove how entirely the prey was in my toils: in less than an hour he had quadrupled his debt. For some time his countenance had been losing the florid tinge lent it by the wine; but now, to my astonishment, I perceived that it had grown to a pallor truly fearful. I say, to my astonishment. Glendenning had been represented to my eager inquiries as immeasurably wealthy; and the sums which he had as yet lost, although in themselves vast, could not, I supposed, very seriously annoy, much less so violently affect him. That he was overcome by the wine just swallowed, was the idea which most readily presented itself; and, rather with a view to the preservation of my own character in the eyes of my associates, than from any less interested motive, I was about to insist, peremptorily, upon a discontinuance of the play, when some expressions at my elbow from among the company, and an ejaculation evincing utter despair on the part of Glendenning, gave me to understand that I had effected his total ruin under circumstances which, rendering him an object for the pity of all, should have protected him from the ill offices even of a fiend.

What now might have been my conduct it is difficult to say. The pitiable condition of my dupe had thrown an air of embarrassed gloom over all; and, for some moments, a profound silence was maintained, during which I could not help feeling my cheeks tingle with the many burning glances of scorn or reproach cast upon me by the less abandoned of the party. I will even own that an intolerable weight of anxiety was for a brief instant lifted from my bosom by the sudden and extraordinary interruption which ensued. The wide, heavy folding doors of the apartment were all at once thrown open, to their full extent, with a vigorous and rushing impetuosity that extinguished, as if by magic, every candle in the room. Their light in dying, enabled us just to perceive that a stranger had entered, about my own height, and closely muffled in a cloak. The darkness, however, was not total; and we could only feel *that* he was standing in our midst. Before any one of us could recover from the extreme astonishment into which this rudeness had thrown all, we heard the voice of the intruder.

"Gentlemen," he said, in a low, distinct, and never-to-be-forgotten *whisper* which thrilled to the very marrow of my bones, "gentlemen, I made no apology for this behavior, because in thus behaving, I am fulfilling a duty. You are, beyond doubt, uninformed of the true character of the person who has to-night won at *écarté* a large sum of money from Lord Glendenning. I will therefore put you upon an expeditious and decisive plan of obtaining this very necessary information. Please to examine, at your leisure, the inner linings of the cuff of his left sleeve, and

the several little packages which may be found in the somewhat capacious pockets of his embroidered morning wrapper."

While he spoke, so profound was the stillness that one might have heard a pin drop upon the floor. In ceasing, he departed at once, and as abruptly as he had entered. Can I — shall I describe my sensations? Must I say that I felt all the horrors of the damned? Most assuredly I had a little time for reflection. Many hands roughly seized me upon the spot, and lights were immediately reproduced. A search ensued. In the lining of my sleeve were found all the court cards essential in écarté, and in the pockets of my wrapper, a number of packs, fac-similes of those used at our sittings, with the single exception that mine were of the species called, technically, *arrondées*; the honors being slightly convex at the ends, the lower cards slightly convex at the sides. In this disposition, the dupe who cuts, as customary, at the length of the pack, will invariably find that he cuts his antagonist an honor; while the gambler, cutting at the breadth, will, as certainly, cut nothing for his victim which may count in the records of the game.

Any burst of indigation upon this discovery would have affected me less than the silent contempt, or the sarcastic composure, with which it was received.

"Mr. Wilson," said our host, stooping to remove from beneath his feet an exceedingly luxurious cloak of rare furs, "Mr. Wilson, this is your property." (The weather was cold; and, upon quitting my own room, I had thrown a cloak over my dressing wrapper, putting it off upon reaching the scene of play.) "I presume it is supererogatory to seek here (eyeing the folds of the garment with a bitter smile) for any farther evidence of your skill. Indeed, we have had enough. You will see the necessity, I hope, of quitting Oxford — at all events, of quitting instantly my chambers."

Abased, humbled to the dust as I then was, it is probable that I should have resented this galling language by immediate personal violence, had not my whole attention been at the moment arrested by a fact of the most startling character. The cloak which I had worn was of a rare description of fur; how rare, how extravagantly costly, I shall not venture to say. Its fashion, too, was of my own fantastic invention; for I was fastidious to an absurd degree of coxcombry, in matters of this frivolous nature. When, therefore, Mr. Preston reached me that which he had picked up upon the floor, and near the folding-doors of the apartment, it was with an astonishment nearly bordering upon terror, that I perceived my own already hanging on my arm, (where I had no doubt unwittingly placed it,) and that the one presented me was but its exact counterpart in every, in even the minutest possible particular. The singular being who had so disastrously exposed me, had been muffled, I remembered, in a cloak; and none had been worn at all by any of the members of our party, with the exception of myself. Retaining some

presence of mind, I took the one offered me by Preston; placed it, unnoticed, over my own; left the apartment with a resolute scowl of defiance; and, next morning ere dawn of day, commenced a hurried journey from Oxford to the continent, in a perfect agony of horror and of shame.

I fled in vain. My evil destiny pursued me as if in exultation, and proved, indeed, that the exercise of its mysterious dominion had as yet only begun. Scarcely had I set foot in Paris, ere I had fresh evidence of the detestable interest taken by this Wilson in my concerns. Years flew, while I experienced no relief. Villain! — at Rome, with how untimely, yet with how spectral an officiousness, stepped he in between me and my ambition! at Vienna, too — at Berlin — and at Moscow! Where, in truth, had I *not* bitter cause to curse him within my heart? From his inscrutable tyranny did I at length flee, panic-stricken, as from a pestilence; and to the very ends of the earth *I fled in vain.*

And again, and again, in secret communion with my own spirit, would I demand the questions "Who is he? — whence came he? — and what are his objects?" But no answer was there found. And now I scrutinized, with a minute scrutiny, the forms, and the methods, and the leading traits of his impertinent supervision. But even here there was very little upon which to base a conjecture. It was noticeable, indeed, that, in no one of the multiplied instances in which he had of late crossed my path, had he so crossed it except to frustrate those schemes, or to disturb those actions, which, if fully carried out, might have resulted in bitter mischief. Poor justification this, in truth, for an authority so imperiously assumed! Poor indemnity for natural rights of self-agency so pertinaciously, so insultingly denied!

I had also been forced to notice that my tormentor, for a very long period of time, (while scrupulously and with miraculous dexterity maintaining his whim of an identity of apparel with myself,) had so contrived it, in the execution of his varied interference with my will, that I saw not, at any moment, the features of his face. Be Wilson what he might, *this*, at least, was but the veriest of affectation, or of folly. Could he, for an instant, have supposed that, in my admonisher at Eton — in the destroyer of my honor at Oxford, — in him who thwarted my ambition at Rome, my revenge at Paris, my passionate love at Naples, or what he falsely termed my avarice in Egypt, — that in this, my arch-enemy and evil genius, I could fail to recognize the William Wilson of my school-boy days, — the name-sake, the companion, the rival, — the hated and dreaded rival at Dr. Bransby's? Impossible! — But let me hasten to the last eventful scene of the drama.

Thus far I had succumbed supinely to this imperious dominion. The sentiment of deep awe with which I habitually regarded the elevated character, the majestic wisdom, the apparent omnipresence and omnipotence of Wilson, added to a feeling of even terror, with which certain other traits in his nature and assumptions inspired me, had operated,

hitherto, to impress me with an idea of my own utter weakness and help-lessness, and to suggest an implicit, although bitterly reluctant submis-sion to his arbitrary will. But, of late days, I had given myself up en-tirely to wine; and its maddening influence upon my hereditary temper rendered me more and more impatient of control. I began to murmur, — to hesitate, — to resist. And was it only fancy which induced me to believe that, with the increase of my own firmness, that of my tormentor underwent a proportional diminution? Be this as it may, I now began to feel the inspiration of a burning hope, and at length nurtured in my secret thoughts a stern and desperate resolution that I would submit no longer to be enslaved.

It was at Rome, during the Carnival of 18 —, that I attended a mas-querade in the palazzo of the Neapolitan Duke Di Broglio. I had in-dulged more freely than usual in the excesses of the wine-table; and now the suffocating atmosphere of the crowded rooms irritated me be-yond endurance. The difficulty, too, of forcing my way through the mazes of the company contributed not a little to the ruffling of my temper; for I was anxiously seeking (let me not say with what unworthy motive) the young, the gay, the beautiful wife of the aged and doting Di Broglio. With a too unscrupulous confidence she had previously com-municated to me the secret of the costume in which she would be habited, and now, having caught a glimpse of her person, I was hurrying to make my way into her presence. At this moment I felt a light hand placed upon my shoulder, and that ever-remembered, low, damnable *whisper* within my ear.

In an absolute phrenzy of wrath, I turned at once upon him who had thus interrupted me, and seized him violently by the collar. He was attired, as I had expected, in a costume altogether similar to my own; wearing a Spanish cloak of blue velvet, begirt about the waist with a crim-son belt sustaining a rapier. A mask of black silk entirely covered his face.

"Scoundrel!" I said, in a voice husky with rage, while every syllable I uttered seemed as new fuel to my fury; "scoundrel! impostor! accursed villain! you shall not — you *shall not* dog me unto death! Follow me, or I stab you where you stand!" — and I broke my way from the ball-room into a small ante-chamber adjoining, dragging him unresistingly with me as I went.

Upon entering, I thrust him furiously from me. He staggered against the wall, while I closed the door with an oath, and commanded him to draw. He hesitated but for an instant; then, with a slight sigh, drew in silence, and put himself upon his defence.

The contest was brief indeed. I was frantic with every species of wild excitement, and felt within my single arm the energy and power of a multitude. In a few seconds I forced him by sheer strength against the wainscotting, and thus, getting him at mercy, plunged my sword, with brute ferocity, repeatedly through and through his bosom.

At that instant some person tried the latch of the door. I hastened to prevent an intrusion, and then immediately returned to my dying antagonist. But what human language can adequately portray *that* astonishment, *that* horror which possessed me at the spectacle then presented to view? The brief moment in which I averted my eyes had been sufficient to produce, apparently, a material change in the arrangements at the upper or farther end of the room. A large mirror, — so at first it seemed to me in my confusion — now stood where none had been perceptible before; and as I stepped up to it in extremity of terror, mine own image, but with features all pale and dabbled in blood, advanced to meet me with a feeble and tottering gait.

Thus it appeared, I say, but was not. It was my antagonist — it was Wilson, who then stood before me in the agonies of his dissolution. His mask and cloak lay, where he had thrown them, upon the floor. Not a thread in all his raiment — not a line in all the marked and singular lineaments of his face which was not, even in the most absolute identity, *mine own!*

It was Wilson; but he spoke no longer in a whisper, and I could have fancied that I myself was speaking while he said:

"*You have conquered, and I yield. Yet henceforward art thou also dead — dead to the World, to Heaven, and to Hope! In me didst thou exist — and, in my death, see by this image, which is thine own, how utterly thou hast murdered thyself.*"

The Conversation of Eiros and Charmion

Πυρ σοι προσοισω

I will bring fire to thee.

E u r i p i d e s Andiom.

Eiros. Why do you call me Eiros?

Charmion. So henceforth will you always be called. You must forget, too, my earthly name, and speak to me as Charmion.

Eiros. This is indeed no dream!

Charmion. Dreams are with us no more; but of these mysteries anon. I rejoice to see you looking like-life and rational. The film of the shadow has already passed from off your eyes. Be of heart and fear nothing. Your allotted days of stupor have expired; and, to-morrow, I will myself induct you into the full joys and wonders of your novel existence.

Eiros. True, I feel no stupor, none at all. The wild sickness and the terrible darkness have left me, and I hear no longer that mad, rushing,

horrible sound, like the "voice of many waters." Yet my senses are be-wildered, Charmion, with the keenness of their perception of *the new*.

CHARMION. A few days will remove all this; — but I fully understand you, and feel for you. It is now ten earthly years since I underwent what you undergo, yet the remembrance of it hangs by me still. You have now suffered all of pain, however, which you will suffer in Aidenn.

EIROS. In Aidenn?

CHARMION. In Aidenn.

EIROS. Oh, God! — pity me, Charmion! — I am overburthened with the majesty of all things — of the unknown now known — of the specu-lative Future merged in the august and certain Present.

CHARMION. Grapple not now with such thoughts. Tomorrow we will speak of this. Your mind wavers, and its agitation will find relief in the exercise of simple memories. Look not around, nor forward — but back. I am burning with anxiety to hear the details of that stupendous event which threw you among us. Tell me of it. Let us converse of familiar things, in the old familiar language of the world which has so fearfully perished.

EIROS. Most fearfully, fearfully! — this is indeed no dream.

CHARMION. Dreams are no more. Was I much mourned, my Eiros?

EIROS. Mourned, Charmion? — oh deeply. To that last hour of all, there hung a cloud of intense gloom and devout sorrow over your household.

CHARMION. And that last hour — speak of it. Remember that, be-yond the naked fact of the catastrophe itself, I know nothing. When, coming out from among mankind, I passed into Night through the Grave — at that period, if I remember aright, the calamity which over-whelmed you was utterly unanticipated. But, indeed, I knew little of the speculative philosophy of the day.

EIROS. The individual calamity was, as you say, entirely unanticipated; but analogous misfortunes had been long a subject of discussion with astronomers. I need scarce tell you, my friend, that, even when you left us, men had agreed to understand those passages in the most holy writ-ings which speak of the final destruction of all things by fire, as having reference to the orb of the earth alone. But in regard to the immediate agency of the ruin, speculation had been at fault from that epoch in astronomical knowledge in which the comets were divested of the ter-rors of flame. The very moderate density of these bodies had been well established. They had been observed to pass among the satellites of Jupiter, without bringing about any sensible alteration either in the masses or in the orbits of these secondary planets. We had long re-garded the wanderers as vapory creations of inconceivable tenuity, and as altogether incapable of doing injury to our substantial globe, even in the event of contact. But contact was not in any degree dreaded; for the elements of all the comets were accurately known. That among *them* we

should look for the agency of the threatened fiery destruction had been for many years considered an inadmissible idea. But wonders and wild fancies had been, of late days, strangely rife among mankind; and although it was only with a few of the ignorant that actual apprehension prevailed, upon the announcement by astronomers of a *new* comet, yet this announcement was generally received with I know not what of agitation and mistrust.

The elements of the strange orb were immediately calculated, and it was at once conceded by all observers, that its path, at perihelion, would bring it into very close proximity with the earth. There were two or three astronomers, of secondary note, who resolutely maintained that a contact was inevitable. I cannot very well express to you the effect of this intelligence upon the people. For a few short days they would not believe an assertion which their intellect, so long employed among worldly considerations, could not in any manner grasp. But the truth of a vitally important fact soon makes its way into the understanding of even the most stolid. Finally, all men saw that astronomical knowledge lied not, and they awaited the comet. Its approach was not, at first, seemingly rapid; nor was its appearance of very unusual character. It was of a dull red, and had little perceptible train. For seven or eight days we saw no material increase in its apparent diameter, and but a partial alteration in its color. Meantime the ordinary affairs of men were discarded, and all interests absorbed in a growing discussion, instituted by the philosophic, in respect to the cometary nature. Even the grossly ignorant aroused their sluggish capacities to such considerations. The learned *now* gave their intellect — their soul — to no such points as the allaying of fear, or to the sustenance of loved theory. They sought — they panted for right views. They groaned for perfected knowledge. *Truth* arose in the purity of her strength and exceeding majsty, and the wise bowed down and adored.

That material injury to our globe or to its inhabitants would result from the apprehended contact, was an opinion which hourly lost ground among the wise; and the wise were now freely permitted to rule the reason and the fancy of the crowd. It was demonstrated, that the density of the comet's *nucleus* was far less than that of our rarest gas; and the harmless passage of a similar visitor among the satellites of Jupiter was a point strongly insisted upon, and which served greatly to allay terror. Theologists, with an earnestness fear-enkindled, dwelt upon the biblical prophecies, and expounded them to the people with a directness and simplicity of which no previous instance had been known. That the final destruction of the earth must be brought about by the agency of fire, was urged with a spirit that enforced everywhere conviction; and that the comets were of no fiery nature (as all men now knew) was a truth which relieved all, in a great measure, from the apprehension of the great calamity foretold. It is noticeable that the popular prejudices and

vulgar errors in regard to pestilences and wars — errors which were wont to prevail upon every appearance of a comet — were now altogether unknown. As if by some sudden convulsive exertion, reason had at once hurled superstition from her throne. The feeblest intellect had derived vigor from excessive interest.

What minor evils might arise from the contact were points of elaborate question. The learned spoke of slight geological disturbances, of probable alterations in climate, and consequently in vegetation; of possible magnetic and electric influences. Many held that no visible or perceptible effect would in any manner be produced. While such discussions were going on, their subject gradually approached, growing larger in apparent diameter, and of a more brilliant lustre. Mankind grew paler as it came. All human operations were suspended. There was an epoch in the course of the general sentiment when the comet had attained, at length, a size surpassing that of any previously recorded visitation. The people now, dismissing any lingering hope that the astronomers were wrong, experienced all the certainty of evil. The chimerical aspect of their terror was gone. The hearts of the stoutest of our race beat violently within their bosoms. A very few days sufficed, however, to merge even such feelings in sentiments more unendurable. We could no longer apply to the strange orb any *accustomed* thoughts. Its historical attributes had disappeared. It oppressed us with a hideous *novelty* of emotion. We saw it not as an astronomical phenomenon in the heavens, but as an incubus upon our hearts, and a shadow upon our brains. It had taken, with inconceivable rapidity, the character of a gigantic mantle of rare flame, extending from horizon to horizon.

Yet a day, and men breathed with greater freedom. It was clear that we were already within the influence of the comet; yet we lived. We even felt an unusual elasticity of frame and vivacity of mind. The exceeding tenuity of the object of our dread was apparent; for all heavenly objects were plainly visible through it. Meantime, our vegetation had perceptibly altered; and we gained faith, from this predicted circumstance, in the foresight of the wise. A wild luxuriance of foliage, utterly unknown before, burst out upon every vegetable thing.

Yet another day — and the evil was not altogether upon us. It was now evident that its nucleus would first reach us. A wild change had come over all men; and the first sense of *pain* was the wild signal for general lamentation and horror. This first sense of pain lay in a rigorous constriction of the breast and lungs, and an insufferable dryness of the skin. It could not be denied that our atmosphere was radically affected; the conformation of this atmosphere and the possible modifications to which it might be subjected, were now the topics of discussion. The result of investigation sent an electric thrill of the intensest terror through the universal heart of man.

It had been long known that the air which encircled us was a com-

pound of oxygen and nitrogen gases, in the proportion of twenty-one measures of oxygen, and seventy-nine of nitrogen, in every one hundred of the atmosphere. Oxygen, which was the principle of combustion, and the vehicle of heat, was absolutely necessary to the support of animal life, and was the most powerful and energetic agent in nature. Nitrogen, on the contrary, was incapable of supporting either animal life or flame. An unnatural excess of oxygen would result, it had been ascertained, in just such an elevation of the animal spirits as we had latterly experienced. It was the pursuit, the extension of the idea, which had engendered awe. What would be the result of *a total extraction of the nitrogen?* A combustion irresistible, all-devouring, omni-prevalent, immediate; — the entire fulfillment, in all their minute and terrible details, of the fiery and horror-inspiring denunciations of the prophecies of the Holy Book.

Why need I paint, Charmion, the now disenchained frenzy of mankind? That tenuity in the comet which had previously inspired us with hope, was now the source of the bitterness of despair. In its impalpable gaseous character we clearly perceived the consummation of Fate. Meantime a day again passed, bearing away with it the last shadow of Hope. We gasped in the rapid modification of the air. The red blood bounded tumultuously through its strict channels. A furious delirium possessed all men; and, with arms rigidly outstretched toward the threatening heavens, they trembled and shrieked aloud. But the nucleus of the destroyer was now upon us; even here in Aidenn, I shudder while I speak. Let me be brief — brief as the ruin that overwhelmed. For a moment there was a wild lurid light alone, visiting and penetrating all things. Then — let us bow down, Charmion, before the excessive majesty of the great God! — then, there came a shouting and pervading sound, as if from the mouth itself of HIM; while the whole incumbent mass of ether in which we existed, burst at once into a species of intense flame, for whose surpassing brilliancy and all-fervid heat even the angels in the high Heaven of pure knowledge have no name. Thus ended all.

Why the Little Frenchman Wears His Hand in a Sling

IT'S on my visiting cards sure enough (and it's them that's all o' pink satin paper) that inny gintleman that plases may behould the intheristhin words, "Sir Pathrick O'Grandison, Barronitt, 39 Southampton Row, Russell Square, Parrish o' Bloomsbury." And shud ye be wantin'

to diskiver who is the pink of purliteness quite, and the laider of the hot tun in the houl city o' Lonon — why it's jist mesilf. And fait that same is no wonder at all at all (so be plased to stop curlin your nose), for every inch o' the six wakes that I've been a gintleman, and left aff wid the bogthrothing to take up wid the Barronissy, it's Pathrick that's been living like a houly imperor, and gitting the iddication and the graces. Och! and wouldn't it be a blessed thing for your spirrits if ye cud lay your two peepers jist, upon Sir Pathrick O'Grandison, Barronitt, when he is all riddy drissed for the hopperer, or stipping into the Brisky for the drive into the Hyde Park. But it's the illigant big figgur that I ave, for the rason o' which all the ladies fall in love wid me. Isn't it my own swate silf now that'll missure the six fut, and the three inches more nor that, in me stockins, and that am excadingly will proportioned all over to match? And it is ralelly more than three fut and a bit that there is, inny how, of the little ould furrener Frinchman that lives jist over the way, and that's a oggling and a goggling the houl day, (and bad luck to him,) at the purty widdy Misthress Tracle that's my own nixt-door neighbor, (God bliss her!) and a most particuller frind and acquaintance? You percave the little spalpeen is summat down in the mouth, and wears his lift hand in a sling; and it's for that same thing, by yur lave, that I'm going to give you the good rason.

The truth of the houl matter is jist simple enough; for the very first day that I com'd from Connaught, and showd my swate little silf in the strait to the widdy, who was looking through the windy, it was a gone case althegither with the heart o' the purty Misthress Tracle. I percaved it, ye see, all at once, and no mistake, and that's God's truth. First of all it was up wid the windy in a jiffy, and thin she threw open her two peepers to the itmost, and thin it was a little gould spy-glass that she clapped tight to one o' them and divil may burn me if it didn't spake to me as plain as a peeper cud spake, and says it, through the spy-glass: "Och! the tip o' the mornin' to ye, Sir Patrick O'Grandison, Barronitt, mavourneen; and it's a nate gintleman that ye are, sure enough, and it's mesilf and me forten jist that'll be at yur sarvice, dear, inny time o' day at all at all for the asking." And it's not mesilf ye wud have to be bate in the purliteness; so I made her a bow that wud ha' broken yur heart altegither to behould, and thin I pulled aff me hat with a flourish, and thin I winked at her hard wid both eyes, as much as to say, "True for you, yer a swate little crature, Mrs. Tracle, me darlint, and I wish I may be drownthed dead in a bog, if it's not mesilf, Sir Pathrick O'Grandison, Barronitt, that'll make a houl bushel o' love to yur leddyship, in the twinkling o' the eye of a Londonderry purraty."

And it was the nixt mornin', sure, jist as I was making up me mind whither it wouldn't be the purlite thing to sind a bit o' writin' to the widdy by way of a love-litter, when up com'd the delivery servant wid an illigant card, and he tould me that the name on it (for I niver could

rade the copperplate printin on account of being lift handed) was all about Mounseer, the Count, A Goose, Look-aisy, Maiter-di-dauns, and that the houl of the divilish lingo was the spalpeeny long name of the little ould furrener Frinchman as lived over the way.

And jist wid that in cum'd the little willian himself, and then be made me a broth of a bow, and thin he said he had ounly taken the liberty of doing me the honor of the giving me a call, and thin he went on to palaver at a great rate, and divil the bit did I comprehind what he wud be afther the tilling me at all at all, excipting and saving that he said "pully wou, woolly wou," and tould me, among a bushel o' lies, bad luck to him, that he was mad for the love o' my widdy Misthress Tracle, and that my widdy Mrs. Tracle had a puncheon for *him*.

At the hearin' of this, ye may swear, though, I was as mad as a grass-hopper, but I remimbered that I was Sir Pathrick O'Grandison, Bar-ronitt, and that it wasn't althegither gentaal to lit the anger git the upper hand o' the purliteness, so I made light o' the matter and kipt dark, and got quite sociable wid the little chap, and afther a while what did he do but ask me to go wid him to the widdy's, saying he wud give me the feshionable inthroduction to her leddyship.

"Is it there ye are?" said I thin to mesilf, "and it's thrue for you, Pathrick, that ye're the fortunittest mortal in life. We'll soon see now whither it's your swate silf, or whither it's little Mounseer Maiter-di-dauns, that Misthress Tracle is head and ears in the love wid."

Wid that we wint aff to the widdy's, next door, and ye may well say it was an illigant place; so it was. There was a carpet all over the floor, and in one corner there was a forty-pinny and a jew's harp and the divil knows what ilse, and in another corner was a sofy, the beautifullest thing in all natur, and sitting on the sofy, sure enough, there was the swate little angel, Misthress Tracle.

"The tip o' the mornin' to ye," says I, "Mrs. Tracle," and thin I made sich an illigant obaysance that it wud ha quite althegither bewildered the brain o' ye.

"Wully woo, pully woo, plump in the mud," says the little furrenner Frinchman, "and sure Mrs. Tracle," says he, that he did, "isn't this gintleman here jist his reverence Sir Pathrick O'Grandison, Barronitt, and isn't he althegither and entirely the most particular frind and ac-quaintance that I have in the houl world?"

And wid that the widdy, she gits up from the sofy, and makes the swatest curthchy nor iver was seen; and thin down she sits like an angel; and thin, by the powers, it was that little spalpeen Mounseer Maiter-di-dauns that plumped his silf right down by the right side of her. Och hon! I ixpicted the two eyes o' me wud ha cum'd out of my head on the spot, I was so dispirate mad! Howiver, "Bait who!" says I, after awhile. "Is it there ye are, Mounseer Maiter-di-dauns?" and so down I plumped on the lift side of her leddyship, to be aven with the willain. Botheration!

it wud ha done your heart good to percave the illigant double wink that I gived her jist thin right in the face with both eyes.

But the little ould Frinchman he niver beginned to suspict me at all at all, and disperate hard it was he made the love to her leddyship. "Woully wou," says he, "Pully wou," says he, "Plump in the mud," says he.

"That's all to no use, Mounseer Frog, mavourneen," thinks I; and I talked as hard and as fast as I could all the while, and throth it was mesilf jist that divarted her leddyship complately and intirely, by rason of the illigant conversation that I kipt up wid her all about the dear bogs of Connaught. And by and by she gived me such a swate smile, from one ind of her mouth to the ither, that it made me as bould as a pig, and I jist took hould of the ind of her little finger in the most dillikitest manner in natur, looking at her all the while out o' the whites of my eyes.

And then ounly percave the cuteness of the swate angel, for no sooner did she obsarve that I was afther the squazing of her flipper, than she up wid it in a jiffy, and put it away behind her back, jist as much as to say, "Now thin, Sir Pathrick O'Grandison, there's a bitther chance for ye, mavourneen, for it's not altogether the gentaal thing to be afther the squazing of my flipper right full in the sight of that little furrenner Frinchman, Mounseer Maiter-di-dauns."

Wid that I giv'd her a big wink jist to say, "lit Sir Pathrick alone for the likes o' them thricks," and thin I wint aisy to work, and you'd have died wid the divarsion to behould how cliverly I slipped my right arm betwane the back o' the sofy, and the back of her leddyship, and there, sure enough, I found a swate little flipper all a waiting to say, "the tip o' the mornin' to ye, Sir Pathrick O'Grandison, Barronitt." And wasn't it mesilf, sure, that jist giv'd it the laste little bit of a squaze in the world, all in the way of a commincement, and not to be too rough wid her leddyship? and och, botheration, wasn't it the gentaalest and dilikittest of all the little squazes that I got in return? "Blood and thunder, Sir Pathrick, mavourneen," thinks I to mesilf, "fait it's jist the mother's son of you, and nobody else at all at all, that's the handsomest and the fortunittest young bog-throtter that ever cum'd out of Connaught!" And with that I giv'd the flipper a big squaze, and a big squaze it was, by the powers, that her leddyship giv'd to me back. But it would ha split the seven sides of you wid the laffin' to behould, jist then all at once, the consated behavior of Mounseer Maiter-di-dauns. The likes o' sich a jabbering, and a smirking, and a parley-wouing as he begin'd wid her leddyship, niver was known before upon arth; and divil may burn me if it wasn't me own very two peepers that cotch'd him tipping her the wink out of one eye. Och, hon! if it wasn't mesilf thin that was mad as a Kilkenny cat I shud like to be tould who it was!

"Let me infarm you, Mounseer Maiter-di-dauns," said I, as purlite as iver ye seed, "that it's not the gintaal thing at all at all, and not for the

likes o' you inny how, to be afther the oggling and a goggling at her leddyship in that fashion," and jist wid that such another squaze as it was I giv'd her flipper, all as much as to say, "isn't it Sir Pathrick now, my jewel, that'll be able to the proticting o' you, my darlint?" and then there cum'd another squaze back, all by way of the answer. "Thrue for you, Sir Pathrick," it said as plain as iver a squaze said in the world, "Thrue for you, Sir Pathrick, mavourneen, and it's a proper nate gintleman ye are — that's God's truth," and with that she opened her two beautiful peepers till I belaved they wud ha' cum'd out of her hid althegither and intirely, and she looked first as mad as a cat at Mounseer Frog, and thin as smiling as all out o' doors at mesilf.

"Thin," says he, the willian, "Och hon! and a wolly-wou, pully-wou," and then wid that he shoved up his two shoulders till the divil the bit of his hid was to be diskivered, and then he let down the two corners of his purraty-trap, and thin not a haporth more of the satisfaction could I git out o' the spalpeen.

Belave me, my jewel, it was Sir Pathrick that was unreasonable mad thin, and the more by token that the Frinchman kipt an wid his winking at the widdy; and the widdy she kept an wid the squazing of my flipper, as much as to say, "At him again, Sir Pathrick O'Grandison, mavourneen:" so I just ripped out wid a big oath, and says I;

"Ye little spalpeeny frog of a bog-throtting son of a bloody noun!" — and jist thin what d'ye think it was that her leddyship did? Troth she jumped up from the sofy as if she was bit, and made off through the door, while I turned my head round afther her, in a complate bewilderment and botheration, and followed her wid me two peepers. You percave I had a reason of my own for knowing that she couldn't git down the stares althegither and intirely; for I knew very well that I had hould of her hand, for the divil the bit had I iver lit it go. And says I;

"Isn't it the laste little bit of a mistake in the world that ye've been afther the making, yer leddyship? Come back now, that's a darlint, and I'll give ye yur flipper." But aff she wint down the stairs like a shot, and thin I turned round to the little Frinch furrener. Och hon! if it wasn't his spalpeeny little paw that I had hould of in my own — why thin — thin it wasn't — that's all.

And maybe it wasn't mesilf that jist died then outright wid the laffin', to behold the little chap when he found out that it wasn't the widdy at all at all that he had had hould of all the time, but only Sir Pathrick O'Grandison. The ould divil himself niver behild sich a long face as he pet an! As for Sir Pathrick O'Grandison, Barronitt, it wasn't for the likes of his riverence to be afther the minding of a thrifle of a mistake. Ye may jist say, though (for it's God's thruth), that afore I left hould of the flipper of the spalpeen (which was not till afther her leddyship's futman had kicked us both down the stairs, I giv'd it such a nate little broth of a squaze as made it all up into raspberry jam.

"Woully wou," says he, "pully wou," says he — "Cot tam!"

And that's jist the thruth of the rason why he wears his lift hand in a sling.

<div align="right">LITTLETON BARRY.</div>

The Business Man

Method is the soul of business.

<div align="right">OLD SAYING.</div>

I AM a business man. I am a methodical man. Method is *the* thing, after all. But there are no people I more heartily despise than your eccentric fools who prate about method without understanding it; attending strictly to its letter, and violating its spirit. These fellows are always doing the most out-of-the-way things in what they call an orderly manner. Now here, I conceive, is a positive paradox. True method appertains to the ordinary and the obvious alone, and cannot be applied to the *outré*. What definite idea can a body attach to such expressions as "methodical Jack o' Dandy," or "a systematical Will o' the Wisp"?

My notions upon this head might not have been so clear as they are, but for a fortunate accident which happened to me when I was a very little boy. A good-hearted old Irish nurse (whom I shall not forget in my will) took me up one day by the heels, when I was making more noise than was necessary, and swinging me round two or three times, "d——d my eyes for a skreeking little spalpeen," and then knocked my head into a cocked hat against the bedpost. This, I say, decided my fate, and made my fortune. A bump arose at once on my sinciput, and turned out to be as pretty an organ of *order* as one shall see on a summer's day. Hence that positive appetite for system and regularity which has made me the distinguished man of business that I am.

If there is any thing on earth I hate, it is a genius. Your geniuses are all arrant asses — the greater the genius the greater the ass — and to this rule there is no exception whatever. Especially, you cannot make a man of business out of a genius, any more than money out of a Jew, or the best nutmegs out of pine-knots. The creatures are always going off at a tangent into some fantastic employment, or ridiculous speculation, entirely at variance with the "fitness of things," and having no business whatever to be considered as a business at all. Thus you may tell these characters immediately by the nature of their occupations. If you ever perceive a man setting up as a merchant or a manufacturer; or going into the cotton or tobacco trade, or any of those eccentric pursuits; or getting to be a drygoods dealer, or soap-boiler, or something of that kind; or

pretending to be a lawyer, or a blacksmith, or a physician — any thing
out of the usual way — you may set him down at once as a genius, and
then, according to the rule-of-three, he's an ass.

Now I am not in any respect a genius, but a regular business man. My
Day-book and Ledger will evince this in a minute. They are well kept,
though I say it myself; and, in my general habits of accuracy and punctu-
ality, I am not to be beat by a clock. Moreover, my occupations have
been always made to chime in with the ordinary habitudes of my fellow-
men. Not that I feel the least indebted, upon this score, to my exceed-
ingly weak-minded parents, who, beyond doubt, would have made an
arrant genius of me at last, if my guardian angel had not come, in good
time, to the rescue. In biography the truth is every thing, and in auto-
biography it is especially so — yet I scarcely hope to be believed when I
state, however solemnly, that my poor father put me, when I was about
fifteen years of age, into the counting-house of what he termed "a
respectable hardware and commission merchant doing a capital bit of
business!" A capital bit of fiddlestick! However, the consequence of this
folly was, that in two or three days, I had to be sent home to my button-
headed family in a high state of fever, and with a most violent and dan-
gerous pain in the sinciput, all around about my organ of order. It was
nearly a gone case with me then — just touch-and-go for six weeks —
the physicians giving me up and all that sort of thing. But, although I
suffered much, I was a thankful boy in the main. I was saved from being
a "respectable hardware and commission merchant, doing a capital bit
of business," and I felt grateful to the protuberance which had been the
means of my salvation, as well as to the kindhearted female who had
originally put these means within my reach.

The most of boys run away from home at ten or twelve years of age,
but I waited till I was sixteen. I don't know that I should have gone even
then, if I had not happened to hear my old mother talk about setting me
up on my own hook in the grocery way. The *grocery* way! — only think
of that! I resolved to be off forthwith, and try and establish myself in
some *decent* occupation, without dancing attendance any longer upon
the caprices of these eccentric old people, and running the risk of being
made a genius of in the end. In this project I succeeded perfectly well at
the first effort, and by the time I was fairly eighteen, found myself doing
an extensive and profitable business in the Tailor's Walking-Advertise-
ment line.

I was enabled to discharge the onerous duties of this profession, only
by that rigid adherence to system which formed the leading feature of
my mind. A scrupulous *method* characterized my actions as well as my
accounts. In my case it was method — not money — which made the
man: at least all of him that was not made by the tailor whom I served.
At nine, every morning, I called upon that individual for the clothes
of the day. Ten o'clock found me in some fashionable promenade or

other place of public amusement. The precise regularity with which I turned my handsome person about, so as to bring successively into view every portion of the suit upon my back, was the admiration of all the knowing men in the trade. Noon never passed without my bringing home a customer to the house of my employers, Messrs. Cut & Comeagain. I say this proudly, but with tears in my eyes — for the firm proved themselves the basest of ingrates. The little account, about which we quarreled and finally parted, cannot, in any item, be thought overcharged, by gentlemen really conversant with the nature of the business. Upon this point, however, I feel a degree of proud satisfaction in permitting the reader to judge for himself. My bill ran thus:

Messrs. Cut & Comeagain,
Merchant Tailors.
To Peter Proffit, Walking Advertiser,

	Drs.
July 10. — to promenade, as usual and customer brought home. .	$oo 25
July 11. — To do do do	25
July 12. — To one lie, second class; damaged black cloth sold for invisible green	25
July 13. — To one lie, first class, extra quality and size; recommending milled satinet as broadcloth	75
July 20. — To purchasing bran new paper shirt collar or dickey, to set off gray Petersham	02
Aug. 15. — To wearing double-padded bobtail frock, (thermometer 106 in the shade.)	25
Aug. 16. — Standing on one leg three hours, to show off new-style strapped pants at 12½ cents per leg per hour	37½
Aug. 17. — To promenade, as usual, and large customer brought (fat man)	50
Aug. 18. — To do do (medium size)	25
Aug. 19. — To do do (small man and bad pay)	06
	[sic] $2 96½

The item chiefly disputed in this bill was the very moderate charge of two pennies for the dickey. Upon my word of honor, this *was not* an unreasonable price for that dickey. It was one of the cleanest and prettiest little dickeys I ever saw; and I have good reason to believe that it effected the sale of three Petershams. The elder partner of the firm, however, would allow me only one penny of the charge, and took it upon himself to show in what manner four of the same sized conveniences could be got out of a sheet of foolscap. But it is needless to say that I stood upon the *principle* of the thing. Business is business, and should be done in a business way. There was no *system* whatever in swindling

me out of a penny — a clear fraud of fifty per cent. — no *method* in any respect. I left at once the employment of Messrs. Cut & Comeagain, and set up in the Eye-Sore line by myself — one of the most lucrative, respectable, and independent of the ordinary occupations.

My strict integrity, economy, and rigorous business habits, here again came into play. I found myself driving a flourishing trade, and soon became a marked man upon 'Change. The truth is, I never dabbled in flashy matters, but jogged on in the good old sober routine of the calling — a calling in which I should, no doubt, have remained to the present hour, but for a little accident which happened to me in the prosecution of one of the usual business operations of the profession. Whenever a rich old hunks or prodigal heir or bankrupt corporation gets into the notion of putting up a palace, there is no such thing in the world as stopping either of them, and this every intelligent person knows. The fact in question is indeed the basis of the Eye-Sore trade. As soon, therefore, as a building-project is fairly afoot by one of these parties, we merchants secure a nice corner of the lot in contemplation, or a prime little situation just adjoining, or right in front. This done, we wait until the palace is half-way up, and then we pay some tasty architect to run us up an ornamental mud hovel, right against it; or a Down-East or Dutch Pagoda, or a pig-sty, or an ingenious little bit of fancy work, either Esquimau, Kickapoo, or Hottentot. Of course we can't afford to take these structures down under a bonus of five hundred per cent. upon the prime cost of our lot and plaster. *Can* we? I ask the question. I ask it of business men. It would be irrational to suppose that we can. And yet there was a rascally corporation which asked me to do this very thing — this *very thing!* I did not reply to their absurd proposition, of course; but I felt it a duty to go that same night, and lamp-black the whole of their palace. For this the unreasonable villains clapped me into jail; and the gentlemen of the Eye-Sore trade could not well avoid cutting my connection when I came out.

The Assault-and-Battery business, into which I was now forced to adventure for a livelihood, was somewhat ill-adapted to the delicate nature of my constitution; but I went to work in it with a good heart, and found my account here, as heretofore, in those stern habits of methodical accuracy which had been thumped into me by that delightful old nurse — I would indeed be the basest of men not to remember her well in my will. By observing, as I say, the strictest system in all my dealings, and keeping a well-regulated set of books, I was enabled to get over many serious difficulties, and, in the end, to establish myself very decently in the profession. The truth is, that few individuals, in any line, did a snugger little busines than I. I will just copy a page or so out of my Day-Book; and this will save me the necessity of blowing my own trumpet — a contemptible practice of which no high-minded man will be guilty. Now, the Day-Book is a thing that don't lie.

"Jan. 1.— New Year's Day. Met Snap in the street, groggy. Mem — he'll do. Met Gruff shortly afterward, blind drunk. Mem — he'll answer, too. Entered both gentlemen in my Ledger, and opened a running account with each.

"Jan. 2. — Saw Snap at the Exchange, and went up and trod on his toe. Doubled his fist and knocked me down. Good! — got up again. Some trifling difficulty with Bag, my attorney. I want the damages at a thousand, but he says that for so simple a knock down we can't lay them at more than five hundred. Mem — must get rid of Bag — no *system* at all.

"Jan. 3. — Went to the theatre, to look for Gruff. Saw him sitting in a side box, in the second tier, between a fat lady and a lean one. Quizzed the whole party through an opera-glass, till I saw the fat lady blush and whisper to G. Went round, then, into the box, and put my nose within reach of his hand. Wouldn't pull it — no go. Blew it, and tried again — no go. Sat down then, and winked at the lean lady, when I had the high satisfaction of finding him lift me up by the nape of the neck, and fling me over into the pit. Neck dislocated, and right leg capitally splintered. Went home in high glee, drank a bottle of champagne, and booked the young man for five thousand. Bag says it'll do.

"Feb. 15. — Compromised the case of Mr. Snap. Amount entered in Journal — fifty cents — which see.

"Feb. 16. — Cast by that ruffian, Gruff, who made me a present of five dollars. Costs of suit, four dollars and twenty-five cents. Nett profit, — see Journal, — seventy-five cents."

Now, here is a clear gain, in a very brief period, of no less than one dollar and twenty-five cents — this is in the mere cases of Snap and Gruff; and I solemnly assure the reader that these extracts are taken at random from my Day-Book.

It's an old saying, and a true one, however, that money is nothing in comparison with health. I found the exactions of the profession somewhat too much for my delicate state of body; and, discovering, at last, that I was knocked all out of shape, so that I didn't know very well what to make of the matter, and so that my friends, when they met me in the street, couldn't tell that I was Peter Proffit at all, it occurred to me that the best expedient I could adopt was to alter my line of business. I turned my attention, therefore, to Mud-Dabbling, and continued it for some years.

The worst of this occupation is, that too many people take a fancy to it, and the competition is in consequence excessive. Every ignoramus of a fellow who finds that he hasn't brains in sufficient quantity to make his way as a walking advertiser, or an eye-sore prig, or a salt-and-batter man, thinks, of course, that he'll answer very well as a dabbler of mud. But there never was entertained a more erroneous idea than that it requires no brains to mud-dabble. Especially, there is nothing to be made

in this way without *method*. I did only a retail business myself, but my old habits of *system* carried me swimmingly along. I selected my street-crossing, in the first place, with great deliberation, and I never put down a broom in any part of the town *but that*. I took care, too, to have a nice little puddle at hand, which I could get at in a minute. By these means I got to be well known as a man to be trusted; and this is one-half the battle, let me tell you, in trade. Nobody ever failed to pitch *me* a copper, and got over *my* crossing with a clean pair of pantaloons. And, as my business habits, in this respect, were sufficiently understood, I never met with any attempt at imposition. I wouldn't have put up with it, if I had. Never imposing upon any one myself, I suffered no one to play the possum with me. The frauds of the banks of course I couldn't help. Their suspension put me to ruinous inconvenience. These, how-ever, are not individuals, but corporations; and corporations, it is very well known, have neither bodies to be kicked nor souls to be damned.

I was making money at this business when, in an evil moment, I was induced to merge it in the Cur-Spattering — a somewhat analogous, but, by no means, so respectable a profession. My location, to be sure, was an excellent one, being central, and I had capital blacking and brushes. My little dog, too, was quite fat and up to all varieties of snuff. He had been in the trade a long time, and, I may say, understood it. Our general routine was this: — Pompey, having rolled himself well in the mud, sat upon end at the shop door, until he observed a dandy approaching in bright boots. He then proceeded to meet him, and gave the Wellingtons a rub or two with his wool. Then the dandy swore very much, and looked about for a boot-black. There I was, full in his view, with blacking and brushes. It was only a minute's work, and then came a sixpence. This did moderately well for a time; — in fact, I was not avaricious, but my dog was. I allowed him a third of the profit, but he was advised to insist upon half. This I couldn't stand — so we quarrelled and parted.

I next tried my hand at the Organ-Grinding for a while, and may say that I made out pretty well. It is a plain, straightforward business, and requires no particular abilities. You can get a music-mill for a mere song, and to put it in order, you have but to open the works, and give them three or four smart raps with a hammer. In improves the tone of the thing, for business purposes, more than you can imagine. This done, you have only to stroll along, with the mill on your back, until you see tan-bark in the street, and a knocker wrapped up in buckskin. Then you stop and grind; looking as if you meant to stop and grind till doomsday. Pres-ently a window opens, and somebody pitches you a sixpence, with a request to "Hush up and go on," etc. I am aware that some grinders have actually afforded to "go on" for this sum; but for my part, I found the necessary outlay of capital too great to permit of my "going on" under a shilling.

At this occupation I did a good deal; but, somehow, I was not quite satisfied, and so finally abandoned it. The truth is, I labored under the disadvantage of having no monkey — and American streets are *so* muddy, and a Democratic rabble is *so* obstrusive, and so full of demnition mischievous little boys.

I was now out of employment for some months, but at length succeeded, by dint of great interest, in procuring a situation in the Sham-Post. The duties, here, are simple, and not altogether unprofitable. For example: — very early in the morning I had to make up my packet of sham letters. Upon the inside of each of these I had to scrawl a few lines — on any subject which occurred to me as sufficiently mysterious — signing all the epistles Tom Dobson, or Bobby Tompkins, or anything in that way. Having folded and sealed all, and stamped them with sham post-marks — New Orleans, Bengal, Botany Bay, or any other place a great way off — I set out, forthwith, upon my daily route, as if in a very great hurry. I always called at the big houses to deliver the letters, and receive the postage. Nobody hesitates at paying for a letter — especially for a double one — people *are* such fools — and it was no trouble to get round a corner before there was time to open the epistles. The worst of this profession was, that I had to walk so much and so fast; and so frequently to vary my route. Besides, I had serious scruples of conscience. I can't bear to hear innocent individuals abused — and the way the whole town took to cursing Tom Dobson and Bobby Tompkins was really awful to hear. I washed my hands of the matter in disgust.

My eighth and last speculation has been in the Cat-Growing way. I I have found that a most pleasant and lucrative business, and, really, no trouble at all. The country, it is well known, has become infested with cats — so much so of late, that a petition for relief, most numerously and respectably signed, was brought before the Legislature at its late memorable session. The Assembly, at this epoch, was unusually well-informed, and, having passed many other wise and wholesome enactments, it crowned all with the Cat-Act. In its original form, this law offered a premium for cat-*heads* (fourpence a-piece), but the Senate succeeded in amending the main clause, so as to substitute the word "*tails*" for "heads." This amendment was so obviously proper, that the House concurred in it *nem. con.*

As soon as the governor had signed the bill, I invested my whole estate in the purchase of Toms and Tabbies. At first I could only afford to feed them upon mice (which are cheap), but they fulfilled the scriptural injunction at so marvellous a rate, that I at length considered it my best policy to be liberal, and so indulged them in oysters and turtle. Their tails, at a legislative price, now bring me in a good income; for I have discovered a way, in which, by means of Macassar oil, I can force three crops in a year. It delights me to find, too, that the animals soon get

accustomed to the thing, and would rather have the appendages cut off
than otherwise. I consider myself, therefore, a made man, and am bar-
gaining for a country seat on the Hudson.

The Man of the Crowd

Ce grand malheur, de ne pouvoir être seul.

LA BRUYÈRE.

I T was well said of a certain German book that *"er lasst sich nicht lesen"*
— it does not permit itself to be read. There are some secrets which do
not permit themselves to be told. Men die nightly in their beds, wringing
the hands of ghostly confessors, and looking them piteously in the eyes —
die with despair of heart and convulsion of throat, on account of the
hideousness of mysteries which will not *suffer themselves to be revealed*.
Now and then, alas, the conscience of man takes up a burden so heavy
in horror that it can be thrown down only into the grave. And thus the
essence of all crime is undivulged.

Not long ago, about the closing in of an evening in autumn, I sat at
the large bow-window of the D—— Coffee-House in London. For some
months I had been ill in health, but was now convalescent, and, with
returning strength, found myself in one of those happy moods which are
so precisely the converse of *ennui* — moods of the keenest appetency,
when the film from the mental vision departs — αχλυs οs πριν επηεν
— and the intellect, electrified, surpasses as greatly its everyday
condition, as does the vivid yet candid reason of Leibnitz, the mad and
flimsy rhetoric of Gorgias. Merely to breathe was enjoyment; and I de-
rived positive pleasure even from many of the legitimate sources of pain.
I felt a calm but inquisitive interest in every thing. With a cigar in my
mouth and a newspaper in my lap, I had been amusing myself for the
greater part of the afternoon, now in poring over advertisements, now
in observing the promiscuous company in the room, and now in peering
through the smoky panes into the street.

This latter is one of the principal thoroughfares of the city, and had
been very much crowded during the whole day. But, as the darkness came
on, the throng momently increased; and, by the time the lamps were
well lighted, two dense and continuous tides of population were rush-
ing past the door. At this particular period of the evening I had never
before been in a similar situation, and the tumultuous sea of human
heads filled me, therefore, with a delicious novelty of emotion. I gave

up, at length, all care of things within the hotel, and became absorbed in contemplation of the scene without.

At first my observations took an abstract and generalizing turn. I looked at the passengers in masses, and thought of them in their aggregate relations. Soon, however, I descended to details, and regarded with minute interest the innumerable varieties of figure, dress, air, gait, visage, and expression of countenance.

By far the greater number of those who went by had a satisfied, business-like demeanor, and seemed to be thinking only of making their way through the press. Their brows were knit, and their eyes rolled quickly; when pushed against by fellow-wayfarers they evinced no symptom of impatience, but adjusted their clothes and hurried on. Others, still a numerous class, were restless in their movements, had flushed faces, and talked and gesticulated to themselves, as if feeling in solitude on account of the very denseness of the company around. When impeded in their progress, these people suddenly ceased muttering; but redoubled their gesticulations, and awaited, with an absent and overdone smile upon their lips, the course of the persons impeding them. If jostled, they bowed profusely to the jostlers, and appeared overwhelmed with confusion. — There was nothing very distinctive about these two large classes beyond what I have noted. Their habiliments belonged to that order which is pointedly termed the decent. They were undoubtedly noblemen, merchants, attorneys, tradesmen, stock-jobbers — the Eupatrids and the common-places of society — men of leisure and men actively engaged in affairs of their own — conducting business upon their own responsibility. They did not greatly excite my attention.

The tribe of clerks was an obvious one; and here I discerned two remarkable divisions. There were the junior clerks of flash houses — young gentlemen with tight coats, bright boots, well-oiled hair, and supercilious lips. Setting aside a certain dapperness of carriage, which may be termed *deskism* for want of a better word, the manner of these persons seemed to be an exact facsimile of what had been the perfection of *bon ton* about twelve or eighteen months before. They wore the cast-off graces of the gentry; — and this, I believe, involves the best definition of the class.

The division of the upper clerks of staunch firms, or of the "steady old fellows," it was not possible to mistake. These were known by their coats and pantaloons of black or brown, made to sit comfortably, with white cravats and waistcoats, broad solid-looking shoes, and thick hose or gaiters. They had all slightly bald heads, from which the right ears, long used to pen-holding, had an odd habit of standing off on end. I observed that they always removed or settled their hats with both hands, and wore watches, with short gold chains of a substantial and ancient pattern. Theirs was the affectation of respectability — if indeed there be an affectation so honorable.

There were many individuals of dashing appearance, whom I easily understood as belonging to the race of swell pick-pockets, with which all great cities are infested. I watched these gentry with much inquisitiveness, and found it difficult to imagine how they should ever be mistaken for gentlemen by gentlemen themselves. Their voluminousness of wristband, with an air of excessive frankness, should betray them at once.

The gamblers, of whom I descried not a few, were still more easily recognizable. They wore every variety of dress, from that of the desperate thimble-rig bully, with velvet waistcoat, fancy neckerchief, gilt chains, and filagreed buttons, to that of the scrupulously inornate clergyman, than which nothing could be less liable to suspicion. Still all were distinguished by a certain sodden swarthiness of complexion, a filmy dimness of eye, and pallor and compression of lip. There were two other traits, moreover, by which I could always detect them: a guarded lowness of tone in conversation, and a more than ordinary extension of the thumb in a direction at right angles with the fingers. Very often, in company with these sharpers, I observed an order of men somewhat different in habits, but still birds of a kindred feather. They may be defined as the gentlemen who live by their wits. They seem to prey upon the public in two battalions — that of the dandies and that of the military men. Of the first grade the leading features are long locks and smiles; of the second, frogged coats and frowns.

Descending in the scale of what is termed gentility, I found darker and deeper themes for speculation. I saw Jew pedlars, with hawk eyes flashing from countenances whose every other feature wore only an expression of abject humility; sturdy professional street beggars scowling upon mendicants of a better stamp, whom despair alone had driven forth into the night for charity; feeble and ghastly invalids, upon whom death had placed a sure hand, and who sidled and tottered through the mob, looking every one beseechingly in the face, as if in search of some chance consolation, some lost hope; modest young girls returning from long and late labor to a cheerless home, and shrinking more tearfully than indignantly from the glances of ruffians, whose direct contact, even, could not be avoided; women of the town of all kinds and of all ages — the unequivocal beauty in the prime of her womanhood, putting one in mind of the statue in Lucian, with the surface of Parian marble, and the interior filled with filth — the loathsome and utterly lost leper in rags — the wrinkled, bejewelled, and paint-begrimed beldame, making a last effort at youth — the mere child of immature form, yet, from long association, an adept in the dreadful coquetries of her trade, and burning with a rabid ambition to be ranked the equal of her elders in vice; drunkards innumerable and indescribable — some in shreds and patches, reeling, inarticulate, with bruised visage and lack-lustre eyes — some in whole although filthy garments, with a slightly unsteady swagger, thick sensual lips, and hearty-looking rubicund faces — others clothed in materials

which had once been good, and which even now were scrupulously well
brushed — men who walked with a more than naturally firm and springy
step, but whose countenances were fearfully pale, and whose eyes were
hideously wild and red; and who clutched with quivering fingers, as they
strode through the crowd, at every object which came within their reach;
beside these, pie-men, porters, coal-heavers, sweeps; organ-grinders,
monkey-exhibitors, and ballad-mongers, those who vended with those
who sang; ragged artizans and exhausted laborers of every description, and
all full of a noisy and inordinate vivacity which jarred discordantly upon
the ear, and gave an aching sensation to the eye.

As the night deepened, so deepened to me the interest of the scene;
for not only did the general character of the crowd materially alter (its
gentler features retiring in the gradual withdrawal of the more orderly
portion of the people, and its harsher ones coming out into bolder relief,
as the late hour brought forth every species of infamy from its den), but
the rays of the gas-lamps, feeble at first in their struggle with the dying
day, had now at length gained ascendancy, and threw over every thing a
fitful and garish lustre. All was dark yet splendid — as that ebony to which
has been likened the style of Tertullian.

The wild effects of the light enchained me to an examination of in-
dividual faces; and although the rapidity with which the world of light
flitted before the window prevented me from casting more than a glance
upon each visage, still it seemed that, in my then peculiar mental state,
I could frequently read, even in that brief interval of a glance, the history
of long years.

With my brow to the glass, I was thus occupied in scrutinizing the
mob, when suddenly there came into view a countenance (that of a
decrepid old man, some sixty-five or seventy years of age) — a counte-
nance which at once arrested and absorbed my whole attention, on ac-
count of the absolute idiosyncrasy of its expression. Any thing even
remotely resembling that expression I had never seen before. I well
remember that my first thought, upon beholding it, was that Retszch,
had he viewed it, would have greatly preferred it to his own pictural
incarnations of the fiend. As I endeavored, during the brief minute of
my original survey, to form some analysis of the meaning conveyed, there
arose confusedly and paradoxically within my mind, the ideas of vast
mental power, of caution, of penuriousness, of avarice, of coolness, of
malice, of blood-thirstiness, of triumph, of merriment, of excessive terror,
of intense — of supreme despair. I felt singularly aroused, startled, fas-
cinated. "How wild a history," I said to myself, "is written within that
bosom!" Then came a craving desire to keep the man in view — to know
more of him. Hurriedly putting on an overcoat, and seizing my hat and
cane, I made my way into the street, and pushed through the crowd in
the direction which I had seen him take; for he had already disappeared.
With some little difficulty I at length came within sight of him, ap-

proached, and followed him closely, yet cautiously, so as not to attract his attention.

I had now a good opportunity of examining his person. He was short in stature, very thin, and apparently very feeble. His clothes, generally, were filthy and ragged; but as he came, now and then, within the strong glare of a lamp, I perceived that his linen, although dirty, was of beautiful texture; and my vision deceived me, or, through a rent in a closely-buttoned and evidently second-handed *roquelaire* which enveloped him, I caught a glimpse both of a diamond and of a dagger. These observations heightened my curiosity, and I resolved to follow the stranger whithersoever he should go.

It was now fully night-fall, and a thick humid fog hung over the city, soon ending in a settled and heavy rain. This change of weather had an odd effect upon the crowd, the whole of which was at once put into new commotion, and overshadowed by a world of umbrellas. The waver, the jostle, and the hum increased in a tenfold degree. For my own part I did not much regard the rain — the lurking of an old fever in my system rendering the moisture somewhat too dangerously pleasant. Tying a handkerchief about my mouth, I kept on. For half an hour the old man held his way with difficulty along the great thoroughfare; and I here walked close at his elbow through fear of losing sight of him. Never once turning his head to look back, he did not observe me. By and by he passed into a cross street, which, although densely filled with people, was not quite so much thronged as the main one he had quitted. Here a change in his demeanor became evident. He walked more slowly and with less object than before — more hesitatingly. He crossed and re-crossed the way repeatedly, without apparent aim; and the press was still so thick, that, at every such movement, I was obliged to follow him closely. The street was a narrow and long one, and his course lay within it for nearly an hour, during which the passengers had gradually diminished to about that number which is ordinarily seen at noon in Broadway near the park — so vast a difference is there between a London populace and that of the most frequented American city. A second turn brought us into a square, brilliantly lighted, and overflowing with life. The old manner of the stranger reappeared. His chin fell upon his breast, while his eyes rolled wildly from under his knit brows, in every direction, upon those who hemmed him in. He urged his way steadily and perseveringly. I was surprised, however, to find, upon his having made the circuit of the square, that he turned and retraced his steps. Still more was I astonished to see him repeat the same walk several times — once nearly detecting me as he came around with a sudden movement.

In this exercise he spent another hour, at the end of which we met with far less interruption from passengers than at first. The rain fell fast; the air grew cool; and the people were retiring to their homes. With a gesture of impatience, the wanderer passed into a by-street comparatively de-

serted. Down this, some quarter of a mile long, he rushed with an activity I could not have dreamed of seeing in one so aged, and which put me to much trouble in pursuit. A few minutes brought us to a large and busy bazaar, with the localities of which the stranger appeared well acquainted, and where his original demeanor again became apparent, as he forced his way to and fro, without aim, among the host of buyers and sellers.

During the hour and a half, or thereabouts, which we passed in this place, it required much caution on my part to keep him within reach without attracting his observation. Luckily I wore a pair of caoutchouc overshoes, and could move about in perfect silence. At no moment did he see that I watched him. He entered shop after shop, priced nothing, spoke no word, and looked at all objects with a wild and vacant stare. I was now utterly amazed at his behavior, and firmly resolved that we should not part until I had satisfied myself in some measure respecting him.

A loud-toned clock struck eleven, and the company were fast deserting the bazaar. A shop-keeper, in putting up a shutter, jostled the old man, and at the instant I saw a strong shudder come over his frame. He hurried into the street, looked anxiously around him for an instant, and then ran with incredible swiftness through many crooked and peopleless lanes, until we emerged once more upon the great thoroughfare whence we had started — the street of the D—— Hotel. It no longer wore, however, the same aspect. It was still brilliant with gas; but the rain fell fiercely, and there were few persons to be seen. The stranger grew pale. He walked moodily some paces up the once populous avenue, then, with a heavy sigh, turned in the direction of the river, and, plunging through a great variety of devious ways, came out, at length, in view of one of the principal theatres. It was about being closed, and the audience were thronging from the doors. I saw the old man gasp as if for breath while he threw himself amid the crowd; but I thought that the intense agony of his countenance had, in some measure, abated. His head again fell upon his breast; he appeared as I had seen him at first. I observed that he now took the course in which had gone the greater number of the audience — but, upon the whole, I was at a loss to comprehend the waywardness of his actions.

As he proceeded, the company grew more scattered, and his old uneasiness and vacillation were resumed. For some time he followed closely a party of some ten or twelve roisterers; but from this number one by one dropped off, until three only remained together, in a narrow and gloomy lane, little frequented. The stranger paused, and, for a moment, seemed lost in thought; then, with every mark of agitation, pursued rapidly a route which brought us to the verge of the city, amid regions very different from those we had hitherto traversed. It was the most noisome quarter of London, where every thing wore the worst impress of the most deplorable poverty, and of the most desperate crime. By the dim light of an accidental lamp, tall, antique, worm-eaten, wooden tenements were

seen tottering to their fall, in directions so many and capricious, that scarce the semblance of a passage was discernible between them. The paving-stones lay at random, displaced from their beds by the rankly-growing grass. Horrible filth festered in the dammed-up gutters. The whole atmosphere teemed with desolation. Yet, as we proceeded, the sounds of human life revived by sure degrees, and at length large bands of the most abandoned of a London populace were seen reeling to and fro. The spirits of the old man again flickered up, as a lamp which is near its death-hour. Once more he strode onward with elastic tread. Suddenly a corner was turned, a blaze of light burst upon our sight, and we stood before one of the huge suburban temples of Intemperance — one of the palaces of the fiend, Gin.

It was now nearly daybreak; but a number of wretched inebriates still pressed in and out of the flaunting entrance. With a half shriek of joy the old man forced a passage within, resumed at once his original bearing, and stalked backward and forward, without apparent object, among the throng. He had not been thus long occupied, however, before a rush to the doors gave token that the host was closing them for the night. It was something even more intense than despair that I then observed upon the countenance of the singular being whom I had watched so pertinaciously. Yet he did not hesitate in his career, but, with a mad energy, retraced his steps at once, to the heart of the mighty London. Long and swiftly he fled, while I followed him in the wildest amazement, resolute not to abandon a scrutiny in which I now felt an interest all-absorbing. The sun arose while we proceeded, and, when we had once again reached that most thronged mart of the populous town, the street of the D—— Hotel, it presented an appearance of human bustle and activity scarcely inferior to what I had seen on the evening before. And here, long, amid the momently increasing confusion, did I persist in my pursuit of the stranger. But, as usual, he walked to and fro, and during the day did not pass from out the turmoil of that street. And, as the shades of the second evening came on, I grew wearied unto death, and, stopping fully in front of the wanderer, gazed at him steadfastly in the face. He noticed me not, but resumed his solemn walk, while I, ceasing to follow, remained absorbed in contemplation. "This old man," I said at length, "is the type and the genius of deep crime. He refuses to be alone. *He is the man of the crowd.* It will be in vain to follow; for I shall learn no more of him, nor of his deeds. The worst heart of the world is a grosser book than the 'Hortulus Animæ,' * and perhaps it is but one of the great mercies of God that *"er lasst sich nicht lesen."*

* The "*Hortulus Animae cum Oratiunculis Aliquibus Superadditis*" of Grün-ninger.

The Murders in the Rue Morgue

WHAT SONG *the Syrens sang, or what name Achilles assumed when he hid himself among women, although puzzling questions, are not beyond all conjecture.*
 SIR THOMAS BROWNE.

THE MENTAL features discoursed of as the analytical, are, in themselves, but little susceptible of analysis. We appreciate them only in their effects. We know of them, among other things, that they are always to their possessor, when inordinately possessed, a source of the liveliest enjoyment. As the strong man exults in his physical ability, delighting in such exercises as call his muscles into action, so glories the analyst in that moral activity which *disentangles*. He derives pleasure from even the most trivial occupations bringing his talent into play. He is fond of enigmas, of conundrums, hieroglyphics; exhibiting in his solutions of each a degree of *acumen* which appears to the ordinary apprehension præternatural. His results, brought about by the very soul and essence of method, have, in truth, the whole air of intuition.

The faculty of re-solution is possibly much invigorated by mathematical study, and especially by that highest branch of it which, unjustly, and merely on account of its retrograde operations, has been called, as if *par excellence*, analysis. Yet to calculate is not in itself to analyze. A chess player, for example, does the one, without effort at the other. It follows that the game of chess, in its effects upon mental character, is greatly misunderstood. I am not now writing a treatise, but simply prefacing a somewhat peculiar narrative by observations very much at random; I will, therefore, take occasion to assert that the higher powers of the reflective intellect are more decidedly and more usefully tasked by the unostentatious game of draughts than by all the elaborate frivolity of chess. In this latter, where the pieces have different and *bizarre* motions, with various and variable values, what is only complex, is mistaken (a not unusual error) for what is profound. The *attention* is here called powerfully into play. If it flag for an instant, an oversight is committed, resulting in injury or defeat. The possible moves being not only manifold, but involute, the chances of such oversights are multiplied; and in nine cases out of ten, it is the more concentrative rather than the more acute player who conquers. In draughts, on the contrary, where the moves are *unique* and have but little variation, the probabilities of inadvertence are diminished, and the mere attention being left comparatively unemployed, what advantages are obtained by either party are obtained by superior *acumen*. To be less abstract, let us suppose a game of draughts where the pieces are reduced to four kings, and where, of course, no oversight is to be

expected. It is obvious that here the victory can be decided (the players being at all equal) only by some *recherché* movement, the result of some strong exertion of the intellect. Deprived of ordinary resources, the analyst throws himself into the spirit of his opponent, identifies himself therewith, and not unfrequently sees thus, at a glance, the sole methods (sometimes indeed absurdly simple ones) by which he may seduce into error or hurry into miscalculation.

Whist has long been noted for its influence upon what is termed the calculating power; and men of the highest order of intellect have been known to take an apparently unaccountable delight in it, while eschewing chess as frivolous. Beyond doubt there is nothing of a similar nature so greatly tasking the faculty of analysis. The best chess-player in Christendom *may* be little more than the best player of chess; but proficiency in whist implies capacity for success in all those more important undertakings where mind struggles with mind. When I say proficiency, I mean that perfection in the game which includes a comprehension of *all* the sources whence legitimate advantage may be derived. These are not only manifold, but multiform, and lie frequently among recesses of thought altogether inaccessible to the ordinary understanding. To observe attentively is to remember distinctly; and, so far, the concentrative chess-player will do very well at whist; while the rules of Hoyle (themselves based upon the mere mechanism of the game) are sufficiently and generally comprehensible. Thus to have a retentive memory, and proceed by "the book" are points commonly regarded as the sum total of good playing. But it is in matters beyond the limits of mere rule that the skill of the analyst is evinced. He makes, in silence, a host of observations and inferences. So, perhaps, do his companions; and the difference in the extent of the information obtained, lies not so much in the validity of the inference as in the quality of the observation. The necessary knowledge is that of *what* to observe. Our player confines himself not at all; nor, because the game is the object, does he reject deductions from things external to the game. He examines the countenance of his partner, comparing it carefully with that of each of his opponents. He considers the mode of assorting the cards in each hand; often counting trump by trump, and honor by honor, through the glances bestowed by their holders upon each. He notes every variation of face as the play progresses, gathering a fund of thought from the differences in the expression of certainty, of surprise, of triumph, or chagrin. From the manner of gathering up a trick he judges whether the person taking it, can make another in the suit. He recognises what is played through feint, by the air with which it is thrown upon the table. A casual or inadvertent word; the accidental dropping or turning of a card, with the accompanying anxiety or carelessness in regard to its concealment; the counting of the tricks, with the order of their arrangement; embarrassment, hesitation, eagerness, or trepidation — all

afford, to his aparently intuitive perception, indications of the true state of affairs. The first two or three rounds having been played, he is in full possession of the contents of each hand, and thenceforward puts down his cards with as absolute a precision of purpose as if the rest of the party had turned outward the faces of their own.

The analytical power should not be confounded with simple ingenuity; for while the analyst is necessarily ingenious, the ingenious man is often remarkably incapable of analysis. The constructive or combining power, by which ingenuity is usually manifested, and to which the phrenologists (I believe erroneously) have assigned a separate organ, supposing it a primitive faculty, has been so frequently seen in those whose intellect bordered otherwise upon idiocy, as to have attracted general observation among writers on morals. Between ingenuity and the analytic ability there exists a difference far greater, indeed, than that between the fancy and the imagination, but of a character very strictly analogous. It will be found, in fact, that the ingenious are always fanciful, and the *truly* imaginative never otherwise than analytic.

The narrative which follows will appear to the reader somewhat in the light of a commentary upon the propositions just advanced.

Residing in Paris during the spring and part of the summer of 18—, I there became acquainted with a Monsieur C. Auguste Dupin. This young gentleman was of an excellent, indeed of an illustrious family, but, by a variety of untoward events, had been reduced to such poverty that the energy of his character succumbed beneath it, and he ceased to bestir himself in the world, or to care for the retrieval of his fortunes. By courtesy of his creditors, there still remained in his possession a small remnant of his patrimony; and, upon the income arising from this, he managed, by means of a rigorous economy, to procure the necessaries of life, without troubling himself about its superfluities. Books, indeed, were his sole luxuries, and in Paris these are easily obtained.

Our first meeting was at an obscure library in the Rue Montmartre, where the accident of our both being in search of the same very rare and very remarkable volume, brought us into closer communion. We saw each other again and again. I was deeply interested in the little family history which he detailed to me with all that candor which a Frenchman indulges whenever mere self is his theme. I was astonished, too, at the vast extent of his reading; and, above all, I felt my soul enkindled within me by the wild fervor, and the vivid freshness of his imagination. Seeking in Paris the objects I then sought, I felt that the society of such a man would be to me a treasure beyond price; and this feeling I frankly confided to him. It was at length arranged that we should live together during my stay in the city; and as my worldly circumstances were somewhat less embarrassed than his own, I was permitted to be at the expense of renting, and furnishing in a style which suited the rather fantastic gloom of our com-

mon temper, a time-eaten and grotesque mansion, long deserted through superstitions into which we did not inquire, and tottering to its fall in a retired and desolate portion of the Faubourg St. Germain.

Had the routine of our life at this place been known to the world, we should have been regarded as madmen — although, perhaps, as madmen of a harmless nature. Our seclusion was perfect. We admitted no visitors. Indeed the locality of our retirement had been carefully kept a secret from my own former associates; and it had been many years since Dupin had ceased to know or be known in Paris. We existed within ourselves alone.

It was a freak of fancy in my friend (for what else shall I call it?) to be enamored of the night for her own sake; and into this *bizarrerie*, as into all his others, I quietly fell; giving myself up to his wild whims with a perfect *abandon*. The sable divinity would not herself dwell with us always; but we could counterfeit her presence. At the first dawn of the morning we closed all the massy shutters of our old building; lighting a couple of tapers which, strongly perfumed, threw out only the ghastliest and feeblest of rays. By the aid of these we then busied our souls in dreams — reading, writing, or conversing, until warned by the clock of the advent of the true Darkness. Then we sallied forth into the streets, arm in arm, continuing the topics of the day, or roaming far and wide until a late hour, seeking, amid the wild lights and shadows of the populous city, that infinity of mental excitement which quiet observation can afford.

At such times I could not help remarking and admiring (although from his rich ideality I had been prepared to expect it) a peculiar analytic ability in Dupin. He seemed, too, to take an eager delight in its exercise — if not exactly in its display — and did not hesitate to confess the pleasure thus derived. He boasted to me, with a low chuckling laugh, that most men, in respect to himself, wore windows in their bosoms, and was wont to follow up such assertions by direct and very startling proofs of his intimate knowledge of my own. His manner at these moments was frigid and abstract; his eyes were vacant in expression; while his voice, usually a rich tenor, rose into a treble which would have sounded petulantly but for the deliberateness and entire distinctness of the enunciation. Observing him in these moods, I often dwelt meditatively upon the old philosophy of the Bi-Part Soul, and amused myself with the fancy of a double Dupin — the creative and the resolvent.

Let it not be supposed, from what I have just said, that I am detailing any mystery, or penning any romance. What I have described in the Frenchman was merely the result of an excited, or perhaps of a diseased, intelligence, but of the character of his remarks at the periods in question an example will best convey the idea.

We were strolling one night down a long dirty street, in the vicinity of the Palais Royal. Being both, apparently, occupied with thought, neither

of us had spoken a syllable for fifteen minutes at least. All at once Dupin broke forth with these words:

"He is a very little fellow, that's true, and would do better for the *Théâtre des Variétés*."

"There can be no doubt of that," I replied, unwittingly, and not at first observing (so much had I been absorbed in reflection) the extraordinary manner in which the speaker had chimed in with my meditations. In an instant afterward I recollected myself, and my astonishment was profound.

"Dupin," said I, gravely, "this is beyond my comprehension. I do not hesitate to say that I am amazed, and can scarcely credit my senses. How was it possible you should know I was thinking of ——?" Here I paused, to ascertain beyond a doubt whether he really knew of whom I thought.

" —— of Chantilly," said he, "why do you pause? You were remarking to yourself that his diminutive figure unfitted him for tragedy."

This was precisely what had formed the subject of my reflections. Chantilly was a *quondam* cobbler of the Rue St. Dennis, who, becoming stage-mad, had attempted the *rôle* of Xerxes, Crébillon's tragedy so called, and been notoriously Pasquinaded for his pains.

"Tell me, for Heaven's sake," I exclaimed, "the method — if method there is — by which you have been enabled to fathom my soul in this matter." In fact, I was even more startled than I would have been willing to express.

"It was the fruiterer," replied my friend, "who brought you to the conclusion that the mender of soles was not of sufficient height for Xerxes *et id genus omne*."

"The fruiterer! — you astonish me — I know no fruiterer whomsoever."

"The man who ran up against you as we entered the street — it may have been fifteen minutes ago."

I now remembered that, in fact, a fruiterer, carrying upon his head a large basket of apples, had nearly thrown me down, by accident, as we passed from the Rue C—— into the thoroughfare where we stood; but what this had to do with Chantilly I could not possibly understand.

There was not a particle of *charlatânerie* about Dupin. "I will explain," he said, "and that you may comprehend all clearly, we will first retrace the course of your meditations, from the moment in which I spoke to you until that of the *rencontre* with the fruiterer in question. The larger links of the chain run thus — Chantilly, Orion, Dr. Nichols, Epicurus, Stereotomy, the street stones, the fruiterer."

There are few persons who have not, at some period of their lives, amused themselves in retracing their steps by which particular conclusions of their own minds have been attained. The occupation is often full of interest; and he who attempts it for the first time is astonished by the apparently illimitable distance and incoherence between the starting-

point and the goal. What, then, must have been my amazement, when I heard the Frenchman speak what he had just spoken, and I could not help acknowledging that he had spoken the truth. He continued:

"We had been talking of horses, if I remember aright, just before leaving the Rue C———. This was the last subject we discussed. As we crossed into this street, a fruiterer, with a large basket upon his head, brushing quickly past us, thrust you upon a pile of paving-stones collected at a spot where the causeway is undergoing repair. You stepped upon one of the loose fragments, slipped, slightly strained your ankle, appeared vexed or sulky, muttered a few words, turned to look at the pile, and then proceeded in silence. I was not particularly attentive to what you did; but observation has become with me, of late, a species of necessity.

"You kept your eyes upon the ground — glancing, with a petulant expression, at the holes and ruts in the pavement, (so that I saw you were still thinking of the stones,) until we reached the little alley called Lamartine, which has been paved, by way of experiment, with the overlapping and riveted blocks. Here your countenance brightened up, and, perceiving your lips move, I could not doubt that you murmured the word 'stereotomy,' a term very affectedly applied to this species of pavement. I knew that you could not say to yourself 'stereotomy' without being brought to think of atomies, and thus of the theories of Epicurus; and since, when we discussed this subject not very long ago, I mentioned to you how singularly, yet with how little notice, the vague guesses of that noble Greek had met with confirmation in the late nebular cosmogony, I felt that you could not avoid casting your eyes upward to the great *nebula* in Orion, and I certainly expected that you would do so. You did look up; and I was now assured that I had correctly followed your steps. But in that bitter *tirade* upon Chantilly, which appeared in yesterday's 'Musée,' the satirist, making some disgraceful allusions to the cobbler's change of name upon assuming the buskin, quoted a Latin line about which we have often conversed. I mean the line

Perdidit antiquum litera prima sonum.

I had told you that this was in reference to Orion, formerly written Urion; and, from certain pungencies connected with this explanation, I was aware that you could not have forgotten it. It was clear, therefore, that you would not fail to combine the two ideas of Orion and Chantilly. That you did combine them I saw by the character of the smile which passed over your lips. You thought of the poor cobbler's immolation. So far, you had been stooping in your gait; but now I saw you draw yourself up to your full height. I was then sure that you reflected upon the diminutive figure of Chantilly. At this point I interrupted your meditations to remark that as, in fact, he *was* a very little fellow — that Chantilly — he would do better at the *Théâtre des Variétés*."

Not long after this, we were looking over an evening edition of the

Gazette des Tribunaux, when the following paragraphs arrested our attention.

"EXTRAORDINARY MURDERS. — This morning, about three o'clock, the inhabitants of the Quartier St. Roch were roused from sleep by a succession of terrific shrieks, issuing, apparently, from the fourth story of a house in the Rue Morgue, known to be in the sole occupancy of one Madame L'Espanaye, and her daughter, Mademoiselle Camille L'Espanaye. After some delay, occasioned by a fruitless attempt to procure admission in the usual manner, the gateway was broken in with a crowbar, and eight or ten of the neighbors entered, accompanied by two *gendarmes.* By this time the cries had ceased; but, as the party rushed up the first flight of stairs, two or more rough voices, in angry contention, were distinguished, and seemed to proceed from the upper part of the house. As the second landing was reached, these sounds, also, had ceased, and every thing remained perfectly quiet. The party spread themselves, and hurried from room to room. Upon arriving at a large back chamber in the fourth story, (the door of which, being found locked, with the key inside, was forced open,) a spectacle presented itself which struck every one present not less with horror than with astonishment.

"The apartment was in the wildest disorder — the furniture broken and thrown about in all directions. There was only one bedstead; and from this the bed had been removed, and thrown into the middle of the floor. On a chair lay a razor, besmeared with blood. On the hearth were two or three long and thick tresses of gray human hair, also dabbled with blood, and seeming to have been pulled out by the roots. Upon the floor were found four Napoleons, an ear-ring of topaz, three large silver spoons, three smaller of *métal d'Alger,* and two bags, containing nearly four thousand francs in gold. The drawers of a *bureau,* which stood in one corner, were open, and had been, apparently, rifled, although many articles still remained in them. A small iron safe was discovered under the *bed* (not under the bedstead). It was open, with the key still in the door. It had no contents beyond a few old letters, and other papers of little consequence.

"Of Madame L'Espanaye no traces were here seen; but an unusual quantity of soot being observed in the fireplace, a search was made in the chimney, and (horrible to relate!) the corpse of the daughter, head downward, was dragged therefrom; it having been thus forced up the narrow aperture for a considerable distance. The body was quite warm. Upon examining it, many excoriations were perceived, no doubt occasioned by the violence with which it had been thrust up and disengaged. Upon the face were many severe scratches, and, upon the throat, dark bruises, and deep indentations of finger nails, as if the deceased had been throttled to death.

"After a thorough investigation of every portion of the house without farther discovery, the party made its way into a small paved yard in the rear of the building, where lay the corpse of the old lady, with her throat

so entirely cut that, upon an attempt to raise her, the head fell off. The body, as well as the head, was fearfully mutilated — the former so much so as scarcely to retain any semblance of humanity.

"To this horrible mystery there is not as yet, we believe, the slightest clew."

The next day's paper had these additional particulars:

"*The Tragedy in the Rue Morgue.* — Many individuals have been examined in relation to this most extraordinary and frightful affair," [the word '*affaire*' has not yet, in France, that levity of import which it conveys with us] "but nothing whatever has transpired to throw light upon it. We give below all the material testimony elicited.

"*Pauline Dubourg,* laundress, deposes that she has known both the deceased for three years, having washed for them during that period. The old lady and her daughter seemed on good terms — very affectionate toward each other. They were excellent pay. Could not speak in regard to their mode or means of living. Believed that Madame L. told fortunes for a living. Was reputed to have money put by. Never met any person in the house when she called for the clothes or took them home. Was sure that they had no servant in employ. There appeared to be no furniture in any part of the building except in the fourth story.

"*Pierre Moreau,* tobacconist, deposes that he has been in the habit of selling small quantities of tobacco and snuff to Madame L'Espanaye for nearly four years. Was born in the neighborhood, and has always resided there. The deceased and her daughter had occupied the house in which the corpses were found, for more than six years. It was formerly occupied by a jeweller, who under-let the upper rooms to various persons. The house was the property of Madame L. She became dissatisfied with the abuse of the premises by her tenant, and moved into them herself, refusing to let any portion. The old lady was childish. Witness had seen the daughter some five or six times during the six years. The two lived an exceedingly retired life — were reputed to have money. Had heard it said among the neighbors that Madame L. told fortunes — did not believe it. Had never seen any person enter the door except the old lady and her daughter, a porter once or twice, and a physician some eight or ten times.

"Many other persons, neighbors, gave evidence to the same effect. No one was spoken of as frequenting the house. It was not known whether there were any living connections of Madame L. and her daughter. The shutters of the front windows were seldom opened. Those in the rear were always closed, with the exception of the large back room, fourth story. The house was a good house — not very old.

"*Isidore Musèt, gendarme,* deposes that he was called to the house about three o'clock in the morning, and found some twenty or thirty persons at the gateway, endeavoring to gain admittance. Forced it open, at length, with a bayonet — not with a crowbar. Had but little difficulty in

getting it open, on account of its being a double or folding gate, and bolted neither at bottom nor top. The shrieks were continued until the gate was forced — and then suddenly ceased. They seemed to be screams of some person (or persons) in great agony — were loud and drawn out, not short and quick. Witness led the way up stairs. Upon reaching the first landing, heard two voices in loud and angry contention — the one a gruff voice, the other much shriller — a very strange voice. Could distinguish some words of the former, which was that of a Frenchman. Was positive that it was not a woman's voice. Could distinguish the words '*sacré*' and '*diable.*' The shrill voice was that of a foreigner. Could not be sure whether it was the voice of a man or of a woman. Could not make out what was said, but believed the language to be Spanish. The state of the room and of the bodies was described by this witness as we described them yesterday.

"*Henri Duval*, a neighbor, and by trade a silver-smith, deposes that he was one of the party who first entered the house. Corroborates the testimony of Musèt in general. As soon as they forced an entrance, they re-closed the door, to keep out the crowd, which collected very fast, notwithstanding the lateness of the hour. The shrill voice, this witness thinks, was that of an Italian. Was certain it was not French. Could not be sure that it was a man's voice. It might have been a woman's. Was not acquainted with the Italian language. Could not distinguish the words, but was convinced by the intonation that the speaker was an Italian. Knew Madame L. and her daughter. Had conversed with both frequently. Was sure that the shrill voice was not that of either of the deceased.

" —— *Odenheimer, restaurateur.* — This witness volunteered his testimony. Not speaking French, was examined through an interpreter. Is a native of Amsterdam. Was passing the house at the time of the shrieks. They lasted for several minutes — probably ten. They were long and loud — very awful and distressing. Was one of those who entered the building. Corroborated the previous evidence in every respect but one. Was sure that the shrill voice was that of a man — of a Frenchman. Could not distinguish the words uttered. They were loud and quick — unequal — spoken apparently in fear as well as in anger. The voice was harsh — not so much shrill as harsh. Could not call it a shrill voice. The gruff voice said repeatedly, '*sacré*,' '*diable*,' and once '*mon Dieu*.'

"*Jules Mignaud*, banker, of the firm of Mignaud et Fils, Rue Deloraine. Is the elder Mignaud. Madame L'Espanaye had some property. Had opened an account with his banking house in the spring of the year — (eight years previously). Made frequent deposits in small sums. Had checked for nothing until the third day before her death, when she took out in person the sum of 4000 francs. This sum was paid in gold, and a clerk sent home with the money.

"*Adolphe Le Bon*, clerk to Mignaud et Fils, deposes that on the day in question, about noon, he accompanied Madame L'Espanaye to her

residence with the 4000 francs, put up in two bags. Upon the door being opened, Mademoiselle L. appeared and took from his hands one of the bags, while the old lady relieved him of the other. He then bowed and departed. Did not see any person in the street at the time. It is a by-street — very lonely.

"*William Bird*, tailor, deposes that he was one of the party who entered the house. Is an Englishman. Has lived in Paris two years. Was one of the first to ascend the stairs. Heard the voices in contention. The gruff voice was that of a Frenchman. Could make out several words, but cannot now remember all. Heard distinctly '*sacré*' and '*mon Dieu*.' There was a sound at the moment as if of several persons struggling — a scraping and scuffling sound. The shrill voice was very loud — louder than the gruff one. Is sure that it was not the voice of an Englishman. Appeared to be that of a German. Might have been a woman's voice. Does not understand German.

"Four of the above-named witnesses being recalled, deposed that the door of the chamber in which was found the body of Mademoiselle L. was locked on the inside when the party reached it. Every thing was perfectly silent — no groans or noises of any kind. Upon forcing the door no person was seen. The windows, both of the back and front room, were down and firmly fastened from within. A door between the two rooms was closed but not locked. The door leading from the front room into the passage was locked, with the key on the inside. A small room in the front of the house, on the fourth story, at the head of the passage, was open, the door being ajar. This room was crowded with old beds, boxes, and so forth. These were carefully removed and searched. There was not an inch of any portion of the house which was not carefully searched. Sweeps were sent up and down the chimneys. The house was a four-story one, with garrets (*mansardes*). A trap-door on the roof was nailed down very securely — did not appear to have been opened for years. The time elapsing between the hearing of the voices in contention and the breaking open of the room door was variously stated by the witnesses. Some made it as short as three minutes — some as long as five. The door was opened with difficulty.

"*Alfonzo Garcio*, undertaker, deposes that he resides in the Rue Morgue. Is a native of Spain. Was one of the party who entered the house. Did not proceed up stairs. Is nervous, and was apprehensive of the consequences of agitation. Heard the voices in contention. The gruff voice was that of a Frenchman. Could not distinguish what was said. The shrill voice was that of an Englishman — is sure of this. Does not understand the English language, but judges by the intonation.

"*Alberto Montani*, confectioner, deposes that he was among the first to ascend the stairs. Heard the voices in question. The gruff voice was that of a Frenchman. Distinguished several words. The speaker appeared to be expostulating. Could not make out the words of the shrill voice.

Spoke quick and unevenly. Thinks it the voice of a Russian. Corroborates the general testimony. Is an Italian. Never conversed with a native of Russia.

"Several witnesses, recalled, here testified that the chimneys of all the rooms on the fourth story were too narrow to admit the passage of a human being. By 'sweeps' were meant cylindrical sweeping-brushes, such as are employed by those who clean chimneys. These brushes were passed up and down every flue in the house. There is no back passage by which any one could have descended while the party proceeded up stairs. The body of Mademoiselle L'Espanaye was so firmly wedged in the chimney that it could not be got down until four or five of the party united their strength.

"*Paul Dumas*, physician, deposes that he was called to view the bodies about daybreak. They were both then lying on the sacking of the bedstead in the chamber where Mademoiselle L. was found. The corpse of the young lady was much bruised and excoriated. The fact that it had been thrust up the chimney would sufficiently account for these appearances. The throat was greatly chafed. There were several deep scratches just below the chin, together with a series of livid spots which were evidently the impression of fingers. The face was fearfully discolored, and the eyeballs protruded. The tongue had been partially bitten through. A large bruise was discovered upon the pit of the stomach, produced, apparently, by the pressure of a knee. In the opinion of M. Dumas, Mademoiselle L'Espanaye had been throttled to death by some person or persons unknown. The corpse of the mother was horribly mutilated. All the bones of the right leg and arm were more or less shattered. The left *tibia* much splintered, as well as all the ribs of the left side. Whole body dreadfully bruised and discolored. It was not possible to say how the injuries had been inflicted. A heavy club of wood, or a broad bar of iron — a chair — any large, heavy, and obtuse weapon would have produced such results, if wielded by the hands of a very powerful man. No woman could have inflicted the blows with any weapon. The head of the deceased, when seen by witness, was entirely separated from the body, and was also greatly shattered. The throat had evidently been cut with some very sharp instrument — probably with a razor.

"*Alexandre Etienne*, surgeon, was called with M. Dumas to view the bodies. Corroborated the testimony and the opinions of M. Dumas.

"Nothing further of importance was elicited, although several other persons were examined. A murder so mysterious, and so perplexing in all its particulars, was never before committed in Paris — if indeed a murder has been committed at all. The police are entirely at fault — an unusual occurrence in affairs of this nature. There is not, however, the shadow of a clew apparent."

The evening edition of the paper stated that the greatest excitement still continued in the Quartier St. Roch — that the premises in question

had been carefully re-searched, and fresh examinations of witnesses instituted, but all to no purpose. A postscript, however, mentioned that Adolphe Le Bon had been arrested and imprisoned — although nothing appeared to criminate him beyond the facts already detailed.

Dupin seemed singularly interested in the progress of this affair — at least so I judged from his manner, for he made no comments. It was only after the announcement that Le Bon had been imprisoned, that he asked me my opinion respecting the murders.

I could merely agree with all Paris in considering them an insoluble mystery. I saw no means by which it would be possible to trace the murderer.

"We must not judge of the means," said Dupin, "by this shell of an examination. The Parisian police, so much extolled for *acumen*, are cunning, but no more. There is no method in their proceedings, beyond the method of the moment. They make a vast parade of measures; but, not unfrequently, these are so ill-adapted to the objects proposed, as to put us in mind of Monsieur Jourdain's calling for his *robe-de-chambre — pour mieux entendre la musique*. The results attained by them are not unfrequently surprising, but, for the most part, are brought about by simple diligence and activity. When these qualities are unavailing, their schemes fail. Vidocq, for example, was a good guesser, and a persevering man. But, without educated thought, he erred continually by the very intensity of his investigations. He impaired his vision by holding the object too close. He might see, perhaps, one or two points with unusual clearness, but in so doing he, necessarily, lost sight of the matter as a whole. Thus there is such a thing as being too profound. Truth is not always in a well. In fact, as regards the more important knowledge, I do believe that she is invariably superficial. The depth lies in the valleys where we seek her, and not upon the mountain-tops where she is found. The modes and sources of this kind of error are well typified in the contemplation of the heavenly bodies. To look at a star by glances — to view it in a side-long way, by turning toward it the exterior portions of the *retina* (more susceptible of feeble impressions of light than the interior), is to behold the star distinctly — is to have the best appreciation of its lustre — a lustre which grows dim just in proportion as we turn our vision *fully* upon it. A greater number of rays actually fall upon the eye in the latter case, but in the former, there is the more refined capacity for comprehension. By undue profundity we perplex and enfeeble thought; and it is possible to make even Venus herself vanish from the firmament by a scrutiny too sustained, too concentrated, or too direct.

"As for these murders, let us enter into some examinations for ourselves, before we make up an opinion respecting them. An inquiry will afford us amusement," [I thought this an odd term, so applied, but said nothing] "and besides, Le Bon once rendered me a service for which I am not ungrateful. We will go and see the premises with our own eyes, I know

G——, the Prefect of Police, and shall have no difficulty in obtaining the necessary permission."

The permission was obtained, and we proceeded at once to the Rue Morgue. This is one of those miserable thoroughfares which intervene between the Rue Richelieu and the Rue St. Roch. It was late in the afternoon when we reached it, as this quarter is at a great distance from that in which we resided. The house was readily found; for there were still many persons gazing up at the closed shutters, with an objectless curiosity, from the opposite side of the way. It was an ordinary Parisian house, with a gateway, on one side of which was a glazed watch-box, with a sliding panel in the window, indicating a *loge de concierge*. Before going in we walked up the street, turned down an alley, and then, again turning, passed in the rear of the building — Dupin, meanwhile, examining the whole neighborhood, as well as the house, with a minuteness of attention for which I could see no possible object.

Retracing our steps we came again to the front of the dwelling, rang, and having shown our credentials, were admitted by the agents in charge. We went up stairs — into the chamber where the body of Mademoiselle L'Espanaye had been found, and where both the deceased still lay. The disorders of the room had, as usual, been suffered to exist. I saw nothing beyond what had been stated in the *Gazette des Tribunaux*. Dupin scrutinized every thing — not excepting the bodies of the victims. We then went into the other rooms, and into the yard; a *gendarme* accompanying us throughout. The examination occupied us until dark, when we took our departure. On our way home my companion stepped in for a moment at the office of one of the daily papers.

I have said that the whims of my friend were manifold, and that *Je les ménageais:* — for this phrase there is no English equivalent. It was his humor, now, to decline all conversation on the subject of the murder, until about noon the next day. He then asked me, suddenly, if I had observed any thing *peculiar* at the scene of the atrocity.

There was something in his manner of emphasizing the word "peculiar," which caused me to shudder, without knowing why.

"No, nothing *peculiar*," I said; "nothing more, at least, than we both saw stated in the paper."

"The *Gazette*," he replied, "has not entered, I fear, into the unusual horror of the thing. But dismiss the idle opinions of this print. It appears to me that this mystery is considered insoluble, for the very reason which should cause it to be regarded as easy of solution — I mean for the *outré* character of its features. The police are confounded by the seeming absence of motive — not for the murder itself — but for the atrocity of the murder. They are puzzled, too, by the seeming impossibility of reconciling the voices heard in contention, with the facts that no one was discovered upstairs but the assassinated Mademoiselle L'Espanaye, and that there were no means of egress without the notice of the party ascend-

ing. The wild disorder of the room; the corpse thrust, with the head downward, up the chimney; the frightful mutilation of the body of the old lady; these considerations, with those just mentioned, and others which I need not mention, have sufficed to paralyze the powers, by putting completely at fault the boasted *acumen*, of the government agents. They have fallen into the gross but common error of confounding the unusual with the abstruse. But it is by these deviations from the plane of the ordinary, that reason feels its way, if at all, in its search for the true. In investigations such as we are now pursuing, it should not be so much asked 'what has occurred,' as 'what has occurred that has never occurred before.' In fact, the facility with which I shall arrive, or have arrived, at the solution of this mystery, is in the direct ratio of its apparent insolubility in the eyes of the police."

I stared at the speaker in mute astonishment.

"I am now awaiting," continued he, looking toward the door of our apartment — "I am now awaiting a person who, although perhaps not the perpetrator of these butcheries, must have been in some measure implicated in their perpetration. Of the worst portion of the crimes committed, it is probable that he is innocent. I hope that I am right in this supposition; for upon it I build my expectation of reading the entire riddle. I look for the man here — in this room — every moment. It is true that he may not arrive; but the probability is that he will. Should he come, it will be necessary to detain him. Here are pistols; and we both know how to use them when occasion demands their use."

I took the pistols, scarcely knowing what I did, or believing what I heard, while Dupin went on, very much as if in a soliloquy. I have already spoken of his abstract manner at such times. His discourse was addressed to myself; but his voice, although by no means loud, had that intonation which is commonly employed in speaking to some one at a great distance. His eyes, vacant in expression, regarded only the wall.

"That the voices heard in contention," he said, "by the party upon the stairs, were not the voices of the women themselves, was fully proved by the evidence. This relieves us of all doubt upon the question whether the old lady could have first destroyed the daughter, and afterward have committed suicide. I speak of this point chiefly for the sake of method; for the strength of Madame L'Espanaye would have been utterly unequal to the task of thrusting her daughter's corpse up the chimney as it was found; and the nature of the wounds upon her own person entirely precludes the idea of self-destruction. Murder, then, has been committed by some third party; and the voices of this third party were those heard in contention. Let me now advert — not to the whole testimony respecting these voices — but to what was *peculiar* in that testimony. Did you observe any thing peculiar about it?"

I remarked that, while all the witnesses agreed in supposing the gruff

voice to be that of a Frenchman, there was much disagreement in regard to the shrill, or, as one individual termed it, the harsh voice.

"That was the evidence itself," said Dupin, "but it was not the peculiarity of the evidence. You have observed nothing distinctive. Yet there *was* something to be observed. The witnesses, as you remark, agreed about the gruff voice; they were here unanimous. But in regard to the shrill voice, the peculiarity is — not that they disagreed — but that, while an Italian, an Englishman, a Spaniard, a Hollander, and a Frenchman attempted to describe it, each one spoke of it as that *of a foreigner.* Each is sure that it was not the voice of one of his own countrymen. Each likens it — not to the voice of an individual of any nation with whose language he is conversant — but the converse. The Frenchman supposes it the voice of a Spaniard, and 'might have distinguished some words *had he been acquainted with the Spanish.*' The Dutchman maintains it to have been that of a Frenchman; but we find it stated that '*not understanding French this witness was examined through an interpreter.*' The Englishman thinks it the voice of a German, and '*does not understand German.*' The Spaniard 'is sure' that it was that of an Englishman, but 'judges by the intonation' altogether, '*as he has no knowledge of the English.*' The Italian believes it the voice of a Russian, but '*has never conversed with a native of Russia.*' A second Frenchman differs, moreover, with the first, and is positive that the voice was that of an Italian; but, *not being cognizant of that tongue,* is, like the Spaniard, 'convinced by the intonation.' Now, how strangely unusual must that voice have really been, about which such testimony as this *could* have been elicited! — in whose *tones,* even, denizens of the five great divisions of Europe could recognize nothing familiar! You will say that it might have been the voice of an Asiatic — of an African. Neither Asiatics nor Africans abound in Paris; but, without denying the inference, I will now merely call your attention to three points. The voice is termed by one witness 'harsh rather than shrill.' It is represented by two others to have been 'quick and *unequal.*' No words — no sounds resembling words — were by any witness mentioned as distinguishable.

"I know not," continued Dupin, "what impression I may have made, so far, upon your own understanding; but I do not hesitate to say that legitimate deductions even from this portion of the testimony — the portion respecting the gruff and shrill voices — are in themselves sufficient to engender a suspicion which should give direction to all farther progress in the investigation of the mystery. I said 'legitimate deductions'; but my meaning is not thus fully expressed. I designed to imply that the deductions are the *sole* proper ones, and that the suspicion arises *inevitably* from them as the single result. What the suspicion is, however, I will not say just yet. I merely wish you to bear in mind that, with myself, it was sufficiently forcible to give a definite form — a certain tendency — to my inquiries in the chamber.

"Let us now transport ourselves, in fancy, to this chamber. What shall we first seek here? The means of egress employed by the murderers. It is not too much to say that neither of us believe in præternatural events. Madame and Mademoiselle L'Espanaye were not destroyed by spirits. The doers of the deed were material and escaped materially. Then how? Fortunately there is but one mode of reasoning upon the point, and that mode *must* lead us to a definite decision. Let us examine, each by each, the possible means of egress. It is clear that the assassins were in the room where Mademoiselle L'Espanaye was found, or at least in the room adjoining, when the party ascended the stairs. It is, then, only from these two apartments that we have to seek issues. The police have laid bare the floors, the ceiling, and the masonry of the walls, in every direction. No *secret* issues could have escaped their vigilance. But, not trusting to *their* eyes, I examined with my own. There were, then, *no* secret issues. Both doors leading from the rooms into the passage were securely locked, with the keys inside. Let us turn to the chimneys. These, although of ordinary width for some eight or ten feet above the hearths, will not admit, throughout their extent, the body of a large cat. The impossibility of egress, by means already stated, being thus absolute, we are reduced to the windows. Through those of the front room no one could have escaped without notice from the crowd in the street. The murderers *must* have passed, then, through those of the back room. Now, brought to this conclusion in so unequivocal a manner as we are, it is not our part, as reasoners, to reject it on account of apparent impossibilities. It is only left for us to prove that these apparent 'impossibilities' are, in reality, not such.

"There are two windows in the chamber. One of them is unobstructed by furniture, and is wholly visible. The lower portion of the other is hidden from view by the head of the unwieldy bedstead which is thrust close up against it. The former was found securely fastened from within. It resisted the utmost force of those who endeavored to raise it. A large gimlet-hole had been pierced in its frame to the left, and a very stout nail was found fitted therein, nearly to the head. Upon examining the other window, a similar nail was seen similarly fitted in it; and a vigorous attempt to raise this sash failed also. The police were now entirely satisfied that egress had not been in these directions. And, *therefore*, it was thought a matter of supererogation to withdraw the nails and open the windows.

"My own examination was somewhat more particular, and was so for the reason I have just given — because here it was, I knew, that all apparent impossibilities *must* be proved to be not such in reality.

"I proceeded to think thus — *a posteriori*. The murderers *did* escape from one of these windows. This being so, they could not have re-fastened the sashes from the inside, as they were found fastened — the consideration which put a stop, through its obviousness, to the scrutiny of the

police in this quarter. Yet the sashes *were* fastened. They *must*, then, have the power of fastening themselves. There was no escape from this conclusion. I stepped to the unobstructed casement, withdrew the nail with some difficulty, and attempted to raise the sash. It resisted all my efforts, as I had anticipated. A concealed spring must, I now knew, exist; and this corroboration of my idea convinced me that my premises, at least, were correct, however mysterious still appeared the circumstances attending the nails. A careful search soon brought to light the hidden spring. I pressed it, and, satisfied with the discovery, forbore to upraise the sash.

"I now replaced the nail and regarded it attentively. A person passing out through this window might have reclosed it, and the spring would have caught — but the nail could not have been replaced. The conclusion was plain, and again narrowed in the field of my investigations. The assassins *must* have escaped through the other window. Supposing, then, the springs upon each sash to be the same, as was probable, there *must* be found a difference between the nails, or at least between the modes of their fixture. Getting upon the sacking of the bedstead, I looked over the head-board minutely at the second casement. Passing my hand down behind the board, I readily discovered and pressed the spring, which was, as I had supposed, identical in character with its neighbor. I now looked at the nail. It was as stout as the other, and apparently fitted in the same manner — driven in nearly up to the head.

"You will say that I was puzzled; but, if you think so, you must have misunderstood the nature of the inductions. To use a sporting phrase, I had not been once 'at fault.' The scent had never for an instant been lost. There was no flaw in any link of the chain. I had traced the secret to its ultimate result, — and that result was *the nail*. It had, I say, in every respect, the appearance of its fellow in the other window; but this fact was an absolute nullity (conclusive as it might seem to be) when compared with the consideration that here, at this point, terminated the clew. 'There *must* be something wrong,' I said, 'about the nail.' I touched it; and the head, with about a quarter of an inch of the shank came off in my fingers. The rest of the shank was in the gimlet-hole, where it had been broken off. The fracture was an old one (for its edges were incrusted with rust), and had apparently been accomplished by the blow of a hammer, which had partially imbedded, in the top of the bottom sash, the head portion of the nail. I now carefully replaced this head portion in the indentation whence I had taken it, and the resemblance to a perfect nail was complete — the fissure was invisible. Pressing the spring, I gently raised the sash for a few inches; the head went up with it, remaining firm in its bed. I closed the window, and the semblance of the whole nail was again perfect.

"This riddle, so far, was now unriddled. The assassin had escaped through the window which looked upon the bed. Dropping of its own

accord upon his exit (or perhaps purposely closed), it had become fastened by the spring; and it was the retention of this spring which had been mistaken by the police for that of the nail, — farther inquiry being thus considered unnecessary.

"The next question is that of the mode of descent. Upon this point I had been satisfied in my walk with you around the building. About five feet and a half from the casement in question there runs a lightning-rod. From this rod it would have been impossible for any one to reach the window itself, to say nothing of entering it. I observed, however, that the shutters of the fourth story were of the peculiar kind called by Parisian carpenters *ferrades* — a kind rarely employed at the present day, but frequently seen upon very old mansions at Lyons and Bourdeaux. They are in the form of an ordinary door (a single, not a folding door), except that the upper half is latticed or worked in open trellis — thus affording an excellent hold for the hands. In the present instance these shutters are fully three feet and a half broad. When we saw them from the rear of the house, they were both about half open — that is to say, they stood off at right angles from the wall. It is probable that the police, as well as myself, examined the back of the tenement; but, if so, in looking at these *ferrades* in the line of their breadth (as they must have done), they did not perceive this great breadth itself, or, at all events, failed to take it into due consideration. In fact, having once satisfied themselves that no egress could have been made in this quarter, they would naturally bestow here a very cursory examination. It was clear to me, however, that the shutter belonging to the window at the head of the bed, would, if swung fully back to the wall, reach to within two feet of the lightning-rod. It was also evident that, by exertion of a very unusual degree of activity and courage, an entrance into the window, from the rod, might have been thus effected. By reaching to the distance of two feet and a half (we now suppose the shutter open to its whole extent) a robber might have taken a firm grasp upon the trellis-work. Letting go, then, his hold upon the rod, placing his feet securely against the wall, and springing boldly from it, he might have swung the shutter so as to close it, and, if we imagine the window open at the time, might even have swung himself into the room.

"I wish you to bear especially in mind that I have spoken of a *very* unusual degree of activity as requisite to success in so hazardous and so difficult a feat. It is my design to show you first, that the thing might possibly have been accomplished: — but, secondly and *chiefly*, I wish to impress upon your understanding the *very extraordinary* — the almost præternatural character of that agility which could have accomplished it.

"You will say, no doubt, using the language of the law, that 'to make out my case,' I should rather undervalue, than insist upon a full estimation of the activity required in this matter. This may be the practice in law, but it is not the usage of reason. My ultimate object is only the

truth. My immediate purpose is to lead you to place in juxtaposition, that *very unusual* activity of which I have just spoken, with that *very peculiar* shrill (or harsh) and *unequal* voice, about whose nationality no two persons could be found to agree, and in whose utterance no syllabification could be detected."

At these words a vague and half-formed conception of the meaning of Dupin flitted over my mind. I seemed to be upon the verge of comprehension, without power to comprehend — as men, at times, find themselves upon the brink of remembrance, without being able, in the end, to remember. My friend went on with his discourse.

"You will see," he said, "that I have shifted the question from the mode of egress to that of ingress. It was my design to convey the idea that both were effected in the same manner, at the same point. Let us now revert to the interior of the room. Let us survey the appearances here. The drawers of the bureau, it is said, had been rifled, although many articles of apparel still remained within them. The conclusion here is absurd. It is a mere guess — a very silly one — and no more. How are we to know that the articles found in the drawers were not all these drawers had originally contained? Madame L'Espanaye and her daughter lived an exceedingly retired life — saw no company — seldom went out — had little use for numerous changes of habiliment. Those found were at least of as good quality as any likely to be possessed by these ladies. If a thief had taken any, why did he not take the best — why did he not take all? In a word, why did he abandon four thousand francs in gold to encumber himself with a bundle of linen? The gold *was* abandoned. Nearly the whole sum mentioned by Monsieur Mignaud, the banker, was discovered, in bags, upon the floor. I wish you therefore, to discard from your thoughts the blundering idea of *motive*, engendered in the brains of the police by that portion of the evidence which speaks of money delivered at the door of the house. Coincidences ten times as remarkable as this (the delivery of the money, and murder committed within three days upon the party receiving it), happen to all of us every hour of our lives, without attracting even momentary notice. Coincidences, in general, are great stumbling-blocks in the way of that class of thinkers who have been educated to know nothing of the theory of probabilities — that theory to which the most glorious objects of human research are indebted for the most glorious of illustration. In the present instance, had the gold been gone, the fact of its delivery three days before would have formed something more than a coincidence. It would have been corroborative of this idea of motive. But, under the real circumstances of the case, if we are to suppose gold the motive of this outrage, we must also imagine the perpetrator so vacillating an idiot as to have abandoned his gold and his motive together.

"Keeping now steadily in mind the points to which I have drawn your attention — that peculiar voice, that unusual agility, and that startling

absence of motive in a murder so singularly atrocious as this — let us glance at the butchery itself. Here is a woman strangled to death by manual strength, and thrust up a chimney head downward. Ordinary assassins employ no such mode of murder as this. Least of all, do they thus dispose of the murdered. In this manner of thrusting the corpse up the chimney, you will admit that there was something *excessively outré* — something altogether irreconcilable with our common notions of human action, even when we suppose the actors the most depraved of men. Think, too, how great must have been that strength which could have thrust the body *up* such an aperture so forcibly that the united vigor of several persons was found barely sufficient to drag it *down!*

"Turn, now, to other indications of the employment of a vigor most marvellous. On the hearth were thick tresses — very thick tresses — of gray human hair. These had been torn out by the roots. You are aware of the great force necessary in tearing thus from the head even twenty or thirty hairs together. You saw the locks in question as well as myself. Their roots (a hideous sight!) were clotted with fragments of the flesh of the scalp — sure token of the prodigious power which had been exerted in uprooting perhaps half a million of hairs at a time. The throat of the old lady was not merely cut, but the head absolutely severed from the body: the instrument was a mere razor. I wish you also to look at the *brutal* ferocity of these deeds. Of the bruises upon the body of Madame L'Espanaye I do not speak. Monsieur Dumas, and his worthy co-adjutor Monsieur Etienne, have pronounced that they were inflicted by some obtuse instrument; and so far these gentlemen are very correct. The obtuse instrument was clearly the stone pavement in the yard, upon which the victim had fallen from the window which looked in upon the bed. This idea, however simple it may now seem, escaped the police for the same reason that the breadth of the shutters escaped them — because, by the affair of the nails, their perceptions had been hermetically sealed against the possibilty of the windows having ever been opened at all.

"If now, in addition to all these things, you have properly reflected upon the odd disorder of the chamber, we have gone so far as to combine the ideas of an agility astounding, a strength superhuman, a ferocity brutal, a butchery without motive, a *grotesquerie* in horror absolutely alien from humanity, and a voice foreign in tone to the ears of men of many nations, and devoid of all distinct or intelligible syllabification. What result, then, has ensued? What impression have I made upon your fancy?"

I felt a creeping of the flesh as Dupin asked me the question. "A madman," I said, "has done this deed — some raving maniac, escaping from a neighboring *Maison de Santé.*"

"In some respects," he replied, "your idea is not irrelevant. But the voices of madmen, even in their wildest paroxysms, are never found to tally with that peculiar voice heard upon the stairs. Madmen are of some

nation, and their language, however incoherent in its words, has always the coherence of syllabification. Besides, the hair of a madman is not such as I now hold in my hand. I disentangled this little tuft from the rigidly clutched fingers of Madame L'Espanaye. Tell me what you can make of it."

"Dupin!" I said, completely unnerved; "this hair is most unusual — this is no *human* hair."

"I have not asserted that it is," said he; "but, before we decide this point, I wish you to glance at the little sketch I have here traced upon this paper. It it a *fac-simile* drawing of what has been described in one portion of the testimony as 'dark bruises and deep indentations of finger nails' upon the throat of Mademoiselle L'Espanaye, and in another (by Messrs. Dumas and Etienne) as a 'series of livid spots, evidently the impressions of fingers.'

"You will perceive," continued my friend, spreading out the paper upon the table before us, "that this drawing gives the idea of a firm and fixed hold. There is no *slipping* apparent. Each finger has retained — possibly until the death of the victim — the fearful grasp by which it originally imbedded itself. Attempt, now, to place all your fingers, at the same time, in the respective impressions as you see them."

I made the attempt in vain.

"We are possibly not giving this matter a fair trial," he said. "The paper is spread out upon a plane surface; but the human throat is cylindrical. Here is a billet of wood, the circumference of which is about that of the throat. Wrap the drawing around it, and try the experiment again."

I did so; but the difficulty was even more obvious than before. "This," I said, "is the mark of no human hand."

"Read now," replied Dupin, "this passage from Cuvier."

It was a minute anatomical and generally descriptive account of the large fulvous Ourang-Outang of the East Indian islands. The gigantic stature, the prodigious strength and activity, the wild ferocity, and the imitative propensities of these mammalia are sufficiently well known to all. I understood the full horrors of the murder at once.

"The description of the digits," said I, as I made an end of reading, "is in exact accordance with this drawing. I see that no animal but an Ourang-Outang, of the species here mentioned, could have impressed the indentations as you have traced them. This tuft of tawny hair, too, is identical in character with that of the beast of Cuvier. But I cannot possibly comprehend the particulars of this frightful mystery. Besides, there were *two* voices heard in contention, and one of them was unquestionably the voice of a Frenchman."

"True; and you will remember an expression attributed almost unanimously, by the evidence, to this voice, — the expression, '*mon Dieu!*' This, under the circumstances, has been justly characterized by one of the witnesses (Montani, the confectioner) as an expression of remon-

strance or expostulation. Upon these two words, therefore, I have mainly built my hopes of a full solution of the riddle. A Frenchman was cognizant of the murder. It is possible — indeed it is far more than probable — that he was innocent of all participation in the bloody transaction which took place. The Ourang-Outang may have escaped from him. He may have traced it to the chamber; but, under the agitating circumstances which ensued, he could never have recaptured it. It is still at large. I will not pursue these guesses — for I have no right to call them more — since the shades of reflection upon which they are based are scarcely of sufficient depth to be appreciable by my own intellect, and since I could not pretend to make them intelligible to the understanding of another. We will call them guesses, then, and speak of them as such. If the Frenchman in question is indeed, as I suppose, innocent of this atrocity, this advertisement, which I left last night upon our return home, at the office of *Le Monde* (a paper devoted to the shipping interest, and much sought by sailors), will bring him to our residence."

He handed me a paper, and I read thus:

CAUGHT — *In the Bois de Boulogne, early in the morning of the —— inst.* (the morning of the murder), *a very large, tawny Ourang-Outang of the Bornese species. The owner (who is ascertained to be a sailor, belonging to a Maltese vessel) may have the animal again, upon identifying it satisfactorily, and paying a few charges arising from its capture and keeping. Call at No. —— Rue ——, Faubourg St. Germain — au troisième."*

"How was it possible," I asked, "that you should know the man to be a sailor, and belonging to a Maltese vessel?"

"I do *not know* it," said Dupin. "I am not *sure* of it. Here, however, is a small piece of ribbon, which from its form, and from its greasy appearance, has evidently been used in tying the hair in one of those long *queues* of which sailors are so fond. Moreover, this knot is one which few besides sailors can tie, and it is peculiar to the Maltese. I picked the ribbon up at the foot of the lightning-rod. It could not have belonged to either of the deceased. Now if, after all, I am wrong in my induction from this ribbon, that the Frenchman was a sailor belonging to a Maltese vessel, still I can have done no harm in saying what I did in the advertisement. If I am right, a great point is gained. Cognizant although innocent of the murder, the Frenchman will naturally hesitate about replying to the advertisement — about demanding the Ourang-Outang. He will reason thus: — 'I am innocent; I am poor; my Ourang-Outang is of great value — to one in my circumstances a fortune of itself — why should I lose it through idle apprehensions of danger? Here it is, within my grasp. It was found in the Bois de Boulogne — at a vast distance from the scene of that butchery. How can it ever be suspected that a brute beast should have done the deed? The police are at fault — they have failed to procure the slightest clew. Should they even trace the animal, it would be

impossible to prove me cognizant of the murder, or to implicate me in guilt on account of that cognizance. Above all, *I am known*. The advertiser designates me as the possessor of the beast. I am not sure to what limit his knowledge may extend. Should I avoid claiming a property of so great value, which it is known that I possess, I will render the animal at least, liable to suspicion. It is not my policy to attract attention either to myself or to the beast. I will answer the advertisement, get the Ourang-Outang, and keep it close until this matter has blown over.'"

At this moment we heard a step upon the stairs.

"Be ready," said Dupin, "with your pistols, but neither use them nor show them until at a signal from myself."

The front door of the house had been left open, and the visitor had entered, without ringing, and advanced several steps upon the staircase. Now, however, he seemed to hesitate. Presently we heard him descending. Dupin was moving quickly to the door, when we again heard him coming up. He did not turn back a second time, but stepped up with decision, and rapped at the door of our chamber.

"Come in," said Dupin, in a cheerful and hearty tone.

A man entered. He was a sailor, evidently, — a tall, stout, and muscular-looking person, with a certain daredevil expression of countenance, not altogether unprepossessing. His face, greatly sunburnt, was more than half hidden by whisker and *mustachio*. He had with him a huge oaken cudgel, but appeared to be otherwise unarmed. He bowed awkwardly, and bade us "good evening," in French accents, which, although somewhat Neufchatelish, were still sufficiently indicative of a Parisian origin.

"Sit down, my friend," said Dupin. "I suppose you have called about the Ourang-Outang. Upon my word, I almost envy you the possession of him; a remarkably fine, and no doubt a very valuable animal. How old do you suppose him to be?"

The sailor drew a long breath, with the air of a man relieved of some intolerable burden, and then replied, in an assured tone:

"I have no way of telling — but he can't be more than four or five years old. Have you got him here?"

"Oh, no; we had no conveniences for keeping him here. He is at a livery stable in the Rue Dubourg, just by. You can get him in the morning. Of course you are prepared to identify the property?"

"To be sure I am, sir."

"I shall be sorry to part with him," said Dupin.

"I don't mean that you should be at all this trouble for nothing, sir," said the man. "Couldn't expect it. Am very willing to pay a reward for the finding of the animal — that is to say, anything in reason."

"Well," replied my friend, "that is all very fair, to be sure. Let me think! — what should I have? Oh! I will tell you. My reward shall be this. You shall give me all the information in your power about these murders in the Rue Morgue."

Dupin said the last words in a very low tone, and very quietly. Just as quietly, too, he walked toward the door, locked it, and put the key in his pocket. He then drew a pistol from his bosom and placed it, without the least flurry, upon the table.

The sailor's face flushed up as if he were struggling with suffocation. He started to his feet and grasped his cudgel; but the next moment he fell back into his seat, trembling violently, and with the countenance of death itself. He spoke not a word. I pitied him from the bottom of my heart.

"My friend," said Dupin, in a kind tone, "you are alarming yourself unnecessarily — you are indeed. We mean you no harm whatever. I pledge you the honor of a gentleman, and of a Frenchman, that we intend you no injury. I perfectly well know that you are innocent of the atrocities in the Rue Morgue. It will not do, however, to deny that you are in some measure implicated in them. From what I have already said, you must know that I have had means of information about this matter — means of which you could never have dreamed. Now the thing stands thus. You have done nothing which you could have avoided — nothing, certainly, which renders you culpable. You are not even guilty of robbery, when you might have robbed with impunity. You have nothing to conceal. You have no reason for concealment. On the other hand, you are bound by every principle of honor to confess all you know. An innocent man is now imprisoned, charged with that crime of which you can point out the perpetrator."

The sailor had recovered his presence of mind, in a great measure, while Dupin uttered these words; but his original boldness of bearing was all gone.

"So help me God!" said he, after a brief pause, "I *will* tell you all I know about this affair; — but I do not expect you to believe one half I say — I would be a fool indeed if I did. Still, I *am* innocent, and I will make a clean breast if I die for it."

What he stated was, in substance, this. He had lately made a voyage to the Indian Archipelago. A party, of which he formed one, landed at Borneo, and passed into the interior on an excursion of pleasure. Himself and a companion had captured the Ourang-Outang. This companion dying, the animal fell into his own exclusive possession. After a great trouble, occasioned by the intractable ferocity of his captive during the home voyage, he at length succeeded in lodging it safely at his own residence in Paris, where, not to attract toward himself the unpleasant curiosity of his neighbors, he kept it carefully secluded, until such time as it should recover from a wound in the foot, received from a splinter on board ship. His ultimate design was to sell it.

Returning home from some sailor's frolic on the night, or rather in the morning, of the murder, he found the beast occupying his own bed-

room, into which it had broken from a closet adjoining, where it had been, as was thought, securely confined. Razor in hand, and fully lathered, it was sitting before a looking-glass, attempting the operation of shaving, in which it had no doubt previously watched its master through the key-hole of the closet. Terrified at the sight of so dangerous a weapon in the possession of an animal so ferocious, and so well able to use it, the man, for some moments, was at a loss what to do. He had been accustomed, however, to quiet the creature, even in its fiercest moods, by the use of a whip, and to this he now resorted. Upon sight of it, the Ourang-Outang sprang at once through the door of the chamber, down the stairs, and thence, through a window, unfortunately open, into the street.

The Frenchman followed in despair; the ape, razor still in hand, occasionally stopping to look back and gesticulate at his pursuer, until the latter had nearly come up with it. It then again made off. In this manner the chase continued for a long time. The streets were profoundly quiet, as it was nearly three o'clock in the morning. In passing down an alley in the rear of the Rue Morgue, the fugitive's attention was arrested by a light gleaming from the open window of Madame L'Espanaye's chamber, in the fourth story of her house. Rushing to the building, it perceived the lightning-rod, clambered up with inconceivable agility, grasped the shutter, which was thrown fully back against the wall, and, by its means, swung itself directly upon the headboard of the bed. The whole feat did not occupy a minute. The shutter was kicked open again by the Ourang-Outang as it entered the room.

The sailor, in the meantime, was both rejoiced and perplexed. He had strong hopes of now recapturing the brute, as it could scarcely escape from the trap into which it had ventured, except by the rod, where it might be intercepted as it came down. On the other hand, there was much cause for anxiety as to what it might do in the house. This latter reflection urged the man still to follow the fugitive. A lightning-rod is ascended without difficulty, especially by a sailor; but, when he had arrived as high as the window, which lay far to his left, his career was stopped; the most that he could accomplish was to reach over so as to obtain a glimpse of the interior of the room. At this glimpse he nearly fell from his hold through excess of horror. Now it was that those hideous shrieks arose upon the night, which had startled from slumber the inmates of the Rue Morgue. Madame L'Espanaye and her daughter, habited in their night clothes, had apparently been occupied in arranging some papers in the iron chest already mentioned, which had been wheeled into the middle of the room. It was open, and its contents lay beside it on the floor. The victims must have been sitting with their backs toward the window; and, from the time elapsing between the ingress of the beast and the screams, it seems probable that it was not immediately perceived. The flapping to of the shutter would naturally have been attributed to the wind.

As the sailor looked in, the gigantic animal had seized Madame L'Espanaye by the hair (which was loose, as she had been combing it), and was flourishing the razor about her face, in imitation of the motions of a barber. The daughter lay prostrate and motionless; she had swooned. The screams and struggles of the old lady (during which the hair was torn from her head) had the effect of changing the probably pacific purposes of the Ourang-Outang into those of wrath. With one determined sweep of its muscular arm it nearly severed her head from her body. The sight of blood inflamed its anger into phrenzy. Gnashing its teeth, and flashing fire from its eyes, it flew upon the body of the girl and embedded its fearful talons in her throat, retaining its grasp until she expired. Its wandering and wild glances fell at this moment upon the head of the bed, over which the face of its master, rigid with horror, was just discernible. The fury of the beast, who no doubt bore still in mind the dreaded whip, was instantly converted into fear. Conscious of having deserved punishment, it seemed desirous of concealing its bloody deeds, and skipped about the chamber in an agony of nervous agitation; throwing down and breaking the furniture as it moved, and dragging the bed from the bedstead. In conclusion, it seized first the corpse of the daughter, and thrust it up the chimney, as it was found; then that of the old lady, which, it immediately hurled through the window headlong.

As the ape approached the casement with its mutilated burden, the sailor shrank aghast to the rod, and, rather gliding than clambering down it, hurried at once home — dreading the consequences of the butchery, and gladly abandoning, in his terror, all solicitude about the fate of the Ourang-Outang. The words heard by the party upon the staircase were the Frenchman's exclamations of horror and affright, commingled with the fiendish jabberings of the brute.

I have scarcely any thing to add. The Ourang-Outang must have escaped from the chamber, by the rod, just before the breaking of the door. It must have closed the window as it passed through it. It was subsequently caught by the owner himself, who obtained for it a very large sum at the *Jardin des Plantes*. Le Bon was instantly released, upon our narration of the circumstances (with some comments from Dupin) at the *bureau* of the Prefect of Police. This functionary, however, well disposed to my friend, could not altogether conceal his chagrin at the turn which affairs had taken, and was fain to indulge in a sarcasm or two about the propriety of every person minding his own business.

"Let him talk," said Dupin, who had not thought it necessary to reply. "Let him discourse; it will ease his conscience. I am satisfied with having defeated him in his own castle. Nevertheless, that he failed in the solution of this mystery, is by no means that matter for wonder which he supposes it; for, in truth, our friend the prefect is somewhat too cunning to be profound. In his wisdom is no *stamen*. It is all head and no body, like the pictures of the Goddess Laverna — or, at best, all head and

shoulders, like a codfish. But he is a good creature after all. I like him especially for one master stroke of cant, by which he has attained his reputation for ingenuity, I mean the way he has '*de nier ce qui est, et d'expliquer ce qui n'est pas.*' " *

A Descent into the Maelström

THE WAYS *of God in Nature, as in Providence, are not as our ways; nor are the models that we frame in any way commensurate to the vastness, profundity, and unsearchableness of His works,* which have a depth in them greater than the well of Democritus.

JOSEPH GLANVILLE.

Wᴇ had now reached the summit of the loftiest crag. For some minutes the old man seemed too much exhausted to speak.

"Not long ago," said he at length, "and I could have guided you on this route as well as the youngest of my sons; but, about three years past, there happened to me an event such as never happened before to mortal man — or at least such as no man ever survived to tell of — and the six hours of deadly terror which I then endured have broken me up body and soul. You suppose me a *very* old man — but I am not. It took less than a single day to change these hairs from a jetty black to white, to weaken my limbs, and to unstring my nerves, so that I tremble at the least exertion, and am frightened at a shadow. Do you know I can scarcely look over this little cliff without getting giddy?"

The "little cliff," upon whose edge he had so carelessly thrown himself down to rest that the weightier portion of his body hung over it, while he was only kept from falling by the tenure of his elbow on its extreme and slippery edge — this "little cliff" arose, a sheer unobstructed precipice of black shining rock, some fifteen or sixteen hundred feet from the world of crags beneath us. Nothing would have tempted me to be within half dozen yards of its brink. In truth so deeply was I excited by the perilous position of my companion, that I fell at full length upon the ground, clung to the shrubs around me, and dared not even glance upward at the sky — while I struggled in vain to divest myself of the idea that the foundations of the mountain were in danger from the fury of the winds. It was long before I could reason myself into sufficient courage to sit up and look out into the distance.

"You must get over these fancies," said the guide, "for I have brought

* Rousseau — Nouvelle Heloise.

you here that you might have the best possible view of the scene of that event I mentioned — and to tell you the whole story with the spot just under your eye."

"We are now," he continued, in that particularizing manner which distinguished him — "we are now close upon the Norwegian coast — in the sixty-eighth degree of latitude — in the great province of Nordland — and in the dreary district of Lofoden. The mountain upon whose top we sit is Helseggen, the Cloudy. Now raise yourself up a little higher — hold on to the grass if you feel giddy — so — and look out, beyond the belt of vapor beneath us, into the sea."

I looked dizzily, and beheld a wide expanse of ocean, whose waters wore so inky a hue as to bring at once to my mind the Nubian geographer's account of the *Mare Tenebrarum*. A panorama more deplorably desolate no human imagination can conceive. To the right and left, as far as the eye could reach, there lay outstretched, like ramparts of the world, lines of horridly black and beetling cliff, whose character of gloom was but the more forcibly illustrated by the surf which reared high up against it its white and ghastly crest, howling and shrieking for ever. Just opposite the promontory upon whose apex we were placed, and at a distance of some five or six miles out at sea, there was visible a small, bleak-looking island; or, more properly, its position was discernible through the wilderness of surge in which it was enveloped. About two miles nearer the land, arose another of smaller size; hideously craggy and barren, and encompassed at various intervals by a cluster of dark rocks.

The appearance of the ocean, in the space between the more distant island and the shore, had something very unusual about it. Although, at the time, so strong a gale was blowing landward that a brig in the remote offing lay to under a double-reefed trysail, and constantly plunged her whole hull out of sight, still there was here nothing like a regular swell, but only a short, quick, angry cross dashing of water in every direction — as well in the teeth of the wind as otherwise. Of foam there was little except in the immediate vicinity of the rocks.

"The island in the distance," resumed the old man, "is called by the Norwegians Vurrgh. The one midway is Moskoe. That a mile to the northward is Ambaaren. Yonder are Islesen, Hotholm, Keildhelm, Suarven, and Buckholm. Further off — between Moskoe and Vurrgh — are Otterholm, Flimen, Sandflesen, and Stockholm. These are the true names of the places — but why it has been thought necessary to name them at all, is more than either you or I can understand. Do you hear anything? Do you see any change in the water?"

We had now been about ten minutes upon the top of Helseggen, to which we had ascended from the interior of Lofoden so that we had caught no glimpse of the sea until it had burst upon us from the summit. As the old man spoke, I became aware of a loud and gradually increasing sound, like the moaning of a vast herd of buffaloes upon an American

prairie; and at the same moment I perceived that what seamen term the *chopping* character of the ocean beneath us, was rapidly changing into a current which set to the eastward. Even while I gazed, this current acquired a monstrous velocity. Each moment added to its speed — to its headlong impetuosity. In five minutes the whole sea, as far as Vurrgh, was lashed into ungovernable fury; but it was between Moskoe and the coast that the main uproar held its sway. Here the vast bed of the waters, seamed and scarred into a thousand conflicting channels, burst suddenly into phrensied convulsion — heaving, boiling, hissing — gyrating in gigantic and innumerable vortices, and all whirling and plunging on to the eastward with a rapidity which water never elsewhere assumes, except in precipitous descents.

In a few minutes more, there came over the scene another radical alteration. The general surface grew somewhat more smooth, and the whirlpools, one by one, disappeared, while prodigious streaks of foam became apparent where none had been seen before. These streaks, at length, spreading out to a great distance, and entering into combination, took unto themselves the gyratory motion of the subsided vortices, and seemed to form the germ of another more vast. Suddenly — very suddenly — this assumed a distinct and definite existence, in a circle of more than a mile in diameter. The edge of the whirl was represented by a broad belt of gleaming spray; but no particle of this slipped into the mouth of the terrific funnel, whose interior, as far as the eye could fathom it, was a smooth, shining, and jet-black wall of water, inclined to the horizon at an angle of some forty-five degrees, speeding dizzily round and round with a swaying and sweltering motion, and sending forth to the winds an appalling voice, half shriek, half roar, such as not even the mighty cataract of Niagara ever lifts up in its agony to Heaven.

The mountain trembled to its very base, and the rock rocked. I threw myself upon my face, and clung to the scant herbage in an excess of nervous agitation.

"This," said I at length, to the old man — "this *can* be nothing else than the great whirlpool of the Maelström."

"So it is sometimes termed," said he. "We Norwegians call it the Moskoe-ström, from the island of Moskoe in the midway."

The ordinary accounts of this vortex had by no means prepared me for what I saw. That of Jonas Ramus, which is perhaps the most circumstantial of any, cannot impart the faintest conception either of the magnificence, or of the horror of the scene — or of the wild bewildering sense of *the novel* which confounds the beholder. I am not sure from what point of view the writer in question surveyed it, nor at what time; but it could neither have been from the summit of Helseggen, nor during a storm. There are some passages of his description, nevertheless, which may be quoted for their details, although their effect is exceedingly feeble in conveying an impression of the spectacle.

"Between Lofoden and Moskoe," he says, "the depth of the water is between thirty-six and forty fathoms; but on the other side, toward Ver (Vurrgh) this depth decreases so as not to afford a convenient passage for a vessel, without the risk of splitting on the rocks, which happens even in the calmest weather. When it is flood, the stream runs up the country between Lofoden and Moskoe with a boisterous rapidity; but the roar of its impetuous ebb to the sea is scarce equalled by the loudest and most dreadful cataracts; the noise being heard several leagues off, and the vortices or pits are of such an extent and depth, that if a ship comes within its attraction, it is inevitably absorbed and carried down to the bottom, and there beat to pieces against the rocks; and when the water relaxes, the fragments thereof are thrown up again. But these intervals of tranquility are only at the turn of the ebb and flood, and in calm weather, and last but a quarter of an hour, its violence gradually returning. When the stream is most boisterous, and its fury heightened by a storm, it is dangerous to come within a Norway mile of it. Boats, yachts, and ships have been carried away by not guarding against it before they were within its reach. It likewise happens frequently, that whales come too near the stream, and are overpowered by its violence; and then it is impossible to describe their howlings and bellowings in their fruitless struggles to disengage themselves. A bear once, attempting to swim from Lofoden to Moskoe, was caught by the stream and borne down, while he roared terribly, so as to be heard on shore. Large stocks of firs and pine trees, after being absorbed by the current, rise again broken and torn to such a degree as if bristles grew upon them. This plainly shows the bottom to consist of craggy rocks, among which they are whirled to and fro. This stream is regulated by the flux and reflux of the sea — it being constantly high and low water every six hours. In the year 1645, early in the morning of Sexagesima Sunday, it raged with such noise and impetuosity that the very stones of the houses on the coast fell to the ground."

In regard to the depth of the water, I could not see how this could have been ascertained at all in the immediate vicinity of the vortex. The "forty fathoms" must have reference only to portions of the channel close upon the shore either of Moskoe or Lofoden. The depth in the centre of the Moskoe-ström must be unmeasurably greater: and no better proof of this fact is necessary than can be obtained from even the sidelong glance into the abyss of the whirl which may be had from the highest crag of Helseggen. Looking down from this pinnacle upon the howling Phlegethon below, I could not help smiling at the simplicity with which the honest Jonas Ramus records, as a matter difficult of belief, the anecdotes of the whales and the bears, for it appeared to me, in fact, a self-evident thing, that the largest ships of the line in existence, coming within the influence of that deadly attraction, could resist it as little as a feather the hurricane, and must disappear bodily and at once.

The attempts to account for the phenomenon — some of which I re-

member, seemed to me sufficiently plausible in perusal — now wore a very different and unsatisfactory aspect. The idea generally received is that this, as well as three smaller vortices among the Ferroe Islands, "have no other cause than the collision of waves rising and falling, at flux and reflux, against a ridge of rocks and shelves, which confines the water so that it precipitates itself like a cataract; and thus the higher the flood rises, the deeper must the fall be, and the natural result of all is a whirl-pool or vortex, the prodigious suction of which is sufficiently known by lesser experiments." — These are the words of the Encylcopaedia Brittanica. Kircher and others imagine that in the centre of the channel of the Maelström is an abyss penetrating the globe, and issuing in some very remote part — the Gulf of Bothnia being somewhat decidedly named in one instance. This opinion, idle in itself, was the one to which, as I gazed, my imagination most readily assented; and, mentioning it to the guide, I was rather surprised to hear him say that, although it was the view almost universally entertained of the subject by the Norwegians, it nevertheless was not his own. As to the former notion he confessed his inability to comprehend it; and here I agreed with him — for, however conclusive on paper, it becomes altogether unintelligible, and even absurd, amid the thunder of the abyss.

"You have had a good look at the whirl now," said the old man, "and if you will creep round this crag, so as to get in its lee, and deaden the roar of the water, I will tell you a story that will convince you I ought to know something of the Moskoe-ström."

I placed myself as desired, and he proceeded.

"Myself and my two brothers once owned a schooner-rigged smack of about seventy tons burthen, with which we were in the habit of fishing among the islands beyond Moskoe, nearly to Vurrgh. In all violent eddies at sea there is good fishing, at proper opportunities, if one has only the courage to attempt it; but among the whole of the Lofoden coastmen, we three were the only ones who made a regular business of going out to the islands, as I tell you. The usual grounds are a great way lower down to the southward. There fish can be got at all hours, without much risk, and therefore these places are preferred. The choice spots over here among the rocks, however, not only yield the finest variety, but in far greater abundance; so that we often got in a single day, what the more timid of the craft could not scrape together in a week. In fact, we made it a matter of desperate speculation — the risk of life standing instead of labor, and courage answering for capital.

"We kept the smack in a cove about five miles higher up the coast than this; and it was our practice, in fine weather, to take advantage of the fifteen minutes' slack to push across the main channel of the Moskoe-ström, far above the pool, and then drop down upon anchorage somewhere near Otterholm, or Sandflesen, where the eddies are not so violent as elsewhere. Here we used to remain until nearly time for slack water

again, when we weighed and made for home. We never set out upon
this expedition without a steady side wind for going and coming — one
that we felt sure would not fail us before our return — and we seldom
made a mis-calculation upon this point. Twice, during six years, we were
forced to stay all night at anchor on account of a dead calm, which is
a rare thing indeed just about here; and once we had to remain on the
grounds nearly a week, starving to death, owing to a gale which blew up
shortly after our arrival, and made the channel too boisterous to be
thought of. Upon this occasion we should have been driven out to sea
in spite of every thing, (for the whirlpools threw us round and round so
violently, that, at length we fouled our anchor and dragged it) if it had
not been that we drifted into one of the innumerable cross currents —
here today and gone tomorrow — which drove us under the lee of Flimen,
where, by good luck, we brought up.

"I could not tell you the twentieth part of the difficulties we encoun-
tered 'on the grounds' — it is a bad spot to be in, even in good weather —
but we make shift always to run the gauntlet of the Moskoe-ström itself
without accident; although at times my heart has been in my mouth
when we happened to be a minute or so behind or before the slack.
The wind sometimes was not as strong as we thought it at starting, and
then we made rather less way than we could wish, while the current
rendered the smack unmanageable. My eldest brother had a son eighteen
years old, and I had two stout boys of my own. These would have been
of great assistance at such times, in using the sweeps as well as afterward
in fishing — but somehow, although we ran the risk ourselves, we had
not the heart to let the young ones get into the danger — for, after all is
said and done, it *was* a horrible danger, and that is the truth.

"It is now within a few days of three years since what I am going to
tell you occurred. It was on the tenth day of July, 18—, a day which the
people of this part of the world will never forget — for it was one in
which blew the most terrible hurricane that ever came out of the heavens.
And yet all the morning and indeed until late in the afternoon, there
was a gentle and steady breeze from the south-west, while the sun shone
brightly, so that the oldest seaman among us could not have foreseen
what was to follow.

"The three of us — my two brothers and myself — had crossed over
to the islands about two o'clock P. M., and had soon nearly loaded the
smack with fine fish, which, we all remarked, were more plenty that
day than we had ever known them. It was just seven, *by my watch*,
when we weighed and started for home, so as to make the worst of the
Ström at slack water, which we knew would be at eight.

"We set out with a fresh wind on our starboard quarter, and for some
time spanked along at a great rate, never dreaming of danger, for indeed
we saw not the slightest reason to apprehend it. All at once we were

taken aback by a breeze from over Helseggen. This was most unusual — something that had never happened to us before — and I began to feel a little uneasy, without exactly knowing why. We put the boat on the wind, but could make no headway at all for the eddies, and I was upon the point of proposing to return to the anchorage, when looking astern, we saw the whole horizon covered with a singular copper-colored cloud that rose with the most amazing velocity.

"In the meantime the breeze that had headed us off fell away and we were dead becalmed, drifting about in every direction. This state of things, however, did not last long enough to give us time to think about it. In less than a minute the storm was upon us — in less than two the sky was entirely overcast — and what with this and the driving spray, it became suddenly so dark that we could not see each other in the smack.

"Such a hurricane as then blew it is folly to attempt describing. The oldest seaman in Norway never experienced any thing like it. We had let our sails go by the run before it cleverly took us; but, at the first puff, both our masts went by the board as if they had been sawed off — the mainmast taking with it my youngest brother, who had lashed himself to it for safety.

"Our boat was the lightest feather of a thing that ever sat upon water. It had a complete flush deck, with only a small hatch near the bow, and this hatch it had always been our custom to batten down when about to cross the Ström, by way of precaution against the chopping seas. But for this circumstance we should have foundered at once — for we lay entirely buried for some moments. How my elder brother escaped destruction I cannot say, for I never had an opportunity of ascertaining. For my part, as soon as I had let the foresail run, I threw myself flat on deck, with my feet against the narrow gunwale of the bow, and with my hands grasping a ring-bolt near the foot of the foremast. It was mere instinct that prompted me to do this — which was undoubtedly the very best thing I could have done — for I was too much flurried to think.

"For some moments we were completely deluged, as I say, and all this time I held my breath, and clung to the bolt. When I could stand it no longer I raised myself upon my knees, still keeping hold with my hands, and thus got my head clear. Presently our little boat gave herself a shake, just as a dog does in coming out of the water, and thus rid herself, in some measure, of the sea. I was now trying to get the better of the stupor that had come over me, and to collect my senses so as to see what was to be done, when I felt somebody grasp my arm. It was my elder brother, and my heart leaped for joy, for I had made sure that he was overboard — but the next moment all this joy was turned into horror — for he put his mouth close to my ear, and screamed out the word '*Moskoe-ström!*'

"No one will ever know what my feelings were at that moment. I shook from head to foot as if I had had the most violent fit of the ague.

I knew what he meant by that one word well enough — I knew what he wished to make me understand. With the wind that now drove us on, we were bound for the whirl of the Ström, and nothing could save us!

"You perceive that in crossing the Ström *channel*, we always went a long way up above the whirl, even in the calmest weather, and then had to wait and watch carefully for the slack — but now we were driving right upon the pool itself, and in such a hurricane as this! 'To be sure,' I thought, 'we shall get there just about the slack — there is some little hope in that' — but in the next moment I cursed myself for being so great a fool as to dream of hope at all. I knew very well that we were doomed, had we been ten times a ninety-gun ship.

"By this time the first fury of the tempest had spent itself, or perhaps we did not feel it so much, as we scudded before it, but at all events the seas, which at first had been kept down by the wind, and lay flat and frothing, now got up into absolute mountains. A singular change, too had come over the heavens. Around in every direction it was still as black as pitch, but nearly overhead there burst out, all at once, a circular rift of clear sky — as clear as I ever saw — and of a deep bright blue — and through it there blazed forth the full moon with a lustre that I never before knew her to wear. She lit up everything about us with the greatest distinctness — but, oh God, what a scene it was to light up!

"I now made one or two attempts to speak to my brother — but in some manner which I could not understand, the din had so increased that I could not make him hear a single word, although I screamed at the top of my voice in his ear. Presently he shook his head, looking as pale as death, and held up one of his fingers, as if to say '*listen!*'

"At first I could not make out what he meant — but soon a hideous thought flashed upon me. I dragged my watch from its fob. It was not going. I glanced at its face by the moonlight, and then burst into tears as I flung it far away into the ocean. *It had run down at seven o'clock! We were behind the time of the slack, and the whirl of the Ström was in full fury!*

"When a boat is well built, properly trimmed, and not deep laden, the waves in a strong gale, when she is going large, seem always to slip from beneath her — which appears strange to a landsman — and this is what is called *riding*, in sea phrase. Well, so far we had ridden the swells very cleverly; but presently a gigantic sea happened to take us right under the counter, and bore us with it as it rose — up — up — as if into the sky. I would not have believed that any wave could rise so high. And then down we came with a sweep, a slide, and a plunge that made me feel sick and dizzy, as if I was falling from some lofty mountaintop in a dream. But while we were up I had thrown a quick glance around — and that one glance was all-sufficient. I saw our exact position in an instant. The Moskoe-ström whirlpool was about a quarter of a mile dead ahead — but no more like the every-day Moskoe-ström than the

whirl, as you now see it, is like a mill-race. If I had not known where we were, and what we had to expect, I should not have recognized the place at all. As it was, I involuntarily closed my eyes in horror. The lids clenched themselves together as if in a spasm.

"It could not have been more than two minutes afterwards until we suddenly felt the waves subside, and were enveloped in foam. The boat made a sharp half turn to larboard, and then shot off in its new direction like a thunderbolt. At the same moment the roaring noise of the water was completely drowned in a kind of shrill shriek — such a sound as you might imagine given out by the waste-pipes of many thousand steam-vessels letting off their steam all together. We were now in the belt of surf that always surrounds the whirl; and I thought, of course, that an-other moment would plunge us into the abyss, down which we could only see indistinctly on account of the amazing velocity with which we were borne along. The boat did not seem to sink into the water at all, but to skim like an air-bubble upon the surface of the surge. Her star-board side was next the whirl, and on the larboard arose the world of ocean we had left. It stood like a huge writhing wall between us and the horizon.

"It may appear strange, but now, when we were in the very jaws of the gulf, I felt more composed than when we were only approaching it. Having made up my mind to hope no more, I got rid of a great deal of that terror which unmanned me at first. I supposed it was despair that strung my nerves.

"It may look like boasting — but what I tell you is truth — I began to reflect how magnificent a thing it was to die in such a manner, and how foolish it was in me to think of so paltry a consideration as my own individual life, in view of so wonderful a manifestation of God's power. I do believe that I blushed with shame when this idea crossed my mind. After a little while I became possessed with the keenest curiosity about the whirl itself. I positively felt a *wish* to explore its depths, even at the sacrifice I was going to make; and my principal grief was that I should never be able to tell my old companions on shore about the mysteries I should see. These, no doubt, were singular fancies to occupy a man's mind in such extremity — and I have often thought since, that the revo-lutions of the boat around the pool might have rendered me a little light-headed.

"There was another circumstance which tended to restore my self-possession; and this was the cessation of the wind, which could not reach us in our present situation — for, as you saw yourself, the belt of the surf is considerably lower than the general bed of the ocean, and this latter now towered above us, a high black, mountainous ridge. If you have never been at sea in a heavy gale, you can form no idea of the confusion of mind occasioned by the wind and spray together. They blind, deafen, and strangle you, and take away all power of action or

reflection. But we were now, in a great measure, rid of these annoyances — just as death-condemned felons in prison are allowed petty indulgences, forbidden them while their doom is yet uncertain.

"How often we made the circuit of the belt it is impossible to say. We careered round and round for perhaps an hour, flying rather than floating, getting gradually more and more into the middle of the surge, and then nearer and nearer to its horrible inner edge. All this time I had never let go of the ring-bolt. My brother was at the stern, holding on to a small empty water-cask which had been securely lashed under the coop of the counters, and was the only thing on deck that had not been swept overboard when the gale first took us. As we approached the brink of the pit he let go his hold upon this, and made for the ring, from which, in the agony of his terror, he endeavored to force my hands, as it was not large enough to afford us both a secure grasp. I never felt deeper grief than when I saw him attempt this act — although I knew he was a madman when he did it — a raving maniac through sheer fright. I did not care, however, to contest the point with him. I knew it could make no difference whether either of us held on at all; so I let him have the bolt, and went astern to the cask. This there was no great difficulty in doing; for the smack flew round steadily enough, and upon an even keel — only swaying to and fro with the immense sweeps and swelters of the whirl. Scarcely had I secured myself in my new position, when we gave a wild lurch to starboard, and rushed headlong into the abyss. I muttered a hurried prayer to God, and thought all was over.

"As I felt the sickening sweep of the descent, I had instinctively tightened my hold upon the barrel, and closed my eyes. For some seconds I dared not open them — while I expected instant destruction, and wondered that I was not already in my death-struggles with the water. But moment after moment elapsed. I still lived. The sense of falling had ceased; and the motion of the vessel seemed much as it had been before, while in the belt of foam, with the exception that she now lay more along. I took courage and looked once again upon the scene.

"Never shall I forget the sensation of awe, horror, and admiration with which I gazed about me. The boat appeared to be hanging, as if by magic, midway down, upon the interior surface of a funnel vast in circumference, prodigious in depth, and whose perfectly smooth sides might have been mistaken for ebony, but for the bewildering rapidity with which they spun around, and for the gleaming and ghastly radiance they shot forth, as the rays of the full moon, from that circular rift amid the clouds which I have already described, streamed in a flood of golden glory along the black walls, and far away down into the inmost recesses of the abyss.

"At first I was too much confused to observe any thing accurately. The general burst of terrific grandeur was all that I beheld. When I recovered myself a little, however, my gaze fell instinctively downward.

In this direction I was able to obtain an unobstructed view, from the manner in which the smack hung on the inclined surface of the pool. She was quite upon an even keel — that is to say, her deck lay in a plane parallel with that of the water — but this latter sloped at an angle of more than forty-five degrees, so that we seemed to be lying upon our beam-ends. I could not help observing, nevertheless, that I had scarcely more difficulty in maintaining my hold and footing in this situation, than if we had been upon a dead level; and this, I suppose, was owing to the speed at which we revolved.

"The rays of the moon seemed to search the very bottom of the profound gulf; but still I could make out nothing distinctly on account of a thick mist in which there hung a magnificent rainbow, like that narrow and tottering bridge which Mussulmen say is the only pathway between Time and Eternity. This mist, or spray, was no doubt occasioned by the clashing of the great walls of the funnel, as they all met together at the bottom — but the yell that went up to the Heavens from out of that mist I dare not attempt to describe.

"Our first slide into the abyss itself, from the belt of foam above, had carried us to a great distance down the slope; but our farther descent was by no means proportionate. Round and round we swept — not with any uniform movement — but in dizzying swings and jerks, that sent us sometimes only a few hundred yards — sometimes nearly the complete circuit of the whirl. Our progress downward, at each revolution, was slow, but very perceptible.

"Looking about me upon the wide waste of liquid ebony on which we were thus borne, I perceived that our boat was not the only object in the embrace of the whirl. Both above and below us were visible fragments of vessels, large masses of building-timber and trunks of trees, with many smaller articles, such as pieces of house furniture, broken boxes, barrels and staves. I have already described the unnatural curiosity which had taken the place of my original terrors. It appeared to grow upon me as I drew nearer and nearer to my dreadful doom. I now began to watch with a strange interest, the numerous things that floated in our company. I *must* have been delirious, for I even sought *amusement* in speculating upon the relative velocities of their several descents toward the foam below. 'This fir-tree,' I found myself at one time saying, 'will certainly be the next thing that takes the awful plunge and disappears,' — and then I was disappointed to find that the wreck of a Dutch merchant ship overtook it and went down before. At length, after making several guesses of this nature, and being deceived in all — this fact — the fact of my invariable miscalculation, set me upon a train of reflection that made my limbs again tremble, and my heart beat heavily once more.

"It was not a new terror that thus affected me, but the dawn of a more exciting *hope*. This hope arose partly from memory, and partly from pres-

ent observation. I called to mind the great variety of buoyant matter that strewed the coast of Lofoden, having been absorbed and then thrown forth by the Moskoe-ström. By far the greater number of the articles were shattered in the most extraordinary way — so chafed and roughened as to have the appearance of being stuck full of splinters — but then I distinctly recollected that there were *some* of them which were not disfigured at all. Now I could not account for this difference except by supposing that the roughened fragments were the only ones which had been *completely* absorbed — that the others had entered the whirl at so late a period of the tide, or, from some reason, had descended so slowly after entering, that they did not reach the bottom before the turn of the flood came, or the ebb, as the case might be. I conceived it possible, in either instance, that they might thus be whirled up again to the level of the ocean, without undergoing the fate of those which had been drawn in more early or absorbed more rapidly. I made, also, three important observations. The first was, that as a general rule, the larger the bodies were, the more rapid their descent — the second, that, between two masses of equal extent, the one spherical, and the other *of any other shape*, the superiority in speed of descent was with the sphere — the third, that, between two masses of equal size, the one cylindrical, and the other of any other shape, the cylinder was absorbed the more slowly. Since my escape, I have had several conversations on this subject with an old school-master of the district; and it was from him that I learned the use of the words 'cylinder' and 'sphere.' He explained to me — although I have forgotten the explanation — how what I observed was, in fact, the natural consequence of the forms of the floating fragments — and showed me how it happened that a cylinder, swimming in a vortex, offered more resistance to its suction, and was drawn in with greater difficulty than an equally bulky body, of any form whatever.*

"There was one startling circumstance which went a great way in enforcing these observations, and rendering me anxious to turn them to account, and this was that, at every revolution, we passed something like a barrel, or else the yard or the mast of a vessel, while many of these things, which had been on our level when I first opened my eyes upon the wonders of the whirlpool, were now high up above us, and seemed to have moved but little from their original station.

"I no longer hesitated what to do. I resolved to lash myself securely to the water-cask upon which I now held, to cut it loose from the counter, and to throw myself with it into the water. I attracted my brother's attention by signs, pointed to the floating barrels that came near us, and did everything in my power to make him understand what I was about to do. I thought at length that he comprehended my design — but, whether this was the case or not, he shook his head despairingly,

* See Archimedes, "*De Incidentibus in Fluido.*" — lib. 2.

and refused to move from his station by the ring-bolt. It was impossible to reach him; the emergency admitted of no delay; and so, with a bitter struggle, I resigned him to his fate, fastened myself to the cask by means of the lashings which secured it to the counter, and precipitated myself with it into the sea, without another moment's hesitation.

"The result was precisely what I had hoped it might be. As it is myself who now tell you this tale — as you see that I *did* escape — and as you are already in possession of the mode in which this escape was effected, and must therefore anticipate all that I have farther to say — I will bring my story quickly to conclusion. It might have been an hour, or thereabout, after my quitting the smack, when, having descended to a vast distance beneath me, it made three or four wild gyrations in rapid succession, and, bearing my loved brother with it, plunged headlong, at once and forever, into the chaos of foam below. The barrel to which I was attached sunk very little farther than half the distance between the bottom of the gulf and the spot at which I leaped overboard before a great change took place in the character of the whirlpool. The slope of the sides of the vast funnel became momently less and less steep. The gyrations of the whirl grew, gradually, less and less violent. By degrees, the froth and the rainbow disappeared, and the bottom of the gulf seemed slowly to uprise. The sky was clear, and the winds had gone down, and the full moon was setting radiantly in the west, when I found myself on the surface of the ocean, in full view of the shores of Lofoden, and above the spot where the pool of the Moskoe-ström *had been*. It was the hour of the slack — but the sea still heaved in mountainous waves from the effects of the hurricane. I was borne violently into the channel of the Ström, and in a few minutes, was hurried down the coast into the 'grounds' of the fishermen. A boat picked me up — exhausted from fatigue — and (now that the danger was removed) speechless from the memory of its horror. Those who drew me on board were my old mates and daily companions — but they knew me no more than they would have known a traveller from the spirit-land. My hair, which had been raven black the day before, was as white as you see it now. They say too that the whole expression of my countenance had changed. I told them my story — they did not believe it. I now tell it to *you* — and I can scarcely expect you to put more faith in it than did the merry fishermen of Lofoden."

The Island of the Fay

Nullus enim locus sine genio est.

<div style="text-align: right;">SERVIUS</div>

L a musique," says Marmontel, in those "Contes Moraux" * which in all our translations, we have insisted upon calling "Moral Tales," as if in mockery of their spirit — "*la musique est le seul des talents qui jouissent de lui-même; tous les autres veulent des temoins.*" He here confounds the pleasure derivable from sweet sounds with the capacity for creating them. No more than any other *talent*, is that for music susceptible of complete enjoyment, where there is no second party to appreciate its exercise. And it is only in common with other talents that it produces *effects* which may be fully enjoyed in solitude. The idea which the *raconteur* has either failed to entertain clearly, or has sacrificed in its expression to his national love of *point*, is, doubtless, the very tenable one that the higher order of music is the most thoroughly estimated when we are exclusively alone. The proposition, in this form, will be admitted at once by those who love the lyre for its own sake, and for its spiritual uses. But there is one pleasure still within the reach of fallen mortality — and perhaps only one — which owes even more than does music to the accessory sentiment of seclusion. I mean the happiness experienced in the contemplation of natural scenery. In truth, the man who would behold aright the glory of God upon earth must in solitude behold that glory. To me, at least, the presence — not of human life only, but of life in any other form than that of the green things which grow upon the soil and are voiceless — is a stain upon the landscape — is at war with the genius of the scene. I love, indeed, to regard the dark valleys, and the gray rocks, and the waters that silently smile, and the forests that sigh in uneasy slumbers, and the proud watchful mountains that look down upon all, — I love to regard these as themselves but the colossal members of one vast animate and sentient whole — a whole whose form (that of the sphere) is the most perfect and most inclusive of all; whose path is among associate planets; whose meek handmaiden is the moon, whose mediate sovereign is the sun; whose life is eternity; whose thought is that of a God; whose enjoyment is knowledge; whose destinies are lost in immensity; whose cognizance of ourselves is akin with our own cognizance of the *animalculæ* which infest the brain — a being which we, in consequence, regard as purely inanimate and ma-

* Moraux is here derived from *mœurs*, and its meaning is "*fashionable*" or more strictly "of manners."

terial, much in the same manner as these *animalculæ* must thus regard us.

Our telescopes and our mathematical investigations assure us on every hand — notwithstanding the cant of the more ignorant of the priesthood — that space, and therefore that bulk, is an important consideration in the eyes of the Almighty. The cycles in which the stars move are those best adapted for the evolution, without collision, of the greatest possible number of bodies. The forms of those bodies are accurately such as, within a given surface, to include the greatest possible amount of matter; — while the surfaces themselves are so disposed as to accommodate a denser population than could be accommodated on the same surfaces otherwise arranged. Nor is it any argument against bulk being an object with God, that space itself is infinite; for there may be an infinity of matter to fill it. And since we see clearly that the endowment of matter with vitality is a principle — indeed, as far as our judgments extend, the *leading* principle in the operations of Deity, — it is scarcely logical to imagine it confined to the regions of the minute, where we daily trace it, and not extending to those of the august. As we find cycle within cycle without end, — yet all revolving around one far-distant centre which is the God-head, may we not analogically suppose in the same manner, life within life, the less within the greater, and all within the Spirit Divine? In short, we are madly erring, through self-esteem, in believing man, in either his temporal or future destinies, to be of more moment in the universe than that vast "clod of the valley" which he tills and contemns, and to which he denies a soul for no more profound reason than that he does not behold it in operation.*

These fancies, and such as these, have always given to my meditations among the mountains and the forests, by the rivers and the ocean, a tinge of what the everyday world would not fail to term fantastic. My wanderings amid such scenes have been many, and far-searching, and often solitary; and the interest with which I have strayed through many a dim, deep valley, or gazed into the reflected Heaven of many a bright lake, has been an interest greatly deepened by the thought that I have strayed and gazed *alone*. What flippant Frenchman was it who said in allusion to the well-known work of Zimmerman, that, "*la solitude est une belle chose; mais il faut quelqu'un pour vous dire que la solitude est une belle chose?*" The epigram cannot be gainsayed; but the necessity is a thing that does not exist.

It was during one of my lonely journeyings, amid a far distant region of mountain locked within mountain, and sad rivers and melancholy tarns writhing or sleeping within all — that I chanced upon a certain rivulet and island. I came upon them suddenly in the leafy June, and threw myself upon the turf, beneath the branches of an unknown odorous

* Speaking of the tides, Pomponius Mela, in his treatise "*De Situ Orbis*," says "either the world is a great animal, or" etc.

shrub, that I might doze as I contemplated the scene. I felt that thus only should I look upon it — such was the character of phantasm which it wore.

On all sides — save to the west, where the sun was about sinking — arose the verdant walls of the forest. The little river which turned sharply in its course, and was thus immediately lost to sight, seemed to have no exit from its prison, but to be absorbed by the deep green foliage of the trees to the east — while in the opposite quarter (so it appeared to me as I lay at length and glanced upward) there poured down noise-lessly and continuously into the valley, a rich golden and crimson water-fall from the sunset fountains of the sky.

About midway in the short vista which my dreamy vision took in, one small circular island, profusely verdured, reposed upon the bosom of the stream.

> So blended bank and shadow there
> That each seemed pendulous in air —

so mirror-like was the glassy water, that it was scarcely possible to say at what point upon the slope of the emerald turf its crystal dominion began.

My position enabled me to include in a single view both the eastern and western extremities of the islet; and I observed a singularly-marked difference in their aspects. The latter was all one radiant harem of garden beauties. It glowed and blushed beneath the eyes of the slant sunlight, and fairly laughed with flowers. The grass was short, springy, sweet-scented, and Asphodel-interspersed. The trees were lithe, mirthful, erect — bright, slender, and graceful, — of eastern figure and foliage, with bark smooth, glossy, and parti-colored. There seemed a deep sense of life and joy about all; and although no airs blew from out the heavens, yet every thing had motion through the gentle sweepings to and fro of innumer-able butterflies, that might have been mistaken for tulips with wings.*

The other or eastern end of the isle was whelmed in the blackest shade. A sombre, yet beautiful and peaceful gloom here pervaded all things. The trees were dark in color, and mournful in form and attitude, wreathing themselves into sad, solemn, and spectral shapes that conveyed ideas of mortal sorrow and untimely death. The grass wore the deep tint of the cypress, and the heads of its blades hung droopingly, and hither and thither among it were many small unsightly hillocks, low and narrow, and not very long, that had the aspect of graves, but were not; although over and all about them the rue and the rosemary clambered. The shade of the trees fell heavily upon the water, and seemed to bury itself therein, impregnating the depths of the element with darkness. I fancied

* Florem putares nare per liquidum æthera. — *P. Commire.*

that each shadow, as the sun descended lower and lower, separated itself sullenly from the trunk that gave it birth, and thus became absorbed by the stream; while other shadows issued momently from the trees, taking the place of their predecessors thus entombed.

This idea, having once seized upon my fancy, greatly excited it, and I lost myself forthwith in revery. "If ever island were enchanted," said I to myself, "this is it. This is the haunt of the few gentle Fays who remain from the wreck of the race. Are these green tombs theirs? — or do they yield up their sweet lives as mankind yield up their own? In dying, do they not rather waste away mournfully, rendering unto God, little by little, their existence, as these trees render up shadow after shadow, exhausting their substance unto dissolution? What the wasting tree is to the water that imbibes its shade, growing thus blacker by what it preys upon, may not the life of the Fay be to the death which engulfs it?"

As I thus mused, with half-shut eyes, while the sun sank rapidly to rest, and eddying currents careered round and round the island, bearing upon their bosom large, dazzling, white flakes of the bark of the sycamore — flakes which, in their multiform positions upon the water, a quick imagination might have converted into any thing it pleased, — while I thus mused, it appeared to me that the form of one of those very Fays about whom I had been pondering made its way slowly into the darkness from out the light at the western end of the island. She stood erect in a singularly fragile canoe, and urged it with the mere phantom of an oar. While within the influence of the lingering sunbeams, her attitude seemed indicative of joy — but sorrow deformed it as she passed within the shade. Slowly she glided along, and at length rounded the islet and re-entered the region of light. "The revolution which has just been made by the Fay," continued I, musingly, "is the cycle of the brief year of her life. She has floated through her winter and through her summer. She is a year nearer unto Death; for I did not fail to see that, as she came into the shade, her shadow fell from her, and was swallowed up in the dark water, making its blackness more black."

And again the boat appeared and the Fay, but about the attitude of the latter there was more of care and uncertainty and less of elastic joy. She floated again from out the light and into the gloom (which deepened momently) and again her shadow fell from her into the ebony water, and became absorbed into its blackness. And again and again she made the circuit of the island, (while the sun rushed down to his slumbers), and at each issuing into the light there was more sorrow about her person, while it grew feebler and far fainter and more indistinct, and at each passage into the gloom there fell from her a darker shade, which became whelmed in a shadow more black. But at length when the sun had utterly departed, the Fay, now the mere ghost of her former self,

went disconsolately with her boat into the region of the ebony flood, and that she issued thence at all I cannot say, for darkness fell over all things and I beheld her magical figure no more.

The Colloquy of Monos and Una

Μέλλοντα ταυτα

SOPHOCLES — Antig:

These things are in the future.

UNA. "Born again?"

MONOS. Yes, fairest and best beloved Una, "born again." These were the words upon whose mystical meaning I had so long pondered, rejecting the explanations of the priesthood, until Death itself resolved for me the secret.

UNA. Death!

MONOS. How strangely, sweet Una, you echo my words! I observe, too, a vacillation in your step, a joyous inquietude in your eyes. You are confused and oppressed by the majestic novelty of the Life Eternal. Yes, it was of Death I spoke. And here how singularly sounds that word which of old was wont to bring terror to all hearts, throwing a mildew upon all pleasures!

UNA. Ah, Death, the spectre which sate at all feasts! How often, Monos, did we lose ourselves in speculations upon its nature! How mysteriously did it act as a check to human bliss, saying unto it "thus far and no further!" That earnest mutual love, my own Monos, which burned within our bosoms — how vainly did we flatter ourselves, feeling happy in its first upspringing, that our happiness would strengthen with its strength! Alas! as it grew, so grew in our hearts the dread of that evil hour which was hurrying to separate us forever! Thus, in time, it became painful to love. Hate would have been mercy then.

MONOS. Speak not here of these griefs, dear Una — mine, mine, forever now!

UNA. But the memory of past sorrow — is it not present joy? I have much to say yet of the things which have been. Above all, I burn to know the incidents of your own passage through the dark Valley and Shadow.

MONOS. And when did the radiant Una ask any thing of her Monos in vain? I will be minute in relating all — but at what point shall the weird narrative begin?

UNA. At what point?

MONOS. You have said.

UNA. Monos, I comprehend you. In Death we have both learned the propensity of man to define the indefinable. I will not say, then, commence with the moment of life's cessation — but commence with that sad, sad instant when, the fever having abandoned you, you sank into a breathless and motionless torpor, and I pressed down your pallid eyelids with the passionate fingers of love.

MONOS. One word first, my Una, in regard to man's general condition at this epoch. You will remember that one or two of the wise among our forefathers — wise in fact, although not in the world's esteem — had ventured to doubt the propriety of the term "improvement," as applied to the progress of our civilization. There were periods in each of the five or six centuries immediately preceding our dissolution, when arose some vigorous intellect, boldly contending for those principles whose truth appears now, to our disenfranchised reason, so utterly obvious — principles which should have taught our race to submit to the guidance of the natural laws, rather than attempt their control. At long intervals some master-minds appeared, looking upon each advance in practical science as a retro-gradation in the true utility. Occasionally the poetic intellect — that intellect which we now feel to have been the most exalted of all — since those truths which to us were of the most enduring importance could only be reached by that *analogy* which speaks in proof-tones to the imagination alone, and to the unaided reason bears no weight — occasionally did this poetic intellect proceed a step farther in the evolving of the vague idea of the philosophic, and find in the mystic parable that tells of the tree of knowledge, and of its forbidden fruit, death-producing, a distinct intimation that knowledge was not meet for man in the infant condition of his soul. And these men, the poets, living and perishing amid the scorn of the "utilitarians" — or rough pedants, who arrogated to themselves a title which could have been properly applied only to the scorned — these men, the poets, ponder piningly, yet not unwisely, upon the ancient days when our wants were not more simple than our enjoyments were keen — days when *mirth* was a word unknown, so solemnly deeptoned was happiness — holy, august and blissful days, when blue rivers ran undammed, between hills unhewn, into far forest solitudes, primeval, odorous, and unexplored.

Yet these noble exceptions from the general misrule served but to strengthen it by opposition. Alas! we had fallen upon the most evil of all our evil days. The great "movement" — that was the cant term — went on: a diseased commotion, moral and physical. Art — the Arts — arose supreme, and, once enthroned, cast chains upon the intellect which had elevated them to power. Man, because he could not but acknowledge the majesty of Nature, fell into childish exultation at his acquired and still-increasing dominion over her elements. Even while he stalked a God in his own fancy, an infantine imbecility came over him. As might be sup-

posed from the origin of his disorder, he grew infected with system, and with abstraction. He enwrapped himself in generalities. Among other odd ideas, that of universal equality gained ground; and in the face of analogy and of God — in despite of the loud warning voice of the laws of *gradation* so visibly pervading all things in Earth and Heaven — wild attempts at an omni-prevalent Democracy were made. Yet this evil sprang necessarily from the leading evil — Knowledge. Man could not both know and succumb. Meantime huge smoking cities arose, innumerable. Green leaves shrank before the hot breath of furnaces. The fair face of Nature was deformed as with the ravages of some loathsome disease. And me-thinks, sweet Una, even our slumbering sense of the forced and of the farfetched might have arrested us here. But now it appears that we had worked out our own destruction in the perversion of our *taste*, or rather in the blind neglect of its culture in the schools. For, in truth, it was at this crisis that taste alone — that faculty which, holding a middle position between the pure intellect and the moral sense, could never safely have been disregarded — it was now that taste alone could have led us gently back to Beauty, to Nature, and to Life. But alas for the pure contempla-tive spirit and majestic intuition of Plato! Alas for the μουσικη which he justly regarded as an all sufficient education for the soul! Alas for him and for it! — since both were most desperately needed when both were most entirely forgotten or despised.*

Pascal, a philosopher whom we both love, has said, how truly! — "*que tout notre raisonnement se réduit à céder au sentiment;*" and it is not im-possible that the sentiment of the natural, had time permitted it, would have regained its old ascendancy over the harsh mathematical reason of the schools. But this thing was not to be. Prematurely induced by intem-perance of knowledge, the old age of the world drew on. This thé mass of mankind saw not, or, living lustily although unhappily, affected not to see. But, for myself, the Earth's records had taught me to look for widest ruin as the price of highest civilization. I had imbibed a prescience of our Fate from comparison of China the simple and enduring, with

* It will be hard to discover a better [method of education] than that which the experience of so many ages has al-ready discovered; and this may be summed up as consisting in gymnastics for the body and *music* for the soul." — Repub. lib. 2. "For this reason is a musi-cal education most essential; since it causes Rhythm and Harmony to pene-trate most intimately into the soul, taking the strangest hold upon it, filling it with *beauty* and making the man *beautiful-minded* . . . He will praise and admire *the beautiful*; will receive it with joy into his soul, will feed upon it. and *assimilate his own condition with it.*" Ibid. lib. 3. Music μουσικη had, among the Atheni-ans, a far more comprehensive significa-tion than with us. It included not only the harmonies of time and of tune, but the poetic diction, sentiment and creation each in its widest sense. The study of *music* was with them in fact, the general cultivation of the taste — of that which recognizes the beautiful — in contra-dis-tinction from reason, which deals only with the true.

Assyria the architect, with Egypt the astrologer, with Nubia, more crafty than either, the turbulent mother of all Arts. In history * of these regions I met with a ray from the Future. The individual artificialities of the three latter were local diseases of the Earth, and in their individual over-throws we had seen local remedies applied; but for the infected world at large I could anticipate no regeneration save in death. That man, as a race, should not become extinct, I saw that he must be *"born again."*

And now it was, fairest and dearest, that we wrapped our spirits, daily, in dreams. Now it was that, in twilight, we discoursed of the days to come, when the Art-scarred surface of the Earth, having undergone that purification † which alone could efface its rectangular obscenities, should clothe itself anew in the verdure and the mountain-slopes and the smiling waters of Paradise, and be rendered at length a fit dwelling-place for man: — for man the Death-purged — for man to whose now exalted intellect there should be poison in knowledge no more — for the redeemed, regen-erated, blissful, and now immortal, but still for the *material*, man.

UNA. Well do I remember these conversations, dear Monos; but the epoch of the fiery overthrow was not so near at hand as we believed, and as the corruption you indicate did surely warrant us in believing. Men lived; and died individually. You yourself sickened, and passed into the grave; and thither your constant Una speedily followed you. And though the century which has since elapsed, and whose conclusion brings us thus together once more, tortured our slumbering senses with no impatience of duration, yet, my Monos, it was a century still.

MONOS. Say, rather, a point in the vague infinity. Unquestionably, it was in the Earth's dotage that I died. Wearied at heart with anxieties which had their origin in the general turmoil and decay, I succumbed to the fierce fever. After some few days of pain, and many of dreamy delirium replete with ecstasy, the manifestations of which you mistook for pain, while I longed but was impotent to undeceive you — after some days there came upon me, as you have said, a breathless and motionless torpor; and this was termed *Death* by those who stood around me.

Words are vague things. My condition did not deprive me of sentience. It appeared to me not greatly dissimilar to the extreme quiescence of him, who, having slumbered long and profoundly, lying motionless and fully prostrate in a midsummer noon, begins to steal slowly back into con-sciousness, through the mere sufficiency of his sleep, and without being awakened by external disturbances.

I breathed no longer. The pulses were still. The heart had ceased to beat. Volition had not departed, but was powerless. The senses were un-usually active, although eccentrically so — assuming often each other's functions at random. The taste and the smell were inextricably con-

* "History," from ιστορειν, to contemplate.

† The word *"purification"* seems here to be used with reference to its root in the Greek, πυρ, fire.

founded, and became one sentiment, abnormal and intense. The rose-water with which your tenderness had moistened my lips to the last, affected me with sweet fancies of flowers — fantastic flowers, far more lovely than any of the old Earth, but whose prototypes we have here blooming around us. The eyelids, transparent and bloodless, offered no complete impediment to vision. As volition was in abeyance the balls could not roll in their sockets — but all objects within the range of the visual hemisphere were seen with more or less distinctness; the rays which fell upon the external retina, or into the corner of the eye, producing a more vivid effect than those which struck the front or anterior surface. Yet, in the former instance, this effect was so far anomalous that I appreciated it only as *sound* — sound sweet or discordant as the matters presenting themselves at my side were light or dark in shade — curved or angular in outline. The hearing at the same time, although excited in degree, was not irregular in action — estimating real sounds with an extravagance of precision, not less than of sensibility. Touch had undergone a modification more peculiar. Its impressions were tardily received, but pertinaciously retained, and resulted always in the highest physical pleasure. Thus the pressure of your sweet fingers upon my eyelids, at first only recognized through vision, at length, long after their removal, filled my whole being with a sensual delight immeasurable. I say with a sensual delight. *All* my perceptions were purely sensual. The materials furnished the passive brain by the senses were not in the least degree wrought into shape by the deceased understanding. Of pain there was some little; of pleasure there was much; but of moral pain or pleasure none at all. Thus your wild sobs floated into my ears with all their mournful cadences, and were appreciated in their every variation of sad tone; but they were soft musical sounds and no more; they conveyed to the extinct reason no intimation of the sorrows which gave them birth; while the large and constant tears which fell upon my face, telling the bystanders of a heart which broke, thrilled every fibre of my frame with ecstasy alone. And this was in truth the *Death* of which these by-standers spoke reverently, in low whispers — you, sweet Una, gaspingly, with loud cries.

They attired me for the coffin — three or four dark figures which flitted busily to and fro. As these crossed the direct line of my vision they affected me as *forms*; but upon passing to my side their images impressed me with the idea of shrieks, groans, and other dismal expressions of terror, of horror, or of wo. You alone, habited in a white robe, passed in all directions musically about me.

The day waned; and, as its light faded away, I became possessed by a vague uneasiness — an anxiety such as the sleeper feels when sad real sounds fall continuously within his ear — low distant bell tones, solemn, at long but equal intervals, and commingling with melancholy dreams. Night arrived; and with its shadows a heavy discomfort. It oppressed my limbs with the oppression of some dull weight, and was palpable. There

was also a moaning sound, not unlike the distant reverberation of surf, but more continuous, which beginning with the first twilight, had grown in strength with the darkness. Suddenly lights were brought into the room, and this reverberation became forthwith interrupted into frequent unequal bursts of the same sound, but less dreary and less distinct. The ponderous oppression was in a great measure relieved; and, issuing from the flame of each lamp, (for there were many,) there flowed unbrokenly into my ears a strain of melodious monotone. And when now, dear Una, approaching the bed upon which I lay outstretched, you sat gently by my side, breathing odor from your sweet lips, and pressing them upon my brow, there arose tremulously within my bosom, and mingling with the merely physical sensations which circumstances had called forth, a some- thing akin to sentiment itself — a feeling that, half appreciating, half responded to your earnest love and sorrow; but this feeling took no root in the pulseless heart, and seemed indeed rather a shadow than a reality, and faded quickly away, first into extreme quiescence, and then into a purely sensual pleasure as before.

And now, from the wreck and the chaos of the usual senses, there ap- peared to have arisen within me a sixth, all perfect. In its exercise I found a wild delight — yet a delight still physical, inasmuch as the understand- ing had in it no part. Motion in the animal frame had fully ceased. No muscle quivered; no nerve thrilled; no artery throbbed. But there seemed to have sprung up in the brain, *that* of which no words could convey to the merely human intelligence even an indistinct conception. Let me term it a mental pendulous pulsation. It was the moral embodiment of man's abstract idea of *Time*. By the absolute equalization of this move- ment — or of such as this — had the cycles of the firmamental orbs them- selves, been adjusted. By its aid I measured the irregularities of the clock upon the mantel, and of the watches of the attendants. Their tickings came sonorously to my ears. The slightest deviation from the true pro- portion — and these deviations were omni-prevalent — affected me just as violations of abstract truth were wont, on earth, to affect the moral sense. Although no two of the time-pieces in the chamber struck individual seconds accurately together, yet I had no difficulty in holding steadily in mind the tones, and the respective momentary errors of each. And this — this keen, perfect, self-existing sentiment of *duration* — this senti- ment existing (as man could not possibly have conceived it to exist) in- dependently of any succession of events — this idea — this sixth sense, upspringing from the ashes of the rest, was the first obvious and certain step of the intemporal soul upon the threshold of the temporal Eternity.

It was midnight; and you still sat by my side. All others had departed from the chamber of Death. They had deposited me in the coffin. The lamps burned flickeringly; for this I knew by the tremulousness of the monotonous strains. But, suddenly these strains diminished in distinct- ness and in volume. Finally they ceased. The perfume in my nostrils died

away. Forms affected my vision no longer. The oppression of the Dark-
ness uplifted itself from my bosom. A dull shock like that of electricity
pervaded my frame, and was followed by total loss of the idea of contact.
All of what man has termed sense was merged in the sole consciousness
of entity, and in the one abiding sentiment of duration. The mortal body
had been at length stricken with the hand of the deadly *Decay*.

Yet had not all of sentience departed; for the consciousness and the
sentiment remaining supplied some of its functions by a lethargic intui-
tion. I appreciated the direful change now in operation upon the flesh,
and, as the dreamer is sometimes aware of the bodily presence of one who
leans over him, so, sweet Una, I still dully felt that you sat by my side.
So, too, when the noon of the second day came, I was not unconscious
of those movements which displaced you from my side, which confined
me within the coffin, which deposited me within the hearse, which bore
me to the grave, which lowered me within it, which heaped heavily the
mould upon me, and which thus left me, in blackness and corruption,
to my sad and solemn slumbers with the worm.

And here, in the prison-house which has few secrets to disclose, they
rolled away days and weeks and months; and the soul watched narrowly
each second as it flew, and, without effort, took record of its flight —
without effort and without object.

A year passed. The consciousness of *being* had grown hourly more in-
distinct, and that of mere *locality* had, in great measure, usurped its posi-
tion. The idea of entity was becoming merged in that of *place*. The nar-
row space immediately surrounding what had been the body, was now
growing to be the body itself. At length, as often happens to the sleeper
(by sleep and its world alone is *Death* imaged) — at length, as sometimes
happened on Earth to the deep slumberer, when some flitting light half
startled him into awaking, yet left him half enveloped in dreams — so to
me, in the strict embrace of the *Shadow*, came *that* light which alone
might have had power to startle — the light of enduring *Love*. Men toiled
at the grave in which I lay darkling. They upthrew the damp earth. Upon
my mouldering bones there descended the coffin of Una.

And now again all was void. That nebulous light had been extin-
guished. That feeble thrill had vibrated itself into quiescence. Many
lustra had supervened. Dust had returned to dust. The worm had food
no more. The sense of being at length utterly departed, and there reigned
in its stead — instead of all things — dominant and perpetual — the auto-
crats *Place* and *Time*. For *that* which *was* not — for that which had no
form — for that which had no thought — for that which had no sentience
— for that which was soulless, yet of which matter formed no portion —
for all this nothingness, yet for all this immortality, the grave was still
a home, and the corrosive hours, co-mates.

Never Bet the Devil Your Head

A TALE WITH A MORAL

Con *tal que las costumbres de un autor*," says Don Thomas de las Torres, in the preface to his "Amatory Poems" "*sean puras y castas, importo muy poco que no sean igualmente severas sus obras*" — meaning, in plain English, that, provided the morals of an author are pure personally, it signifies nothing what are the morals of his books. We presume that Don Thomas is now in Purgatory for the assertion. It would be a clever thing, too, in the way of poetical justice, to keep him there until his "Amatory Poems" get out of print, or are laid definitely upon the shelf through lack of readers. Every fiction *should have* a moral; and, what is more to the purpose, the critics have discovered that every fiction *has*. Philip Melanchthon, some time ago, wrote a commentary upon the "Batrachomyomachia," and proved that the poet's object was to excite a distaste for sedition. Pierre la Seine, going a step farther, shows that the intention was to recommend to young men temperance in eating and drinking. Just so, too, Jacobus Hugo has satisfied himself that, by Euenis, Homer meant to insinuate John Calvin; by Antinous, Martin Luther; by the Lotophagi, Protestants in general; and, by the Harpies, the Dutch. Our more modern Scholiasts are equally acute. These fellows demonstrate a hidden meaning in "The Antediluvians," a parable in "Powhatan," new views in "Cock Robin," and transcendentalism in "Hop O' My Thumb." In short, it has been shown that no man can sit down to write without a very profound design. Thus to authors in general much trouble is spared. A novelist, for example, need have no care of his moral. It is there — that is to say, it is somewhere — and the moral and the critics can take care of themselves. When the proper time arrives, all that the gentleman intended, and all that he did not intend, will be brought to light, in the "Dial," or the "Down-Easter," together with all that he ought to have intended, and the rest that he clearly meant to intend: — so that it will all come very straight in the end.

There is no just ground, therefore, for the charge brought against me by certain ignoramuses — that I have never written a moral tale, or, in more precise words, a tale with a moral. They are not the critics predestined to bring me out, and *develop* my morals: — that is the secret. By and by the "North American Quarterly Humdrum" will make them ashamed of their stupidity. In the meantime, by way of staying execution — by way of mitigating the accusations against me — I offer the sad history appended, — a history about whose obvious moral there can be no question whatever, since he who runs may read it in the large capitals which form the title of the tale. I should have credit for this

arrangement — a far wiser one than that of La Fontaine and others, who reserve the impression to be conveyed until the last moment, and thus sneak it in at the fag end of their fables.

Defuncti injuriâ ne afficiantur was a law of the twelve tables, and *De mortuis nil nisi bonum* is an excellent injunction — even if the dead in question be nothing but dead small beer. It is not my design, therefore, to vituperate my deceased friend, Toby Dammit. He was a sad dog, it is true, and a dog's death it was that he died; but he himself was not to blame for his vices. They grew out of a personal defect in his mother. She did her best in the way of flogging him while an infant — for duties to her well-regulated mind were always pleasures, and babies, like tough steaks, or the modern Greek olive trees, are invariably the better for beating — but, poor woman! she had the misfortune to be left-handed, and a child flogged left-handedly had better be left un-flogged. The world revolves from right to left. It will not do to whip a baby from left to right. If each blow in the proper direction drives an evil propensity out, it follows that every thump in an opposite one knocks its quota of wickedness in. I was often present at Toby's chastisements, and, even by the way in which he kicked, I could perceive that he was getting worse and worse every day. At last I saw, through the tears in my eyes, that there was no hope of the villain at all, and one day when he had been cuffed until he grew so black in the face that one might have mistaken him for a little African, and no effect had been produced beyond that of making him wriggle himself into a fit, I could stand it no longer, but went down upon my knees forthwith, and, uplifting my voice, made prophecy of his ruin.

The fact is that his precocity in vice was awful. At five months of age he used to get into such passions that he was unable to articulate. At six months, I caught him gnawing a pack of cards. At seven months he was in the constant habit of catching and kissing the female babies. At eight months he peremptorily refused to put his signature to the Temperance pledge. Thus he went on increasing in iniquity, month after month, until, at the close of the first year, he not only insisted upon wearing *moustaches*, but had contracted a propensity for cursing and swearing, and for backing his assertions by bets.

Through this latter most ungentlemanly practice, the ruin which I had predicted to Toby Dammit overtook him at last. The fashion had "grown with his growth and strengthened with his strength," so that, when he came to be a man, he could scarcely utter a sentence without interlarding it with a proposition to gamble. Not that he actually *laid* wagers — no. I will do my friend the justice to say that he would as soon have laid eggs. With him the thing was a mere formula — nothing more. His expressions on this head had no meaning attached to them whatever. They were simple if not altogether innocent expletives — imaginative phrases wherewith to round off a sentence. When he said

"I'll bet you so and so," nobody ever thought of taking him up; but still I could not help thinking it my duty to put him down. The habit was an immoral one, and so I told him. It was a vulgar one — this I begged him to believe. It was discountenanced by society — here I said nothing but the truth. It was forbidden by act of Congress — here I had not the slightest intention of telling a lie. I remonstrated — but to no purpose. I demonstrated — in vain. I entreated — he smiled. I implored — he laughed. I preached — he sneered. I threatened — he swore. I kicked him — he called for the police. I pulled his nose — he blew it, and offered to bet the Devil his head that I would not venture to try that experiment again.

Poverty was another vice which the peculiar physical deficiency of Dammit's mother had entailed upon her son. He was detestably poor; and this was the reason, no doubt, that his expletive expressions about betting, seldom took a pecuniary turn. I will not be bound to say that I ever heard him make use of such a figure of speech as "I'll bet you a dollar." It was usually "I'll bet you what you please," or "I'll bet you what you dare," or "I'll bet you a trifle," or else, more significantly still, *"I'll bet the Devil my head."*

This latter form seemed to please him best; — perhaps because it involved the least risk; for Dammit had become excessively parsimonious. Had any one taken him up, his head was small, and thus his loss would have been small too. But these are my own reflections, and I am by no means sure that I am right in attributing them to him. At all events the phrase in question grew daily in favor, notwithstanding the gross impropriety of a man betting his brains like bank-notes: — but this was a point which my friend's perversity of disposition would not permit him to comprehend. In the end, he abandoned all other forms of wager, and gave himself up to *"I'll bet the Devil my head,"* with a pertinacity and exclusiveness of devotion that displeased not less than it surprised me. I am always displeased by circumstances for which I cannot account. Mysteries force a man to think, and so injure his health. The truth is, there was something in *the air* with which Mr. Dammit was wont to give utterance to his offensive expression — something in his *manner* of enunciation — which at first interested, and afterwards made me very uneasy — something which, for want of a more definite term at present, I must be permitted to call *queer*; but which Mr. Coleridge would have called mystical, Mr. Kant pantheistical, Mr. Carlyle twistical, and Mr. Emerson hyperquizzitistical. I began not to like it at all. Mr. Dammit's soul was in a perilous state. I resolved to bring all my eloquence into play to save it. I vowed to serve him as St. Patrick, in the Irish chronicle, is said to have served the toad, — that is to say, "awaken him to a sense of his situation." I addressed myself to the task forthwith. Once more I betook myself to remonstrance. Again I collected my energies for a final attempt at expostulation.

When I had made an end of my lecture, Mr. Dammit indulged him-
self in some very equivocal behavior. For some moments he remained
silent, merely looking me inquisitively in the face. But presently he
threw his head to one side, and elevated his eyebrows to a great extent.
Then he spread out the palms of his hands and shrugged up his shoulders.
Then he winked with the right eye. Then he repeated the operation with
the left. Then he shut them both up very tight. Then he opened them
both so very wide that I became seriously alarmed for the consequences.
Then, applying his thumb to his nose, he thought proper to make an
indescribable movement with the rest of his fingers. Finally, setting his
arms a-kimbo, he condescended to reply.

I can call to mind only the heads of his discourse. He would be
obliged to me if I would hold my tongue. He wished none of my advice.
He despised all my insinuations. He was old enough to take care of
himself. Did I still think him baby Dammit? Did I mean to say any
thing against his character? Did I intend to insult him? Was I a fool?
Was my maternal parent aware, in a word, of my absence from the
domiciliary residence? He would put this latter question to me as to a
man of veracity, and he would bind himself to abide by my reply. Once
more he would demand explicitly if my mother knew that I was out.
My confusion, he said, betrayed me, and he would be willing to bet the
Devil his head that she did not.

Mr. Dammit did not pause for my rejoinder. Turning upon his heel,
he left my presence with undignified precipitation. It was well for him
that he did so. My feelings had been wounded. Even my anger had been
aroused. For once I would have taken him up upon his insulting wager.
I would have won for the Arch-Enemy Mr. Dammit's little head — for
the fact is, my mamma *was* very well aware of my merely temporary
absence from home.

But *Khoda shefa midêhed* — Heaven gives relief — as the Mussul-
mans say when you tread upon their toes. It was in pursuance of my
duty that I had been insulted, and I bore the insult like a man. It now
seemed to me, however, that I had done all that could be required of me,
in the case of this miserable individual, and I resolved to trouble him
no longer with my counsel, but to leave him to his conscience and him-
self. But although I forebore to intrude with my advice, I could not
bring myself to give up his society altogether. I even went so far as to
humor some of his less reprehensible propensities; and there were times
when I found myself lauding his wicked jokes, as epicures do mustard,
with tears in my eyes: — so profoundly did it grieve me to hear his
evil talk.

One fine day, having strolled out together, arm in arm, our route led
us in the direction of a river. There was a bridge, and we resolved to
cross it. It was roofed over, by way of protection from the weather, and
the archway, having but few windows, was thus very uncomfortably dark.

As we entered the passage, the contrast between the external glare and the interior gloom struck heavily upon my spirits. Not so upon those of the unhappy Dammit, who offered to bet the Devil his head that I was hipped. He seemed to be in an unusual good humor. He was excessively lively — so much so that I entertained I know not what of uneasy suspicion. It is not impossible that he was affected with the transcendentals. I am not well enough versed, however, in the diagnosis of this disease to speak with decision upon the point; and unhappily there were none of my friends of the "Dial" present. I suggest the idea, nevertheless, because of a certain species of austere Merry-Andrewism which seemed to beset my poor friend, and caused him to make quite a Tom-Fool of himself. Nothing would serve him but wriggling and skipping about under and over every thing that came in his way; now shouting out, and now lisping out, all manner of odd little and big words, yet preserving the gravest face in the world all the time. I really could not make up my mind whether to kick or to pity him. At length, having passed nearly across the bridge, we approached the termination of the footway, when our progress was impeded by a turnstile of some height. Through this I made my way quietly, pushing it around as usual. But this turn would not serve the turn of Mr. Dammit. He insisted upon leaping the stile, and said he could cut a pigeon-wing over it in the air. Now this, conscientiously speaking, I did not think he could do. The best pigeon-winger over all kinds of style was my friend Mr. Carlyle, and as I knew *he* could not do it, I would not believe that it could be done by Toby Dammit. I therefore told him, in so many words, that he was a braggadocio, and could not do what he said. For this I had reason to be sorry afterward; — for he straightway offered to *bet the Devil his head* that he could.

I was about to reply, notwithstanding my previous resolutions, with some remonstrance against his impiety, when I heard, close at my elbow, a slight cough, which sounded very much like the ejaculation *"ahem!"* I started, and looked about me in surprise. My glance at length fell into a nook of the frame-work of the bridge, and upon the figure of a little lame old gentleman of venerable aspect. Nothing could be more reverend than his whole appearance; for he not only had on a full suit of black, but his shirt was perfectly clean and the collar turned very neatly down over a white cravat, while his hair was parted in front like a girl's. His hands were clasped pensively together over his stomach, and his two eyes were carefully rolled up into the top of his head.

Upon observing him more closely, I perceived that he wore a black silk apron over his small-clothes; and this was a thing which I thought very odd. Before I had time to make any remark, however, upon so singular a circumstance, he interrupted me with a second *"ahem!"*

To this observation I was not immediately prepared to reply. The fact is, remarks of this laconic nature are nearly unanswerable. I have

known a Quarterly Review *non-plussed* by the word *"Fudge!"* I am not ashamed to say, therefore, that I turned to Mr. Dammit for assistance.

"Dammit," said I, "what are you about? don't you hear? — the gentleman says '*ahem!*' " I looked sternly at my friend while I thus addressed him; for, to say the truth, I felt particularly puzzled, and when a man is particularly puzzled he must knit his brows and look savage, or else he is pretty sure to look like a fool.

"Dammit," observed I — although this sounded very much like an oath, than which nothing was further from my thoughts — "Dammit," I suggested — "the gentleman says '*ahem!*' "

I do not attempt to defend my remark on the score of profundity; I did not think it profound myself; but I have noticed that the effect of our speeches is not always proportionate with their importance in our own eyes; and if I had shot Mr. D. through and through with a Paixhan bomb, or knocked him in the head with the "Poets and Poetry of America," he could hardly have been more discomfited than when I addressed him with those simple words: "Dammit, what are you about? — don't you hear? — the gentleman says '*ahem!*' "

"You don't say so?" gasped he at length, after turning more colors than a pirate runs up, one after the other, when chased by a man-of-war. "Are you quite sure he said *that?* Well, at all events I am in for it now, and may as well put a bold face upon the matter. Here goes, then — *ahem!*"

At this the little old gentleman seemed pleased — God only knows why. He left his station at the nook of the bridge, limped forward with a gracious air, took Dammit by the hand and shook it cordially, looking all the while straight up in his face with an air of the most unadulterated benignity which it is possible for the mind of man to imagine.

"I am quite sure you will win it, Dammit," said he, with the frankest of all smiles, "but we are obliged to have a trial, you know, for the sake of mere form."

"Ahem!" replied my friend, taking off his coat, with a deep sigh, tying a pocket-handkerchief around his waist, and producing an unaccountable alteration in his countenance by twisting up his eyes and bringing down the corners of his mouth — "ahem!" And "ahem!" said he again, after a pause; and not another word more than "ahem!" did I ever know him to say after that. "Aha!" thought I, without expressing myself aloud — "this is quite a remarkable silence on the part of Toby Dammit, and is no doubt a consequence of his verbosity upon a previous occasion. One extreme induces another. I wonder if he has forgotten the many unanswerable questions which he propounded to me so fluently on the day when I gave him my last lecture? At all events, he is cured of the transcendentals."

"Ahem!" here replied Toby, just as if he had been reading my thoughts, and looking like a very old sheep in a revery.

The old gentleman now took him by the arm, and led him more into the shade of the bridge — a few paces back from the turnstile. "My good fellow," said he, "I make it a point of conscience to allow you this much run. Wait here, till I take my place by the stile, so that I may see whether you go over it handsomely, and transcendentally, and don't omit any flourishes of the pigeon-wing. A mere form, you know. I will say 'one, two, three, and away.' Mind you, start at the word 'away.'" Here he took his position by the stile, paused a moment as if in profound reflection, then *looked up* and, I thought, smiled very slightly, then tightened the strings of his apron, then took a long look at Dammit, and finally gave the word as agreed upon —

One — two — three — and — away!

Punctually at the word "away," my poor friend set off in a strong gallop. The stile was not very high, like Mr. Lord's — nor yet very low, like that of Mr. Lord's reviewers, but upon the whole I made sure that he would clear it. And then what if he did not? — ah, that was the question — what if he did not? "What right," said I, "had the old gentleman to make any other gentleman jump? The little old dot-and-carry-one! who is *he?* If he asks *me* to jump, I won't do it, that's flat, and I don't care who *the devil he is.*" The bridge, as I say, was arched and covered in, in a very ridiculous manner, and there was a most uncomfortable echo about it at all times — an echo which I never before so particularly observed as when I uttered the four last words of my remark.

But what I said, or what I thought, or what I heard, occupied only an instant. In less than five seconds from his starting, my poor Toby had taken the leap. I saw him run nimbly, and spring grandly from the floor of the bridge, cutting the most awful flourishes with his legs as he went up. I saw him high in the air, pigeon-winging it to admiration just over the top of the stile; and of course I thought it an unusually singular thing that he did not *continue* to go over. But the whole leap was the affair of a moment, and, before I had a chance to make any profound reflections, down came Mr. Dammit on the flat of his back, on the same side of the stile from which he had started. At the same instant I saw the old gentleman limping off at the top of his speed, having caught and wrapt up in his apron something that fell heavily into it from the darkness of the arch just over the turnstile. At all this I was much astonished; but I had no leisure to think, for Dammit lay particularly still, and I concluded that his feelings had been hurt, and that he stood in need of my assistance. I hurried up to him and found that he had received what might be termed a serious injury. The truth is, he had been deprived of his head, which after a close search I could not find anywhere; so I determined to take him home and send for the homœopathists. In the meantime a thought struck me, and I threw open an adjacent win-

dow of the bridge, when the sad truth flashed upon me at once. About
five feet just above the top of the turnstile, and crossing the arch of
the foot-path so as to constitute a brace, there extended a flat iron bar,
lying with its breadth horizontally, and forming one of a series that
served to strengthen the structure throughout its extent. With the edge
of this brace it appeared evident that the neck of my unfortunate friend
had come precisely in contact.

He did not long survive his terrible loss. The homœopathists did not
give him little enough physic, and what little they did give him he hesi-
tated to take. So in the end he grew worse, and at length died, a lesson
to all riotous livers. I bedewed his grave with my tears, worked a *bar*
sinister on his family escutcheon, and, for the general expenses of his
funeral, sent in my very moderate bill to the transcendentalists. The
scoundrels refused to pay it, so I had Mr. Dammit dug up at once, and
sold him for dog's meat.

Eleonora

Sub conservatione formæ specificæ salva anima.

RAYMOND LULLY.

I AM come of a race noted for vigor of fancy and ardor of passion. Men
have called me mad; but the question is not yet settled, whether madness
is or is not the loftiest intelligence — whether much that is glorious —
whether all that is profound — does not spring from disease of thought
— from *moods* of mind exalted at the expense of the general intellect.
They who dream by day are cognizant of many things which escape
those who dream only by night. In their gray visions they obtain glimpses
of eternity, and thrill, in awakening, to find that they have been upon the
verge of the great secret. In snatches, they learn something of the wis-
dom which is of good, and more of the mere knowledge which is of evil.
They penetrate, however, rudderless or compassless into the vast ocean
of the "light ineffable," and again, like the adventures of the Nubian
geographer, "*agressi sunt mare tenebrarum, quid in eo esset exploraturi.*"

We will say, then, that I am mad. I grant, at least, that there are two
distinct conditions of my mental existence — the condition of a lucid
reason, not to be disputed, and belonging to the memory of events form-
ing the first epoch of my life — and a condition of shadow and doubt,
appertaining to the present, and to the recollection of what constitutes
the second great era of my being. Therefore, what I shall tell of the
earlier period, believe; and to what I may relate of the later time, give

only such credit as may seem due; or doubt it altogether; or, if doubt it ye cannot, then play unto its riddle the Œdipus.

She whom I loved in youth, and of whom I now pen calmly and distinctly these remembrances, was the sole daughter of the only sister of my mother long departed. Eleonora was the name of my cousin. We had always dwelled together, beneath a tropical sun, in the Valley of the Many-Colored Grass. No unguided footstep ever came upon that vale; for it lay away up among a range of giant hills that hung beetling around about it, shutting out the sunlight from its sweetest recesses. No path was trodden in its vicinity; and, to reach our happy home, there was need of putting back, with force, the foliage of many thousands of forest trees, and of crushing to death the glories of many millions of fragrant flowers. Thus it was that we lived all alone, knowing nothing of the world without the valley — I, and my cousin, and her mother.

From the dim regions beyond the mountains at the upper end of our encircled domain, there crept out a narrow and deep river, brighter than all save the eyes of Eleonora; and, winding stealthily about in mazy courses, it passed away, at length, through a shadowy gorge, among hills still dimmer than those whence it had issued. We called it the "River of Silence"; for there seemed to be a hushing influence in its flow. No murmur arose from its bed, and so gently it wandered along, that the pearly pebbles upon which we loved to gaze, far down within its bosom, stirred not at all, but lay in a motionless content, each in its own old station, shining on gloriously forever.

The margin of the river, and of the many dazzling rivulets that glided through devious ways into its channel, as well as the spaces that extended from the margins away down into the depths of the streams until they reached the bed of pebbles at the bottom, — these spots, not less than the whole surface of the valley, from the river to the mountains that girdled it in, were carpeted all by a soft green grass, thick, short, perfectly even, and vanilla-perfumed, but so besprinkled throughout with the yellow buttercup, the white daisy, the purple violet, and the ruby-red asphodel, that its exceeding beauty spoke to our hearts in loud tones, of the love and of the glory of God.

And, here and there, in groves about this grass, like wildernesses of dreams, sprang up fantastic trees, whose tall slender stems stood not upright, but slanted gracefully toward the light that peered at noon-day into the centre of the valley. Their mark was speckled with the vivid alternate splendor of ebony and silver, and was smoother than all save the cheeks of Eleonora; so that, but for the brilliant green of the huge leaves that spread from their summits in long, tremulous lines, dallying with the Zephyrs, one might have fancied them giant serpents of Syria doing homage to their sovereign the Sun.

Hand in hand about this valley, for fifteen years, roamed I with Eleonora before Love entered within our hearts. It was one evening at

the close of the third lustrum of her life, and of the fourth of my own, that we sat, locked in each other's embrace, beneath the serpent-like trees, and looked down within the water of the River of Silence at our images therein. We spoke no words during the rest of that sweet day; and our words even upon the morrow were tremulous and few. We had drawn the God Eros from that wave, and now we felt that he had enkindled within us the fiery souls of our forefathers. The passions which had for centuries distinguished our race, came thronging with the fancies for which they had been equally noted, and together breathed a delirious bliss over the Valley of the Many-Colored Grass. A change fell upon all things. Strange, brilliant flowers, star-shaped, burst out upon the trees where no flowers had been known before. The tints of the green carpet deepened; and when, one by one, the white daisies shrank away, there sprang up in place of them, ten by ten of the ruby-red asphodel. And life arose in our paths; for the tall flamingo, hitherto unseen, with all gay glowing birds, flaunted his scarlet plumage before us. The golden and silver fish haunted the river, out of the bosom of which issued, little by little, a murmur that swelled, at length, into a lulling melody more divine than that of the harp of Æolus — sweeter than all save the voice of Eleonora. And now, too, a voluminous cloud, which we had long watched in the regions of Hesper, floated out thence, all gorgeous in crimson and gold, and settling in peace above us, sank, day by day, lower and lower, until its edges rested upon the tops of the mountains, turning all their dimness into magnificence, and shutting us up, as if forever, within a magic prison-house of grandeur and of glory.

The loveliness of Eleonora was that of the Seraphim; but she was a maiden artless and innocent as the brief life she had led among the flowers. No guile disguised the fervor of love which animated her heart, and she examined with me its inmost recesses as we walked together in the Valley of the Many-Colored Grass, and discoursed of the mighty changes which had lately taken place therein.

At length, having spoken one day, in tears, of the last sad change which must befall Humanity, she thenceforward dwelt only upon this one sorrowful theme, interweaving it into all our converse, as, in the songs of the bard of Schiraz, the same images are found occurring, again and again, in every impressive variation of phrase.

She had seen that the finger of Death was upon her bosom — that, like the ephemeron, she had been made perfect in loveliness only to die; but the terrors of the grave to her lay solely in a consideration which she revealed to me, one evening at twilight, by the banks of the River of Silence. She grieved to think that, having entombed her in the Valley of the Many-Colored Grass, I would quit forever its happy recesses, transferring the love which now was so passionately her own to some maiden of the outer and everyday world. And, then and there, I threw myself hurriedly at the feet of Eleonora, and offered up a vow, to herself and

to Heaven, that I would never bind myself in marriage to any daughter of Earth — that I would in no manner prove recreant to her dear memory, or to the memory of the devout affection with which she had blessed me. And I called the Mighty Ruler of the Universe to witness the pious solemnity of my vow. And the curse which I invoked of *Him* and of her, a saint in Helusion should I prove traitorous to that promise, involved a penalty the exceeding great horror of which will not permit me to make record of it here. And the bright eyes of Eleonora grew brighter at my words; and she sighed as if a deadly burthen had been taken from her breast; and she trembled and very bitterly wept; but she made acceptance of the vow, (for what was she but a child?) and it made easy to her the bed of her death. And she said to me, not many days afterward, tranquilly dying, that, because of what I had done for the comfort of her spirit she would watch over me in that spirit when departed, and, if so it were permitted her return to me visibly in the watches of the night; but, if this thing were, indeed, beyond the power of the souls in Paradise, that she would, at least, give me frequent indications of her presence; sighing upon me in the evening winds, or filling the air which I breathed with perfume from the censers of the angels. And, with these words upon her lips, she yielded up her innocent life, putting an end to the first epoch of my own.

Thus far I have faithfully said. But as I pass the barrier in Time's path, formed by the death of my beloved, and proceed with the second era of my existence, I feel that a shadow gathers over my brain, and I mistrust the perfect sanity of the record. But let me on. — Years dragged themselves along heavily, and still I dwelled within the Valley of the Many-Colored Grass; but a second change had come upon all things. The star-shaped flowers shrank into the stems of the trees, and appeared no more. The tints of the green carpet faded; and, one by one, the ruby-red asphodels withered away; and there sprang up, in place of them, ten by ten, dark, eye-like violets, that writhed uneasily and were ever encumbered with dew. And Life departed from our paths; for the tall flamingo flaunted no longer his scarlet plumage before us, but flew sadly from the vale into the hills, with all the gay glowing birds that had arrived in his company. And the golden and silver fish swam down through the gorge at the lower end of our domain and bedecked the sweet river never again. And the lulling melody that had been softer than the wind-harp of Æolus, and more divine than all save the voice of Eleonora, it died little by little away, in murmurs growing lower and lower, until the stream returned, at length, utterly, into the solemnity of its original silence. And then, lastly, the voluminous cloud uprose, and, abandoning the tops of the mountains to the dimness of old, fell back into the regions of Hesper, and took away all its manifold golden and gorgeous glories from the Valley of the Many-Colored Grass.

Yet the promises of Eleonora were not forgotten; for I heard the

sounds of the swinging of the censers of the angels; and streams of a holy perfume floated ever and ever about the valley; and at lone hours, when my heart beat heavily, the winds that bathed my brow came unto me laden with soft sighs; and indistinct murmurs filled often the night air; and once — oh, but once only! I was awakened from a slumber, like the slumber of death, by the pressing of spiritual lips upon my own.

But the void within my heart refused, even thus, to be filled. I longed for the love which had before filled it to overflowing. At length the valley *pained* me through its memories of Eleonora, and I left it for ever for the vanities and the turbulent triumphs of the world.

I found myself within a strange city, where all things might have served to blot from recollection the sweet dreams I had dreamed so long in the Valley of the Many-Colored Grass. The pomps and pageantries of a stately court, and the mad clangor of arms, and the radiant loveliness of women, bewildered and intoxicated my brain. But as yet my soul had proved true to its vows, and the indications of the presence of Eleonora were still given me in the silent hours of the night. Suddenly these manifestations they ceased, and the world grew dark before mine eyes, and I stood aghast at the burning thoughts which possessed, at the terrible temptations which beset me; for there came from some far, far distant and unknown land, into the gay court of the king I served, a maiden to whose beauty my whole recreant heart yielded at once — at whose footstool I bowed down without a struggle, in the most ardent, in the most abject worship of love. What, indeed, was my passion for the young girl of the valley in comparison with the fervor, and the delirium, and the spirit-lifting ecstasy of adoration with which I poured out my whole soul in tears at the feet of the ethereal Ermengarde? — Oh, bright was the seraph Ermengarde! and in that knowledge I had room for none other. — Oh, divine was the angel Ermengarde! and as I looked down into the depths of her memorial eyes, I thought only of them — and *of her.*

I wedded; — nor dreaded the curse I had invoked; and its bitterness was not visited upon me. And once — but once again in the silence of the night; there came through my lattice the soft sighs which had forsaken me; and they modelled themselves into familiar and sweet voice, saying:

"Sleep in peace! — for the Spirit of Love reigneth and ruleth, and, in taking to thy passionate heart her who is Ermengarde, thou art absolved, for reasons which shall be made known to thee in Heaven, of thy vows unto Eleonora."

Three Sundays in a Week

Yᴏᴜ hard-headed, dunder-headed, obstinate, rusty, crusty, musty, fusty, old savage!" said I, in fancy, one afternoon, to my grand uncle Rumgudgeon — shaking my fist at him in imagination.

Only in imagination. The fact is, some trivial discrepancy *did* exist, just then, between what I said and what I had not the courage to say — between what I did and what I had half a mind to do.

The old porpoise, as I opened the drawing-room door, was sitting with his feet upon the mantel-piece, and a bumper of port in his paw, making strenuous efforts to accomplish the ditty.

> *Remplis ton verre vide!*
> *Vide ton verre plein!*

"My *dear* uncle," said I, closing the door gently, and approaching him with the blandest of smiles, "you are always so *very* kind and considerate, and have evinced your benevolence in so many — so *very* many ways — that — that I feel I have only to suggest this little point to you once more to make sure of your full acquiescence."

"Hem!" said he, "good boy! go on!"

"I am sure, my dearest uncle [you confounded old rascal!], that you have no design really, seriously, to oppose my union with Kate. This is merely a joke of yours, I know — ha! ha! ha! — how *very* pleasant you are at times."

"Ha! ha! ha!" said he, "curse you! yes!"

"To be sure — of course! I *knew* you were jesting. Now, uncle, all that Kate and myself wish at present, is that you would oblige us with your advice as — as regards the *time* — *you* know, uncle — in short, when will it be most convenient for yourself, that the wedding shall — shall — come off, you know?"

"Come off, you scoundrel! — what do you mean by that? — Better wait till it goes on."

"Ha! ha! ha! — he! he! he! — hi! hi! hi! — ho! ho! ho! — hu! hu! hu! — oh, that's good! — oh that's capital — *such* a wit! But all we want just *now*, you know, uncle, is that you would indicate the time precisely."

"Ah! — precisely?"

"Yes, uncle — that is, if it would be quite agreeable to yourself."

"Wouldn't it answer, Bobby, if I were to leave it at random — some time within a year or so, for example? — *must* I say precisely?"

"*If* you please, uncle — precisely."

"Well, then, Bobby, my boy — you're a fine fellow, aren't you? — since you *will* have the exact time I'll — why I'll oblige you for once."

"Dear uncle!"

"Hush, sir!" [drowning my voice] — I'll oblige you for once. You shall have my consent — and the *plum*, we mus'n't forget the plum — let me see! when shall it be? To-day's Sunday — isn't it? Well, then, you shall be married precisely — *precisely*, now mind! — *when three Sundays come together in a week!* Do you hear me, sir! *What* are you gaping at? I say, you shall have Kate and her plum when three Sundays come together in a week — but not *till* then — you young scapegrace — not *till* then, if I die for it. You know me — *I'm a man of my word* — now be off!" Here he swallowed his bumper of port, while I rushed from the room in despair.

A very "fine old English gentleman," was my grand-uncle Rumgudgeon, but unlike him of the song, he had his weak points. He was a little, pursy, pompous, passionate semicircular somebody, with a red nose, a thick scull, [sic] a long purse, and a strong sense of his own consequence. With the best heart in the world, he contrived, through a predominant whim of *contradiction*, to earn for himself, among those who only knew him superficially, the character of a curmudgeon. Like many excellent people, he seemed possessed with a spirit of *tantalization*, which might easily, at a casual glance, have been mistaken for malevolence. To every request, a positive "No!" was his immediate answer; but in the end — in the long, long end — there were exceedingly few requests which he refused. Against all attacks upon his purse he made the most sturdy defence; but the amount extorted from him, at last, was generally in direct ratio with the length of the siege and the stubbornness of the resistance. In charity no one gave more liberally or with a worse grace.

For the fine arts, and especially for the belles-lettres, he entertained a profound contempt. With this he had been inspired by Casimir Perier, whose pert little query "*A quoi un poete est il bon?*" he was in the habit of quoting, with a very droll pronunciation, as the *ne plus ultra* of logical wit. Thus my own inkling for the Muses had excited his entire displeasure. He assured me one day, when I asked him for a new copy of Horace, that the translation of "*Poeta nascitur non fit*" was "a nasty poet for nothing fit" — a remark which I took in high dudgeon. His repugnance to "the humanities" had, also, much increased of late, by an accidental bias in favor of what he supposed to be natural science. Somebody had accosted him in the street, mistaking him for no less a personage than Doctor Dubble L. Dee, the lecturer upon quack physics. This set him off at a tangent; and just at the epoch of this story — for story it is getting to be after all — my grand-uncle Rumgudgeon was accessible and pacific only upon points which happened to chime in with the caprioles of the hobby he was riding. For the rest, he laughed with his arms and legs, and his politics were stubborn and easily understood. He thought, with Horsley, that "the people have nothing to do with the laws but to obey them."

I had lived with the old gentleman all my life. My parents, in dying, had bequeathed me to him as a rich legacy. I believe the old villain loved me as his own child — nearly if not quite as well as he loved Kate — but it was a dog's existence that he led me, after all. From my first year until my fifth, he obliged me with very regular floggings. From five to fifteen, he threatened me, hourly, with the House of Correction. From fifteen to twenty, not a day passed in which he did not promise to cut me off with a shilling. I was a sad dog, it is true — but then it was a part of my nature — a point of my faith. In Kate, however, I had a firm friend, and I knew it. She was a good girl, and told me very sweetly that I might have her (plum and all) whenever I could badger my grand-uncle Rumgudgeon, into the necessary consent. Poor girl! — she was barely fifteen, and without this consent, her little amount in the funds was not come-at-able until five immeasurable summers had "dragged their slow length along." What, then, to do? At fifteen, or even at twenty-one [for I had now passed my fifth olympiad] five years in prospect are very much the same as five hundred. In vain we besieged the old gentleman with importunities. Here was a *piece de resistance* (as Messieurs Ude and Careme would say) which suited his perverse fancy to a T. It would have stirred the indignation of Job himself, to see how much like an old mouser he behaved to us two poor wretched little mice. In his heart he wished for nothing more ardently than our union. He had made up his mind to this all along. In fact, he would have given ten thousand pounds from his own pocket (Kate's plum was *her own*) if he could have invented any thing like an excuse for complying with our very natural wishes. But then we had been so imprudent as to broach the subject *ourselves*. Not to oppose it under such circumstances, I sincerely believe, was not in his power.

I have said already that he had his weak points; but in speaking of these, I must not be understood as referring to his obstinacy: which was one of his strong points — "*assurement ce n' etait pas sa foible.*" When I mention his weakness I have allusion to a *bizarre* old-womanish superstition which beset him. He was great in dreams, portents, *et id genus omne* of rigmarole. He was excessively punctilious, too, upon small points of honor, and, after his own fashion, was a man of his word, beyond doubt. This was, in fact, one of his hobbies. The *spirit* of his vows he made no scruple of setting at naught, but the *letter* was a bond inviolable. Now it was this latter peculiarity in his disposition, of which Kate's ingenuity enabled us one fine day, not long after our interview in the dining-room, to take a very unexpected advantage, and, having thus, in the fashion of all modern bards and orators, exhausted in *prolegomena*, all the time at my command, and nearly all the room at my disposal, I will sum up in a few words what constitutes the whole pith of the story.

It happened then — so the Fates ordered it — that among the naval acquaintances of my betrothed, were two gentlemen who had just set foot upon the shores of England, after a year's absence, each, in foreign

travel. In company with these gentlemen, my cousin and I, preconcert-edly paid uncle Rumgudgeon a visit on the afternoon of Sunday, October the tenth, — just three weeks after the memorable decision which had so cruelly defeated our hopes. For about half an hour the conversation ran upon ordinary topics, but at last, we contrived, quite naturally, to give it the following turn:

CAPT. PRATT. "Well I have been absent just one year. — Just one year to-day, as I live — let me see! yes! — this is October the tenth. You re-member, Mr. Rumgudgeon, I called, this day year to bid you good-bye. And by the way, it *does* seem something like a coincidence, does it not — that our friend, Captain Smitherton, here, has been absent exactly a year also — a year to-day!"

SMITHERTON. "Yes! just one year to a fraction. You will remember, Mr. Rumgudgeon, that I called with Capt. Pratol on this very day, last year, to pay my parting respects."

UNCLE. "Yes, yes, yes — I remember it very well — very queer indeed! Both of you gone just one year. A very strange coincidence, indeed! Just what Doctor Dubble L. Dee would denominate an extraordinary concur-rence of events. Doctor Dub — "

KATE. [*Interrupting.*] "To be sure, papa, it *is* something strange; but then Captain Pratt and Captain Smitherton didn't go altogether the same route, and that makes a difference, you know."

UNCLE. "I don't know any such thing, you huzzy! How should I? I think it only makes the matter more remarkable, Doctor Dubble L. Dee — "

KATE. "Why, papa, Captain Pratt went round Cape Horn, and Cap-tain Smitherton doubled the Cape of Good Hope."

UNCLE. "Precisely! — the one went east and the other went west, you jade, and they both have gone quite round the world. By the by, Doctor Dubble L. Dee — "

MYSELF. [*Hurriedly.*] "Captain Pratt, you must come and spend the evening with us to-morrow — you and Smitherton — you can tell us all about your voyage, and we'll have a game of whist and — "

PRATT. "Whist, my dear fellow — you forget. To-morrow will be Sun-day. Some other evening — "

KATE. "Oh, no. fie! — Robert's not *quite* so bad as that. *To-day's* Sun-day."

UNCLE. "To be sure — to be sure!"

PRATT. "I beg both your pardons — but I can't be so much mistaken. I know to-morrow's Sunday, because — "

SMITHERTON. [*Much surprised.*] "What *are* you all thinking about? Wasn't *yesterday* Sunday, I should like to know?"

ALL. "Yesterday, indeed! you *are* out!"

UNCLE. "To-day's Sunday, I say — don't *I* know?"

PRATT. "Oh no! — to-morrow's Sunday."

SMITHERTON. "You are *all* mad — every one of you. I am as positive that yesterday was Sunday as I am that I sit upon this chair."

KATE. [*Jumping up eagerly.*] "I see it — I see it all. Papa, this is a judgment upon you, about — about you know what. Let me alone, and I'll explain it all in a minute. It's a very simple thing, indeed. Captain Smitherton says that yesterday was Sunday: so it was; he is right. Cousin Bobby, and uncle and I say that to-day is Sunday: so it is; we are right. Captain Pratt maintains that to-morrow will be Sunday: so it will; he is right, too. The fact is, we are all right, and thus *three Sundays have come together in a week*."

SMITHERTON. [*After a pause.*] "By the by, Pratt, Kate has us completely. What fools we two are! Mr. Rumgudgeon, the matter stands thus: the earth, you know, is twenty-four thousand miles in circumference. Now this globe of the earth turns upon its own axis — revolves — spins round — these twenty-four thousand miles of extent, going from west to east, in precisely twenty-four hours. Do you understand Mr. Rumgudgeon? — "

UNCLE. "To be sure — to be sure — Doctor Dub — "

SMITHERTON. [*Drowning his voice.*] "Well, sir; that is at the rate of one thousand miles per hour. Now, suppose that I sail from this position a thousand miles east. Of course I anticipate the rising of the sun here at London by just one hour. I see the sun rise one hour before you do. Proceeding, in the same direction, yet another thousand miles, I anticipate the rising by two hours — another thousand, and I anticipate it by three hours, and so on, until I go entirely round the globe, and back to this spot, when, having gone twenty-four thousand miles east, I anticipate the rising of the London sun by no less than twenty-four hours; that is to say, I am a day *in advance* of your time. Understand, eh?"

UNCLE. "But Double L. Dee — "

SMITHERTON. [*Speaking very loud.*] "Captain Pratt, on the contrary, when he had sailed a thousand miles west of this position, was an hour, and when he had sailed twenty-four thousand miles west, was twenty-four hours, or one day, *behind* the time at London. Thus, with me, yesterday was Sunday — thus, with you, to-day is Sunday — and thus, with Pratt, to-morrow will be Sunday. And what is more, Mr. Rumgudgeon, it is positively clear that we are *all right*; for there can be no philosophical reason assigned why the idea of one of us should have preference over that of the other."

UNCLE. "My eyes! — well, Kate — well, Bobby! — this *is* a judgment upon me, as you say. But I am a man of my word — *mark that!* you shall have her, boy, (plum and all), when you please. Done up, by Jove! Three Sundays all in a row! I'll go, and take Dubble L. Dee's opinion upon *that*."

The Oval Portrait

THE CHATEAU into which my valet had ventured to make forcible entrance, rather than permit me, in my desperately wounded condition, to pass a night in the open air, was one of those piles of commingled gloom and grandeur which have so long frowned among the Appennines, not less in fact than in the fancy of Mrs. Radcliffe. To all appearance it had been temporarily and very lately abandoned. We established ourselves in one of the smallest and least sumptuously furnished apartments. It lay in a remote turret of the building. Its decorations were rich, yet tattered and antique. Its walls were hung with tapestry and bedecked with manifold and multiform armorial trophies, together with an unusually great number of very spirited modern paintings in frames of rich golden arabesque. In these paintings, which depended from the walls not only in their main surfaces, but in very many nooks which the bizarre architecture of the chateau rendered necessary — in these paintings my incipient delirium, perhaps, had caused me to take deep interest; so that I bade Pedro to close the heavy shutters of the room — since it was already night — to light the tongues of a tall candelabrum which stood by the head of my bed — and to throw open far and wide the fringed curtains of black velvet which enveloped the bed itself. I wished all this done that I might resign myself, if not to sleep, at least alternately to the contemplation of these pictures, and the perusal of a small volume which had been found upon the pillow, and which purported to criticise and describe them.

Long — long I read — and devoutly, devotedly I gazed. Rapidly and gloriously the hours flew by and the deep midnight came. The position of the candelabrum displeased me, and outreaching my hand with difficulty, rather than disturb my slumbering valet, I placed it so as to throw its rays more fully upon the book.

But the action produced an effect altogether unanticipated. The rays of the numerous candles (for there were many) now fell within a niche of the room which had hitherto been thrown into deep shade by one of the bed-posts. I thus saw in vivid light a picture all unnoticed before. It was the portrait of a young girl just ripening into womanhood. I glanced at the painting hurriedly, and then closed my eyes. Why I did this was not at first apparent even to my own perception. But while my lids remained thus shut, I ran over in my mind my reason for so shutting them. It was an impulsive movement to gain time for thought — to make sure that my vision had not deceived me — to calm and subdue my fancy for a more sober and more certain gaze. In a very few moments I again looked fixedly at the painting.

That I now saw aright I could not and would not doubt; for the first flashing of the candles upon that canvas had seemed to dissipate the dreamy stupor which was stealing over my senses, and to startle me at once into waking life.

The portrait, I have already said, was that of a young girl. It was a mere head and shoulders, done in what is technically termed a *vignette* manner; much in the style of the favorite heads of Sully. The arms, the bosom, and even the ends of the radiant hair melted imperceptibly into the vague yet deep shadow which formed the back-ground of the whole. The frame was oval, richly gilded and filigreed in *Moresque*. As a thing of art nothing could be more admirable than the painting itself. But it could have been neither the execution of the work, nor the immortal beauty of the countenance, which had so suddenly and so vehemently moved me. Least of all, could it have been that my fancy, shaken from its half slumber, had mistaken the head for that of a living person. I saw at once that the peculiarities of the design, of the *vignetting*, and of the frame, must have instantly dispelled such idea — must have prevented even its momentary entertainment. Thinking earnestly upon these points, I remained, for an hour perhaps, half sitting, half reclining, with my vision riveted upon the portrait. At length, satisfied with the true secret of its effect, I fell back within the bed. I had found the spell of the picture in an absolute *life-likeliness* of expression, which, at first startling, finally confounded, subdued, and appalled me. With deep and reverent awe I replaced the candelabrum in its former position. The cause of my deep agitation being thus shut from view, I sought eagerly the volume which discussed the paintings and their histories. Turning to the number which designated the oval portrait, I there read the vague and quaint words which follow:

"She was a maiden of rarest beauty, and not more lovely than full of glee. And evil was the hour when she saw, and loved, and wedded the painter. He, passionate, studious, austere, and having already a bride in his Art; she a maiden of rarest beauty, and not more lovely than full of glee; all light and smiles, and frolicsome as the young fawn; loving and cherishing all things; hating only the Art which was her rival; dreading only the pallet and brushes and other untoward instruments which deprived her of the countenance of her lover. It was thus a terrible thing for this lady to hear the painter speak of his desire to pourtray even his young bride. But she was humble and obedient, and sat meekly for many weeks in the dark, high turret-chamber where the light dripped upon the pale canvas only from overhead. But he, the painter, took glory in his work, which went on from hour to hour, and from day to day. And he was a passionate, and wild, and moody man, who became lost in reveries; so that he *would* not see that the light which fell so ghastly in that lone turret withered the health and the spirits of his bride, who pined visibly to all but him. Yet she smiled on and still on, uncomplain-

ingly, because she saw that the painter (who had high renown) took a fervid and burning pleasure in his task, and wrought day and night to depict her who so loved him, yet who grew daily more dispirited and weak. And in sooth some who beheld the portrait spoke of its resemblance in low words, as of a mighty marvel, and a proof not less of the power of the painter than of his deep love for her whom he depicted so surpassingly well. But at length, as the labor drew nearer to its conclusion, there were admitted none into the turret; for the painter had grown wild with the ardor of his work, and turned his eyes from canvas rarely, even to regard the countenance of his wife. And he *would* not see that the tints which he spread upon the canvas were drawn from the cheeks of her who sate beside him. And when many weeks had passed, and but little remained to do, save one brush upon the mouth and one tint upon the eye, the spirit of the lady again flickered up as the flame within the socket of the lamp. And then the brush was given, and then the tint was placed; and, for one moment, the painter stood entranced before the work which he had wrought; but in the next, while he yet gazed, he grew tremulous and very pallid, and aghast, and crying with a loud voice, 'This is indeed *Life* itself!' turned suddenly to regard his beloved: — *She was dead!*"

The Masque of the Red Death

THE "Red Death" had long devastated the country. No pestilence had ever been so fatal, or so hideous. Blood was its Avatar and its seal — the redness and the horror of blood. There were sharp pains, and sudden dizziness, and then profuse bleeding at the pores, with dissolution. The scarlet stains upon the body and especially upon the face of the victim, were the pest ban which shut him out from the aid and from the sympathy of his fellow-men. And the whole seizure, progress, and termination of the disease, were the incidents of half an hour.

But the Prince Prospero was happy and dauntless and sagacious. When his dominions were half depopulated, he summoned to his presence a thousand hale and light-hearted friends from among the knights and dames of his court, and with these retired to the deep seclusion of one of his castellated abbeys. This was an extensive and magnificent structure, the creation of the prince's own eccentric yet august taste. A strong and lofty wall girdled it in. This wall had gates of iron. The courtiers, having entered, brought furnaces and massy hammers and welded the bolts. They resolved to leave means neither of ingress or egress to the sudden impulses of despair or of frenzy from within. The abbey was amply provisioned. With such precautions the courtiers might bid defiance to

contagion. The external world could take care of itself. In the meantime it was folly to grieve, or to think. The prince had provided all the appliances of pleasure. There were buffoons, there were improvisatori, there were ballet-dancers, there were musicians, there was Beauty, there was wine. All these and security were within. Without was the "Red Death."

It was toward the close of the fifth or sixth month of his seclusion, and while the pestilence raged most furiously abroad, that the Prince Prospero entertained his thousand friends at a masked ball of the most unusual magnificence.

It was a voluptuous scene, that masquerade. But first let me tell of the rooms in which it was held. There were seven — an imperial suite. In many palaces, however, such suites form a long and straight vista, while the folding doors slide back nearly to the walls on either hand, so that the view of the whole extent is scarcely impeded. Here the case was very different; as might have been expected from the duke's love of the *bizarre*. The apartments were so irregularly disposed that the vision embraced but little more than one at a time. There was a sharp turn at every twenty or thirty yards, and at each turn a novel effect. To the right and left, in the middle of each wall, a tall and narrow Gothic window looked out upon a closed corridor which pursued the windings of the suite. These windows were of stained glass whose color varied in accordance with the prevailing hue of the decorations of the chamber into which it opened. That at the eastern extremity was hung, for example in blue — and vividly blue were its windows. The second chamber was purple in its ornaments and tapestries, and here the panes were purple. The third was green throughout, and so were the casements. The fourth was furnished and lighted with orange — the fifth with white — the sixth with violet. The seventh apartment was closely shrouded in black velvet tapestries that hung all over the ceiling and down the walls, falling in heavy folds upon a carpet of the same material and hue. But in this chamber only, the color of the windows failed to correspond with the decorations. The panes here were scarlet — a deep blood color. Now in no one of the seven apartments was there any lamp or candelabrum, amid the profusion of golden ornaments that lay scattered to and fro or depended from the roof. There was no light of any kind emanating from the lamp or candle within the suite of chambers. But in the corridors that followed the suite, there stood, opposite to each window, a heavy tripod, bearing a brazier of fire, that projected its rays through the tinted glass and so glaringly illumined the room. And thus were produced a multitude of gaudy and fantastic appearances. But in the western or black chamber the effect of the firelight that streamed upon the dark hangings through the blood-tinted panes was ghastly in the extreme, and produced so wild a look upon the countenances of those who entered, that there were few of the company bold enough to set foot within its precincts at all.

It was in this apartment, also, that there stood against the western

wall, a gigantic clock of ebony. Its pendulum swung to and fro with a dull, heavy, monotonous clang; and when the minute-hand made the circuit of the face, and the hour was to be stricken, there came from the brazen lungs of the clock a sound which was clear and loud and deep and exceedingly musical, but of so peculiar a note and emphasis that, at each lapse of an hour, the musicians of the orchestra were constrained to pause, momentarily, in their performance, to hearken to the sound; and thus the waltzers perforce ceased their evolutions; and there was a brief disconcert of the whole gay company; and, while the chimes of the clock yet rang, it was observed that the giddiest grew pale, and the more aged and sedate passed their hands over their brows as if in confused revery or meditation. But when the echoes had fully ceased, a light laughter at once pervaded the assembly; the musicians looked at each other and smiled as if at their own nervousness and folly, and made whispering vows, each to the other, that the next chiming of the clock should produce in them no similar emotion; and then, after the lapse of sixty minutes (which embrace three thousand and six hundred seconds of the Time that flies), there came yet another chiming of the clock, and then were the same disconcert and tremulousness and meditation as before.

But, in spite of these things, it was a gay and magnificent revel. The tastes of the duke were peculiar. He had a fine eye for colors and effects. He disregarded the *decora* of mere fashion. His plans were bold and fiery, and his conceptions glowed with barbaric lustre. There are some who would have thought him mad. His followers felt that he was not. It was necessary to hear and see and touch him to be *sure* that he was not.

He had directed, in great part, the movable embellishments of the seven chambers, upon occasion of this great *fête*; and it was his own guiding taste which had given character to the masqueraders. Be sure they were grotesque. There were much glare and glitter and piquancy and phantasm — much of what has been since seen in "Hernani." There were arabesque figures with unsuited limbs and appointments.

There were delirious fancies such as the madman fashions. There were much of the beautiful, much of the wanton, much of the *bizarre*, something of the terrible, and not a little of that which might have excited disgust. To and fro in the seven chambers there stalked, in fact, a multitude of dreams. And these — the dreams — writhed in and about, taking hue from the rooms, and causing the wild music of the orchestra to seem as the echo of their steps. And, anon, there strikes the ebony clock which stands in the hall of the velvet. And then, for a moment, all is still, and all is silent save the voice of the clock. The dreams are stiff-frozen as they stand. But the echoes of the chime die away — they have endured but an instant — and a light, half-subdued laughter floats after them as they depart. And now again the music swells, and the dreams live, and writhe to and fro more merrily than ever, taking hue from the many-tinted windows through which stream the rays from the tripods. But to the

chamber which lies most westwardly of the seven there are now none of the maskers who venture; for the night is waning away; and there flows a ruddier light through the blood-colored panes; and the blackness of the sable drapery appalls; and to him whose foot falls upon the sable carpet, there comes from the near clock of ebony a muffled peal more solemnly emphatic than any which reaches *their* ears who indulge in the more remote gaieties of the other apartments.

But these other apartments were densely crowded, and in them beat feverishly the heart of life. And the revel went whirlingly on, until at length there commenced the sounding of midnight upon the clock. And then the music ceased, as I have told; and the evolutions of the waltzers were quieted; and there was an uneasy cessation of all things as before. But now there were twelve strokes to be sounded by the bell of the clock; and thus it happened, perhaps that more of thought crept, with more of time, into the meditations of the thoughtful among those who revelled. And thus too, it happened, perhaps, that before the last echoes of the last chime had utterly sunk into silence, there were many individuals in the crowd who had found leisure to become aware of the presence of a masked figure which had arrested the attention of no single individual before. And the rumor of this new presence having spread itself whisper-ingly around, there arose at length from the whole company a buzz, or murmur, expressive of disapprobation and surprise — then, finally, of terror, of horror, and of disgust.

In an assembly of phantasms such as I have painted, it may well be supposed that no ordinary appearance could have excited such sensa-tion. In truth the masquerade license of the night was nearly unlimited; but the figure in question had out-Heroded Herod, and gone beyond the bounds of even the prince's indefinite decorum. There are chords in the hearts of the most reckless which cannot be touched without emotion.

Even with the utterly lost, to whom life and death are equally jests, there are matters of which no jest can be made. The whole company, in-deed, seemed now deeply to feel that in the costume and bearing of the stranger neither wit nor propriety existed. The figure was tall and gaunt, and shrouded from head to foot in the habiliments of the grave. The mask which concealed the visage was made so nearly to resemble the countenance of a stiffened corpse that the closest scrutiny must have had difficulty in detecting the cheat. And yet all this might have been en-dured, if not approved, by the mad revellers around. But the mummer had gone so far as to assume the type of the Red Death. His vesture was dabbled in *blood* — and his broad brow, with all the features of the face, was besprinkled with the scarlet horror.

When the eyes of Prince Prospero fell upon this spectral image (which, with a slow and solemn movement, as if more fully to sustain its *rôle*, stalked to and fro among the waltzers) he was seen to be convulsed, in

the first moment with a strong shudder either of terror or distaste; but, in the next, his brow reddened with rage.

"Who dares" — he demanded hoarsely of the courtiers who stood near him — "who dares insult us with this blasphemous mockery? Seize him and unmask him — that we may know whom we have to hang, at sunrise, from the battlements!"

It was in the eastern or blue chamber in which stood the Prince Prospero as he uttered these words. They rang throughout the seven rooms loudly and clearly, for the prince was a bold and robust man, and the music had become hushed at the waving of his hand.

It was in the blue room where stood the prince, with a group of pale courtiers by his side. At first, as he spoke, there was a slight rushing movement of this group in the direction of the intruder, who, at the moment was also near at hand, and now, with deliberate and stately step, made closer approach to the speaker. But from a certain nameless awe with which the mad assumptions of the mummer had inspired the whole party, there were found none who put forth hand to seize him; so that, unimpeded, he passed within a yard of the prince's person; and, while the vast assembly, as if with one impulse, shrank from the centres of the rooms to the walls, he made his way uninterruptedly, but with the same solemn and measured step, which had distinguished him from the first, through the blue chamber to the purple — through the purple to the green — through the green to the orange — through this again to the white — and even thence to the violet, ere a decided movement had been made to arrest him. It was then, however, that the Prince Prospero, maddening with rage and the shame of his own momentary cowardice, rushed hurriedly through the six chambers, while none followed him on account of a deadly terror that had seized upon all. He bore aloft a drawn dagger, and had approached, in rapid impetuosity, to within three or four feet of the retreating figure, when the latter, having attained the extremity of the velvet apartment, turned suddenly and confronted his pursuer. There was a sharp cry — and the dagger dropped gleaming upon the sable carpet, upon which, instantly afterward, fell prostrate in death the Prince Prospero. Then, summoning the wild courage of despair, a throng of the revellers at once threw themselves into the black apartment, and, seizing the mummer, whose tall figure stood erect and motionless within the shadow of the ebony clock, gasped in unutterable horror at finding the grave-cerements and corpse-like mask, which they handled with so violent a rudeness, untenanted by any tangible form.

And now was acknowledged the presence of the Red Death. He had come like a thief in the night. And one by one dropped the revellers in the blood-bedewed halls of their revel, and died each in the despairing posture of his fall. And the life of the ebony clock went out with that of the last of the gay. And the flames of the tripods expired. And Darkness and Decay and the Red Death held illimitable dominion over all.

The Landscape Garden

The garden like a lady fair was cut
That lay as if she slumbered in delight,
And to the open skies her eyes did shut;
The azure fields of heaven were 'sembled right
In a large round set with the flow'rs of light:
The flowers de luce and the round sparks of dew
That hung upon their azure leaves, did show
Like twinkling stars that sparkle in the ev'ning blue.

GILES FLETCHER.

No more remarkable man ever lived than my friend, the young Ellison. He was remarkable in the entire and continuous profusion of good gifts ever lavished upon him by fortune. From his cradle to his grave, a gale of the blandest prosperity bore him along. Nor do I use the word Prosperity in its mere wordly or external sense. I mean it as synonymous with happiness. The person of whom I speak, seemed born for the purpose of foreshadowing the wild doctrines of Turgot, Price, Priestley, and Condorcet — of exemplifying, by individual instance, what has been deemed the mere chimera of the perfectionists. In the brief existence of Ellison, I fancy, that I have seen refuted the dogma — that in man's physical and spiritual nature, lies some hidden principle, the antagonist of Bliss. An intimate and anxious examination of his career, has taught me to understand that, in general, from the violation of a few simple laws of Humanity, arises the Wretchedness of mankind; that, as a species, we have in our possession the as yet unwrought elements of Content; and that even now, in the present blindness and darkness of all idea on the great question of the Social Condition, it is not impossible that Man, the individual, under certain unusual and highly fortuitous conditions, may be happy.

With opinions such as these was my young friend fully imbued; and thus is it especially worthy of observation that the uninterrupted enjoyment which distinguished his life was in great part the result of preconcert. It is, indeed evident, that with less of the instinctive philosophy which, now and then, stands so well in the stead of experience, Mr. Ellison would have found himself precipitated, by the very extraordinary successes of his life, into the common vortex of Unhappiness which yawns for those of preeminent endowments. But it is by no means my present object to pen an essay on Happiness. The ideas of my friend may be summed up in a few words. He admitted but four unvarying laws, or rather elementary principles, of Bliss. That which he considered chief,

was (strange to say!) the simple and purely physical one of free exercise in the open air. "The health," he said, "attainable by other means than this is scarcely worth the name." He pointed to the tillers of the earth — the only people who, as a class, are proverbially more happy than others — and then he instanced the high ecstasies of the fox-hunter. His second principle was the love of woman. His third was the contempt of ambition. His fourth was an object of unceasing pursuit; and he held that, other things being equal, the extent of happiness was proportioned to the spirituality of this object.

I have said that Ellison was remarkable in the continuous profusion of good gifts lavished upon him by Fortune. In personal grace and beauty he exceeded all men. His intellect was of that order to which the attainment of knowledge is less a labor than a necessity and an intuition. His family was one of the most illustrious of the empire. His bride was the loveliest and most devoted of women. His possessions had been always ample; but, upon the attainment of his one and twentieth year, it was discovered that one of those extraordinary freaks of Fate had been played in his behalf which startle the whole social world amid which they occur, and seldom fail radically to alter the entire moral constitution of those who are their objects. It appears that about one hundred years prior to Mr. Ellison's attainment of his marjority, there had died, in a remote province, one Mr. Seabright Ellison. This gentlemen had amassed a princely fortune, and, having no very immediate connexions, conceived the whim of suffering his wealth to accumulate for a century after his decease. Minutely and sagaciously directing the various modes of investment, he bequeathed the aggregate amount to the nearest of blood, bearing the name Ellison, who should be alive at the end of the hundred years. Many futile attempts had been made to set aside this singular bequest; their *ex post facto* character rendered them abortive; but the attention of a jealous government was aroused, and a decree finally obtained, forbidding all similar accumulations. This act did not prevent young Ellison, upon his twenty-first birth-day, from entering into possession, as the heir of his ancestor, Seabright, of a fortune of *four hundred and fifty millions of dollars.**

When it had become definitely known that such was the enormous wealth inherited, there were, of course, many speculations as to the mode of its disposal. The gigantic magnitude and the immediately available

* An incident similar in outline to the one here imagined, occurred, not very long ago, in England. The name of the fortunate heir (who still lives,) is Thelluson. I first saw an account of this matter in the "Tour" of Prince Puckler Muskau. He makes the sum received ninety millions of pounds, and observes, with much force, that, "in the contemplation of so vast a sum, and of the services, to which it might be applied, there is something even of the sublime." To suit the views of this article, I have followed the Prince's statement — a grossly exaggerated one, no doubt,

nature of the sum, dazzled and bewildered all who thought upon the topic. The possessor of any *appreciable* amount of money might have been imagined to perform any one of a thousand things. With riches merely surpassing those of any citizen, it would have been easy to suppose him engaging to supreme excess in the fashionable extravagances of his time; or busying himself with political intrigues; or aiming at ministerial power; or purchasing increase of nobility; or devising gorgeous architectural piles; or collecting large specimens of Virtù; or playing the munificent patron of Letters and Art; or endowing and bestowing his name upon extensive institutions of charity. But, for the inconceivable wealth in the actual possession of the young heir, these objects and all ordinary objects were felt to be inadequate. Recourse was had to figures; and figures but sufficed to confound. It was seen, that even at three per cent, the annual income of the inheritance amounted to no less than thirteen millions and five hundred thousand dollars; which was one million and one hundred and twenty-five thousand per month; or thirty-six thousand, nine hundred and eighty-six per day, or one thousand five hundred and forty-one per hour; or six and twenty dollars for every minute that flew. Thus the usual track of supposition was thoroughly broken up. Men knew not what to imagine. There were some who even conceived that Mr. Ellison would divest himself forthwith of at least two-thirds of his fortune as of utterly superfluous opulence; enriching whole troops of his relatives by division of his superabundance.

I was not surprised, however, to perceive that he had long made up his mind upon a topic which had occasioned so much of discussion to his friends. Nor was I greatly astonished at the nature of his decision. In the widest and noblest sense, he was a poet. He comprehended, moreover, the true character, the august aims, the supreme majesty and dignity of the poetic sentiment. The proper gratification of the sentiment he instinctively felt to lie in the *creation of novel forms of Beauty*. Some peculiarities, either in his early education, or in the nature of his intellect, had tinged with what is termed materialism the whole cast of his ethical speculations; and it was this bias, perhaps, which imperceptibly led him to perceive that the most advantageous, if not the sole legitimate field for the exercise of the poetic sentiment, was to be found in the creation of novel moods of purely *physical* loveliness. Thus it happened that he became neither musician nor poet; if we use this latter term in its every-day acceptation. Or it might have been that he became neither the one nor the other, in pursuance of an idea of his which I have already mentioned — the idea, that in the contempt of ambition lay one of the essential principles of happiness on earth. Is it not, indeed, possible that while a *high* order of genius is necessarily ambitious, the *highest* is invariably *above* that which is termed ambition? And may it not thus happen that many far greater than Milton, have contentedly remained "mute and inglorious?" I believe the world has never yet seen, and that,

unless through some series of accidents goading the noblest order of mind into distasteful exertion, the world will *never* behold, that full extent of triumphant execution, in the richer productions of Art, of which the human nature is absolutely capable.

Mr. Ellison became neither musician nor poet; although no man lived more profoundly enamored both of Music and the Muse. Under other circumstances than those which invested him, it is not impossible that he would have become a painter. The field of sculpture, although in its nature rigidly poetical, was too limited in its extent and in its consequences, to have occupied, at any time, much of his attention. And I have now mentioned *all* the provinces in which even the most liberal understanding of the poetic sentiment has declared this sentiment capable of expatiating. I mean the most liberal public or recognized conception of the idea involved in the phrase "poetic sentiment." But Mr. Ellison imagined that the richest, and altogether the most natural and most suitable province, had been blindly neglected. No definition had spoken of the *Landscape-Gardener*, as of the poet; yet my friend could not fail to perceive that the creation of the Landscape-Garden offered to the true muse the most magnificent of opportunities. Here was, indeed, the fairest field for the display of invention, or imagination, in the endless combining of forms of novel Beauty; the elements which should enter into combination being, at all times, and by a vast superiority, the most glorious which the earth could afford. In the multiform of the tree, and in the multicolor of the flower, he recognized the most direct and the most energetic efforts of Nature at physical loveliness. And in the direction or concentration of this effort, or, still more properly, in its adaption to the eyes which were to behold it upon earth, he perceived that he should be employing the best means — laboring to the greatest advantage — in the fulfilment of his destiny as Poet.

"Its adaptation to the eyes which were to behold it upon earth." In his explanation of this phraseology, Mr. Ellison did much towards solving what has always seemed to me an enigma. I mean the fact (which none but the ignorant dispute,) that no such combinations of scenery exist in Nature as the painter of genius has in his power to produce. No such Paradises are to be found in reality as have glowed upon the canvass of Claude. In the most enchanting of natural landscapes, there will always be found a defect or an excess — many excesses and defects. While the component parts may exceed, individually, the highest skill of the artist, the arrangement of the parts will always be susceptible of improvement. In short, no position can be attained, from which an artistical eye, looking steadily, will not find matter of offence, in what is technically termed the *composition* of a natural landscape. And yet how unintelligible is this! In all other matters we are justly instructed to regard Nature as supreme. With her details we shrink from competition. Who shall presume to imitate the colors of the tulip, or to improve the proportions

of the lily of the valley? The criticism which says, of sculpture or of portraiture, that "Nature is to be exalted rather than imitated," is in error. No pictorial or sculptural combinations of *points* of human loveliness, do more than approach the living and breathing human beauty as it gladdens our daily path. Byron, who often erred, erred not in saying,

> I've seen more living beauty, ripe and real,
> Than all the nonsense of their stone ideal.

In landscape alone is the principle of the critic true; and, having felt its truth here, it is but the headlong spirit of generalization which has induced him to pronounce it true throughout *all* the domains of Art. Having, I say, *felt* its truth here. For the feeling is no affectation or chimera. The mathematics afford no more absolute demonstrations, than the *sentiment* of his Art yields to the artist. He not only believes, but positively *knows*, that such and such apparently arbitrary arrangements of matter, or form, constitute, and alone constitute, the true Beauty. Yet his reasons have not yet been matured into expression. It remains for a more profound analysis than the world has yet seen, fully to investigate and express them. Nevertheless is he confirmed in his instinctive opinions, by the concurrence of all his compeers. Let a composition be defective; let an emendation be wrought in its mere arrangement of form; let this emendation be submitted to every artist in the world; by each will its necessity be admitted. And even far more than this; in remedy of the defective composition, each insulated member of the fraternity will *suggest* the identical emendation.

I repeat that in landscape arrangements, or collocations alone, is the *physical* Nature susceptible of "exaltation," and that, therefore, her susceptibility of improvement at this one point, was a mystery which, hitherto I had been unable to solve. It was Mr. Ellison who first suggested the idea that what we regarded as improvement or exaltation of the natural beauty, was really such, as respected only the mortal or human *point of view*; that each alteration or disturbance of the primitive scenery might possibly effect a blemish in the picture, if we could suppose this picture viewed *at large* from some remote point in the heavens. "It is easily understood," says Mr. Ellison, "that what might improve a closely scrutinized detail, might, at the same time, injure a general and more distantly-observed effect." He spoke upon this topic with warmth: regarding not so much its immediate or obvious importance, (which is little,) as the character of the conclusions to which it might lead, or of the collateral propositions which it might serve to corroborate or sustain. There *might be* a class of beings, human once, but now to humanity invisible, for whose scrutiny and for whose refined appreciation of the beautiful, more especially than for our own, had been set in order by God the great landscape-garden of the *whole earth*.

In the course of our discussion, my young friend took occasion to

quote some passages from a writer who has been supposed to have well treated this theme.

"There are, properly," he writes, "but two styles of landscape-gardening, the natural and the artificial. One seeks to recall the original beauty of the country, by adapting its means to the surrounding scenery; cultivating trees in harmony with the hills or plain of the neighboring land; detecting and bringing into practice those nice relations of size, proportion and color which, hid from the common observer, are revealed everywhere to the experienced student of nature. The result of the natural style of gardening, is seen rather in the absence of all defects and incongruities — in the prevalence of a beautiful harmony and order, than in the creation of any special wonders or miracles. The artificial style has as many varieties as there are different tastes to gratify. It has a certain general relation to the various styles of building. There are the stately avenues and retirements of Versailles; Italian terraces; and a various mixed old English style, which bears some relation to the domestic Gothic or English Elizabethan architecture. Whatever may be said against the abuses of the artificial landscape-gardening, a mixture of pure art in a garden scene, adds to it a great beauty. This is partly pleasing to the eye, by the show of order and design, and partly moral. A terrace, with an old moss-covered balustrade, calls up at once to the eye, the fair forms that have passed there in other days. The slightest exhibition of art is an evidence of care and human interest."

"From what I have already observed," said Mr. Ellison, "you will understand that I reject the idea, here expressed, of 'recalling the original beauty of the country.' The original beauty is never so great as that which may be introduced. Of course, much depends upon the selection of a spot with *capabilities*. What is said in respect to the 'detecting and bringing into practice those nice relations of size, proportion and color,' is a mere vagueness of speech, which may mean much, or little, or nothing, and which guides in no degree. That the true 'result of the natural style of gardening is seen rather in the absence of all defects and incongruities, than in the creation of any special wonders or miracles,' is a proposition better suited to the grovelling apprehension of the herd, than to the fervid dreams of the man of genius. The merit suggested is, at best, negative, and appertains to that hobbling criticism which, in letters, would elevate Addison into apotheosis. In truth, while that merit which consists in the mere avoiding demerit, appeals directly to the understanding, and can thus be foreshadowed in *Rule*, the loftier merit, which breathes and flames in invention or creation, can be apprehended solely in its results. Rule applies but to the excellences of avoidance — to the virtues which deny or refrain. Beyond these the critical art can but suggest. We may be instructed to build an Odyssey, but it is in vain that we are told *how* to conceive a 'Tempest,' an 'Inferno,' a 'Prometheus Bound,' a 'Nightingale,' such as that of Keats, or the 'Sensitive Plant' of Shelley.

But, the thing done, the wonder accomplished, and the capacity for apprehension becomes universal. The sophists of the *negative* school, who, through inability to create, have scoffed at creation, are now found the loudest in applause. What, in its chrysalis condition of principle, affronted their demure reason, never fails, in its maturity of accomplishment, to extort admiration from their instinct of the beautiful or of the sublime.

"Our author's observations on the artificial style of gardening," continued Mr. Ellison, "are less objectionable. 'A mixture of pure art in a garden scene, adds to it a great beauty.' This is just; and the reference to the sense of human interest is equally so. I repeat that the principle here expressed, is incontrovertible; but there *may be* something even beyond it. There may be an object in full keeping with the principle suggested — an object unattainable by the means ordinarily in possession of mankind, yet which, if attained, would lend a charm to the landscape-garden immeasurably surpassing that which a merely *human* interest could bestow. The true poet possessed of very unusual pecuniary resources, might possibly, while retaining the necessary idea of *art* or *interest* or *culture*, so imbue his designs at once with extent and novelty of Beauty, as to convey the sentiment of *spiritual* interference. It will be seen that, in bringing about such result, he secures all the advantages of *interest* or *design*, while relieving his work of all the harshness and technicality of Art. In the most rugged of wildernesses — in the most savage of the scenes of pure Nature — there is apparent the *art* of a Creator; yet is *this* art apparent only to reflection; in no respect has it the obvious force of a feeling. Now, if we imagine this sense of the Almighty Design to be *harmonized* in a measurable degree; if we suppose a landscape whose combined *strangeness*, vastness, definitiveness, and magnificence, shall inspire the idea of culture, or care, or superintendence, on the part of intelligences superior yet akin to humanity — then the sentiment of *interest* is preserved, while the Art is made to assume the air of an intermediate or secondary Nature — a Nature which is not God, nor an emanation of God, but which still is Nature, in the sense that it is the handiwork of the angels that hover betwen man and God."

It was in devoting his gigantic wealth to the practical embodiment of a vision such as this — in the free exercise in the open air, which resulted from personal direction of his plans — in the continuous and unceasing *object* which these plans afford — in the contempt of ambition which it enabled him more to feel than to affect — and, lastly, it was in the companionship and sympathy of a devoted wife, that Ellison thought to find, *and found*, an exemption from the ordinary cares of Humanity, with a far greater amount of positive happiness than ever glowed in the rapt day-dreams of De Staël.

The Mystery of Marie Roget *

A SEQUEL TO "THE MURDERS IN THE RUE MORGUE"

Es GIEBT *eine Reihe idealischer Begebenheiten, die der Wirklichkeit parallel lauft. Selten fallen sie zusammen. Menchen und zufalle modificiren gewohulich die idealische Begebenheit, so dass sie unvollkommen erscheint, und ihre Felgen gleichfalls unvollkommen sind. So bei der Reformation; statt des Protestantismus kam das Lutherum hervor.*

THERE ARE *ideal series of events which run parallel with the real ones. They rarely coincide. Men and circumstances generally modify the ideal train of events, so that it seems imperfect, and its consequences are equally imperfect. Thus with the Reformation; instead of Protestantism came Lutheranism.*

NOVALIS.† Moral Ansichten.

THERE ARE few persons, even among the calmest thinkers, who have not occasionally been startled into a vague yet thrilling half-credence in the supernatural, by *coincidences* of so seemingly marvellous a character that, as *mere* coincidences, the intellect has been unable to receive them. Such sentiments — for the half-credences of which I speak have never the full force of *thought* — such sentiments are seldom thoroughly stifled unless by reference to the doctrine of chance, or, as it is technically termed, the Calculus of Probabilities. Now this Calculus is, in its essence, purely mathematical; and thus we have the anomaly of the most rigidly

* Upon the original publication of "Marie Roget," the footnotes now appended were considered unnecessary; but the lapse of several years since the tragedy upon which the tale is based, renders it expedient to give them, and also to say a few words in explanation of the general design. A young girl, *Mary Cecilia Rogers*, was murdered in the vicinity of New York; and although her death occasioned an intense and long-enduring excitement, the mystery attending it had remained unsolved at the period when the present paper was written and published (November, 1842). Herein, under pretence of relating the fate of a Parisian *grisette*, the author has followed, in minute detail, the essential, while merely paralleling the inessential, facts of the real murder of Mary Rogers. Thus all argument founded upon the fiction is applicable to the truth:

and the investigation of the truth was the object.

The "Mystery of Marie Roget" was composed at a distance from the scene of the atrocity, and with no other means of investigation than the newspapers afforded. Thus much escaped the writer of which he could have availed himself had he been upon the spot and visited the localities. It may not be improper to record, nevertheless, that the confessions of *two* persons (one of them the Madame Deluc of the narrative), made, at different periods, long subsequent to the publication, confirmed, in full, not only the general conclusion, but absolutely *all* the chief hypothetical details by which that conclusion was attained.

† The *nom de plume* of Von Hardenburg.

exact in science applied to the shadow and spirituality of the most intangible in speculation.

The extraordinary details which I am now called upon to make public, will be found to form, as regards sequence of time, the primary branch of a series of scarcely intelligible *coincidences*, whose secondary or concluding branch will be recognized by all readers in the late murder of MARY CECILIA ROGERS, at New York.

When, in an article entitled "The Murders in the Rue Morgue," I endeavored, about a year ago, to depict some very remarkable features in the mental character of my friend, the Chevalier C. Auguste Dupin, it did not occur to me that I should ever resume the subject. This depicting of character constituted my design; and this design was thoroughly fulfilled in the wild train of circumstances brought to instance Dupin's idiosyncrasy. I might have adduced other examples, but I should have proven no more. Late events, however, in their surprising development, have startled me into some farther details, which will carry with them the air of extorted confession. Hearing what I have lately heard, it would be indeed strange should I remain silent in regard to what I both heard and saw so long ago.

Upon the winding up of the tragedy involved in the deaths of Madame L'Espanaye and her daughter, the Chevalier dismissed the affair at once from his attention, and relapsed into his old habits of moody revery. Prone, at all times, to abstraction, I readily fell in with his humor; and continuing to occupy our chambers in the Faubourg Saint Germain, we gave the Future to the winds, and slumbered tranquilly in the Present, weaving the dull world around us into dreams.

But these dreams were not altogether uninterrupted. It may readily be supposed that the part played by my friend, in the drama at the Rue Morgue had not failed of its impression upon the fancies of the Parisian police. With its emissaries, the name of Dupin had grown into a household word. The simple character of those inductions by which he had disentangled the mystery never having been explained even to the Prefect, or to any other individual than myself, of course it is not surprising that the affair was regarded as little less than miraculous, or that the Chevalier's analytical abilities acquired for him the credit of intuition. His frankness would have led him to disabuse every inquirer of such prejudice; but his indolent humor forbade all further agitation of a topic whose interest to himself had long ceased. It thus happened that he found himself the cynosure of the political eyes; and the cases were not few in which attempt was made to engage his services at the Prefecture. One of the most remarkable instances was that of the murder of a young girl named Marie Rogêt.

This event occurred about two years after the atrocity in the Rue Morgue. Marie, whose Christian and family name will at once arrest attention from their resemblance to those of the unfortunate "cigar-girl,"

was the only daughter of the widow Estelle Rogêt. The father had died during the child's infancy, and from the period of his death, until within eighteen months before the assassination which forms the subject of our narrative, the mother and daughter had dwelt together in the Rue Pavée Saint Andrée; * Madame there keeping a *pension*, assisted by Marie. Affairs went on thus until the latter had attained her twenty-second year, when her great beauty attracted the notice of a perfumer, who occupied one of the shops in the basement of the Palais Royal, and whose custom lay, chiefly among the desperate adventurers infesting that neighborhood. Monsieur Le Blanc † was not unaware of the advantages to be derived from the attendance of the fair Marie in his perfumery; and his liberal proposals were accepted eagerly by the girl, although with somewhat more of hesitation by Madame.

The anticipations of the shopkeeper were realized, and his rooms soon became notorious through the charms of the sprightly *grisette*. She had been in his employ about a year, when her admirers were thrown into confusion by her sudden disappearance from the shop. Monsieur Le Blanc was unable to account for her absence, and Madame Rogêt was distracted with anxiety and terror. The public papers immediately took up the theme, and the police were upon the point of making serious investigations, when, one fine morning, after the lapse of a week, Marie, in good health, but with a somewhat saddened air, made her re-appearance at her usual counter in the perfumery. All inquiry, except that of a private character, was of course, immediately hushed. Monsieur Le Blanc professed total ignorance, as before. Marie, with Madame, replied to all questions, that the last week had been spent at the house of a relation in the country. Thus the affair died away, and was generally forgotten; for the girl, ostensibly to relieve herself from the impertinence of curiosity soon bade a final adieu to the perfumer, and sought the shelter of her mother's residence in the Rue Pavée Saint Andrée.

It was about five months after this return home, that her friends were alarmed by her sudden disappearance for the second time. Three days elapsed, and nothing was heard of her. On the fourth her corpse was found floating in the Seine,‡ near the shore which is opposite the Quartier of the Rue Saint Andre, and at a point not very far distant from the secluded neighborhood of the Barrière du Roule.§

The atrocity of this murder (for it was at once evident that murder had been committed), the youth and beauty of the victim, and, above all her previous notoriety, conspired to produce intense excitement in the minds of the sensitive Parisians. I can call to mind no similar occurrence producing so general and so intense an effect. For several weeks, in the discussion of this one absorbing theme, even the momentous political topics of the day were forgotten. The Prefect made unusual exertions;

* Nassau Street. ‡ The Hudson.
† Anderson. § Weehawken.

and the powers of the whole Parisian police were, of course, tasked to the utmost extent.

Upon the first discovery of the corpse, it was not supposed that the murderer would be able to elude, for more than a very brief period, the inquisition which was immediately set on foot. It was not until the expiration of a week that it was deemed necessary to offer a reward; and even then this reward was limited to a thousand francs. In the meantime the investigation proceeded with vigor, if not always with judgment, and numerous individuals were examined to no purpose; while, owing to the continual absence of all clew to the mystery, the popular excitement greatly increased. At the end of the tenth day it was thought advisable to double the sum originally proposed; and, at length, the second week having elapsed without leading to any discoveries, and the prejudice which always exists in Paris against the Police having given vent to itself in several serious *émeutes,* the Prefect took it upon himself to offer the sum of twenty thousand francs "for the conviction of the assassin," or, if more than one should prove to have been implicated, "for the conviction of any one of the assassins." In the proclamation setting forth this reward, a full pardon was promised to any accomplice who should come forward in evidence against his fellow; and to the whole was appended, wherever it appeared, the private placard of a committee of citizens, offering ten thousand francs, in addition to the amount proposed by the Prefecture. The entire reward thus stood at no less than thirty thousand francs, which will be regarded as an extraordinary sum when we consider the humble condition of the girl, and the great frequency, in large cities, of such atrocities as the one described.

No one doubted now that the mystery of this murder would be immediately brought to light. But although, in one or two instances, arrests were made which promised elucidation, yet nothing was elicited which could implicate the parties suspected; and they were discharged forthwith. Strange as it may appear, the third week from the discovery of the body had passed, and passed without any light being thrown upon the subject, before even a rumor of the events which had so agitated the public mind reached the ears of Dupin and myself. Engaged in researches which had absorbed our whole attention, it had been nearly a month since either of us had gone abroad, or received a visiter, or more than glanced at the leading political articles in one of the daily papers. The first intelligence of the murder was brought us by G——, in person. He called upon us early in the afternoon of the thirteenth of July, 18—, and remained with us until late in the night. He had been piqued by the failure of all his endeavors to ferret out the assassins. His reputation — so he said with a peculiarly Parisian air — was at stake. Even his honor was concerned. The eyes of the public were upon him; and there was really no sacrifice which he would not be willing to make for the development of the mystery. He concluded a somewhat droll speech with a compli-

ment upon what he was pleased to term the *tact* of Dupin, and made him a direct and certainly a liberal proposition, the precise nature of which I do not feel myself at liberty to disclose, but which has no bearing upon the proper subject of my narrative.

The compliment my friend rebutted as best he could, but the proposition he accepted at once, although its advantages were altogether provisional. This point being settled, the Prefect broke forth at once into explanations of his own views, interspersing them with long comments upon the evidence; of which latter we were not yet in possession. He discoursed much and, beyond doubt, learnedly; while I hazarded an occasional suggestion as the night wore drowsily away. Dupin, sitting steadily in his accustomed armchair, was the embodiment of respectful attention. He wore spectacles, during the whole interview; and an occasional glance beneath their green glasses sufficed to convince me that he slept not the less soundly, because silently, throughout the seven or eight leaden-footed hours which immediately preceded the departure of the Prefect.

In the morning, I procured, at the Prefecture, a full report of all the evidence elicited, and, at the various newspaper offices, a copy of every paper in which, from first to last, had been published any decisive information in regard to this sad affair. Freed from all that was positively disproved, this mass of information stood thus:

Marie Rogêt left the residence of her mother, in the Rue Pavée St. Andrée, about nine o'clock in the morning of Sunday, June the twenty-second, 18—. In going out, she gave notice to a Monsieur Jacques St. Eustache,* and to him only, of her intention to spend the day with an aunt, who resided in the Rue des Drômes. The Rue des Drômes is a short and narrow but populous thoroughfare, not far from the banks of the river, and at a distance of some two miles, in the most direct course possible, from the *pension* of Madame Rogêt. St. Eustache was the accepted suitor of Marie, and lodged, as well as took his meals, at the *pension*. He was to have gone for his betrothed at dusk, and to have escorted her home. In the afternoon, however, it came on to rain heavily; and, supposing that she would remain all night at her aunt's (as she had done under similar circumstances before), he did not think it necessary to keep his promise. As night drew on, Madame Rogêt (who was an infirm old lady, seventy years of age) was heard to express a fear "that she should never see Marie again;" but this observation attracted little attention at the time.

On Monday it was ascertained that the girl had not been to the Rue des Drômes; and when the day elapsed without tidings of her, a tardy search was instituted at several points in the city and its environs. It was not, however, until the fourth day from the period of her disappearance that any thing satisfactory was ascertained respecting her. On this day

* Payne.

(Wednesday, the twenty-fifth of June) a Monsieur Beauvais,* who, with a friend, had been making inquiries for Marie near the Barrière du Roule, on the shore of the Seine which is opposite the Rue Pavée St. Andrée, was informed that a corpse had just been towed ashore by some fishermen, who had found it floating in the river. Upon seeing the body, Beauvais, after some hesitation, identified it as that of the perfumery-girl. His friend recognized it more promptly.

The face was suffused with dark blood, some of which issued from the mouth. No foam was seen, as in the case of the merely drowned. There was no discoloration in the cellular tissue. About the throat were bruises and impressions of fingers. The arms were bent over on the chest, and were rigid. The right hand was clenched; the left partially open. On the left wrist were two circular excoriations, apparently the effect of ropes, or of a rope in more than one volution. A part of the right wrist, also, was much chafed, as well as the back throughout its extent, but more especially at the shoulder-blades. In bringing the body to the shore the fishermen had attached to it a rope, but none of the excorations had been effected by this. The flesh of the neck was much swollen. There were no cuts apparent, or bruises which appeared the effect of blows. A piece of lace was found tied so tightly around the neck as to be hidden from sight; it was completely buried in the flesh, and was fastened by a knot which lay just under the left ear. This alone would have sufficed to produce death. The medical testimony spoke confidently of the virtuous character of the deceased. She had been subjected, it said, to brutal violence. The corpse was in such condition when found, that there could have been no difficulty in its recognition by friends.

The dress was much torn and otherwise disordered. In the outer garment, a slip, about a foot wide, had been torn upward from the bottom hem to the waist, but not torn off. It was wound three times around the waist, and secured by a sort of hitch in the back. The dress immediately beneath the frock was of fine muslin; and from this a slip eighteen inches wide had been torn entirely out — torn very evenly and with great care. It was found around her neck, fitting loosely, and secured with a hard knot. Over this muslin slip and the slip of lace the strings of a bonnet were attached, the bonnet being appended. The knot by which the strings of the bonnet were fastened was not a lady's, but a slip or sailor's knot.

After the recognition of the corpse, it was not, as usual, taken to the Morgue (this formality being superfluous), but hastily interred not far from the spot at which it was brought ashore. Through the exertions of Beauvais, the matter was industriously hushed up, as far as possible; and several days had elapsed before any public emotion resulted. A weekly paper,† however, at length took up the theme; the corpse was disinterred,

* Crommelin. † The New York Mercury.

and a re-examination instituted; but nothing was elicited beyond what has been already noted. The clothes, however, were now submitted to the mother and friends of the deceased, and fully identified as those worn by the girl upon leaving home.

Meantime, the excitement increased hourly. Several individuals were arrested and discharged. St. Eustache fell especially under suspicion; and he failed, at first, to give an intelligible account of his whereabouts during the Sunday on which Marie left home. Subsequently, however, he submitted to Monsieur G——, affidavits, accounting satisfactorily for every hour of the day in question. As time passed and no discovery ensued, a thousand contradictory rumors were circulated, and journalists busied themselves in *suggestions*. Among these, the one which attracted the most notice, was the idea that Marie Rogêt still lived — that the corpse found in the Seine was that of some other unfortunate. It will be proper that I submit to the reader some passages which embody the suggestion alluded to. These passages are *literal* translations from L'Etoile,* a paper conducted, in general, with much ability.

"Mademoiselle Rogêt left her mother's house on Sunday morning, June the twenty-second, 18—, with the ostensible purpose of going to see her aunt, or some other connection, in the Rue des Drômes. From that hour, nobody is proved to have seen her. There is no trace or tidings of her at all. . . . There has no person, whatever, come forward, so far, who saw her at all, in that day, after she left her mother's door. . . . Now, though we have no evidence that Marie Rogêt was in the land of the living after nine o'clock on Sunday, June the twenty-second, we have proof that, up to that hour, she was alive. On Wednesday noon, at twelve, a female body was discovered afloat on the shore of the Barrière du Roule. This was, even if we presume that Marie Rogêt was thrown into the river within three hours after she left her mother's house, only three days from the time she left her home — three days to an hour. But it is folly to suppose that the murder, if murder was committed on her body, could have been consummated soon enough to have enabled her murderers to throw the body into the river before midnight. Those who are guilty of such horrid crimes choose darkness rather than light. . . . Thus we see that if the body found in the river *was* that of Marie Rogêt, it could only have been in the water two and a half days, or three at the outside. All experience has shown that drowned bodies, or bodies thrown into the water immediately after death by violence, require from six to ten days for sufficient decomposition to take place to bring them to the top of the water. Even where a cannon is fired over a corpse, and it rises before at least five or six days' immersion, it sinks again, if left alone. Now, we ask, what was there in this case to cause a departure from the ordinary course of nature? . . . If the body had been kept in its mangled state on shore until Tuesday night, some trace would be found in shore of the mur-

* The New York Brother Jonathan, edited by H. Hastings Weld, Esq.

derers. It is a doubtful point, also, whether the body would be so soon afloat, even were it thrown in after having been dead two days. And, furthermore, it is exceedingly improbable that any villains who had committed such a murder as is here supposed, would have thrown the body in without weight to sink it, when such a precaution could have so easily been taken."

The editor here proceeds to argue that the body must have been in the water "not three days merely, but, at least, five times three days," because it was so far decomposed that Beauvais had great difficulty in recognizing it. This latter point, however, was fully disproved. I continue the translation:

"What, then, are the facts on which M. Beauvais says that he had no doubt the body was that of Marie Rogêt? He ripped up the gown sleeve, and says he found marks which satisfied him of the identity. The public generally supposed those marks to have consisted of some description of scars. He rubbed the arm and found *hair* upon it — something as indefinite, we think, as can readily be imagined — as little conclusive as finding an arm in the sleeve. M. Beauvais did not return that night, but sent word to Madame Rogêt, at seven o'clock, on Wednesday evening, that an investigation was still in progress respecting her daughter. If we allow that Madame Rogêt, from her age and grief, could not go over (which is allowing a great deal), there certainly must have been some one who would have thought it worth while to go over and attend the investigation, if they thought the body was that of Marie. Nobody went over. There was nothing said or heard about the matter in the Rue Pavée St. Andrée, that reached even the occupants of the same building. M. St. Eustache, the lover and intended husband of Marie, who boarded in her mother's house, deposes that he did not hear of the discovery of the body of his intended until the next morning, when M. Beauvais came into his chamber and told him of it. For an item of news like this, it strikes us it was very coolly received."

In this way the journal endeavored to create the impression of an apathy on the part of the relatives of Marie, inconsistent with the supposition that these relatives believed the corpse to be hers. Its insinuations amount to this: — that Marie, with the connivance of her friends, had absented herself from the city for reasons involving a charge against her chastity; and that these friends upon the discovery of a corpse in the Seine, somewhat resembling that of the girl, had availed themselves of the opportunity to impress the public with the belief of her death. But L'Etoile was again overhasty. It was distinctly proved that no apathy, such as was imagined, existed; that the old lady was exceedingly feeble, and so agitated as to be unable to attend to any duty; that St. Eustache, so far from receiving the news coolly, was distracted with grief, and bore himself so frantically, that M. Beauvais prevailed upon a friend and relative to take charge of him, and prevent his attending the examination

at the disinterment. Moreover, although it was stated by L'Etoile, that
the corpse was re-interred at the public expense, — that an advantageous
offer of private sepulture was absolutely declined by the family, — and
that no member of the family attended the ceremonial: — although, I
say, all this was asserted by L'Etoile in furtherance of the impression it
designed to convey — yet *all* this was satisfactorily disproved. In a sub-
sequent number of the paper, an attempt was made to throw suspicion
upon Beauvais himself. The editor says:

"Now, then, a change comes over the matter. We are told that, on
one occasion, while a Madame B—— was at Madame Rogêt's house, M.
Beauvais, who was going out, told her that a *gendarme* was expected
there, and that she, Madame B., must not say any thing to the *gendarme*
until he returned, but let the matter be for him. . . . In the present pos-
ture of affairs, M. Beauvais appears to have the whole matter locked up
in his head. A single step cannot be taken without M. Beauvais, for, go
which way you will, you run against him. . . . For some reason he deter-
mined that nobody shall have anything to do with the proceedings but
himself, and he has elbowed the male relatives out of the way, accord-
ing to their representations, in a very singular manner. He seems
to have been very much averse to permitting the relatives to see the
body."

By the following fact, some color was given to the suspicion thus
thrown upon Beauvais. A visiter at his office, a few days prior to the
girl's disappearance, and during the absence of its occupant, had observed
a rose in the key-hole of the door, and the name "*Marie*" inscribed upon
a slate which hung near at hand.

The general impression, so far as we were enabled to glean it from the
newspapers, seemed to be, that Marie had been the victim of *a gang* of
desperadoes — that by these she had been borne across the river, mal-
treated, and murdered. Le Commerciel,* however, a print of extensive
influence, was earnest in combatting this popular idea. I quote a passage
or two from its columns:

"We are persuaded that pursuit has hitherto been on a false scent,
so far as it has been directed to the Barrière du Roule. It is impossible
that a person so well known to thousands as this young woman was,
should have passed three blocks without some one having seen her; and
any one who saw her would have remembered it, for she interested all
who knew her. It was when the streets were full of people, when she went
out. . . . It is impossible that she could have gone to the Barrière du
Roule, or to the Rue des Drômes, without being recognized by a dozen
persons; yet no one has come forward who saw her outside of her mother's
door, and there is no evidence, except the testimony concerning her *ex-
pressed intentions,* that she did go out at all. Her gown was torn, bound

* New York Journal of Commerce.

round her, and tied; and by that the body was carried as a bundle. If the murder had been committed at the Barrière du Roule, there would have been no necessity for any such arrangement. The fact that the body was found floating near the Barrière, is no proof as to where it was thrown into the water. . . . A piece of one of the unfortunate girl's petticoats, two feet long and one foot wide, was torn out and tied under her chin around the back of her head, probably to prevent screams. This was done by fellows who had no pocket-handkerchief."

A day or two before the Prefect called upon us, however, some important information reached the police, which seemed to overthrow, at least, the chief portion of Le Commerciel's argument. Two small boys, sons of a Madame Deluc, while roaming among the woods near the Barrière du Roule, chanced to penetrate a close thicket, within which were three or four large stones, forming a kind of seat with a back and footstool. On the upper stone lay a white petticoat; on the second, a silk scarf. A parasol, gloves, and a pocket-handkerchief were also here found. The handkerchief bore the name "Marie Roget." Fragments of dress were discovered on the brambles around. The earth was trampled, the bushes were broken, and there was every evidence of a struggle. Between the thicket and the river, the fences were found taken down, and the ground bore evidence of some heavy burthen having been dragged along it.

A weekly paper, Le Soleil,* had the following comments upon this discovery — comments which merely echoed the sentiment of the whole Parisian press:

"The things had all evidently been there at least three or four weeks; they were all mildewed down hard with the action of the rain, and stuck together from mildew. The grass had grown around and over some of them. The silk on the parasol was strong, but the threads of it were run together within. The upper part, where it had been doubled and folded, was all mildewed and rotten, and tore on its being opened. . . . The pieces of her frock torn out by the bushes were about three inches wide and six inches long. One part was the hem of the frock, and it had been mended; the other piece was part of the skirt, not the hem. They looked like strips torn off, and were on the thorn bush, about a foot from the ground. . . . There can be no doubt, therefore, that the spot of this appalling outrage has been discovered."

Consequent upon this discovery, new evidence appeared. Madame Deluc testified that she keeps a roadside inn not far from the bank of the river, opposite the Barrière du Roule. The neighborhood is secluded — particularly so. It is the usual Sunday resort of blackguards from the city, who cross the river in boats. About three o'clock, in the afternoon of the Sunday in question, a young girl arrived at the inn, accompanied by a young man of dark complexion. The two remained here for some

* Philadelphia Saturday Evening Post, edited by C. I. Peterson, Esq.

time. On their departure, they took the road to some thick woods in the
vicinity. Madame Deluc's attention was called to the dress worn by the
girl, on account of its resemblance to one worn by a deceased relative.
A scarf was particularly noticed. Soon after the departure of the couple,
a gang of miscreants made their appearance, behaved boisterously, ate
and drank without making payment, followed in the route of the young
man and girl, returned to the inn about dusk, and re-crossed the river as
if in great haste.

It was soon after dark, upon this same evening, that Madame Deluc,
as well as her eldest son, heard the screams of a female in the vicinity of
the inn. The screams were violent but brief. Madame D. recognized not
only the scarf which was found in the thicket, but the dress which was
discovered upon the corpse. An omnibus-driver, Valence,* now also tes-
tified that he saw Marie Rogêt cross a ferry on the Seine, on the Sunday
in question, in company with a young man of dark complexion. He,
Valence, knew Marie, and could not be mistaken in her identity. The
articles found in the thicket were fully identified by the relatives of Marie.

The items of evidence and information thus collected by myself, from
the newspapers, at the suggestion of Dupin, embraced only one more
point — but this was a point of seemingly vast consequence. It appears
that, immediately after the discovery of the clothes as above described,
the lifeless or nearly lifeless body of St. Eustache, Marie's betrothed, was
found in the vicinity of what all now supposed the scene of the outrage.
A phial labelled "laudanum," and emptied, was found near him. His
breath gave evidence of the poison. He died without speaking. Upon his
person was found a letter, briefly stating his love for Marie, with his
design of self-destruction.

"I need scarcely tell you," said Dupin, as he finished the perusal of
my notes, "that this is a far more intricate case than that of the Rue
Morgue; from which it differs in one important respect. This is an *ordi-
nary*, although an atrocious, instance of crime. There is nothing peculiarly
outré about it. You will observe that, for this reason, the mystery has been
considered easy, when, for this reason, it should have been considered
difficult, of solution. Thus, at first, it was thought unnecessary to offer a
reward. The myrmidons of G—— were able at once to comprehend how
and why such an atrocity *might have been* committed. They could pic-
ture to their imaginations a mode — many modes — and a motive —
many motives; and because it was not impossible that either of these
numerous modes or motives *could* have been the actual one, they have
taken it for granted that one of them *must*. But the ease with which these
variable fancies were entertained, and the very plausibility which each as-
sumed, should have been understood as indicative rather of the difficulties

* Adam.

than of the facilities which must attend elucidation. I have before observed that it is by prominences above the plane of the ordinary, that reason feels her way, if at all, in her search for the true, and that the proper question in cases such as this, is not so much 'what has occurred?' as 'what has occurred that has never occurred before?' In the investigations at the house of Madame L'Espanaye,* the agents of G—— were discouraged and confounded by that very *unusualness* which, to a properly regulated intellect, would have afforded the surest omen of success; while this same intellect might have been plunged in despair at the ordinary character of all that met the eye in the case of the perfumery-girl, and yet told of nothing but easy triumph to the functionaries of the Prefecture.

"In the case of Madame L'Espanaye and her daughter, there was, even at the begining of our investigation, no doubt that murder had been committed. The idea of suicide was excluded at once. Here, too, we are freed, at the commencement, from all supposition of self-murder. The body found at the Barrière du Roule was found under such circumstances as to leave us no room for embarrassment upon this important point. But it has been suggested that the corpse discovered is not that of the Marie Rogêt for the conviction of whose assassin, or assassins, the reward is offered, and respecting whom, solely, our agreement has been arranged with the Prefect. We both know this gentleman well. It will not do to trust him too far. If, dating our inquiries from the body found, and then tracing a murderer, we yet discover this body to be that of some other individual than Marie; or if, starting from the living Marie, we find her, yet find her unassassinated — in either case we lose our labor; since it is Monsieur G—— with whom we have to deal. For our own purpose, therefore, if not for the purpose of justice, it is indispensable that our first step should be the determination of the identity of the corpse with the Marie Rogêt who is missing.

"With the public the arguments of L'Etoile have had weight; and that the journal itself is convinced of their importance would appear from the manner in which it commences one of its essays upon the subject — 'Several of the morning papers of the day,' it says, 'speak of the *conclusive* article in Monday's Etoile.' To me, this article appears conclusive of little beyond the zeal of its inditer. We should bear in mind that, in general, it is the object of our newspapers rather to create a sensation — to make a point — than to further the cause of truth. The latter end is only pursued when it seems coincident with the former. The print which merely falls in with ordinary opinion (however well founded this opinion may be) earns for itself no credit with the mob. The mass of the people regard as profound only him who suggests *pungent contradictions*

* See "Murders in the Rue Morgue."

of the general idea. In ratiocination, not less than in literature, it is the *epigram* which is the most immediately and the most universally appreciated. In both, it is of the lowest order of merit.

"What I mean to say is, that it is the mingled epigram and melodrame of the idea, that Marie Rogêt still lives, rather than any true plausibility in this idea, which have suggested it to L'Etoile, and secured it a favorable reception with the public. Let us examine the heads of this journal's argument; endeavoring to avoid the incoherence with which it is originally set forth.

"The first aim of the writer is to show, from the brevity of the interval between Marie's disappearance and the finding of the floating corpse, that this corpse cannot be that of Marie. The reduction of this interval to its smallest possible dimension, becomes thus, at once, an object with the reasoner. In the rash pursuit of this object, he rushes into mere assumption at the outset. 'It is folly to suppose,' he says, 'that the murder, if murder was committed on her body, could have been consummated soon enough to have enabled her murderers to throw the body into the river before midnight.' We demand at once, and very naturally, *why?* Why is it folly to suppose that the murder was committed *within five minutes* after the girl's quitting her mother's house? Why is it folly to suppose that the murder was committed at any given period of the day? There have been assassinations at all hours. But, had the murder taken place at any moment between nine o'clock in the morning of Sunday and a quarter before midnight, there would still have been time enough 'to throw the body into the river before midnight.' This assumption, then, amounts precisely to this — that the murder was not committed on Sunday at all — and, if we allow L'Etoile to assume this, we may permit it any liberties whatever. The paragraph beginning 'It is folly to suppose that the murder, etc.,' however it appears as printed in L'Etoile, may be imagined to have existed actually *thus* in the brain of its inditer: 'It is folly to suppose that the murder, if murder was committed on the body, could have been committed soon enough to have enabled her murderers to throw the body into the river before midnight; it is folly, we say, to suppose all this, and to suppose at the same time, (as we are resolved to suppose), that the body was *not* thrown in until *after* midnight' — a sentence sufficiently inconsequential in itself, but not so utterly preposterous as the one printed.

"Were it my purpose," continued Dupin, "merely to *make out a case* against this passage of L'Etoile's argument, I might safely leave it where it is. It is not, however, with L'Etoile that we have to do, but with truth. The sentence in question has but one meaning, as it stands; and this meaning I have fairly stated; but it is material that we go behind the mere words, for an idea which these words have obviously intended, and failed to convey. It was the design of the journalists to say that at whatever period of the day or night of Sunday this murder was committed, it

was improbable that the assassins would have ventured to bear the corpse to the river before midnight. And herein lies, really, the assumption of which I complain. It is assumed that the murder was committed at such a position, and under such circumstances, that *the bearing it* to the river became necessary. Now, the assassination might have taken place upon the river's brink, or on the river itself; and, thus, the throwing the corpse in the water might have been resorted to at any period of the day or night, as the most obvious and most immediate mode of disposal. You will understand that I suggest nothing here as probable, or as coincident with my own opinion. My design, so far, has no reference to the *facts* of the case. I wish merely to caution you against the whole tone of L'Etoile's *suggestion*, by calling your attention to its *ex-parte* character at the outset.

"Having prescribed thus a limit to suit its own preconceived notions; having assumed that, if this were the body of Marie, it could have been in the water but a very brief time, the journal goes on to say:

All experience has shown that drowned bodies, or bodies thrown into the water immediately after death by violence, require from six to ten days for sufficient decomposition to take place to bring them to the top of the water. Even when a cannon is fired over a corpse, and it rises before at least five or six days' immersion, it sinks again if let alone.

"These assertions have been tacitly received by every paper in Paris, with the exception of Le Moniteur.* This latter print endeavors to combat that portion of the paragraph which has reference to 'drowned bodies' only, by citing some five or six instances in which the bodies of individuals known to be drowned were found floating after the lapse of less time than is insisted upon by L'Etoile. But there is something excessively unphilosophical in the attempt, on the part of Le Moniteur, to rebut the general assertion of L'Etoile, by a citation of particular instances militating against that assertion. Had it been possible to adduce fifty instead of five examples of bodies found floating at the end of two or three days, these fifty examples could still have been properly regarded only as exceptions to L'Etoile's rule, until such time as the rule itself should be confuted. Admitting the rule, (and this Le Moniteur does not deny, insisting merely upon its exceptions,) the argument of L'Etoile is suffered to remain in full force; for this argument does not pretend to involve more than a question of the *probability* of the body having risen to the surface in less than three days; and this probability will be in favor of L'Etoile's position until the instances so childishly adduced shall be sufficient in number to establish an antagonistical rule.

"You will see at once that all argument upon this head should be urged, if at all, against the rule itself; and for this end we must examine

* The New York Commercial Advertiser, edited by Col. Stone.

the *rationale* of the rule. Now the human body, in general, is neither much lighter nor much heavier than the water of the Seine; that is to say, the specific gravity of the human body, in its natural condition, is about equal to the bulk of fresh water which it displaces. The bodies of fat and fleshy persons, with small bones, and of women generally, are lighter than those of the lean and large-boned, and of men; and the specific gravity of the water of a river is somewhat influenced by the presence of the tide from the sea. But, leaving this tide out of the question, it may be said that *very* few human bodies will sink at all, even in fresh water, *of their own accord*. Almost any one, falling into a river, will be enabled to float, if he suffer the specific gravity of the water fairly to be adduced in comparison with his own — that is to say, if he suffer his whole person to be immersed, with as little exception as possible. The proper position for one who cannot swim, is the upright position of the walker on land, with the head thrown fully back, and immersed; the mouth and nostrils alone remaining above the surface. Thus circumstanced, we shall find that we float without difficulty and without exertion. It is evident, however, that the gravities of the body, and of the bulk of water displaced, are very nicely balanced, and that a trifle will cause either to preponderate. An arm, for instance, uplifted from the water, and thus deprived of its support, is an additional weight sufficient to immerse the whole head, while the accidental aid of the smallest piece of timber will enable us to elevate the head so as to look about. Now, in the struggles of one unused to swimming, the arms are invariably thrown upward, while an attempt is made to keep the head in its usual perpendicular position. The result is the immersion of the mouth and nostrils, and the inception, during efforts to breathe while beneath the surface, of water into the lungs. Much is also received into the stomach, and the whole body becomes heavier by the difference between the weight of the air originally distending these cavities, and that of the fluid which now fills them. This difference is sufficient to cause the body to sink, as a general rule; but is insufficient in the case of individuals with small bones and an abnormal quantity of flaccid or fatty matter. Such individuals float even after drowning.

"The corpse, being supposed at the bottom of the river, will there remain until, by some means, its specific gravity again becomes less than that of the bulk of water which it displaces. This effect is brought about by decomposition, or otherwise. The result of decomposition is the generation of gas, distending the cellular tissues and all the cavities, and giving the *puffed* appearance which is so horrible. When this distension has so far progressed that the bulk of the corpse is materially increased without a corresponding increase of *mass* or weight, its specific gravity becomes less than that of the water displaced, and it forthwith makes its appearance at the surface. But decomposition is modified by innumerable circumstances — is hastened or retarded by innumerable agencies; for example, by the heat or cold of the season, by the mineral

impregnation or purity of the water, by its depth or shallowness, by its currency or stagnation, by the temperament of the body, by its infection or freedom from disease before death. Thus it is evident that we can assign no period, with anything like accuracy, at which the corpse shall rise through decomposition. Under certain conditions this result would be brought about within an hour; under others it might not take place at all. There are chemical infusions by which the animal frame can be preserved *forever* from corruption; the Bi-chloride of Mercury is one. But, apart from decomposition, there may be, and very usually is, a generation of gas within the stomach, from the acetous fermentation of vegetable matter (or within other cavities from other causes), sufficient to induce a distension which will bring the body to the surface. The effect produced by the firing of a cannon is that of simple vibration. This may either loosen the corpse from the soft mud or ooze in which it is imbedded, thus permitting it to rise when other agencies have already prepared it for so doing; or it may overcome the tenacity of some putrescent portions of the cellular tissue, allowing the cavities to distend under the influence of the gas.

"Having thus before us the whole philosophy of this subject, we can easily test by it the assertions of L'Etoile. 'All experience shows,' says this paper, 'that drowned bodies, or bodies thrown into the water immediately after death by violence, require from six to ten days for sufficient decomposition to take place to bring them to the top of the water. Even when a cannon is fired over a corpse, and it rises before at least five or six days' immersion, it sinks again if let alone.'

"The whole of this paragraph must now appear a tissue of inconsequence and incoherence. All experience does *not* show that 'drowned bodies' *require* from six to ten days for sufficient decomposition to take place to bring them to the surface. Both science and experience show that the period of their rising is, and necessarily must be, indeterminate. If, moreover, a body has risen to the surface through firing of cannon, it will *not* 'sink again if let alone,' until decomposition has so far progressed as to permit the escape of the generated gas. But I wish to call your attention to the distinction which is made between 'drowned bodies,' and 'bodies thrown into the water immediately after death by violence.' Although the writer admits the distinction, he yet includes them all in the same category. I have shown how it is that the body of a drowning man becomes specifically heavier than its bulk of water, and that he would not sink at all, except for the struggle by which he elevates his arms above the surface, and his gasps for breath while beneath the surface — gasps which supply by water the place of the original air in the lungs. But these struggles and these gasps would not occur in the body 'thrown into the water immediately after death by violence.' Thus, in the latter instance, *the body, as a general rule, would not sink at all* — a fact of which L'Etoile is evidently ignorant. When decomposition had pro-

ceeded to a very great extent — when the flesh had in a great measure left the bones — then, indeed, but not *till* then, should we lose sight of the corpse.

"And now what are we to make of the argument, that the body found could not be that of Marie Rogêt, because, three days only having elapsed, this body was found floating? If drowned, being a woman, she might never have sunk; or, having sunk, might have reappeared in twenty-four hours or less. But no one supposes her to have been drowned; and, dying before being thrown into the river, she might have been found floating at any period afterwards whatever.

" 'But,' says L'Etoile, 'if the body had been kept in its mangled state on shore until Tuesday night, some trace would be found on shore of the murderers.' Here it is at first difficult to perceive the intention of the reasoner. He means to anticipate what he imagines would be an objection to his theory — viz.: that the body was kept on shore two days, suffering rapid decomposition — *more* rapid than if immersed in water. He supposes that, had this been the case, it *might* have appeared at the surface on the Wednesday, and thinks that *only* under such circumstances it could so have appeared. He is accordingly in haste to show that it *was not* kept on shore; for, if so, 'some trace would be found on shore of the murderers.' I presume you smile at the *sequitur*. You cannot be made to see how the mere *duration* of the corpse on the shore could operate to *multiply traces* of the assassins. Nor can I.

" 'And furthermore it is exceedingly improbable," continues our journal, 'that any villains who had committed such a murder as is here supposed, would have thrown the body in without weight to sink it, when such a precaution could have so easily been taken.' Observe, here, the laughable confusion of thought! No one — not even L'Etoile — disputes the murder committed *on the body found*. The marks of violence are too obvious. It is our reasoner's object merely to show that this body is not Marie's. He wishes to prove that *Marie* is not assassinated — not that the corpse was not. Yet his observation proves only the latter point. Here is a corpse without weight attached. Murderers, casting it in, would not have failed to attach a weight. Therefore it was not thrown in by murderers. This is all which is proved, if any thing is. The question of identity is not even approached, and L'Etoile has been at great pains merely to gainsay now what it has admitted only a moment before. 'We are perfectly convinced,' it says, 'that the body found was that of a murdered female.'

"Nor is this the sole instance, even in this division of the subject, where our reasoner unwittingly reasons against himself. His evident object, I have already said, is to reduce, as much as possible, the interval between Marie's disappearance and the finding of the corpse. Yet we find him *urging* the point that no person saw the girl from the moment of her leaving her mother's house. 'We have no evidence,' he says, 'that Marie

Rogêt was in the land of the living after nine o'clock on Sunday, June the twenty-second.' As his argument is obviously an *ex-parte* one, he should, at least, have left this matter out of sight; for had any one been known to see Marie, say on Monday, or on Tuesday, the interval in question would have been much reduced, and, by his own ratiocination, the probability much diminished of the corpse being that of the *grisette*. It is, nevertheless, amusing to observe that L'Etoile insists upon its point in the full belief of its furthering its general argument.

"Reperuse now that portion of this argument which has reference to the identification of the corpse by Beauvais. In regard to the *hair* upon the arm, L'Etoile has been obviously disingenuous. M. Beauvais, not being an idiot, could never have urged in identification of the corpse, simply *hair upon its arm*. No arm is *without* hair. The *generality* of the expression of L'Etoile is a mere perversion of the witness' phraseology. He must have spoken of some *peculiarity* in this hair. It must have been a peculiarity of color, of quantity, of length, or of situation.

" 'Her foot,' says the journal, 'was small — so are thousands of feet. Her garter is no proof whatever — nor is her shoe — for shoes and garters are sold in packages. The same may be said of the flowers in her hat. One thing upon which M. Beauvais strongly insists is, that the clasp on the garter found had been set back to take it in. This amounts to nothing; for most women find it proper to take a pair of garters home and ,fit them to the size of the limbs they are to encircle, rather than to try them in the store where they purchase.' Here it is difficult to suppose the reasoner in earnest. Had M. Beauvais, in his search for the body of Marie, discovered a corpse corresponding in general size and appearance to the missing girl, he would have been warranted (without reference to the question of habiliment at all) in forming an opinion that his search had been successful. If, in addition to the point of general size and contour, he had found upon the arm a peculiar hairy appearance which he had observed upon the living Marie, his opinion might have been justly strengthened; and the increase of positiveness might well have been in the ratio of the peculiarity, or unusualness, of the hairy mark. If, the feet of Marie being small, those of the corpse were also small, the increase of probability that the body was that of Marie would not be an increase in a ratio merely arithmetical, but in one highly geometrical, or accumulative. Add to all this shoes such as she had been known to wear upon the day of her disappearance, and, although these shoes may be 'sold in packages,' you so far augment the probability as to verge upon the certain. What, of itself, would be no evidence of identity, becomes through its corroborative position, proof most sure. Give us, then, flowers in the hat corresponding to those worn by the missing girl, and we seek for nothing farther. If only *one* flower, we seek for nothing farther — what then if two or three, or more? Each successive one is multiple evidence — proof not *added* to proof, but *multiplied*

by hundreds or thousands. Let us now discover, upon the deceased, garters such as the living used, and it is almost folly to proceed. But these garters are found to be tightened, by the setting back of a clasp, in just such a manner as her own had been tightened by Marie shortly previous to her leaving home. It is now madness or hypocrisy to doubt. What L'Etoile says in respect to this abbreviation of the garter's being an unusual occurrence, shows nothing beyond its own pertinacity in error. The elastic nature of the clasp-garter is self-demonstration of the *unusualness* of the abbreviation. What is made to adjust itself, must of necessity require foreign adjustment but rarely. It must have been by an accident, in its strictest sense, that these garters of Marie needed the tightening described. They alone would have amply established her identity. But it is not that the corpse was found to have the garters of the missing girl, or found to have her shoes, or her bonnet, or the flowers of her bonnet, or her feet, or a peculiar mark upon the arm, or her general size and appearance — it is that the corpse had each and *all collectively*. Could it be proved that the editor of L'Etoile *really* entertained a doubt, under the circumstances, there would be no need, in his case, of a commission *de lunatico inquirendo*. He has thought it sagacious to echo the small talk of the lawyers, who, for the most part, content themselves with echoing the rectangular precepts of the courts. I would here observe that very much of what is rejected as evidence by a court, is the best of evidence to the intellect. For the court, guiding itself by the general principles of evidence — the recognized and *booked* principles — is averse from swerving at particular instances. And this steadfast adherence to principle, with rigorous disregard of the conflicting exception, is a sure mode of attaining the *maximum* of attainable truth, in any long sequence of time. The practice, *in mass*, is therefore philosophical; but it is not the less certain that it engenders vast individual error.*

"In respect to the insinuations levelled at Beauvais, you will be willing to dismiss them in a breath. You have already fathomed the true character of this good gentleman. He is a *busy-body*, with much of romance and little of wit. Any one so constituted will readily so conduct himself, upon occasion of *real* excitement, as to render himself liable to suspicion on the part of the over-acute, or the ill-disposed. M. Beauvais (as it appears from your notes) had some personal interviews with the editor of L'Etoile, and offended him by venturing an opinion that the corpse, notwithstanding the theory of the editor, was, in sober fact, that

* "A theory based on the qualities of an object, will prevent its being unfolded according to its objects; and he who arranges topics in reference to their causes, will cease to value them according to their results. Thus the jurisprudence of every nation will show that, when law becomes a science and a system, it ceases to be justice. The errors into which a blind devotion to *principles* of classification has led the common law, will be seen by observing how often the legislature has been obliged to come forward to restore the equity its scheme had lost." — *Landor*.

of Marie. 'He persists,' says the paper, 'in asserting the corpse to be that of Marie, but cannot give a circumstance, in addition to those which we have commented upon, to make others believe.' Now, without re-adverting to the fact that stronger evidence 'to make others believe,' could *never* have been adduced, it may be remarked that a man may very well be understood to believe, in a case of this kind, without the ability to advance a single reason for the belief of a second party. Nothing is more vague than impressions of individual identity. Each man recognizes his neighbor, yet there are few instances in which any one is prepared *to give a reason* for his recognition. The editor of L'Etoile had no right to be offended at M. Beauvais' unreasoning belief.

"The suspicious circumstances which invest him, will be found to tally much better with my hypothesis of *romantic busy-bodyism*, than with the reasoner's suggestion of guilt. Once adopting the more charitable interpretation, we shall find no difficulty in comprehending the rose in the key-hole; the 'Marie' upon the slate; the 'elbowing the male relatives out of the way'; the 'aversion to permitting them to see the body'; the caution given to Madame B——, that she must hold no conversation with the *gendarme* until his return (Beauvais'); and, lastly, his apparent determination 'that nobody should have any thing to do with the proceedings except himself.' It seems to be unquestionable that Beauvais was a suitor of Marie's; that she coquetted with him; and that he was ambitious of being thought to enjoy her fullest intimacy and confidence. I shall say nothing more upon this point; and, as the evidence fully rebuts the assertion of L'Etoile, touching the matter of *apathy* on the part of the mother and other relatives — an apathy inconsistent with the supposition of their believing the corpse to be that of the perfumery-girl — we shall now proceed as if the question of *identity* were settled to our perfect satisfaction."

"And what," I here demanded, "do you think of the opinions of Le Commerciel?"

"That, in spirit, they are far more worthy of attention than any which have been promulgated upon the subject. The deductions from the premises are philosophical and acute; but the premises, in two instances, at least, are founded in imperfect observation. Le Commerciel wishes to intimate that Marie was seized by some gang of low ruffians not far from her mother's door. 'It is impossible,' it urges, 'that a person so well known to thousands as this young woman was, should have passed three blocks without some one having seen her.' This is the idea of a man long resident in Paris — a public man — and one whose walks to and fro in the city have been mostly limited to the vicinity of the public offices. He is aware that he seldom passes so far as a dozen blocks from his own *bureau*, without being recognized and accosted. And, knowing the extent of his personal acquaintance with others, and of others with him, he compares his notoriety with that of the perfumery-

girl, finds no great difference between them, and reaches at once the conclusion that she, in her walks, would be equally liable to recognition with himself in his. This could only be the case were her walks of the same unvarying, methodical character, and within the same *species* of limited region as are his own. He passes to and fro, at regular intervals, within a confined periphery, abounding in individuals who are led to observation of his person through interest in the kindred nature of his occupation with their own. But the walks of Marie may, in general, be supposed discursive. In this particular instance, it will be understood as most probable, that she proceeded upon a route of more than average diversity from her accustomed ones. The parallel which we imagine to have existed in the mind of Le Commerciel would only be sustained in the event of the two individuals traversing the whole city. In this case, granting the personal acquaintances to be equal, the chances would be also equal that an equal number of personal rencounters would be made. For my own part, I should hold it not only as possible, but as very far more probable, that Marie might have proceeded, at any given period, by any one of the many routes between her own residence and that of her aunt, without meeting a single individual whom she knew, or by whom she was known. In viewing this question in its full and proper light, we must hold steadily in mind the great disproportion between the personal acquaintances of even the most noted individual in Paris, and the entire population of Paris itself.

"But whatever force there may still appear to be in the suggestion of Le Commerciel, will be much diminished when we take into consideration *the hour* at which the girl went abroad. 'It was when the streets were full of people,' says Le Commerciel, 'that she went out.' But not so. It was at nine o'clock in the morning. Now at nine o'clock of every morning in the week, *with the exception of Sunday*, the streets of the city are, it is true, thronged with people. At nine on Sunday, the populace are chiefly within doors *preparing for church*. No observing person can have failed to notice the peculiarly deserted air of the town, from about eight until ten on the morning of every Sabbath. Between ten and eleven the streets are thronged, but not at so early a period as that designated.

"There is another point at which there seems a deficiency of *observation* on the part of Le Commerciel. 'A piece,' it says, 'of one of the unfortunate girl's petticoats, two feet long, and one foot wide, was torn out and tied under her chin, and around the back of her head, probably to prevent screams. This was done by fellows who had no pocket-handkerchiefs.' Whether this idea is or is not well founded, we will endeavor to see hereafter; but by 'fellows who have no pocket-handkerchiefs,' the editor intends the lowest class of ruffians. These, however, are the very description of people who will always be found to have handkerchiefs even when destitute of shirts. You must have had occasion

to observe how absolutely indispensable, of late years, to the thorough blackguard, has become the pocket-handkerchief."

"And what are we to think," I asked, "of the article in Le Soleil?"

"That it is a vast pity its inditer was not born a parrot — in which case he would have been the most illustrious parrot of his race. He has merely repeated the individual items of the already published opinion; collecting them, with a laudable industry, from this paper and from that. 'The things had all *evidently* been there,' he says, 'at least three or four weeks, and there can be *no doubt* that the spot of this appalling outrage has been discovered.' The facts here re-stated by Le Soleil, are very far indeed from removing my own doubts upon this subject, and we will examine them more particularly hereafter in connection with another division of the theme.

"At present we must occupy ourselves with other investigations. You cannot fail to have remarked the extreme laxity of the examination of the corpse. To be sure, the question of identity was readily determined, or should have been; but there were other points to be ascertained. Had the body been in any respect *despoiled*? Had the deceased any articles of jewelry about her person upon leaving home? If so, had she any when found? These are important questions utterly untouched by the evidence; and there are others of equal moment, which have met with no attention. We must endeavor to satisfy ourselves by personal inquiry. The case of St. Eustache must be re-examined. I have no suspicion of this person; but let us proceed methodically. We will ascertain beyond a doubt the validity of the *affidavits* in regard to his whereabouts on the Sunday. Affidavits of this character are readily made matter of mystification. Should there be nothing wrong here, however, we will dismiss St. Eustache from our investigations. His suicide, however, corroborative of suspicion, were there found to be deceit in the affidavits, is, without such deceit, in no respect an unaccountable circumstance, or one which need cause us to deflect from the line of ordinary analysis.

"In that which I now propose, we will discard the interior points of this tragedy, and concentrate our attention upon its outskirts. Not the least usual error in investigations such as this is the limiting of inquiry to the immediate, with total disregard of the collateral or circumstantial events. It is the malpractice of the courts to confine evidence and discussion to the bounds of apparent relevancy. Yet experience has shown, and a true philosophy will always show, that a vast, perhaps the larger, portion of truth arises from the seemingly irrelevant. It is through the spirit of this principle, if not precisely through its letter, that modern science has resolved to *calculate upon the unforeseen*. But perhaps you do not comprehend me. The history of human knowledge has so uninterruptedly shown that to collateral, or incidental, or accidental events we are indebted for the most numerous and most valuable discoveries, that it has at length become necessary, in any prospective view of im-

provement, to make not only large, but the largest, allowances for inventions that shall arise by chance, and quite out of the range of ordinary expectation. It is no longer philosophical to base upon what has been a vision of what is to be. *Accident* is admitted as a portion of the substructure. We make chance a matter of absolute calculation. We subject the unlooked for and unimagined to the mathematical *formulæ* of the schools.

"I repeat that it is no more than fact that the *larger* portion of all truth has sprung from the collateral; and it is but in accordance with the spirit of the principle involved in this fact that I would divert inquiry, in the present case, from the trodden and hitherto unfruitful ground of the event itself to the contemporary circumstances which surround it. While you ascertain the validity of the affidavits, I will examine the newspapers more generally than you have as yet done. So far, we have only reconnoitred the field of investigation; but it will be strange, indeed, if a comprehensive survey, such as I propose, of the public prints will not afford us some minute points which shall establish a *direction* for inquiry."

In pursuance of Dupin's suggestion, I made scrupulous examination of the affair of the affidavits. The result was a firm conviction of their validity, and of the consequent innocence of St. Eustache. In the meantime my friend occupied himself, with what seemed to me a minuteness altogether objectless, in a scrutiny of the various newspaper files. At the end of a week he placed before me the following extracts:

"About three years and a half ago, a disturbance very similar to the present was caused by the disappearance of this same Marie Rogêt from the *parfumerie* of Monsieur Le Blanc, in the Palais Royal. At the end of a week, however, she re-appeared at her customary *comptoir*, as well as ever, with the exception of a slight paleness not altogether usual. It was given out by Monsieur Le Blanc and her mother that she had merely been on a visit to some friend in the country; and the affair was speedily hushed up. We presume that the present absence is a freak of the same nature, and that, at the expiration of a week or, perhaps, of a month, we shall have her among us again." — *Evening Paper*, Monday, June 23.*

"An evening journal of yesterday refers to a former mysterious disappearance of Mademoiselle Rogêt. It is well known that, during the week of her absence from Le Blanc's *parfumerie*, she was in the company of a young naval officer much noted for his debaucheries. A quarrel, it is supposed, providentially, led to her return home. We have the name of the Lothario in question, who is at present stationed in Paris, but for obvious reasons forbear to make it public." — *Le Mercure*, Tuesday Morning, June 24.†

"An outrage of the most atrocious character was perpetrated near this

* New York Express. † New York Herald.

city the day before yesterday. A gentleman, with his wife and daughter, engaged, about dusk, the services of six young men, who were idly rowing a boat to and fro near the banks of the Seine, to convey him across the river. Upon reaching the opposite shore the three passengers stepped out, and had proceeded so far as to be beyond the view of the boat, when the daughter discovered that she had left in it her parasol. She returned for it, was seized by the gang, carried out into the stream, gagged, brutally treated, and finally taken to the shore at a point not far from that at which she had originally entered the boat with her parents. The villains have escaped for the time, but the police are upon their trail, and some of them will soon be taken." — *Morning Paper*, June 25.*

"We have received one or two communications, the object of which is to fasten the crime of the late atrocity upon Mennais; † but as this gentleman has been fully exonerated by a legal inquiry, and as the arguments of our several correspondents appear to be more zealous than profound, we do not think it advisable to make them public." — *Morning Paper*, June 28.‡

"We have received several forcibly written communications, apparently from various sources, and which go far to render it a matter of certainty that the unfortunate Marie Roget has become a victim of one of the numerous bands of blackguards which infest the vicinity of the city upon Sunday. Our own opinion is decidedly in favor of this supposition. We shall endeavor to make room for some of these arguments hereafter." — *Evening Paper*, Tuesday, June 31.§

"On Monday, one of the bargemen connected with the revenue service saw an empty boat floating down the Seine. Sails were lying in the bottom of the boat. The bargeman towed it under the barge office. The next morning it was taken from thence without the knowledge of any of the officers. The rudder is now at the barge office." — *Le Diligence*, Thursday, June 26.||

Upon reading these various extracts, they not only seemed to me irrelevant, but I could perceive no mode in which any one of them could be brought to bear upon the matter in hand. I waited for some explanation from Dupin.

"It is not my present design," he said, "to *dwell* upon the first and second of these extracts. I have copied them chiefly to show you the extreme remissness of the police, who, as far as I can understand from the Prefect, have not troubled themselves, in any respect, with an examination of the naval officer alluded to. Yet it is mere folly to say that between the first and second disappearance of Marie there is no *supposable* connection. Let us admit the first elopement to have resulted

* New York Courier and Inquirer.

† Mennais was one of the parties originally suspected and arrested, but discharged through total lack of evidence.

‡ New York Courier and Inquirer.

§ New York Evening Post.

|| New York Standard.

in a quarrel between the lovers, and the return home of the betrayed. We are now prepared to view a second *elopement* (if we *know* that an elopement has again taken place) as indicating a renewal of the betrayer's advances, rather than as the result of new proposals by a second individual — we are prepared to regard it as a 'making up' of the old *amour*, rather than as the commencement of a new one. The chances are ten to one, that he who had once eloped with Marie would again propose an elopement, rather than that she to whom proposals of an elopement had been made by one individual, should have them made to her by another. And here let me call your attention to the fact, that the time elapsing between the first ascertained and the second supposed elopement is a few months more than the general period of the cruises of our men-of-war. Had the lover been interrupted in his first villainy by the necessity of departure to sea, and had he seized the first moment of his return to renew the base designs not yet altogether accomplished — or not yet altogether accomplished *by him?* Of all these things we know nothing.

"You will say, however, that, in the second instance, there was *no* elopement as imagined. Certainly not — but are we prepared to say that there was not the frustrated design? Beyond St. Eustache, and perhaps Beauvais, we find no recognized, no open, no honorable suitors of Marie. Of none other is there any thing said. Who, then, is the secret lover, of whom the relatives (*at least most of them*) know nothing, but whom Marie meets upon the morning of Sunday, and who is so deeply in her confidence, that she hesitates not to remain with him until the shades of the evening descend, amid the solitary groves of the Barrière du Roule? Who is that secret lover, I ask, of whom, at least, *most* of the relatives know nothing? And what means the singular prophecy of Madam Rogêt on the morning of Marie's departure? — 'I fear that I shall never see Marie again.'

"But if we cannot imagine Madame Rogêt privy to the design of elopement, may we not at least suppose this design entertained by the girl? Upon quitting home, she gave it to be understood that she was about to visit her aunt in the Rue des Drômes, and St. Eustache was requested to call for her at dark. Now, at first glance, this fact strongly militates against my suggestion; — but let us reflect. That she *did* meet some companion, and proceed with him across the river, reaching the Barrière du Roule at so late an hour as three o'clock in the afternoon, is known. But in consenting so to accompany this individual, (*for whatever purpose — to her mother known or unknown,*) she must have thought of her expressed intention when leaving home, and of the surprise and suspicion aroused in the bosom of her affianced suitor, St. Eustache, when, calling for her, at the hour appointed, in the Rue des Drômes, he should find that she had not been there, and when, moreover, upon returning to the *pension* with this alarming intelligence, he

should become aware of her continued absence from home. She must have thought of these things, I say. She must have foreseen the chagrin of St. Eustache, the suspicion of all. She could not have thought of returning to brave this suspicion; but the suspicion becomes a point of trivial importance to her, if we suppose her *not* intending to return.

"We may imagine her thinking thus — 'I am to meet a certain person for the purpose of elopement, or for certain other purposes known only to myself. It is necessary that there be no chance of interruption — there must be sufficient time given us to elude pursuit — I will give it to be understood that I shall visit and spend the day with my aunt at the Rue des Drômes — I will tell St. Eustache not to call for me until dark — in this way, my absence from home for the longest possible period, without causing suspicion or anxiety, will be accounted for, and I shall gain more time than in any other manner. If I bid St. Eustache call for me at dark, he will be sure not to call before; but if I wholly neglect to bid him call, my time for escape will be diminished, since it will be expected that I return the earlier, and my absence will the sooner excite anxiety. Now, if it were my design to return *at all* — if I had in contemplation merely a stroll with the individual in question — it would not be my policy to bid St. Eustache call; for, calling, he will be *sure* to ascertain that I have played him false — a fact of which I might keep him forever in ignorance, by leaving home without notifying him of my intention, by returning before dark, and by then stating that I had been to visit my aunt in the Rue des Drômes. But, as it is my design *never* to return — or not for some weeks — or not until certain concealments are effected — the gaining of time is the only point about which I need give myself any concern.'

"You have observed, in your notes, that the most general opinion in relation to this sad affair is, and was from the first, that the girl had been the victim of *a gang* of blackguards. Now, the popular opinion, under certain conditions, is not to be disregarded. When arising of itself — when manifesting itself in a strictly spontaneous manner — we should look upon it as analogous with that *intuition* which is the idiosyncrasy of the individual man of genius. In ninety-nine cases from the hundred I would abide by its decision. But it is important that we find no palpable traces of *suggestion*. The opinion must be rigorously *the public's own*; and the distinction is often exceedingly difficult to perceive and to maintain. In the present instance, it appears to me that this 'public opinion,' in respect to *a gang*, has been superinduced by the collateral event which is detailed in the third of my extracts. All Paris is excited by the discovered corpse of Marie, a girl young, beautiful, and notorious. This corpse is found, bearing marks of violence, and floating in the river. But it is now made known that, at the very period, or about the very period, in which it is supposed that the girl was assassinated, an outrage similar in nature to that endured by the deceased, although less in extent, was

perpetrated by a gang of young ruffians, upon the person of a second young female. Is it wonderful that the one known atrocity should influence the popular judgment in regard to the other unknown? This judgment awaited direction, and the known outrage seemed so opportunely to afford it! Marie, too, was found in the river; and upon this very river was this known outrage committed. The connection of the two events had about it so much of the palpable, that the true wonder would have been a *failure* of the populace to appreciate and to seize it. But, in fact, the one atrocity, known to be so committed, is, if any thing, evidence that the other, committed at a time nearly coincident, was *not* so committed. It would have been a miracle indeed, if, while a gang of ruffians were perpetrating, at a given locality, a most unheard-of wrong, there should have been another similar gang, in a similar locality, in the same city, under the same circumstances, with the same means and appliances, engaged in a wrong of precisely the same aspect, at precisely the same period of time! Yet in what, if not in this marvellous train of coincidence, does the accidentally *suggested* opinion of the populace call upon us to believe?

"Before proceeding farther, let us consider the supposed scene of the assassination, in the thicket at the Barrière du Roule. This thicket, although dense, was in the close vicinity of a public road. Within were three or four large stones, forming a kind of seat with a back and a footstool. On the upper stone was discovered a white petticoat; on the second, a silk scarf. A parasol, gloves, and a pocket-handkerchief were also here found. The handkerchief bore the name 'Marie Rogêt.' Fragments of dress were seen on the branches around. The earth was trampled, the bushes were broken, and there was every evidence of a violent struggle.

"Notwithstanding the acclamation with which the discovery of this thicket was received by the press, and the unanimity with which it was supposed to indicate the precise scene of the outrage, it must be admitted that there was some very good reason for doubt. That it *was* the scene, I may or I may not believe — but there was excellent reason for doubt. Had the *true* scene been, as Le Commerciel suggested, in the neighborhood of the Rue Pavée St. Andrée, the perpetrators of the crime, supposing them still resident in Paris, would naturally have been stricken with terror at the public attention thus acutely directed into the proper channel; and, in certain classes of minds, there would have arisen, at once, a sense of the necessity of some exertion to re-divert this attention. And thus, the thicket of the Barrière du Roule having been already suspected, the idea of placing the articles where they were found, might have been naturally entertained. There is no real evidence, although Le Soleil so supposes, that the articles discovered had been more than a very few days in the thicket; while there is much circumstantial proof that they could not have remained there, without attracting atten-

tion, during the twenty days elapsing between the fatal Sunday and the afternoon upon which they were found by the boys. 'They were all *mildewed* down hard,' says Le Soleil, adopting the opinions of its predecessors, 'with the action of the rain and stuck together from *mildew*. The grass had grown around and over some of them. The silk of the parasol was strong, but the threads of it were run together within. The upper part, where it had been doubled and folded, was all *mildewed* and rotten, and tore on being opened.' In respect to the grass having 'grown around and over some of them,' it is obvious that the fact could only have been ascertained from the words, and thus from the recollections, of two small boys; for these boys removed the articles and took them home before they had been seen by a third party. But the grass will grow, especially in warm and damp weather (such as was that of the period of the murder), as much as two or three inches in a single day. A parasol lying upon a newly turfed ground, might, in a single week, be entirely concealed from sight by the upspringing grass. And touching that *mildew* upon which the editor of Le Soleil so pertinaciously insists, that he employs the word no less than three times in the brief paragraph just quoted, is he really unaware of the nature of this *mildew?* Is he to be told that it is one of the many classes of *fungus*, of which the most ordinary feature is its upspringing and decadence within twenty-four hours?

"Thus we see, at a glance, that what has been most triumphantly adduced in support of the idea that the articles had been 'for at least three or four weeks' in the thicket, is most absurdly null as regards any evidence of that fact. On the other hand, it is exceedingly difficult to believe that these articles could have remained in the thicket specified for a longer period than a single week — for a longer period than from one Sunday to the next. Those who know any thing of the vicinity of Paris, know the extreme difficulty of finding *seclusion*, unless at a great distance from its suburbs. Such a thing as an unexplored or even an unfrequently visited recess, amid its woods or groves, is not for a moment to be imagined. Let any one who, being at heart a lover of nature, is yet chained by duty to the dust and heat of this great metropolis — let any such one attempt, even during the week-days, to slake his thirst for solitude amid the scenes of natural loveliness which immediately surround us. At every second step, he will find the growing charm dispelled by the voice and personal intrusion of some ruffian or party of carousing blackguards. He will seek privacy amid the densest foliage, all in vain. Here are the very nooks where the unwashed most abound — here are the temples most desecrate. With sickness of the heart the wanderer will flee back to the polluted Paris as to a less odious because less incongruous sink of pollution. But if the vicinity of the city is so beset during the working days of the week, how much more so on the Sabbath! It is now especially that, released from the claims of labor, or deprived

of the customary opportunities of crime, the town blackguard seeks the precincts of the town, not through love of the rural, which in his heart he despises, but by way of escape from the restraints and conventionalities of society. He desires less the fresh air and the green trees, than the utter *license* of the country. Here, at the road-side inn, or beneath the foliage of the woods, he indulges unchecked by any eye except those of his boon companions, in all the mad excess of a counterfeit hilarity — the joint offspring of liberty and of rum. I say nothing more than what must be obvious to every dispassionate observer, when I repeat that the circumstance of the articles in question having remained undiscovered, for a longer period than from one Sunday to another, in *any* thicket in the immediate neighborhood of Paris, is to be looked upon as little less than miraculous.

"But there are not wanting other grounds for the suspicion that the articles were placed in the thicket with the view of diverting attention from the real scene of the outrage. And first, let me direct your notice to the *date* of the discovery of the articles. Collate this with the date of the fifth extract made by myself from the newspapers. You will find that the discovery followed, almost immediately, the urgent communications sent to the evening paper. These communications, although various, and apparently from various sources, tended all to the same point — viz., the directing of attention to *a gang* as the perpetrators of the outrage, and to the neighborhood of the Barrière du Roule as its scene. Now, here, of course, the suspicion is not that, in consequence of these communications, or of the public attention by them directed, the articles were found by the boys; but the suspicion might and may well have been, that the articles were not *before* found by the boys, for the reason that the articles had not before been in the thicket; having been deposited there only at so late a period as at the date, or shortly prior to the date of the communications, by the guilty authors of these communications themselves.

"This thicket was a singular — an exceedingly singular one. It was unusually dense. Within its naturally walled enclosure were three extraordinary stones, *forming a seat with a back and a footstool*. And this thicket, so full of art, was in the immediate vicinity, *within a few rods*, of the dwelling of Madame Deluc, whose boys were in the habit of closely examining the shrubberies about them in search of the bark of the sassafras. Would it be a rash wager — a wager of one thousand to one — that *a day* never passed over the heads of these boys without finding at least one of them ensconced in the umbrageous hall, and enthroned upon its natural throne? Those who would hesitate at such a wager, have either never been boys themselves, or have forgotten the boyish nature. I repeat — it is exceedingly hard to comprehend how the articles could have remained in this thicket undiscovered, for a longer period than one or two days; and that thus there is good ground for

suspicion, in spite of the dogmatic ignorance of Le Soleil, that they were, at a comparatively late date, deposited where found.

"But there are still other and stronger reasons for believing them so deposited, than any which I have as yet urged. And, now, let me beg your notice to the highly artificial arrangement of the articles. On the *upper* stone lay a white petticoat; on the *second*, a silk scarf; scattered around, were a parasol, gloves, and a pocket-handkerchief bearing the name 'Marie Rogêt.' Here is just such an arrangement as would *naturally* be made by a not over-acute person wishing to dispose the articles *naturally*. But it is by no means a *really* natural arrangement. I should rather have looked to see the things *all* lying on the ground and trampled under foot. In the narrow limits of that bower, it would have been scarcely possible that the petticoat and scarf should have retained a position upon the stones, when subjected to the brushing to and fro of many struggling persons. 'There was evidence,' it is said, 'of a struggle; and the earth was trampled, the bushes were broken,' — but the petticoat and the scarf are found deposited as if upon shelves. 'The pieces of the frock torn out by the bushes were about three inches wide and six inches long. One part was the hem of the frock and it had been mended. They *looked like strips torn off*.' Here, inadvertently, Le Soleil has employed an exceedingly suspicious phrase. The pieces, as described, do indeed 'look like strips torn off'; but purposely and by hand. It is one of the rarest of accidents that a piece is 'torn off,' from any garment such as is now in question, by the agency *of a thorn*. From the very nature of such fabrics, a thorn or nail becoming tangled in them, tears them rectangularly — divides them into two longitudinal rents, at right angles with each other, and meeting at an apex where the thorn enters — but it is scarcely possible to conceive the piece 'torn off.' I never so knew it, nor did you. To tear a piece *off* from such fabric, two distinct forces, in different directions, will be, in almost every case, required. If there be two edges to the fabric — if, for example, it be a pocket-handkerchief, and it is desired to tear from it a slip, then, and then only, will the one force serve the purpose. But in the present case the question is of a dress, presenting but one edge. To tear a piece from the interior, where no edge is presented, could only be effected by a miracle through the agency of thorns, and no *one* thorn could accomplish it. But, even where an edge is presented, two thorns will be necessary, operating, the one in two distinct directions, and the other in one. And this in the supposition that the edge is unhemmed. If hemmed, the matter is nearly out of the question. We thus see the numerous and great obstacles in the way of pieces being 'torn off' through the simple agency of 'thorns'; yet we are required to believe not only that one piece but that many have been so torn. 'And one part,' too, '*was the hem of the frock*'! Another piece was '*part of the skirt, not the hem*,' — that is to say, was torn completely out, through the agency of thorns, from the unedged interior

of the dress! These, I say, are things which one may well be pardoned for disbelieving; yet, taken collectedly, they form, perhaps, less of reasonable ground for suspicion, than the one startling circumstance of the articles having been left in this thicket at all, by any *murderers* who had enough precaution to think of removing the corpse. You will not have apprehended me rightly, however, if you suppose it my design to *deny* this thicket as the scene of the outrage. There might have been a wrong *here*, or more possibly, an accident at Madame Deluc's. But, in fact, this is a point of minor importance. We are not engaged in an attempt to discover the scene, but to produce the perpetrators of the murder. What I have adduced, notwithstanding the minuteness with which I have adduced it, has been with the view, first, to show the folly of the positive and headlong assertions of Le Soleil, but secondly and chiefly, to bring you, by the most natural route, to a further contemplation of the doubt whether this assassination has, or has not, been the work of *a gang*.

"We will resume this question by mere allusion to the revolting details of the surgeon examined at the inquest. It is only necessary to say that his published *inferences*, in regard to the number of the ruffians, have been properly ridiculed as unjust and totally baseless, by all the reputable anatomists of Paris. Not that the matter *might not* have been as inferred, but that there was no ground for the inference: — was there not much for another?

"Let us reflect now upon 'the traces of a struggle'; and let me ask what these traces have been supposed to demonstrate. A gang. But do they not rather demonstrate the absence of a gang? What *struggle* could have taken place — what struggle so violent and so enduring as to have left its 'traces' in all directions — between a weak and defenceless girl and *a gang* of ruffians imagined? The silent grasp of a few rough arms and all would have been over. The victim must have been absolutely passive at their will. You will here bear in mind that the arguments urged against the thicket as the scene, are applicable, in chief part, only against it as the scene of an outrage committed by *more than a single individual*. If we imagine but *one* violator, we can conceive, and thus only conceive, the struggle of so violent and so obstinate a nature as to have left the 'traces' apparent.

"And again. I have already mentioned the suspicion to be excited by the fact that the articles in question were suffered to remain *at all* in the thicket where discovered. It seems almost impossible that these evidences of guilt should have been accidentally left where found. There was sufficient presence of mind (it is supposed) to remove the corpse; and yet a more positive evidence than the corpse itself (whose features might have been quickly obliterated by decay), is allowed to lie conspicuously in the scene of the outrage — I allude to the handkerchief with the *name* of the deceased. If this was accident, it was not the acci-

dent *of a gang*. We can imagine it only the accident of an individual. Let us see. An individual has committed the murder. He is alone with the ghost of the departed. He is appalled by what lies motionless before him. The fury of his passion is over, and there is abundant room in his heart for the natural awe of the deed. His is none of that confidence which the presence of numbers inevitably inspires. He is *alone* with the dead. He trembles and is bewildered. Yet there is a necessity for disposing of the corpse. He bears it to the river, and leaves behind him the other evidences of his guilt; for it is difficult, if not impossible to carry all the burthen at once, and it will be easy to return for what is left. But in his toilsome journey to the water his fears redouble within him. The sounds of life encompass his path. A dozen times he hears or fancies he hears the step of an observer. Even the very lights from the city bewilder him. Yet, in time, and by long and frequent pauses of deep agony, he reaches the river's brink, and disposes of his ghastly charge — perhaps through the medium of a boat. But *now* what treasure does the world hold — what threat of vengeance could it hold out — which would have power to urge the return of that lonely murderer over that toilsome and perilous path, to the thicket and its blood-chilling recollections? He returns *not*, let the consequences be what they may. He *could* not return if he would. His sole thought is immediate escape. He turns his back *forever* upon those dreadful shrubberies, and flees as from the wrath to come.

"But how with a gang? Their number would have inspired them with confidence; if, indeed, confidence is ever wanting in the breast of the arrant blackguard; and of arrant blackguards alone are the supposed *gangs* ever constituted. Their number, I say, would have prevented the bewildering and unreasoning terror which I have imagined to paralyze the single man. Could we suppose an oversight in one, or two, or three, this oversight would have been remedied by a fourth. They would have left nothing behind them; for their number would have enabled them to carry *all* at once. There would have been no need of *return*.

"Consider now the circumstance that, in the outer garment of the corpse when found, 'a slip, about a foot wide, had been torn upward from the bottom hem to the waist, wound three times around the waist, and secured by a sort of hitch in the back.' This was done with the obvious design of affording *a handle* by which to carry the body. But would any *number* of men have dreamed of resorting to such an expedient? To three or four, the limbs of the corpse would have afforded not only a sufficient, but the best possible, hold. The device is that of a single individual; and this brings us to the fact that 'between the thicket and the river, the rails of the fences were found taken down, and the ground bore evident traces of some heavy burden having been dragged along it!' But would a *number* of men have put themselves to the superfluous trouble of taking down a fence, for the purpose of drag-

ging through it a corpse which they might have *lifted over* any fence in an instant? Would a *number* of men have so *dragged* a corpse at all as to have left evident *traces* of the dragging?

"And here we must refer to an observation of Le Commerciel; an observation upon which I have already, in some measure, commented. 'A piece,' says this journal, 'of one of the unfortunate girl's petticoats was torn out and tied under her chin, and around the back of her head, probably to prevent screams. This was done by fellows who had no pocket-handkerchiefs.'

"I have before suggested that a genuine blackguard is never *without* a pocket-handkerchief. But it is not to this fact that I now especially advert. That it was not through want of a handkerchief for the purpose imagined by Le Commerciel, that this bandage was employed, is rendered apparent by the handkerchief left in the thicket; and that the object was not 'to prevent screams' appears, also, from the bandage having been employed in preference to what would so much better have answered the purpose. But the language of the evidence speaks of the strip in question as 'found around the neck, fitting loosely, and secured with a hard knot.' These words are sufficiently vague, but differ materially from those of Le Commerciel. The slip was eighteen inches wide, and therefore, although of muslin, would form a strong band when folded or rumpled longitudinally. And thus rumpled it was discovered. My inference is this. The solitary murderer, having borne the corpse for some distance (whether from the thicket or elsewhere) by means of the bandage *hitched* around its middle, found the weight, in this mode of procedure, too much for his strength. He resolved to drag the burthen — the evidence goes to show that it *was* dragged. With this object in view, it became necessary to attach something like a rope to one of the extremities. It could be best attached about the neck, where the head would prevent it slipping off. And now the murderer bethought him, unquestionably, of the bandage about the loins. He would have used this, but for its volution about the corpse, the *hitch* which embarrassed it, and the reflection that it had not been 'torn off' from the garment. It was easier to tear a new slip from the petticoat. He tore it, made it fast about the neck, and so *dragged* his victim to the brink of the river. That this 'bandage,' only attainable with trouble and delay, and but imperfectly answering its purpose — that this bandage was employed *at all*, demonstrates that the necessity for its employment sprang from circumstances arising at a period when the handkerchief was no longer attainable — that is to say, arising, as we have imagined, after quitting the thicket (if the thicket it was), and on the road between the thicket and the river.

"But the evidence, you will say, of Madame Deluc(!) points especially to the presence of *a gang* in the vicinity of the thicket, at or about the epoch of the murder. This I grant. I doubt if there were not a

dozen gangs, such as described by Madame Deluc, in and about the vicinity of the Barrière du Roule at *or about* the period of this tragedy. But the gang which has drawn upon itself the pointed animadversion, although the somewhat tardy and very suspicious evidence, of Madame Deluc, is the *only* gang which is represented by that honest and scrupulous old lady as having eaten her cakes and swallowed her brandy, without putting themselves to the trouble of making her payment. *Et hinc illæ iræ?*

"But what *is* the precise evidence of Madame Deluc? 'A gang of miscreants made their appearance, behaved boisterously, ate and drank without making payment, followed in the route of the young man and the girl, returned to the inn *about dusk*, and re-crossed the river as if in great haste.'

"Now this 'great haste' very possibly seemed *greater* haste in the eyes of Madame Deluc, since she dwelt lingeringly and lamentingly upon her violated cakes and ale, — cakes and ale for which she might still have entertained a faint hope of compensation. Why, otherwise, since it was *about dusk*, should she make a point of the *haste?* It is no cause for wonder, surely, that even a gang of blackguards should make *haste* to get home when a wide river is to be crossed in small boats, when storm impends, and when night *approaches*.

"I say *approaches*; for the night had *not yet arrived*. It was only *about dusk* that the indecent haste of these 'miscreants' offended the sober eyes of Madame Deluc. But we are told that it was upon this very evening that Madame Deluc, as well as her eldest son, 'heard the screams of a female in the vicinity of the inn.' And in what words does Madame Deluc designate the period of the evening at which these screams were heard? 'It was *soon after dark*,' she says. But 'soon after dark' is, at least, *dark*; and '*about dusk*' is as certainly daylight. Thus it is abundantly clear that the gang quitted the Barrière du Roule *prior* to the screams overheard(?) by Madame Deluc. And although, in all the many reports of the evidence, the relative expressions in question are distinctly and invariably employed just as I have employed them in this conversation with yourself, no notice whatever of the gross discrepancy has, as yet, been taken by any of the public journals, or by any of the myrmidons of police.

"I shall add but one to the arguments against *a gang*; but this *one* has, to my own understanding at least, a weight altogether irresistible. Under the circumstances of large reward offered, and full pardon to any king's evidence, it is not to be imagined, for a moment, that some member of *a gang* of low ruffians, or of any body of men would not long ago have betrayed his accomplices. Each one of a gang, so placed, is not so much greedy of reward, or anxious for escape, as *fearful of betrayal*. He betrays eagerly and early that *he may not himself be betrayed*. That the secret has not been divulged is the very best of proof that it is, in fact,

a secret. The horrors of this dark deed are known only to *one*, or two, living human beings, and to God.

"Let us sum up now the meagre yet certain fruits of our long analysis. We have attained the idea either of a fatal accident under the roof of Madame Deluc, or of a murder perpetrated, in the thicket at the Barrière du Roule, by a lover, or at least by an intimate and secret associate of the deceased. This associate is of swarthy complexion. This complexion, the 'hitch' in the bandage, and the 'sailor's knot' with which the bonnet-ribbon is tied, point to a seaman. His companionship with the deceased, a gay but not an abject young girl, designates him as above the grade of the common sailor. Here the well-written and urgent communications to the journals are much in the way of corroboration. The circumstance of the first elopement, as mentioned by Le Mercurie, tends to blend the idea of this seaman with that of that 'naval officer' who is first known to have led the unfortunate into crime.

"And here, most fitly, comes the consideration of the continued absence of him of the dark complexion. Let me pause to observe that the complexion of this man is dark and swarthy; it was no common swarthiness which constituted the *sole* point of remembrance, both as regards Valence and Madame Deluc. But why is this man absent? Was he murdered by the gang? If so, why are there only *traces* of the assassinated *girl?* The scene of the two outrages will naturally be supposed identical. And where is his corpse? The assassins would most probably have disposed of both in the same way. But it may be said that this man lives, and is deterred from making himself known, through dread of being charged with the murder. This consideration might be supposed to operate upon him now — at this late period — since it has been given in evidence that he was seen with Marie — but it would have had no force at the period of the deed. The first impulse of an innocent man would have been to announce the outrage, and to aid in identifying the ruffians. This, *policy* would have suggested. He had been seen with the girl. He had crossed the river with her in an open ferry-boat. The denouncing of the assassins would have appeared, even to an idiot, the surest and sole means of relieving himself from suspicion. We cannot suppose him, on the night of the fatal Sunday, both innocent himself and incognizant of an outrage committed. Yet only under such circumstances is it possible to imagine that he would have failed, if alive, in the denouncement of the assassins.

"And what means are ours of attaining the truth? We shall find these means multiplying and gathering distinctness as we proceed. Let us sift to the bottom this affair of the first elopement. Let us know the full history of 'the officer,' with his present circumstances, and his whereabouts at the precise period of the murder. Let us carefully compare with each other the various communications sent to the evening paper,

in which the object was to inculpate *a gang*. This done, let us compare these communications, both as regards style and MS., with those sent to the morning paper, at a previous period, and insisting so vehemently upon the guilt of Mennais. And, all this done, let us again compare these various communications with the known MSS. of the officer. Let us endeavor to ascertain, by repeated questionings of Madame Deluc and her boys, as well as of the omnibus-driver, Valence, something more of the personal appearance and bearing of the 'man of dark complexion.' Queries, skillfully directed will not fail to elicit, from some of these parties, information on this particular point (or upon others) — information which the parties themselves may not even be aware of possessing. And let us now trace *the boat* picked up by the bargeman on the morning of Monday the twenty-third of June, and which was removed from the barge-office, without the cognizance of the officer in attendance, and *without the rudder*, at some period prior to the discovery of the corpse. With a proper caution and perseverance we shall infallibly trace this boat; for not only can the bargeman who picked it up identify it, but the *rudder is at hand*. The rudder *of a sail boat* would not have been abandoned, without inquiry, by one altogether at ease in heart. And here let me pause to insinuate a question. There was no *advertisement* of the picking up of this boat. It was silently taken to the barge-office and as silently removed. But its owner or employer — how *happened* he, at so early a period as Tuesday morning, to be informed, without the agency of advertisement, of the locality of the boat taken up on Monday, unless we imagine some connection with the *navy* — some personal permanent connexion leading to cognizance of its minute interests — its petty local news?

"In speaking of the lonely assassin dragging his burden to the shore, I have already suggested the probability of his availing himself *of a boat*. Now we are to understand that Marie Rogêt *was* precipitated from a boat. This would naturally have been the case. The corpse could not have been trusted to the shallow waters of the shore. The peculiar marks on the back and shoulders of the victim tell of the bottom ribs of a boat. That the body was found without weight is also corroborative of the idea. If thrown from the shore a weight would have been attached. We can only account for its absence by supposing the murderer to have neglected the precaution of supplying himself with it before pushing off. In the act of consigning the corpse to the water, he would unquestionably have noticed his oversight; but then no remedy would have been at hand. Any risk would have been preferred to a return to that accursed shore. Having rid himself of his ghastly charge, the murderer would have hastened to the city. There, at some obscure wharf, he would have leaped on land. But the boat — would he have secured it? He would have been in too great haste for such things as securing a boat. More-

over, in fastening it to the wharf, he would have felt as if securing evidence against himself. His natural thought would have been to cast from him, as far as possible, all that had held connection with his crime. He would not only have fled from the wharf, but he would not have permitted *the boat* to remain. Assuredly he would have cast it adrift. Let us pursue our fancies. — In the morning, the wretch is stricken with unutterable horror at finding that the boat has been picked up and detained at a locality which he is in the daily habit of frequenting — at a locality, perhaps, which his duty compels him to frequent. The next night, *without daring to ask for the rudder*, he removes it. Now *where* is that rudderless boat? Let it be one of our first purposes to discover. With the first glimpse we obtain of it, the dawn of our success shall begin. This boat shall guide us, with a rapidity which will surprise even ourselves, to him who employed it in the midnight of the fatal Sabbath. Corroboration will rise upon corroboration, and the murderer will be traced."

[For reasons which we shall not specify, but which to many readers will appear obvious, we have taken the liberty of here omitting, from the MSS. placed in our hands, such portion as details the *following up* of the apparently slight clew obtained by Dupin. We feel it advisable only to state, in brief, that the result desired was brought to pass; and that the Prefect fulfilled punctually, although with reluctance, the terms of his compact with the Chevalier. Mr. Poe's article concludes with the following words. — Eds.*]

It will be understood that I speak of coincidences and *no more*. What I have said above upon this topic must suffice. In my own heart there dwells no faith in præter-nature. That Nature and its God are two, no man who thinks will deny. That the latter, creating the former, can, at will, control or modify it, is also unquestionable. I say "at will"; for the question is of will, and not, as the insanity of logic has assumed, of power. It is not that the Deity *cannot* modify his laws, but that we insult him in imagining a possible necessity for modification. In their origin these laws were fashioned to embrace *all* contingencies which *could* lie in the Future. With God all is *Now*.

I repeat, then, that I speak of these things only as of coincidences. And further: in what I relate it will be seen that between the fate of the unhappy Mary Cecilia Rogers, so far as that fate is known, and the fate of one Marie Rogêt up to a certain epoch in her history, there has existed a parallel in the contemplation of whose wonderful exactitude the reason becomes embarrassed. I say all this will be seen. But let it not for a moment be supposed that, in proceeding with the sad narrative of Marie from the epoch just mentioned, and in tracing to its *dénouement* the mystery which enshrouded her, it is my covert design to hint at an extension of the parallel, or even to suggest that the measures

* Of the Magazine in which the article was originally published.

adopted in Paris for the discovery of the assassin of a grisette, or measures founded in any similar ratiocination would produce any similar result.

For, in respect to the latter branch of the supposition, it should be considered that the most trifling variation in the facts of the two cases might give rise to the most important miscalculations, by diverting thoroughly the two courses of events; very much as, in arithmetic, an error which, in its own individuality, may be inappreciable, produces, at length, by dint of multiplication at all points of the process, a result enormously at variance with truth. And, in regard to the former branch, we must not fail to hold in view that the very Calculus of Probabilities to which I have referred, forbids all idea of the extension of the parallel, — forbids it with a positiveness strong and decided just in proportion as this parallel has already been long-drawn and exact. This is one of those anomalous propositions which, seemingly appealing to thought altogether apart from the mathematical, is yet one which only the mathematician can fully entertain. Nothing, for example, is more difficult than to convince the merely general reader that the fact of sixes having been thrown twice in succession by a player at dice, is sufficient cause for betting the largest odds that sixes will not be thrown in the third attempt. A suggestion to this effect is usually rejected by the intellect at once. It does not appear that the two throws which have been completed, and which lie now absolutely in the Past, can have influence upon the throw which exists only in the Future. The chance for throwing sixes seems to be precisely as it was at any ordinary time — that is to say, subject only to the influence of the various other throws which may be made by the dice. And this is a reflection which appears so exceedingly obvious that attempts to controvert it are received more frequently with a derisive smile than with any thing like respectful attention. The error here involved — a gross error redolent of mischief — I cannot pretend to expose within the limits assigned me at present; and with the philosophical it needs no exposure. It may be sufficient here to say that it forms one of an infinite series of mistakes which arise in the path of Reason through her propensity for seeking truth *in detail*.

The Pit and the Pendulum

Impia tortorum longas hic turba furores
Sanguinis innocui, non satiata, aluit.
Sospite nunc patria, fracto nunc funeris antro,
Mors ubi dira fuit vita salusque patent.

[Quatrain composed for the gates of a market to be erected upon the site of the
Jacobin Club House at Paris.]

I WAS sick — sick unto death with that long agony; and when they at
length unbound me, and I was permitted to sit, I felt that my senses
were leaving me. The sentence — the dread sentence of death — was the
last of distinct accentuation which reached my ears. After that, the sound
of the inquisitorial voices seemed merged in one dreamy indeterminate
hum. It conveyed to my soul the idea of *revolution* — perhaps from its
association in fancy with the burr of a mill-wheel. This only for a brief
period, for presently I heard no more. Yet, for a while, I saw — but with
how terrible an exaggeration! I saw the lips of the black-robed judges.
They appeared to me white — whiter than the sheet upon which I trace
these words — and thin even to grotesqueness; thin with the intensity
of their expression of firmness — of immovable resolution — of stern
contempt of human torture. I saw that the decrees of what to me was
Fate were still issuing from those lips. I saw them writhe with a deadly
locution. I saw them fashion the syllables of my name; and I shuddered
because no sound succeeded. I saw, too, for a few moments of delirious
horror, the soft and nearly imperceptible waving of the sable draperies
which enwrapped the walls of the apartment. And then my vision fell
upon the seven tall candles upon the table. At first they wore the aspect
of charity, and seemed white slender angels who would save me; but
then, all at once, there came a most deadly nausea over my spirit, and
I felt every fibre in my frame thrill as if I had touched the wire of a
galvanic battery, while the angel forms became meaningless spectres,
with heads of flame, and I saw that from them there would be no help.
And then there stole into my fancy, like a rich musical note, the thought
of what sweet rest there must be in the grave. The thought came gently
and stealthily, and it seemed long before it attained full appreciation;
but just as my spirit came at length properly to feel and entertain it,
the figures of the judges vanished, as if magically, from before me; the
tall candles sank into nothingness! their flames went out utterly; the
blackness of darkness supervened; all sensations appeared swallowed up

in a mad rushing descent as of the soul into Hades. Then silence, and stillness, and night were the universe.

I had swooned; but still will not say that all of consciousness was lost. What of it there remained I will not attempt to define, or even to describe; yet all was not lost. In the deepest slumber— no! In delirium — no! In a swoon — no! In death — no! even in the grave all *is not* lost. Else there is no immortality for man. Arousing from the most profound of slumbers, we break the gossamer web of *some* dream. Yet in a second afterward, (so frail may that web have been) we remember not that we have dreamed. In the return to life from the swoon there are two stages: first, that of the sense of mental or spiritual; secondly, that of the sense of physical, existence. It seems probable that if, upon reaching the second stage, we could recall the impressions of the first, we should find these impressions eloquent in memories of the gulf beyond. And that gulf is — what? How at least shall we distinguish its shadows from those of the tomb? But if the impressions of what I have termed the first stage are not, at will, recalled, yet, after long interval, do they not come unbidden, while we marvel whence they come? He who has [never] swooned, is not he who finds strange palaces and wildly familiar faces in coals that glow; is not he who beholds floating in mid-air the sad visions that the many may not view; is not he who ponders over the perfume of some novel flower; is not he whose brain grows bewildered with the meaning of some musical cadence which has never before arrested his attention.

Amid frequent and thoughtful endeavors to remember, amid earnest struggles to regather some token of the state of seeming nothingness into which my soul had lapsed, there have been moments when I have dreamed of success; there have been brief, very brief periods when I have conjured up remembrances which the lucid reason of a later epoch assures me could have had reference only to that condition of seeming unconsciousness. These shadows of memory tell, indistinctly, of tall figures that lifted and bore me in silence down — down — still down — till a hideous dizziness oppressed me at the mere idea of the interminableness of the descent. They tell also of a vague horror at my heart, on account of that heart's unnatural stillness. Then comes a sense of sudden motionlessness throughout all things; as if those who bore me (a ghastly train!) had outrun, in their descent, the limits of the limitless, and paused from the wearisomeness of their toil. After this I call to mind flatness and dampness; and then all is *madness* — the madness of a memory which busies itself among forbidden things.

Very suddenly there came back to my soul motion and sound — the tumultuous motion of the heart, and, in my ears, the sound of its beating. Then a pause in which all is blank. Then again sound, and motion, and touch — a tingling sensation pervading my frame. Then the mere consciousness of existence, without thought — a condition which lasted

long. Then, very suddenly, *thought,* and shuddering terror, and earnest endeavor to comprehend my true state. Then a strong desire to lapse into insensibility. Then a rushing revival of soul and a successful effort to move. And now a full memory of the trial, of the judges, of the sable draperies, of the sentence, of the sickness, of the swoon. Then entire forgetfulness of all that followed; of all that a later day and much earnestness of endeavor have enabled me vaguely to recall.

So far, I had not opened my eyes. I felt that I lay upon my back, unbound. I reached out my hand, and it fell heavily upon something damp and hard. There I suffered it to remain for many minutes, while I strove to imagine where and *what* I could be. I longed, yet dared not, to employ my vision. I dreaded the first glance at objects around me. It was not that I feared to look upon things horrible, but that I grew aghast lest there should be *nothing* to see. At length, with a wild desperation at heart, I quickly unclosed my eyes. My worst thoughts, then, were confirmed. The blackness of eternal night encompassed me. I struggled for breath. The intensity of the darkness seemed to oppress and stifle me. The atmosphere was intolerably close. I still lay quietly, and made effort to exercise my reason. I brought to mind the inquisitorial proceedings, and attempted from that point to deduce my real condition. The sentence had passed; and it appeared to me that a very long interval of time had since elapsed. Yet not for a moment did I suppose myself actually dead. Such a supposition, notwithstanding what we read in fiction, is altogether inconsistent with real existence; — but where and in what state was I? The condemned to death, I knew, perished usually at the *auto-da-fes,* and one of these had been held on the very night of the day of my trial. Had I been remanded to my dungeon, to await the next sacrifice, which would not take place for many months? This I at once saw could not be. Victims had been in immediate demand. Moreover, my dungeon, as well as all the condemned cells at Toledo, had stone floors, and light was not altogether excluded.

A fearful idea now suddenly drove the blood in torrents upon my heart, and for a brief period I once more relapsed into insensibility. Upon recovering, I at once started to my feet, trembling convulsively in every fibre. I thrust my arms wildly above and around me in all directions. I felt nothing; yet dreaded to move a step, lest I should be impeded by the walls of a *tomb.* Perspiration burst from every pore, and stood in cold big beads upon my forehead. The agony of suspense grew at length intolerable, and I cautiously moved forward, with my arms extended, and my eyes straining from their sockets in the hope of catching some faint ray of light. I proceeded for many paces; but still all was blackness and vacancy. I breathed more freely. It seemed evident that mine was not, at least, the most hideous of fates.

And now, as I still continued to step cautiously onward, there came thronging upon my recollection a thousand vague rumors of the horrors

of Toledo. Of the dungeons there had been strange things narrated — fables I had always deemed them, — but yet strange, and too ghastly to repeat, save in a whisper. Was I left to perish of starvation in the subterranean world of darkness; or what fate, perhaps even more fearful, awaited me? That the result would be death, and a death of more than customary bitterness, I knew too well the character of my judges to doubt. The mode and the hour were all that occupied or distracted me.

My outstretched hands at length encountered some solid obstruction. It was a wall, seemingly of stone masonry — very smooth, slimy, and cold. I followed it up; stepping with all the careful distrust with which certain antique narratives had inspired me. This process, however, afforded me no means of ascertaining the dimensions of my dungeon, as I might make its circuit and return to the point whence I set out without being aware of the fact, so perfectly uniform seemed the wall. I therefore sought the knife which had been in my pocket when led into the inquisitorial chamber; but it was gone; my clothes had been exchanged for a wrapper of coarse serge. I had thought of forcing the blade in some minute crevice of the masonry, so as to identify my point of departure. The difficulty, nevertheless, was but trivial; although, in the disorder of my fancy, it seemed at first insuperable. I tore a part of the hem from the robe and placed the fragment at full length, and at right angles to the wall. In groping my way around the prison, I could not fail to encounter this rag upon completing the circuit. So, at least, I thought; but I had not counted upon the extent of the dungeon, or upon my own weakness. The ground was moist and slippery. I staggered onward for some time, when I stumbled and fell. My excessive fatigue induced me to remain prostrate; and sleep soon overtook me as I lay.

Upon awaking, and stretching forth an arm, I found beside me a loaf and a pitcher with water. I was too much exhausted to reflect upon this circumstance, but ate and drank with avidity. Shortly afterward, I resumed my tour around the prison, and with much toil, came at last upon the fragment of the serge. Up to the period when I fell, I had counted fifty-two paces, and, upon resuming my walk, I had counted forty-eight more; — when I arrived at the rag. There were in all, then, a hundred paces; and, admitting two paces to the yard, I presumed the dungeon to be fifty yards in circuit. I had met, however with many angles in the wall, and thus I could form no guess at the shape of the vault, for vault I could not help supposing it to be.

I had little object — certainly no hope — in these researches; but a vague curiosity prompted me to continue them. Quitting the wall, I resolved to cross the area of the enclosure. At first, I proceeded with extreme caution, for the floor, although seemingly of solid material, was treacherous with slime. At length, however, I took courage, and did not hesitate to step firmly — endeavoring to cross in as direct a line as possible. I had advanced some ten or twelve paces in this manner, when the

remnant of the torn hem of my robe became entangled between my legs. I stepped on it, and fell violently on my face.

In the confusion attending my fall, I did not immediately apprehend a somewhat startling circumstance, which yet, in a few seconds after-ward, and while I still lay prostrate, arrested my attention. It was this — my chin rested upon the floor of the prison, but my lips, and the upper portion of my head, although seemingly at a less elevation than the chin, touched nothing. At the same time, my forehead seemed bathed in a clammy vapor, and the peculiar smell of decayed fungus arose to my nos-trils. I put forward my arm, and shuddered to find that I had fallen at the very brink of a circular pit, whose extent, of course, I had no means of ascertaining at the moment. Groping about the masonry just below the margin, I succeeded in dislodging a small fragment, and let it fall into the abyss. For many seconds I hearkened to its reverberations as it dashed against the sides of the chasm in its descent; at length, there was a sullen plunge into water, succeeded by loud echoes. At the same mo-ment, there came a sound resembling the quick opening and as rapid closing of a door overhead, while a faint gleam of light flashed suddenly through the gloom, and as suddenly faded away.

I saw clearly the doom which had been prepared for me, and congratu-lated myself upon the timely accident by which I had escaped. Another step before my fall, and the world had seen me no more. And the death just avoided was of that very character which I had regarded as fabulous and frivolous in the tales respecting the Inquisition. To the victims of its tyranny, there was the choice of death with its direst physical agonies, or death with its most hideous moral horrors. I had been reserved for the latter. By long suffering my nerves had been unstrung, until I trembled at the sound of my own voice, and had become in every respect a fitting subject for the species of torture which awaited me.

Shaking in every limb, I groped my way back to the wall; resolving there to perish rather than risk the terrors of the wells, of which my imagination now pictured many in various position about the dungeon. In other con-ditions of mind, I might have had courage to end my misery at once, by a plunge into one of these abysses; but now I was the veriest of cowards. Neither could I forget what I had read of these pits — that the *sudden* extinction of life formed no part of their most horrible plan.

Agitation of spirit kept me awake for many long hours, but at length I again slumbered. Upon arousing, I found by my side, as before, a loaf and a pitcher of water. A burning thirst consumed me, and I emptied the vessel at a draught. It must have been drugged; for scarcely had I drunk, before I became irresistibly drowsy. A deep sleep fell upon me — a sleep like that of death. How long it lasted, of course I know not; but when, once again, I unclosed my eyes, the objects around me were visible. By a wild, sulphurous lustre, the origin of which I could not at first determine, I was enabled to see the extent and aspect of the prison.

In its size I had been greatly mistaken. The whole circuit of its walls did not exceed twenty-five yards. For some minutes this fact occasioned me a world of vain trouble; vain indeed! for what could be of less importance, under the terrible circumstances which environed me, than the mere dimensions of my dungeon? But my soul took a wild interest in trifles, and I busied myself in endeavors to account for the error I had committed in my measurement. The truth at length flashed upon me. In my first attempt at exploration I had counted fifty-two paces, up to the period when I fell; I must then have been within a pace or two of the fragment of serge; in fact, I had nearly performed the circuit of the vault. I then slept and, upon awaking, I must have returned upon my steps — thus supposing the circuit nearly double what it actually was. My confusion of mind prevented me from observing that I began my tour with the wall to the left, and ended it with the wall to the right.

I had been deceived, too, in respect to the shape of the enclosure. In feeling my way I had found many angles, and thus deduced an idea of great irregularity; so potent is the effect of total darkness upon one arousing from lethargy or sleep! The angles were simply those of a few slight depressions, or niches, at odd intervals. The general shape of the prison was square. What I had taken for masonry seemed now to be iron, or some other metal, in huge plates, whose sutures or joints occasioned the depression. The entire surface of this metallic enclosure was rudely daubed in all the hideous and repulsive devices to which the charnal superstition of the monks has given rise. The figures of fiends in aspects of menace, with skeleton forms, and other more really fearful images, overspread and disfigured the walls. I observed that the outlines of these monstrosities were sufficiently distinct, but that the colors seemed faded and blurred, as if from the effects of a damp atmosphere. I now noticed the floor, too, which was of stone. In the centre yawned the circular pit from whose jaws I had escaped; but it was the only one in the dungeon.

All this I saw indistinctly and by much effort: for my personal condition had been greatly changed during slumber. I now lay upon my back, and at full length, on a species of low framework of wood. To this I was securely bound by a long strap resembling a surcingle. It passed in many convolutions about my limbs and body, leaving at liberty only my head, and my left arm to such extent, that I could, by dint of much exertion, supply myself with food from an earthen dish which lay by my side on the floor. I saw, to my horror, that the pitcher had been removed. I say to my horror; for I was consumed with intolerable thirst. This thirst it appeared to be the design of my persecutors to stimulate — for the food in the dish was meat pungently seasoned.

Looking upward, I surveyed the ceiling of my prison. It was some thirty or forty feet overhead, and constructed much as the side walls. In one of its panels a very singular figure riveted my whole attention. It was the painted figure of Time as he is commonly represented, save that, in lieu

of a scythe, he held what, at a casual glance, I supposed to be the pictured image of a huge pendulum, such as we see on antique clocks. There was something, however, in the appearance of this machine which caused me to regard it more attentively. While I gazed directly upward at it (for its position was immediately over my own) I fancied that I saw it in motion. In an instant afterward the fancy was confirmed. Its sweep was brief, and of course slow. I watched it for some minutes somewhat in fear, but more in wonder. Wearied at length with observing its dull movement, I turned my eyes upon the other objects in the cell.

A slight noise attracted my notice, and, looking to the floor, I saw several enormous rats traversing it. They had issued from the well which lay just within view to my right. Even then, while I gazed, they came up in troops, hurriedly, with ravenous eyes, allured by the scent of the meat. From this it required much effort and attention to scare them away.

It might have been half an hour, perhaps, even an hour (for I could take but imperfect note of time), before I again cast my eyes upward. What I then saw confounded and amazed me. The sweep of the pendulum had increased in extent by nearly a yard. As a natural consequence its velocity was also much greater. But what mainly disturbed me was the idea that it had perceptibly *descended*. I now observed — with what horror it is needless to say — that its nether extremity was formed of a crescent of glittering steel, about a foot in length from horn to horn; the horns upward, and the under edge evidently as keen as that of a razor. Like a razor also, it seemed massy and heavy, tapering from the edge into a solid and broad structure above. It was appended to a weighty rod of brass, and the whole *hissed* as it swung through the air.

I could no longer doubt the doom prepared for me by monkish ingenuity in torture. My cognizance of the pit had become known to the inquisitorial agents — *the pit*, whose horrors had been destined for so bold a recusant as myself — *the pit*, typical of hell and regarded by rumor as the Ultima Thule of all their punishments. The plunge into this pit I had avoided by the merest of accidents, and I knew that surprise, or entrapment into torment, formed an important portion of all the grotesquerie of these dungeon deaths. Having failed to fall, it was no part of the demon plan to hurl me into the abyss, and thus (there being no alternative) a different and a milder destruction awaited me. Milder! I half smiled in my agony as I thought of such application of such a term.

What boots it to tell of the long, long hours of horror more than mortal, during which I counted the rushing vibrations of the steel! Inch by inch — line by line — with a descent only appreciable at intervals that seemed ages — down and still down it came! Days passed — it might have been that many days passed — ere it swept so closely over me as to fan me with its acrid breath. The odor of the sharp steel forced itself into my nostrils. I prayed — I wearied heaven with my prayer for its more speedy descent. I grew frantically mad, and struggled to force myself up-

ward against the sweep of the fearful scimitar. And then I fell suddenly calm, and lay smiling at the glittering death, as a child at some rare bauble.

There was another interval of utter insensibility; it was brief; for, upon again lapsing into life, there had been no perceptible descent in the pendulum. But it might have been long — for I knew there were demons who took note of my swoon, and who could have arrested the vibration at pleasure. Upon my recovery, too, I felt very — oh! inexpressibly — sick and weak, as if through long inanition. Even amid the agonies of that period, the human nature craved food. With painful effort I outstretched my left arm as far as my bonds permitted, and took possession of the small remnant which had been spared me by the rats. As I put a portion of it within my lips, there rushed to my mind a half-formed thought of joy — of hope. Yet what business had I with hope? It was, as I say, a half-formed thought — man has many such, which are never completed. I felt that it was of joy — of hope; but I felt also that it had perished in its formation. In vain I struggled to perfect — to regain it. Long suffering had nearly annihilated all my ordinary powers of mind. I was an imbecile — an idiot.

The vibration of the pendulum was at right angles to my length. I saw that the crescent was designed to cross the region of the heart. It would fray the serge of my robe — it would return and repeat its operations — again — and again. Notwithstanding its terrifically wide sweep (some thirty feet or more), and the hissing vigor of its descent, sufficient to sunder these very walls of iron, still the fraying of my robe would be all that, for several minutes, it would accomplish. And at this thought I paused. I dared not go further than this reflection. I dwelt upon it with a pertinacity of attention — as if, in so dwelling, I could arrest *here* the descent of the steel. I forced myself to ponder upon the sound of the crescent as it should pass across the garment — upon the peculiar thrilling sensation which the friction of cloth produces on the nerves. I pondered upon all this frivolity until my teeth were on edge.

Down — steadily down it crept. I took a frenzied pleasure in contrasting its downward with its lateral velocity. To the right — to the left — far and wide — with the shriek of a damned spirit! to my heart, with the stealthy pace of the tiger! I alternately laughed and howled, as the one or the other idea grew predominant.

Down — certainly, relentlessly down! It vibrated within three inches of my bosom! I struggled violently — furiously — to free my left arm. This was free only from the elbow to the hand. I could reach the latter, from the platter beside me, to my mouth, with great effort, but no farther. Could I have broken the fastenings above the elbow, I would have seized and attempted to arrest the pendulum. I might as well have attempted to arrest an avalanche!

Down — still unceasingly — still inevitably down! I gasped and struggled at each vibration. I shrunk convulsively at its every sweep. My eyes

followed its outward or upward whorls with the eagerness of the most unmeaning despair; they closed themselves spasmodically at the descent, although death would have been a relief, oh, how unspeakable! Still I quivered in every nerve to think how slight a sinking of the machinery would precipitate that keen, glistening axe upon my bosom. It was *hope* that prompted the nerve to quiver — the frame to shrink. It was *hope* — the hope that triumphs on the rack — that whispers to the death-condemned even in the dungeons of the Inquisition.

I saw that some ten or twelve vibrations would bring the steel in actual contact with my robe, and with this observation there suddenly came over my spirit all the keen, collected calmness of despair. For the first time during many hours — or perhaps days — I *thought*. It now occurred to me, that the bandage, or surcingle, which enveloped me, was *unique*. I was tied by no separate cord. The first stroke of the razor-like crescent athwart any portion of the band would so detach it that it might be unwound from my person by means of my left hand. But how fearful, in that case, the proximity of the steel! The result of the slightest struggle, how deadly! Was it likely, moreover, that the minions of the torturer had not foreseen and provided for this possibility? Was it probable that the bandage crossed my bosom in the track of the pendulum? Dreading to find my faint and, as it seemed, my last hope frustrated, I so far elevated my head as to obtain a distinct view of my breast. The surcingle enveloped my limbs and body close in all directions — *save in the path of the destroying crescent*.

Scarcely had I dropped my head back into its original position, when there flashed upon my mind what I cannot better describe than as the unformed half of that idea of deliverance to which I had previously alluded, and of which a moiety only floated indeterminately through my brain when I raised food to my burning lips. The whole thought was now present — feeble, scarcely sane, scarcely definite — but still entire. I proceeded at once, with the nervous energy of despair, to attempt its execution.

For many hours the immediate vicinity of the low framework upon which I lay had been literally swarming with rats. They were wild, bold, ravenous — their red eyes glaring upon me as if they waited but for motionlessness on my part to make me their prey. "To what food," I thought, "have they been accustomed in the well?"

They had devoured, in spite of all my efforts to prevent them, all but a small remnant of the contents of the dish. I had fallen into an habitual see-saw or wave of the hand about the platter; and, at length, the unconscious uniformity of the movement deprived it of effect. In their voracity, the vermin frequently fastened their sharp fangs in my fingers. With the particles of the oily and spicy viand which now remained, I thoroughly rubbed the bandage wherever I could reach it; then, raising my hand from the floor, I lay breathlessly still.

At first, the ravenous animals were startled and terrified at the change — at the cessation of movement. They shrank alarmedly back; many sought the well. But this was only for a moment. I had not counted in vain upon their voracity. Observing that I remained without motion, one or two of the boldest leaped upon the framework, and smelt at the surcingle. This seemed the signal for a general rush. Forth from the well they hurried in fresh troops. They clung to the wood — they overran it, and leaped in hundreds upon my person. The measured movement of the pendulum disturbed them not at all. Avoiding its strokes, they busied themselves with the anointed bandage. They pressed — they swarmed upon me in ever accumulating heaps. They writhed upon my throat; their cold lips sought my own; I was half stifled by their thronging pressure; disgust, for which the world has no name, swelled my bosom, and chilled, with a heavy clamminess, my heart. Yet one minute, and I felt that the struggle would be over. Plainly I perceived the loosening of the bandage. I knew that in more than one place it must be already severed. With a more than human resolution I lay *still*.

Nor had I erred in my calculations — nor had I endured in vain. I at length felt that I was *free*. The surcingle hung in ribands from my body. But the stroke of the pendulum already pressed upon my bosom. It had divided the serge of the robe. It had cut through the linen beneath. Twice again it swung, and a sharp sense of pain shot through every nerve. But the moment of escape had arrived. At a wave of my hand my deliverers hurried tumultuously away. With a steady movement — cautious, sidelong, shrinking, and slow — I slid from the embrace of the bandage and beyond the reach of the scimitar. For the moment, at least, *I was free*.

Free! — and in the grasp of the Inquisition! I had scarcely stepped from my wooden bed of horror upon the stone floor of the prison, when the motion of the hellish machine ceased, and I beheld it drawn up, by some invisible force, through the ceiling. This was a lesson which I took desperately to heart. My every motion was undoubtedly watched. Free! — I had but escaped death in one form of agony, to be delivered unto worse than death in some other. With that thought I rolled my eyes nervously around on the barriers of iron that hemmed me in. Something unusual — some change which at first, I could not appreciate distinctly — it was obvious, had taken place in the apartment. For many minutes of a dreamy and trembling abstraction, I busied myself in vain, unconnected conjecture. During this period, I became aware, for the first time, of the origin of the sulphurous light which illumined the cell. It proceeded from a fissure, about half an inch in width, extending entirely around the prison at the base of the walls, which thus appeared, and were completely separated from the floor. I endeavored, but of course in vain, to look through the aperture.

As I arose from the attempt, the mystery of the alteration in the cham-

ber broke at once upon my understanding. I had observed that, although the outlines of the figures upon the walls were sufficiently distinct, yet the colors seemed blurred and indefinite. These colors had now assumed, and were momentarily assuming, a startling and most intense brilliancy, that gave to the spectral and fiendish portraitures an aspect that might have thrilled even firmer nerves than my own. Demon eyes, of a wild and ghastly vivacity, glared upon me in a thousand directions where none had been visible before, and gleamed with the lurid lustre of a fire that I could not force my imagination to regard as unreal.

Unreal! — even while I breathed there came to my nostrils the breath of the vapor of heated iron! A suffocating odor pervaded the prison! A deeper glow settled each moment in the eyes that glared at my agonies! A richer tint of crimson diffused itself over the pictured horrors of blood. I panted! I gasped for breath! There could be no doubt of the design of my tormenters — oh! most unrelenting! oh! most demoniac of men! I shrank from the glowing metal to the centre of the cell. Amid the thought of the fiery destruction that impended, the idea of the coolness of the well came over my soul like balm. I rushed to its deadly brink. I threw my straining vision below. The glare from the enkindled roof illumined its inmost recesses. Yet, for a wild moment, did my spirit refuse to comprehend the meaning of what I saw. At length it forced — it wrestled its way into my soul — it burned itself in upon my shuddering reason. — Oh! for a voice to speak! — oh! horror! — oh! any horror but this! With a shriek, I rushed from the margin, and buried my face in my hands — weeping bitterly.

The heat rapidly increased, and once again I looked up, shuddering as with a fit of the ague. There had been a second change in the cell — and now the change was obviously in the *form*. As before, it was in vain that I at first endeavored to appreciate or understand what was taking place. But not long was I left in doubt. The Inquisitorial vengeance had been hurried by my two-fold escape, and there was to be no more dallying with the King of Terrors. The room had been square. I saw that two of its iron angles were now acute — two, consequently, obtuse. The fearful difference quickly increased with a low rumbling or moaning sound. In an instant the apartment had shifted its form into that of a lozenge. But the alteration stopped not here — I neither hoped nor desired it to stop. I could have clasped the red walls to my bosom as a garment of eternal peace. "Death," I said, "any death but that of the pit!" Fool! might I not have known that *into the pit* it was the object of the burning iron to urge me? Could I resist its glow? or if even that, could I withstand its pressure? And now, flatter and flatter, grew the lozenge, with a rapidity that left me no time for contemplation. Its centre, and of course its greatest width, came just over the yawning gulf. I shrank back — but the closing walls pressed me resistlessly onward. At length for my seared and writhing body there was no longer an inch of foothold on the firm floor of

the prison. I struggled no more, but the agony of my soul found vent in one loud, long, and final scream of despair. I felt that I tottered upon the brink — I averted my eyes —

There was a discordant hum of human voices! There was a loud blast as of many trumpets! There was a harsh grating as of a thousand thunders! The fiery walls rushed back! An outstretched arm caught my own as I fell, fainting, into the abyss. It was that of General Lasalle. The French army had entered Toledo. The Inquisition was in the hands of its enemies.

The Tell-Tale Heart

T RUE! — nervous — very, very dreadfully nervous I had been and am! but why *will* you say that I am mad? The disease had sharpened my senses — not destroyed — not dulled them. Above all was the sense of hearing acute. I heard all things in the heaven and in the earth. I heard many things in hell. How, then, am I mad? Hearken! and observe how healthily — how calmly I can tell you the whole story.

It is impossible to say how first the idea entered my brain; but once conceived, it haunted me day and night. Object there was none. Passion there was none. I loved the old man. He had never wronged me. He had never given me insult. For his gold I had no desire. I think it was his eye! yes, it was this! He had the eye of a vulture — a pale blue eye, with a film over it.Whenever it fell upon me, my blood ran cold; and so by degrees — very gradually — I made up my mind to take the life of the old man, and thus rid myself of the eye forever.

Now this is the point. You fancy me mad. Madmen know nothing. But you should have seen *me*. You should have seen how wisely I proceeded — with what caution — with what foresight — with what dissimulation I went to work!

I was never kinder to the old man than during the whole week before I killed him. And every night, about midnight, I turned the latch of his door and opened it — oh, so gently! And then, when I had made an opening sufficient for my head, I put in a dark lantern, all closed, closed, so that no light shone out, and then I thrust in my head. Oh, you would have laughed to see how cunningly I thrust it in! I moved it slowly — very, very slowly, so that I might not disturb the old man's sleep. It took me an hour to place my whole head within the opening so far that I could see him as he lay upon his bed. Ha! — would a madman have been so wise as this? And then, when my head was well in the room, I undid the lantern cautiously — oh, so cautiously — cautiously (for the hinges creaked) — I undid it just so much that a single thin ray fell upon the vulture eye. And this I did for seven long nights — every night just at

midnight — but I found the eye always closed; and so it was impossible to do the work; for it was not the old man who vexed me, but his Evil Eye. And every morning, when the day broke, I went boldly into the chamber, and spoke courageously to him, calling him by name in a hearty tone, and inquiring how he had passed the night. So you see he would have been a very profound old man, indeed, to suspect that every night, just at twelve, I looked in upon him while he slept.

Upon the eighth night I was more than usually cautious in opening the door. A watch's minute hand moves more quickly than did mine. Never before that night had I *felt* the extent of my own powers — of my sagacity. I could scarcely contain my feelings of triumph. To think that there I was, opening the door, little by little, and he not even to dream of my secret deeds or thoughts. I fairly chuckled at the idea; and perhaps he heard me; for he moved on the bed suddenly, as if startled. Now you may think that I drew back — but no. His room was as black as pitch with the thick darkness (for the shutters were close fastened, through fear of robbers), and so I knew that he could not see the opening of the door, and I kept pushing it on steadily, steadily.

I had my head in, and was about to open the lantern, when my thumb slipped upon the tin fastening, and the old man sprang up in the bed, crying out — "Who's there?"

I kept quite still and said nothing. For a whole hour I did not move a muscle, and in the meantime I did not hear him lie down. He was still sitting up in the bed listening; — just as I have done, night after night, hearkening to the death watches in the wall.

Presently I heard a slight groan, and I knew it was the groan of mortal terror. It was not a groan of pain or of grief — oh no! — it was the low stifled sound that arises from the bottom of the soul when overcharged with awe. I knew the sound well. Many a night, just at midnight, when all the world slept, it has welled up from my own bosom, deepening, with its dreadful echo, the terrors that distracted me. I say I knew it well. I knew what the old man felt, and pitied him, although I chuckled at heart. I knew that he had been lying awake ever since the first slight noise, when he had turned in the bed. His fears had been ever since growing upon him. He had been trying to fancy them causeless, but could not. He had been saying to himself — "It is nothing but the wind in the chimney — it is only a mouse crossing the floor," or "it is merely a cricket which has made a single chirp." Yes, he has been trying to comfort himself with these suppositions; but he had found all in vain. *All in vain*; because Death, in approaching him, had stalked with his black shadow before him, and enveloped the victim. And it was the mournful influence of the unperceived shadow that caused him to feel — although he neither saw nor heard — to *feel* the presence of my head within the room.

When I had waited a long time, very patiently, without hearing him lie down, I resolved to open a little — a very, very little crevice in the

lantern. So I opened it — you cannot imagine how stealthily, stealthily — until, at length, a single dim ray, like the thread of the spider, shot from out the crevice and fell full upon the vulture eye.

It was open — wide, wide open — and I grew furious as I gazed upon it. I saw it with perfect distinctness — all a dull blue, with a hideous veil over it that chilled the very marrow in my bones; but I could see nothing else of the old man's face or person: for I had directed the ray as if by instinct, precisely upon the damned spot.

And now have I not told you that what you mistake for madness is but over-acuteness of the senses? — now, I say, there came to my ears a low, dull, quick sound, such as a watch makes when enveloped in cotton. I knew *that* sound well too. It was the beating of the old man's heart. It increased my fury, as the beating of a drum stimulates the soldier into courage.

But even yet I refrained and kept still. I scarcely breathed. I held the lantern motionless. I tried how steadily I could maintain the ray upon the eye. Meantime the hellish tattoo of the heart increased. It grew quicker and quicker, and louder and louder every instant. The old man's terror *must* have been extreme! It grew louder, I say, louder every moment! — do you mark me well? I have told you that I am nervous: so I am. And now at the dead hour of the night, amid the dreadful silence of that old house, so strange a noise as this excited me to uncontrollable terror. Yet, for some minutes longer I refrained and stood still. But the beating grew louder, louder! I thought the heart must burst. And now a new anxiety seized me — the sound would be heard by a neighbor! The old man's hour had come! With a loud yell, I threw open the lantern and leaped into the room. He shrieked once — once only. In an instant I dragged him to the floor, and pulled the heavy bed over him. I then smiled gaily, to find the deed so far done. But, for many minutes, the heart beat on with a muffled sound. This, however, did not vex me; it would not be heard through the wall. At length it ceased. The old man was dead. I removed the bed and examined the corpse. Yes, he was stone, stone dead. I placed my hand upon the heart and held it there many minutes. There was no pulsation. He was stone dead. His eye would trouble me no more.

If still you think me mad, you will think so no longer when I describe the wise precautions I took for the concealment of the body. The night waned, and I worked hastily, but in silence. First of all I dismembered the corpse. I cut off the head and the arms and the legs.

I then took up three planks from the flooring of the chamber, and deposited all between the scantlings. I then replaced the boards so cleverly, so cunningly, that no human eye — not even *his* — could have detected any thing wrong. There was nothing to wash out — no stain of any kind — no blood-spot whatever. I had been too wary for that. A tub had caught all — ha! ha!

When I made an end of these labors, it was four o'clock — still dark

as midnight. As the bell sounded the hour, there came a knocking at the street door. I went down to open it with a light heart, — for what had I *now* to fear? There entered three men, who introduced themselves, with perfect suavity, as officers of the police. A shriek had been heard by a neighbor during the night: suspicion of foul play had been aroused; information had been lodged at the police office, and they (the officers) had been deputed to search the premises.

I smiled, — for *what* had I to fear? I bade the gentlemen welcome. The shriek, I said, was my own in a dream. The old man, I mentioned, was absent in the country. I took my visitors all over the house. I bade them search — search *well*. I led them, at length, to *his* chamber. I showed them his treasures, secure, undisturbed. In the enthusiasm of my confidence, I brought chairs into the room, and desired them *here* to rest from their fatigues, while I myself, in the wild audacity of my perfect triumph, placed my own seat upon the very spot beneath which reposed the corpse of the victim.

The officers were satisfied. My *manner* had convinced them. I was singularly at ease. They sat, and while I answered cheerily, they chatted of familiar things. But, ere long, I felt myself getting pale and wished them gone. My head ached, and I fancied a ringing in my ears: but still they sat and still chatted. The ringing became more distinct: — it continued and became more distinct: I talked more freely to get rid of the feeling: but it continued and gained definitiveness — until at length, I found that the noise was *not* within my ears.

No doubt I now grew *very* pale; — but I talked more fluently, and with a heightened voice. Yet the sound increased — and what could I do? It was *a low, dull, quick sound — much such a sound as a watch makes when enveloped in cotton*. I gasped for breath — and yet the officers heard it not. I talked more quickly — more vehemently; but the noise steadily increased. I arose and argued about trifles, in a high key and with violent gesticulations, but the noise steadily increased. Why *would* they not be gone? I paced the floor to and fro with heavy strides, as if excited to fury by the observation of the men — but the noise steadily increased. Oh God! what *could* I do? I foamed — I raved — I swore. I swung the chair upon which I had been sitting, and grated it upon the boards, but the noise arose over all and continually increased. It grew louder — louder — *louder!* And still the men chatted pleasantly, and smiled. Was it possible they heard not? Almighty God! — no, no! They heard! — they suspected! — they *knew!* — they were making a *mockery* of my horror! — this I thought, and this I think. But any thing was better than this agony! Any thing was more tolerable than this derision! I could bear those hypocritical smiles no longer! I felt that I must scream or die! — and now — again! — hark! louder! louder! *louder!* —

"Villains!" I shrieked, "dissemble no more! I admit the deed! — tear up the planks! — here, here! — it is the beating of his hideous heart!"

The Gold Bug

What ho! what ho! this fellow is dancing mad!
He hath been bitten by the Tarantula.

ALL IN THE WRONG.

MANY years ago, I contracted an intimacy with a Mr. William Legrand. He was of an ancient Huguenot family, and had once been wealthy; but a series of misfortunes had reduced him to want. To avoid the mortification consequent upon his disasters, he left New Orleans, the city of his forefathers, and took up his residence at Sullivan's Island, near Charleston, South Carolina.

This Island is a very singular one. It consists of little else than the sea sand, and is about three miles long. Its breadth at no point exceeds a quarter of a mile. It is separated from the mainland by a scarcely perceptible creek, oozing its way through a wilderness of reeds and slime, a favorite resort of the marsh-hen. The vegetation, as might be supposed, is scant, or at least dwarfish. No trees of any magnitude are to be seen. Near the western extremity, where Fort Moultrie stands, and where are some miserable frame buildings, tenanted, during summer, by the fugitives from Charleston dust and fever, may be found, indeed, the bristly palmetto; but the whole island, with the exception of this western point, and a line of hard, white beach on the sea-coast, is covered with a dense undergrowth of the sweet myrtle so much prized by the horticulturists of England. The shrub here often attains the height of fifteen or twenty feet, and forms an almost impenetrable coppice, burdening the air with its fragrance.

In the inmost recesses of this coppice, not far from the eastern or more remote end of the island, Legrand had built himself a small hut, which he occupied when I first, by mere accident, made his acquaintance. This soon ripened into friendship — for there was much in the recluse to excite interest and esteem. I found him well educated, with unusual powers of mind, but infected with misanthropy, and subject to perverse moods of alternate enthusiasm and melancholy. He had with him many books, but rarely employed them. His chief amusements were gunning and fishing, or sauntering along the beach and through the myrtles, in quest of shells or entomological specimens; — his collection of the latter might have been envied by a Swammerdamm. In these excursions he was usually accompanied by an old negro, called Jupiter, who had been manumitted before the reverses of the family, but who could be induced, neither by threats nor by promises, to abandon what he considered his right of attendance upon the footsteps of his young "Massa Will." It is not im-

probable that the relatives of Legrand, conceiving him to be somewhat unsettled in intellect, had contrived to instill this obstinacy into Jupiter, with a view to the supervision and guardianship of the wanderer.

The winters in the latitude of Sullivan's Island are seldom very severe, and in the fall of the year it is a rare event indeed when a fire is considered necessary. About the middle of October, 18—, there occurred, however, a day of remarkable chilliness. Just before sunset I scrambled my way through the evergreens to the hut of my friend, whom I had not visited for several weeks — my residence being, at that time, in Charleston, a distance of nine miles from the island, while the facilities of passage and re-passage were very far behind those of the present day. Upon reaching the hut I rapped, as was my custom, and getting no reply, sought for the key where I knew it was secreted, unlocked the door, and went in. A fine fire was blazing upon the hearth. It was a novelty, and by no means an ungrateful one. I threw off an overcoat, took an arm-chair by the crackling logs, and awaited patiently the arrival of my hosts.

Soon after dark they arrived, and gave me a most cordial welcome. Jupiter, grinning from ear to ear, bustled about to prepare some marsh-hens for supper. Legrand was in one of his fits — how else shall I term them? — of enthusiasm. He had found an unknown bivalve, forming a new genus, and, more than this, he had hunted down and secured, with Jupiter's assistance a *scarabæus* which he believed to be totally new, but in respect to which he wished to have my opinion on the morrow.

"And why not to-night?" I asked, rubbing my hands over the blaze, and wishing the whole tribe of *scarabæi* at the devil.

"Ah, if I had only known you were here!" said Legrand, "but it's so long since I saw you; and how could I foresee that you would pay me a visit this very night of all others? As I was coming home I met Lieutenant G——, from the fort, and, very foolishly, I lent him the bug; so it will be impossible for you to see it until the morning. Stay here to-night, and I will send Jup down for it at sunrise. It is the loveliest thing in creation!"

"What? — sunrise?"

"Nonsense! no! — the bug. It is of a brilliant gold color — about the size of a large hickory-nut — with two jet black spots near one extremity of the back, and another, somewhat longer, at the other. The *antennæ* are —"

"Dey ain't *no* tin in him, Massa Will, I keep a tellin' on you," here interrupted Jupiter; "de bug is a goole-bug, solid, ebery bit of him, inside and all, sep him wing — neber feel half so hebby a bug in my life."

"Well, suppose it is, Jup," replied Legrand, somewhat more earnestly, it seemed to me, than the case demanded; "is that any reason for your letting the birds burn? The color" — here he turned to me — "is really almost enough to warrant Jupiter's idea. You never saw a more brilliant metallic lustre that the scales emit — but of this you cannot judge till to-morrow. In the meantime I can give you some idea of the shape."

Saying this, he seated himself at a small table, on which were a pen and ink, but no paper. He looked for some in a drawer, but found none.

"Never mind," he said at length, "this will answer;" and he drew from his waistcoat pocket a scrap of what I took to be very dirty foolscap, and made upon it a rough drawing with the pen. While he did this, I retained my seat by the fire, for I was still chilly. When the design was complete, he handed it to me without rising. As I received it, a loud growl was heard, succeeded by a scratching at the door. Jupiter opened it, and a large Newfoundland, belonging to Legrand, rushed in, leaped upon my shoulders, and loaded me with caresses; for I had shown him much attention during previous visits. When his gambols were over, I looked at the paper, and, to speak the truth, found myself not a little puzzled at what my friend had depicted.

"Well!" I said, after contemplating it for some minutes, "This *is* a strange *scarabæus*, I must confess; new to me; never saw anything like it before — unless it was a skull, or a death's-head, which it more nearly resembles than anything else that has come under *my* observation."

"A death's-head!" echoed Legrand. "Oh — yes — well, it has something of that appearance upon paper, no doubt. The two upper black spots look like eyes, eh? and the longer one at the bottom like a mouth — and then the shape of the whole is oval."

"Perhaps so," said I; "but, Legrand, I fear you are no artist. I must wait until I see the beetle itself, if I am to form any idea of its personal appearance."

"Well, I don't know," said he, a little nettled, "I draw tolerably — *should* do it at least — have had good masters, and flatter myself that I am not quite a blockhead."

"But, my dear fellow, you are joking, then," said I, "this is a very passable *skull* — indeed, I may say that it is a very *excellent* skull, according to the vulgar notions about such specimens of physiology — and your *scarabæus* must be the queerest *scarabæus* in the world if it resembles it. Why, we may get up a very thrilling bit of superstition upon this hint. I presume you will call the bug *scarabæus caput hominis*, or something of that kind — there are many similar titles in the Natural Histories. But where are the *antennæ* you spoke of?"

"The *antennæ!*" said Legrand, who seemed to be getting unaccountably warm upon the subject; "I am sure you must see the *antennæ*. I made them as distinct as they are in the original insect, and I presume that is sufficient."

"Well, well," I said, "perhaps you have — still I don't see them;" and I handed him the paper without additional remark, not wishing to ruffle his temper; but I was much surprised at the turn affairs had taken; his ill humor puzzled me — and, as for the drawing of the beetle, there were positively *no antennæ* visible, and the whole *did* bear a very close resemblance to the ordinary cuts of a death's-head.

He received the paper very peevishly, and was about to crumple it, apparently to throw it in the fire, when a casual glance at the design seemed suddenly to rivet his attention. In an instant his face grew violently red — in another excessively pale. For some minutes he continued to scrutinize the drawing minutely where he sat. At length he arose, took a candle from the table, and proceeded to seat himself upon a sea-chest in the farthest corner of the room. Here again he made an anxious examination of the paper; turning it in all directions. He said nothing however, and his conduct greatly astonished me; yet I thought it prudent not to exacerbate the growing moodiness of his temper by any comment. Presently he took from his coat-pocket a wallet, placed the paper carefully in it, and deposited both in a writing-desk, which he locked. He now grew more composed in his demeanor; but his original air of enthusiasm had quite disappeared. Yet he seemed not so much sulky as abstracted. As the evening wore away he became more and more absorbed in revery, from which no sallies of mine could arouse him. It had been my intention to pass the night at the hut, as I had frequently done before, but, seeing my host in this mood, I deemed it proper to take leave. He did not press me to remain, but, as I departed, he shook my hand with even more than his usual cordiality.

It was about a month after this (and during the interval I had seen nothing of Legrand) when I received a visit, at Charleston, from his man, Jupiter. I had never seen the good old negro look so dispirited, and I feared that some serious disaster had befallen my friend.

"Well, Jup," said I, "what is the matter now? — how is your master?"

"Why, to speak the troof, massa, him not so berry well as mought be."

"Not well! I am truly sorry to hear it. What does he complain of?"

"Dar! dat's it! — him neber plain of notin — but him berry sick for all dat."

"Very sick, Jupiter! — why didn't you say so at once? Is he confined to bed?"

"No, dat he aint! — he aint find nowhar — dat's just whar he shoe pinch — my mind is got to be berry hebby bout poor Massa Will."

"Jupiter, I should like to understand what it is you are talking about. You say your master is sick. Hasn't he told you what ails him?"

"Why, massa, taint worf while for to git mad about de matter — Massa Will say noffin at all aint de matter wid him — but den what make him go about looking dis here way, wid he head down and he soldiers up, and as white as a gose? And den he keep a syphon all de time —"

"Keeps a what, Jupiter?"

"Keeps a syphon wid de figgurs on de slate — de queerest figgurs I ebber did see. Ise gittin to be skeered, I tell you. Hab for to keep mighty tight eye pon him noovers. Todder day he gib me slip fore de sun up and was gone de whole ob de blessed day. I had a big stick ready cut

for to gib him deuced good beating when he did come — but Ise sich a fool dat I hadn't de heart arter all — he looked so berry poorly."

"Eh? — what? — ah yes! — upon the whole I think you had better not be too severe with the poor fellow — don't flog him, Jupiter — he can't very well stand it — but can you form no idea of what has occasioned this illness, or rather this change of conduct? Has anything unpleasant happened since I saw you?"

"No, massa, dey aint bin noffin onpleasant *since* den — 'twas *fore* den I'm feared — 'twas be berry day you was dare."

"How? what do you mean?"

"Why, massa, I mean de bug — dare now."

"That what?"

"De bug — I'm berry sartain dat Massa Will bin bit somewhere 'bout he head by dat goole-bug."

"And what cause have you, Jupiter, for such a supposition."

"Claws enuff, massa, and mouff, too. I never did see sich a deuced bug — he kick and he bite ebery ting what cum near him. Massa Will cotch him fuss, but had for to let him go gin mighty quick, I tell you — den was de time he must ha got de bite. I didn't like de look ob de bug mouff, myself, no how, so I wouldn't take hold ob him wid my finger, but I cotch him wid a piece of paper dat I found. I rap him up in de paper and stuff a piece of it in he mouff — dat was de way."

"And you think then, that your master was really bitten by the beetle, and that the bite made him sick?"

"I don't think noffin about it — I nose it. What make him dream bout de goole so much, if taint cause he bit by the goole-bug? Ise heered bout dem goole-bugs fore dis."

"But how do you know he dreams about gold?"

"How I know? why, cause he talk about it in he sleep — dat's how I nose."

"Well, Jup, perhaps you are right; but to what fortunate circumstance am I to attribute the honor of a visit from you to-day?"

"What de matter, massa?"

"Did you bring any message from Mr. Legrand?"

"No, massa, I bring dis here pissel;" and here Jupiter handed me a note which ran thus:

"MY DEAR ——

"Why have I not seen you for so long a time? I hope you have not been so foolish as to take offence at any little *brusquerie* of mine; but no, that is improbable.

"Since I saw you I have had great cause for anxiety. I have something to tell you, yet scarcely know how to tell it, or whether I should tell it at all.

"I have not been quite well for some days past, and poor old Jup

annoys me, almost beyond endurance, by his well-meant attentions. Would you believe it? — he had prepared a huge stick, the other day, with which to chastise me for giving him the slip, and spending the day, *solus*, among the hills on the mainland. I verily believe that my ill looks alone saved me a flogging.

"I have made no addition to my cabinet since we met.

"If you can, in any way, make it convenient, come over with Jupiter. *Do* come. I wish to see you *to-night*, upon business of importance. I assure you that it is of the *highest* importance.

<div style="text-align:right">"Ever yours,
"William Legrand."</div>

There was something in the tone of this note which gave me great uneasiness. Its whole style differed materially from that of Legrand. What could he be dreaming of? What new crotchet possessed his excitable brain? What "business of the highest importance" could *he* possibly have to transact? Jupiter's account of him boded no good. I dreaded lest the continued pressure of misfortune had, at length, fairly unsettled the reason of my friend. Without a moment's hesitation, therefore, I prepared to accompany the negro.

Upon reaching the wharf, I noticed a scythe and three spades, all apparently new, lying in the bottom of the boat in which we were to embark.

"What is the meaning of all this, Jup?" I inquired.

"Him syfe, massa, and spade."

"Very true; but what are they doing here?"

"Him de syfe and de spade what Massa Will sis pon my buying for him in de town, and de debbils own lot of money I had to gib for em."

"But what, in the name of all that is mysterious, is your 'Massa Will' going to do with scythes and spades?"

"Dat's more dan I know, and debbil take me if I don't blieve 'tis more dan he know too. But it's all cum ob de bug."

Finding that no satisfaction was to be obtained of Jupiter, whose whole intellect seemed to be absorbed by "de bug," I now stepped into the boat, and made sail. With a fair and strong breeze we soon ran into the little cove to the northward of Fort Moultrie, and a walk of some two miles brought us to the hut. It was about three in the afternoon when we arrived. Legrand had been awaiting us in eager expectation. He grasped my hand with a nervous *empressement* which alarmed me and strengthened the suspicions already entertained. His countenance was pale even to ghastliness, and his deep-set eyes glared with unnatural lustre. After some inquiries respecting his health, I asked him, not knowing what better to say, if he had yet obtained the *scarabæus* from Lieutenant G——,

"Oh, yes," he replied, coloring violently, "I got it from him the next morning. Nothing should tempt me to part with that *scarabæus*. Do you know that Jupiter is quite right about it?"

"In what way?" I asked, with a sad foreboding at heart.

"In supposing it to be a bug of *real gold*." He said this with an air of profound seriousness, and I felt inexpressibly shocked.

"This bug is to make my fortune," he continued, with a triumphant smile; "to reinstate me in my family possessions. Is it any wonder, then, that I prize it? Since Fortune has thought fit to bestow it upon me, I have only to use it properly, and I shall arrive at the gold of which it is the index. Jupiter, bring me that *scarabæus!*"

"What! de bug, massa? I'd rudder not go fer trubble dat bug; you mus git him for your own self." Hereupon Legrand arose, with a grave and stately air, and brought me the beetle from a glass case in which it was enclosed. It was a beautiful *scarabæus*, and, at that time, unknown to naturalists — of course a great prize in a scientific point of view. There were two round black spots near one extremity of the back, and a long one near the other. The scales were exceedingly hard and glossy, with all the appearance of burnished gold. The weight of the insect was very remarkable, and, taking all things into consideration, I could hardly blame Jupiter for his opinion respecting it; but what to make of Legrand's concordance with that opinion, I could not, for the life of me, tell.

"I sent for you," said he, in a grandiloquent tone, when I had completed my examination of the beetle, "I sent for you that I might have your counsel and assistance in furthering the views of Fate and of the bug — "

"My dear Legrand," I cried, interrupting him, "you are certainly unwell, and had better use some little precautions. You shall go to bed, and I will remain with you a few days, until you get over this. You are feverish and — "

"Feel my pulse," said he.

I felt it, and, to say the truth, found not the slightest indication of fever.

"But you may be ill and yet have no fever. Allow me this once to prescribe for you. In the first place go to bed. In the next — "

"You are mistaken," he interposed, "I am as well as I can expect to be under the excitement which I suffer. If you really wish me well, you will relieve this excitement."

"And how is this to be done?"

"Very easily. Jupiter and myself are going upon an expedition into the hills, upon the main land, and, in this expedition, we shall need the aid of some person in whom we can confide. You are the only one we can trust. Whether we succeed or fail, the excitement which you now perceive in me will be equally allayed."

"I am anxious to oblige you in any way," I replied; "but do you mean to say that this infernal beetle has any connection with your expedition into the hills?"

"It has."

"Then, Legrand, I can become a party to no such absurd proceeding."

"I am sorry — very sorry — for we shall have to try it by ourselves."

"Try it by yourselves! The man is surely mad! — but stay! — how long do you propose to be absent?"

"Probably all night. We shall start immediately, and be back, at all events, by sunrise."

"And will you promise me, upon your honor, that when this freak of yours is over, and the bug business (good God!) settled to your satisfaction, you will then return home and follow my advice implicitly, as that of your physician? "

"Yes; I promise; and now let us be off, for we have no time to lose."

With a heavy heart I accompanied my friend. We started about four o'clock — Legrand, Jupiter, the dog, and myself. Jupiter had with him the scythe and spades — the whole of which he insisted upon carrying — more through fear, it seemed to me, of trusting either of the implements within reach of his master, than from any excess of industry or complaisance. His demeanor was dogged in the extreme, and "dat deuced bug" were the sole words which escaped his lips during the journey. For my own part, I had charge of a couple of dark lanterns, while Legrand contented himself with the *scarabæus*, which he carried attached to the end of a bit of whipcord: twirling it to and fro, with the air of a conjuror, as he went. When I observed this last, plain evidence of my friend's aberration of mind, I could scarcely refrain from tears. I thought it best, however, to humor his fancy, at least for the present, or until I could adopt some more energetic measures with a chance of success. In the meantime I endeavored, but all in vain, to sound him in regard to the object of the expedition. Having succeeded in inducing me to accompany him, he seemed unwilling to hold conversation upon any topic of minor importance, and to all my questions vouchsafed no other reply than "we shall see!"

We crossed the creek at the head of the island by means of a skiff, and, ascending the high grounds on the shore of the main land, proceeded in a northwesterly direction, through a tract of country excessively wild and desolate, where no trace of a human footstep was to be seen. Legrand led the way with decision; pausing only for an instant, here and there, to consult what appeared to be certain landmarks of his own contrivance upon a former occasion.

In this manner we journeyed for about two hours, and the sun was just setting when we entered a region infinitely more dreary than any yet seen. It was a species of tableland, near the summit of an almost

inaccessible hill, densely wooded from base to pinnacle, and interspersed with huge crags that appeared to lie loosely upon the soil, and in many cases were prevented from precipitating themselves into the valleys below, merely by the support of the trees against which they reclined. Deep ravines, in various directions, gave an air of still sterner solemnity to the scene.

The natural platform to which we had clambered was thickly overgrown with brambles, through which we soon discovered that it would have been impossible to force our way but for the scythe; and Jupiter, by direction of his master, proceeded to clear for us a path to the foot of an enormously tall tulip-tree, which stood, with some eight or ten oaks, upon the level, and far surpassed them all, and all other trees which I had then ever seen, in the beauty of its foliage and form, in the wide spread of its branches, and in the general majesty of its appearance. When we reached this tree, Legrand turned to Jupiter, and asked him if he thought he could climb it. The old man seemed a little staggered by the question, and for some moments made no reply. At length he approached the huge trunk, walked slowly around it, and examined it with minute attention. When he had completed his scrutiny, he merely said:

"Yes, massa, Jup climb any tree he ebber see in he life."

"Then up with you as soon as possible, for it will soon be too dark to see what we are about."

"How far mus go up, massa?" inquired Jupiter.

"Get up the main trunk first, and then I will tell you which way to go — and here — stop! take this beetle with you."

"De bug, Massa Will! — de goole-bug!" cried the negro, drawing back in dismay — "What for mus tote de bug way up de tree? — d—n if I do!"

"If you are afraid, Jup, a great big negro like you, to take hold of a hamless little dead beetle, why you can carry it up by this string — but, if you do not take it up with you in some way, I shall be under the necessity of breaking your head with this shovel."

"What de matter now, massa?" said Jup, evidently shamed into compliance; "always want for to raise fuss wid old nigger. Was only funnin anyhow. *Me* feered de bug! what I keer for de bug?" Here he took cautiously hold of the extreme end of the string, and, maintaining the insect as far from his person as circumstances would permit, prepared to ascend the tree.

In youth, the tulip-tree, or *Liriodendron Tulipiferum*, the most magnificent of American foresters, has a trunk peculiarly smooth, and often rises to a great height without lateral branches; but, in its riper age, the bark becomes gnarled and uneven, while many short limbs make their appearance on the stem. Thus the difficulty of ascension, in the present case, lay more in semblance than in reality. Embracing the huge cylinder, as closely as possible, with his arms and knees, seizing with his

hands some projections, and resting his naked toes upon others, Jupiter, after one or two narrow escapes from falling, at length wriggled himself into the first great fork, and seemed to consider the whole business as virtually accomplished. The *risk* of the achievement was, in fact, now over, although the climber was some sixty or seventy feet from the ground.

"Which way mus go now, Massa Will?" he asked.

"Keep up the largest branch — the one on this side," said Legrand. The negro obeyed him promptly, and apparently with but little trouble; ascending higher and higher, until no glimpse of his squat figure could be obtained through the dense foliage which enveloped it. Presently his voice was heard in a sort of halloo.

"How much fudder is got for go?"

"How high up are you?" asked Legrand.

"Ebber so fur," replied the negro; "can see de sky fru de top ob de tree."

"Never mind the sky, but attend to what I say. Look down the trunk and count the limbs below you on this side. How many limbs have you passed?"

"One, two, tree, four, fibe — I done pass fibe big limb, massa, pon dis side."

"Then go one limb higher."

In a few minutes the voice was heard again, announcing that the seventh limb was attained.

"Now, Jup," cried Legrand, evidently much excited, "I want you to work your way out upon that limb as far as you can. If you see anything strange let me know."

By this time what little doubt I might have entertained of my poor friend's insanity was put finally at rest. I had no alternative but to conclude him stricken with lunacy, and I became seriously anxious about getting him home. While I was pondering upon what was best to be done, Jupiter's voice was again heard.

"Mos feered for to ventur pon dis limb berry far — 'tis dead limb putty much all de way."

"Did you say it was a *dead* limb, Jupiter?" cried Legrand in a quavering voice.

"Yes, massa, him dead as de doornail — done up for sartain — done departed dis here life."

"What in the name of heaven shall I do?" asked Legrand, seemingly in the greatest distress.

"Do!" said I, glad of an opportunity to interpose a word, "why come home and go to bed. Come now! — that's a fine fellow. It's getting late, and, besides, you remember your promise."

"Jupiter," cried he, without heeding me in the least, "do you hear me?"

"Yes, Massa Will, hear you ebber so plain."

"Try the wood well, then, with your knife, and see if you think it *very* rotten."

"Him rotten, massa, sure nuff," replied the negro in a few moments, "but not so berry rotten as mought be. Mought venture out leetle way pon de limb by myself, dat's true."

"By yourself! — what do you mean?"

"Why, I mean de bug. 'Tis *berry* hebby bug. Spose I drop him down fuss, and den de limb won't break wid just de weight of one nigger."

"You infernal scoundrel!" cried Legrand, apparently much relieved, "what do you mean by telling me such nonsense as that? As sure as you drop that beetle I'll break your neck. Look here, Jupiter, do you hear me?"

"Yess, massa, needn't hollo at poor nigger dat style."

"Well! now listen! — if you will venture out on the limb as far as you think safe, and not let go the beetle, I'll make you a present of a silver dollar as soon as you get down."

"I'm gwine, Massa Will — deed I is," replied the negro very promptly — "mos out to the eend now."

"*Out to the end!*" here fairly screamed Legrand; "do you say you are out to the end of that limb?"

"Soon be to de eend, massa — o-o-o-o-oh! Lor-gol-a-marcy! what *is* dis here pon de tree?"

"Well!" cried Legrand, highly delighted, "what is it?"

"Why 'taint noffin but a skull — somebody bin lef him head up de tree, and de crows done gobble ebery bit ob de meat off."

"A skull, you say! — very well, — how is it fastened to the limb? — what holds it on?"

"Sure nuff, massa; mus look. Why dis berry curious sarcumstance, pon my word — dare's a great big nail in de skull, what fastens ob it on to de tree."

"Well now, Jupiter, do exactly as I tell you — do you hear?"

"Yes, massa."

"Pay attention, then — find the left eye of the skull."

"Hum! hoo! dat's good! why dare ain't no eye lef at all."

"Curst your stupidity! do you know your right hand from your left?"

"Yes, I nose dat — nose all about dat — tis my lef hand what I chops de wood wid."

"To be sure! you are left-handed; and your left eye is on the same side as your left hand. Now, I suppose, you can find the left eye of the skull, or the place where the left eye has been. Have you found it?"

Here was a long pause. At length the negro asked.

"Is de lef eye of de skull pon de same side as de lef hand of de skull too? — cause de skull aint got not a bit ob a hand at all — nebber mind! I got de lef eye now — here de lef eye! what mus do wid it?"

"Let the beetle drop through it, as far as the string will reach — but be careful and not let go your hold of the string."

"All dat done, Massa Will; mighty easy ting for to put de bug fru de hole — look out for him dare below!"

During this colloquy no portion of Jupiter's person could be seen; but the beetle, which he had suffered to descend, was now visible at the end of the string, and glistened, like a globe of burnished gold, in the last rays of the setting sun, some of which still faintly illumined the eminence upon which we stood. The *scarabæus* hung quite clear of any branches, and, if allowed to fall, would have fallen at our feet. Legrand immediately took the scythe, and cleared with it a circular space, three or four yards in diameter, just beneath the insect, and, having accomplished this, ordered Jupiter to let go the string and come down from the tree.

Driving a peg, with great nicety, into the ground, at the precise spot where the beetle fell, my friend now produced from his pocket a tape-measure. Fastening one end of this at that point of the trunk of the tree which was nearest the peg, he unrolled it till it reached the peg, and thence farther unrolled it, in the direction already established by the two points of the tree and the peg, for the distance of fifty feet — Jupiter clearing away the brambles with the scythe. At the spot thus attained a second peg was driven, and about this, as a centre, a rude circle, about four feet in diameter, described. Taking now a spade himself, and giving one to Jupiter and one to me, Legrand begged us to set about digging as quickly as possible.

To speak the truth, I had no especial relish for such amusement at any time, and, at that particular moment, would willingly have declined it; for the night was coming on, and I felt much fatigued with the exercise already taken; but I saw no mode of escape, and was fearful of disturbing my poor friend's equanimity by a refusal. Could I have depended, indeed upon Jupiter's aid, I would have had no hesitation in attempting to get the lunatic home by force; but I was too well assured of the old negro's disposition, to hope that he would assist me, under any circumstances, in a personal contest with his master. I made no doubt that the latter had been infected with some of the innumerable Southern superstitions about money buried, and that his phantasy had received confirmation by the finding of the *scarabæus*, or, perhaps, by Jupiter's obstinacy in maintaining it to be "a bug of real gold." A mind disposed to lunacy would readily be led away by such suggestions — especially if chiming in with favorite preconceived ideas — and then I called to mind the poor fellow's speech about the bettle's being "the index of his fortune." Upon the whole, I was sadly vexed and puzzled, but, at length, I concluded to make a virtue of necessity — to dig with a good will, and thus the sooner to convince the visionary, by ocular demonstration, of the fallacy of the opinions he entertained.

The lanterns having been lit, we all fell to work with a zeal worthy a more rational çause; and, as the glare fell upon our persons and imple-

ments, I could not help thinking how picturesque a group we composed, and how strange and suspicious our labors must have appeared to any interloper who, by chance, might have stumbled upon our whereabouts.

We dug very steadily for two hours. Little was said; and our chief embarrassment lay in the yelpings of the dog, who took exceeding interest in our proceedings. He, at length, became so obstreperous that we grew fearful of his giving the alarm to some stragglers in the vicinity, — or, rather, this was the apprehension of Legrand; — for myself, I should have rejoiced at any interruption which might have enabled me to get the wanderer home. The noise was, at length, very effectually silenced by Jupiter, who, getting out of the hole with a dogged air of deliberation, tied the brute's mouth up with one of his suspenders, and then returned, with a grave chuckle, to his task.

When the time mentioned had expired, we had reached a depth of five feet, and yet no sign of any treasure became manifest. A general pause ensued, and I began to hope that the farce was at an end. Legrand, however, although evidently much disconcerted, wiped his brow thoughtfully and recommenced. We had excavated the entire circle of four feet diameter, and now we slightly enlarged the limit, and went to the farther depth of two feet. Still nothing appeared. The gold-seeker, whom I sincerely pitied, at length clambered from the pit, with the bitterest disappointment imprinted upon every feature, and proceeded, slowly and reluctantly, to put on his coat, which he had thrown off at the beginning of his labor. In the meantime I made no remark. Jupiter, at a signal from his master, began to gather up his tools. This done, and the dog having been unmuzzled, we turned in profound silence toward home.

We had taken, perhaps, a dozen steps in this direction, when, with a loud oath, Legrand strode up to Jupiter, and seized him by the collar. The astonished negro opened his eyes and mouth to the fullest extent, let fall the spades, and fell upon his knees.

"You scoundrel!" said Legrand, hissing out the syllables from between his clenched teeth — "you infernal black villain! — speak, I tell you! — answer me this instant, without prevarication! — which — which is your left eye?"

"Oh, my golly, Massa Will! aint dis here my lef eye for sartain?" roared the terrified Jupiter, placing his hand upon his *right* organ of vision, and holding it there with a desperate pertinacity, as if in immediate dread of his master's attempt at a gouge.

"I thought so! — I knew it! hurrah!" vociferated Legrand, letting the negro go and executing a series of curvets and caracols, much to the astonishment of his valet, who, arising from his knees, looked, mutely, from his master to myself, and then from myself to his master.

"Come! we must go back," said the latter, "the game's not up yet"; and he again led the way to the tulip-tree.

"Jupiter," said he, when we reached its foot, "come here! Was the skull nailed to the limb with the face outward, or with the face to the limb?"

"De face was out, massa, so dat de crows could get at de eyes good, widout any trouble."

"Well, then, was it this eye or that through which you dropped the beetle?" here Legrand touched each of Jupiter's eyes.

"Twas dis eye, massa — de lef eye — jis as you tell me," and here it was his right eye that the negro indicated.

"That will do — we must try it again."

Here my friend, about whose madness I now saw, or fancied that I saw, certain indications of method, removed the peg which marked the spot where the beetle fell, to a spot about three inches to the westward of its former position. Taking, now, the tape measure from the nearest point of the trunk to the peg, as before, and continuing the extension in a straight line to the distance of fifty feet, a spot was indicated, removed, by several yards, from the point at which we had been digging.

Around the new position a circle, somewhat larger than in the former instance, was now described, and we again set to work with the spades. I was dreadfully weary, but, scarcely understanding what had occasioned the change in my thoughts, I felt no longer any great aversion from the labor imposed. I had become most unaccountably interested — nay, even excited. Perhaps there was something, amid all the extravagant demeanor of Legrand — some air of forethought, or of deliberation, which impressed me. I dug eagerly, and now and then caught myself actually looking, with something that very much resembled expectation, for the fancied treasure, the vision of which had demented my unfortunate companion. At a period when such vagaries of thought most fully possessed me, and when we had been at work perhaps an hour and a half, we were again interrupted by the violent howlings of the dog. His uneasiness, in the first instance, had been, evidently, but the result of playfulness or caprice, but he now assumed a bitter and serious tone. Upon Jupiter's again attempting to muzzle him, he made furious resistance, and, leaping into the hole, tore up the mould frantically with his claws. In a few seconds he had uncovered a mass of human bones, forming two complete skeletons, intermingled with several buttons of metal, and what appeared to be the dust of decayed woolen. One or two strokes of a spade upturned the blade of a large Spanish knife, and, as we dug farther, three or four loose pieces of gold and silver coin came to light.

At sight of these the joy of Jupiter could scarcely be restrained, but the countenance of his master wore an air of extreme disappointment. He urged us, however, to continue our exertions, and the words were hardly uttered when I stumbled and fell forward, having caught the toe of my boot in a large ring of iron that lay half buried in the loose earth.

We now worked in earnest, and never did I pass ten minutes of more

intense excitement. During this interval we had fairly unearthed an oblong chest of wood, which, from its perfect preservation and wonderful hardness, had plainly been subjected to some mineralizing process — perhaps that of the Bi-chloride of Mercury. This box was three feet and a half long, three feet broad, and two and a half feet deep. It was firmly secured by bands of wrought iron, riveted, and forming a kind of open trellis-work over the whole. On each side of the chest, near the top, were three rings of iron — six in all — by means of which a firm hold could be obtained by six persons. Our utmost united endeavors served only to disturb the coffer very slightly in its bed. We at once saw the impossibility of removing so great a weight. Luckily, the sole fastenings of the lid consisted of two sliding bolts. These we drew back — trembling and panting with anxiety. In an instant, a treasure of incalculable value lay gleaming before us. As the rays of the lanterns fell within the pit, there flashed upwards a glow and a glare, from a confused heap of gold and jewels, that absolutely dazzled our eyes.

I shall not pretend to describe the feelings with which I gazed. Amazement was, of course, predominant. Legrand appeared exhausted with excitement, and spoke very few words. Jupiter's countenance wore, for some minutes, as deadly a pallor as it is possible, in the nature of things, for any negro's visage to assume. He seemed stupefied — thunderstricken. Presently he fell upon his knees in the pit, and burying his naked arms up to the elbows in gold, let them there remain, as if enjoying the luxury of a bath. At length, with a deep sigh, he exclaimed, as if in a soliloquy:

"And dis all cum ob de goole-bug! de putty goole-bug! de poor little goole-bug, what I boosed in dat sabage kind ob style! Aint you shamed ob yourself, nigger? — answer me dat!"

It became necessary, at last, that I should arouse both master and valet to the expediency of removing the treasure. It was growing late, and it behooved us to make exertion, that we might get every thing housed before daylight. It was difficult to say what should be done, and much time was spent in deliberation — so confused were the ideas of all. We, finally, lightened the box by removing two-thirds of its contents, when we were enabled, with some trouble to raise it from the hole. The articles taken out were deposited among the brambles, and the dog left to guard them, with strict orders from Jupiter neither, upon any pretence, to stir from the spot, nor to open his mouth until our return. We then hurriedly made for home with the chest; reaching the hut in safety, but after excessive toil, at one o'clock in the morning. Worn out as we were, it was not in human nature to do more immediately. We rested until two, and had supper; starting for the hills immediately afterward, armed with three stout sacks, which, by good luck, were upon the premises. A little before four we arrived at the pit, divided the remainder of the booty, as equally as might be, among us, and, leaving the holes unfilled, again set out for the hut, at which, for the second time, we deposited our

golden burthens, just as the first faint streaks of the dawn gleamed from over the tree-tops in the East.

We were now thoroughly broken down; but the intense excitement of the time denied us repose. After an unquiet slumber of some three or four hours' duration, we arose, as if by preconcert, to make examination of our treasure.

The chest had been full to the brim, and we spent the whole day, and the greater part of the next night, in a scrutiny of its contents. There had been nothing like order or arrangement. Everything had been heaped in promiscuously. Having assorted all with care we found ourselves possessed of even vaster wealth than we had at first supposed. In coin there was rather more than four hundred and fifty thousand dollars — estimating the value of the pieces, as accurately as we could, by the tables of the period. There was not a particle of silver. All was gold of antique date and of great variety — French, Spanish, and German money, with a few English guineas, and some counters, of which we had never seen specimens before. There were several very large and heavy coins, so worn that we could make nothing of their inscriptions. There was no American money. The value of the jewels we found more difficulty in estimating. There were diamonds — some of them exceedingly large and fine — a hundred and ten in all, and not one of them small; eighteen rubies of remarkable brilliancy; — three hundred and ten emeralds, all very beautiful; and twenty-one sapphires, with an opal. These stones had all been broken from their settings and thrown loose in the chest. The settings themselves, which we picked out from among the other gold, appeared to have been beaten up with hammers, as if to prevent identification. Besides all this, there was a vast quantity of solid gold ornaments; nearly two hundred massive finger and earrings; rich chains — thirty of these, if I remember; eighty-three very large and heavy crucifixes; five gold censers of great value; a prodigious golden punch-bowl, ornamented with richly chased vine-leaves and Bacchanalian figures; with two sword-handles exquisitely embossed, and many other smaller articles which I cannot recollect. The weight of these valuables exceeded three hundred and fifty pounds avoirdupois; and in this estimate I have not included one hundred and ninety-seven superb gold watches; three of the number being worth each five hundred dollars, if one. Many of them were very old, and as timekeepers valueless; the works having suffered, more or less, from corrosion — but all were richly jewelled and in cases of great worth. We estimated the entire contents of the chest, that night, at a million and a half of dollars; and upon the subsequent disposal of the trinkets and jewels (a few being retained for our own use), it was found that we had greatly under-valued the treasure.

When, at length, we had concluded our examination, and the intense excitement of the time had, in some measure, subsided, Legrand, who saw that I was dying with impatience for a solution of this most extraor-

dinary riddle, entered into a full detail of all the circumstances connected with it.

"You remember," said he, "the night when I handed you the rough sketch I had made of the *scarabæus*. You recollect also, that I became quite vexed at you for insisting that my drawing resembled a death's-head. When you first made this assertion I thought you were jesting; but afterwards I called to mind the peculiar spots on the back of the insect, and admitted to myself that your remark had some little foundation in fact. Still, the sneer at my graphic powers irritated me — for I am considered a good artist — and, therefore, when you handed me the scrap of parchment, I was about to crumple it up and throw it angrily into the fire."

"The scrap of paper, you mean," said I.

"No; it had much of the appearance of paper, and at first I supposed it to be such, but when I came to draw upon it, I discovered it at once to be a piece of very thin parchment. It was quite dirty, you remember. Well, as I was in the very act of crumpling it up, my glance fell upon the sketch at which you had been looking, and you may imagine my astonishment when I perceived, in fact, the figure of a death's-head just where, it seemed to me, I had made the drawing of the beetle. For a moment I was too much amazed to think with accuracy. I knew that my design was very different in detail from this — although there was a certain similarity in general outline. Presently I took a candle, and seating myself at the other end of the room, proceeded to scrutinize the parchment more closely. Upon turning it over, I saw my own sketch upon the reverse, just as I had made it. My first idea, now, was mere surprise at the really remarkable similarity of outline — at the singular coincidence involved in the fact that, unknown to me, there should have been a skull upon the other side of the parchment, immediately beneath my figure of the *scarabæus*, and that this skull, not only in outline, but in size, should so closely resemble my drawing. I say the singularity of this coincidence absolutely stupefied me for a time. This is the usual effect of such coincidences. The mind struggles to establish a connexion — a sequence of cause and effect — and, being unable to do so, suffers a species of temporary paralysis. But, when I recovered from this stupor, there dawned upon me gradually a conviction which startled me even far more than the coincidence. I began distinctly, positively, to remember that there had been *no* drawing upon the parchment, when I made my sketch of the *scarabæus*. I became perfectly certain of this; for I recollected turning up first one side and then the other, in search of the cleanest spot. Had the skull been then there, of course I could not have failed to notice it. Here was indeed a mystery which I felt it impossible to explain; but, even at that early moment, there seemed to glimmer, faintly, within the most remote and secret chambers of my intellect, a glow-worm-like conception of that truth which last night's adventure

brought to so magnificent a demonstration. I arose at once, and putting the parchment securely away, dismissed all further reflection until I should be alone.

"When you had gone, and when Jupiter was fast asleep, I betook myself to a more methodical investigation of the affair. In the first place I considered the manner in which the parchment had come into my possession. The spot where we discovered the *scarabæus* was on the coast of the mainland, about a mile eastward of the island, and but a short distance above high-water mark. Upon my taking hold of it, it gave me a sharp bite, which caused me to let it drop. Jupiter, with his accustomed caution, before seizing the insect, which had flown toward him, looked about him for a leaf, or something of that nature, by which to take hold of it. It was at this moment that his eyes, and mine also, fell upon the scrap of parchment, which I then supposed to be paper. It was lying half buried in the sand, a corner sticking up. Near the spot where we found it, I observed the remnants of the hull of what appeared to have been a ship's long boat. The wreck seemed to have been there for a very great while; for the resemblance to boat timbers could scarcely be traced.

"Well, Jupiter picked up the parchment, wrapped the beetle in it, and gave it to me. Soon afterward we turned to go home, and on the way met Lieutenant G——. I showed him the insect, and he begged me to let him take it to the fort. Upon my consenting, he thrust it forthwith into his waistcoat pocket, without the parchment in which it had been wrapped, and which I had continued to hold in my hand during his inspection. Perhaps he dreaded my changing my mind, and thought it best to make sure of the prize at once — you know how enthusiastic he is on all subjects connected with Natural History. At the same time, without being conscious of it, I must have deposited the parchment in my own pocket.

"You remember that when I went to the table, for the purpose of making a sketch of the beetle, I found no paper where it was usually kept. I looked in the drawer, and found none there. I searched my pockets, hoping to find an old letter, when my hand fell upon the parchment. I thus detail the precise mode in which it came into my possession; for the circumstances impressed me with a peculiar force.

"No doubt you will think me fanciful — but I had already established a kind of *connexion*. I had put together two links of a great chain. There was a boat lying upon a sea-coast, and not far from the boat was a parchment — *not a paper* — with a skull depicted upon it. You will, of course, ask 'where is the connexion?' I reply that the skull, or death's-head, is the well-known emblem of the pirate. The flag of the death's-head is hoisted in all engagements.

"I have said that the scrap was parchment, and not paper. Parchment is durable — almost imperishable. Matters of little moment are rarely consigned to parchment; since, for the mere ordinary purposes of draw-

ing or writing, it is not nearly so well adapted as paper. This reflection suggested some meaning — some relevancy — in the death's-head. I did not fail to observe, also, the *form* of the parchment. Although one of its corners had been, by some accident, destroyed, it could be seen that the original form was oblong. It was just such a slip, indeed, as might have been chosen for a memorandum — for a record of something to be long remembered and carefully preserved."

"But," I interposed, "you say that the skull was *not* upon the parchment when you made the drawing of the beetle. How then do you trace any connexion between the boat and the skull — since this latter, according to your own admission, must have been designed (God only knows how or by whom) at some period subsequent to your sketching the *scarabæus?*"

"Ah, hereupon turns the whole mystery; although the secret, at this point, I had comparatively little difficulty in solving. My steps were sure, and could afford but a single result. I reasoned, for example, thus: When I drew the *scarabæus*, there was no skull apparent upon the parchment. When I had completed the drawing I gave it to you, and observed you narrowly until you returned it. *You*, therefore, did not design the skull, and no one else was present to do it. Then it was not done by human agency. And nevertheless it was done.

"At this stage of my reflections I endeavored to remember, and *did* remember, with entire distinctness, every incident which occurred about the period in question. The weather was chilly (oh, rare and happy accident!), and a fire was blazing upon the hearth. I was heated with exercise and sat near the table. You, however, had drawn a chair close to the chimney. Just as I placed the parchment in your hand, and as you were in the act of inspecting it, Wolf, the Newfoundland, entered, and leaped upon your shoulders. With your left hand you caressed him and kept him off, while your right, holding the parchment, was permitted to fall listlessly between your knees, and in close proximity to the fire. At one moment I thought the blaze had caught it, and was about to caution you, but, before I could speak, you had withdrawn it, and were engaged in its examination. When I considered all these particulars, I doubted not for a moment that *heat* had been the agent in bringing to light, upon the parchment, the skull which I saw designed upon it. You are well aware that chemical preparations exist, and have existed time out of mind, by means of which it is possible to write upon either paper or vellum, so that the characters shall become visible only when subjected to the action of fire. Zaffre, digested in *aqua regia*, and diluted with four times its weight of water, is sometimes employed; a green tint results. The regulus of cobalt, dissolved in spirit of nitre, gives a red. These colors disappear at longer or shorter intervals after the material written upon cools, but again become apparent upon the re-application of heat.

"I now scrutinized the death's-head with care. Its outer edges — the

edges of the drawing nearest the edge of the vellum — were far more *distinct* than the others. It was clear that the action of the caloric had been imperfect or unequal. I immediately kindled a fire, and subjected every portion of the parchment to a glowing heat. At first, the only effect was the strengthening of the faint lines in the skull; but, upon persevering in the experiment, there became visible, at the corner of the slip, diagonally opposite to the spot in which the death's-head was deline-ated, the figure of what I at first supposed to be a goat. A closer scrutiny, however, satisfied me that it was intended for a kid."

"Ha! ha!" said I, "to be sure I have no right to laugh at you — a million and a half of money is too serious a matter for mirth — but you are not about to establish a third link in your chain — you will not find any especial connexion between your pirates and a goat — pirates, you know, have nothing to do with goats; they appertain to the farming interest."

"But I have just said that the figure was *not* that of a goat."

"Well, a kid then — pretty much the same thing."

"Pretty much, but not altogether," said Legrand. "You may have heard of one *Captain* Kidd. I at once looked upon the figure of the ani-mal as a kind of punning or hieroglyphical signature. I say signature; because its position upon the vellum suggested this idea. The death's-head at the corner diagonally opposite, had, in the same manner, the air of a stamp, or seal. But I was sorely put out by the absence of all else — of the body to my imagined instrument — of the text for my context."

"I presume you expected to find a letter between the stamp and the signature."

"Something of that kind. The fact is, I felt irresistibly impressed with a presentiment of some vast good fortune impending. I can scarcely say why. Perhaps, after all, it was rather a desire than an actual belief; — but do you know that Jupiter's silly words, about the bug being of solid gold, had a remarkable effect upon my fancy? And then the series of accidents and coincidents — these were so *very* extraordinary. Do you observe how mere an accident it was that these events should have occurred upon the *sole* day of all the year in which it has been, or may be sufficiently cool for fire, and that without the fire, or without the inter-vention of the dog at the precise moment in which he appeared, I should never have become aware of the death's-head, and so never the possessor of the treasure."

"But proceed — I am all impatience."

"Well; you have heard, of course, the many stories current — the thousand vague rumors afloat about money buried, somewhere upon the Atlantic coast, by Kidd and his associates. These rumors must have had some foundation in fact. And that the rumors have existed so long and so continuous, could have resulted, it appeared to me, only from the cir-

cumstance of the buried treasures still *remaining* entombed. Had Kidd concealed his plunder for a time, and afterward reclaimed it, the rumors would scarcely have reached us in their present unvarying form. You will observe that the stories told are all about money-seekers, not about money-finders. Had the pirate recovered his money, there the affair would have dropped. It seemed to me that some accident — say the loss of a memorandum indicating its locality — had deprived him of the means of recovering it, and that this accident had become known to his followers, who otherwise might never have heard that the treasure had been concealed at all, and who, busying themselves in vain, because unguided, attempts to regain it, had given first birth, and then universal currency, to the reports which are now so common. Have you ever heard of any important treasure being unearthed along the coast?"

"Never."

"But that Kidd's accumulations were immense, is well known. I took it for granted, therefore, that the earth still held them; and you will scarcely be surprised when I tell you that I felt a hope, nearly amounting to certainty, that the parchment so strangely found involved a lost record of the place of deposit."

"But how did you proceed?"

"I held the vellum again to the fire, after increasing the heat, but nothing appeared. I now thought it possible that the coating of dirt might have something to do with the failure: so I carefully rinsed the parchment by pouring warm water over it, and, having done this, I placed it in a tin pan, with the skull downward, and put the pan upon a furnace of lighted charcoal. In a few minutes, the pan having become thoroughly heated, I removed the slip, and, to my inexpressible joy, found it spotted, in several places, with what appeared to be figures arranged in lines. Again I placed it in the pan, and suffered it to remain another minute. Upon taking it off, the whole was just as you see it now."

Here Legrand, having re-heated the parchment, submitted it to my inspection. The following characters were rudely traced, in a red tint, between the death's head and the goat:

53‡‡†305))6*;4826)4‡.)4‡);806*;48†8¶60))
85;1‡(;:‡*8†83(88)5*†;46(;88*96*?;8)*‡(;48
5);5*†2:*‡(;4956*2(5*—4)8¶8*;4069285);)6†
8)4‡‡;1(‡9;48081;8:8‡1;48†85;4)485†528806*
81(‡9;48;(88;4(‡?34;48)4‡;161;:188;‡?;

"But," said I, returning him the slip, "I am as much in the dark as ever. Were all the jewels of Golconda awaiting me upon my solution of this enigma, I am quite sure that I should be unable to earn them."

"And yet," said Legrand, "the solution is by no means so difficult as you might be led to imagine from the first hasty inspection of the char-

acters. These characters, as any one might readily guess, form a cipher —
that is to say, they convey a meaning; but then from what is known
of Kidd, I could not suppose him capable of constructing any of the
more abstruse cryptographs. I made up my mind, at once, that this was
a simple species — such, however, as would appear, to the crude intel-
lect of the sailor, absolutely insoluble without the key."

"And you really solved it?"

"Readily; I have solved others of an abstruseness ten thousand times
greater. Circumstances, and a certain bias of mind, have led me to take
interest in such riddles, and it may well be doubted whether human in-
genuity can construct an enigma of the kind which human ingenuity
may not, by proper application, resolve. In fact, having once established
connected and legible characters, I scarcely gave a thought to the mere
difficulty of developing their import.

"In the present case — indeed in all cases of secret writing — the first
question regards the *language* of the cipher; for the principles of solu-
tion, so far, especially, as the more simple ciphers are concerned, depend
upon, and are varied by, the genius of the particular idiom. In general,
there is no alternative but experiment (directed by probabilities) of
every tongue known to him who attempts the solution, until the true
one be attained. But, with the cipher now before us all difficulty was re-
moved by the signature. The pun upon the word 'Kidd' is appreciable
in no other language than the English. But for this consideration I should
have begun my attempts with the Spanish and French, as the tongues
in which a secret of this kind would most naturally have been written
by a pirate of the Spanish main. As it was, I assumed the cryptograph
to be English.

"You observe there are no divisions between the words. Had there
been divisions the task would have been comparatively easy. In such
cases I should have commenced with a collation and analysis of the
shorter words, and, had a word of a single letter occurred, as is most
likely, (*a* or *I*, for example,) I should have considered the solution as
assured. But, there being no division, my first step was to ascertain the
predominant letters, as well as the least frequent. Counting all, I con-
structed a table thus:

Of the character 8 there are 33.

;	"	26.
4	"	19.
‡)	"	16.
*	"	13.
5	"	12.
6	"	11.
† 1	"	8.
0	"	6.

Of the character 9 2 there are 5.

 : 3 " 4.

 ? " 3.

 ¶ " 2.

 — . " 1.

"Now, in English, the letter which most frequently occurs is *e*. Afterward, the succession runs thus: *a o i d h n r s t u y c f g l m w b k p q x z.* E predominates so remarkably, that an individual sentence of any length is rarely seen, in which it is not the prevailing character.

"Here, then, we have, in the very beginning, the groundwork for something more than a mere guess. The general use which may be made of the table is obvious — but, in this particular cipher, we shall only very partially require its aid. As our predominant character is 8, we will commence by assuming it as the *e* of the natural alphabet. To verify the supposition, let us observe if the 8 be seen often in couples — for *e* is doubled with great frequency in English — in such words, for example, as 'meet,' 'fleet,' 'speed,' 'seen,' 'been,' 'agree,' &c. In the present instance we see it doubled no less than five times, although the cryptograph is brief.

"Let us assume 8, then, as *e*. Now, of all *words* in the language, 'the' is most usual; let us see, therefore, whether there are not repetitions of any three characters, in the same order of collocation, the last of them being 8. If we discover repetitions of such letters, so arranged, they will most probably represent the word 'the.' Upon inspection, we find no less than seven such arrangements, the characters being ;48. We may, therefore, assume that ; represents *t*, 4 represents *h*, and 8 represents *e* — the last being now well confirmed. Thus a great step has been taken.

"But, having established a single word, we are enabled/to establish a vastly important point; that is to say, several commencements and terminations of other words. Let us refer, for example, to the last instance but one, in which the combination ;48 occurs — not far from the end of the cipher. We know that the ; immediately ensuing is the commencement of a word, and, of the six characters succeeding this 'the,' we are cognizant of no less than five. Let us set these characters down, thus, by the letters we know them to represent, leaving a space for the unknown —

t eeth

"Here we are enabled, at once, to discard the '*th*,' as forming no portion of the word commencing with the first *t*; since, by experiment of the entire alphabet for a letter adapted to the vacancy, we perceive that no word can be formed of which this *th* can be a part. We are thus narrowed into

t ee

and, going through the alphabet, if necessary, as before, we arrive at the word 'tree,' as the sole possible reading. We thus gain another letter, *r*, represented by (, with the words 'the tree' in juxtaposition.

"Looking beyond these words, for a short distance, we again see the combination ;48, and employ it by way of *termination* to what immediately precedes. We have thus this arrangement:

the tree ;4(‡?34 the,

or, substituting the natural letters, where known, it reads thus:

the tree thr‡?3h the.

"Now, if, in place of the unknown characters, we leave blank spaces, or substitute dots, we read thus:

the tree thr...h the,

when the word *'through'* makes itself evident at once. But this discovery gives us three new letters, *o*, *u*, and *g*, represented by ‡, ?, and 3.

"Looking now, narrowly, through the cipher for combinations of known characters, we find, not very far from the beginning, this arrangement,

83(88, or egree,

which plainly, is the conclusion of the word 'degree,' and gives us another letter, *d*, represented by †.

"Four letters beyond the word 'degree,' we perceive the combination

;46(;88.

"Translating the known characters, and representing the unknown by dots, as before, we read thus:

th.rtee

an arrangement immediately suggestive of the word 'thirteen,' and again furnishing us with two new characters, *i* and *n*, represented by 6 and *.

"Referring, now, to the beginning of the cryptograph, we find the combination,

53‡‡†.

"Translating as before, we obtain

.good,

which assures us that the first letter is A, and that the first two words are 'A good.'

"It is now time that we arrange our key, as far as discovered, in a tabular form, to avoid confusion. It will stand thus:

5	represents	a
†	"	d
8	"	e
3	"	g
4	"	h
6	"	i
*	"	n
‡	"	o
("	r
;	"	t

"We have therefore, no less than ten of the most important letters represented, and it will be unnecessary to proceed with the details of the solution. I have said enough to convince you that ciphers of this nature are readily soluble, and to give you some insight into the *rationale* of their development. But be assured that the specimen before us appertains to the very simplest species of cryptograph. It now only remains to give you the full translation of the characters upon the parchment, as unriddled. Here it is:

'A good glass in the bishop's hostel in the devil's seat forty-one degrees and thirteen minutes northeast and by north main branch seventh limb east side shoot from the left eye of the death's-head a bee line from the tree through the shot fifty feet out.'"

"But," said I, "the enigma seems still in as bad condition as ever. How is it possible to extort a meaning from all this jargon about 'devil's seats,' 'death's-heads,' and 'bishop's hotels?' "

"I confess," replied Legrand, "that the matter still wears a serious aspect, when regarded with a casual glance. My first endeavor was to divide the sentence into the natural division intended by the cryptographist."

"You mean, to punctuate it?"

"Something of that kind."

"But how was it possible to effect this?"

I reflected that it had been a *point* with the writer to run his words together without division, so as to increase the difficulty of solution. Now, a not over-acute man, in pursuing such an object, would be nearly certain to overdo the matter. When, in the course of his composition, he arrived at a break in his subject which would naturally require a pause, or a point, he would be exceedingly apt to run his characters, at this place, more than usually close together. If you will observe the MS., in the present instance, you will easily detect five such cases of unusual crowding. Acting upon this hint, I made the division thus:

"*A good glass in the Bishop's hostel in the Devil's seat — forty-one degrees and thirteen minutes — northeast and by north — main branch seventh limb east side — shoot from the left eye of the death's-head — a bee-line from the tree through the shot fifty feet out.*"

"Even this division," said I, "leaves me still in the dark."

"It left me also in the dark," replied Legrand, "for a few days; during which I made diligent inquiry in the neighborhood of Sullivan's Island, for any building which went by the name of the 'Bishop's Hotel'; for, of course, I dropped the obsolete word 'hostel.' Gaining no information on the subject, I was on the point of extending my sphere of search, and proceeding in a more systematic manner, when, one morning, it entered into my head, quite suddenly, that this 'Bishop's Hostel' might have some reference to an old family, of the name of Bessop, which, time out of mind, had held possession of an ancient manor-house, about four miles to the northward of the Island. I accordingly went over to the plantation, and re-instituted my inquiries among the older negroes of the place. At length one of the most aged of the women said that she had heard of such a place as *Bessop's Castle*, and thought that she could guide me to it, but that it was not a castle, nor a tavern, but a high rock.

"I offered to pay her well for her trouble, and, after some demur, she consented to accompany me to the spot. We found it without much difficulty, when, dismissing her, I proceeded to examine the place. The 'castle' consisted of an irregular assemblage of cliffs and rocks — one of the latter being quite remarkable for its height as well as for its insulated and artificial appearance. I clambered to its apex, and then felt much at a loss as to what should be next done.

"While I was busied in reflection, my eyes fell upon a narrow ledge in the eastern face of the rock, perhaps a yard below the summit upon which I stood. This ledge projected about eighteen inches, and was not more than a foot wide, while a niche in the cliff just above it gave it a rude resemblance to one of the hollow-backed chairs used by our ancestors. I made no doubt that here was the 'devil's-seat' alluded to in the MS., and now I seemed to grasp the full secret of the riddle.

"The 'good glass,' I knew, could have reference to nothing but a telescope; for the word 'glass' is rarely employed in any other sense by seamen. Now here, I at once saw, was a telescope to be used, and a definite point of view, *admitting no variation*, from which to use it. Nor did I hesitate to believe that the phrases 'forty-one degrees and thirteen minutes,' and 'northeast and by north,' were intended as directions for the levelling of the glass. Greatly excited by these discoveries, I hurried home, procured a telescope, and returned to the rock.

"I let myself down to the ledge, and found that it was impossible to retain a seat upon it except in one particular position. This fact con-

firmed my preconceived idea. I proceeded to use the glass. Of course, the 'forty-one degrees and thirteen minutes' could allude to nothing but elevation above the visible horizon, since the horizontal direction was clearly indicated by the words, 'northeast and by north.' This latter direction I at once established by means of a pocket-compass; then, pointing the glass as nearly at an angle of forty-one degrees of elevation as I could do it by guess, I moved it cautiously up or down, until my attention was arrested by a circular rift or opening in the foliage of a large tree that overtopped its fellows in the distance. In the centre of this rift I perceived a white spot, but could not, at first, distinguish what it was. Adjusting the focus of the telescope, I again looked, and now made it out to be a human skull.

"Upon this discovery I was so sanguine as to consider the enigma solved; for the phrase 'main branch, seventh limb, east side,' could refer only to the position of the skull upon the tree, while 'shoot from the left eye of the death's-head' admitted, also, of but one interpretation, in regard to a search for buried treasure. I perceived that the design was to drop a bullet from the left eye of the skull, and that a bee-line, or, in other words, a straight line, drawn from the nearest point of the trunk through 'the shot' (or the spot where the bullet fell), and thence extended to a distance of fifty feet, would indicate a definite point — and beneath this point I thought it at least *possible* that a deposit of value lay concealed."

"All this," I said, "is exceedingly clear, and, although ingenious, still simple and explicit. When you left the Bishop's Hotel, what then?"

"Why, having carefuly taken the bearings of the tree, I turned homeward. The instant that I left 'the devil's-seat,' however, the circular rift vanished; nor could I get a glimpse of it afterward, turn as I would. What seems to me the chief ingenuity in this whole business, is the fact (for repeated experiment has convinced me it *is* a fact) that the circular opening in question is visible from no other attainable point of view than that afforded by the narrow ledge upon the face of the rock.

"In this expedition to the 'Bishop's Hotel' I had been attended by Jupiter, who had, no doubt, observed, for some weeks past, the abstraction of my demeanor, and took especial care not to leave me alone. But, on the next day, getting up very early, I contrived to give him the slip, and went into the hills in search of the tree. After much toil I found it. When I came home at night my valet proposed to give me a flogging. With the rest of the adventure I believe you are as well acquainted as myself."

"I suppose," said I, "you missed the spot, in the first attempt at digging, through Jupiter's stupidity in letting the bug fall through the right instead of through the left eye of the skull."

"Precisely. This mistake made a difference of about two inches and a half in the 'shot' — that is to say, in the position of the peg nearest the

tree; and had the treasure been *beneath* the 'shot,' the error would have been of little moment; but 'the shot,' together with the nearest point of the tree, were merely two points for the establishment of a line of direction; of course the error, however trivial in the beginning, increased as we proceeded with the line, and by the time we had gone fifty feet threw us quite off the scent. But for my deep-seated impressions that treasure was here somewhere actually buried, we might have had all our labor in vain."

"But your grandiloquence, and your conduct in swinging the beetle — how excessively odd! I was sure you were mad. And why did you insist upon letting fall the bug, instead of a bullet, from the skull?"

"Why, to be frank, I felt somewhat annoyed by your evident suspicions touching my sanity, and so resolved to punish you quietly, in my own way, by a little bit of sober mystification. For this reason I swung the beetle, and for this reason I let it fall from the tree. An observation of yours about its great weight suggested the latter idea."

"Yes, I perceive; and now there is only one point which puzzles me. What are we to make of the skeletons found in the hole?"

"That is a question I am no more able to answer than yourself. There seems, however, only one plausible way of accounting for them — and yet it is dreadful to believe in such atrocity as my suggestion would imply. It is clear that Kidd — if Kidd indeed secreted this treasure, which I doubt not — it is clear that he must have had assistance in the labor. But this labor concluded, he may have thought it expedient to remove all participants in his secret. Perhaps a couple of blows with a mattock were sufficient, while his coadjutors were busy in the pit; perhaps it required a dozen — who shall tell?"

The Black Cat

For the most wild yet most homely narrative which I am about to pen, I neither expect nor solicit belief. Mad indeed would I be to expect it, in a case where my very senses reject their own evidence. Yet, mad am I not — and very surely do I not dream. But to-morrow I die, and to-day I would unburthen my soul. My immediate purpose is to place before the world, plainly, succinctly, and without comment, a series of mere household events. In their consequences, these events have terrified — have tortured — have destroyed me. Yet I will not attempt to expound them. To me, they have presented little but horror — to many they will seem less terrible than *barroques*. Hereafter, perhaps, some intellect

may be found which will reduce my phantasm to the commonplace — some intellect more calm, more logical, and far less excitable than my own, which will perceive, in the circumstances I detail with awe, nothing more than an ordinary succession of very natural causes and effects.

From my infancy I was noted for the docility and humanity of my disposition. My tenderness of heart was even so conspicuous as to make me the jest of my companions. I was especially fond of animals, and was indulged by my parents with a great variety of pets. With these I spent most of my time, and never was so happy as when feeding and caressing them. This peculiarity of character grew with my growth, and, in my manhood, I derived from it one of my principal sources of pleasure. To those who have cherished an affection for a faithful and sagacious dog, I need hardly be at the trouble of explaining the nature or the intensity of the gratification thus derivable. There is something in the unselfish and self-sacrificing love of a brute, which goes directly to the heart of him who has had frequent occasion to test the paltry friendship and gossamer fidelity of mere *Man*.

I married early, and was happy to find in my wife a disposition not uncongenial with my own. Observing my partiality for domestic pets, she lost no opportunity of procuring those of the most agreeable kind. We had birds, gold-fish, a fine dog, rabbits, a small monkey, and a *cat*.

This latter was a remarkably large and beautiful animal, entirely black, and sagacious to an astonishing degree. In speaking of his intelligence, my wife, who at heart was not a little tinctured with superstition, made frequent allusions to the ancient popular notion, which regarded all black cats as witches in disguise. Not that she was ever *serious* upon this point — and I mention the matter at all for no better reason than that it happens, just now, to be remembered.

Pluto — this was the cat's name — was my favorite pet and playmate. I alone fed him, and he attended me wherever I went about the house. It was even with difficulty that I could prevent him from following me through the streets.

Our friendship lasted, in this manner, for several years, during which my general temperament and character — through the instrumentality of the Fiend Intemperance — had (I blush to confess it) experienced a radical alteration for the worse. I grew, day by day, more moody, more irritable, more regardless of the feelings of others. I suffered myself to use intemperate language to my wife. At length, I even offered her personal violence. My pets, of course, were made to feel the change in my disposition. I not only neglected, but ill-used them. For Pluto, however, I still retained sufficient regard to restrain me from maltreating him, as I made no scruple of maltreating the rabbits, the monkey, or even the dog, when, by accident, or through affection, they came in my way. But my disease grew upon me — for what disease is like Alcohol! — and at

length even Pluto, who was now becoming old, and consequently somewhat peevish — even Pluto began to experience the effects of my ill temper.

One night, returning home, much intoxicated, from one of my haunts about town, I fancied that the cat avoided my presence. I seized him; when, in his fright at my violence, he inflicted a slight wound upon my hand with his teeth. The fury of a demon instantly possessed me. I knew myself no longer. My original soul seemed, at once, to take its flight from my body; and a more than fiendish malevolence, gin-nurtured, thrilled every fibre of my frame. I took from my waistcoat-pocket a penknife, opened it, grasped the poor beast by the throat, and deliberately cut one of its eyes from the socket! I blush, I burn, I shudder, while I pen the damnable atrocity.

When reason returned with the morning — when I had slept off the fumes of the night's debauch — I experienced a sentiment half of horror, half of remorse, for the crime of which I had been guilty; but it was, at best, a feeble and equivocal feeling, and the soul remained untouched. I again plunged into excess, and soon drowned in wine all memory of the deed.

In the meantime the cat slowly recovered. The socket of the lost eye presented, it is true, a frightful appearance, but he no longer appeared to suffer any pain. He went about the house as usual, but, as might be expected, fled in extreme terror at my approach. I had so much of my old heart left, as to be at first grieved by this evident dislike on the part of a creature which had once so loved me. But this feeling soon gave place to irritation. And then came, as if to my final and irrevocable overthrow, the spirit of PERVERSENESS. Of this spirit philosophy takes no account. Yet I am not more sure that my soul lives, than I am that perverseness is one of the primitive impulses of the human heart — one of the indivisible primary faculties, or sentiments, which give direction to the character of Man. Who has not, a hundred times, found himself committing a vile or a silly action, for no other reason than because he knows he should *not*? Have we not a perpetual inclination, in the teeth of our best judgment, to violate that which is *Law*, merely because we understand it to be such? This spirit of perverseness, I say, came to my final overthrow. It was this unfathomable longing of the soul to vex *itself* — to offer violence to its own nature — to do wrong for the wrong's sake only — that urged me to continue and finally to consummate the injury I had inflicted upon the unoffending brute. One morning, in cool blood, I slipped a noose about its neck and hung it to the limb of a tree — hung it with the tears streaming from my eyes, and with the bitterest remorse at my heart — hung it *because* I knew that it had loved me, and *because* I felt it had given me no reason of offence; — hung it *because* I knew that in so doing I was committing a sin — a deadly sin that would so jeopardize my immortal soul as to place it —

if such a thing were possible — even beyond the reach of the infinite mercy of the Most Merciful and Most Terrible God.

On the night of the day on which this cruel deed was done, I was aroused from sleep by the cry of fire. The curtains of my bed were in flames. The whole house was blazing. It was with great difficulty that my wife, a servant, and myself, made our escape from the conflagration. The destruction was complete. My entire worldly wealth was swallowed up, and I resigned myself thenceforward to despair.

I am above the weakness of seeking to establish a sequence of cause and effect, between the disaster and the atrocity. But I am detailing a chain of facts — and wish not to leave even a possible link imperfect. On the day succeeding the fire, I visited the ruins. The walls, with one exception, had fallen in. This exception was found in a compartment wall, not very thick, which stood about the middle of the house, and against which had rested the head of my bed. The plastering had here, in great measure, resisted the action of the fire — a fact which I attributed to its having been recently spread. About this wall a dense crowd were collected, and many persons seemed to be examining a particular portion of it with very minute and eager attention. The words "strange!" "singular!" and other similar expressions, excited my curiosity. I approached and saw, as if graven in *bas-relief* upon the white surface, the figure of a gigantic *cat*. The impression was given with an accuracy truly marvellous. There was a rope about the animal's neck.

When I first beheld this apparition — for I could scarcely regard it as less — my wonder and my terror were extreme. But at length reflection came to my aid. The cat, I remembered, had been hung in a garden adjacent to the house. Upon the alarm of fire, this garden had been immediately filled by the crowd — by some one of whom the animal must have been cut from the tree and thrown, through an open window, into my chamber. This had probably been done with the view of arousing me from sleep. The falling of other walls had compressed the victim of my cruelty into the substance of the freshly-spread plaster; the lime of which, with the flames, and the *ammonia* from the carcass, had then accomplished the portraiture as I saw it.

Although I thus readily accounted to my reason, if not altogether to my conscience, for the startling fact just detailed, it did not the less fail to make a deep impression upon my fancy. For months I could not rid myself of the phantasm of the cat; and, during this period, there came back into my spirit a half-sentiment that seemed, but was not, remorse. I went so far as to regret the loss of the animal, and to look about me, among the vile haunts which I now habitually frequented, for another pet of the same species, and of somewhat similar appearance, with which to supply its place.

One night as I sat, half stupefied, in a den of more than infamy, my attention was suddenly drawn to some black object, reposing upon the

head of one of the immense hogsheads of Gin, or of Rum, which constituted the chief furniture of the apartment. I had been looking steadily at the top of this hogshead for some minutes, and what now caused me surprise was the fact that I had not sooner perceived the object thereupon. I approached it, and touched it with my hand. It was a black cat — a very large one — fully as large as Pluto, and closely resembling him in every respect but one. Pluto had not a white hair upon any portion of his body; but this cat had a large, although indefinite splotch of white, covering nearly the whole region of the breast.

Upon my touching him, he immediately arose, purred loudly, rubbed against my hand, and appeared delighted with my notice. This, then, was the very creature of which I was in search. I at once offered to purchase it of the landlord; but this person made no claim to it — knew nothing of it — had never seen it before.

I continued my caresses, and when I prepared to go home, the animal evinced a disposition to accompany me. I permitted it to do so; occasionally stooping and patting it as I proceeded. When it reached the house it domesticated itself at once, and became immediately a great favorite with my wife.

For my own part, I soon found a dislike to it arising within me. This was just the reverse of what I had anticipated; but — I know not how or why it was — its evident fondness for myself rather disgusted and annoyed. By slow degrees these feelings of disgust and annoyance rose into the bitterness of hatred. I avoided the creature; a certain sense of shame, and the remembrance of my former deed of cruelty, prevented me from physically abusing it. I did not, for some weeks, strike, or otherwise violently ill use it; but gradually — very gradually — I came to look upon it with unutterable loathing, and to flee silently from its odious presence, as from the breath of a pestilence.

What added, no doubt, to my hatred of the beast, was the discovery, on the morning after I brought it home, that, like Pluto, it also had been deprived of one of its eyes. This circumstance, however, only endeared it to my wife, who, as I have already said, possessed, in a high degree, that humanity of feeling which had once been my distinguishing trait, and the source of many of my simplest and purest pleasures.

With my aversion to this cat, however, its partiality for myself seemed to increase. It followed my footsteps with a pertinacity which it would be difficult to make the reader comprehend. Wherever I sat, it would crouch beneath my chair, or spring upon my knees, covering me with its loathsome caresses. If I arose to walk it would get between my feet and thus nearly throw me down, or, fastening its long and sharp claws in my dress, clamber, in this manner, to my breast. At such times, although I longed to destroy it with a blow, I was yet withheld from so doing, partly by a memory of my former crime, but chiefly — let me confess it at once — by absolute *dread* of the beast.

This dread was not exactly a dread of physical evil — and yet I should be at a loss how otherwise to define it. I am almost ashamed to own — yes, even in this felon's cell, I am almost ashamed to own — that the terror and horror with which the animal inspired me, had been heightened by one of the merest chimeras it would be possible to conceive. My wife had called my attention, more than once, to the character of the mark of white hair, of which I have spoken, and which constituted the sole visible difference between the strange beast and the one I had destroyed. The reader will remember that this mark, although large, had been originally very indefinite; but, by slow degrees — degrees nearly imperceptible, and which for a long time my reason struggled to reject as fanciful — it had, at length, assumed a rigorous distinctness of outline. It was now the representation of an object that I shudder to name — and for this, above all, I loathed, and dreaded, and would have rid myself of the monster *had I dared* — it was now, I say, the image of a hideous — of a ghastly thing — of the GALLOWS! — oh, mournful and terrible engine of Horror and of Crime — of Agony and of Death!

And now I was indeed wretched beyond the wretchedness of mere Humanity. And *a brute beast* — whose fellow I had contemptuously destroyed — *a brute beast* to work out for *me* — for me, a man fashioned in the image of the High God — so much of insufferable wo! Alas! neither by day nor by night knew I the blessing of Rest any more! During the former the creature left me no moment alone, and in the latter I started hourly from dreams of unutterable fear to find the hot breath of *the thing* upon my face, and its vast weight — an incarnate Night-Mare that I had no power to shake off — incumbent eternally upon my *heart!*

Beneath the pressure of torments such as these the feeble remnant of the good within me succumbed. Evil thoughts became my sole intimates —the darkest and most evil of thoughts. The moodiness of my usual temper increased to hatred of all things and of all mankind; while from the sudden, frequent, and ungovernable outbursts of a fury to which I now blindly abandoned myself, my uncomplaining wife, alas! was the most usual and the most patient of sufferers.

One day she accompanied me, upon some household errand, into the cellar of the old building which our poverty compelled us to inhabit. The cat followed me down the steep stairs, and, nearly throwing me headlong, exasperated me to madness. Uplifting an axe, and forgetting in my wrath the childish dread which had hitherto stayed my hand, I aimed a blow at the animal, which, of course, would have proved instantly fatal had it descended as I wished. But this blow was arrested by the hand of my wife. Goaded by the interference into a rage more than demoniacal, I withdrew my arm from her grasp and buried the axe in her brain. She fell dead upon the spot without a groan.

This hideous murder accomplished, I set myself forthwith, and with entire deliberation, to the task of concealing the body. I knew that I

could not remove it from the house, either by day or night, without the risk of being observed by the neighbors. Many projects entered my mind. At one period I thought of cutting the corpse into minute fragments, and destroying them by fire. At another, I resolved to dig a grave for it in the floor of the cellar. Again, I deliberated about casting it in the well in the yard — about packing it in a box, as if merchandise, with the usual arrangements, and so getting a porter to take it from the house. Finally I hit upon what I considered a far better expedient than either of these. I determined to wall it up in the cellar — as the monks of the Middle Ages are recorded to have walled up their victims.

For a purpose such as this the cellar was well adapted. Its walls were loosely constructed, and had lately been plastered throughout with a rough plaster, which the dampness of the atmosphere had prevented from hardening. Moreover, in one of the walls was a projection, caused by a false chimney, or fire-place, that had been filled up and made to resemble the rest of the cellar. I made no doubt that I could readily displace the bricks at this point, insert the corpse, and wall the whole up as before, so that no eye could detect any thing suspicious.

And in this calculation I was not deceived. By means of a crow-bar I easily dislodged the bricks, and, having carefully deposited the body against the inner wall, I propped it in that position, while with little trouble I relaid the whole structure as it originally stood. Having procured mortar, sand, and hair, with every possible precaution, I prepared a plaster which could not be distinguished from the old, and with this I very carefully went over the new brick-work. When I had finished, I felt satisfied that all was right. The wall did not present the slightest appearance of having been disturbed. The rubbish on the floor was picked up with the minutest care. I looked around triumphantly, and said to myself — "Here at least, then, my labor has not been in vain."

My next step was to look for the beast which had been the cause of so much wickedness; for I had, at length, firmly resolved to put it to death. Had I been able to meet with it at the moment, there could have been no doubt of its fate; but it appeared that the crafty animal had been alarmed at the violence of my previous anger, and forebore to present itself in my present mood. It is impossible to describe or to imagine the deep, the blissful sense of relief which the absence of the detested creature occasioned in my bosom. It did not make its appearance during the night — and thus for one night, at least, since its introduction into the house, I soundly and tranquilly slept; aye, *slept* even with the burden of murder upon my soul.

The second and the third day passed, and still my tormentor came not. Once again I breathed as a free man. The monster, in terror, had fled the premises for ever! I should behold it no more! My happiness was supreme! The guilt of my dark deed disturbed me but little. Some few inquiries had been made, but these had been readily answered. Even a

search had been instituted — but of course nothing was to be discovered. I looked upon my future felicity as secured.

Upon the fourth day of the assassination, a party of the police came, very unexpectedly, into the house, and proceeded again to make rigorous investigation of the premises. Secure, however, in the inscrutability of my place of concealment, I felt no embarrassment whatever. The officers bade me accompany them in their search. They left no nook or corner unexplored. At length, for the third or fourth time, they descended into the cellar. I quivered not in a muscle. My heart beat calmly as that of one who slumbers in innocence. I walked the cellar from end to end. I folded my arms upon my bosom, and roamed easily to and fro. The police were thoroughly satisfied and prepared to depart. The glee at my heart was too strong to be restrained. I burned to say if but one word, by way of triumph, and to render doubly sure their assurance of my guiltlessness.

"Gentlemen," I said at last, as the party ascended the steps, "I delight to have allayed your suspicions. I wish you all health and a little more courtesy. By the bye, gentlemen, this — this is a very well-constructed house," (in the rabid desire to say something easily, I scarcely knew what I uttered at all), — "I may say an *excellently* well-constructed house. These walls — are you going, gentlemen? — these walls are solidly put together"; and here, through the mere frenzy of bravado, I rapped heavily with a cane which I held in my hand, upon that very portion of the brickwork behind which stood the corpse of the wife of my bosom.

But may God shield and deliver me from the fangs of the Arch-Fiend! No sooner had the reverberation of my blows sunk into silence, than I was answered by a voice from within the tomb! — by a cry, at first muffled and broken, like the sobbing of a child, and then quickly swelling into one long, loud and continuous scream, utterly anomalous and inhuman — a howl — a wailing shriek, half of horror and half of triumph, such as might have arisen only out of hell, conjointly from the throats of the damned in their agony and of the demons that exult in the damnation.

Of my own thoughts it is folly to speak. Swooning, I staggered to the opposite wall. For one instant the party on the stairs remained motionless through extremity of terror and awe. In the next a dozen stout arms were toiling at the wall. It fell bodily. The corpse, already greatly decayed and clotted with gore, stood erect before the eyes of the spectators. Upon its head, with red extended mouth and solitary eye of fire, sat the hideous beast whose craft had seduced me into murder, and whose informing voice had consigned me to the hangman. I had walled the monster up within the tomb.

Diddling

CONSIDERED AS ONE OF THE EXACT SCIENCES

Hey, diddle diddle,
The cat and the fiddle.

SINCE the world began there have been two Jeremys. The one wrote a
Jeremiad about usury, and was called Jeremy Bentham. He has been
much admired by Mr. John Neal, and was a great man in a small way.
The other gave name to the most important of the Exact Sciences, and
was a great man in a *great* way — I may say, indeed, in the very greatest
of ways.

Diddling — or the abstract idea conveyed by the verb to diddle — is
sufficiently well understood. Yet the fact, the deed, the thing *diddling,*
is somewhat difficult to define. We may get, however, at a tolerably
distinct conception of the matter in hand, by defining — not the thing,
diddling, in itself — but man, as an animal that diddles. Had Plato but
hit upon this, he would have been spared the affront of the picked
chicken.

Very pertinently it was demanded of Plato, why a picked chicken,
which was clearly "a biped without feathers," was not, according to his
own definition, a man? But I am not to be bothered by any similar query.
Man is an animal that diddles, and there is *no* animal that diddles *but*
man. It will take an entire hen-coop of picked chickens to get over that.

What constitutes the essence, the nare, the principle of diddling is,
in fact, peculiar to the class of creatures that wear coats and pantaloons.
A crow thieves; a fox cheats; a weasel outwits; a man diddles. To diddle
is his destiny. "Man was made to mourn," says the poet. But not so: —
he was made to diddle. This is his aim — his object — his *end.* And for
this reason when a man's diddled we say he's *"done."*

Diddling, rightly considered, is a compound, of which the ingredients
are minuteness, interest, perseverance, ingenuity, audacity, *nonchalance,*
originality, impertinence, and *grin.*

Minuteness: — Your diddler is minute. His operations are upon a small
scale. His business is retail, for cash, or approved paper at sight. Should
he ever be tempted into magnificent speculation, he then, at once, loses
his distinctive features, and becomes what we term "financier." This lat-
ter word conveys the diddling idea in every respect except that of mag-
nitude. A diddler may thus be regarded as a banker *in petto* — a "financial
operation," as a diddle at Brobdignag. The one is to the other, as Homer
to "Flaccus" — as a Mastodon to a mouse — as the tail of a comet to
that of a pig.

Interest: — Your diddler is guided by self-interest. He scorns to diddle for the mere *sake* of the diddle. He has an object in view — his pocket — and yours. He regards always the main chance. He looks to Number One. You are Number Two, and must look to yourself.

Perseverance: — Your diddler perseveres. He is not readily discouraged. Should even the banks break, he cares nothing about it. He steadily pursues his end, and

> *Ut canis a corio nunquam absterrebitur uncto.*

so he never lets go of his game.

Ingenuity: — Your diddler is ingenious. He has constructiveness large. He understands plot. He invents and circumvents. Were he not Alexander he would be Diogenes. Were he not a diddler, he would be a maker of patent rat-traps or an angler for trout.

Audacity: — Your diddler is audacious. — He is a bold man. He carries the war into Africa. He conquers all by assault. He would not fear the daggers of Frey Herren. With a little more prudence Dick Turpin would have made a good diddler; with a trifle less blarney, Daniel O'Connell; with a pound or two more brains Charles the Twelfth.

Nonchalance: — Your diddler is *nonchalant.* He is not at all nervous. He never *had* any nerves. He is never seduced into a flurry. He is never put out — unless put out of doors. He is cool — cool as a cucumber. He is calm — "calm as a smile from Lady Bury." He is easy — easy as an old glove, or the damsels of ancient Baiæ.

Originality: — Your diddler is original — conscientiously so. His thoughts are his own. He would scorn to employ those of another. A stale trick is his aversion. He would return a purse, I am sure, upon discovering that he had obtained it by an unoriginal diddle.

Impertinence: — Your diddler is impertinent. He swaggers. He sets his arms a-kimbo. He thrusts his hands in your trowsers' pockets. He sneers in your face. He treads on your corns. He eats your dinner, he drinks your wine, he borrows your money, he pulls your nose, he kicks your poodle, and he kisses your wife.

Grin: — Your *true* diddler winds up all with a grin. But this nobody sees but himself. He grins when his daily work is done — when his allotted labors are accomplished — at night in his own closet, and altogether for his own private entertainment. He goes home. He locks his door. He divests himself of his clothes. He puts out his candle. He gets into bed. He places his head upon the pillow. All this done, and your diddler *grins.* This is no hypothesis. It is a matter of course. I reason *à priori,* and a diddle would be *no* diddle without a grin.

The origin of the diddle is referrable to the infancy of the Human Race. Perhaps the first diddler was Adam. At all events, we can trace the science back to a very remote period of antiquity. The moderns, however, have brought it to a perfection never dreamed of by our thickheaded progenitors. Without pausing to speak of the "old saws," there-

fore, I shall content myself with a compendious account of some of the
more "modern instances."

A very good diddle is this. A housekeeper in want of a sofa, for in-
stance, is seen to go in and out of several cabinet warehouses. At length
she arrives at one offering an excellent variety. She is accosted, and in-
vited to enter, by a polite and voluble individual at the door. She finds
a sofa well adapted to her views, and upon inquiring the price, is sur-
prised and delighted to hear a sum named at least twenty per cent. lower
than her expectations. She hastens to make the purchase, gets a bill and
receipt, leaves her address, with a request that the article be sent home
as speedily as possible, and retires amid a profusion of bows from the
shopkeeper. The night arrives and no sofa. A servant is sent to make
inquiry about the delay. The whole transaction is denied. No sofa has
been sold — no money received — except by the diddler, who played
shop-keeper for the nonce.

Our cabinet warehouses are left entirely unattended, and thus afford
every facility for a trick of this kind. Visiters enter, look at furniture,
and depart unheeded and unseen. Should any one wish to purchase, or
to inquire the price of an article, a bell is at hand, and this is considered
amply sufficient.

Again, quite a respectable diddle is this. A well-dressed individual en-
ters a shop; makes a purchase to the value of a dollar; finds, much to his
vexation, that he has left his pocket-book in another coat pocket; and
so says to the shopkeeper —

"My dear sir, never mind; just oblige me, will you, by sending the
bundle home? But stay! I really believe that I have nothing less than a
five dollar bill, even *there*. However, you can send four dollars in change
with the bundle, you know."

"Very good, sir," replies the shop-keeper, who entertains, at once, a
lofty opinion of the high-mindedness of his customer. "I know fellows,"
he says to himself, "who would just have put the goods under their arm,
and walked off with a promise to call and pay the dollar as they came
by in the afternoon."

A boy is sent with the parcel and change. On the route, quite acci-
dentally, he is met by the purchaser, who exclaims:

"Ah! this is my bundle, I see — I thought you had been home with it,
long ago. Well, go on! My wife, Mrs. Trotter, will give you the five dol-
lars — I left instructions with her to that effect. The change you might
as well give to *me* — I shall want some silver for the Post Office. Very
good! One, two, is this a good quarter? — three, four — quite right! Say
to Mrs. Trotter that you met me, and be sure now and *do* not loiter on
the way."

The boy doesn't loiter at all — but he is a very long time in getting
back from his errand — for no lady of the precise name of Mrs. Trotter
is to be discovered. He consoles himself, however, that he has not been

such a fool as to leave the goods without the money, and re-entering his shop with a self-satisfied air, feels sensibly hurt and indignant when his master asks him what has become of the change.

A very simple diddle, indeed, is this. The captain of a ship, which is about to sail, is presented by an official looking person with an unusually moderate bill of city charges. Glad to get off so easily, and confused by a hundred duties pressing upon him all at once, he discharges the claim forthwith. In about fifteen minutes, another and less reasonable bill is handed him by one who soon makes it evident that the first collector was a diddler, and the original collection a diddle.

And here, too, is a somewhat similar thing. A steamboat is casting loose from the wharf. A traveller, portmanteau in hand, is discovered running toward the wharf, at full speed. Suddenly, he makes a dead halt, stoops, and picks up something from the ground in a very agitated manner. It is a pocket-book, and — "Has any gentleman lost a pocket-book?" he cries. No one can say that he has exactly lost a pocket-book; but a great excitement ensues, when the treasure trove is found to be of value. The boat, however, must not be detained.

"Time and tide wait for no man," says the captain.

"For God's sake, stay only a few minutes," says the finder of the book — "the true claimant will presently appear."

"Can't wait!" replies the man in authority; "cast off there, d'ye hear?"

"What *am* I to do?" asks the finder, in great tribulation. "I am about to leave the country for some years, and I cannot conscientiously retain this large amount in my possession. I beg your pardon, sir," [here he addresses a gentleman on shore,] "but you have the air of an honest man. *Will* you confer upon me the favor of taking charge of this pocket-book — I *know* I can trust you — and of advertising it? The notes, you see, amount to a very considerable sum. The owner will, no doubt, insist upon rewarding you for your trouble — "

"*Me!* — no, *you!* — it was *you* who found the book."

"Well, if you *must* have it so — *I* will take a small reward — just to satisfy your scruples. Let me see — why these notes are all hundreds — bless my soul! a hundred is too much to take — fifty would be quite enough, I am sure — "

"Cast off there!" says the captain.

"But then I have no change for a hundred, and upon the whole, *you* had better — "

"Cast off there!" says the captain.

"Never mind!" cries the gentleman on shore, who has been examining his own pocket-book for the last minute or so — "never mind! *I* can fix it — here is a fifty on the Bank of North America — throw me the book."

And the over-conscientious finder takes the fifty with marked reluctance, and throws the gentleman the book, as desired, while the steamboat fumes and fizzes on her way. In about half an hour after her de-

parture, the "large amount" is seen to be a "counterfeit presentment," and the whole thing a capital diddle.

A bold diddle is this. A camp-meeting, or something similar, is to be held at a certain spot which is accessible only by means of a free bridge. A diddler stations himself upon this bridge, respectfully informs all passers by of the new county law, which establishes a toll of one cent for foot passengers, two for horses and donkeys, and so forth, and so forth. Some grumble but all submit, and the diddler goes home a wealthier man by some fifty or sixty dollars well earned. This taking a toll from a great crowd of people is an excessively troublesome thing.

A neat diddle is this. A friend holds one of the diddler's promises to pay, filled up and signed in due form, upon the ordinary blanks printed in red ink. The diddler purchases one or two dozen of these blanks, and every day dips one of them in his soup, makes his dog jump for it, and finally gives it to him as a *bonne bouche*. The note arriving at maturity, the diddler, with the diddler's dog, calls upon the friend, and the promise to pay is made the topic of discussion. The friend produces it from his *escritoire*, and is in the act of reaching it to the diddler, when up jumps the diddler's dog and devours it forthwith. The diddler is not only surprised but vexed and incensed at the absurd behavior of his dog, and expresses his entire readiness to cancel the obligation at any moment when the evidence of the obligation shall be forthcoming.

A very mean diddle is this. A lady is insulted in the street by a diddler's accomplice. The diddler himself flies to her assistance, and, giving his friend a comfortable thrashing, insists upon attending the lady to her own door. He bows, with his hand upon his heart, and most respectfully bids her adieu. She entreats him, as her deliverer, to walk in and be introduced to her big brother and her papa. With a sigh, he declines to do so. "Is there no way, then, sir," she murmurs, "in which I may be permitted to testify my gratitude?"

"Why, yes, madam, there is. Will you be kind enough to lend me a couple of shillings?"

In the first excitement of the moment the lady decides upon fainting outright. Upon second thought, however, she opens her purse-strings and delivers the specie. Now this, I say, is a diddle minute — for one entire moiety of the sum borrowed has to be paid to the gentleman who had the trouble of performing the insult, and who had then to stand still and be thrashed for performing it.

Rather a small, but still a scientific diddle is this. The diddler approaches the bar of a tavern, and demands a couple of twists of tobacco. These are handed to him, when, having slightly examined them, he says:

"I don't much like this tobacco. Here, take it back, and give me a glass of brandy and water in its place."

The brandy and water is furnished and imbibed, and the diddler makes his way to the door. But the voice of the tavern-keeper arrests him.

"I believe, sir, you have forgotten to pay for your brandy and water."

"Pay for my brandy and water! — didn't I give you the tobacco for the brandy and water? What more would you have?"

"But, sir, if you please, I don't remember that you paid me for the tobacco."

"What do you mean by that, you scoundrel? — Didn't I give you back your tobacco? Isn't *that* your tobacco lying *there?* Do you expect me to pay for what I did not take?"

"But, sir," says the publican, now rather at a loss what to say, "but sir — "

"But me no buts, sir," interrupts the diddler, apparently in very high dudgeon, and slamming the door after him, as he makes his escape. — "But me no buts, sir, and none of your tricks upon travellers."

Here again is a very clever diddle, of which the simplicity is not its least recommendation. A purse, or pocket-book, being really lost, the loser inserts in *one* of the daily papers of a large city a fully descriptive advertisement.

Whereupon our diddler copies the *facts* of this advertisement, with a change of heading, of general phraseology and *address*. The original, for instance, is long, and verbose, is headed "A Pocket-Book Lost!" and requires the treasure, when found, to be left at No. 1 Tom Street. The copy is brief, and being headed with "Lost" only, indicates No. 2 Dick, or No. 3 Harry Street, as the locality at which the owner may be seen. Moreover, it is inserted in at least five or six of the daily papers of the day, while in point of time, it makes its appearance only a few hours after the original. Should it be read by the loser of the purse, he would hardly suspect it to have any reference to his own misfortune. But, of course, the chances are five or six to one, that the finder will repair to the address given by the diddler, rather than to that pointed out by the rightful proprietor. The former pays the reward, pockets the treasure and decamps.

Quite an analogous diddle is this. A lady of *ton* has dropped, some where in the street, a diamond ring of very unusual value. For its recovery, she offers some forty or fifty dollars reward — giving, in her advertisement, a very minute description of the gem, and of its settings, and declaring that, on its restoration at No. so and so, in such and such Avenue, the reward would be paid *instanter*, without a single question being asked. During the lady's absence from home, a day or two afterwards, a ring is heard at the door of No. so and so, in such and such Avenue; a servant appears; the lady of the house is asked for and is declared to be out, at which astounding information, the visitor expresses the most poignant regret. His business is of importance and concerns the lady herself. In fact, he had the good fortune to find her diamond ring. But perhaps it would be as well that he should call again. "By no means!" says the servant; and "By no means!" says the lady's sister and

the lady's sister-in-law, who are summoned forthwith. The ring is clamorously identified, the reward is paid, and the finder nearly thrust out of doors. The lady returns and expresses some little dissatisfaction with her sister and sister-in-law, because they happen to have paid forty or fifty dollars for a *fac-simile* of her diamond ring — a *fac-simile* made out of real pinch-beck and unquestionable paste.

But as there is really no end to diddling, so there would be none to this essay, were I even to hint at half the variations, or inflections, of which this science is susceptible. I must bring this paper, perforce, to a conclusion, and this I cannot do better than by a summary notice of a very decent, but rather elaborate diddle, of which our own city was made the theatre, not very long ago, and which was subsequently repeated with success, in other still more verdant localities of the Union. A middle-aged gentleman arrives in town from parts unknown. He is remarkably precise, cautious, staid, and deliberate in his demeanor. His dress is scrupulously neat, but plain, unostentatious. He wears a white cravat, an ample waistcoat, made with an eye to comfort alone; thick-soled cosy-looking shoes, and pantaloons without straps. He has the whole air, in fact, of your well-to-do, sober-sided, exact, and respectable "man of business," *par excellence* — one of the stern and outwardly hard, internally soft, sort of people that we see in the crack high comedies — fellows whose words are so many bonds, and who are noted for giving away guineas, in charity, with the one hand, while, in the way of mere bargain, they exact the uttermost fraction of a farthing with the other.

He makes much ado before he can get suited with a boarding house. He dislikes children. He has been accustomed to quiet. His habits are methodical — and then he would prefer getting into a private and respectable small family, piously inclined. Terms, however, are no object — only he must insist upon settling his bill on the first of every month, (it is now the second) and begs his landlady, when he finally obtains one to his mind, *not* on any account to forget his instructions upon this point — but to send in a bill, *and* receipt, precisely at ten o'clock, on the *first* day of every month, and under no circumstances to put it off to the second.

These arrangements made, our man of business rents an office in a reputable rather than a fashionable quarter of the town. There is nothing he more despises than pretense. "Where there is much show," he says, "there is seldom any thing very solid behind" — an observation which so profoundly impresses his landlady's fancy, that she makes a pencil memorandum of it forthwith, in her great family Bible, on the broad margin of the Proverbs of Solomon.

The next step is to advertise, after some such fashion as this, in the principal business six-pennies of the city — the pennies are eschewed as not "respectable" — and as demanding payment for all advertisements in

advance. Our man of business holds it as a point of his faith that work should never be paid for until done.

"WANTED. — The advertisers, being about to commence extensive business operations in this city, will require the services of three or four intelligent and competent clerks, to whom a liberal salary will be paid. The very best recommendations, not so much for capacity, as for integrity, will be expected. Indeed, as the duties to be performed involve high responsibilities, and large amounts of money must necessarily pass through the hands of those engaged, it is deemed advisable to demand a deposit of fifty dollars from each clerk employed. No person need apply, therefore, who is not prepared to leave this sum in the possession of the advertisers, and who cannot furnish the most satisfactory testimonials of morality. Young gentlemen piously inclined will be preferred. Application should be made between the hours of ten and eleven A. M., and four and five P. M., of Messrs.

"BOGS, HOGS, LOGS, FROGS & CO.,
"No. 110 Dog Street."

By the thirty-first day of the month, this advertisement has brought to the office of Messrs. Bogs, Hogs, Logs, Frogs, and Company, some fifteen or twenty young gentlemen piously inclined. But our man of business is in no hurry to conclude a contract with any — no man of business is *ever* precipitate — and it is not until the most rigid catechism in respect to the piety of each young gentleman's inclination, that his services are engaged and his fifty dollars receipted for, *just* by way of proper precaution, on the part of the respectable firm of Bogs, Hogs, Logs, Frogs, and Company. On the morning of the first day of the next month, the landlady does *not* present her bill, according to promise — a piece of neglect for which the comfortable head of the house ending in *ogs* would no doubt have chided her severely, could he have been prevailed upon to remain in town a day or two for that purpose.

As it is, the constables have had a sad time of it, running hither and thither, and all they can do is to declare the man of business most emphatically, a "hen knee high" — by which some persons imagine them to imply that, in fact, he is n. e. i. — by which again the very classical phrase *non est inventus*, is supposed to be understood. In the meantime the young gentlemen, one and all, are somewhat less piously inclined than before, while the landlady purchases a shilling's worth of the Indian rubber, and very carefully obliterates the pencil memorandum that some fool has made in her great family Bible, on the broad margin of the Proverbs of Solomon.

Morning on the Wissahiccon

THE NATURAL scenery of America has often been contrasted, in its general features as well as in detail, with the landscape of the Old World — more especially of Europe — and not deeper has been the enthusiasm, than wide the dissension, of the supporters of each region. The discussion is one not likely to be soon closed, for, although much has been said on both sides, a word more yet remains to be said.

The most conspicuous of the British tourists who have attempted a comparison, seem to regard our northern and eastern seaboard, comparatively speaking, as all of America, at least, as all of the United States, worthy consideration. They say little, because they have seen less, of the gorgeous interior scenery of some of our western and southern districts — of the vast valley of Louisiana, for example, — a realization of the wildest dreams of paradise. For the most part, these travellers content themselves with a hasty inspection of the natural *lions* of the land — the Hudson, Niagara, the Catskills, Harper's Ferry, the lakes of New York, the Ohio, the prairies, and the Mississippi. These, indeed, are objects well worthy the contemplation even of him who has just clambered by the castellated Rhine, or roamed

By the blue rushing of the arrowy Rhone;

but these are not *all* of which we can boast; and, indeed, I will be so hardy as to assert that there are innumerable quiet, obscure, and scarcely explored nooks, within the limits of the United States, that, by the true artist, or cultivated lover of the grand and beautiful amid the works of God, will be preferred to each *and to all* of the chronicled and better accredited scenes to which I have referred.

In fact, the real Edens of the land lie far away from the track of our own most deliberate tourists — how very far, then, beyond the reach of the foreigner, who, having made with his publisher at home arrangements for a certain amount of comment upon America, to be furnished in a stipulated period, can hope to fulfil his agreement in no other manner than by steaming it, memorandum-book in hand, through only the most beaten thoroughfares of the country!

I mentioned, just above, the valley of Louisiana. Of all extensive areas of natural loveliness, this is perhaps the most lovely. No fiction has approached it. The most gorgeous imagination might derive suggestions from its exuberant beauty. And *beauty* is, indeed, its sole character. It has little, or rather nothing, of the sublime. Gentle undulations of soil, interwreathed with fantastic crystallic streams, banked by flowery slopes, and backed by a forest vegetation, gigantic, glossy, multicoloured,

sparkling with gay birds and burthened with perfume — these features make up, in the vale of Louisiana, the most voluptuous natural scenery upon earth.

But, even of this delicious region, the sweeter portions are reached only by the bypaths. Indeed, in America generally, the traveller who would behold the finest landscapes, must seek them not by the railroad, nor by the steamboat, not by the stage-coach, nor in his private carriage, not yet even on horseback — but on foot. He must *walk*, he must leap ravines, he must risk his neck among precipices, or he must leave unseen the truest, the richest, and most unspeakable glories of the land.

Now in the greater portion of Europe no such necessity exists. In England it exists not at all. The merest dandy of a tourist may there visit every nook worth visiting without detriment to his silk stockings; so thoroughly known are all points of interest, and so well-arranged are the means of attaining them. This consideration has never been allowed its due weight, in comparisons of the natural scenery of the Old and New Worlds. The entire loveliness of the former is collated with only the most noted, and with by no means the most eminent items in the general loveliness of the latter.

River scenery has, unquestionably, within itself, all the main elements of beauty, and, time out of mind, has been the favourite theme of the poet. But much of this fame is attributable to the predominance of travel in fluvial over that in mountainous districts. In the same way, large rivers, because usually highways, have, in all countries, absorbed an undue share of admiration. They are more observed, and, consequently, made more the subject of discourse, than less important, but often more interesting streams.

A singular exemplification of my remarks upon this head may be found in the Wissahiccon, a brook, (for more it can scarcely be called,) which empties itself into the Schuylkill, about six miles westward of Philadelphia. Now the Wissahiccon is of so remarkable a loveliness that, were it flowing in England, it would be the theme of every bard, and the common topic of every tongue, if, indeed, its banks were not parcelled off in lots, at an exorbitant price, as building-sites for the villas of the opulent. Yet it is only within a very few years that any one has more than heard of the Wissahiccon, while the broader and more navigable water into which it flows, has been long celebrated as one of the finest specimens of American river scenery. The Schuylkill, whose beauties have been much exaggerated, and whose banks, at least in the neighborhood of Philadelphia, are marshy like those of the Delaware, is not at all comparable, as an object of picturesque interest, with the more humble and less notorious rivulet of which we speak.

It was not until Fanny Kemble, in her droll book about the United States, pointed out to the Philadelphians the rare loveliness of a stream which lay at their own doors, that this loveliness was more than sus-

pected by a few adventurous pedestrians of the vicinity. But, the "Journal" having opened all eyes, the Wissahiccon, to a certain extent, rolled at once into notoriety. I say "to a certain extent," for, in fact, the true beauty of the stream lies far above the *route* of the Philadelphian picturesque-hunters, who rarely proceed farther than a mile or two above the mouth of the rivulet — for the very excellent reason that here the carriage-road stops. I would advise the adventurer who would behold its finest points to take the Ridge Road, running westwardly from the city, and, having reached the second lane beyond the sixth mile-stone, to follow this lane to its termination. He will thus strike the Wissahiccon, at one of its best reaches, and, in a skiff, or by clambering along its banks, he can go up or down the stream, as best suits his fancy, and in either direction will meet his reward.

I have already said, or should have said, that the brook is narrow. Its banks are generally, indeed almost universally, precipitous, and consist of high hills, clothed with noble shrubbery near the water, and crowned at a greater elevation, with some of the most magnificent forest trees of America, among which stands conspicuous the *liriodendron tulipiferum.* The immediate shores, however, are of granite, sharply-defined or moss-covered, against which the pellucid water lolls in its gentle flow, as the blue waves of the Mediterranean upon the steps of her palaces of marble. Occasionally in front of the cliffs, extends a small definite *plateau* of richly herbaged land, affording the most picturesque position for a cottage and garden which the richest imagination could conceive. The windings of the stream are many and abrupt, as is usually the case where banks are precipitous, and thus the impression conveyed to the voyager's eye, as he proceeds, is that of an endless succession of infinitely varied small lakes, or, more properly speaking, tarns. The Wissahiccon, however, should be visited, not like "fair Melrose," by moonlight, or even in cloudy weather, but amid the brightest glare of a noonday sun; for the narrowness of the gorge through which it flows, the height of the hills on either hand, and the density of the foliage, conspire to produce a gloominess, if not an absolute dreariness of effect, which, unless relieved by a bright general light, detracts from the mere beauty of the scene.

Not long ago I visited the stream by the route described, and spent the better part of a sultry day in floating in a skiff upon its bosom. The heat gradually overcame me, and, resigning myself to the influence of the scenes and of the weather, and of the gentle moving current, I sank into a half slumber, during which my imagination revelled in visions of the Wissahiccon of ancient days — of the "good old days" when the Demon of the Engine was not, when pic-nics were undreamed of, when "water privileges" were neither bought nor sold, and when the red man trod alone, with the elk, upon the ridges that now towered above. And, while gradually these conceits took possession of my mind, the lazy brook

had borne me, inch by inch, around one promontory and within full view of another that bounded the prospect at the distance of forty or fifty yards. It was a steep rocky cliff, abutting far into the stream, and presenting much more of the Salvator character than any portion of the shore hitherto passed. What I saw upon this cliff, although surely an object of very extraordinary nature, the place and season considered, at first neither startled nor amazed me — so thoroughly and appropriately did it chime in with the half-slumberous fancies that enwrapped me. I saw, or dreamed that I saw, standing upon the extreme verge of the precipice, with neck outstretched, with ears erect, and the whole attitude indicative of profound and melancholy inquisitiveness, one of the oldest and boldest of those identical elks which had been coupled with the red men of my vision.

I say that, for a few moments, this apparition neither startled nor amazed me. During this interval my whole soul was bound up in intense sympathy alone. I fancied the elk repining, not less than wondering, at the manifest alterations for the worse, wrought upon the brook and its vicinage, even within the last few years, by the stern hand of the utilitarian. But a slight movement of the animal's head at once dispelled the dreaminess which invested me, and aroused me to a full sense of novelty of the adventure. I arose upon one knee within the skiff, and, while I hesitated whether to stop my career, or let myself float nearer to the object of my wonder, I heard the words "hist!" "hist!" ejaculated quickly but cautiously, from the shrubbery overhead. In an instant afterwards, a negro emerged from the thicket, putting aside the bushes with care, and treading stealthily. He bore in one hand a quantity of salt, and, holding it towards the elk, gently yet steadily approached. The noble animal, although a little fluttered, made no attempt at escape. The negro advanced; offered the salt; and spoke a few words of encouragement or conciliation. Presently, the elk bowed and stamped, and then lay quietly down and was secured with a halter.

Thus ended my romance of the elk. It was a *pet* of great age and very domestic habits, and belonged to an English family occupying a villa in the vicinity.

The Spectacles

M ANY years ago, it was the fashion to ridicule the idea of "love at first sight;" but those who think, not less than those who feel deeply, have always advocated its existence. Modern discoveries, indeed, in what may be termed ethical magnetism or magnetoesthetics, render it probable that the most natural, and, consequently, the truest and most in-

tense of the human affections are those which arise in the heart as if by electric sympathy — in a word, that the brightest and most enduring of the psychal fetters are those which are riveted by a glance. The confession I am about to make will add another to the already almost innumerable instances of the truth of the position.

My story requires that I should be somewhat minute. I am still a very young man — not yet twenty-two years of age. My name, at present, is a very usual and rather plebeian one — Simpson. I say "at present;" for it is only lately that I have been so called — having legislatively adopted this surname within the last year in order to receive a large inheritance left me by a distant male relative, Adolphus Simpson, Esq. The bequest was conditioned upon my taking the name of the testator; — the family, not the Christian name; my Christian name is Napoleon Bonaparte — or, more properly, these are my first and middle appellations.

I assumed the name, Simpson, with some reluctance, as in my true patronym, Froissart, I felt a very pardonable pride — believing that I could trace a descent from the immortal author of the "Chronicles." While on the subject of names, by the bye, I may mention a singular coincidence of sound attending the names of some of my immediate predecessors. My father was a Monsieur Froissart, of Paris. His wife — my mother, whom he married at fifteen — was a Mademoiselle Croissart, eldest daughter of Croissart the banker; whose wife, again, being only sixteen when married, was the eldest daughter of one Victor Voissart. Monsieur Voissart, very singularly, had married a lady of similar name — a Mademoiselle Moissart. She, too, was quite a child when married; and her mother, also, Madame Moissart, was only fourteen when led to the altar. These early marriages are usual in France. Here, however, are Moissart, Voissart, Croissart, and Froissart, all in the direct line of descent. My own name, though, as I say, became Simpson, by act of Legislature, and with so much repugnance on my part, that, at one period, I actually hesitated about accepting the legacy with the useless and annoying *proviso* attached.

As to personal endowments, I am by no means deficient. On the contrary, I believe that I am well made, and possess what nine tenths of the world would call a handsome face. In height I am five feet eleven. My hair is black and curling. My nose is sufficiently good. My eyes are large and gray; and although, in fact, they are weak to a very inconvenient degree, still no defect in this regard would be suspected from their appearance. The weakness itself, however, has always much annoyed me, and I have resorted to every remedy — short of wearing glasses. Being youthful and good-looking, I naturally dislike these, and have resolutely refused to employ them. I know nothing, indeed, which so disfigures the countenance of a young person, or so impresses every feature with an air of demureness, if not altogether of sanctimoniousness

and of age. An eyeglass, on the other hand, has a savor of downright foppery and affectation. I have hitherto managed as well as I could without either. But something too much of these merely personal details, which, after all, are of little importance. I will content myself with saying, in addition, that my temperament is sanguine, rash, ardent, enthusiastic — and that all my life I have been a devoted admirer of the women.

One night last winter I entered a box at the P—— Theatre, in company with a friend, Mr. Talbot. It was an opera night, and the bills presented a very rare attraction, so that the house was excessively crowded. We were in time, however, to obtain the front seats which had been reserved for us, and into which, with some little difficulty, we elbowed our way.

For two hours my companion, who was a musical *fanatico*, gave his undivided attention to the stage; and, in the meantime, I amused myself by observing the audience, which consisted, in chief part, of the very *elite* of the city. Having satisfied myself upon this point, I was about turning my eyes to the *prima donna*, when they were arrested and riveted by a figure in one of the private boxes which had escaped my observation.

If I live a thousand years, I can never forget the intense emotion with which I regarded this figure. It was that of a female, the most exquisite I had ever beheld. The face was so far turned toward the stage that, for some minutes, I could not obtain a view of it — but the form was *divine;* no other word can sufficiently express its magnificent proportion — and even the term "divine" seems ridiculously feeble as I write it.

The magic of a lovely form in woman — the necromancy of female gracefulness — was always a power which I had found it impossible to resist; but here was grace personified, incarnate, the *beau idéal* of my wildest and most enthusiastic visions. The figure, almost all of which the construction of the box permitted to be seen, was somewhat above the medium height, and nearly approached, without positively reaching, the majestic. Its perfect fullness and *tournure* were delicious. The head of which only the back was visible, rivalled in outline that of the Greek Psyche, and was rather displayed than concealed by an elegant cap of *gaze äerienne*, which put me in mind of the *ventum textilem* of Apuleius. The right arm hung over the balustrade of the box, and thrilled every nerve of my frame with its exquisite symmetry. Its upper portion was draperied by one of the loose open sleeves now in fashion. This extended but little below the elbow. Beneath it was worn an under one of some frail material, close-fitting, and terminated by a cuff of rich lace, which fell gracefully over the top of the hand, revealing only the delicate fingers, upon one of which sparkled a diamond ring, which I at once saw was of extraordinary value. The admirable roundness of the wrist was well set off by a bracelet which encircled it, and which also was ornamented

and clasped by a magnificent *aigrette* of jewels — telling, in words that could not be mistaken, at once of the wealth and fastidious taste of the wearer.

I gazed at this queenly apparition for at least half an hour, as if I had been suddenly converted to stone; and, during this period, I felt the full force and truth of all that has been said or sung concerning "love at first sight." My feelings were totally different from any which I had hitherto experienced, in the presence of even the most celebrated specimens of female loveliness. An unaccountable, and what I am compelled to consider a *magnetic*, sympathy of soul for soul, seemed to rivet, not only my vision, but my whole powers of thought and feeling, upon the admirable object before me. I saw — I felt — I knew that I was deeply, madly, irrevocably in love — and this even before seeing the face of the person beloved. So intense, indeed, was the passion that consumed me, that I really believe it would have received little if any abatement had the features, yet unseen, proved of merely ordinary character; so anomalous is the nature of the only true love — of the love at first sight — and so little really dependent is it upon the external conditions which only seem to create and control it.

While I was thus wrapped in admiration of this lovely vision, a sudden disturbance among the audience caused her to turn her head partially toward me, so that I beheld the entire profile of the face. Its beauty even exceeded my anticipations — and yet there was something about it which disappointed me without my being able to tell exactly what it was. I said "disappointed," but this is not altogether the word. My sentiments were at once quieted and exalted. They partook less of transport and more of calm enthusiasm — of enthusiastic repose. This state of feeling arose, perhaps, from the Madonna-like and matronly air of the face; and yet I at once understood that it could not have arisen entirely from this. There was something else — some mystery which I could not develope — some expression about the countenance which slightly disturbed me while it greatly heightened my interest. In fact, I was just in that condition of mind which prepares a young and susceptible man for any act of extravagance. Had the lady been alone, I should undoubtedly have entered her box and accosted her at all hazards; but, fortunately, she was attended by two companions — a gentleman, and a strikingly beautiful woman, to all appearance a few years younger than herself.

I revolved in my mind a thousand schemes by which I might obtain, hereafter, an introduction to the elder lady, or, for the present, at all events, a more distinct view of her beauty. I would have removed my position to one nearer her own, but the crowded state of the theatre rendered this impossible; and the stern decrees of Fashion had, of late, imperatively prohibited the use of the opera-glass in a case such as this, even had I been so fortunate as to have one with me — but I had not — and was thus in despair.

At length I bethought me of applying to my companion.

"Talbot," I said, "*you* have an opera-glass. Let me have it."

"An opera-glass! — no! — what do you suppose *I* would be doing with an opera-glass?" Here he turned impatiently toward the stage.

"But, Talbot," I continued, pulling him by the shoulder, "listen to me will you? Do you see the stage-box? — there! — no, the next. — did you ever behold as lovely a woman?"

"She is very beautiful, no doubt," he said.

"I wonder who she can be?"

"Why, in the name of all that is angelic, don't you *know* who she is? 'Not to know her argues yourself unknown.' She is the celebrated Madame Lalande — the beauty of the day *par excellence*, and the talk of the whole town. Immensely wealthy too — a widow, and a great match — has just arrived from Paris."

"Do you know her?"

"Yes; I have the honor."

"Will you introduce me?"

"Assuredly; with the greatest pleasure; when shall it be?"

"To-morrow, at one, I will call upon you at B——'s."

"Very good; and now do hold your tongue, *if* you can."

In this latter respect I was forced to take Talbot's advice; for he remained obstinately deaf to every further question or suggestion, and occupied himself exclusively for the rest of the evening with what was transacting upon the stage.

In the meantime I kept my eyes riveted on Madame Lalande, and at length had the good fortune to obtain a full front view of her face. It was exquisitely lovely — this, of course, my heart had told me before, even had not Talbot fully satisfied me upon the point — but still the unintelligible something disturbed me. I finally concluded that my senses were impressed by a certain air of gravity, sadness, or, still more properly, of weariness, which took something from the youth and freshness of the countenance, only to endow it with a seraphic tenderness and majesty, and thus, of course, to my enthusiastic and romantic temperament, with an interest tenfold.

While I thus feasted my eyes, I perceived, at last, to my great trepidation, by an almost imperceptible start on the part of the lady, that she had become suddenly aware of the intensity of my gaze. Still, I was absolutely fascinated, and could not withdraw it, even for an instant. She turned aside her face, and again I saw only the chiselled contour of the back portion of the head. After some minutes, as if urged by curiosity to see if I was still looking, she gradually brought her face again around and again encountered my burning gaze. Her large dark eyes fell instantly, and a deep blush mantled her cheek. But what was my astonishment at perceiving that she not only did not a second time avert her head, but that she actually took from her girdle a double eye-

glass — elevated it — adjusted it — and then regarded me through it, in-
tently and deliberately, for the space of several minutes.

Had a thunderbolt fallen at my feet I could not have been more
thoroughly astounded — astounded *only* — not offended or disgusted in
the slightest degree; although an action so bold in any other woman
would have been likely to offend or disgust. But the whole thing was
done with so much quietude — so much *nonchalance* — so much repose
— with so evident an air of the highest breeding, in short — that nothing
of mere effrontery was perceptbile, and my sole sentiments were those
of admiration and surprise.

I observed that, upon her first elevation of the glass, she had seemed
satisfied with a momentary inspection of my person, and was withdraw-
ing the instrument, when, as if struck by a second thought, she resumed
it, and so continued to regard me with fixed attention for the space of
several minutes — for five minutes, at the very least, I am sure.

This action, so remarkable in an American theatre, attracted very
general observation, and gave rise to an indefinite movement, or *buzz*,
among the audience, which for a moment filled me with confusion, but
produced no visible effect upon the countenance of Madame Lalande.

Having satisfied her curiosity — if such it was — she dropped the glass,
and quietly gave her attention again to the stage; her profile now being
turned toward myself, as before. I continued to watch her unremittingly,
although I was fully conscious of my rudeness in so doing. Presently I
saw the head slowly and slightly change its position; and soon I became
convinced that the lady, while pretending to look at the stage was, in
fact, attentively regarding myself. It is needless to say what effect this
conduct, on the part of so fascinating a woman, had upon my excitable
mind.

Having thus scrutinized me for perhaps a quarter of an hour, the
fair object of my passion addressed the gentleman who attended her, and
while she spoke, I saw distinctly, by the glances of both, that the con-
versation had reference to myself.

Upon its conclusion, Madame Lalande again turned toward the stage,
and, for a few minutes, seemed absorbed in the performance. At the ex-
piration of this period, however, I was thrown into an extremity of agita-
tion by seeing her unfold, for the second time, the eye-glass which hung
at her side, fully confront me as before, and, disregarding the renewed
buzz of the audience, survey me, from head to foot, with the same
miraculous composure which had previously so delighted and con-
founded my soul.

This extraordinary behavior, by throwing me into a perfect fever of
excitement — into an absolute delirium of love — served rather to em-
bolden than to disconcert me. In the mad intensity of my devotion, I
forgot everything but the presence and the majestic loveliness of the
vision which confronted my gaze. Watching my opportunity, when I

thought the audience were fully engaged with the opera, I at length caught the eyes of Madame Lalande, and, upon the instant, made a slight but unmistakable bow.

She blushed very deeply — then averted her eyes — then slowly and cautiously looked around, apparently to see if my rash action had been noticed — then leaned over toward the gentleman who sat by her side.

I now felt a burning sense of the impropriety I had committed, and expected nothing less than instant exposure; while a vision of pistols upon the morrow floated rapidly and uncomfortably through my brain. I was greatly and immediately relieved, however, when I saw the lady merely hand the gentleman a play-bill, without speaking, but the reader may form some feeble conception of my astonishment — of my profound amazement — my delirious bewilderment of heart and soul — when, instantly afterward, having again glanced furtively around, she allowed her bright eyes to set fully and steadily upon my own, and then, with a faint smile, disclosing a bright line of her pearly teeth, made two distinct, pointed, and unequivocal affirmative inclinations of the head.

It is useless, of course, to dwell upon my joy — upon my transport — upon my illimitable ecstasy of heart. If ever man was mad with excess of happiness, it was myself at that moment. I loved. This was my *first* love — so I felt it to be. It was love supreme — indescribable. It was "love at first sight;" and at first sight, too, it had been appreciated and — *returned*.

Yes, returned. How and why should I doubt it for an instant. What other construction could I possibly put upon such conduct, on the part of a lady so beautiful — so wealthy — evidently so accomplished — of so high breeding — of so lofty a position in society — in every regard so entirely respectable as I felt assured was Madame Lalande? Yes, she loved me — she returned the enthusiasm of my love, with an enthusiasm as blind — as uncompromising — as uncalculating — as abandoned — and as utterly unbounded as my own! These delicious fancies and reflections, however, were now interrupted by the falling of the drop-curtain. The audience arose; and the usual tumult immediately supervened. Quitting Talbot abruptly, I made every effort to force my way into closer proximity with Madame Lalande. Having failed in this, on account of the crowd, I at length gave up the chase, and bent my steps homeward; consoling myself for my disappointment in not having been able to touch even the hem of her robe, by the reflection that I should be introduced by Talbot, in due form, upon the morrow.

This morrow at last came; that is to say, a day finally dawned upon a long and weary night of impatience; and then the hours until "one" were snail-paced, dreary, and innumerable. But even Stamboul, it is said, shall have an end, and there came an end to this long delay. The clock struck. As the last echo ceased, I stepped into B——'s and inquired for Talbot.

"Out," said the footman — Talbot's own.

"Out!" I replied, staggering back half a dozen paces — "let me tell you, my fine fellow, that this thing is thoroughly impossible and impracticable; Mr. Talbot is *not* out. What do you mean?"

"Nothing, sir; only Mr. Talbot is not in, that's all. He rode over to S——, immediately after breakfast, and left word that he would not be in town again for a week."

I stood petrified with horror and rage. I endeavored to reply, but my tongue refused its office. At length I turned on my heel, livid with wrath, and inwardly consigning the whole tribe of the Talbots to the innermost regions of Erebus. It was evident that my considerate friend, *il fanatico*, had quite forgotten his appointment with myself — had forgotten it as soon as it was made. At no time was he a very scrupulous man of his word. There was no help for it; so smothering my vexation as well as I could, I strolled moodily up the street, propounding futile inquiries about Madame Lalande to every male acquaintance I met. By report she was known, I found, to all — to many by sight — but she had been in town only a few weeks, and there were very few, therefore, who claimed her personal acquaintance. These few, being still comparatively strangers, could not, or would not, take the liberty of introducing me through the formality of a morning call. While I stood thus in despair, conversing with a trio of friends upon the all absorbing subject of my heart, it so happened that the subject itself passed by.

"As I live, there she is!" cried one.

"Surprisingly beautiful!" exclaimed a second.

"An angel upon earth!" ejaculated a third.

I looked; and in an open carriage which approached us, passing slowly down the street, sat the enchanting vision of the opera, accompanied by the younger lady who had occupied a portion of her box.

"Her companion also wears remarkably well," said the one of my trio who had spoken first.

"Astonishingly," said the second; "still quite a brilliant air; but art will do wonders. Upon my word, she looks better than she did at Paris five years ago. A beautiful woman still; — don't you think so, Froissart? — Simpson, I mean."

"*Still!*" said I, "and why shouldn't she be? But compared with her friend she is as a rush-light to the evening star — a glow-worm to Antares."

"Ha! ha! ha! — why, Simpson, you have an astonishing tact at making discoveries — original ones, I mean." And here we separated, while one of the trio began humming a gay *vaudeville*, of which I caught only the lines —

Ninon, Ninon, Ninon à bas —
A bas Ninon De L'Enclos!

During this little scene, however, one thing had served greatly to console me, although it fed the passion by which I was consumed. As the carriage of Madame Lalande rolled by our group, I had observed that she recognized me; and more than this, she had blessed me, by the most seraphic of all imaginable smiles, with no equivocal mark of the recognition.

As for an introduction, I was obliged to abandon all hope of it, until such time as Talbot should think proper to return from the country. In the meantime I perseveringly frequented every reputable place of public amusement; and, at length, at the theatre, where I first saw her, I had the supreme bliss of meeting her, and of exchanging glances with her once again. This did not occur, however, until the lapse of a fortnight. Every day, in the *interim*, I had inquired for Talbot at his hotel, and every day had been thrown into a spasm of wrath by the everlasting "Not come home yet" of his footman.

Upon the evening in question, therefore, I was in a condition little short of madness. Madame Lalande, I had been told, was a Parisian — had lately arrived from Paris — might she not suddenly return? — return before Talbot came back — and might she not be thus lost to me forever? The thought was too terrible to bear. Since my future happiness was at issue, I resolved to act with a manly decision. In a word, upon the breaking up of the play, I traced the lady to her residence, noted the address, and the next morning sent her a full and elaborate letter, in which I poured out my whole heart.

I spoke boldly, freely — in a word, I spoke with passion. I concealed nothing — nothing even of my weakness. I alluded to the romantic circumstances of our first meeting — even to the glances which had passed between us. I went so far as to say that I felt assured of her love; while I offered this assurance, and my own intensity of devotion, as two excuses for my otherwise unpardonable conduct. As a third, I spoke of my fear that she might quit the city before I could have the opportunity of a formal introduction. I concluded the most wildly enthusiastic epistle ever penned, with a frank declaration of my worldly circumstances — of my affluence — and with an offer of my heart and of my hand.

In an agony of expectation I awaited the reply. After what seemed the lapse of a century it came.

Yes, *actually came*. Romantic as all this may appear, I really received a letter from Madame Lalande — the beautiful, the wealthy, the idolized Madame Lalande. Her eyes — her magnificent eyes, had not belied her noble heart. Like a true Frenchwoman as she was she had obeyed the frank dictates of her reason — the generous impulses of her nature — despising the conventional pruderies of the world. She had *not* scorned my proposals. She had *not* sheltered herself in silence. She had *not* returned my letter unopened. She had even sent me, in reply, one penned by her own exquisite fingers. It ran thus:

"Monsieur Simpson vill pardonne me for not compose de butefulle tong of his contrée so vell as might. It is only de late dat I am arrive, and not yet ave do opportunité for to — l'étudier.

"Vid dis apologie for the manière, I vill now say dat, hélas! — Monsieur Simpson ave guess but de too true. Need I say de more? Hélas! am I not ready speak de too moshe?

"EUGÉNIE LALANDE."

This noble-spirited note I kissed a million times, and committed, no doubt, on its account, a thousand other extravagances that have now escaped my memory. Still Talbot *would* not return. Alas! could he have formed even the vaguest idea of the suffering his absence had occasioned his friend, would not his sympathizing nature have flown immediately to my relief? Still, however, he came *not*. I wrote. He replied. He was detained by urgent business — but would shortly return. He begged me not to be impatient — to moderate my transports — to read soothing books — to drink nothing stronger than Hock — and to bring the consolations of philosophy to my aid. The fool! if he could not come himself, why, in the name of every thing rational, could he not have enclosed me a letter of presentation? I wrote him again, entreating him to forward one forthwith. My letter was returned by *that* footman, with the following endorsement in pencil. The scoundrel had joined his master in the country:

"Left S—— yesterday, for parts unknown — did not say where — or when be back — so thought best to return letter, knowing your handwriting, and as how you is always, more or less, in a hurry.

"Yours sincerely,
"STUBBS."

After this, it is needless to say, that I devoted to the infernal deities both master and valet: — but there was little use in anger, and no consolation at all in complaint.

But I had yet a resource left, in my constitutional audacity. Hitherto it had served me well, and I now resolved to make it avail me to the end. Besides, after the correspondence which had passed between us, what act of mere informality *could I* commit, within bounds, that ought to be regarded as indecorous by Madame Lalande? Since the affair of the letter, I had been in the habit of watching her house, and thus discovered that, about twilight, it was her custom to promenade, attended only by a negro in livery, in a public square overlooked by her windows. Here, amid the luxuriant and shadowing groves, in the gray gloom of a sweet midsummer evening, I observed my opportunity and accosted her.

The better to deceive the servant in attendance, I did this with the assured air of an old and familiar acquaintance. With a presence of mind truly Parisian, she took the cue at once, and, to greet me, held out the

most bewitchingly little of hands. The valet at once fell into the rear; and now, with hearts full to overflowing, we discoursed long and unreservedly of our love.

As Madame Lalande spoke English even less fluently than she wrote it, our conversation was necessarily in French. In this sweet tongue, so adapted to passion, I gave loose to the impetuous enthusiasm of my nature, and, with all the eloquence I could command, besought her to consent to an immediate marriage.

At this impatience she smiled. She urged the old story of decorum — that bug-bear which deters so many from bliss until the opportunity for bliss has forever gone by. I had most imprudently made it known among my friends, she observed, that I desired her acquaintance — thus that I did not possess it — thus, again, there was no possibility of concealing the date of our first knowledge of each other. And then she adverted, with a blush, to the extreme recency of this date. To wed immediately would be improper — would be indecorous — would be *outré*. All this she said with a charming air of *naiveté* which enraptured while it grieved and convinced me. She went even so far as to accuse me, laughingly, of rashness — of imprudence. She bade me remember that I really even know not who she was — what were her prospects, her connections, her standing in society. She begged me, but with a sigh, to reconsider my proposal, and termed my love an infatuation — a will o' the wisp — a fancy or fantasy of the moment — a baseless and unstable creation rather of the imagination than of the heart. These things she uttered as the shadows of the sweet twilight gathered darkly and more darkly around us — and then, with a gentle pressure of her fairy-like hand, overthrew, in a single sweet instant, all the argumentative fabric she had reared.

I replied as best I could — as only a true lover can. I spoke at length, and perseveringly of my devotion, of my passion — of her exceeding beauty, and of my own enthusiastic admiration. In conclusion, I dwelt, with a convincing energy, upon the perils that encompass the course of love — that course of true love that never did run smooth — and thus deduced the manifest danger of rendering that course unnecessarily long.

This latter argument seemed finally to soften the rigor of her determination. She relented; but there was yet an obstacle, she said, which she felt assured I had not properly considered. This was a delicate point — for a woman to urge, especially so; in mentioning it, she saw that she must make a sacrifice of her feelings; still, for *me*, every sacrifice should be made. She alluded to the topic of *age*. Was I aware — was I fully aware of the discrepancy between us? That the age of the husband, should surpass by a few years — even by fifteen or twenty — the age of the wife, was regarded by the world as admissible, and, indeed, as even proper; but she had always entertained the belief that the years of the wife should *never* exceed in number those of the husband. A discrepancy of this unnatural kind gave rise, too frequently, alas! to a life of unhappiness. Now

she was aware that my own age did not exceed two and twenty; and I, on the contrary, perhaps, was *not* aware that the years of my Eugénie extended very considerably beyond that sum.

About all this there was a nobility of soul — a dignity of candor — which delighted — which enchanted me — which eternally riveted my chains. I could scarcely restrain the excessive transport which possessed me.

"My sweetest Eugénie," I cried, "what is all this about which you are discoursing? Your years surpass in some measure my own. But what then? The customs of the world are so many conventional follies. To those who love as ourselves, in what respect differs a year from an hour? I am twenty-two, you say, granted: indeed, you may as well call me, at once, twenty-three. Now you yourself, my dearest Eugénie, can have numbered no more than — can have numbered no more than — no more than — than — than — than — "

Here I paused for an instant, in the expectation that Madame Lalande would interrupt me by supplying her true age. But a Frenchwoman is seldom direct, and has always, by way of answer to an embarrassing query, some little practical reply of her own. In the present instance, Eugénie, who for a few moments past had seemed to be searching for something in her bosom, at length let fall upon the grass a miniature, which I immediately picked up and presented to her.

"Keep it!" she said, with one of her most ravishing smiles. "Keep it for my sake — for the sake of her whom it too flatteringly represents. Besides, upon the back of the trinket you may discover, perhaps, the very information you seem to desire. It is now, to be sure, growing rather dark — but you can examine it at your leisure in the morning. In the meantime, you shall be my escort home to-night. My friends are about holding a little musical *levée*. I can promise you, too, some good singing. We French are not nearly so punctilious as you Americans, and I shall have no difficulty in smuggling you in, in the character of an old acquaintance."

With this, she took my arm, and I attended her home. The mansion was quite a fine one, and, I believe, furnished in good taste. Of this latter point, however, I am scarcely qualified to judge; for it was just dark as we arrived; and in American mansions of the better sort lights seldom, during the heat of summer, make their appearance at this, the most pleasant period of the day. In about an hour after my arrival, to be sure, a single shaded solar lamp was lit in the principal drawing-room; and this apartment, I could thus see, was arranged with unusual good taste and even splendor; but two other rooms of the suite, and in which the company chiefly assembled, remained, during the whole evening, in a very agreeable shadow. This is a well-conceived custom, giving the party at least a choice of light or shade, and one which our friends over the water could not do better than immediately adopt.

The evening thus spent was unquestionably the most delicious of my life. Madame Lalande had not overrated the musical abilities of her friends; and the singing I here heard I had never heard excelled in any private circle out of Vienna. The instrumental performers were many and of superior talents. The vocalists were chiefly ladies, and no individual sang less than well. At length, upon a peremptory call for "Madame Lalande," she arose at once, without affectation or demur, from the *chaise longue* upon which she had sat by my side, and, accompanied by one or two gentlemen and her female friend of the opera, repaired to the piano in the main drawing-room. I would have escorted her myself, but felt that, under the circumstances of my introduction to the house, I had better remain unobserved where I was. I was thus deprived of the pleasure of seeing, although not of hearing, her sing.

The impression she produced upon the company seemed electrical — but the effect upon myself was something even more. I know not how adequately to describe it. It arose in part, no doubt, from the sentiment of love with which I was imbued; but chiefly from my conviction of the extreme sensibility of the singer. It is beyond the reach of art to endow either air or recitative with more impassioned *expression* than was hers. Her utterance of the romance in Otello — the tone with which she gave the words "*Sul mio sasso*," in the Capuletti — is ringing in my memory yet. Her lower tones were absolutely miraculous. Her voice embraced three complete octaves, extending from the contralto D to the D upper soprano, and, though sufficiently powerful to have filled the San Carlos, executed, with the minutest precision, every difficulty of vocal composition — ascending and descending scales, cadences, or *fiorituri*. In the final of the Somnambula, she brought about a most remarkable effect at the words:

Ah! non guinge uman pensiero
Al contento ond 'io son piena.

Here, in imitation of Malibran, she modified the original phrase of Bellini, so as to let her voice descend to the tenor G, when, by a rapid transition, she struck the G above the treble stave, springing over an interval of two octaves.

Upon rising from the piano after these miracles of vocal execution, she resumed her seat by my side; when I expressed to her, in terms of the deepest enthusiasm, my delight at her performance. Of my surprise I said nothing, and yet was I most unfeignedly surprised; for a certain feebleness, or rather a certain tremulous indecision of voice in ordinary conversation, had prepared me to anticipate that, in singing, she would not acquit herself with any remarkable ability.

Our conversation was now long, earnest, uninterrupted, and totally unreserved. She made me relate many of the earlier passages of my life, and listened with breathless attention to every word of the narrative.

I concealed nothing — felt that I had a right to conceal nothing — from her confiding affection. Encouraged by her candor upon the delicate point of her age, I entered, with perfect frankness, not only into a detail of my many minor vices, but made full confession of those moral and even of those physical infirmities, the disclosure of which, in demanding so much higher a degree of courage, is so much surer an evidence of love. I touched upon my college indiscretions — upon my extravagances — upon my carousals — upon my debts — upon my flirtations. I even went so far as to speak of a slightly hectic cough with which, at one time, I had been troubled — of a chronic rheumatism — of a twinge of hereditary gout — and, in conclusion, of the disagreeable and inconvenient, but hitherto carefully concealed, weakness of my eyes.

"Upon this latter point," said Madame Lalande, laughingly, "you have been surely injudicious in coming to confession; for, without the confession, I take it for granted that no one would have accused you of the crime. By the by," she continued, "have you any recollection — " and here I fancied that a blush, even through the gloom of the apartment, became distinctly visible upon her cheek — "have you any recollection, *mon cher ami*, of this little ocular assistant, which now depends from my neck?"

As she spoke she twirled in her fingers the identical double eye-glass which had so overwhelmed me with confusion at the opera.

"Full well — alas! do I remember it," I exclaimed, pressing passionately the delicate hand which offered the glasses for my inspection. They formed a complex and magnificent toy, richly chased and filigreed, and gleaming with jewels, which, even in the deficient light, I could not help perceiving were of high value.

"*Eh bien! mon ami*," she resumed with a certain *empressment* of manner that rather surprised me — "*Eh bien! mon ami*, you have earnestly besought of me a favor which you have been pleased to denominate priceless. You have demanded of me my hand upon the morrow. Should I yield to your entreaties — and, I may add, to the pleadings of my own bosom — would I not be entitled to demand of you a very — a very little boon in return?"

"Name it!" I exclaimed with an energy that had nearly drawn upon us the observation of the company, and restrained by their presence alone from throwing myself impetuously at her feet. "Name it, my beloved, my Eugénie, my own! — name it! — but, alas! it is already yielded ere named."

"You shall conquer, then, *mon ami*," said she, "for the sake of the Eugénie whom you love, this little weakness which you have at last confessed — this weakness more moral than physical — and which, let me assure you, is so unbecoming the nobility of your real nature — so inconsistent with the candor of your usual character — and which, if permitted further control, will assuredly involve you, sooner or later, in some very

disagreeable scrape. You shall conquer, for my sake, this affectation which leads you, as you yourself acknowledge, to the tacit or implied denial of your infirmity of vision. For, this infirmity you virtually deny, in refusing to employ the customary means for its relief. You will understand me to say, then, that I wish you to wear spectacles; — ah, hush! — you have already consented to wear them, *for my sake*. You shall accept the little toy which I now hold in my hand, and which, though admirable as an aid to vision, is really of no very immense value as a gem. You perceive that, by a trifling modification thus — or thus — it can be adapted to the eyes in the form of spectacles, or worn in the waistcoat pocket as an eye-glass. It is in the former mode, however, and habitually, that you have already consented to wear it *for my sake*."

This request — must I confess it? — confused me in no little degree. But the condition with which it was coupled rendered hesitation, of course, a matter altogether out of the question.

"It is done!" I cried, with all the enthusiasm that I could muster at the moment. "It is done — it is most cheerfully agreed. I sacrifice every feeling for your sake. To-night I wear this dear eye-glass, *as* an eye-glass, and upon my heart; but with the earliest dawn of that morning which gives me the pleasure of calling you wife, I will place it upon my — upon my nose, — and there wear it ever afterward, in the less romantic, and less fashionable, but certainly in the more serviceable, form which you desire."

Our conversation now turned upon the details of our arrangements for the morrow. Talbot, I learned from my betrothed, had just arrived in town. I was to see him at once, and procure a carriage. The *soirée* would scarcely break up before two; and by this hour the vehicle was to be at the door; when, in the confusion occasioned by the departure of the company, Madame L. could easily enter it unobserved. We were then to call at the house of a clergyman who would be in waiting; there be married, drop Talbot, and proceed on a short tour to the East, leaving the fashionable world at home to make whatever comments upon the matter it thought best.

Having planned all this, I immediately took leave, and went in search of Talbot, but, on the way, I could not refrain from stepping into a hotel, for the purpose of inspecting the miniature; and this I did by the powerful aid of the glasses. The countenance was a surpassingly beautiful one! Those large luminous eyes! — that proud Grecian nose! — those dark luxuriant curls! — "Ah!" said I, exultingly to myself, "this is indeed the speaking image of my beloved!" I turned the reverse, and discovered the words — "Eugénie Lalande — aged twenty-seven years and seven months."

I found Talbot at home, and proceeded at once to acquaint him with my good fortune. He professed excessive astonishment, of course, but congratulated me most cordially, and proffered every assistance in his power. In a word, we carried out our arrangement to the letter, and, at

two in the morning, just ten minutes after the ceremony, I found myself in a close carriage with Madame Lalande — with Mrs. Simpson, I should say — and driving at a great rate out of town, in a direction Northeast by North, half-North.

It had been determined for us by Talbot, that, as we were to be up all night, we should make our first stop at C——, a village about twenty miles from the city, and there get an early breakfast and some repose, before proceeding upon our route. At four precisely, therefore, the carriage drew up at the door of the principal inn. I handed my adored wife out, and ordered breakfast forthwith. In the meantime we were shown into a small parlor, and sat down.

It was now nearly if not altogether daylight; and, as I gazed, enraptured, at the angel by my side, the singular idea came, all at once, into my head, that this was really the very first moment since my acquaintance with the celebrated loveliness of Madame Lalande, that I had enjoyed a near inspection of that loveliness by daylight at all.

"And now, *mon ami*," said she, taking my hand, and so interrupting this train of reflection, "and now, *mon cher ami*, since we are indissolubly one — since I have yielded to your passionate entreaties, and performed my portion of our agreement — I presume you have not forgotten that you also have a little favor to bestow — a little promise which it is your intention to keep. Ah! let me see! Let me remember! Yes; full easily do I call to mind the precise words of the dear promise you made to Eugénie last night. Listen! You spoke thus: 'It is done! — it is most cheerfully agreed! I sacrifice every feeling for your sake. To-night I wear this dear eye-glass *as* an eye-glass, and upon my heart; but with the earliest dawn of that morning which gives me the privilege of calling you wife, I will place it upon my — upon my nose, — and there wear it ever afterward, in the less romantic, and less fashionable, but certainly in the more serviceable, form which you desire.' These were the exact words, my beloved husband, were they not?"

"They were," I said; "you have an excellent memory; and assuredly, my beautiful Eugénie, there is no disposition on my part to evade the performance of the trivial promise they imply. See! Behold! they are becoming — rather — are they not?" And here, having arranged the glasses in the ordinary form of spectacles, I applied them gingerly in their proper position; while Madame Simpson, adjusting her cap, and folding her arms, sat bolt upright in her chair, in a somewhat stiff and prim, and indeed, in a somewhat undignified position.

"Goodness gracious me!" I exclaimed, almost at the very instant that the rim of the spectacles had settled upon my nose — "*My!* goodness gracious me! — why, what *can* be the matter with these glasses?" and taking them quickly off, I wiped them carefully with a silk handkerchief, and adjusted them again.

But if, in the first instance, there had occurred something which occa-

sioned me surprise, in the second, this surprise became elevated into astonishment; and this astonishment was profound — was extreme — indeed I may say it was horrific. What, in the name of everything hideous, did this mean? Could I believe my eyes? — *could* I? — that was the question. Was that — was that — was that *rouge*? And were those — and were those — were those *wrinkles*, upon the visage of Eugénie Lalande? And oh! Jupiter, and every one of the gods and goddesses, little and big! what — what — what — *what* had become of her teeth? I dashed the spectacles violently to the ground, and, leaping to my feet, stood erect in the middle of the floor, confronting Mrs. Simpson, with my arms set a-kimbo, and grinning and foaming, but, at the same time, utterly speechless with terror and with rage.

Now I have already said that Madame Eugénie Lalande — that is to say, Simpson — spoke the English language but very little better than she wrote it; and for this reason she very properly never attempted to speak it upon ordinary occasions. But rage will carry a lady to any extreme; and in the present case it carried Mrs. Simpson to the very extraordinary extreme of attempting to hold a conversation in a tongue that she did not altogether understand.

"Vell, Monsieur," said she, after surveying me, in great apparent astonishment, for some moments — "Vell, Monsieur? — and vat den? — vat de matter now? Is it de dance of de Saint Vitusse dat you ave? If not like me, vat for vy buy de pig in the poke?"

"You wretch!" said I, catching my breath — "you — you — you villainous old hag!"

"Ag? — ole? — me not so *ver* ole, after all! Me not one single day more dan de eighty-doo."

"Eighty-two!" I ejaculated, staggering to the wall — "eighty-two hundred thousand baboons! The miniature said twenty-seven years and seven months!"

"To be sure! — dat is so! — ver true! but den de portraite has been take for dese fifty-five year. Ven I go marry my segonde usbande, Monsieur Lalande, at dat time I had de portraite take for my daughter by my first usbande, Monsieur Moissart!"

"Moissart!" said I.

"Yes, Moissart," said she, mimicking my pronunciation, which, to speak the truth, was none of the best; "and vat den? Vat *you* know about de Moissart?"

"Nothing, you old fright! — I know nothing about him at all; only I had an ancestor of that name, once upon a time."

"Dat name! and vat you ave for say to dat name? 'Tis ver *goot* name; and so is Voissart — dat is ver goot name too. My daughter, Mademoiselle Moissart, she marry von Monsieur Voissart; and de name is bot *ver* respectaable name."

"Moissart?" I exclaimed, "and Voissart! Why, what is it you mean?"

"Vat I mean? — I mean Moissart and Voissart; and for de matter of dat, I mean Croissart and Froissart, too, if I only tink proper to mean it. My daughter's daughter, Mademoiselle Voissart, she marry von Monsieur Croissart, and den again, my daughter's grande daughter, Mademoiselle Croissart, she marry von Monsieur Froissart; and I suppose you say dat *dat* is not von *ver* respectaable name."

"Froissart!" said I, beginning to faint, "why, surely you don't say Moissart, and Voissart, and Croissart, and Froissart?"

"Yes," she replied, leaning fully back in her chair, and stretching out her lower limbs at great length; "yes, Moissart, and Voissart, and Croissart, and Froissart. But Monsieur Froissart, he vas von *ver* big vat you call fool — he vas von ver great big donce like yourself — for he lef *la belle France* for come to dis stupide Amérique — and ven he get here he went and ave von *ver* stupide, von *ver*, *ver* stupide sonn, so I hear, dough I not yet av ad de plaisir to meet vid him — neither me nor my companion, de Madame Stephanie Lalande. He is name de Napoleon Bonaparte Froissart, and I suppose you say dat *dat*, too, is not von *ver* respectable name."

Either the length or the nature of this speech, had the effect of working up Mrs. Simpson into a very extraordinary passion indeed; and as she made an end of it, with great labor, she jumped up from her chair like somebody bewitched, dropping upon the floor an entire universe of bustle as she jumped. Once upon her feet, she gnashed her gums, brandished her arms, rolled up her sleeves, shook her fist in my face, and concluded the performance by tearing the cap from her head, and with it an immense wig of the most valuable and beautiful black hair, the whole of which she dashed upon the ground with a yell, and there trampled and danced a fandango upon it, in an absolute ecstasy and agony of rage.

Meantime I sank aghast into the chair which she had vacated. "Moissart and Voissart!" I repeated, thoughtfully, as she cut one of her pigeon-wings, and "Croissart and Froissart!" as she completed another — "Moissart and Voissart and Croissart and Napoleon Bonaparte Froissart! — why, you ineffable old serpent, that's *me* — that's *me* — d'ye hear? — that's *me*" — here I screamed at the top of my voice — "that's *me-e-e!* I am Napoleon Bonaparte Froissart! and if I havn't married my great, great, grandmother, I wish I may be everlastingly confounded!"

Madame Eugénie Lalande, *quasi* Simpson — formerly Moissart — was, in sober fact, my great, great, grandmother. In her youth she had been beautiful, and even at eighty-two, retained the majestic height, the sculptural contour of head, the fine eyes and the Grecian nose of her girlhood. By the aid of these, of pearl-powder, of rouge, of false hair, false teeth, and false *tournure*, as well as of the most skilful modistes of Paris, she contrived to hold a respectable footing among the beauties *en peu passées* of the French metropolis. In this respect, indeed, she might have been regarded as little less than the equal of the celebrated Ninon De L'Enclos.

She was immensely wealthy, and being left, for the second time, a widow without children, she bethought herself of my existence in America, and for the purpose of making me her heir, paid a visit to the United States, in company with a distant and exceedingly lovely relative of her second husband's — a Madame Stephanie Lalande.

At the opera, my great, great, grandmother's atttention was arrested by my notice; and, upon surveying me through her eye-glass, she was struck with a certain family resemblance to herself. Thus interested, and knowing that the heir she sought was actually in the city, she made inquiries of her party respecting me. The gentleman who attended her knew my person, and told her who I was. The information thus obtained induced her to renew her scrutiny; and this scrutiny it was which so emboldened me that I behaved in the absurd manner already detailed. She returned my bow, however, under the impression that, by some odd accident, I had discovered her identity. When, deceived by my weakness of vision, and the arts of the toilet, in respect to the age and charms of the strange lady, I demanded so enthusiastically of Talbot who she was, he concluded that I meant the younger beauty, as a matter of course, and so informed me, with perfect truth, that she was "the celebrated widow, Madame Lalande."

In the street, next morning, my great, great, grandmother encountered Talbot, an old Parisian acquaintance; and the conversation, very naturally, turned upon myself. My deficiencies of vision were then explained; for these were notorious, although I was entirely ignorant of their notoriety; and my good old relative discovered, much to her chagrin, that she had been deceived in supposing me aware of her identity, and that I had been merely making a fool of myself in making open love, in a theatre, to an old woman unknown. By way of punishing me for this imprudence, she concocted with Talbot a plot. He purposely kept out of my way to avoid giving me the introduction. My street inquiries about "the lovely widow, Madame Lalande," were supposed to refer to the younger lady, of course; and thus the conversation with the three gentlemen whom I encountered shortly after leaving Talbot's hotel will be easily explained, as also their allusion to Ninon De L'Enclos. I had no opportunity of seeing Madame Lalande closely during daylight; and, at her musical *soirée*, my silly weakness in refusing the aid of glasses effectually prevented me from making a discovery of her age. When "Madame Lalande" was called upon to sing, the younger lady was intended; and it was she who arose to obey the call; my great, great, grandmother, to further the deception, arising at the same moment and accompanying her to the piano in the main drawing-room. Had I decided upon escorting her thither, it had been her design to suggest the propriety of my remaining where I was; but my own prudential views rendered this unnecessary. The songs which I so much admired, and which so confirmed my impression of the youth of my mistress, were executed by Madame Stephanie Lalande. The eye-

glass was presented by way of adding a reproof to the hoax — a sting to the epigram of the deception. Its presentation afforded an opportunity for the lecture upon affectation with which I was so especially edified. It is almost superfluous to add that the glasses of the instrument, as worn by the old lady, had been exchanged by her for a pair better adapted to my years. They suited me, in fact, to a T.

The clergyman, who merely pretended to tie the fatal knot, was a boon companion of Talbot's, and no priest. He was an excellent "whip," however; and having doffed his cassock to put on a great-coat, he drove the hack which conveyed the "happy couple" out of town. Talbot took a seat at his side. The two scoundrels were thus "in at the death," and through a half-open window of the back parlor of the inn, amused themselves in grinning at the *dénouement* of the drama. I believe I shall be forced to call them both out.

Nevertheless, I am *not* the husband of my great, great, grandmother; and this is a reflection which affords me infinite relief; — but I *am* the husband of Madame Lalande — of Madame Stephanie Lalande —with whom my good old relative, besides making me her sole heir when she dies — if she ever does — has been at the trouble of concocting me a match. In conclusion: I am done forever with *billets doux* and am never to be met without SPECTACLES.

A Tale of the Ragged Mountains

DURING the fall of the year 1827, while residing near Charlottesville, Virginia, I casually made the acquaintance of Mr. Augustus Bedloe. This young gentleman was remarkable in every respect, and excited in me a profound interest and curiosity. I found it impossible to comprehend him either in his moral or his physical relations. Of his family I could obtain no satisfactory account. Whence he came, I never ascertained. Even about his age — although I call him a young gentleman — there was something which perplexed me in no little degree. He certainly *seemed* young — and he made a point of speaking about his youth — yet there were moments when I should have had little trouble in imagining him a hundred years of age. But in no regard was he more peculiar than in his personal appearance. He was singularly tall and thin. He stooped much. His limbs were exceedingly long and emaciated. His forehead was broad and low. His complexion was absolutely bloodless. His mouth was large and flexible, and his teeth were more wildly uneven, although sound, than I had ever before seen teeth in a human head. The expression of his smile, however, was by no means unpleasing, as might be supposed; but it had no variation whatever. It was one of profound melancholy — of a phase-

less and unceasing gloom. His eyes were abnormally large, and round like those of a cat. The pupils, too, upon any accession or diminution of light, underwent contraction or dilation, just such as is observed in the feline tribe. In moments of excitement the orbs grew bright to a degree almost inconceivable; seeming to emit luminous rays, not of a reflected but of an intrinsic lustre, as does a candle or the sun; yet their ordinary condition was so totally vapid, filmy, and dull, as to convey the idea of the eyes of a long-interred corpse.

These peculiarities of person appeared to cause him much annoyance, and he was continually alluding to them in a sort of half explanatory, half apologetic strain, which, when I first heard it, impressed me very painfully. I soon, however, grew accustomed to it, and my uneasiness wore off. It seemed to be his design rather to insinuate than directly to assert that, physically, he had not always been what he was — that a long series of neuralgic attacks had reduced him from a condition of more than usual personal beauty, to that which I saw. For many years past he had been attended by a physician, named Templeton — an old gentleman, perhaps seventy years of age — whom he had first encountered at Saratoga, and from whose attention, while there, he either received, or fancied that he received, great benefit. The result was that Bedloe, who was wealthy, had made an arrangement with Dr. Templeton, by which the latter, in consideration of a liberal annual allowance, had consented to devote his time and medical experience exclusively to the care of the invalid.

Doctor Templeton had been a traveller in his younger days, and at Paris had become a convert, in great measure, to the doctrines of Mesmer. It was altogether by means of magnetic remedies that he had succeeded in alleviating the acute pains of his patient; and this success had very naturally inspired the latter with a certain degree of confidence in the opinions from which the remedies had been educed. The Doctor, however, like all enthusiasts, had struggled hard to make a thorough convert of his pupil, and finally so far gained his point as to induce the sufferer to submit to numerous experiments. By a frequent repetition of these, a result had arisen, which of late days has become so common as to attract little or no attention, but which, at the period of which I write, had very rarely been known in America. I mean to say, that between Doctor Templeton and Bedloe there had grown up, little by little, a very distinct and strongly marked *rapport*, or magnetic relation. I am not prepared to assert, however, that this *rapport* extended beyond the limits of the simple sleep-producing power; but this power itself had attained great intensity. At the first attempt to induce the magnetic somnolency, the mesmerist entirely failed. In the fifth or sixth he succeeded very partially, and after long continued effort. Only at the twelfth was the triumph complete. After this the will of the patient succumbed rapidly to that of the physician, so that, when I first became acquainted with

the two, sleep was brought about almost instantaneously by the mere volition of the operator, even when the invalid was unaware of his presence. It is only now, in the year 1845, when similar miracles are witnessed daily by thousands, that I dare venture to record this apparent impossibility as a matter of serious fact.

The temperature of Bedloe was, in the highest degree sensitive, excitable, enthusiastic. His imagination was singularly vigorous and creative; and no doubt it derived additional force from the habitual use of morphine, which he swallowed in great quantity, and without which he would have found it impossible to exist. It was his practice to take a very large dose of it immediately after breakfast each morning — or, rather, immediately after a cup of strong coffee, for he ate nothing in the forenoon — and then set forth alone, or attended only by a dog, upon a long ramble among the chain of wild and dreary hills that lie westward and southward of Charlottesville, and are there dignified by the title of the Ragged Mountains.

Upon a dim, warm, misty day, toward the close of November, and during the strange *interregnum* of the seasons which in America is termed the Indian Summer, Mr. Bedloe departed as usual for the hills. The day passed, and still he did not return.

About eight o'clock at night, having become seriously alarmed at his protracted absence, we were about setting out in search of him, when he unexpectedly made his appearance, in health no worse than usual, and in rather more than ordinary spirits. The account which he gave of his expedition, and of the events which had detained him, was a singular one indeed.

"You will remember," said he, "that it was about nine in the morning when I left Charlottesville. I bent my steps immediately to the mountains, and, about ten, entered a gorge which was entirely new to me. I followed the windings of this pass with much interest. The scenery which presented itself on all sides, although scarcely entitled to be called grand, had about it an indescribable and to me a delicious aspect of dreary desolation. The solitude seemed absolutely virgin. I could not help believing that the green sods and the gray rocks upon which I trod had been trodden never before by the foot of a human being. So entirely secluded, and in fact inaccessible, except through a series of accidents, is the entrance of the ravine, that it is by no means impossible that I was indeed the first adventurer — the very first and sole adventurer who had ever penetrated its recesses.

"The thick and peculiar mist, or smoke, which distinguishes the Indian Summer, and which now hung heavily over all objects, served, no doubt, to deepen the vague impressions which these objects created. So dense was this pleasant fog that I could at no time see more than a dozen yards of the path before me. This path was excessively sinuous, and as the sun could not be seen, I soon lost all idea of the direction in which I jour-

neyed. In the meantime the morphine had its customary effect — that of enduing all the external world with an intensity of interest. In the quivering of a leaf — in the hue of a blade of grass — in the shape of a trefoil — in the humming of a bee — in the gleaming of a dew-drop — in the breathing of the wind — in the faint odors that came from the forest — there came a whole universe of suggestion — a gay and motley train of rhapsodical and immethodical thought.

"Busied in this, I walked on for several hours, during which the mist deepened around me to so great an extent that at length I was reduced to an absolute groping of the way. And now an indescribable uneasiness possessed me — a species of nervous hesitation and tremor. I feared to tread, lest I should be precipitated into some abyss. I remembered, too, strange stories told about these Ragged Hills, and of the uncouth and fierce races of men who tenanted their groves and caverns. A thousand vague fancies oppressed and disconcerted me — fancies the more distressing because vague. Very suddenly my attention was arrested by the loud beating of a drum.

"My amazement was, of course, extreme. A drum in these hills was a thing unknown. I could not have been more surprised at the sound of the trump of the Archangel. But a new and still more astounding source of interest and perplexity arose. There came a wild rattling or jingling sound, as if of a bunch of large keys, and upon the instant a dusky-visaged and half-naked man rushed past me with a shriek. He came so close to my person that I felt his hot breath upon my face. He bore in one hand an instrument composed of an assemblage of steel rings, and shook them vigorously as he ran. Scarcely had he disappeared in the mist before, panting after him, with open mouth and glaring eyes, there darted a huge beast. I could not be mistaken in its character. It was a hyena.

"The sight of this monster rather relieved than heightened my terrors — for I now made sure that I dreamed, and endeavored to arouse myself to waking consciousness. I stepped boldly and briskly forward. I rubbed my eyes. I called aloud. I pinched my limbs. A small spring of water presented itself to my view, and here, stooping, I bathed my hands and my head and neck. This seemed to dissipate the equivocal sensations which had hitherto annoyed me. I arose, as I thought, a new man, and proceeded steadily and complacently on my unknown way.

"At length, quite overcome by exertion, and by a certain oppressive closeness of the atmosphere, I seated myself beneath a tree. Presently there came a feeble gleam of sunshine, and the shadow of the leaves of the tree fell faintly but definitely upon the grass. At this shadow I gazed wonderingly for many minutes. Its character stupefied me with astonishment. I looked upward. The tree was a palm.

"I now arose hurriedly, and in a state of fearful agitation — for the fancy that I dreamed would serve me no longer. I saw — I felt that I had perfect command of my senses — and these senses now brought to my

soul a world of novel and singular sensation. The heat became all at once intolerable. A strange odor loaded the breeze. A low, continuous murmur, like that arising from a full, but gently flowing river, came to my ears, intermingled with the peculiar hum of multitudinous human voices.

"While I listened in an extremity of astonishment which I need not attempt to describe, a strong and brief gust of wind bore off the incumbent fog as if by the wand of an enchanter.

"I found myself at the foot of a high mountain, and looking down into a vast plain, through which wound a majestic river. On the margin of this river stood an Eastern-looking city, such as we read of in the Arabian Tales, but of a character even more singular than any there described. From my position, which was far above the level of the town, I could perceive its every nook and corner, as if delineated on a map. The streets seemed innumerable, and crossed each other irregularly in all directions, but were rather long winding alleys than streets, and absolutely swarmed with inhabitants. The houses were wildly picturesque. On every hand was a wilderness of balconies, of verandas, of minarets, of shrines, and fantastically carved oriels. Bazaars abounded; and in these were displayed rich wares in infinite variety and profusion — silks, muslins, the most dazzling cutlery, the most magnificent jewels and gems. Besides these things, were seen, on all sides, banners and palanquins, litters with stately dames close veiled, elephants gorgeously caparisoned, idols grotesquely hewn, drums, banners, and gongs, spears, silver and gilded maces. And amid the crowd, and the clamor, and the general intricacy and confusion — amid the million of black and yellow men, turbaned and robed, and of flowing beard, there roamed a countless multitude of holy filleted bulls, while vast legions of the filthy but sacred ape clambered, chattering and shrieking, about the cornices of the mosques, or clung to the minarets and oriels. From the swarming streets to the banks of the river, there descended innumerable flights of steps leading to bathing places, while the river itself seemed to force a passage with difficulty through the vast fleets of deeply-burthened ships that far and wide encountered its surface. Beyond the limits of the city arose, in frequent majestic groups, the palm and the cocoa, with other gigantic and weird trees of vast age; and here and there might be seen a field of rice, the thatched hut of a peasant, a tank, a stray temple, a gypsy camp, or a solitary graceful maiden taking her way, with a pitcher upon her head, to the banks of the magnificent river.

"You will say now, of course, that I dreamed; but not so. What I saw — what I heard — what I felt — what I thought — had about it nothing of the unmistakable idiosyncrasy of the dream. All was rigorously self-consistent. At first, doubting that I was really awake, I entered into a series of tests, which soon convinced me that I really was. Now, when one dreams, and, in the dream, suspects that he dreams, the suspicion *never fails to confirm* itself, and the sleeper is almost immediately aroused. Thus

Novalis errs not in saying that 'we are near waking when we dream that we dream.' Had the vision occurred to me as I describe it, without my suspecting it as a dream, then a dream it might absolutely have been, but, occurring as it did, and suspected and tested as it was, I am forced to class it among other phenomena."

"In this I am not sure that you are wrong," observed Dr. Templeton, "but proceed. You arose and descended into the city."

"I arose," continued Bedloe, regarding the Doctor with an air of profound astonishment, "I arose, as you say, and descended into the city. On my way I fell in with an immense populace, crowding through every avenue, all in the same direction, and exhibiting in every action the wildest excitement. Very suddenly, and by some inconceivable impulse, I became intensely imbued with personal interest in what was going on. I seemed to feel that I had an important part to play, without exactly understanding what it was. Against the crowd which environed me, however, I experienced a deep sentiment of animosity. I shrank from amid them, and, swiftly, by a circuitous path, reached and entered the city. Here all was the wildest tumult and contention. A small party of men, clad in garments half-Indian, half-European, and officered by gentlemen in a uniform partly British, were engaged, at great odds, with the swarming rabble of the alleys. I joined the weaker party, arming myself with the weapons of a fallen officer, and fighting I knew not whom with the nervous ferocity of despair. We were soon overpowered by numbers, and driven to seek refuge in a species of kiosk. Here we barricaded ourselves, and, for the present, were secure. From a loop-hole near the summit of the kiosk, I perceived a vast crowd, in furious agitation, surrounding and assaulting a gay palace that overhung the river. Presently, from an upper window of this place, there descended an effeminate-looking person, by means of a string made of the turbans of his attendants. A boat was at hand, in which he escaped to the opposite bank of the river.

"And now a new object took possession of my soul. I spoke a few hurried but energetic words to my companions, and, having succeeded in gaining over a few of them to my purpose made a frantic sally from the kiosk. We rushed amid the crowd that surrounded it. They retreated, at first, before us. They rallied, fought madly, and retreated again. In the mean time we were borne far from the kiosk, and became bewildered and entangled among the narrow streets of tall, overhanging houses, into the recesses of which the sun had never been able to shine. The rabble pressed impetuously upon us, harrassing us with their spears, and overwhelming us with flights of arrows. These latter were very remarkable, and resembled in some respects the writhing creese of the Malay. They were made to imitate the body of a creeping serpent, and were long and black, with a poisoned barb. One of them struck me upon the right temple. I reeled and fell. An instantaneous and dreadful sickness seized me. I struggled — I gasped — I died."

"You will hardly persist *now*," said I smiling, "that the whole of your adventure was not a dream. You are not prepared to maintain that you are dead?"

When I said these words, I of course expected some lively sally from Bedloe in reply; but, to my astonishment, he hesitated, trembled, became fearfully pallid, and remained silent. I looked toward Templeton. He sat erect and rigid in his chair — his teeth chattered, and his eyes were starting from their sockets. "Proceed!" he at length said hoarsely to Bedloe.

"For many minutes," continued the latter, "my sole sentiment — my sole feeling — was that of darkness and nonentity, with the consciousness of death. At length there seemed to pass a violent and sudden shock through my soul, as if of electricity. With it came the sense of elasticity and of light. This latter I felt — not saw. In an instant I seemed to rise from the ground. But I had no bodily, no visible, audible, or palpable presence. The crowd had departed. The tumult had ceased. The city was in comparative repose. Beneath me lay my corpse, with the arrow in my temple, the whole head greatly swollen and disfigured. But all these things I felt — not saw. I took interest in nothing. Even the corpse seemed a matter in which I had no concern. Volition I had none, but appeared to be impelled into motion, and flitted buoyantly out of the city, retracing the circuitous path by which I had entered it. When I had attained that point of the ravine in the mountains at which I had encountered the hyena, I again experienced a shock as of a galvanic battery; the sense of weight, of volition, of substance, returned. I became my original self, and bent my steps eagerly homeward — but the past had not lost the vividness of the real — and not now, even for an instant, can I compel my understanding to regard it as a dream."

"Nor was it," said Templeton, with an air of deep solemnity, "yet it would be difficult to say how otherwise it should be termed. Let us suppose only, that the soul of the man of to-day is upon the verge of some stupendous psychal discoveries. Let us content ourselves with this supposition. For the rest I have some explanation to make. Here is a water-color drawing, which I should have shown you before, but which an unaccountable sentiment of horror has hitherto prevented me from showing."

We looked at the picture which he presented. I saw nothing in it of an extraordinary character; but its effect upon Bedloe was prodigious. He nearly fainted as he gazed. And yet it was but a miniature portrait — a miraculously accurate one, to be sure — of his own very remarkable features. At least this was my thought as I regarded it.

"You will perceive," said Templeton, "the date of this picture — it is here, scarcely visible, in this corner — 1780. In this year was the portrait taken. It is the likeness of a dead friend — a Mr. Oldeb — to whom I became much attached at Calcutta, during the administration of Warren

Hastings. I was then only twenty years old. When I first saw you, Mr. Bedloe, at Saratoga, it was the miraculous similarity which existed between yourself and the painting which induced me to accost you, to seek your friendship, and to bring about those arrangements which resulted in my becoming your constant companion. In accomplishing this point, I was urged partly. and perhaps principally, by a regretful memory of the deceased, but also, in part, by an uneasy, and not altogether horrorless curiosity respecting yourself.

"In your detail of the vision which presented itself to you amid the hills, you have described, with the minutest accuracy, the Indian city of Benares, upon the Holy River. The riots, the combat, the massacre, were the actual events of the insurrection of Cheyte Sing, which took place in 1780, when Hastings was put in imminent peril of his life. The man escaping by the string of turbans was Cheyte Sing himself. The party in the kiosk were sepoys and British officers, headed by Hastings. Of this party I was one, and did all I could to prevent the rash and fatal sally of the officer who fell, in the crowded alleys, by the poisoned arrow of a Bengalee. That officer was my dearest friend. It was Oldeb. You will perceive by these manuscripts," (here the speaker produced a note-book in which several pages appeared to have been freshly written,) "that at the very period in which you fancied these things amid the hills, I was engaged in detailing them upon paper here at home."

In about a week after this conversation, the following paragraphs appeared in a Charlottesville paper:

"We have the painful duty of announcing the death of MR. AUGUSTUS BEDLO, a gentleman whose amiable manners and many virtues have long endeared him to the citizens of Charlottesville.

"Mr. B., for some years past, has been subject to neuralgia, which has often threatened to terminate fatally; but this can be regarded only as the mediate cause of his decease. The proximate cause was one of especial singularity. In an excursion to the Ragged Mountains, a few days since, a slight cold and fever were contracted, attended with great determination of blood to the head. To relieve this, Dr. Templeton resorted to topical bleeding. Leeches were applied to the temples. In a fearfully brief period the patient died, when it appeared that in the jar containing the leeches, had been introduced, by accident, one of the venomous vermicular sangsues which are now and then found in the neighboring ponds. This creature fastened itself upon a small artery in the right temple. Its close resemblance to the medicinal leech caused the mistake to be overlooked until too late.

"N. B. The poisonous sangsue of Charlottesville may always be distinguished from the medicinal leech by its blackness, and especially by its writhing or vermicular motions, which very nearly resemble those of a snake."

I was speaking with the editor of the paper in question, upon the

topic of this remarkable accident, when it occurred to me to ask how it happened that the name of the deceased had been given as Bedlo.

"I presume," I said, "you have authority for this spelling, but I have always supposed the name to be written with an *e* at the end."

"Authority? — no," he replied. "It is a mere typographical error. The name is Bedlo with an *e*, all the world over, and I never knew it to be spelt otherwise in my life."

"Then," said I mutteringly, as I turned upon my heel, "then indeed has it come to pass that one truth is stranger than any fiction — for Bedloe, without the *e*, what is it but Oldeb conversed! And this man tells me that it is a typographical error."

The Balloon-Hoax

ASTOUNDING NEWS BY EXPRESS, *VIA* NORFOLK! — The Atlantic Crossed in Three Days! — Signal Triumph of Mr. Monck Mason's Flying Machine! — Arrival at Sullivan's Island, near Charlestown, S. C., of Mr. Mason, Mr. Robert Holland, Mr. Henson, Mr. Harrison Ainsworth, and four others, in the Steering Balloon, *Victoria*, after a Passage of Seventy-five Hours from Land to Land! Full Particulars of the Voyage!

The subjoined jeu d'esprit with the preceding heading in magnificent capitals, well interspersed with notes of admiration, was originally published, as matter of fact, in the New York Sun, a daily newspaper, and therein fully subserved the purpose of creating indigestible aliment for the quidnuncs during the few hours intervening between a couple of the Charleston mails. The rush for the "sole paper which had the news" was something beyond even the prodigious; and, in fact, if (as some assert) the Victoria did not absolutely accomplish the voyage recorded it will be difficult to assign a reason why she should not have accomplished it. E. A. P.

T HE GREAT problem is at length solved! The air, as well as the earth and the ocean, has been subdued by science, and will become a common and convenient highway for mankind. *The Atlantic has been actually crossed in a Balloon!* and this too without difficulty — without any great apparent danger — with thorough control of the machine — and in the inconceivably brief period of seventy-five hours from shore to shore! By the energy of an agent at Charleston, S. C., we are enabled to be the first to furnish the public with a detailed account of this most extraordinary voyage, which was performed between Saturday, the 6th instant, at 11 A. M. and 2 P. M., on Tuesday, the 9th instant, by Sir Everard Bringhurst; Mr. Osborne, a nephew of Lord Bentinck's; Mr. Monck Mason and Mr. Robert Holland, the well-known aeronauts; Mr. Harrison Ains-

worth, author of "Jack Sheppard," etc.; and Mr. Henson, the projector of the late unsuccessful flying machine — with two seamen from Woolwich — in all, eight persons. The particulars furnished below may be relied on as authentic and accurate in every respect, as, with a slight exception, they are copied *verbatim* from the joint diaries of Mr. Monck Mason and Mr. Harrison Ainsworth, to whose politeness our agent is also indebted for much verbal information respecting the balloon itself, its construction, and other matters of interest. The only alteration in the MS. received, has been made for the purpose of throwing the hurried account of our agent, Mr. Forsyth, into a connected and intelligible form.

THE BALLOON

Two very decided failures, of late, — those of Mr. Henson and Sir George Cayley, — had much weakened the public interest in the subject of aerial navigation. Mr. Henson's scheme (which at first was considered very feasible even by men of science) was founded upon the principle of an inclined plane, started from an eminence by an extrinsic force, applied and continued by the revolution of impinging vanes, in form and number resembling the vanes of a windmill. But, in all the experiments made with models at the Adelaide Gallery, it was found that the operation of these fans not only did not propel the machine, but actually impeded its flight. The only propelling force it ever exhibited, was the mere *impetus* acquired from the descent of the inclined plane; and this *impetus* carried the machine farther when the vanes were at rest, than when they were in motion — a fact which sufficiently demonstrates their inutility; and in the absence of the propelling, which was also the *sustaining*, power, the whole fabric would necessarily descend. This consideration led Sir George Cayley to think only of adapting a propeller to some machine having of itself an independent power of support — in a word, to a balloon; the idea, however, being novel, or original, with Sir George, only so far as regards the mode of its application to practice. He exhibited a model of his invention at the Polytechnic Institution. The propelling principle, or power, was here, also, applied to interrupted surfaces, or vanes, put in revolution. These vanes were four in number, but were found entirely ineffectual in moving the balloon, or in aiding its ascending power. The whole project was thus a complete failure.

It was at this juncture that Mr. Monck Mason (whose voyage from Dover to Weilburg in the balloon Nassau occasioned so much excitement in 1837) conceived the idea of employing the principle of the Archimedean screw for the purpose of propulsion through the air — rightly attributing the failure of Mr. Henson's scheme, and of Sir George Cayley's to the interruption of surface in the independent vanes. He made the first public experiment at Willis's Rooms, but afterward removed his model to the Adelaide Gallery.

Like Sir George Cayley's balloon, his own was an ellipsoid. Its length was 13 feet 6 inches — height, 6 feet 8 inches. It contained about 320 cubic feet of gas, which, if pure hydrogen, would support 21 pounds upon its first inflation, before the gas has time to deteriorate or escape. The weight of the whole machine and apparatus was 17 pounds — leaving about 4 pounds to spare. Beneath the centre of the balloon, was a frame of light wood, about 9 feet long, and rigged on to the balloon itself with a net-work in the customary manner. From this framework was suspended a wicker basket or car.

The screw consists of an axis of hollow brass tube, 18 inches in length, through which, upon a semi-spiral inclined at 15 degrees, pass a series of steel-wire radii, 2 feet long, and thus projecting a foot on either side. These radii are connected at the outer extremities by 2 bands of flattened wire; the whole in this manner forming the framework of the screw, which is completed by a covering of oiled silk cut into gores, and tightened so as to present a tolerably uniform surface. At each end of its axis this screw is supported by pillars of hollow brass tube descending from the hoop. In the lower ends of these tubes are holes in which the pivots of the axis revolve. From the end of the axis which is next the car, proceeds a shaft of steel, connecting the screw with the pinion of a piece of spring machinery fixed in the car. By the operation of this spring, the screw is made to revolve with great rapidity, communicating a progressive motion to the whole. By means of the rudder, the machine was readily turned in any direction. The spring was of great power, compared with its dimensions, being capable of raising 45 pounds upon a barrel of 4 inches diameter, after the first turn, and gradually increasing as it was wound up. It weighed, altogether, eight pounds six ounces. The rudder was a light frame of cane covered with silk, shaped somewhat like a battledoor, and was about 3 feet long, and at the widest, one foot. Its weight was about 2 ounces. It could be turned *flat*, and directed upward or downward, as well as to the right or left; and thus enabled the aeronaut to transfer the resistance of the air which in an inclined position it must generate in its passage, to any side upon which he might desire to act; thus determining the balloon in the opposite direction.

This model (which, through want of time, we have necessarily described in an imperfect manner) was put in action at the Adelaide Gallery, where it accomplished a velocity of 5 miles per hour; although, strange to say, it excited very little interest in comparison with the previous complex machine of Mr. Henson — so resolute is the world to despise anything which carries with it an air of simplicity. To accomplish the great desideratum of aerial navigation, it was very generally supposed that some exceedingly complicated application must be made of some unusually profound principle in dynamics.

So well satisfied, however, was Mr. Mason of the ultimate success of his invention, that he determined to construct immediately, if possible,

a balloon of sufficient capacity to test the question by a voyage of some extent; the original design being to cross the British Channel, as before, in the Nassau balloon. To carry out his views, he solicited and obtained the patronage of Sir Everard Bringhurst and Mr. Osborne, two gentlemen well known for scientific acquirement, and especially for the interest they have exhibited in the progress of aerostation. The project, at the desire of Mr. Osborne, was kept a profound secret from the public — the only persons entrusted with the design being those actually engaged in the construction of the machine, which was built (under the superintendence of Mr. Mason, Mr. Holland, Sir Everard Bringhurst, and Mr. Osborne) at the seat of the latter gentleman near Penstruthal, in Wales. Mr. Henson, accompanied by his friend Mr. Ainsworth, was admitted to a private view of the balloon, on Saturday last; when the two gentlemen made final arrangements to be included in the adventure. We are not informed for what reason the two seamen were also included in the party — but, in the course of a day or two, we shall put our readers in possession of the minutest particulars respecting this extraordinary voyage.

The balloon is composed of silk, varnished with the liquid gum caoutchouc. It is of vast dimensions, containing more than 40,000 cubic feet of gas; but as coal gas was employed in place of the more expensive and inconvenient hydrogen, the supporting power of the machine, when fully inflated, and immediately after inflation, is not more than about 2500 pounds. The coal gas is not only much less costly, but is easily procured and managed.

For its introduction into common use for purposes of aerostation, we are indebted to Mr. Charles Green. Up to his discovery, the process of inflation was not only exceedingly expensive, but uncertain. Two and even three days have frequently been wasted in futile attempts to procure a sufficiency of hydrogen to fill a balloon, from which it had great tendency to escape, owing to its extreme subtlety, and its affinity for the surrounding atmosphere. In a balloon sufficiently perfect to retain its contents of coal gas unaltered, in quantity or amount, for six months, an equal quantity of hydrogen could not be maintained in equal purity for six weeks.

The supporting power being estimated at 2500 pounds, and the united weights of the party amounting only to about 1200, there was left a surplus of 1300, of which again 1200 was exhausted by ballast, arranged in bags of different sizes, with their respective weights marked upon them — by cordage, barometers, telescopes, barrels containing provision for a fortnight, water-casks, cloaks, carpet-bags, and various other indispensable matters, including a coffee-warmer, contrived for warming coffee by means of slack-lime, so as to dispense altogether with fire, if it should be judged prudent to do so. All these articles, with the exception of the ballast, and a few trifles, were suspended from the hoop overhead. The

car is much smaller and lighter, in proportion, than the one appended to the model. It is formed of a light wicker, and is wonderfully strong, for so frail looking a machine. Its rim is about 4 feet deep. The rudder is also very much larger, in proportion, than that of the model; and the screw is considerably smaller. The balloon is furnished besides with a grapnel, and a guide-rope; which latter is of the most indispensable importance. A few words, in explanation, will here be necessary for such of our readers as are not conversant with the details of aerostation.

As soon as the balloon quits the earth, it is subjected to the influence of many circumstances tending to create a difference in its weight; augmenting or diminishing its ascending power. For example, there may be a deposition of dew upon the silk, to the extent, even, of several hundred pounds; ballast has then to be thrown out, or the machine may descend. This ballast being discarded, and a clear sunshine evaporating the dew, and at the same time expanding the gas in the silk, the whole will again rapidly ascend. To check this ascent, the only recourse is (or rather *was*, until Mr. Green's invention of the guide-rope) the permission of the escape of gas from the valve; but, in the loss of gas, is a proportionate general loss of ascending power; so that, in a comparatively brief period, the best-constructed balloon must necessarily exhaust all its resources, and come to the earth. This was the great obstacle to voyages of length.

The guide-rope remedies the difficulty in the simplest manner conceivable. It is merely a very long rope which is suffered to trail from the car, and the effect of which is to prevent the balloon from changing its level in any material degree. If, for example, there should be a deposition of moisture upon the silk, and the machine begins to descend in consequence, there will be no necessity for discharging ballast to remedy the increase of weight, for it is remedied, or counteracted, in an exactly just proportion, by the deposit on the ground of just so much of the end of the rope as is necessary. If, on the other hand, any circumstances should cause undue levity, and consequent ascent, this levity is immediately counteracted by the additional weight of rope upraised from the earth. Thus, the balloon can neither ascend nor descend, except within very narrow limits, and its resources, either in gas or ballast, remain comparatively unimpaired. When passing over an expanse of water, it becomes necessary to employ small kegs of copper or wood, filled with liquid ballast of a lighter nature than water. These float, and serve all the purposes of a mere rope on land. Another most important office of the guide-rope, is to point out the *direction* of the balloon. The rope *drags*, either on land or sea, while the balloon is free; the latter, consequently, is always in advance, when any progress whatever is made, a comparison, therefore, by means of the compass, of the relative positions of the two objects, will always indicate the *course*. In the same way, the angle formed by the rope with the vertical axis of the machine, indicates the *velocity*. When there is *no*

angle — in other words, when the rope hangs perpendicularly, the whole apparatus is stationary; but the larger the angle, that is to say, the farther the balloon precedes the end of the rope, the greater the velocity; and the converse.

As the original design was to cross the British Channel, and alight as near Paris as possible, the voyagers had taken the precaution to prepare themselves with passports directed to all parts of the Continent, specifying the nature of the expedition, as in the case of the Nassau voyage, and entitling the adventurers to exemption from the usual formalities of office; unexpected events, however, rendered these passports superfluous.

The inflation was commenced very quietly at day-break, on Saturday morning, the 6th instant, in the courtyard of Wheal-Vor House, Mr. Osborne's seat, about a mile from Penstruthal, in North Wales; and at 7 minutes past 11, everything being ready for departure, the balloon was set free, rising gently but steadily, in a direction nearly South; no use being made, for the first half hour, of either the screw or the rudder. We proceed now with the journal, as transcribed by Mr. Forsyth from the joint MSS. of Mr. Monck Mason and Mr. Ainsworth. The body of the journal, as given, is in the handwriting of Mr. Mason, and a P. S. is appended, each day, by Mr. Ainsworth, who has in preparation, and will shortly give the public a more minute and, no doubt, a thrillingly interesting account of the voyage.

THE JOURNAL

Saturday, April the 6th. — Every preparation likely to embarrass us having been made overnight, we commenced the inflation this morning at daybreak; but owing to a thick fog, which encumbered the folds of the silk and rendered it unmanageable, we did not get through before nearly eleven o'clock. Cut loose, then, in high spirits, and rose gently but steadily, with a light breeze at North, which bore us in the direction of the Bristol Channel. Found the ascending force greater than we had expected; and as we arose higher and so got clear of the cliffs, and more in the sun's rays, our ascent became very rapid. I did not wish, however, to lose gas at so early a period of the adventure, and so concluded to ascend for the present. We soon ran out our guide-rope; but even when we had raised it clear of the earth, we still went up very rapidly. The balloon was unusually steady, and looked beautifully. In about 10 minutes after starting, the barometer indicated an altitude of 15,000 feet. The weather was remarkably fine, and the view of the subjacent country — a most romantic one when seen from any point — was now especially sublime. The numerous deep gorges presented the appearance of lakes, on account of the dense vapors with which they were filled, and the pinnacles and crags to the South East, piled in inextricable confusion, resembling nothing so much as the giant cities of Eastern fable. We were

rapidly approaching the mountains in the South, but our elevation was more than sufficient to enable us to pass them in safety. In a few minutes we soared over them in fine style; and Mr. Ainsworth, with the seamen, was surprised at their apparent want of altitude when viewed from the car, the tendency of great elevation in a balloon being to reduce inequalities of the surface below, to nearly a dead level. At half-past eleven still proceeding nearly South, we obtained our first view of the Bristol Channel; and, in fifteen minutes afterward, the line of breakers on the coast appeared immediately beneath us, and we were fairly out at sea. We now resolved to let off enough gas to bring our guide-rope, with the buoys affixed, into the water. This was immediately done, and we commenced a gradual descent. In about 20 minutes our first buoy dipped, and at the touch of the second soon afterward, we remained stationary as to elevation. We were all now anxious to test the efficiency of the rudder and screw, and we put them both into requisition forthwith, for the purpose of altering our direction more to the eastward, and in a line for Paris. By means of the rudder we instantly effected the necessary change of direction, and our course was brought nearly at right angles to that of the wind; when we set in motion the spring of the screw, and were rejoiced to find it propel us readily as desired. Upon this we gave nine hearty cheers, and dropped in the sea a bottle, inclosing a slip of parchment with a brief account of the principle of the invention. Hardly, however, had we done with our rejoicings, when an unforeseen accident occurred which discouraged us in no little degree. The steel rod connecting the spring with the propeller was suddenly jerked out of place, at the car end, (by a swaying of the car through some movement of one of the two seamen we had taken up,) and in an instant hung dangling out of reach, from the pivot of the axis of the screw. While we were endeavoring to regain it, our attention being completely absorbed, we became involved in a strong current of wind from the East, which bore us, with rapidly increasing force, toward the Atlantic. We soon found ourselves driving out to sea at the rate of not less, certainly, than 50 or 60 miles an hour, so that we came up with Cape Clear, at some 40 miles to our North, before we had secured the rod, and had time to think what we were about. It was now that Mr. Ainsworth made an extraordinary but, to my fancy, a by no means unreasonable or chimerical proposition, in which he was instantly seconded by Mr. Holland — viz.: that we should take advantage of the strong gale which bore us on, and in place of beating back to Paris, make an attempt to reach the coast of North America. After slight reflection, I gave a willing assent to this bold proposition, which (strange to say) met with objection from the two seamen only. As the stronger party, however, we overruled their fears, and kept resolutely upon our course. We steered due West; but as the trailing of the buoys materially impeded our progress, and we had the balloon abundantly at command, either for ascent or descent, we first

threw out fifty pounds of ballast, and then wound up (by means of a windlass) so much of the rope as brought it quite clear of the sea. We perceived the effect of this manœuvre immediately, in a vastly increased rate of progress; and, as the gale freshened, we flew with a velocity nearly inconceivable; the guide-rope flying out behind the car, like a streamer from a vessel. It is needless to say that a very short time sufficed us to lose sight of the coast. We passed over innumerable vessels of all kinds, a few of which were endeavoring to beat up, but the most of them lying to. We occasioned the greatest excitement on board all — an excitement greatly relished by ourselves, and especially by our two men, who, now under the influence of a dram of Geneva, seemed resolved to give all scruple, or fear, to the wind. Many of the vessels fired signal guns; and in all we were saluted with loud cheers (which we heard with surprising distinctness) and the waving of caps and handkerchiefs. We kept on in this manner throughout the day with no material incident, and, as the shades of night closed around us, we made a rough estimate of the distance traversed. It could not have been less than 500 miles, and was probably much more. The propeller was kept in constant operation, and, no doubt, aided our progress materially. As the sun went down, the gale freshened into an absolute hurricane, and the ocean beneath was clearly visible on account of its phosphorescence. The wind was from the East all night, and gave us the brightest omen of success. We suffered no little from cold, and the dampness of the atmosphere was most unpleasant; but the ample space in the car enabled us to lie down, and by means of cloaks and a few blankets we did sufficiently well.

P. S. [by Mr. Ainsworth.] The last nine hours have been unquestionably the most exciting of my life. I can conceive nothing more sublimating than the strange peril and novelty of an adventure such as this. May God grant that we succeed! I ask not success for mere safety to my insignificant person, but for the sake of human knowledge and — for the vastness of the triumph. And yet the feat is only so evidently feasible that the sole wonder is why men have scrupled to attempt it before. One single gale such as now befriends us — let such a tempest whirl forward a balloon for 4 or 5 days (these gales often last longer) and the voyager will be easily borne, in that period, from coast to coast. In view of such a gale the broad Atlantic becomes a mere lake. I am more struck, just now, with the supreme silence which reigns in the sea beneath us, notwithstanding its agitation, than with any other phenomenon presenting itself. The waters give up no voice to the Heavens. The immense flaming ocean writhes and is tortured uncomplainingly. The mountainous surges suggest the idea of innumerable dumb gigantic fiends struggling in impotent agony. In a night such as is this to me, a man *lives* — lives a whole century of ordinary life — nor would I forego this rapturous delight for that of a whole century of ordinary existence.

Sunday, the 7th. [Mr. Mason's MS.] This morning the gale, by 10,

had subsided to an eight- or nine-knot breeze (for a vessel at sea), and bears us, perhaps, 30 miles per hour, or more. It has veered, however, very considerably to the North; and now, at sundown, we are holding our course due West, principally by the screw and rudder, which answer their purposes to admiration. I regard the project as thoroughly successful, and the easy navigation of the air in any direction (not exactly in the teeth of a gale) as no longer problematical. We could not have made head against the strong wind of yesterday; but, by ascending, we might have got out of its influence, if requisite. Against a pretty stiff breeze, I feel convinced, we can make our way with the propeller. At noon, to-day, ascended to an elevation of nearly 25,000 feet, (about the height of Cotopaxi) by discharging ballast. Did this to search for a more direct current, but found none so favorable as the one we are now in. We have an abundance of gas to take us across this small pond, even should the voyage last 3 weeks. I have not the slightest fear for the result. The difficulty has been strangely exaggerated and misapprehended. I can choose my current, and should I find *all* currents against me, I can make very tolerable headway with the propeller. We have had no incidents worth recording. The night promises fair.

P. S. [By Mr. Ainsworth.] I have little to record, except the fact (to me quite a surprising one) that, at an elevation equal to that of Cotopaxi, I experienced neither very intense cold, nor headache, nor difficulty of breathing; neither, I find, did Mr. Mason, nor Mr. Holland, nor Sir Everard. Mr. Osborne complained of constriction of the chest — but this soon wore off. We have flown at a great rate during the day, and we must be more than half way across the Atlantic. We have passed over some 20 or 30 vessels of various kinds, and all seem to be delightfully astonished. Crossing the ocean in a balloon is not so difficult a feat after all. *Omne ignotum pro magnifico. Mem.*: at 25,000 feet elevation the sky appears nearly black, and the stars are distinctly visible; while the sea does not seem convex (as one might suppose) but absolutely and most unequivocally *concave.**

* "Mr. Ainsworth has not attempted to account for this phenomenon, which however, is quite susceptible of explanation. A line dropped from an elevation of 25,000 feet, perpendicularly to the surface of the earth (or sea), would form the perpendicular of a right-angled triangle, of which the base would extend from the right angle to the horizon, and the hypotenuse from the horizon to the balloon. But the 25,000 feet of altitude is little or nothing, in comparison with the extent of the prospect. In other words, the base and hypotenuse of the supposed triangle would be so long, when compared with the perpendicular, that the two former may be regarded as nearly parallel. In this manner the horizon of the aeronaut would appear to be *on a level* with the car. But, as the point immediately beneath him seems, and is, at a great distance below him, it seems, of course, also, at a great distance below the horizon. Hence the impression of *concavity*; and this impression must remain, until the elevation shall bear so great a proportion to the extent of prospect, that the apparent parallelism of the base and hypotenuse disappears — when the earth's real convexity must appear.

Monday, the 8th. [Mr. Mason's MS.] This morning we had again some little trouble with the rod of the propeller, which must be entirely remodelled, for fear of serious accident — I mean the steel rod, not the vanes. The latter could not be improved. The wind has been blowing steadily and strongly from the North-East all day; and so far fortune seems bent upon favoring us. Just before day, we were all somewhat alarmed at some odd noises and concussions in the balloon, accompanied with the apparent rapid subsidence of the whole machine. These phenomena were occasioned by the expansion of the gas, through increase of heat in the atmosphere, and the consequent disruption of the minute particles of ice with which the network had become encrusted during the night. Threw down several bottles to the vessels below. Saw one of them picked up by a large ship — seemingly one of the New York line packets. Endeavored to make out her name, but could not be sure of it. Mr. Osborne's telescope made it out something like "Atalanta." It is now 12 at night, and we are still going nearly West, at a rapid pace. The sea is peculiarly phosphorescent.

P. S. [By Mr. Ainsworth.] It is now 2 A. M., and nearly calm, as well as I can judge — but it is very difficult to determine this point, since we move *with* the air so completely. I have not slept since quitting Wheal-Vor, but can stand it no longer, and must take a nap. We cannot be far from the American coast.

Tuesday, the 9th. [Mr. Ainsworth's MS.] One, P. M. *We are in full view of the low coast of South Carolina.* The great problem is accomplished. We have crossed the Atlantic — fairly and *easily* crossed it in a balloon! God be praised! Who shall say that anything is impossible hereafter?

The Journal here ceases. Some particulars of the descent were communicated, however, by Mr. Ainsworth to Mr. Forsyth. It was nearly dead calm when the voyagers first came in view of the coast, which was immediately recognized by both the seamen, and by Mr. Osborne. The latter gentleman having acquaintances at Fort Moultrie, it was immediately resolved to descend in its vicinity. The balloon was brought over the beach (the tide being out and the sand hard, smooth, and admirably adapted for a descent), and the grapnel let go, which took firm hold at once. The inhabitants of the Island, and of the Fort, thronged out, of course, to see the balloon; but it was with the greatest difficulty that any one could be made to credit the actual voyage — *the crossing of the Atlantic.* The grapnel caught at 2 P. M. precisely; and thus the whole voyage was completed in 75 hours; or rather less, counting from shore to shore. No serious accident occurred. No real danger was at any time apprehended. The balloon was exhausted and secured without trouble; and when the MS. from which this narrative is compiled was despatched from Charleston, the party were still at Fort Moultrie. Their

further intentions were not ascertained; but we can safely promise our
readers some additional information either on Monday or in the course
of the next day, at furthest.

This is unquestionably the most stupendous, the most interesting, and
the most important undertaking ever accomplished or even attempted
by man. What magnificent events may ensue, it would be useless now
to think of determining.

The Premature Burial

THERE are certain themes of which the interest is all-absorbing, but
which are too entirely horrible for the purposes of legitimate fiction.
These the mere romanticist must eschew, if he do not wish to offend or
to disgust. They are with propriety handled only when the severity and
majesty of Truth sanctify and sustain them. We thrill, for example, with
the most intense of "pleasurable pain" over the accounts of the Passage
of the Beresina, of the Earthquake at Lisbon, of the Plague at London,
of the Massacre of St. Bartholomew, or of the stifling of the hundred
and twenty-three prisoners in the Black Hole at Calcutta. But in these
accounts it is the fact — it is the reality — it is the history which excites.
As inventions, we should regard them with simple abhorrence.

I have mentioned some few of the more prominent and august calami-
ties on record; but in these it is the extent, not less than the character
of the calamity, which so vividly impresses the fancy. I need not remind
the reader that, from the long and weird catalogue of human miseries,
I might have selected many individual instances more replete with essen-
tial suffering than any of these vast generalities of disaster. The true
wretchedness, indeed — the ultimate woe — is particular, not diffuse.
That the ghastly extremes of agony are endured by man the unit, and
never by man the mass — for this let us thank a merciful God!

To be buried while alive is, beyond question, the most terrific of
these extremes which has ever fallen to the lot of mere mortality. That
it has frequently, very frequently, so fallen will scarcely be denied by
those who think. The boundaries which divide Life from Death are at
best shadowy and vague. Who shall say where the one ends, and where
the other begins? We know that there are diseases in which occur total
cessations of all the apparent functions of vitality, and yet in which these
cessations are merely suspensions, properly so called. They are only tem-
porary pauses in the incomprehensible mechanism. A certain period
elapses, and some unseen mysterious principle again sets in motion the
magic pinions and the wizard wheels. The silver cord was not for ever

loosed, nor the golden bowl irreparably broken. But where, meantime, was the soul?

Apart, however, from the inevitable conclusion, *à priori* that such causes must produce such effects — that the well-known occurrence of such cases of suspended animation must naturally give rise, now and then, to premature interments — apart from this consideration, we have the direct testimony of medical and ordinary experience to prove that a vast number of such interments have actually taken place. I might refer at once, if necessary to a hundred well authenticated instances. One of very remarkable character, and of which the circumstances may be fresh in the memory of some of my readers, occurred, not very long ago, in the neighboring city of Baltimore, where it occasioned a painful, intense, and widely-extended excitement. The wife of one of the most respectable citizens — a lawyer of eminence and a member of Congress — was seized with a sudden and unaccountable illness, which completely baffled the skill of her physicians. After much suffering she died, or was supposed to die. No one suspected, indeed, or had reason to suspect, that she was not actually dead. She presented all the ordinary appearances of death. The face assumed the usual pinched and sunken outline. The lips were of the usual marble pallor. The eyes were lustreless. There was no warmth. Pulsation had ceased. For three days the body was preserved unburied, during which it had acquired a stony rigidity. The funeral, in short, was hastened, on account of the rapid advance of what was supposed to be decomposition.

The lady was deposited in her family vault, which, for three subsequent years, was undisturbed. At the expiration of this term it was opened for the reception of a sarcophagus; — but, alas! how fearful a shock awaited the husband, who, personally, threw open the door! As its portals swung outwardly back, some white-apparelled object fell rattling within his arms. It was the skeleton of his wife in her yet unmoulded shroud.

A careful investigation rendered it evident that she had revived within two days after her entombment; that her struggles within the coffin had caused it to fall from a ledge, or shelf to the floor, where it was so broken as to permit her escape. A lamp which had been accidentally left, full of oil, within the tomb, was found empty; it might have been exhausted, however, by evaporation. On the uttermost of the steps which led down into the dread chamber was a large fragment of the coffin, with which, it seemed, that she had endeavored to arrest attention by striking the iron door. While thus occupied, she probably swooned, or possibly died, through sheer terror; and, in falling, her shroud became entangled in some iron-work which projected interiorly. Thus she remained, and thus she rotted, erect.

In the year 1810, a case of living inhumation happened in France, attended with circumstances which go far to warrant the assertion that

truth is, indeed, stranger than fiction. The heroine of the story was a Mademoiselle Victorine Lafourcade, a young girl of illustrious family, of wealth, and of great personal beauty. Among her numerous suitors was Julien Bossuet, a poor *littérateur*, or journalist of Paris. His talents and general amiability had recommended him to the notice of the heiress, by whom he seems to have been truly beloved; but her pride of birth decided her, finally, to reject him, and to wed a Monsieur Rénelle, a banker and a diplomatist of some eminence. After marriage, however, this gentleman neglected, and, perhaps, even more positively ill-treated her. Having passed with him some wretched years, she died, — at least her condition so closely resembled death as to deceive every one who saw her. She was buried — not in a vault, but in an ordinary grave in the village of her nativity. Filled with despair, and still inflamed by the memory of a profound attachment, the lover journeys from the capital to the remote province in which the village lies, with the romantic purpose of disinterring the corpse, and possessing himself of its luxuriant tresses. He reaches the grave. At midnight he unearths the coffin, opens it, and is in the act of detaching the hair, when he is arrested by the unclosing of the beloved eyes. In fact, the lady had been buried alive. Vitality had not altogether departed, and she was aroused by the caresses of her lover from the lethargy which had been mistaken for death. He bore her frantically to his lodgings in the village. He employed certain powerful restoratives suggested by no little medical learning. In fine, she revived. She recognized her preserver. She remained with him until, by slow degrees, she fully recovered her original health. Her woman's heart was not adamant, and this last lesson of love sufficed to soften it. She bestowed it upon Bossuet. She returned no more to her husband, but, concealing from him her resurrection, fled with her lover to America. Twenty years afterward, the two returned to France, in the persuasion that time had so greatly altered the lady's appearance that her friends would be unable to recognize her. They were mistaken, however; for, at the first meeting, Monsieur Rénelle did actually recognize and make claim to his wife. This claim she resisted, and a judicial tribunal sustained her in her resistance, deciding that the peculiar circumstances, with the long lapse of years, had extinguished, not only equitably, but legally, the authority of the husband.

The "Chirurgical Journal" of Leipsic — a periodical of high authority and merit, which some American bookseller would do well to translate and republish, records in a late number a very distressing event of the character in question.

An officer of artillery, a man of gigantic stature and of robust health, being thrown from an unmanageable horse, received a very severe contusion upon the head, which rendered him insensible at once; the skull was slightly fractured, but no immediate danger was apprehended. Trepanning was accomplished successfully. He was bled, and many other

of the ordinary means of relief were adopted. Gradually, however, he fell into a more and more hopeless state of stupor, and, finally, it was thought that he died.

The weather was warm, and he was buried with indecent haste in one of the public cemeteries. His funeral took place on Thursday. On the Sunday following, the grounds of the cemetery were, as usual, much thronged with visiters, and about noon an intense excitement was created by the declaration of a peasant that, while sitting upon the grave of the officer, he had distinctly felt a commotion of the earth, as if occasioned by some one struggling beneath. At first little attention was paid to the man's asseveration; but his evident terror, and the dogged obstinacy with which he persisted in his story, had at length their natural effect upon the crowd. Spades were hurriedly procured, and the grave, which was shamefully shallow, was in a few minutes so far thrown open that the head of its occupant appeared. He was then seemingly dead; but he sat nearly erect within his coffin, the lid of which, in his furious struggles, he had partially uplifted.

He was forthwith conveyed to the nearest hospital, and there pronounced to be still living, although in an asphytic condition. After some hours he revived, recognized individuals of his acquaintance, and, in broken sentences spoke of his agonies in the grave.

From what he related, it was clear that he must have been conscious of life for more than an hour, while inhumed, before lapsing into insensibility. The grave was carelessly and loosely filled with an exceedingly porous soil; and thus some air was necessarily admitted. He heard the footsteps of the crowd overhead, and endeavored to make himself heard in turn. It was the tumult within the grounds of the cemetery, he said, which appeared to awaken him from a deep sleep, but no sooner was he awake than he became fully aware of the awful horrors of his position.

This patient, it is recorded, was doing well, and seemed to be in a fair way of ultimate recovery, but fell a victim to the quackeries of medical experiment. The galvanic battery was applied, and he suddenly expired in one of those ecstatic paroxysms which, occasionally, it superinduces.

The mention of the galvanic battery, nevertheless, recalls to my memory a well known and very extraordinary case in point, where its action proved the means of restoring to animation a young attorney of London, who had been interred for two days. This occurred in 1831, and created, at the time, a very profound sensation wherever it was made the subject of converse.

The patient, Mr. Edward Stapleton, had died, apparently of typhus fever, accompanied with some anomalous symptoms which had excited the curiosity of his medical attendants. Upon his seeming decease, his friends were requested to sanction a *post-mortem* examination, but declined to permit it. As often happens, when such refusals are made, the

practitioners resolved to disinter the body and dissect it at leisure, in private. Arrangements were easily effected with some of the numerous corps of body-snatchers, with which London abounds; and, upon the third night after the funeral, the supposed corpse was unearthed from a grave eight feet deep, and deposited in the operating chamber of one of the private hospitals.

An incision of some extent had been actually made in the abdomen, when the fresh and undecayed appearance of the subject suggested an application of the battery. One experiment succeeded another, and the customary effects supervened, with nothing to characterize them in any respect, except, upon one or two occasions, a more than ordinary degree of life-likeness in the convulsive action.

It grew late. The day was about to dawn; and it was thought expedient, at length, to proceed at once to the dissection. A student, however, was especially desirous of testing a theory of his own, and insisted upon applying the battery to one of the pectoral muscles. A rough gash was made, and a wire hastily brought in contact; when the patient, with a hurried but quite unconvulsive movement, arose from the table, stepped into the middle of the floor, gazed about him uneasily for a few seconds, and then — spoke. What he said was unintelligible; but words were uttered; the syllabification was distinct. Having spoken, he fell heavily to the floor.

For some moments all were paralyzed with awe — but the urgency of the case soon restored them their presence of mind. It was seen that Mr. Stapleton was alive, although in a swoon. Upon exhibition of ether he revived and was rapidly restored to health, and to the society of his friends — from whom, however, all knowledge of his resuscitation was withheld, until a relapse was no longer to be apprehended. Their wonder — their rapturous astonishment — may be conceived.

The most thrilling peculiarity of this incident, nevertheless, is involved in what Mr. S. himself asserts. He declares that at no period was he altogether insensible — that, dully and confusedly, he was aware of everything which happened to him, from the moment in which he was pronounced *dead* by his physicians, to that in which he fell swooning to the floor of the hospital. "I am alive," were the uncomprehended words which, upon recognizing the locality of the dissecting-room, he had endeavored, in his extremity, to utter.

It were an easy matter to multiply such histories as these — but I forbear — for, indeed, we have no need of such to establish the fact that premature interments occur. When we reflect how very rarely, from the nature of the case, we have it in our power to detect them, we must admit that they may *frequently* occur without our cognizance. Scarcely, in truth, is a graveyard ever encroached upon, for any purpose, to any great extent, that skeletons are not found in postures which suggest the most fearful of suspicions.

Fearful indeed the suspicion — but more fearful the doom! It may be asserted, without hesitation, that *no* event is so terribly well adapted to inspire the supremeness of bodily and of mental distress, as is burial before death. The unendurable oppression of the lungs — the stifling fumes from the damp earth — the clinging to the death garments — the rigid embrace of the narrow house — the blackness of the absolute Night — the silence like a sea that overwhelms — the unseen but palpable presence of the Conqueror Worm — these things, with the thoughts of the air and grass above, with memory of dear friends who would fly to save us if but informed of our fate, and with consciousness that of this fate they can *never* be informed — that our hopeless portion is that of the really dead — these considerations, I say, carry into the heart, which still palpitates, a degree of appalling and intolerable horror from which the most daring imagination must recoil. We know of nothing so agonizing upon Earth — we can dream of nothing half so hideous in the realms of the nethermost Hell. And thus all narratives upon this topic have an interest profound; an interest, nevertheless, which, through the sacred awe of the topic itself, very properly and very peculiarly depends upon our conviction of the *truth* of the matter narrated. What I have now to tell is of my own actual knowledge — of my own positive and personal experience.

For several years I had been subject to attacks of the singular disorder which physicians have agreed to term catalepsy, in default of a more definitive title. Although both the immediate and the predisposing causes, and even the actual diagnosis, of this disease are still mysterious, its obvious and apparent character is sufficiently well understood. Its variations seem to be chiefly of degree. Sometimes the patient lies, for a day only, or even for a shorter period, in a species of exaggerated lethargy. He is senseless and externally motionless; but the pulsation of the heart is still faintly perceptible; some traces of warmth remain; a slight color lingers within the centre of the cheek; and, upon application of a mirror to the lips, we can detect a torpid, unequal, and vacillating action of the lungs. Then again the duration of the trance is for weeks — even for months; while the closest scrutiny, and the most rigorous medical tests, fail to establish any material distinction between the state of the sufferer and what we conceive of absolute death. Very usually he is saved from premature interment solely by the knowledge of his friends that he has been previously subject to catalepsy, by the consequent suspicion excited, and, above all, by the non-appearance of decay. The advances of the malady are, luckily, gradual. The first manifestations, although marked, are unequivocal. The fits grow successively more and more distinctive, and endure each for a longer term than the preceding. In this lies the principal security from inhumation. The unfortunate whose *first* attack should be of the extreme character which is occasionally seen, would almost inevitably be consigned alive to the tomb.

My own case differed in no important particular from those mentioned in medical books. Sometimes, without any apparent cause, I sank, little by little, into a condition of hemi-syncope, or half swoon; and, in this condition, without pain, without ability to stir, or, strictly speaking, to think, but with a dull lethargic consciousness of life and of the presence of those who surrounded my bed, I remained, until the crisis of the disease restored me, suddenly, to perfect sensation. At other times I was quickly and impetuously smitten. I grew sick, and numb, and chilly, and dizzy, and so fell prostrate at once. Then, for weeks, all was void, and black, and silent, and Nothing became the universe. Total annihilation could be no more. From these latter attacks I awoke, however, with a gradation slow in proportion to the suddenness of the seizure. Just as the day dawns to the friendless and houseless beggar who roams the streets throughout the long desolate winter night — just so tardily — just so wearily — just so cheerily came back the light of the Soul to me.

Apart from the tendency to trance, however, my general health appeared to be good; nor could I perceive that it was at all affected by the one prevalent malady — unless, indeed, an idiosyncrasy in my ordinary *sleep* may be looked upon as superinduced. Upon awaking from slumber, I could never gain, at once, thorough possession of my senses, and always remained, for many minutes, in much bewilderment and perplexity; — the mental faculties in general, but the memory in especial, being in a condition of absolute abeyance.

In all that I endured there was no physical suffering, but of moral distress an infinitude. My fancy grew charnel, I talked "of worms, of tombs, and epitaphs." I was lost in reveries of death, and the idea of premature burial held continual possession of my brain. The ghastly Danger to which I was subjected haunted me day and night. In the former, the torture of meditation was excessive — in the latter, supreme. When the grim Darkness overspread the Earth, then, with every horror of thought, I shook — shook as the quivering plumes upon the hearse. When Nature could endure wakefulness no longer, it was with a struggle that I consented to sleep — for I shuddered to reflect that, upon awaking, I might find myself the tenant of a grave. And when, finally, I sank into slumber, it was only to rush at once into a world of phantasms, above which, with vast, sable, overshadowing wing, hovered, predominant, the one sepulchral Idea.

From the innumerable images of gloom which thus oppressed me in dreams, I select for record but a solitary vision. Methought I was immersed in a cataleptic trance of more than usual duration and profundity. Suddenly there came an icy hand upon my forehead, and an impatient, gibbering voice whispered the word "Arise!" within my ear.

I sat erect. The darkness was total. I could not see the figure of him who had aroused me. I could call to mind neither the period at which I had fallen into the trance, nor the locality in which I then lay. While I re-

mained motionless, and busied in endeavors to collect my thought, the cold hand grasped me fiercely by the wrist, shaking it petulantly, while the gibbering voice said again:

"Arise! did I not bid thee arise?"

"And who," I demanded, "art thou?"

"I have no name in the regions which I inhabit," replied the voice, mournfully; "I was mortal, but am fiend. I was merciless, but am pitiful. Thou dost feel that I shudder. — My teeth chatter as I speak, yet it is not with the chilliness of the night — of the night without end. But this hideousness is insufferable. How canst *thou* tranquilly sleep? I cannot rest for the cry of these great agonies. These sights are more than I can bear. Get thee up! Come with me into the outer Night, and let me unfold to thee the graves. Is not this a spectacle of woe? — Behold!"

I looked; and the unseen figure, which still grasped me by the wrist, had caused to be thrown open the graves of all mankind; and from each issued the faint phosphoric radiance of decay; so that I could see into the innermost recesses, and there view the shrouded bodies in their sad and solemn slumbers with the worm. But alas! the real sleepers were fewer, by many millions, than those who slumbered not at all; and there was a feeble struggling; and there was a general sad unrest; and from out the depths of the countless pits there came a melancholy rustling from the garments of the buried. And of those who seemed tranquilly to repose, I saw that a vast number had changed, in a greater or less degree, the rigid and uneasy position in which they had originally been entombed. And the voice again said to me as I gazed:

"Is it not — oh! is it *not* a pitiful sight?" — but, before I could find words to reply, the figure had ceased to grasp my wrist, the phosphoric lights expired, and the graves were closed with a sudden violence, while from out them arose a tumult of despairing cries, saying again: "Is it not — O, God, is it *not* a very pitiful sight?"

Phantasies such as these, presenting themselves at night, extended their terrific influence far into my waking hours. My nerves became thoroughly unstrung, and I fell a prey to perpetual horror. I hesitated to ride, or to walk, or to indulge in any exercise that would carry me from home. In fact, I no longer dared trust myself out of the immediate presence of those who were aware of my proneness to catalepsy, lest, falling into one of my usual fits, I should be buried before my real condition could be ascertained. I doubted the care, the fidelity of my dearest friends. I dreaded that, in some trance of more than customary duration, they might be prevailed upon to regard me as irrecoverable. I even went so far as to fear that, as I occasioned much trouble, they might be glad to consider any very protracted attack as sufficient excuse for getting rid of me altogether. It was in vain they endeavored to reassure me by the most solemn promises. I exacted the most sacred oaths, that under no circumstances they would bury me until decomposition had so materi-

ally advanced as to render farther preservation impossible. And, even then, my mortal terrors would listen to no reason — would accept no consolation. I entered into a series of elaborate precautions. Among other things, I had the family vault so remodelled as to admit of being readily opened from within. The slightest pressure upon a long lever that extended far into the tomb would cause the iron portals to fly back. There were arrangements also for the free admission of air and light, and convenient receptacles for food and water, within immediate reach of the coffin intended for my reception. This coffin was warmly and softly padded, and was provided with a lid, fashioned upon the principle of the vault-door, with the addition of springs so contrived that the feeblest movement of the body would be sufficient to set it at liberty. Besides all this, there was suspended from the roof of the tomb, a large bell, the rope of which, it was designed, should extend through a hole in the coffin, and so be fastened to one of the hands of the corpse. But, alas! what avails the vigilance against the Destiny of man? Not even these well-contrived securities sufficed to save from the uttermost agonies of living inhumation, a wretch to these agonies foredoomed!

There arrived an epoch — as often before there had arrived — in which I found myself emerging from total unconsciousness into the first feeble and indefinite sense of existence. Slowly — with a tortoise gradation — approached the faint gray dawn of the psychal day. A torpid uneasiness. An apathetic endurance of dull pain. No care — no hope — no effort. Then, after a long interval, a ringing in the ears; then, after a lapse still longer, a prickling or tingling sensation in the extremities; then a seemingly eternal period of pleasurable quiescence, during which the awakening feelings are struggling into thought; then a brief re-sinking into non-entity; then a sudden recovery. At length the slight quivering of an eyelid, and immediately thereupon, an electric shock of a terror, deadly and indefinite, which sends the blood in torrents from the temples to the heart. And now the first positive effort to think. And now the first endeavor to remember. And now a partial and evanescent success. And now the memory has so far regained its dominion, that, in some measure, I am cognizant of my state. I feel that I am not awaking from ordinary sleep. I recollect that I have been subject to catalepsy. And now, at last, as if by the rush of an ocean, my shuddering spirit is overwhelmed by the one grim Danger — by the one spectral and ever-prevalent idea.

For some minutes after this fancy possessed me, I remained without motion. And why? I could not summon courage to move. I dared not make the effort which was to satisfy me of my fate — and yet there was something at my heart which whispered me *it was sure*. Despair — such as no other species of wretchedness ever calls into being — despair alone urged me, after long irresolution, to uplift the heavy lids of my eyes. I uplifted them. It was dark — all dark. I knew that the fit was over. I knew

that the crisis of my disorder had long passed. I knew that I had now fully recovered the use of my visual faculties — and yet it was dark — all dark — the intense and utter raylessness of the Night that endureth for evermore.

I endeavored to shriek; and my lips and my parched tongue moved convulsively together in the attempt — but no voice issued from the cavernous lungs, which oppressed as if by the weight of some incumbent mountain, gasped and palpitated, with the heart, at every elaborate and struggling inspiration.

The movement of the jaws, in this effort to cry aloud, showed me that they were bound up, as is usual with the dead. I felt, too, that I lay upon some hard substance; and by something similar my sides were, also, closely compressed. So far, I had not ventured to stir any of my limbs — but now I violently threw up my arms, which had been lying at length, with the wrists crossed. They struck a solid wooden substance, which extended above my person at an elevation of not more than six inches from my face. I could no longer doubt that I reposed within a coffin at last.

And now, amid all my infinite miseries, came sweetly the cherub Hope — for I thought of my precautions. I writhed, and made spasmodic exertions to force open the lid: it would not move. I felt my wrists for the bell-rope: it was not to be found. And now the Comforter fled for ever, and a still sterner Despair reigned triumphant; for I could not help perceiving the absence of the paddings which I had so carefully prepared — and then, too, there came suddenly to my nostrils the strong peculiar odor of moist earth. The conclusion was irresistible. I was *not* within the vault. I had fallen into a trance while absent from home — while among strangers — when, or how, I could not remember — and it was they who had buried me as a dog — nailed up in some common coffin — and thrust deep, deep, and for ever, into some ordinary and nameless *grave*.

As this awful conviction forced itself, thus, into the innermost chambers of my soul, I once again struggled to cry aloud. And in this second endeavor I succeeded. A long, wild, and continuous shriek, or yell, of agony, resounded through the realms of the subterranean Night.

"Hillo! hillo, there!" said a gruff voice, in reply.

"What the devil's the matter now!" said a second.

"Get out o' that!" said a third.

"What do you mean by yowling in that ere kind of style, like a cattymount?" said a fourth; and hereupon I was seized and shaken without ceremony, for several minutes, by a junto of very rough-looking individuals. They did not arouse me from my slumber — for I was wide-awake when I screamed — but they restored me to the full possession of my memory.

This adventure occurred near Richmond, in Virginia. Accompanied

by a friend, I had proceeded, upon a gunning expedition, some miles down the banks of the James River. Night approached, and we were overtaken by a storm. The cabin of a small sloop lying at anchor in the stream, and laden with garden mould, afforded us the only available shelter. We made the best of it, and passed the night on board. I slept in one of the only two berths in the vessel — and the berths of a sloop of sixty or seventy tons need scarcely be described. That which I occupied had no bedding of any kind. Its extreme width was eighteen inches. The distance of its bottom from the deck overhead was precisely the same. I found it a matter of exceeding difficulty to squeeze myself in. Nevertheless, I slept soundly; and the whole of my vision — for it was no dream, and no nightmare — arose naturally from the circumstances of my position — from my ordinary bias of thought — and from the difficulty, to which I have alluded, of collecting my senses, and especially of regaining my memory, for a long time after awaking from slumber. The men who shook me were the crew of the sloop, and some laborers engaged to unload it. From the load itself came the earthly smell. The bandage about the jaws was a silk handkerchief in which I had bound up my head, in default of my customary nightcap.

The tortures endured, however, were indubitably quite equal, for the time, to those of actual sepulture. They were fearfully — they were inconceivably hideous; but out of Evil proceeded Good; for their very excess wrought in my spirit an inevitable revulsion. My soul acquired tone — acquired temper. I went abroad. I took vigorous exercise. I breathed the free air of Heaven. I thought upon other subjects than Death. I discarded my medical books. "Buchan" I burned. I read no "Night Thoughts" — no fustian about churchyards — no bugaboo tales — *such as this*. In short, I became a new man, and lived a man's life. From that memorable night, I dismissed forever my charnel apprehensions, and with them vanished the cataleptic disorder, of which, perhaps, they had been less the consequence than the cause.

There are moments when, even to the sober eye of Reason, the world of our sad Humanity may assume the semblance of a Hell — but the imagination of man is no Carathis, to explore with impunity its every cavern. Alas! the grim legion of sepulchral terrors cannot be regarded as altogether fanciful — but, like the Demons in whose company Afrasiab made his voyage down the Oxus, they must sleep, or they will devour us — they must be suffered to slumber, or we perish.

Mesmeric Revelation

W<small>HATEVER</small> doubt may still envelop the *rationale* of mesmerism, its startling *facts* are now almost universally admitted. Of these latter, those who doubt, are your mere doubters by profession — an unprofitable and disreputable tribe. There can be no more absolute waste of time than the attempt to *prove*, at the present day, that man, by mere exercise of will, can so impress his fellow as to cast him into an abnormal condition, of which the phenomena resemble very closely those of *death*, or at least resemble them more nearly than they do the phenomena of any other normal condition within our cognizance; that, while in this state, the person so impressed employs only with effort, and then feebly, the external organs of sense, yet perceives, with keenly refined perception, and through channels supposed unknown, matters beyond the scope of the physical organs; that, moreover, his intellectual faculties are wonderfully exalted and invigorated; that his sympathies with the person so impressing him are profound; and, finally, that his susceptibility to the impression increases with its frequency, while in the same proportion, the peculiar phenomena elicited are more extended and more *pronounced*.

I say that these — which are the laws of mesmerism in its general features — it would be supererogation to demonstrate; nor shall I inflict upon my readers so needless a demonstration to-day. My purpose at present is a very different one indeed. I am impelled, even in the teeth of a world of prejudice, to detail, without comment, the very remarkable substance of a colloquy occurring between a sleep-waker and myself.

I had long been in the habit of mesmerizing the person in question (Mr. Vankirk), and the usual acute susceptibility and exaltation of the mesmeric perception had supervened. For many months he had been laboring under confirmed phthisis, the more distressing effects of which had been relieved by my manipulations; and on the night of Wednesday, the fifteenth instant, I was summoned to his bedside.

The invalid was suffering with acute pain in the region of the heart, and breathed with great difficulty, having all the ordinary symptoms of asthma. In spasms such as these he had usually found relief from the application of mustard to the nervous centres, but to-night this had been attempted in vain.

As I entered his room he greeted me with a cheerful smile, and although evidently in much bodily pain, appeared to be, mentally, quite at ease.

"I sent for you to-night," he said, "not so much to administer to my bodily ailment, as to satisfy me concerning certain physical impressions

which, of late, have occasioned me much anxiety and surprise. I need not tell you how skeptical I have hitherto been on the topic of the soul's immortality. I cannot deny that there has always existed, as if in that very soul which I have been denying, a vague half-sentiment of its own existence. But this half-sentiment at no time amounted to conviction. With it my reason had nothing to do. All attempts at logical inquiry resulted, indeed, in leaving me more sceptical than before. I had been advised to study Cousin. I studied him in his own works as well as in those of his European and American echoes. The 'Charles Elwood' of Mr. Brownson for example, was placed in my hands. I read it with profound attention. Throughout I found it logical, but the portions which were not *merely* logical were unhappily the initial arguments of the disbelieving hero of the book. In his summing up it seemed evident to me that the reasoner had not even succeeded in convincing himself. His end had plainly forgotten his beginning, like the government of Trinculo. In short, I was not long in perceiving that if man is to be intellectually convinced of his own immortality, he will never be so convinced by the mere abstractions which have been so long the fashion of the moralists of England, of France, and of Germany. Abstractions may amuse and exercise, but take no hold on the mind. Here upon earth, at least, philosophy, I am persuaded, will always in vain call upon us to look upon qualities as things. The will may assent — the soul — the intellect, never.

"I repeat, then, that I only half felt, and never intellectually believed. But latterly there has been a certain deepening of the feeling, until it has come so nearly to resemble the acquiescence of reason, that I find it difficult to distinguish between the two. I am enabled, too, plainly to trace this effect to the mesmeric influence. I cannot better explain my meaning than by the hypothesis that the mesmeric exaltation enables me to perceive a train of ratiocination which, in my abnormal existence, convinces, but which, in full accordance with the mesmeric phenomena, does not extend, except through its *effect*, into my normal condition. In sleep-waking, the reasoning and its conclusion — the cause and its effect — are present together. In my natural state, the cause vanishes, the effect only, and perhaps only partially, remains.

"These considerations have led me to think that some good results might ensue from a series of well-directed questions propounded to me while mesmerized. You have often observed the profound self-cognizance evinced by the sleep-waker — the extensive knowledge he displays upon all points relating to the mesmeric condition itself; and from this self-cognizance may be deduced hints for the proper conduct of a catechism."

I consented of course to make this experiment. A few passes threw Mr. Vankirk into the mesmeric sleep. His breathing became immediately more easy, and he seemed to suffer no physical uneasiness. The following conversation then ensued: — V. in the dialogue representing the patient, and P. myself.

P. Are you asleep?

V. Yes — no; I would rather sleep more soundly.

P. [*After a few more passes.*] Do you sleep now?

V. Yes.

P. How do you think your present illness will result?

V. [*After a long hesitation and speaking as if with effort.*] I must die.

P. Does the idea of death afflict you?

V. [*Very quickly.*] No — no!

P. Are you pleased with the prospect?

V. If I were awake I should like to die, but now it is no matter. The mesmeric condition is so near death as to content me.

P. I wish you would explain yourself, Mr. Vankirk.

V. I am willing to do so, but it requires more effort than I feel able to make. You do not question me properly.

P. What then shall I ask?

V. You must begin at the beginning.

P. The beginning! But where is the beginning?

V. You know that the beginning is GOD. [*This was said in a low, fluctuating tone, and with every sign of the most profound veneration.*]

P. What, then, is God?

V. [*Hesitating for many minutes.*] I cannot tell.

P. Is not God spirit?

V. While I was awake I knew what you meant by "spirit," but now it seems only a word — such, for instance, as truth, beauty — a quality, I mean.

P. Is not God immaterial?

V. There is no immateriality — it is a mere word. That which is not matter, is not at all — unless qualities are things.

P. Is God, then, material?

V. No. [*This reply startled me very much.*]

P. What, then, is he?

V. [*After a long pause, and mutteringly.*] I see — but it is a thing difficult to tell. [*Another long pause.*] He is not spirit, for he exists. Nor is he matter, *as you understand it*. But there are *gradations* of matter of which man knows nothing; the grosser impelling the finer, the finer pervading the grosser. The atmosphere, for example, impels the electric principle, while the electric principle permeates the atmosphere. These gradations of matter increase in rarity or fineness until we arrive at a matter *unparticled* — without particles — indivisible — *one;* and here the law of impulsion and permeation is modified. The ultimate or unparticled matter not only permeates all things, but impels all things; and thus *is* all things within itself. This matter is God. What men attempt to embody in the word "thought," is this matter in motion.

P. The metaphysicians maintain that all action is reducible to motion and thinking, and that the latter is the origin of the former.

V. Yes; and I now see the confusion of idea. Motion is the action of *mind*, not of *thinking*. The unparticled matter, or God, in quiescence is (as nearly as we can conceive it) what men call mind. And the power of self-movement (equivalent in effect to human volition) is, in the unparticled matter, the result of its unity and omniprevalence; *how*, I know not, and now clearly see that I shall never 'know. But the unparticled matter, set in motion by a law or quality existing within itself, is thinking.

P. Can you give me no more precise idea of what you term the unparticled matter?

V. The matters of which man is cognizant escape the senses in gradation. We have, for example, a metal, a piece of wood, a drop of water, the atmosphere, a gas, caloric, electricity, the luminiferous ether. Now, we call all these things matter, and embrace all matter in one general definition; but in spite of this, there can be no two ideas more essentially distinct than that which we attach to a metal, and that which we attach to the luminiferous ether. When we reach the latter, we feel an almost irresistible inclination to class it with spirit, or with nihility. The only consideration which restrains us is our conception of its atomc constitution; and here, even, we have to seek aid from our notion of an atom, as something possessing in infinite minuteness, solidity, palpability, weight. Destroy the idea of the atomic constitution and we should no longer be able to regard the ether as an entity, or, at least, as matter. For want of a better word we might term it spirit. Take, now, a step beyond the luminiferous ether — conceive a matter as much more rare than the ether, as this ether is more rare than the metal, and we arrive at once (in spite of all the school dogmas) at a unique mass — an unparticled matter. For although we may admit infinite littleness in the atoms themselves, the infinitude of littleness in the spaces between them is an absurdity. There will be a point — there will be a degree of rarity at which, if the atoms are sufficiently numerous, the interspaces must vanish, and the mass absolutely coalesce. But the consideration of the atomic constitution being now taken away, the nature of the mass inevitably glides into what we conceive of spirit. It is clear, however, that it is as fully matter as before. The truth is, it is impossible to conceive spirit, since it is impossible to imagine what is not. When we flatter ourselves that we have formed its conception, we have merely deceived our understanding by the consideration of infinitely rarefied matter.

P. There seems to me an insurmountable objection to the idea of absolute coalescence; — and that is the very slight resistance experienced by the heavenly bodies in their revolutions through space — a resistance now ascertained, it is true, to exist in *some* degree, but which is, nevertheless, so slight as to have been quite overlooked by the sagacity even of Newton. We know that the resistance of bodies is, chiefly, in proportion to their density. Absolute coalescence is absolute density. Where there are no

interspaces, there can be no yielding. An ether, absolutely dense, would put an infinitely more effectual stop to the progress of a star than would an ether of adamant or of iron.

V. Your objection is answered with an ease which is nearly in the ratio of its apparent unanswerability. — As regards the progress of the star, it can make no difference whether the star passes through the ether *or the ether through it.* There is no astronomical error more unaccountable than that which reconciles the known retardation of the comets with the idea of their passage through an ether; for, however rare this ether be supposed, it would put a stop to all sidereal revolution in a very far briefer period than has been admitted by those astronomers who have endeavored to slur over a point which they found it impossible to comprehend. The retardation actually experienced is, on the other hand, about that which might be expected from the *friction* of the ether in the instantaneous passage through the orb. In the one case, the retarding force is momentary and complete within itself — in the other it is endlessly accumulative.

P. But in all this — in this identification of mere matter with God — is there nothing of irreverence? [*I was forced to repeat this question before the sleep-waker fully comprehended my meaning.*]

V. Can you say *why* matter should be less reverenced than mind? But you forget that the matter of which "mind" or "spirit" of the schools, so far as regards its high capacities, and is, moreover, the "matter" of these schools at the same time. God, with all the powers attributed to spirit, is but the perfection of matter.

P. You assert, then, that the unparticled matter, in motion, is thought.

V. In general, this motion is the universal thought of the universal mind. This thought creates. All created things are but the thoughts of God.

P. You say, "in general."

V. Yes. The universal mind is God. For new individualities, *matter* is necessary.

P. But you now speak of "mind" and "matter" as do the metaphysicians.

V. Yes — to avoid confusion. When I say "mind," I mean the unparticled or ultimate matter; by "matter," I intend all else.

P. You were saying that "for new individualities matter is necessary."

V. Yes; for mind, existing unincorporate, is merely God. To create individual, thinking beings, it was necessary to incarnate portions of the divine mind. Thus man is individualized. Divested of corporate investiture, he were God. Now the particular motion of the incarnated portions of the unparticled matter is the thought of man; as the motion of the whole is that of God.

P. You say that divested of the body man will be God?

V. [*After much hesitation.*] I could not have said this; it is an absurdity.

P. [*Referring to my notes.*] You *did* say that "divested of corporate investiture man were God."

V. And this is true. Man thus divested *would* be God — would be un-individualized. But he can never be thus divested — at least never *will be* — else we must imagine an action of God returning upon itself — a purposeless and futile action. Man is a creature. Creatures are thoughts of God. It is the nature of thought to be irrevocable.

P. I do not comprehend. You say that man will never put off the body?

V. I say that he will never be bodiless.

P. Explain.

V. There are two bodies — the rudimental and the complete, corresponding with the two conditions of the worm and the butterfly. What we call "death," is but the painful metamorphosis. Our present incarnation is progressive, preparatory, temporary. Our future is perfected, ultimate, immortal. The ultimate life is the full design.

P. But of the worm's metamorphosis we are palpably cognizant.

V. *We*, certainly — but not the worm. The matter of which our rudimental body is composed, is within the ken of the organs of that body; or, more distinctly, our rudimental organs are adapted to the matter of which is formed the rudimental body; but not to that of which the ultimate is composed. The ultimate body thus escapes our rudimental senses, and we perceive only the shell which falls, in decaying, from the inner form, not that inner form itself; but this inner form as well as the shell, is appreciable by those who have already acquired the ultimate life.

P. *You* have often said that the mesmeric state very nearly resembles death. How is this?

V. When I say that it resembles death, I mean that it resembles the ultimate life; for when I am entranced the senses of my rudimental life are in abeyance and I perceive external things directly, without organs, through a medium which I shall employ in the ultimate, unorganized life.

P. Unorganized?

V. Yes; organs are contrivances by which the individual is brought into sensible relation with particular classes and forms of matter, to the exclusion of other classes and forms. The organs of man are adapted to his rudimental condition, and to that only; his ultimate condition, being unorganized, is of unlimited comprehension in all points but one — the nature of the volition of God — that is to say, the motion of the unparticled matter. You may have a distinct idea of the ultimate body by conceiving it to be entire brain. This it is *not*; but a conception of this nature will bring you near a comprehension of what it *is*. A luminous body imparts vibration to the luminiferous ether. The vibrations generate similar ones within the retina; these again communicate similar ones to the optic nerve. The nerve conveys similar ones to the brain; the brain, also, similar ones to the unparticled matter which permeates it. The motion of

this latter is thought, of which perception is the first undulation. This is the mode by which the mind of the rudimental life communicates with the external world; and this external world is, to the rudimental life, limited, through the idiosyncrasy of its organs. But in the ultimate, unorganized life, the external world reaches the whole body, (which is of a substance having affinity to brain, as I have said,) with no other intervention than that of an infinitely rarer ether than even the luminiferous; and to this ether — in unison with it — the whole body vibrates, setting in motion the unparticled matter which permeates it. It is to the absence of idiosyncratic organs, therefore, that we must attribute the nearly unlimited perception of the ultimate life. To rudimental beings, organs are the cages necessary to confine them until fledged.

P. You speak of rudimental "beings." Are there other rudimental thinking beings than man?

V. The multitudinous conglomeration of rare matter into nebulæ, planets, suns, and other bodies which are neither nebulæ, suns, nor planets, is for the sole purpose of supplying *pabulum* for the idiosyncrasy of the organs of an infinity of rudimental beings. But for the necessity of the rudimental, prior to the ultimate life, there would have been no bodies such as these. Each of these is tenanted by a distinct variety of organic rudimental, thinking creatures. In all, the organs vary with the features of the place tenanted. At death, or metamorphosis, these creatures, enjoying the ultimate life — immortality — and cognizant of all secrets but *the one*, act all things and pass every where by mere volition: — indwelling, not the stars, which to us seem the sole palpabilities, and for the accommodation of which we blindly deem space created — but that SPACE itself — that infinity of which the truly substantive vastness swallows up the star-shadows — blotting them out as non-entities from the perception of the angels.

P. You say that "but for the *necessity* of the rudimental life, there would have been no stars. But why this necessity?

V. In the inorganic life, as well as in the inorganic matter generally, there is nothing to impede the action of one simple *unique* law — the Divine Volition. With the view of producing impediment, the organic life and matter (complex, substantial, and law-encumbered) were contrived.

P. But again — why need this impediment have been produced?

V. The result of law inviolate is perfection — right — negative happiness. The result of law violate is imperfection, wrong, positive pain. Through the impediments afforded by the number, complexity, and substantiality of the laws of organic life and matter, the violation of law is rendered, to a certain extent, practicable. Thus pain, which is the inorganic life is impossible, is possible in the organic.

P. But to what good end is pain thus rendered possible?

V. All things are either good or bad by comparison. A sufficient analysis

will show that pleasure, in all cases, is but the contrast of pain. *Positive* pleasure is a mere idea. To be happy at any one point we must have suffered at the same. Never to suffer would have been never to have been blessed. But it has been shown that, in the inorganic life, pain cannot be; thus the necessity for the organic. The pain of the primitive life of Earth, is the sole basis of the bliss of the ultimate life in Heaven.

P. Still, there is one of your expressions which I find it impossible to comprehend — "the truly *substantive* vastness of infinity."

V. This, probably, is because you have no sufficiently generic conception of the term *"substance"* itself. We must not regard it as a quality, but as a sentiment: — it is the perception, in thinking beings, of the adaptation of matter to their organization. There are many things on the Earth, which would be nihility to the inhabitants of Venus — many things visible and tangible in Venus, which we could not be brought to appreciate as existing at all. But to the inorganic beings — to the angels — the whole of the unparticled matter is substance; that is to say, the whole of what we term "space," is to them the truest substantiality; — the stars, meantime, through what we consider their materiality, escaping the angelic sense, just in proportion as the unparticled matter, through what we consider its immateriality, eludes the organic.

As the sleep-waker pronounced these latter words, in a feeble tone, I observed on his countenance a singular expression, which somewhat alarmed me, and induced me to awake him at once. No sooner had I done this than, with a bright smile irradiating all his features, he fell back upon his pillow and expired. I noticed that in less than a minute afterward his corpse had all the stern rigidity of stone. His brow was of the coldness of ice. Thus, ordinarily, should it have appeared, only after long pressure from Azrael's hand. Had the sleep-waker, indeed, during the latter portion of his discourse, been addressing me from out the regions of the shadows?

The Oblong Box

SOME years ago, I engaged passage from Charleston, S. C., to the city of New York, in the fine packet-ship "Independence," Captain Hardy. We were to sail on the fifteenth of the month (June), weather permitting; and on the fourteenth, I went on board to arrange some matters in my state-room.

I found that we were to have a great many passengers, including a more than usual number of ladies. On the list were several of my acquaintances; and among other names, I was rejoiced to see that of Mr. Cornelius Wyatt, a young artist, for whom I entertained feelings of warm friend-

ship. He had been with me a fellow-student at C—— University, where we were very much together. He had the ordinary temperament of genius, and was a compound of misanthropy, sensibility, and enthusiasm. To these qualities he united the warmest and truest heart which ever beat in a human bosom.

I observed that his name was carded upon *three* state-rooms; and, upon again referring to the list of passengers, I found that he had engaged passage for himself, wife, and two sisters — his own. The state-rooms were sufficiently roomy, and each had two berths, one above the other. These berths, to be sure, were so exceedingly narrow as to be insufficient for more than one person; still, I could not comprehend why there were *three* state-rooms for these four persons. I was, just at that epoch, in one of those moody frames of mind which make a man abnormally inquisitive about trifles: and I confess, with shame, that I busied myself in a variety of ill-bred and preposterous conjectures about this matter of the supernumerary state-room. It was no business of mine, to be sure; but with none the less pertinacity did I occupy myself in attempts to resolve the enigma. At last I reached a conclusion which wrought in me great wonder why I had not arrived at it before. "It is a servant, of course," I said; "what a fool I am, not sooner to have thought of so obvious a solution!" And then I again repaired to the list — but here I saw distinctly that *no* servant was to come with the party; although, in fact, it had been the original design to bring one — for the words "and servant" had been first written and then overscored. "Oh, extra baggage, to be sure," I now said to myself — "something he wishes not to be put in the hold — something to be kept under his own eye — ah, I have it — a painting or so — and this is what he has been bargaining about with Nicolino, the Italian Jew." This idea satisfied me, and I dismissed my curiosity for the nonce.

Wyatt's two sisters I knew very well, and most amiable and clever girls they were. His wife he had newly married, and I had never yet seen her. He had often talked about her in my presence, however, and in his usual style of enthusiasm. He described her as of surpassing beauty, wit, and accomplishment. I was, therefore, quite anxious to make her acquaintance.

On the day in which I visited the ship (the fourteenth), Wyatt and party were also to visit it — so the captain informed me — and I waited on board an hour longer than I had designed, in hope of being presented to the bride, but then an apology came. "Mrs. W. was a little indisposed, and would decline coming on board until to-morrow, at the hour of sailing."

The morrow having arrived, I was going from my hotel to the wharf, when Captain Hardy met me and said that, "owing to circumstances" (a stupid but convenient phrase), "he rather thought the 'Independence' would not sail for a day or two, and that when all was ready, he would send up and let me know." This I thought strange, for there was a stiff

southerly breeze; but as "the circumstances" were not forthcoming, although I pumped for them with much perseverance, I had nothing to do but to return home and digest my impatience at leisure.

I did not receive the expected message from the captain for nearly a week. It came at length, however, and I immediately went on board. The ship was crowded with passengers, and every thing was in the bustle attendant upon making sail. Wyatt's party arrived in about ten minutes after myself. There were the two sisters, the bride, and the artist — the latter in one of his customary fits of moody misanthropy. I was too well used to these, however, to pay them any special attention. He did not even introduce me to his wife — this courtesy devolving, per force, upon his sister Marian — a very sweet and intelligent girl, who, in a few hurried words, made us acquainted.

Mrs. Wyatt had been closely veiled; and when she raised her veil, in acknowledging my bow, I confess that I was very profoundly astonished. I should have been much more so, however, had not long experience advised me not to trust, with too implicit a reliance, the enthusiastic descriptions of my friend, the artist, when indulging in comments upon the loveliness of woman. When beauty was the theme, I well knew with what facility he soared into the regions of the purely ideal.

The truth is, I could not help regarding Mrs. Wyatt as a decidedly plain-looking woman. If not positively ugly, she was not, I think, very far from it. She was dressed, however, in exquisite taste — and then I had no doubt that she had captivated my friend's heart by the more enduring graces of the intellect and soul. She said very few words, and passed at once into her state-room with Mr. W.

My old inquisitiveness now returned. There was *no* servant — *that* was a settled point. I looked, therefore, for the extra baggage. After some delay, a cart arrived at the wharf, with an oblong pine box, which was every thing that seemed to be expected. Immediately upon its arrival we made sail, and in a short time were safely over the bar and standing out to sea.

The box in question was, as I say, oblong. It was about six feet in length by two and a half in breadth; I observed it attentively, and like to be precise. Now this shape was *peculiar*; and no sooner had I seen it, than I took credit to myself for the accuracy of my guessing. I had reached the conclusion, it will be remembered, that the extra baggage of my friend, the artist, would prove to be pictures, or at least a picture; for I knew he had been for several weeks in conference with Nicolino: — and now here was a box, which, from its shape, *could* possibly contain nothing in the world but a copy of Leonardo's "Last Supper;" and a copy of this very "Last Supper," done by Rubini the younger, at Florence, I had known, for some time, to be in the possession of Nicolino. This point, therefore, I considered as sufficiently settled. I chuckled excessively when I thought of my acumen. It was the first time I had ever known Wyatt

to keep from me any of his artistical secrets; but here he evidently intended to steal a march upon me, and smuggle a fine picture to New York, under my very nose; expecting me to know nothing of the matter. I resolved to quiz him *well*, now and hereafter.

One thing, however, annoyed me not a little. The box did *not* go into the extra state-room. It was deposited in Wyatt's own; and there, too, it remained, occupying very nearly the whole of the floor — no doubt to the exceeding discomfort of the artist and his wife; — this the more especially as the tar or paint with which it was lettered in sprawling capitals, emitted a strong, disagreeable, and, to *my* fancy, a peculiarly disgusting odor. On the lid were painted the words — *"Mrs. Adelaide Curtis, Albany, New York. Charge of Cornelius Wyatt, Esq. This side up. To be handled with care."*

Now, I was aware that Mrs. Adelaide Curtis, of Albany, was the artist's wife's mother; — but then I looked upon the whole address as a mystification, intended especially for myself. I made up my mind, of course, that the box and contents would never get farther north than the studio of my misanthropic friend, in Chambers Street, New York.

For the first three or four days we had fine weather, although the wind was dead ahead; having chopped round to the northward, immediately upon our losing sight of the coast. The passengers were, consequently, in high spirits and disposed to be social. I *must* except, however, Wyatt and his sisters, who behaved stiffly, and, I could not help thinking, uncourteously to the rest of the party. *Wyatt's* conduct I did not so much regard. He was gloomy, even beyond his usual habit — in fact he was *morose* — but in him I was prepared for eccentricity. For the sisters, however, I could make no excuse. They secluded themselves in their state-rooms during the greater part of the passage, and absolutely refused, although I repeatedly urged them, to hold communication with any person on board.

Mrs. Wyatt herself was far more agreeable. That is to say, she was *chatty*; and to be chatty is no slight recommendation at sea. She became *excessively* intimate with most of the ladies; and, to my profound astonishment, evinced no equivocal disposition to coquet with the men. She amused us all very much. I say *"amused"* — and scarcely know how to explain myself. The truth is, I soon found that Mrs. W. was far oftener laughed *at* than *with*. The gentlemen said little about her; but the ladies, in a little while, pronounced her "a good-hearted thing, rather indifferent-looking, totally uneducated, and decidedly vulgar." The great wonder was, how Wyatt had been entrapped into such a match. Wealth was the general solution — but this I knew to be no solution at all; for Wyatt had told me that she neither brought him a dollar nor had any expectations from any source whatever. "He had married," he said, "for love, and for love only; and his bride was far more than worthy of his love." When I thought of these expressions, on the part of my friend, I confess

that I felt indescribably puzzled. Could it be possible that he was taking leave of his senses? What else could I think? *He*, so refined, so intellectual, so fastidious, with so exquisite a perception of the faulty, and so keen an appreciation of the beautiful! To be sure, the lady seemed especially fond of *him* — particularly so in his absence — when she made herself ridiculous by frequent quotations of what had been said by her "beloved husband, Mr. Wyatt." The word "husband" seemed forever — to use one of her own delicate expressions — forever "on the tip of her tongue." In the meantime, it was observed by all on board, that he avoided *her* in the most pointed manner, and, for the most part, shut himself up alone in his state-room, where, in fact, he might have been said to live altogether, leaving his wife at full liberty to amuse herself as she thought best, in the public society of the main cabin.

My conclusion, from what I saw and heard, was, that the artist, by some unaccountable freak of fate, or perhaps in some fit of enthusiastic and fanciful passion, had been induced to unite himself with a person altogether beneath him, and that the natural result, entire and speedy disgust, had ensued. I pitied him from the bottom of my heart — but could not, for that reason, quite forgive his incommunicativeness in the matter of the "Last Supper." For this I resolved to have my revenge.

One day he came upon deck, and, taking his arm as had been my wont, I sauntered with him backward and forward. His gloom, however (which I considerd quite natural under the circumstances), seemed entirely unabated. He said little, and that moodily, and with evident effort. I ventured a jest or two, and he made a sickening attempt at a smile. Poor fellow! — as I thought of *his wife*, I wondered that he could have heart to put on even the semblance of mirth. I determined to commence a series of covert insinuations, or innuendoes, about the oblong box — just to let him perceive, gradually, that I was *not* altogether the butt, or victim, of his little bit of pleasant mystification. My first observation was by way of opening a masked battery. I said something about the "peculiar shape of *that* box;" and, as I spoke the words, I smiled knowingly, winked, and touched him gently with my forefinger in the ribs.

The manner in which Wyatt received this harmless pleasantry convinced me, at once, that he was mad. At first he stared at me as if he found it impossible to comprehend the witticism of my remark; but as its point seemed slowly to make its way into his brain, his eyes, in the same proportion, seemed protruding from their sockets. Then he grew very red — then hideously pale — then, as if highly amused with what I had insinuated, he began a loud and boisterous laugh, which, to my astonishment, he kept up, with gradually increasing vigor, for ten minutes or more. In conclusion, he fell flat and heavily upon the deck. When I ran to uplift him, to all appearance he was *dead*.

I called assistance, and, with much difficulty, we brought him to himself. Upon reviving he spoke incoherently for some time. At length we

bled him and put him to bed. The next morning he was quite recovered, so far as regarded his mere bodily health. Of his mind I say nothing, of course. I avoided him during the rest of the passage, by advice of the captain, who seemed to coincide with me altogether in my views of his insanity, but cautioned me to say nothing on this head to any person on board.

Several circumstances occurred immediately after this fit of Wyatt which contributed to heighten the curiosity with which I was already possessed. Among other things, this: I had been nervous — drank too much strong green tea, and slept ill at night — in fact, for two nights I could not be properly said to sleep at all. Now, my state-room opened into the main cabin, or dining-room, as did those of all the single men on board. Wyatt's three rooms were in the after-cabin, which was separated from the main one by a slight sliding door, never locked even at night. As we were almost constantly on a wind, and the breeze was not a little stiff, the ship heeled to leeward very considerably; and whenever her starboard side was to leeward, the sliding door between the cabins slid open, and so remained, nobody taking the trouble to get up and shut it. But my berth was in such a position, that when my own state-room door was open, as well as the sliding door in question, (and my own door was *always* open on account of the heat,) I could see into the after-cabin quite distinctly, and just at that portion of it, too, where were situated the state-rooms of Mr. Wyatt. Well, during two nights (*not* consecutive) while I lay awake, I clearly saw Mrs. W., about eleven o'clock upon each night, steal cautiously from the state-room of Mr. W., and enter the extra room, where she remained until daybreak, when she was called by her husband and went back. That they were virtually separated was clear. They had separate apartments — no doubt in contemplation of a more permanent divorce; and here, after all, I thought was the mystery of the extra state-room.

There was another circumstance, too, which interested me much. During the two wakeful nights in question, and immediately after the disappearance of Mrs. Wyatt into the extra state-room, I was attracted by certain singular cautious, subdued noises in that of her husband. After listening to them for some time, with thoughtful attention, I at length succeeded perfectly in translating their import. They were sounds occasioned by the artist in prying open the oblong box, by means of a chisel and mallet — the latter being apparently muffled, or deadened, by some soft woollen or cotton substance in which its head was enveloped.

In this manner I fancied I could distinguish the precise moment when he fairly disengaged the lid — also, that I could determine when he removed it altogether, and when he deposited it upon the lower berth in his room; this latter point I knew, for example, by certain slight taps which the lid made in striking against the wooden edges of the berth, as he endeavored to lay it down *very* gently — there being no room for it on

the floor. After this there was a dead stillness, and I heard nothing more, upon either occasion, until nearly daybreak; unless, perhaps, I may mention a low sobbing, or murmuring sound, so very much suppressed as to be nearly inaudible — if, indeed, the whole of this latter noise were not rather produced by my own imagination. I say it seemed to *resemble* sobbing or sighing — but, of course, it could not have been either. I rather think it was a ringing in my own ears. Mr. Wyatt, no doubt, according to custom, was merely giving the rein to one of his hobbies — indulging in one of his fits of artistic enthusiasm. He had opened his oblong box, in order to feast his eyes on the pictorial treasure within. There was nothing in this, however, to make him *sob*. I repeat, therefore, that it must have been simply a freak of my own fancy, distempered by good Captain Hardy's green tea. Just before dawn, on each of the two nights of which I speak, I distinctly heard Mr. Wyatt replace the lid upon the oblong box, and force the nails into their old places by means of the muffled mallet. Having done this, he issued from his state-room, fully dressed, and proceeded to call Mrs. W. from hers.

We had been at sea seven days, and were now off Cape Hatteras, when there came a tremendously heavy blow from the southwest. We were, in a measure, prepared for it, however, as the weather had been holding out threats for some time. Every thing was made snug, alow and aloft; and as the wind steadily freshened, we lay to, at length, under spanker and foretopsail, both double-reefed.

In this trim we rode safely enough for forty-eight hours — the ship proving herself an excellent sea-boat in many respects, and shipping no water of any consequence. At the end of this period, however, the gale had freshened into a hurricane, and our after-sail split into ribbons, bringing us so much in the trough of the water that we shipped several prodigious seas, one immediately after the other. By this accident we lost three men overboard with the caboose, and nearly the whole of the larboard bulwarks. Scarcely had we recovered our senses, before the foretopsail went into shreds, when we got up a storm stay-sail, and with this did pretty well for some hours, the ship heading the sea much more steadily than before.

The gale still held on, however, and we saw no signs of its abating. The rigging was found to be ill-fitted, and greatly strained; and on the third day of the blow, about five in the afternoon, our mizzen-mast, in a heavy lurch to windward, went by the board. For an hour or more, we tried in vain to get rid of it, on account of the prodigious rolling of the ship; and, before we had succeeded, the carpenter came aft and announced four feet of water in the hold. To add to our dilemma, we found the pumps choked and nearly useless.

All was now confusion and despair — but an effort was made to lighten the ship by throwing overboard as much of her cargo as could be reached, and by cutting away the two masts that remained. This we at last ac-

complished — but we were still unable to do any thing at the pumps; and, in the meantime, the leak gained on us very fast.

At sundown, the gale had sensibly diminished in violence, and, as the sea went down with it, we still entertained faint hopes of saving ourselves in the boats. At eight P. M., the clouds broke away to windward, and we had the advantage of a full moon — a piece of good fortune which served wonderfully to cheer our drooping spirits.

After incredible labor we succeeded, at length, in getting the long-boat over the side without material accident, and into this we crowded the whole of the crew and most of the passengers. This party made off immediately, and, after undergoing much suffering, finally arrived, in safety, at Ocracoke Inlet, on the third day after the wreck.

Fourteen passengers, with the captain, remained on board, resolving to trust their fortunes to the jolly-boat at the stern. We lowered it without difficulty, although it was only by a miracle that we prevented it from swamping as it touched the water. It contained, when afloat, the captain and his wife, Mr. Wyatt and party, a Mexican officer, wife, four children, and myself, with a negro valet.

We had no room, of course, for any thing except a few positively necessary instruments, some provisions, and the clothes upon our backs. No one had thought of even attempting to save any thing more. What must have been the astonishment of all, then, when having proceeded a few fathoms from the ship, Mr. Wyatt stood up in the stern-sheets, and coolly demanded of Captain Hardy that the boat should be put back for the purpose of taking in his oblong box!

"Sit down, Mr. Wyatt," replied the captain, somewhat sternly, "you will capsize us if you do not sit quite still. Our gunwhale is almost in the water now."

"The box!" vociferated Mr. Wyatt, still standing — "the box, I say! Captain Hardy, you cannot, you *will* not refuse me. Its weight will be but a trifle — it is nothing — mere nothing. By the mother who bore you — for the love of Heaven — by your hope of salvation, I *implore* you to put back for the box!"

The captain, for a moment, seemed touched by the earnest appeal of the artist, but he regained his stern composure, and merely said:

"Mr. Wyatt, you are *mad*. I cannot listen to you. Sit down, I say, or you will swamp the boat. Stay — hold him — seize him! — he is about to spring overboard! There — I knew it — he is over!"

As the captain said this, Mr. Wyatt, in fact, sprang from the boat, and, as we were yet in the lee of the wreck, succeeded, by almost superhuman exertion, in getting hold of a rope which hung from the fore-chains. In another moment he was on board, and rushing frantically down into the cabin.

In the meantime, we had been swept astern of the ship, and being quite out of her lee, were at the mercy of the tremendous sea which was

still running. We made a determined effort to put back, but our little boat was like a feather in the breath of the tempest. We saw at a glance that the doom of the unfortunate artist was sealed.

As our distance from the wreck rapidly increased, the madman (for as such only could we regard him) was seen to emerge from the companion-way, up which by dint of strength that appeared gigantic, he dragged, bodily, the oblong box. While we gazed in the extremity of astonishment, he passed, rapidly, several turns of a three-inch rope, first around the box and then around his body. In another instant both body and box were in the sea — disappearing suddenly, at once and forever.

We lingered awhile sadly upon our oars, with our eyes riveted upon the spot. At length we pulled away. The silence remained unbroken for an hour. Finally, I hazarded a remark.

"Did you observe, captain, how suddenly they sank? Was not that an exceedingly singular thing? I confess that I entertained some feeble hope of his final deliverance, when I saw him lash himself to the box, and commit himself to the sea."

"They sank as a matter of course," replied the captain, "and that like a shot. They will soon rise again, however — *but not till the salt melts.*"

"The salt!" I ejaculated.

"Hush!" said the captain, pointing to the wife and sisters of the deceased. "We must talk of these things at some more appropriate time."

We suffered much, and made a narrow escape; but fortune befriended *us*, as well as our mates in the long-boat. We landed, in fine, more dead than alive, after four days of intense distress, upon the beach opposite Roanoke Island. We remained here a week, were not ill-treated by the wreckers, and at length obtained a passage to New York.

About a month after the loss of the "Independence," I happened to meet Captain Hardy in Broadway. Our conversation turned, naturally, upon the disaster, and especially upon the sad fate of poor Wyatt. I thus learned the following particulars.

The artist had engaged passage for himself, wife, two sisters and a servant. His wife was, indeed, as she had been represented, a most lovely, and most accomplished woman. On the morning of the fourteenth of June (the day in which I first visited the ship), the lady suddenly sickened and died. The young husband was frantic with grief — but circumstances imperatively forbade the deferring his voyage to New York. It was necessary to take to her mother the corpse of his adored wife, and, on the other hand, the universal prejudice which would prevent his doing so openly was well known. Nine-tenths of the passengers would have abandoned the ship rather than take passage with a dead body.

In this dilemma, Captain Hardy arranged that the corpse, being first partially embalmed, and packed, with a large quantity of salt, in a box of suitable dimensions, should be conveyed on board as merchandise. Noth-

ing was to be said of the lady's decease; and, as it was well understood that Mr. Wyatt had engaged passage for his wife, it became necessary that some person should personate her during the voyage. This the deceased lady's-maid was easily prevailed on to do. The extra state-room, originally engaged for this girl, during her mistress' life, was now merely retained. In this state-room the pseudo-wife, slept, of course, every night. In the daytime she performed, to the best of her ability, the part of her mistress — whose person, it had been carefully ascertained, was unknown to any of the passengers on board.

My own mistake arose, naturally enough, through too careless, too inquisitive, and too impulsive a temperament. But of late, it is a rare thing that I sleep soundly at night. There is a countenance which haunts me, turn as I will. There is an hysterical laugh which will forever ring within my ears.

The Angel of the Odd — An Extravaganza

It was a chilly November afternoon. I had just consummated an unusually hearty dinner, of which the dyspeptic *truffe* formed not the least important item, and was sitting alone in the dining-room, with my feet upon the fender, and at my elbow a small table which I had rolled up to the fire, and upon which were some apologies for dessert, with some miscellaneous bottles of wine, spirit, and *liqueur*. In the morning I had been reading Glover's "Leonidas," Wilkie's "Epigoniad," Lamartine's "Pilgrimage," Barlow's "Columbiad," Tuckermann's "Sicily," and Griswold's "Curiosities"; I am willing to confess, therefore, that I now felt a little stupid. I made effort to arouse myself by aid of frequent Lafitte, and, all failing, I betook myself to a stray newspaper in despair. Having carefully perused the column of "houses to let," and the column of "dogs lost," and then the two columns of "wives and apprentices runaway," I attacked with great resolution the editorial matter, and, reading it from beginning to end without understanding a syllable, conceived the possibility of its being Chinese, and so re-read it from the end to the beginning, but with no more satisfactory result. I was about throwing away, in disgust,

> This folio of four pages, happy work
> Which not even poets criticise,

when I felt my attention somewhat aroused by the paragraph which follows:

"The avenues to death are numerous and strange. A London paper mentions the decease of a person from a singular cause. He was playing at 'puff the dart,' which is played with a long needle inserted in some worsted, and blown at a target through a tin tube. He placed the needle at the wrong end of the tube, and drawing his breath strongly to puff the dart forward with force, drew the needle into his throat. It entered the lungs, and in a few days killed him."

Upon seeing this I fell into a great rage, without exactly knowing why. "This thing," I exclaimed, "is a contemptible falsehood — a poor hoax — the lees of the invention of some pitiable penny-a-liner — of some wretched concoctor of accidents in Cocaigne. These fellows, knowing the extravagant gullibility of the age, set their wits to work in the imagination of improbable possibilities — of odd accidents, as they term them; but to a reflecting intellect (like mine," I added, in parenthesis, putting my forefinger unconsciously to the side of my nose), "to a contemplative understanding such as I myself possess, it seems evident at once that the marvelous increase of late in these 'odd accidents' is by far the oddest accident of all. For my own part, I intend to believe nothing henceforward that has anything of the 'singular' about it."

"Mein Gott, den, vat a vool you bees for dat!" replied one of the most remarkable voices I ever heard. At first I took it for a rumbling in my ears — such as man sometimes experiences when getting very drunk — but, upon second thought, I considered the sound as more nearly resembling that which proceeds from an empty barrel beaten with a big stick; and, in fact, this I should have concluded it to be, but for the articulation of the syllables and words. I am by no means naturally nervous, and the very few glasses of Lafitte which I had sipped served to embolden me a little, so that I felt nothing of trepidation, but merely uplifted my eyes with a leisurely movement, and looked carefully around the room for the intruder. I could not, however, perceive any one at all.

"Humph!" resumed the voice, as I continued my survey, "you mus pe so dronk as de pig, den, for not zee me as I zit here at your zide."

Hereupon I bethought me of looking immediately before my nose, and there, sure enough, confronting me at the table sat a personage nondescript, although not altogether indescribable. His body was a wine-pipe, or a rum-puncheon, or something of that character, and had a truly Falstaffian air. In its nether extremity were inserted two kegs, which seemed to answer all the purposes of legs. For arms there dangled from the upper portion of the carcass two tolerably long bottles, with the necks outward for hands. All the head that I saw the monster possessed of was one of those Hessian canteens which resemble a large snuff-box with a hole in the middle of the lid. This canteen (with a funnel on its top, like a cavalier cap slouched over the eyes) was set on edge upon the puncheon, with the hole toward myself; and through this hole, which

seemed puckered up like the mouth of a very precise old maid, the creature was emitting certain rumbling and grumbling noises which he evidently intended for intelligible talk.

"I zay," said he, "you mos pe dronk as de pig, vor zit dare and not zee me zit ere; and I zay, doo, you most pe pigger vool as de goose, vor to dispelief vat iz print in de print. 'Tiz de troof — dat it iz — eberry vord ob it."

"Who are you, pray?" said I, with much dignity, although somewhat puzzled; "how did you get here? and what is it you are talking about?"

"Az vor ow I com'd ere," replied the figure, "dat iz none of your pizzness; and as vor vat I be talking apout, I be talk apout vot I tink proper; and as vor who I be, vy dat is de very ting I com'd here for to let you zee for yourzelf."

"You are a drunken vagabond," said I, "and I shall ring the bell and order my footman to kick you into the street."

"He! he! he!" said the fellow, "hu! hu! hu! dat you can't do."

"Can't do!" said I, "what do you mean? — can't do what?"

"Ring de pell," he replied, attempting a grin with his little villainous mouth.

Upon this I made an effort to get up, in order to put my threat into execution; but the ruffian just reached across the table very deliberately, and hitting me a tap on the forehead with the neck of one of the long bottles, knocked me back into the arm-chair from which I had half arisen. I was utterly astounded; and, for a moment, was quite at a loss what to do. In the meantime, he continued his talk.

"You zee," said he, "it iz te bess vor zit still; and now you shall know who I pe. Look at me! zee! I am te *Angel ov te Odd!*"

"And odd enough, too," I ventured to reply; "but I was always under the impression that an angel had wings."

"Te wing!" he cried, highly incensed, "vat I pe do mit te wing? Mein Gott! do you take me vor a shicken?"

"No — oh, no!" I replied, much alarmed, "you are no chicken — certainly not."

"Well, den, zit still and pehabe yourself, or I'll rap you again mid me vist. It iz te shicken ab te wing, und te owl ab te wing, und te imp ab te wing, und te headteuffel ab te wing. Te angel ab *not* te wing, and I am te *Angel ov te Odd.*"

"And your business with me at present is — is — "

"My pizzness!" ejaculated the thing, "vy vot a low bred puppy you mos pe vor to ask a gentleman und an angel apout his pizzness!"

This language was rather more than I could bear, even from an angel; so, plucking up courage, I seized a salt-cellar which lay within reach, and hurled it at the head of the intruder. Either he dodged, however, or my aim was inaccurate; for all I accomplished was the demolition of the crystal which protected the dial of the clock upon the mantelpiece.

As for the Angel, he evinced his sense of my assault by giving me two or three hard consecutive raps upon the forehead as before. These reduced me at once to submission, and I am almost ashamed to confess that, either through pain or vexation, there came a few tears into my eyes.

"Mein Gott!" said the Angel of the Odd, apparently much softened at my distress; "mein Gott, te man is eder ferry dronck or ferry sorry. You mos not trink it so strong — you mos put de water in te wine. Here, trink dis, like a goot veller, und don't gry now — don't!"

Hereupon the Angel of the Odd replenished my goblet (which was about a third full of Port) with a colorless fluid that he poured from one of his hand bottles. I observed that these bottles had labels about their necks, and that these labels were inscribed "Kirschenwasser."

The considerate kindness of the Angel mollified me in no little measure; and, aided by the water with which he diluted my Port more than once, I at length regained sufficient temper to listen to his very extraordinary discourse. I cannot pretend to recount all that he told me, but I gleaned from what he said that he was the genius who presided over the *contre temps* of mankind, and whose business it was to bring about the *odd accidents* which are continually astonishing the skeptic. Once or twice, upon my venturing to express my total incredulity in respect to his pretensions, he grew very angry indeed, so that at length I considered it the wiser policy to say nothing at all, and let him have his own way. He talked on, therefore, at great length, while I merely leaned back in my chair with my eyes shut, and amused myself with munching raisins and flipping the stems about the room. But, by and bye, the Angel suddenly construed this behavior of mine into contempt. He arose in a terrible passion, slouched his funnel down over his eyes, swore a vast oath, uttered a threat of some character which I did not precisely comprehend, and finally made me a low bow and departed, wishing me, in the language of the archbishop in Gil-Blas, *"beaucoup de bonheur et un peu plus de bon sens."*

His departure afforded me relief. The very few glasses of Lafitte that I had sipped had the effect of rendering me drowsy, and I felt inclined to take a nap of some fifteen or twenty minutes, as is my custom after dinner. At six I had an appointment of consequence, which it was quite indispensable that I should keep. The policy of insurance for my dwelling house had expired the day before; and, some dispute having arisen, it was agreed that, at six, I should meet the board of directors of the company and settle the terms of a renewal. Glancing upward at the clock on the mantel-piece (for I felt too drowsy to take out my watch), I had the pleasure to find that I had still twenty-five minutes to spare. It was half past five; I could easily walk to the insurance office in five minutes; and my usual post prandian siestas had never been known to exceed five and twenty. I felt sufficiently safe, therefore, and composed myself to my slumbers forthwith.

Having completed them to my satisfaction, I again looked toward the time-piece, and was half inclined to believe in the possibility of odd accidents when I found that, instead of my ordinary fifteen or twenty minutes, I had been dozing only three; for it still wanted seven and twenty of the appointed hour. I betook myself again to my nap, and at length a second time awoke, when, to my utter amazement, it still wanted twenty-seven minutes of six. I jumped up to examine the clock, and found that it had ceased running. My watch informed me that it was half past seven; and, of course, having slept two hours, I was too late for my appointment. "It will make no difference," I said; "I can call at the office in the morning and apologize; in the meantime what can be the matter with the clock?" Upon examining it I discovered that one of the raisin-stems which I had been flipping about the room during the discourse of the Angel of the Odd had flown through the fractured crystal, and lodging, singularly enough, in the key-hole, with an end projecting outward, had thus arrested the revolution of the minute-hand.

"Ah!" said I; "I see how it is. This thing speaks for itself. A natural accident, such as *will* happen now and then!"

I gave the matter no further consideration, and at my usual hour retired to bed. Here, having placed a candle upon a reading-stand at the bed-head, and having made an attempt to peruse some pages of the "Omnipresence of the Deity," I unfortunately fell asleep in less than twenty seconds, leaving the light burning as it was.

My dreams were terrifically disturbed by visions of the Angel of the Odd. Methought he stood at the foot of the couch, drew aside the curtains, and, in the hollow, detestable tones of a rum-puncheon, menaced me with the bitterest vengeance for the contempt with which I had treated him. He concluded a long harangue by taking off his funnel-cap, inserting the tube into my gullet, and thus deluging me with an ocean of Kirschenwasser, which he poured, in a continuous flood, from one of the long-necked bottles that stood him instead of an arm. My agony was at length insufferable, and I awoke just in time to perceive that a rat had run off with the lighted candle from the stand, but *not* in season to prevent his making his escape with it through the hole. Very soon, a strong suffocating odor assailed my nostrils; the house, I clearly perceived, was on fire. In a few minutes the blaze broke forth with violence, and in an incredibly brief period the entire building was wrapped in flames. All egress from my chamber, except through a window, was cut off. The crowd, however, quickly procured and raised a long ladder. By means of this I was descending rapidly, and in apparent safety, when a huge hog, about whose rotund stomach, and indeed about whose whole air and physiognomy, there was something which reminded me of the Angel of the Odd, — when this hog, I say, which hitherto had been quietly slumbering in the mud, took it suddenly into his head that his left shoulder needed scratching, and could find no more convenient

rubbing post than that afforded by the foot of the ladder. In an instant I was precipitated, and had the misfortune to fracture my arm.

This accident, with the loss of my insurance, and with the more serious loss of my hair, the whole of which had been singed off by the fire, predisposed me to serious impressions, so that, finally, I made up my mind to take a wife. There was a rich widow disconsolate for the loss of her seventh husband, and to her wounded spirit I offered the balm of my vows. She yielded a reluctant consent to my prayers. I knelt at her feet in gratitude and adoration. She blushed, and bowed her luxuriant tresses into close contact with those supplied me, temporarily, by Grandjean. I know not how the entanglement took place, but so it was. I arose with a shining pate, wigless; she in disdain and wrath, half buried in alien hair. Thus ended my hopes of the widow by an accident which could not have been anticipated, to be sure, but which the natural sequence of events had brought about.

Without despairing, however, I undertook the siege of a less implacable heart. The fates were again propitious for a brief period; but again a trivial incident interfered. Meeting my betrothed in an avenue thronged with the *elite* of the city, I was hastening to greet her with one of my best considered bows, when a small particle of some foreign matter lodging in the corner of my eye, rendered me, for the moment, completely blind. Before I could recover my sight, the lady of my love had disappeared — irreparably affronted at what she chose to consider my premeditated rudeness in passing her by ungreeted. While I stood bewildered at the suddenness of this accident (which might have happened, nevertheless, to any one under the sun), and while I still continued incapable of sight, I was accosted by the Angel of the Odd, who proffered me his aid with a civility which I had no reason to expect. He examined my disordered eye with much gentleness and skill, informed me that I had a drop in it, and (whatever a "drop" was) took it out, and afforded me relief.

I now considered it time to die, (since fortune had so determined to persecute me,) and accordingly made my way to the nearest river. Here, divesting myself of my clothes, (for there is no reason why we cannot die as we were born,) I threw myself headlong into the current; the sole witness of my fate being a solitary crow that had been seduced into the eating of brandy-saturated corn, and so had staggered away from his fellows. No sooner had I entered the water than this bird took it into its head to fly away with the most indispensable portion of my apparel. Postponing, therefore, for the present, my suicidal design, I just slipped my nether extremities into the sleeves of my coat, and betook myself to a pursuit of the felon with all the nimbleness which the case required and its circumstances would admit. But my evil destiny attended me still. As I ran at full speed, with my nose up in the atmosphere, and intent only upon the purloiner of my property, I suddenly perceived

that my feet rested no longer upon *terra firma*; the fact is, I had thrown myself over a precipice, and should inevitably have been dashed to pieces, but for my good fortune in grasping the end of a long guide-rope, which depended from a passing balloon.

As soon as I sufficiently recovered my senses to comprehend the terrific predicament in which I stood or rather hung, I exerted all the power of my lungs to make that predicament known to the aeronaut overhead. But for a long time I exerted myself in vain. Either the fool could not, or the villain would not perceive me. Meantime the machine rapidly soared, while my strength even more rapidly failed. I was soon upon the point of resigning myself to my fate, and dropping quietly into the sea, when my spirits were suddenly revived by hearing a hollow voice from above, which seemed to be lazily humming an opera air. Looking up, I perceived the Angel of the Odd. He was leaning with his arms folded, over the rim of the car; and with a pipe in his mouth, at which he puffed leisurely, seemed to be upon excellent terms with himself and the universe. I was too much exhausted to speak, so I merely regarded him with an imploring air.

For several minutes, although he looked me full in the face, he said nothing. At length removing carefully his meerschaum from the right to the left corner of his mouth, he condescended to speak.

"Who pe you?" he asked, "und what der teuffel you pe do dare?"

To this piece of impudence, cruelty, and affectation, I could reply only by ejaculating the monosyllable "Help!"

"Elp!" echoed the ruffian — "not I. Dare iz te pottle — elp yourself, und pe tam'd!"

With these words he let fall a heavy bottle of Kirschenwasser which, dropping precisely upon the crown of my head, caused me to imagine that my brains were entirely knocked out. Impressed with this idea, I was about to relinquish my hold and give up the ghost with a good grace, when I was arrested by the cry of the Angel, who bade me hold on.

"Old on!" he said; "don't pe in te urry — don't. Will you pe take de odder pottle, or ave you pe got zober yet and come to your zenzes?"

I made haste, hereupon, to nod my head twice — once in the negative, meaning thereby that I would prefer not taking the other bottle at present — and once in the affirmative, intending thus to imply that I *was* sober and *had* positively come to my senses. By these means I somewhat softened the Angel.

"Und you pelief, ten," he inquired, "at te last? You pelief, ten, in te possibilty of te odd?"

I again nodded my head in assent.

"Und you ave pelief in *me*, te Angel of te Odd?"

I nodded again.

"Und you acknowledge tat you pe te blind dronk and te vool?"

I nodded once more.

"Put your right hand into your left hand preeches pocket, ten, in token ov your vull zubmission unto te Angel ov te Odd."

This thing, for very obvious reasons, I found it quite impossible to do. In the first place, my left arm had been broken in my fall from the ladder, and, therefore, had I let go my hold with the right hand, I must have let go altogether. In the second place, I could have no breeches until I came across the crow. I was therefore obliged, much to my regret, to shake my head in the negative — intending thus to give the Angel to understand that I found it inconvenient, just at that moment, to comply with his very reasonable demand! No sooner, however, had I ceased shaking my head than —

"Go to der teuffel, ten!" roared the Angel of the Odd.

In pronouncing these words, he drew a sharp knife across the guiderope by which I was suspended, and as we then happened to be precisely over my own house, (which, during my peregrinations, had been handsomely rebuilt,) it so occurred that I tumbled headlong down the ample chimney and alit upon the dining-room hearth.

Upon coming to my senses, (for the fall had very thoroughly stunned me,) I found it about four o'clock in the morning. I lay outstretched where I had fallen from the balloon. My head grovelled in the ashes of an extinguished fire, while my feet reposed upon the wreck of a small table, overthrown, and amid the fragments of a miscellaneous dessert, intermingled with a newspaper, some broken glass and shattered bottles, and an empty jug of the Schiedam Kirschenwasser. Thus revenged himself the Angel of the Odd.

"Thou Art the Man"

I will now play the Œdipus to the Rattleborough enigma. I will expound to you — as I alone can — the secret of the enginery that effected the Rattelborough miracle — the one, the true, the admitted, the undisputed, the indisputable miracle, which put a definite end to infidelity among the Rattleburghers and converted to the orthodoxy of the grandames all the carnal-minded who had ventured to be sceptical before.

This event — which I should be sorry to discuss in a tone of unsuitable levity — occurred in the summer of 18—. Mr. Barnabas Shuttleworthy — one of the wealthiest and most respectable citizens of the borough — had been missing for several days under circumstances which gave rise to suspicion of foul play. Mr. Shuttleworthy had set out from Rattleborough very early one Saturday morning, on horseback, with the avowed intention of proceeding to the city of ——, about fifteen miles distant, and of returning the night of the same day. Two hours after his de-

parture, however, his horse returned without him, and without the sad-
dle-bags which had been strapped on his back at starting. The animal
was wounded, too, and covered with mud. These circumstances naturally
gave rise to much alarm among the friends of the missing man; and when
it was found, on Sunday morning, that he had not yet made his appear-
ance, the whole borough arose *en masse* to go and look for his body.

The foremost and most energetic in instituting this search was the
bosom friend of Mr. Shuttleworthy — a Mr. Charles Goodfellow, or, as
he was universally called, "Charley Goodfellow," or "Old Charley Good-
fellow." Now, whether it is a marvellous coincidence, or whether it is
that the name itself has an imperceptible effect upon the character, I
have never yet been able to ascertain; but the fact is unquestionable,
that there never yet was any person named Charles who was not an
open, manly, honest, good-natured, and frank-hearted fellow, with a rich,
clear voice, that did you good to hear it, and an eye that looked you al-
ways straight in the face, as much as to say: "I have a clear conscience
myself, am afraid of no man, and am altogether above doing a mean
action." And thus all the hearty, careless, "walking gentlemen" of the
stage are very certain to be called Charles.

Now, "Old Charley Goodfellow," although he had been in Rattle-
borough not longer than six months or thereabouts, and although nobody
knew any thing about him before he came to settle in the neighborhood,
had experienced no difficulty in the world in making the acquaintance
of all the respectable people in the borough. Not a man of them but
would have taken his bare word for a thousand at any moment; and as
for the women, there is no saying what they would not have done to
oblige him. And all this came of his having been christened Charles,
and of his possessing, in consequence, that ingenuous face which is
proverbially the very "best letter of recommendation."

I have already said that Mr. Shuttleworthy was one of the most re-
spectable and, undoubtedly, he was the most wealthy man in Rattle-
borough, while "Old Charley Goodfellow" was upon as intimate terms
with him as if he had been his own brother. The two old gentlemen were
next-door neighbours, and, although Mr. Shuttleworthy seldom, if ever,
visited "Old Charley," and never was known to take a meal in his house,
still this did not prevent the two friends from being exceedingly inti-
mate, as I have just observed; for "Old Charley" never let a day pass
without stepping in three or four times to see how his neighbour came
on, and very often he would stay to breakfast or tea, and almost always
to dinner; and then the amount of wine that was made way with by the
two cronies at a sitting, it would really be a difficult thing to ascertain.
"Old Charley's" favorite beverage was *Chateau-Margaux*, and it appeared
to do Mr. Shuttleworthy's heart good to see the old fellow swallow it,
as he did, quart after quart; so that, one day, when the wine was *in* and
the wit, as a natural consequence, somewhat *out*, he said to his crony, as

he slapped him upon the back — "I tell you what it is, 'Old Charley,' you are, by all odds, the heartiest old fellow I ever came across in all my born days; and, since you love to guzzle the wine at that fashion, I'll be darned if I don't have to make thee a present of a big box of the Chateau-Margaux. Od rot me," — (Mr. Shuttleworthy had a sad habit of swearing, although he seldom went beyond "Od rot me," or "By gosh," or "By the jolly golly,") — "Od rot me," says he, "if I don't send an order to town this very afternoon for a double box of the best that can be got, and I'll make ye a present of it, I will! — ye needn't say a word now — I *will*, I tell ye, and there's an end of it; so look out for it — it will come to hand some of these fine days, precisely when ye are looking for it the least!" I mention this little bit of liberality on the part of Mr. Shuttleworthy, just by way of showing you how *very* intimate an understanding existed between the two friends.

Well, on the Sunday morning in question, when it came to be fairly understood that Mr. Shuttleworthy had met with foul play, I never saw any one so profoundly affected as "Old Charley Goodfellow." When he first heard that the horse had come home without his master, and without his master's saddle-bags, and all bloody from a pistol-shot, that had gone clean through and through the poor animal's chest without quite killing him; when he heard all this, he turned as pale as if the missing man had been his own dear brother or father, and shivered and shook all over as if he had had a fit of the ague.

At first he was too much overpowered with grief to be able to do any thing at all, or to concert upon any plan of action; so that for a long time he endeavoured to dissuade Mr. Shuttleworthy's other friends from making a stir about the matter, thinking it best to wait awhile — say for a week or two, or a month, or two — to see if something wouldn't turn up, or if Mr. Shuttleworthy wouldn't come in the natural way, and explain his reasons for sending his horse on before. I dare say you have often observed this disposition to temporize, or to procrastinate, in people who are labouring under any very poignant sorrow. Their powers of mind seem to be rendered torpid, so that they have a horror of any thing like action, and like nothing in the world so well as to lie quietly in bed and "nurse their grief," as the old ladies express it — that is to say, ruminate over the trouble.

The people of Rattleborough had, indeed, so high an opinion of the wisdom and discretion of "Old Charley," that the greater part of them felt disposed to agree with him, and not make a stir in the business "until something should turn up," as the honest old gentleman worded it; and I believe that, after all, this would have been the general determination, but for the very suspicious interference of Mr. Shuttleworthy's nephew, a young man of very dissipated habits, and otherwise of rather bad character. This nephew, whose name was Pennifeather, would listen to nothing like reason in the matter of "lying quiet," but insisted upon making

immediate search for the "corpse of the murdered man." This was the expression he employed; and Mr. Goodfellow acutely remarked at the time, that it was "a *singular* expression, to say no more." This remark of "Old Charley's," too, had great effect upon the crowd; and one of the party was heard to ask, very impressively, "how it happened that young Mr. Pennifeather was so intimately cognizant of all the circumstances connected with his wealthy uncle's disappearance, as to feel authorized to assert, distinctly and unequivocally, that his uncle *was* 'a murdered man.'" Hereupon some little squibbing and bickering occurred among various members of the crowd, and especially between "Old Charley" and Mr. Pennifeather — although this latter occurrence was, indeed, by no means a novelty, for no good will had subsisted between the parties for the last three or four months; and matters had even gone so far that Mr. Pennifeather had actually knocked down his uncle's friend for some alleged excess of liberty that the latter had taken in the uncle's house, of which the nephew was an inmate. Upon this occasion "Old Charley" is said to have behaved with exemplary moderation and Christian charity. He arose from the blow, adjusted his clothes, and made no attempt at retaliation at all — merely muttering a few words about "taking summary vengeance at the first convenient opportunity," — a natural and very justifiable ebullition of anger, which meant nothing, however, and, beyond doubt, was no sooner given vent to than forgotten.

However these matters may be (which have no reference to the point now at issue), it is quite certain that the people of Rattleborough, principally through the persuasion of Mr. Pennifeather, came at length to the determination of dispersion over the adjacent country in search of the missing Mr. Shuttleworthy. I say they came to this determination in the first instance. After it had been fully resolved that a search should be made, it was considered almost a matter of course that the seekers should disperse — that is to say, distribute themselves in parties — for the more thorough examination of the region round about. I forget, however, by what ingenious train of reasoning it was that "Old Charley" finally convinced the assembly that this was the most injudicious plan that could be pursued. Convince them, however, he did — all except Mr. Pennifeather; and, in the end, it was arranged that a search should be instituted, carefully and very thoroughly, by the burghers *en masse*, "Old Charley" himself leading the way.

As for the matter of that, there could have been no better pioneer than "Old Charley," whom everybody knew to have the eye of a lynx; but, although he led them into all manner of out-of-the-way holes and corners, by routes that nobody had ever suspected of existing in the neighbourhood, and although the search was incessantly kept up day and night for nearly a week, still no trace of Mr. Shuttleworthy could be discovered. When I say no trace, however, I must not be understood to speak literally; for trace, to some extent, there certainly was. The poor gentle-

man had been tracked, by his horse's shoes (which were peculiar), to a spot about three miles to the east of the borough, on the main road leading to the city. Here the track made off into a by-path through a piece of woodland — the path coming out again into the main road, and cutting off about half a mile of the regular distance. Following the shoe-marks down this lane, the party came at length to a pool of stagnant water, half hidden by the brambles, to the right of the lane, and opposite this pool all vestige of the track was lost sight of. It appeared, however, that a struggle of some nature had here taken place, and it seemed as if some large and heavy body, much larger and heavier than a man, had been drawn from the by-path to the pool. This latter was carefully dragged twice, but nothing was found; and the party was upon the point of going away, in despair of coming to any result, when Providence suggested to Mr. Goodfellow the expediency of draining the water off altogether. This project was received with cheers, and many high compliments to "Old Charley" upon his sagacity and consideration. As many of the burghers had brought spades with them, supposing that they might possibly be called upon to disinter a corpse, the drain was easily and speedily effected; and no sooner was the bottom visible, than right in the middle of the mud that remained was discovered a black silk velvet waistcoat, which nearly every one present immediately recognized as the property of Mr. Pennifeather. This waistcoat was much torn and stained with blood, and there were several persons among the party who had a distinct remembrance of its having been worn by its owner on the very morning of Mr. Shuttleworthy's departure for the city; while there were others, again, ready to testify upon oath, if required, that Mr. P. did *not* wear the garment in question at any period during the *remainder* of that memorable day; nor could any one be found to say that he had seen it upon Mr. P.'s person at any period at all subsequent to Mr. Shuttleworthy's disappearance.

Matters now wore a very serious aspect for Mr. Pennifeather, and it was observed, as an indubitable confirmation of the suspicions which were excited against him, that he grew exceedingly pale, and when asked what he had to say for himself, was utterly incapable of saying a word. Hereupon, the few friends his riotous mode of living had left him, deserted him at once to a man, and were even more clamorous than his ancient and avowed enemies for his instantaneous arrest. But, on the other hand, the magnanimity of Mr. Goodfellow shone forth with only the more brilliant lustre through contrast. He made a warm and intensely eloquent defence of Mr. Pennifeather, in which he alluded more than once to his own sincere forgiveness of that wild young gentleman — "the heir of the worthy Mr. Shuttleworthy," — for the insult which he (the young gentleman) had, no doubt in the heat of passion, thought proper to put upon him (Mr. Goodfellow). "He forgave him for it," he said, "from the very bottom of his heart; and for himself (Mr. Goodfellow),

so far from pushing the suspicious circumstances to extremity, which he was sorry to say, really *had* arisen against Mr. Pennifeather, he (Mr. Goodfellow) would make every exertion in his power, would employ all the little eloquence in his possession to — to — to — soften down, as much as he could conscientiously do so, the worst features of this really exceedingly perplexing piece of business."

Mr. Goodfellow went on for some half hour longer in this strain, very much to the credit both of his head and of his heart; but your warm-hearted people are seldom apposite in their observations — they run into all sorts of blunders, *contre-temps* and *mal apropos-isms*, in the hot-headedness of their zeal to serve a friend — thus, often with the kindest intentions in the world, doing infinitely more to prejudice his cause than to advance it.

So, in the present instance, it turned out with all the eloquence of "Old Charley"; for, although he laboured earnestly in behalf of the suspected, yet it so happened, somehow or other, that every syllable he uttered of which the direct but unwitting tendency was not to exalt the speaker in the good opinion of his audience, had the effect to deepen the suspicion already attached to the individual whose cause he pleaded, and to arouse against him the fury of the mob.

One of the most unaccountable errors committed by the orator was his allusion to the suspected as "the heir of the worthy old gentleman Mr. Shuttleworthy." The people had really never thought of this before. They had only remembered certain threats of disinheritance uttered a year or two previously by the uncle (who had no living relative except the nephew), and they had, therefore, always looked upon this disinheritance as a matter that was settled — so single-minded a race of beings were the Rattleburghers; but the remark of "Old Charley" brought them at once to a consideration of this point, and thus gave them to see the possibility of the threats having been nothing *more* than a threat. And straightway hereupon, arose the natural question of *cui bono?* — a question that tended even more than the waistcoat to fasten the terrible crime upon the young man. And here, lest I may be misunderstood, permit me to digress for one moment merely to observe that the exceedingly brief and simple Latin phrase which I have employed, is invariably mistranslated and misconceived. "*Cui bono?*" in all the crack novels and elsewhere, — in those of Mrs. Gore, for example, (the author of "Cecil,") a lady who quotes all tongues from the Chaldæan to Chickasaw, and is helped to her learning, "as needed," upon a systematic plan, by Mr. Beckford, — in *all* the crack novels, I say, from those of Bulwer and Dickens to those of Turnapenny and Ainsworth, the two little Latin words *cui bono* are rendered "to what purpose?" or, (as if *quo bono*,) "to what good." Their true meaning, nevertheless, is "for whose advantage." *Cui*, to whom; *bono*, is it for a benefit. It is a purely legal phrase, and applicable precisely in cases such as we have now under consideration, where

the probability of the doer of a deed hinges upon the probability of the benefit accruing to this individual or to that from the deed's accomplishment. Now in the present instance, the question *cui bono?* very pointedly implicated Mr. Pennifeather. His uncle had threatened him, after making a will in his favour, with disinheritance. But the threat had not been actually kept; the original will, it appeared, had not been altered. *Had* it been altered, the only supposable motive for murder on the part of the suspected would have been the ordinary one of revenge; and even this would have been counteracted by the hope of reinstation into the good graces of the uncle. But the will being unaltered, while the threat to alter remained suspended over the nephew's head, there appears at once the very strongest possible inducement for the atrocity; and so concluded, very sagaciously, the worthy citizens of the borough of Rattle.

Mr. Pennifeather was, accordingly, arrested upon the spot, and the crowd, after some further search, proceeded homeward, having him in custody. On the route, however, another circumstance occurred tending to confirm the suspicion entertained. Mr. Goodfellow, whose zeal led him to be always a little in advance of the party, was seen suddenly to run forward a few paces, stoop, and then apparently to pick up some small object from the grass. Having quickly examined it, he was observed, too, to make a sort of half attempt at concealing it in his coat pocket; but this action was noticed, as I say, and consequently prevented, when the object picked up was found to be a Spanish knife which a dozen persons at once recognized as belonging to Mr. Pennifeather. Moreover, his initials were engraved upon the handle. The blade of this knife was open and bloody.

No doubt now remained of the guilt of the nephew, and immediately upon reaching Rattleborough he was taken before a magistrate for examination.

Here matters again took a most unfavourable turn. The prisoner, being questioned as to his whereabouts on the morning of Mr. Shuttleworthy's disappearance, had absolutely the audacity to acknowledge that on that very morning he had been out with his rifle deer-stalking, in the immediate neighbourhood of the pool where the blood-stained waistcoat had been discovered through the sagacity of Mr. Goodfellow.

This latter now came forward, and, with tears in his eyes, asked permission to be examined. He said that a stern sense of the duty he owed his Maker, not less than his fellow-men, would permit him no longer to remain silent. Hitherto, the sincerest affection for the young man (notwithstanding the latter's ill-treatment of himself, Mr. Goodfellow) had induced him to make every hypothesis which imagination could suggest, by way of endeavouring to account for what appeared suspicious in the circumstances that told so seriously against Mr. Pennifeather; but these circumstances were now altogether *too* convincing — *too* damning; he would hesitate no longer — he would tell all he knew, although his

heart (Mr. Goodfellow's) should absolutely burst asunder in the effort. He then went on to state that, on the afternoon of the day previous to Mr. Shuttleworthy's departure for the city, that worthy old gentleman had mentioned to his nephew, in *his* hearing (Mr. Goodfellow's), that his object in going to town on the morrow was to make a deposit of an unusually large sum of money in the "Farmers and Mechanics' Bank," and that, then and there, the said Mr. Shuttleworthy had distinctly avowed to the said nephew his irrevocable determination of rescinding the will originally made, and of cutting him off with a shilling. He (the witness) now solemnly called upon the accused to state whether what he (the witness) had just stated was or was not the truth in every substantial particular. Much to the astonishment of every one present, Mr. Pennifeather frankly admitted that *it was*.

The magistrate now considered it his duty to send a couple of constables to search the chamber of the accused in the house of his uncle. From this search they almost immediately returned with the well-known steel-bound, russet leather pocket-book which the old gentleman had been in the habit of carrying for years. Its valuable contents, however, had been abstracted, and the magistrate in vain endeavoured to extort from the prisoner the use which had been made of them, or the place of their concealment. Indeed, he obstinately denied all knowledge of the matter. The constables, also, discovered, between the bed and sacking of the unhappy man, a shirt and neck-handkerchief both marked with the initials of his name, and both hideously besmeared with the blood of the victim.

At this juncture, it was announced that the horse of the murdered man had just expired in the stable from the effects of the wound he had received, and it was proposed by Mr. Goodfellow that a *post mortem* examination of the beast should be immediately made, with the view, if possible, of discovering the ball. This was accordingly done; and, as if to demonstrate beyond a question the guilt of the accused, Mr. Goodfellow, after considerable searching in the cavity of the chest, was enabled to detect and to pull forth a bullet of very extraordinary size, which, upon trial, was found to be exactly adapted to the bore of Mr. Pennifeather's rifle, while it was far too large for that of any other person in the borough or its vicinity. To render the matter even surer yet, however, this bullet was discovered to have a flaw or seam at right angles to the usual suture, and upon examination, this seam corresponded precisely with an accidental ridge or elevation in a pair of moulds acknowledged by the accused himself to be his own property. Upon finding of this bullet, the examining magistrate refused to listen to any farther testimony, and immediately committed the prisoner for trial — declining resolutely to take any bail in the case, although against this severity Mr. Goodfellow very warmly remonstrated, and offered to become surety in whatever amount might be required. This generosity on the part of "Old

Charley" was only in accordance with the whole tenour of his amiable and chivalrous conduct during the entire period of his sojourn in the borough of Rattle. In the present instance the worthy man was so entirely carried away by the excessive warmth of his sympathy, that he seemed to have quite forgotten, when he offered to go bail for his young friend, that he himself (Mr. Goodfellow) did not possess a single dollar's worth of property upon the face of the earth.

The result of the committal may be readily foreseen. Mr. Pennifeather, amid the loud execrations of all Rattleborough, was brought to trial at the next criminal sessions, when the chain of circumstantial evidence (strengthened as it was by some additional damning facts, which Mr. Goodfellow's sensitive conscientiousness forbade him to withhold from the court) was considered so unbroken and so thoroughly conclusive, that the jury, without leaving their seats, returned an immediate verdict of "*Guilty of murder in the first degree.*" Soon afterward the unhappy wretch received sentence of death, and was remanded to the county jail to await the inexorable vengeance of the law.

In the meantime, the noble behaviour of "Old Charley Goodfellow" had doubly endeared him to the honest citizens of the borough. He became ten times a greater favorite than ever; and, as a natural result of the hospitality with which he was treated, he relaxed, as it were, perforce, the extremely parsimonious habits which his poverty had hitherto impelled him to observe, and very frequently had little *réunions* at his own house, when wit and jollity reigned supreme — dampened a little, *of course*, by the occasional remembrance of the untoward and melancholy fate which impended over the nephew of the late lamented bosom friend of the generous host.

One fine day, this magnanimous old gentleman was agreeably surprised at the receipt of the following letter: —

"*Charles Goodfellow, Esquire:*

"*Dear Sir — In conformity with an order transmitted to our firm about two months since, by our esteemed correspondent, Mr. Barnabus Shuttleworthy, we have the honour of forwarding this morning, to your address, a double box of Chateau-Margaux, of the antelope brand, violet seal. Box numbered and marked as per margin.*

"*We remain, sir,*

"*Your most ob'nt ser'ts,*

HOGGS, FROGS, BOGS, & Co.

"*City of ——, June 21, 18—.*

"*P. S. — The box will reach you by wagon, on the day after your receipt of this letter. Our respects to Mr. Shuttleworthy.*

"H., F., B., & Co."

Chat. Mar. A — No. 1. —
6 doz. bottles (½ Gross)
From H. F. B. & Co.
Charles Goodfellow, Esq., Rattleborough

The fact is, that Mr. Goodfellow had, since the death of Mr. Shuttle-worthy, given over all expectation of ever receiving the promised Cha-teau-Margaux; and he, therefore, looked upon it *now* as a sort of especial dispensation of Providence in his behalf. He was highly delighted, of course, and in the exuberance of his joy invited a large party of friends to a *petit souper* on the morrow, for the purpose of broaching the good old Mr. Shuttleworthy's present. Not that he *said* any thing about "the good old Mr. Shuttleworthy" when he issued the invitations. The fact is, he thought much and concluded to say nothing at all. He did *not* mention to any one — if I remember aright — that he had received *a present* of Chateau-Margaux. He merely asked his friends to come and help him drink some, of a remarkable fine quality and rich flavour, that he had ordered up from the city a couple of months ago, and of which he would be in the receipt upon the morrow. I have often puzzled myself to imagine *why* it was that "Old Charley" came to the conclusion to say nothing about having received the wine from his old friend, but I could never precisely understand his reason for the silence, although he had *some* excellent and very magnanimous reason, no doubt.

The morrow at length arrived, and with it a very large and highly respectable company at Mr. Goodfellow's house. Indeed, half the bor-ough was there, — I myself among the number, — but, much to the vexation of the host, the Chateau-Margaux did not arrive until a late hour, and when the sumptuous supper supplied by "Old Charley" had been done very ample justice by the guests. It came at length, however, — a monstrously big box of it there was, too — and as the whole party were in excessively good humor, it was decided, *nem. con.*, that it should be lifted upon the table and its contents disembowelled forthwith.

No sooner said than done. I lent a helping hand; and, in a trice we had the box upon the table, in the midst of all the bottles and glasses, not a few of which were demolished in the scuffle. "Old Charley," who was pretty much intoxicated, and excessively red in the face, now took a seat, with an air of mock dignity, at the head of the board, and thumped furi-ously upon it with a decanter, calling upon the company to keep order "during the ceremony of disinterring the treasure."

After some vociferation, quiet was at length fully restored, and, as very often happens in similar cases, a profound and remarkable silence ensued. Being then requested to force open the lid, I complied, of course, "with an infinite deal of pleasure." I inserted a chisel, and giving it a few slight taps with a hammer, the top of the box flew suddenly off, and at the same instant, there sprang up into a sitting position, directly facing the host, the bruised, bloody, and nearly putrid corpse of the murdered Mr. Shuttleworthy himself. It gazed for a few seconds, fixedly and sorrow-fully, with its decaying and lack-lustre eyes, full into the countenance of Mr. Goodfellow; uttered slowly, but clearly and impressively, the words — "Thou art the man!" and then, falling over the side of the

chest as if thoroughly satisfied, stretched out its limbs quiveringly upon the table.

The scene that ensued is altogether beyond description. The rush for the doors and windows was terrific, and many of the most robust *men* in the room fainted outright through sheer horror. But after the first wild, shrieking burst of affright, all eyes were directed to Mr. Goodfellow. If I live a thousand years, I can never forget the more than mortal agony which was depicted in that ghastly face of his, so lately rubicund with triumph and wine. For several minutes he sat rigidly as a statue of marble; his eyes seeming, in the intense vacancy of their gaze, to be turned inward and absorbed in the contemplation of his own miserable, murderous soul. At length their expression appeared to flash suddenly out into the external world, when, with a quick leap, he sprang from his chair, and falling heavily with his head and shoulders upon the table, and in contact with the corpse, poured out rapidly and vehemently a detailed confession of the hideous crime for which Mr. Pennifeather was then imprisoned and doomed to die.

What he recounted was in substance this: — He followed his victim to the vicinity of the pool; there shot his horse with a pistol; despatched its rider with the butt end; possessed himself of the pocket-book; and, supposing the horse dead, dragged it with great labour to the brambles by the pond. Upon his own beast he slung the corpse of Mr. Shuttleworthy, and thus bore it to a secure place of concealment a long distance off through the woods.

The waistcoat, the knife, the pocket-book, and bullet, had been placed by himself where found, with the view of avenging himself upon Mr. Pennifeather. He had also contrived the discovery of the stained handkerchief and shirt.

Towards the end of the blood-chilling recital, the words of the guilty wretch faltered and grew hollow. When the record was finally exhausted, he arose, staggered backward from the table, and fell — *dead*.

The means by which this happily-timed confession was extorted, although efficient, were simple indeed. Mr. Goodfellow's excess of frankness had disgusted me, and excited my suspicions from the first. I was present when Mr. Pennifeather had struck him, and the fiendish expression which then arose upon his countenance, although momentary, assured me that his threat of vengeance would, if possible, be rigidly fulfilled. I was thus prepared to view the *manœuvring* of "Old Charley" in a very different light from that in which it was regarded by the good citizens of Rattleborough. I saw at once that all the criminating discoveries arose, either directly or indirectly, from himself. But the fact which clearly opened my eyes to the true state of the case, was the affair of the bullet, *found* by Mr. G. in the carcass of the horse. *I* had not forgotten, although the Rattleburghers *had*, that there was a hole where the ball

had entered the horse, and another where it *went out*. If it were found in the animal then, after having made its exit, I saw clearly that it must have been deposited by the person who found it. The bloody shirt and handkerchief confirmed the idea suggested by the bullet; for the blood on examination proved to be capital claret, and no more. When I came to think of these things, and also of the late increase of liberality and expenditure on the part of Mr. Goodfellow, I entertained a suspicion which was none the less strong because I kept it altogether to myself.

In the meantime, I instituted a rigorous private search for the corpse of Mr. Shuttleworthy, and, for good reasons, searched in quarters as divergent as possible from those to which Mr. Goodfellow conducted his party. The result was that, after some days, I came across an old dry well, the mouth of which was nearly hidden by brambles; and here, at the bottom, I discovered what I sought.

Now it so happened that I had overheard the colloquy between the two cronies, when Mr. Goodfellow had contrived to cajole his host into the promise of a box of Chateaux-Margaux. Upon this hint I acted. I procured a stiff piece of whalebone, thrust it down the throat of the corpse, and deposited the latter in an old wine box — taking care so to double the body up as to double the whalebone with it. In this manner I had to press forcibly upon the lid to keep it down while I secured it with nails; and I anticipated, of course, that as soon as these latter were removed, the top would fly *off* and the body *up*.

Having thus arranged the box, I marked, numbered, and addressed it as already told; and then writing a letter in the name of the wine merchants with whom Mr. Shuttleworthy dealt, I gave instructions to my servant to wheel the box to Mr. Goodfellow's door, in a barrow, at a given signal from myself. For the words which I intended the corpse to speak, I confidently depended upon my ventriloquial abilities; for their effect, I counted upon the conscience of the murderous wretch.

I believe there is nothing more to be explained. Mr. Pennifeather was released upon the spot, inherited the fortune of his uncle, profited by the lessons of experience, turned over a new leaf, and led happily ever afterward a new life.

Literary Life of Thingum Bob, Esq.

LATE EDITOR OF THE "GOOSETHERUMFOODLE"

BY HIMSELF

I AM now growing in years, and — since I understand that Shakespeare and Mr. Emmons are deceased — it is not impossible that I may even die. It has occurred to me, therefore, that I may as well retire from the field of Letters and repose upon my laurels. But I am ambitious of signalizing my abdication of the literary sceptre by some important bequest to posterity; and, perhaps, I cannot do a better thing than just pen for it an account of my earlier career. My name, indeed, has been so long and so constantly before the public eye, that I am not only willing to admit the naturalness of the interest which it has everywhere excited, but ready to satisfy the extreme curiosity which it has inspired. In fact, it is no more than the duty of him who achieves greatness to leave behind him, in his ascent, such landmarks as may guide others to be great. I propose, therefore, in the present paper (which I had some idea of calling "Memoranda to Serve for the Literary History of America") to give a detail of those important, yet feeble and tottering, first steps, by which, at length, I attained the high road to the pinnacle of human renown.

Of one's *very* remote ancestors it is superfluous to say much. My father, Thomas Bob, Esq., stood for many years at the summit of his profession, which was that of a merchant-barber, in the city of Smug. His warehouse was the resort of all the principal people of the place, and especially of the editorial corps — a body which inspires all about it with profound veneration and awe. For my own part, I regarded them as gods, and drank in with avidity the rich wit and wisdom which continuously flowed from their august mouths during the process of what is styled "lather." My first moment of positive inspiration must be dated from that ever-memorable epoch, when the brilliant conductor of the "Gad-Fly," in the intervals of the important process just mentioned, recited aloud, before a conclave of our apprentices, an inimitable poem in honor of the "Only Genuine Oil-of-Bob" (so called from its talented inventor, my father), and for which effusion the editor of the "Fly" was remunerated with a regal liberality by the firm of Thomas Bob & Company, merchant-barbers.

The genius of the stanzas to the "Oil-of-Bob" first breathed into me, I say, the divine *afflatus*. I resolved at once to become a great man, and to commence by becoming a great poet. That very evening I fell upon my knees at the feet of my father.

"Father," I said, "pardon me! — but I have a soul above lather. It is

my firm intention to cut the shop. I would be an editor — I would be a poet — I would pen stanzas to the 'Oil-of-Bob.' Pardon me and aid me to be great!"

"My dear Thingum," replied father, (I had been christened Thingum after a wealthy relative so surnamed,) "My dear Thingum," he said, raising me from my knees by the ears — "Thingum, my boy, you're a trump, and take after your father in having a soul. You have an immense head, too, and it must hold a great many brains. This I have long seen, and therefore had thoughts of making you a lawyer. The business, however, has grown ungenteel, and that of a politician don't pay. Upon the whole you judge wisely; — the trade of editor is best: — and if you can be a poet at the same time, — as most of the editors are, by the by, — why, you will kill two birds with the one stone. To encourage you in the beginning of things, I will allow you a garret; pen, ink, and paper; a rhyming dictionary; and a copy of the 'Gad-Fly.' I suppose you would scarcely demand any more."

"I would be an ungrateful villain if I did," I replied with enthusiasm. "Your generosity is boundless. I will repay it by making you the father of a genius."

Thus ended my conference with the best of men, and immediately upon its termination, I betook myself with zeal to my poetical labors; as upon these, chiefly, I founded my hopes of ultimate elevation to the editorial chair.

In my first attempts at composition I found the stanzas to "The Oil-of-Bob" rather a drawback than otherwise. Their splendor more dazzled than enlightened me. The contemplation of their excellence tended, naturally, to discourage me by comparison with my own abortions; so that for a long time I labored in vain. At length there came into my head one of those exquisitely original ideas which now and then *will* permeate the brain of a man of genius. It was this: — or, rather, thus was it carried into execution. From the rubbish of an old book-stall, in a very remote corner of the town, I got together several antique and altogether unknown or forgotten volumes. The bookseller sold them to me for a song. From one of these, which purported to be a translation of one Dante's "Inferno," I copied with remarkable neatness a long passage about a man named Ugolino, who had a parcel of brats. From another, which contained a good many old plays by some person whose name I forget, I extracted in the same manner, and with the same care, a great number of lines about "angels" and "ministers saying grace," and "goblins damned," and more besides of that sort. From a third, which was the composition of some blind man or other, either a Greek or a Choctaw — I cannot be at the pains of remembering every trifle exactly, — I took about fifty verses beginning with "Achilles' wrath," and "grease," and something else. From a fourth, which I recollect was also the work of a blind man, I selected a page or two all about "hail" and "holy light";

and, although a blind man has no business to write about light, still the verses were sufficiently good in their way.

Having made fair copies of these poems, I signed every one of them "Oppodeldoc" (a fine sonorous name), and, doing each up nicely in a separate envelope, I dispatched one to each of the four principal Magazines, with a request for speedy insertion and prompt pay. The result of this well-conceived plan, however, (the success of which would have saved me much trouble in after-life,) served to convince me that some editors are not to be bamboozled, and gave the *coup-de-grace* (as they say in France) to my nascent hopes (as they say in the city of the transcendentals).

The fact is, that each and every one of the Magazines in question gave Mr. "Oppodeldoc" a complete using-up, in the "Monthly Notices to Correspondents." The "Hum-Drum" gave him a dressing after this fashion:

" 'Oppodeldoc' (whoever he is) has sent us a long *tirade* concerning a bedlamite whom he styles 'Ugolino,' who had a great many children that should have been all whipped and sent to bed without their suppers. The whole affair is exceedingly tame — not to say *flat*. 'Oppodeldoc' (whoever he is) is entirely devoid of imagination — and imagination, in our humble opinion, is not only the soul of POESY, but also its very heart. 'Oppodeldoc' (whoever he is) has the audacity to demand of us, for his twattle, a 'speedy insertion and prompt pay.' We neither insert not purchase any stuff of the sort. There can be no doubt, however, that he would meet with a ready sale for all the balderdash he can scribble, at the office of either the 'Rowdy-Dow,' the 'Lollipop,' or the 'Goosetherumfoodle.' "

All this, it must be acknowledged, was very severe upon "Oppodeldoc," — but the unkindest cut was putting the word POESY in small caps. In those five pre-eminent letters what a world of bitterness is there not involved!

But "Oppodeldoc" was punished with equal severity in the "Rowdy Dow," which spoke thus:

"We have received a most singular and insolent communication from a person (whoever he is) signing himself 'Oppodeldoc,' — thus desecrating the greatness of the illustrious Roman emperor so named. Accompanying the letter of 'Oppodeldoc' (whoever he is) we find sundry lines of most disgusting and unmeaning rant about 'angels and ministers of grace,' — rant such as no madman short of a Nat Lee, or an 'Oppodeldoc,' could possibly perpetrate. And for this trash of trash, we are modestly requested to 'pay promptly.' No, sir — no! We pay for nothing of *that* sort. Apply to the 'Hum-Drum,' the 'Lollipop,' or the 'Goosetherumfoodle.' These *periodicals* will undoubtedly accept any literary offal you may send them — and as undoubtedly *promise* to pay for it."

This was bitter indeed upon poor "Oppodeldoc"; but, in this instance, the weight of the satire falls upon the "Hum-Drum," the "Lollipop," and the "Goosetherumfoodle," who are pungently styled *"periodicals"* — in Italics, too — a thing that must have cut them to the heart.

Scarcely less savage was the "Lollipop," which thus discoursed:

"Some *individual*, who rejoices in the appellation 'Oppodeldoc,' (to what low uses are the names of the illustrious dead too often applied!) has enclosed us some fifty or sixty *verses* commencing after this fashion:

'Achilles' wrath, to Greece the direful spring
Of woes unnumbered, &c., &c., &c., &c.'

" 'Oppodeldoc' (whoever he is) is respectfully informed that there is not a printer's devil in our office who is not in the daily habit of composing better *lines*. Those of 'Oppodeldoc' will not *scan*. 'Oppodeldoc' should learn to *count*. But why he should have conceived the idea that *we* (of all others, *we!*) would disgrace our pages with his ineffable nonsense is utterly beyond comprehension. Why, the absurd twattle is scarcely good enough for the 'Hum-Drum,' the 'Rowdy-Dow,' the 'Goosetherum-foodle,' — things that are in the practice of publishing 'Mother Goose's Melodies' as original lyrics. And 'Oppodeldoc' (whoever he is) has even the assurance to demand *pay* for this drivel. Does 'Oppodeldoc' (whoever he is) know — is he aware that we could not be paid to insert it?"

As I perused this I felt myself growing gradually smaller and smaller, and when I came to the point at which the editor sneered at the poem as *"verses,"* there was little more than an ounce of me left. As for "Oppodeldoc," I began to experience *compassion* for the poor fellow. But the "Goosetherumfoodle" showed, if possible, less mercy than the "Lollipop." It was the "Goosetherumfoodle" that said —

"A wretched poetaster, who signs himself 'Oppodeldoc,' is silly enough to fancy that *we* will print and *pay for* a medley of incoherent and un-grammatical bombast which he has transmitted to us, and which com-mences with the following most *intelligible* line:

'Hail, Holy Light! Offspring of Heaven, first born.'

"We say, 'most *intelligible*.' 'Oppodeldoc' (whoever he is) will be kind enough to tell us, perhaps, how '*hail*' can be '*holy light*.' We always re-garded it as *frozen rain*. Will he inform us, also, how frozen rain can be, at one and the same time, both 'holy light' (whatever that is) and an 'off-spring'? — which latter term (if we understand anything about Eng-lish) is only employed, with propriety, in reference to small babies of about six weeks old. But it is preposterous to descant upon such absurdity — although 'Oppodeldoc' (whoever he is) has the unparalled effrontery

to suppose that we will not only 'insert' his ignorant ravings, but (absolutely) *pay for them!*

"Now this is fine — it is rich! — and we have half a mind to punish this young scribbler for his egotism by really publishing his effusion *verbatim et literatim*, as he has written it. We could inflict no punishment so severe, and we *would* inflict it, but for the boredom which we should cause our readers in so doing.

"Let 'Oppodeldoc' (whoever he is) send any future *composition* of like character to the 'Hum-Drum,' the 'Lollipop,' or the 'Rowdy-Dow.' *They* will 'insert' it. *They* 'insert' every month just such stuff. Send it to them. WE are not to be insulted with impunity."

This made an end of me; and as for the "Hum-Drum," the "Rowdy-Dow," and the "Lollipop," I never could comprehend how they survived it. The putting *them* in the smallest possible *minion*, (that was the rub — thereby insinuating their lowness — their baseness,) while WE stood looking upon them in gigantic capitals! — oh it was *too* bitter! — it was wormwood — it was gall. Had I been either of these periodicals I would have spared no pains to have the "Goosetherumfoodle" prosecuted. It might have been done under the Act for the "Prevention of Cruelty to Animals." As for Oppodeldoc (whoever he was), I had by this time lost all patience with the fellow, and sympathized with him no longer. He was a fool, beyond doubt, (whoever he was,) and got not a kick more than he deserved.

The result of my experiment with the old books convinced me, in the first place, that "honesty is the best policy," and, in the second, that if I could not write better than Mr. Dante, and the two blind men, and the rest of the old set, it would, at least, be a difficult matter to write worse. I took heart, therefore, and determined to prosecute the "entirely original" (as they say on the covers of the magazines), at whatever cost of study and pains. I again placed before my eyes, as a model, the brilliant stanzas on "The Oil-of-Bob" by the editor of the "Gad-Fly" and resolved to construct an ode on the same sublime theme, in rivalry of what had already been done.

With my first line I had no material difficulty. It ran thus:

"*To pen an Ode upon the 'Oil-of-Bob.'*"

Having carefully looked out, however, all the legitimate rhymes to "Bob," I found it impossible to proceed. In this dilemma I had recourse to paternal aid; and, after some hours of mature thought, my father and myself thus constructed the poem:

"*To pen an Ode upon the 'Oil-of-Bob'*
Is all sorts of a job.
(Signed) SNOB."

To be sure, this composition was of no very great length, — but I "have yet to learn," as they say in the "Edinburgh Review," that the mere ex‑ tent of a literary work has anything to do with its merit. As for the Quar‑ terly cant about "sustained effort," it is impossible to see the sense of it. Upon the whole, therefore, I was satisfied with the success of my maiden attempt, and now the only question regarded the disposal I should make of it. My father suggested that I should send it to the "Gad‑ Fly," — but there were two reasons which operated to prevent me from so doing. I dreaded the jealousy of the editor — and I had ascertained that he did not pay for original contributions. I therefore, after due de‑ liberation, consigned the article to the more dignified pages of the "Lolli‑ pop" and awaited the event in anxiety, but with resignation.

In the very next published number I had the proud satisfaction of seeing my poem printed at length, as the leading article, with the follow‑ ing significant words, prefixed in italics and between brackets:

[*We call the attention of our readers to the subjoined admirable stanzas on "The Oil-of-Bob." We need say nothing of their sublimity, or of their pathos: — it is impossible to peruse them without tears. Those who have been nauseated with a sad dose on the same august topic from the goose-quill of the editor of the "Gad-Fly," will do well to compare the two compositions.*

P. S. — We are consumed with anxiety to probe the mystery which envelops the evident pseudonym "Snob." May we hope for a personal interview?]

All this was scarcely more than justice, but it was, I confess, rather more than I had expected: — I acknowledge this, be it observed, to the everlasting disgrace of my country and of mankind. I lost no time, how‑ ever, in calling upon the editor of the "Lollipop" and had the good fortune to find this gentleman at home. He saluted me with an air of pro‑ found respect, slightly blended with a fatherly and patronizing admira‑ tion, wrought in him, no doubt, by my appearance of extreme youth and inexperience. Begging me to be seated, he entered at once upon the sub‑ ject of my poem; — but modesty will ever forbid me to repeat the thou‑ sand compliments which he lavished upon me. The eulogies of Mr. Crab (such was the editor's name) were, however, by no means fulsomely in‑ discriminate. He analyzed my composition with much freedom and great ability — not hesitating to point out a few trivial defects — a circum‑ stance which elevated him highly in my esteem. The "Gad-Fly" was, of course, brought upon the *tapis*, and I hope never to be subjected to a criticism so searching, or to rebukes so withering, as were bestowed by Mr. Crab upon that unhappy effusion. I had been accustomed to regard the editor of the "Gad-Fly" as something superhuman; but Mr. Crab

soon disabused me of that idea. He set the literary as well as the personal character of the Fly (so Mr. C. satirically designated the rival editor), in its true light. He, the Fly, was very little better than he should be. He had written infamous things. He was a penny-a-liner, and a buffoon. He was a villain. He had composed a tragedy which set the whole country in a guffaw, and a farce which deluged the universe in tears. Besides all this, he had the impudence to pen what he meant for a lampoon upon himself (Mr. Crab), and the temerity to style him "an ass." Should I at any time wish to express my opinion of Mr. Fly, the pages of the "Lollipop," Mr. Crab assured me, were at my unlimited disposal. In the meantime, as it was very certain that I would be attacked in the "Fly" for my attempt at composing a rival poem on the "Oil-of-Bob," he (Mr. Crab) would take it upon himself to attend, pointedly, to my private and personal interests. If I were not made a man of at once, it should not be the fault of himself (Mr. Crab).

Mr. Crab having now paused in his discourse (the latter portion of which I found it impossible to comprehend), I ventured to suggest something about the remuneration which I had been taught to expect for my poem, by an announcement on the cover of the "Lollipop," declaring that it (the "Lollipop") "insisted upon being permitted to pay exorbitant prices for all accepted contributions, — frequently expending more money for a single brief poem than the whole annual cost of the 'Hum-Drum,' the 'Rowdy-Dow,' and the 'Goosetherumfoodle' combined."

As I mentioned the word "remuneration," Mr. Crab first opened his eyes, and then his mouth, to quite a remarkable extent, causing his personal appearance to resemble that of a highly agitated elderly duck in the act of quacking; and in this condition he remained (ever and anon pressing his hinds tightly to his forehead, as if in a state of desperate bewilderment) until I had nearly made an end of what I had to say.

Upon my conclusion, he sank back into his seat, as if much overcome, letting his arms fall lifelessly by his side, but keeping his mouth still rigorously open, after the fashion of the duck. While I remained in speechless astonishment at behavior so alarming he suddenly leaped to his feet and made a rush at the bell-rope; but just as he reached this, he appeared to have altered his intention, whatever it was, for he dived under a table and immediately re-appeared with a cudgel. This he was in the act of uplifting (for what purpose I am at a loss to imagine), when all at once, there came a benign smile over his features, and he sank placidly back in his chair.

"Mr. Bob," he said, (for I had sent up my card before ascending myself,) "Mr. Bob, you are a young man, I presume — *very*?"

I assented; adding that I had not yet concluded my third lustrum.

"Ah!" he replied, "very good! I see how it is — say no more! Touching this matter of compensation, what you observe is very just, — in fact it

is excessively so. But ah — ah — the *first* contribution — the *first*, I say — it is never the Magazine custom to pay for, — you comprehend, eh? The truth is, we are usually the *recipients* in such case." [Mr. Crab smiled blandly as he emphasized the word "recipients."] "for the most part, we are *paid* for the insertion of a maiden attempt — especially in verse. In the second place, Mr. Bob, the Magazine rule is never to disburse what we term in France the *argent comptant:* — I have no doubt you understand. In a quarter or two after publication of the article — or in a year or two — we make no objection to giving our note at nine months; provided, always, that we can so arrange our affairs as to be quite certain of a 'burst up' in six. I really *do* hope, Mr. Bob, that you will look upon this explanation as satisfactory." Here Mr. Crab concluded, and the tears stood in his eyes.

Grieved to the soul at having been, however innocently, the cause of pain to so eminent and so sensitive a man, I hastened to apologize, and to reassure him, by expressing my perfect coincidence with his views, as well as my entire appreciation of the delicacy of his position. Having done all this in a neat speech, I look leave.

One fine morning, very shortly afterwards, "I awoke and found myself famous." The extent of my renown will be best estimated by reference to the editorial opinions of the day. These opinions, it will be seen, were embodied in critical notices of the number of the "Lollipop" containing my poem, and are perfectly satisfactory, conclusive, and clear with the exception, perhaps, of the hieroglyphical marks, "*Sep.* 15 — 1 *t*," appended to each of the critiques.

The "Owl," a journal of profound sagacity, and well known for the deliberate gravity of its literary decisions — the "Owl," I say, spoke as follows:

"The Lollipop! The October number of this delicious Magazine surpasses its predecessors, and sets competition at defiance. In the beauty of its typography and paper — in the number and excellence of its steel plates — as well as in the literary merit of its contributions — the 'Lollipop' compares with its slow-paced rivals as Hyperion with Satyr. The 'Hum-Drum,' the 'Rowdy-Dow,' and the 'Goosetherumfoodle,' excel, it is true, in braggadocio, but in all other points, give us the 'Lollipop'! How this celebrated journal can sustain its evidently tremendous expenses, is more than we can understand. To be sure, it has a circulation of 100,000, and its subscription list has increased one fourth during the last month; but, on the other hand, the sums it disburses constantly for contributions are inconceivable. It is reported that Mr. Slyass received no less than thirty-seven and a half cents for his inimitable paper on 'Pigs.' With Mr. Crab, as editor, and with such names upon the list of contributors as Snob and Slyass, there can be no such word as 'fail' for the 'Lollipop.' Go and subscribe. *Sep.* 15 — 1 *t.*"

I must say that I was gratified with this high-toned notice from a paper so respectable as the "Owl." The placing my name — that is to say, my *nom de guerre* — in priority of station to that of the great Slyass, was a compliment as happy as I felt it to be deserved.

My attention was next arrested by these paragraphs in the "Toad" — a print highly distinguished for its uprightness and independence — for its entire freedom from sycophancy and subservience to the givers of dinners:

"The 'Lollipop' for October is out in advance of all its contemporaries, and infinitely surpasses them, of course, in the splendor of its embellishments, as well as in the richness of its contents. The 'Hum-Drum,' the 'Rowdy-Dow,' and the 'Goosetherumfoodle' excel, we admit, in braggadocio, but, in all other points, give us the 'Lollipop.' How this celebrated Magazine can sustain its evidently tremendous expenses is more than we can understand. To be sure, it has a circulation of 200,000, and its subscription list has increased one third during the last fortnight, but, on the other hand, the sums it disburses, monthly, for contributions, are fearfully great. We learn that Mr. Mumblethumb received no less than fifty cents for his late 'Monody in a Mud-Puddle.'

"Among the original contributors to the present number we notice (besides the eminent editor, Mr. CRAB), such men as SNOB, Slyass, and Mumblethumb. Apart from the editorial matter, the most valuable paper, nevertheless, is, we think, a poetical gem by Snob, on the 'Oil-of-Bob,' — but our readers must not suppose, from the title of this incomparable *bijou*, that it bears any similitude to some balderdash on the same subject by a certain contemptible individual whose name is unmentionable to ears polite. The *present* poem 'On the Oil-of-Bob,' has excited universal anxiety and curiosity in respect to the owner of the evident pseudonym, 'Snob,' — a curiosity which, happily, we have it in our power to satisfy. 'Snob' is the *nom de plume* of Mr. Thingum Bob, of this city, — a relative of the great Mr. Thingum (after whom he is named), and otherwise connected with the most illustrious families of the State. His father, Thomas Bob, Esq., is an opulent merchant in Smug. *Sep. 15 — 1 t.*"

This generous approbation touched me to the heart — the more especially as it emanated from a source so avowedly — so proverbially pure as the "Toad." The word "balderdash," as applied to the "Oil-of-Bob" of the Fly, I considered singularly pungent and appropriate. The words "gem" and "*bijou*," however, used in reference to my composition, struck me as being, in some degree, feeble. They seemed to me to be deficient in force. They were not sufficiently *prononces* (as we have it in France).

I had hardly finished reading the "Toad," when a friend placed in my hands a copy of the "Mole," a daily, enjoying high reputation for the

keenness of its perception about matters in general, and for the open, honest, above-ground style of its editorials. The "Mole" spoke of the "Lollypop" as follows:

"We have just received the 'Lollipop' for October, and *must* say that never before have we perused any single number of any periodical which afforded us a felicity so supreme. We speak advisedly. The 'Hum-Drum,' the 'Rowdy-Dow,' and the 'Goosetherumfoodle' must look well to their laurels. These prints, no doubt, surpass everything in loud-ness of pretension, but, in all other points, give us the 'Lollipop'! How this celebrated Magazine can sustain its evidently tremendous expenses, is more than we can comprehend. To be sure, it has a circulation of 300,000; and its subscription list has increased one half within the last week, but then the sum it disburses, monthly, for contributions, is as-toundingly enormous. We have it upon good authority that Mr. Fatquack received no less than sixty-two cents and a half for his late Domestic Nouvellette, the 'Dish-Clout.'

"The contributors to the number before us are Mr. CRAB (the eminent editor), SNOB, Mumblethumb, Fatquack, and others; but, after the in-imitable compositions of the editor himself, we prefer a diamond-like effusion from the pen of a rising poet who writes over the signature 'Snob' — a *nom de guerre* which we predict will one day extinguish the radiance of 'Boz.' 'SNOB,' we learn, is a Mr. THINGUM BOB, Esq., sole heir of a wealthy merchant of this city, Thomas Bob, Esq., and a near relative of the distinguished Mr. Thingum. The title of Mr. B.'s admirable poem is the 'Oil-of-Bob' — a somewhat unfortunate name, by-the-bye, as some contemptible vagabond connected with the penny press has already dis-gusted the town with a great deal of drivel upon the same topic. There will be no danger, however, of confounding the compositions. *Sep.* 15 —1 *t.*"

The generous approbation of so clear-sighted a journal as the "Mole" penetrated my soul with delight. The only objection which occurred to me was, that the terms "contemptible vagabond" might have been bet-ter written "*odious and* contemptible *wretch, villain, and* vagabond." This would have sounded more graceful, I think. "Diamond-like," also, was scarcely, it will be admitted, of sufficient intensity to express what the "Mole" evidently *thought* of the brilliancy of the "Oil-of-Bob."

On the same afternoon in which I saw these notices in the "Owl," the "Toad," and the "Mole," I happened to meet with a copy of the "Daddy-Long-Legs," a periodical proverbial for the extreme extent of its under-standing. And it was the "Daddy-Long-Legs" which spoke thus:

"The 'Lollipop'!! This gorgeous Magazine is already before the public for October. The question of pre-eminence is forever put to rest, and

hereafter it will be excessively preposterous in the 'Hum-Drum,' the 'Rowdy-Dow,' or the 'Goosetherumfoodle' to make any further spasmodic attempts at competition. These journals may excel the 'Lollipop' in outcry, but, in all other points, give us the 'Lollipop'! How this celebrated Magazine can sustain its evidently tremendous expenses, is past comprehension. To be sure it has a circulation of precisely half a million, and its subscription list has increased seventy-five per cent. within the last couple of days, but then the sums it disburses, monthly, for contributions, are scarcely credible; we are cognizant of the fact, that Mademoiselle Cribalittle received no less than eighty-seven cents and a half for her late valuable Revolutionary Tale, entitled 'The York-Town Katy-Did, and the Bunker-Hill Katy-Didn't.'

"The most able papers in the present number are, of course, those furnished by the editor (the eminent Mr. CRAB), but there are numerous magnificent contributions from such names as SNOB, Mademoiselle Cribalittle, Slyass, Mrs. Fibalittle, Mumblethumb, Mrs. Squibalittle, and last, though not least, Fatquack. The world may well be challenged to produce so rich a galaxy of genius.

"The poem over the signature, 'SNOB' is, we find, attracting universal commendation, and, we are constrained to say, deserves, if possible, even more applause than it has received. The 'Oil-of-Bob' is the title of this masterpiece of eloquence and art. One or two of our readers *may* have a *very* faint, although sufficiently disgusting recollection of a poem (?) similarly entitled, the perpetration of a miserable penny-a-liner, mendicant, and cut-throat, connected in the capacity of scullion, we believe, with one of the indecent prints about the purlieus of the city; we beg them, for God's sake, not to confound the compositions. The author of *the* 'Oil-of-Bob' is, we hear, THINGUM BOB, Esq., a gentleman of high genius, and a scholar. 'Snob' is merely a *nom de guerre. Sep.* 15. — 1 *t.*"

I could scarcely restrain my indignation while I perused the concluding portions of this diatribe. It was clear to me that the yea-nay manner — not to say the gentleness, — the positive forbearance — with which the "Daddy-Long-Legs" spoke of that pig, the editor of the "Gad-Fly," — it was evident to me, I say, that this gentleness of speech could proceed from nothing else than a partiality for the "Fly" — whom it was clearly the intention of the "Daddy-Long-Legs" to elevate into reputation at my expense. Any one, indeed, might perceive, with half an eye, that, had the real design of the "Daddy" been what it wished to appear, it (the "Daddy") might have expressed itself in terms more direct, more pungent, and altogether more to the purpose. The words "penny-a-liner," "mendicant," "scullion," and "cut-throat," were epithets so intentionally inexpressive and equivocal, as to be worse than nothing when applied to the author of the very worst stanzas ever penned by one of the human race. We all know what is meant by "damning with faint praise," and,

on the other hand, who could fail seeing through the covert purpose of the "Daddy," — that of glorifying with feeble abuse?

What the "Daddy" chose to say to the "Fly," however, was no business of mine. What it said of myself *was*. After the noble manner in which the "Owl," the "Toad," the "Mole," had expressed themselves in respect to my ability, it was rather too much to be coolly spoken of by a thing like the "Daddy-Long-Legs," as merely "a gentleman of high genius and a scholar." Gentleman indeed! I made up my mind at once either to get a written apology from the "Daddy-Long-Legs," or to call it out.

Full of this purpose, I looked about me to find a friend whom I could entrust with a message to his "Daddy"ship, and as the editor of the "Lollipop" had given me marked tokens of regard, I at length concluded to seek assistance upon the present occasion.

I have never yet been able to account, in a manner satisfactory to my own understanding, for the *very* peculiar countenance and demeanor with which Mr. Crab listened to me, as I unfolded to him my design. He again went through the scene of the bell-rope and cudgel, and did not omit the duck. At one period I thought he really intended to quack. His fit, nevertheless, finally subsided as before, and he began to act and speak in a rational way. He declined bearing the cartel, however, and in fact, dissuaded me from sending it at all; but was candid enough to admit that the "Daddy-Long-Legs" had been disgracefully in the wrong — more especially in what related to the epithets "gentleman and scholar."

Toward the end of this interview with Mr. Crab, who really appeared to take a paternal interest in my welfare, he suggested to me that I might turn an honest penny, and at the same time, advance my reputation, by occasionally playing Thomas Hawk for the "Lollypop."

I begged Mr. Crab to inform me who was Mr. Thomas Hawk, and how it was expected that I should play him.

Here Mr. Crab again "made great eyes" (as we say in Germany), but at length, recovering himself from a profound attack of astonishment, he assured me that he employed the words "Thomas Hawk" to avoid the colloquialsm, Tommy, which was low — but that the true idea was Tommy Hawk — or tomahawk — and that by "playing tomahawk" he referred to scalping, brow-beating, and otherwise using-up the herd of poor-devil authors.

I assured my patron that, if this was all, I was perfectly resigned to the task of playing Thomas Hawk. Hereupon Mr. Crab desired me to use up the editor of the "Gad-Fly" forthwith, in the fiercest style within the scope of my ability, and as a specimen of my powers. This I did, upon the spot, in a review of the original "Oil-of-Bob," occupying thirty-six pages of the "Lollipop." I found playing Thomas Hawk, indeed, a far less onerous occupation than poetizing; for I went upon *system* altogether, and thus it was easy to do the thing thoroughly well. My practice

was this. I bought auction copies (cheap) of "Lord Brougham's Speeches," "Cobbett's Complete Works," the "New Slang-Syllabus," the "Whole Art of Snubbing," "Prentice's Billingsgate" (folio edition), and "Lewis G. Clarke on Tongue." These works I cut up thoroughly with a curry-comb, and then, throwing the shreds into a sieve, sifted out carefully all that might be thought decent (a mere trifle); reserving the hard phrases, which I threw into a large tin pepper-castor with longitudinal holes, so that an entire sentence could get through without material injury. The mixture was then ready for use. When called upon to play Thomas Hawk, I anointed a sheet of foolscap with the white of a gander's egg; then, shredding the thing to be reviewed as I had previously shredded the books — only with more care, so as to get every word separate — I threw the latter shreds in with the former, screwed on the lid of the castor, gave it a shake, and so dusted out the mixture upon the egged foolscap; where it stuck. The effect was beautiful to behold. It was captivating. Indeed, the reviews I brought to pass by this simple expedient have never been approached, and were the wonder of the world. At first, through bashfulness — the result of inexperience — I was a little put out by a certain inconsistency — a certain air of the *bizarre* (as we say in France), worn by the composition as a whole. All the phrases did not *fit* (as we say in the Anglo-Saxon). Many were quite awry. Some, even, were upside-down; and there were none of them which were not in some measure, injured in regard to effect, by this latter species of accident, when it occurred — with the exception of Mr. Lewis Clarke's paragraphs, which were so vigorous and altogether stout, that they seemed not particularly disconcerted by any extreme of position, but looked equally happy and satisfactory, whether on their heads, or on their heels.

What became of the editor of the "Gad-Fly" after the publication of my criticism on his "Oil-of-Bob," it is somewhat difficult to determine. The most reasonable conclusion is, that he wept himself to death. At all events he disappeared instantaneously from the face of the earth, and no man has seen even the ghost of him since.

This matter having been properly accomplished, and the Furies appeased, I grew at once into high favor with Mr. Crab. He took me into his confidence, gave me a permanent situation as Thomas Hawk of the "Lollipop," and, as for the present, he could afford me no salary, allowed me to profit, at discretion, by his advice.

"My dear Thingum," said he to me one day after dinner, "I respect your abilities and love you as a son. You shall be my heir. When I die I will bequeath you the "Lollipop." In the meantime I will make a man of you — I *will* — provided always that you follow my counsel. The first thing to do is to get rid of the old bore."

"Boar?" said I inquiringly — "pig, eh? — *aper?* (as we say in Latin) — who? — where?"

"Your father," said he.

"Precisely," I replied — "pig."

"You have your fortune to make, Thingum," resumed Mr. Crab, "and that governor of yours is a millstone about your neck. We must cut him at once." [Here I took out my knife.] "We must cut him," continued Mr. Crab, "decidedly and forever. He won't do — he *won't*. Upon second thoughts, you had better kick him, or cane him, or something of that kind."

"What do you say," I suggested modestly, "to my kicking him in the first instance, caning him afterward, and winding up by tweaking his nose?"

Mr. Crab looked at me musingly for some moments, and then answered:

"I think, Mr. Bob, that what you propose would answer sufficiently well — indeed remarkably well — that is to say, as far as it went — but barbers are exceedingly hard to cut, and I think, upon the whole, that, having performed upon Thomas Bob the operations you suggest, it would be advisable to blacken, with your fists, both his eyes, very carefully and thoroughly, to prevent his ever seeing you again in fashionable promenades. After doing this, I really do not perceive that you can do any more. However — it might be just as well to roll him once or twice in the gutter, and then put him in charge of the police. Any time the next morning you can call at the watch-house and swear an assault."

I was much affected by the kindness of feeling toward me personally, which was evinced in this excellent advice of Mr. Crab, and I did not fail to profit by it forthwith. The result was, that I got rid of the old bore, and began to feel a little independent and gentleman-like. The want of money, however, was, for a few weeks, a source of some discomfort; but at length, by carefully putting to use my two eyes, and observing how matters went just in front of my nose, I perceived how the thing was to be brought about. I say "thing" — be it observed — for they tell me in the Latin for it is *rem*. By the way, talking of Latin, can any one tell me the meaning of *quocunque* — or what is the meaning of *modo*?

My plan was exceedingly simple. I bought, for a song, a sixteenth of the "Snapping-Turtle": — that was all. The thing was *done*, and I put money in my purse. There were some trivial arrangements afterward, to be sure; but these formed no portion of the plan. They were a consequence — a result. For example, I bought pen, ink, and paper, and put them into furious activity. Having thus completed a Magazine article, I gave it, for appellation, "FOL LOL, *by the Author of* 'THE OIL-OF-BOB,'" and enveloped it to the "Goosetherumfoodle." That journal, however, having pronounced it "twattle" in the "Monthly Notices to Correspondents," I reheaded the paper " 'Hey-Diddle-Diddle," by THINGUM BOB, Esq., Author of the Ode on 'The Oil-of-Bob,' *and* Editor of the 'Snapping-Turtle.' " With this amendment, I re-enclosed it to the "Goosetherumfoodle," and, while I awaited a reply, published daily, in the "Turtle," six

columns of what may be termed philosophical and analytical investiga-
tion of the literary merits of the "Goosetherumfoodle," as well as of the
personal character of the editor of the "Goosetherumfoodle. At the end
of a week the "Goosetherumfoodle" discovered that it had, by some odd
mistake, "confounded a stupid article, headed 'Hey-Diddle-Diddle,' and
composed by some unknown ignoramus, with a gem of resplendent lus-
tre similarly entitled, the work of Thingum Bob, Esq., the celebrated
author of 'The Oil-of-Bob.'" The "Goosetherumfoodle" deeply "re-
gretted this very natural accident," and promised, moreover, an insertion
of the *genuine* "Hey-Diddle-Diddle" in the very next number of the
Magazine.

The fact is, I *thought* — I *really* thought — I thought at the time — I
thought *then* — and have no reason for thinking otherwise *now* — that
the "Goosetherumfoodle" *did* make a mistake. With the best intentions
in the world, I never knew any thing that made as many singular mis-
takes as the "Goosetherumfoodle." From that day I took a liking to the
"Goosetherumfoodle, and the result was I soon saw into the very depths
of its literary merits, and did not fail to expatiate upon them, in the "Tur-
tle," whenever a fitting opportunity occurred. And it is to be regarded
as a very peculiar coincidence — as one of those positively *remarkable*
coincidences which set a man to serious thinking — that just such a total
revolution of opinion — just such entire *bouleversement* (as we say in
French) — just such thorough *topsiturviness* (if I may be permitted to
employ a rather forcible term of the Choctaws), as happened, *pro* and
con, between myself on the one part, and the "Goosetherumfoodle" on
the other, did actually again happen, in a brief period afterwards, and
with precisely similar circumstances, in the case of myself and the
"Rowdy-Dow," and in the case of myself and the "Hum-Drum."

Thus it was that, by a master-stroke of genius, I at length consummated
my triumphs by "putting money in my purse," and thus may be said really
and fairly to have commenced that brilliant and eventful career which
rendered me illustrious, and which now enables me to say with Chateau-
briand: "I have made history" — "*J'ai fait l' histoire.*"

I have indeed "made history." From the bright epoch which I now re-
cord, my actions — my works — are the property of mankind. They are fa-
miliar to the world. It is, then, needless for me to detail how, soaring
rapidly, I fell heir to the "Lollipop" — how I merged this journal in the
"Hum-Drum" — how again I made purchase of the "Rowdy-Dow," thus
combining the three periodicals — how lastly, I effected a bargain for the
sole remaining rival, and united all the literature of the country in one
magnificent Magazine known everywhere as the

Rowdy-Dow, Lollipop. Hum-Drum,
and
GOOSETHERUMFOODLE.

Yes; I have made history. My fame is universal. It extends to the utter-most ends of the earth. You cannot take up a common newspaper in which you shall not see some allusion to the immortal THINGUM BOB. It is Mr. Thingum Bob said so, and Mr. Thingum Bob wrote this, and Mr. Thingum Bob did that. But I am meek and expire with an humble heart. After all, what is it? — this indescribable something which men will persist in terming "genius"? I agree with Buffon — with Hogarth — it is but *diligence* after all.

Look at *me!* — how I labored — how I toiled — how I wrote! Ye Gods, did I *not* write? I knew not the word "ease." By day I adhered to my desk, and at night, a pale student, I consumed the midnight oil. You should have seen me — you *should*. I leaned to the right. I leaned to the left. I sat forward. I sat backward. I sat *tête baissée* (as they have it in the Kickapoo), bowing my head close to the alabaster page. And, through all, I — *wrote*. Through joy and through sorrow, I — *wrote*. Through hun-ger and through thirst, I — *wrote*. Through good report and through ill report — I *wrote*. Through sunshine and through moonshine, I — *wrote*. *What* I wrote it is unnecessary to say. The *style!* — that was the thing. I caught it from Fatquack — whizz! — fizz! — and I am giving you a specimen of it now.

The Purloined Letter

Nil sapientiae odiosius acumine nimio.

SENECA.

AT Paris, just after dark one gusty evening in the autumn of 18—, I was enjoying the twofold luxury of meditation and a meerschaum, in com-pany with my friend, C. Auguste Dupin, in his little back library, or book-closet, *au troisiême*, No. 33 *Rue Dunôt, Faubourg St. Germain*. For one hour at least we had maintained a profound silence; while each, to any casual observer, might have seemed intently and exclusively occupied with the curling eddies of smoke that oppressed the atmosphere of the chamber. For myself, however, I was mentally discussing certain topics which had formed matter for conversation between us at an earlier period of the evening; I mean the affair of the Rue Morgue, and the mystery attending the murder of Marie Rogêt. I looked upon it, therefore, as something of a coincidence, when the door of our apartment was thrown open and admitted our old acquaintance, Monsieur G——, the Prefect of the Parisian police.

We gave him a hearty welcome; for there was nearly half as much

of the entertaining as of the contemptible about the man, and we had not seen him for several years. We had been sitting in the dark, and Dupin now arose for the purpose of lighting a lamp, but sat down again, without doing so, upon G.'s saying that he had called to consult us, or rather to ask the opinion of my friend, about some official business which had occasioned a great deal of trouble.

"If it is any point requiring reflection," observed Dupin, as he fore-bore to enkindle the wick, "we shall examine it to better purpose in the dark."

"That is another of your odd notions," said the Prefect, who had the fashion of calling every thing "odd" that was beyond his comprehension, and thus lived amid an absolute legion of "oddities."

"Very true," said Dupin, as he supplied his visiter with a pipe, and rolled toward him a comfortable chair.

"And what is the difficulty now?" I asked. "Nothing more in the assassination way I hope?"

"Oh, no; nothing of that nature. The fact is, the business is *very* simple indeed, and I make no doubt that we can manage it sufficiently well ourselves; but then I thought Dupin would like to hear the details of it, because it is so excessively *odd*."

"Simple and odd," said Dupin.

"Why, yes; and not exactly that either. The fact is, we have all been a good deal puzzled because the affair *is* so simple, and yet baffles us altogether."

"Perhaps it is the very simplicity of the thing which puts you at fault," said my friend.

"What nonsense you *do* talk!" replied the Prefect, laughing heartily.

"Perhaps the mystery is a little *too* plain," said Dupin.

"Oh, good heavens! who ever heard of such an idea?"

"A little *too* self-evident."

"Ha! ha! ha! — ha! ha! ha! — ho! ho! ho!" roared our visitor, pro-foundly amused, "oh, Dupin, you will be the death of me yet!"

"And what, after all, *is* the matter on hand?" I asked.

"Why, I will tell you," replied the Prefect, as he gave a long, steady, and contemplative puff, and settled himself in his chair. "I will tell you in a few words; but, before I begin, let me caution you that this is an affair demanding the greatest secrecy, and that I should most probably lose the position I now hold, were it known that I confided it to any one."

"Proceed," said I.

"Or not," said Dupin.

"Well, then; I have received personal information, from a very high quarter, that a certain document of the last importance has been pur-loined from the royal apartments. The individual who purloined it is known; this beyond a doubt; he was seen to take it. It is known, also, that it still remains in his possession."

"How is this known?" asked Dupin.

"It is clearly inferred," replied the Prefect, "from the nature of the document, and from the non-appearance of certain results which would at once arise from its passing *out* of the robber's possession; — that is to say, from his employing it as he must design in the end to employ it."

"Be a little more explicit," I said.

"Well, I may venture so far as to say that the paper gives its holder a certain power in a certain quarter where such power is immensely valuable." The Prefect was fond of the cant of diplomacy.

"Still I do not quite understand," said Dupin.

"No? Well; the disclosure of the document to a third person, who shall be nameless, would bring in question the honor of a personage of most exalted station; and this fact gives the holder of the document an ascendancy over the illustrious personage whose honor and peace are so jeopardized."

"But this ascendancy," I interposed, "would depend upon the robber's knowledge of the loser's knowledge of the robber. Who would dare — "

"The thief," said G., "is the Minister D——, who dares all things, those unbecoming as well as those becoming a man. The method of the theft was not less ingenious than bold. The document in question — a letter, to be frank — had been received by the personage robbed while alone in the royal *boudoir*. During its perusal she was suddenly interrupted by the entrance of the other exalted personage from whom especially it was her wish to conceal it. After a hurried and vain endeavor to thrust it in a drawer, she was forced to place it, open as it was, upon a table. The address, however, was uppermost, and, the contents thus unexposed, the letter escaped notice. At this juncture enters the Minister D——. His lynx eye immediately perceives the paper, recognizes the handwriting of the address, observes the confusion of the personage addressed, and fathoms her secret. After some business transactions, hurried through in his ordinary manner, he produces a letter somewhat similar to the one in question, opens it, pretends to read it, and then places it in close juxtaposition to the other. Again he converses, for some fifteen minutes, upon the public affairs. At length, in taking leave, he takes also from the table the letter to which he had no claim. Its rightful owner saw, but, of course, dared not call attention to the act, in the presence of the third personage who stood at her elbow. The minister decamped; leaving his own letter — one of no importance — upon the table."

"Here, then," said Dupin to me, "you have precisely what you demand to make the ascendancy complete — the robber's knowledge of the loser's knowledge of the robber."

"Yes," replied the Prefect; "and the power thus attained has, for some months past, been wielded, for political purposes, to a very dangerous

extent. The personage robbed is more thoroughly convinced, every day, of the necessity of reclaiming her letter. But this, of course, cannot be done openly. In fine, driven to despair, she has committed the matter to me."

"Than whom," said Dupin, amid a perfect whirlwind of smoke, "no more sagacious agent could, I suppose, be desired, or even imagined."

"You flatter me," replied the Prefect; "but it is possible that some such opinion may have been entertained."

"It is clear," said I, "as you observe, that the letter is still in the possession of the minister; since it is this possession, and not any employment of the letter, which bestows the power. With the employment the power departs."

"True," said G.; "and upon this conviction I proceeded. My first care was to make thorough search of the minister's hotel; and here my chief embarrassment lay in the necessity of searching without his knowledge. Beyond all things, I have been warned of the danger which would result from giving him reason to suspect our design."

"But," said I, "you are quite *au fait* in these investigations. The Parisian police have done this thing often before."

"Oh, yes; and for this reason I did not despair. The habits of the minister gave me, too, a great advantage. He is frequently absent from home all night. His servants are by no means numerous. They sleep at a distance from their master's apartment, and, being chiefly Neapolitans, are readily made drunk. I have keys, as you know, with which I can open any chamber or cabinet in Paris. For three months a night has not passed, during the greater part of which I have not been engaged, personally, in ransacking the D—— Hotel. My honor is interested, and, to mention a great secret, the reward is enormous. So I did not abandon the search until I had become fully satisfied that the thief is a more astute man than myself. I fancy that I have investigated every nook and corner of the premises in which it is possible that the paper can be concealed."

"But is it not possible," I suggested, "that although the letter may be in possession of the minister, as it unquestionably is, he may have concealed it elsewhere than upon his own premises?"

"This is barely possible," said Dupin. "The present peculiar condition of affairs at court, and especially of those intrigues in which D—— is known to be involved, would render the instant availability of the document — its susceptibility of being produced at a moment's notice — a point of nearly equal importance with its possession."

"Its susceptibility of being produced?" said I.

"That is to say, of being *destroyed*," said Dupin.

"True," I observed; "the paper is clearly then upon the premises. As for its being upon the person of the minister, we may consider that as out of the question."

"Entirely," said the Prefect. "He has been twice waylaid, as if by foot-pads, and his person rigorously searched under my own inspection."

"You might have spared yourself this trouble," said Dupin. "D——, I presume, is not altogether a fool, and, if not, must have anticipated these waylayings, as a matter of course."

"Not *altogether* a fool," said G., "but then he is a poet, which I take to be only one remove from a fool."

"True," said Dupin, after a long and thoughtful whiff from his meer-schaum, "although I have been guilty of certain doggerel myself."

"Suppose you detail," said I, "the particulars of your search."

"Why, the fact is, we took our time, and we searched *everywhere*. I have had long experience in these affairs. I took the entire building, room by room; devoting the nights of a whole week to each. We examined, first, the furniture of each apartment. We opened every possible drawer; and I presume you know that, to a properly trained police agent, such a thing as a 'secret' drawer is impossible. Any man is a dolt who permits a 'secret' drawer to escape him in a search of this kind. The thing is *so* plain. There is a certain amount of bulk — of space — to be accounted for in every cabinet. Then we have accurate rules. The fiftieth part of a line could not escape us. After the cabinets we took the chairs. The cushions we probed with the fine long needles you have seen me employ. From the tables we removed the tops."

"Why so?"

"Sometimes the top of a table, or other similarly arranged piece of furniture, is removed by the person wishing to conceal an article; then the leg is excavated, the article deposited within the cavity, and the top replaced. The bottoms and tops of bedposts are employed in the same way."

"But could not the cavity be detected by sounding?" I asked.

"By no means, if, when the article is deposited, a sufficient wadding of cotton be placed around it. Besides, in our case, we were obliged to proceed without noise."

"But you could not have removed — you could not have taken to pieces *all* articles of furniture in which it would have been possible to make a deposit in the manner you mention. A letter may be compressed into a thin spiral roll, not differing much in shape or bulk from a large knitting-needle, and in this form it might be inserted into the rung of a chair, for example. You did not take to pieces all the chairs?"

"Certainly not; but we did better — we examined the rungs of every chair in the hotel, and, indeed, the jointings of every description of furniture, by the aid of a most powerful microscope. Had there been any traces of recent disturbance we should not have failed to detect it instantly. A single grain of gimlet-dust, for example, would have been as obvious as an apple. Any disorder in the gluing — any unusual gaping in the joints — would have sufficed to insure detection."

"I presume you looked to the mirrors, between the boards and the plates, and you probed the beds and the bedclothes, as well as the curtains and carpets."

"That of course; and when we had absolutely completed every particle of the furniture in this way, then we examined the house itself. We divided its entire surface into compartments, which we numbered, so that none might be missed; then we scrutinized each individual square inch throughout the premises, including the two houses immediately adjoining, with the microscope, as before."

"The two houses adjoining!" I exclaimed; "you must have had a great deal of trouble."

"We had; but the reward offered is prodigious."

"You include the *grounds* about the houses?"

"All the grounds are paved with brick. They gave us comparatively little trouble. We examined the moss between the bricks, and found it undisturbed.

"You looked among D——'s papers, of course, and into the books of the library?"

"Certainly; we opened every package and parcel; we not only opened every book, but we turned over every leaf in each volume, not contenting ourselves with a mere shake, according to the fashion of some of our police officers. We also measured the thickness of every book-*cover*, with the most accurate admeasurement, and applied to each the most jealous scrutiny of the microscope. Had any of the bindings been recently meddled with, it would have been utterly impossible that the fact should have escaped observation. Some five or six volumes, just from the hands of the binder, we carefully probed, longitudinally, with the needles."

"You explored the floors beneath the carpets?"

"Beyond doubt. We removed every carpet, and examined the boards with the microscope."

"And the paper on the walls?"

"Yes."

"You looked into the cellars?"

"We did."

"Then," I said, "you have been making a miscalculation, and the letter is *not* upon the premises, as you suppose."

"I fear you are right there," said the Prefect. "And now, Dupin, what would you advise me to do?"

"To make a thorough research of the premises."

"That is absolutely needless," replied G——. "I am not more sure that I breathe than I am that the letter is not at the hotel."

"I have no better advice to give you," said Dupin. "You have, of course, an accurate description of the letter?"

"Oh, yes!" — And here the Prefect, producing a memorandum-book, proceeded to read aloud a minute account of the internal, and especially

of the external appearance of the missing document. Soon after finishing the perusal of this description, he took his departure, more entirely depressed in spirits than I had ever known the good gentleman before.

In about a month afterward he paid us another visit, and found us occupied very nearly as before. He took a pipe and a chair and entered into some ordinary conversation. At length I said:

"Well, but G——, what of the purloined letter? I presume you have at last made up your mind that there is no such thing as overreaching the Minister?"

"Confound him, say I — yes; I made the re-examination, however, as Dupin suggested — but it was all labor lost, as I knew it would be."

"How much was the reward offered, did you say?" asked Dupin.

"Why, a very great deal — a *very* liberal reward — I don't like to say how much, precisely; but one thing I *will* say, that I wouldn't mind giving my individual check for fifty thousand francs to any one who could obtain me that letter. The fact is, it is becoming of more and more importance every day; and the reward has been lately doubled. If it were trebled, however, I could do no more than I have done."

"Why, yes," said Dupin, drawlingly between the whiffs of his meerschaum. "I really — think, G——, you have not exerted yourself — to the utmost in this matter. You might — do a little more, I think, eh?"

"How? — in what way?"

"Why — puff, puff — you might — puff, puff — employ counsel in the matter, eh? — puff, puff, puff. Do you remember the story they tell of Abernethy?"

"No; hang Abernethy!"

"To be sure! hang him and welcome. But, once upon a time, a certain rich miser conceived the design of sponging upon this Abernethy for a medical opinion. Getting up, for this purpose, an ordinary conversation in a private company, he insinuated his case to the physician, as that of an imaginary individual.

" 'We will suppose,' said the miser, 'that his symptoms are such and such; now, doctor, what would *you* have directed him to take?'

" 'Take!' said Abernethy, 'why, take *advice*, to be sure.' "

"But," said the Prefect, a little discomposed, "I am *perfectly* willing to take advice, and to pay for it. I would *really* give fifty thousand francs to any one who would aid me in the matter."

"In that case," replied Dupin, opening a drawer, and producing a check-book, "you may as well fill me up a check for the amount mentioned. When you have signed it, I will hand you the letter."

I was astounded. The Prefect appeared absolutely thunder-stricken. For some minutes he remained speechless and motionless, looking incredulously at my friend with open mouth, and eyes that seemed starting from their sockets; then apparently recovering himself in some measure, he seized a pen, and after several pauses and vacant stares, finally filled

up and signed a check for fifty thousand francs, and handed it across the table to Dupin. The latter examined it carefully and deposited it in his pocket-book; then, unlocking an *escritoire*, took thence a letter and gave it to the Prefect. This functionary grasped it in a perfect agony of joy, opened it with a trembling hand, cast a rapid glance at its contents, and then scrambling and struggling to the door, rushed at length unceremoniously from the room and from the house, without having uttered a syllable since Dupin had requested him to fill up the check.

When he had gone, my friend entered into some explanations.

"The Parisian police," he said, "are exceedingly able in their way. They are persevering, ingenious, cunning, and thoroughly versed in the knowledge which their duties seem chiefly to demand. Thus, when G—— detailed to us his mode of searching the premises at the Hotel D——, I felt entire confidence in his having made a satisfactory investigation — so far as his labors extended."

"So far as his labors extended?" said I.

"Yes," said Dupin. "The measures adopted were not only the best of their kind, but carried out to absolute perfection. Had the letter been deposited within the range of their search, these fellows would, beyond a question, have found it."

I merely laughed — but he seemed quite serious in all that he said.

"The measures then," he continued, "were good in their kind, and well executed; their defect lay in their being inapplicable to the case and to the man. A certain set of highly ingenious resources are, with the Prefect, a sort of Procrustean bed, to which he forcibly adapts his designs. But he perpetually errs by being too deep or too shallow for the matter in hand; and many a schoolboy is a better reasoner than he. I knew one about eight years of age, whose success at guessing in the game of 'even and odd' attracted universal admiration. This game is simple, and is played with marbles. One player holds in his hand a number of these toys, and demands of another whether that number is even or odd. If the guess is right, the guesser wins one; if wrong, he loses one. The boy to whom I allude won all the marbles of the school. Of course he had some principle of guessing; and this lay in mere observation and admeasurement of the astuteness of his opponents. For example, an arrant simpleton is his opponent, and, holding up his closed hand, asks, 'Are they even or odd?' Our schoolboy replies, 'Odd,' and loses; but upon the second trial he wins, for he then says to himself: 'The simpleton had them even upon the first trial, and his amount of cunning is just sufficient to make him have them odd upon the second; I will therefore guess odd"; — he guesses odd, and wins. Now, with a simpleton a degree above the first, he would have reasoned thus: 'This fellow finds that in the first instance I guessed odd, and, in the second, he will propose to himself, upon the first impulse, a simple variation from even to odd, as did the first simpleton; but then a second thought will suggest that this is too

simple a variation, and finally he will decide upon putting it even as before. I will therefore guess even'; — he guesses even, and wins. Now this mode of reasoning in the schoolboy, whom his fellows termed 'lucky,' — what, in its last analysis, is it?"

"It is merely," I said, "an identification of the reasoner's intellect with that of his opponent."

"It is," said Dupin; "and, upon inquiring of the boy by what means he effected the *thorough* identification in which his success consisted, I received answer as follows: 'When I wish to find out how wise, or how stupid, or how good, or how wicked is any one, or what are his thoughts at the moment, I fashion the expression of my face, as accurately as possible, in accordance with the expression of his, and then wait to see what thoughts or sentiments arise in my mind or heart, as if to match or correspond with the expression.' This response of the schoolboy lies at the bottom of all the spurious profundity which has been attributed to Rochefoucault, to La Bougive, to Machiavelli, and to Campanella."

"And the identification," I said, "of the reasoner's intellect with that of his opponent, depends, if I understand you aright, upon the accuracy with which the opponent's intellect is admeasured."

"For its practical value it depends upon this," replied Dupin; "and the Prefect and his cohort fail so frequently, first by default of his identification, and, secondly, by ill-admeasurement, or rather through non-admeasurement, of the intellect with which they are engaged. They consider only their *own* ideas of ingenuity; and, in searching for anything hidden advert only to the modes in which *they* would have hidden it. They are right in this much — that their own ingenuity is a faithful representative of that of *the mass*; but when the cunning of the individual felon is diverse in character from their own, the felon foils them, of course. This always happens when it is above their own, and very usually when it is below. They have no variation of principle in their investigations; at best, when urged by some unusual emergency — by some extraordinary reward — they extend or exaggerate their old modes of *practice*, without touching their principles. What, for example, in this case of D——, has been done to vary the principle of action? What is all this boring, and probing, and sounding, and scrutinizing with the microscope, and dividing the surface of the building into registered square inches — what is it all but an exaggeration *of the application* of the one principle or set of principles of search, which are based upon the one set of notions regarding human ingenuity, to which the Prefect, in the long routine of his duty, has been accustomed? Do you not see he has taken it for granted that *all* men proceed to conceal a letter — not exactly in a gimlet-hole bored in a chair-leg, but, at least, in *some* out-of-the-way hole or corner suggested by the same tenor of thought which would urge a man to secrete a letter in a gimlet-hole bored in a chair-leg? And do you not see also that such *recherchés* nooks for concealment are adapted only

for ordinary occasions, and would be adopted only by ordinary intellects; for, in all cases of concealment, a disposal of the article concealed — a disposal of it in this *recherché* manner, — is in the very first instance, presumable and presumed; and thus its discovery depends, not at all upon the acumen, but altogether upon the mere care, patience, and determination of the seekers; and where the case is of importance — or, what amounts to the same thing in the political eyes, when the reward is of magnitude, — the qualities in question have *never* been known to fail. You will now understand what I meant in suggesting that, had the purloined letter been hidden anywhere within the limits of the Prefect's examination — in other words, had the principle of its concealment been comprehended within the principles of the Prefect — its discovery would have been a matter altogether beyond question. This functionary, however, has been thoroughly mystified; and the remote source of his defeat lies in the supposition that the Minister is a fool, because he has acquired renown as a poet. All fools are poets; this the Prefect feels; and he is merely guilty of a *non distributio medii* in thence inferring that all poets are fools."

"But is this really the poet?" I asked. "There are two brothers, I know; and both have attained reputation in letters. The minister I believe has written learnedly on the Differential Calculus. He is a mathematician, and no poet."

"You are mistaken; I know him well; he is both. As poet *and* mathematician, he would reason well; as mere mathematician, he could not have reasoned at all, and thus would have been at the mercy of the Prefect."

"You surprise me," I said, "by these opinions, which have been contradicted by the voice of the world. You do not mean to set at naught the well-digested idea of centuries. The mathematical reason has long been regarded as *the* reason *par excellence*."

" '*Il y à parièr*,' " replied Dupin, quoting from Chamfort, " '*que toute idée publique, toute convention reçue, est une sottise, car elle a convenue au plus grand nombre*.' The mathematicians, I grant you, have done their best to promulgate the popular error to which you allude, and which is none the less an error for its promulgation as truth. With an art worthy a better cause, for example, they have insinuated the term 'analysis' into application to algebra. The French are the originators of this particular deception; but if a term is of any importance — if words derive any value from applicability — then 'analysis' conveys 'algebra' about as much as, in Latin, '*ambitus*' implies 'ambition,' '*religio*' 'religion,' or '*homines honesti*' a set of *honorable* men."

"You have a quarrel on hand, I see," said I, "with some of the algebraists of Paris; but proceed."

"I dispute the availability, and thus the value, of that reason which is cultivated in any especial form other than the abstractly logical. I dis-

pute, in particular, the reason educed by mathematical study. The mathematics are the science of form and quantity; mathematical reasoning is merely logic applied to observation upon form and quantity. The great error lies in supposing that even the truths of what is called *pure* algebra are abstract or general truths. And this error is so egregious that I am confounded at the universality with which it has been received. Mathematical axioms are *not* axiom; of general truth. What is true of *relation* — of form and quantity — is often grossly false in regard to morals, for example. In this latter science it is very usually *untrue* that the aggregated parts are equal to the whole. In chemistry also the axiom fails. In the consideration of motive it fails; for two motives, each of a given value, have not necessarily, a value when united, equal to the sum of their values apart. There are numerous other mathematical truths which are only truths within the limits of *relation*. But the mathematician argues from his *finite truths*, through habit, as if they were of an absolutely general applicability — as the world indeed imagines them to be. Bryant, in his very learned 'Mythology,' mentions an analogous source of error, when he says that 'although the Pagan fables are not believed, yet we forget ourselves continually, and make inferences from them as existing realities.' With the algebraists, however, who are Pagans themselves, the 'Pagan fables' *are* believed, and the inferences are made, not so much through lapse of memory as through an unaccountable addling of the brains. In short, I never yet encountered the mere mathematician who could be trusted out of equal roots, or one who did not clandestinely hold it as a point of his faith that $x^2 + px$ was absolutely and unconditionally equal to q. Say to one of these gentlemen, by way of experiment, if you please, that you believe occasions may occur where $x^2 + px$ is not altogether equal to q, and, having made him understand what you mean, get out of his reach as speedily as convenient, for, beyond doubt, he will endeavor to knock you down.

"I mean to say," continued Dupin, while I merely laughed at his last observations, "that if the Minister had been no more than a mathematician, the Prefect would have been under no necessity of giving me this check. I knew him, however, as both mathematician and poet, and my measures were adapted to his capacity, with reference to the circumstances by which he was surrounded. I knew him as a courtier, too, and as a bold *intriguant*. Such a man, I considered, could not fail to be aware of the ordinary political modes of action. He could not have failed to anticipate — and events have proved that he did not fail to anticipate — the waylayings to which he was subjected. He must have foreseen, I reflected, the secret investigations of his premises. His frequent absences from home at night, which were hailed by the Prefect as certain aids to his success, I regarded only as *ruses*, to afford opportunity for thorough search to the police, and thus the sooner to impress them with the conviction to which G——, in fact, did finally arrive — the conviction that

the letter was not upon the premises. I felt, also, that the whole train of thought, which I was at some pains in detailing to you just now, concerning the invariable principle of political action in searches for articles concealed — I felt that this whole train of thought would necessarily pass through the mind of the Minister. It would imperatively lead him to despise all the ordinary *nooks* of concealment. *He* could not, I reflected, be so weak as not to see that the most intricate and remote recess of his hotel would be as open as his commonest closets to the eyes, to the probes, to the gimlets, and to the microscopes of the Prefect. I saw, in fine, that he would be driven, as a matter of course, to *simplicity*, if not deliberately induced to it as a matter of choice. You will remember, perhaps, how desperately the Prefect laughed when I suggested, upon our first interview, that it was just possible this mystery troubled him so much on account of its being so *very* self-evident."

"Yes," said I, "I remember his merriment well. I really thought he would have fallen into convulsions."

"The material world," continued Dupin, "abounds with very strict analogies to the immaterial; and thus some color of truth has been given to the rhetorical dogma, that metaphor, or simile, may be made to strengthen an argument as well as to embellish a description. The principle of the *vis inertiæ*, for example, seems to be identical in physics and metaphysics. It is not more true in the former, that a large body is with more difficulty set in motion than a smaller one, and that its subsequent *momentum* is commensurate with this difficulty, than it is, in the latter, that intellects of the vaster capacity, while more forcible, more constant, and more eventful in their movements than those of inferior grade, are yet the less readily moved, and more embarrassed, and full of hesitation in the first few steps of their progress. Again: have you ever noticed which of the street signs, over the shop doors, are the most attractive of attention?"

"I have never given the matter a thought," I said.

"There is a game of puzzles," he resumed, "which is played upon a map. One party playing requires another to find a given word — the name of town, river, state, or empire — any word, in short, upon the motley and perplexed surface of the chart. A novice in the game generally seeks to embarrass his opponents by giving them the most minutely lettered names; but the adept selects such words as stretch, in large characters, from one end of the chart to the other. These, like the over-largely lettered signs and placards of the street, escape observation by dint of being excessively obvious; and here the physical oversight is precisely analogous with the moral inapprehension by which the intellect suffers to pass unnoticed those considerations which are too obtrusively and too palpably self-evident. But this is a point, it appears, somewhat above or beneath the understanding of the Prefect. He never once thought it probable, or possible, that the Minister had deposited the let-

ter immediately beneath the nose of the whole world by way of best preventing any portion of that world from perceiving it.

"But the more I reflected upon the daring, dashing, and discriminating ingenuity of D——; upon the fact that the document must always have been *at hand*, if he intended to use it to good purpose; and upon the decisive evidence, obtained by the Prefect, that it was not hidden within the limits of that dignitary's ordinary search — the more satisfied I became that, to conceal this letter, the Minister had resorted to the comprehensive and sagacious expedient of not attempting to conceal it at all.

"Full of these ideas, I prepared myself with a pair of green spectacles, and called one fine morning quite by accident, at the Ministerial hotel. I found D—— at home, yawning, lounging, and dawdling, as usual, and pretending to be in the last extremity of *ennui*. He is, perhaps, the most really energetic human being now alive — but that is only when nobody sees him.

"To be even with him, I complained of my weak eyes, and lamented the necessity of the spectacles, under cover of which I cautiously and thoroughly surveyed the whole apartment, while seemingly intent only upon the conversation of my host.

"I paid especial attention to a large writing-table near which he sat, and upon which lay confusedly, some miscellaneous letters and other papers, with one or two musical instruments and a few books. Here, however, after a long and very deliberate scrutiny, I saw nothing to excite particular suspicion.

"At length my eyes, in going the circuit of the room, fell upon a trumpery filigree card-rack of pasteboard, that hung dangling by a dirty blue ribbon, from a little brass knob just beneath the middle of the mantel-piece. In this rack, which had three or four compartments, were five or six visiting cards and a solitary letter. This last was much soiled and crumpled. It was torn nearly in two, across the middle — as if a design, in the first instance, to tear it entirely up as worthless, had been altered or stayed in the second. It had a large black seal, bearing the D—— cipher *very* conspicuously, and was addressed, in a diminutive female hand, to D——, the minister, himself. It was thrust carelessly, and even, as it seemed, contemptuously, into one of the uppermost divisions of the rack.

"No sooner had I glanced at this letter than I concluded it to be that of which I was in search. To be sure, it was, to all appearance, radically different from the one of which the Prefect had read us so minutely a description. Here the seal was large and black, with the D—— cipher; there it was small and red, with the ducal arms of the S—— family. Here, the address, to the Minister, was diminutive and feminine; there the superscription, to a certain royal personage, was markedly bold and decided; the size alone formed a point of correspondence. But, then, the

radicalness of these differences, which was excessive; the dirt; the soiled and torn condition of the paper, so inconsistent with the *true* methodical habits of D——, and so suggestive of a design to delude the beholder into an idea of the worthlessness of the document; — these things, together with the hyperobtrusive situation of this document, full in the view of every visiter, and thus exactly in accordance with the conclusions to which I had previously arrived; these things, I say, were strongly corroborative of suspicion, in one who came with the intention to suspect.

"I protracted my visit as long as possible, and, while I maintained a most animated discussion with the Minister, upon a topic which I knew well had never failed to interest and excite him, I kept my attention really riveted upon the letter. In this examination, I committed to memory its external appearance and arrangement in the rack; and also fell, at length, upon a discovery which set at rest whatever trivial doubt I might have entertained. In scrutinizing the edges of the paper, I observed them to be more *chafed* than seemed necessary. They presented the *broken* appearance which is manifested when a stiff paper, having been once folded and pressed with a folder, is refolded in a reversed direction, in the same creases or edges which had formed the original fold. This discovery was sufficient. It was clear to me that the letter had been turned as a glove, inside out, re-directed and re-sealed. I bade the Minister good-morning, and took my departure at once, leaving a gold snuff-box upon the table.

"The next morning I called for the snuff-box, when we resumed, quite eagerly, the conversation of the preceding day. While thus engaged, however, a loud report, as if of a pistol, was heard immediately beneath the windows of the hotel, and was succeeded by a series of fearful screams, and the shoutings of a terrified mob. D—— rushed to a casement, threw it open, and looked out. In the meantime I stepped to the card-rack, took the letter, put it in my pocket, and replaced it by a *fac-simile*, (so far as regards externals) which I had carefully prepared at my lodgings — imitating the D—— cipher, very readily, by means of a seal formed of bread.

"The disturbance in the street had been occasioned by the frantic behavior of a man with a musket. He had fired it among a crowd of women and children. It proved, however, to have been without ball, and the fellow was suffered to go his way as a lunatic or a drunkard. When he had gone, D—— came from the window, whither I had followed him immediately upon securing the object in view. Soon afterward I bade him farewell. The pretended lunatic was a man in my own pay."

"But what purpose had you," I asked, "in replacing the letter by a *fac-simile?* Would it not have been better at the first visit, to have seized it openly, and departed?"

"D——," replied Dupin, "is a desperate man, and a man of nerve. His hotel, too, is not without attendants devoted to his interests. Had

I made the wild attempt you suggest, I might never have left the Min-
isterial presence alive. The good people of Paris might have heard of me
no more. But I had an object apart from these considerations. You know
my political prepossessions. In this matter, I act as a partisan of the lady
concerned. For eighteen months the Minister has had her in his power.
She has now him in hers — since, being unaware that the letter is not in
his possession, he will proceed with his exactions as if it was. Thus will
he inevitably commit himself, at once, to his political destruction. His
downfall, too, will not be more precipitate than awkward. It is all very
well to talk about the *facilis descensus Averni;* but in all kinds of climb-
ing, as Catalani said of singing, it is far more easy to get up than to come
down. In the present instance I have no sympathy — at least no pity —
for him who descends. He is that *monstrum horrendum,* an unprincipled
man of genius. I confess, however, that I should like very well to know
the precise character of his thoughts, when, being defied by her whom
the Prefect terms 'a certain personage,' he is reduced to opening the let-
ter which I left for him in the card-rack."

"How? did you put any thing particular in it?"

"Why — it did not seem altogether right to leave the interior blank
— that would have been insulting. D——, at Vienna once, did me an evil
turn, which I told him, quite good-humoredly, that I should remember.
So, as I knew he would feel some curiosity in regard to the identity of
the person who had outwitted him, I thought it a pity not to give him
a clew. He is well acquainted with my MS., and I just copied into the
middle of the blank sheet the words —

" ' — — Un dessein si funeste,
S'il n'est digne d' Atrée, est digne de Thyeste.'

They are to be found in Crébillon's 'Atrée.' "

The Thousand-and-Second Tale of Scheherazade

Truth is stranger than fiction.

OLD SAYING.

Having had occasion, lately, in the course of some Oriental investiga-
tions, to consult the *Tellmenow Isitsöornot,* a work which (like the
Zohar of Simeon Jochaides) is scarcely known at all, even in Europe;
and which has never been quoted, to my knowledge, by any American —
if we except, perhaps, the author of the "Curiosities of American Lit-

erature"; — having had occasion, I say, to turn over some pages of the first-mentioned very remarkable work, I was not a little astonished to discover that the literary world has hitherto been strangely in error respecting the fate of the vizier's daughter, Scheherazade, as that fate is depicted in the "Arabian Nights"; and that the *dénouement* there given, if not altogether inaccurate, as far as it goes, is at least to blame in not having gone very much farther.

For full information on this interesting topic, I must refer the inquisitive reader to the "Isitsöornot" itself; but in the meantime, I shall be pardoned for giving a summary of what I there discovered.

It will be remembered, that, in the usual version of the tales, a certain monarch having good cause to be jealous of his queen, not only puts her to death, but makes a vow, by his beard and the prophet, to espouse each night the most beautiful maiden in his dominions, and the next morning to deliver her up to the executioner.

Having fulfilled this vow for many years to the letter, and with a religious punctuality and method that conferred great credit upon him as a man of devout feeling and excellent sense, he was interrupted one afternoon (no doubt at his prayers) by a visit from his grand vizier, to whose daughter, it appears, there had occurred an idea.

Her name was Scheherazade, and her idea was, that she would either redeem the land from the depopulating tax upon its beauty, or perish, after the approved fashion of all heroines, in the attempt.

Accordingly, and although we do not find it to be leap-year (which makes the sacrifice more meritorious), she deputes her father, the grand vizier, to make an offer to the king of her hand. This hand the king eagerly accepts — (he had intended to take it at all events, and had put off the matter from day to day, only through fear of the vizier), — but, in accepting it now, he gives all parties very distinctly to understand, that, grand vizier or no grand vizier, he has not the slightest design of giving up one iota of his vow or of his privileges. When, therefore, the fair Scheherazade insisted upon marrying the king, and did actually marry him despite her father's excellent advice not to do any thing of the kind — when she would and did marry him, I say, will I, nill I, it was with her beautiful black eyes as thoroughly open as the nature of the case would allow.

It seems, however, that this politic damsel (who had been reading Machiavelli, beyond doubt), had a very ingenious little plot in her mind. On the night of the wedding, she contrived, upon I forget what specious pretence, to have her sister occupy a couch sufficiently near that of the royal pair to admit of easy conversation from bed to bed; and, a little before cock-crowing, she took care to awaken the good monarch, her husband (who bore her none the worse will because he intended to wring her neck on the morrow), — she managed to awaken him, I say, (although on account of a capital conscience and an easy digestion, he

slept well) by the profound interest of a story (about a rat and a black cat, I think) which she was narrating (all in an undertone, of course) to her sister. When the day broke, it so happened that this history was not altogether finished, and that Scheherazade, in the nature of things could not finish it just then, since it was high time for her to get up and be bowstrung — a thing very little more pleasant than hanging, only a trifle more genteel!

The king's curiosity, however, prevailing, I am sorry to say, even over his sound religious principles, induced him for this once to postpone the fulfilment of his vow until next morning, for the purpose and with the hope of hearing that night how it fared in the end with the black cat (a black cat, I think it was) and the rat.

The night having arrived, however, the lady Scheherazade not only put the finishing stroke to the black cat and the rat (the rat was blue) but before she well knew what she was about, found herself deep in the intricacies of a narration, having reference (if I am not altogether mistaken) to a pink horse (with green wings) that went, in a violent manner, by clockwork, and was wound up with an indigo key. With this history the king was even more profoundly interested than with the other — and, as the day broke before its conclusion (notwithstanding all the queen's endeavors to get through with it in time for the bowstringing), there was again no resource but to postpone that ceremony as before, for twenty-four hours. The next night there happened a similar accident with a similar result; and then the next — and then again the next; so that, in the end, the good monarch, having been unavoidably deprived of all opportunity to keep his vow during a period of no less than one thousand and one nights, either forgets it altogether by the expiration of this time, or gets himself absolved of it in the regular way, or (what is more probable) breaks it outright, as well as the head of his father confessor. At all events, Scheherazade, who, being lineally descended from Eve, fell heir, perhaps, to the whole seven baskets of talk, which the latter lady, we all know, picked up from under the trees in the garden of Eden — Scheherazade, I say, finally triumphed, and the tariff upon beauty was repealed.

Now, this conclusion (which is that of the story as we have it upon record) is, no doubt, excessively proper and pleasant — but alas! like a great many pleasant things, is more pleasant than true; and I am indebted altogether to the "Isitsöornot" for the means of correcting the error. "*Le mieux,*" says a French proverb, "*est l'ennemi du bien,*" and, in mentioning that Scheherazade had inherited the seven baskets of talk, I should have added that she put them out at compound interest until they amounted to seventy-seven.

"My dear sister," said she, on the thousand-and-second night, (I quote the language of the "Isitsöornot" at this point, *verbatim*) "my dear sister," said she, "now that all this little difficulty about the bowstring has

blown over, and that this odious tax is so happily repealed, I feel that I have been guilty of great indiscretion in withholding from you and the king (who I am sorry to say, snores — a thing no gentleman would do) the full conclusion of Sinbad the sailor. This person went through numerous other and more interesting adventures than those which I related; but the truth is, I felt sleepy on the particular night of their narration, and so was seduced into cutting them short — a grievous piece of misconduct, for which I only trust that Allah will forgive me. But even yet it is not too late to remedy my great neglect — and as soon as I have given the king a pinch or two in order to wake him up so far that he may stop making that horrible noise, I will forthwith entertain you (and him if he pleases) with the sequel of this very remarkable story.

Hereupon the sister of Scheherazade, as I have it from the "Isitsöornot," expressed no very particular intensity of gratification; but the king, having been sufficiently pinched, at length ceased snoring, and finally said, "hum!" and then "hoo!" when the queen, understanding these words (which are no doubt Arabic) to signify that he was all attention, and would do his best not to snore any more — the queen, I say, having arranged these matters to her satisfaction, re-entered thus, at once, into the history of Sinbad the sailor:

" 'At length, in my old age, [these are the words of Sinbad himself, as retailed by Scheherazade] — 'at length, in my old age, and after enjoying many years of tranquillity at home, I became once more possessed of a desire of visiting foreign countries; and one day, without acquainting any of my family with my design, I packed up some bundles of such merchandise as was most precious and least bulky, and, engaging a porter to carry them, went with him down to the sea-shore, to await the arrival of any chance vessel that might convey me out of the kingdom into some region which I had not as yet explored.

" 'Having deposited the packages upon the sands, we sat down beneath some trees, and looked out into the ocean in the hope of perceiving a ship, but during several hours we saw none whatever. At length I fancied that I could hear a singular buzzing or humming sound; and the porter, after listening awhile, declared that he also could distinguish it. Presently it grew louder, and then still louder, so that we could have no doubt that the object which caused it was approaching us. At length, on the edge of the horizon, we discovered a black speck, which rapidly increased in size until we made it out to be a vast monster, swimming with a great part of its body above the surface of the sea. It came toward us with inconceivable swiftness, throwing up huge waves of foam around its breast, and illuminating all that part of the sea through which it passed, with a long line of fire that extended far off into the distance.

" 'As the thing drew near we saw it very distinctly. Its length was equal to that of three of the loftiest trees that grow, and it was as wide as the great hall of audience in your palace, O most sublime and munifi-

cent of the Caliphs. Its body, which was unlike that of ordinary fishes, was as solid as a rock, and of a jetty blackness throughout all that portion of it which floated above the water, with the exception of a narrow blood-red streak that completely begirdled it. The belly, which floated beneath the surface, and of which we could get only a glimpse now and then as the monster rose and fell with the billows, was entirely covered with metallic scales, of a color like that of the moon in misty weather. The back was flat and nearly white, and from it there extended upwards of six spines, about half the length of the whole body.

" 'This horrible creature had no mouth that we could perceive; but, as if to make up for this deficiency, it was provided with at least four score of eyes, that protruded from their sockets like those of the green dragon-fly, and were arranged all around the body in two rows, one above the other, and parallel to the blood-red streak, which seemed to answer the purpose of an eyebrow. Two or three of these dreadful eyes were much larger than the others, and had the appearance of solid gold.

" 'Although this beast approached us, as I have before said, with the greatest rapidity, it must have been moved altogether by necromancy — for it had neither fins like a fish nor web-feet like a duck, nor wings like the seashell which is blown along in the manner of a vessel; nor yet did it writhe itself forward as do the eels. Its head and its tail were shaped precisely alike, only, not far from the latter, were two small holes that served for nostrils, and through which the monster puffed out its thick breath with prodigious violence, and with a shrieking, disagreeable noise.

" 'Our terror at beholding this hideous thing was very great, but it was even surpassed by our astonishment, when upon getting a nearer look, we perceived upon the creature's back a vast number of animals about the size and shape of men, and altogether much resembling them, except that they wore no garments (as men do), being supplied (by nature, no doubt) with an ugly uncomfortable covering, a good deal like cloth, but fitting so tight to the skin, as to render the poor wretches laughably awkward, and put them apparently to severe pain. On the very tips of their heads were certain square-looking boxes, which, at first sight, I thought might have been intended to answer as turbans, but I soon discovered that they were excessively heavy and solid, and I therefore concluded they were contrivances designed, by their great weight, to keep the heads of the animals steady and safe upon their shoulders. Around the necks of the creatures were fastened black collars, (badges of servitude, no doubt,) such as we keep on our dogs, only much wider and infinitely stiffer, so that it was quite impossible for these poor victims to move their heads in any direction without moving the body at the same time; and thus they were doomed to perpetual contemplation of their noses — a view puggish and snubby in a wonderful, if not positively in an awful degree.

" 'When the monster had nearly reached the shore where we stood,

it suddenly pushed out one of its eyes to a great extent, and emitted from
it a terrible flash of fire, accompanied by a dense cloud of smoke, and
a noise that I can compare to nothing but thunder. As the smoke cleared
away, we saw one of the odd man-animals standing near the head of the
large beast with a trumpet in his hand, through which (putting it to his
mouth) he presently addressed us in loud, harsh, and disagreeable ac-
cents, that, perhaps, we should have mistaken for language, had they
not come altogether through the nose.

" 'Being thus evidently spoken to, I was at a loss how to reply, as I
could in no manner understand what was said; and in this difficulty I
turned to the porter, who was near swooning through affright, and de-
manded of him his opinion as to what species of monster it was, what
it wanted, and what kind of creatures those were that so swarmed upon
its back. To this the porter replied, as well as he could for trepidation,
that he had once before heard of this sea-beast; that it was a cruel demon,
with bowels of sulphur and blood of fire, created by evil genii as the
means of inflicting misery upon mankind; that the things upon its back
were vermin, such as sometimes infest cats and dogs, only a little larger
and more savage; and that these vermin had their uses, however evil —
for, through the torture they caused the beast by their nibblings and
stingings, it was goaded into that degree of wrath which was requisite
to make it roar and commit ill, and so fulfil the vengeful and malicious
designs of the wicked genii.

" 'This account determined me to take to my heels, and, without
once even looking behind me, I ran at full speed up into the hills,
while the porter ran equally fast, although nearly in an opposite direc-
tion, so that, by these means, he finally made his escape with my bundles,
of which I have no doubt he took excellent care — although this is a
point I cannot determine, as I do not remember that I ever beheld
him again.

" 'For myself, I was so hotly pursued by a swarm of the men-vermin
(who had come to the shore in boats) that I was very soon overtaken,
bound hand and foot, and conveyed to the beast, which immediately
swam out again into the middle of the sea.

" 'I now bitterly repented my folly in quitting a comfortable home
to peril my life in such adventures as this; but regret being useless, I
made the best of my condition, and exerted myself to secure the good-
will of the man-animal that owned the trumpet, and who appeared to
exercise authority over his fellows. I succeeded so well in this endeavor
that, in a few days, the creature bestowed upon me various tokens of
his favor, and in the end even went to the trouble of teaching me the
rudiments of what it was vain enough to denominate its language; so
that, at length, I was enabled to converse with it readily, and came to
make it comprehend the ardent desire I had of seeing the world.

" '*Washish squashish squeak, Sinbad, hey-diddle diddle, grunt unt*

grumble, hiss, fiss, whiss,' said he to me, one day after dinner — but I beg a thousand pardons, I had forgotten that your majesty is not conversant with the dialect of the Cock-neighs (so the man-animals were called; I presume because their language formed the connecting link between that of the horse and that of the rooster). With your permission, I will translate. '*Washish squashish,*' and so forth: — that is to say, 'I am happy to find, my dear Sinbad, that you are really a very excellent fellow; we are now about doing a thing which is called circumnavigating the globe; and since you are so desirous of seeing the world, I will strain a point and give you a free passage upon the back of the beast.' "

When the Lady Scheherazade had proceeded thus far, relates the "Isitsöornot," the king turned over from his left side to his right, and said:

"It is, in fact, *very* surprising, my dear queen, that you omitted, hitherto, these latter adventures of Sinbad. Do you know I think them exceedingly entertaining and strange?"

The king having thus expressed himself, we are told, the fair Scheherazade resumed her history in the following words:

"Sinbad went on in this manner with his narrative to the caliph — 'I thanked the man-animal for its kindness, and soon found myself very much at home on the beast, which swam at a prodigious rate through the ocean; although the surface of the latter is, in that part of the world, by no means flat, but round like a pomegranate, so that we went — so to say — either up hill or down hill all the time.' "

"That, I think, was very singular," interrupted the king.

"Nevertheless, it is quite true," replied Scheherazade.

"I have my doubts," rejoined the king; "but, pray, be so good as to go on with the story."

"I will," said the queen. " 'The beast,' continued Sinbad to the caliph, 'swam, as I have related, up hill and down hill, until, at length, we arrived at an island, many hundreds of miles in circumference, but which, nevertheless, had been built in the middle of the sea by a colony of little things like caterpillars.' " *

"Hum!" said the king.

" 'Leaving this island,' said Sinbad — (for Scheherazade, it must be understood, took no notice of her husband's ill-mannered ejaculation) — 'leaving this island, we came to another where the forests were of solid stone, and so hard that they shivered to pieces the finest-tempered axes with which we endeavoured to cut them down.' " †

* The coralites.

† "One of the most remarkable natural curiosities in Texas is a petrified forest, near the head of Pasigno river. It consists of several hundred trees, in an erect position, all turned to stone. Some trees, now growing, are partly petrified. This is a startling fact for natural philosophers, and must cause them to modify the existing theory of petrification. — *Kennedy.*

This account, at first discredited, has since been corroborated by the discovery of a completely petrified forest, near the

"Hum!" said the king, again; but Scheherazade, paying him no attention, continued in the language of Sinbad.

" 'Passing beyond this last island, we reached a country where there was a cave that ran to the distance of thirty or forty miles within the bowels of the earth, and that contained a greater number of far more spacious and more magnificent palaces than are to be found in all Damascus and Bagdad. From the roofs of these palaces there hung myriads of gems, liked diamonds, but larger than men; and in among the streets of towers and pyramids and temples, there flowed immense rivers as black as ebony, and swarming with fish that had no eyes.' " *

"Hum!" said the king.

" 'We then swam into a region of the sea where we found a lofty mountain, down whose sides there streamed torrents of melted metal, some of which were twelve miles wide and sixty miles long; † while from an abyss on the summit, issued so vast a quantity of ashes that the sun was entirely blotted out from the heavens, and it became darker than the darkest midnight; so that when we were even at the distance of a hundred and fifty miles from the mountain, it was impossible to see the whitest object, however close we held it to our eyes.' " ‡

head waters of the Cheyenne, or Chienne river, which has its source in the Black Hills of the rocky chain.

There is scarcely, perhaps, a spectacle on the surface of the globe more remarkable, either in a geological or picturesque point of view than that presented by the petrified forest, near Cairo. The traveller, having passed the tombs of the caliphs, just beyond the gates of the city, proceeds to the southward, nearly at right angles to the road across the desert to Suez, and after having travelled some ten miles up a low barren valley, covered with sand, gravel, and sea shells, fresh as if the tide had retired but yesterday, crosses a low range of sandhills, which has for some distance run parallel to his path. The scene now presented to him is beyond conception singular and desolate. A mass of fragments of trees, all converted into stone, and when struck by his horse's hoof ringing like cast iron, is seen to extend itself for miles and miles around him, in the form of a decayed and prostrate forest. The wood is of a dark brown hue, but retains its form in perfection, the pieces being from one to fifteen feet in length, and from half a foot to three feet in thickness, strewed so closely together, as far as the eye can reach, that an Egyptian donkey can scarcely thread its way through amongst them, and so natural that, were it in Scotland or Ireland, it might pass without remark for some enormous drained bog, on which the exhumed trees lay rotting in the sun. The roots and rudiments of the branches are, in many cases, nearly perfect, and in some the worm-holes eaten under the bark are readily recognizable. The most delicate of the sap vessels, and all the finer portions of the centre of the wood, are perfectly entire, and bear to be examined with the strongest magnifiers. The whole are so thoroughly silicified as to scratch glass and are capable of receiving the highest polish. — Asiatic Magazine.

* The Mammoth Cave of Kentucky.

† In Iceland, 1783.

‡ "During the eruption of Hecla, in 1766, clouds of this kind produced such a degree of darkness that, at Glaumba, which is more than fifty leagues from the mountain, people could only find their way by groping. During the eruption of Vesuvius, in 1794, at Caserta, four leagues distant, people could only walk by the light of torches. On the first of May, 1812, a cloud of volcanic ashes and sand, coming from a volcano in the island of St. Vincent, covered the whole of Bar-

"Hum!" said the king.

" 'After quitting this coast, the beast continued his voyage until we met with a land in which the nature of things seemed reversed — for we here saw a great lake, at the bottom of which, more than a hundred feet beneath the surface of the water, there flourished in full leaf a forest of tall and luxuriant trees.' " *

"Hoo!" said the king.

" 'Some hundred miles farther on brought us to a climate where the atmosphere was so dense as to sustain iron or steel, just as our own does feather.' " †

"Fiddle de dee," said the king.

" 'Proceeding still in the same direction, we presently arrived at the most magnificent region in the whole world. Through it there meandered a glorious river for several thousands of miles. This river was of unspeakable depth, and of a transparency richer than that of amber. It was from three to six miles in width; and its banks which arose on either side to twelve hundred feet in perpendicular height, were crowned with ever-blossoming trees and perpetual sweet-scented flowers, that made the whole territory one gorgeous garden; but the name of this luxuriant land was the Kingdom of Horror, and to enter it was inevitable death.' " ‡

"Humph!" said the king.

" 'We left this kingdom in great haste, and, after some days, came to another, where we were astonished to perceive myriads of monstrous animals with horns resembling scythes upon their heads. These hideous beasts dig for themselves vast caverns in the soil, of a funnel shape, and line the sides of them with rocks, so disposed one upon the other that they fall instantly, when trodden upon by other animals, thus precipitating them into the monster's dens, where their blood is immediately sucked, and their carcasses afterwards hurled contemptuously out to an immense distance from "the caverns of death." ' " §

"Pooh!" said the king.

badoes, spreading over it so intense a darkness that, at mid-day, in the open air, one could not perceive the trees or other objects near him, or even a white handkerchief placed at the distance of six inches from the eye." — *Murray*, p. 215, *Phil. edit.*

* In the year 1790, in the Caraccas during an earthquake a portion of the granite soil sank and left a lake eight hundred yards in diameter, and from eighty to a hundred feet deep. It was a part of the forest of Aripao which sank, and the trees remained green for several months under the water." — *Murray*, p. 221.

† The hardest steel ever manufactured may, under the action of a blowpipe, be reduced to an impalpable powder, which will float readily in the atmospheric air.

‡ The region of the Niger. See *Simmona's "Colonial Magazine."*

§ The *Myrmeleon* — lion-ant. The term "monster" is equally applicable to small abnormal things and to great, while such epithets as "vast" are merely comparative. The cavern of the myrmeleon is *vast* in comparison with the hole of the common red ant. A grain of silex is also a "rock."

" 'Continuing our progress, we perceived a district with vegetables that grew not upon any soil, but in the air.* There were others that sprang from the substance of other vegetables; † others that derived their substance from the bodies of living animals; ‡ and then again, there were others that glowed all over with intense fire; § others that moved from place to place at pleasure,|| and what was still more wonderful, we discovered flowers that lived and breathed and moved their limbs at will, and had, moreover, the detestable passion of mankind for enslaving other creatures, and confining them in horrid and solitary prisons until the fulfillment of appointed tasks.' " ¶

"Pshaw!" said the king.

" 'Quitting this land, we soon arrived at another in which the bees and the birds are mathematicians of such genius and erudition, that they give daily instructions in the science of geometry to the wise men of

* The *Epidendron, Flos Aeris*, of the family of the *Orchideæ*, grows with merely the surface of its roots attached to a tree or other object, from which it derives no nutriment — subsisting altogether upon air.

† The *Parasites*, such as the wonderful *Rafflesia Arnaldii*.

‡ *Schouw* advocates a class of plants that grow upon living animals — the *Plantæ Epizoæ*. Of this class are the *Fuci* and *Algæ*.

Mr. J. B. Williams, of *Salem, Mass.*, presented the "National Institute," with an insect from New Zealand, with the following description: — " 'The Hotte,' a decided caterpillar, or worm, is found growing at the foot of the *Rata* tree, with a plant growing out of its head. This most peculiar and most extraordinary insect travels up both the *Rata* and *Perriri* trees, and entering into the top, eats its way, perforating the trunk of the tree until it reaches the root, it then comes out of the root, and dies, or remains dormant, and the plant propagates out of its head; the body remains perfect and entire, of a harder substance than when alive. From this insect the natives making a coloring for tattooing."

§ In mines and natural caves we find a species of cryptogamous *fungus* that emits an intense phosphorescence.

|| The orchis, scabius and valisneria.

¶ "The corolla of this flower (*Aristolochia Clematitis*), which is tubular, but terminating upwards in a ligulate limb, is inflated into a globular figure at the base. The tubular part is internally beset with stiff hairs, pointing downwards. The globular part contains the pistil, which consists merely of a germen and stigma, together with the surrounding stamens. But the stamens, being shorter than even the germen, cannot discharge the pollen so as to throw it upon the stigma, as the flower stands always upright till after impregnation. And hence, without some additional and peculiar aid, the pollen must necessarily fall down to the bottom of the flower. Now, the aid that nature has furnished in this case, is that of the *Tiputa Pennicornis*, a small insect, which entering the tube of the corolla in quest of honey, descends to the bottom, and rummages about till it becomes quite covered with pollen; but not being able to force its way out again, owing to the downward position of the hairs, which converge to a point like the wires of a mouse-trap, and being somewhat impatient of its confinement it brushes backwards and forwards, trying every corner, till, after repeatedly traversing the stigma, it covers it with pollen sufficient for its impregnation, in consequence of which the flower soon begins to droop, and the hairs to shrink to the sides of the tube, effecting an easy passage for the escape of the insect." — *Rev. P. Keith — System of Physiological Botany.*

the empire. The king of the place having offered a reward for the solution of two very difficult problems, they were solved upon the spot — the one by the bees, and the other by the birds; but the king keeping their solution a secret, it was only after the most profound researches and labor, and the writing of an infinity of big books, during a long series of years, that the men-mathematicians at length arrived at the identical solutions which had been given upon the spot by the bees and by the birds.' " *

"Oh my!" said the king.

" 'We had scarcely lost sight of this empire when we found ourselves close upon another, from whose shores there flew over our heads a flock of fowls a mile in breadth, and two hundred and forty miles long; so that, although they flew a mile during every minute, it required no less than four hours for the whole flock to pass over us — in which there were several millions of millions of fowl.' " †

"Oh fy!" said the king.

" 'No sooner had we got rid of these birds, which occasioned us great annoyance, than we were terrified by the appearance of a fowl of another kind, and infinitely larger than even the rocs which I met in my former voyages; for it was bigger than the biggest of the domes on your seraglio, oh, most Munificent of Caliphs. This terrible fowl had no head that we could perceive, but was fashioned entirely of belly, which was of a prodigious fatness and roundness, of a soft-looking substance, smooth, shining and striped with various colors. In its talons, the monster was bearing away to his eyrie in the heavens, a house from which it had knocked off the roof, and in the interior of which we distinctly saw human beings, who, beyond doubt, were in a state of frightful despair at the horrible fate which awaited them. We shouted with all our might,

* The bees — ever since bees were — have been constructing their cells with just such sides, in just such number, and at just such inclinations, as it has been demonstrated (in a problem involving the profoundest mathematical principles) are the very sides, in the very number, and at the very angles, which will afford the creatures the most room that is compatible with the greatest stability of structure.

During the latter part of the last century, the question arose among mathematicians — "to determine the best form that can be given to the sails of a windmill, according to their varying distances from the revolving vanes, and likewise from the centres of the revolution." This is an excessively complex problem, for it is, in other words, to find the best possible position at an infinity of varied distances, and at an infinity of points on the arm. There were a thousand futile attempts to answer the query on the part of the most illustrious mathematicians; and when, at length, an undeniable solution was discovered, men found that the wings of a bird had given it with absolute precision ever since the first bird had traversed the air.

† He observed a flock of pigeons passing betwixt Frankfort and the Indian territory, one mile at least in breadth; it took up four hours in passing; which, at the rate of one mile per minute, gives a length of 240 miles; and, supposing three pigeons to each square yard, gives 2,230,-272,000 pigeons. — "Travels in Canada and the United States," by Lieut. F. Hall.

in the hope of frightening the bird into letting go of its prey; but it merely gave a snort or puff, as if of rage and then let fall upon our heads a heavy sack which proved to be filled with sand!' "

"Stuff!" said the king.

" 'It was just after this adventure that we encountered a continent of immense extent and prodigious solidity, but which, nevertheless, was supported entirely upon the back of a sky-blue cow that had no fewer than four hundred horns.' " *

"That, now, I believe," said the king, "because I have read something of the kind before, in a book."

" 'We passed immediately beneath this continent, (swimming in between the legs of the cow, and, after some hours, found ourselves in a wonderful country indeed, which, I was informed by the man-animal, was his own native land, inhabited by things of his own species. This elevated the man-animal very much in my esteem, and in fact, I now began to feel ashamed of the contemptuous familiarity with which I had treated him; for I found that the man-animals in general were a nation of the most powerful magicians, who lived with worms in their brain,† which, no doubt, served to stimulate them by their painful writhings and wrigglings to the most miraculous efforts of imagination.' "

"Nonsense!" said the king.

" 'Among the magicians, were domesticated several animals of very singular kinds; for example, there was a huge horse whose bones were iron and whose blood was boiling water. In place of corn, he had black stones for his usual food; and yet, in spite of so hard a diet, he was so strong and swift that he would drag a load more weighty than the grandest temple in this city, at a rate surpassing that of the flight of most birds.' " ‡

"Twattle!" said the king.

" 'I saw, also, among these people a hen without feathers, but bigger than a camel; instead of flesh and bone she had iron and brick; her blood, like that of the horse, (to whom, in fact, she was nearly related,) was boiling water; and like him she ate nothing but wood or black stones. This hen brought forth very frequently, a hundred chickens in the day; and, after birth, they took up their residence for several weeks within the stomach of their mother.' " §

"Fal lal!" said the king.

" 'One of this nation of mighty conjurors created a man out of brass

* "The earth is upheld by a cow of a blue color, having horns four hundred in number." — Sale's Koran.

† "The Entozoa, or intestinal worms, have repeatedly been observed in the muscles, and in the cerebral substance of men." — See Wyatt's Physiology, p. 143.

‡ On the Great Western Railway, between London and Exeter, a speed of 71 miles per hour has been attained. A train weighing 90 tons was whirled from Paddington to Didcot (53 miles) in 51 minutes.

§ The Eccalobeion.

and wood, and leather, and endowed him with such ingenuity that he would have beaten at chess, all the race of mankind with the exception of the great Caliph, Haroun Alraschid.* Another of these magi constructed (of like material) a creature that put to shame even the genius of him who made it; for so great were its reasoning powers that, in a second, it performed calculations of so vast an extent that they would have required the united labor of fifty thousand fleshy men for a year.† But a still more wonderful conjuror fashioned for himself a mighty thing that was neither man nor beast, but which had brains of lead, intermixed with a black matter like pitch, and fingers that it employed with such incredible speed and dexterity that it would have had no trouble in writing out twenty thousand copies of the Koran in an hour; and this with so exquisite a precision, that in all the copies there should not be found one to vary from another by the breadth of the finest hair. This thing was of prodigious strength, so that it erected or overthrew the mightiest empires at a breath; but its powers were exercised equally for evil and for good.' "

"Ridiculous!" said the king.

" 'Among this nation of necromancers there was also one who had in his veins the blood of the salamanders; for he made no scruple of sitting down to smoke his chibouc in a red-hot oven until his dinner was thoroughly roasted upon its floor.‡ Another had the faculty of converting the common metals into gold, without even looking at them during the process.§ Another had such a delicacy of touch that he made a wire so fine as to be invisible.‖ Another had such quickness of perception that he counted all the separate motions of an elastic body, while it was springing backward and forward at the rate of nine hundred millions of times in a second.' " ¶

"Absurd!" said the king.

" 'Another of these magicians, by means of a fluid that nobody ever yet saw, could make the corpses of his friends brandish their arms, kick out their legs, fight, or even get up and dance at his will.** Another had cultivated his voice to so great an extent that he could have made himself heard from one end of the world to the other.†† Another had so long an arm that he could sit down in Damascus and indite a letter at Bagdad — or indeed at any distance whatsoever.‡‡ Another commanded the

* Maelzel's Automaton Chess-player.

† Babbage's Calculating Machine.

‡ *Chabert*, and since him, a hundred others.

§ The Electrotype.

‖ *Wollaston* made of platinum for the field of views in a telescope a wire one eighteen-thousandth part of an inch in thickness. It could be seen only by means of the microscope.

¶ Newton demonstrated that the retina beneath the influence of the violet ray of the spectrum, vibrated 900,000,-000 of times in a second.

** The Voltaic pile.

†† The Electro Telegraph Printing Apparatus.

‡‡ The Electro telegraph transmits intelligence instantaneously — at least so far as regards any distance upon the earth.

lightning to come down to him out of the heavens, and it came at his call; and served him for a plaything when it came. Another took two loud sounds and out of them made a silence. Another constructed a deep darkness out of two brilliant lights.* Another made ice in a red-hot furnace.† Another directed the sun to paint his portrait, and the sun did.‡ Another took this luminary with the moon and the planets, and having first weighed them with scrupulous accuracy, probed into their depths and found out the solidity of the substance of which they were made. But the whole nation is, indeed, of so surprising a necromantic ability, that not even their infants, nor their commonest cats and dogs have any difficulty in seeing objects that do not exist at all, or that for twenty millions of years before the birth of the nation itself had been blotted out from the face of creation.' " §

"Preposterous!" said the king.

" 'The wives and daughters of these incomparably great and wise magi,' " continued Scheherazade, without being in any manner disturbed by these frequent and most ungentlemanly interruptions on the part of her husband — " 'the wives and daughters of these eminent conjurers are every thing that is accomplished and refined; and would be every thing that is interesting and beautiful, but for an unhappy fatality that besets them, and from which not even the miraculous powers of their husbands and fathers has, hitherto, been adequate to save. Some fatalities

* Common experiments in Natural Philosophy. If two red rays from two luminous points be admitted into a dark chamber so as to fall on a white surface, and differ in their length by 0.0000258 of an inch, their intensity is doubled. So also if the difference in length be any whole-number multiple of that fraction. A multiple by 2¼, 3¼, &c., gives an intensity equal to one ray only; but a multiple by 2½, 3½, &c., gives the result of total darkness. In violet rays similar effects arise when the difference in length is 0.000157 of an inch; and with all other rays the results are the same — the difference varying with a uniform increase from the violet to the red.

Analogous experiments in respect to sound produce analogous results.

† Place a platina crucible over a spirit lamp, and keep it a red heat; pour in some sulphuric acid, which, though the most volatile of bodies at a common temperature, will be found to become completely fixed in a hot crucible, and not a drop evaporates — being surrounded by an atmosphere of its own, it does not, in fact, touch the sides. A few drops of water are now introduced, when the acid, immediately coming in contact with the heated sides of the crucible, flies off in sulphurous acid vapor, and so rapid is its progress, that the caloric of the water passes off with it, which falls a lump of ice to the bottom; by taking advantage of the moment before it is allowed to re-melt, it may be turned out a lump of ice from a red-hot vessel.

‡ The Daguerreotype.

§ Although light travels 167,000 miles in a second, the distance of 61 Cygni (the only star whose distance is ascertained) is so inconceivably great, that its rays would require more than ten years to reach the earth. For stars beyond this, 20 — or even 1000 years — would be a moderate estimate. Thus, if they had been annihilated 20, or 1000 years ago, we might still see them to-day by the light which *started* from their surfaces 20 or 1000 years in the past time. That many which we see daily are really extinct, is not impossible — not even improbable.

come in certain shapes, and some in others — but this of which I speak has come in the shape of a crotchet.' "

"A what?" said the king.

" 'A crotchet,' " said Scheherazade. " 'One of the evil genii, who are perpetually upon the watch to inflict ill, has put it into the heads of these accomplished ladies that the thing which we describe as personal beauty consists altogether in the protuberance of the region which lies not very far below the small of the back. Perfection of loveliness, they say, is in the direct ratio of the extent of this lump. Having been long possessed of this idea, and bolsters being cheap in that country, the days have long gone by since it was possible to distinguish a woman from a drome- dary —— ' "

"Stop!" said the king — "I can't stand that, and I won't. You have already given me a dreadful headache with your lies. The day, too, I perceive, is beginning to break. How long have we been married? —— my conscience is getting to be troublesome again. And then that drome- dary touch — do you take me for a fool? Upon the whole, you might as well get up and be throttled."

These words, as I learn from the "Isitsöornot," both grieved and as- tonished Scheherazade; but, as she knew the king to be a man of scrupu- lous integrity, and quite unlikely to forfeit his word, she submitted to her fate with a good grace. She derived, however, great consolation, (dur- ing the tightening of the bowstring,) from the reflection that much of the history remained still untold, and that the petulance of her brute of a husband had reaped for him a most righteous reward, in depriving him of many inconceivable adventures.

Some Words with a Mummy

THE SYMPOSIUM of the preceding evening had been a little too much for my nerves. I had a wretched headache, and was desperately drowsy. Instead of going out therefore to spend the evening as I had proposed, it occurred to me that I could not do a wiser thing than just eat a mouth- ful of supper and go immediately to bed.

A *light* supper of course. I am exceedingly fond of Welsh rabbit. More than a pound at once, however, may not at all times be advisable. Still, there can be no material objection to two. And really between two and three, there is merely a single unit of difference. I ventured, perhaps, upon four. My wife will have it five; — but, clearly, she has confounded two very distinct affairs. The abstract number, five, I am willing to admit; but, concretely, it has reference to bottles of Brown Stout, without which, in the way of condiment, Welsh rabbit is to be eschewed.

Having thus concluded a frugal meal, and donned my night-cap, with the serene hope of enjoying it till noon the next day, I placed my head upon the pillow, and, through the aid of a capital conscience, fell into a profound slumber forthwith.

But when were the hopes of humanity fulfilled? I could not have completed my third snore when there came a furious ringing at the street-door bell, and then an impatient thumping at the knocker, which awakened me at once. In a minute afterward, and while I was still rubbing my eyes, my wife thrust in my face a note, from my old friend, Doctor Ponnonner. It ran thus:

Come to me, by all means, my dear good friend, as soon as you receive this. Come and help us to rejoice. At last, by long persevering diplomacy, I have gained the assent of the Directors of the City Musum, to my examination of the Mummy — you know the one I mean. I have permission to unswathe it and open it, if desirable. A few friends only will be present — you, of course. The Mummy is now at my house, and we shall begin to unroll it at eleven to-night.

Yours, ever,
PONNONNER.

By the time I had reached the "Ponnonner," it struck me that I was as wide awake as a man need be. I leaped out of bed in an ecstacy, overthrowing all in my way; dressed myself with a rapidity truly marvellous; and set off, at the top of my speed, for the doctor's.

There I found a very eager company assembled. They had been awaiting me with much impatience; the Mummy was extended upon the dining-table; and the moment I entered its examination was commenced.

It was one of a pair brought, several years previously, by Captain Arthur Sabretash, a cousin of Ponnonner's from a tomb near Eleithias, in the Lybian mountains, a considerable distance above Thebes on the Nile. The grottoes at this point, although less magnificent than the Theban sepulchres, are of higher interest, on account of affording more numerous illustrations of the private life of the Egyptians. The chamber from which our specimen was taken, was said to be very rich in such illustrations; the walls being completely covered with fresco paintings and bas-reliefs, while statues, vases, and Mosaic work of rich patterns, indicated the vast wealth of the deceased.

The treasure had been deposited in the Museum precisely in the same condition in which Captain Sabretash had found it; — that is to say, the coffin had not been disturbed. For eight years it had thus stood, subject only externally to public inspection. We had now, therefore, the complete Mummy at our disposal; and to those who are aware how very rarely the unransacked antique reaches our shores, it will be evident, at once that we had great reason to congratulate ourselves upon our good fortune.

Approaching the table, I saw on it a large box, or case, nearly seven

feet long, and perhaps three feet wide, by two feet and a half deep. It was oblong — not coffin-shaped. The material was at first supposed to be the wood of the sycamore (*platanus*), but, upon cutting into it, we found it to be pasteboard, or, more properly, *papier maché*, composed of papyrus. It was thickly ornamented with paintings, representing funeral scenes, and other mournful subjects — interspersed among which, in every variety of position, were certain series of hieroglyphical characters, intended, no doubt, for the name of the departed. By good luck, Mr. Gliddon formed one of our party; and he had no difficulty in translating the letters, which were simply phonetic, and represented the word *Allamistakeo*.

We had some difficulty in getting this case open without injury; but, having at length accomplished the task, we came to a second, coffin-shaped, and very considerably less in size than the exterior one, but resembling it precisely in every other respect. The interval between the two was filled with resin, which had, in some degree, defaced the colors of the interior box.

Upon opening this latter (which we did quite easily), we arrived at a third case, also coffin-shaped, and varying from the second one in no particular, except in that of its material, which was cedar, and still emitted the peculiar and highly aromatic odor of that wood. Between the second and the third case there was no interval — the one fitting accurately within the other.

Removing the third case, we discovered and took out the body itself. We had expected to find it, as usual, enveloped in frequent rolls, or bandages, of linen; but, in place of these, we found a sort of sheath, made of papyrus, and coated with a layer of plaster, thickly gilt and painted. The paintings represented subjects connected with the various supposed duties of the soul, and its presentation to different divinities, with numerous identical human figures, intended, very probably, as portraits of the persons embalmed. Extending from head to foot was a columnar, or perpendicular, inscription, in phonetic hieroglyphics, giving again his name and titles, and the names and titles of his relations.

Around the neck thus ensheathed, was a collar of cylindrical glass beads, diverse in color, and so arranged as to form images of deities, of the scarabæus, etc., with the winged globe. Around the small of the waist was a similar collar or belt.

Stripping off the papyrus, we found the flesh in excellent preservation, with no perceptible odor. The color was reddish. The skin was hard, smooth, and glossy. The teeth and hair were in good condition. The eyes (it seemed) had been removed, and glass ones substituted, which were very beautiful and wonderfully life-like, with the exception of somewhat too determined a stare. The fingers and the nails were brilliantly gilded.

Mr. Gliddon was of opinion, from the redness of the epidermis, that the embalmment had been effected altogether by asphaltum; but,

on scraping the surface with a steel instrument, and throwing into the fire some of the powder thus obtained, the flavor of camphor and other sweet-scented gums became apparent.

We searched the corpse very carefully for the usual openings through which the entrails are extracted, but, to our surprise, we could discover none. No member of the party was at that period aware that entire or unopened mummies are not infrequently met. The brain it was customary to withdraw through the nose; the intestines through an incision in the side; the body was then shaved, washed, and salted; then laid aside for several weeks, when the operation of embalming, properly so called, began.

As no trace of an opening could be found, Doctor Ponnonner was preparing his instruments for dissection, when I observed that it was then past two o'clock. Hereupon it was agreed to postpone the internal examination until the next evening; and we were about to separate for the present, when some one suggested an experiment or two with the Voltaic pile.

The application of electricity to a mummy three or four thousand years old at the least, was an idea, if not very sage, still sufficiently original, and we all caught it at once. About one-tenth in earnest and nine-tenths in jest, we arranged a battery in the Doctor's study, and conveyed thither the Egyptian.

It was only after much trouble that we succeeded in laying bare some portions of the temporal muscle which appeared of less stony rigidity than other parts of the frame, but which, as we had anticipated, of course, gave no indication of galvanic susceptibility when brought in contact with the wire. This, the first trial, indeed, seemed decisive, and, with a hearty laugh at our own absurdity, we were bidding each other good night, when my eyes, happening to fall upon those of the Mummy, were there immediately riveted in amazement. My brief glance, in fact, had sufficed to assure me that the orbs which we had all supposed to be glass, and which were originally noticeable for a certain wild stare, were now so far covered by the lids, that only a small portion of the *tunica albuginea* remained visible.

With a shout I called attention to the fact, and it became immediately obvious to all.

I cannot say that I was *alarmed* at the phenomenon, because "alarmed" is, in my case, not exactly the word. It is possible, however, that, but for the Brown Stout, I might have been a little nervous. As for the rest of the company, they really made no attempt at concealing the downright fright which possessed them. Doctor Ponnonner was a man to be pitied. Mr. Gliddon, by some peculiar process, rendered himself invisible. Mr. Silk Buckingham, I fancy, will scarcely be so bold as to deny that he made his way, upon all fours, under the table.

After the first shock of astonishment, however, we resolved, as a mat-

ter of course, upon further experiment forthwith. Our operations were now directed against the great toe of the right foot. We made an incision over the outside of the exterior *os sesamoideum pollicis pedis,* and thus got at the root of the *abductor* muscle. Readjusting the battery, we now applied the fluid to the bisected nerves — when, with a movement of exceeding life-likeness, the Mummy first drew up its right knee so as to bring it nearly in contact with the abdomen, and then, straightening the limb with inconceivable force, bestowed a kick upon Doctor Ponnonner, which had the effect of discharging that gentleman, like an arrow from a catapult, through a window into the street below.

We rushed out *en masse* to bring in the mangled remains of the victim, but had the happiness to meet him upon the staircase, coming up in an unaccountable hurry, brimful of the most ardent philosophy, and more than ever impressed with the necessity of prosecuting our experiment with vigor and with zeal.

It was by his advice, accordingly, that we made, upon the spot, a profound incision into the tip of the subject's nose, while the Doctor himself, laying violent hands upon it, pulled it into vehement contact with the wire.

Morally and physically — figuratively and literally — was the effect electric. In the first place, the corpse opened its eyes and winked very rapidly for several minutes, as does Mr. Barnes in the pantomime; in the second place, it sneezed; in the third, it sat upon end; in the fourth, it shook its fist in Doctor Ponnonner's face; in the fifth, turning to Messieurs Gliddon and Buckingham, it addressed them, in very capital Egyptian, thus:

"I must say, gentlemen, that I am as much surprised as I am mortified at your behaviour. Of Doctor Ponnonner nothing better was to be expected. He is a poor little fat fool who *knows* no better. I pity and forgive him. But you, Mr. Gliddon — and you, Silk — who have travelled and resided in Egypt until one might imagine you to the manner born — you, I say who have been so much among us that you speak Egyptian fully as well, I think, as you write your mother tongue — you, whom I have always been led to regard as the firm friend of the mummies — I really did anticipate more gentlemanly conduct from *you.* What am I to think of your standing quietly by and seeing me thus unhandsomely used? What am I to suppose by your permitting Tom, Dick, and Harry to strip me of my coffins, and my clothes, in this wretchedly cold climate? In what light (to come to the point) am I to regard your aiding and abetting that miserable little villain, Doctor Ponnonner, in pulling me by the nose?"

It will be taken for granted, no doubt, that upon hearing this speech under the circumstances, we all either made for the door, or fell into violent hysterics, or went off in a general swoon. One of these three things was, I say, to be expected. Indeed each and all of these lines of conduct might have been very plausibly pursued. And, upon my word, I am at a

loss to know how or why it was that we pursued neither the one nor the
other. But, perhaps, the true reason is to be sought in the spirit of the
age, which proceeds by the rule of contraries altogether, and is now usually
admitted as the solution of every thing in the way of paradox and
impossibility. Or, perhaps, after all, it was only the Mummy's exceed-
ingly natural and matter-of-course air that divested his words of the ter-
rible. However this may be, the facts are clear, and no member of our
party betrayed any very particular trepidation, or seemed to consider that
any thing had gone very especially wrong.

For my part I was convinced it was all right, and merely stepped aside,
out of the range of the Egyptian's fist. Doctor Ponnonner thrust his hands
into his breeches' pockets, looked hard at the Mummy, and grew exces-
sively red in the face. Mr. Glidden stroked his whiskers and drew up the
collar of his shirt. Mr. Buckingham hung down his head, and put his
right thumb into the left corner of his mouth.

The Egyptian regarded him with a severe countenance for some min-
utes and at length, with a sneer, said:

"Why don't you speak, Mr. Buckingham? Did you hear what I asked
you, or not? Do take your thumb out of your mouth!"

Mr. Buckingham, hereupon, gave a slight start, took his right thumb
out of the left corner of his mouth, and, by way of indemnification in-
serted his left thumb in the right corner of the aperture above-mentioned.

Not being able to get an answer from Mr. B., the figure turned peev-
ishly to Mr. Glidden, and, in a peremptory tone, demanded in general
terms what we all meant.

Mr. Glidden replied at great length, in phonetics; and but for the
deficiency of American printing-offices in hieroglyphical type, it would
afford me much pleasure to record here, in the original, the whole of his
very excellent speech.

I may as well take this occasion to remark, that all the subsequent con-
versation in which the Mummy took a part, was carried on in primitive
Egyptian, through the medium (so far as concerned myself and other
untravelled members of the company) — through the medium, I say, of
Messieurs Glidden and Buckingham, as interpreters. These gentlemen
spoke the mother tongue of the Mummy with inimitable fluency and
grace; but I could not help observing that (owing, no doubt, to the intro-
duction of images entirely modern, and, of course, entirely novel to the
stranger) the two travellers were reduced, occasionally, to the employ-
ment of sensible forms for the purpose of conveying a particular mean-
ing. Mr. Glidden, at one period, for example, could not make the Egyp-
tian comprehend the term "politics," until he sketched upon the wall,
with a bit of charcoal, a little carbuncle-nosed gentleman, out at elbows,
standing upon a stump, with his left leg drawn back, right arm thrown
forward, with his fist shut, the eyes rolled up toward Heaven, and the

mouth open at an angle of ninety degrees. Just in the same way Mr. Buckingham failed to convey the absolutely modern idea "wig," until (at Doctor Ponnonner's suggestion) he grew very pale in the face, and consented to take off his own.

It will be readily understood that Mr. Gliddon's discourse turned chiefly upon the vast benefits accruing to science from the unrolling and disembowelling of mummies; apologizing, upon this score, for any disturbance that might have been occasioned *him*, in particular, the individual Mummy called Allamistakeo; and concluding with a mere hint (for it could scarcely be considered more) that, as these little matters were now explained, it might be as well to proceed with the investigation intended. Here Doctor Ponnonner made ready his instruments.

In regard to the latter suggestions of the orator, it appears that Allamistakeo had certain scruples of conscience, the nature of which I did not distinctly learn; but he expressed himself satisfied with the apologies tendered, and, getting down from the table, shook hands with the company all round.

When this ceremony was at an end, we immediately busied ourselves in repairing the damages which our subject had sustained from the scalpel. We sewed up the wound in his temple, bandaged his foot, and applied a square inch of black plaster to the tip of his nose.

It was now observed that the Count (this was the title, it seems, of Allamistakeo) had a slight fit of shivering — no doubt from the cold. The Doctor immediately repaired to his wardrobe, and soon returned with a black dress coat, made in Jennings' best manner, a pair of sky-blue plaid pantaloons with straps, a pink gingham *chemise*, a flapped vest of brocade, a white sack overcoat, a walking cane with a hook, a hat with no brim, patent-leather boots, straw-colored kid gloves, an eye-glass, a pair of whiskers, and a waterfall cravat. Owing to the disparity of size between the Count and the doctor (the proportion being as two to one), there was some little difficulty in adjusting these habiliments upon the person of the Egyptian; but when all was arranged, he might have been said to be dressed. Mr. Gliddon, therefore, gave him his arm, and led him to a comfortable chair by the fire, while the Doctor rang the bell upon the spot and ordered a supply of cigars and wine.

The conversation soon grew animated. Much curiosity was, of course, expressed in regard to the somewhat remarkable fact of Allamistakeo's still remaining alive.

"I should have thought," observed Mr. Buckingham, "that it is high time you were dead."

"Why," replied the Count, very much astonished, "I am little more than seven hundred years old! My father lived a thousand, and was by no means in his dotage when he died."

Here ensued a brisk series of questions and computations, by means of

which it became evident that the antiquity of the Mummy had been grossly misjudged. It had been five thousand and fifty years and some months since he had been consigned to the catacombs at Eleithias.

"But my remark," resumed Mr. Buckingham, "had no reference to your age at the period of interment (I am willing to grant, in fact, that you are still a young man), and my illusion was to the immensity of time during which, by your own showing, you must have been done up in asphaltum."

"In what?" said the Count.

"In asphaltum," persisted Mr. B.

"Ah, yes; I have some faint notion of what you mean; it might be made to answer, no doubt — but in my time we employed scarcely any thing else than the Bichloride of Mercury."

"But what we are especially at a loss to understand," said Doctor Ponnonner, "is how it happens that, having been dead and buried in Egypt five thousand years ago, you are here to-day all alive and looking so delightfully well."

"Had I been, as you say, *dead*," replied the Count, "it is more than probable that dead I should still be; for I perceive you are yet in the infancy of Galvanism, and cannot accomplish with it what was a common thing among us in the old days. But the fact is, I fell into catalepsy, and it was considered by my best friends that I was either dead or should be; they accordingly embalmed me at once — I presume you are aware of the chief principle of the embalming process?"

"Why, not altogether."

"Why, I perceive — a deplorable condition of ignorance! Well, I cannot enter into details just now: but it is necessary to explain that to embalm (properly speaking), in Egypt, was to arrest indefinitely *all* the animal functions subjected to the process. I use the word 'animal' in its widest sense, as including the physical not more than the moral and *vital* being. I repeat that the leading principle of embalmment consisted, with us, in the immediately arresting, and holding in perpetual *abeyance*, *all* the animal functions subjected to the process. To be brief, in whatever condition the individual was, at the period of embalmment, in that condition he remained. Now, as it is my good fortune to be of the blood of the Scarabæus, I was embalmed *alive*, as you see me at present."

"The blood of the Scarabæus!" exclaimed Doctor Ponnonner.

"Yes. The Scarabæus was the *insignium*, or the 'arms,' of a very distinguished and very rare patrician family. To be 'of the blood of the Scarabæus,' is merely to be one of that family of which the Scarabæus is the *insignium*. I speak figuratively."

"But what has this to do with you being alive?"

"Why, it is the general custom in Egypt to deprive a corpse, before embalmment, of its bowels and brains; the race of the Scarabæi alone did not coincide with the custom. Had I not been a Scarabæus, therefore,

I should have been without bowels and brains; and without either it is inconvenient to live."

"I perceive that," said Mr. Buckingham, "and I presume that all the *entire* mummies that come to hand are of the race of Scarabæi."

"Beyond doubt."

"I thought," said Mr. Gliddon, very meekly, "that the Scarabæus was one of the Egyptian gods."

"One of the Egyptian *what?*" exclaimed the Mummy, starting to its feet.

"Gods!" repeated the traveller.

"Mr. Gliddon, I really am astonished to hear you talk in this style," said the Count, resuming his chair. "No nation upon the face of the earth has ever acknowledged more than *one* god. The Scarabæus, the Ibis, etc., were with us (as similar creatures have been with others) the symbols, or *media*, through which we offered worship to the Creator too august to be more directly approached."

There was here a pause. At length the colloquy was renewed by Doctor Ponnonner.

"It is not improbable, then, from what you have explained," said he, "that among the catacombs near the Nile there may exist other mummies of the Scarabæus tribe, in a condition of vitality."

"There can be no question of it," replied the Count; "all the Scarabæi embalmed accidentally while alive, are alive now. Even some of those *purposely* so embalmed, may have been overlooked by their executors, and still remain in the tomb."

"Will you be kind enough to explain," I said, "what you mean by 'purposely so embalmed'?"

"With great pleasure," answered the Mummy, after surveying me leisurely through his eye-glass — for it was the first time I had ventured to address him a direct question.

"With great pleasure," he said. "The usual duration of man's life, in my time, was about eight hundred years. Few men died, unless by most extraordinary accident, before the age of six hundred; few lived longer than a decade of centuries; but eight were considered the natural term. After the discovery of the embalming principle, as I have already described it to you, it occurred to our philosophers that a laudable curiosity might be gratified, and, at the same time, the interests of science much advanced, by living this natural term in installments. In the case of history, indeed, experience demonstrated that something of this kind was indispensable. An historian, for example, having attained the age of five hundred, would write a book with great labor and then get himself carefully embalmed; leaving instructions to his executors *pro tem.*, that they should cause him to be revivified after the lapse of a certain period — say five or six hundred years. Resuming existence at the expiration of this time, he would invariably find his great work converted into a species of

hap-hazard note-book — that is to say, into a kind of literary arena for
the conflicting guesses, riddles, and personal squabbles of whole herds of
exasperated commentators. These guesses, etc., which passed under the
name of annotations, or emendations, were found so completely to have
enveloped, distorted, and overwhelmed the text, that the author had to
go about with a lantern to discover his own book. When discovered, it
was never worth the trouble of the search. After re-writing it throughout,
it was regarded as the bounden duty of the historian to set himself to
work immediately in correcting, from his own private knowledge and
experience, the traditions of the day concerning the epoch at which he
had originally lived. Now this process of re-scription and personal rectifi-
cation, pursued by various individual sages from time to time, had the
effect of preventing our history from degenerating into absolute fable."

"I beg your pardon," said Doctor Ponnonner at this point, laying his
hand gently upon the arm of the Egyptian — "I beg your pardon, sir,
but may I presume to interrupt you for one moment?"

"By all means, *sir*," replied the Count, drawing up.

"I merely wished to ask you a question," said the Doctor. "You men-
tioned the historian's personal correction of *traditions* respecting his
own epoch. Pray, sir, upon an average what proportion of these Kabbala
were usually found to be right?"

"The Kabbala, as you properly term them, sir, were generally discov-
ered to be precisely on a par with the facts recorded in the un-re-written
histories themselves; — that is to say, not one individual iota of either
was ever known, under any circumstances, to be not totally and radically
wrong."

"But since it is quite clear," resumed the Doctor, "that at least five
thousand years have elapsed since your entombment, I take it for granted
that your histories at that period, if not your traditions were sufficiently
explicit on that one topic of universal interest, the Creation, which took
place, as I presume you are aware, only about ten centuries before."

"Sir!" said the Count Allamistakeo.

The Doctor repeated his remarks, but it was only after much addi-
tional explanation that the foreigner could be made to comprehend them.
The latter at length said, hesitatingly:

"The ideas you have suggested are to me, I confess, utterly novel. Dur-
ing my time I never knew any one to entertain so singular a fancy as that
the universe (or this world if you will have it so) ever had a beginning
at all. I remember once, and once only, hearing something remotely
hinted, by a man of many speculations, concerning the origin *of the
human race*; and by this individual, the very word *Adam* (or Red Earth),
which you make use of, was employed. He employed it, however, in a
generical sense, with reference to the spontaneous germination from rank
soil (just as a thousand of the lower *genera* of creatures are germinated)
— the spontaneous germination, I say, of five vast hordes of men, simul·

taneously upspringing in five distinct and nearly equal divisions of the globe."

Here, in general, the company shrugged their shoulders, and one or two of us touched our foreheads with a very significant air. Mr. Silk Buckingham, first glancing slightly at the occiput and then at the sinciput of Allamistakeo, spoke as follows:

"The long duration of human life in your time, together with the occasional practice of passing it, as you have explained, in installments, must have had, indeed, a strong tendency to the general development and conglomeration of knowledge. I presume, therefore, that we are to attribute the marked inferiority of the old Egyptians in all particulars of science, when compared with the moderns, and more especially with the Yankees, altogether to the superior solidity of the Egyptian skull."

"I confess again," replied the Count, with much suavity, "that I am somewhat at a loss to comprehend you; pray, to what particulars of science do you allude?"

Here our whole party, joining voices, detailed, at great length, the assumptions of phrenology and the marvels of animal magnetism.

Having heard us to an end, the Count proceeded to relate a few anecdotes, which rendered it evident that prototypes of Gall and Spurzheim had flourished and faded in Egypt so long ago as to have been nearly forgotten, and that the manœuvres of Mesmer were really very contemptible tricks when put in collation with the positive miracles of the Theban *savans*, who created lice and a great many other similar things.

I here asked the Count if his people were able to calculate eclipses. He smiled rather contemptuously, and said they were.

This put me a little out, but I began to make other inquiries in regard to his astronomical knowledge, when a member of the company, who had never as yet opened his mouth, whispered in my ear, that for information on this head, I had better consult Ptolemy (whoever Ptolemy is), as well as one Plutarch *de facie lunæ*.

I then questioned the Mummy about burning-glasses and lenses, and, in general, about the manufacture of glass; but I had not made an end of my queries before the silent member again touched me quietly on the elbow, and begged me for God's sake to take a peep at Diodorus Siculus. As for the Count, he merely asked me, in the way of reply, if we moderns possessed any such microscopes as would enable us to cut cameos in the style of the Egyptians. While I was thinking how I should answer this question, little Doctor Ponnonner committed himself in a very extraordinary way.

"Look at our architecture!" he exclaimed, greatly to the indignation of both the travellers, who pinched him black and blue to no purpose.

"Look," he cried with enthusiasm, "at the Bowling-Green Fountain in New York! or if this be too vast a contemplation, regard for a moment the Capitol at Washington, D. C.!" — and the good little medical man

went on to detail, very minutely, the proportions of the fabric to which he referred. He explained that the portico alone was adorned with no less than four and twenty columns, five feet in diameter, and ten feet apart.

The Count said that he regretted not being able to remember, just at that moment, the precise dimensions of any one of the principal buildings of the city of Aznac, whose foundations were laid in the night of Time, but the ruins of which were still standing, at the epoch of his entombment, in a vast plain of sand to the westward of Thebes. He recollected, however, (talking of the porticoes,) that one affixed to an inferior palace in a kind of suburb called Carnac, consisted of a hundred and forty-four columns, thirty-seven feet in circumference, and twenty-five feet apart. The approach to this portico, from the Nile, was through an avenue two miles long, composed of sphynxes, statues, and obelisks, twenty, sixty, and a hundred feet in height. The palace itself (as well as he could remember) was, in one direction, two miles long, and might have been altogether about seven in circuit. Its walls were richly painted all over, within and without, with hieroglyphics. He would not pretend to *assert* that even fifty or sixty of the Doctor's Capitols might have been built within these walls, but he was by no means sure that two or three hundred of them might not have been squeezed in with some trouble. That palace at Carnac was an insignificant little building after all. He (the Count), however, could not conscientiously refuse to admit the ingenuity, magnificence, and superiority of the Fountain at the Bowling-Green, as described by the Doctor. Nothing like it, he was forced to allow, had ever been seen in Egypt or elsewhere.

I here asked the Count what he had to say to our railroads.

"Nothing," he replied, "in particular." They were rather slight, rather ill-conceived, and clumsily put together. They could not be compared, of course, with the vast, level, direct, iron-grooved causeways upon which the Egyptians conveyed entire temples and solid obelisks of a hundred and fifty feet in altitude.

I spoke of our gigantic mechanical forces.

He agreed that we knew something in that way, but inquired how I should have gone to work in getting up the imposts on the lintels of even the little palace at Carnac.

This question I concluded not to hear, and demanded if he had any idea of Artesian wells; but he simply raised his eyebrows; while Mr. Gliddon winked at me very hard and said, in a low tone, that one had been recently discovered by the engineers employed to bore for water in the Great Oasis.

I then mentioned our steel; but the foreigner elevated his nose, and asked me if our steel could have executed the sharp carved work seen on the obelisks, and which was wrought altogether by edge-tools of copper.

This disconcerted us so greatly that we thought it advisable to vary the attack to Metaphysics. We sent for a copy of a book called the "Dial,"

and read out of it a chapter or two about something that is not very clear, but which the Bostonians call the Great Movement of Progress.

The Count merely said that Great Movements were awfully common things in his day, and as for Progress, it was at one time quite a nuisance, but it never progressed.

We then spoke of the great beauty and importance of Democracy, and were at much trouble in impressing the Count with a due sense of the advantages we enjoyed in living where there was suffrage *ad libitum*, and no king.

He listened with marked interest, and in fact seemed not a little amused. When we had done, he said that, a great while ago, there had occurred something of a very similar sort. Thirteen Egyptian provinces determined all at once to be free, and to set a magnificent example to the rest of mankind. They assembled their wise men, and concocted the most ingenious constitution it is possible to conceive. For a while they managed remarkably well; only their habit of bragging was prodigious. The thing ended, however, in the consolidation of the thirteen states, with some fifteen or twenty others, in the most odious and insupportable despotism that was ever heard of upon the face of the Earth.

I asked what was the name of the usurping tyrant.

As well as the Count could recollect, it was *Mob*.

Not knowing what to say to this, I raised my voice, and deplored the Egyptian ignorance of steam.

The Count looked at me with much astonishment, but made no answer. The silent gentleman, however, gave me a violent nudge in the ribs with his elbows — told me I had sufficiently exposed myself for once — and demanded if I was really such a fool as not to know that the modern steam-engine is derived from the invention of Hero, through Solomon de Caus.

We were now in imminent danger of being discomfited; but, as good luck would have it, Doctor Ponnonner, having rallied, returned to our rescue, and inquired if the people of Egypt would seriously pretend to rival the moderns in the all-important particular of dress.

The Count, at this, glanced downward to the straps of his pantaloons, and then taking hold of the end of one of his coat-tails, held it up close to his eyes for some minutes. Letting it fall, at last, his mouth extended itself very gradually from ear to ear; but I do not remember that he said any thing in the way of reply.

Hereupon we recovered our spirits, and the Doctor, approaching the Mummy with great dignity, desired it to say candidly, upon its honor as a gentleman, if the Egyptians had comprehended, at *any* period, the manufacture of either Ponnonner's lozenges or Brandreth's pills.

We looked, with profound anxiety, for an answer — but in vain. It was not forthcoming. The Egyptian blushed and hung down his head. Never was triumph more consummate; never was defeat borne with so ill a

grace. Indeed, I could not endure the spectacle of the poor Mummy's mortification. I reached my hat, bowed to him stiffly, and took leave.

Upon getting home I found it past four o'clock, and went immediately to bed. It is now ten A.M. I have been up since seven, penning these memoranda for the benefit of my family and of mankind. The former I shall behold no more. My wife is a shrew. The truth is, I am heartily sick of this life and of the nineteenth century in general. I am convinced that every thing is going wrong. Besides, I am anxious to know who will be President in 2045. As soon, therefore, as I shave and swallow a cup of coffee, I shall just step over to Ponnonner's and get embalmed for a couple of hundred years.

The Power of Words

OINOS. Pardon, Agathos, the weakness of a spirit new-fledged with immortality!

AGATHOS. You have spoken nothing, my Oinos, for which pardon is to be demanded. Not even here is knowledge a thing of intuition. For wisdom, ask of the angels freely, that it may be given!

OINOS. But in this existence, I dreamed that I should be at once cognizant of all things, and thus at once be happy in being cognizant of all.

AGATHOS. Ah, not in knowledge is happiness, but in the acquisition of knowledge! In for ever knowing, we are for ever blessed; but to know all, were the curse of a fiend.

OINOS. But does not The Most High know all?

AGATHOS. *That* (since he is The Most Happy) must be still the *one* thing unknown even to HIM.

OINOS. But, since we grow hourly in knowledge, must not at *last* all things be known?

AGATHOS. Look down into the abysmal distances! — attempt to force the gaze down the multitudinous vistas of the stars, as we sweep slowly through them thus — and thus — and thus! Even the spiritual vision, is it not at all points arrested by the continuous golden walls of the universe? — the walls of the myriads of the shining bodies that mere number has appeared to blend into unity?

OINOS. I clearly perceive that the infinity of matter is no dream.

AGATHOS. There are *no* dreams in Aidenn — but it is here whispered that, of this infinity of matter, the *sole* purpose is to afford infinite springs, at which the soul may allay the thirst *to know*, which is for ever unquench-

able within it — since to quench it, would be to extinguish the soul's self. Question me then, my Oinos, freely and without fear. Come! we will leave to the left the loud harmony of the Pleiades, and swoop outward from the throne into the starry meadows beyond Orion, where, for pansies and violets, and heart's-ease, are the beds of the triplicate and triple-tinted suns.

Oinos. And now, Agathos, as we proceed, instruct me! — speak to me in the earth's familiar tones. I understand not what you hinted to me, just now, of the modes or of the method of what, during mortality, we were accustomed to call Creation. Do you mean to say that the Creator is not God?

Agathos. I mean to say that the Deity does not create.

Oinos. Explain.

Agathos. In the beginning *only*, he created. The seeming creatures which are now, throughout the universe, so perpetually springing into being, can only be considered as the mediate or indirect, not as the direct or immediate results of the Divine creative power.

Oinos. Among men, my Agathos, this idea would be considered heretical in the extreme.

Agathos. Among angels, my Oinos, it is seen to be simply true.

Oinos. I can comprehend you thus far — that certain operations of what we term Nature, or the natural laws, will, under certain conditions, give rise to that which has all the *appearance* of creation. Shortly before the final overthrow of the earth, there were, I well remember, many very successful experiments in what some philosophers were weak enough to denominate the creation of animalculæ.

Agathos. The cases of which you speak were, in fact, instances of the secondary creation — and of the *only* species of creation which has ever been, since the first word spoke into existence the first law.

Oinos. Are not the starry worlds that, from the abyss of nonentity, burst hourly forth into the heavens — are not these stars, Agathos, the immediate handiwork of the King?

Agathos. Let me endeavor, my Oinos, to lead you, step by step, to the conception I intend. You are well aware that, as no thought can perish, so no act is without infinite result. We moved our hands, for example, when we were dwellers on the earth, and, in so doing, we gave vibration to the atmosphere which engirdled it. This vibration was indefinitely extended, till it gave impulse to every particle of the earth's air, which thenceforward, *and for ever*, was actuated by the one movement of the hand. This fact the mathematicians of our globe well knew. They made the special effects, indeed, wrought in the fluid by special impulses, the subject of exact calculation — so that it became easy to determine in what precise period an impulse of given extent would engirdle the orb, and impress (for ever) every atom of the atmosphere circumambient. Retrograding, they found no difficulty, from a given effect, under given

conditions, in determining the value of the original impulse. Now the mathematicians who saw that the results of any given impulse were absolutely endless — and who saw that a portion of these results were accurately traceable through the agency of algebraic analysis — who saw, too, the facility of the retrogradation — these men saw, at the same time, that this species of analysis itself, had within itself a capacity for indefinite progress — that there were no bounds conceivable to its advancement and applicability, except within the intellect of him who advanced or applied it. But at this point our mathematicians paused.

Oinos. And why, Agathos, should they have proceeded?

Agathos. Because there were some considerations of deep interest beyond. It was deducible from what they knew, that to a being of infinite understanding — one to whom the *perfection* of the algebraic analysis lay unfolded — there could be no difficulty in tracing every impulse given the air — and the ether through the air — to the remotest consequences at any even infinitely remote epoch of time. It is indeed demonstrable that every such impulse *given the air, must, in the end,* impress every individual thing that exists *within the universe;* — and the being of infinite understanding — the being whom we have imagined — might trace the remote undulations of the impulse — trace them upward and onward in their influences upon all particles of all matter — upward and onward for ever in their modifications of old forms — or, in other words, *in their creation of new* — until he found them reflected — unimpressive *at last* — back from the throne of the Godhead. And not only could such a thing do this, but at any epoch, should a given result be afforded him — should one of these numberless comets, for example, be presented to his inspection — he could have no difficulty in determining, by the analytic retrogradation, to what original impulse it was due. This power of retrogradation in its absolute fulness and perfection — this faculty of referring at *all* epochs, *all* effects to *all* causes — is of course the prerogative of the Deity alone — but in every variety of degree, short of the absolute perfection, is the power itself exercised by the whole host of the Angelic intelligences.

Oinos. But you speak merely of impulses upon the air.

Agathos. In speaking of the air, I referred only to the earth; but the general proposition has reference to impulses upon the ether — which, since it pervades, and alone pervades all space, is thus the great medium of *creation.*

Oinos. Then all motion, of whatever nature, creates?

Agathos. It must: but a true philosophy has long taught that the source of all motion is thought — and the source of all thought is ——

Oinos. God.

Agathos. I have spoken to you, Oinos, as to a child of the fair Earth which lately perished — of impulses upon the atmosphere of the Earth.

Oinos. You did.

AGATHOS. And while I thus spoke, did there not cross your mind some thought of the *physical power of words?* Is not every word an impulse on the air?

OINOS. But why, Agathos, do you weep — and why, oh why do your wings droop as we hover above this fair star — which is the greenest and yet most terrible of all we have encountered in our flight? Its brilliant flowers look like a fairy dream — but its fierce volcanoes like the passions of a turbulent heart.

AGATHOS. They *are!* — they *are!* This wild star — it is now three centuries since, with clasped hands, and with streaming eyes, at the feet of my beloved — I spoke it — with a few passionate sentences — into birth. Its brilliant flowers *are* the dearest of all unfulfilled dreams, and its raging volcanoes *are* the passions of the most turbulent and unhallowed of hearts.

The Imp of the Perverse

IN the consideration of the faculties and impulses — of the *prima mobilia* of the human soul, the phrenologists have failed to make room for a propensity which, although obviously existing as a radical, primitive, irreducible sentiment, has been equally overlooked by all the moralists who have preceded them. In the pure arrogance of the reason, we have all overlooked it. We have suffered its existence to escape our senses, solely through want of belief — of faith; — whether it be faith in Revelation, or faith in the Kabbala. The idea of it has never occurred to us, simply because of its supererogation. We saw no *need* of the impulse — for the propensity. We could not perceive its necessity. We could not understand, that is to say, we could not have understood, had the notion of this *primum mobile* ever obtruded itself; — we could not have understood in what manner it might be made to further the objects of humanity, either temporal or eternal. It cannot be denied that phrenology and, in great measure, all metaphysicianism have been concocted *à priori.* The intellectual or logical man, rather than the understanding or observant man, set himself to imagine designs — to dictate purposes to God. Having thus fathomed, to his satisfaction, the intentions of Jehovah, out of these intentions he built his innumerable systems of mind. In the matter of phrenology, for example, we first determined, naturally enough, that it was the design of the Deity that man should eat. We then assigned to man an organ of alimentiveness, and this organ is the scourge with which the Deity compels man, will-I nill-I, into eating. Secondly, having settled it to be God's will that man should continue his species, we discovered an organ of amativeness, forthwith. And so with

combativeness, with ideality, with causality, with constructiveness, — so, in short, with every organ, whether representing a propensity, a moral sentiment, or a faculty of the pure intellect. And in these arrangements of the *principia* of human action, the Spurzheimites, whether right or wrong, in part, or upon the whole, have but followed, in principle, the footsteps of their predecessors: deducing and establishing every thing from the preconceived destiny of man, and upon the ground of the objects of his Creator.

It would have been wiser, it would have been safer, to classify (if classify we must) upon the basis of what man usually or occasionally did, and was always occasionally doing, rather than upon the basis of what we took it for granted the Deity intended him to do. If we cannot comprehend God in his visible works, how then in his inconceivable thoughts, that call the works into being? If we cannot understand him in his objective creatures, how then in his substantive moods and phases of creation?

Induction, *à posteriori*, would have brought phrenology to admit, as an innate and primitive principle of human action, a paradoxical something, which we may call *perverseness*, for want of a more characteristic term. In the sense I intend, it is, in fact, a *mobile* without motive, a motive not *motivirt*. Through its promptings we act without comprehensible object; or, if this shall be understood as a contradiction in terms, we may so far modify the proposition as to say, that through its promptings we act, for the reason that we should *not*. In theory, no reason can be more unreasonable; but, in fact, there is none more strong. With certain minds, under certain conditions, it becomes absolutely irresistible. I am not more certain that I breathe, than that the assurance of the wrong or error of any action is often the one unconquerable *force* which impels us, and alone impels us to its prosecution. Nor will this overwhelming tendency to do wrong for the wrong's sake, admit of analysis, or resolution into ulterior elements. It is a radical, a primitive impulse — elementary. It will be said, I am aware, that when we persist in acts because we feel we should *not* persist in them, our conduct is but a modification of that which ordinarily springs from the *combativeness* of phrenology. But a glance will show the fallacy of this idea. The phrenological combativeness has for its essence, the necessity of self-defence. It is our safeguard against injury. Its principle regards our well-being; and thus the desire to be well is excited simultaneously with its development. It follows, that the desire to be well must be excited simultaneously with any principle which shall be merely a modification of combativeness, but in the case of that something which I term *perverseness*, the desire to be well is not only not aroused, but a strongly antagonistical sentiment exists.

An appeal to one's own heart is, after all, the best reply to the sophistry just noticed. No one who trustingly consults and thoroughly ques-

tions his own soul, will be disposed to deny the entire radicalness of the propensity in question. It is not more incomprehensible than distinctive. There lives no man who at some period has not been tormented, for example, by an earnest desire to tantalize a listener by circumlocution. The speaker is aware that he displeases; he has every intention to please, he is usually curt, precise, and clear; the most laconic and luminous language is struggling for utterance upon his tongue; it is only with difficulty that he restrains himself from giving it flow; he dreads and deprecates the anger of him whom he addresses; yet, the thought strikes him, that by certain involutions and parentheses this anger may be engendered. That single thought is enough. The impulse increases to a wish, the wish to a desire, the desire to an uncontrollable longing, and the longing (to the deep regret and mortification of the speaker, and in defiance of all consequences) is indulged.

We have a task before us which must be speedily performed. We know that it will be ruinous to make delay. The most important crisis of our life calls, trumpet-tongued, for immediate energy and action. We glow, we are consumed with eagerness to commence the work, with the anticipation of whose glorious result our whole souls are on fire. It must, it shall be undertaken to-day, and yet we put it off until to-morrow; and why? There is no answer, except that we feel *perverse*, using the word with no comprehension of the principle. To-morrow arrives, and with it a more impatient anxiety to do our duty, but with this very increase of anxiety arrives, also, a nameless, a positively fearful, because unfathomable, craving for delay. This craving gathers strength as the moments fly. The last hour for action is at hand. We tremble with the violence of the conflict within us, — of the definite with the indefinite — of the substance with the shadow. But, if the contest have proceeded thus far, it is the shadow which prevails, — we struggle in vain. The clock strikes, and is the knell of our welfare. At the same time, it is the chanticleer-note to the ghost that has so long overawed us. It flies — it disappears — we are free. The old energy returns. We will labor *now*. Alas, it is *too late!*

We stand upon the brink of a precipice. We peer into the abyss — we grow sick and dizzy. Our first impulse is to shrink from the danger. Unaccountably we remain. By slow degrees our sickness and dizziness and horror become merged in a cloud of unnamable feeling. By gradations, still more imperceptible, this cloud assumes shape, as did the vapor from the bottle out of which arose the genius in the Arabian Nights. But out of this *our* cloud upon the precipice's edge, there grows into palpability, a shape, far more terrible than any genius or any demon of a tale, and yet it is but a thought, although a fearful one, and one which chills the very marrow of our bones with the fierceness of the delight of its horror. It is merely the idea of what would be our sensations during the sweeping precipitancy of a fall from such a height. And this fall — this rush-

ing annihilation — for the very reason that it involves that one most ghastly and loathsome of all the most ghastly and loathsome images of death and suffering which have ever presented themselves to our imagination — for this very cause do we now the most vividly desire it. And because our reason violently deters us from the brink, *therefore* do we the most impetuously approach it. There is no passion in nature so demoniacally impatient, as that of him who, shuddering upon the edge of a precipice, thus meditates a plunge. To indulge, for a moment, in any attempt at *thought*, is to be inevitably lost; for reflection but urges us to forbear, and *therefore* it is, I say, that we *cannot*. If there be no friendly arm to check us, or if we fail in a sudden effort to prostrate ourselves backward from the abyss, we plunge, and are destroyed.

Examine these similar actions as we will, we shall find them resulting solely from the spirit of the *Perverse*. We perpetrate them because we feel that we should *not*. Beyond or behind this there is no intelligible principle; and we might, indeed, deem this perverseness a direct instigation of the Arch-Fiend, were it not occasionally known to operate in furtherance of good.

I have said thus much, that in some measure I may answer your question, that I may explain to you why I am here, that I may assign to you something that shall have at least the faint aspect of a cause for my wearing these fetters, and for my tenanting this cell of the condemned. Had I not been thus prolix, you might either have misunderstood me altogether; or, with the rabble, have fancied me mad. As it is, you will easily perceive that I am one of the many uncounted victims of the Imp of the Perverse.

It is impossible that any deed could have been wrought with a more thorough deliberation. For weeks, for months, I pondered upon the means of the murder. I rejected a thousand schemes, because their accomplishment involved a *chance* of detection. At length, in reading some French Memoirs, I found an account of a nearly fatal illness that occurred to Madame Pilau, through the agency of a candle accidentally poisoned. The idea struck my fancy at once. I knew my victim's habit of reading in bed. I knew, too, that his apartment was narrow and ill-ventilated. But I need not vex you with impertinent details. I need not describe the easy artifices by which I substituted, in his bed-room candle-stand, a wax-light of my own making for the one which I there found. The next morning he was discovered dead in his bed, and the Coroner's verdict was — "Death by the visitation of God."

Having inherited his estate, all went well with me for years. The idea of detection never once entered my brain. Of the remains of the fatal taper I had myself carefully disposed. I had left no shadow of a clew by which it would be possible to convict, or even to suspect, me of the crime. It is inconceivable how rich a sentiment of satisfaction arose in my bosom as I reflected upon my absolute security. For a very long period

of time I was accustomed to revel in this sentiment. It afforded me more real delight than all the mere worldly advantages accruing from my sin. But there arrived at length an epoch, from which the pleasurable feeling grew, by scarcely perceptible gradations, into a haunting and harassing thought. It harassed because it haunted. I could scarcely get rid of it for an instant. It is quite a common thing to be thus annoyed with the ringing in our ears, or rather in our memories, of the burthen of some ordinary song, or some unimpressive snatches from an opera. Nor will we be the less tormented if the song in itself be good, or the opera air meritorious. In this manner, at last, I would perpetually catch myself pondering upon my security, and repeating. in a low undertone, the phrase, "I am safe."

One day, whilst sauntering along the streets, I arrested myself in the act of murmuring, half aloud, these customary syllables. In a fit of petulance, I remodelled them thus; "I am safe — I am safe — yes — if I be not fool enough to make open confession!"

No sooner had I spoken these words, than I felt an icy chill creep to my heart. I had had some experience in these fits of perversity, (whose nature I have been at some trouble to explain), and I remembered well that in no instance I had successfully resisted their attacks. And now my own casual self-suggestion that I might possibly be fool enough to confess the murder of which I had been guilty, confronted me, as if the very ghost of him whom I had murdered — and beckoned me on to death.

At first, I made an effort to shake off this nightmare of the soul. I walked vigorously — faster — still faster — at length I ran. I felt a maddening desire to shriek aloud. Every succeeding wave of thought overwhelmed me with new terror, for, alas! I well, too well understood that to *think*, in my situation, was to be lost. I still quickened my pace. I bounded like a madman through the crowded thoroughfares. At length, the populace took the alarm, and pursued me. I felt *then* the consummation of my fate. Could I have torn out my tongue, I would have done it, but a rough voice resounded in my ears — a rougher grasp seized me by the shoulder. I turned — I gasped for breath. For a moment I experienced all the pangs of suffocation; I became blind, and deaf, and giddy; and then some invisible fiend, I thought, struck me with his broad palm upon the back. The long imprisoned secret burst forth from my soul.

They say that I spoke with a distinct enunciation, but with marked emphasis and passionate hurry, as if in dread of interruption before concluding the brief, but pregnant sentences that consigned me to the hangman and to hell.

Having related all that was necessary for the fullest judicial conviction, I fell prostrate in a swoon.

But why shall I say more? To-day I wear these chains, and am *here!* To-morrow I shall be fetterless! — *but where?*

The System of Dr. Tarr and Prof. Fether

DURING the autumn of 18—, while on a tour through the extreme southern provinces of France, my route led me within a few miles of a certain *Maison de Santé* or private mad-house, about which I had heard much in Paris from my medical friends. As I had never visited a place of the kind, I thought the opportunity too good to be lost; and so proposed to my travelling companion (a gentleman with whom I had made casual acquaintance a few days before) that we should turn aside, for an hour or so, and look through the establishment. To this he objected — pleading haste in the first place, and, in the second, a very usual horror at the sight of a lunatic. He begged me, however, not to let any mere courtesy towards himself interfere with the gratification of my curiosity, and said that he would ride on leisurely, so that I might overtake him during the day, or, at all events, during the next. As he bade me good-bye, I bethought me that there might be some difficulty in obtaining access to the premises, and mentioned my fears on this point. He replied that, in fact, unless I had personal knowledge of the superintendent, Monsieur Maillard, or some credential in the way of a letter, a difficulty might be found to exist, as the regulations of these private mad-houses were more rigid than the public hospital laws. For himself, he added, he had, some years since, made the acquaintance of Maillard, and would so far assist me as to ride up to the door and introduce me; although his feelings on the subject of lunacy would not permit of his entering the house.

I thanked him, and, turning from the main road, we entered a grass-grown by-path, which, in half an hour, nearly lost itself in a dense forest, clothing the base of a mountain. Through this dank and gloomy wood we rode some two miles, when the *Maison de Santé* came in view. It was a fantastic *château*, much dilapidated, and indeed scarcely tenantable through age and neglect. Its aspect inspired me with absolute dread, and, checking my horse, I half resolved to turn back. I soon, however, grew ashamed of my weakness, and proceeded.

As we rode up to the gate-way, I perceived it slightly open, and the visage of a man peering through. In an instant afterward, this man came forth, accosted my companion by name, shook him cordially by the hand, and begged him to alight. It was Monsieur Maillard himself. He was a portly, fine-looking gentleman of the old school, with a polished manner, and a certain air of gravity, dignity, and authority which was very impressive.

My friend, having presented me, mentioned my desire to inspect the establishment, and received Monsieur Maillard's assurance that he would show me all attention, now took leave, and I saw him no more.

When he had gone, the superintendent ushered me into a small and exceedingly neat parlor, containing, among other indications of refined taste, many books, drawings, pots of flowers, and musical instruments. A cheerful fire blazed upon the hearth. At a piano, singing an aria from Bellini, sat a young and very beautiful woman, who, at my entrance, paused in her song, and received me with graceful courtesy. Her voice was low, and her whole manner subdued. I thought, too, that I perceived the traces of sorrow in her countenance, which was excessively, although to my taste, not unpleasingly, pale. She was attired in deep mourning, and excited in my bosom a feeling of mingled respect, interest, and admiration.

I had heard, at Paris, that the institution of Monsieur Maillard was managed upon what is vulgarly termed the "system of soothing" — that all punishments were avoided — that even confinement was seldom resorted to — that the patients, while secretly watched, were left much apparent liberty, and that most of them were permitted to roam about the house and grounds in the ordinary apparel of persons in right mind.

Keeping these impressions in view, I was cautious in what I said before the young lady; for I could not be sure that she was sane; and, in fact, there was a certain restless brilliancy about her eyes which half led me to imagine she was not. I confined my remarks, therefore, to general topics, and to such as I thought would not be displeasing or exciting even to a lunatic. She replied in a perfectly rational manner to all that I said; and even her original observations were marked with the soundest good sense; but a long acquaintance with the metaphysics of *mania*, had taught me to put no faith in such evidence of sanity, and I continued to practise, throughout the interview, the caution with which I commenced it.

Presently a smart footman in livery brought in a tray with fruit, wine, and other refreshments, of which I partook, the lady soon afterward leaving the room. As she departed I turned my eyes in an inquiring manner toward my host.

"No," he said, "oh, no — a member of my family — my niece, and a most accomplished woman."

"I beg a thousand pardons for the suspicion," I replied, "but of course you will know how to excuse me. The excellent administration of your affairs here is well understood in Paris, and I thought it just possible, you know —"

"Yes, yes — say no more — or rather it is myself who should thank you for the commendable prudence you have displayed. We seldom find so much of forethought in young men; and, more than once, some unhappy *contre-temps* has occurred in consequence of thoughtlessness on the part of our visitors. While my former system was in operation, and my patients were permitted the privilege of roaming to and fro at will, they were often aroused to a dangerous frenzy by injudicious persons who

called to inspect the house. Hence I was obliged to enforce a rigid system of exclusion; and none obtained access to the premises upon whose discretion I could not rely."

"While your *former* system was in operation!" I said, repeating his words — "do I understand you, then, to say that the 'soothing system' of which I have heard so much is no longer in force?"

"It is now," he replied, "several weeks since we have concluded to renounce it forever."

"Indeed! you astonish me!"

"We found it, sir," he said, with a sigh, "absolutely necessary to return to the old usages. The *danger* of the soothing system was, at all times, appalling; and its advantages have been much overrated. I believe, sir, that in this house it has been given a fair trial, if ever in any. We did every thing that rational humanity could suggest. I am sorry that you could not have paid us a visit at an earlier period, that you might have judged for yourself. But I presume you are conversant with the soothing practice — with its details."

"Not altogether. What I have heard has been at third or fourth hand."

"I may state the system, then, in general terms, as one in which the patients were *menages* — humored. We contradicted *no* fancies which entered the brains of the mad. On the contrary, we not only indulged but encouraged them; and many of our most permanent cures have been thus effected. There is no argument which so touches the feeble reason of the madman as the *argumentum ad absurdum*. We have had men, for example, who fancied themselves chickens. The cure was, to insist upon the thing as a fact — to accuse the patient of stupidity in not sufficiently perceiving it to be a fact — and thus to refuse him any other diet for a week than that which properly appertains to a chicken. In this manner a little corn and gravel were made to perform wonders."

"But was this species of acquiescence all?"

"By no means. We put much faith in amusements of a simple kind, such as music, dancing, gymnastic exercises generally, cards, certain classes of books, and so forth. We affected to treat each individual as if for some ordinary physical disorder; and the word 'lunacy' was never employed. A great point was to set each lunatic to guard the actions of all the others. To repose confidence in the understanding or discretion of a madman, is to gain him body and soul. In this way we were enabled to dispense with an expensive body of keepers."

"And you had no punishments of any kind?"

"None."

"And you never confined your patients?"

"Very rarely. Now and then, the malady of some individual growing to a crisis, or taking a sudden turn of fury, we conveyed him to a secret cell, lest his disorder should infect the rest, and there kept him until we

could dismiss him to his friends — for with the raging maniac we have nothing to do. He is usually removed to the public hospitals."

"And you have now changed all this — and you think for the better?"

"Decidedly. The system had its disadvantages, and even its dangers. It is now, happily, exploded throughout all the *Maisons de Santé* of France."

"I am very much surprised," I said, "at what you tell me; for I made sure that, at this moment, no other method of treatment for mania existed in any portion of the country."

"You are young yet, my friend," replied my host, "but the time will arrive when you will learn to judge for yourself of what is going on in the world, without trusting to the gossip of others. Believe nothing you hear, and only one-half that you see. Now about our *Maisons de Santé*, it is clear that some ignoramus has misled you. After dinner, however, when you have sufficiently recovered from the fatigue of your ride, I will be happy to take you over the house, and introduce to you a system which, in my opinion, and in that of every one who has witnessed its operation, is incomparably the most effectual as yet devised."

"Your own?" I inquired — "one of your own invention?"

"I am proud," he replied, "to acknowledge that it is — at least in some measure."

In this manner I conversed with Monsieur Maillard for an hour or two, during which he showed me the gardens and conservatories of the place.

"I cannot let you see my patients," he said, "just at present. To a sensitive mind there is always more or less of the shocking in such exhibitions; and I do not wish to spoil your appetite for dinner. We will dine. I can give you some veal *à la Menehoult*, with cauliflowers in *velouté* sauce — after that a glass of *Clos de Vougeôt* — then your nerves will be sufficiently steadied."

At six, dinner was announced; and my host conducted me into a large *salle à manger*, where a very numerous company were assembled — twenty-five or thirty in all. They were, apparently, people of rank — certainly of high breeding — although their habiliments, I thought, were extravagantly rich, partaking somewhat too much of the ostentatious finery of the *vielle cour*. I noticed that at least two-thirds of these guests were ladies; and some of the latter were by no means accoutred in what a Parisian would consider good taste at the present day. Many females, for example, whose age could not have been less than seventy, were bedecked with a profusion of jewelry, such as rings, bracelets, and earrings, and wore their bosoms and arms shamefully bare. I observed, too, that very few of the dresses were well made — or, at least, that very few of them fitted the wearers. In looking about, I discovered the interesting girl to whom Monsieur Maillard had presented me in the little parlor; but my surprise was great to see her wearing a hoop and far-

thingale, with high-heeled shoes, and a dirty cap of Brussels lace, so much too large for her that it gave her face a ridiculously diminutive expression. When I had first seen her, she was attired, most becomingly, in deep mourning. There was an air of oddity, in short, about the dress of the whole party, which, at first, caused me to recur to my original idea of the "soothing system," and to fancy that Monsieur Maillard had been willing to deceive me until after dinner, that I might experience no uncomfortable feelings during the repast, at finding myself dining with lunatics; but I remembered having been informed, in Paris, that the southern provincialists were a peculiarly eccentric people, with a vast number of antiquated notions; and then, too, upon conversing with several members of the company, my apprehensions were immediately and fully dispelled.

The dining-room itself, although perhaps sufficiently comfortable and of good dimensions, had nothing too much of elegance about it. For example, the floor was uncarpeted; in France, however, a carpet is frequently dispensed with. The windows, too, were without curtains; the shutters, being shut, were securely fastened with iron bars, applied diagonally, after the fashion of our ordinary shop-shutters. The apartment, I observed, formed, in itself, a wing of the *château*, and thus the windows were on three sides of the parallelogram, the door being at the other. There were no less than ten windows in all.

The table was superbly set out. It was loaded with plate, and more than loaded with delicacies. The profusion was absolutely barbaric. There were meats enough to have feasted the Anakim. Never, in all my life, had I witnessed so lavish, so wasteful an expenditure of the good things of life. There seemed very little taste, however, in the arrangements; and my eyes, accustomed to quiet lights, were sadly offended by the prodigious glare of a multitude of wax candles, which, in silver *candelabra*, were deposited upon the table, and all about the room, wherever it was possible to find a place. There were several active servants in attendance; and, upon a large table, at the farther end of the apartment, were seated seven or eight people with fiddles, fifes, trombones, and a drum. These fellows annoyed me very much, at intervals, during the repast, by an infinite variety of noises, which were intended for music, and which appeared to afford much entertainment to all present, with the exception of myself.

Upon the whole, I could not help thinking that there was much of the *bizarre* about every thing I saw — but then the world is made up of all kinds of persons, with all modes of thought, and all sorts of conventional customs. I had travelled, too, so much, as to be quite an adept at the *nil admirari*; so I took my seat very coolly at the right hand of my host, and, having an excellent appetite, did justice to the good cheer set before me.

The conversation, in the meantime, was spirited and general. The ladies, as usual, talked a great deal. I soon found that nearly all the company were well educated; and my host was a world of good-humored anecdote in himself. He seemed quite willing to speak of his position as superintendent of a *Maison de Santé*; and, indeed, the topic of lunacy was, much to my surprise, a favorite one with all present. A great many amusing stories were told, having reference to the *whims* of the patients.

"We had a fellow here once," said a fat little gentleman, who sat at my right, — "a fellow that fancied himself a tea-pot; and by the way, is it not especially singular how often this particular crotchet has entered the brain of the lunatic? There is scarcely an insane asylum in France which cannot supply a human tea-pot. *Our* gentleman was a Britannia-ware tea-pot, and was careful to polish himself every morning with buckskin and whiting."

"And then," said a tall man just opposite, "we had here, not long ago, a person who had taken it into his head that he was a donkey — which allegorically speaking, you will say, was quite true. He was a troublesome patient; and we had much ado to keep him within bounds. For a long time he would eat nothing but thistles; but of this idea we soon cured him by insisting upon his eating nothing else. Then he was perpetually kicking out his heels — so — so — "

"Mr. De Kock! I will thank you to behave yourself!" here interrupted an old lady, who sat next to the speaker. "Please keep your feet to yourself! You have spoiled my brocade! Is it necessary, pray, to illustrate a remark in so practical a style? Our friend here can surely comprehend you without all this. Upon my word, you are nearly as great a donkey as the poor unfortunate imagined himself. Your acting is very natural, as I live."

"*Mille pardons! Ma'm'selle!*" replied Monsieur De Kock, thus addressed — "a thousand pardons! I had no intention of offending. Ma'm'selle Laplace — Monsieur De Kock will do himself the honor of taking wine with you."

Here Monsieur De Kock bowed low, kissed his hand with much ceremony, and took wine with Ma'm'selle Laplace.

"Allow me, *mon ami*," now said Monsieur Maillard, addressing myself, "allow me to send you a morsel of this veal *à la St. Menhoult* — you will find it particularly fine."

At this instant three sturdy waiters had just succeeded in depositing safely upon the table an enormous dish, or trencher, containing what I supposed to be the "*monstrum horrendum, informe, ingens, cui lumen ademptum.*" A closer scrutiny assured me, however, that it was only a small calf roasted whole, and set upon its knees, with an apple in its mouth, as is the English fashion of dressing a hare.

"Thank you, no," I replied; "to say the truth, I am not particularly

partial to veal *à la St.* —— what is it? — for I do not find that it alto-
gether agrees with me. I will change my plate, however, and try some
of the rabbit."

There were several side-dishes on the table, containing what appeared
to be the ordinary French rabbit — a very delicious *morceau*, which I can
recommend.

"Pierre," cried the host, "change this gentleman's plate, and give him
a side-piece of this rabbit *au-chat*."

"This what?" said I.

"This rabbit *au-chat*."

"Why, thank you — upon second thoughts, no. I will just help myself
to some of the ham."

There is no knowing what one eats, thought I to myself, at the tables
of these people of the province. I will have none of their rabbit *au-chat* —
and, for the matter of that, none of their *cat-au-rabbit* either.

"And then," said a cadaverous looking personage, near the foot of the
table, taking up the thread of the conversation where it had been broken
off, — "and then, among other oddities, we had a patient, once upon a
time, who very pertinaciously maintained himself to be a Cordova
cheese, and went about, with a knife in his hand, soliciting his friends
to try a small slice from the middle of his leg."

"He was a great fool, beyond doubt," interposed some one, "but not
to be compared with a certain individual whom we all know, with the
exception of this strange gentleman. I mean the man who took himself
for a bottle of champagne, and always went off with a pop and a fizz, in
this fashion."

Here the speaker, very rudely, as I thought, put his right thumb in
his left cheek, withdrew it with a sound resembling the popping of a
cork, and then, by a dexterous movement of the tongue upon the teeth,
created a sharp hissing and fizzing, which lasted for several minutes,
in imitation of the frothing of champagne. This behavior, I saw plainly,
was not very pleasing to Monsieur Maillard; but that gentleman said
nothing, and the conversation was resumed by a very lean little man in
a big wig.

"And then there was an ignoramus," said he, "who mistook himself
for a frog; which, by the way, he resembled in no little degree. I wish
you could have seen him, sir," — here the speaker addressed myself —
"it would have done your heart good to see the natural airs that he put
on. Sir, if that man was *not* a frog, I can only observe that it is a pity he
was not. His croak thus — o-o-o-o-gh — o-o-o-o-gh! was the finest note in
the world — B flat; and when he put his elbows upon the table thus —
after taking a glass or two of wine — and distended his mouth, thus, and
rolled up his eyes, thus, and winked them with excessive rapidity, thus,
why then, sir, I take it upon myself to say, positively, that you would
have been lost in admiration of the genius of the man."

"I have no doubt of it," I said.

"And then," said somebody else, "then there was Petit Gaillard, who thought himself a pinch of snuff, and was truly distressed because he could not take himself between his own finger and thumb."

"And then there was Jules Desoulières, who was a very singular genius, indeed, and went mad with the idea that he was a pumpkin. He persecuted the cook to make him up into pies — a thing which the cook indignantly refused to do. For my part, I am by no means sure that a pumpkin pie *à la Desoulières* would not have been very capital eating indeed!"

"You astonish me!" said I; and I looked inquisitively at Monsieur Maillard.

"Ha! ha! ha!" said that gentleman — "he! he! he! — hi! hi! hi! — ho! ho! ho! — hu! hu! hu! — very good indeed! You must not be astonished, *mon ami*; our friend here is a wit — a *drôle* — you must not understand him to the letter."

"And then," said some other one of the party, — "then there was Bouffon Le Grand — another extraordinary personage in his way. He grew deranged through love, and fancied himself possessed of two heads. One of these he maintained to be the head of Cicero; the other he imagined a composite one, being Demosthenes' from the top of the forehead to the mouth, and Lord Brougham's from the mouth to the chin. It is not impossible that he was wrong; but he would have convinced you of his being in the right; for he was a man of great eloquence. He had an absolute passion for oratory, and could not refrain from display. For example, he used to leap upon the dinner-table thus, and — and — "

Here a friend, at the side of the speaker, put a hand upon his shoulder and whispered a few words in his ear; upon which he ceased talking with great suddenness, and sank back within his chair.

"And then," said the friend who had whispered, "there was Boullard, the tee-totum. I call him the tee-totum because, in fact, he was seized with the droll, but not altogether irrational, crotchet, that he had been converted into a tee-totum. You would have roared with laughter to see him spin. He would turn round upon one heel by the hour, in this manner — so — "

Here the friend whom he had just interrupted by a whisper, performed an exactly similar office for himself.

"But then," cried the old lady, at the top of her voice, "your Monsieur Boullard was a madman, and a very silly madman at best; for who, allow me to ask you, ever heard of a human tee-totum? The thing is absurd. Madame Joyeuse was a more sensible person, as you know. She had a crotchet, but it was instinct with common sense, and gave pleasure to all who had the honor of her acquaintance. She found, upon mature deliberation, that, by some accident, she had been turned into a chicken-cock; but, as such, she behaved with propriety. She flapped her wings

with prodigious effect — so — so — so — and, as for her crow, it was delicious! Cock-a-doodle-doo! — cock-a-doodle-doo! — cock-a-doodle-de-doo-doo-dooo-do-o-o-o-o-o-o!"

"Madame Joyeuse, I will thank you to behave yourself!" here interrupted our host, very angrily. "You can either conduct yourself as a lady should do, or you can quit the table forthwith — take your choice."

The lady (whom I was much astonished to hear addressed as Madame Joyeuse, after the description of Madame Joyeuse she had just given) blushed up to the eyebrows, and seemed exceedingly abashed at the reproof. She hung down her head, and said not a syllable in reply. But another and younger lady resumed the theme. It was my beautiful girl of the little parlor.

"Oh, Madame Joyeuse *was* a fool!" she exclaimed, "but there was really much sound sense, after all, in the opinion of Eugénie Salsafette. She was a very beautiful and painfully modest young lady, who thought the ordinary mode of habiliment indecent, and wished to dress herself, always, by getting outside instead of inside of her clothes. It is a thing very easily done, after all. You have only to do so — and then so — so — so — and then so — so — so — and then — "

"Mon dieu! Ma'm'selle Salsafette!" here cried a dozen voices at once. "What *are* you about? — forbear! — that is sufficient! — we see, very plainly, how it is done! — hold! hold!" and several persons were already leaping from their seats to withhold Ma'm'selle Salsafette from putting herself upon a par with the Medicean Venus, when the point was very effectually and suddenly accomplished by a series of loud screams, or yells, from some portion of the main body of the *château*.

My nerves were very much affected, indeed, by these yells: but the rest of the company I really pitied. I never saw any set of reasonable people so thoroughly frightened in my life. They all grew as pale as so many corpses, and, shrinking within their seats, sat quivering and gibbering with terror, and listening for a repetition of the sound. It came again — louder and seemingly nearer — and then a third time *very* loud, and then a fourth time with a vigor evidently diminished. At this apparent dying away of the noise, the spirits of the company were immediately regained, and all was life and anecdote as before. I now ventured to inquire the cause of the disturbance.

"A mere *bagatelle*," said Monsieur Maillard. "We are used to these things, and care really very little about them. The lunatics, every now and then, get up a howl in concert; one starting another, as is sometimes the case with a bevy of dogs at night. It occasionally happens, however, that the *concerto* yells are succeeded by a simultaneous effort at breaking loose; when, of course, some little danger is to be apprehended."

"And how many have you in charge?"

"At present we have not more than ten, altogether."

"Principally females, I presume?"

"Oh, no — every one of them men, and stout fellows, too, I can tell you."

"Indeed! I have always understood that the majority of lunatics were of the gentler sex."

"It is generally so, but not always. Some time ago, there were about twenty-seven patients here; and, of that number, no less than eighteen were women; but, lately, matters have changed very much, as you see."

"Yes — have changed very much, as you see," here interrupted the gentleman who had broken the shins of Ma'm'selle Laplace.

"Yes — have changed very much, as you see!" chimed in the whole company at once.

"Hold your tongues, every one of you!" said my host, in a great rage. Whereupon the whole company maintained a dead silence for nearly a minute. As for one lady, she obeyed Monsieur Maillard to the letter, and thrusting out her tongue, which was an excessively long one, held it very resignedly, with both hands, until the end of the entertainment.

"And this gentlewoman," said I, to Monsieur Maillard, bending over and addressing him in a whisper — "this good lady who has just spoken, and who gives us the cock-a-doodle-de-doo — she, I presume, is harmless — quite harmless, eh?"

"Harmless!" ejaculated he, in unfeigned surprise, "why — why, what *can* you mean?"

"Only slightly touched?" said I, touching my head. "I take it for granted that she is not particularly — not dangerously affected, eh?"

"*Mon dieu!* what *is* it you imagine? This lady, my particular old friend Madame Joyeuse, is as absolutely sane as myself. She has her little eccentricities, to be sure — but then, you know, all old women — all *very* old women — are more or less eccentric!"

"To be sure," said I, — "to be sure — and then the rest of these ladies and gentlemen — "

"Are my friends and keepers," interrupted Monsieur Maillard, drawing himself up with *hauteur*, — "my very good friends and assistants."

"What! all of them?" I asked, — "the women and all?"

"Assuredly," he said, — "we could not do at all without the women; they are the best lunatic nurses in the world; they have a way of their own, you know; their bright eyes have a marvellous effect; — something like the fascination of the snake, you know."

"To be sure," said I, — "to be sure! They behave a little odd, eh? — they are a little *queer*, eh? — don't you think so?"

"Odd! — queer! — why, do you *really* think so? We are not very prudish, to be sure, here in the South — do pretty much as we please — enjoy life, and all that sort of thing, you know — "

"To be sure," said I, — "to be sure."

"And then, perhaps, this *Clos de Vougeôt* is a little heady, you know — a little *strong* — you understand, eh?"

"To be sure," said I, — "to be sure. By the bye, Monsieur, did I understand you to say that the system you have adopted, in place of the celebrated soothing system, was one of very rigorous severity?"

"By no means. Our confinement is necessarily close; but the treatment — the medical treatment, I mean — is rather agreeable to the patients than otherwise."

"And the new system is one of your own invention?"

"Not altogether. Some portions of it are referable to Professor Tarr, of whom you have, necessarily, heard; and, again, there are modifications in my plan which I am happy to acknowledge as belonging of right to the celebrated Fether, with whom, if I mistake not, you have the honor of an intimate acquaintance."

"I am quite ashamed to confess," I replied, "that I have never even heard the names of either gentleman before."

"Good heavens!" ejaculated my host, drawing back his chair abruptly, and uplifting his hands. "I surely do not hear you aright! You did not intend to say, eh? that you had never *heard* either of the learned Doctor Tarr, or of the celebrated Professor Fether?"

"I am forced to acknowledge my ignorance," I replied; "but the truth should be held inviolate above all things. Nevertheless, I feel humbled to the dust, not to be acquainted with the works of these, no doubt, extraordinary men. I will seek out their writings forthwith, and peruse them with deliberate care. Monsieur Maillard, you have really — I must confess it — you have *really* — made me ashamed of myself!"

And this was the fact.

"Say no more, my good young friend," he said kindly, pressing my hand, — "join me now in a glass of Sauterne."

We drank. The company followed our example without stint. They chatted — they jested — they laughed — they perpetrated a thousand absurdities — the fiddles shrieked — the drum row-de-dowed — the trombones bellowed like so many brazen bulls of Phalaris — and the whole scene, growing gradually worse and worse, as the wines gained the ascendancy, became at length a sort of pandemonium *in petto*. In the meantime, Monsieur Maillard and myself, with some bottles of Sauterne and Vougeôt between us, continued our conversation at the top of the voice. A word spoken in an ordinary key stood no more chance of being heard than the voice of a fish from the bottom of Niagara Falls.

"And, sir," said I, screaming in his ear, "you mentioned something before dinner about the danger incurred in the old system of soothing. How is that?"

"Yes," he replied, "there was, occasionally, very great danger indeed. There is no accounting for the caprices of madmen; and, in my opinion as well as in that of Dr. Tarr and Professor Fether, it is *never* safe to permit them to run at large unattended. A lunatic may be 'soothed,' as it is called, for a time, but, in the end, he is very apt to become obstrep-

erous. His cunning, too, is proverbial and great. If he has a project in view, he conceals his design with a marvellous wisdom; and the dexterity with which he counterfeits sanity, presents, to the metaphysician, one of the most singular problems in the study of mind. When a madman appears *thoroughly* sane, indeed, it is high time to put him in a strait-jacket."

"But the *danger*, my dear sir, of which you were speaking, in your own experience — during your control of this house — have you had practical reason to think liberty hazardous in the case of a lunatic?"

"Here? — in my own experience? — why, I may say, yes. For example: — no *very* long while ago, a singular circumstance occurred in this very house. The 'soothing system,' you know, was then in operation, and the patients were at large. They behaved remarkably well — especially so, — any one of sense might have known that some devilish scheme was brewing from that particular fact, that the fellows behaved so *remarkably* well. And, sure enough, one fine morning the keepers found themselves pinioned hand and foot, and thrown into the cells, where they were attended, as if *they* were the lunatics, by the lunatics themselves, who had usurped the offices of the keepers."

"You don't tell me so! I never heard of any thing so absurd in my life!"

"Fact — it all came to pass by means of a stupid fellow — a lunatic — who, by some means, had taken it into his head that he had invented a better system of government than any ever heard of before — of lunatic government, I mean. He wished to give his invention a trial, I suppose, and so he persuaded the rest of the patients to join him in a conspiracy for the overthrow of the reigning powers."

"And he really succeeded?"

"No doubt of it. The keepers and kept were soon made to exchange places. Not that exactly either — for the madmen had been free, but the keepers were shut up in cells forthwith, and treated, I am sorry to say, in a very cavalier manner."

"But I presume a counter-revolution was soon effected. This condition of things could not have long existed. The country people in the neighborhood — visiters coming to see the establishment — would have given the alarm."

"There you are out. The head rebel was too cunning for that. He admitted no visiters at all — with the exception, one day, of a very stupid-looking young gentleman of whom he had no reason to be afraid. He let him in to see the place — just by way of variety, — to have a little fun with him. As soon as he had gammoned him sufficiently, he let him out, and sent him about his business."

"And *how* long, then, did the madmen reign?"

"Oh, a very long time, indeed — a month certainly — how much longer I can't precisely say. In the meantime, the lunatics had a jolly

season of it — that you may swear. They doffed their own shabby clothes, and made free with the family wardrobe and jewels. The cellars of the *château* were well stocked with wine; and these madmen are just the devils that know how to drink it. They lived well, I can tell you."

"And the treatment — what was the particular species of treatment which the leader of the rebels put into operation?"

"Why, as for that, a madman is not necessarily a fool, as I have already observed; and it is my honest opinion that his treatment was a much better treatment than that which it superseded. It was a very capital system indeed — simple — neat — no trouble at all — in fact it was delicious — it was — "

Here my host's observations were cut short by another series of yells, of the same character as those which had previously disconcerted us. This time, however, they seemed to proceed from persons rapidly approaching.

"Gracious heavens!" I ejaculated — "the lunatics have most undoubtedly broken loose."

"I very much fear it is so," replied Monsieur Maillard, now becoming excessively pale. He had scarcely finished the sentence, before loud shouts and imprecations were heard beneath the windows; and, immediately afterward, it became evident that some persons outside were endeavoring to gain entrance into the room. The door was beaten with what appeared to be a sledge-hammer, and the shutters were wrenched and shaken with prodigious violence.

A scene of the most terrible confusion ensued. Monsieur Maillard, to my excessive astonishment, threw himself under the side-board. I had expected more resolution at his hands. The members of the orchestra, who, for the last fifteen minutes, had been seemingly too much intoxicated to do duty, now sprang all at once to their feet and to their instruments, and, scrambling upon their table, broke out, with one accord, into, "Yankee Doodle," which they performed, if not exactly in tune, at least with an energy superhuman, during the whole of the uproar.

Meantime, upon the main dining-table, among the bottles and glasses, leaped the gentleman who, with such difficulty, had been restrained from leaping there before. As soon as he fairly settled himself, he commenced an oration, which, no doubt, was a very capital one, if it could only have been heard. At the same moment, the man with the tee-totum predilection, set himself to spinning around the apartment, with immense energy, and with arms outstretched at right angles with his body; so that he had all the air of a tee-totum in fact, and knocked everybody down that happened to get in his way. And now, too, hearing an incredible popping and fizzing of champagne, I discovered at length, that it proceeded from the person who performed the bottle of that delicate drink during dinner. And then, again, the frog-man croaked away as if the salvation of his soul depended upon every note that he uttered.

And, in the midst of all this, the continuous braying of a donkey arose over all. As for my old friend, Madame Joyeuse, I really could have wept for the poor lady, she appeared so terribly perplexed. All she did, however, was to stand up in a corner, by the fireplace, and sing out incessantly at the top of her voice, "Cock-a-doodle-de-dooooooh!"

And now came the climax — the catastrophe of the drama. As no resistance, beyond whooping and yelling and cock-a-doodling, was offered to the encroachments of the party without, the ten windows were very speedily, and almost simultaneously, broken in. But I shall never forget the emotions of wonder and horror with which I gazed, when, leaping through these windows, and down among us *pêle-mêle*, fighting, stamping, scratching, and howling, there rushed a perfect army of what I took to be Chimpanzees, Ourang-Outangs, or big black baboons of the Cape of Good Hope.

I received a terrible beating — after which I rolled under a sofa and lay still. After lying there some fifteen minutes, during which time I listened with all my ears to what was going on in the room, I came to same satisfactory *dénouement* of this tragedy. Monsieur Maillard, it appeared, in giving me the account of the lunatic who had excited his fellows to rebellion, had been merely relating his own exploits. This gentleman had, indeed, some two or three years before, been the superintendent of the establishment; but grew crazy himself, and so became a patient. This fact was unknown to the travelling companion who introduced me. The keepers, ten in number, having been suddenly overpowered, were first well tarred, then carefully feathered, and then shut up in underground cells. They had been so imprisoned for more than a month, during which period Monsieur Maillard had generously allowed them not only the tar and feathers (which constituted his "system"), but some bread and abundance of water. The latter was pumped on them daily. At length, one escaping through a sewer, gave freedom to all the rest.

The "soothing system," with important modifications, has been resumed at the *château;* yet I cannot help agreeing with Monsieur Maillard, that his own "treatment" was a very capital one of its kind. As he justly observed, it was "simple — neat — and gave no trouble at all — not the least."

I have only to add that, although I have searched every library in Europe for the works of Doctor *Tarr* and Professor *Fether*, I have, up to the present day, utterly failed in my endeavors at procuring an edition.

The Facts in the Case of M. Valdemar

O<small>F</small> course I shall not pretend to consider it any matter for wonder, that the extraordinary case of M. Valdemar has excited discussion. It would have been a miracle had it not — especially under the circumstances. Through the desire of all parties concerned, to keep the affair from the public, at least for the present, or until we had further opportunities for investigation — through our endeavors to effect this — a garbled or exaggerated account made its way into society, and became the source of many unpleasant misrepresentations; and, very naturally, of a great deal of disbelief.

It is now rendered necessary that I give the *facts* — as far as I comprehend them myself. They are, succinctly, these:

My attention, for the last three years, had been repeatedly drawn to the subject of Mesmerism; and, about nine months ago, it occurred to me, quite suddenly, that in the series of experiments made hitherto, there had been a very remarkable and most unaccountable omission: — no person had as yet been mesmerized *in articulo mortis*. It remained to be seen, first, whether, in such condition, there existed in the patient any susceptibility to the magnetic influence; secondly, whether, if any existed, it was impaired or increased by the condition; thirdly, to what extent, or for how long a period, the encroachments of Death might be arrested by the process. There were other points to be ascertained, but these most excited my curiosity — the last in especial, from the immensely important character of its consequences.

In looking around me for some subject by whose means I might test these particulars, I was brought to think of my friend, M. Ernest Valdemar, the well-known compiler of the "Bibliotheca Forensica," and author (under the *nom de plume* of Issachar Marx) of the Polish versions of "Wallenstein" and "Gargantua." M. Valdemar, who has resided principally at Harlem, N. Y., since the year 1839, is (or was) particularly noticeable for the extreme spareness of his person — his lower limbs much resembling those of John Randolph; and, also, for the whiteness of his whiskers, in violent contrast to the blackness of his hair — the latter, in consequence, being very generally mistaken for a wig. His temperament was markedly nervous, and rendered him a good subject for mesmeric experiment. On two or three occasions I had put him to sleep with little difficulty, but was disappointed in other results which his peculiar constitution had naturally led me to anticipate. His will was at no period positively, or thoroughly, under my control, and in regard to *clairvoyance*, I could accomplish with him nothing to be relied upon. I always attributed my failure at these points to the disordered state of

his health. For some months previous to my becoming acquainted with him, his physicians had declared him in a confirmed phthisis. It was his custom, indeed, to speak calmly of his approaching dissolution, as of a matter neither to be avoided nor regretted.

When the ideas to which I have alluded first occurred to me, it was of course very natural that I should think of M. Valdemar. I knew the steady philosophy of the man too well to apprehend any scruples from *him*; and he had no relatives in America who would be likely to interfere. I spoke to him frankly upon the subject; and, to my surprise, his interest seemed vividly excited. I say to my surprise, for, although he had always yielded his person freely to my experiments, he had never before given me any tokens of sympathy with what I did. His disease was of that character which would admit of exact calculation in respect to the epoch of its termination in death; and it was finally arranged between us that he would send for me about twenty-four hours before the period announced by his physicians as that of his decease.

It is now rather more than seven months since I received, from M. Valdemar himself, the subjoined note:

"My Dear P——.

"You may as well come *now*. D—— and F—— are agreed that I cannot hold out beyond to-morrow midnight; and I think they have hit the time very nearly. Valdemar."

I received this note within half an hour after it was written, and in fifteen minutes more I was in the dying man's chamber. I had not seen him for ten days, and was appalled by the fearful alteration which the brief interval had wrought in him. His face wore a leaden hue; the eyes were utterly lustreless; and the emaciation was so extreme, that the skin had been broken through by the cheek-bones. His expectoration was excessive. The pulse was barely perceptible. He retained, nevertheless, in a very remarkable manner, both his mental power and a certain degree of physical strength. He spoke with distinctness — took some palliative medicines without aid — and, when I entered the room, was occupied in penciling memoranda in a pocket-book. He was propped up in the bed by pillows. Doctors D—— and F—— were in attendance.

After pressing Valdemar's hand, I took these gentlemen aside, and obtained from them a minute account of the patient's condition. The left lung had been for eighteen months in a semi-osseous or cartilaginous state, and was, of course, entirely useless for all purposes of vitality. The right, in its upper portion, was also partially, if not thoroughly, ossified, while the lower region was merely a mass of purulent tubercles, running one into another. Several extensive perforations existed; and, at one point, permanent adhesion to the ribs had taken place. These appearances in the right lobe were of comparatively recent date. The ossification had proceeded with very unusual rapidity; no sign of it had been

discovered a month before, and the adhesion had only been observed during the three previous days. Independently of the phthisis, the patient was suspected of aneurism of the aorta; but on this point the osseous symptoms rendered an exact diagnosis impossible. It was the opinion of both physicians that M. Valdemar would die about midnight on the morrow (Sunday). It was then seven o'clock on Saturday evening.

On quitting the invalid's bed-side to hold conversation with myself, Doctors D—— and F—— had bidden him a final farewell. It had not been their intention to return; but, at my request, they agreed to look in upon the patient about ten the next night.

When they had gone, I spoke freely with M. Valdemar on the subject of his approaching dissolution, as well as, more particularly, of the experiment proposed. He still professed himself quite willing and even anxious to have it made, and urged me to commence it at once. A male and a female nurse were in attendance; but I did not feel myself altogether at liberty to engage in a task of this character with no more reliable witnesses than these people, in case of sudden accident, might prove. I therefore postponed operations until about eight the next night, when the arrival of a medical student with whom I had some acquaintance (Mr. Theodore L——l), relieved me from farther embarrassment. It had been my design, originally, to wait for the physicians; but I was induced to proceed, first, by the urgent entreaties of M. Valdemar, and secondly, by my conviction that I had not a moment to lose, as he was evidently sinking fast.

Mr. L——l was so kind as to accede to my desire that he would take notes of all that occurred; and it is from his memoranda that what I now have to relate is, for the most part, either condensed or copied *verbatim*.

It wanted about five minutes of eight when, taking the patient's hand, I begged him to state, as distinctly as he could, to Mr. L——l, whether he (M. Valdemar) was entirely willing that I should make the experiment of mesmerizing him in his then condition.

He replied feebly, yet quite audibly: "Yes, I wish to be mesmerized" — adding immediately afterward: "I fear you have deferred it too long."

While he spoke thus, I commenced the passes which I had already found most effectual in subduing him. He was evidently influenced with the first lateral stroke of my hand across his forehead; but, although I exerted all my powers, no farther perceptible effect was induced until some minutes after ten o'clock, when Doctors D—— and F—— called, according to appointment. I explained to them, in a few words, what I designed, and as they opposed no objection, saying that the patient was already in the death agony, I proceeded without hesitation — exchanging, however, the lateral passes for downward ones, and directing my gaze entirely into the right eye of the sufferer.

By this time his pulse was imperceptible and his breathing was stertorous, and at intervals of half a minute.

This condition was nearly unaltered for a quarter of an hour. At the expiration of this period, however, a natural although a very deep sigh escaped the bosom of the dying man, and the stertorous breathing ceased — that is to say, its stertorousness was no longer apparent; the intervals were undiminished. The patient's extremities were of an icy coldness.

At five minutes before eleven, I perceived unequivocal signs of the mesmeric influence. The glassy roll of the eye was changed for that expression of uneasy *inward* examination which is never seen except in cases of sleep-waking, and which it is quite impossible to mistake. With a few rapid lateral passes I made the lids quiver, as in incipient sleep, and with a few more I closed them altogether. I was not satisfied, however, with this, but continued the manipulations vigorously, and with the fullest exertion of the will, until I had completely stiffened the limbs of the slumberer, after placing them in a seemingly easy position. The legs were at full length; the arms were nearly so, and reposed on the bed at a moderate distance from the loins. The head was very slightly elevated.

When I had accomplished this, it was fully midnight, and I requested the gentlemen present to examine M. Valdemar's condition. After a few experiments, they admitted him to be in an unusually perfect state of mesmeric trance. The curiosity of both the physicians was greatly excited. Dr. D—— resolved at once to remain with the patient all night, while Dr. F—— took leave with a promise to return at daybreak. Mr. L——l and the nurses remained.

We left M. Valdemar entirely undisturbed until about three o'clock in the morning, when I approached him and found him in precisely the same condition as when Dr. F—— went away — that is to say, he lay in the same position; the pulse was imperceptible; the breathing was gentle (scarcely noticeable, unless through the application of a mirror to the lips); the eyes were closed naturally; and the limbs were as rigid and as cold as marble. Still, the general appearance was certainly not that of death.

As I approached M. Valdemar I made a kind of half effort to influence his right arm into pursuit of my own, as I passed the latter gently to and fro above his person. In such experiments with this patient, I had never perfectly succeeded before, and assuredly I had little thought of succeeding now; but to my astonishment, his arm very readily, although feebly, followed every direction I assigned it with mine. I determined to hazard a few words of conversation.

"M. Valdemar," I said, "are you asleep?" He made no answer, but I perceived a tremor about the lips, and was thus induced to repeat the question, again and again. At its third repetition, his whole frame was agitated by a very slight quivering; the eyelids unclosed themselves so far as to display a white line of a ball; the lips moved

sluggishly, and from between them, in a barely audible whisper, issued the words:

"Yes — asleep now. Do not wake me! — let me die so!"

I here felt the limbs, and found them as rigid as ever. The right arm, as before, obeyed the direction of my hand. I questioned the sleep-waker again:

"Do you still feel pain in the breast, M. Valdemar?"

The answer now was immediate, but even less audible than before:

"No pain — I am dying!"

I did not think it advisable to disturb him farther just then, and nothing more was said or done until the arrival of Dr. F——, who came a little before sunrise, and expressed unbounded astonishment at finding the patient still alive. After feeling the pulse and applying a mirror to the lips, he requested me to speak to the sleep-waker again. I did so, saying:

"M. Valdemar, do you still sleep?"

As before, some minutes elapsed ere a reply was made; and during the interval the dying man seemed to be collecting his energies to speak. At my fourth repetition of the question, he said very faintly, almost inaudibly:

"Yes; still asleep — dying."

It was now the opinion, or rather the wish, of the physicians, that M. Valdemar should be suffered to remain undisturbed in his present apparently tranquil condition, until death should supervene — and this, it was generally agreed, must now take place within a few minutes. I concluded, however, to speak to him once more, and merely repeated my previous question.

While I spoke, there came a marked change over the countenance of the sleep-waker. The eyes rolled themselves slowly open, the pupils disappearing upwardly; the skin generally assumed a cadaverous hue, resembling not so much parchment as white paper; and the circular hectic spots which, hitherto, had been strongly defined in the centre of each cheek, *went out* at once. I use this expression, because the suddenness of their departure put me in mind of nothing so much as the extinguishment of a candle by a puff of the breath. The upper lip, at the same time, writhed itself away from the teeth, which it had previously covered completely; while the lower jaw fell with an audible jerk, leaving the mouth widely extended, and disclosing in full view the swollen and blackened tongue. I presume that no member of the party then present had been unaccustomed to death-bed horrors; but so hideous beyond conception was the appearance of M. Valdemar at this moment, that there was a general shrinking back from the region of the bed.

I now feel that I have reached a point of this narrative at which every reader will be startled into positive disbelief. It is my business, however, simply to proceed.

There was no longer the faintest sign of vitality in M. Valdemar; and

concluding him to be dead, we were consigning him to the charge of the nurses, when a strong vibratory motion was observable in the tongue. This continued for perhaps a minute. At the expiration of this period, there issued from the distended and motionless jaws a voice — such as it would be madness in me to attempt describing. There are, indeed, two or three epithets which might be considered as applicable to it in part; I might say, for example, that the sound was harsh, and broken and hollow; but the hideous whole is indescribable, for the simple reason that no similar sounds have ever jarred upon the ear of humanity. There were two particulars, nevertheless, which I thought then, and still think, might fairly be stated as characteristic of the intonation — as well adapted to convey some idea of its unearthly peculiarity. In the first place, the voice seemed to reach our ears — at least mine — from a vast distance, or from some deep cavern within the earth. In the second place, it impressed me (I fear, indeed, that it will be impossible to make myself comprehended) as gelatinous or glutinous matters impress the sense of touch.

I have spoken both of "sound" and of "voice." I mean to say that the sound was one of distinct — of even wonderfully, thrillingly distinct — syllabification. M. Valdemar *spoke* — obviously in reply to the question I had propounded to him a few minutes before. I had asked him, it will be remembered, if he still slept. He now said:

"Yes! — no; — I *have been* sleeping — and now — now — *I am dead.*"

No person present even affected to deny, or attempted to repress, the unutterable, shuddering horror which these few words, thus uttered, were so well calculated to convey. Mr. L——l (the student) swooned. The nurses immediately left the chamber, and could not be induced to return. My own impressions I would not pretend to render intelligible to the reader. For nearly an hour, we busied ourselves, silently — without the utterance of a word — in endeavors to revive Mr. L——l. When he came to himself, we addressed ourselves again to an investigation of M. Valdemar's condition.

It remained in all respects as I have last described it, with the exception that the mirror no longer afforded evidence of respiration. An attempt to draw blood from the arm failed. I should mention, too, that this limb was no further subject to my will. I endeavored in vain to make it follow the direction of my hand. The only real indication, indeed, of the mesmeric influence, was now found in the vibratory movement of the tongue, whenever I addressed M. Valdemar a question. He seemed to be making an effort to reply, but had no longer sufficient volition. To queries put to him by any other person than myself he seemed utterly insensible — although I endeavored to place each member of the company in mesmeric *rapport* with him. I believe that I have now related all that is necessary to an understanding of the sleep-waker's state at this epoch. Other nurses were procured; and at ten o'clock I left the house in company with the two physicians and Mr. L——l.

In the afternoon we all called again to see the patient. His condition remained precisely the same. We had now some discussion as to the propriety and feasibility of awakening him; but we had little difficulty in agreeing that no good purpose would be served by so doing. It was evident that, so far, death (or what is usually termed death) had been arrested by the mesmeric process. It seemed clear to us all that to awaken M. Valdemar would be merely to insure his instant, or at least his speedy, dissolution.

From this period until the close of last week — *an interval of nearly seven months* — we continued to make daily calls at M. Valdemar's house, accompanied, now and then, by medical and other friends. All this time the sleep-waker remained *exactly* as I have last described him. The nurses' attentions were continual.

It was on Friday last that we finally resolved to make the experiment of awakening, or attempting to awaken him; and it is the (perhaps) unfortunate result of this latter experiment which has given rise to so much discussion in private circles — to so much of what I cannot help thinking unwarranted popular feeling.

For the purpose of relieving M. Valdemar from the mesmeric trance, I made use of the customary passes. These for a time were unsuccessful. The first indication of revival was afforded by a partial descent of the iris. It was observed, as especially remarkable, that this lowering of the pupil was accompanied by the profuse outflowing of a yellowish ichor (from beneath the lids) of a pungent and highly offensive odor.

It was now suggested that I should attempt to influence the patient's arm as heretofore. I made the attempt and failed. Dr. F—— then intimated a desire to have me put a question. I did so, as follows:

"M. Valdemar, can you explain to us what are your feelings or wishes now?"

There was an instant return of the hectic circles on the cheeks: the tongue quivered, or rather rolled violently in the mouth (although the jaws and lips remained rigid as before), and at length the same hideous voice which I have already described, broke forth:

"For God's sake! — quick! — quick! — put me to sleep — or, quick! — waken me! — quick! — *I say to you that I am dead!*"

I was thoroughly unnerved, and for an instant remained undecided what to do. At first I made an endeavor to recompose the patient; but, failing in this through total abeyance of the will, I retracted my steps and as earnestly struggled to awaken him. In this attempt I soon saw that I should be successful — or at least I soon fancied that my success would be complete — and I am sure that all in the room were prepared to see the patient awaken.

For what really occurred, however, it is quite impossible that any human being could have been prepared.

As I rapidly made the mesmeric passes, amid ejaculations of "dead!

dead!" absolutely *bursting* from the tongue and not from the lips of the sufferer, his whole frame at once — within the space of a single minute, or even less, shrunk — crumbled, absolutely *rotted* away beneath my hands. Upon the bed, before that whole company, there lay a nearly liquid mass of loathsome — of detestable putridity.

The Sphinx

Dᴜʀɪɴɢ the dread reign of the Cholera in New York, I had accepted the invitation of a relative to spend a fortnight with him in the retirement of his *cottage ornée* on the banks of the Hudson. We had here around us all the ordinary means of summer amusement; and what with rambling in the woods, sketching, boating, fishing, bathing, music, and books, we should have passed the time pleasantly enough, but for the fearful intelligence which reached us every morning from the populous city. Not a day elapsed which did not bring us news of the decease of some acquaintance. Then as the fatality increased, we learned to expect daily the loss of some friend. At length we trembled at the approach of every messenger. The very air from the South seemed to us redolent with death. That palsying thought, indeed, took entire posession of my soul. I could neither speak, think, nor dream of any thing else. My host was of a less excitable temperament, and, although greatly depressed in spirits, exerted himself to sustain my own. His richly philosophical intellect was not at any time affected by unrealities. To the substances of terror he was sufficiently alive, but of its shadows he had no apprehension.

His endeavors to arouse me from the condition of abnormal gloom into which I had fallen, were frustrated, in great measure, by certain volumes which I had found in his library. These were of a character to force into germination whatever seeds of hereditary superstition lay latent in my bosom. I had been reading these books without his knowledge, and thus he was often at a loss to account for the forcible impressions which had been made upon my fancy.

A favorite topic with me was the popular belief in omens — a belief which, at this one epoch of my life, I was almost seriously disposed to defend. On this subject we had long and animated discussions — he maintaining the utter groundlessness of faith in such matters, — I contending that a popular sentiment arising with absolute spontaneity — that is to say, without apparent traces of suggestion — had in itself the unmistakable elements of truth, and was entitled to as much respect as that intuition which is the idiosyncrasy of the individual man of genius.

The fact is, that soon after my arrival at the cottage there had occurred to myself an incident so entirely inexplicable, and which had in it so

much of the portentous character, that I might well have been excused for regarding it as an omen. It appalled, and at the same time so confounded and bewildered me, that many days elapsed before I could make up my mind to communicate the circumstances to my friend.

Near the close of an exceedingly warm day, I was sitting, book in hand, at an open window, commanding, through a long vista of the river banks, a view of a distant hill, the face of which nearest my position had been denuded by what is termed a land-slide, of the principal portion of its trees. My thoughts had been long wandering from the volume before me to the gloom and desolation of the neighboring city. Uplifting my eyes from the page, they fell upon the naked face of the hill, and upon an object — upon some living monster of hideous conformation, which very rapidly made its way from the summit to the bottom, disappearing finally in the dense forest below. As this creature first came in sight, I doubted my own sanity — or at least the evidence of my own eyes; and many minutes passed before I succeeded in convincing myself that I was neither mad nor in a dream. Yet when I described the monster (which I distinctly saw, and calmly surveyed through the whole period of its progress), my readers, I fear, will feel more difficulty in being convinced of these points than even I did myself.

Estimating the size of the creature by comparison with the diameter of the large trees near which it passed — the few giants of the forest which had escaped the fury of the land-slide — I concluded it to be far larger than any ship of the line in existence. I say ship of the line, because the shape of the monster suggested the idea — the hull of one of our seventy-four might convey a very tolerable conception of the general outline. The mouth of the animal was situated at the extremity of a proboscis some sixty or seventy feet in length, and about as thick as the body of an ordinary elephant. Near the root of this trunk was an immense quantity of black shaggy hair — more than could have been supplied by the coats of a score of buffaloes; and projecting from this hair downwardly and laterally, sprang two gleaming tusks not unlike those of the wild boar, but of infinitely greater dimensions. Extending forward, parallel with the proboscis, and on each side of it, was a gigantic staff, thirty or forty feet in length, formed seemingly of pure crystal, and in shape a perfect prism, — it reflected in the most gorgeous manner the rays of the declining sun. The trunk was fashioned like a wedge with the apex to the earth. From it there were outspread two pairs of wings — each wing nearly one hundred yards in length — one pair being placed above the other, and all thickly covered with metal scales; each scale apparently some ten or twelve feet in diameter. I observed that the upper and lower tiers of wings were connected by a strong chain. But the chief peculiarity of this horrible thing was the representation of a *Death's Head*, which covered nearly the whole surface of its breast, and which was as accurately traced in glaring white, upon the dark ground of the

body, as if it had been there carefully designed by an artist. While I re-garded the terrific animal, and more especially the appearance on its breast, with a feeling or horror and awe — with a sentiment of forth-coming evil, which I found it impossible to quell by any effort of the reason, I perceived the huge jaws at the extremity of the proboscis sud-denly expand themselves, and from them there proceeded a sound so loud and so expressive of wo, that it struck upon my nerves like a knell, and as the monster disappeared at the foot of the hill, I fell at once, faint-ing, to the floor.

Upon recovering, my first impulse, of course, was to inform my friend of what I had seen and heard — and I can scarcely explain what feeling of repugnance it was which, in the end, operated to prevent me.

At length, one evening, some three or four days after the occurrence, we were sitting together in the room in which I had seen the apparition — I occupying the same seat at the same window, and he lounging on a sofa near at hand. The association of the place and time impelled me to give him an account of the phenomenon. He heard me to the end — at first laughed heartily — and then lapsed into an excessively grave demeanor, as if my insanity was a thing beyond suspicion. At this instant I again had a distinct view of the monster — to which, with a shout of absolute terror, I now directed his attention. He looked eagerly — but maintained that he saw nothing — although I designated minutely the course of the creature, as it made its way down the naked face of the hill.

I was now immeasurably alarmed, for I considered the vision either as an omen of my death, or, worse, as the fore-runner of an attack of mania. I threw myself passionately back in my chair, and for some mo-ments buried my face in my hands. When I uncovered my eyes, the ap-parition was no longer apparent.

My host, however, had in some degree resumed the calmness of his demeanor, and questioned me very rigorously in respect to the conforma-tion of the visionary creature. When I had fully satisfied him on this head, he sighed deeply, as if relieved of some intolerable burden, and went on to talk, with what I thought a cruel calmness, of various points of speculative philosophy, which had heretofore formed subject of discus-sion between us. I remember his insisting very especially (among other things) upon the idea that the principle source of error in all human investigations lay in the liability of the understanding to under-rate or to over-value the importance of an object, through mere mis-admeasure-ment of its propinquity. "To estimate properly, for example," he said, "the influence to be exercised on mankind at large by the thorough dif-fusion of Democracy, the distance of the epoch at which such diffusion may possibly be accomplished should not fail to form an item in the estimate. Yet can you tell me one writer on the subject of government who has ever thought this particular branch of the subject worthy of discussion at all?"

He here paused for a moment, stepped to a book-case, and brought forth one of the ordinary synopses of Natural History. Requesting me then to exchange seats with him, that he might the better distinguish the fine print of the volume, he took my armchair at the window, and, opening the book, resumed his discourse very much in the same tone as before.

"But for your exceeding minuteness," he said, "in describing the monster, I might never have had it in my power to demonstrate to you what it was. In the first place, let me read to you a schoolboy account of the genus *Sphinx*, of the family *Crepuscularia*, of the order *Lepidoptera*, of the class of *Insecta* — or insects. The account runs thus:

" 'Four membranous wings covered with little colored scales of metallic appearance; mouth forming a rolled proboscis, produced by an elongation of the jaws, upon the sides of which are found the rudiments of mandibles and downy palpi; the inferior wings retained to the superior by a stiff hair; antennae in the form of an elongated club, prismatic; abdomen pointed, The Death's-headed Sphinx has occasioned much terror among the vulgar, at times, by the melancholy kind of cry which it utters, and the insignia of death which it wears upon its corslet.' "

He here closed the book and leaned forward in the chair, placing himself accurately in the position which I had occupied at the moment of beholding "the monster."

"Ah, here it is," he presently exclaimed — "it is reascending the face of the hill, and a very remarkable looking creature I admit it to be. Still, it is by no means so large or so distant as you imagined it; for the fact is that, as it wriggles its way up this thread, which some spider has wrought along the window-sash, I find it to be about the sixteenth of an inch in its extreme length, and also about the sixteenth of an inch distant from the pupil of my eye."

The Cask of Amontillado

THE THOUSAND injuries of Fortunato I had borne as I best could, but when he ventured upon insult, I vowed revenge. You, who so well know the nature of my soul, will not suppose, however, that I gave utterance to a threat. *At length* I would be avenged; this was a point definitely settled — but the very definitiveness with which it was resolved, precluded the idea of risk. I must not only punish, but punish with impunity. A wrong is unredressed when retribution overtakes its redresser. It is equally unredressed when the avenger fails to make himself felt as such to him who has done the wrong.

It must be understood that neither by word nor deed had I given Fortunato cause to doubt my good will. I continued as was my wont, to

smile in his face, and he did not perceive that my smile *now* was at the thought of his immolation.

He had a weak point — this Fortunato — although in other regards he was a man to be respected and even feared. He prided himself on his connoisseurship in wine. Few Italians have the true virtuoso spirit. For the most part their enthusiasm is adapted to suit the time and opportunity — to practice imposture upon the British and Austrian *millionaires*. In painting and gemmary Fortunato, like his country men, was a quack — but in the matter of old wines he was sincere. In this respect I did not differ from him materially: I was skilful in the Italian vintages myself, and bought largely whenever I could.

It was about dusk, one evening during the supreme madness of the carnival season, that I encountered my friend. He accosted me with excessive warmth, for he had been drinking much. The man wore motley. He had on a tight-fitting parti-striped dress, and his head was surmounted by the conical cap and bells. I was so pleased to see him, that I thought I should never have done wringing his hand.

I said to him: "My dear Fortunato, you are luckily met. How remarkably well you are looking to-day! But I have received a pipe of what passes for Amontillado, and I have my doubts."

"How?" said he. "Amontillado? A pipe? Impossible! And in the middle of the carnival!"

"I have my doubts," I replied; "and I was silly enough to pay the full Amontillado price without consulting you in the matter. You were not to be found, and I was fearful of losing a bargain."

"Amontillado!"

"I have my doubts."

"Amontillado!"

"And I must satisfy them."

"Amontillado!"

"As you are engaged, I am on my way to Luchesi. If any one has a critical turn, it is he. He will tell me —— "

"Luchesi cannot tell Amontillado from Sherry."

"And yet some fools will have it that his taste is a match for your own."

"Come, let us go."

"Whither?"

"To your vaults."

"My friend, no; I will not impose upon your good nature. I perceive you have an engagement. Luchesi —— "

"I have no engagement; — come."

"My friend, no. It is not the engagement, but the severe cold with which I perceive you are afflicted. The vaults are insufferably damp. They are encrusted with nitre."

"Let us go, nevertheless. The cold is merely nothing. Amontillado!

You have been imposed upon. And as for Luchesi, he cannot distinguish Sherry from Amontillado."

Thus speaking, Fortunato possessed himself of my arm. Putting on a mask of black silk, and drawing a *roquelaire* closely about my person, I suffered him to hurry me to my palazzo.

There were no attendants at home; they had absconded to make merry in honor of the time. I had told them that I should not return until the morning, and had given them explicit orders not to stir from the house. These orders were sufficient, I well knew, to insure their immediate disappearance, one and all, as soon as my back was turned.

I took from their sconces two flambeaux, and giving one to Fortunato, bowed him through several suites of rooms to the archway that led into the vaults. I passed down a long and winding staircase, requesting him to be cautious as he followed. We came at length to the foot of the descent, and stood together on the damp ground of the catacombs of the Montresors.

The gait of my friend was unsteady, and the bells upon his cap jingled as he strode.

"The pipe?" said he.

"It is farther on," said I; "but observe the white web-work which gleams from these cavern walls."

He turned toward me, and looked into my eyes with two filmy orbs that distilled the rheum of intoxication.

"Nitre?" he asked, at length.

"Nitre," I replied. "How long have you had that cough?"

"Ugh! ugh! ugh! — ugh! ugh! ugh! — ugh! ugh! ugh! — ugh! ugh! ugh! — ugh! ugh! ugh!"

My poor friend found it impossible to reply for many minutes.

"It is nothing," he said, at last.

"Come," I said, with decision, "we will go back; your health is precious. You are rich, respected, admired, beloved; you are happy, as once I was. You are a man to be missed. For me it is no matter. We will go back; you will be ill, and I cannot be responsible. Besides, there is Luchesi —— "

"Enough," he said; "the cough is a mere nothing; it will not kill me. I shall not die of a cough."

"True — true," I replied; "and, indeed, I had no intention of alarming you unnecessarily — but you should use all proper caution. A draught of this Medoc will defend us from the damps."

Here I knocked off the neck of a bottle which I drew from a long row of its fellows that lay upon the mould.

"Drink," I said, presenting him the wine.

He raised it to his lips with a leer. He paused and nodded to me familiarly, while his bells jingled.

"I drink," he said, "to the buried that repose around us."

"And I to your long life."

He again took my arm, and we proceeded.

"These vaults," he said, "are extensive."

"The Montresors," I replied, "were a great and numerous family."

"I forget your arms."

"A huge human foot d'or, in a field azure; the foot crushes a serpent rampant whose fangs are imbedded in the heel."

"And the motto?"

"*Nemo me impune lacessit.*"

"Good!" he said.

The wine sparkled in his eyes and the bells jingled. My own fancy grew warm with the Medoc. We had passed through walls of piled bones, with casks and puncheons intermingling, into the inmost recesses of the catacombs. I paused again, and this time I made bold to seize Fortunato by an arm above the elbow.

"The nitre!" I said; "see, it increases. It hangs like moss upon the vaults. We are below the river's bed. The drops of moisture trickle among the bones. Come, we will go back ere it is too late. Your cough —— "

"It is nothing," he said; "let us go on. But first, another draught of the Medoc."

I broke and reached him a flagon of De Grave. He emptied it at a breath. His eyes flashed with a fierce light. He laughed and threw the bottle upward with a gesticulation I did not understand.

I looked at him in surprise. He repeated the movement — a grotesque one.

"You do not comprehend?" he said.

"Not I," I replied.

"Then you are not of the brotherhood."

"How?"

"You are not of the masons."

"Yes, yes," I said; "yes, yes."

"You? Impossible! A mason?"

"A mason," I replied.

"A sign," he said.

"It is this," I answered, producing a trowel from beneath the folds of my *roquelaire.*

"You jest," he exclaimed, recoiling a few paces. "But let us proceed to the Amontillado."

"Be it so," I said, replacing the tool beneath the cloak, and again offering him my arm. He leaned upon it heavily. We continued our route in search of the Amontillado. We passed through a range of low arches, descended, passed on, and descending again, arrived at a deep crypt, in which the foulness of the air caused our flambeaux rather to glow than flame.

At the most remote end of the crypt there appeared another less spacious. Its walls had been lined with human remains, piled to the vault overhead, in the fashion of the great catacombs of Paris. Three sides of this interior crypt were still ornamented in this manner. From the fourth the bones had been thrown down, and lay promiscuously upon the earth, forming at one point a mound of some size. Within the wall thus exposed by the displacing of the bones, we perceived a still interior recess, in depth about four feet, in width three, in height six or seven. It seemed to have been constructed for no especial use within itself, but formed merely the interval between two of the colossal supports of the roof of the catacombs, and was backed by one of their circumscribing walls of solid granite.

It was in vain that Fortunato, uplifting his dull torch, endeavored to pry into the depth of the recess. Its termination the feeble light did not enable us to see.

"Proceed," I said; "herein is the Amontillado. As for Luchesi —— "

"He is an ignoramus," interrupted my friend, as he stepped unsteadily forward, while I followed immediately at his heels. In an instant he had reached the extremity of the niche, and finding his progress arrested by the rock, stood stupidly bewildered. A moment more and I had fettered him to the granite. In its surface were two iron staples, distant from each other about two feet, horizontally. From one of these depended a short chain, from the other a padlock. Throwing the links about his waist, it was but the work of a few seconds to secure it. He was too much astounded to resist. Withdrawing the key I stepped back from the recess.

"Pass your hand," I said, "over the wall; you cannot help feeling the nitre. Indeed it is *very* damp. Once more let me *implore* you to return. No? Then I must positively leave you. But I must first render you all the little attentions in my power."

"The Amontillado!" ejaculated my friend, not yet recovered from his astonishment.

"True," I replied; "the Amontillado."

As I said these words I busied myself among the pile of bones of which I have before spoken. Throwing them aside, I soon uncovered a quantity of building stone and mortar. With these materials and with the aid of my trowel, I began vigorously to wall up the entrance of the niche.

I had scarcely laid the first tier of the masonry when I discovered that the intoxication of Fortunato had in a great measure worn off. The earliest indication I had of this was a low moaning cry from the depth of the recess. It was *not* the cry of a drunken man. There was then a long and obstinate silence. I laid the second tier, and the third, and the fourth; and then I heard the furious vibrations of the chain. The noise lasted for several minutes, during which, that I might hearken to it with the more satisfaction, I ceased my labors and sat down upon the bones.

When at last the clanking subsided, I resumed the trowel, and finished without interruption the fifth, the sixth, and the seventh tier. The wall was now nearly upon a level with my breast. I again paused, and holding the flambeaux over the mason-work, threw a few feeble rays upon the figure within.

A succession of loud and shrill screams, bursting suddenly from the throat of the chained form, seemed to thrust me violently back. For a brief moment I hesitated — I trembled. Unsheathing my rapier, I began to grope with it about the recess; but the thought of an instant reassured me. I placed my hand upon the solid fabric of the catacombs, and felt satisfied. I reapproached the wall. I replied to the yells of him who clamored. I re-echoed — I aided — I surpassed them in volume and in strength. I did this, and the clamorer grew still.

It was now midnight, and my task was drawing to a close. I had completed the eighth, the ninth, and the tenth tier. I had finished a portion of the last and the eleventh; there remained but a single stone to be fitted and plastered in. I struggled with its weight; I placed it partially in its destined position. But now there came from out the niche a low laugh that erected the hairs upon my head. It was succeeded by a sad voice, which I had difficulty in recognizing as that of the noble Fortunato. The voice said —

"Ha! ha! ha! — he! he! — a very good joke indeed — an excellent jest. We will have many a rich laugh about it at the palazzo — he! he! he! — —— over our wine — he! he! he!"

"The Amontillado!" I said.

"He! he! he! — he! he! he! — yes, the Amontillado. But is it not getting late? Will not they be awaiting us at the palazzo, the Lady Fortunato and the rest? Let us be gone."

"Yes," I said, "let us be gone."

"*For the love of God, Montresor!*"

"Yes," I said, "for the love of God!"

But to these words I hearkened in vain for a reply. I grew impatient. I called aloud;

"Fortunato!"

No answer. I called again;

"Fortunato!"

No answer still. I thrust a torch through the remaining aperture and let it fall within. There came forth in return only a jingling of the bells. My heart grew sick — on account of the dampness of the catacombs. I hastened to make an end of my labor. I forced the last stone into its position; I plastered it up. Against the new masonry I re-erected the old rampart of bones. For the half of a century no mortal has disturbed them. *In pace requiescat!*

The Domain of Arnheim

The garden like a lady fair was cut,
That lay as if she slumbered in delight,
And to the open skies her eyes did shut.
The azure fields of Heaven were 'sembled right
In a large round, set with the flowers of light.
The flowers de luce, and the round sparks of dew.
That hung upon their azure leaves did shew
Like twinkling stars that sparkle in the evening blue.
 Giles Fletcher.

FROM his cradle to his grave a gale of prosperity bore my friend Ellison along. Nor do I use the word prosperity in its mere worldly sense. I mean it as synonymous with happiness. The person of whom I speak seemed born for the purpose of foreshadowing the doctrines of Turgôt, Price, Priestley, and Condorcêt — of exemplifying by individual instance what has been deemed the chimera of the perfectionists. In the brief existence of Ellison I fancy that I have seen refuted the dogma, that in man's very nature lies some hidden principle, the antagonist of bliss. An anxious examination of his career has given me to understand that in general, from the violation of a few simple laws of humanity arises the wretchedness of mankind — that as a species we have in our possession the as yet unwrought elements of content — and that, even now, in the present darkness and madness of all thought on the great question of the social condition, it is not impossible that man, the individual, under certain unusual and highly fortuitous conditions, may be happy.

With opinions such as these my young friend, too, was fully imbued, and thus it is worthy of observation that the uninterrupted enjoyment which distinguished his life was, in great measure, the result of preconcert. It is indeed evident that with less of the instinctive philosophy which, now and then, stands so well in the stead of experience, Mr. Ellison would have found himself precipitated, by the very extraordinary success of his life, into the common vortex of unhappiness which yawns for those of pre-eminent endowments. But it is by no means my object to pen an essay on happiness. The ideas of my friend may be summed up in a few words. He admitted but four elementary principles, or more strictly, conditions of bliss. That which he considered chief was (strange to say!) the simple and purely physical one of free exercise in the open air. "The health," he said, "attainable by other means is scarcely worth the name." He instanced the ecstasies of the fox-hunter, and pointed to the tillers of the earth, the only people who, as a class, can be fairly

considered happier than others. His second condition was the love of woman. His third, and most difficult of realization, was the contempt of ambition. His fourth was an object of unceasing pursuit; and he held that, other things being equal, the extent of attainable happiness was in proportion to the spirituality of this object.

Ellison was remarkable in the continuous profusion of good gifts lavished upon him by fortune. In personal grace and beauty he exceeded all men. His intellect was of that order to which the acquisition of knowledge is less a labor than an intuition and a necessity. His family was one of the most illustrious of the empire. His bride was the loveliest and most devoted of women. His possessions had been always ample; but on the attainment of his majority, it was discovered that one of those extraordinary freaks of fate had been played in his behalf which startle the whole social world amid which they occur, and seldom fail radically to alter the moral constitution of those who are their objects.

It appears that about a hundred years before Mr. Ellison's coming of age, there had died, in a remote province, one Mr. Seabright Ellison. This gentleman had amassed a princely fortune, and, having no immediate connections, conceived the whim of suffering his wealth to accumulate for a century after his decease. Minutely and sagaciously directing the various modes of investment, he bequeathed the aggregate amount to the nearest of blood, bearing the name of Ellison, who should be alive at the end of the hundred years. Many attempts had been made to set aside this singular bequest; their *ex post facto* character rendered them abortive; but the attention of a jealous government was aroused, and a legislative act finally obtained, forbidding all similar accumulations. This act, however, did not prevent young Ellison from entering into possession, on his twenty-first birthday, as the heir of his ancestor Seabright, of a fortune of *four hundred and fifty millions of dollars.**

When it had become known that such was the enormous wealth inherited, there were, of course, many speculations as to the mode of its disposal. The magnitude and the immediate availability of the sum bewildered all who thought on the topic. The possessor of any *appreciable* amount of money might have been imagined to perform any one of a thousand things. With riches merely surpassing those of any citizen, it would have been easy to suppose him engaging to supreme excess in the

* An incident, similar in outline to the one here imagined, occurred, not very long ago, in England. The name of the fortunate heir was Thelluson. I first saw an account of this matter in the "Tour" of Prince Puckler Muskau, who makes the sum inherited *ninety millions of pounds,* and justly observes that "in the contemplation of so vast a sum, and of the services to which it might be applied, there is something even of the sublime." To suit the views of this article I have followed the Prince's statement, although a grossly exaggerated one. The germ, and in fact, the commencement of the present paper was published many years ago — previous to the issue of the first number of Sue's admirable "*Juif Errant*," which may possibly have been suggested to him by Muskau's account.

fashionable extravagances of his time — or busying himself with political intrigue — or aiming at ministerial power — or purchasing increase of nobility — or collecting large museums of *virtu* — or playing the munificent patron of letters, of science, of art — or endowing, and bestowing his name upon extensive institutions of charity. But for the inconceivable wealth in the actual possession of the heir, these objects and all ordinary objects were felt to afford too limited a field. Recourse was had to figures, and these but sufficed to confound. It was seen that, even at three per cent., the annual income of the inheritance amounted to no less than thirteen millions and five hundred thousand dollars; which was one million and one hundred and twenty-five thousand per month; or thirty-six thousand nine hundred and eighty-six per day; or one thousand five hundred and forty-one per hour; or six and twenty dollars for every minute that flew. Thus the usual track of supposition was thoroughly broken up. Men knew not what to imagine. There were some who even conceived that Mr. Ellison would divest himself of at least one-half of his fortune, as of utterly superfluous opulence — enriching whole troops of his relatives by division of his superabundance. To the nearest of these he did, in fact, abandon the very unusual wealth which was his own before the inheritance.

I was not surprised, however, to perceive that he had long made up his mind on a point which had occasioned so much discussion to his friends. Nor was I greatly astonished at the nature of his decision. In regard to individual charities he had satisfied his conscience. In the possibility of any improvement, properly so called, being effected by man himself in the general condition of man, he had (I am sorry to confess it) little faith. Upon the whole, whether happily or unhappily, he was thrown back, in very great measure, upon self.

In the widest and noblest sense he was a poet. He comprehended, moreover, the true character, the august aims, the supreme majesty and dignity of the poetic sentiment. The fullest, if not the sole proper satisfaction of this sentiment he instinctively felt to lie in the creation of novel forms of beauty. Some peculiarities, either in his early education, or in the nature of his intellect, had tinged with what is termed materialism all his ethical speculations; and it was this bias, perhaps, which led him to believe that the most advantageous at least, if not the sole legitimate field for the poetic exercise, lies in the creation of novel moods of purely *physical* loveliness. Thus it happened he became neither musician nor poet — if we use this latter term in its every-day acceptation. Or it might have been that he neglected to become either, merely in pursuance of his idea that in contempt of ambition is to be found one of the essential principles of happiness on earth. Is it not indeed, possible that, while a high order of genius is necessarily ambitious, the highest is above that which is termed ambition? And may it not thus happen that many far greater than Milton have contentedly remained "mute and

inglorious?" I believe that the world has never seen — and that, unless through some series of accidents goading the noblest order of mind into distasteful exertion, the world will never see — that full extent of triumphant execution, in the richer domains of art, of which the human nature is absolutely capable.

Ellison became neither musician nor poet; although no man lived more profoundly enamored of music and poetry. Under other circum stances than those which invested him, it is not impossible that he would have become a painter. Sculpture, although in its nature rigorously poetical, was too limited in its extent and consequences, to have occupied, at any time, much of his attention. And I have now mentioned all the provinces in which the common understanding of the poetic sentiment has declared it capable of expatiating. But Ellison maintained that the richest, the truest, and most natural, if not altogether the most extensive province, had been unaccountably neglected. No definition had spoken of the landscape-gardener as of the poet; yet it seemed to my friend that the creation of the landscape-garden offered to the proper Muse the most magnificent of opportunities. Here, indeed, was the fairest field for the display of imagination in the endless combining of forms of novel beauty; the elements to enter into combination being, by a vast superiority, the most glorious which the earth could afford. In the multiform and multicolor of the flowers and the trees, he recognised the most direct and energetic efforts of Nature at physical loveliness. And in the direction or concentration of this effort — or, more properly, in its adaptation to the eyes which were to behold it on earth — he perceived that he should be employing the best means — laboring to the greatest advantage — in the fulfilment, not only of his own destiny as poet, but of the august purposes for which the Deity had implanted the poetic sentiment in man.

"Its adaptation to the eyes which were to behold it on earth." In his explanation of this phraseology, Mr. Ellison did much toward solving what has always seemed to me an enigma: — I mean the fact (which none but the ignorant dispute) that no such combination of scenery exists in nature as the painter of genius may produce. No such paradises are to be found in reality as have glowed on the canvas of Claude. In the most enchanting of natural landscapes, there will always be found a defect or an excess — many excesses and defects. While the component parts may defy, individually, the highest skill of the artist, the arrangement of these parts will always be susceptible of improvement. In short, no position can be attained on the wide surface of the *natural* earth, from which an artistical eye, looking steadily, will not find matter of offence in what is termed the "composition" of the landscape. And yet how unintelligible is this! In all other matters we are justly instructed to regard nature as supreme. With her details we shrink from competition. Who shall presume to imitate the colors of the tulip, or to improve

the proportions of the lily of the valley? The criticism which says, of sculpture or portraiture, that here nature is to be exalted or idealized rather than imitated, is in error. No pictorial or sculptural combinations of points of human liveliness do more than approach the living and breathing beauty. In landscape alone is the principle of the critic true; and, having felt its truth here, it is but the headlong spirit of generalization which has led him to pronounce it true throughout all the domains of art. Having, I say, *felt* its truth here; for the feeling is no affectation or chimera. The mathematics afford no more absolute demonstrations than the sentiments of his art yields the artist. He not only believes, but positively knows, that such and such apparently arbitrary arrangements of matter constitute and alone constitute the true beauty. His reasons, however, have not yet been matured into expression. It remains for a more profound analysis than the world has yet seen, fully to investigate and express them. Nevertheless he is confirmed in his instinctive opinions by the voice of all his brethren. Let a "composition" be defective; let an emendation be wrought in its mere arrangement of form; let this emendation be submitted to every artist in the world; by each will its necessity be admitted. And even far more than this: — in remedy of the defective composition, each insulated member of the fraternity would have suggested the identical emendation.

I repeat that in landscape arrangements alone is the physical nature susceptible of exaltation, and that, therefore, her susceptibility of improvement at this one point, was a mystery I had been unable to solve. My own thoughts on the subject had rested in the idea that the primitive intention of nature would have so arranged the earth's surface as to have fulfilled at all points man's sense of perfection in the beautiful, the sublime, or the picturesque; but that this primitive intention had been frustrated by the known geological disturbances — disturbances of form and color-grouping, in the correction or allaying of which lies the soul of art. The force of this idea was much weakened, however, by the necessity which it involved of considering the disturbances abnormal and unadapted to any purpose. It was Ellison who suggested that they were prognostic of *death*. He thus explained: — Admit the earthly immortality of man to have been the first intention. We have then the primitive arrangement of the earth's surface adapted to his blissful estate, as not existent but designed. The disturbances were the preparations for his subsequently conceived deathful condition.

"Now," said my friend, "what we regard as exaltation of the landscape may be really such, as respects only the moral or human *point of view*. Each alteration of the natural scenery may possibly effect a blemish in the picture, if we can suppose this picture viewed at large — in mass — from some point distant from the earth's surface, although not beyond the limits of its atmosphere. It is easily understood that what might improve a closely scrutinized detail, may at the same time injure a general

or more distantly observed effect. There *may* be a class of beings, human once, but now invisible to humanity, to whom, from afar, our disorder may seem order — our unpicturesqueness picturesque; in a word, the earth-angels, for whose scrutiny more especially than our own, and for whose death-refined appreciation of the beautiful, may have been set in array by God the wide landscape-gardens of the hemispheres."

In the course of discussion, my friend quoted some passages from a writer on landscape-gardening, who has been supposed to have well treated his theme:

"There are properly but two styles of landscape-gardening, the natural and the artificial. One seeks to recall the original beauty of the country, by adapting its means to the surrounding scenery; cultivating trees in harmony with the hills or plain of the neighboring land; detecting and bringing into practice those nice relations of size, proportion, and color which, hid from the common observer, are revealed everywhere to the experienced student of nature. The result of the natural style of gardening, is seen rather in the absence of all defects and incongruities — in the prevalence of a healthy harmony and order — than in the creation of any special wonders or miracles. The artificial style has as many varieties as there are different tastes to gratify. It has a certain general relation to the various styles of building. There are the stately avenues and retirements of Versailles; Italian terraces; and a various mixed old English style, which bears some relation to the domestic Gothic or English Elizabethan architecture. Whatever may be said against the abuses of the artificial landscape-gardening, a mixture of pure art in a garden scene adds to it a great beauty. This is partly pleasing to the eye, by the show of order and design, and partly moral. A terrace, with an old moss-covered balustrade, calls up at once to the eye the fair forms that have passed there in other days. The slightest exhibition of art is an evidence of care and human interest."

"From what I have already observed," said Ellison, "you will understand that I reject the idea, here expressed, of recalling the original beauty of the country. The original beauty is never so great as that which may be introduced. Of course, every thing depends on the selection of a spot with capabilities. What is said about detecting and bringing into practice nice relations of size, proportion, and color, is one of those mere vaguenesses of speech which serve to veil inaccuracy of thought. The phrase quoted may mean any thing, or nothing, and guides in no degree. That the true result of the natural style of gardening is seen rather in the absence of all defects and incongruities than in the creation of any special wonders or miracles, is a proposition better suited to the grovelling apprehension of the herd than to the fervid dreams of the man of genius. The negative merit suggested appertains to that hobbling criticism which, in letters, would elevate Addison into apotheosis. In truth, while that virtue which consists in the mere avoidance of vice appeals

directly to the understanding, and can thus be circumscribed in *rule*, the loftier virtue, which flames in creation, can be apprehended in its results alone. Rule applies but to the merits of denial — to the excellencies which refrain. Beyond these, the critical art can but suggest. We may be instructed to build a "Cato," but we are in vain told *how* to conceive a Parthenon or an "Inferno." The thing done, however; the wonder accomplished; and the capacity for apprehension becomes universal. The sophists of the negative school who, through inability to create, have scoffed at creation, are now found the loudest in applause. What, in its chrysalis condition of principle, affronted their demure reason, never fails, in its maturity of accomplishment, to extort admiration from their instinct of beauty.

"The author's observations on the artificial style," continued Ellison, "are less objectionable. A mixture of pure art in a garden scene adds to it a great beauty. This is just; as also is the reference to the sense of human interest. The principle expressed is incontrovertible — but there *may* be something beyond it. There may be an object in keeping with the principle — an object unattainable by the means ordinarily possessed by individuals, yet which, if attained, would lend a charm to the landscape-garden far surpassing that which a sense of merely human interest could bestow. A poet, having very unusual pecuniary resources, might, while retaining the necessary idea of art or culture, or, as our author expresses it, of interest, so imbue his designs at once with extent and novelty of beauty, as to convey the sentiment of spiritual interference. It will be seen that, in bringing about such result, he secures all the advantages of interest or *design*, while relieving his work of the harshness or technicality of the worldly *art*. In the most rugged of wildernesses — in the most savage of the scenes of pure nature — there is apparent the *art* of a creator; yet this art is apparent to reflection only; in no respect has it the obvious force of a feeling. Now let us suppose this sense of the Almighty design to be *one step depressed* — to be brought into something like harmony or consistency with the sense of human art — to form an intermedium between the two: — let us imagine, for example, a landscape whose combined vastness and definitiveness — whose united beauty, magnificence, and *strangeness*, shall convey the idea of care, or culture, or superintendence, on the part of beings superior, yet akin to humanity — then the sentiment of *interest* is preserved, while the art intervolved is made to assume the air of an intermediate or secondary nature — a nature which is not God, nor an emanation from God, but which still is nature in the sense of the handiwork of the angels that hover between man and God."

It was in devoting his enormous wealth to the embodiment of a vision such as this — in the free exercise in the open air ensured by the personal superintendence of his plans — in the unceasing object which these plans afforded — in the high spirituality of the object — in the contempt of

ambition which it enabled him truly to feel — in the perennial springs with which it gratified, without possibility of satiating, that one master passion of his soul, the thirst for beauty; above all, it was in the sympathy of a woman, not unwomanly, whose loveliness and love enveloped his existence in the purple atmosphere of Paradise, that Ellison thought to find, *and found*, exemption from the ordinary cares of humanity, with a far greater amount of positive happiness than ever glowed in the rapt day-dreams of De Stäel.

I despair of conveying to the reader any distinct conception of the marvels which my friend did actually accomplish. I wish to describe, but am disheartened by the difficulty of description, and hesitate between detail and generality. Perhaps the better course will be to unite the two in their extremes.

Mr. Ellison's first step regarded, of course, the choice of a locality; and scarcely had he commenced thinking on this point, when the luxuriant nature of the Pacific Islands arrested his attention. In fact, he had made up his mind for a voyage to the South Seas, when a night's reflection induced him to abandon the idea. "Were I misanthropic," he said, "such a *locale* would suit me. The thoroughness of its insulation and seclusion, and the difficulty of ingress and egress, would in such case be the charm of charms; but as yet I am not Timon. I wish the composure but not the depression of solitude. There must remain with me a certain control over the extent and duration of my repose. There will be frequent hours in which I shall need, too, the sympathy of the poetic in what I have done. Let me seek, then, a spot not far from a populous city — whose vicinity, also, will best enable me to execute my plans."

In search of a suitable place so situated, Ellison travelled for several years, and I was permitted to accompany him. A thousand spots with which I was enraptured he rejected without hesitation, for reasons which satisfied me, in the end, that he was right. We came at length to an elevated table-land of wonderful fertility and beauty, affording a panoramic prospect very little less in extent than that of Ætna, and, in Ellison's opinion as well as my own, surpassing the far-famed view from that mountain in all the true elements of the picturesque.

"I am aware," said the traveller, as he drew a sigh of deep delight after gazing on this scene, entranced, for nearly an hour, "I know that here, in my circumstances, nine-tenths of the most fastidious of men would rest content. This panorama is indeed glorious, and I should rejoice in it but for the excess of its glory. The taste of all the architects I have ever known leads them, for the sake of 'prospect,' to put up buildings on hill-tops. The error is obvious. Grandeur in any of its moods, but especially in that of extent, startles, excites — and then fatigues, depresses. For the occasional scene nothing can be better — for the constant view nothing worse. And, in the constant view, the most objectionable phase of grandeur is that of extent; the worst phase of extent, that

of distance. It is at war with the sentiment and with the sense of *seclusion* — the sentiment and sense which we seek to humor in 'retiring to the country.' In looking from the summit of a mountain we cannot help feeling *abroad* in the world. The heart-sick avoid distant prospects as a pestilence."

It was not until toward the close of the fourth year of our search that we found a locality with which Ellison professed himself satisfied. It is, of course, needless to say *where* was the locality. The late death of my friend, in causing his domain to be thrown open to certain classes of visiters, has given to *Arnheim* a species of secret and subdued if not solemn celebrity, similar in kind, although infinitely superior in degree, to that which so long distinguished Fonthill.

The usual approach to Arnheim was by the river. The visiter left the city in the early morning. During the forenoon he passed between shores of a tranquil and domestic beauty, on which grazed innumerable sheep, their white fleeces spotting the vivid green of rolling meadows. By degrees the idea of cultivation subsided into that of merely pastoral care. This slowly became merged in a sense of retirement — this again in a consciousness of solitude. As the evening approached, the channel grew more narrow; the banks more and more precipitous; and these latter were clothed in rich, more profuse, and more sombre foliage. The water increased in transparency. The stream took a thousand turns, so that at no moment could its gleaming surface be seen for a greater distance than a furlong. At every instant the vessel seemed imprisoned within an enchanted circle, having insuperable and impenetrable walls of foliage, a roof of ultramarine satin, and *no* floor — the keel balancing itself with admirable nicety on that of a phantom bark which, by some accident having been turned upside down, floated in constant company with the substantial one, for the purpose of sustaining it. The channel now became a *gorge* — although the term is somewhat inapplicable, and I employ it merely because the language has no word which better represents the most striking — not the most distinctive — feature of the scene. The character of gorge was maintained only in the height and parallelism of the shores; it was lost altogether in their other traits. The walls of the ravine (through which the clear water still tranquilly flowed) arose to an elevation of a hundred and occasionally of a hundred and fifty feet, and inclined so much toward each other as, in a great measure, to shut out the light of day; while the long plume-like moss which depended densely from the intertwining shrubberies overhead, gave the whole chasm an air of funereal gloom. The windings became more frequent and intricate, and seemed often as if returning in upon themselves, so that the voyager had long lost all idea of direction. He was, moreover, enwrapt in an exquisite sense of the strange. The thought of nature still remained, but her character seemed to have undergone modification, there was a weird symmetry, a thrilling uniformity, a wizard propriety

in these her works. Not a dead branch — not a withered leaf — not a stray pebble — not a patch of the brown earth was anywhere visible. The crystal water welled up against the clean granite, or the unblemished moss, with a sharpness of outline that delighted while it bewildered the eye.

Having threaded the mazes of this channel for some hours, the gloom deepening every moment, a sharp and unexpected turn of the vessel brought it suddenly, as if dropped from heaven, into a circular basin of very considerable extent when compared with the width of the gorge. It was about two hundred yards in diameter, and girt in at all points but one — that immediately fronting the vessel as it entered — by hills equal in general height to the walls of the chasm, although of a thoroughly different character. Their sides sloped from the water's edge at an angle of some forty-five degrees, and they were clothed from base to summit — not a perceptible point escaping — in a drapery of the most gorgeous flower-blossoms; scarcely a green leaf being visible among the sea of odorous and fluctuating color. This basin was of great depth, but so transparent was the water that the bottom, which seemed to consist of a thick mass of small round alabaster pebbles, was distinctly visible by glimpses — that is to say, whenever the eye could permit itself *not* to see, far down in the inverted heaven, the duplicate blooming of the hills. On these latter there were no trees, nor even shrubs of any size. The impressions wrought on the observer were those of richness, warmth, color, quietude, uniformity, softness, delicacy, daintiness, voluptuousness, and a miraculous extremeness of culture that suggested dreams of a new race of fairies, laborious, tasteful, magnificent, and fastidious; but as the eye traced upward the myriad-tinted slope, from its sharp junction with the water to its vague termination amid the folds of overhanging cloud, it became, indeed, difficult not to fancy a panoramic cataract of rubies, sapphires, opals, and golden onyxes, rolling silently out of the sky.

The visiter, shooting suddenly into this bay from out the gloom of the ravine, is delighted but astounded by the full orb of the declining sun, which he had supposed to be already far below the horizon, but which now confronts him, and forms the sole termination of an otherwise limitless vista seen through another chasm-like rift in the hills.

But here the voyager quits the vessel which has borne him so far, and descends into a light canoe of ivory, stained with arabesque devices in vivid scarlet, both within and without. The poop and beak of this boat arise high above the water, with sharp points, so that the general form is that of an irregular crescent. It lies on the surface of the bay with the proud grace of a swan. On its ermined floor reposes a single feathery paddle of satin-wood; but no oarsmen or attendant is to be seen. The guest is bidden to be of good cheer — that the fates will take care of him. The larger vessel disappears, and he is left alone in the canoe, which lies apparently motionless in the middle of the lake. While he considers what

course to pursue, however, he becomes aware of a gentle movement in the fairy bark. It slowly swings itself around until its prow points toward the sun. It advances with a gentle but gradually accelerated velocity, while the slight ripples it creates seem to break about the ivory side in divinest melody — seem to offer the only possible explanation of the soothing yet melancholy music for whose unseen origin the bewildered voyager looks around him in vain.

The canoe steadily proceeds, and the rocky gate of the vista is approached, so that its depths can be more distinctly seen. To the right arise a chain of lofty hills rudely and luxuriantly wooded. It is observed, however, that the trait of exquisite *cleanness* where the bank dips into the water, still prevails. There is not one token of the usual river *débris*. To the left the character of the scene is softer and more obviously artificial. Here the bank slopes upward from the stream in a very gentle ascent, forming a broad sward of grass of a texture resembling nothing so much as velvet, and of a brilliancy of green which would bear comparison with the tint of the purest emerald. This *plateau* varies in width from ten to three hundred yards; reaching from the river-bank to a wall, fifty feet high, which extends, in an infinity of curves, but following the general direction of the river, until lost in the distance to the westward. This wall is of one continuous rock, and has been formed by cutting perpendicularly the once rugged precipice of the stream's southern bank; but no trace of the labor has been suffered to remain. The chiselled stone has the hue of ages, and is profusely overhung and overspread with the ivy, the coral honeysuckle, the eglantine, and the clematis. The uniformity of the top and bottom lines of the wall is fully relieved by occasional trees of gigantic height, growing singly or in small groups, both along the *plateau* and in the domain behind the wall, but in close proximity to it; so that frequent limbs (of the black walnut especially) reach over and dip their pendent extremities into the water. Farther back within the domain, the vision is impeded by an impenetrable screen of foliage.

These things are observed during the canoe's gradual approach to what I have called the gate of the vista. On drawing nearer to this, however, its chasm-like appearance vanishes; a new outlet from the bay is discovered to the left — in which direction the wall is also seen to sweep, still following the general course of the stream. Down this new opening the eye cannot penetrate very far; for the stream, accompanied by the wall, still bends to the left, until both are swallowed up by the leaves.

The boat, nevertheless, glides magically into the winding channel; and here the shore opposite the wall is found to resemble that opposite the wall in the straight vista. Lofty hills, rising occasionally into mountains, and covered with vegetation in wild luxuriance, still shut in the scene.

Floating gently onward, but with a velocity slightly augmented, the

voyager, after many short turns, finds his progress apparently barred by a gigantic gate or rather door of burnished gold, elaborately carved and fretted, and reflecting the direct rays of the now fast-sinking sun with an effulgence that seems to wreath the whole surrounding forest in flames. This gate is inserted in the lofty wall; which here appears to cross the river at right angles. In a few moments, however, it is seen that the main body of the water still sweeps in a gentle and extensive curve to the left, the wall following it as before, while a stream of considerable volume, diverging from the principal one, makes its way, with a slight ripple, under the door, and is thus hidden from sight. The canoe falls into the lesser channel and approaches the gate. Its ponderous wings are slowly and musically expanded. The boat glides between them, and commences a rapid descent into a vast amphitheatre entirely begirt with purple mountains, whose bases are laved by a gleaming river throughout the full extent of their circuit. Meantime the whole Paradise of Arnheim bursts upon the view. There is a gush of entrancing melody; there is an oppressive sense of strange sweet odor; — there is a dream-like inter-mingling to the eye of tall slender Eastern trees — bosky shrubberies — flocks of golden and crimson birds — lily-fringed lakes — meadows of violets, tulips, poppies, hyacinths, and tuberoses — long intertangled lines of silver streamlets — and, upspringing confusedly from amid all, a mass of semi-Gothic, semi-Saracenic architecture sustaining itself by miracle in mid-air; glittering in the red sunlight with a hundred oriels, minarets, and pinnacles; and seeming the phantom handiwork, conjointly, of the Sylphs, of the Fairies, of the Genii, and of the Gnomes.

Mellonta Tauta

To the Editors of the Lady's Book: *I have the honor of sending you, for your magazine, an article which I hope you will be able to comprehend rather more distinctly than I do myself. It is a translation, by my friend, Martin Van Buren Mavis, (sometimes called the "Toughkeepsie Seer") of an odd-looking MS. which I found, about a year ago, tightly corked up in a jug floating in the Mare Tenebrarum — a sea well described by the Nubian geographer, but seldom visited now-a-days, except for the transcendentalists and divers for crotchets.*

Truly yours,

E D G A R A. P O E

ON BOARD BALLOON "SKYLARK"

APRIL 1, 2848

Now, my dear friend — now, for your sins, you are to suffer the in-fliction of a long gossiping letter. I tell you distinctly that I am going to punish you for all your impertinences by being as tedious, as dis-

cursive, as incoherent, and as unsatisfactory as possible. Besides, here I am, cooped up in a dirty balloon, with some one or two hundred of the *canaille*, all bound on a *pleasure* excursion, (what a funny idea some people have of pleasure!) and I have no prospect of touching *terra firma* for a month at least. Nobody to talk to. Nothing to do. When one has nothing to do, then is the time to correspond with one's friends. You perceive, then, why it is that I write you this letter — it is on account of my *ennui* and your sins.

Get ready your spectacles and make up your mind to be annoyed. I mean to write at you every day during this odious voyage.

Heigho! when will any *Invention* visit the human pericranium? Are we forever to be doomed to the thousand inconveniences of the balloon? Will *nobody* contrive a more expeditious mode of progress? The jog-trot movement, to my thinking, is little less than positive torture. Upon my word we have not made more than a hundred miles the hour since leaving home! The very birds beat us — at least some of them. I assure you that I do not exaggerate at all. Our motion, no doubt, seems slower than it actually is — this on account of our having no objects about us by which to estimate our velocity, and on account of our going *with* the wind. To be sure, whenever we meet a balloon we have a chance of perceiving our rate, and then, I admit, things do not appear so very bad. Accustomed as I am to this mode of travelling, I cannot get over a kind of giddiness whenever a balloon passes us in a current directly overhead. It always seems to me like an immense bird of prey about to pounce upon us and carry us off in its claws. One went over us this morning about sunrise, and so nearly overhead that its drag-rope actually brushed the network suspending our car, and caused us very serious apprehension. Our captain said that if the material of the bag had been the trumpery varnished "silk" of five hundred or a thousand years ago, we should inevitably have been damaged. This silk, as he explained it to me, was a fabric composed of the entrails of a species of earth-worm. The worm was carefully fed on mulberries — a kind of fruit resembling a water-melon — and, when sufficiently fat, was crushed in a mill. The paste thus arising was called *papyrus* in its primary state, and went through a variety of processes until it finally became "silk." Singular to relate, it was once much admired as an article of *female dress!* Balloons were also very generally constructed from it. A better kind of material, it appears, was subsequently found in the down surrounding the seed-vessels of a plant vulgarly called *euphorbium*, and at that time botanically termed milk-weed. This latter kind of silk was designated as silk-buckingham, on account of its superior durability, and was usually prepared for use by being varnished with a solution of gum caoutchouc — a substance which in some respects must have resembled the *gutta percha* now in common use. This caoutchouc was occasionally called Indian

rubber or rubber of twist, and was no doubt one of the numerous *fungi*. Never tell me again that I am not at heart an antiquarian.

Talking of drag-ropes — our own, it seems, has this moment knocked a man overboard from one of the small magnetic propellers that swarm in ocean below us — a boat of about six thousand tons, and, from all accounts, shamefully crowded. These diminutive barques should be prohibited from carrying more than a definite number of passengers. The man, of course, was not permitted to get on board again, and was soon out of sight, he and his life-preserver. I rejoice, my dear friend, that we live in an age so enlightened that no such a thing as an individual is supposed to exist. It is the mass for which the true Humanity cares. By-the-by, talking of Humanity, do you know that our immortal Wiggins is not so original in his views of the Social Condition and so forth, as his contemporaries are inclined to suppose? Pundit assures me that the same ideas were put nearly in the same way, about a thousand years ago, by an Irish philosopher called Furrier, on account of his keeping a retail shop for cat peltries and other furs. Pundit *knows*, you know; there can be no mistake about it. How very wonderfully do we see verified every day, the profound observation of the Hindoo Aries Tottle (as quoted by Pundit) — "Thus must we say that, not once or twice, or a few times, but with almost infinite repetitions, the same opinions come round in a circle among men."

April 2. — Spoke to-day the magnetic cutter in charge of the middle section of floating telegraph wires. I learn that when this species of telegraph was first put into operation by Horse, it was considered quite impossible to convey the wires over sea, but now we are at a loss to comprehend where the difficulty lay! So wags the world. *Tempora mutantur* — excuse me for quoting the Etruscan. What *would* we do without the Atalantic telegraph? (Pundit says Atlantic was the ancient adjective.) We lay to a few minutes to ask the cutter some questions, and learned, among other glorious news, that civil war is raging in Africa, while the plague is doing its good work beautifully both in Yurope and Ayesher. Is it not truly remarkable that, before the magnificent light shed upon philosophy by Humanity, the world was accustomed to regard War and Pestilence as calamities? Do you know that prayers were actually offered up in the ancient temples to the end that these *evils* (!) might not be visited upon mankind? Is it not really difficult to comprehend upon what principle of interest our forefathers acted? Were they so blind as not to perceive that the destruction of a myriad of individuals is only so much positive advantage to the mass!

April 3. — It is really a very fine amusement to ascend the rope-ladder leading to the summit of the balloon-bag, and thence survey the surrounding world. From the car below you know the prospect is not so comprehensive — you can see little vertically. But seated here (where I

write this) in the luxuriously-cushioned open piazza of the summit, one can see everything that is going on in all directions. Just now there is quite a crowd of balloons in sight, and they present a very animated appearance, while the air is resonant with the hum of so many millions of human voices. I have heard it asserted that when Yellow or (Pundit *will* have it) Violet, who is supposed to have been the first æronaut, maintained the practicability of traversing the atmosphere in all directions, by merely ascending or descending until a favorable current was attained, he was scarcely hearkened to at all by his contemporaries, who looked upon him as merely an ingenious sort of madman, because the philosophers (?) of the day declared the thing impossible. Really now it does seem to me *quite* unaccountable how any thing so obviously feasible could have escaped the sagacity of the ancient *savans*. But in all ages the great obstacles to advancement in Art have been opposed by the so-called men of science. To be sure, *our* men of science are not quite so bigoted as those of old: — oh, I have something *so* queer to tell you on this topic. Do you know that it is not more than a thousand years ago since the metaphysicians consented to relieve the people of the singular fancy that there existed but *two possible roads for the attainment of Truth!* Believe it if you can! It appears that long, long ago, in the night of Time, there lived a Turkish philosopher (or Hindoo possibly) called Aries Tottle. This person introduced, or at all events propagated what was termed the deductive or *à priori* mode of investigation. He started with what he maintained to be *axioms* or "self-evident truths," and thence proceeded "logically" to results. His greatest disciples were one Neuclid, and one Cant. Well, Aries Tottle flourished supreme until advent of one Hog, surnamed the "Ettrick Shepherd," who preached an entirely different system, which he called the *à posteriori* or *inductive.* His plan referred altogether to Sensation. He proceeded by observing, analyzing, and classifying facts — *instantiæ naturæ*, as they were affectedly called — into general laws. Aries Tottle's mode, in a word, was based on *noumena*; Hog's on *phenomena*. Well, so great was the admiration excited by this latter system that, at its first introduction, Aries Tottle fell into disrepute; but finally he recovered ground and was permitted to divide the realm of Truth with his more modern rival. The *savans* now maintained the Aristotelian and *Baconian* roads were the sole possible avenues to knowledge. "Baconian," you must know, was an adjective invented as equivalent to Hog-ian and more euphonious and dignified.

Now, my dear friend, I do assure you, most positively, that I represent this matter fairly, on the soundest authority; and you can easily understand how a notion so absurd on its very face must have operated to retard the progress of all true knowledge — which makes its advances almost invariably by intuitive bounds. The ancient idea confined investigations to *crawling*; and for hundreds of years so great was the infatuation about Hog especially, that a virtual end was put to all thinking,

properly so called. No man dared utter a truth to which he felt himself indebted to his *Soul* alone. It mattered not whether the truth was even *demonstrably* a truth, for the bullet-headed *savans* of the time regarded only *the road* by which he had attained it. They would not even *look* at the end. "Let us see the means," they cried, "the means!" If, upon investigation of the means, it was found to come under neither the category Aries (that is to say Ram) nor under the category Hog, why then the savans went no farther, but pronounced the "theorist" a fool, and would have nothing to do with him or his truth.

Now, it cannot be maintained, even, that by the crawling system the greatest amount of truth would be attained in any long series of ages, for the repression of *imagination* was an evil not to be compensated for by any superior *certainty* in the ancient modes of investigation. The error of these Jurmains, these Vrinch, these Inglitch, and these Amriccans (the latter, by the way, were our own immediate progenitors), was an error quite analogous with that of the wiseacre who fancies that he must necessarily see an object the better the more closely he holds it to his eyes. These people blinded themselves by details. When they proceeded Hoggishly, their "facts" were by no means always facts — a matter of little consequence had it not been for assuming that they *were* facts and must be facts because they appeared to be such. When they proceeded on the path of the Ram, their course was scarcely as straight as a ram's horn, for they *never had* an axiom which was an axiom at all. They must have been very blind not to see this, even in their own day; for even in their own day many of the long "established" axioms had been rejected. For example — "*Ex nihilo nihil fit*"; "a body cannot act where it is not"; "there cannot exist antipodes"; "darkness cannot come out of light" — all these, and a dozen other similar propositions, formerly admitted without hesitation as axioms, were, even at the period of which I speak, seen to be untenable. How absurd in these people, then, to persist in putting faith in "axioms" as immutable bases of Truth! But even out of the mouths of their soundest reasoners it is easy to demonstrate the futility, the impalpability of their axioms in general. Who *was* the soundest of their logicians? Let me see! I will go and ask Pundit and be back in a minute. . . . Ah, here we have it! Here is a book written nearly a thousand years ago and lately translated from the Inglitch — which, by the way, appears to have been the rudiment of the Amriccan. Pundit says it is decidedly the cleverest ancient work on its topic, Logic. The author (who was much thought of in his day) was one Miller, or Mill; and we find it recorded of him, as a point of some importance, that he had a mill-horse called Bentham. But let us glance at the treatise!

Ah! — "Ability or inability to conceive," says Mr. Mill, very properly, "is in no case to be received as a criterion of axiomatic truth." What *modern* in his senses would ever think of disputing this truism? The only wonder with us must be, how it happened that Mr. Mill conceived it

necessary even to hint at any thing so obvious. So far good — but let us turn over another paper. What have we here? — "Contradictories cannot both be true — that is, cannot co-exist in nature." Here Mr. Mill means, for example, that a tree must be either a tree or not a tree — that it cannot be at the same time a tree and not a tree. Very well; but I ask him *why*. His reply is this — and never pretends to be any thing else than this — "Because it is impossible to conceive that contradictories can both be true." But this is no answer at all, by his own showing; for has he not just admitted as a truism that "ability or inability to conceive is *in no case* to be received as a criterion of axiomatic truth."

Now I do not complain of these ancients so much because their logic is, by their own showing, utterly baseless, worthless and fantastic altogether, as because of their pompous and imbecile proscription of all *other* roads of Truth, of all *other* means for its attainment than the two preposterous paths — the one of creeping and the one of crawling — to which they have dared to confine the Soul that loves nothing so well as to *soar*.

By the by, my dear friend, do you not think it would have puzzled these ancient dogmaticians to have determined by which of their two roads it was that the most important and most sublime of *all* their truths was, in effect, attained? I mean the truth of Gravitation. Newton owed it to Kepler. Kepler admitted that his three laws were *guessed at* — these three laws of all laws which led the great Inglitch mathematician to his principle, the basis of all physical principle — to go behind which we must enter the Kingdom of Metaphysics. Kepler guessed — that is to say *imagined*. He was essentially a "theorist" — that word now of so much sanctity, formerly an epithet of contempt. Would it not have puzzled these old moles too, to have explained by which of the two "roads" a cryptographist unriddles a cryptograph of more than usual secrecy, or by which of the two roads Champollion directed mankind to those enduring and almost innumerable truths which resulted from his deciphering the Hieroglyphics.

One word more on this topic and I will be done boring you. Is it not *passing* strange that, with their eternal prattling about *roads* to Truth, these bigoted people missed what we now so clearly perceive to be the great highway — that of Consistency? Does it not seem singular how they should have failed to deduce from the works of God the vital fact that a perfect consistency *must be* an absolute truth! How plain has been our progress since the late announcement of this proposition! Investigation has been taken out of the hands of the ground-moles and given, as a task, to the true and only true thinkers, the men of ardent imagination. These latter *theorize*. Can you not fancy the shout of scorn with which my words would be received by our progenitors were it possible for them to be now looking over my shoulder? These men, I say, *theorize*; and their theories are simply corrected, reduced, systematized — cleared, little

by little, of their dross of inconsistency — until, finally, a perfect consistency stands apparent which even the most stolid admit, because it *is* a consistency, to be an absolute and an unquestionable *truth*.

April 4. — The new gas is doing wonders, in conjunction with the new improvement with gutta percha. How very safe, commodious, manageable, and in every respect convenient are our modern balloons! Here is an immense one approaching us at the rate of at least a hundred and fifty miles an hour. It seems to be crowded with people — perhaps there are three or four hundred passengers — and yet it soars to an elevation of nearly a mile, looking down upon poor us with sovereign contempt. Still a hundred or even two hundred miles an hour is slow travelling after all. Do you remember our flight on the railroad across the Kanadaw continent? — fully three hundred miles the hour — *that* was travelling. Nothing to be seen though — nothing to be done but flirt, feast and dance in the magnificent saloons. Do you remember what an odd sensation was experienced when, by chance, we caught a glimpse of external objects while the cars were in full flight? Every thing seemed unique — in one mass. For my part, I cannot say but that I preferred the travelling by the slow train of a hundred miles the hour. Here we were permitted to have glass windows — even to have them open — and something like a distinct view of the country was attainable. . . . Pundit says that *the route* for the great Kanadaw railroad must have been in some measure marked out about nine hundred years ago! In fact, he goes so far as to assert that actual traces of a road are still discernible — traces referable to a period quite as remote as that mentioned. The track, it appears was *double* only; ours, you know, has twelve paths; and three or four new ones are in preparation. The ancient rails were very slight, and placed so close together as to be, according to modern notions, quite frivolous, if not dangerous in the extreme. The present width of track — fifty feet — is considered, indeed, scarcely secure enough. For my part, I make no doubt that a track of some sort *must* have existed in very remote times, as Pundit asserts; for nothing can be clearer, to my mind, than that, at some period — not less than seven centuries ago, certainly — the Northern and Southern Kanadaw continents were *united*; the Kanawdians, then, would have been driven, by necessity, to a great railroad across the continent.

April 5. — I am almost devoured by *ennui*. Pundit is the only conversible person on board; and he, poor soul! can speak of nothing but antiquities. He has been occupied all the day in the attempt to convince me that the ancient Amriccans *governed themselves!* — did ever anybody hear of such an absurdity? — that they existed in a sort of every-man-for-himself confederacy, after the fashion of the "prairie dogs" that we read of in fable. He says that they started with the queerest idea conceivable, viz: that all men are born free and equal — this in the very teeth of the laws of *gradation* so visibly impressed upon all things both in the moral

and physical universe. Every man "voted," as they called it — that is to
say meddled with public affairs — until, at length, it was discovered that
what is everybody's business is nobody's, and that the "Republic" (so the
absurd thing was called) was without a government at all. It is related,
however, that the first circumstance which disturbed, very particularly,
the self-complacency of the philosophers who constructed this "Repub-
lic," was the startling discovery that universal suffrage gave opportunity
for fraudulent schemes, by means of which any desired number of votes
might at any time be polled, without the possibility of prevention or even
detection, by any party which should be merely villainous enough not to
be ashamed of the fraud. A little reflection upon this discovery sufficed
to render evident the consequences, which were that rascality *must* pre-
dominate — in a word, that a republican government *could* never be any
thing but a rascally one. While the philosophers, however, were busied
in blushing at their stupidity in not having foreseen these inevitable
evils, and intent upon the invention of new theories, the matter was put
to an abrupt issue by a fellow of the name of *Mob*, who took every thing
into his own hands and set up a despotism, in comparison with which
those of the fabulous Zeros and Hellofagabaluses were respectable and
delectable. This Mob (a foreigner, by-the-by), is said to have been the
most odious of all men that ever encumbered the earth. He was a giant
in stature — insolent, rapacious, filthy; had the gall of a bullock with the
heart of a hyena and the brains of a peacock. He died, at length, by dint
of his own energies, which exhausted him. Nevertheless, he had his uses,
as every thing has, however vile, and taught mankind a lesson which to
this day it is in no danger of forgetting — never to run directly contrary
to the natural analogies. As for Republicanism, no analogy could be
found for it upon the face of the earth — unless we except the case of the
"prairie dogs," an exception which seems to demonstrate, if anything,
that democracy is a very admirable form of government — for dogs.

April 6. — Last night had a fine view of Alpha Lyræ, whose disk,
through our captain's spy-glass, subtends an angle of half a degree, look-
ing very much as our sun does to the naked eye on a misty day. Alpha Lyræ,
although so *very* much larger than our sun, by the by, resembles him
closely as regards its spots, its atmosphere, and in many other particulars.
It is only within the last century, Pundit tells me, that the binary relation
existing between these two orbs began even to be suspected. The evident
motion of our system in the heavens was (strange to say!) referred to an
orbit about a prodigious star in the centre of the galaxy. About this star,
or at all events about a centre of gravity common to all the globes of
the Milky Way and supposed to be near Alcyone in the Pleiades, every
one of these globes was declared to be revolving, our own performing the
circuit in a period of 117,000,000 of years! *We*, with our present lights,
our vast telescopic improvements, and so forth, of course find it difficult
to comprehend *the ground* of an idea such as this. Its first propagator

was one Mudler. He was led, we must presume, to this wild hypothesis by mere analogy in the first instance; but, this being the case, he should have at least adhered to analogy in its development. A great central orb *was*, in fact, suggested; so far Mudler was consistent. This central orb, however, dynamically, should have been greater than all its surrounding orbs taken together. The question might then have been asked — "Why do we not see it?" — *we*, especially, who occupy the mid region of the cluster — the very locality *near* which, at least, must be situated this inconceivable central sun. The astronomer, perhaps, at this point, took refuge in the suggestion of non-luminosity; and here analogy was suddenly let fall. But even admitting the central orb non-luminous, how did he manage to explain its failure to be rendered visible by the incalculable host of glorious suns glaring in all directions about it? No doubt what he finally maintained was merely a centre of gravity common to all the revolving orbs — but here again analogy must have been let fall. Our system revolves, it is true, about a common centre of gravity, but it does this in connection with and in consequence of a material sun whose mass more than counterbalances the rest of the system. The mathematical circle is a curve composed of an infinity of straight lines; but this idea of the circle — this idea of it which, in regard to all earthly geometry, we consider as merely the mathematical, in contradistinction from the practical, idea — is, in sober fact, the *practical* conception which alone we have any right to entertain in respect to those Titanic circles with which we have to deal, at least in fancy, when we suppose our system, with its fellows, revolving about a point in the centre of the galaxy. Let the most vigorous of human imaginations but attempt to take a single step toward the comprehension of a circuit so unutterable! I would scarcely be paradoxical to say that a flash of lightning itself, travelling *forever* upon the circumference of this inconceivable circle, would still *forever* be travelling in a straight line. That the path of our sun along such a circumference — that the direction of our system in such an orbit — would, to any human perception, deviate in the slightest degree from a straight line even in a million of years, is a proposition not to be entertained; and yet these ancient astronomers were absolutely cajoled, it appears, into believing that a decisive curvature had become apparent during the brief period of their astronomical history — during the mere point — during the utter nothingness of two or three thousand years! How incomprehensible, that considerations such as this did not at once indicate to them the true state of affairs — that of the binary revolution of our sun and Alpha Lyræ around a common centre of gravity!

April 7. — Continued last night our astronomical amusements. Had a fine view of the five Neptunian asteroids, and watched with much interest the putting up of a huge impost on a couple of lintels in the new temple at Daphnis in the moon. It was amusing to think that creatures so diminutive as the lunarians, and bearing so little resemblance to

humanity, yet evinced a mechanical ingenuity so much superior to our own. One finds it difficult, too, to conceive the vast masses which these people handle so easily, to be as light as our own reason tells us they actually are.

April 8. — Eureka! Pundit is in his glory. A balloon from Kanadaw spoke us to-day and threw on board several late papers; they contain some exceedingly curious information relative to Kanawdian or rather Amriccan antiquities. You know, I presume, that laborers have for some months been employed in preparing the ground for a new fountain at Paradise, the Emperor's principal pleasure garden. Paradise, it appears, has been, *literally* speaking, an island time out of mind — that is to say, its northern boundary was always (as far back as any record extends) a rivulet, or rather a very narrow arm of the sea. This arm was gradually widened until it attained its present breadth — a mile. The whole length of the island is nine miles; the breadth varies materially. The entire area (so Pundit says) was, about eight hundred years ago, densely packed with houses, some of them twenty stories high; land (for some most unaccountable reason) being considered as especially precious just in this vicinity. The disastrous earthquake, however, of the year 2050, so totally uprooted and overwhelmed the town (for it was almost too large to be called a village) that the most indefatigable of our antiquarians have never yet been able to obtain from the site any sufficient data (in the shape of coins, medals or inscriptions) wherewith to build up even the ghost of a theory concerning the manners, customs, &c., &c., &c., of the aboriginal inhabitants. Nearly all that we have hitherto known of them is, that they were a portion of the Knickerbocker tribe of savages infesting the continent at its first discovery by Recorder Riker, a knight of the Golden Fleece. They were by no means uncivilized, however, but cultivated various arts and even sciences after a fashion of their own. It is related of them that they were acute in many respects, but were oddly afflicted with monomania for building what, in the ancient Amriccan, was denominated "churches" — a kind of pagoda instituted for the worship of two idols that went by the names of Wealth and Fashion. In the end, it is said, the island became, nine tenths of it, church. The women, too, it appears, were oddly deformed by a natural protuberance of the region just below the small of the back — although, most unaccountably, this deformity was looked upon altogether in the light of a beauty. One or two pictures of these singular women have in fact, been miraculously preserved. They look very odd, *very* — like something between a turkey-cock and a dromedary.

Well, these few details are nearly all that have descended to us respecting the ancient Knickerbockers. It seems, however, that while digging in the centre of the emperor's garden, (which, you know, covers the whole island), some of the workmen unearthed a cubical and evidently chiseled block of granite, weighing several hundred pounds. It

was in good preservation, having received, apparently, little injury from the convulsion which entombed it. On one of its surfaces was a marble slab with (only think of it!) *an inscription — a legible inscription.* Pundit is in ecstacies. Upon detaching the slab, a cavity appeared, containing a leaden box filled with various coins, a long scroll of names, several documents which appear to resemble newspapers, with other matters of intense interest to the antiquarian! There can be no doubt that all these are genuine Amriccan relics belonging to the tribe called Knickerbocker. The papers thrown on board our balloon are filled with fac-similes of the coins, MSS., typography, &c., &c. I copy for your amusement the Knickerbocker inscription on the marble slab: —

> THIS CORNER STONE OF A MONUMENT TO
> THE MEMORY OF
> ## GEORGE WASHINGTON
> WAS LAID WITH APPROPRIATE CEREMONIES
> ON THE
> 19TH DAY OF OCTOBER, 1847
> THE ANNIVERSARY OF THE SURRENDER OF
> LORD CORNWALLIS
> TO GENERAL WASHINGTON AT YORKTOWN
> A. D. 1781
> UNDER THE AUSPICES OF THE
> WASHINGTON MONUMENT ASSOCIATION OF
> THE CITY OF NEW YORK

This, as I give it, is a verbatim translation done by Pundit himself, so there *can* be no mistake about it. From the few words thus preserved, we glean several important items of knowledge, not the least interesting of which is the fact that a thousand years ago *actual* monuments had fallen into disuse — as was all very proper — the people contenting themselves, as we do now, with a mere indication of the design to erect a monument at some future time; a corner-stone being cautiously laid by itself "solitary and alone" (excuse me for quoting the great American poet Benton!), as a guarantee of the magnanimous *intention.* We ascertain, too, very distinctly, from this admirable inscription, the how as well as the where and the what, of the great surrender in question. As to the *where,* it was Yorktown (wherever that was), and as to the *what,* it was General Cornwallis (no doubt some wealthy dealer in corn). *He* was surrendered. The inscription commemorates the surrender of — what? why, "of Lord Cornwallis." The only question is what could the savages wish him surrendered for. But when we remember that these savages were undoubtedly cannibals, we are led to the conclusion that they intended him for

sausage. As to the *how* of the surrender, no language can be more explicit. Lord Cornwallis was surrendered (for sausage) "under the auspices of the Washington Monument Association" — no doubt a charitable institution for the depositing of corner-stones. —— But, Heaven bless me! what is the matter? Ah, I see — the balloon has collapsed, and we shall have a tumble into the sea. I have, therefore, only time enough to add that, from a hasty inspection of the fac-similes of newspapers, &c., &c., I find that *the* great men in those days among the Amriccans, were one John, a smith, and one Zacchary, a tailor.

Good-bye, until I see you again. Whether you ever get this letter or not is point of little importance, as I write altogether for my own amusement. I shall cork the MS. up in a bottle, however, and throw it into the sea.

Yours everlastingly,
PUNDITA.

Hop-Frog: or, the Eight Chained Ourang-Outangs

I NEVER knew anyone so keenly alive to a joke as the king was. He seemed to live only for joking. To tell a good story of the joke kind, and to tell it well, was the surest road to his favor. Thus it happened that his seven ministers were all noted for their accomplishments as jokers. They all took after the king, too, in being large, corpulent, oily men, as well as inimitable jokers. Whether people grow fat by joking, or whether there is something in fat itself which predisposes to a joke, I have never been quite able to determine; but certain it is that a lean joker is a *rara avis in terris.*

About the refinements, or, as he called them, the 'ghost' of wit, the king troubled himself very little. He had an especial admiration for *breadth* in a jest, and would often put up with *length*, for the sake of it. Over-niceties wearied him. He would have preferred Rabelais' 'Gargantua' to the 'Zadig' of Voltaire: and, upon the whole, practical jokes suited his taste far better than verbal ones.

At the date of my narrative, professing jesters had not altogether gone out of fashion at court. Several of the great continental 'powers' still retain their 'fools,' who wore motley, with caps and bells, and who were expected to be always ready with sharp witticisms, at a moment's notice, in consideration of the crumbs that fell from the royal table.

Our king, as a matter of course, retained his 'fool.' The fact is, he *required* something in the way of folly — if only to counterbalance the

heavy wisdom of the seven wise men who were his ministers — not to mention himself.

His fool, or professional jester, was not *only* a fool, however. His value was trebled in the eyes of the king, by the fact of his being also a dwarf and a cripple. Dwarfs were as common at court, in those days, as fools; and many monarchs would have found it difficult to get through their days (days are rather longer at court than elsewhere) without both a jester to laugh *with*, and a dwarf to laugh *at*. But, as I have already observed, your jesters, in ninety-nine cases out of a hundred, are fat, round, and unwieldy — so that it was no small source of self-gratulation with our king that, in Hop-Frog (this was the fool's name), he possessed a triplicate treasure in one person.

I believe the name 'Hop-Frog' was *not* that given to the dwarf by his sponsors at baptism, but it was conferred upon him, by general consent of the several ministers, on account of his inability to walk as other men do. In fact, Hop-Frog could only get along by a sort of interjectional gait — something between a leap and a wriggle — a movement that afforded illimitable amusement, and of course consolation, to the king, for (notwithstanding the protuberance of his stomach and a constitutional swelling of the head) the king, by his whole court, was accounted a capital figure.

But although Hop-Frog, through the distortion of his legs, could move only with great pain and difficulty along a road or floor, the prodigious muscular power which nature seemed to have bestowed upon his arms, by way of compensation for deficiency in the lower limbs, enabled him to perform many feats of wonderful dexterity, where trees or ropes were in question, or any thing else to climb. At such exercises he certainly much more resembled a squirrel, or a small monkey, than a frog.

I am not able to say, with precision, from what country Hop-Frog originally came. It was from some barbarous region, however, that no person ever heard of — a vast distance from the court of our king. Hop-Frog, and a young girl very little less dwarfish than himself (although of exquisite proportions, and a marvellous dancer), had been forcibly carried off from their respective homes in adjoining provinces, and sent as presents to the king, by one of his ever-victorious generals.

Under these circumstances, it is not to be wondered at that a close intimacy arose between the two little captives. Indeed, they soon became sworn friends. Hop-Frog, who, although he made a great deal of sport, was by no means popular, had it not in his power to render Trippetta many services; but *she*, on account of her grace and exquisite beauty (although a dwarf), was universally admired and petted; so she possessed much influence; and never failed to use it, whenever she could, for the benefit of Hop-Frog.

On some grand state occasion — I forgot what — the king determined to have a masquerade, and whenever a masquerade or any thing of that

kind, occurred at our court, then the talents, both of Hop-Frog and
Trippetta were sure to be called into play. Hop-Frog, in especial, was so
inventive in the way of getting up pageants, suggesting novel characters,
and arranging costumes, for masked balls, that nothing could be done,
it seems, without his assistance.

The night appointed for the fête had arrived. A gorgeous hall had been
fitted up, under Trippetta's eye, with every kind of device which could
possibly give *éclât* to a masquerade. The whole court was in a fever of
expectation. As for costumes and characters, it might well be supposed
that everybody had come to a decision on such points. Many had made
up their minds (as to what *rôles* they should assume) a week, or even
a month, in advance; and, in fact, there was not a particle of indecision
anywhere — except in the case of the king and his seven minsters. Why
they hesitated I never could tell, unless they did it by way of a joke.
More probably, they found it difficult, on account of being so fat, to make
up their minds. At all events, time flew; and, as a last resort, they sent for
Trippetta and Hop-Frog.

When the two little friends obeyed the summons of the king, they
found him sitting at his wine with the seven members of his cabinet
council; but the monarch appeared to be in a very ill humor. He knew
that Hop-Frog was not fond of wine; for it excited the poor cripple
almost to madness; and madness is no comfortable feeling. But the king
loved his practical jokes, and took pleasure in forcing Hop-Frog to drink
and (as the king called it) 'to be merry.'

'Come here, Hop-Frog,' said he, as the jester and his friend entered
the room; 'swallow this bumper to the health of your absent friends,
[here Hop-Frog sighed,] and then let us have the benefit of your inven-
tion. We want characters — *characters*, man — something novel — out
of the way. We are wearied with this everlasting sameness. Come, drink!
the wine will brighten your wits.'

Hop-Frog endeavored, as usual, to get up a jest in reply to these ad-
vances from the king; but the effort was too much. It happened to be the
poor dwarf's birthday, and the command to drink to his 'absent friends'
forced the tears to his eyes. Many large, bitter drops fell into the goblet
as he took it, humbly, from the hand of the tyrant.

'Ah! ha! ha! ha!' roared the latter, as the dwarf reluctantly drained
the beaker. — 'See what a glass of good wine can do! Why, your eyes
are shining already!'

Poor fellow! his large eyes *gleamed*, rather than shone; for the effect
of wine on his excitable brain was not more powerful than instantaneous.
He placed the goblet nervously on the table, and looked round upon the
company with a half-insane stare. They all seemed highly amused at the
success of the king's 'jóke.'

'And now to business,' said the prime minister, a *very* fat man.

'Yes,' said the king; 'Come, Hop-Frog, lend us your assistance. Char-

acters, my fine fellow; we stand in need of characters — all of us — ha! ha! ha!' and as this was seriously meant for a joke, his laugh was chorused by the seven.

Hop-Frog also laughed although feebly and somewhat vacantly.

'Come, come,' said the king, impatiently, 'have you nothing to suggest?'

'I am endeavoring to think of something *novel*,' replied the dwarf, abstractedly, for he was quite bewildered by the wine.

'Endeavoring!' cried the tyrant, fiercely; 'what do you mean by *that?* Ah, I perceive. You are sulky, and want more wine. Here, drink this!' and he poured out another goblet full and offered it to the cripple, who merely gazed at it, gasping for breath.

'Drink, I say!' shouted the monster, 'or by the fiends —— '

The dwarf hesitated. The king grew purple with rage. The courtiers smirked. Trippetta, pale as a corpse, advanced to the monarch's seat, and, falling on her knees before him, implored him to spare her friend.

The tyrant regarded her, for some moments, in evident wonder at her audacity. He seemed quite at a loss what to do or say — how most becomingly to express his indignation. At last, without uttering a syllable, he pushed her violently from him, and threw the contents of the brimming goblet in her face.

The poor girl got up the best she could, and, not daring even to sigh, resumed her position at the foot of the table.

There was a dead silence for about half a minute, during which the falling of a leaf, or of a feather, might have been heard. It was interrupted by a low, but harsh and protracted *grating* sound which seemed to come at once from every corner of the room.

'What — what — *what* are you making that noise for?' demanded the king, turning furiously to the dwarf.

The latter seemed to have recovered, in great measure, from his intoxication, and looking fixedly but quietly into the tyrant's face, merely ejaculated:

'I — I? How could it have been me?'

'The sound appeared to come from without,' observed one of the courtiers. 'I fancy it was the parrot at the window, whetting his bill upon his cage-wires.'

'True,' replied the monarch, as if much relieved by the suggestion; 'but, on the honor of a knight, I could have sworn that it was the gritting of this vagabond's teeth.'

Hereupon the dwarf laughed (the king was too confirmed a joker to object to any one's laughing), and displayed a set of large, powerful, and very repulsive teeth. Moreover, he avowed his perfect willingness to swallow as much wine as desired. The monarch was pacified; and having drained another bumper with no very perceptible ill effect, Hop-Frog entered at once, and with spirit, into the plans for the masquerade.

'I cannot tell what was the association of idea,' observed he, very tranquilly, and as if he had never tasted wine in his life, 'but *just after* your majesty had struck the girl and thrown the wine in her face — *just after* your majesty had done this, and while the parrot was making that odd noise outside the window, there came into my mind a capital diversion — one of my own country frolics — often enacted among us, at our masquerades: but here it will be new altogether. Unfortunately, however, it requires a company of eight persons and —— "

'Here we *are!*' cried the king, laughing at his acute discovery of the coincidence; 'eight to a fraction — I and my seven ministers. Come! what is the diversion?'

'We call it,' replied the cripple, 'the Eight Chained Ourang-Outangs, and it really is excellent sport if well enacted.'

'*We* will enact it,' remarked the king, drawing himself up, and lowering his eyelids.

'The beauty of the game,' continued Hop-Frog, 'lies in the fright it occasions among the women.'

'Capital!' roared in chorus the monarch and his ministry.

'*I* will equip you as ourang-outangs,' proceeded the dwarf; 'leave all that to me. The resemblance shall be so striking, that the company of masqueraders will take you for real beasts — and of course, they will be as much terrified as astonished.'

'Oh, this is exquisite!' exclaimed the king. 'Hop-Frog! I will make a man of you.'

'The chains are for the purpose of increasing the confusion by their jangling. You are supposed to have escaped, *en masse*, from your keepers. Your majesty cannot conceive the *effect* produced, at a masquerade, by eight chained ourang-outangs, imagined to be real ones by most of the company; and rushing in with savage cries, among the crowd of delicately and gorgeously habited men and women. The *contrast* is inimitable.'

'It *must* be,' said the king: and the council arose hurriedly (as it was growing late), to put in execution the scheme of Hop-Frog.

His mode of equipping the party as ourang-outangs was very simple, but effective enough for his purposes. The animals in question had, at the epoch of my story, very rarely been seen in any part of the civilized world; and as the imitations made by the dwarf were sufficiently beast-like and more than sufficiently hideous, their truthfulness to nature was thus thought to be secured.

The king and his ministers were first encased in tight-fitting stockinet shirts and drawers. They were then saturated with tar. At this stage of the process, some one of the party suggested feathers; but the suggestion was at once overruled by the dwarf, who soon convinced the eight, by ocular demonstration, that the hair of such a brute as the ourang-outang was much more efficiently represented by *flax*. A thick coating

of the latter was accordingly plastered upon the coating of tar. A long chain was now procured. First, it was passed about the waist of the king, *and tied*; then about another of the party, and also tied; then about all successively, in the same manner. When this chaining arrangement was complete, and the party stood as far apart from each other as possible, they formed a circle; and to make all things appear natural, Hop-Frog passed the residue of the chain in two diameters, at right angles, across the circle, after the fashion adopted, at the present day, by those who capture Chimpanzees, or other large apes, in Borneo.

The grand saloon in which the masquerade was to take place, was a circular room, very lofty, and receiving the light of the sun only through a single window at top. At night (the season for which the apartment was especially designed) it was illuminated principally by a large chandelier, depending by a chain from the centre of the sky-light, and lowered, or elevated, by means of a counter-balance as usual; but (in order not to look unsightly) this latter passed outside the cupola and over the roof.

The arrangements of the room had been left to Trippetta's superintendence; but, in some particulars, it seems, she had been guided by the calmer judgment of her friend the dwarf. At his suggestion it was that, on this occasion, the chandelier was removed. Its waxen drippings (which, in weather so warm, it was quite impossible to prevent) would have been seriously detrimental to the rich dresses of the guests, who, on account of the crowded state of the saloon, could not *all* be expected to keep from out its centre; that is to say, from under the chandelier. Additional sconces were set in various parts of the hall, out of the way; and a flambeau, emitting sweet odor, was placed in the right hand of each of the Caryatides that stood against the wall — some fifty or sixty altogether.

The eight ourang-outangs, taking Hop-Frog's advice, waited patiently until midnight (when the room was thoroughly filled with masqueraders) before making their appearance. No sooner had the clock ceased striking, however, than they rushed, or rather rolled in, all together — for the impediments of their chains caused most of the party to fall, and all to stumble as they entered.

The excitement among the masqueraders was prodigious, and filled the heart of the king with glee. As had been anticipated, there were not a few of the guests who supposed the ferocious-looking creatures to be beasts of *some* kind in reality, if not precisely ourang-outangs. Many of the women swooned with affright; and had not the king taken the precaution to exclude all weapons from the saloon, his party might soon have expiated their frolic in their blood. As it was, a general rush was made for the doors; but the king had ordered them to be locked immediately upon his entrance; and, at the dwarf's suggestion, the keys had been deposited with *him*.

While the tumult was at its height, and each masquerader attentive only to his own safety (for, in fact, there was much *real* danger from the pressure of the excited crowd), the chain by which the chandelier ordinarily hung, and which had been drawn up on its removal, might have been seen very gradually to descend, until its hooked extremity came within three feet of the floor.

Soon after this, the king and his seven friends having reeled about the hall in all directions, found themselves, at length, in its centre, and, of course, in immediate contact with the chain. While they were thus situated, the dwarf, who had followed noiselessly at their heels, inciting them to keep up the commotion, took hold of their own chain at the intersection of the two portions which crossed the circle diametrically and at right angles. Here, with the rapidity of thought, he inserted the hook from which the chandelier had been wont to depend; and, in an instant, by some unseen agency, the chandelier-chain was drawn so far upward as to take the hook out of reach, and, as an inevitable consequence, to drag the ourang-outangs together in close connection, and face to face.

The masqueraders, by this time, had recovered, in some measure, from their alarm; and, beginning to regard the whole matter as a well-contrived pleasantry, set up a loud shout of laughter at the predicament of the apes.

'Leave them to *me!*' now screamed Hop-Frog, his shrill voice making itself easily heard through all the din. 'Leave them to *me*. I fancy *I* know them. If I can only get a good look at them, *I* can soon tell who they are.'

Here, scrambling over the heads of the crowd, he managed to get to the wall; when, seizing a flambeau from one of the Caryatides, he returned, as he went, to the centre of the room — leaping, with the agility of a monkey, upon the king's head, and thence clambered a few feet up the chain; holding down the torch to examine the group of ourang-outangs, and still screaming: 'I shall soon find out who they are!'

And now, while the whole assembly (the apes included) were convulsed with laughter, the jester suddenly uttered a shrill whistle; when the chain flew violently up for about thirty feet — dragging with it the dismayed and struggling ourang-outangs, and leaving them suspended in mid-air between the sky-light and the floor. Hop-Frog, clinging to the chain as it rose, still maintained his relative position in respect to the eight maskers, and still (as if nothing were the matter) continued to thrust his torch down toward them, as though endeavoring to discover who they were.

So thoroughly astonished was the whole company at this ascent, that a dead silence, of about a minute's duration, ensued. It was broken by just such a low, harsh, *grating* sound, as had before attracted the attention of the king and his councillors when the former threw the wine in

the face of Trippetta. But, on the present occasion, there could be no question as to *whence* the sound issued. It came from the fang-like teeth of the dwarf, who ground them and gnashed them as he foamed at the mouth, and glared, with an expression of maniacal rage, into the up-turned countenances of the king and his seven companions.

'Ah, ha!' said at length the infuriated jester. 'Ah, ha! I begin to see who these people *are* now!' Here, pretending to scrutinize the king more closely, he held the flambeau to the flaxen coat which enveloped him, and which instantly burst into a sheet of vivid flame. In less than half a minute the whole eight ourang-outangs were blazing fiercely, amid the shrieks of the multitude who gazed at them from below, horror-stricken, and without the power to render them the slightest assistance.

At length the flames, suddenly increasing in virulence, forced the jester to climb higher up the chain, to be out of their reach; and, as he made this movement, the crowd again sank, for a brief instant, into silence. The dwarf seized his opportunity, and once more spoke:

'I now see *distinctly*,' he said, 'what manner of people these maskers are. They are a great king and his seven privy-councillors, — a king who does not scruple to strike a defenceless girl, and his seven councillors who abet him in the outrage. As for myself, I am simply Hop-Frog, the jester — and *this is my last jest*.'

Owing to the high combustibility of both the flax and the tar to which it adhered, the dwarf had scarcely made an end of his brief speech before the work of vengeance was complete. The eight corpses swung in their chains, a fetid, blackened, hideous, and indistinguishable mass. The crip-ple hurled his torch at them, clambered leisurely to the ceiling, and dis-appeared through the sky-light.

It is supposed that Trippetta, stationed on the roof of the saloon, had been the accomplice of her friend in his fiery revenge, and that, together, they effected their escape to their own country: for neither was seen again.

Von Kempelen and His Discovery

AFTER the very minute and elaborate paper by Arago, to say nothing of the summary in 'Silliman's Journal,' with the detailed statement just published by Lieutenant Maury, it will not be supposed, of course, that in offering a few hurried remarks in reference to Von Kempelen's dis-covery, I have any design to look at the subject in a *scientific* point of view. My object is simply, in the first place, to say a few words of Von Kempelen himself (with whom, some years ago, I had the honor of a

slight personal acquaintance), since every thing which concerns him must necessarily, at this moment, be of interest; and, in the second place, to look in a general way, and speculatively, at the *results* of the discovery.

It may be as well, however, to premise the cursory observations which I have to offer, by denying, very decidedly, what seems to be a general impression (gleaned, as usual in a case of this kind, from the newspapers), viz.: that this discovery, astounding as it unquestionably is, is *unanticipated*.

By reference to the 'Diary of Sir Humphrey Davy' (Cottle and Munroe, London, pp. 150), it will be seen at pp. 53 and 82, that this illustrious chemist had not only conceived the idea now in question, but had actually made *no inconsiderable progress, experimentally*, in the very *identical analysis* now so triumphantly brought to an issue by Von Kempelen, who although he makes not the slightest allusion to it, is, *without doubt* (I say it unhesitatingly, and can prove it, if required), indebted to the 'Diary' for at least the first hint of his own undertaking. Although a little technical, I cannot refrain from appending two passages from the 'Diary,' with one of Sir Humphrey's equations. [As we have not the algebraic signs necessary and as the 'Diary' is to be found at the Athenaeum Library, we omit here a small portion of Mr. Poe's manuscript. — ED.]

The paragraph from the 'Courier and Enquirer,' which is now going the rounds of the press, and which purports to claim the invention for a Mr. Kissam, of Brunswick, Maine, appears to me, I confess, a little apocryphal, for several reasons; although there is nothing either impossible or very improbable in the statement made. I need not go into details. My opinion of the paragraph is founded principally upon its *manner*. It does not *look* true. Persons who are narrating *facts*, are seldom so particular as Mr. Kissam seems to be, about day and date and precise location. Besides, if Mr. Kissam actually *did* come upon the discovery he says he did, at the period designated — nearly eight years ago — how happens it that he took no steps, *on the instant*, to reap the immense benefits which the merest bumpkin must have known would have resulted to him individually, if not to the world at large, from the discovery? It seems to me quite incredible that any man of common understanding could have discovered what Mr. Kissam says he did, and yet have subsequently acted so like a baby — so like an owl — as Mr. Kissam *admits* that he did. By-the-way, who *is* Mr. Kissam? and is not the whole paragraph in the 'Courier and Enquirer' a fabrication got up to 'make a talk'? It must be confessed that it has an amazingly moon-hoaxy-air. Very little dependence is to be placed upon it, in my humble opinion; and if I were not well aware, from experience, how very easily men of science are *mystified*, on points out of their usual range of inquiry, I should be profoundly astonished at finding so eminent a chemist as

Professor Draper, discussing Mr. Kissam's (or is it Mr. Quizzem's?) pretensions to the discovery, in so serious a tone.

But to return to the 'Diary' of Sir Humphrey Davy. This pamphlet was *not* designed for the public eye, even upon the decease of the writer, as any person at all conversant with authorship may satisfy himself at once by the slightest inspection of the style. At page 13, for example, near the middle, we read, in reference to his researches about the protoxide of azote: 'In less than half a minute the respiration being continued, diminished gradually and *were* succeeded by analogous to gentle pressure on all the muscles.' That the *respiration* was not 'diminished,' is not only clear by the subsequent context, but by the use of the plural, 'were.' The sentence, no doubt, was thus intended: 'In less than half a minute, the respiration [being continued, these feelings] diminished gradually, and were succeeded by [a sensation] analogous to gentle pressure on all the muscles.' A hundred similar instances go to show that the MS. so inconsiderately published, was merely a *rough note-book*, meant only for the writer's own eye; but an inspection of the pamphlet will convince almost any thinking person of the truth of my suggestion. The fact is, Sir Humphrey Davy was about the last man in the world to *commit himself* on scientific topics. Not only had he a more than ordinary dislike to quackery, but he was morbidly afraid of *appearing* empirical; so that, however fully he might have been convinced that he was on the right track in the matter now in question, he would never have spoken *out*, until he had every thing ready for the most practical demonstration. I verily believe that his last moments would have been rendered wretched, could he have suspected that his wishes in regard to burning this 'Diary' (full of crude speculations) would have been unattended to; as, it seems, they were. I say 'his wishes,' for that he meant to include this note-book among the miscellaneous papers directed 'to be burnt,' I think there can be no manner of doubt. Whether it escaped the flames by good fortune or by bad, yet remains to be seen. That the passages quoted above, with the other similar ones referred to, gave Von Kempelen *the hint*, I do not in the slightest degree question; but I repeat, it yet remains to be seen whether this momentous discovery itself (*momentous* under any circumstances) will be of service or disservice to mankind at large. That Von Kempelen and his immediate friends will reap a rich harvest, it would be folly to doubt for a moment. They will scarcely be so weak as not to '*realize*,' in time, by large purchases of houses and land, with other property of *intrinsic* value.

In the brief account of Von Kempelen which appeared in the 'Home Journal,' and has since been extensively copied, several misapprehensions of the German original seem to have been made by the translator, who professes to have taken the passage from a late number of the Presburg 'Schnellpost.' 'Viele' has evidently been misconceived (as it

often is), and what the translator renders by 'sorrows,' is probably *'lieden,'* which, in its true version, 'sufferings,' would give a totally different complexion to the whole account; but, of course, much of this is merely guess, on my part.

Von Kempelen, however, is by no means 'a misanthrope,' in appearance, at least, whatever he may be in fact. My acquaintance with him was casual altogether; and I am scarcely warranted in saying that I know him at all; but to have seen and conversed with a man of so *prodigious* a notoriety as he has attained, or *will* attain in a few days, is not a small matter, as times go.

'The Literary World' speaks of him, confidently, as a *native* of Presburg (misled, perhaps, by the account in 'The Home Journal') but I am pleased in being able to state *positively*, since I have it from his own lips, that he was born in Utica, in the State of New York, although both his parents, I believe, are of Presburg descent. The family is connected, in some way, with Maelzel, of Automaton-chess-player memory. [If we are not mistaken, the name of the *inventor* of the chess-player was either Kempelen, Von Kempelen, or something like it. ED.] In person, he is short and stout, with large, *fat*, blue eyes, sandy hair and whiskers, a wide but pleasing mouth, fine teeth, and I think a Roman nose. There is some defect in one of his feet. His address is frank, and his whole manner noticeable for *bonhomie*. Altogether, he looks, speaks, and acts as little like 'a misanthrope' as any man I ever saw. We were fellow-sojourners for a week about six years ago, at Earl's Hotel, in Providence, Rhode Island; and I presume that I conversed with him, at various times, for some three or four hours altogether. His principal topics were those of the day; and nothing that fell from him led me to suspect his scientific attainments. He left the hotel before me, intending to go to New York, and thence to Bremen; it was in the latter city that his great discovery was first made public; or, rather, it was there that he was first suspected of having made it. This is about all that I personally know of the now immortal Von Kempelen; but I have thought that even these few details would have interest for the public.

There can be little question that most of the marvellous rumors afloat about this affair are pure inventions, entitled to about as much credit as the story of Aladdin's lamp; and yet, in a case of this kind, as in the case of the discoveries in California, it is clear that the truth *may be* stranger than fiction. The following anecdote, at least, is so well authenticated, that we may receive it implicitly.

Von Kempelen had never been even tolerably well off during his residence at Bremen; and often, it was well known, he had been put to extreme shifts in order to raise trifling sums. When the great excitement occurred about the forgery on the house of Gutsmuth & Co., suspicion was directed toward Von Kempelen, on account of his having purchased a considerable property in Gasperitch Lane, and his refusing, when ques-

tioned, to explain how he became possessed of the purchase money. He was at length arrested, but nothing decisive appearing against him, was in the end set at liberty. The police, however, kept a strict watch upon his movements, and thus discovered that he left home frequently, taking always the same road, and invariably giving his watchers the slip in the neighborhood of that labyrinth of narrow and crooked passages known by the flash name of the 'Dondergat.' Finally, by dint of great perseverance, they traced him to a garret in an old house of seven stories, in an alley called Flatzplatz; and, coming upon him suddenly, found him, as they imagined, in the midst of his counterfeiting operations. His agitation is represented as so excessive that the officers had not the slightest doubt of his guilt. After hand-cuffing him, they searched his room, or rather rooms, for it appears he occupied all the *mansarde.*

Opening into the garret where they caught him, was a closet, ten feet by eight, fitted up with some chemical apparatus, of which the object has not yet been ascertained. In one corner of the closet was a very small furnace, with a glowing fire in it, and on the fire a kind of duplicate crucible — two crucibles connected by a tube. One of these crucibles was nearly full of *lead* in a state of fusion, but not reaching up to the aperture of the tube, which was close to the brim. The other crucible had some liquid in it, which, as the officers entered, seemed to be furiously dissipating in vapor. They relate that, on finding himself taken, Kempelen seized the crucibles with both hands (which were encased in gloves that afterwards turned out to be asbestic), and threw the contents on the tiled floor. It was now that they hand-cuffed him; and before proceeding to ransack the premises they searched his person, but nothing unusual was found about him, excepting a paper parcel, in his coat-pocket, containing what was afterward ascertained to be a mixture of antimony and some *unknown substance,* in nearly, but not quite, equal proportions. All attempts at analyzing the unknown substance have, so far, failed, but that it will ultimately be analyzed, is not to be doubted.

Passing out of the closet with their prisoner, the officers went through a sort of ante-chamber, in which nothing material was found, to the chemist's sleeping-room. They here rummaged some drawers and boxes, but discovered only a few papers, of no importance, and some good coin, silver and gold. At length, looking under the bed, they saw *a large, common hair trunk, without hinges, hasp, or lock,* and with the top lying carelessly *across* the bottom portion. Upon attempting to draw this trunk out from under the bed, they found that, with their united strength (there were three of them, all powerful men), they 'could not stir it one inch.' Much astonished at this, one of them crawled under the bed, and looking into the trunk, said:

'No wonder we couldn't move it — why it's full to the brim of old bits of brass!'

Putting his feet, now, against the wall, so as to get a good purchase,

and pushing with all his force, while his companions pulled with all theirs, the trunk, with much difficulty, was slid out from under the bed, and its contents examined. The supposed brass with which it was filled was all in small, smooth pieces, varying from the size of a pea to that of a dollar; but the pieces were irregular in shape, although more or less flat — looking, upon the whole, 'very much as lead looks when thrown upon the ground in a molten state, and there suffered to grow cool.' Now, not one of these officers for a moment suspected this metal to be any thing *but* brass. The idea of its being *gold* never entered their brains, of course; how *could* such a wild fancy have entered it? And their astonishment may be well conceived, when the next day it became known, all over Bremen, that the 'lot of brass' which they had carted so contemptuously to the police office, without putting themselves to the trouble of pocketing the smallest scrap, was not only gold — real gold — but gold far finer than any employed in coinage — gold, in fact, absolutely pure, virgin, without the slightest appreciable alloy.

I need not go over the details of Von Kempelen's confession (as far as it went) and release, for these are familiar to the public. That he has actually realized, in spirit and in effect, if not to the letter, the old chimaera of the philosopher's stone, no sane person is at liberty to doubt. The opinions of Arago are, of course, entitled to the greatest consideration; but he is by no means infallible; and what he says of *bismuth*, in his report to the Academy, must be taken *cum grano salis*. The simple truth is, that up to this period *all* analysis has failed; and until Von Kempelen chooses to let us have the key to his own published enigma, it is more than probable that the matter will remain, for years, *in statu quo*. All that as yet can fairly be said to be known is, that *'Pure gold can be made at will, and very readily from lead in connection with certain other substances, in kind and in proportions, unknown.'*

Speculation, of course, is busy as to the immediate and ultimate results of this discovery — a discovery which few thinking persons will hesitate in referring to an increased interest in the matter of gold generally, by the late developments in California; and this reflection brings us inevitably to another — the exceeding *inopportuneness* of Von Kempelen's analysis. If many were prevented from adventuring to California, by the mere apprehension that gold would so materially diminish in value, on account of its plentifulness in the mines there, as to render the speculation of going so far in search of it a doubtful one — what impression will be wrought *now*, upon the minds of those about to emigrate, and especially upon the minds of those actually in the mineral region, by the announcement of this astounding discovery of Von Kempelen? a discovery which declares, in so many words, that beyond its intrinsic worth for manufacturing purposes (whatever that worth may be), gold now is, or at least soon will be (for it cannot be supposed that Von Kempelen can *long* retain his secret), of no greater *value* than lead, and

of far inferior value to silver. It is, indeed, exceedingly difficult to specu-late prospectively upon the consequences of the discovery; but one thing may be positively maintained — that the announcement of the discov-ery six months ago would have had material influence in regard to the settlement of California.

In Europe, as yet, the most noticeable results have been a rise of two hundred per cent. in the price of lead, and nearly twenty-five per cent. in that of silver.

X-ing a Paragrab

As it is well known that the 'wise men' came 'from the East,' and as Mr. Touch-and-go Bullet-head came from the East, it follows that Mr. Bullet-head was a wise man; and if collateral proof of the matter be needed, here we have it — Mr. B. was an editor. Irascibility was his sole foible; for in fact the obstinacy of which men accused him was anything but his *foible*, since he justly considered it his forte. It was his strong point — his virtue; and it would have required all the logic of a Brown-son to convince him that it was 'anything else.'

I have shown that Touch-and-go Bullet-head was a wise man; and the only occasion on which he did not prove infallible, was when, abandon-ing that legitimate home for all wise men, the East, he migrated to the city of Alexander-the-Great-o-nopolis, or some place of a similar title, out West.

I must do him the justice to say, however, that when he made up his mind finally to settle in that town, it was under the impression that no newspaper, and consequently no editor, existed in that particular section of the country. In establishing 'The Tea-Pot' he expected to have the field all to himself. I feel confident he never would have dreamed of taking up his residence in Alexander-the-Great-o-nopolis had he been aware that, in Alexander-the-Great-o-nopolis, there lived a gentleman named John Smith (if I rightly remember), who for many years had there quietly grown fat in editing and publishing the 'Alexander-the-Great-o-nopolis Gazette.' It was solely, therefore, on account of having been misinformed, that Mr. Bullet-head found himself in Alex—— sup-pose we call it Nopolis, 'for short' — but, as he *did* find himself there, he determined to keep up his character for obst — for firmness, and re-main. So remain he did; and he did more; he unpacked his press, type, etc., etc., rented an office exactly opposite to that of the 'Gazette,' and, on the third morning after his arrival, issued the first number of 'The Alexan' — that is to say, of 'The Nopolis Tea-Pot' — as nearly as I can recollect, this was the name of the new paper.

The leading article, I must admit, was brilliant — not to say severe. It was especially bitter about things in general — and as for the editor of 'The Gazette,' he was torn all to pieces in particular. Some of Bullet-head's remarks were really so fiery that I have always, since that time, been forced to look upon John Smith, who is still alive, in the light of a salamander. I cannot pretend to give *all* the 'Tea-Pot's' paragraphs *verbatim*, but one of them runs thus:

'Oh, yes! — Oh, we perceive! Oh, no doubt! The editor over the way is a genius — O, my! Oh, goodness, gracious! — what *is* this world coming to? *Oh, tempora! Oh, Moses!*'

A philippic at once so caustic and so classical, alighted like a bomb-shell among the hitherto peaceful citizens of Nopolis. Groups of excited individuals gathered at the corners of the streets. Every one awaited, with heartfelt anxiety, the reply of the dignified Smith. Next morning it appeared as follows:

'We quote from "The Tea-Pot" of yesterday the subjoined paragraph: "*Oh*, yes! *Oh*, we perceive! *Oh*, no doubt! *Oh*, my! *Oh*, goodness! *Oh*, tempora! *Oh*, Moses!" Why, the fellow is all O! That accounts for his reasoning in a circle, and explains why there is neither beginning nor end to him, nor to anything he says. We really do not believe the vagabond can write a word that hasn't an O in it. Wonder if this O-ing is a habit of his? By-the-by, he came away from Down-East in a great hurry. Wonder if he O's as much there as he does here? "O! it is pitiful." '

The indignation of Mr. Bullet-head at these scandalous insinuations, I shall not attempt to describe. On the eel-skinning principle, however, he did not seem to be so much incensed at the attack upon his integrity as one might have imagined. It was the sneer at his *style* that drove him to desperation. What! — *he* Touch-and-go Bullet-head! — not able to write a word without an O in it! He would soon let the jackanapes see that he was mistaken. Yes! he would let him see how *much* he was mistaken, the puppy! He, Touch-and-go Bullet-head, of Frogpondium, would let Mr. John Smith perceive that he, Bullet-head, could indite, if it so pleased him, a whole paragraph — aye! a whole article — in which that contemptible vowel should not *once* — not even *once* — make its appearance. But no; — that would be yielding a point to the said John Smith. *He*, Bullet-head, would make *no* alteration in his style, to suit the caprices of any Mr. Smith in Christendom. Perish so vile a thought! The O forever; He would persist in the O. He would be as O-wy as O-wy could be.

Burning with the chivalry of this determination, the great Touch-and-go, in the next 'Tea-Pot,' came out merely with this simple but resolute paragraph, in reference to this unhappy affair:

'The editor of the "Tea-Pot" has the *honor* of advising the editor of the "Gazette" that he (the "Tea-Pot") will take an opportunity in to-morrow morning's paper, of convincing him (the "Gazette") that he

(the "Tea-Pot") both can and will be *his own master*, as regards style; —
he (the "Tea-Pot") intending to show him (the "Gazette") the su-
preme, and indeed the withering contempt with which the criticism of
him (the "Gazette") inspires the independent bosom of him (the "Tea-
Pot") by composing for the especial gratification (?) of him (the
"Gazette") a leading article, of some extent, in which the beautiful
vowel — the emblem of Eternity — yet so offensive to the hyper-exqui-
site delicacy of him (the "Gazette") shall most certainly *not be avoided*
by his (the "Gazette's") most obedient, humble servant, the "Tea-Pot."
"So much for Buckingham!" '

In fulfilment of the awful threat thus darkly intimated rather than
decidedly enunciated, the great Bullet-head, turning a deaf ear to all
entreaties for 'copy,' and simply requesting his foreman to 'go to the
d——l,' when he (the foreman) assured him (the 'Tea-Pot'!) that it
was high time to 'go to press': turning a deaf ear to everything, I say,
the great Bullet-head sat up until day-break, consuming the midnight
oil, and absorbed in the composition of the really unparalleled paragraph,
which follows: —

'So ho, John! how now? Told you so, you know. Don't crow, another
time, before you're out of the woods! Does your mother *know* you're
out? Oh, no, no! — so go home at once, now, John, to your odious old
woods of Concord! Go home to your woods, old owl, — go! You won't!
Oh, poh, poh, John, don't do so! You've *got* to go, you know! So go at
once, and don't go slow; for nobody owns you here, you know! Oh!
John, John, if you *don't* go you're no *homo* — no! You're only a fowl,
an owl; a cow, a sow; a doll, a poll; a poor, old, good-for-nothing-to-
nobody, log, dog, hog, or frog, come out of a Concord bog. Cool, now —
cool! *Do* be cool, you fool! None of your crowing, old cock! Don't frown
so — don't! Don't hollo, nor howl, nor growl, nor bow-wow-wow! Good
Lord, John, how you *do* look! Told you so, you know — but stop rolling
your goose of an old poll about so, and go and drown your sorrows
in a bowl!'

Exhausted, very naturally, by so stupendous an effort, the great Touch-
and-go could attend to nothing farther that night. Firmly, composedly,
yet with an air of conscious power, he handed his MS. to the devil in
waiting, and then, walking leisurely home, retired, with ineffable dignity
to bed.

Meantime the devil, to whom the copy was entrusted, ran up stairs
to his 'case,' in an unutterable hurry, and forthwith made a commence-
ment at 'setting' the MS. 'up.'

In the first place, of course, — as the opening word was 'So,' — he
made a plunge into the capital S hole and came out in triumph with a
capital S. Elated by this success, he immediately threw himself upon the
little-*o* box with a blindfold impetuosity — but who shall describe his
horror when his fingers came up without the anticipated letter in their

clutch? who shall paint his astonishment and rage at perceiving, as he rubbed his knuckles, that he had been only thumping them to no purpose, against the bottom of an *empty* box. Not a single little-*o* was in the little-*o* hole; and, glancing fearfully at the capital-O partition, he found *that* to his extreme terror, in a precisely similar predicament. Awe-stricken, his first impulse was to rush to the foreman.

'Sir!' said he, gasping for breath, 'I can't never set up nothing without no o's.'

'*What* do you mean by that?' growled the foreman, who was in a very ill humor at being kept so late.

'Why, sir, there beant an *o* in the office, neither a big un nor a little un!'

'What — what the d—l has become of all that were in the case?'

'*I* don't know, sir,' said the boy, 'but one of them ere "G'zette" devils is bin prowling 'bout here all night, and I spect *he's* gone and cabbaged 'em every one.'

'Dod rot him! I haven't a doubt of it,' replied the foreman, getting purple with rage — 'but I tell you what you do, Bob, that's a good boy — you go over the first chance you get and hook every one of their i's and (d—n them!) their izzards.'

'Jist so,' replied Bob, with a wink and a frown — '*I'll* be into 'em, *I'll* let 'em know a thing or two; but in de meantime, that ere para-grab? *Mus* go in to-night, you know — else there'll be the d—l to pay, and —'

'And not a *bit* of pitch hot,' interrupted the foreman, with a deep sigh, and an emphasis on the 'bit.' 'Is it a long paragraph, Bob?'

'Shouldn't call it a *wery* long paragrab,' said Bob.

'Ah, well, then! do the best you can with it! We *must* get to press,' said the foreman, who was over head and ears in work; 'just stick in some other letter for *o*; nobody's going to read the fellow's trash anyhow.'

'*Wery* well,' replied Bob, 'here goes it!' and off he hurried to his case; muttering as he went: 'Considdeble vell, them ere expressions, perticcler for a man as doesn't swar. So I's to gouge out all their eyes, eh? and d—n all their gizzards! Vell! this here's the chap as is just able *for* to do it.' The fact is that although Bob was but twelve years old and four feet high, he was equal to any amount of fight, in a small way.

The exigency here described is by no means of rare occurrence in printing-offices; and I cannot tell how to account for it, but the fact is indisputable, that when the exigency *does* occur, it almost always happens that *x* is adopted as a substitute for the letter deficient. The true reason, perhaps, is that *x* is rather the most superabundant letter in the cases, or at least *was* so in the old times — long enough to render the substitution in question an habitual thing with printers. As for Bob, he would have considered it heretical to employ any other character, in a case of this kind, than the *x* to which he had been accustomed.

'I *shell* have to x this ere paragrab,' said he to himself, as he read it over in astonishment, 'but it's jest about the awfulest o-wy paragrab I ever *did* see': so x it he did, unflinchingly, and to press it went *x-ed*.

Next morning the population of Nopolis were taken all aback by reading in 'The Tea-Pot,' the following extraordinary leader:

'Sx hx, Jxhn! hxw nxw? Txld yxu sx, yxu knxw. Dxn't crxw, anxther time, befxre yxu're xut xf the wxxds! Dxes yxur mxther *knxw* yxu're xut? Xh, nx, nx! — sx gx hxme at xnce, nxw, Jxhn, tx yxur xdixus xld wxxds xf Cxncxrd! Gx hxme tx yxur wxxds, xld xwl, — gx! Yxu wxn't? Xh, pxh, pxh, Jxhn, dxn't dx sx! Yxu've *gxt* tx gx, yxu knxw; sx gx at xnce, and dxn't gx slxw; fxr nxbxdy xwns yxu here, yxu knxw. Xh, Jxhn, Jxhn, if yxu *dxn't* gx yxu're nx *hxmx* — nx! Yxu're xnly a fxwl, an xwl; a cxw, a sxw; a dxll, a pxll; a pxxr xld gxxd-fxr-nxthing-tx-nxbxdy, lxg, dxg, hxg, xr frxg, cxme xut xf a Cxncxrd bxg. Cxxl, nxw — cxxl! Dx be cxxl, yxu fxxl! Nxne xf yxur crxwing, xld cxck! Dxn't frxwn sx — dxn't! Dxn't hxllx, nxr hxwl, nxr grxwl, nxr bxw-wxw-wxw! Gxxd Lxrd, Jxhn, hxw yxu dx lxxk! Txld yxu sx, yxu knxw, — but stxp rxlling yxur gxxse xf an xld pxll abxut sx, and gx and drxwn yxur sxrrxws in a bxwl!'

The uproar occasioned by this mystical and cabalistical article, is not to be conceived. The first definite idea entertained by the populace was, that some diabolical treason lay concealed in the hieroglyphics; and there was a general rush to Bullet-head's residence, for the purpose of riding him on a rail; but that gentleman was nowhere to be found. He had vanished, no one could tell how; and not even the ghost of him has ever been seen since.

Unable to discover its legitimate object, the popular fury at length subsided; leaving behind it, by way of sediment, quite a medley of opinion about this unhappy affair.

One gentleman thought the whole an X-ellent joke.

Another said that, indeed, Bullet-head had shown much X-uberance of fancy.

A third admitted him X-entric, but no more.

A fourth could only suppose it the Yankee's design to X-press, in a general way, his X-asperation.

'Say, rather, to set an X-ample to posterity,' suggested a fifth.

That Bullet-head had been driven to an extremity, was clear to all; and in fact, since *that* editor could not be found, there was some talk about lynching the other one.

The more common conclusion, however, was that the affair was, simply, X-traordinary and in-X-plicable. Even the town mathematician confessed that he could make nothing of so dark a problem. X, everybody knew, was an unknown quantity; but in this case (as he properly observed), there was an unknown quantity of X.

The opinion of Bob, the devil (who kept dark about his having 'X-ed the paragrab'), did not meet with so much attention as I think

it deserved, although it was very openly and very fearlessly expressed. He said that, for his part, he had no doubt about the matter at all, that it was a clear case, that Mr. Bullet-head 'never *could* be persvaded fur to drink like other folks, but vas *continually* a-svigging o' that ere blessed XXX ale, and as a naiteral consekvence, it just puffed him up savage, and made him X (cross) in the X-treme.'

Landor's Cottage

A PENDANT TO "THE DOMAIN OF ARNHEIM"

DURING a pedestrian trip last summer, through one or two of the river counties of New York, I found myself, as the day declined, somewhat embarrassed about the road I was pursuing. The land undulated very remarkably; and my path, for the last hour, had wound about and about so confusedly, in its effort to keep in the valleys, that I no longer knew in what direction lay the sweet village of B——, where I had determined to stop for the night. The sun had scarcely *shone* — strictly speaking — during the day, which nevertheless, had been unpleasantly warm. A smoky mist, resembling that of the Indian summer, enveloped all things, and of course, added to my uncertainty. Not that I cared much about the matter. If I did not hit upon the village before sunset, or even before dark, it was more than possible that a little Dutch farmhouse, or something of that kind, would soon make its appearance — although, in fact, the neighborhood (perhaps on account of being more picturesque than fertile) was very sparsely inhabited. At all events, with my knapsack for a pillow, and my hound as a sentry, a bivouac in the open air was just the thing which would have amused me. I sauntered on, therefore, quite at ease — Ponto taking charge of my gun — until at length, just as I had begun to consider whether the numerous little glades that led hither and thither, were intended to be paths at all, I was conducted by one of them into an unquestionable carriage track. There could be no mistaking it. The traces of light wheels were evident; and although the tall shrubberies and overgrown undergrowth met overhead, there was no obstruction whatever below, even to the passage of a Virginian mountain wagon — the most aspiring vehicle, I take it, of its kind. The road, however, except in being open through the wood — if wood be not too weighty a name for such an assemblage of light trees — and except in the particulars of evident wheel-tracks — bore no resemblance to any road I had before seen. The tracks of which I speak were but faintly perceptible — having been impressed upon the firm, yet pleasantly moist surface of — what looked more like green Genoese velvet than any thing

else. It was grass, clearly — but grass such as we seldom see out of England — so short, so thick, so even, and so vivid in color. Not a single impediment lay in the wheel-route — not even a chip or dead twig. The stones that once obstructed the way had been carefully *placed* — not thrown — along the sides of the lane, so as to define its boundaries at bottom with a kind of half-precise, half-negligent, and wholly picturesque definition. Clumps of wild flowers grew everywhere, luxuriantly, in the interspaces.

What to make of all this, of course I knew not. Here was *art* undoubtedly — *that* did not surprise me — all roads, in the ordinary sense, are works of art; nor can I say that there was much to wonder at in the mere *excess* of art manifested; all that seemed to have been done, might have been done *here* — with such natural "capabilities" (as they have it in the books on Landscape Gardening) — with very little labor and expense. No; it was not the amount but the *character* of the art which caused me to take a seat on one of the blossomy stones and gaze up and down this fairy-like avenue for half an hour or more in bewildered admiration. One thing became more and more evident the longer I gazed: an artist, and one with a most scrupulous eye for form, had superintended all these arrangements. The greatest care had been taken to preserve a due medium between the neat and graceful on the one hand, and the *pittoresque*, in the true sense of the Italian term, on the other. There were few straight, and no long uninterrupted lines. The same effect of curvature or of color appeared twice, usually, but not oftener, at any one point of view. Everywhere was variety in uniformity. It was a piece of "composition," in which the most fastidiously critical taste could scarcely have suggested an emendation.

I had turned to the right as I entered this road, and now, arising, I continued in the same direction. The path was so serpentine, that at no moment could I trace its course for more than two or three paces in advance. Its character did not undergo any material change.

Presently the murmur of water fell gently upon my ear — and in a few moments afterward, as I turned with the road somewhat more abruptly than hitherto, I became aware that a building of some kind lay at the foot of a gentle declivity just before me. I could see nothing distinctly on account of the mist which occupied all the little valley below. A gentle breeze, however, now arose, as the sun was about descending; and while I remained standing on the brow of the slope, the fog gradually became dissipated into wreaths, and so floated over the scene.

As it came fully into view — thus *gradually* as I describe it — piece by piece, here a tree, there a glimpse of water, and here again the summit of a chimney, I could scarcely help fancying that the whole was one of the ingenious illusions sometimes exhibited under the name of "vanishing pictures."

By the time, however, that the fog had thoroughly disappeared, the

sun had made its way down behind the gentle hills, and thence, as it with a slight *chassez* to the south, had come again fully into sight, glaring with a purplish lustre through a chasm that entered the valley from the west. Suddenly, therefore — and as if by the hand of magic — this whole valley and every thing in it became brilliantly visible.

The first *coup d'œil*, as the sun slid into the position described, impressed me very much as I have been impressed, when a boy, by the concluding scene of some well-arranged theatrical spectacle or melodrama. Not even the monstrosity of color was wanting; for the sunlight came out through the chasm, tinted all orange and purple; while the vivid green of the grass in the valley was reflected more or less upon all objects from the curtain of vapor that still hung overhead, as if loth to take its total departure from a scene so enchantingly beautiful.

The little vale into which I thus peered down from under the fog-canopy could not have been more than four hundred yards long; while in breadth it varied from fifty to one hundred and fifty or perhaps two hundred. It was most narrow at its northern extremity, opening out as it tended southwardly, but with no very precise regularity. The widest portion was within eighty yards of the southern extreme. The slopes which encompassed the vale could not fairly be called hills, unless at their northern face. Here a precipitous ledge of granite arose to a height of some ninety feet; and, as I have mentioned, the valley at this point was not more than fifty feet wide; but as the visiter proceeded southwardly from the cliff, he found on his right hand and on his left, declivities at once less high, less precipitous, and less rocky. All, in a word, sloped and softened to the south; and yet the whole vale was engirdled by eminences, more or less high, except at two points. One of these I have already spoken of. It lay considerably to the north of west, and was where the setting sun made its way, as I have before described, into the amphitheatre, through a cleanly cut natural cleft in the granite embankment; this fissure might have been ten yards wide at its widest point, so far as the eye could trace it. It seemed to lead up, up like a natural causeway, into the recesses of unexplored mountains and forests. The other opening was directly at the southern end of the vale. Here, generally, the slopes were nothing more than gentle inclinations, extending from east to west about one hundred and fifty yards. In the middle of this extent was a depression, level with the ordinary floor of the valley. As regards vegetation, as well as in respect to every thing else, the scene *softened and sloped* to the south. To the north — on the craggy precipice — a few paces from the verge — up sprang the magnificent trunks of numerous hickories, black walnuts, and chestnuts, interspersed with occasional oak; and the strong lateral branches thrown out by the walnuts especially, spread far over the edge of the cliff. Proceeding southwardly, the explorer saw, at first, the same class of trees, but less and less lofty and Salvatorish in character; then he saw the gentler

elm, succeeded by the sassafras and locust — these again by the softer linden, red-bud, catalpa, and maple — these yet again by still more graceful and more modest varieties. The whole face of the southern declivity was covered with wild shrubbery alone — an occasional silver willow or white poplar excepted. In the bottom of the valley itself — (for it must be borne in mind that the vegetation hitherto mentioned grew only on the cliffs or hillsides) — were to be seen three insulated trees. One was an elm of fine size and exquisite form: it stood guard over the southern gate of the vale. Another was a hickory, much larger than the elm, and altogether a much finer tree, although both were exceedingly beautiful: it seemed to have taken charge of the northwestern entrance, springing from a group of rocks in the very jaws of the ravine, and throwing its graceful body, at an angle of nearly forty-five degrees, far out into the sunshine of the amphitheatre. About thirty yards east of this tree stood, however, the pride of the valley, and beyond all question the most magnificent tree I have ever seen, unless, perhaps, among the cypresses of the Itchiatuckanee. It was a triple-stemmed tulip-tree — the *Liriodendron Tulipiferum* — one of the natural order of magnolias. Its three trunks separated from the parent at about three feet from the soil, and diverging very slightly and gradually, were not more than four feet apart at the point where the largest stem shot out into foliage: this was at an elevation of about eighty feet. The whole height of the principal division was one hundred and twenty feet. Nothing can surpass in beauty the form, or the glossy, vivid green of the leaves of the tulip-tree. In the present instance they were fully eight inches wide; but their glory was altogether eclipsed by the gorgeous splendor of the profuse blossoms. Conceive, closely congregated, a million of the largest and most resplendent tulips! Only thus can the reader get any idea of the picture I would convey. And then the stately grace of the clean, delicately-granulated columnar stems, the largest four feet in diameter, at twenty from the ground. The innumerable blossoms, mingling with those of other trees scarcely less beautiful, although infinitely less majestic, filled the valley with more than Arabian perfumes.

The general floor of the amphitheatre was *grass* of the same character as that I had found in the road; if anything, more deliciously soft, thick, velvety, and miraculously green. It was hard to conceive how all this beauty had been attained.

I have spoken of two openings into the vale. From the one to the northwest issued a rivulet, which came, gently murmuring and slightly foaming, down the ravine, until it dashed against the group of rocks out of which sprang the insulated hickory. Here, after encircling the tree, it passed on a little to the north of east, leaving the tulip tree some twenty feet to the south, and making no decided alteration in its course until it came near the midway between the eastern and western boundaries of the valley. At this point, after a series of sweeps, it turned off

at right angles and pursued a generally southern direction — meandering as it went — until it became lost in a small lake of irregular figure (although roughly oval), that lay gleaming near the lower extremity of the vale. This lakelet was, perhaps, a hundred yards in diameter at its widest part. No crystal could be clearer than its waters. Its bottom, which could be distinctly seen, consisted altogether of pebbles brilliantly white. Its banks, of the emerald grass already described, *rounded*, rather than sloped, off into the clear heaven below; and so clear was this heaven, so perfectly, at times, did it reflect all objects above it, that where the true bank ended and where the mimic one commenced, it was a point of no little difficulty to determine. The trout, and some other varieties of fish, with which this pond seemed to be almost inconveniently crowded, had all the appearance of veritable flying-fish. It was almost impossible to believe that they were not absolutely suspended in the air. A light birch canoe that lay placidly on the water, was reflected in its minutest fibres with a fidelity unsurpassed by the most exquisitely polished mirror. A small island, fairly laughing with flowers in full bloom, and affording little more space than just enough for a picturesque little building, seemingly a fowl-house — arose from the lake not far from its northern shore — to which it was connected by means of an inconceivably light-looking and yet very primitive bridge. It was formed of a single, broad and thick plank of the tulip wood. This was forty feet long, and spanned the interval between shore and shore with a slight but very perceptible arch, preventing all oscillation. From the southern extreme of the lake issued a continuation of the rivulet, which, after meandering for, perhaps, thirty yards, finally passed through the "depression" (already described) in the middle of the southern declivity, and tumbling down a sheer precipice of a hundred feet, made its devious and unnoticed way to the Hudson.

The lake was deep — at some points thirty feet — but the rivulet seldom exceeded three, while its greatest width was about eight. Its bottom and banks were as those of the pond — if a defect could have been attributed, in point of picturesqueness, it was that of excessive *neatness*.

The expanse of the green turf was relieved, here and there, by an occasional showy shrub, such as the hydrangea, or the common snowball, or the aromatic seringa; or, more frequently, by a clump of geraniums blossoming gorgeously in great varieties. These latter grew in pots which were carefully buried in the soil, so as to give the plants the appearance of being indigenous. Besides all this, the lawn's velvet was exquisitely spotted with sheep — a considerable flock of which roamed about the vale, in company with three tamed deer, and a vast number of brilliantly-plumed ducks. A very large mastiff seemed to be in vigilant attendance upon these animals, each and all.

Along the eastern and western cliffs — where, toward the upper portion of the amphitheatre, the boundaries were more or less precipitous

— grew ivy in great profusion — so that only here and there could even a glimpse of the naked rock be obtained. The northern precipice, in like manner, was almost entirely clothed by grape-vines of rare luxuriance; some springing from the soil at the base of the cliff, and others from ledges on its face.

The slight elevation which formed the lower boundary of this little domain, was crowned by a neat stone wall, of sufficient height to prevent the escape of the deer. Nothing of the fence kind was observable elsewhere; for nowhere else was an artificial enclosure needed: — any stray sheep, for example, which should attempt to make its way out of the vale by means of the ravine, would find its progress arrested, after a few yards' advance, by the precipitous ledge of rock over which tumbled the cascade that had arrested my attention as I first drew near the domain. In short, the only ingress or egress was through a gate occupying a rocky pass in the road, a few paces below the point at which I stopped to reconnoitre the scene.

I have described the brook as meandering very irregularly through the whole of its course. Its two *general* directions, as I have said, were first from west to east, and then from north to south. At the *turn*, the stream, sweeping backward, made an almost circular *loop*, so as to form a peninsula which was very nearly an island, and which included about the sixteenth of an acre. On this peninsula stood a dwelling-house — and when I say that this house, like the infernal terrace seen by Vathek, *"était d'une architecture inconnue dans les annales de la terre,"* I mean, merely, that its *tout ensemble* struck me with the keenest sense of combined novelty and propriety — in a word, of *poetry* — (for, than in the words just employed, I could scarcely give, of poetry in the abstract, a more rigorous definition) — and I do *not* mean that merely *outré* was perceptible in any respect.

In fact nothing could well be more simple — more utterly unpretending than this cottage. Its marvellous *effect* lay altogether in its artistic arrangement *as a picture*. I could have fancied, while I looked at it, that some eminent landscape-painter had built it with his brush.

The point of view from which I first saw the valley, was not *altogether*, although it was nearly, the best point from which to survey the house. I will therefore describe it as I afterwards saw it — from a position on the stone wall at the southern extreme of the amphitheatre.

The main building was about twenty-four feet long and sixteen broad — certainly not more. Its total height, from the ground to the apex of the roof, could not have exceeded eighteen feet. To the west end of this structure was attached one about a third smaller in all its proportions: — the line of its front standing back about two yards from that of the larger house; and the line of its roof, of course, being considerably depressed below that of the roof adjoining. At right angles to these buildings, and from the rear of the main one — not exactly in the middle — extended a

third compartment, very small — being, in general, one-third less than the western wing. The roofs of the two larger were very steep — sweeping down from the ridge-beam with a long concave curve, and extending at least four feet beyond the walls in front, so as to form the roofs of two piazzas. These latter roofs, of course, needed no support; but as they had the *air* of needing it, slight and perfectly plain pillars were inserted at the corners alone. The roof of the northern wing was merely an extension of a portion of the main roof. Between the chief building and western wing arose a very tall and rather slender square chimney of hard Dutch bricks, alternately black and red: — a slight cornice of projecting bricks at the top. Over the gables the roofs also projected very much: — in the main building about four feet to the east and two to the west. The principal door was not exactly in the main division, being a little to the east — while the two windows were to the west. These latter did not extend to the floor, but were much longer and narrower than usual — they had single shutters like doors — the panes were of lozenge form, but quite large. The door itself had its upper half of glass, also in lozenge panes — a movable shutter secured it at night. The door to the west wing was in its gable, and quite simple — a single window looked out to the south. There was no external door to the north wing, and it also had only one window to the east.

The blank wall of the eastern gable was relieved by stairs (with a balustrade) running diagonally across it — the ascent being from the south. Under cover of the widely projecting eave these steps gave access to a door leading to the garret, or rather loft — for it was lighted only by a single window to the north, and seemed to have been intended as a store-room.

The piazzas of the main building and western wing had no floors, as is usual; but at the doors and at each window, large, flat irregular slabs of granite lay imbedded in the delicious turf, affording comfortable footing in all weather. Excellent paths of the same material — not *nicely* adapted, but with the velvety sod filling frequent intervals between the stones, led hither and thither from the house, to a crystal spring about five paces off, to the road, or to one or two out-houses that lay to the north, beyond the brook, and were thoroughly concealed by a few locusts and catalpas.

Not more than six steps from the main door of the cottage stood the dead trunk of a fantastic pear-tree, so clothed from head to foot in the gorgeous bignonia blossoms that one required no little scrutiny to determine what manner of sweet thing it could be. From various arms of this tree hung cages of different kinds. In one, a large wicker cylinder with a ring at top, revelled a mocking bird; in another an oriole; in a third the impudent bobolink — while three or four more delicate prisons were loudly vocal with canaries.

The pillars of the piazza were enwreathed in jasmine and sweet honeysuckle; while from the angle formed by the main structure and its west wing, in front, sprang a grape-vine of unexampled luxuriance. Scorning

all restraint, it had clambered first to the lower roof — then to the higher; and along the ridge of this latter it continued to writhe on, throwing out tendrils to the right and left, until at length it fairly attained the east gable, and fell trailing over the stairs.

The whole house, with its wings, was constructed of the old-fashioned Dutch shingles — broad, and with unrounded corners. It is a peculiarity of this material to give houses built of it the appearance of being wider at bottom than at top — after the manner of Egyptian architecture; and in the present instance, this exceedingly picturesque effect was aided by numerous pots of gorgeous flowers that almost encompassed the base of the buildings.

The shingles were painted a dull gray; and the happiness with which this neutral tint melted into the vivid green of the tulip tree leaves that partially overshadowed the cottage, can readily be conceived by an artist.

From the position near the stone wall, as described, the buildings were seen at great advantage — for the southeastern angle was thrown forward — so that the eye took in at once the whole of the two fronts, with the picturesque eastern gable, and at the same time obtained just a sufficient glimpse of the northern wing, with parts of a pretty roof to the spring-house, and nearly half of a light bridge that spanned the brook in the near vicinity of the main buildings.

I did not remain very long on the brow of the hill, although long enough to make a thorough survey of the scene at my feet. It was clear that I had wandered from the road to the village, and I had thus good traveller's excuse to open the gate before me, and inquire my way, at all events; so, without more ado, I proceeded.

The road, after passing the gate, seemed to lie upon a natural ledge, sloping gradually down along the face of the north-eastern cliffs. It led me on to the foot of the northern precipice, and thence over the bridge, round by the eastern gable to the front door. In this progress, I took notice that no sight of the out-houses could be obtained.

As I turned the corner of the gable, the mastiff bounded towards me in stern silence, but with the eye and the whole air of a tiger. I held him out my hand, however, in token of amity — and I never yet knew the dog who was proof against such an appeal to his courtesy. He not only shut his mouth and wagged his tail, but absolutely offered me his paw — afterward extending his civilities to Ponto.

As no bell was discernible, I rapped with my stick against the door, which stood half open. Instantly a figure advanced to the threshold — that of a young woman about twenty-eight years of age — slender, or rather slight, and somewhat above the medium height. As she approached, with a certain *modest decision* of step altogether indescribable. I said to myself, "Surely here I have found the perfection of natural, in contradistinction from artificial *grace*." The second impression which she made on me, but by far the more vivid of the two, was that of

enthusiasm. So intense an expression of *romance*, perhaps I should call it, or of unworldliness, as that which gleamed from her deep-set eyes, had never so sunk into my heart of hearts before. I know not how it is, but this peculiar expression of the eye, wreathing itself occasionally into the lips, is the most powerful, if not absolutely the *sole* spell, which rivets my interest in woman. "*Romance*," provided my readers fully comprehended what I would here imply by the word — "romance" and "womanliness" seem to me convertible terms: and, after all, what man truly *loves* in woman, is simply her *womanhood*. The eyes of Annie (I heard some one from the interior call her "Annie, darling!") were "spiritual gray;" her hair, a light chestnut: this is all I had time to observe of her.

At her most courteous of invitations, I entered — passing first into a tolerably wide vestibule. Having come mainly to *observe*, I took notice that to my right as I stepped in, was a window, such as those in front of the house; to the left, a door leading into the principal room; while, opposite me, an *open* door enabled me to see a small apartment, just the size of the vestibule, arranged as a study, and having a large *bow* window looking out to the north.

Passing into the parlor, I found myself with *Mr. Landor* — for this, I afterwards found, was his name. He was civil, even cordial in his manner; but just then, I was more intent on observing the arrangements of the dwelling which had so much interested me, than the personal appearance of the tenant.

The north wing, I now saw, was a bed-chamber; its door opened into the parlor. West of this door was a single window, looking toward the brook. At the west end of the parlor, were a fireplace, and a door leading into the west wing — probably a kitchen.

Nothing could be more rigorously simple than the furniture of the parlor. On the floor was an ingrain carpet, of excellent texture — a white ground, spotted with small circular green figures. At the windows were curtains of snowy white jaconet muslin: they were tolerably full, and hung *decisively*, perhaps rather formally in sharp, parallel plaits to the floor — *just* to the floor. The walls were prepared with a French paper of great delicacy, a silver ground, with a faint green cord running zig-zag throughout. Its expanse was relieved merely by three of Julien's exquisite lithographs *à trois crayons*, fastened to the wall without frames. One of these drawings was a scene of Oriental luxury, or rather voluptuousness; another was a "carnival piece," spirited beyond compare; the third was a Greek female head — a face so divinely beautiful, and yet of an expression so provokingly indeterminate, never before arrested my attention.

The more substantial furniture consisted of a round table, a few chairs (including a large rocking-chair), and a sofa, or rather "settee;" its material was plain maple painted a creamy white, slightly interstriped with green; the seat of cane. The chairs and table were "to match," but the

forms of all had evidently been designed by the same brain which planned "the grounds;" it is impossible to conceive anything more graceful.

On the table were a few books, a large, square, crystal bottle of some novel perfume, a plain ground-glass *astral* (not solar) lamp with an Italian shade, and a large vase of resplendently-blooming flowers. Flowers, indeed, of gorgeous colours and delicate odour formed the sole mere *decoration* of the apartment. The fire-place was nearly filled with a vase of brilliant geranium. On a triangular shelf in each angle of the room stood also a similar vase, varied only as to its lovely contents. One or two smaller *bouquets* adorned the mantel, and late violets clustered about the open windows.

It is not the purpose of this work to do more than give in detail, a picture of Mr. Landor's residence — *as I found it*. How he made it what it was — and *why* — with some particulars of Mr. Landor himself — may, *possibly* form the subject of another article.

IV

THE NARRATIVE
OF
ARTHUR GORDON PYM
OF NANTUCKET

PREFACE

Upon my return to the United States a few months ago, after the extraordinary series of adventure in the South Seas and elsewhere, of which an account is given in the following pages, accident threw me into the society of several gentlemen in Richmond, Va., who felt deep interest in all matters relating to the regions I had visited, and who were constantly urging it upon me, as a duty, to give my narrative to the public. I had several reasons, however, for declining to do so, some of which were of a nature altogether private, and concern no person but myself; others not so much so. One consideration which deterred me was, that,

having kept no journal during a greater portion of the time in which I was absent, I feared I should not be able to write, from mere memory, a statement so minute and connected as to have the *appearance* of that truth it would really possess, barring only the natural and unavoidable exaggeration to which all of us are prone when detailing events which have had powerful influence in exciting the imaginative faculties. Another reason was, that the incidents to be narrated were of a nature so positively marvellous, that, unsupported as my assertions must necessarily be (except by the evidence of a single individual, and he a half-breed Indian), I could only hope for belief among my family, and those of my friends who have had reason, through life, to put faith in my veracity — the probability being that the public at large would regard what I should put forth as merely an impudent and ingenious fiction. A distrust in my own abilities as a writer was, nevertheless, one of the principal causes which prevented me from complying with the suggestion of my advisers.

Among those gentlemen in Virginia who expressed the greatest interest in my statement, more particularly in regard to that portion of it which related to the Antarctic Ocean, was Mr. Poe, lately editor of the *Southern Literary Messenger*, a monthly magazine, published by Mr. Thomas W. White, in the city of Richmond. He strongly advised me, among others, to prepare at once a full account of what I had seen and undergone, and trust to the shrewdness and common sense of the public — insisting, with great plausibility, that however roughly, as regards mere authorship, my book should be got up, its very uncouthness, if there were any, would give it all the better chance of being received as truth.

Notwithstanding this representation, I did not make up my mind to do as he suggested. He afterward proposed (finding that I would not stir in the matter) that I should allow him to draw up, in his own words, a narrative of the earlier portion of my adventures, from facts afforded by myself, publishing it in the *Southern Messenger under the garb of fiction*. To this, perceiving no objection, I consented, stipulating only that my real name should be retained. Two numbers of the pretended fiction appeared, consequently, in the *Messenger* for January and February, (1837), and, in order that it might certainly be regarded as fiction, the name of Mr. Poe was affixed to the articles in the table of contents of the magazine.

The manner in which this *ruse* was received has induced me at length to undertake a regular compilation and publication of the adventures in question; for I found that, in spite of the air of fable which had been so ingeniously thrown around that portion of my statement which appeared in the *Messenger* (without altering or distorting a single fact), the public were still not at all disposed to receive it as fable, and several letters were sent to Mr. P.'s address. distinctly expressing a conviction to

the contrary. I thence concluded that the facts of my narrative would prove of such a nature as to carry with them sufficient evidence of their own authenticity, and that I had consequently little to fear on the score of popular incredulity.

This *exposé* being made, it will be seen at once how much of what follows I claim to be my own writing; and it will also be understood that no fact is misrepresented in the first few pages which were written by Mr. Poe. Even to those readers who have not seen the *Messenger*, it will be unnecessary to point out where his portion ends and my own commences; the difference in point of style will be readily perceived.

<div style="text-align: right;">A. G. PYM.</div>

New-York, July, 1838.

CHAPTER I

My name is Arthur Gordon Pym. My father was a respectable trader in sea-stores at Nantucket, where I was born. My maternal grandfather was an attorney in good practice. He was fortunate in every thing, and had speculated very successfully in stocks of the Edgarton New Bank, as it was formerly called. By these and other means he had managed to lay by a tolerable sum of money. He was more attached to myself, I believe, than to any other person in the world, and I expected to inherit the most of his property at his death. He sent me, at six years of age, to the school of old Mr. Ricketts, a gentleman with only one arm, and of eccentric manners — he is well known to almost every person who has visited New Bedford. I stayed at his school until I was sixteen, when I left him for Mr. E. Ronald's academy on the hill. Here I became intimate with the son of Mr. Barnard, a sea-captain, who generally sailed in the employ of Lloyd and Vredenburgh — Mr. Barnard is also very well known in New Bedford, and has many relations, I am certain, in Edgarton. His son was named Augustus, and he was nearly two years older than myself. He had been on a whaling voyage with his father in the John Donaldson, and was always talking to me of his adventures in the South Pacific Ocean. I used frequently to go home with him, and remain all day, and sometimes all night. We occupied the same bed, and he would be sure to keep me awake until almost light, telling me stories of the natives of the Island of Tinian, and other places he had visited in his travels. At last I could not help being interested in what he said, and by degrees I felt the greatest desire to go to sea. I owned a sailboat called the Ariel, and worth about seventy-five dollars. She had a half-deck or cuddy, and was rigged sloop-fashion — I forget her tonnage, but she would hold ten persons without much crowding. In this boat we were in the habit of going on some of the maddest freaks in the world; and, when I now think of them, it appears to me a thousand wonders that I am alive to-day.

I will relate one of these adventures by way of introduction to a longer

and more momentous narrative. One night there was a party at Mr. Barnard's, and both Augustus and myself were not a little intoxicated toward the close of it. As usual, in such cases, I took part of his bed in preference to going home. He went to sleep, as I thought, very quietly (it being near one when the party broke up), and without saying a word on his favorite topic. It might have been half an hour from the time of our getting in bed, and I was just about falling into a doze, when he suddenly started up, and swore with a terrible oath that he would not go to sleep for any Arthur Pym in Christendom, when there was so glorious a breeze from the southwest. I never was so astonished in my life, not knowing what he intended, and thinking that the wines and liquors he had drunk had set him entirely beside himself. He proceeded to talk very coolly, however, saying he knew that I supposed him intoxicated, but that he was never more sober in his life. He was only tired, he added, of lying in bed on such a fine night like a dog, and was determined to get up and dress, and go out on a frolic with the boat. I can hardly tell what possessed me, but the words were no sooner out of his mouth than I felt a thrill of the greatest excitement and pleasure, and thought his mad idea one of the most delightful and most reasonable things in the world. It was blowing almost a gale, and the weather was very cold — it being late in October. I sprang out of bed, nevertheless, in a kind of ecstasy, and told him I was quite as brave as himself, and quite as tired as he was of lying in bed like a dog, and quite as ready for any fun or frolic as any Augustus Barnard in Nantucket.

We lost no time in getting on our clothes and hurrying down to the boat. She was lying at the old decayed wharf by the lumber-yard of Pankey & Co., and almost thumping her side out against the rough logs. Augustus got into her and bailed her, for she was nearly half full of water. This being done, we hoisted jib and mainsail, kept full, and started boldly out to sea.

The wind, as I before said, blew freshly from the southwest. The night was very clear and cold. Augustus had taken the helm, and I stationed myself by the mast, on the deck of the cuddy. We flew along at a great rate — neither of us having said a word since casting loose from the wharf. I now asked my companion what course he intended to steer, and what time he thought it probable we should get back. He whistled for a few minutes, and then said crustily: "I am going to sea — *you* may go home if you think proper." Turning my eyes upon him, I perceived at once that, in spite of his assumed *nonchalance*, he was greatly agitated. I could see him distinctly by the light of the moon — his face was paler than any marble, and his hand shook so excessively that he could scarcely retain hold of the tiller. I found that something had gone wrong, and became seriously alarmed. At this period I knew little about the management of a boat, and was now depending entirely upon the nautical skill of my friend. The wind, too, had suddenly increased, as we were

fast getting out of the lee of the land — still I was ashamed to betray any trepidation, and for almost half an hour maintained a resolute silence. I could stand it no longer, however, and spoke to Augustus about the propriety of turning back. As before, it was nearly a minute before he made answer, or took any notice of my suggestion. "By-and-by," said he at length — "time enough — home by-and-by." I had expected a similar reply, but there was something in the tone of these words which filled me with an indescribable feeling of dread. I again looked at the speaker attentively. His lips were perfectly livid, and his knees shook so violently together that he seemed scarcely able to stand. "For God's sake, Augustus," I screamed, now heartily frightened, "what ails you? — what is the matter? — what *are* you going to do?" "Matter!" he stammered, in the greatest apparent surprise, letting go the tiller at the same moment, and falling forward into the bottom of the boat — "matter — why, nothing is the — matter — going home — d — d — don't you see?" The whole truth now flashed upon me. I flew to him and raised him up. He was drunk — beastly drunk — he could no longer either stand, speak or see. His eyes were perfectly glazed; and as I let him go in the extremity of my despair, he rolled like a mere log into the bilge-water, from which I had lifted him. It was evident that, during the evening, he had drunk far more than I suspected, and that his conduct in bed had been the result of a highly-concentrated state of intoxication — a state which, like madness, frequently enables the victim to imitate the outward demeanour of one in perfect possession of his senses. The coolness of the night air, however, had had its usual effect — the mental energy began to yield before its influence — and the confused perception which he no doubt then had of his perilous situation had assisted in hastening the catastrophe. He was now thoroughly insensible, and there was no probability that he would be otherwise for many hours.

It is hardly possible to conceive the extremity of my terror. The fumes of the wine lately taken had evaporated, leaving me doubly timid and irresolute. I knew that I was altogether incapable of managing the boat, and that a fierce wind and strong ebb tide were hurrying us to destruction. A storm was evidently gathering behind us; we had neither compass nor provisions; and it was clear that, if we held our present course, we should be out of sight of land before daybreak. These thoughts, with a crowd of others equally fearful, flashed through my mind with a bewildering rapidity, and for some moments paralyzed me beyond the possibility of making any exertion. The boat was going through the water at a terrible rate — full before the wind — no reef in either jib or mainsail — running her bows completely under the foam. It was a thousand wonders she did not broach to — Augustus having let go the tiller, as I said before, and I being too much agitated to think of taking it myself. By good luck, however, she kept steady, and gradually I recovered some degree of presence of mind. Still the wind was increasing fearfully; and

whenever we rose from a plunge forward, the sea behind fell combing over our counter, and deluged us with water. I was so utterly benumbed, too, in every limb, as to be nearly unconscious of sensation. At length I summoned up the resolution of despair, and rushing to the mainsail, let it go by the run. As might have been expected, it flew over the bows, and, getting drenched with water, carried away the mast short off by the board. This latter accident alone saved me from instant destruction. Under the jib only, I now boomed along before the wind, shipping heavy seas occasionally over the counter, but relieved from the terror of immediate death. I took the helm, and breathed with greater freedom as I found that there yet remained to us a chance of ultimate escape. Augustus still lay senseless in the bottom of the boat; and as there was imminent danger of his drowning (the water being nearly a foot deep just where he fell), I contrived to raise him partially up, and keep him in a sitting position, by passing a rope round his waist, and lashing it to a ringbolt in the deck of the cuddy. Having thus arranged every thing as well as I could in my chilled and agitated condition, I recommended myself to God, and made up my mind to bear whatever might happen with all the fortitude in my power.

Hardly had I come to this resolution, when, suddenly, a loud and long scream or yell, as if from the throats of a thousand demons, seemed to pervade the whole atmosphere around and above the boat. Never while I live shall I forget the intense agony of terror I experienced at that moment. My hair stood erect on my head — I felt the blood congealing in my veins — my heart ceased utterly to beat, and without having once raised my eyes to learn the source of my alarm, I tumbled headlong and insensible upon the body of my fallen companion.

I found myself, upon reviving, in the cabin of a large whaling-ship (the Penguin) bound to Nantucket. Several persons were standing over me, and Augustus, paler than death, was busily occupied in chafing my hands. Upon seeing me open my eyes, his exclamations of gratitude and joy excited alternate laughter and tears from the rough-looking personages who were present. The mystery of our being in existence was now soon explained. We had been run down by the whaling-ship, which was close-hauled, beating up to Nantucket with every sail she could venture to set, and consequently running almost at right angles to our own course. Several men were on the look-out forward, but did not perceive our boat until it was an impossibility to avoid coming in contact — their shouts of warning upon seeing us were what so terribly alarmed me. The huge ship, I was told, rode immediately over us with as much ease as our own little vessel would have passed over a feather, and without the least perceptible impediment to her progress. Not a scream arose from the deck of the victim — there was a slight grating sound to be heard mingling with the roar of wind and water, as the frail bark which was swallowed up rubbed for a moment along the keel of her destroyer

— but this was all. Thinking our boat (which it will be remembered was dismasted) some mere shell cut adrift as useless, the captain (Captain E. T. V. Block, of New London) was for proceeding on his course without troubling himself further about the matter. Luckily, there were two of the look-out who swore positively to having seen some person at our helm, and represented the possibility of yet saving him. A discussion ensued, when Block grew angry, and, after a while, said that "it was no business of his to be eternally watching for egg-shells; that the ship should *not* put about for any such nonsense; and if there was a man run down, it was nobody's fault but his own — he might drown and be d—d," or some language to that effect. Henderson, the first mate, now took the matter up, being justly indignant, as well as the whole ship's crew, at a speech evincing so base a degree of heartless atrocity. He spoke plainly, seeing himself upheld by the men, told the captain he considered him a fit subject for the gallows, and that he would disobey his orders if he were hanged for it the moment he set his foot on shore. He strode aft, jostling Block (who turned pale and made no answer) on one side, and seizing the helm, gave the word, in a firm voice, *Hard-a-lee!* The men flew to their posts, and the ship went cleverly about. All this had occupied nearly five minutes, and it was supposed to be hardly within the bounds of possibility that any individual could be saved — allowing any to have been on board the boat. Yet, as the reader has seen, both Augustus and myself were rescued; and our deliverance seemed to have been brought about by two of those almost inconceivable pieces of good fortune which are attributed by the wise and pious to the special interference of Providence.

While the ship was yet in stays, the mate lowered the jolly-boat and jumped into her with the very two men, I believe, who spoke up as having seen me at the helm. They had just left the lee of the vessel (the moon still shining brightly) when she made a long and heavy roll to windward, and Henderson, at the same moment, starting up in his seat, bawled out to his crew to *back water*. He would say nothing else — repeating his cry impatiently, *back water! back water!* The men put back as speedily as possible; but by this time the ship had gone round, and gotten fully under headway, although all hands on board were making great exertions to take in sail. In despite of the danger of the attempt, the mate clung to the main-chains as soon as they came within his reach. Another huge lurch now brought the starboard side of the vessel out of water nearly as far as her keel, when the cause of his anxiety was rendered obvious enough. The body of a man was seen to be affixed in the most singular manner to the smooth and shining bottom (the Penguin was coppered and copper-fastened), and beating violently against it with every movement of the hull. After several ineffectual efforts, made during the lurches of the ship, and at the imminent risk of swamping the boat, I was finally disengaged from my perilous situation and taken on board

— for the body proved to be my own. It appeared that one of the timber-bolts having started and broken a passage through the copper, it had arrested my progress as I passed under the ship, and fastened me in so extraordinary a manner to her bottom. The head of the bolt had made its way through the collar of the green baize jacket I had on, and through the back part of my neck, forcing itself out between two sinews and just below the right ear. I was immediately put to bed — although life seemed to be totally extinct. There was no surgeon on board. The captain, however, treated me with every attention — to make amends, I presume, in the eyes of his crew, for his atrocious behaviour in the previous portion of the adventure.

In the meantime, Henderson had again put off from the ship, although the wind was now blowing almost a hurricane. He had not been gone many minutes when he fell in with some fragments of our boat, and shortly afterward one of the men with him asserted that he could distinguish a cry for help at intervals amid the roaring of the tempest. This induced the hardy seamen to persevere in their search for more than half an hour, although repeated signals to return were made them by Captain Block, and although every moment on the water in so frail a boat was fraught to them with the most imminent and deadly peril. Indeed, it is nearly impossible to conceive how the small jolly they were in could have escaped destruction for a single instant. She was built, however, for the whaling service, and was fitted, as I have since had reason to believe, with air-boxes, in the manner of some life-boats used on the coast of Wales.

After searching in vain for about the period of time just mentioned, it was determined to get back to the ship. They had scarcely made this resolve when a feeble cry arose from a dark object that floated rapidly by. They pursued and soon overtook it. It proved to be the entire deck of the Ariel's cuddy. Augustus was struggling near it, apparently in the last agonies. Upon getting hold of him it was found that he was attached by a rope to the floating timber. This rope, it will be remembered, I had myself tied around his waist, and made fast to a ringbolt, for the purpose of keeping him in an upright position, and my so doing, it appeared, had been ultimately the means of preserving his life. The Ariel was slightly put together, and in going down her frame naturally went to pieces; the deck of the cuddy, as might have been expected, was lifted, by the force of the water rushing in, entirely from the main timbers, and floated (with other fragments, no doubt) to the surface — Augustus was buoyed up with it, and thus escaped a terrible death.

It was more than an hour after being taken on board the Penguin before he could give any account of himself, or be made to comprehend the nature of the accident which had befallen our boat. At length he became thoroughly aroused, and spoke much of his sensations while in the water. Upon his first attaining any degree of consciousness, he found

himself beneath the surface, whirling round and round with inconceiv·
able rapidity, and with a rope wrapped in three or four folds tightly about
his neck. In an instant afterward he felt himself going rapidly upward,
when, his head striking violently against a hard substance, he again re-
lapsed into insensibility. Upon once more reviving he was in fuller pos-
session of his reason — this was still, however, in the greatest degree
clouded and confused. He now knew that some accident had occurred,
and that he was in the water, although his mouth was above the surface,
and he could breathe with some freedom. Possibly, at this period the
deck was drifting rapidly before the wind, and drawing him after it, as
he floated upon his back. Of course, as long as he could have retained this
position, it would have been nearly impossible that he should be
drowned. Presently a surge threw him directly athwart the deck; and this
post he endeavored to maintain, screaming at intervals for help. Just
before he was discovered by Mr. Henderson, he had been obliged to
relax his hold through exhaustion, and, falling into the sea, had given
himself up for lost. During the whole period of his struggles he had not
the faintest recollection of the Ariel, nor of the matters in connexion
with the source of his disaster. A vague feeling of terror and despair had
taken entire possession of his faculties. When he was finally picked up,
every power of his mind had failed him; and, as before said, it was nearly
an hour after getting on board the Penguin before he became fully
aware of his condition. In regard to myself — I was resuscitated from
a state bordering very nearly upon death (and after every other means
had been tried in vain for three hours and a half) by vigorous friction
with flannels bathed in hot oil — a proceeding suggested by Augustus.
The wound in my neck, although of an ugly appearance, proved of little
real consequence, and I soon recovered from its effects.

The Penguin got into port about nine o'clock in the morning, after
encountering one of the severest gales ever experienced off Nantucket.
Both Augustus and myself managed to appear at Mr. Barnard's in time
for breakfast — which, luckily, was somewhat late, owing to the party
over night. I suppose all at the table were too much fatigued themselves
to notice our jaded appearance — of course, it would not have borne a
very rigid scrutiny. Schoolboys, however, can accomplish wonders in the
way of deception, and I verily believe not one of our friends in Nan-
tucket had the slightest suspicion that the terrible story told by some
sailors in town of their having run down a vessel at sea and drowned
some thirty or forty poor devils, had reference either to the Ariel, my
companion, or myself. We two have since very frequently talked the
matter over — but never without a shudder. In one of our conversations
Augustus frankly confessed to me, that in his whole life he had at no
time experienced so excruciating a sense of dismay, as when on board our
little boat he first discovered the extent of his intoxication, and felt him·
self sinking beneath its influence.

CHAPTER II

In no affairs of mere prejudice, *pro* or *con*, do we deduce inferences with entire certainty, even from the most simple data. It might be supposed that a catastrophe such as I have just related would have effectually cooled my incipient passion for the sea. On the contrary, I never experienced a more ardent longing for the wild adventures incident to the life of a navigator than within a week after our miraculous deliverance. This short period proved amply long enough to erase from my memory the shadows, and bring out in vivid light all the pleasurably exciting points of color, all the picturesqueness, of the late perilous accident. My conversations with Augustus grew daily more frequent and more intensely full of interest. He had a manner of relating his stories of the ocean (more than one half of which I now suspect to have been sheer fabrications) well adapted to have weight with one of my enthusiastic temperament and somewhat gloomy although glowing imagination. It is strange, too, that he most strongly enlisted my feelings in behalf of the life of a seaman, when he depicted his more terrible moments of suffering and despair. For the bright side of the painting I had a limited sympathy. My visions were of shipwreck and famine; of death or captivity among barbarian hordes; of a lifetime dragged out in sorrow and tears, upon some gray and desolate rock, in an ocean unapproachable and unknown. Such visions or desires — for they amounted to desires — are common, I have since been assured, to the whole numerous race of the melancholy among men — at the time of which I speak I regarded them only as prophetic glimpses of a destiny which I felt myself in a measure bound to fulfil. Augustus thoroughly entered into my state of mind. It is probable, indeed, that our intimate communion had resulted in a partial interchange of character.

About eighteen months after the period of the Ariel's disaster, the firm of Lloyd and Vredenburgh (a house connected in some manner with the Messieurs Enderby, I believe, of Liverpool) were engaged in repairing and fitting out the brig Grampus for a whaling voyage. She was an old hulk, and scarcely seaworthy when all was done to her that could be done. I hardly know why she was chosen in preference to other good vessels belonging to the same owners — but so it was. Mr. Barnard was appointed to command her, and Augustus was going with him. While the brig was getting ready, he frequently urged upon me the excellency of the opportunity now offered for indulging my desire of travel. He found me by no means an unwilling listener — yet the matter could not be so easily arranged. My father made no direct opposition; but my mother went into hysterics at the bare mention of the design; and, more than all, my grandfather, from whom I expected much, vowed to cut me off with a shilling if I should ever broach the subject to him again. These difficulties, however, so far from abating my desire, only added

fuel to the flame. I determined to go at all hazards; and, having made known my intentions to Augustus, we set about arranging a plan by which it might be accomplished. In the meantime I forbore speaking to any of my relations in regard to the voyage, and, as I busied myself ostensibly with my usual studies, it was supposed that I had abandoned the design. I have since frequently examined my conduct on this occasion with sentiments of displeasure as well as of surprise. The intense hypocrisy I made use of for the furtherance of my project — an hypocrisy pervading every word and action of my life for so long a period of time — could only have been rendered tolerable to myself by the wild and burning expectation with which I looked forward to the fulfilment of my long-cherished visions of travel.

In pursuance of my scheme of deception, I was necessarily obliged to leave much to the management of Augustus, who was employed for the greater part of every day on board the Grampus, attending to some arrangements for his father in the cabin and cabin hold. At night, however, we were sure to have a conference and talk over our hopes. After nearly a month passed in this manner, without our hitting upon any plan we thought likely to succeed, he told me at last that he had determined upon everything necessary. I had a relation living in New Bedford, a Mr. Ross, at whose house I was in the habit of spending occasionally two or three weeks at a time. The brig was to sail about the middle of June (June, 1827), and it was agreed that, a day or two before her putting to sea, my father was to receive a note, as usual, from Mr. Ross, asking me to come over and spend a fortnight with Robert and Emmet (his sons). Augustus charged himself with the inditing of this note and getting it delivered. Having set out, as supposed, for New Bedford, I was then to report myself to my companion, who would contrive a hiding-place for me in the Grampus. This hiding-place, he assured me, would be rendered sufficiently comfortable for a residence of many days, during which I was not to make my appearance. When the brig had proceeded so far on her course as to make any turning back a matter out of question, I should then, he said, be formally installed in all the comforts of the cabin; and as to his father, he would only laugh heartily at the joke. Vessels enough would be met with by which a letter might be sent home explaining the adventure to my parents.

The middle of June at length arrived, and every thing had been matured. The note was written and delivered, and on a Monday morning I left the house for the New Bedford packet, as supposed. I went, however, straight to Augustus, who was waiting for me at the corner of a street. It had been our original plan that I should keep out of the way until dark, and then slip on board the brig; but, as there was now a thick fog in our favor, it was agreed to lose no time in secreting me. Augustus led the way to the wharf, and I followed at a little distance, enveloped in a thick seaman's cloak, which he had brought with him, so that my

person might not be easily recognized. Just as we turned the second corner, after passing Mr. Edmund's well, who should appear, standing right in front of me, and looking me full in the face, but old Mr. Peterson, my grandfather. "Why, bless my soul, Gordon," said he, after a long pause, "why, why, — *whose* dirty cloak is that you have on?" "Sir!" I replied, assuming, as well as I could, in the exigency of the moment, an air of offended surprise, and talking in the gruffest of all imaginable tones — "sir! you are a sum'mat mistaken — my name, in the first place, bee'nt nothing at all like Goddin, and I'd want you for to know better, you blackguard, than to call my new obercoat a darty one." For my life I could hardly refrain from screaming with laughter at the odd manner in which the old gentleman received this handsome rebuke. He started back two or three steps, turned first pale and then excessively red, threw up his spectacles, then, putting them down, ran full tilt at me, with his umbrella uplifted. He stopped short, however, in his career, as if struck with a sudden recollection; and presently, turning round, hobbled off down the street, shaking all the while with rage, and muttering between his teeth: "Won't do — new glasses — thought it was Gordon — d—d good-for-nothing salt water Long Tom."

After this narrow escape we proceeded with greater caution, and arrived at our point of destination in safety. There were only one or two of the hands on board, and these were busy forward, doing something to the forecastle combings. Captain Barnard, we knew very well, was engaged at Lloyd and Vredenburgh's, and would remain there until late in the evening, so we had little to apprehend on his account. Augustus went first up the vessel's side, and in a short while I followed him, without being noticed by the men at work. We proceeded at once into the cabin, and found no person there. It was fitted up in the most comfortable style — a thing somewhat unusual in a whaling-vessel. There were four very excellent staterooms, with wide and convenient berths. There was also a large stove, I took notice, and a remarkably thick and valuable carpet covering the floor of both the cabin and staterooms. The ceiling was full seven feet high, and, in short, every thing appeared of a more roomy and agreeable nature than I had anticipated. Augustus, however, would allow me but little time for observation, insisting upon the necessity of my concealing myself as soon as possible. He led the way into his own stateroom, which was on the starboard side of the brig, and next to the bulkheads. Upon entering, he closed the door and bolted it. I thought I had never seen a nicer little room than the one in which I now found myself. It was about ten feet long, and had only one berth, which, as I said before, was wide and convenient. In that portion of the closet nearest the bulkheads there was a space of four feet square, containing a table, a chair, and a set of hanging shelves full of books, chiefly books of voyages and travels. There were many other little comforts in the room, among which I ought not to forget a kind of safe or refrigerator,

in which Augustus pointed out to me a host of delicacies, both in the eating and drinking department.

He now pressed with his knuckles upon a certain spot of the carpet in one corner of the space just mentioned, letting me know that a portion of the flooring, about sixteen inches square, had been neatly cut out and again adjusted. As he pressed, this portion rose up at one end sufficiently to allow the passage of his finger beneath. In this manner he raised the mouth of the trap (to which the carpet was still fastened by tacks), and I found that it led into the after hold. He next lit a small taper by means of a phosphorous match, and, placing the light in a dark lantern, descended with it through the opening, bidding me follow. I did so, and he then pulled the cover upon the hole, by means of a nail driven into the under side — the carpet, of course, resuming its original position on the floor of the stateroom, and all traces of the aperture being concealed.

The taper gave out so feeble a ray that it was with the greatest difficulty I could grope my way through the confused mass of lumber among which I now found myself. By degrees, however, my eyes became accustomed to the gloom, and I proceeded with less trouble, holding on to the skirts of my friend's coat. He brought me, at length, after creeping and winding through innumerable narrow passages, to an iron-bound box, such as is used sometimes for packing fine earthenware. It was nearly four feet high, and full six long, but very narrow. Two large empty oil-casks lay on the top of it, and above these, again, a vast quantity of straw matting, piled up as high as the floor of the cabin. In every other direction around was wedged as closely as possible, even up to the ceiling, a complete chaos of almost every species of ship-furniture, together with a heterogeneous medley of crates, hampers, barrels, and bales, so that it seemed a matter no less than miraculous that we had discovered any passage at all to the box. I afterward found that Augustus had purposely arranged the stowage in this hold with a view to affording me a thorough concealment, having had only one assistant in the labour, a man not going out in the brig.

My companion now showed me that one of the ends of the box could be removed at pleasure. He slipped it aside and displayed the interior, at which I was excessively amused. A mattress from one of the cabin berths covered the whole of its bottom, and it contained almost every article of mere comfort which could be crowded into so small a space, allowing me, at the same time, sufficient room for my accommodation, either in a sitting position or lying at full length. Among other things, there were some books, pen, ink, and paper, three blankets, a large jug full of water, a keg of sea-biscuit, three or four immense Bologna sausages, an enormous ham, a cold leg of roast mutton, and half a dozen bottles of cordials and liqueurs. I proceeded immediately to take possession of my little apartment, and this with feelings of higher satisfaction, I am sure, than

any monarch ever experienced upon entering a new palace. Augustus now pointed out to me the method of fastening the open end of the box, and then, holding the taper close to the deck, showed me a piece of dark whipcord lying along it. This, he said, extended from my hiding-place throughout all the necessary windings among the lumber, to a nail which was driven into the deck of the hold, immediately beneath the trap-door leading into his stateroom. By means of this cord I should be enabled readily to trace my way out without his guidance, provided any unlooked-for accident should render such a step necessary. He now took his departure, leaving with me the lantern, together with a copious supply of tapers and phosphorous, and promising to pay me a visit as often as he could contrive to do so without observation. This was on the seventeenth of June.

I remained three days and nights (as nearly as I could guess) in my hiding-place without getting out of it at all, except twice for the purpose of stretching my limbs by standing erect between two crates just opposite the opening. During the whole period I saw nothing of Augustus; but this occasioned me little uneasiness, as I knew the brig was expected to put to sea every hour, and in the bustle he would not easily find opportunities of coming down to me. At length I heard the trap open and shut, and presently he called in a low voice; asking if all was well, and if there was any thing I wanted. "Nothing," I replied; "I am as comfortable as can be; when will the brig sail?" "She will be under weigh in less than half an hour," he answered. "I came to let you know, and for fear you should be uneasy at my absence. I shall not have a chance of coming down again for some time — perhaps for three or four days more. All is going on right aboveboard. After I go up and close the trap, do you creep along by the whipcord to where the nail is driven in. You will find my watch there — it may be useful to you, as you have no daylight to keep time by. I suppose you can't tell how long you have been buried — only three days — this is the twentieth. I would bring the watch to your box, but am afraid of being missed." With this he went up.

In about an hour after he had gone I distinctly felt the brig in motion, and congratulated myself upon having at length fairly commenced a voyage. Satisfied with this idea, I determined to make my mind as easy as possible, and await the course of events until I should be permitted to exchange the box for the more roomy, although hardly more comfortable, accommodations of the cabin. My first care was to get the watch. Leaving the taper burning, I groped along in the dark, following the cord through windings innumerable, in some of which I discovered that, after toiling a long distance, I was brought back within a foot or two of a former position. At length I reached the nail, and securing the object of my journey, returned with it in safety. I now looked over the books which had been so thoughtfully provided, and selected the expedition of Lewis and Clarke to the mouth of the Colum-

bia. With this I amused myself for some time, when, growing sleepy, I extinguished the light with great care, and soon fell into a sound slumber.

Upon awakening I felt strangely confused in mind, and some time elapsed before I could bring to recollection all the various circumstances of my situation. By degrees, however, I remembered all. Striking a light, I looked at the watch; but it was run down, and there were, consequently, no means of determining how long I slept. My limbs were greatly cramped, and I was forced to relieve them by standing between the crates. Presently feeling an almost ravenous appetite, I bethought myself of the cold mutton, some of which I had eaten just before going to sleep, and found excellent. What was my astonishment in discovering it to be in a state of absolute putrefaction! This circumstance occasioned me great disquietude; for, connecting it with the disorder of mind I experienced upon awakening, I began to suppose that I must have slept for an inordinately long period of time. The close atmosphere of the hold might have had something to do with this, and might, in the end, be productive of the most serious results. My head ached excessively; I fancied that I drew every breath with difficulty; and, in short, I was oppressed with a multitude of gloomy feelings. Still I could not venture to make any disturbance by opening the trap or otherwise, and, having wound up the watch, contented myself as well as possible.

Throughout the whole of the next tedious twenty-four hours no person came to my relief, and I could not help accusing Augustus of the grossest inattention. What alarmed me chiefly was, that the water in my jug was reduced to about half a pint, and I was suffering much from thirst, having eaten freely of the Bologna sausages after the loss of my mutton. I became very uneasy, and could no longer take any interest in my books. I was overpowered, too, with a desire to sleep, yet trembled at the thought of indulging it, lest there might exist some pernicious influence, like that of burning charcoal, in the confined air of the hold. In the meantime the roll of the brig told me that we were far in the main ocean, and a dull humming sound, which reached my ears as if from an immense distance, convinced me no ordinary gale was blowing. I could not imagine a reason for the absence of Augustus. We were surely far enough advanced on our voyage to allow of my going up. Some accident might have happened to him — but I could think of none which would account for his suffering me to remain so long a prisoner, except, indeed, his having suddenly died or fallen overboard, and upon this idea I could not dwell with any degree of patience. It was possible that we had been baffled by head winds, and were still in the near vicinity of Nantucket. This notion, however, I was forced to abandon; for such being the case, the brig must have frequently gone about; and I was entirely satisfied, from her continual inclination to the larboard, that she had been sailing all along with a steady breeze on her starboard

quarter. Besides, granting that we were still in the neighborhood of the
island, why should not Augustus have visited me and informed me of
the circumstance? Pondering in this manner upon the difficulties of my
solitary and cheerless condition, I resolved to wait yet another twenty-
four hours, when, if no relief were obtained, I would make my way to
the trap, and endeavour either to hold a parley with my friend, or get at
least a little fresh air through the opening, and a further supply of water
from the stateroom. While occupied with this thought, however, I fell,
in spite of every exertion to the contrary, into a state of profound sleep,
or rather stupor. My dreams were of the most terrific description. Every
species of calamity and horror befell me. Among other miseries I was
smothered to death between huge pillows, by demons of the most ghastly
and ferocious aspect. Immense serpents held me in their embrace, and
looked earnestly in my face with their fearfully shining eyes. Then
deserts, limitless, and of the most forlorn and awe-inspiring character,
spread themselves out before me. Immensely tall trunks of trees, gray
and leafless, rose up in endless succession as far as the eye could reach.
Their roots were concealed in wide-spreading morasses, whose dreary
water lay intensely black, still, and altogether terrible, beneath. And
the strange trees seemed endowed with a human vitality, and waving to
and fro their skeleton arms, were crying to the silent waters for mercy,
in the shrill and piercing accents of the most acute agony and despair.
The scene changed; and I stood, naked and alone, amidst the burning
sand-plains of Sahara. At my feet lay crouched a fierce lion of the tropics.
Suddenly his wild eyes opened and fell upon me. With a conculsive
bound he sprang to his feet, and laid bare his horrible teeth. In another
instant there burst from his red throat a roar like the thunder of the
firmament, and I fell impetuously to the earth. Stifling in a paroxysm of
terror, I at last found myself partially awake. My dream, then, was not
all a dream. Now, at least, I was in possession of my senses. The paws
of some huge and real monster were pressing heavily upon my bosom —
his hot breath was in my ear — and his white and ghastly fangs were
gleaming upon me through the gloom.

Had a thousand lives hung upon the movement of a limb or the ut-
terance of a syllable, I could have neither stirred nor spoken. The beast,
whatever it was, retained his position without attempting any immedi-
ate violence, while I lay in an utterly helpless, and, I fancied, a dying
condition beneath him. I felt that my powers of body and mind were
fast leaving me — in a word, that I was perishing, and perishing of sheer
fright. My brain swam — I grew deadly sick — my vision failed — even
the glaring eyeballs above me grew dim. Making a last strong effort, I
at length breathed a faint ejaculation to God, and resigned myself to
die. The sound of my voice seemed to arouse all the latent fury of the
animal. He precipitated himself at full length upon my body; but what
was my astonishment, when, with a long and low whine, he commenced

licking my face and hands with the greatest eagerness, and with the most extravagant demonstration of affection and joy! I was bewildered, utterly lost in amazement — but I could not forget the peculiar whine of my Newfoundland dog Tiger, and the odd manner of his caresses I well knew. It was he. I experienced a sudden rush of blood to my temples — a giddy and overpowering sense of deliverance and reanimation. I rose hurriedly from the mattress upon which I had been lying, and, throwing myself upon the neck of my faithful follower and friend, relieved the long oppression of my bosom in a flood of the most passionate tears.

As upon a former occasion my conceptions were in a state of the greatest indistinctness and confusion after leaving the mattress. For a long time I found it nearly impossible to connect any ideas; but, by very slow degrees, my thinking faculties returned, and I again called to memory the several incidents of my condition. For the presence of Tiger I tried in vain to account; and after busying myself with a thousand different conjectures respecting him, was forced to content myself with rejoicing that he was with me to share my dreary solitude, and render me comfort by his caresses. Most people love their dogs, but for Tiger I had an affection far more ardent than common; and never, certainly, did any creature more truly deserve it. For seven years he had been my inseparable companion, and in a multitude of instances had given evidence of all the noble qualities for which we value the animal. I had rescued him, when a puppy, from the clutches of a malignant little villain in Nantucket who was leading him, with a rope around his neck, to the water; and the grown dog repaid the obligation, about three years afterward, by saving me from the bludgeon of a street robber.

Getting now hold of the watch, I found, upon applying it to my ear, that it had again run down; but at this I was not at all surprised, being convinced, from the peculiar state of my feelings, that I had slept, as before, for a very long period of time; how long, it was of course impossible to say. I was burning up with fever, and my thirst was almost intolerable. I felt about the box for my little remaining supply of water, for I had no light, the taper having burnt to the socket of the lantern, and the phosphorus-box not coming readily to hand. Upon finding the jug, however, I discovered it to be empty — Tiger, no doubt, having been tempted to drink it, as well as to devour the remnant of mutton, the bone of which lay, well picked, by the opening of the box. The spoiled meat I could well spare, but my heart sank as I thought of the water. I was feeble in the extreme — so much so that I shook all over, as with an ague, at the slightest movement or exertion. To add to my troubles, the brig was pitching and rolling with great violence, and the oil-casks which lay upon my box were in momentary danger of falling down, so as to block up the only way of ingress or egress. I felt, also, terrible sufferings from sea-sickness. These considerations determined me to make my way, at all hazards, to the trap, and obtain immediate relief, before

I should be incapacitated from doing so altogether. Having come to this resolve, I again felt about for the phosphorus-box and tapers. The former I found after some little trouble; but, not discovering the tapers as soon as I had expected (for I remembered very nearly the spot in which I had placed them), I gave up the search for the present, and bidding Tiger lie quiet, began at once my journey toward the trap.

In this attempt my great feebleness became more than ever apparent. It was with the utmost difficulty I could crawl along at all, and very frequently my limbs sank suddenly from beneath me; when, falling prostrate on my face, I would remain for some minutes in a state bordering on insensibility. Still I struggled forward by slow degrees, dreading every moment that I should swoon amid the narrow and intricate windings of the lumber, in which event I had nothing but death to expect as the result. At length, upon making a push forward with all the energy I could command, I struck my forehead violently against the sharp corner of an iron-bound crate. The accident only stunned me for a few moments; but I found, to my inexpressible grief, that the quick and violent roll of the vessel had thrown the crate entirely across my path, so as effectually to block up the passage. With my utmost exertions I could not move it a single inch from its position, it being closely wedged in among the surrounding boxes and ship-furniture. It became necessary, therefore, enfeebled as I was, either to leave the guidance of the whip-cord and seek out a new passage, or to climb over the obstacle, and resume the path on the other side. The former alternative presented too many difficulties and dangers to be thought of without a shudder. In my present weak state of both mind and body, I should infallibly lose my way if I attempted it, and perish miserably amid the dismal and disgusting labyrinths of the hold. I proceeded, therefore, without hesitation, to summon up all my remaining strength and fortitude, and endeavour, as I best might, to clamber over the crate.

Upon standing erect, with this end in view, I found the undertaking even a more serious task than my fears had led me to imagine. On each side of the narrow passage arose a complete wall of various heavy lumber, which the least blunder on my part might be the means of bringing down upon my head; or, if this accident did not occur, the path might be effectually blocked up against my return by the descending mass, as it was in front by the obstacle there. The crate itself was a long and unwieldy box, upon which no foothold could be obtained. In vain I attempted, by every means in my power, to reach the top, with the hope of being thus enabled to draw myself up. Had I succeeded in reaching it, it is certain that my strength would have proved utterly inadequate to the task of getting over, and it was better in every respect that I failed. At length, in a desperate effort to force the crate from its ground, I felt a strong vibration in the side next me. I thrust my hand eagerly to the edge of the planks, and found that a very large one was loose. With my

pocket-knife, which, luckily, I had with me, I succeeded, after great labour, in prying it entirely off; and getting it through the aperture, discovered, to my exceeding joy, that there were no boards on the opposite side — in other words, that the top was wanting, it being the bottom through which I had forced my way. I now met with no important difficulty in proceeding along the line until I finally reached the nail. With a beating heart I stood erect, and with a gentle touch pressed against the cover of the trap. It did not rise as soon as I had expected, and I pressed it with somewhat more determination, still dreading lest some other person than Augustus might be in his state-room. The door, however, to my astonishment, remained steady, and I became somewhat uneasy, for I knew that it had formerly required but little or no effort to remove it. I pushed it strongly — it was nevertheless firm: with all my strength — it still did not give way: with rage, with fury, with despair — it set at defiance my utmost efforts; and it was evident, from the unyielding nature of the resistance, that the hole had either been discovered and effectually nailed up, or that some immense weight had been placed upon it, which it was useless to think of removing.

My sensations were those of extreme horror and dismay. In vain I attempted to reason on the probable cause of my being thus entombed. I could summon up no connected chain of reflection, and, sinking on the floor, gave way, unresistingly, to the most gloomy imaginings, in which the dreadful deaths of thirst, famine, suffocation, and premature interment crowded upon me as the prominent disasters to be encountered. At length there returned to me some portion of presence of mind. I arose, and felt with my fingers for the seams or cracks of the aperture. Having found them, I examined them closely to ascertain if they emitted any light from the state-room; but none was visible. I then forced the blade of my pen-knife through them, until I met with some hard obstacle. Scraping against it, I discovered it to be a solid mass of iron, which, from its peculiar wavy feel as I passed the blade along it, I concluded to be a chain-cable. The only course now left me was to retrace my way to the box, and there either yield to my sad fate, or try so to tranquilize my mind as to admit of my arranging some plan of escape. I immediately set about the attempt, and succeeded, after innumerable difficulties, in getting back. As I sank, utterly exhausted, upon the mattress, Tiger threw himself at full length by my side, and seemed as if desirous, by his caresses, of consoling me in my troubles, and urging me to bear them with fortitude.

The singularity of his behavior at length forcibly arrested my attention. After licking my face and hands for some minutes, he would suddenly cease doing so, and utter a low whine. Upon reaching out my hand toward him, I then invariably found him lying on his back, with his paws uplifted. This conduct, so frequently repeated, appeared strange, and I could in no manner account for it. As the dog seemed distressed,

I concluded that he had received some injury; and, taking his paws in my hands, I examined them one by one, but found no sign of any hurt. I then supposed him hungry, and gave him a large piece of ham, which he devoured with avidity — afterward, however, resuming his extraordinary manœuvres. I now imagined that he was suffering, like myself, the torments of thirst, and was about adopting this conclusion as the true one, when the idea occurred to me that I had as yet only examined his paws, and that there might possibly be a wound upon some portion of his body or head. The latter I felt carefully over, but found nothing. On passing my hand, however, along his back, I perceived a slight erection of the hair extending completely across it. Probing this with my finger, I discovered a string, and tracing it up, found that it encircled the whole body. Upon a closer scrutiny, I came across a small slip of what had the feeling of letter paper, through which the string had been fastened in such a manner as to bring it immediately beneath the left shoulder of the animal.

CHAPTER III

The thought instantly occurred to me that the paper was a note from Augustus, and that some unaccountable accident having happened to prevent his relieving me from my dungeon, he had devised this method of acquainting me with the true state of affairs. Trembling with eagerness, I now commenced another search for my phosphorus matches and tapers. I had a confused recollection of having put them carefully away just before falling asleep; and, indeed, previously to my last journey to the trap, I had been able to remember the exact spot where I had deposited them. But now I endeavored in vain to call it to mind, and busied myself for a full hour in a fruitless and vexatious search for the missing articles; never, surely, was there a more tantalizing state of anxiety and suspense. At length, while groping about, with my head close to the ballast, near the opening of the box, and outside of it, I perceived a faint glimmering of light in the direction of the steerage. Greatly surprised, I endeavored to make my way toward it, as it appeared to be but a few feet from my position. Scarcely had I moved with this intention, when I lost sight of the glimmer entirely, and, before I could bring it into view again, was obliged to feel along by the box until I had exactly resumed my original situation. Now, moving my head with caution to and fro, I found that, by proceeding slowly, with great care, in an opposite direction to that in which I had at first started, I was enabled to draw near the light, still keeping it in view. Presently I came directly upon it (having squeezed my way through innumerable narrow windings), and found that it proceeded from some fragments of my matches lying in an empty barrel turned upon its side. I was wondering how they came in such a place, when my hand fell upon two or three pieces of taper wax, which had been evidently mumbled by the dog. I concluded at

once that he had devoured the whole of my supply of candles, and I felt hopeless of being ever able to read the note of Augustus. The small remnants of the wax were so mashed up among other rubbish in the barrel, that I despaired of deriving any service from them, and left them as they were. The phosphorus, of which there was only a speck or two, I gathered up as well as I could, and returned with it, after much difficulty, to my box, where Tiger had all the while remained.

What to do next I could not tell. The hold was so intensely dark that I could not see my hand, however close I would hold it to my face. The white slip of paper could barely be discerned, and not even that when I looked at it directly; by turning the exterior portions of the retina toward it — that is to say, by surveying it slightly askance, I found that it became in some measure perceptible. Thus the gloom of my prison may be imagined, and the note of my friend, if indeed it were a note from him, seemed only likely to throw me into further trouble, by disquieting to no purpose my already enfeebled and agitated mind. In vain I revolved in my brain a multitude of absurd expedients for procuring light — such expedients precisely as a man in the perturbed sleep occasioned by opium would be apt to fall upon for a similar purpose — each and all of which appear by turns to the dreamer the most reasonable and the most preposterous of conceptions, just as the reasoning or imaginative faculties flicker, alternately, one above the other. At last an idea occurred to me which seemed rational, and which gave me cause to wonder, very justly, that I had not entertained it before. I placed the slip of paper on the back of a book, and, collecting the fragments of the phosporus matches which I had brought from the barrel, laid them together upon the paper. I then, with the palm of my hand, rubbed the whole over quickly, yet steadily. A clear light diffused itself immediately throughout the whole surface; and had there been any writing upon it, I should not have experienced the least difficulty, I am sure, in reading it. Not a syllable was there, however — nothing but a dreary and unsatisfactory blank; the illumination died away in a few seconds, and my heart died away within me as it went.

I have before stated more than once that my intellect, for some period prior to this, had been in a condition nearly bordering on idiocy. There were, to be sure, momentary intervals of perfect sanity, and, now and then, even of energy; but these were few. It must be remembered that I had been, for many days certainly, inhaling the almost pestilential atmosphere of a close hold in a whaling vessel, and for a long portion of that time but scantily supplied with water. For the last fourteen or fifteen hours I had none — nor had I slept during that time. Salt provisions of the most exciting kind had been my chief, and, indeed, since the loss of the mutton, my only supply of food, with the exception of the sea-biscuit; and these latter were utterly useless to me, as they were too dry and hard to be swallowed in the swollen and parched condition

of my throat. I was now in a high state of fever, and in every respect exceedingly ill. This will account for the fact that many miserable hours of despondency elapsed after my last adventure with the phosphorus, before the thought suggested itself that I had examined only one side of the paper. I shall not attempt to describe my feelings of rage (for I believe I was more angry than any thing else) when the egregious oversight I had committed flashed suddenly upon my perception. The blunder itself would have been unimportant, had not my own folly and impetuosity rendered it otherwise — in my disappointment at not finding some words upon the slip, I had childishly torn it in pieces and thrown it away, it was impossible to say where.

From the worst part of this dilemma I was relieved by the sagacity of Tiger. Having got, after a long search, a small piece of the note, I put it to the dog's nose, and endeavored to make him understand that he must bring me the rest of it. To my astonishment, (for I had taught him none of the usual tricks for which his breed are famous,) he seemed to enter at once into my meaning, and, rummaging about for a few moments, soon found another considerable portion. Bringing me this, he paused awhile, and, rubbing his nose against my hand, appeared to be waiting for my approval of what he had done. I patted him on the head, when he immediately made off again. It was now some minutes before he came back — but when he did come, he brought with him a large slip, which proved to be all the paper missing — it having been torn, it seems, only into three pieces. Luckily, I had no trouble in finding what few fragments of the phosphorus were left — being guided by the indistinct glow one or two of the particles still emitted. My difficulties had taught me the necessity of caution, and I now took time to reflect upon what I was about to do. It was very probable, I considered, that some words were written upon that side of the paper which had not been examined — but which side was that? Fitting the pieces together gave me no clew in this respect, although it assured me that the words (if there were any) would be found all on one side, and connected in a proper manner, as written. There was the greater necessity of ascertaining the point in question beyond a doubt, as the phosphorus remaining would be altogether insufficient for a third attempt, should I fail in the one I was now about to make. I placed the paper on a book as before, and sat for some minutes thoughtfully revolving the matter over in my mind. At last I thought it barely possible that the written side might have some unevenness on its surface, which a delicate sense of feeling might enable me to detect. I determined to make the experiment, and passed my finger very carefully over the side which first presented itself. Nothing, however, was perceptible, and I turned the paper, adjusting it on the book. I now again carried my forefinger cautiously along, when I was aware of an exceedingly slight, but still discernible glow, which followed as it proceeded. This, I knew, must arise from some very minute remaining

Arthur Gordon Pym

particles of the phosphorus with which I had covered the paper in my previous attempt. The other, or under side, then, was that on which lay the writing, if writing there should finally prove to be. Again I turned the note, and went to work as I had previously done. Having rubbed in the phosphorus, a brilliancy ensued as before — but this time several lines of MS. in a large hand, and apparently in red ink, became distinctly visible. The glimmer, although sufficiently bright, was but momentary. Still, had I not been too greatly excited, there would have been ample time enough for me to peruse the whole three sentences before me — for I saw there were three. In my anxiety, however, to read all at once, I succeeded only in reading the seven concluding words, which thus appeared — "*blood — your life depends upon lying close.*"

Had I been able to ascertain the entire contents of the note — the full meaning of the admonition which my friend had thus attempted to convey, that admonition, even although it should have revealed a story of disaster the most unspeakable, could not, I am firmly convinced, have imbued my mind with one tithe of the harrowing and yet indefinable horror with which I was inspired by the fragmentary warning thus received. And '*blood*," too, that word of all words — so rife at all times with mystery, and suffering, and terror — how trebly full of import did it now appear — how chilly and heavily (disjointed, as it thus was, from any foregoing words to qualify or render it distinct) did its vague syllables fall, amid the deep gloom of my prison, into the innermost recesses of my soul!

Augustus had, undoubtedly, good reasons for wishing me to remain concealed, and I formed a thousand surmises as to what they could be — but I could think of nothing affording a satisfactory solution of the mystery. Just after returning from my last journey to the trap, and before my attention had been otherwise directed by the singular conduct of Tiger, I had come to the resolution of making myself heard at all events by those on board, or, if I could not succeed in this directly, of trying to cut my way through the orlop deck. The half certainty which I felt of being able to accomplish one of these two purposes in the last emergency, had given me courage (which I should not otherwise have had) to endure the evils of my situation. The few words I had been able to read, however, had cut me off from these final resources, and I now, for the first time, felt all the misery of my fate. In a paroxysm of despair I threw myself again upon the mattress, where, for about the period of a day and night, I lay in a kind of stupor, relieved only by momentary intervals of reason and recollection.

At length I once more arose, and busied myself in reflection upon the horrors which encompassed me. For another twenty-four hours it was barely possible that I might exist without water — for a longer time I could not do so. During the first portion of my imprisonment I had made free use of the cordials with which Augustus had supplied me, but

they only served to excite fever, without in the least degree assuaging my thirst. I had now only about a gill left, and this was of a species of strong peach liqueur at which my stomach revolted. The sausages were entirely consumed; of the ham nothing remained but a small piece of the skin; and all the biscuit, except a few fragments of one, had been eaten by Tiger. To add to my troubles, I found that my headache was increasing momentarily, and with it the species of delirium which had distressed me more or less since my first falling asleep. For some hours past it had been with the greatest difficulty I could breathe at all, and now each attempt at so doing was attended with the most depressing spasmodic action of the chest. But there was still another and very different source of disquietude, and one, indeed, whose harassing terrors had been the chief means of arousing me to exertion from my stupor on the mattress. It arose from the demeanor of the dog.

I first observed an alteration in his conduct while rubbing in the phosphorus on the paper in my last attempt. As I rubbed, he ran his nose against my hand with a slight snarl; but I was too greatly excited at the time to pay much attention to the circumstance. Soon afterward, it will be remembered, I threw myself on the mattress, and fell into a species of lethargy. Presently I became aware of a singular hissing sound close at my ears, and discovered it to proceed from Tiger, who was panting and wheezing in a state of the greatest apparent excitement, his eyeballs flashing fiercely through the gloom. I spoke to him, when he replied with a low growl, and then remained quiet. Presently I relapsed into my stupor, from which I was again awakened in a similar manner. This was repeated three or four times, until finally his behaviour inspired me with so great a degree of fear, that I became fully aroused. He was now lying close by the door of the box, snarling fearfully, although in a kind of undertone, and grinding his teeth as if strongly convulsed. I had no doubt whatever that the want of water or the confined atmosphere of the hold had driven him mad, and I was at a loss what course to pursue. I could not endure the thought of killing him, yet it seemed absolutely necessary for my own safety. I could distinctly perceive his eyes fastened upon me with an expression of the most deadly animosity, and I expected every instant that he would attack me. At last I could endure my terrible situation no longer, and determined to make my way from the box at all hazards, and dispatch him, if his opposition should render it necessary for me to do so. To get out, I had to pass directly over his body, and he already seemed to anticipate my design — raising himself upon his forelegs (as I perceived by the altered position of his eyes), and displayed the whole of his white fangs, which were easily discernible. I took the remains of the ham-skin, and the bottle containing the liqueur, and secured them about my person, together with a large carving-knife which Augustus had left me — then, folding my cloak around me as closely as possible, I made a movement toward the mouth of the box. No sooner

did I do this, than the dog sprang with a loud growl toward my throat. The whole weight of his body struck me on the right shoulder, and I fell violently to the left, while the enraged animal passed entirely over me. I had fallen upon my knees, with my head buried among the blankets, and these protected me from a second furious assault, during which I felt the sharp teeth pressing vigorously upon the woollen which enveloped my neck — yet, luckily, without being able to penetrate all the folds. I was now beneath the dog, and a few moments would place me completely in his power. Despair gave me strength, and I rose boldly up, shaking him from me by main force, and dragging with me the blankets from the mattress. These I now threw over him, and before he could extricate himself, I had got through the door and closed it effectually against his pursuit. In this struggle, however, I had been forced to drop the morsel of ham-skin, and I now found my whole stock of provisions reduced to a single gill of liqueur. As this reflection crossed my mind, I felt myself actuated by one of those fits of perverseness which might be supposed to influence a spoiled child in similar circumstances, and, raising the bottle to my lips, I drained it to the last drop, and dashed it furiously upon the floor.

Scarcely had the echo of the crash died away, when I heard my name pronounced in an eager but subdued voice, issuing from the direction of the steerage. So unexpected was anything of the kind, and so intense was the emotion excited within me by the sound, that I endeavoured in vain to reply. My powers of speech totally failed, and in an agony of terror lest my friend should conclude me dead, and return without attempting to reach me, I stood up between the crates near the door of the box, trembling convulsively, and gasping and struggling for utterance. Had a thousand words depended upon a syllable, I could not have spoken it. There was a slight movement now audible among the lumber somewhere forward of my station. The sound presently grew less distinct, then again less so, and still less. Shall I ever forget my feelings at this moment? He was going — my friend, my companion, from whom I had a right to expect so much — he was going — he would abandon me — he was gone! He would leave me to perish miserably, to expire in the most horrible and loathesome of dungeons — and one word, one little syllable, would save me — yet that single syllable I could not utter! I felt, I am sure, more than ten thousand times the agonies of death itself. My brain reeled, and I fell, deadly sick, against the end of the box.

As I fell, the carving-knife was shaken out from the waist-band of my pantaloons, and dropped with a rattling sound to the floor. Never did any strain of the richest melody come so sweetly to my ears! With the intensest anxiety I listened to ascertain the effect of the noise upon Augustus — for I knew that the person who called my name could be no one but himself. All was silent for some moments. At length I again heard the word "Arthur!" repeated in a low tone, and one full of hesi-

tation. Reviving hope loosened at once my powers of speech, and I now
screamed at the top of my voice, "*Augustus! oh, Augustus!*" "Hush! for
God's sake be silent!" he replied, in a voice trembling with agitation;
"I will be with you immediately — as soon as I can make my way through
the hold." For a long time I heard him moving among the lumber, and
every moment seemed to me an age. At length I felt his hand upon my
shoulder, and he placed, at the same moment, a bottle of water to my
lips. Those only who have been suddenly redeemed from the jaws of the
tomb, or who have known the insufferable torments of thirst under cir-
cumstances as aggravated as those which encompassed me in my dreary
prison, can form any idea of the unutterable transports which that one
long draught of the richest of all physical luxuries afforded.

When I had in some degree satisfied my thirst, Augustus produced
from his pocket three or four boiled potatoes, which I devoured with the
greatest avidity. He had brought with him a light in a dark lantern, and
the grateful rays afforded me scarcely less comfort than the food and
drink. But I was impatient to learn the cause of his protracted absence,
and he proceeded to recount what had happened on board during my
incarceration.

CHAPTER IV

The brig put to sea, as I had supposed, in about an hour after he had
left the watch. This was on the twentieth of June. It will be remembered
that I had then been in the hold for three days; and, during this period,
there was so constant a bustle on board, and so much running to and
fro, especially in the cabin and staterooms, that he had had no chance
of visiting me without the risk of having the secret of the trap discovered.
When at length he did come, I had assured him that I was doing as well
as possible; and, therefore, for the two next days he felt but little uneasi-
ness on my account — still, however, watching an opportunity of going
down. It was not *until the fourth day* that he found one. Several times
during this interval he had made up his mind to let his father know of
the adventure, and have me come up at once; but we were still within
reaching distance of Nantucket, and it was doubtful, from some expres-
sions which had escaped Captain Barnard, whether he would not im-
mediately put back if he discovered me to be on board. Besides, upon
thinking the matter over, Augustus, so he told me, could not imagine
that I was in immediate want, or that I would hesitate, in such case, to
make myself heard at the trap. When, therefore, he considered every-
thing he concluded to let me stay until he could meet with an oppor-
tunity of visiting me unobserved. This, as I said before, did not occur
until the fourth day after his bringing me the watch, and the seventh
since I had first entered the hold. He then went down without taking
with him any water or provisions, intending in the first place merely
to call my attention, and get me to come from the box to the trap, —

when he would go up to the stateroom and thence hand me down a supply. When he descended for this purpose he found that I was asleep, for it seems that I was snoring very loudly. From all the calculations I can make on the subject, this must have been the slumber into which I fell just after my return from the trap with the watch, and which, consequently, must have lasted *for more than three entire days and nights* at the very least. Latterly, I have had reason both from my own experience and the assurance of others, to be acquainted with the strong soporific effects of the stench arising from old fish-oil when closely confined; and when I think of the condition of the hold in which I was imprisoned, and the long period during which the brig had been used as a whaling vessel, I am more inclined to wonder that I awoke at all, after once falling asleep, than that I should have slept uninterruptedly for the period specified above.

Augustus called to me at first in a low voice and without closing the trap — but I made him no reply. He then shut the trap, and spoke to me in a louder, and finally in a very loud tone — still I continued to snore. He was now at a loss what to do. It would take him some time to make his way through the lumber to my box, and in the meanwhile his absence would be noticed by Captain Barnard, who had occasion for his services every minute, in arranging and copying papers connected with the business of the voyage. He determined, therefore, upon reflection, to ascend, and await another opportunity of visiting me. He was the more easily induced to this resolve, as my slumber appeared to be of the most tranquil nature, and he could not suppose that I had undergone any inconvenience from my incarceration. He had just made up his mind on these points when his attention was arrested by an unusual bustle, the sound of which proceeded apparently from the cabin. He sprang through the trap as quickly as possible, closed it, and threw open the door of his stateroom. No sooner had he put his foot over the threshold than a pistol flashed in his face, and he was knocked down, at the same moment, by a blow from a handspike.

A strong hand held him on the cabin floor, with a tight grasp upon his throat; still he was able to see what was going on around him. His father was tied hand and foot, and lying along the steps of the companion-way, with his head down, and a deep wound in the forehead, from which the blood was flowing in a continued stream. He spoke not a word, and was apparently dying. Over him stood the first mate, eyeing him with an expression of fiendish derision, and deliberately searching his pockets, from which he presently drew forth a large wallet and a chronometer. Seven of the crew (among whom was the cook, a negro) were rummaging the staterooms on the larboard for arms, where they soon equipped themselves with muskets and ammunition. Besides Augustus and Captain Barnard, there were nine men altogether in the cabin, and these among the most ruffianly of the brig's company. The villains now went

upon deck, taking my friend with them after having secured his arms behind his back. They proceeded straight to the forecastle, which was fastened down — two of the mutineers standing by it with axes — two also at the main hatch. The mate called out in a loud voice: "Do you hear there below? tumble up with you, one by one — now, mark that — and no grumbling!" It was some minutes before any one appeared: — at last an Englishman, who had shipped as a raw hand, came up, weeping piteously, and entreating the mate, in the most humble manner, to spare his life. The only reply was a blow on the forehead from an axe. The poor fellow fell to the deck without a groan, and the black cook lifted him up in his arms as he would a child, and tossed him deliberately into the sea. Hearing the blow and the plunge of the body, the men below could now be induced to venture on deck neither by threats nor promises, until a proposition was made to smoke them out. A general rush then ensued, and for a moment it seemed possible that the brig might be retaken. The mutineers, however, succeeded at last in closing the forecastle effectually before more than six of their opponents could get up. These six, finding themselves so greatly outnumbered and without arms, submitted after a brief struggle. The mate gave them fair words — no doubt with a view of inducing those below to yield, for they had no difficulty in hearing all that was said on deck. The result proved his sagacity, no less than his diabolical villainy. All in the forecastle presently signified their intention of submitting, and, ascending one by one, were pinioned and then thrown on their backs, together with the first six — there being in all, of the crew who were not concerned in the mutiny, twenty-seven.

A scene of the most horrible butchery ensued. The bound seamen were dragged to the gangway. Here the cook stood with an axe, striking each victim on the head as he was forced over the side of the vessel by the other mutineers. In this manner twenty-two perished, and Augustus had given himself up for lost, expecting every moment his own turn to come next. But it seemed that the villains were now either weary, or in some measure disgusted with their bloody labour; for the four remaining prisoners, together with my friend, who had been thrown on the deck with the rest, were respited while the mate sent below for rum, and the whole murderous party held a drunken carouse, which lasted until sunset. They now fell to disputing in regard to the fate of the survivers, who lay not more than four paces off, and could distinguish every word said. Upon some of the mutineers the liquor appeared to have a softening effect, for several voices were heard in favor of releasing the captives altogether, on condition of joining the mutiny and sharing the profits. The black cook, however (who in all respects was a perfect demon, and who seemed to exert as much influence, if not more, than the mate himself), would listen to no proposition of the kind, and rose repeatedly for the purpose of resuming his work at the gangway. Fortunately he was so far overcome by intoxication as to be easily restrained by the less bloodthirsty

of the party, among whom was a line-manager, who went by the name of Dirk Peters. This man was the son of an Indian squaw of the tribe of Upsarokas, who live among the fastnesses of the Black Hills, near the source of the Missouri. His father was a fur-trader, I believe, or at least connected in some manner with the Indian trading-posts on Lewis river. Peter himself was one of the most ferocious-looking men I ever beheld. He was short in stature, not more than four feet eight inches high, but his limbs were of Herculean mould. His hands, especially, were so enormously thick and broad as hardly to retain a human shape. His arms, as well as legs, were *bowed* in the most singular manner, and appeared to possess no flexibility whatever. His head was equally deformed, being of immense size, with an indentation on the crown (like that on the head of most negroes), and entirely bald. To conceal this latter deficiency, which did not proceed from old age, he usually wore a wig formed of any hair-like material which presented itself — occasionally the skin of a Spanish dog or American grizzly bear. At the time spoken of, he had on a portion of one of these bearskins; and it added no little to the natural ferocity of his countenance, which betook of the Upsaroka character. The mouth extended nearly from ear to ear; the lips were thin, and seemed, like some other portions of his frame, to be devoid of natural pliancy, so that the ruling expression never varied under the influence of any emotion whatever. This ruling expression may be conceived when it is considered that the teeth were exceedingly long and protruding, and never even partially covered, in any instance, by the lips. To pass this man with a casual glance, one might imagine him to be convulsed with laughter; but a second look would induce a shuddering acknowledgment, that if such an expression were indicative of merriment, the merriment must be that of a demon. Of this singular being many anecdotes were prevalent among the seafaring men of Nantucket. These anecdotes went to prove his prodigious strength when under excitement, and some of them had given rise to a doubt of his sanity. But on board the Grampus, it seems, he was regarded, at the time of the mutiny, with feelings more of derision than of anything else. I have been thus particular in speaking of Dirk Peters, because, ferocious as he appeared, he proved the main instrument in preserving the life of Augustus, and because I shall have frequent occasion to mention him hereafter in the course of my narrative — a narrative, let me here say, which, in its latter portions, will be found to include incidents of a nature so entirely out of the range of human experience, and for this reason so far beyond the limits of human credulity, that I proceed in utter hopelessness of obtaining credence for all that I shall tell, yet confidently trusting in time and progressing science to verify some of the most important and most improbable of my statements.

After much indecision and two or three violent quarrels, it was determined at last that all the prisoners (with the exception of Augustus, whom Peters insisted in a jocular manner upon keeping as his clerk)

should be set adrift in one of the smallest whaleboats. The mate went down into the cabin to see if Captain Barnard was still living — for, it will be remembered, he was left below when the mutineers came up. Presently the two made their appearance, the captain pale as death, but somewhat recovered from the effects of his wound. He spoke to the men in a voice hardly articulate, entreated them not to set him adrift, but to return to their duty, and promising to land them wherever they chose, and to take no steps for bringing them to justice. He might as well have spoken to the winds. Two of the ruffians seized him by the arms and hurled him over the brig's side into the boat, which had been lowered while the mate went below. The four men who were lying on the deck were then untied and ordered to follow, which they did without attempting any resistance — Augustus being still left in his painful position, although he struggled and prayed only for the poor satisfaction of being permitted to bid his father farewell. A handful of sea-biscuit and a jug of water were now handed down; but neither mast, sail, oar, nor compass. The boat was towed astern for a few minutes, during which the mutineers held another consultation — it was then finally cut adrift. By this time night had come on — there were neither moon nor stars visible — and a short and ugly sea was running, although there was no great deal of wind. The boat was instantly out of sight, and little hope could be entertained for the unfortunate sufferers who were in it. This event happened, however, in latitude 35° 30′ north, longitude 61° 20′ west, and consequently at no very great distance from the Bermuda Islands. Augustus therefore endeavored to console himself with the idea that the boat might either succeed in reaching the land, or come sufficiently near to be fallen in with by vessels off the coast.

All sail was now put upon the brig, and she continued her original course to the southwest — the mutineers being bent upon some piratical expedition, in which, from all that could be understood, a ship was to be intercepted on her way from the Cape Verd Islands to Porto Rico. No attention was paid to Augustus, who was untied and suffered to go about anywhere forward of the cabin companion-way. Dirk Peters treated him with some degree of kindness, and on one occasion saved him from the brutality of the cook. His situation was still one of the most precarious, as the men were continually intoxicated, and there was no relying upon their continued good-humor or carelessness in regard to himself. His anxiety on my account he represented, however, as the most distressing result of his condition; and, indeed, I had never reason to doubt the sincerity of his friendship. More than once he had resolved to acquaint the mutineers with the secret of my being on board, but was restrained from so doing, partly through recollection of the atrocities he had already beheld, and partly through a hope of being able soon to bring me relief. For the latter purpose he was constantly on the watch; but, in spite of the most constant vigilance, three days elapsed after the

boat was cut adrift before any chance occurred. At length, on the night of the third day, there came on a heavy blow from the eastward, and all hands were called up to take in sail. During the confusion which ensued, he made his way below unobserved, and into the stateroom. What was his grief and horror in discovering that the latter had been rendered a place of deposit for a variety of sea-stores and ship-furniture, and that several fathoms of old chain-cable, which had been stowed away beneath the companion-ladder, had been dragged thence to make room for a chest, and were now lying immediately upon the trap! To remove it without discovery was impossible, and he returned on deck as quickly as he could. As he came up, the mate seized him by the throat, and demanding what he had been doing in the cabin, was about flinging him over the larboard bulwark, when his life was again preserved through the interference of Dirk Peters. Augustus was now put in handcuffs (of which there were several pairs on board), and his feet lashed tightly together. He was then taken into the steerage, and thrown into a lower berth next to the forecastle bulkheads, with the assurance that he should never put his foot on deck again "until the brig was no longer a brig." This was the expression of the cook, who threw him into the berth — it is hardly possible to say what precise meaning was intended by the phrase. The whole affair, however, proved the ultimate means of my relief, as will presently appear.

CHAPTER V

For some minutes after the cook had left the forecastle, Augustus abandoned himself to despair, never hoping to leave the berth alive. He now came to the resolution of acquainting the first of the men who should come down with my situation, thinking it better to let me take my chance with the mutineers than perish of thirst in the hold, — for it had been ten days since I was first imprisoned, and my jug of water was not a plentiful supply even for four. As he was thinking on this subject, the idea came all at once into his head that it might be possible to communicate with me by the way of the main hold. In any other circumstances, the difficulty and hazard of the undertaking would have prevented him from attempting it; but now he had, at all events, little prospect of life, and consequently little to lose; he bent his whole mind, therefore, upon the task.

His handcuffs were the first consideration. At first he saw no method of removing them, and feared that he should thus be baffled in the very outset; but upon a closer scrutiny he discovered that the irons could be slipped off and on at pleasure, with very little effort or inconvenience, merely by squeezing his hands through them, — this species of manacle being altogether ineffectual in confining young persons, in whom the smaller bones readily yield to pressure. He now untied his feet, and, leaving the cord in such a manner that it could easily be readjusted in the

event of any person's coming down, proceeded to examine the bulkhead where it joined the berth. The partition here was of soft pine board, an inch thick, and he saw that he should have little trouble in cutting his way through. A voice was now heard at the forecastle companion-way, and he had just time to put his right hand into its handcuff (the left had not been removed) and to draw the rope in a slipknot around his ankle, when Dirk Peters came below, followed by Tiger, who immediately leaped into the berth and lay down. The dog had been brought on board by Augustus, who knew my attachment to the animal, and thought it would give me pleasure to have him with me during the voyage. He went up to our house for him immediately after first taking me into the hold, but did not think of mentioning the circumstance upon his bringing the watch. Since the mutiny, Augustus had not seen him before his appearance with Dirk Peters, and had given him up for lost, supposing him to have been thrown overboard by some of the malignant villains belonging to the mate's gang. It appeared afterward that he had crawled into a hole beneath a whale-boat, from which, not having room to turn round, he could not extricate himself. Peters at last let him out, and, with a species of good feeling which my friend knew well how to appreciate, had now brought him to him in the forecastle as a companion, leaving at the same time some salt junk and potatoes, with a can of water; he then went on deck, promising to come down with something more to eat on the next day.

When he had gone, Augustus freed both hands from the manacles and unfastened his feet. He then turned down the head of the mattress on which he had been lying, and with his penknife (for the ruffians had not thought it worth while to search him) commenced cutting vigorously across one of the partition planks, as closely as possible to the floor of the berth. He chose to cut here, because, if suddenly interrupted, he would be able to conceal what had been done by letting the head of the mattress fall into its proper position. For the remainder of the day, however, no disturbance occurred, and by night he had completely divided the plank. It should here be observed that none of the crew occupied the forecastle as a sleeping-place, living altogether in the cabin since the mutiny, drinking the wines and feasting on the sea-stores of Captain Barnard, and giving no more heed than was absolutely necessary to the navigation of the brig. These circumstances proved fortunate both for myself and Augustus; for, had matters been otherwise, he would have found it impossible to reach me. As it was, he proceeded with confidence in his design. It was near daybreak, however, before he completed the second division of the board (which was about a foot above the first cut), thus making an aperture quite large enough to admit his passage through with facility to the main orlop deck. Having got here, he made his way with but little trouble to the lower main hatch, although in so doing he had to scramble over tiers of oil-casks piled nearly as high as the upper

deck, there being barely room enough left for his body. Upon reaching the hatch he found that Tiger had followed him below, squeezing between two rows of the casks. It was now too late, however, to attempt getting to me before dawn, as the chief difficulty lay in passing through the close stowage in the lower hold. He therefore resolved to return, and wait till the next night. With this design, he proceeded to loosen the hatch, so that he might have as little detention as possible when he should come again. No sooner had he loosened it than Tiger sprang eagerly to the small opening produced, snuffed for a moment, and then uttered a long whine, scratching at the same time, as if anxious to remove the covering with his paws. There could be no doubt, from his behaviour, that he was aware of my being in the hold, and Augustus thought it possible that he would be able to get to me if he put him down. He now hit upon the expedient of sending the note, as it was especially desirable that I should make no attempt at forcing my way out, at least under existing circumstances, and there could be no certainty of his getting to me himself on the morrow as he intended. After-events proved how fortunate it was that the idea occurred to him as it did; for, had it not been for the receipt of the note, I should undoubtedly have fallen upon some plan, however desperate, of alarming the crew, and both our lives would most probably have been sacrificed in consequence.

Having concluded to write, the difficulty was now to procure the materials for so doing. An old toothpick was soon made into a pen; and this by means of feeling altogether, for the between-decks was as dark as pitch. Paper enough was obtained from the back of a letter — a duplicate of the forged letter from Mr. Ross. This had been the original draught; but the handwriting not being sufficiently well imitated, Augustus had written another, thrusting the first, by good fortune, into his coat-pocket, where it was now most opportunely discovered. Ink alone was thus wanting, and a substitute was immediately found for this by means of a slight incision with the penknife on the back of a finger just above the nail — a copious flow of blood ensuing, as usual, from wounds in that vicinity. The note was now written, as well as it could be in the dark and under the circumstances. It briefly explained that a mutiny had taken place; that Captain Barnard was set adrift; and that I might expect immediate relief as far as provisions were concerned, but must not venture upon making any disturbance. It concluded with these words: *"I have scrawled this with blood — your life depends upon lying close."*

This slip of paper being tied upon the dog, he was now put down the hatchway, and Augustus made the best of his way back to the forecastle, where he found no reason to believe that any of the crew had been in his absence. To conceal the hole in the partition, he drove his knife in just above it, and hung up a pea-jacket which he found in the berth. His handcuffs were then replaced, and also the rope around his ankles.

These arrangements were scarcely completed when Dirk Peters came

below, very drunk, but in excellent humour, and bringing with him my friend's allowance of provision for the day. This consisted of a dozen large Irish potatoes roasted, and a pitcher of water. He sat for some time on a chest by the berth, and talked freely about the mate and the general concerns of the brig. His demeanour was exceedingly capricious, and even grotesque. At one time Augustus was much alarmed by his odd conduct. At last, however, he went on deck, muttering a promise to bring his prisoner a good dinner on the morrow. During the day two of the crew (harpooners) came down, accompanied by the cook, all three in nearly the last stage of intoxication. Like Peters, they made no scruple of talking unreservedly about their plans. It appeared that they were much divided among themselves as to their ultimate course, agreeing in no point, except the attack on the ship from the Cape Verd Islands, with which they were in hourly expectation of meeting. As far as could be ascertained, the mutiny had not been brought about altogether for the sake of booty; a private pique of the chief mate's against Captain Barnard having been the main instigation. There now seemed to be two principal factions among the crew — one headed by the mate, the other by the cook. The former party were for seizing the first suitable vessel which should present itself, and equipping it at some of the West India Islands for a piratical cruise. The latter division, however, which was the stronger, and included Dirk Peters among its partisans, were bent upon pursuing the course originally laid out for the brig into the South Pacific; there either to take whale, or act otherwise, as circumstances should suggest. The representations of Peters, who had frequently visited these regions, had great weight, apparently, with the mutineers, wavering, as they were, between half-engendered notions of profit and pleasure. He dwelt on the world of novelty and amusement to be found among the innumerable islands of the Pacific, on the perfect security and freedom from all restraint to be enjoyed, but, more particularly, on the deliciousness of the climate, on the abundant means of good living, and on the voluptuous beauty of the women. As yet, nothing had been absolutely determined upon; but the pictures of the hybrid line-manager were taking strong hold upon the ardent imaginations of the seamen, and there was every possibility that his intentions would be finally carried into effect.

The three men went away in about an hour, and no one else entered the forecastle all day. Augustus lay quiet until nearly night. He then freed himself from the rope and irons, and prepared for his attempt. A bottle was found in one of the berths, and this he filled with water from the pitcher left by Peters, storing his pockets at the same time with cold potatoes. To his great joy he also came across a lantern, with a small piece of tallow candle in it. This he could light at any moment, as he had in his possession a box of phosphorus matches. When it was quite dark, he got through the hole in the bulkhead, having taken the precaution to arrange the bedclothes in the berth

so as to convey the idea of a person covered up. When through, he hung up the pea-jacket on his knife, as before, to conceal the aperture — this manœuvre being easily effected, as he did not readjust the piece of plank taken out until afterward. He was now on the main orlop deck, and proceeded to make his way, as before, between the upper deck and the oil-casks to the main hatchway. Having reached this, he lit the piece of candle, and descended, groping with extreme difficulty among the compact stowage of the hold. In a few moments he became alarmed at the insufferable stench and the closeness of the atmosphere. He could not think it possible that I had survived my confinement for so long a period breathing so oppressive an air. He called my name repeatedly, but I made him no reply, and his apprehensions seemed thus to be confirmed. The brig was rolling violently, and there was so much noise in consequence, that it was useless to listen for any weak sound, such as those of my breathing or snoring. He threw open the lantern, and held it as high as possible, whenever an opportunity occurred, in order that, by observing the light, I might, if alive, be aware that succor was approaching. Still nothing was heard from me, and the supposition of my death began to assume the character of certainty. He determined, nevertheless, to force a passage, if possible, to the box, and at least ascertain beyond a doubt the truth of his surmises. He pushed on for some time in a most pitiable state of anxiety, until, at length, he found the pathway utterly blocked up, and that there was no possibility of making any farther way by the course in which he had set out. Overcome now by his feelings, he threw himself among the lumber in despair, and wept like a child. It was at this period that he heard the crash occasioned by the bottle which I had thrown down. Fortunate, indeed, was it that the incident occurred — for, upon this incident, trivial as it appears, the thread of my destiny depended. Many years elapsed, however, before I was aware of this fact. A natural shame and regret for his weakness and indecision prevented Augustus from confiding to me at once what a more intimate and unreserved communion afterward induced him to reveal. Upon finding his further progress in the hold impeded by obstacles which he could not overcome, he had resolved to abandon his attempt at reaching me, and return at once to the forecastle. Before condemning him entirely on this head, the harassing circumstances which embarrassed him should be taken into consideration. The night was fast wearing away, and his absence from the forecastle might be discovered; and indeed would necessarily be so, if he should fail to get back to the berth by daybreak. His candle was expiring in the socket, and there would be the greatest difficulty in retracing his way to the hatchway in the dark. It must be allowed, too, that he had every good reason to believe me dead; in which event no benefit could result to me from his reaching the box, and a world of danger would be encountered to no purpose by himself. He had repeatedly called, and I had made him no answer. I had been now eleven

days and nights with no more water than that contained in the jug which he had left with me — a supply which it was not at all probable I had hoarded in the beginning of my confinement, as I had every cause to expect a speedy release. The atmosphere of the hold, too, must have appeared to him, coming from the comparatively open air of the steerage, of a nature absolutely poisonous, and by far more intolerable than it had seemed to me upon my first taking up my quarters in the box — the hatchways at that time having been constantly open for many months previous. Add to these considerations that of the scene of bloodshed and terror so lately witnessed by my friend; his confinement, privations, and narrow escapes from death, together with the frail and equivocal tenure by which he still existed — circumstances all so well calculated to prostrate every energy of mind — and the reader will be easily brought, as I have been, to regard his apparent falling off in friendship and in faith with sentiments rather of sorrow than of anger.

The crash of the bottle was distinctly heard, yet Augustus was not sure that it proceeded from the hold. The doubt, however, was sufficient inducement to persevere. He clambered up nearly to the orlop deck by means of the stowage, and then, watching for a lull in the pitchings of the vessel, he called out to me in as loud a tone as he could command, regardless, for the moment, of being overheard by the crew. It will be remembered that on this occasion the voice reached me, but I was so entirely overcome by violent agitation as to be incapable of reply. Confident, now, that his worst apprehensions were well founded, he descended, with a view of getting back to the forecastle without loss of time. In his haste some small boxes were thrown down, the noise occasioned by which I heard, as will be recollected. He had made considerable progress on his return when the fall of the knife again caused him to hesitate. He retraced his steps immediately, and, clambering up the stowage a second time, called out my name, loudly as before, having watched for a lull. This time I found voice to answer. Overjoyed at discovering me to be still alive, he now resolved to brave every difficulty and danger in reaching me. Having extricated himself as quickly as possible from the labyrinth of lumber by which he was hemmed in, he at length struck into an opening which promised better, and finally, after a series of struggles, arrived at the box in a state of utter exhaustion.

CHAPTER VI

The leading particulars of this narration were all that Augustus communicated to me while we remained near the box. It was not until afterward that he entered fully into all the details. He was apprehensive of being missed, and I was wild with impatience to leave my detested place of confinement. We resolved to make our way at once to the hole in the bulkhead, near which I was to remain for the present, while he went through to reconnoiter. To leave Tiger in the box was what neither of

us could endure to think of; yet, how to act otherwise was the question. He now seemed to be perfectly quiet, and we could not even distinguish the sound of his breathing upon applying our ears closely to the box. I was convinced that he was dead, and determined to open the door. We found him lying at full length, apparently in a deep stupor, yet still alive. No time was to be lost, yet I could not bring myself to abandon an animal who had now been twice instrumental in saving my life, without some attempt at preserving him. We therefore dragged him along with us as well as we could, although with the greatest difficulty and fatigue; Augustus, during part of the time, being forced to clamber over the impediments in our way with the huge dog in his arms — a feat to which the feebleness of my frame rendered me totally inadequate. At length we succeeded in reaching the hole, when Augustus got through, and Tiger was pushed in afterward. All was found to be safe, and we did not fail to return sincere thanks to God for our deliverance from the imminent danger we had escaped. For the present, it was agreed that I should remain near the opening, through which my companion could readily supply me with a part of his daily provision, and where I could have the advantages of breathing an atmosphere comparatively pure.

In explanation of some portions of this narrative, wherein I have spoken of the stowage of the brig, and which may appear ambiguous to some of my readers who may have seen a proper or regular stowage, I must here state that the manner in which this most important duty had been performed on board the Grampus was a most shameful piece of neglect on the part of Captain Barnard, who was by no means as careful or as experienced a seaman as the hazardous nature of the service on which he was employed would seem necessarily to demand. A proper stowage cannot be accomplished in a careless manner, and many most disastrous accidents, even within the limits of my own experience, have arisen from neglect or ignorance in this particular. Coasting vessels, in the frequent hurry and bustle attendant upon taking in or discharging cargo, are the most liable to mishap from the want of a proper attention to stowage. The great point is to allow no possibility of the cargo or ballast shifting position even in the most violent rollings of the vessel. With this end, great attention must be paid, not only to the bulk taken in, but to the nature of the bulk, and whether there be a full or only a partial cargo. In most kinds of freight the stowage is accomplished by means of a screw. Thus, in a load of tobacco or flour, the whole is screwed so tightly into the hold of the vessel that the barrels or hogsheads, upon discharging, are found to be completely flattened, and take some time to regain their original shape. This screwing, however, is resorted to principally with a view of obtaining more room in the hold; for in a *full* load of any such commodities as flour or tobacco, there can be no danger of any shifting whatever, at least none from which inconvenience can result. There have been instances, indeed, where this method of screwing has resulted in the

most lamentable consequences, arising from a cause altogether distinct from the danger attendant upon a shifting of cargo. A load of cotton, for example, tightly screwed while in certain conditions, has been known, through the expansion of its bulk, to rend a vessel asunder at sea. There can be no doubt, either that the same result would ensue in the case of tobacco, while undergoing its usual course of fermentation, were it not for the interstices consequent upon the rotundity of the hogsheads.

It is when a partial cargo is received that danger is chiefly to be apprehended from shifting, and that precautions should be always taken to guard against such misfortune. Only those who have encountered a violent gale of wind, or rather who have experienced the rolling of a vessel in a sudden calm after the gale, can form an idea of the tremendous force of the plunges, and of the consequent terrible impetus given to all loose articles in the vessel. It is then that the necessity of a cautious stowage, when there is a partial cargo, becomes obvious. When lying-to (especially with a small head sail), a vessel which is not properly modelled in the bows is frequently thrown upon her beam-ends; this occurring even every fifteen or twenty minutes upon an average, yet without any serious consequences resulting, provided *there be a proper stowage*. If this, however, has not been strictly attended to, in the first of these heavy lurches the whole of the cargo tumbles over to the side of the vessel which lies upon the water, and, being thus prevented from regaining her equilibrium, as she would otherwise necessarily do, she is certain to fill in a few seconds and go down. It is not too much to say that at least one-half of the instances in which vessels have foundered in heavy gales at sea may be attributed to a shifting of cargo or of ballast.

When a partial cargo of any kind is taken on board, the whole, after being first stowed as compactly as may be, should be covered with a layer of stout shifting-boards, extending completely across the vessel. Upon these boards strong temporary stanchions should be erected, reaching to the timbers above, and thus securing every thing in its place. In cargoes consisting of grain, or any similar matter, additional precautions are requisite. A hold filled entirely with grain upon leaving port will be found not more than three fourths full upon reaching its destination — this, too, although the freight, when measured bushel by bushel by the consignee, will overrun by a vast deal (on account of the swelling of the grain) the quantity consigned. This result is occasioned by *settling* during the voyage, and is the more perceptible in proportion to the roughness of the weather experienced. If grain loosely thrown in a vessel, then, is ever so well secured by shifting-boards and stanchions, it will be liable to shift in a long passage so greatly as to bring about the most distressing calamities. To prevent these, every method should be employed before leaving port to *settle* the cargo as much as possible; and for this there are many contrivances, among which may be mentioned the driving of wedges into the grain. Even after all this is done, and unusual pains taken to

secure the shifting-boards, no seaman who knows what he is about will feel altogether secure in a gale of any violence with a cargo of grain on board, and, least of all, with a partial cargo. Yet there are hundreds of our coasting vessels, and, it is likely, many more from the ports of Europe, which sail daily with partial cargoes, even of the most dangerous species, and without any precaution whatever. The wonder is that no more accidents occur than do actually happen. A lamentable instance of this heedlessness occurred to my knowledge in the case of Captain Joel Rice of the schooner Firefly, which sailed from Richmond, Virginia, to Madeira, with a cargo of corn, in the year 1825. The captain had gone many voyages without serious accident, although he was in the habit of paying no attention whatever to his stowage, more than to secure it in the ordinary manner. He had never before sailed with a cargo of grain, and on this occasion had the corn thrown on board loosely, when it did not much more than half fill the vessel. For the first portion of the voyage he met with nothing more than light breezes; but when within a day's sail of Madeira there came on a strong gale from the N. N. E. which forced him to lie-to. He brought the schooner to the wind under a double-reefed foresail alone, when she rode as well as any vessel could be expected to do, and shipped not a drop of water. Toward night the gale somewhat abated, and she rolled with more unsteadiness than before, but still did very well, until a heavy lurch threw her upon her beam-ends to starboard. The corn was then heard to shift bodily, the force of the movement bursting open the main hatchway. The vessel went down like a shot. This happened within hail of a small sloop from Madeira, which picked up one of the crew (the only person saved), and which rode out the gale in perfect security, as indeed a jolly boat might have done under proper management.

The stowage on board the Grampus was most clumsily done, if stowage that could be called which was little better than a promiscuous huddling together of oil-casks * and ship furniture. I have already spoken of the condition of articles in the hold. On the orlop deck there was space enough for my body (as I have stated) between the oil-casks and the upper deck; a space was left open around the main hatchway; and several other large spaces were left in the stowage. Near the hole cut through the bulkhead by Augustus there was room enough for an entire cask, and in this space I found myself comfortably situated for the present.

By the time my friend had got safely into the berth, and readjusted his handcuffs and the rope, it was broad daylight. We had made a narrow escape indeed; for scarcely had he arranged all matters, when the mate came below, with Dirk Peters and the cook. They talked for some time about the vessel from the Cape Verds, and seemed to be excessively anxious for her appearance. At length the cook came to the berth in

* Whaling vessels are usually fitted with iron oil-tanks — why the Grampus was not I have never been able to ascertain.

which Augustus was lying, and seated himself in it near the head. I could see and hear every thing from my hiding-place, for the piece cut out had not been put back, and I was in momentary expectation that the negro would fall against the pea-jacket, which was hung up to conceal the aperture, in which case all would have been discovered, and our lives would, no doubt, have been instantly sacrificed. Our good fortune prevailed, however; and although he frequently touched it as the vessel rolled, he never pressed against it sufficiently to bring about a discovery. The bottom of the jacket had been carefully fastened to the bulkhead, so that the hole might not be seen by its swinging to one side. All this time Tiger was lying in the foot of the berth, and appeared to have recovered in some measure his faculties, for I could see him occasionally open his eyes and draw a long breath.

After a few minutes the mate and cook went above, leaving Dirk Peters behind, who, as soon as they were gone, came and sat himself down in the place just occupied by the mate. He began to talk very sociably with Augustus, and we could now see that the greater part of his apparent intoxication, while the two others were with him, was a feint. He answered all my companion's questions with perfect freedom; told him that he had no doubt of his father's having been picked up, as there were no less than five sail in sight just before sundown on the day he was cut adrift; and used other language of a consolatory nature, which occasioned me no less surprise than pleasure. Indeed, I began to entertain hopes, that through the instrumentality of Peters we might be finally enabled to regain possession of the brig, and this idea I mentioned to Augustus as soon as I found an opportunity. He thought the matter possible, but urged the necessity of the greatest caution in making the attempt, as the conduct of the hybrid appeared to be instigated by the most arbitrary caprice alone; and, indeed, it was difficult to say if he was at any moment of sound mind. Peters went upon deck in about an hour, and did not return again until noon, when he brought Augustus a plentiful supply of junk beef and pudding. Of this, when we were left alone, I partook heartily, without returning through the hole. No one else came down into the forecastle during the day, and at night, I got into Augustus' berth, where I slept soundly and sweetly until nearly daybreak, when he awakened me upon hearing a stir upon deck, and I regained my hiding-place as quickly as possible. When the day was fully broke, we found that Tiger had recovered his strength almost entirely, and gave no indications of hydrophobia, drinking a little water that was offered him with great apparent eagerness. During the day he regained all his former vigour and appetite. His strange conduct had been brought on, no doubt, by the deleterious quality of the air of the hold, and had no connexion with canine madness. I could not sufficiently rejoice that I had persisted in bringing him with me from the box. This day was the thirtieth of June, and the thirteenth since the Grampus made sail from Nantucket.

On the second of July the mate came below drunk as usual, and in an excessively good-humor. He came to Augustus's berth, and, giving him a slap on the back, asked him if he thought he could behave himself if he let him loose, and whether he would promise not to be going into the cabin again. To this, of course, my friend answered in the affirmative, when the ruffian set him at liberty, after making him drink from a flask of rum which he drew from his coat-pocket. Both now went on deck, and I did not see Augustus for about three hours. He then came below with the good news that he had obtained permission to go about the brig as he pleased anywhere forward of the mainmast, and that he had been ordered to sleep, as usual, in the forecastle. He brought me, too, a good dinner, and a plentiful supply of water. The brig was still cruising for the vessel from the Cape Verds, and a sail was now in sight, which was thought to be the one in question. As the events of the ensuing eight days were of little importance, and had no direct bearing upon the main incidents of my narrative, I will here throw them into the form of a journal, as I do not wish to omit them altogether.

July 3. — Augustus furnished me with three blankets, with which I contrived a comfortable bed in my hiding-place. No one came below, except my companion, during the day. Tiger took his station in the berth just by the aperture, and slept heavily, as if not yet entirely recovered from the effects of his sickness. Toward night a flaw of wind struck the brig before sail could be taken in, and very nearly capsized her. The puff died away immediately, however, and no damage was done beyond the splitting of the foretopsail. Dirk Peters treated Augustus all this day with great kindness and entered into a long conversation with him respecting the Pacific Ocean, and the islands he had visited in that region. He asked him whether he would not like to go with the mutineers on a kind of exploring and pleasure voyage in those quarters, and said that the men were gradually coming over to the mate's views. To this Augustus thought it best to reply that he would be glad to go on such an adventure, since nothing better could be done, and that any thing was preferable to a piratical life.

July 4. — The vessel in sight proved to be a small brig from Liverpool, and was allowed to pass unmolested. Augustus spent most of his time on deck, with a view of obtaining all the information in his power respecting the intentions of the mutineers. They had frequent and violent quarrels among themselves, in one of which a harpooner, Jim Bonner, was thrown overboard. The party of the mate was gaining ground. Jim Bonner belonged to the cook's gang, of which Peters was a partisan.

July 5. — About daybreak there came on a stiff breeze from the west, which at noon freshened into a gale, so that the brig could carry nothing more than her trysail and foresail. In taking in the foretopsail, Simms, one of the common hands, and belonging also to the cook's gang, fell overboard, being very much in liquor, and was drowned — no attempt

being made to save him. The whole number of persons on board was now thirteen, to wit: Dirk Peters; Seymour, the black cook; —— Jones; —— Greely; Hartman Rogers; and William Allen, of the cook's party; the mate, whose name I never learned; Absalom Hicks; —— Wilson; John Hunt; and Richard Parker, of the mate's party; — besides Augustus and myself.

July 6. — The gale lasted all this day, blowing in heavy squalls, accompanied with rain. The brig took in a good deal of water through her seams, and one of the pumps was kept continually going, Augustus being forced to take his turn. Just at twilight a large ship passed close by us, without having been discovered until within hail. The ship was supposed to be the one for which the mutineers were on the lookout. The mate hailed her, but the reply was drowned in the roaring of the gale. At eleven, a sea was shipped amidships, which tore away a great portion of the larboard bulwarks, and did some other slight damage. Toward morning the weather moderated, and at sunrise there was very little wind.

July 7. — There was a heavy swell running all this day, during which the brig, being light, rolled excessively, and many articles broke loose in the hold, as I could hear distinctly from my hiding-place. I suffered a great deal from sea-sickness. Peters had a long conversation this day with Augustus, and told him that two of his gang, Greely and Allen, had gone over to the mate, and were resolved to turn pirates. He put several questions to Augustus which he did not then exactly understand. During a part of this evening the leak gained upon the vessel; and little could be done to remedy it, as it was occasioned by the brig's straining, and taking in the water through her seams. A sail was thrummed, and got under the bows, which aided us in some measure, so that we began to gain upon the leak.

July 8. — A light breeze sprang up at sunrise from the eastward, when the mate headed the brig to the southwest, with the intention of making some of the West India islands in pursuance of his piratical designs. No opposition was made by Peters or the cook — at least none in the hearing of Augustus. All idea of taking the vessel from the Cape Verds was abandoned. The leak was now easily kept under by one pump going every three quarters of an hour. The sail was drawn from beneath the bows. Spoke two small schooners during the day.

July 9. — Fine weather. All hands employed in repairing bulwarks. Peters had again a long conversation with Augustus, and spoke more plainly than he had done heretofore. He said nothing should induce him to come into the mate's views, and even hinted his intention of taking the brig out of his hands. He asked my friend if he could depend upon his aid in such case, to which Augustus said, "Yes," without hesitation. Peters then said he would sound the others of his party upon the subject, and went away. During the remainder of the day Augustus had no opportunity of speaking with him privately.

July 10. — Spoke a brig from Rio, bound to Norfolk. Weather hazy, with a light baffling wind from the eastward. To-day Hartman Rogers died, having been attacked on the eighth with spasms after drinking a glass of grog. This man was of the cook's party, and one upon whom Peters placed his main reliance. He told Augustus that he believed the mate had poisoned him, and that he expected, if he did not be on the look-out, his own turn would come shortly. There were now only himself, Jones, and the cook belonging to his own gang — on the other side there were five. He had spoken to Jones about taking the command from the mate; but the project having been coolly received, he had been deterred from pressing the matter any further, or from saying any thing to the cook. It was well, as it happened, that he was so prudent, for in the afternoon the cook expressed his determination of siding with the mate, and went over formally to that party; while Jones took an opportunity of quarrelling with Peters, and hinted that he would let the mate know of the plan in agitation. There was now, evidently, no time to be lost, and Peters expressed his determination of attempting to take the vessel at all hazards, provided Augustus would lend him his aid. My friend at once assured him of his willingness to enter into any plan for that purpose, and, thinking the opportunity a favourable one, made known the fact of my being on board. At this the hybrid was not more astonished than delighted, as he had no reliance whatever upon Jones, whom he already considered as belonging to the party of the mate. They went below immediately, when Augustus called to me by name, and Peters and myself were soon made acquainted. It was agreed that we should attempt to retake the vessel upon the first good opportunity, leaving Jones altogether out of our councils. In the event of success, we were to run the brig into the first port that offered, and deliver her up. The desertion of his party had frustrated Peters' design of going into the Pacific — an adventure which could not be accomplished without a crew, and he depended upon either getting acquitted upon trial, on the score of insanity (which he solemnly averred had actuated him in lending his aid to the mutiny), or upon obtaining a pardon, if found guilty, through the representations of Augustus and myself. Our deliberations were interrupted for the present by the cry of, "All hands take in sail," and Peters and Augustus ran up on deck.

As usual, the crew were nearly all drunk; and, before sail could be properly taken in, a violent squall laid the brig on her beam-ends. By keeping her away, however, she righted, having shipped a good deal of water. Scarcely was everything secure, when another squall took the vessel, and immediately afterward another — no damage being done. There was every appearance of a gale of wind, which, indeed, shortly came on, with great fury, from the northward and westward. All was

made as snug as possible, and we laid-to, as usual, under a close-reefed foresail. As night drew on, the wind increased in violence, with a remarkably heavy sea. Peters now came into the forecastle with Augustus, and we resumed our deliberations.

We agreed that no opportunity could be more favourable than the present for carrying our designs into effect, as an attempt at such a moment would never be anticipated. As the brig was snugly laid-to, there would be no necessity of manœuvring her until good weather, when, if we succeeded in our attempt, we might liberate one, or perhaps two of the men, to aid us in taking her into port. The main difficulty was the great disproportion in our forces. There were only three of us, and in the cabin there were nine. All the arms on board, too, were in their possession, with the exception of a pair of small pistols which Peters had concealed about his person, and the large seaman's knife which he always wore in the waistband of his pantaloons. From certain indications, too — such, for example, as there being no such thing as an axe or a handspike lying in their customary places — we began to fear that the mate had his suspicions, at least in regard to Peters, and that he would let slip no opportunity of getting rid of him. It was clear, indeed, that what we should determine to do could not be done too soon. Still the odds were too much against us to allow of our proceeding without the greatest caution.

Peters proposed that he should go up on deck, and enter into conversation with the watch (Allen), when he would be able to throw him into the sea without trouble, and without making any disturbance, by seizing a good opportunity; that Augustus and myself should then come up, and endeavour to provide ourselves with some kind of weapons from the deck; and that we should then make a rush together, and secure the companion-way before any opposition could be offered. I objected to this, because I could not believe that the mate (who was a cunning fellow in all matters which did not affect his superstitious prejudices) would suffer himself to be so easily entrapped. The very fact of there being a watch on deck at all was sufficient proof that he was upon the alert, — it not being usual, except in vessels where discipline is most rigidly enforced, to station a watch on deck when a vessel is lying-to in a gale of wind. As I address myself principally, if not altogether, to persons who have never been to sea, it may be as well to state the exact condition of a vessel under such circumstances. Lying-to, or, in sea-parlance, "laying-to," is a measure resorted to for various purposes, and effected in various manners. In moderate weather it is frequently done with a view of merely bringing the vessel to a stand-still, to wait for another vessel, or any similar object. If the vessel which lies-to is under full sail, the manœuvre is usually accomplished by throwing round some portion of her sails, so as to let the wind take them aback, when she becomes stationary. But we are now speaking of lying-to in a gale of wind. This is

done when the wind is ahead, and too violent to admit of carrying sail without danger of capsizing; and sometimes even when the wind is fair, but the sea too heavy for the vessel to be put before it. If a vessel be suffered to scud before the wind in a very heavy sea, much damage is usually done her by the shipping of water over her stern, and sometimes by the violent plunges she makes forward. This manœuvre, then, is seldom resorted to in such case, unless through necessity. When the vessel is in a leaky condition she is often put before the wind even in the heaviest seas; for, when lying-to, her seams are sure to be greatly opened by her violent straining, and it is not so much the case when scudding. Often, too, it becomes necessary to scud a vessel, either when the blast is so exceedingly furious as to tear in pieces the sail which is employed with a view of bringing her head to the wind, or when, through the false modelling of the frame or other causes, this main object cannot be effected.

Vessels in a gale of wind are laid-to in different manners, according to their peculiar construction. Some lie-to best under a foresail, and this, I believe, is the sail most usually employed. Large square-rigged vessels have sails for the express purpose, called storm-staysails. But the jib is occasionally employed by itself, — sometimes the jib and foresail, or a double-reefed foresail, and not unfrequently the after-sails, are made use of. Foretopsails are very often found to answer the purpose better than any other species of sail. The Grampus was generally laid-to under a close-reefed foresail.

When a vessel is to be laid-to, her head is brought up to the wind just so nearly as to fill the sail under which she lies when hauled flat aft, that is, when brought diagonally across the vessel. This being done, the bows point within a few degrees of the direction from which the wind issues, and the windward bow of course receives the shock of the waves. In this situation a good vessel will ride out a very heavy gale of wind without shipping a drop of water, and without any further attention being requisite on the part of the crew. The helm is usually lashed down, but this is altogether unnecessary (except on account of the noise it makes when loose), for the rudder has no effect upon the vessel when lying-to. Indeed, the helm had far better be left loose than lashed very fast, for the rudder is apt to be torn off by heavy seas if there be no room for the helm to play. As long as the sail holds, a well modelled vessel will maintain her situation, and ride every sea, as if instinct with life and reason. If the violence of the wind, however, should tear the sail into pieces (a feat which it requires a perfect hurricane to accomplish under ordinary circumstances), there is then imminent danger. The vessel falls off from the wind, and, coming broadside to the sea, is completely at its mercy: the only resource in this case is to put her quietly before the wind, letting her scud until some other sail can be set. Some vessels will lie-to under no sail whatever, but such are not to be trusted at sea.

But to return from this digression. It had never been customary with the mate to have any watch on deck when lying-to in a gale of wind, and the fact that he had now one, coupled with the circumstance of the missing axes and handspikes, fully convinced us that the crew were too well on the watch to be taken by surprise in the manner Peters had suggested. Something, however, was to be done, and that with as little delay as practicable, for there could be no doubt that a suspicion having been once entertained against Peters, he would be sacrificed upon the earliest occasion, and one would certainly be either found or made upon the breaking of the gale.

Augustus now suggested that if Peters could contrive to remove, under any pretext, the piece of chain-cable which lay over the trap in the stateroom, we might possibly be able to come upon them unawares by means of the hold; but a little reflection convinced us that the vessel rolled and pitched too violently for any attempt of that nature.

By good fortune I at length hit upon the idea of working upon the superstitious terrors and guilty conscience of the mate. It will be remembered that one of the crew, Hartman Rogers, had died during the morning, having been attacked two days before with spasms after drinking some spirits and water. Peters had expressed to us his opinion that this man had been poisoned by the mate, and for this belief he had reasons, so he said, which were incontrovertible, but which he could not be prevailed upon to explain to us — this wayward refusal being only in keeping with other points of his singular character. But whether or not he had any better grounds for suspecting the mate than we had ourselves, we were easily led to fall in with his suspicion, and determined to act accordingly.

Rogers had died about eleven in the forenoon, in violent convulsions; and the corpse presented in a few minutes after death one of the most horrid and loathsome spectacles I ever remember to have seen. The stomach was swollen immensely, like that of a man who has been drowned and lain under water for many weeks. The hands were in the same condition, while the face was shrunken, shrivelled, and of a chalky whiteness, except where relieved by two or three glaring red blotches like those occasioned by the erysipelas: one of these blotches extended diagonally across the face, completely covering up an eye as if with a band of red velvet. In this disgusting condition the body had been brought up from the cabin at noon to be thrown overboard, when the mate getting a glimpse of it (for he now saw it for the first time), and being either touched with remorse for his crime or struck with terror at so horrible a sight, ordered the men to sew the body up in its hammock, and allow it the usual rites of sea-burial. Having given these directions, he went below, as if to avoid any further sight of his victim. While preparations were making to obey his orders, the gale came on with great fury, and the design was abandoned for the present. The corpse, left to iself, was

washed into the larboard scuppers, where it still lay at the time of which I speak, floundering about with the furious lurches of the brig.

Having arranged our plan, we set about putting it in execution as speedily as possible. Peters went upon deck, and, as he had anticipated, was immediately accosted by Allen, who appeared to be stationed more as a watch upon the forecastle than for any other purpose. The fate of this villain, however, was speedily and silently decided; for Peters, approaching him in a careless manner, as if about to address him, seized him by the throat, and, before he could utter a single cry, tossed him over the bulwarks. He then called to us, and we came up. Our first precaution was to look about for something with which to arm ourselves, and in doing this we had to proceed with great care, for it was impossible to stand on deck an instant without holding fast, and violent seas broke over the vessel at every plunge forward. It was indispensable, too, that we should be quick in our operations, for every minute we expected the mate to be up to set the pumps going, as it was evident the brig must be taking in water very fast. After searching about for some time, we could find nothing more fit for our purpose than the two pump-handles, one of which Augustus took, and I the other. Having secured these, we stripped off the shirt of the corpse and dropped the body overboard. Peters and myself then went below, leaving Augustus to watch upon deck, where he took his station just where Allen had been placed, and with his back to the cabin companion-way, so that, if any of the mate's gang should come up, he might suppose it was the watch.

As soon as I got below I commenced disguising myself so as to represent the corpse of Rogers. The shirt which we had taken from the body aided us very much, for it was of singular form and character, and easily recognizable — a kind of smock, which the deceased wore over his other clothing. It was a blue stockinett, with large white stripes running across. Having put this on, I proceeded to equip myself with a false stomach, in imitation of the horrible deformity of the swollen corpse. This was soon effected by means of stuffing with some bedclothes. I then gave the same appearance to my hands by drawing on a pair of white woollen mittens, and filling them in with any kind of rags that offered themselves. Peters then arranged my face, first rubbing it well over with white chalk, and afterward blotching it with blood, which he took from a cut in his finger. The streak across the eye was not forgotten and presented a most shocking appearance.

CHAPTER VIII

As I viewed myself in a fragment of looking-glass which hung up in the cabin, and by the dim light of a kind of battle-lantern, I was so impressed with a sense of vague awe at my appearance, and at the recollection of the terrific reality which I was thus representing, that I was

seized with a violent tremour, and could scarcely summon resolution to go on with my part. It was necessary, however, to act with decision, and Peters and myself went upon deck.

We there found everything safe, and, keeping close to the bulwarks, the three of us crept to the cabin companion-way. It was only partially closed, precautions having been taken to prevent its being suddenly pushed to from without, by means of placing billets of wood on the upper step so as to interfere with the shutting. We found no difficulty in getting a full view of the interior of the cabin through the cracks where the hinges were placed. It now proved to have been very fortunate for us that we had not attempted to take them by surprise, for they were evidently on the alert. Only one was asleep, and he lying just at the foot of the companion-ladder, with a musket by his side. The rest were seated on several mattresses, which had been taken from the berths and thrown on the floor. They were engaged in earnest conversation; and although they had been carousing, as appeared from two empty jugs, with some tin tumblers which lay about, they were not as much intoxicated as usual. All had knives, one or two of them pistols, and a great many muskets were lying in a berth close at hand.

We listened to their conversation for some time before we could make up our minds how to act, having as yet resolved on nothing determinate, except that we would attempt to paralyze their exertions, when we should attack them, by means of the apparition of Rogers. They were discussing their piratical plans, in which all we could hear distinctly was, that they would unite with the crew of a schooner Hornet, and, if possible, get the schooner herself into their possession preparatory to some attempt on a large scale, the particulars of which could not be made out by either of us.

One of the men spoke of Peters, when the mate replied to him in a low voice which could not be distinguished, and afterward added more loudly, that "he could not understand his being so much forward with the captain's brat in the forecastle, and he thought the sooner both of them were overboard the better." To this no answer was made, but we could easily perceive that the hint was well received by the whole party, and more particularly by Jones. At this period I was excessively agitated, the more so as I could see that neither Augustus nor Peters could determine how to act. I made up my mind, however, to sell my life as dearly as possible, and not to suffer myself to be overcome by any feelings of trepidation.

The tremendous noise made by the roaring of the wind in the rigging, and the washing of the sea over the deck, prevented us from hearing what was said, except during momentary lulls. In one of these, we all distinctly heard the mate tell one of the men to "go forward, and order the d—d lubbers to come into the cabin, where he could have an eye upon them, for he wanted no such secret doings on board the brig." It

was well for us that the pitching of the vessel at this moment was so violent as to prevent this order from being carried into instant execution. The cook got up from his mattress to go for us, when a tremendous lurch, which I thought would carry away the masts, threw him headlong against one of the larboard stateroom doors, bursting it open, and creating a good deal of other confusion. Luckily, neither of our party was thrown from his position, and we had time to make a precipitate retreat to the forecastle, and arrange a hurried plan of action before the messenger made his appearance, or rather before he put his head out of the companion-hatch, for he did not come on deck. From this station he could not notice the absence of Allen, and he accordingly bawled out, as if to him, repeating the orders of the mate. Peters cried out, "Ay, ay," in a disguised voice, and the cook immediately went below, without entertaining a suspicion that all was not right.

My two companions now proceeded boldly aft and down into the cabin, Peters closing the door after him in the same manner he had found it. The mate received them with feigned cordiality, and told Augustus that, since he had behaved himself so well of late, he might take up his quarters in the cabin and be one of them for the future. He then poured him out a tumbler half full of rum, and made him drink it. All this I saw and heard, for I followed my friends to the cabin as soon as the door was shut, and took up my old point of observation. I had brought with me the two pump-handles, one of which I secured near the companion-way, to be ready for use when required.

I now steadied myself as well as possible so as to have a good view of all that was passing within, and endeavoured to nerve myself to the task of descending among the mutineers when Peters should make a signal to me, as agreed upon. Presently he contrived to turn the conversation upon the bloody deeds of the mutiny, and by degrees led the men to talk of the thousand superstitions which are so universally current among seamen. I could not make out all that was said, but I could plainly see the effects of the conversation in the countenances of those present. The mate was evidently much agitated, and presently, when some one mentioned the terrific appearance of Rogers' corpse, I thought he was upon the point of swooning. Peters now asked him if he did not think it would be better to have the body thrown overboard at once as it was too horrible a sight to see it floundering about in the scuppers. At this the villain absolutely gasped for breath, and turned his head slowly round upon his companions, as if imploring some one to go up and perform the task. No one, however, stirred, and it was quite evident that the whole party were wound up to the highest pitch of nervous excitement. Peters now made me the signal. I immediately threw open the door of the companion-way, and, descending, without uttering a syllable, stood erect in the midst of the party.

The intense effect produced by this sudden apparition is not at all

to be wondered at when the various circumstances are taken into consideration. Usually, in cases of a similar nature, there is left in the mind of the spectator some glimmering of doubt as to the reality of the vision before his eyes; a degree of hope, however feeble, that he is the victim of chicanery, and that the apparition is not actually a visitant from the old world of shadows. It is not too much to say that such remnants of doubt have been at the bottom of almost every such visitation, and that the appalling horror which has sometimes been brought about, is to be attributed, even in the cases most in point, and where most suffering has been experienced, more to a kind of anticipative horror, lest the apparition *might possibly be* real, than to an unwavering belief in its reality. But, in the present instance, it will be seen immediately, that in the minds of the mutineers there was not even the shadow of a basis upon which to rest a doubt that the apparition of Rogers was indeed a revivification of his disgusting corpse, or at least its spiritual image. The isolated situation of the brig, with its entire inaccessibility on account of the gale, confined the apparently possible means of deception within such narrow and definite limits, that they must have thought themselves enabled to survey them all at a glance. They had now been at sea twenty-four days, without holding more than a speaking communication with any vessel whatever. The whole of the crew, too — at least all whom they had the most remote reason for suspecting to be on board — were assembled in the cabin, with the exception of Allen, the watch; and his gigantic stature (he was six feet six inches high) was too familiar in their eyes to permit the notion that he was the apparition before them to enter their minds even for an instant. Add to these considerations the awe-inspiring nature of the tempest, and that of the conversation brought about by Peters; the deep impression which the loathsomeness of the actual corpse had made in the morning upon the imaginations of the men; the excellence of the imitation in my person, and the uncertain and wavering light in which they beheld me, as the glare of the cabin lantern, swinging violently to and fro, fell dubiously and fitfully upon my figure, and there will be no reason to wonder that the deception had even more than the entire effect which we had anticipated. The mate sprang up from the mattress on which he was lying, and, without uttering a syllable, fell back, stone dead, upon the cabin floor, and was hurled to the leeward like a log by a heavy roll of the brig. Of the remaining seven, there were but three who had at first any degree of presence of mind. The four others sat for some time rooted apparently to the floor, the most pitiable objects of horror and utter despair my eyes ever encountered. The only opposition we experienced at all was from the cook, John Hunt, and Richard Parker; but they made but a feeble and irresolute defence. The two former were shot instantly by Peters, and I felled Parker with a blow on the head from the pump-handle which I had brought with me. In the meantime, Augustus seized one of the muskets

lying on the floor and shot another mutineer (—— Wilson) through the breast. There were now but three remaining; but by this time they had become aroused from their lethargy, and perhaps began to see that a deception had been practised upon them, for they fought with great resolution and fury, and, but for the immense muscular strength of Peters, might have ultimately got the better of us. These three men were —— Jones, —— Greeley, and Absalom Hicks. Jones had thrown Augustus on the floor, stabbed him in several places along the right arm, and would no doubt have soon dispatched him (as neither Peters nor myself could immediately get rid of our own antagonists) had it not been for the timely aid of a friend, upon whose assistance we, surely, had never depended. This friend was no other than Tiger. With a low growl, he bounded into the cabin, at a most critical moment for Augustus, and throwing himself upon Jones, pinned him to the floor in an instant. My friend, however, was now too much injured to render us any aid whatever, and I was so encumbered with my disguise that I could do but little. The dog would not leave his hold upon the throat of Jones — Peters, nevertheless, was far more than a match for the two men who remained, and would, no doubt, have dispatched them sooner, had it not been for the narrow space in which he had to act, and the tremendous lurches of the vessel. Presently he was enabled to get hold of a heavy stool, several of which lay about the floor. With this he beat out the brains of Greely as he was in the act of discharging a musket at me, and immediately afterward a roll of the brig throwing him in contact with Hicks, he seized him by the throat, and, by dint of sheer strength, strangled him instantaneously. Thus, in far less time than I have taken to tell it, we found ourselves masters of the brig.

The only person of our opponents who was left alive was Richard Parker. This man, it will be remembered, I had knocked down with a blow from the pump-handle at the commencement of the attack. He now lay motionless by the door of the shattered stateroom; but, upon Peters touching him with his foot, he spoke, and entreated for mercy. His head was only slightly cut, and otherwise he had received no injury, having been merely stunned by the blow. He now got up, and, for the present, we secured his hands behind his back. The dog was still growling over Jones; but, upon examination, we found him completely dead, the blood issuing in a stream from a deep wound in the throat, inflicted, no doubt, by the sharp teeth of the animal.

It was now about one o'clock in the morning, and the wind was still blowing tremendously. The brig evidently laboured much more than usual, and it became absolutely necessary that something should be done with a view of easing her in some measure. At almost every roll to leeward she shipped a sea, several of which came partially down into the cabin during our scuffle, the hatchway having been left open by myself when I descended. The entire range of bulwarks to larboard had

been swept away, as well as the caboose, together with the jollyboat from the counter. The creaking and working of the mainmast, too, gave indication that it was nearly sprung. To make room for more stowage in the afterhold, the heel of this mast had been stepped between decks (a very reprehensible practice, occasionally resorted to by ignorant ship-builders), so that it was in imminent danger of working from its step. But, to crown all our difficulties, we plummed the well, and found no less than seven feet of water.

Leaving the bodies of the crew lying in the cabin, we got to work immediately at the pumps — Parker, of course, being set at liberty to assist us in the labour. Augustus's arm was bound up as well as we could effect it, and he did what he could, but that was not much. However, we found that we could just manage to keep the leak from gaining upon us by having one pump constantly going. As there were only four of us, this was severe labour; but we endeavoured to keep up our spirits, and looked anxiously for daybreak, when we hoped to lighten the brig by cutting away the mainmast.

In this manner we passed a night of terrible anxiety and fatigue, and, when the day at length broke, the gale had neither abated in the least, nor were there any signs of its abating. We now dragged the bodies on deck and threw them overboard. Our next care was to get rid of the mainmast. The necessary preparations having been made, Peters cut away at the mast (having found axes in the cabin), while the rest of us stood by the stays and lanyards. As the brig gave a tremendous lee-lurch, the word was given to cut away the weather-lanyards, which being done, the whole mass of wood and rigging plunged into the sea, clear of the brig, and without doing any material injury. We now found that the vessel did not labour quite as much as before, but our situation was still exceedingly precarious, and in spite of the utmost exertions, we could not gain upon the leak without the aid of both pumps. The little assistance which Augustus could render us was not really of any importance. To add to our distress, a heavy sea, striking the brig to the windward, threw her off several points from the wind, and, before she could regain her position, another broke completely over her, and hurled her full upon her beam-ends. The ballast now shifted in a mass to leeward (the stowage had been knocking about perfectly at random for some time), and for a few moments we thought nothing could save us from capsizing. Presently, however, we partially righted; but the ballast still retaining its place to larboard, we lay so much along that it was useless to think of working the pumps, which indeed we could not have done much longer in any case, as our hands were entirely raw with the excessive labour we had undergone, and were bleeding in the most horrible manner.

Contrary to Parker's advice, we now proceeded to cut away the fore-mast, and at length accomplished it after much difficulty, owing to the

position in which we lay. In going overboard the wreck took with it the bowsprit, and left us a complete hulk.

So far we had had reason to rejoice in the escape of our longboat, which had received no damage from any of the huge seas which had come on board. But we had not long to congratulate ourselves; for the foremast having gone, and, of course, the foresail with it, by which the brig had been steadied, every sea now made a complete breach over us, and in five minutes our deck was swept from stem to stern, the longboat and starboard bulwarks torn off, and even the windlass shattered into fragments. It was, indeed, hardly possible for us to be in a more pitiable condition.

At noon there seemed to be some slight appearance of the gale's abating, but in this we were sadly disappointed, for it only lulled for a few minutes to blow with redoubled fury. About four in the afternoon it was utterly impossible to stand up against the violence of the blast; and, as the night closed in upon us, I had not a shadow of hope that the vessel would hold together until morning.

By midnight we had settled very deep in the water, which was now up to the orlop deck. The rudder went soon afterward, the sea which tore it away lifting the after portion of the brig entirely from the water, against which she thumped in her descent with such a concussion as would be occasioned by going ashore. We had all calculated that the rudder would hold its own to the last, as it was unusually strong, being rigged as I have never seen one rigged either before or since. Down its main timber there ran a succession of stout iron hooks, and others in the same manner down the stern-post. Through these hooks there extended a very thick wrought-iron rod, the rudder being thus held to the stern-post and swinging freely on the rod. The tremendous force of the sea which tore it off may be estimated by the fact, that the hooks in the stern-post, which ran entirely through it, being clinched on the inside, were drawn every one of them completely out of the solid wood.

We had scarcely time to draw breath after the violence of this shock, when one of the most tremendous waves I had then ever known broke right on board of us, sweeping the companion-way clear off, bursting in the hatchways, and filling every inch of the vessel with water.

CHAPTER IX

Luckily, just before night, all four of us had lashed ourselves firmly to the fragments of the windlass, lying in this manner as flat upon the deck as possible. This precaution alone saved us from destruction. As it was, we were all more or less stunned by the immense weight of water which tumbled upon us, and which did not roll from above us until we were nearly exhausted. As soon as I could recover breath, I called aloud to my companions. Augustus alone replied, saying: "It is all over with us, and may God have mercy upon our souls!" By-and-by both the others were

enabled to speak, when they exhorted us to take courage, as there was still hope; it being impossible, from the nature of the cargo, that the brig could go down, and there being every chance that the gale would blow over by the morning. These words inspired me with new life; for, strange as it may seem, although it was obvious that a vessel with a cargo of empty oil-casks would not sink, I had been hitherto so confused in mind as to have overlooked this consideration altogether; and the danger which I had for some time regarded as the most imminent was that of foundering. As hope revived within me, I made use of every opportunity to strengthen the lashings which held me to the remains of the windlass, and in this occupation I soon discovered that my companions were also busy. The night was as dark as it could possibly be, and the horrible shrieking din and confusion which surrounded us it is useless to attempt describing. Our deck lay level with the sea, or rather we were encircled with a towering ridge of foam, a portion of which swept over us every instant. It is not too much to say that our heads were not fairly out of the water more than one second in three. Although we lay close together, no one of us could see the other, or, indeed, any portion of the brig itself, upon which we were so tempestuously hurled about. At intervals we called one to the other, thus endeavouring to keep alive hope, and render consolation and encouragement to such of us as stood most in need of it. The feeble condition of Augustus made him an object of solicitude with us all; and as, from the lacerated condition of his right arm, it must have been impossible for him to secure his lashings with any degree of firmness, we were in momentary expectation of finding that he had gone overboard — yet to render him aid was a thing altogether out of the question. Fortunately, his station was more secure than that of any of the rest of us; for the upper part of his body lying just beneath a portion of the shattered windlass, the seas, as they tumbled in upon him, were greatly broken in their violence. In any other situation than this (into which he had been accidentally thrown after having lashed himself in a very exposed spot) he must inevitably have perished before morning. Owing to the brig's lying so much along, we were all less liable to be washed off than otherwise would have been the case. The heel, as I have before stated, was to larboard, about one half of the deck being constantly under water. The seas, therefore, which struck us to starboard were much broken, by the vessel's side, only reaching us in fragments as we lay flat on our faces; while those which came from larboard being what are called back-water seas, and obtaining little hold upon us on account of our posture, had not sufficient force to drag us from our fastenings.

In this frightful situation we lay until the day broke so as to show us more fully the horrors which surrounded us. The brig was a mere log, rolling about at the mercy of every wave; the gale was upon the increase, if any thing, blowing indeed a complete hurricane, and there appeared

to us no earthly prospect of deliverance. For several hours we held on in silence, expecting every moment that our lashings would either give way, that the remains of the windlass would go by the board, or that some of the huge seas, which roared in every direction around us and above us, would drive the hulk so far beneath the water that we should be drowned before it could regain the surface. By the mercy of God, however, we were preserved from these imminent dangers, and about midday were cheered by the light of the blessed sun. Shortly afterward we could perceive a sensible diminution in the force of the wind, when, now for the first time since the latter part of the evening before, Augustus spoke, asking Peters, who lay closest to him, if he thought there was any possibility of our being saved. As no reply was at first made to this question, we all concluded that the hybrid had been drowned where he lay; but presently, to our great joy, he spoke, although very feebly, saying that he was in great pain, being so cut by the tightness of his lashings across the stomach, that he must either find means of loosening them or perish, as it was impossible that he could endure his misery much longer. This occasioned us great distress, as it was altogether useless to think of aiding him in any manner while the sea continued washing over us as it did. We exhorted him to bear his sufferings with fortitude, and promised to seize the first opportunity which should offer itself to relieve him. He replied that it would soon be too late; that it would be all over with him before we could help him; and then, after moaning for some minutes, lay silent, when we concluded that he had perished.

As the evening drew on, the sea had fallen so much that scarcely more than one wave broke over the hulk from windward in the course of five minutes, and the wind had abated a great deal, although still blowing a severe gale. I had not heard any of my companions speak for hours, and now called to Augustus. He replied, although very feebly, so that I could not distinguish what he said. I then spoke to Peters and to Parker, neither of whom returned any answer.

Shortly after this period I fell into a state of partial insensibility, during which the most pleasing images floated in my imagination; such as green trees, waving meadows of ripe grain, processions of dancing girls, troops of cavalry, and other phantasies. I now remember that, in all which passed before my mind's eye, *motion* was a predominant idea. Thus, I never fancied any stationary object, such as a house, a mountain, or any thing of that kind; but windmills, ships, large birds, balloons, people on horseback, carriages driving furiously, and similar moving objects, presented themselves in endless succession. When I recovered from this state, the sun was, as near as I could guess, an hour high. I had the greatest difficulty in bringing to recollection the various circumstances connected with my situation, and for some time remained firmly convinced that I was still in the hold of the brig, near the box, and that the body of Parker was that of Tiger.

When I at length completely came to my senses, I found that the wind blew no more than a moderate breeze, and that the sea was comparatively calm; so much so that it only washed over the brig amidships. My left arm had broken loose from its lashings, and was much cut about the elbow; my right was entirely benumbed, and the hand and wrist swollen prodigiously by the pressure of the rope, which had worked from the shoulder downward. I was also in great pain from another rope which went about my waist, and had been drawn to an insufferable degree of tightness. Looking round upon my companions, I saw that Peters still lived, although a thick line was pulled so forcibly around his loins as to give him the appearance of being cut nearly in two; as I stirred, he made a feeble motion to me with his hand, pointing to the rope. Augustus gave no indication of life whatever, and was bent nearly double across a splinter of the windlass. Parker spoke to me when he saw me moving, and asked me if I had not sufficient strength to release him from his situation, saying that if I would summon up what spirits I could, and contrive to untie him, we might yet save our lives; but that otherwise we must all perish. I told him to take courage, and I would endeavor to free him. Feeling in my pantaloons' pocket, I got hold of my penknife, and, after several ineffectual attempts, at length succeeded in opening it. I then, with my left hand, managed to free my right from its fastenings, and afterward cut the other ropes which held me. Upon attempting, however, to move from my position, I found that my legs failed me altogether, and that I could not get up; neither could I move my right arm in any direction. Upon mentioning this to Parker, he advised me to lie quiet for a few minutes, holding on to the windlass with my left hand, so as to allow time for the blood to circulate. Doing this, the numbness presently began to die away so that I could move first one of my legs, and then the other, and, shortly afterward I regained the partial use of my right arm. I now crawled with great caution toward Parker, without getting on my legs, and soon cut loose all the lashings about him, when, after a short delay, he also recovered the partial use of his limbs. We now lost no time in getting loose the rope from Peters. It had cut a deep gash through the waistband of his woollen pantaloons, and through two shirts, and made its way into his groin, from which the blood flowed out copiously as we removed the cordage. No sooner had we removed it, however, than he spoke, and seemed to experience instant relief — being able to move with much greater ease than either Parker or myself — this was no doubt owing to the discharge of blood.

We had little hopes that Augustus would recover, as he evinced no signs of life; but, upon getting to him, we discovered that he had merely swooned from the loss of blood, the bandages we had placed around his wounded arm having been torn off by the water; none of the ropes which held him to the windlass were drawn sufficiently tight to occasion his death. Having relieved him from the fastenings, and got him clear of

the broken wood about the windlass, we secured him in a dry place to windward, with his head somewhat lower than his body, and all three of us busied ourselves in chafing his limbs. In about half an hour he came to himself, although it was not until the next morning that he gave signs of recognizing any of us, or had sufficient strength to speak. By the time we had thus got clear of our lashings it was quite dark, and it began to cloud up, so that we were again in the greatest agony lest it should come on to blow hard, in which event nothing could have saved us from perishing, exhausted as we were. By good fortune it continued very moderate during the night, the sea subsiding every minute, which gave us great hopes of ultimate preservation. A gentle breeze still blew from the N. W., but the weather was not at all cold. Augustus was lashed carefully to windward in such a manner as to prevent him from slipping overboard with the rolls of the vessel, as he was still too weak to hold on at all. For ourselves there was no such necessity. We sat close together, supporting each other with the aid of the broken ropes about the windlass, and devising methods of escape from our frightful situation. We derived much comfort from taking off our clothes and wringing the water from them. When we put them on after this, they felt remarkably warm and pleasant, and served to invigorate us in no little degree. We helped Augustus off with his, and wrung them for him, when he experienced the same comfort.

Our chief sufferings were now those of hunger and thirst, and when we looked forward to the means of relief in this respect, our hearts sunk within us, and we were induced to regret that we had escaped the less dreadful perils of the sea. We endeavoured, however, to console ourselves with the hope of being speedily picked up by some vessel and encouraged each other to bear with fortitude the evils that might happen.

The morning of the fourteenth at length dawned, and the weather still continued clear and pleasant, with a steady but very light breeze from the N. W. The sea was now quite smooth, and as, from some cause which we could not determine, the brig did not lie so much along as she had done before, the deck was comparatively dry, and we could move about with freedom. We had now been better than three entire days and nights without either food or drink, and it became absolutely necessary that we should make an attempt to get up something from below. As the brig was completely full of water, we went to this work despondently, and with but little expectation of being able to obtain anything. We made a kind of drag by driving some nails which we broke out from the remains of the companion-hatch into two pieces of wood. Tying these across each other, and fastening them to the end of a rope, we threw them into the cabin, and dragged them to and fro, in the faint hope of being thus able to entangle some article which might be of use to us for food, or which might at least render us assistance in getting it. We spent the greater part of the morning in this labour without effect, fishing up nothing more than a few bedclothes, which were readily caught by the

nails. Indeed, our contrivance was so very clumsy that any greater success was hardly to be anticipated.

We now tried the forecastle, but equally in vain, and were upon the brink of despair, when Peters proposed that we should fasten a rope to his body, and let him make an attempt to get up something by diving into the cabin. This proposition we hailed with all the delight which reviving hope could inspire. He proceeded immediately to strip off his clothes with the exception of his pantaloons; and a strong rope was then carefully fastened around his middle, being brought up over his shoulders in such a manner that there was no possibility of its slipping. The undertaking was one of great difficulty and danger; for, as we could hardly expect to find much, if any, provision in the cabin itself, it was necessary that the diver, after letting himself down, should make a turn to the right, and proceed under water a distance of ten or twelve feet, in a narrow passage, to the storeroom, and return, without drawing breath.

Everything being ready, Peters now descended in the cabin, going down the companion-ladder until the water reached his chin. He then plunged in, head first, turning to the right as he plunged, and endeavouring to make his way to the storeroom. In this first attempt, however, he was altogether unsuccessful. In less than half a minute after his going down we felt the rope jerked violently (the signal we had agreed upon when he desired to be drawn up). We accordingly drew him up instantly, but so incautiously as to bruise him badly against the ladder. He had brought nothing with him, and had been unable to penetrate more than a very little way into the passage, owing to the constant exertions he found it necessary to make in order to keep himself from floating up against the deck. Upon getting out he was very much exhausted, and had to rest full fifteen minutes before he could again venture to descend.

The second attempt met with even worse success; for he remained so long under water without giving the signal, that, becoming alarmed for his safety, we drew him out without it, and found that he was almost at the last gasp, having, as he said, repeatedly jerked at the rope without our feeling it. This was probably owing to a portion of it having become entangled in the balustrade at the foot of the ladder. This balustrade was, indeed, so much in the way, that we determined to remove it, if possible, before proceeding with our design. As we had no means of getting it away except by main force, we all descended into the water as far as we could on the ladder, and giving a pull against it with our united strength, succeeded in breaking it down.

The third attempt was equally unsuccessful with the two first, and it now became evident that nothing could be done in this manner without the aid of some weight with which the diver might steady himself, and keep to the floor of the cabin while making his search. For a long time we looked about in vain for something which might answer this purpose;

but at length, to our great joy, we discovered one of the weather-forechains so loose that we had not the least difficulty in wrenching it off. Having fastened this securely to one of his ankles, Peters now made his fourth descent into the cabin, and this time succeeded in making his way to the door of the steward's room. To his inexpressible grief, however, he found it locked, and was obliged to return without effecting an entrance, as, with the greatest exertion, he could remain under water not more, at the utmost extent, than a single minute. Our affairs now looked gloomy indeed, and neither Augustus nor myself could refrain from bursting into tears, as we thought of the host of difficulties which encompassed us, and the slight probability which existed of our finally making an escape. But this weakness was not of long duration. Throwing ourselves on our knees to God, we implored His aid in the many dangers which beset us; and arose with renewed hope and vigor to think what could yet be done by mortal means toward accomplishing our deliverance.

CHAPTER X

Shortly afterward an incident occurred which I am induced to look upon as more intensely productive of emotion, as far more replete with the extremes first of delight and then of horror, than even any of the thousand chances which afterward befell me in nine long years, crowded with events of the most startling and, in many cases, of the most unconceived and unconceivable character. We were lying on the deck near the companion-way, and debating the possibility of yet making our way into the storeroom, when, looking toward Augustus, who lay fronting myself, I perceived that he had become all at once deadly pale, and that his lips were quivering in the most singular and unaccountable manner. Greatly alarmed, I spoke to him, but he made me no reply, and I was beginning to think that he was suddenly taken ill, when I took notice of his eyes, which were glaring apparently at some object behind me. I turned my head, and shall never forget the ecstatic joy which thrilled through every particle of my frame, when I perceived a large brig bearing down upon us, and not more than a couple of miles off. I sprung to my feet as if a musket bullet had suddenly struck me to the heart; and, stretching out my arms in the direction of the vessel, stood in this manner, motionless, and unable to articulate a syllable. Peters and Parker were equally affected, although in different ways. The former danced about the deck like a madman, uttering the most extravagant rhodomontades, intermingled with howls and imprecations, while the latter burst into tears, and continued for many minutes weeping like a child.

The vessel in sight was a large hermaphrodite brig, of a Dutch build, and painted black, with a tawdry gilt figure-head. She had evidently seen a good deal of rough weather, and, we supposed, had suffered much in the gale which had proved so disastrous to ourselves; for her foretopmast was gone, and some of her starboard bulwarks. When we first saw her,

she was, as I have already said, about two miles off and to windward, bearing down upon us. The breeze was very gentle, and what astonished us chiefly was, that she had no other sails set than her foremast and mainsail, with a flying jib — of course she came down but slowly, and our impatience amounted nearly to phrensy. The awkward manner in which she steered, too, was remarked by all of us, even excited as we were. She yawed about so considerably, that once or twice we thought it impossible she could see us, or imagined that, having seen us, and discovered no person on board, she was about to tack and make off in another direction. Upon each of these occasions we screamed and shouted at the top of our voices, when the stranger would appear to change for a moment her intention, and again hold on toward us — this singular conduct being repeated two or three times, so that at last we could think of no other manner of accounting for it than by supposing the helmsman to be in liquor.

No person was seen upon her decks until she arrived within about a quarter of a mile of us. We then saw three seamen, whom by their dress we took to be Hollanders. Two of these were lying on some old sails near the forecastle, and the third, who appeared to be looking at us with great curiosity, was leaning over the starboard bow near the bowsprit. This last was a stout and tall man, with a very dark skin. He seemed by his manner to be encouraging us to have patience, nodding to us in a cheerful although rather odd way, and smiling constantly, so as to display a set of the most brilliantly white teeth. As his vessel drew nearer, we saw a red flannel cap which he had on fall from his head into the water; but of this he took little or no notice, continuing his odd smiles and gesticulations. I relate these things and circumstances minutely, and I relate them, it must be understood, precisely as they *appeared* to us.

The brig came on slowly, and now more steadily than before, and — I cannot speak calmly of this event — our hearts leaped up wildly within us, and we poured out our whole souls in shouts and thanksgiving to God for the complete, unexpected, and glorious deliverance that was so palpably at hand. Of a sudden, and all at once, there came wafted over the ocean from the strange vessel (which was now close upon us) a smell, a stench, such as the whole world has no name for — no conception of — hellish — utterly suffocating — insufferable, inconceivable. I gasped for breath, and turning to my companions, perceived that they were paler than marble. But we had now no time left for question or surmise — the brig was within fifty feet of us, and it seemed to be her intention to run under our counter, that we might board her without putting out a boat. We rushed aft, when, suddenly, a wide yaw threw her off full five or six points from the course she had been running, and, as she passed under our stern at the distance of about twenty feet, we had a full view of her decks. Shall I ever forget the triple horror of that spectacle? Twenty-five or thirty human bodies, among whom were several females, lay scattered about

between the counter and the galley in the last and most loathsome state of putrefaction. We plainly saw that not a soul lived in that fated vessel! Yet we could not help shouting to the dead for help! Yes, long and loudly did we beg, in the agony of the moment, that those silent and disgusting images would stay for us, would not abandon us to become like them, would receive us among their goodly company! We were raving with horror and despair — thoroughly mad through the anguish of our grievous disappointment.

As our first loud yell of terror broke forth, it was replied to by something, from near the bowsprit of the stranger, so closely resembling the scream of a human voice that the nicest ear might have been startled and deceived. At this instant another sudden yaw brought the region of the forecastle for a moment into view, and we beheld at once the origin of the sound. We saw the tall stout figure still leaning on the bulwark, and still nodding his head to and fro, but his face was now turned from us so that we could not behold it. His arms were extended over the rail, and the palms of his hands fell outward. His knees were lodged upon a stout rope, tightly stretched, and reaching from the heel of the bowsprit to a cathead. On his back, from which a portion of the shirt had been torn, leaving it bare, there sat a huge sea-gull, busily gorging itself with the horrible flesh, its bill and talons deep buried, and its white plumage spattered all over with blood. As the brig moved farther round so as to bring us close in view, the bird, with much apparent difficulty, drew out its crimsoned head, and, after eyeing us for a moment as if stupefied, arose lazily from the body upon which it had been feasting, and, flying directly above our deck, hovered there a while with a portion of clotted and liver-like substance in its beak. The horrid morsel dropped at length with a sullen splash immediately at the feet of Parker. May God forgive me, but now, for the first time, there flashed through my mind a thought, a thought which I will not mention, and I felt myself making a step toward the ensanguined spot. I looked upward, and the eyes of Augustus met my own with a degree of intense and eager meaning which immediately brought me to my senses. I sprang forward quickly, and, with a deep shudder, threw the frightful thing into the sea.

The body from which it had been taken, resting as it did upon the rope, had been easily swayed to and fro by the exertions of the carnivorous bird, and it was this motion which had at first impressed us with the belief of its being alive. As the gull relieved it of its weight, it swung round and fell partially over, so that the face was fully discovered. Never, surely, was any object so terribly full of awe! The eyes were gone, and the whole flesh around the mouth, leaving the teeth utterly naked. This, then, was the smile which had cheered us on to hope! this the — but I forbear. The brig, as I have already told, passed under our stern, and made its way slowly but steadily to leeward. With her and with her terrible crew went all our gay visions of deliverance and joy. Deliberately as she went by,

we might possibly have found means of boarding her, had not our sudden disappointment, and the appalling nature of the discovery which accompanied it, laid entirely prostrate every active faculty of mind and body. We had seen and felt, but we could neither think nor act, until, alas! too late. How much our intellects had been weakened by this incident may be estimated by the fact, that when the vessel had proceeded so far that we could perceive no more than the half of her hull, the proposition was seriously entertained of attempting to overtake her by swimming!

I have, since this period, vainly endeavoured to obtain some clew to the hideous uncertainty which enveloped the fate of the stranger. Her build and general appearance, as I have before stated, led us to the belief that she was a Dutch trader, and the dresses of the crew also sustained this opinion. We might have easily seen the name upon her stern, and, indeed, taken other observations, which would have guided us in making out her character; but the intense excitement of the moment blinded us to every thing of that nature. From the saffron-like hue of such of the corpses as were not entirely decayed, we concluded that the whole of her company had perished by the yellow fever, or some other virulent disease of the same fearful kind. If such were the case (and I know not what else to imagine), death, to judge from the positions of the bodies, must have come upon them in a manner awfully sudden and overwhelming, in a way totally distinct from that which generally characterizes even the most deadly pestilences with which mankind are acquainted. It is possible, indeed, that poison, accidentally introduced into some of their sea-stores, may have brought about the disaster; or that the eating of some unknown venomous species of fish, or other marine animal, or oceanic bird, might have induced it, — but it is utterly useless to form conjectures where all is involved, and will, no doubt, remain for ever involved, in the most appalling and unfathomable mystery.

<div align="center">CHAPTER XI</div>

We spent the remainder of the day in a condition of stupid lethargy, gazing after the retreating vessel until the darkness, hiding her from our sight, recalled us in some measure to our senses. The pangs of hunger and thirst then returned, absorbing all other cares and considerations. Nothing, however, could be done until the morning, and, securing ourselves as well as possible, we endeavoured to snatch a little repose. In this I succeeded beyond my expectations, sleeping until my companions, who had not been so fortunate, aroused me at daybreak to renew our attempts at getting up provisions from the hull.

It was now a dead calm, with the sea as smooth as I have ever known it, — the weather warm and pleasant. The brig was out of sight. We commenced our operations by wrenching off, with some trouble, another of the forechains; and having fastened both to Peters' feet, he again made an endeavour to reach the door of the storeroom, thinking it possible that

he might be able to force it open, provided he could get at it in sufficient time; and this he hoped to do, as the hulk lay much more steadily than before.

He succeeded very quickly in reaching the door, when, loosening one of the chains from his ankle, he made every exertion to force the passage with it, but in vain, the framework of the room being far stronger than was anticipated. He was quite exhausted with his long stay under water, and it became absolutely necessary that some other one of us should take his place. For this service Parker immediately volunteered; but, after making three ineffectual efforts, found that he could never even succeed in getting near the door. The condition of Augustus's wounded arm rendered it useless for him to attempt going down, as he would be unable to force the room open should he reach it, and it accordingly now devolved upon me to exert myself for our common deliverance.

Peters had left one of the chains in the passage, and I found, upon plunging in, that I had not sufficient balance to keep me firmly down. I determined, therefore, to attempt no more, in my first effort, than merely to recover the other chain. In groping along the floor of the passage for this, I felt a hard substance, which I immediately grasped, not having time to ascertain what it was, but returning and ascending instantly to the surface. The prize proved to be a bottle, and our joy may be conceived when I say that it was found to be full of port wine. Giving thanks to God for this timely and cheering assistance, we immediately drew the cork with my penknife, and, each taking a moderate sup, felt the most indescribable comfort from the warmth, strength, and spirits with which it inspired us. We then carefully recorked the bottle, and, by means of a handkerchief, swung it in such a manner that there was no possibility of its getting broken.

Having rested a while after this fortunate discovery, I again descended, and now recovered the chain, with which I instantly came up. I then fastened it on and went down for the third time, when I became fully satisfied that no exertions whatever, in that situation, would enable me to force open the door of the storeroom. I therefore returned in despair.

There seemed now to be no longer any room for hope, and I could perceive in the countenances of my companions that they had made up their minds to perish. The wine had evidently produced in them a species of delirium, which, perhaps, I had been prevented from feeling by the immersion I had undergone since drinking it. They talked incoherently, and about matters unconnected with our condition, Peters repeatedly asking me questions about Nantucket. Augustus, too, I remember, approached me with a serious air, and requested me to lend him a pocketcomb, as his hair was full of fish-scales, and he wished to get them out before going on shore. Parker appeared somewhat less affected, and urged me to dive at random into the cabin, and bring up any article which might come to hand. To this I consented, and, in the first attempt, after staying

under a full minute, brought up a small leather trunk belonging to Captain Barnard. This was immediately opened in the faint hope that it might contain something to eat or drink. We found nothing, however, except a box of razors and two linen shirts. I now went down again, and returned without any success. As my head came above water I heard a crash on deck, and, upon getting up, saw that my companions had ungratefully taken advantage of my absence to drink the remainder of the wine, having let the bottle fall in the endeavour to replace it before I saw them. I remonstrated with them on the heartlessness of their conduct, when Augustus burst into tears. The other two endeavoured to laugh the matter off as a joke, but I hope never again to behold laughter of such a species: the distortion of countenance was absolutely frightful. Indeed, it was apparent that the stimulus, in the empty state of their stomachs, had taken instant and violent effect, and that they were all exceedingly intoxicated. With great difficulty I prevailed upon them to lie down, when they fell very soon into a heavy slumber, accompanied with loud stertorous breathing. I now found myself, as it were, alone in the brig, and my reflections, to be sure, were of the most fearful and gloomy nature. No prospect offered itself to my view but a lingering death by famine, or, at the best, by being overwhelmed in the first gale which should spring up, for in our present exhausted condition we could have no hope of living through another.

The gnawing hunger which I now experienced was nearly insupportable, and I felt myself capable of going to any lengths in order to appease it. With my knife I cut off a small portion of the leather trunk, and endeavoured to eat it, but found it utterly impossible to swallow a single morsel, although I fancied that some little alleviation of my suffering was obtained by chewing small pieces of it and spitting them out. Toward night my companions awoke, one by one, each in an indescribable state of weakness and horror, brought on by the wine, whose fumes had now evaporated. They shook as if with a violent ague, and uttered the most lamentable cries for water. Their condition affected me in the most lively degree, at the same time causing me to rejoice in the fortunate train of circumstances which had prevented me from indulging in the wine, and consequently from sharing their melancholy and most distressing sensations. Their conduct, however, gave me great uneasiness and alarm; for it was evident that, unless some favourable change took place, they could afford me no assistance in providing for our common safety. I had not yet abandoned all idea of being able to get up something from below; but the attempt could not possibly be resumed until some one of them was sufficiently master of himself to aid me by holding the end of the rope while I went down. Parker appeared to be somewhat more in possession of his senses than the others, and I endeavoured, by every means in my power, to rouse him. Thinking that a plunge in the sea-water might have a beneficial effect, I contrived to fasten the end of a rope around his body, and

then, leading him to the companion-way (he remaining quite passive all the while), pushed him in, and immediately drew him out. I had good reason to congratulate myself upon having made this experiment; for he appeared much revived and invigorated, and, upon getting out, asked me, in a rational manner, why I had so served him. Having explained my object, he expressed himself indebted to me, and said that he felt greatly better from the immersion, afterward conversing sensibly upon our situation. We then resolved to treat Augustus and Peters in the same way, which we immediately did, when they both experienced much benefit from the shock. This idea of sudden immersion had been suggested to me by reading in some medical work the good effect of the shower-bath in a case where the patient was suffering from *mania a potu.*

Finding that I could now trust my companions to hold the end of the rope, I again made three or four plunges into the cabin, although it was now quite dark, and a gentle but long swell from the northward rendered the hulk somewhat unsteady. In the course of these attempts I succeeded in bringing up two case-knives, a three-gallon jug, empty, and a blanket, but nothing which could serve us for food. I continued my efforts, after getting these articles, until I was completely exhausted, but brought up nothing else. During the night Parker and Peters occupied themselves by turns in the same manner; but nothing coming to hand, we now gave up this attempt in despair, concluding that we were exhausting ourselves in vain.

We passed the remainder of this night in a state of the most intense mental and bodily anguish that can possibly be imagined. The morning of the sixteenth at length dawned, and we looked eagerly around the horizon for relief, but to no purpose. The sea was still smooth, with only a long swell from the northward, as on yesterday. This was the sixth day since we had tasted either food or drink, with the exception of the bottle of port wine, and it was clear that we could hold out but a very little while longer unless something could be obtained. I never saw before, nor wish to see again, human beings so utterly emaciated as Peters and Augustus. Had I met them on shore in their present condition I should not have had the slightest suspicion that I had ever beheld them. Their countenances were totally changed in character, so that I could not bring myself to believe them really the same individuals with whom I had been in company but a few days before. Parker, although sadly reduced, and so feeble that he could not raise his head from his bosom, was not so far gone as the other two. He suffered with great patience, making no complaint, and endeavouring to inspire us with hope in every manner he could devise. For myself, although at the commencement of the voyage I had been in bad health, and was at all times of a delicate constitution, I suffered less than any of us, being much less reduced in frame, and retaining my powers of mind in a surprising degree, while the rest were completely prostrated in intellect, and seemed to be brought to a species

of second childhood, generally simpering in their expressions, with idiotic smiles, and uttering the most absurd platitudes. At intervals, however, they would appear to revive suddenly, as if inspired all at once with a consciousness of their condition, when they would spring upon their feet in a momentary flash of vigour, and speak, for a short period, of their prospects, in a manner altogether rational, although full of the most intense despair. It is possible, however, that my companions may have entertained the same opinion of their own condition as I did of mine, and that I may have unwittingly been guilty of the same extravagances and imbecilities as themselves — this is a matter which cannot be determined.

About noon Parker declared that he saw land off the larboard quarter, and it was with the utmost difficulty I could restrain him from plunging into the sea with the view of swimming toward it. Peters and Augustus took little notice of what he said, being apparently wrapped up in moody contemplation. Upon looking in the direction pointed out, I could not perceive the faintest appearance of the shore — indeed, I was too well aware that we were far from any land to indulge in a hope of that nature. It was a long time, nevertheless, before I could convince Parker of his mistake. He then burst into a flood of tears, weeping like a child, with loud cries and sobs, for two or three hours, when becoming exhausted, he fell asleep.

Peters and Augustus now made several ineffectual efforts to swallow portions of the leather. I advised them to chew it and spit it out; but they were too excessively debilitated to be able to follow my advice. I continued to chew pieces of it at intervals, and found some relief from so doing; my chief distress was for water, and I was only prevented from taking a draught from the sea by remembering the horrible consequences which thus have resulted to others who were similarly situated with ourselves.

The day wore on in this manner, when I suddenly discovered a sail to the eastward, and on our larboard bow. She appeared to be a large ship, and was coming nearly athwart us, being probably twelve or fifteen miles distant. None of my companions had as yet discovered her, and I forbore to tell them of her for the present, lest we might again be disappointed of relief. At length upon her getting nearer, I saw distinctly that she was heading immediately for us, with her light sails filled. I could now contain myself no longer, and pointed her out to my fellow-sufferers. They immediately sprang to their feet, again indulging in the most extravagant demonstrations of joy, weeping, laughing in an idiotic manner, jumping, stamping upon the deck, tearing their hair, and praying and cursing by turns. I was so affected by their conduct, as well as by what I considered a sure prospect of deliverance, that I could not refrain from joining in with their madness, and gave way to the impulses of my gratitude and ecstasy by lying and rolling on the deck, clapping my hands, shouting, and other similar acts, until I was suddenly called to my recol-

lection, and once more to the extreme human misery and despair, by perceiving the ship all at once with her stern fully presented toward us, and steering in a direction nearly opposite to that in which I had at first perceived her.

It was some time before I could induce my poor companions to believe that this sad reverse in our prospects had actually taken place. They replied to all my assertions with a stare and a gesture implying that they were not to be deceived by such misrepresentations. The conduct of Augustus most sensibly affected me. In spite of all I could say or do to the contrary, he persisted in saying that the ship was rapidly nearing us, and in making preparations to go on board of her. Some seaweed floating by the brig, he maintained that it was the ship's boat, and endeavoured to throw himself upon it, howling and shrieking in the most heartrending manner, when I forcibly restrained him from thus casting himself into the sea.

Having become in some degree pacified, we continued to watch the ship until we finally lost sight of her, the weather becoming hazy, with a light breeze springing up. As soon as she was entirely gone, Parker turned suddenly toward me with an expression of countenance which made me shudder. There was about him an air of self-possession which I had not noticed in him until now, and before he opened his lips my heart told me what he would say. He proposed, in a few words, that one of us should die to preserve the existence of the others.

<center>CHAPTER XII</center>

I had for some time past, dwelt upon the prospect of our being reduced to this last horrible extremity, and had secretly made up my mind to suffer death in any shape or under any circumstances rather than resort to such a course. Nor was this resolution in any degree weakened by the present intensity of hunger under which I laboured. The proposition had not been heard by either Peters or Augustus. I therefore took Parker aside; and mentally praying to God for power to dissuade him from the horrible purpose he entertained, I expostulated with him for a long time, and in the most supplicating manner, begging him in the name of every thing which he held sacred, and urging him by every species of argument which the extremity of the case suggested, to abandon the idea, and not to mention it to either of the other two.

He heard all I said without attempting to controvert any of my arguments, and I had begun to hope that he would be prevailed upon to do as I desired. But when I had ceased speaking, he said that he knew very well all I had said was true, and that to resort to such a course was the most horrible alternative which could enter into the mind of man; but that he had now held out as long as human nature could be sustained; that it was unnecessary for all to perish, when, by the death of one, it was possible, and even probable, that the rest might be finally preserved;

adding that I might save myself the trouble of trying to turn him from his purpose, his mind having been thoroughly made up on the subject even before the appearance of the ship, and that only her heaving in sight had prevented him from mentioning his intention at an earlier period.

I now begged him, if he would not be prevailed upon to abandon his design, at least to defer it for another day, when some vessel might come to our relief; again reiterating every argument I could devise, and which I thought likely to have influence with one of his rough nature. He said, in reply, that he had not spoken until the very last possible moment, that he could exist no longer without sustenance of some kind, and that therefore in another day his suggestion would be too late, as regarded himself at least.

Finding that he was not to be moved by anything I could say in a mild tone, I now assumed a different demeanor, and told him that he must be aware I had suffered less than any of us from our calamities; that my health and strength, consequently, were at that moment far better than his own, or than that either of Peters or Augustus; in short, that I was in a condition to have my own way by force if I found it necessary; and that if he attempted in any manner to acquaint the others with his bloody and cannibal designs, I would not hesitate to throw him into the sea. Upon this he immediately seized me by the throat, and drawing a knife, made several ineffectual efforts to stab me in the stomach; an atrocity which his excessive debility alone prevented him from accomplishing. In the meantime, being roused to a high pitch of anger, I forced him to the vessel's side, with the full intention of throwing him overboard. He was saved from his fate, however, by the interference of Peters, who now approached and separated us, asking the cause of the disturbance. This Parker told before I could find means in any manner to prevent him.

The effect of his words was even more terrible than what I had anticipated. Both Augustus and Peters, who, it seems, had long secretly entertained the same fearful idea which Parker had been merely the first to broach, joined with him in his design and insisted upon its immediately being carried into effect. I had calculated that one at least of the two former would be found still possessed of sufficient strength of mind to side with myself in resisting any attempt to execute so dreadful a purpose; and, with the aid of either one of them, I had no fear of being able to prevent its accomplishment. Being disappointed in this expectation, it became absolutely necessary that I should attend to my own safety, as a further resistance on my part might possibly be considered by men in their frightful condition a sufficient excuse for refusing me fair play in the tragedy that I knew would speedily be enacted.

I now told them I was willing to submit to the proposal, merely requesting a delay of about one hour, in order that the fog which had gathered around us might have an opportunity of lifting, when it was possible that the ship we had seen might be again in sight. After great

difficulty I obtained from them a promise to wait thus long; and, as I had anticipated (a breeze rapidly coming in), the fog lifted before the hour had expired, when, no vessel appearing in sight, we prepared to draw lots.

It is with extreme reluctance that I dwell upon the appalling scene which ensued; a scene which, with its minutest details, no after events have been able to efface in the slightest degree from my memory, and whose stern recollection will embitter every future moment of my existence. Let me run over this portion of my narrative with as much haste as the nature of the events to be spoken of will permit. The only method we could devise for the terrific lottery, in which we were to take each a chance, was that of drawing straws. Small splinters of wood were made to answer our purpose, and it was agreed that I should be the holder. I retired to one end of the hulk, while my poor companions silently took up their station in the other with their backs turned toward me. The bitterest anxiety which I endured at any period of this fearful drama was while I occupied myself in the arrangement of the lots. There are few conditions into which man can possibly fall where he will not feel a deep interest in the preservation of his existence; an interest momentarily increasing with the frailness of the tenure by which that existence may be held. But now that the silent, definite, and stern nature of the business in which I was engaged (so different from the tumultuous dangers of the storm or the gradually approaching horrors of famine) allowed me to reflect on the few chances I had of escaping the most appalling of deaths — a death for the most appalling of purposes — every particle of that energy which had so long buoyed me up departed like feathers before the wind, leaving me a helpless prey to the most abject and pitiable terror. I could not, at first, even summon up sufficient strength to tear and fit together the small splinters of wood, my fingers absolutely refusing their office, and my knees knocking violently against each other. My mind ran over rapidly a thousand absurd projects by which to avoid becoming a partner in the awful speculation. I thought of falling on my knees to my companions, and entreating them to let me escape this necessity; of suddenly rushing upon them, and, by putting one of them to death, of rendering the decision by lot useless — in short, of every thing but of going through with the matter I had in hand. At last, after wasting a long time in this imbecile conduct, I was recalled to my senses by the voice of Parker, who urged me to relieve them at once from the terrible anxiety they were enduring. Even then I could not bring myself to arrange the splinters upon the spot, but thought over every species of finesse by which I could trick some one of my fellow-sufferers to draw the short straw, as it had been agreed that whoever drew the shortest of four splinters from my hand was to die for the preservation of the rest. Before any one condemn me for this apparent heartlessness, let him be placed in a situation precisely similar to my own.

At length delay was no longer possible, and, with a heart almost burst-

ing from my bosom, I advanced to the region of the forecastle, where my companions were awaiting me. I held out my hand with the splinters, and Peters immediately drew. He was free — *his*, at least, was not the shortest; and there was now another chance against my escape. I summoned up all my strength, and passed the lots to Augustus. He also drew immediately, and he also was free; and now, whether I should live or die, the chances were no more than precisely even. At this moment all the fierceness of the tiger possessed my bosom, and I felt toward my poor fellow-creature, Parker, the most intense, the most diabolical hatred. But the feeling did not last; and, at length, with a convulsive shudder and closed eyes, I held out the two remaining splinters toward him. It was fully five minutes before he could summon resolution to draw, during which period of heartrending suspense I never once opened my eyes. Presently one of the two lots was quickly drawn from my hand. The decision was then over, yet I knew not whether it was for me or against me. No one spoke, and still I dared not satisfy myself by looking at the splinter I held. Peters at length took me by the hand, and I forced myself to look up, when I immediately saw by the countenance of Parker that I was safe, and that he it was who had been doomed to suffer. Gasping for breath, I fell senseless to the deck.

I recovered from my swoon in time to behold the consummation of the tragedy in the death of him who had been chiefly instrumental in bringing it about. He made no resistance whatever, and was stabbed in the back by Peters, when he fell instantly dead. I must not dwell upon the fearful repast which immediately ensued. Such things may be imagined, but words have no power to impress the mind with the exquisite horror of their reality. Let it suffice to say that, having in some measure appeased the raging thirst which consumed us by the blood of the victim, and having by common consent taken off the hands, feet, and head, throwing them together with the entrails, into the sea, we devoured the rest of the body, piecemeal, during the four ever memorable days of the seventeenth, eighteenth, nineteenth, and twentieth of the month.

On the nineteenth, there coming on a smart shower which lasted fifteen or twenty minutes, we contrived to catch some water by means of a sheet which had been fished up from the cabin by our drag just after the gale. The quantity we took in all did not amount to more than half a gallon; but even this scanty allowance supplied us with comparative strength and hope.

On the twenty-first we were again reduced to the last necessity. The weather still remained warm and pleasant, with occasional fogs and light breezes, most usually from N. to W.

On the twenty-second, as we were sitting close huddled together, gloomily revolving over our lamentable condition, there flashed through my mind all at once an idea which inspired me with a bright gleam of hope. I remembered that, when the foremast had been cut away, Peters,

being in the windward chains, passed one of the axes into my hand, requesting me to put it, if possible, in a place of security, and that a few minutes before the last heavy sea struck the brig and filled her I had taken this axe into the forecastle and laid it in one of the larboard berths. I now thought it possible that, by getting at this axe, we might cut through the deck over the storeroom, and thus readily supply ourselves with provisions.

When I communicated this object to my companions, they uttered a feeble shout of joy, and we all proceeded forthwith to the forecastle. The difficulty of descending here was greater than that of going down in the cabin, the opening being much smaller, for it will be remembered that the whole framework about the cabin companion-hatch had been carried away, whereas the forecastle-way, being a simple hatch of only about three feet square, had remained uninjured. I did not hesitate, however, to attempt the descent; and a rope being fastened round my body as before, I plunged boldly in, feet foremost, made my way quickly to the berth, and at the first attempt brought up the axe. It was hailed with the most ecstatic joy and triumph, and the ease with which it had been obtained was regarded as an omen of our ultimate preservation.

We now commenced cutting at the deck with all the energy of re-kindled hope, Peters and myself taking the axe by turns, Augustus's wounded arm not permitting him to aid us in any degree. As we were still so feeble as to be scarcely able to stand unsupported, and could consequently work but a minute or two without resting, it soon became evident that many long hours would be necessary to accomplish our task — that is, to cut an opening sufficiently large to admit of a free access to the storeroom. This consideration, however, did not discourage us; and, working all night by the light of the moon, we succeeded in effecting our purpose by daybreak on the morning of the twenty-third.

Peters now volunteered to go down; and, having made all arrangements as before, he descended, and soon returned bringing up with him a small jar, which, to our great joy, proved to be full of olives. Having shared these among us, and devoured them with the greatest avidity, we proceeded to let him down again. This time he succeeded beyond our utmost expectations, returning instantly with a large ham and a bottle of Madeira wine. Of the latter we each took a moderate sup, having learned by experience the pernicious consequences of indulging too freely. The ham, except about two pounds near the bone, was not in a condition to be eaten, having been entirely spoiled by the salt water. The sound part was divided among us. Peters and Augustus, not being able to restrain their appetite, swallowed theirs upon the instant; but I was more cautious, and ate but a small portion of mine, dreading the thirst which I knew would ensue. We now rested a while from our labors, which had been intolerably severe.

By noon, feeling somewhat strengthened and refreshed, we again re-

newed our attempt at getting up provisions, Peters and myself going down alternately, and always with more or less success, until sundown. During this interval we had the good fortune to bring up, altogether, four more small jars of olives, another ham, a carboy containing nearly three gallons of excellent Cape Madeira wine, and, what gave us still more delight, a small tortoise of the Gallipago breed, several of which had been taken on board by Captain Barnard, as the Grampus was leaving port, from the schooner Mary Pitts, just returned from a sealing voyage in the Pacific.

In a subsequent portion of this narrative I shall have frequent occasion to mention this species of tortoise. It is found principally, as most of my readers may know, in the group of islands called the Gallipagos, which, indeed, derive their name from the animal — the Spanish word Gallipago meaning a fresh-water terrapin. From the peculiarity of their shape and action they have been sometimes called the elephant tortoise. They are frequently found of an enormous size. I have myself seen several which would weigh from twelve to fifteen hundred pounds, although I do not remember that any navigator speaks of having seen them weighing more than eight hundred. Their appearance is singular, and even disgusting. Their steps are very slow, measured, and heavy, their bodies being carried about a foot from the ground. Their neck is long, and exceedingly slender; from eighteen inches to two feet is a very common length, and I killed one, where the distance from the shoulder to the extremity of the head was no less than three feet ten inches. The head has a striking resemblance to that of a serpent. They can exist without food for an almost incredible length of time, instances having been known where they have been thrown into the hold of a vessel and lain two years without nourishment of any kind — being as fat, and, in every respect, in as good order at the expiration of the time as when they were first put in. In one particular these extraordinary animals bear a resemblance to the dromedary, or camel of the desert. In a bag at the root of the neck they carry with them a constant supply of water. In some instances, upon killing them after a full year's deprivation of all nourishment, as much as three gallons of perfectly sweet and fresh water have been found in their bags. Their food is chiefly wild parsley and celery, with purslain, sea-kelp, and prickly pears, upon which latter vegetable they thrive wonderfully, a great quantity of it being usually found on the hillsides near the shore wherever the animal itself is discovered. They are excellent and highly nutritious food, and have, no doubt, been the means of preserving the lives of thousands of seamen employed in the whale-fishery and other pursuits in the Pacific.

The one which we had the good fortune to bring up from the storeroom was not of a large size, weighing probably sixty-five or seventy pounds. It was a female, and in excellent condition, being exceedingly fat, and having more than a quart of limpid and sweet water in its bag.

This was indeed a treasure; and, falling on our knees with one accord, we returned fervent thanks to God for so seasonable a relief.

We had great difficulty in getting the animal up through the opening, as its struggles were fierce and its strength prodigious. It was upon the point of making its escape from Peter's grasp, and slipping back into the water, when Augustus, throwing a rope with a slipknot around its throat, held it up in this manner until I jumped into the hole by the side of Peters, and assisted him in lifting it out.

The water we drew carefully from the bag into the jug; which, it will be remembered, had been brought up before from the cabin. Having done this, we broke off the neck of a bottle so as to form, with the cork, a kind of glass, holding not quite half a gill. We then each drank one of these measures full, and resolved to limit ourselves to this quantity per day as long as it should hold out.

During the last two or three days, the weather having been dry and pleasant, the bedding we had obtained from the cabin, as well as our clothing, had become thoroughly dry, so that we passed this night (that of the twenty-third) in comparative comfort, enjoying a tranquil repose, after having supped plentifully on olives and ham, with a small allowance of the wine. Being afraid of losing some of our stores overboard during the night, in the event of a breeze springing up, we secured them as well as possible with cordage to the fragments of the windlass. Our tortoise, which we were anxious to preserve alive as long as we could, we threw on its back, and otherwise carefully fastened.

<div align="center">CHAPTER XIII</div>

July 24. — This morning saw us wonderfully recruited in spirits and strength. Notwithstanding the perilous situation in which we were still placed, ignorant of our position, although certainly at a great distance from land, without more food than would last us for a fortnight even with great care, almost entirely without water, and floating about at the mercy of every wind and wave on the merest wreck in the world, still the infinitely more terrible distresses and dangers from which we had so lately and so providentially been delivered caused us to regard what we now endured as but little more than an ordinary evil — so strictly comparative is either good or ill.

At sunrise we were preparing to renew our attempts at getting up something from the storeroom, when, a smart shower coming on, with some lightning, we turn our attention to the catching of water by means of the sheet we had used before for this purpose. We had no other means of collecting the rain than by holding the sheet spread out with one of the forechain-plates in the middle of it. The water, thus conducted to the centre, was drained through into our jug. We had nearly filled it in this manner, when, a heavy squall coming on from the northward, obliged us to desist, as the hulk began once more to roll so violently

that we could no longer keep our feet. We now went forward, and, lashing ourselves securely to the remnant of the windlass as before, awaited the event with far more calmness than could have been antici-pated or would have been imagined possible under the circumstances. At noon the wind had freshened into a two-reef breeze, and by night into a stiff gale, accompanied with a tremendously heavy swell. Experi-ence having taught us, however, the best method of arranging our lash-ings, we weathered this dreary night in tolerable security, although thor-oughly drenched at almost every instant by the sea, and in momentary dread of being washed off. Fortunately, the weather was so warm as to render the water rather grateful than otherwise.

July 25. — This morning the gale had diminished to a mere ten-knot breeze, and the sea had gone down with it so considerably that we were able to keep ourselves dry upon the deck. To our great grief, however, we found that two jars of our olives, as well as the whole of our ham, had been washed overboard, in spite of the careful manner in which they had been fastened. We determined not to kill the tortoise as yet, and contented ourselves for the present with a breakfast on a few of the olives, and a measure of water each, which latter we mixed half and half, with wine, finding great relief and strength from the mixture, with-out the distressing intoxication which had ensued upon drinking the port. The sea was still far too rough for the renewal of our efforts at getting up provision from the storeroom. Several articles, of no impor-tance to us in our present situation, floated up through the opening during the day, and were immediately washed overboard. We also now observed that the hulk lay more along than ever, so that we could not stand an instant without lashing ourselves. On this account we passed a gloomy and uncomfortable day. At noon the sun appeared to be nearly vertical, and we had no doubt that we had been driven down by the long succession of northward and northwesterly winds into the near vicinity of the equator. Toward evening saw several sharks, and were somewhat alarmed by the audacious manner in which an enormously large one approached us. At one time, a lurch throwing the deck very far beneath the water, the monster actually swam in upon us, floundering for some moments just over the companion-hatch, and striking Peters violently with his tail. A heavy sea at length hurled him overboard, much to our relief. In moderate weather we might have easily captured him.

July 26. — This morning, the wind having greatly abated, and the sea not being very rough, we determined to renew our exertions in the store-room. After a great deal of hard labor during the whole day, we found that nothing further was to be expected from this quarter, the partitions of the room having been stove during the night, and its contents swept into the hold. This discovery, as may be supposed, filled us with despair.

July 27. — The sea nearly smooth, with a light wind, and still from the

northward and westward. The sun coming out hotly in the afternoon, we occupied ourselves in drying our clothes. Found great relief from thirst, and much comfort otherwise, by bathing in the sea; in this, however, we were forced to use great caution, being afraid of sharks, several of which were seen swimming around the brig during the day.

July 28. — Good weather still. The brig now began to lie along so alarmingly that we feared she would eventually roll bottom up. Prepared ourselves as well as we could for this emergency, lashing our tortoise, waterjug, and two remaining jars of olives as far as possible over to the windward, placing them outside the hull, below the main-chains. The sea very smooth all day, with little or no wind.

July 29. — A continuance of the same weather. Augustus's wounded arm began to evince symptoms of mortification. He complained of drowsiness and excessive thirst, but no acute pain. Nothing could be done for his relief beyond rubbing his wounds with a little of the vinegar from the olives, and from this no benefit seemed to be experienced. We did every thing in our power for his comfort, and trebled his allowance of water.

July 30. — An excessively hot day, with no wind. An enormous shark kept close by the hulk during the whole of the forenoon. We made several unsuccessful attempts to capture him by means of a noose. Augustus much worse, and evidently sinking as much from want of proper nourishment as from the effect of his wounds. He constantly prayed to be relieved from his sufferings, wishing for nothing but death. This evening we ate the last of our olives, and found the water in our jug so putrid that we could not swallow it at all without the addition of wine. Determined to kill our tortoise in the morning.

July 31. — After a night of excessive anxiety and fatigue, owing to the position of the hulk, we set about killing and cutting up our tortoise. He proved to be much smaller than we had supposed, although in good condition, — the whole meat about him not amounting to more than ten pounds. With a view of preserving a portion of this as long as possible, we cut it into fine pieces, and filled with them our three remaining olive jars and the wine-bottle (all of which had been kept), pouring in afterward the vinegar from the olives. In this manner we put away about three pounds of the tortoise, intending not to touch it until we had consumed the rest. We concluded to restrict ourselves to about four ounces of the meat per day; the whole would thus last us thirteen days. A brisk shower, with severe thunder and lightning, came on about dusk, but lasted so short a time that we only succeeded in catching about half a pint of water. The whole of this, by common consent, was given to Augustus, who now appeared to be in the last extremity. He drank the water from the sheet as we caught it (we holding it above him as he lay so as to let it run into his mouth), for we had now nothing left capable of holding water, unless we had chosen to empty out our wine from the

carboy, or the stale water from the jug. Either of these expedients would have been resorted to had the shower lasted.

The sufferer seemed to derive but little benefit from the draught. His arm was completely black from the wrist to the shoulder, and his feet were like ice. We expected every moment to see him breathe his last. He was frightfully emaciated; so much so that, although he weighed a hundred and twenty-seven pounds upon his leaving Nantucket, he now did not weigh more than *forty or fifty at the farthest*. His eyes were sunk far in his head, being scarcely perceptible, and the skin of his cheeks hung so loosely as to prevent his masticating any food, or even swallowing any liquid, without great difficulty.

August 1. — A continuance of the same calm weather, with an oppressively hot sun. Suffered exceedingly from thirst, the water in the jug being absolutely putrid and swarming with vermin. We contrived, nevertheless, to swallow a portion of it by mixing it with wine; our thirst, however, was but little abated. We found more relief by bathing in the sea, but could not avail ourselves of this expedient except at long intervals, on account of the continual presence of sharks. We now saw clearly that Augustus could not be saved; that he was evidently dying. We could do nothing to relieve his sufferings, which appeared to be great. About twelve o'clock he expired in strong convulsions, and without having spoken for several days. His death filled us with the most gloomy forebodings, and had so great an effect upon our spirits that we sat motionless by the corpse during the whole day, and never addressed each other except in a whisper. It was not until some time after dark that we took courage to get up and throw the body overboard. It was then loathsome beyond expression, and so far decayed that, as Peters attempted to lift it, an entire leg came off in his grasp. As the mass of putrefaction slipped over the vessel's side into the water, the glare of phosphoric light with which it was surrounded plainly discovered to us seven or eight large sharks, the clashing of whose horrible teeth, as their prey was torn to pieces among them, might have been heard at the distance of a mile. We shrunk within ourselves in the extremity of horror at the sound.

August 2. — The same fearfully calm and hot weather. The dawn found us in a state of pitiable dejection as well as bodily exhaustion. The water in the jug was now absolutely useless, being a thick gelatinous mass; nothing but frightful-looking worms mingled with slime. We threw it out, and washed the jug well in the sea, afterward pouring a little vinegar in it from our bottles of pickled tortoise. Our thirst could now scarcely be endured, and we tried in vain to relieve it by wine, which seemed only to add fuel to the flame, and excited us to a high degree of intoxication. We afterward endeavoured to relieve our sufferings by mixing the wine with seawater; but this instantly brought about the most violent retchings, so that we never again attempted it. During the whole day we anxiously sought an opportunity of bathing, but to no purpose;

for the hulk was now entirely besieged on all sides with sharks — no doubt the identical monsters who had devoured our poor companion on the evening before, and who were in momentary expectation of another similar feast. This circumstance occasioned us the most bitter regret and filled us with the most depressing and melancholy forebodings. We had experienced indescribable relief in bathing, and to have this resource cut off in so frightful a manner was more than we could bear. Nor, indeed, were we altogether free from the apprehension of immediate danger, for the least slip or false movement would have thrown us at once within reach of those voracious fish, who frequently thrust themselves directly upon us, swimming up to leeward. No shouts or exertions on our part seemed to alarm them. Even when one of the largest was struck with an axe by Peters and much wounded, he persisted in his attempts to push in where we were. A cloud came up at dusk, but, to our extreme anguish, passed over without discharging itself. It is quite impossible to conceive our sufferings from thirst at this period. We passed a sleepless night, both on this account and through dread of the sharks.

August 3. — No prospect of relief, and the brig lying still more and more along, so that now we could not maintain a footing upon deck at all. Busied ourselves in securing our wine and tortoise-meat, so that we might not lose them in the event of our rolling over. Got out two stout spikes from the forechains, and, by means of the axe, drove them into the hull to windward within a couple of feet of the water; this not being very far from the keel, as we were nearly upon our beam-ends. To these spikes we now lashed our provisions, as being more secure than their former position beneath the chains. Suffered great agony from thirst during the whole day — no chance of bathing on account of the sharks, which never left us for a moment. Found it impossible to sleep.

August 4. — A little before daybreak we perceived that the hulk was heeling over, and aroused ourselves to prevent being thrown off by the movement. At first the roll was slow and gradual, and we contrived to clamber over to windward very well, having taken the precaution to leave ropes hanging from the spikes we had driven in for the provision. But we had not calculated sufficiently upon the acceleration of the impetus; for, presently the heel became too violent to allow of our keeping pace with it; and, before either of us knew what was to happen, we found ourselves hurled furiously into the sea, and struggling several fathoms beneath the surface, with the huge hull immediately above us.

In going under the water I had been obliged to let go my hold upon the rope; and finding that I was completely beneath the vessel, and my strength nearly exhausted, I scarcely made a struggle for life, and resigned myself, in a few seconds, to die. But here again I was deceived, not having taken into consideration the natural rebound of the hull to windward. The whirl of the water upward, which the vessel occasioned in rolling partially back, brought me to the surface still more violently than

I had been plunged beneath. Upon coming up I found myself about twenty yards from the hulk, as near as I could judge. She was lying keel up, rocking furiously from side to side, and the sea in all directions around was much agitated, and full of strong whirlpools. I could see nothing of Peters. An oil-cask was floating within a few feet of me, and various other articles from the brig were scattered about.

My principal terror was now on account of the sharks, which I knew to be in my vicinity. In order to deter these, if possible, from approaching me, I splashed the water vigorously with both hands and feet as I swam towards the hulk, creating a body of foam. I have no doubt that to this expedient, simple as it was, I was indebted for my preservation; for the sea all round the brig, just before her rolling over, was so crowded with these monsters, that I must have been, and really was, in actual contact with some of them during my progress. By great good fortune, however, I reached the side of the vessel in safety, although so utterly weakened by the violent exertion I had used that I should never have been able to get upon it but for the timely assistance of Peters, who, now, to my great joy, made his appearance (having scrambled up to the keel from the opposite side of the hull), and threw me the end of a rope — one of those which had been attached to the spikes.

Having barely escaped this danger, our attention was now directed to the dreadful imminency of another — that of absolute starvation. Our whole stock of provision had been swept overboard in spite of all our care in securing it; and seeing no longer the remotest possibility of obtaining more, we gave way both of us to despair, weeping aloud like children, and neither of us attempting to offer consolation to the other. Such weakness can scarcely be conceived, and to those who have never been similarly situated will, no doubt, appear unnatural; but it must be remembered that our intellects were so entirely disordered by the long course of privation and terror to which we had been subjected, that we could not justly be considered, at that period, in the light of rational beings. In subsequent perils, nearly as great, if not greater, I bore up with fortitude against all the evils of my situation, and Peters, it will be seen, evinced a stoical philosophy nearly as incredible as his present childlike supineness and imbecility — the mental condition made the difference.

The overturning of the brig, even with the consequent loss of the wine and turtle, would not, in fact, have rendered our situation more deplorable than before, except for the disappearance of the bedclothes by which we had been hitherto enabled to catch rainwater, and of the jug in which we had kept it when caught; for we found the whole bottom, from within two or three feet of the bends as far as the keel, together with the keel itself, *thickly covered with large barnacles, which proved to be excellent and highly nutritious food.* Thus, in two important respects, the accident we had so greatly dreaded proved to be a benefit rather than an injury; it had opened to us a supply of provisions which

we could not have exhausted, using it moderately, in a month; and it had greatly contributed to our comfort as regards position, we being much more at ease, and in infinitely less danger, than before.

The difficulty, however, of now obtaining water blinded us to all the benefits of the change in our condition. That we might be ready to avail ourselves, as far as possible, of any shower which might fall, we took off our shirts, to make use of them as we had of the sheets — not hoping, of course, to get more in this way, even under the most favorable circumstances, than half a gill at a time. No signs of a cloud appeared during the day, and the agonies of our thirst were nearly intolerable. At night, Peters obtained about an hour's disturbed sleep, but my intense sufferings would not permit me to close my eyes for a single moment.

August 5. — To-day, a gentle breeze springing up carried us through a vast quantity of seaweed, among which we were so fortunate as to find eleven small crabs, which afforded us several delicious meals. Their shells being quite soft, we ate them entire, and found that they irritated our thirst far less than the barnacles. Seeing no trace of sharks among the seaweed, we also ventured to bathe, and remained in the water for four or five hours, during which we experienced a very sensible diminution of our thirst. Were greatly refreshed, and spent the night somewhat more comfortably than before, both of us snatching a little sleep.

August 6. — This day we were blessed by a brisk and continual rain, lasting from about noon until after dark. Bitterly did we now regret the loss of our jug and carboy; for, in spite of the little means we had of catching the water, we might have filled one, if not both of them. As it was, we contrived to satisfy the cravings of thirst by suffering the shirts to become saturated, and then wringing them so as to let the grateful fluid trickle into our mouths. In this occupation we passed the entire day.

August 7. — Just at daybreak we both at the same instant descried a sail to the eastward, and *evidently coming towards us!* We hailed the glorious sight with a long, although feeble shout of rapture; and began instantly to make every signal in our power, by flaring the shirts in the air, leaping as high as our weak condition would permit, and even by hallooing with all the strength of our lungs, although the vessel could not have been less than fifteen miles distant. However, she still continued to near our hulk, and we felt that, if she but held her present course, she must eventually come so close as to perceive us. In about an hour after we first discovered her, we could clearly see the people on her decks. She was a long, low, and rakish-looking topsail schooner, with a black ball in her foretopsail, and had, apparently, a full crew. We now became alarmed, for we could hardly imagine it possible that she did not observe us, and were apprehensive that she meant to leave us to perish as we were — an act of fiendish barbarity, which, however incredible it may appear, has been repeatedly perpetuated at sea, under circumstances very nearly similar, and by beings who were regarded as belonging to

the human species.* In this instance, however, by the mercy of God, we were destined to be most happily deceived; for, presently we were aware of a sudden commotion on the deck of the stranger, who immediately afterward ran up a British flag, and, hauling her wind, bore up directly upon us. In half an hour more we found ourselves in her cabin. She proved to be the Jane Guy, of Liverpool, Captain Guy, bound on a sealing and trading voyage to the South Seas and Pacific.

CHAPTER XIV

The Jane Guy was a fine-looking topsail schooner of a hundred and eighty tons burden. She was unusually sharp in the bows, and on a wind, in moderate weather, the fastest sailer I have ever seen. Her qualities, however, as a rough sea-boat, were not so good, and her draught of water was by far too great for the trade to which she was destined. For this peculiar service, a larger vessel, and one of a light proportionate draught, is desirable — say a vessel of from three hundred to three hundred and fifty tons. She should be bark-rigged, and in other respects of a different construction from the usual South Sea ships. It is absolutely necessary that she should be well armed. She should have, say ten or twelve twelve-pound carronades, and two or three long twelves, with brass blunder-busses, and water-tight arm-chests for each top. Her anchors and cables should be of far greater strength than is required for any other species of trade, and, above all, her crew should be numerous and efficient — not less, for such a vessel as I have described, than fifty or sixty able-bodied

* The case of the brig Polly, of Boston, is one so much in point, and her fate, in many respects, so remarkably similar to our own, that I cannot forbear alluding to it here. This vessel, of one hundred and thirty tons burden, sailed from Boston, with a cargo of lumber and provisions, for Santa Croix, on the twelfth of December, 1811, under the command of Captain Casneau. There were eight souls on board besides the captain — the mate, four seamen, and the cook, together with a Mr. Hunt, and a negro girl belonging to him. On the fifteenth, having cleared the shoal of Georges, she sprung a leak in a gale of wind from the southeast, and was finally capsized; but, the masts going by the board, she afterward righted. They remained in this situation, without fire, and with very little provision, for the period of one hundred and ninety-one days (from December the fifteenth to June the twentieth), when Captain Casneau and Samuel Badger, the only survivors, were taken off the wreck by the Fame, of Hull, Captain Featherstone, bound home from Rio Janeiro. When picked up, they were in latitude 28° N., longitude 13° W., *having drifted above two thousand miles!* On the ninth of July the Fame fell in with the brig Dromero, Captain Perkins, who landed the two sufferers in Kennebeck. The narrative from which we gather these details ends in the following words:

"It is natural to inquire how they could float such a vast distance, upon the most frequented part of the Atlantic, and not be discovered all this time. *They were passed by more than a dozen sail, one of which came so nigh them that they could distinctly see the people on deck and on the rigging looking at them; but, to the inexpressible disappointment of the starving and freezing men, they stifled the dictates of compassion, hoisted sail, and cruelly abandoned them to their fate.*"

men. The Jane Guy had a crew of thirty-five, all able seamen, besides the captain and mate, but she was not altogether as well armed or otherwise equipped, as a navigator acquainted with the difficulties and dangers of the trade could have desired.

Captain Guy was a gentleman of great urbanity of manner, and of considerable experience in the southern traffic, to which he had devoted a great portion of his life. He was deficient, however, in energy, and, consequently, in that spirit of enterprise which is here so absolutely requisite. He was part owner of the vessel in which he sailed, and was invested with discretionary powers to cruise in the South Seas for any cargo which might come most readily to hand. He had on board, as usual in such voyages, beads, looking-glasses, tinder-works, axes, hatchets, saws, adzes, planes, chisels, gouges, gimlets, files, spokeshaves, rasps, hammers, nails, knives, scissors, razors, needles, thread, crockery-ware, calico, trinkets, and other similar articles.

The schooner sailed from Liverpool on the tenth of July, crossed the Tropic of Cancer on the twenty-fifth, in longitude twenty degrees west, and reached Sal, one of the Cape Verd islands, on the twenty-ninth, where she took in salt and other necessaries for the voyage. On the third of August, she left the Cape Verds and steered southwest, stretching over toward the coast of Brazil, so as to cross the equator between the meridians of twenty-eight and thirty degrees west longitude. This is the course usually taken by vessels bound from Europe to the Cape of Good Hope, or by that route to the East Indies. By proceeding thus they avoid the calms and strong contrary currents which continually prevail on the coast of Guinea, while, in the end, it is found to be the shortest track, as westerly winds are never wanting afterward by which to reach the Cape. It was Captain Guy's intention to make his first stoppage at Kerguelen's Land — I hardly know for what reason. On the day we were picked up the schooner was off Cape St. Roque, in longitude thirty-one degrees west; so that, when found, we had drifted probably, from north to south, *not less than five-and-twenty degrees!*

On board the Jane Guy we were treated with all the kindness our distressed situation demanded. In about a fortnight, during which time we continued steering to the southeast, with gentle breezes and fine weather, both Peters and myself recovered entirely from the effects of our late privation and dreadful sufferings, and we began to remember what had passed rather as a frightful dream from which we had been happily awakened, than as events which had taken place in sober and naked reality. I have since found that this species of partial oblivion is usually brought about by sudden transition, whether from joy to sorrow or from sorrow to joy — the degree of forgetfulness being proportioned to the degree of difference in the exchange. Thus, in my own case, I now feel it impossible to realize the full extent of the misery which I endured during the days spent upon the hulk. The incidents are remembered,

but not the feelings which the incidents elicited at the time of their occurrence. I only know, that when they did occur, I *then* thought human nature could sustain nothing more of agony.

We continued our voyage for some weeks without any incidents of greater moment than the occasional meeting with whaling-ships, and more frequently with the black or right whale, so called in contradistinction to the spermaceti. These, however, were chiefly found south of the twenty-fifth parallel. On the sixteenth of September, being in the vicinity of the Cape of Good Hope, the schooner encountered her first gale of any violence since leaving Liverpool. In this neighborhood, but more frequently to the south and east of the promontory (we were to the westward), navigators have often to contend with storms from the northward, which rage with great fury. They always bring with them a heavy sea, and one of their most dangerous features is the instantaneous chopping round of the wind, an occurrence almost certain to take place during the greatest force of the gale. A perfect hurricane will be blowing at one moment from the northward or northeast, and in the next not a breath of wind will be felt in that direction, while from the southwest it will come out all at once with a violence almost inconceivable. A bright spot to the southward is the sure forerunner of the change, and vessels are thus enabled to take the proper precautions.

It was about six in the morning when the blow came on with a white squall, and, as usual, from the northward. By eight it had increased very much, and brought down upon us one of the most tremendous seas I had then ever beheld. Every thing had been made as snug as possible, but the schooner laboured excessively, and gave evidence of her bad qualities as a seaboat, pitching her forecastle under at every plunge and with the greatest difficulty struggling up from one wave before she was buried in another. Just before sunset the bright spot for which we had been on the look-out made its appearance in the southwest, and in an hour afterward we perceived the little headsail we carried flapping listlessly against the mast. In two minutes more, in spite of every preparation, we were hurled on our beam-ends, as if by magic, and a perfect wilderness of foam made a clear breach over us as we lay. The blow from the southwest, however, luckily proved to be nothing more than a squall, and we had the good fortune to right the vessel without the loss of a spar. A heavy cross sea gave us great trouble for a few hours after this, but toward morning we found ourselves in nearly as good condition as before the gale. Captain Guy considered that he had made an escape little less than miraculous.

On the thirteenth of October we came in sight of Prince Edward's Island, in latitude 46° 53′ S., longitude 37° 46′ E. Two days afterward we found ourselves near Possession Island, and presently passed the islands of Crozet, in latitude 42° 59′ S., longitude 48° E. On the eighteenth we made Kerguelen's or Desolation Island, in the Southern Indian

Ocean, and came to anchor in Christmas Harbour, having four fathoms of water.

This island, or rather group of islands, bears southeast from the Cape of Good Hope, and is distant therefrom nearly eight hundred leagues. It was first discovered in 1772, by the Baron de Kergulen, or Kerguelen, a Frenchman, who, thinking the land to form a portion of an extensive southern continent carried home information to that effect, which produced much excitement at the time. The government, taking the matter up, sent the baron back in the following year for the purpose of giving his new discovery a critical examination, when the mistake was discovered. In 1777, Captain Cook fell in with the same group, and gave to the principal one the name of Desolation Island, a title which it certainly well deserves. Upon approaching the land, however, the navigator might be induced to suppose otherwise, as the sides of most of the hills, from September to March, are clothed with very brilliant verdure. This deceitful appearance is caused by a small plant resembling saxifrage, which is abundant, growing in large patches on a species of crumbling moss. Besides this plant there is scarcely a sign of vegetation on the island, if we except some coarse rank grass near the harbor, some lichen, and a shrub which bears resemblance to a cabbage shooting into seed, and which has a bitter and acrid taste.

The face of the country is hilly, although none of the hills can be called lofty. Their tops are perpetually covered with snow. There are several harbors, of which Christmas Harbour is the most convenient. It is the first to be met with on the northeast side of the island after passing Cape Francois, which forms the northern shore, and, by its peculiar shape, serves to distinguish the harbour. Its projecting point terminates in a high rock, through which is a large hole, forming a natural arch. The entrance is in latitude 48° 40′ S., longitude 69° 6′ E. Passing in here, good anchorage may be found under the shelter of several small islands, which form a sufficient protection from all easterly winds. Proceeding on eastwardly from this anchorage you come to Wasp Bay, at the head of the harbour. This is a small basin, completely landlocked, into which you can go with four fathoms, and find anchorage in from ten to three, hard clay bottom. A ship might lie here with her best bower ahead all the year round without risk. To the westward, at the head of Wasp Bay, is a small stream of excellent water, easily procured.

Some seal of the fur and hair species are still to be found on Kerguelen's Island, and sea elephants abound. The feathered tribes are discovered in great numbers. Penguins are very plenty, and of these there are four different kinds. The royal penguin, so called from its size and beautiful plumage, is the largest. The upper part of the body is usually gray, sometimes of a lilac tint; the under portion of the purest white imaginable. The head is of a glossy and most brilliant black, the feet also. The chief beauty of plumage, however, consists in two broad stripes of a gold

color, which pass along from the head to the breast. The bill is long, and either pink or bright scarlet. These birds walk erect; with a stately carriage. They carry their heads high with their wings drooping like two arms, and, as their tails project from their body in a line with the legs, the resemblance to a human figure is very striking, and would be apt to deceive the spectator at a casual glance or in the gloom of the evening. The royal penguins which we met with on Kerguelen's Land were rather larger than a goose. The other kinds are the macaroni, the jackass, and the rookery penguin. These are much smaller, less beautiful in plumage, and different in other respects.

Besides the penguin many other birds are here to be found, among which may be mentioned sea-hens, blue peterels, teal, ducks, Port Egmont hens, shags, Cape pigeons, the nelly, sea swallows, terns, sea gulls, Mother Carey's chickens, Mother Carey's geese, or the great peterel, and, lastly, the albatross.

The great peterel is as large as the common albatross, and is carnivorous. It is frequently called the break-bones, or osprey peterel. They are not at all shy, and, when properly cooked, are palatable food. In flying they sometimes sail very close to the surface of the water, with the wings expanded, without appearing to move them in the least degree, or make any exertion with them whatever.

The albatross is one of the largest and fiercest of the South Sea birds. It is of the gull species, and takes its prey on the wing, never coming on land except for the purpose of breeding. Between this bird and the penguin the most singular friendship exists. Their nests are constructed with great uniformity upon a plan concerted between the two species — that of the albatross being placed in the centre of a little square formed by the nests of four penguins. Navigators have agreed in calling an assemblage of such encampments *a rookery*. These rookeries have been often described, but as my readers may not all have seen these descriptions, and as I shall have occasion hereafter to speak of the penguin and albatross, it will not be amiss to say something here of their mode of building and living.

When the season for incubation arrives, the birds assemble in vast numbers, and for some days appear to be deliberating upon the proper course to be pursued. At length they proceed to action. A level piece of ground is selected, of suitable extent, usually comprising three or four acres, and situated as near the sea as possible, being still beyond its reach. The spot is chosen with reference to its evenness of surface, and that is preferred which is the least encumbered with stones. This matter being arranged, the birds proceed, with one accord, and actuated apparently by one mind, to trace out, with mathematical accuracy, either a square or other parallelogram, as may best suit the nature of the ground, and of just sufficient size to accommodate easily all the birds assembled, and no more — in this particular seeming determined upon preventing the ac-

cess of future stragglers who have not participated in the labor of the encampment. One side of the place thus marked out runs parallel with the water's edge, and is left open for ingress or egress.

Having defined the limits of the rookery, the colony now begin to clear it of every species of rubbish, picking up stone by stone, and carrying them outside of the lines, and close by them, so as to form a wall on the three inland sides. Just within this wall a perfectly level and smooth walk is formed, from six to eight feet wide, and extending around the encampment — thus serving the purpose of a general promenade.

The next process is to partition out the whole area into small squares exactly equal in size. This is done by forming narrow paths, very smooth, and crossing each other at right angles throughout the entire extent of the rookery. At each intersection of these paths the nest of an albatross is constructed, and a penguin's nest in the centre of each square — thus every penguin is surrounded by four albatrosses, and each albatross by a like number of penguins. The penguin's nest consists of a hole in the earth, very shallow, being only just of sufficient depth to keep her single egg from rolling. The albatross is somewhat less simple in her arrangements, erecting a hillock about a foot high and two in diameter. This is made of earth, seaweed, and shells. On its summit she builds her nest.

The birds take especial care never to leave their nests unoccupied for an instant during the period of incubation, or, indeed, until the young progeny are sufficiently strong to take care of themselves. While the male is absent at sea in search of food, the female remains on duty, and it is only upon the return of her partner that she ventures abroad. The eggs are never left uncovered at all — while one bird leaves the nest the other nestling in by its side. This precaution is rendered necessary by the thieving propensities prevalent in the rookery, the inhabitants making no scruple to purloin each other's eggs at every good opportunity.

Although there are some rookeries in which the penguin and albatross are the sole population, yet in most of them a variety of oceanic birds are to be met with, enjoying all the privileges of citizenship, and scattering their nests here and there, wherever they can find room, never interfering, however, with the stations of the larger species. The appearance of such encampments, when seen from a distance, is exceedingly singular. The whole atmosphere just above the settlement is darkened with the immense number of the albatross (mingled with the smaller tribes) which are continually hovering over it, either going to the ocean or returning home. At the same time a crowd of penguins are to be observed, some passing to and fro in the narrow alleys, and some marching with the military strut so peculiar to them, around the general promenade ground which encircles the rookery. In short, survey it as we will, nothing can be more astonishing than the spirit of reflection evinced by these feathered beings, and nothing surely can be better calculated to elicit reflection in every well-regulated human intellect.

On the morning after our arrival in Christmas Harbour the chief mate, Mr. Patterson, took the boats, and (although it was somewhat early in the season) went in scarch of seal, leaving the captain and a young relation of his on a point of barren land to the westward, they having some business, whose nature I could not ascertain, to transact in the interior of the island. Captain Guy took with him a bottle, in which was a sealed letter, and made his way from the point on which he was set on shore toward one of the highest peaks in the place. It is probable that his design was to leave the letter on that height for some vessel which he expected to come after him. As soon as we lost sight of him we proceeded (Peters and myself being in the mate's boat) on our cruise around the coast, looking for seal. In this business we were occupied about three weeks, examining with great care every nook and corner, not only of Kerguelen's Land, but of the several small islands in the vicinity. Our labours, however, were not crowned with any important success. We saw a great many fur seal, but they were exceedingly shy, and with the greatest exertions, we could only procure three hundred and fifty skins in all. Sea elephants were abundant, especially on the western coast of the mainland, but of these we killed only twenty, and this with great difficulty. On the smaller islands we discovered a good many of the hair seal, but did not molest them. We returned to the schooner on the eleventh, where we found Captain Guy and his nephew, who gave a very bad account of the interior, representing it as one of the most dreary and utterly barren countries in the world. They had remained two nights on the island, owing to some misunderstanding, on the part of the second mate, in regard to the sending a jollyboat from the schooner to take them off.

CHAPTER XV

On the twelfth we made sail from Christmas Harbour retracing our way to the westward, and leaving Marion's Island, one of Crozet's group, on the larboard. We afterward passed Prince Edward's Island, leaving it also on our left; then, steering more to the northward, made, in fifteen days, the islands of Tristan d'Acunha, in latitude 37° 8′ S., longitude 12° 8′ W.

This group, now so well known, and which consists of three circular islands, was first discovered by the Portuguese, and was visited afterward by the Dutch in 1643, and by the French in 1767. The three islands together form a triangle, and are distant from each other about ten miles, there being fine open passages between. The land in all of them is very high, especially in Tristan d'Acunha, properly so called. This is the largest of the group, being fifteen miles in circumference, and so elevated that it can be seen in clear weathcr at the distance of eighty or ninety miles. A part of the land toward the north rises more than a thousand feet perpendicularly from the sea. A tableland at this height extends

back nearly to the centre of the island, and from this tableland arises a lofty cone like that of Teneriffe. The lower half of this cone is clothed with trees of good size, but the upper region is barren rock, usually hidden among the clouds, and covered with snow during the greater part of the year. There are no shoals or other dangers about the island, the shores being remarkably bold and the water deep. On the northwestern coast is a bay, with a beach of black sand where a landing with boats can be easily effected, provided there be a southerly wind. Plenty of excellent water may here be readily procured; also cod and other fish may be taken with hook and line.

The next island in point of size, and the most westwardly of the group, is that called the Inaccessible. Its precise situation is 37° 17′ S. latitude, longitude 12° 24′ W. It is seven or eight miles in circumference, and on all sides presents a forbidding and precipitous aspect. Its top is perfectly flat, and the whole region is sterile, nothing growing upon it except a few stunted shrubs.

Nightingale Island, the smallest and most southerly, is in latitude 37° 26′ S., longitude 12° 12′ W. Off its southern extremity is a high ledge of rocky islets; a few also of a similar appearance are seen to the northeast. The ground is irregular and sterile, and a deep valley partially separates it.

The shores of these islands abound, in the proper season, with sea lions, sea elephants, the hair and fur seal, together with a great variety of oceanic birds. Whales are also plenty in their vicinity. Owing to the ease with which these various animals were here formerly taken, the group has been much visited since its discovery. The Dutch and French frequented it at a very early period. In 1790, Captain Patten, of the ship Industry, of Philadelphia, made Tristan d'Acunha, where he remained seven months (from August, 1790, to April, 1791) for the purpose of collecting sealskins. In this time he gathered no less than five thousand six hundred, and says that he would have had no difficulty in loading a large ship with oil in three weeks. Upon his arrival he found no quadrupeds, with the exception of a few wild goats; the island now abounds with all our most valuable domestic animals, which have been introduced by subsequent navigators.

I believe it was not long after Captain Patten's visit that Captain Colquhoun, of the American brig Betsey, touched at the largest of the islands for the purpose of refreshment. He planted onions, potatoes, cabbages, and a great many other vegetables, an abundance of all which is now to be met with.

In 1811, a Captain Haywood, in the Nereus, visited Tristan. He found there three Americans, who were residing upon the island to prepare sealskins and oil. One of these men was named Jonathan Lambert, and he called himself the sovereign of the country. He had cleared and cultivated about sixty acres of land, and turned his attention to raising

the coffee-plant and sugar-cane, with which he had been furnished by the American Minister at Rio Janeiro. This settlement, however, was finally abandoned, and in 1817 the islands were taken possession of by the British Government, who sent a detachment for that purpose from the Cape of Good Hope. They did not, however, retain them long; but, upon the evacuation of the country as a British possession, two or three English families took up their residence there independently of the Government. On the twenty-fifth of March, 1824, the Berwick, Captain Jeffrey, from London to Van Diemen's Land, arrived at the place, where they found an Englishman of the name of Glass, formerly a corporal in the British artillery. He claimed to be supreme governor of the islands, and had under his control twenty-one men and three women. He gave a very favourable account of the salubrity of the climate and of the productiveness of the soil. The population occupied themselves chiefly in collecting sealskins and sea elephant oil, with which they traded to the Cape of Good Hope, Glass owning a small schooner. At the period of our arrival the governor was still a resident, but his little community had multiplied, there being fifty-six persons upon Tristan, besides a smaller settlement of seven on Nightingale Island. We had no difficulty in procuring almost every kind of refreshment which we required — sheep, hogs, bullocks, rabbits, poultry, goats, fish in great variety, and vegetables were abundant. Having come to anchor close in with the large island, in eighteen fathoms, we took all we wanted on board very conveniently. Captain Guy also purchased of Glass five hundred sealskins and some ivory. We remained here a week, during which the prevailing winds were from the northward and westward, and the weather somewhat hazy. On the fifth of November we made sail to the southward and westward, with the intention of having a thorough search for a group of islands called the Auroras, respecting whose existence a great diversity of opinion has existed.

These islands are said to have been discovered as early as 1762, by the commander of the ship Aurora. In 1790, Captain Manuel de Oyarvido, in the ship Princess, belonging to the Royal Philippine Company, sailed, as he asserts, directly among them. In 1794, the Spanish corvette Atrevida went with the determination of ascertaining their precise situation, and, in a paper published by the Royal Hydrographical Society of Madrid in the year 1809, the following language is used respecting this expedition: "The corvette Atrevida practised, in their immediate vicinity, from the twenty-first to the twenty-seventh of January, all the necessary observations, and measured by chronometers the difference of longitude between these islands and the port of Soledad in the Manillas. The islands are three; they are very nearly in the same meridian; the centre one is rather low, and the other two may be seen at nine leagues' distance." The observations made on board the Atrevida give the following results as the precise situation of each island. The most northern is

in latitude 52° 37′ 24″ S., longitude 47° 43′ 15″ W.; the middle one in latitude 53° 2′ 40″ S., longitude 47° 55′ 15″ W.; and the most southern in latitude 53° 15′ 22″ S., longitude 47° 57′ 15″ W.

On the twenty-seventh of January, 1820, Captain James Weddel, of the British navy, sailed from Staten Land also in search of the Auroras. He reports that, having made the most diligent search and passed not only immediately over the spots indicated by the commander of the Atrevida, but in every direction throughout the vicinity of these spots, he could discover no indication of land. These conflicting statements have induced other navigators to look out for the islands; and, strange to say, while some have sailed through every inch of sea where they are supposed to lie without finding them, there have been not a few who declare positively that they have seen them; and even been close in with their shores. It was Captain Guy's intention to make every exertion within his power to settle the question so oddly in dispute.*

We kept on our course, between the south and west, with variable weather, until the twentieth of the month, when we found ourselves on the debated ground, being in latitude 53° 15′ S., longitude 47° 58′ W. — that is to say, very nearly upon the spot indicated as the situation of the most southern of the group. Not perceiving any sign of land, we continued to the westward of the parallel of fifty-three degrees south, as far as the meridian of fifty degrees west. We then stood to the north as far as the parallel of fifty-two degrees south, when we turned to the eastward, and kept our parallel by double altitudes, morning and evening, and meridian altitudes of the planets and moon. Having thus gone eastwardly to the meridian of the western coast of Georgia, we kept that meridian until we were in the latitude from which we set out. We then took diagonal courses throughout the entire extent of sea circumscribed, keeping a lookout constantly at the masthead, and repeating our examination with the greatest care for a period of three weeks, during which the weather was remarkably pleasant and fair, with no haze whatsoever. Of course we were thoroughly satisfied that, whatever islands might have existed in this vicinity at any former period, no vestige of them remained at the present day. Since my return home I find that the same ground was traced over, with equal care, in 1822, by Captain Johnson, of the American schooner Henry, and by Captain Morrell, in the American schooner Wasp — in both cases with the same result as in our own.

CHAPTER XVI

It had been Captain Guy's original intention, after satisfying himself about the Auroras, to proceed through the Strait of Magellan, and up

* Among the vessels which at various times have professed to meet with the Auroras may be mentioned the ship San Miguel, in 1769; the ship Aurora, in 1774; the brig Pearl, in 1779; and the ship Dolores, in 1790. They all agree in giving the mean latitude fifty-three degrees south.

along the western coast of Patagonia; but information received at Tristan d'Acunha induced him to steer to the southward, in the hope of falling in with some small islands said to lie about the parallel of 60° S., longitude 41° 20′ W. In the event of his not discovering these lands, he designed, should the season prove favourable, to push on toward the pole. Accordingly, on the twelfth of December, we made sail in that direction. On the eighteenth we found ourselves about the station indicated by Glass, and cruised for three days in that neighborhood without finding any traces of the islands he had mentioned. On the twenty-first, the weather being unusually pleasant, we again made sail to the southward, with the resolution of penetrating in that course as far as possible. Before entering upon this portion of my narrative, it may be as well, for the information of those readers who have paid little attention to the progress of discovery in these regions, to give some brief account of the very few attempts at reaching the southern pole which have hitherto been made.

That of Captain Cook was the first of which we have any distinct account. In 1772 he sailed to the south in the Resolution, accompanied by Lieutenant Furneaux in the Adventure. In December he found himself as far as the fifty-eighth parallel of south latitude, and in longitude 26° 57′ E. Here he met with narrow fields of ice, about eight or ten inches thick, and running northwest and southeast. This ice was in large cakes, and usually it was packed so closely that the vessel had great difficulty in forcing a passage. At this period Captain Cook supposed, from the vast number of birds to be seen, and from other indications, that he was in the near vicinity of land. He kept on to the southward, the weather being exceedingly cold, until he reached the sixty-fourth parallel, in longitude 38° 14′ E. Here he had mild weather, with gentle breezes, for five days, the thermometer being at thirty-six. In January, 1773, the vessels crossed the Antarctic circle, but did not succeed in penetrating much farther; for upon reaching latitude 67° 15′ they found all farther progress impeded by an immense body of ice, extending all along the southern horizon as far as the eye could reach. This ice was of every variety — and some large floes of it, miles in extent, formed a compact mass, rising eighteen or twenty feet above the water. It being late in the season, and no hope entertained of rounding these obstructions, Captain Cook now reluctantly turned to the northward.

In the November following he renewed his search in the Antarctic. In latitude 59° 40′ he met with a strong current setting to the southward. In December, when the vessels were in latitude 67° 31′, longitude 142° 54′ W., the cold was excessive, with heavy gales and fog. Here also birds were abundant; the albatross, the penguin, and the peterel especially. In latitude 70° 23′ some large islands of ice were encountered, and shortly afterward the clouds to the southward were observed to be of a snowy whiteness, indicating the vicinity of field ice. In latitude 71° 10′, longi-

tude 106° 54′ W., the navigators were stopped, as before, by an immense frozen expanse, which filled the whole area of the southern horizon. The northern edge of this expanse was ragged and broken, so firmly wedged together as to be utterly impassible, and extending about a mile to the southward. Behind it the frozen surface was comparatively smooth for some distance, until terminated in the extreme background by gigantic ranges of ice mountains, the one towering above the other. Captain Cook concluded that this vast field reached the southern pole or was joined to a continent. Mr. J. N. Reynolds, whose great exertions and perseverance have at length succeeded in getting set on foot a national expedition, partly for the purpose of exploring these regions, thus speaks of the attempt of the Resolution. "We are not surprised that Captain Cook was unable to go beyond 71° 10′, but we are astonished that he did attain that point on the meridian of 106° 54′ west longitude. Palmer's Land lies south of the Shetland, latitude sixty-four degrees, and tends to the southward and westward farther than any navigator has yet penetrated. Cook was standing for this land when his progress was arrested by the ice; which, we apprehend, must always be the case in that point, and so early in the season as the sixth of January — and we should not be surprised if a portion of the icy mountains described was attached to the main body of Palmer's Land, or to some other portions of land lying farther to the southward and westward."

In 1803, Captains Kreutzenstern and Lisiausky were dispatched by Alexander of Russia for the purpose of circumnavigating the globe. In endeavouring to get south, they made no farther than 59° 58′, in longitude 70° 15′ W. They here met with strong currents setting eastwardly. Whales were abundant, but they saw no ice. In regard to this voyage, Mr. Reynolds observes that, if Kreutzenstern had arrived where he did earlier in the season, he must have encountered ice — it was March when he reached the latitude specified. The winds, prevailing, as they do, from the southward and westward, had carried the floes, aided by currents, into that icy region bounded on the north by Georgia, east by Sandwich Land and the South Orkneys, and west by the South Shetland islands.

In 1822, Captain James Weddell, of the British navy, with two very small vessels, penetrated farther to the south than any previous navigator, and this, too, without encountering extraordinary difficulties. He states that although he was frequently hemmed in by ice *before* reaching the seventy-second parallel, yet, upon attaining it, not a particle was to be discovered, and that, upon arriving at the latitude of 74° 15′, no fields, and only three islands of ice were visible. It is somewhat remarkable that, although vast flocks of birds were seen, and other usual indications of land, and although, south of the Shetlands, unknown coasts were observed from the masthead tending southwardly, Weddell discourages the idea of land existing in the polar regions of the south.

On the 11th of January, 1823, Captain Benjamin Morrell, of the American schooner Wasp, sailed from Kerguelen's Land with a view of penetrating as far south as possible. On the first of February he found himself in latitude 64° 52′ S., longitude 118° 27′ E. The following passage is extracted from his journal of that date. "The wind soon freshened to an eleven-knot breeze, and we embraced this opportunity of making to the west; being however convinced that the farther we went south beyond latitude sixty-four degrees, the less ice was to be apprehended, we steered a little to the southward, until we crossed the Antarctic circle, and were in latitude 69° 15′ E. In this latitude there was *no field ice*, and very few ice islands in sight.

Under the date of March fourteenth I find also this entry. "The sea was now entirely free of field ice, and there were not more than a dozen ice islands in sight. At the same time the temperature of the air and water was at least thirteen degrees higher (more mild) than we had ever found it between the parallels of sixty and sixty-two south. We were now in latitude 70° 14′ S., and the temperature of the air was forty-seven, and that of the water forty-four. In this situation I found the variation to be 14° 27′ easterly, per azimuth. . . . I have several times passed within the Antarctic circle, on different meridians, and have uniformly found the temperature, both of the air and the water, to become more and more mild the farther I advanced beyond the sixty-fifth degree of south latitude, and that the variation decreases in the same proportion. While north of this latitude, say between sixty and sixty-five south, we frequently had great difficulty in finding a passage for the vessel between the immense and almost innumerable ice islands, some of which were from one to two miles in circumference, and more than five hundred feet above the surface of the water."

Being nearly destitute of fuel and water, and without proper instruments, it being also late in the season, Captain Morrell was now obliged to put back, without attempting any further progress to the westward, although an entirely open sea lay before him. He expresses the opinion that, had not these overruling considerations obliged him to retreat, he could have penetrated, if not to the pole itself, at least to the eighty-fifth parallel. I have given his ideas respecting these matters somewhat at length, that the reader may have an opportunity of seeing how far they were borne out by my own subsequent experience.

In 1831, Captain Briscoe, in the employ of the Messieurs Enderby, whale-ship owners of London, sailed in the brig Lively for the South Seas, accompanied by the cutter Tula. On the twenty-eighth of February, being in latitude 66° 30′ S., longitude 47° 31′ E., he descried land, and "clearly discovered through the snow the black peaks of a range of mountains running E. S. E." He remained in this neighbourhood during the whole of the following month, but was unable to approach the coast nearer than within ten leagues, owing to the boisterous state of the

weather. Finding it impossible to make further discovery during this season, he returned northward to winter in Van Diemen's Land.

In the beginning of 1832 he again proceeded southwardly, and on the fourth of February was seen to the southeast in latitude 67° 15′, longitude 69° 29′ W. This was soon found to be an island near the headland of the country he had first discovered. On the twenty-first of the month he succeeded in landing on the latter, and took possession of it in the name of William IV, calling it Adelaide's Island, in honour of the English queen. These particulars being made known to the Royal Geographical Society of London, the conclusion was drawn by that body "that there is a continuous tract of land extending from 47° 30′ E. to 69° 29′ W. longitude, running the parallel of from sixty-six to sixty-seven degrees south latitude." In respect to this conclusion Mr. Reynolds observes: "In the correctness of it we by no means concur; nor do the discoveries of Briscoe warrant any such inference. It was within these limits that Weddel proceeded south on a meridian to the east of Georgia, Sandwich Land, and the South Orkney and Shetland islands." My own experience will be found to testify most directly to the falsity of the conclusion arrived at by the society.

These are the principal attempts which have been made at penetrating to a high southern latitude, and it will now be seen that there remained, previous to the voyage of the Jane, nearly three hundred degrees of longitude in which the Antarctic circle had not been crossed at all. Of course a wide field lay before us for discovery, and it was with feelings of most intense interest that I heard Captain Guy express his resolution of pushing boldly to the southward.

CHAPTER XVII

We kept our course southwardly for four days after giving up the search for Glass's islands, without meeting with any ice at all. On the twenty-sixth, at noon, we were in latitude 63° 23′ S., longitude 41° 25′ W. We now saw several large ice islands, and a floe of field ice, not, however, of any great extent. The winds generally blew from the southeast, or the northeast, but were very light. Whenever we had a westerly wind, which was seldom, it was invariably attended with a rain squall. Every day we had more or less snow. The thermometer, on the twenty-seventh stood at thirty-five.

January 1, 1828. — This day we found ourselves completely hemmed in by the ice, and our prospects looked cheerless indeed. A strong gale blew, during the whole forenoon, from the northeast, and drove large cakes of the drift against the rudder and counter with such violence that we all trembled for the consequences. Toward evening, the gale still blowing with fury, a large field in front separated, and we were enabled, by carrying a press of sail, to force a passage through the smaller flakes into some open water beyond. As we approached this space we took in

sail by degrees, and having at length got clear, lay-to under a single-reefed foresail.

January 2. — We had now tolerably pleasant weather. At noon we found ourselves in latitude 69° 10′ S., longitude 42° 20′ W., having crossed the Antarctic circle. Very little ice was to be seen to the southward, although large fields of it lay behind us. This day we rigged some sounding gear, using a large iron pot capable of holding twenty gallons, and a line of two hundred fathoms. We found the current setting to the north, about a quarter of a mile per hour. The temperature of the air was now about thirty-three. Here we found the variation to be 14° 28′ easterly, per azimuth.

January 5. — We had still held on to the southward without any very great impediments. On this morning, however, being in latitude 73° 15′ E., longitude 42° 10′ W., we were again brought to a stand by an immense expanse of firm ice. We saw, nevertheless, much open water to the southward, and felt no doubt of being able to reach it eventually. Standing to the eastward along the edge of the floe, we at length came to a passage of about a mile in width, through which we warped our way by sundown. The sea in which we now were was thickly covered with ice islands, but had no field ice, and we pushed on boldly as before. The cold did not seem to increase, although we had snow very frequently, and now and then hail squalls of great violence. Immense flocks of the albratross flew over the schooner this day, going from southeast to northwest.

January 7. — The sea still remained pretty well open, so that we had no difficulty in holding on our course. To the westward we saw some icebergs of incredible size, and in the afternoon passed very near one whose summit could not have been less than four hundred fathoms from the surface of the ocean. Its girth was probably, at the base, three-quarters of a league, and several streams of water were running from crevices in its sides. We remained in sight of this island two days, and then only lost it in a fog.

January 10. — Early this morning we had the misfortune to lose a man overboard. He was an American named Peter Vredenburgh, a native of New York, and was one of the most valuable hands on board the schooner. In going over the bows his foot slipped, and he fell between two cakes of ice, never rising again. At noon of this day we were in latitude 78° 30′, longitude 40° 15′ W. The cold was now excessive, and we had hail squalls continually from the northward and eastward. In this direction also we saw several more immense icebergs, and the whole horizon to the eastward appeared to be blocked up with field ice, rising in tiers, one mass above the other. Some driftwood floated by during the evening, and a great quantity of birds flew over, among which were nellies, peterels, albatrosses, and a large bird of a brilliant blue plumage. The variation

here, per azimuth, was less than it had been previously to our passing the Antartic circle.

January 12. — Our passage to the south again looked doubtful, as nothing was to be seen in the direction of the pole but one apparently limitless floe, backed by absolute mountains of ragged ice, one precipice of which arose frowningly above the other. We stood to the westward until the fourteenth, in the hope of finding an entrance.

January 14. — This morning we reached the western extremity of the field which had impeded us, and, weathering it, came to an open sea, without a particle of ice. Upon sounding with two hundred fathoms, we here found a current setting southwardly at the rate of half a mile per hour. The temperature of the air was forty-seven, that of the water thirty-four. We now sailed to the southward without meeting any interruption of moment until the sixteenth, when, at noon, we were in latitude 81° 21′, longitude 42° W. We here again sounded, and found a current setting still southwardly, and at the rate of three quarters of a mile per hour. The variation per azimuth had diminished, and the temperature of the air was mild and pleasant, the thermometer being as high as fifty-one. At this period not a particle of ice was to be discovered. All hands on board now felt certain of attaining the pole.

January 17. — This day was full of incident. Innumerable flights of birds flew over us from the southward, and several were shot from the deck; one of them, a species of pelican, proved to be excellent eating. About midday a small floe of ice was seen from the masthead off the larboard bow, and upon it there appeared to be some large animal. As the weather was good and nearly calm, Captain Guy ordered out two of the boats to see what it was. Dirk Peters and myself accompanied the mate in the larger boat. Upon coming up with the floe, we perceived that it was in the possession of a gigantic creature of the race of the Arctic bear, but far exceeding in size the largest of these animals. Being well armed, we made no scruple of attacking it at once. Several shots were fired in quick succession, the most of which took effect, apparently, in the head and body. Nothing discouraged, however, the monster threw himself from the ice, and swam with open jaws, to the boat in which were Peters and myself. Owing to the confusion which ensued among us at this unexpected turn of the adventure, no person was ready immediately with a second shot, and the bear had actually succeeded in getting half his vast bulk across our gunwale, and seizing one of the men by the small of his back, before any efficient means were taken to repel him. In this extremity nothing but the promptness and agility of Peters saved us from destruction. Leaping upon the back of the huge beast, he plunged the blade of a knife behind the neck, reaching the spinal marrow at a blow. The brute tumbled into the sea lifeless, and without a struggle, rolling over Peters as he fell. The latter soon recovered himself,

and a rope being thrown him, he secured the carcass before entering the boat. We then returned in triumph to the schooner, towing our trophy behind us. This bear, upon admeasurement, proved to be full fifteen feet in his greatest length. His wool was perfectly white, and very coarse, curling tightly. The eyes were of a blood red, and larger than those of the Arctic bear; the snout also more rounded, rather resembling the snout of the bulldog. The meat was tender, but excessively rank and fishy, although the men devoured it with avidity, and declared it excellent eating.

Scarcely had we got our prize alongside, when the man at the masthead gave the joyful shout of "*land on the starboard bow!*" All hands were now upon the alert, and, a breeze springing up very opportunely from the northward and eastward, we were soon close in with the coast. It proved to be a low rocky islet, of about a league in circumference, and altogether destitute of vegetation, if we except a species of prickly pear. In approaching it from the northward, a singular ledge of rock is seen projecting into the sea, and bearing a strong resemblance to corded bales of cotton. Around this ledge to the westward is a small bay, at the bottom of which our boats effected a convenient landing.

It did not take us long to explore every portion of the island, but, with one exception, we found nothing worthy of our observation. In the southern extremity, we picked up near the shore, half buried in a pile of loose stones, a piece of wood, which seemed to have formed the prow of a canoe. There had been evidently some attempt at carving upon it, and Captain Guy fancied that he made out the figure of a tortoise, but the resemblance did not strike me very forcibly. Besides this prow, if such it were, we found no other token that any living creature had ever been here before. Around the coast we discovered occasional small floes of ice — but these were very few. The exact situation of the islet (to which Captain Guy gave the name of Bennet's Islet, in honour of his partner in the ownership of the schooner) is 82° 50′ S. latitude, 42° 20′ W. longitude.

We had now advanced to the southward more than eight degrees farther than any previous navigators, and the sea still lay perfectly open before us. We found, too, that the variation uniformly decreased as we proceeded, and, what was still more surprising, that the temperature of the air, and latterly of the water, became milder. The weather might even be called pleasant, and we had a steady but very gentle breeze always from some northern point of the compass. The sky was usually clear, with now and then a slight appearance of thin vapour in the southern horizon — this, however, was invariably of brief duration. Two difficulties alone presented themselves to our view; we were getting short of fuel, and symptoms of scurvy had occurred among several of the crew. These considerations began to impress upon Captain Guy the necessity of returning, and he spoke of it frequently. For my own part, confident as I

was of soon arriving at land of some description upon the course we were pursuing, and having every reason to believe, from present appearances, that we should not find it the sterile soil met with in the higher Arctic latitudes, I warmly pressed upon him the expediency of persevering, at least for a few days longer, in the direction we were now holding. So tempting an opportunity of solving the great problem in regard to an Antarctic continent had never yet been afforded to man, and I confess that I felt myself bursting with indignation at the timid and ill-timed suggestions of our commander. I believe, indeed, that what I could not refrain from saying to him on this head had the effect of inducing him to push on. While, therefore, I cannot but lament the most unfortunate and bloody events which immediately arose from my advice, I must still be allowed to feel some degree of gratification at having been instrumental, however remotely, in opening to the eye of science one of the most intensely exciting secrets which has ever engrossed its attention.

CHAPTER XVIII

January 18. — This morning * we continued to the southward, with the same pleasant weather as before. The sea was entirely smooth, the air tolerably warm and from the northeast, the temperature of the water fifty-three. We now again got our sounding-gear in order, and, with a hundred and fifty fathoms of line, found the current setting toward the pole at the rate of a mile an hour. This constant tendency to the southward, both in the wind and current, caused some degree of speculation, and even of alarm, in different quarters of the schooner, and I saw distinctly that no little impression had been made upon the mind of Captain Guy. He was exceedingly sensitive to ridicule, however, and I finally succeeded in laughing him out of his apprehensions. The variation was now very trivial. In the course of the day we saw several large whales of the right species, and innumerable flights of the albatross passed over the vessel. We also picked up a bush, full of red berries, like those of the hawthorn, and the carcass of a singular-looking land-animal. It was three feet in length, and but six inches in height, with four very short legs, the feet armed with long claws of a brilliant scarlet, and resembling coral in substance. The body was covered with a straight silky hair, perfectly white. The tail was peaked like that of a rat, and about a foot and a half long. The head resembled a cat's, with the exception of the ears — these were

* The terms *morning* and *evening*, which I have made use of to avoid confusion in my narrative, as far as possible, must not, of course, be taken in their ordinary sense. For a long time past we had had no night at all, the daylight being continual. The dates throughout are according to nautical time, and the bearings must be understood as per compass. I would also remark, in this place, that I cannot, in the first portion of what is here written, pretend to strict accuracy in respect to dates, or latitudes and longitudes, having kept no regular journal until after the period of which this first portion treats. In many instances I have relied altogether upon memory.

flopped like the ears of a dog. The *teeth* were of the same brilliant scarlet as the claws.

January 19. — To-day, being in latitude 83° 20', longitude 43° 5' W. (the sea being of an extraordinarily dark colour), we again saw land from the masthead, and, upon a closer scrutiny, found it to be one of a group of very large islands. The shore was precipitous, and the interior seemed to be well wooded, a circumstance which occasioned us great joy. In about four hours from our first discovering the land we came to anchor in ten fathoms, sandy bottom, a league from the coast, as a high surf, with strong ripples here and there, rendered a nearer approach of doubtful expediency. The two largest boats were now ordered out, and a party, well armed (among whom were Peters and myself), proceeded to look for an opening in the reef which appeared to encircle the island. After searching about for some time, we discovered an inlet, which we were entering, when we saw four large canoes put off from the shore, filled with men who seemed to be well armed. We waited for them to come up, and, as they moved with great rapidity, they were soon within hail. Captain Guy now held up a white handkerchief on the blade of an oar, when the strangers made a full stop, and commenced a loud jabbering all at once, intermingled with occasional shouts, in which we could distinguish the words *Anamoo-moo!* and *Lama-Lama!* They continued this for at least half an hour, during which we had a good opportunity of observing their appearance.

In the four canoes, which might have been fifty feet long and five broad, there were a hundred and ten savages in all. They were about the ordinary stature of Europeans, but of a more muscular and brawny frame. Their complexion a jet black, with thick and long woolly hair. They were clothed in skins of an unknown black animal, shaggy and silky, and made to fit the body with some degree of skill, the hair being inside, except where turned out about the neck, wrists, and ankles. Their arms consisted principally of clubs, of a dark, and apparently very heavy wood. Some spears, however, were observed among them, headed with flint, and a few slings. The bottoms of the canoes were full of black stones about the size of a large egg.

When they had concluded their harangue (for it was clear they intended their jabbering for such), one of them who seemed to be the chief stood up in the prow of his canoe, and made signs for us to bring our boats alongside of him. This hint we pretended not to understand, thinking it the wiser plan to maintain, if possible, the interval between us, as their number more than quadrupled our own. Finding this to be the case, the chief ordered the three other canoes to hold back, while he advanced toward us with his own. As soon as he came up with us he leaped on board the largest of our boats, and seated himself by the side of Captain Guy, pointing at the same time to the schooner, and

repeating the word *Anamoo-moo!* and *Lama-Lama!* We now put back to the vessel, the four canoes following at a little distance.

Upon getting alongside, the chief evinced symptoms of extreme surprise and delight, clapping his hands, slapping his thighs and breast, and laughing obstreperously. His followers behind joined in his merriment, and for some minutes the din was so excessive as to be absolutely deafening. Quiet being at length restored, Captain Guy ordered the boats to be hoisted up, as a necessary precaution, and gave the chief (whose name we soon found to be *Too-wit*) to understand that we could admit no more than twenty of his men on deck at one time. With this arrangement he appeared perfectly satisfied, and gave some directions to the canoes, when one of them approached, the rest remaining about fifty yards off. Twenty of the savages now got on board, and proceeded to ramble over every part of the deck, and scramble about among the rigging, making themselves much at home, and examining every article with great inquisitiveness.

It was quite evident that they had never before seen any of the white race — from whose complexion, indeed, they appeared to recoil. They believed the Jane to be a living creature, and seemed to be afraid of hurting it with the points of their spears, carefully turning them up. Our crew were much amused with the conduct of Too-wit in one instance. The cook was splitting some wood near the galley, and, by accident, struck his axe into the deck, making a gash of considerable depth. The chief immediately ran up, and pushing the cook on one side rather roughly, commenced a half whine, half howl, strongly indicative of sympathy in what he considered the sufferings of the schooner, patting and smoothing the gash with his hand, and washing it from a bucket of seawater which stood by. This was a degree of ignorance for which we were not prepared, and for my part I could not help thinking some of it affected.

When the visitors had satisfied, as well as they could, their curiosity in regard to our upper works, they were admitted below, when their amazement exceeded all bounds. Their astonishment now appeared to be far too deep for words, for they roamed about in silence, broken only by low ejaculations. The arms afforded them much food for speculation, and they were suffered to handle and examine them at leisure. I do not believe that they had the least suspicion of their actual use, but rather took them for idols, seeing the care we had of them, and the attention with which we watched their movements while handling them. At the great guns their wonder was redoubled. They approached them with every mark of the profoundest reverence and awe, but forbore to examine them minutely. There were two large mirrors in the cabin, and here was the acme of their amazement. Too-wit was the first to approach them, and he had got in the middle of the cabin, with his face to one and his back to the other, before he fairly perceived them. Upon raising his eyes and

seeing his reflected self in the glass, I thought the savage would go mad; but, upon turning short round to make a retreat, and beholding himself a second time in the opposite direction, I was afraid he would expire upon the spot. No persuasion could prevail upon him to take another look; but, throwing himself upon the floor, with his face buried in his hands, he remained thus until we were obliged to drag him upon deck.

The whole of the savages were admitted on board in this manner, twenty at a time, Too-wit being suffered to remain during the entire period. We saw no disposition to thievery among them, nor did we miss a single article after their departure. Throughout the whole of their visit they evinced the most friendly manner. There were, however, some points in their demeanour which we found it impossible to understand; for example, we could not get them to approach several very harmless objects — such as the schooner's sails, an egg, an open book, or a pan of flour. We endeavoured to ascertain if they had among them any articles which might be turned to account in the way of traffic, but found great difficulty in being comprehended. We made out, nevertheless, what greatly astonished us, that the islands abounded in the large tortoise of the Gallipagos, one of which we saw in the canoe of Too-wit. We saw also some *biche de mer* in the hands of one of the savages, who was greedily devouring it in its natural state. These anomalies — for they were such when considered in regard to the latitude — induced Captain Guy to wish for a thorough investigation of the country, in the hope of making a profitable speculation in his discovery. For my own part, anxious as I was to know something more of these islands, I was still more earnestly bent on prosecuting the voyage to the southward without delay. We had now fine weather, but there was no telling how long it would last; and being already in the eighty-fourth parallel, with an open sea before us, a current setting strongly to the southward, and the wind fair, I could not listen with any patience to a proposition of stopping longer than was absolutely necessary for the health of the crew and the taking on board a proper supply of fuel and fresh provisions. I represented to the captain that we might easily make this group on our return, and winter here in the event of being blocked up by the ice. He at length came into my views (for in some way, hardly known to myself, I had acquired much influence over him), and it was finally resolved that, even in the event of our finding *biche de mer*, we should only stay here a week to recruit, and then push on to the southward while we might. Accordingly we made every necessary preparation, and, under the guidance of Too-wit, got the Jane through the reef in safety, coming to anchor about a mile from the shore, in an excellent bay, completely landlocked, on the southeastern coast of the main island, and in ten fathoms of water, black sandy bottom. At the head of this bay there were three fine springs (we were told) of good water, and we saw abundance of wood in the vicinity. The four canoes followed us in, keeping, however, at a respectful distance. Too-wit himself remained on

board, and, upon our dropping anchor, invited us to accompany him on shore, and visit his village in the interior. To this Captain Guy consented; and ten savages being left on board as hostages, a party of us, twelve in all, got in readiness to attend the chief. We took care to be well armed, yet without evincing any distrust. The schooner had her guns run out, her boarding-nettings up, and every other proper precaution was taken to guard against surprise. Directions were left with the chief mate to admit no person on board during our absence, and, in the event of our not appearing in twelve hours, to send the cutter, with a swivel, around the island in search of us.

At every step we took inland the conviction forced itself upon us that we were in a country differing essentially from any hitherto visited by civilized men. We saw nothing with which we had been formerly conversant. The trees resembled no growth of either the torrid, the temperate, of the northern frigid zones, and were altogether unlike those of the lower southern latitudes we had already traversed. The very rocks were novel in their mass, their color, and their stratification; and the streams themselves, utterly incredible as it may appear, had so little in common with those of other climates, that we were scrupulous of tasting them, and, indeed, had difficulty in bringing ourselves to believe that their qualities were purely those of nature. At a small brook which crossed our path (the first we had reached) Too-wit and his attendants halted to drink. On account of the singular character of the water, we refused to taste it, supposing it to be polluted; and it was not until some time afterward we came to understand that such was the appearance of the streams throughout the whole group. I am at a loss to give a distinct idea of the nature of this liquid, and cannot do so without many words. Although it flowed with rapidity in all declivities where common water would do so, yet never, except when falling in a cascade, had it the customary appearance of *limpidity*. It was, nevertheless, in point of fact, as perfectly limpid as any limestone water in existence, the difference being only in appearance. At first sight, and especially in cases where little declivity was found, it bore resemblance, as regards consistency, to a thick infusion of gum arabic in common water. But this was only the least remarkable of its extraordinary qualities. It was *not* colourless, nor was it of any one uniform colour — presenting to the eye, as it flowed, every possible shade of purple; like the hues of a changeable silk. This variation in shade was produced in a manner which excited as profound astonishment in the minds of our party as the mirror had done in the case of Too-wit. Upon collecting a basinful, and allowing it to settle thoroughly, we perceived that the whole mass of liquid was made up of a number of distinct veins, each of a distinct hue; that these veins did not commingle; and that their cohesion was perfect in regard to their own particles among themselves, and imperfect in regard to neighbouring veins. Upon passing the blade of a knife athwart the veins, the water closed over it immediately, as with us, and also, in

withdrawing it, all traces of the passage of the knife were instantly ob-
literated. If, however, the blade was passed down accurately between the
two veins, a perfect separation was effected, which the power of cohesion
did not immediately rectify. The phenomena of this water formed the
first definite link in that vast chain of apparent miracles with which I was
destined to be at length encircled.

<div align="center">CHAPTER XIX</div>

We were nearly three hours in reaching the village, it being more than
nine miles in the interior, and the path lying through a rugged country.
As we passed along, the party of Too-wit (the whole hundred and ten
savages of the canoes) was momentarily strengthened by smaller detach-
ments, of from two to six or seven, which joined us, as if by accident, at
different turns of the road. There appeared so much of system in this that
I could not help feeling distrust, and I spoke to Captain Guy of my
apprehensions. It was now too late, however, to recede, and we concluded
that our best security lay in evincing a perfect confidence in the good
faith of Too-wit. We accordingly went on, keeping a wary eye upon the
manœuvres of the savages, and not permitting them to divide our num-
bers by pushing in between. In this way, passing through a precipitous
ravine, we at length reached what we were told was the only collection
of habitations upon the island. As we came in sight of them, the chief set
up a shout, and frequently repeated the word *Klock-klock*, which we sup-
posed to be the name of the village, or perhaps the generic name for
villages.

The dwellings were of the most miserable description imaginable, and,
unlike those of even the lowest of the savage races with which mankind
are acquainted, were of no uniform plan. Some of them (and these we
found belonged to the *Wampoos* or *Yampoos*, the great men of the land)
consisted of a tree cut down at about four feet from the root, with a large
black skin thrown over it, and hanging in loose folds upon the ground.
Under this the savage nestled. Others were formed by means of rough
limbs of trees, with the withered foliage upon them, made to recline, at
an angle of forty-five degrees, against a bank of clay, heaped up, with-
out regular form, to the height of five or six feet. Others, again, were mere
holes dug in the earth perpendicularly, and covered over with similar
branches, these being removed when the tenant was about to enter, and
pulled on again when he had entered. A few were built among the forked
limbs of trees as they stood, the upper limbs being partially cut through,
so as to bend over upon the lower, thus forming thicker shelter from the
weather. The greater number, however, consisted of small shallow cav-
erns, apparently scratched in the face of a precipitous ledge of dark stone,
resembling fuller's earth, with which three sides of the village were
bounded. At the door of each of these primitive caverns was a small rock,
which the tenant carefully placed before the entrance upon leaving his

residence, for what purpose I could not ascertain, as the stone itself was never of sufficient size to close up more than a third of the opening.

This village, if it were worthy of the name, lay in a valley of some depth, and could only be approached from the southward, the precipitous ledge of which I have already spoken cutting off all access in other directions. Through the middle of the valley ran a brawling stream of the same magical-looking water which has been described. We saw several strange animals about the dwellings, all appearing to be thoroughly domesticated. The largest of these creatures resembled our common hog in the structure of the body and snout; the tail, however, was bushy, and the legs slender as those of the antelope. Its motion was exceedingly awkward and indecisive, and we never saw it attempt to run. We noticed also several animals very similar in appearance, but of a greater length of body, and covered with a black wool. There were a great variety of tame fowls running about, and these seemed to constitute the chief food of the natives. To our astonishment we saw black albatross among these birds in a state of entire domestication, going to sea periodically for food, but always returning to the village as a home, and using the southern shore in the vicinity as a place of incubation. There they were joined by their friends the pelicans as usual, but these latter never followed them to the dwellings of the savages. Among the other kinds of tame fowls were ducks, differing very little from the canvass-back of our own country, black gannets, and a large bird not unlike the buzzard in appearance, but not carnivorous. Of fish there seemed to be a great abundance. We saw, during our visit, a quantity of dried salmon, rock cod, blue dolphins, mackerel, blackfish, skate, conger eels, elephantfish, mullets, soles, parrotfish, leather-jackets, gurnards, hake, flounders, paracutas, and innumerable other varieties. We noticed, too, that most of them were similar to the fish about the group of Lord Auckland Islands, in a latitude as low as fifty-one degrees south. The Gallipago tortoise was also very plentiful. We saw but few wild animals, and none of a large size, or of a species with which we were familiar. One or two serpents of a formidable aspect crossed our path, but the natives paid them little attention, and we concluded that they were not venomous.

As we approached the village with Too-wit and his party, a vast crowd of the people rushed out to meet us, with loud shouts, among which we could only distinguish the everlasting *Anamoo-moo!* and *Lama-Lama!* We were much surprised at perceiving that, with one or two exceptions, these new comers were entirely naked, and skins being used only by the men of the canoes. All the weapons of the country seemed also to be in the possession of the latter, for there was no appearance of any among the villagers. There were a great many women and children, the former not altogether wanting in what might be termed personal beauty. They were straight, tall, and well formed, with a grace and freedom of carriage not to be found in civilized society. Their lips, however, like those of the

men, were thick and clumsy, so that, even when laughing, the teeth were never disclosed. Their hair was of a finer texture than that of the males. Among these naked villagers there might have been ten or twelve who were clothed, like the party of Too-wit, in dresses of black skin, and armed with lances and heavy clubs. These appeared to have great influence among the rest, and were always addressed by the title *Wampoo*. These, too, were the tenants of the black skin palaces. That of Too-wit was situated in the centre of the village, and was much larger and somewhat better constructed than others of its kind. The tree which formed its support was cut off at a distance of twelve feet or thereabouts from the root, and there were several branches left just below the cut, these serving to extend the covering, and in this way prevent its flapping about the trunk. The covering, too, which consisted of four very large skins fastened together with wooden skewers, was secured at the bottom with pegs driven through it and into the ground. The floor was strewed with a quantity of dry leaves by way of carpet.

To this hut we were conducted with great solemnity, and as many of the natives crowded in after us as possible. Too-wit seated himself on the leaves, and made signs that we should follow his example. This we did, and presently found ourselves in a situation peculiarly uncomfortable, if not indeed critical. We were on the ground, twelve in number, with the savages, as many as forty, sitting on their hams so closely around us that, if any disturbance had arisen, we should have found it impossible to make use of our arms, or indeed to have risen to our feet. The pressure was not only inside the tent, but outside, where probably was every individual on the whole island, the crowd being prevented from trampling us to death only by the incessant exertions and vociferations of Too-wit. Our chief security lay, however, in the presence of Too-wit himself among us, and we resolved to stick by him closely, as the best chance of extricating ourselves from the dilemma, sacrificing him immediately upon the first appearance of hostile design.

After some trouble a certain degree of quiet was restored, when the chief addressed us in a speech of great length, and very nearly resembling the one delivered in the canoes, with the exception that the *Anamoo-moos!* were now somewhat more strenuously insisted upon than the *Lama-Lamas!* We listened in profound silence until the conclusion of this harangue, when Captain Guy replied by assuring the chief of his eternal friendship and goodwill, concluding what he had to say be a present of several strings of blue beads and a knife. At the former the monarch, much to our surprise, turned up his nose with some expression of contempt; but the knife gave him the most unlimited satisfaction, and he immediately ordered dinner. This was handed into the tent over the heads of the attendants, and consisted of the palpitating entrails of a specials of unknown animal, probably one of the slim-legged hogs which we had observed in our approach to the village. Seeing us at a loss how

to proceed, he began, by way of setting us an example, to devour yard after yard of the enticing food, until we could positively stand it no longer, and evinced such manifest symptoms of rebellion of stomach as inspired his majesty with a degree of astonishment only inferior to that brought about by the looking-glasses. We declined, however, partaking of the delicacies before us, and endeavoured to make him understand that we had no appetite whatever, having just finished a hearty *déjeuner*.

When the monarch had made an end of his meal, we commenced a series of cross-questioning in every ingenious manner we could devise, with a view of discovering what were the chief productions of the country, and whether any of them might be turned to profit. At length he seemed to have some idea of our meaning, and offered to accompany us to a part of of the coast where he assured us the *biche de mer* (pointing to a specimen of that animal) was to be found in great abundance. We were glad of this early opportunity of escaping from the oppression of the crowd, and signified our eagerness to proceed. We now left the tent, and, accompanied by the whole population of the village, followed the chief to the southeastern extremity of the island, nor far from the bay where our vessel lay at anchor. We waited here for about an hour, until the four canoes were brought around by some of the savages to our station. The whole of our party then getting into one of them, we were paddled along the edge of the reef before mentioned, and of another still farther out, where we saw a far greater quantity of *biche de mer* than the oldest seamen among us had ever seen in those groups of the lower latitudes most celebrated for this article of commerce. We stayed near these reefs only long enough to satisfy ourselves that we could easily load a dozen vessels with the animal if necessary, when we were taken alongside the schooner, and parted with Too-wit, after obtaining from him a promise that he would bring us, in the course of twenty-four hours, as many of the canvassback ducks and Gallipago tortoises as his canoes would hold. In the whole of this adventure we saw nothing in the demeanour of the natives calculated to create suspicion, with the single exception of the systematic manner in which their party was strengthened during our route from the schooner to the village.

CHAPTER XX

The chief was as good as his word, and we were soon plentifully supplied with fresh provisions. We found the tortoises as fine as we had ever seen, and the ducks surpassed our best species of wild fowl, being exceedingly tender, juicy, and well-flavoured. Besides these, the savages brought us, upon our making them comprehend our wishes, a vast quantity of brown celery and scurvy grass, with a canoe-load of fresh fish and some dried. The celery was a treat indeed, and the scurvy grass proved of incalculable benefit in restoring those of our men who had shown symptoms of disease. In a very short time we had not a single person on the

sick-list. We had also plenty of other kinds of fresh provisions, among which may be mentioned a species of shellfish resembling the mussel in shape, but with the taste of an oyster. Shrimps, too, and prawns were abundant, and albatross and other birds' eggs with dark shells. We took in, too, a plentiful stock of the flesh of the hog which I have mentioned before. Most of the men found it a palpatable food, but I thought it fishy and otherwise disagreeable. In return for these good things we presented the natives with blue beads, brass trinkets, nails, knives, and pieces of red cloth, they being fully delighted in the exchange. We established a regular market on shore, just under the guns of the schooner, where our barterings were carried on with every appearance of good faith, and a degree of order which their conduct at the village of *Klock-klock* had not led us to expect from the savages.

Matters went on thus very amicably for several days, during which parties of the natives were frequently on board the schooner, and parties of our men frequently on shore, making long excursions into the interior, and receiving no molestation whatever. Finding the ease with which the vessel might be loaded with *biche de mer*, owing to the friendly disposition of the islanders, and the readiness with which they would render us assistance in collecting it, Captain Guy resolved to enter into negotiations with Too-wit for the erection of suitable houses in which to cure the article, and for the services of himself and tribe in gathering as much as possible, while he himself took advantage of the fine weather to prosecute his voyage to the southward. Upon mentioning this project to the chief he seemed very willing to enter into an agreement. A bargain was accordingly struck, perfectly satisfactory to both parties, by which it was arranged that, after making the necessary preparations, such as laying off the proper grounds, erecting a portion of the buildings, and doing some other work in which the whole of our crew would be required, the schooner should proceed on her route, leaving three of her men on the island to superintend the fulfilment of the project, and instruct the natives in drying the *biche de mer*. In regard to terms, these were made to depend upon the exertions of the savages in our absence. They were to receive a stipulated quantity of blue beads, knives, red cloth, and so forth, for every certain number of piculs of the *biche de mer* which should be ready on our return.

A description of the nature of this important article of commerce, and the method of preparing it, may prove of some interest to my readers, and I can find no more suitable place than this for introducing an account of it. The following comprehensive notice of the substance is taken from a modern history of a voyage to the South Seas.

"It is that *mollusca* from the Indian Seas which is known to commerce by the French name *bouche de mer* (a nice morsel from the sea). If I am not much mistaken, the celebrated Cuvier calls it *gasteropeda pulmonifera*. It is abundantly gathered in the coasts of the Pacific islands,

and gathered especially for the Chinese market, where it commands a great price, perhaps as much as their much-talked-of edible birds' nests, which are properly made up of the gelatinous matter picked up by a species of swallow from the body of these molluscæ. They have no shell, no legs, nor any prominent part, except an *absorbing* and an *excretory*, opposite organs; but, by their elastic wings, like caterpillars or worms, they creep in shallow waters, in which, when low, they can be seen by a kind of swallow, the sharp bill of which, inserted in the soft animal, draws a gummy and filamentous substance, which, by drying, can be wrought into the solid walls of their nest. Hence the name of *gasteropeda pulmonifera.*

"This mollusca is oblong, and of different sizes, from three to eighteen inches in length; and I have seen a few that were not less than two feet long. They were nearly round, a little flattish on one side, which lies next to the bottom of the sea; and they are from one to eight inches thick. They crawl up into shallow water at particular seasons of the year, probably for the purpose of gendering, as we often find them in pairs. It is when the sun has the most power on the water, rendering it tepid, that they approach the shore; and they often go up into places so shallow that, on the tide's receding, they are left dry, exposed to the heat of the sun. But they do not bring forth their young in shallow water, as we never see any of their progeny, and full-grown ones are always observed coming in from deep water. They feed principally on that class of zoophytes which produce the coral.

"The *biche de mer* is generally taken in three or four feet of water; after which they are brought on shore, and split at one end with a knife, the incision being one inch or more, according to the size of the mollusca. Through this opening the entrails are forced out by pressure, and they are much like those of any other small tenant of the deep. The article is then washed, and afterward boiled to a certain degree, which must not be too much or too little. They are then buried in the ground for four hours, then boiled again for a short time, after which they are dried, either by the fire or the sun. Those cured by the sun are worth the most; but where one picul (133⅓ lbs.) can be cured that way, I can cure thirty piculs by the fire. When once properly cured, they can be kept in a dry place for two or three years without any risk; but they should be examined once in every few months, say four times a year, to see if any dampness is likely to affect them.

"The Chinese, as before stated, consider *biche de mer* a very great luxury, believing that it wonderfully strengthens and nourishes the system, and renews the exhausted system of the immoderate voluptuary. The first quality commands a high price in Canton, being worth ninety dollars a picul; the second quality, seventy-five dollars; the third, fifty dollars; the fourth, thirty dollars; the fifth, twenty dollars; the sixth, twelve dollars; the seventh, eight dollars; and the eighth, four dollars; small

cargoes, however, will often bring more in Manilla, Singapore, and Batavia."

An agreement having been thus entered into, we proceeded immediately to land everything necessary for preparing the buildings and clearing the ground. A large flat space near the eastern shore of the bay was selected, where there was plenty of both wood and water, and within a convenient distance of the principal reefs on which the *biche de mer* was to be procured. We now all set to work in good earnest, and soon, to the great astonishment of the savages, had felled a sufficient number of trees for our purpose, getting them quickly in order for the framework of the houses, which in two or three days were so far under way that we could safely trust the rest of the work to the three men whom we intended to leave behind. These were John Carson, Alfred Harris, —— Peterson (all natives of London, I believe), who volunteered their services in this respect.

By the last of the month we had everything in readiness for departure. We had agreed, however, to pay a formal visit of leave-taking to the village, and Too-wit insisted so pertinaciously upon our keeping the promise that we did not think it advisable to run the risk of offending him by a final refusal. I believe that not one of us had at this time the slightest suspicion of the good faith of the savages. They had uniformly behaved with the greatest decorum, aiding us with alacrity in our work, offering us their commodities, frequently without price, and never, in any instance, pilfering a single article, although the high value they set upon the goods we had with us was evident by the extravagant demonstrations of joy always manifested upon our making them a present. The women especially were most obliging in every respect, and, upon the whole, we should have been the most suspicious of human beings had we entertained a single thought of perfidy on the part of a people who treated us so well. A very short while sufficed to prove that this apparent kindness of disposition was only the result of a deeply laid plan for our destruction, and that the islanders for whom we entertained such inordinate feelings of esteem, were among the most barbarous, subtle, and bloodthirsty wretches that ever contaminated the face of the globe.

It was on the first of February that we went on shore for the purpose of visiting the village. Although, as said before, we entertained not the slightest suspicion, still no proper precaution was neglected. Six men were left in the schooner, with instructions to permit none of the savages to approach the vessel during our absence, under any pretence whatever, and to remain constantly on deck. The boarding-nettings were up, the guns double-shotted with grape and canister, and the swivels loaded with canisters of musket-balls. She lay, with her anchor apeak, about a mile from the shore, and no canoe could approach her in any direction without being distinctly seen and exposed to the 'full fire of our swivels immediately.

The six men being left on board, our shore-party consisted of thirty-two persons in all. We were armed to the teeth, having with us muskets, pistols, and cutlasses; besides, each had a long kind of seaman's knife, somewhat resembling the bowie knife now so much used throughout our western and southern country. A hundred of the black skin warriors met us at the landing for the purpose of accompanying us on our way. We noticed, however, with some surprise, that they were now entirely without arms; and, upon questioning Too-wit in relation to this circumstance, he merely answered that *Mattee non we pa pa si* — meaning that there was no need of arms where all were brothers. We took this in good part, and proceeded.

We had passed the spring and rivulet of which I before spoke, and were now entering upon a narrow gorge leading through the chain of soapstone hills among which the village was situated. This gorge was very rocky and uneven, so much so that it was with no little difficulty we scrambled through it on our first visit to Klock-klock. The whole length of the ravine might have been a mile and a half, or probably two miles. It wound in every possible direction through the hills (having apparently formed, at some remote period, the bed of a torrent), in no instance proceeding more than twenty yards without an abrupt turn. The sides of this dell would have averaged, I am sure, seventy or eighty feet in perpendicular altitude throughout the whole of their extent, and in some portions they arose to an astonishing height, overshadowing the pass so completely that but little of the light of day could penetrate. The general width was about forty feet, and occasionally it diminished so as not to allow the passage of more than five or six persons abreast. In short, there could be no place in the world better adapted for the consummation of an ambuscade, and it was no more than natural that we should look carefully to our arms as we entered upon it. When I now think of our egregious folly, the chief subject of astonishment seems to be, that we should have ever ventured, under any circumstances, so completely into the power of unknown savages as to permit them to march both before and behind us in our progress through this ravine. Yet such was the order we blindly took up, trusting foolishly to the force of our party, the unarmed condition of Too-wit and his men, the certain efficacy of our firearms (whose effect was yet a secret to the natives), and, more than all, to the long-sustained pretension of friendship kept up by these infamous wretches. Five or six of them went on before, as if to lead the way, ostentatiously busying themselves in removing the larger stones and rubbish from the path. Next came our own party. We walked closely together, taking care only to prevent separation. Behind followed the main body of the savages, observing unusual order and decorum.

Dirk Peters, a man named Wilson Allen, and myself were on the right of our companions, examining, as we went along, the singular stratification of the precipice which overhung us. A fissure in the soft rock at-

tracted our attention. It was about wide enough for one person to enter without squeezing, and extended back into the hill some eighteen or twenty feet in a straight course, sloping afterward to the left. The height of the opening, as far as we could see into it from the main gorge, was perhaps sixty or seventy feet. There were one or two stunted shrubs growing from the crevices, bearing a species of filbert which I felt some curiosity to examine, and pushed in briskly for that purpose, gathering five or six of the nuts at a grasp, and then hastily retreating. As I turned, I found that Peters and Allen had followed me. I desired them to go back, as there was not room for two persons to pass, saying they should have some of my nuts. They accordingly turned, and were scrambling back, Allen being close to the mouth of the fissure, when I was suddenly aware of a concussion resembling nothing I had ever before experienced, and which impressed me with a vague conception, if indeed I then thought of anything, that the whole foundations of the solid globe were suddenly rent asunder, and that the day of universal dissolution was at hand.

CHAPTER XXI

As soon as I could collect my scattered senses, I found myself nearly suffocated, and grovelling in utter darkness among a quantity of loose earth, which was also falling upon me heavily in every direction, threatening to bury me entirely. Horribly alarmed at this idea, I struggled to gain my feet, and at last succeeded. I then remained motionless for some moments, endeavouring to conceive what had happened to me, and where I was. Presently I heard a deep groan just at my ear, and afterward the smothered voice of Peters calling to me for aid in the name of God. I scrambled one or two paces forward, when I fell directly over the head and shoulders of my companion, who, I soon discovered, was buried in a loose mass of earth as far as his middle, and struggling desperately to free himself from the pressure. I tore the dirt from around him with all the energy I could command, and at length succeeded in getting him out.

As soon as we sufficiently recovered from our fright and surprise to be capable of conversing rationally, we both came to the conclusion that the walls of the fissure in which we had ventured had, by some convulsion of nature, or probably from their own weight, caved in overhead, and that we were consequently lost for ever, being thus entombed alive. For a long time we gave up supinely to the most intense agony and despair, such as cannot be adequately imagined by those who have never been in a similar position. I firmly believed that no incident ever occurring in the course of human events is more adapted to inspire the supremeness of mental and bodily distress than a case like our own, of living inhumation. The blackness of darkness which envelops the victim, the terrific oppression of lungs, the stifling fumes from the damp earth, unite with the ghastly considerations that we are beyond the remotest

confines of hope, and that such is the allotted portion of *the dead*, to carry into the human heart a degree of appalling awe and horror not to be tolerated — never to be conceived.

At length Peters proposed that we should endeavour to ascertain precisely the extent of our calamity, and grope about our prison; it being barely possible, he observed, that some opening might yet be left us for escape. I caught eagerly at this hope, and, arousing myself to exertion, attempted to force my way through the loose earth. Hardly had I advanced a single step before a glimmer of light became perceptible, enough to convince me that, at all events, we should not immediately perish for want of air. We now took some degree of heart, and encouraged each other to hope for the best. Having scrambled over a bank of rubbish which impeded our farther progress in the direction of the light, we found less difficulty in advancing and also experienced some relief from the excessive oppression of lungs which had tormented us. Presently we were enabled to obtain a glimpse of the objects around, and discovered that we were near the extremity of the straight portion of the fissure, where it made a turn to the left. A few struggles more, and we reached the bend, when to our inexpressible joy, there appeared a long seam or crack extending upward a vast distance, generally at an angle of about forty-five degrees, although sometimes much more precipitous. We could not see through the whole extent of this opening; but, as a good deal of light came down it, we had little doubt of finding at the top of it (if we could by any means reach the top) a clear passage into the open air.

I now called to mind that three of us had entered the fissure from the main gorge, and that our companion, Allen, was still missing; we determined at once to retrace our steps and look for him. After a long search, and much danger from the farther caving in of the earth above us, Peters at length cried out to me that he had hold of our companion's foot, and that his whole body was deeply buried beneath the rubbish beyond the possibility of extricating him. I soon found that what he said was too true, and that, of course, life had been long extinct. With sorrowful hearts, therefore, we left the corpse to its fate, and again made our way to the bend.

The breadth of the seam was barely sufficient to admit us, and, after one or two ineffectual efforts at getting up, we began once more to despair. I have before said that the chain of hills through which ran the main gorge was composed of a species of soft rock resembling soapstone. The sides of the cleft we were now attempting to ascend were of the same material, and so excessively slippery, being wet, that we could get but little foothold upon them even in their least precipitous parts; in some places, where the ascent was nearly perpendicular, the difficulty was, of course, much aggravated; and, indeed, for some time we thought insurmountable. We took courage, however, from despair; and what, by

dint of cutting steps in the soft stone with our bowie knives, and swing-
ing at the risk of our lives, to small projecting points of a harder species
of slaty rock which now and then protruded from the general mass, we
at length reached a natural platform, from which was perceptible a
patch of blue sky, at the extremity of a thickly-wooded ravine. Looking
back now, with somewhat more leisure, at the passage through which
we had thus far proceeded, we clearly saw from the appearance of its
sides, that it was of late formation, and we concluded that the concus-
sion, whatever it was, which had so unexpectedly overwhelmed us, had
also, at the same moment, laid open this path for escape. Being quite
exhausted with exertion, and indeed, so weak that we were scarcely able
to stand or articulate, Peters now proposed that we should endeavour to
bring our companions to the rescue by firing the pistols which still re-
mained in our girdles — the muskets as well as cutlasses had been lost
among the loose earth at the bottom of the chasm. Subsequent events
proved that, had we fired, we should have sorely repented it, but luckily
a half suspicion of foul play had by this time arisen in my mind, and
we forbore to let the savages know of our whereabouts.

After having reposed for about an hour, we pushed on slowly up the
ravine, and had gone no great way before we heard a succession of tre-
mendous yells. At length we reached what might be called the surface of
the ground; for our path hitherto, since leaving the platform, had lain
beneath an archway of high rock and foliage, at a vast distance over-
head. With great caution we stole to a narrow opening, through which
we had a clear sight of the surrounding country, when the whole dreadful
secret of the concussion broke upon us in one moment and at one view.

The spot from which we looked was not far from the summit of the
highest peak in the range of the soapstone hills. The gorge in which our
party of thirty-two had entered ran within fifty feet to the left of us. But,
for at least one hundred yards, the channel or bed of this gorge was en-
tirely filled up with the chaotic ruins of more than a million tons of earth
and stone that had been artificially tumbled within it. The means by
which the vast mass had been precipitated were not more simple than
evident, for sure traces of the murderous work were yet remaining. In
several spots along the top of the eastern side of the gorge (we were now
on the western) might be seen stakes of wood driven into the earth.
In these spots the earth had not given way; but throughout the whole
extent of the face of the precipice from which the mass *had* fallen, it
was clear, from marks left in the soil resembling those made by the drill
of the rock blaster, that stakes similar to those we saw standing had been
inserted, at not more than a yard apart, for the length of perhaps three
hundred feet, and ranging at about ten feet back from the edge of the
gulf. Strong cords of grape vine were attached to the stakes still remain-
ing on the hill, and it was evident that such cords had also been attached
to each of the other stakes. I have already spoken of the singular strati-

fication of these soapstone hills; and the description just given of the narrow and deep fissure through which we effected our escape from inhumation will afford a further conception of its nature. This was such that almost every natural convulsion would be sure to split the soil into perpendicular layers or ridges running parallel with one another; and a very moderate exertion of art would be sufficient for effecting the same purpose. Of this stratification the savages had availed themselves to accomplish their treacherous ends. There can be no doubt that, by the continuous line of stakes, a partial rupture of the soil had been brought about, probably to the depth of one or two feet, when by means of a savage pulling at the end of each of the cords (these cords being attached to the tops of the stakes, and extending back from the edge of the cliff), a vast leverage power was obtained, capable of hurling the whole face of the hill, upon a given signal, into the bosom of the abyss below. The fate of our poor companions was no longer a matter of uncertainty. We alone had escaped from the tempest of that overwhelming destruction. We were the only living white men upon the island.

<div align="center">CHAPTER XXII</div>

Our situation, as it now appeared, was scarcely less dreadful than when we had conceived ourselves entombed forever. We saw before us no prospect but that of being put to death by the savages, or of dragging out a miserable existence in capitivity among them. We might, to be sure, conceal ourselves for a time from their observation among the fastnesses of the hills, and, as a final resort, in the chasm from which we had just issued; but we must either perish in the long polar winter through cold and famine, or be ultimately discovered in our efforts to obtain relief.

The whole country around us seemed to be swarming with savages, crowds of whom, we now perceived, had come over from the islands to the southward on flat rafts, doubtless with a view of lending their aid in the capture and plunder of the Jane. The vessel still lay calmly at anchor in the bay, those on board being apparently quite unconscious of any danger awaiting them. How we longed at that moment to be with them! either to aid in effecting their escape, or to perish with them in attempting a defence. We saw no chance even of warning them of their danger without bringing immediate destruction upon our own heads, with but a remote hope of benefit to them. A pistol fired might suffice to apprise them that something wrong had occurred; but the report could not possibly inform them that their only prospect of safety lay in getting out of the harbour forthwith — nor tell them no principles of honour now bound them to remain, that their companions were no longer among the living. Upon hearing the discharge they could not be more thoroughly prepared to meet the foe, who were now getting ready to attack, than they already were, and always had been. No good, there-

fore, and infinite harm, would result from our firing, and after mature deliberation, we forbore.

Our next thought was to attempt to rush toward the vessel, to seize one of the four canoes which lay at the head of the bay, and endeavour to force a passage on board. But the utter impossibility of succeeding in this desperate task soon became evident. The country, as I said before, was literally swarming with the natives, skulking among the bushes and recesses of the hills, so as not to be observed from the schooner. In our immediate vicinity especially, and blockading the sole path by which we could hope to attain the shore at the proper point were stationed the whole party of the black skin warriors, with Too-wit at their head, and apparently only waiting for some re-enforcement to commence his onset upon the Jane. The canoes, too, which lay at the head of the bay, were manned with savages, unarmed, it is true, but who undoubtedly had arms within reach. We were forced, therefore, however unwillingly, to remain in our place of concealment, mere spectators of the conflict which presently ensued.

In about half an hour we saw some sixty or seventy rafts, or flatboats, with outriggers, filled with savages, and coming round the southern bight of the harbor. They appeared to have no arms except short clubs, and stones which lay in the bottom of the rafts. Immediately afterward another detachment, still larger, appeared in an opposite direction, and with similar weapons. The four canoes, too, were now quickly filled with natives, starting up from the bushes at the head of the bay, and put off swiftly to join the other parties. Thus, in less time than I have taken to tell it, and as if by magic, the Jane saw herself surrounded by an immense multitude of desperadoes evidently bent upon capturing her at all hazards.

That they would succeed in so doing could not be doubted for an instant. The six men left in the vessel, however resolutely they might engage in her defence, were altogether unequal to the proper management of the guns, or in any manner to sustain a contest at such odds. I could hardly imagine that they would make resistance at all, but in this was deceived; for presently I saw them get springs upon the cable, and bring the vessel's starboard broadside to bear upon the canoes, which by this time were within pistol range, the rafts being nearly a quarter of a mile to windward. Owing to some cause unknown, but most probably to the agitation of our poor friends at seeing themselves in so hopeless a situation, the discharge was an entire failure. Not a canoe was hit or a single savage injured, the shots striking short and *ricochêting* over their heads. The only effect produced upon them was astonishment at the unexpected report and smoke, which was so excessive that for some moments I almost thought they would abandon their design entirely, and return to the shore. And this they would most likely have done had our men followed up their broadside by a discharge of small arms, in

which, as the canoes were now so near at hand, they could not have failed in doing some execution, sufficient, at least, to deter this party from a farther advance, until they could have given the rafts also a broadside. But, in place of this, they left the canoe party to recover from their panic, and, by looking about them, to see that no injury had been sustained, while they flew to the larboard to get ready for the rafts.

The discharge to larboard produced the most terrible effect. The star and double-headed shot of the large guns cut seven or eight of the rafts completely asunder, and killed, perhaps, thirty or forty of the savages outright, while a hundred of them, at least, were thrown into the water, the most of them dreadfully wounded. The remainder, frightened out of their senses, commenced at once a precipitate retreat, not even waiting to pick up their maimed companions, who were swimming about in every direction, screaming and yelling for aid. This great success, however, came too late for the salvation of our devoted people. The canoe party were already on board the schooner to the number of more than a hundred and fifty, the most of them having succeeded in scrambling up the chains and over the boarding-netting even before the matches had been applied to the larboard guns. Nothing now could withstand their brute rage. Our men were borne down at once, overwhelmed, trodden under foot, and absolutely torn to pieces in an instant.

Seeing this, the savages on the rafts got the better of their fears, and came up in shoals to the plunder. In five minutes the Jane was a pitiable scene indeed of havoc and tumultuous outrage. The decks were split open and ripped up; the cordage, sails, and everything movable on deck demolished as if by magic; while, by dint of pushing at the stern, towing with the canoes, and hauling at the sides, as they swam in thousands around the vessel, the wretches finally forced her on shore (the cable having been slipped), and delivered her over to the good offices of Too-wit, who, during the whole of the engagement, had maintained, like a skilful general, his post of security and reconnaissance among the hills, but, now that the victory was completed to his satisfaction, condescended to scamper down with his warriors of the black skin, and become a partaker in the spoils.

Too-wit's descent left us at liberty to quit our hiding place and reconnoitre the hill in the vicinity of the chasm. At about fifty yards from the mouth of it we saw a small spring of water, at which we slaked the burning thirst that now consumed us. Not far from the spring we discovered several of the filbert-bushes which I mentioned before. Upon tasting the nuts we found them palatable, and very nearly resembling in flavour the common English filbert. We collected our hats full immediately, deposited them within the ravine, and returned for more. While we were busily employed in gathering these, a rustling in the bushes alarmed us, and we were upon the point of stealing back to our covert, when a large black bird of the bittern species strugglingly and slowly arose above the

shrubs. I was so much startled that I could do nothing, but Peters had sufficient presence of mind to run up to it before it could make its escape, and seize it by the neck. Its struggles and screams were tremendous, and we had thoughts of letting it go, lest the noise should alarm some of the savages who might be still lurking in the neighbourhood. A stab with a bowie knife, however, at length brought it to the ground, and we dragged it into the ravine, congratulating ourselves that, at all events, we had thus obtained a supply of food enough to last us for a week.

We now went out again to look about us, and ventured a considerable distance down the southern declivity of the hill, but met with nothing else which could serve us for food. We therefore collected a quantity of dry wood and returned, seeing one or two large parties of the natives on their way to the village, laden with the plunder of the vessel, and who, we were apprehensive, might discover us in passing beneath the hill.

Our next care was to render our place of concealment as secure as possible, and with this object, we arranged some brushwood over the aperture which I have before spoken of as the one through which we saw the patch of blue sky, on reaching the platform from the interior of the chasm. We left only a very small opening just wide enough to admit of our seeing the bay, without the risk of being discovered from below. Having done this, we congratulated ourselves upon the security of the position; for we were now completely excluded from observation, as long as we chose to remain within the ravine itself, and not venture out upon the hill. We could perceive no traces of the savages having ever been within this hollow; but, indeed, when we came to reflect upon the probability that the fissure through which we attained it had been only just now created by the fall of the cliff opposite, and that no other way of attaining it could be perceived, we were not so much rejoiced at the thought of being secure from molestation as fearful lest there should be absolutely no means left us for descent. We resolved to explore the summit of the hill thoroughly, when a good opportunity should offer. In the meantime we watched the motions of the savages through our loophole.

They had already made a complete wreck of the vessel, and were now preparing to set her on fire. In a little while we saw the smoke ascending in huge volumes from her main hatchway, and, shortly afterward, a dense mass of flame burst up from the forecastle. The rigging, masts and what remained of the sails caught immediately, and the fire spread rapidly along the decks. Still a great many of the savages retained their stations about her, hammering with large stones, axes, and cannon balls at the bolts and other iron and copper work. On the beach, and in canoes and rafts, there were not less, altogether, in the immediate vicinity of the schooner, than ten thousand natives, besides the shoals of them who, laden with booty, were making their way inland and over to the neighbouring islands. We now anticipated a catastrophe, and were not

disappointed. First of all there came a smart shock (which we felt as distinctly where we were as if we had been slightly galvanized), but unattended with any visible signs of an explosion. The savages were evidently startled, and paused for an instant from their labours and yellings. They were upon the point of recommencing, when suddenly a mass of smoke puffed up from the decks, resembling a black and heavy thundercloud — then, as if from its bowels, arose a tall stream of vivid fire to the height, apparently, of a quarter of a mile — then there came a sudden circular expansion of the flame — then the whole atmosphere was magically crowded, in a single instant, with a wild chaos of wood, and metal, and human limbs — and, lastly, came the concussion in its fullest fury, which hurled us impetuously from our feet, while the hills echoed and re-echoed the tumult, and a dense shower of the minutest fragments of the ruins tumbled headlong in every direction around us.

The havoc among the savages far exceeded our utmost expectation, and they had now, indeed, reaped the full and perfect fruits of their treachery. Perhaps a thousand perished by the explosion, while at least an equal number were desperately mangled. The whole surface of the bay was literally strewn with the struggling and drowning wretches, and on shore matters were even worse. They seemed utterly appalled by the suddenness and completeness of their discomfiture, and made no efforts at assisting one another. At length we observed a total change in their demeanour. From absolute stupor, they appeared to be, all at once, aroused to the highest pitch of excitement, and rushed wildly about, going to and from a certain point on the beach, with the strangest expressions of mingled horror, rage, and intense curiosity depicted on their countenances, and shouting, at the top of their voices, *"Tekeli-li! Tekeli-li!"*

Presently we saw a large body go off into the hills, whence they returned in a short time, carrying stakes of wood. These they brought to the station where the crowd was the thickest, which now separated so as to afford us a view of the object of all this excitement. We perceived something white lying upon the ground, but could not immediately make out what it was. At length we saw that it was the carcass of the strange animal with the scarlet teeth and claws which the schooner had picked up at sea on the eighteenth of January. Captain Guy had had the body preserved for the purpose of stuffing the skin and taking it to England. I remember he had given some directions about it just before our making the island, and it had been brought into the cabin and stowed away in one of the lockers. It had now been thrown on shore by the explosion; but why it had occasioned so much concern among the savages was more than we could comprehend. Although they crowded around the carcass at a little distance, none of them seemed willing to approach it closely. By-and-by the men with the stakes drove them in a

circle around it, and no sooner was this arrangement completed, than the whole of the vast assemblage rushed into the interior of the island, with loud screams of *"Tekeli-li! Tekeli-li!"*

CHAPTER XXIII

During the six or seven days immediately following we remained in our hiding-place upon the hill, going out only occasionally, and then with the greatest precaution, for water and filberts. We had made a kind of penthouse on the platform, furnishing it with a bed of dry leaves, and placing in it three large flat stones, which served us for both fireplace and table. We kindled a fire without difficulty by rubbing two pieces of dry wood together, the one soft, the other hard. The bird we had taken in such good season proved excellent eating, although somewhat tough. It was not an oceanic fowl, but a species of bittern, with jet black and grizzly plumage, and diminutive wings in proportion to its bulk. We afterward saw three of the same kind in the vicinity of the ravine, apparently seeking for the one we had captured; but, as they never alighted, we had no opportunity of catching them.

As long as this fowl lasted we suffered nothing from our situation, but it was now entirely consumed, and it became absolutely necessary that we should look out for provision. The filberts would not satisfy the cravings of hunger, afflicting us, too, with severe gripings of the bowels, and, if freely indulged in, with violent headache. We had seen several large tortoises near the seashore to the eastward of the hill, and perceived they might be easily taken, if we could get at them without the observation of the natives. It was resolved, therefore, to make an attempt at descending.

We commenced by going down the southern declivity, which seemed to offer the fewest difficulties, but had not proceeded a hundred yards before (as we had anticipated from appearances on the hilltop) our progress was entirely arrested by a branch of the gorge in which our companions had perished. We now passed along the edge of this for about a quarter of a mile, when we were again stopped by a precipice of immense depth, and, not being able to make our way along the brink of it, we were forced to retrace our steps by the main ravine.

We now pushed over to the eastward, but with precisely similar fortune. After an hour's scramble, at the risk of breaking our necks, we discovered that we had merely descended into a vast pit of black granite, with fine dust at the bottom, and whence the only egress was by the rugged path in which we had come down. Toiling again up this path, we now tried the northern edge of the hill. Here we were obliged to use the greatest possible caution in our manœuvres, as the least indiscretion would expose us to the full view of the savages in the village. We crawled along, therefore, on our hands and knees, and, occasionally, were even forced to throw ourselves at full length, dragging our bodies along by

means of the shrubbery. In this careful manner we had proceeded but a little way, when we arrived at a chasm far deeper than any we had yet seen, and leading directly into the main gorge. Thus our fears were fully confirmed, and we found ourselves cut off entirely from access to the world below. Thoroughly exhausted by our exertions, we made the best of our way back to the platform, and throwing ourselves upon the bed of leaves, slept sweetly and soundly for some hours.

For several days after this fruitless search we were occupied in ex· ploring every part of the summit of the hill, in order to inform ourselves of its actual resources. We found that it would afford us no food, with the exception of the unwholesome filberts, and a rank species of scurvy grass, which grew in a little patch of not more than four rods square, and would be soon exhausted. On the fifteenth of February, as near as I can remember, there was not a blade of this left, and the nuts were growing scarce; our situation, therefore, could hardly be more lamentable.* On the sixteenth we again went round the walls of our prison, in hope of finding some avenue of escape; but to no purpose. We also descended the chasm in which we had been overwhelmed, with the faint expectation of discovering, through this channel, some opening to the main ravine. Here, too, we were disappointed, although we found and brought up with us a musket.

On the seventeenth we set out with the determination of examining more thoroughly the chasm of black granite into which we had made our way in the first search. We remembered that one of the fissures in the sides of this pit had been but partially looked into, and we were anxious to explore it, although with no expectation of discovering here any opening.

We found no great difficulty in reaching the bottom of the hollow as before, and were now sufficiently calm to survey it with some attention. It was, indeed, one of the most singular-looking places imaginable, and we could scarcely bring ourselves to believe it altogether the work of nature. The pit, from its eastern to its western extremity, was about five hundred yards in length, when all its windings were threaded; the distance from east to west in a straight line not being more (I should suppose, having no means of accurate examination) than forty or fifty yards. Upon first descending into the chasm, that is to say, for a hundred feet downward from the summit of the hill, the sides of the abyss bore little resemblance to each other, and, apparently, had at no time been connected, the one surface being of the soapstone, and the other of marl, granulated with some metallic matter. The average breadth or interval between the two cliffs was probably here sixty feet, but there seemed to be no regularity of formation. Passing down, however, beyond the limit spoken of, the interval rapidly contracted, and the sides began to run

* This day was rendered remarkable by our observing in the south several huge wreaths of the grayish vapour I have spoken of.

parallel, although, for some distance farther, they were still dissimilar in their material and form of surface. Upon arriving within fifty feet of the bottom, a perfect regularity commenced. The sides were now entirely uniform in substance, in colour, and in lateral direction, the material being a very black and shining granite, and the distance between the two sides, at all points facing each other, exactly twenty yards. The precise formation of the chasm will be best understood by means of a delineation taken upon the spot; for I had luckily with me a pocketbook and pencil, which I preserved with great care through a long series of subsequent adventure, and to which I am indebted for memoranda of many subjects which would otherwise have been crowded from my remembrance.

FIG. 1. FIG. 2.

This figure (see fig. 1) gives the general outlines of the chasm, without the minor cavities in the sides, of which there were several, each cavity having a corresponding protuberance opposite. The bottom of the gulf was covered to the depth of three or four inches with a powder almost impalpable, beneath which we found a continuation of the black granite. To the right, at the lower extremity, will be noticed the appearance of a small opening; this is the fissure alluded to above, and to examine which more minutely than before was the object of our second visit. We now pushed into it with vigor, cutting away a quantity of brambles which impeded us, and removing a vast heap of sharp flints somewhat resembling arrowheads in shape. We were encouraged to persevere, however, by perceiving some little light proceeding from the farther end. We at length squeezed our way for about thirty feet, and found that the aperture was a low and regularly formed arch, having a bottom of the same impalpable powder as that in the main chasm. A strong light now broke upon us, and, turning a short bend, we found ourselves in another lofty chamber, similar to the one we had left in every respect but longitudinal form. Its general figure is here given. (See fig. 2.)

The total length of this chasm, commencing at the opening a and proceeding round the curve b to the extremity d, is five hundred and fifty yards. At c we discovered a small aperture similar to the one through which we had issued from the other chasm, and this was choked up in the same manner with brambles and a quantity of the white arrowhead flints. We forced our way through it, finding it about forty feet long,

and emerged into a third chasm. This, too, was precisely like the first, except in its longitudinal shape, which was thus. (See fig. 3.)

We found the entire length of the third chasm three hundred and twenty yards. At the point *a* was an opening about six feet wide, and extending fifteen feet into the rock, where it terminated in a bed of marl, there being no other chasm beyond, as we had expected. We were about leaving this fissure, into which very little light was admitted, when Peters called my attention to a range of singular-looking indentures in the surface of the marl forming the termination of the *cul-de-sac*. With a very slight exertion of the imagination, the left, or most northern of these indentures might have been taken for the intentional, although rude, representation of a human figure standing erect, with outstretched arm. The rest of them bore also some little resemblance to alphabetical characters, and Peters was willing, at all events, to adopt the idle opinion

FIG. 3. FIG. 5. FIG. 4.

that they were really such. I convinced him of his error, finally, by directing his attention to the floor of the fissure, where, among the powder, we picked up, piece by piece, several large flakes of the marl, which had evidently been broken off by some convulsion from the surface where the indentures were found, and which had projecting points exactly fitting the indentures; thus proving them to have been the work of nature. Fig. 4 presents an accurate copy of the whole.

After satisfying ourselves that these singular caverns afforded us no means of escape from our prison, we made our way back, dejected and dispirited, to the summit of the hill. Nothing worth mentioning occurred during the next twenty-four hours, except that, in examining the ground to the eastward of the third chasm, we found two triangular holes of great depth, and also with black granite sides. Into these holes we did not think it worth while to attempt descending, as they had the appearance of mere natural wells, without outlet. They were each about twenty yards in circumference, and their shape, as well as relative position in regard to the third chasm, is shown in figure 5.

CHAPTER XXIV

On the twentieth of the month, finding it altogether impossible to subsist any longer upon the filberts, the use of which occasioned us the most excruciating torment, we resolved to make a desperate attempt at descending the southern declivity of the hill. The face of the precipice was here of the softest species of soapstone, although nearly perpendicu-

lar throughout its whole extent (a depth of a hundred and fifty feet at the least), and in many places even overarching. After long search we discovered a narrow ledge about twenty feet below the brink of the gulf; upon this Peters contrived to leap, with what assistance I could render him by means of our pocket-handkerchiefs tied together. With somewhat more difficulty I also got down; and we then saw the possibility of descending the whole way by the process in which we had clambered up from the chasm when we had been buried by the fall of the hill — that is, by cutting steps in the face of the soapstone with our knives. The extreme hazard of the attempt can scarcely be conceived; but, as there was no other resource, we determined to undertake it.

Upon the ledge where we stood there grew some filbert bushes; and to one of these we made fast an end of our rope of handkerchiefs. The other end being tied round Peters' waist, I lowered him down over the edge of the precipice until the handkerchiefs were stretched tight. He now proceeded to dig a deep hole in the soapstone (as far in as eight or ten inches), sloping away the rock above to the height of a foot, or thereabout, so as to allow of his driving, with the butt of a pistol, a tolerably strong peg into the levelled surface. I then drew him up for about four feet, when he made a hole similar to the one below, driving in a peg as before and having thus a resting place for both feet and hands. I now unfastened the handkerchiefs from the bush, throwing him the end, which he tied to the peg in the uppermost hole, letting himself down gently to a station about three feet lower than he had yet been — that is, to the full extent of the handkerchiefs. Here he dug another hole, and drove another peg. He then drew himself up, so as to rest his feet in the hole just cut, taking hold with his hands upon the peg in the one above. It was now necessary to untie the handkerchiefs from the topmost peg, with the view of fastening them to the second; and here he found that an error had been committed in cutting the holes at so great a distance apart. However, after one or two unsuccessful and dangerous attempts at reaching the knot (having to hold on with his left hand while he laboured to undo the fastening with his right), he at length cut the string, leaving six inches of it affixed to the peg. Tying the handkerchiefs now to the second peg, he descended to a station below the third, taking care not to go too far down. By these means (means which I should never have conceived of myself, and for which we were indebted altogether to Peters' ingenuity and resolution) my companion finally succeeded, with the occasional aid of projections in the cliff, in reaching the bottom without accident.

It was some time before I could summon sufficient resolution to follow him; but I did at length attempt it. Peters had taken off his shirt before descending, and this, with my own, formed the rope necessary for the adventure. After throwing down the musket found in the chasm, I fastened this rope to the bushes, and let myself down rapidly, striving,

by the vigour of my movements, to banish the trepidation which I could overcome in no other manner. This answered sufficiently well for the first four or five steps; but presently I found my imagination growing terribly excited by thoughts of the vast depths yet to be descended, and the precarious nature of the pegs and soapstone holes which were my only support. It was in vain I endeavoured to banish these reflections, and to keep my eyes steadily bent upon the flat surface of the cliff before me. The more earnestly I struggled *not to think*, the more intensely vivid became my conceptions, and the more horribly distinct. At length arrived that crisis of fancy, so fearful in all similar cases, the crisis in which we begin to anticipate the feelings with which we *shall* fall — to picture to ourselves the sickness, and dizziness, and the last struggle, and the half swoon, and the final bitterness of the rushing and headlong descent. And now I found these fancies creating their own realities, and all imagined horrors crowding upon me in fact. I felt my knees strike violently together, while my fingers were gradually but certainly relaxing their grasp. There was a ringing in my ears, and I said, "This is my knell of death!" And now I was consumed with the irrepressible desire of looking below. I could not, I would not, confine my glances to the cliff; and, with a wild, indefinable emotion, half of horror, half of a relieved oppression, I threw my vision far down into the abyss. For one moment my fingers clutched convulsively upon their hold, while, with the movement, the faintest possible idea of ultimate escape wandered, like a shadow, through my mind — in the next my whole soul was pervaded with a *longing to fall*; a desire, a yearning, a passion utterly uncontrollable. I let go at once my grasp upon the peg, and, turning half round from the precipice, remained tottering for an instant against its naked face. But now there came a spinning of the brain; a shrill-sounding and phantom voice screamed within my ears; a dusky, fiendish, and filmy figure stood immediately beneath me; and, sighing, I sunk down with a bursting heart, and plunged within its arms.

I had swooned, and Peters had caught me as I fell. He had observed my proceedings from his station at the bottom of the cliff; and perceiving my imminent danger, had endeavoured to inspire me with courage by every suggestion he could devise; although my confusion of mind had been so great as to prevent my hearing what he said, or being conscious that he had even spoken to me at all. At length, seeing me totter, he hastened to ascend to my rescue, and arrived just in time for my preservation. Had I fallen with my full weight, the rope of linen would inevitably have snapped, and I should have been precipitated into the abyss; as it was, he contrived to let me down gently, so as to remain suspended without danger until animation returned. This was in about fifteen minutes. On recovery, my trepidation had entirely vanished; I felt a new being, and, with some little further aid from my companion, reached the bottom also in safety.

We now found ourselves not far from the ravine which had proved the tomb of our friends, and to the southward of the spot where the hill had fallen. The place was one of singular wildness, and its aspect brought to my mind the descriptions given by travellers of those dreary regions marking the site of degraded Babylon. Not to speak of the ruins of the disrupted cliff, which formed a chaotic barrier in the vista to the northward, the surface of the ground in every other direction was strewn with huge tumuli, apparently the wreck of some gigantic structures of art; although, in detail, no semblance of art could be detected. Scoria were abundant, and large shapeless blocks of the black granite, intermingled with others of marl,* and both granulated with metal. Of vegetation there were no traces whatsoever throughout the whole of the desolate area within sight. Several immense scorpions were seen, and various reptiles not elsewhere to be found in the high latitudes.

As food was our most immediate object, we resolved to make our way to the seacoast, distant not more than half a mile, with a view of catching turtle, several of which we had observed from our place of concealment on the hill. We had proceeded some hundred yards, threading our route cautiously between the huge rocks and tumuli, when, upon turning a corner, five savages sprung upon us from a small cavern, felling Peters to the ground with a blow from a club. As he fell the whole party rushed upon him to secure their victim, leaving me time to recover from my astonishment. I still had the musket, but the barrel had received so much injury in being thrown from the precipice that I cast it aside as useless, preferring to trust my pistols, which had been carefully preserved in order. With these I advanced upon the assailants, firing one after the other in quick succession. Two savages fell, and one, who was in the act of thrusting a spear into Peters, sprung to his feet without accomplishing his purpose. My companion being thus released, we had no further difficulty. He had his pistols also, but prudently declined using them, confiding in his great personal strength, which far exceeded that of any person I have ever known. Seizing a club from one of the savages who had fallen, he dashed out the brains of the three who remained, killing each instantaneously with a single blow of the weapon, and leaving us completely masters of the field.

So rapidly had these events passed, that we could scarcely believe in their reality, and were standing over the bodies of the dead in a species of stupid contemplation, when we were brought to recollection by the sound of shouts in the distance. It was clear that the savages had been alarmed by the firing, and that we had little chance of avoiding discovery. To regain the cliff, it would be necessary to proceed in the direction of the shouts; and even should we succeed in arriving at its base, we should never be able to ascend it without being seen. Our situation was

* The marl was also black; indeed, we noticed no light-coloured substances of any kind upon the island.

one of the greatest peril, and we were hesitating in which path to commence a flight, when one of the savages whom I had shot, and supposed dead, sprang briskly to his feet, and attempted to make his escape. We overtook him, however, before he had advanced many paces, and were about to put him to death, when Peters suggested that we might derive some benefit from forcing him to accompany us in our attempt to escape. We therefore dragged him with us, making him understand that we would shoot him if he offered resistance. In a few minutes he was perfectly submissive, and ran by our sides as we pushed in among the rocks, making for the seashore.

So far, the irregularities of the ground we had been traversing hid the sea, except at intervals, from our sight, and, when we first had it fairly in view, it was perhaps, two hundred yards distant. As we emerged into the open beach we saw, to our great dismay, an immense crowd of the natives pouring from the village, and from all visible quarters of the island, making toward us with gesticulations of extreme fury, and howling like wild beasts. We were upon the point of turning upon our steps, and trying to secure a retreat among the fastnesses of the rougher ground, when I discovered the bows of two canoes projecting from behind a large rock which ran out into the water. Toward these we now ran with all speed, and, reaching them, found them unguarded, and without any other freight than three of the large Gallipago turtles and the usual supply of paddles for sixty rowers. We instantly took possession of one of them, and, forcing our captive on board, pushed out to sea with all the strength we could command.

We had not made, however, more than fifty yards from the shore before we became sufficiently calm to perceive the great oversight of which we had been guilty in leaving the other canoe in the power of the savages, who, by this time, were not more than twice as far from the beach as ourselves, and were rapidly advancing to the pursuit. No time was now to be lost. Our hope was, at best, a forlorn one, but we had none other. It was very doubtful whether, with the utmost exertion, we could get back in time to anticipate them in taking possession of the canoe; but yet there was a chance that we could. We might save ourselves if we succeeded, while not to make the attempt was to resign ourselves to inevitable butchery.

The canoe was modelled with the bow and stern alike, and, in place of turning it round, we merely changed our position in paddling. As soon as the savages perceived this they redoubled their yells, as well as their speed, and approached with inconceivable rapidity. We pulled, however, with all the energy of desperation, and arrived at the contested point before more than one of the natives had attained it. This man paid dearly for his superior agility, Peters shooting him through the head with a pistol as he approached the shore. The foremost among the rest of his party were probably some twenty or thirty paces distant as we

seized upon the canoe. We at first endeavoured to pull her into the deep
water, beyond the reach of the savages, but, finding her too firmly
aground, and there being no time to spare, Peters, with one or two
heavy strokes from the butt of the musket, succeeded in dashing out a
large portion of the bow and of one side. We then pushed off. Two of
the natives by this time had got hold of our boat, obstinately refusing
to let go, until we were forced to despatch them with our knives. We
were now clear off, and making great way out to sea. The main body
of the savages, upon reaching the broken canoe, set up the most tre-
mendous yell of rage and disappointment conceivable. In truth, from
every thing I could see of these wretches, they appeared to be the most
wicked, hypocritical, vindictive, bloodthirsty, and altogether fiendish race
of men upon the face of the globe. It is clear we should have had no
mercy had we fallen into their hands. They made a mad attempt at fol-
lowing us in the fractured canoe, but, finding it useless, again vented
their rage in a series of hideous vociferations, and rushed up into the
hills.

We were thus relieved from immediate danger, but our situation was
still sufficiently gloomy. We knew that four canoes of the kind we had
were at one time in the possession of the savages, and were not aware of
the fact (afterward ascertained from our captive) that two of these had
been blown to pieces in the explosion of the Jane Guy. We calculated,
therefore, upon being yet pursued, as soon as our enemies could get
round to the bay (distant about three miles) where the boats were usu-
ally laid up. Fearing this, we made every exertion to leave the island
behind us, and went rapidly through the water, forcing the prisoner to
take a paddle. In about half an hour, when we had gained, probably, five
or six miles to the southward, a large fleet of the flat-bottomed canoes
or rafts were seen to emerge from the bay evidently with the design of
pursuit. Presently they put back, despairing to overtake us.

CHAPTER XXV

We now found ourselves in the wide and desolate Antarctic Ocean,
in a latitude exceeding eighty-four degrees, in a frail canoe, and with
no provision but the three turtles. The long polar winter, too, could not
be considered as far distant, and it became necessary that we should
deliberate well upon the course to be pursued. There were six or seven
islands in sight belonging to the same group, and distant from each
other about five or six leagues; but upon neither of these had we any
intention to venture. In coming from the northward in the Jane Guy
we had been gradually leaving behind us the severest regions of ice —
this, however little it may be in accordance with the generally received
notions respecting the Antarctic, was a fact experience would not permit
us to deny. To attempt, therefore, getting back would be folly — espe-
cially at so late a period of the season. Only one course seemed to be

left open for hope. We resolved to steer boldly to the southward, where there was at least a probability of discovering lands, and more than a probability of finding a still milder climate.

So far we had found the Antarctic, like the Arctic Ocean, peculiarly free from violent storms or immoderately rough water; but our canoe was, at best, of frail structure, although large, and we set busily to work with a view of rendering her as safe as the limited means in our possession would admit. The body of the boat was of no better material than bark — the bark of a tree unknown. The ribs were of a tough osier, well adapted to the purpose for which it was used. We had fifty feet room from stem to stern, from four to six in breadth, and in depth throughout four feet and a half — the boats thus differing vastly in shape from those of any other inhabitants of the Southern Ocean with whom civilized nations are acquainted. We never did believe them the workmanship of the ignorant islanders who owned them; and some days after this period discovered, by questioning our captive, that they were in fact made by the natives of a group to the southwest of the country where we found them, having fallen accidentally into the hands of our barbarians. What we could do for the security of our boat was very little indeed. Several wide rents were discovered near both ends, and these we contrived to patch up with pieces of woollen jacket. With the help of the superfluous paddles, of which there were a great many, we erected a kind of framework about the bow, so as to break the force of any seas which might threaten to fill us in that quarter. We also set up two paddle-blades for masts, placing them opposite each other, one by each gunwale, thus saving the necessity of a yard. To these masts we attached a sail made of our shirts — doing this with some difficulty, as here we could get no assistance from our prisoner whatever, although he had been willing enough to labour in all the other operations. The sight of the linen seemed to affect him in a very singular manner. He could not be prevailed upon to touch it or go near it, shuddering when we attempted to force him, and shrieking out, "*Tekeli-li!*"

Having completed our arrangements in regard to the security of the canoe, we now set sail to the south southeast for the present, with the view of weathering the most southerly of the group in sight. This being done, we turned the bow full to the southward. The weather could by no means be considered disagreeable. We had a prevailing and very gentle wind from the northward, a smooth sea, and continual daylight. No ice whatever was to be seen; *nor did I ever see one particle of this after leaving the parallel of Bennet's Islet.* Indeed, the temperature of the water was here far too warm for its existence in any quantity. Having killed the largest of our tortoises, and obtained from him not only food but a copious supply of water, we continued on our course, without any incident of moment, for perhaps seven or eight days, during which period we must have proceeded a vast distance to the southward, as the wind

blew constantly with us, and a very strong current set continually in the direction we were pursuing.

March 1.* — Many unusual phenomena now indicated that we were entering upon a region of novelty and wonder. A high range of light gray vapour appeared constantly in the southern horizon, flaring up occasionally in lofty streaks, now darting from east to west, now from west to east, and again presenting a level and uniform summit — in short, having all the wild variations of the Aurora Borealis. The average height of this vapour, as apparent from our station, was about twenty-five degrees. The temperature of the sea seemed to be increasing momentarily, and there was a very perceptible alteration in its colour.

March 2. — To-day by repeated questioning of our captive, we came to the knowledge of many particulars in regard to the island of the massacre, its inhabitants, and customs — but with these how can I *now* detain the reader? I may say, however, that we learned there were eight islands in the group — that they were governed by a common king, named *Tsalemon* or *Psalemoun*, who resided in one of the smallest of the islands; that the black skins forming the dress of the warriors came from an animal of huge size to be found only in a valley near the court of the king — that the inhabitants of the group fabricated no other boats than the flat-bottomed rafts; the four canoes being all of the kind in their possession, and these having been obtained, by mere accident, from some large island in the southwest — that his own name was Nu-Nu — that he had no knowledge of Bennet's Islet — and that the appellation of the island he had left was *Tsalal*. The commencement of the words *Tsalemon* and *Tsalal* was given with a prolonged hissing sound, which we found it impossible to imitate, even after repeated endeavours, and which was precisely the same with the note of the black bittern we had eaten up on the summit of the hill.

March 3. — The heat of the water was now truly remarkable, and in colour was undergoing a rapid change, being no longer transparent, but of a milky consistency and hue. In our immediate vicinity it was usually smooth, never so rough as to endanger the canoe — but we were frequently surprised at perceiving, to our right and left, at different distances, sudden and extensive agitations of the surface — these, we at length noticed, were always preceded by wild flickerings in the region of vapour to the southward.

March 4. — To-day, with the view of widening our sail, the breeze from the northward dying away perceptibly, I took from my coat-pocket a white handkerchief. Nu-Nu was seated at my elbow, and the linen accidentally flaring in his face, he became violently affected with convulsions.

* For obvious reasons I cannot pretend to strict accuracy in these dates. They are given principally with a view to perspicuity of narration, and as set down in my pencil memorandum.

These were succeeded by drowsiness and stupor, and low murmurings of "*Tekeli-li! Tekeli-li!*"

March 5. — The wind had entirely ceased, but it was evident that we were still hurrying on to the southward, under the influence of a powerful current. And now, indeed, it would seem reasonable that we should experience some alarm at the turn events were taking — but we felt none. The countenance of Peters indicated nothing of this nature, although it wore at times an expression I could not fathom. The polar winter appeared to be coming on — but coming without its terrors. I felt a *numbness* of body and mind — a dreaminess of sensation — but this was all.

March 6. — The gray vapour had now arisen many more degrees above the horizon, and was gradually losing its grayness of tint. The heat of the water was extreme, even unpleasant to the touch, and its milky hue was more evident than ever. To-day a violent agitation of the water occurred very close to the canoe. It was attended, as usual, with a wild flaring up of the vapour at its summit, and a momentary division at its base. A fine white powder, resembling ashes — but certainly not such — fell over the canoe and over a large surface of the water, as the flickering died away among the vapour and the commotion subsided in the sea. Nu-Nu now threw himself on his face in the bottom of the boat, and no persuasions could induce him to arise.

March 7. — This day we questioned Nu-Nu concerning the motives of his countrymen in destroying our companions; but he appeared to be too utterly overcome by terror to afford us any rational reply. He still obstinately lay in the bottom of the boat; and, upon reiterating the questions as to the motive, made use only of idiotic gesticulations, such as raising with his forefinger the upper lip, and displaying the teeth which lay beneath it. These were black. We had never before seen the teeth of an inhabitant of Tsalal.

March 8. — To-day there floated by us one of the white animals whose appearance upon the beach at Tsalal had occasioned so wild a commotion among the savages. I would have picked it up, but there came over me a sudden listlessness, and I forbore. The heat of the water still increased, and the hand could no longer be endured within it. Peters spoke little, and I knew not what to think of his apathy. Nu-Nu breathed, and no more.

March 9. — The whole ashy material fell now continually around us, and in vast quantities. The range of vapour to the southward had arisen prodigiously in the horizon, and began to assume more distinctness of form. I can liken it to nothing but a limitless cataract, rolling silently into the sea from some immense and far-distant rampart in the heaven. The gigantic curtain ranged along the whole extent of the southern horizon. It emitted no sound.

March 21. — A sullen darkness now hovered above us — but from out

the milky depths of the ocean a luminous glare arose, and stole up along the bulwarks of the boat. We were nearly overwhelmed by the white ashy shower which settled upon us and upon the canoe, but melted into the water as it fell. The summit of the cataract was utterly lost in the dimness and the distance. Yet we were evidently approaching it with a hideous velocity. At intervals there were visible in it wide, yawning, but momentary rents, and from out these rents, within which was a chaos of flitting and indistinct images, there came rushing and mighty, but soundless winds, tearing up the enkindled ocean in their course.

March 22. — The darkness had materially increased, relieved only by the glare of the water thrown back from the white curtain before us. Many gigantic and pallidly white birds flew continuously now from beyond the veil, and their scream was the eternal *Tekeli-li!* as they retreated from our vision. Hereupon Nu-Nu stirred in the bottom of the boat; but upon touching him, we found his spirit departed. And now we rushed into the embraces of the cataract, where a chasm threw itself open to receive us. But there arose in our pathway a shrouded human figure, very far larger in its proportions than any dweller among men. And the hue of the skin of the figure was of the perfect whiteness of the snow.

NOTE

The circumstances connected with the late sudden and distressing death of Mr. Pym are already well known to the public through the medium of the daily press. It is feared that the few remaining chapters which were to have completed his narrative, and which were retained by him, while the above were in type, for the purpose of revision, have been irrecoverably lost through the accident by which he perished himself. This, however, may prove not to be the case, and the papers, if ultimately found, will be given to the public.

No means have been left untried to remedy the deficiency. The gentleman whose name is mentioned in the preface, and who, from the statement there made, might be supposed able to fill the vacuum, has declined the task — this for satisfactory reasons connected with the general inaccuracy of the details afforded him, and his disbelief in the entire truth of the latter portions of the narration. Peters, from whom some information might be expected, is still alive, and a resident of Illinois, but cannot be met with at present. He may hereafter be found, and will, no doubt, afford material for a conclusion of Mr. Pym's account.

The loss of the two or three final chapters (for there were but two or three) is the more deeply to be regretted, as, it cannot be doubted, they contained matter relative to the Pole itself, or at least to regions in its very near proximity; and as, too, the statements of the author in relation to these regions may shortly be verified or contradicted by means of the governmental expedition now preparing for the Southern Ocean.

On one point in the Narrative some remarks may be well offered; and it would afford the writer of this appendix much pleasure if what he may here observe should have a tendency to throw credit, in any degree, upon

the very singular pages now published. We allude to the chasms found in the island of Tsalal, and to the whole of the figures upon pages 842, 843.

Mr. Pym has given the figures of the chasm without comment, and speaks decidedly of the *indentures* found at the extremity of the most easterly of these chasms as having but a fanciful resemblance to alphabetical characters, and, in short, as being positively *not such*. This assertion is made in a manner so simple, and sustained by a species of demonstration so conclusive (viz., the fitting of the projections of the fragments found among the dust into the indentures upon the wall), that we are forced to believe the writer in earnest; and no reasonable reader should suppose otherwise. But as the facts in relation to *all* the figures are most singular (especially when taken in connexion with statements made in the body of the narrative), it may be as well to say a word or two concerning them all — this, too, the more especially as the facts in question have, beyond doubt, escaped the attention of Mr. Poe.

Figure 1, then figure 2, figure 3, and figure 5, when conjoined with one another in the precise order which the chasms themselves presented, and when deprived of the small lateral branches or arches (which, it will be remembered, served only as means of communication between the main chambers, and were of totally distinct character), constitute an Ethiopian verbal root — the root ልሕⶩ "To be shady" — whence all the inflections of shadow or darkness.

In regard to the "left or most northwardly" of the indentures in figure 4, it is more than probable that the opinion of Peters was correct, and that the hieroglyphical appearance was really the work of art, and intended as the representation of a human form. The delineation is before the reader, and he may, or may not, perceive the resemblance suggested; but the rest of the indentures afford strong confirmation of Peters' idea. The upper range is evidently the Arabic verbal root ⲥⲛⲥⲥⲛ "To be white," whence all the inflections of brilliancy and whiteness. The lower range is not so immediately perspicuous. The characters are somewhat broken and disjointed; nevertheless, it cannot be doubted that, in their perfect state, they formed the full Egyptian word Π&ⴞΥΡΗⲤ., "The region of the south." It should be observed that these interpretations confirm the opinion of Peters in regard to the "most northwardly" of the figures. The arm is outstretched towards the south.

Conclusions such as these open a wide field for speculation and exciting conjecture. They should be regarded, perhaps, in connexion with some of the most faintly-detailed incidents of the narrative; although in no visible manner is this chain of connexion complete. Tekeli-li! was the cry of the affrighted natives of Tsalal upon discovering the carcass of the *white* animal picked up at sea. This also was the shuddering exclamation of the captive Tsalalian upon encountering the *white* materials in possession of Mr. Pym. This also was the shriek of the swift-flying, *white*, and gigantic birds which issued from the vapoury *white* curtain of the South. Nothing *white* was to be found at Tsalal, and nothing otherwise in the subsequent voyage to the region beyond. It is not impossible that "Tsalal," the appellation of the island of the chasms, may

be found, upon minute philological scrutiny, to betray either some alliance with the chasms themselves, or some reference to the Ethiopian characters so mysteriously written in their windings.

"*I have graven it within the hills, and my vengeance upon the dust within the rock.*"

V

CRITICISM

Letter to B_____*

It has been said that a good critique on a poem may be written by one who is no poet himself. This, according to *your* idea and *mine* of poetry, I feel to be false — the less poetical the critic, the less just the critique, and the converse. On this account, and because there are but few B——s in the world, I would be as much ashamed of the world's good opinion as proud of your own. Another than yourself might here

* These detached passages form part of the preface to a small volume printed some years ago for private circulation. They have vigor and much originality — but of course we shall not be called upon to endorse all the writer's opinions. — *Ed.*

observe, "Shakespeare is in possession of the world's good opinion, anc
yet Shakespeare is the greatest of poets. It appears then that as the world
judges correctly, why should you be ashamed of their favourable judg-
ment?" The difficulty lies in the interpretation of the word "judgment"
or "opinion." The opinion is the world's, truly, but it may be called theirs
as a man would call a book his, having bought it; he did not write the
book, but it is his; they did not originate the opinion, but it is theirs. A
fool, for example, thinks Shakespeare a great poet — yet the fool has
never read Shakespeare. But the fool's neighbor, who is a step higher
on the Andes of the mind, whose head (that is to say, his more exalted
thought) is too far above the fool to be seen or understood, but whose
feet (by which I mean his every-day actions) are sufficiently near to be
discerned, and by means of which that superiority is ascertained, which
but for them would never have been discovered — this neighbor asserts
that Shakespeare is a great poet — the fool believes him, and it is hence-
forward his *opinion*. This neighbor's own opinion has, in like manner,
been adopted from one above *him*, and so, ascendingly, to a few gifted
individuals who kneel around the summit, beholding, face to face, the
master spirit who stands upon the pinnacle. . . .

You are aware of the great barrier in the path of an American writer.
He is read, if at all, in preference to the combined and established wit
of the world. I say established; for it is with literature as with law or
empire — an established name is an estate in tenure, or a throne in posses-
sion. Besides, one might suppose that books, like their authors, improve
by travel — their having crossed the sea is, with us, so great a distinction.
Our antiquaries abandon time for distance; our very fops glance from
the binding to the bottom of the title-page, where the mystic characters
which spell London, Paris, or Genoa, are precisely so many letters of
recommendation.

* * * * *

I mentioned just now a vulgar error as regards criticism. I think the
notion that no poet can form a correct estimate of his own writings is
another. I remarked before that in proportion to the poetical talent would
be the justice of a critique upon poetry. Therefore a bad poet would,
I grant, make a false critique, and his self-love would infallibly bias his
little judgment in his favour; but a poet, who is indeed a poet, could not,
I think, fail of making a just critique; whatever should be deducted on the
score of self-love might be replaced on account of his intimate acquaint-
ance with the subject; in short, we have more instances of false criticism
than of just where one's own writings are the test, simply because we
have more bad poets than good. There are, of course, many objections

to what I say: Milton is a great example of the contrary; but his opinion with respect to the Paradise Regained is by no means fairly ascertained. By what trivial circumstances men are often led to assert what they do not really believe! Perhaps an inadvertent world has descended to posterity. But, in fact, the Paradise Regained is little, if at all, inferior to the Paradise Lost, and is only supposed so to be because men do not like epics, whatever they may say to the contrary, and reading those of Milton in their natural order, are too much wearied with the first to derive any pleasure from the second.

I dare say Milton preferred Comos to either — if so — justly.

As I am speaking of poetry, it will not be amiss to touch slightly upon the most singular heresy in its modern history — the heresy of what is called, very foolishly, the Lake School. Some years ago I might have been induced, by an occasion like the present, to attempt a formal refutation of their doctrine; at present it would be a work of supererogation. The wise must bow to the wisdom of such men as Coleridge and Southey, but being wise, have laughed at poetical theories so prosaically exemplified.

Aristotle, with singular assurance, has declared poetry the most philosophical of all writings — but it required a Wordsworth to pronounce it the most metaphysical. He seems to think that the end of poetry is, or should be, instruction; yet it is a truism that the end of our existence is happiness; if so, the end of every separate part of our existence, everything connected with our existence, should be still happiness. Therefore the end of instruction should be happiness; and happiness is another name for pleasure; — therefore the end of instruction should be pleasure; yet we see the above-mentioned opinion implies precisely the reverse.

To proceed: ceteris paribus, he who pleases is of more importance to his fellow-men than he who instructs, since utility is happiness, and pleasure is the end already obtained while instruction is merely the means of obtaining.

I see no reason, then, why our metaphysical poets should plume themselves so much on the utility of their works, unless indeed they refer to instruction with eternity in view; in which case, sincere respect for their piety would not allow me to express my contempt for their judgment; contempt which it would be difficult to conceal, since their writings are professedly to be understood by the few, and it is the many who stand in need of salvation. In such case I should no doubt be tempted to think of the devil in "Melmoth," who labours indefatigably, through three octavo volumes, to accomplish the destruction of one or two souls, while any common devil would have demolished one or two thousand.

* * * * *

Against the subtleties which would make poetry a study — not a passion — it becomes the metaphysician to reason — but the poet to protest. Yet Wordsworth and Coleridge are men in years; the one imbued in contemplation from his childhood; the other a giant in intellect and learning. The diffidence, then, with which I venture to dispute their authority would be overwhelming did I not feel, from the bottom of my heart, that learning has little to do with the imagination — intellect with the passions — or age with poetry.

> Trifles, like straws, upon the surface flow;
> He who would search for pearls must dive below,

are lines which have done much mischief. As regards the greater truths, men oftener err by seeking them at the bottom than at the top; Truth lies in the huge abysses where wisdom is sought — not in the palpable palaces where she is found. The ancients were not always right in hiding the goddess in a well; witness the light which Bacon has thrown upon philosophy; witness the principles of our divine faith — that moral mechanism by which the simplicity of a child may overbalance the wisdom of a man.

We see an instance of Coleridge's liability to err, in his *Biographia Literaria* — professedly his literary life and opinions, but, in fact, a treatise *de omni scibili et quibusdam aliis*. He goes wrong by reason of his very profundity, and of his error we have a natural type in the contemplation of a star. He who regards it directly and intensely sees, it is true, the star, but it is the star without a ray — while he who surveys it less inquisitively is conscious of all for which the star is useful to us below — its brilliancy and its beauty.

As to Wordsworth, I have no faith in him. That he had in youth the feelings of a poet I believe — for there are glimpses of extreme delicacy in his writings — (and delicacy is the poet's own kingdom — his *El Dorado*) — but they have the appearance of a better day recollected; and glimpses, at best, are little evidence of present poetic fire — we know that a few straggling flowers spring up daily in the crevices of the glacier.

He was to blame in wearing away his youth in contemplation with the end of poetizing in his manhood. With the increase of his judgment the light which should make it apparent has faded away. His judgment consequently is too correct. This may not be understood, — but the old Goths of Germany would have understood it, who used to debate matters of importance to their State twice, once when drunk, and once when sober — sober that they might not be deficient in formality — drunk lest they should be destitute of vigour.

The long wordy discussions by which he tries to reason us into admira-

tion of his poetry, speak very little in his favour: they are full of such assertions as this (I have opened one of his volumes at random) — "Of genius the only proof is the act of doing well what is worthy to be done, and what was never done before"; — indeed? then it follows that in doing what is *unworthy* to be done, or what *has* been done before, no genius can be evinced; yet the picking of pockets is an unworthy act, pockets have been picked time immemorial, and Barrington, the pickpocket, in point of genius, would have thought hard of a comparison with William Wordsworth, the poet.

Again — in estimating the merit of certain poems, whether they be Ossian's or M'Pherson's, can surely be of little consequence, yet, in order to prove their worthlessness, Mr. W. has expended many pages in the controversy. *Tantæne animis?* Can great minds descend to such absurdity? But worse still: that he may bear down every argument in favour of these poems, he triumphantly drags forward a passage in his abomination with which he expects the reader to sympathise. It is the beginning of the epic poem "Temora." "The blue waves of Ullin roll in light; the green hills are covered with day; trees shake their dusty heads in the breeze." And this — this gorgeous, yet simple imagery, where all is alive and panting with immortality — this, William Wordsworth, the author of "Peter Bell," has *selected* for his contempt. We shall see what better he, in his own person, has to offer. Imprimis:

> And now she's at the pony's tail,
> And now she's at the pony's head,
> On that side now, and now on this;
> And, almost stifled with her bliss,
> A few sad tears does Betty shed. . . .
> She pats the pony, where or when
> She knows not . . . happy Betty Foy!
> Oh, Johnny, never mind the doctor!

Secondly:

> The dew was falling fast, the — stars began to blink;
> I heard a voice: it said — "Drink, pretty creature, drink!"
> And, looking o'er the hedge, be — fore me I espied
> A snow-white mountain lamb, with a — maiden at its side.
> No other sheep was near, — the lamb was all alone,
> And by a slender cord was — tether'd to a stone.

Now, we have no doubt this is all true; we *will* believe it, indeed we will, Mr. W. Is it sympathy for the sheep you wish to excite? I love a sheep from the bottom of my heart.

* * * * *

But there *are* occasions, dear B——, there are occasions when even Wordsworth is reasonable. Even Stamboul, it is said, shall have an end, and the most unlucky blunders must come to a conclusion. Here is an extract from his preface: —

"Those who have been accustomed to the phraseology of modern writers, if they persist in reading this book to a conclusion (*impossible!*) will, no doubt, have to struggle with feelings of awkwardness; (ha! ha! ha!) they will look round for poetry (ha! ha! ha! ha!), and will be induced to inquire by what species of courtesy these attempts have been permitted to assume that title." Ha! ha! ha! ha! ha!

Yet, let not Mr. W. despair; he has given immortality to a wagon, and the bee Sophocles has transmitted to eternity a sore toe, and dignified a tragedy with a chorus of turkeys.

* * * * *

Of Coleridge, I cannot speak but with reverence. His towering intellect! his gigantic power! He is one more evidence of the fact *"que la plupart des sectes ont raison dans une bonne partie de ce qu'elles avancent, mais non pas en ce qu'elles nient."* He has imprisoned his own conceptions by the barrier he has erected against those of others. It is lamentable to think that such a mind should be buried in metaphysics, and, like the Nyctanthes, waste its perfume upon the night alone. In reading that man's poetry, I tremble like one who stands upon a volcano, conscious from the very darkness bursting from the crater, of the fire and the light that are weltering below.

* * * * *

What is Poetry? — Poetry! that Proteus-like idea, with as many appellations as the nine-titled Corcyra! Give me, I demanded of a scholar some time ago, give me a definition of poetry. *"Très-volontiers"*; and he proceeded to his library, brought me a Dr. Johnson, and overwhelmed me with a definition. Shade of the immortal Shakespeare! I imagine to myself the scowl of your spiritual eye upon the profanity of the scurrilous Ursa Major. Think of poetry, dear B——, think of poetry, and then think of Dr. Samuel Johnson! Think of all that is airy and fairy-like, and then of all that is hideous and unwieldy; think of his huge bulk, the Elephant! and then — and then think of the Tempest — the Midsummer Night's Dream — Prospero — Oberon — and Titania!

* * * * *

A poem, in my opinion, is opposed to a work of science by having, for its *immediate* object, pleasure, not truth; to romance, by having for its object, an *indefinite* instead of a *definite* pleasure, being a poem only so far as this object is attained; romance presenting perceptible images with definite poetry with *indefinite* sensations, to which end music is an *essential*, since the comprehension of sweet sound is our most indefinite conception. Music, when combined with a pleasurable idea, is poetry; music, without the idea, is simply music; the idea, without the music, is prose, from its very definitiveness.

What was meant by the invective against him who had no music in his soul?

* * * * *

To sum up this long rigmarole, I have, dear B——, what you, no doubt, perceive, for the metaphysical poets *as* poets, the most sovereign contempt. That they have followers proves nothing —

> No Indian prince has to his palace
> More followers than a thief to the gallows.

The Culprit Fay, and Other Poems
Joseph Rodman Drake

Alnwick Castle, with Other Poems
Fitz-Greene Halleck

Before entering upon the detailed notice which we propose of the volumes before us, we wish to speak a few words in regard to the present state of American criticism.

It must be visible to all who meddle with literary matters, that of late years a thorough revolution has been effected in the censorship of our press. That this revolution is infinitely for the worse we believe. There was a time, it is true, when we cringed to foreign opinion — let us even say when we paid most servile deference to British critical dicta. That an American book could, by any possibility, be worthy perusal, was an idea by no means extensively prevalent in the land; and if we were in-

duced to read at all the productions of our native writers, it was only after repeated assurances from England that such productions were not altogether contemptible. But there was, at all events, a shadow of excuse, and a slight basis of reason for a subserviency so grotesque. Even now, perhaps, it would not be far wrong to assert that such basis of reason may still exist. Let us grant that in many of the abstract sciences — that even in Theology, in Medicine, in Law, in Oratory, in the Mechanical Arts, we have no competitors whatever, still nothing but the most egregious national vanity would assign us a place, in the matter of Polite Literature, upon a level with the elder and riper climes of Europe, the earliest steps of whose children are among the groves of magnificently endowed Academies, and whose innumerable men of leisure, and of consequent learning, drink daily from those august fountains of inspiration which burst around them everywhere from out the tombs of their immortal dead, and from out their hoary and trophied monuments of chivalry and song. In paying then, as a nation, a respectful and not undue deference to a supremacy rarely questioned but by prejudice or ignorance, we should, of course, be doing nothing more than acting in a rational manner. The *excess* of our subserviency was blamable — but, as we have before said, this very excess might have found a shadow of excuse in the strict justice, if properly regulated, of the principle from which it issued. Not so, however, with our present follies. We are becoming boisterous and arrogant in the pride of a too speedily assumed literary freedom. We throw off, with the most presumptuous and unmeaning hauteur, *all* deference whatever to foreign opinion — we forget, in the puerile inflation of vanity, that *the world* is the true theatre of the biblical histrio — we get up a hue and cry about the necessity of encouraging native writers of merit — we blindly fancy that we can accomplish this by indiscriminate puffing of good, bad, and indifferent, without taking the trouble to consider that what we choose to denominate encouragement is thus, by its general application, rendered precisely the reverse. In a word, so far from being ashamed of the many disgraceful literary failures to which our own inordinate vanities and misapplied patriotism have lately given birth, and so far from deeply lamenting that these daily puerilities are of home manufacture, we adhere pertinaciously to our original blindly conceived idea, and thus often find ourselves involved in the gross paradox of liking a stupid book the better, because, sure enough, its stupidity is American.*

Deeply lamenting this unjustifiable state of public feeling, it has been our constant endeavor, since assuming the Editorial duties of this Jour-

* This charge of indiscriminate puffing will, of course, only apply to the *general* character of our criticism — there are some noble exceptions. We wish also especially to discriminate between those *notices* of new works which are intended merely to call public attention to them, and deliberate criticism on the works themselves.

nal, to stem, with what little abilities we possess, a current so disastrously undermining the health and prosperity of our literature.

We have seen our efforts applauded by men whose applauses we value. From all quarters we have received abundant private as well as public testimonials in favor of our *Critical Notices*, and, until very lately, have heard from no respectable source one word impugning their integrity or candor. In looking over, however, a number of the New York Commercial Advertiser, we meet with the following paragraph.

" 'The last number of the Southern Literary Messenger is very readable and respectable. The contributions to the Messenger are much better than the original matter. The critical department of this work — much as it would seem to boast itself of impartiality and discernment, — is in our opinion decidedly *quacky*. There is in it a great assumption of acumen, which is completely unsustained. Many a work has been slashingly condemned therein, of which the critic himself could not write a page, were he to die for it. This affectation of eccentric sternness in criticism, without the power to back one's suit withal, so far from deserving praise, as some suppose, merits the strongest reprehension. *Philadelphia Gazette.*'

"We are entirely of opinion with the Philadelphia Gazette in relation to the Southern Literary Messenger, and take this occasion to express our total dissent from the numerous and lavish encomiums we have seen bestowed upon its critical notices. Some few of them have been judicious, fair and candid; bestowing praise and censure with judgment and impartiality; but by far the greater number of those we have read, have been flippant, unjust, untenable and uncritical. The duty of the critic is to act as judge, not as enemy, of the writer whom he reviews; a distinction of which the Zoilus of the Messenger seems not to be aware. It is possible to review a book sincerely, without bestowing opprobrious epithets upon the writer; to condemn with courtesy, if not with kindness. The critic of the Messenger has been eulogized for his scorching and scarifying abilities, and he thinks it incumbent upon him to keep up his reputation in that line, by sneers, sarcasm and downright abuse; by straining his vision with microscopic intensity in search of faults, and shutting his eyes, with all his might to beauties. Moreover, we have detected him, more than once, in blunders quite as gross as those on which it was his pleasure to descant." *

In the paragraph from the Philadelphia Gazette, (which is edited by

* In addition to these things we observe, in the New York Mirror, what follows: "Those who have read the Notices of American books in a certain Southern Monthly, which is striving to gain notoriety by the loudness of its abuse, may find amusement in the sketch on another page, entitled "The Successful Novel." The Southern Literary Messenger knows *by experience* what it is to write a successless novel." We have, in this case, only to deny, flatly, the assertion of the Mirror. The Editor of the Messenger never in his life wrote or published, or attempted to publish, a novel either successful or successless.

Mr. Willis Gaylord Clark, one of the editors of the Knickerbocker) we find nothing at which we have any desire to take exception. Mr. C. has a right to think us *quacky* if he pleases, and we do not remember having assumed for a moment that we could write a single line of the works we have reviewed. But there is something equivocal, to say the least, in the remarks of Col. Stone. He acknowledges that "*some* of our notices have been judicious, fair, and candid bestowing praise and censure with judgment and impartiality." This being the case, how can he reconcile his *total* dissent from the public verdict in our favor, with the dictates of justice? We are accused too of bestowing "opprobrious epithets" upon writers whom we review and in the paragraphs so accusing us are called nothing less than "flippant, unjust, and uncritical."

But there is another point of which we disapprove. While in our reviews we have at all times been particularly careful *not* to deal in generalities, and have never, if we remember aright, advanced in any single instance an unsupported assertion, our accuser has forgotten to give us any better evidence of our flippancy, injustice, personality, and gross blundering, than the solitary *dictum* of Col. Stone. We call upon the Colonel for assistance in this dilemma. We wish to be shown our blunders that we may correct them — to be made aware of our flippancy that we may avoid it hereafter — and above all to have our personalities pointed out that we may proceed forthwith with a repentant spirit, to make the *amende honorable*. In default of this aid from the Editor of the Commercial we shall take it for granted that we are neither blunderers, flippant, personal, nor unjust.

Who will deny that in regard to individual poems no definitive opinions can exist, so long as to Poetry in the abstract we attach no definitive idea? Yet it is a common thing to hear our critics, day after day, pronounce, with a positive air, laudatory or condemnatory sentences, *en masse*, upon material works of whose merits or demerits they have, in the first place, virtually confessed an utter ignorance, in confessing ignorance of all determinate principles by which to regulate a decision. Poetry has never been defined to the satisfaction of all parties. Perhaps, in the present condition of language it never will be. Words cannot hem it in. Its intangible and purely spiritual nature refuses to be bound down within the widest horizon of mere sounds. But it is not, therefore, misunderstood — at least, not by all men is it misunderstood. Very far from it. If, indeed, there be any one circle of thought distinctly and palpably marked out from amid the jarring and tumultuous chaos of human intelligence, it is that evergreen and radiant Paradise which the true poet knows, and knows alone, as the limited realm of his authority — as the circumscribed Eden of his dreams. But a definition is a thing of words — a conception of ideas. And thus while we readily believe that Poesy, the term, it will be troublesome, if not impossible to define — still, with its image vividly existing in the world, we apprehend no difficulty in so

describing Poesy, the Sentiment, as to imbue even the most obtuse intellect with a comprehension of it sufficiently distinct for all the purposes of practical analysis.

To look upwards from any existence, material or immaterial, to its *design*, is, perhaps, the most direct, and the most unerring method of attaining a just notion of the nature of the existence itself. Nor is the principle at fault when we turn our eyes from Nature even to Nature's God. We find certain faculties, implanted within us, and arrive at a more plausible conception of the character and attributes of those faculties, by considering, with what finite judgment we possess, the *intention* of the Deity in so implanting them within us, than by any actual investigation of their powers, or any speculative deductions from their visible and material effects. Thus, for example, we discover in all men a disposition to look with reverence upon superiority, whether real or supposititious. In some, this disposition is to be recognized with difficulty, and, in very peculiar cases, we are occasionally even led to doubt its existence altogether, until circumstances beyond the common routine bring it accidentally into development. In others again it forms a prominent and distinctive feature of character, and is rendered palpably evident in its excesses. But in all human beings it is, in a greater or less degree, finally perceptible. It has been, therefore, justly considered a primitive sentiment. Phrenologists call it Veneration. It is, indeed, the instinct given to man by God as security for his own worship. And although, preserving its nature, it becomes perverted from its principal purpose, and although swerving from that purpose, it serves to modify the relations of human society — the relations of father and child, of master and slave, of the ruler and the ruled — its primitive essence is nevertheless the same, and by a reference to primal causes, may at any moment be determined.

Very nearly akin to this feeling, and liable to the same analysis, is the Faculty of Ideality — which is the sentiment of Poesy. This sentiment is the sense of the beautiful, of the sublime, and of the mystical.* Thence spring immediately admiration of the fair flowers, the fairer forests, the bright valleys and rivers and mountains of the Earth — and love of the gleaming stars and other burning glories of Heaven — and, mingled up inextricably with this love and this admiration of Heaven and of Earth, the unconquerable desire — *to know*. Poesy is the sentiment of Intellectual Happiness here, and the Hope of a higher Intellectual Happiness hereafter.†

* We separate the sublime and the mystical — for, despite of high authorities, we are firmly convinced that the latter *may* exist, in the most vivid degree, without giving rise to the sense of the former.

† The consciousness of this truth was possessed by no mortal more fully than by Shelley, although he has only once especially alluded to it. In his *Hymn to Intellectual Beauty* we find these lines.

While yet a boy I sought for ghosts, and sped
 Through many a listening chamber, cave and ruin,

Imagination is its soul.‡ With the *passions* of mankind — although it may modify them greatly — although it may exalt, or inflame, or purify, or control them — it would require little ingenuity to prove that it has no inevitable, and indeed no necessary co-existence. We have hitherto spoken of poetry in the abstract: we come now to speak of it in its everyday acceptation — that is to say, of the practical result arising from the sentiment we have considered.

And now it appears evident, that since Poetry, in this new sense, *is* the practical result, expressed in language, of this Poetic Sentiment in certain individuals, the only proper method of testing the merits of a poem is by measuring its capabilities of exciting the Poetic Sentiments in others. And to this end we have many aids — in observation, in experience, in ethical analysis, and in the dictates of common sense. Hence the *Poeta nascitur*, which is indisputably true if we consider the Poetic Sentiment, becomes the merest of absurdities when we regard it in reference to the practical result. We do not hesitate to say that a man highly endowed with the powers of Causality — that is to say, a man of metaphysical acumen — will, even with a very deficient share of Ideality, compose a finer poem (if we test it, as we should, by its measure of exciting the Poetic Sentiment) than one who, without such metaphysical acumen, shall be gifted, in the most extraordinary degree, with the faculty of Ideality. For a poem is not the Poetic faculty, but the *means* of exciting it in mankind. Now these means the metaphysician may discover by analysis of their effects in other cases than his own, without even conceiving the nature of these effects — thus arriving at a result which the unaided Ideality of his competitor would be utterly unable, except

And starlight wood, with fearful steps pursuing
Hopes of high talk with the departed dead:
I called on poisonous names with which our youth is fed:
I was not heard: I saw them not.
When musing deeply on the lot
Of life at that sweet time when birds are wooing
All vital things that wake to bring
News of buds and blossoming,
Sudden thy shadow fell on me —
I shrieked and clasped my hands in ecstasy!

I vow'd that I would dedicate my powers
To thee and thine: have I not kept the vow?
With beating heart and streaming eyes, even now
I call the phantoms of a thousand hours

Each from his voiceless grave: they have in vision'd bowers
Of studious zeal or love's delight
Outwatch'd with me the envious night:
They know that never joy illum'd my brow,
Unlink'd with hope that thou wouldst free,
This world from its dark slavery,
That thou, O awful *Loveliness*,
Wouldst give whate'er these words cannot express.

‡ Imagination is, possibly in man, a lesser degree of the creative power in God. What the Deity imagines, *is*, but *was not* before. What man imagines, *is*, but *was* also. The mind of man cannot imagine what *is not*. This latter point may be demonstrated. — See *Les Premiers Traits de L'Erudition Universelle, par* M. *Le Baron de Biefield,* 1767.

by accident, to attain. It is more than possible that the man who, of all writers, living or dead, has been most successful in writing the purest of all poems — that is to say, poems which excite more purely, most exclusively, and most powerfully the imaginative faculties in men — owed his extraordinary and almost magical pre-eminence rather to metaphysical than poetical powers. We allude to the author of Christabel, of the Rime of the Auncient Mariner, and of Love — to Coleridge — whose head, if we mistake not its character, gave no great phrenological tokens of Ideality, while the organs of Causality and Comparison were most singularly developed.

Perhaps at this particular moment there are no American poems held in so high estimation by our countrymen, as the poems of Drake, and of Halleck. The exertions of Mr. George Dearborn have no doubt a far greater share in creating this feeling than the lovers of literature for its own sake and spiritual uses would be willing to admit. We have indeed seldom seen more beautiful volumes than the volumes now before us. But an adventitious interest of a loftier nature — the interest of the living in the memory of the beloved dead — attaches itself to the few literary remains of Drake. The poems which are now given to us with his name are nineteen in number; and whether all, or whether even the best of his writings, it is our present purpose to speak of these alone, since upon this edition his poetical reputation to all time will most probably depend.

It is only lately that we have read *The Culprit Fay*. This is a poem of six hundred and forty irregular lines, generally iambic, and divided into thirty-six stanzas, of unequal length. The scene of the narrative, as we ascertain from the single line,

The moon looks down on old *Cronest*,

is principally in the vicinity of West Point on the Hudson. The plot is as follows. An Ouphe, one of the race of Fairies, has "broken his vestal vow,"

He has loved an earthly maid
And left for her his woodland shade;
He has lain upon her lip of dew,
And sunned him in her eye of blue,
Fann'd her cheek with his wing of air,
Play'd with the ringlets of her hair,
And, nestling on her snowy breast,
Forgot the lily-king's behest —

in short, he has broken Fairy-law in becoming enamored of a mortal. The result of this misdemeanor we could not express so well as the poet, and will therefore make use of the language put into the mouth of the Fairy-King who reprimands the criminal.

Fairy! Fairy! list and mark,
 Thou hast broke thine elfin chain,
Thy flame-wood lamp is quench'd and dark
 And thy wings are dyed with a deadly stain.

The Ouphe being in this predicament, it has become necessary that
his case and crime should be investigated by a jury of his fellows, and to
this end the "shadowy tribes of air" are summoned by the "sentry elve"
who has been awakened by the "wood-tick" — are summoned we say to
the "elfin-court" at midnight to hear the doom of the *Culprit Fay.*

"Had a stain been found on the earthly fair," whose blandishments
so bewildered the little Ouphe, his punishment would have been severe
indeed. In such case he would have been (as we learn from the Fairy
judge's exposition of the criminal code,)

Tied to the hornet's shardy wings;
Tossed on the pricks of nettles' stings;
Or seven long ages doomed to dwell
With the lazy worm in the walnut shell;
Or every night to writhe and bleed
Beneath the tread of the centipede;
Or bound in a cobweb dungeon dim
His jailer a spider huge and grim,
Amid the carrion bodies to lie
Of the worm and the bug and the murdered fly —

Fortunately, however, for the Culprit, his mistress is proved to be of
"sinless mind" and under such redeeming circumstances the sentence is,
mildly, as follows —

Thou shalt seek the beach of sand
Where the water bounds the elfin land,
Thou shalt watch the oozy brine
Till the sturgeon leaps in the bright moonshine,
Then dart the glistening arch below,
And catch a drop from his silver bow.

If the spray-bead be won
 The stain of thy wing is washed away,
But another errand must be done
 Ere thy crime be lost for aye;
Thy flame-wood lamp is quenched and dark,
 Thou must re-illume its spark.
Mount thy steed and spur him high
To the heaven's blue canopy;

And when thou seest a shooting star
Follow it fast and follow it far —
The last faint spark of its burning train
Shall light the elfin lamp again.

Upon this sin, and upon this sentence, depends the web of the nar·
rative, which is now occupied with the elfin difficulties overcome by the
Ouphe in washing away the stain of his wing, and re-illuming his flame-
wood lamp. His soiled pinion having lost its power, he is under the
necessity of wending his way on foot from the Elfin court upon Cronest
to the river beach at its base. His path is encumbered at every step with
"bog and briar," with "brook and mire," with "beds of tangled fern,"
with "groves of night-shade," and with the minor evils of ant and snake.
Happily, however, a spotted toad coming in sight, our adventurer jumps
upon her back, and "bridling her mouth with a silk-weed twist" bounds
merrily along

Till the mountain's magic verge is past
And the beach of sand is reached at last.

Alighting now from his "courser-toad" the Ouphe folds his wings
around his bosom, springs on a rock, breathes a prayer, throws his arms
above his head,

Then tosses a tiny curve in air
And plunges in the waters blue.

Here, however, a host of difficulties await him by far too multitudi-
nous to enumerate. We will content ourselves with simply stating the
names of his most respectable assailants. These are the "spirits of the
waves" dressed in "snail-plate armor" and aided by the "mailed shrimp,"
the "prickly prong," the "blood-red leech," the "stony star-fish," the
"jellied quarl," the "soldier-crab," and the "lancing squab." But the hopes
of our hero are high, and his limbs are strong, so

He spreads his arms like the swallow's wing,
And throws his feet with a frog-like fling.

All, however, is to no purpose.

On his thigh the leech has fixed his hold,
The quarl's long arms are round him roll'd,
The prickly prong has pierced his skin,
And the squab has thrown his javelin,
The gritty star has rubb'd him raw,
And the crab has struck with his giant claw;
He bawls with rage, and he shrieks with pain
He strikes around but his blows are vain —

So then,

> He turns him round and flies amain
> With hurry and dash to the beach again.

Arrived safely on land our Fairy friend now gathers the dew from the "sorrel-leaf and henbane-bud" and bathing therewith his wounds, finally ties them up with cobweb. Thus recruited, he

> — treads the fatal shore
> As fresh and vigorous as before.

At length espying a "purple-muscle shell" upon the beach, he determines to use it as a boat, and thus evade the animosity of the water spirits whose powers extend not above the wave. Making a "sculler's notch" in the stern, and providing himself with an oar of the bootle-blade, the Ouphe a second time ventures upon the deep. His perils are now diminished, but still great. The imps of the river heave the billows up before the prow of the boat, dash the surges against her side, and strike against her keel. The quarl uprears "his island-back" in her path, and the scallop, floating in the rear of the vessel, spatters it all over with water. Our adventurer, however, bails it out with the colen bell (which he has luckily provided for the purpose of catching the drop from the silver bow of the sturgeon,) and keeping his little bark warily trimmed, holds on his course undiscomfited.

The object of his first adventure is at length discovered in a "brown-backed sturgeon," who

> Like the heaven-shot javelin
> Springs above the waters blue,
> And, instant as the star-fall light
> Plunges him in the deep again,
> But leaves an arch of silver bright,
> The rainbow of the moony main.

From this rainbow our Ouphe succeeds in catching, by means of his colen bell cup, a "droplet of the sparkling dew." One half of his task is accordingly done —

> His wings are pure, for the gem is won.

On his return to land, the ripples divide before him, while the water-spirits, so rancorous before, are obsequiously attentive to his comfort. Having tarried a moment on the beach to breathe a prayer, he "spreads his wings of gilded blue" and takes his way to the elfin court — there resting until the cricket, at two in the morning, rouses him up for the second portion of his penance.

His equipments are now an "acorn-helmet," a "thistle-down plume," a corslet of the "wild-bee's" skin, a cloak of the "wings of butterflies,"

a shield of the "shell of the lady-bug," for lance "the sting of a wasp," for sword a "blade of grass," for horse "a fire-fly," and for spurs a couple of "cockle seed." Thus accoutred,

> Away like a glance of thought he flies
> To skim the heavens and follow far
> The fiery trail of the rocket-star.

In the Heavens he has new dangers to encounter. The "shapes of air" have begun their work — a "drizzly mist" is cast around him — "storm, darkness, sleet and shade" assail him — "shadowy hands" twitch at his bridle-rein — "flame-shot tongues" play around him — "fiendish eyes" glare upon him — and

> Yells of rage and shrieks of fear
> Come screaming on his startled ear.

Still our adventurer is nothing daunted.

> He thrusts before, and he strikes behind,
> Till he pierces the cloudy bodies through
> And gashes the shadowy limbs of mind.

and the Elfin makes no stop, until he reaches the "bank of the milky way." He there checks his courser, and watches "for the glimpse of the planet shoot." While thus engaged, however, an unexpected adventure befalls him. He is approached by a company of the "sylphs of Heaven attired in sunset's crimson pall." They dance around him, and "skip before him on the plain." One receiving his "wasp-sting lance," and another taking his bridle-rein,

> With warblings wild they lead him on,
> To where, through clouds of amber seen,
> Studded with stars resplendent shone
> The palace of the sylphid queen.

A glowing description of the queen's beauty follows: and as the form of an earthly Fay had never been seen before in the bowers of light, she is represented as falling desperately in love at first sight with our adventurous Ouphe. He returns the compliment in some measure, of course; but, although "his heart bent fitfully," the "earthly form imprinted there" was a security against a too vivid impression. He declines, consequently, the invitation of the queen to remain with her and amuse himself by "lying within the fleecy drift," "hanging upon the rainbow's rim," having his "brow adorned with all the jewels of the sky," "sitting within the Pleiad ring," "resting upon Orion's belt," "riding upon the

lightning's gleam," "dancing upon the orbed moon," and "swimming within the milky way."

> Lady, he cries, I have sworn to-night
> On the word of a fairy knight
> To do my sentence task aright.

The queen, therefore, contents herself with bidding the Fay an affectionate farewell — having first directed him carefully to that particular portion of the sky where a star is about to fall. He reaches this point in safety, and in despite of the "fiends of the cloud," who "bellow very loud," succeeds finally in catching a "glimmering spark" with which he returns triumphantly to Fairy-land. The poem closes with an Io Paean chaunted by the elves in honor of these glorious adventures.

It is more than probable that from ten readers of the *Culprit Fay*, nine would immediately pronounce it a poem betokening the most extraordinary powers of imagination, and of these nine, perhaps five or six, poets themselves, and fully impressed with the truth of what we have already assumed, that Ideality is indeed the soul of the Poetic Sentiment, would feel embarrassed between a half-consciousness that they *ought* to admire the production, and a wonder that they *do not*. This embarrassment would then arise from an indistinct conception of the results in which Ideality is rendered manifest. Of these results some few are seen in the *Culprit Fay*, but the greater part of it is utterly destitute of any evidence of imagination whatever. The general character of the poem will, we think, be sufficiently understood by any one who may have taken the trouble to read our foregoing compendium of the narrative. It will be there seen that what is so frequently termed the imaginative power of this story, lies especially — we should have rather said is thought to lie — in the passages we have quoted, or in others of a precisely similar nature. These passages embody, principally, mere specifications of qualities, of habiliments, of punishments, of occupations, of circumstances, &c., which the poet has believed in unison with the size, firstly, and secondly with the nature of his Fairies. To all which may be added specifications of other animal existences (such as the toad, the beetle, the lance-fly, the fire-fly and the like) supposed also to be in accordance. An example will best illustrate our meaning upon this point — we take it from page 20.

> He put his acorn helmet on;
> It was plumed of the silk of the thistle down:
> The corslet plate that guarded his breast
> Was once the wild bee's golden vest;
> His cloak of a thousand mingled dyes,
> Was formed of the wings of butterflies;
> His shield was the shell of a lady-bug queen,

> Studs of gold on a ground of green; *
> And the quivering lance which he brandished bright
> Was the sting of a wasp he had slain in fight.

We shall now be understood. Were any of the admirers of the *Culprit Fay* asked their opinion of these lines, they would most probably speak in high terms of the *imagination* they display. Yet let the most stolid and the most confessedly unpoetical of these admirers only try the experiment, and he will find, possibly to his extreme surprise, that he himself will have no difficulty whatever in substituting for the equipments of the Fairy, as assigned by the poet, other equipments equally comfortable, no doubt, and equally in unison with the preconceived size, character, and other qualities of the equipped. Why we could accoutre him as well ourselves — let us see.

> His blue-bell helmet, we have heard
> Was plumed with the down of the humming-bird,
> The corslet on his bosom bold
> Was once the locust's coat of gold,
> His cloak, of a thousand mingled hues,
> Was the velvet violet, wet with dews,
> His target was the crescent shell
> Of the small sea Sidrophel,
> And a glittering beam from a maiden's eye
> Was the lance which he proudly wav'd on high.

The truth is, that the only requisite for writing verses of this nature, *ad libitum*, is a tolerable acquaintance with the qualities of the objects to be detailed, and a very moderate endowment of the faculty of Comparison — which is the chief constituent of *Fancy* or the powers of combination. A thousand such lines may be composed without exercising in the least degree the Poetic Sentiment, which is Ideality, Imagination, or the creative ability. And, as we have before said, the greater portion of the *Culprit Fay* is occupied with these, or similiar things, and upon such, depends very nearly, if not altogether, its reputation. We select another example from page 25.

> But oh! how fair the shape that lay
> Beneath a rainbow bending bright,
> She seem'd to the entranced Fay
> The loveliest of the forms of light;
> Her mantle was the purple rolled
> At twilight in the west afar;

* Chestnut color, or more slack,
Gold upon a ground of black.
 Ben Jonson.

'Twas tied with threads of dawning gold,
 And button'd with a sparkling star.
Her face was like the lily roon
 That veils the vestal planet's hue;
Her eyes, two beamlets from the moon
 Set floating in the welkin blue.
Her hair is like the sunny beam,
And the diamond gems which round it gleam
Are the pure drops of dewy even,
That ne'er have left their native heaven.

Here again the faculty of Comparison is alone exercised, and no mind possessing the faculty in any ordinary degree would find a difficulty in substituting for the materials employed by the poet other materials equally as good. But viewed as mere efforts of the Fancy and without reference to Ideality, the lines just quoted are much worse than those which were taken from page 20. A congruity was observable in the accoutrements of the Ouphe, and we had no trouble in forming a distinct conception of his appearance when so accoutred. But the most vivid powers of Comparison can attach no definitive idea to even "the loveliest form of light," when habited in a mantle of "rolled purple tied with threads of dawn and buttoned with a star," and sitting at the same time under a rainbow with "beamlet" eyes and a visage of "lily roon."

But if these things evince no Ideality in their author, do they not excite it in others? — if so, we must conclude, that without being himself imbued with the Poetic Sentiment, he has still succeeded in writing a fine poem — a supposition as we have before endeavored to show, not altogether paradoxical. Most assuredly we think not. In the case of a great majority of readers the only sentiment aroused by compositions of this order is a species of vague wonder at the writer's *ingenuity*, and it is this indeterminate sense of wonder which passes but too frequently current for the proper influence of the Poetic power. For our own part we plead guilty to a predominant sense of the ludicrous while occupied in the perusal of the poem before us — a sense whose promptings we sincerely and honestly endeavored to quell, perhaps not altogether successfully, while penning our compend of the narrative. That a feeling of this nature is utterly at war with the Poetic Sentiment, will not be disputed by those who comprehend the character of the sentiment itself. This character is finely shadowed out in that popular although vague idea so prevalent throughout all time, that a species of melancholy is inseparably connected with the higher manifestations of the beautiful. But with the numerous and seriously-adduced incongruities of the Culprit Fay, we find it generally impossible to connect other ideas than those of the ridiculous. We are bidden, in the first place, and in a tone of sentiment and language adapted to the loftiest breathings of the Muse,

to imagine a race of Fairies in the vicinity of West Point. We are told, with a grave air, of their camp, of their king, and especially of their sentry, who is a wood-tick. We are informed that an Ouphe of about an inch in height has committed a deadly sin in falling in love with a mortal maiden, who may, very possibly, be six feet in her stockings. The consequence to the Ouphe is — what? Why, that he has "dyed his wings," "broken his elfin chain," and "quenched his flame-wood lamp." And he is therefore sentenced to what? To catch a spark from the tail of a falling star, and a drop of water from the belly of a sturgeon. What are his equipments for the first adventure? An acorn-helmet, a thistle-down plume, a butterfly cloak, a lady-bug shield, cockle-seed spurs, and a fire-fly horse. How does he ride to the second? On the back of a bull-frog. What are his opponents in the one? "Drizzly-mists," "sulphur and smoke," "shadowy hands and flame-shot tongues." What in the other? "Mailed shrimps," "prickly prongs," "blood-red leeches," "jellied quarls," "stony star fishes," "lancing squabs" and "soldier crabs." Is that all? No — Although only an inch high he is in imminent danger of seduction from a "sylphid queen," dressed in a mantle of "rolled purple," "tied with threads of dawning gold," "buttoned with a sparkling star," and sitting under a rainbow with "beamlet eyes" and a countenance of "lily roon." In our account of all this matter we have had reference to the book — and to the book alone. It will be difficult to prove us guilty in any degree of distortion or exaggeration. Yet such are the puerilities we daily find ourselves called upon to admire, as among the loftiest efforts of the human mind, and which not to assign a rank with the proud trophies of the matured and vigorous genius of England, is to prove ourselves at once a fool, a maligner, and no patriot.*

As an instance of what may be termed the sublimely ridiculous we quote the following lines from page 17.

> With sweeping tail and quivering fin,
> Through the wave the sturgeon flew,
> And like the heaven-shot javelin,
> He sprung above the waters blue.
>
> Instant as the star-fall light,
> He plunged into the deep again,
> But left an arch of silver bright
> The rainbow of the moony main.

* A review of Drake's poems, emanating from one of our proudest Universities, does not scruple to make use of the following language in relation to the *Culprit Fay*. "It is, to say the least, an elegant production, the purest specimen of Ideality* we have ever met with, sustaining in each incident a most bewitching interest. Its very title is enough," &c. &c. We quote these expressions as a fair specimen of the general unphilosophical and adulatory tenor of our criticism.

> *It was a strange and lovely sight*
> *To see the puny goblin there;*
> *He seemed an angel form of light*
> *With azure wing and sunny hair,*
> *Throned on a cloud of purple fair*
> *Circled with blue and edged with white*
> *And sitting at the fall of even*
> *Beneath the bow of summer heaven.*

The verses here italicized, if considered without their context, have a certain air of dignity, elegance, and chastity of thought. If however we apply the context, we are immediately overwhelmed with the grotesque. It is impossible to read without laughing, such expressions as "It was a strange and lovely sight" — "He seemed an angel form of light" — "And sitting at the fall of even, beneath the bow of summer heaven" to a Fairy — a goblin — an Ouphe — half an inch high, dressed in an acorn helmet and butterfly-cloak, and sitting on the water in a muscle-shell, with a "brown-backed sturgeon" turning somersets over his head.

In a world where evil is a mere consequence of good, and good a mere consequence of evil — in short where all of which we have any conception is good or bad only by comparison — we have never yet been fully able to appreciate the validity of that decision which would debar the critic from enforcing upon his readers the merits or demerits of a work by placing it in juxtaposition with another. It seems to us that an adage based in the purest ignorance has had more to do with this popular feeling than any just reason founded upon common sense. Thinking thus, we shall have no scruple in illustrating our opinion in regard to what *is not* Ideality or the Poetic Power, by an example of what *is*.*

We have already given the description of the Sylphid Queen in the *Culprit Fay*. In the *Queen Mab* of Shelley a Fairy is thus introduced —

> Those who had looked upon the sight
> Passing all human glory,
> Saw not the yellow moon,
> Saw not the mortal scene,
> Heard not the night wind's rush,
> Heard not an earthly sound,
> Saw but the fairy pageant,
> Heard but the heavenly strains
> That filled the lonely dwelling —

* As examples of entire poems of the purest ideality, we would cite the *Prometheus Vinctus* of Æchylus, the *Inferno* of Dante, Cervantes' *Destruction of Numantia*, the *Comus* of Milton, Pope's *Rape of the Lock*, Burns' *Tam O' Shanter*, the *Auncient Mariner*, the *Christabel*, and the *Kubla Khan* of Coleridge; and most especially the *Sensitive Plant* of Shelley, and the *Nightingale* of Keats. We have seen American poems evincing the faculty in the highest degree.

and thus described —

> The Fairy's frame was slight; yon fibrous cloud
> That catches but the faintest tinge of even,
> And which the straining eye can hardly seize
> When melting into eastern twilight's shadow,
> Were scarce so thin, so slight; but the fair star
> That gems the glittering coronet of morn,
> *Sheds not a light so mild, so powerful,*
> *As that which, bursting from the Fairy's form,*
> *Spread a purpureal halo round the scene,*
> *Yet with an undulating motion,*
> *Swayed to her outline gracefully.*

In these exquisite lines the Faculty of mere Comparison is but little exercised — that of Ideality in a wonderful degree. It is probable that in a similar case the poet we are now reviewing would have formed the face of the Fairy of the "fibrous cloud," her arms of the "pale tinge of even," her eyes of the "fair stars," and her body of the "twilight shadow." Having so done, his admirers would have congratulated him upon his *imagination,* not taking the trouble to think that they themselves could at any moment *imagine* a Fairy of materials equally as good, and conveying an equally distinct idea. Their mistake would be precisely analogous to that of many a schoolboy who admires the imagination displayed in *Jack the Giant-Killer,* and is finally rejoiced at discovering his own imagination to surpass that of the author, since the monsters destroyed by Jack are only about forty feet in height, and he himself has no trouble in imagining some of one hundred and forty. It will be seen that the Fairy of Shelley is not a mere compound of incongruous natural objects, inartificially put together, and unaccompanied by any *moral* sentiment — but a being, in the illustration of whose nature some physical elements are used collaterally as adjuncts, while the main conception springs immediately *or thus apparently springs,* from the brain of the poet, enveloped in the moral sentiments of grace, of color, of motion — of the beautiful, of the mystical, of the august — in short of *the ideal.**

It is by no means our intention to deny that in the *Culprit Fay* are passages of a different order from those to which we have objected — passages evincing a degree of imagination not to be discovered in the plot, conception, or general execution of the poem. The opening stanza will afford us a tolerable example.

* Among things, which not only in our opinion, but in the opinion of far wiser and better men, are to be ranked with the mere prettinesses of the Muse, are the positive similes so abundant in the writings of antiquity, and so much insisted upon by the critics of the reign of Queen Anne.

'Tis the middle watch of a summer's night —
The earth is dark but the heavens are bright
Naught is seen in the vault on high
But the moon, and the stars, and the cloudless sky,
And the flood which rolls its milky hue
A river of light on the welkin blue.
The moon looks down on old Cronest,
She mellows the shades of his shaggy breast,
And seems his huge gray form to throw
In a silver cone on the wave below;
His sides are broken by spots of shade,
By the walnut bow and the cedar made,
And through their clustering branches dark
Glimmers and dies the fire-fly's spark —
Like starry twinkles that momently break
Through the rifts of the gathering tempest rack.

There is Ideality in these lines — but except in the case of the words
italicized — it is Ideality *not of a high order*. We have, it is true, a col-
lection of natural objects, each individually of great beauty, and, if actu-
ally seen as in nature, capable of exciting in any mind, through the means
of the Poetic Sentiment more or less inherent in all, a certain sense of
the beautiful. But to view such natural objects as they exist, and to be-
hold them through the medium of words, are different things. Let us
pursue the idea that such a collection as we have here will produce,
of necessity, the Poetic Sentiment, and we may as well make up our
minds to believe that a catalogue of such expressions as moon, sky, trees,
rivers, mountains, &c., shall be capable of exciting it, — it is merely an
extension of the principle. But in the line "the earth is dark, *but* the
heavens are bright" besides the simple mention of the "dark earth"
"and the bright heaven," we have, directly, the moral sentiment
of the brightness of the sky compensating for the darkness of the
earth — and thus, indirectly, of the happiness of a future state com-
pensating for the miseries of the present. All this is effected by the
simple introduction of the word *but* between the "dark earth" and
the "bright heaven" — this introduction, however, was prompted by
the Poetic Sentiment, and by the Poetic Sentiment alone. The case
is analogous in the expression " glimmers and dies," where the imagi-
nation is exalted by the moral sentiment of beauty heightened in
dissolution.

In one or two shorter passages of the *Culprit Fay* the poet will recog-
nize the purely ideal, and be able at a glance to distinguish it from that
baser alloy upon which we have descanted. We give them without farther
comment.

The winds *are whist*, and the owl is still,
 The bat in the shelvy rock *is hid*
And naught is heard on the *lonely* hill
But the cricket's chirp and the answer *shrill*
 Of the gauze-winged katydid;
And the plaint of the *wailing* whippoorwill
 Who mourns *unseen*, and ceaseless sings
Ever a note of wail and wo —

Up to the vaulted firmament
His path the fire-fly courser bent,
And at every gallop on the wind
He flung a glittering spark behind.

He blessed the force of the charmed line
 And he banned the water-goblins' spite,
For he saw around in the *sweet moonshine,*
Their little wee faces above the brine,
Grinning and laughing with all their might
At the piteous hap of the Fairy wight.

The poem "To a Friend" consists of fourteen Spenserian stanzas. They are fine spirited verses, and probably were not supposed by their author to be more. Stanza the fourth, although beginning nobly, concludes with that very common exemplification of the bathos, the illustrating natural objects of beauty or grandeur by references to the tinsel of artificiality.

Oh! for a seat on Appalachia's brow,
That I might scan the glorious prospects round,
Wild waving woods, and rolling floods below,
Smooth level glades and fields with grain embrowned,
High heaving hills, with tufted forests crowned,
Rearing their tall tops to the heaven's blue dome,
And emerald isles, *like banners green un-wound,*
Floating along the lake, while round them roam
Bright helms of billowy blue, and plumes of dancing foam.

In the *Extracts from Leon* are passages not often surpassed in vigor of passionate thought and expression — and which induce us to believe not only that their author would have succeeded better in prose romance than in poetry, but that his attention would have naturally fallen into the former direction, had the Destroyer only spared him a little longer.

This poem contains also lines of far greater poetic power than any to be found in the *Culprit Fay.* For example —

The stars have lit in heaven their lamps of gold,
The *viewless* dew falls lightly on the world;
The gentle air *that softly sweeps the leaves*
A strain of faint unearthly music weaves:
As when the harp of heaven *remotely* plays,
Or sygnets *wail* — or song of *sorrowing* fays
That *float amid the moonshine glimmerings pale,*
On wings of woven air in some enchanted vale.*

Niagara is objectionable in many respects, and in none more so than in its frequent inversions of language, and the artificial character of its versification. The invocation,

Roar, raging torrent! and thou, mighty river,
Pour thy white foam on the valley below!
Frown ye dark mountains, &c.

is ludicrous — and nothing more. In general, all such invocations have an air of the burlesque. In the present instance we may fancy the majestic Niagara replying, "Most assuredly I will roar, whether, worm! thou tellest me or not."

The American Flag commences with a collection of those bald conceits, which we have already shown to have no dependence whatever upon the Poetic Power — springing altogether from Comparison.

When Freedom from her mountain height
 Unfurled her standard to the air,
She tore the azure robe of night
 And set the stars of glory there.
She mingled with its gorgeous dyes
The milky baldric of the skies,
And striped its pure celestrial white
With streakings of the morning light;
Then from his mansion in the sun
She called her eagle bearer down
And gave into his mighty hand
 The symbol of her chosen land.

Let us reduce all this to plain English, and we have — what? Why, a flag, consisting of the "azure robe of night," "set with stars of glory," interspersed with "streaks of morning light," relieved with a few pieces of "milky way," and the whole carried by an "eagle bearer," that is to say, an eagle ensign, who bears aloft this "symbol of our chosen land" in his "mighty hand," by which we are to understand his claw. In the

* The expression "woven air," much insisted upon by the friends of Drake, seems to be accredited to him as original. It is to be found in many English writers — and can be traced back to Apuleius, who calls fine drapery *ventum textilem.*

second stanza, "the thunder-drum of Heaven" is bathetic and grotesque in the highest degree — a commingling of the most sublime music of Heaven with the most utterly contemptible and common-place of Earth. The two concluding verses are in a better spirit, and might almost be supposed to be from a different hand. The images contained in the lines

> When Death careering on the gale
> Sweeps darkly round the bellied sail,
> And frighted waves rush wildly back,
> Before the broadside's reeling rack,

are of the highest order of Ideality. The deficiencies of the whole poem may be best estimated by reading it in connection with "Scots wha hae," with the "Mariners of England," or with "Hohenlinden." It is indebted for its high and most undeserved reputation to our patriotism — not to our judgment.

The remaining poems in Mr. Dearborn's edition of Drake, are three Songs; Lines in an Album; Lines to a Lady; Lines on leaving New Rochelle; Hope; A Fragment; To ——; To Eva; To a Lady; To Sarah; and Bronx. These are all poems of little compass, and with the exception of Bronx and a portion of the Fragment, they have no character distinctive from the mass of our current poetical literature. Bronx, however, is in our opinion, not only the best of the writings of Drake, but altogether a lofty and beautiful poem, upon which his admirers would do better to found a hope of the writer's ultimate reputation than upon the *niaiseries* of the *Culprit Fay*. In the *Fragment* is to be found the finest individual passage in the volume before us, and we quote it as a proper finale to our review.

> Yes! thou art lovelier now than ever;
> How sweet 't would be *when all the air*
> *In moonlight swims*, along thy river
> To couch upon the grass, and hear
> Niagara's everlasting voice
> Far in the deep blue west away;
> That dreamy and poetic noise
> We mark not in the glare of day,
> Oh! how unlike its torrent-cry,
> When o'er the brink the tide is driven,
> As if the vast and sheeted sky
> In thunder fell from Heaven.

Halleck's poetical powers appear to us essentially inferior, upon the whole, to those of his friend Drake. He has written nothing at all comparable to *Bronx*. By the hackneyed phrase, *sportive elegance*, we might

possibly designate at once the general character of his writings and the very loftiest praise to which he is justly entitled.

Alnwick Castle is an irregular poem of one hundred and twenty-eight lines — was written, as we are informed, in October 1822 — and is descriptive of a seat of the Duke of Northumberland, in Northumberland-shire, England. The effect of the first stanza is materially impaired by a defect in its grammatical arrangement. The fine lines,

> Home of the Percy's high-born race,
> Home of their beautiful and brave,
> Alike their birth and burial place,
> Their cradle and their grave!

are of the nature of an invocation, and thus require a continuation of the address to the "Home, &c." We are consequently disappointed when the stanza proceeds with —

> Still sternly o'er the castle gate
> *Their* house's Lion stands in state
> As in *his* proud departed hours;
> And warriors frown in stone on high,
> And feudal banners "flout the sky"
> Above *his* princely towers.

The objects of allusion here vary, in an awkward manner, from the castle to the Lion, and from the Lion to the towers. By writing the verses thus the difficulty would be remedied.

> Still sternly o'er the castle gate
> *Thy* house's Lion stands in state,
> As in his proud departed hours;
> And warriors frown in stone on high,
> And feudal banners "flout the sky"
> Above *thy* princely towers.

The second stanza, without evincing in any measure the loftier powers of a poet, has that quiet air of grace, both in thought and expression, which seems to be the prevailing feature of the Muse of Halleck.

> A gentle hill its side inclines,
> Lovely in England's fadeless green,
> To meet the quiet stream which winds
> Through this romantic scene
> As silently and sweetly still,
> As when, at evening, on that hill,
> While summer's wind blew soft and low,
> Seated by gallant Hotspur's side
> His Katherine was a happy bride
> A thousand years ago.

There are one or two brief passages in the poem evincing a degree of rich imagination not elsewhere perceptible throughout the book. For example —

> Gaze on the Abbey's ruined pile:
>> Does not the succoring Ivy keeping,
> Her watch around it seem to smile
>> As o'er a lov'd one sleeping?

and,

>> One solitary turret gray
>>> Still tells in melancholy glory
>> The legend of the Cheviot day.

The commencement of the fourth stanza is of the highest order of Poetry, and partakes, in a happy manner, of that quaintness of expression so effective an adjunct to Ideality, when employed by the Shelleys, the Coleridges and the Tennysons, but so frequently debased, and rendered ridiculous, by the herd of brainless imitators.

> Wild roses by the abbey towers
>> Are gay in their young bud and bloom:
> *They were born of a race of funeral flowers,*
> That garlanded in long-gone hours,
>> A Templar's knightly tomb.

The tone employed in the concluding portions of Alnwick Castle, is, we sincerely think, reprehensible, and unworthy of Halleck. No true poet can unite in any manner the low burlesque with the ideal, and not be conscious of incongruity and of a profanation. Such verses as

> Men in the coal and cattle line
> From Tevoit's bard and hero land,
> From royal Berwick's beach of sand,
> From Wooller, Morpeth, Hexham, and
>> Newcastle upon Tyne.

may lay claim to oddity — but no more. These things are the defects and not the beauties of *Don Juan.* They are totally out of keeping with the graceful and delicate manner of the initial portions of *Alnwick Castle,* and serve no better purpose than to deprive the entire poem of all unity of effect. If a poet must be farcical, let him be just that, and nothing else. To be drolly sentimental is bad enough, as we have just seen in certain passages of the *Culprit Fay,* but to be sentimentally droll is a thing intolerable to men, and Gods, and columns.

Marco Bozzaris appears to have much lyrical without any high order of *ideal* beauty. *Force* is its prevailing character — a force, however, consisting more in a well ordered and sonorous arrangement of this metre,

and a judicious disposal of what may be called the circumstances of the poem, than in the true *material* of lyric vigor. We are introduced, first, to the Turk who dreams, at midnight, in his guarded tent,

> of the hour
> When Greece her knee in suppliance bent,
> Should tremble at his power —

He is represented as revelling in the visions of ambition.

> In dreams through camp and court he bore
> The trophies of a conqueror;
> In dreams his song of triumph heard;
> Then wore his monarch's signet ring;
> Then pressed that monarch's throne — a king;
> As wild his thoughts and gay of wing
> As Eden's garden bird.

In direct contrast to this we have Bozzaris watchful in the forest, and ranging his band of Suliotes on the ground, and amid the memories of Plataea. An hour elapses, and the Turk awakes from his visions of false glory — to die. But Bozzaris dies — to awake. He dies in the flush of victory to awake, in death, to an ultimate certainty of Freedom. Then follows an invocation to death. His terrors under ordinary circumstances are contrasted with the glories of the dissolution of Bozzaris, in which the approach of the Destroyer is

> welcome as the cry
> That told the Indian isles were nigh
> To the world-seeking Genoese,
> When the land-wind from woods of palm,
> And orange groves and fields of balm,
> Blew o'er the Haytian seas.

The poem closes with the poetical apotheosis of Marco Bozzaris as

> One of the few, the immortal names
> That are not born to die.

It will be seen that these arrangements of the subject are skillfully contrived — perhaps they are a little too evident, and we are enabled too readily by the perusal of one passage, to anticipate the succeeding. The rhythm is highly artificial. The stanzas are well adapted for vigorous expression — the fifth will afford a just specimen of the versification of the whole poem.

> Come to the bridal Chamber, Death!
> Come to the mother's when she feels
> For the first time her first born's breath;

Come when the blessed seals
That close the pestilence are broke,
And crowded cities wail its stroke;
Come in consumption's ghastly form,
The earthquake shock, the ocean storm;
Come when the heart beats high and warm,
 With banquet song, and dance, and wine;
And thou art terrible — the tear,
The groan, the knell, the pall, the bier;
And all we know, or dream, or fear
 Of agony, are thine.

Granting, however, to *Marco Bozzaris*, the minor excellences we have pointed out, we should be doing our conscience great wrong in calling it, upon the whole, any more than a very ordinary matter. It is surpassed, even as a lyric, by a multitude of foreign and by many American compositions of a similar character. To Ideality it has few pretensions, and the finest portion of the poem is probably to be found in the verses we have quoted elsewhere —

Thy grasp is welcome as the hand
Of brother in a foreign land;
Thy summons welcome as the cry
That told the Indian isles were nigh
 To the world-seeking Genoese,
When the land-wind from woods of palm
And orange groves, and fields of balm
Blew o'er the Haytian seas.

The verses entitled *Burns* consist of thirty-eight quatrains — the three first lines of each quatrain being of four feet, the fourth of three. This poem has many of the traits of *Alnwick Castle*, and bears also a strong resemblance to some of the writings of Wordsworth. Its chief merits, and indeed the chief merit, so we think, of all the poems of Halleck is the merit of *expression*. In the brief extracts from *Burns* which follow, our readers will recognize the peculiar character of which we speak.

Wild Rose of Alloway! my thanks:
 Thou mind'st me of that *autumn noon*
When first we met upon "the banks
 And braes o' bonny Doon" —

Like thine, beneath the thorn-tree's bough,
 My sunny hour was glad and brief —
We've crossed the winter sea, *and thou*
 Art withered — flower and leaf,

There have been loftier themes than his,
 And longer scrolls and louder lyres
And lays lit up with Poesy's
 Purer and holier fires.

———————

And when he breathes his master-lay
 Of Alloway's witch-haunted wall
All passions in our frames of clay
 Come thronging at his call.

———————

Such graves as his are pilgrim-shrines,
 Shrines to no code or creed confined —
The Delphian vales, the Palestines,
 The Meccas of the mind.

———————

They linger by the Doon's low trees,
 And pastoral Nith, and wooded Ayr,
And round thy Sepulchres, Dumfries!
 The Poet's tomb is there.

Wyoming is composed of nine Spenserian stanzas. With some unusual excellences, it has some of the worst faults of Halleck. The lines which follow are of great beauty.

I then but dreamed: thou art before me now,
In life — a vision of the brain no more,
I've stood upon the wooded mountain's brow,
That beetles high thy lovely valley o'er;
And now, *where winds thy river's greenest shore,*
Within a bower of sycamores am laid;
And winds as soft and sweet as ever bore
The fragrance of wild flowers through sun and shade
Are singing in the trees, whose low boughs press my head.

The poem, however, is disfigured with the mere burlesque of some portions of Alnwick Castle — with such things as

he would look *particularly droll*
In his Iberian boot and Spanish plume;

and

A girl of sweet sixteen
Love-darting eyes and tresses like the morn
Without a shoe or stocking — hoeing corn,

mingled up in a pitiable manner with images of real beauty.

The Field of the Grounded Arms contains twenty-four quatrains, without rhyme, and, we think, of a disagreeable versification. In this poem are to be observed some of the finest passages of Halleck. For example —

> Strangers! your eyes are on that valley fixed
> Intently, as we gaze on vacancy,
>> *When the mind's wings o'erspread*
>> *The spirit world of dreams.*

and again —

>> *O'er sleepless seas of grass whose waves are flowers.*

Red-Jacket has much power of expression with little evidence of poetical ability. Its humor is very fine, and does not interfere, in any great degree, with the general tone of the poem.

A *Sketch* should have been omitted from the edition as altogether unworthy of its author.

The remaining pieces in the volume are *Twilight; Psalm cxxxvii; To . . . ; Love; Domestic Happiness; Magdalen; From the Italian; Woman; Connecticut; Music; On the Death of Lieut. William Howard Allen; A Poet's Daughter;* and *On the Death of Joseph Rodman Drake.* Of the majority of these we deem it unnecessary to say more than that they partake, in a more or less degree, of the general character observable in the poems of Halleck. *The Poet's Daughter* appears to us a particularly happy specimen of that general character, and we doubt whether it be not the favorite of its author. We are glad to see the vulgarity of

> I'm busy in the cotton trade
> And sugar line,

omitted in the present edition. The eleventh stanza is certainly not English as it stands — and besides it is altogether unintelligible. What is the meaning of this?

> But her who asks, though first among
> The good, the beautiful, the young
> The birthright of a spell more strong
> Than these have brought her.

The Lines on the Death of Joseph Rodman Drake, we prefer to any of the writings of Halleck. It has that rare merit in composition of this kind — the union of tender sentiment and simplicity. This poem consists merely of six quatrains, and we quote them in full.

> Green be the turf above thee,
>> Friend of my better days!
> None knew thee but to love thee,
>> Nor named thee but to praise.

> Tears fell when thou wert dying,
>> From eyes unused to weep,
> And long, where thou art lying,
>> Will tears the cold turf steep.

When hearts whose truth was proven,
 Like thine are laid in earth,
There should a wreath be woven
 To tell the world their worth.

And I, who woke each morrow
 To clasp thy hand in mine,
Who shared thy joy and sorrow,
 Whose weal and woe were thine —

It should be mine to braid it
 Around thy faded brow,
But I've in vain essayed it,
 And feel I cannot now.

While memory bids me weep thee,
 Nor thoughts nor words are free,
The grief is fixed too deeply,
 That mourns a man like thee.

If we are to judge from the subject of these verses, they are a work of some care and reflection. Yet they abound in faults. In the line,

Tears fell when thou wert dying;

wert is not English.

Will tears the cold turf steep,

is an exceedingly rough verse. The metonymy involved in

There should a wreath be woven
To *tell* the world their worth,

is unjust. The quatrain beginning,

And I who woke each morrow,

is ungrammatical in its construction when viewed in connection with the quatrain which immediately follows. "Weep thee" and "deeply" are inaccurate rhymes — and the whole of the first quatrain,

Green be the turf, &c.

although beautiful, bears too close a resemblance to the still more beautiful lines of William Wordsworth,

She dwelt among the untrodden ways
 Beside the springs of Dove,
A maid whom there were none to praise
 And very few to love.

As a versifier Halleck is by no means equal to his friend, all of whose poems evince an ear finely attuned to the delicacies of melody. We seldom meet with more inharmonious lines than those, generally, of the author of *Alnwick Castle*. At every step such verses occur as,

> And *the* monk's hymn and minstrel's song —
> True *as* the steel of *their* tried blades —
> For him the joy of *her* young years —
> Where *the* Bard-peasant first drew breath —
> And withered *my* life's leaf like thine —

in which the proper course of the rhythm would demand an accent upon syllables too unimportant to sustain it. Not infrequently, too, we meet with lines such as this,

> Like torn branch from death's leafless tree,

in which the multiplicity of consonants renders the pronunciation of the words at all, a matter of no inconsiderable difficulty.

But we must bring our notice to a close. It will be seen that while we are willing to admire in many respects the poems before us, we feel obliged to dissent materially from that public opinion (perhaps not fairly ascertained) which would assign them a very brilliant rank in the empire of Poesy. That we have among us poets of the loftiest order we believe — but we do *not* believe that these poets are Drake and Halleck.

Bryant's Poems

Mr. Bryant's poetical reputation, both at home and abroad, is greater, we presume, than that of any other American. British critics have frequently awarded him high praise; and here, the public press have been unanimous in approbation. We can call to mind no dissenting voice. Yet the nature, and, most especially the manner, of the expressed opinions in this case, should be considered as somewhat equivocal, and but too frequently must have borne to the mind of the poet doubts and dissatisfaction. The edition now before us may be supposed to embrace all such of his poems as he deems not unworthy his name. These (amounting to about one hundred) have been "carefully revised." With the exception of some few, about which nothing could well be said, we will speak briefly of them one by one, but in such order as we may find convenient.

The Ages, a didactic piece of thirty-five Spenserian stanzas, is the first and longest in the volume. It was originally printed in 1821, with about half a dozen others now included in this collection. The design of the author in this poem is "from a survey of the past ages of the world, and of the successive advances of mankind in knowledge and virtue, to justify and confirm the hopes of the philanthropist for the future destinies of the

human race." It is, indeed, an essay on the perfectibility of man, wherein, among other better arguments some in the very teeth of analogy, are deduced from the eternal *cycles* of physical nature, to sustain a hope of *progression* in happiness. But it is only as a poem that we wish to examine *The Ages.* Its commencement is impressive. The four initial lines arrest the attention at once by a quiet dignity of manner, an air of placid contemplation, and a versification combining the extremes of melody and force —

> When to the common rest that crowns our days,
> Called in the noon of life, the good man goes,
> Or full of years, and ripe in wisdom, lays
> His silver temples in their last repose —

The five concluding lines of the stanza, however, are not equally effective —

> When, o'er the buds of youth, the death-wind blows,
> And blights the fairest; when our bitterest tears
> Stream, as the eyes of those that love us close,
> We think on what they were, with many fears
> Lest goodness die with them, and leave the coming years.

The defects, here, are all of a metrical and of course minor nature, but are still defects. The line

> When o'er the buds of youth the death-wind blows,

is impeded in its flow by the final *th* in *youth,* and especially in *death* where *w* follows. The word *tears* cannot readily be pronounced after the final *st* in *bitterest;* and its own final consonants, *rs,* in like manner render an effort necessary in the utterance of *stream* which commences the next line. In the verse

> We think on what they were, with many fears

the word *many* is, from its nature, too rapidly pronounced for the fulfilment of the *time* necessary to give weight to the foot of two syllables. All words of two syllables do not necessarily constitute a foot (we speak now of the Pentameter here employed) even although the syllables be entirely distinct, as in *many, very, often,* and the like. Such as, without effort, cannot employ in their pronunciation the *time* demanded by each of the preceding and succeeding feet of the verse, and occasionally of a preceding verse, will never fail to offend. It is the perception of this fact which so frequently forces the versifier of delicate ear to employ feet exceeding what are unjustly called legitimate dimensions. For example. At page 21 of the volume before us we have the following lines —

> Lo! to the smiling Arno's classic side,
> The emulous nations of the West repair!

These verses are exceedingly forcible, yet, upon scanning the latter we find a syllable too many. We shall be told possibly that there should be an elision of the *e* in *the* at the commencement. But no — this was not intended. Both *the* and *emulous* demand a perfect accentuation. The verse commencing *Lo!*

> Lo! to the smiling Arno's classic side,

has, it will be observed, a Trochee in its first foot. As is usually the case, the whole line partakes, in consequence, of a stately and emphatic enunciation, and to equalize the time in the verse succeeding, something more is necessary than the succession of Iambuses which constitute the ordinary English Pentameter. The equalization is therefore judiciously effected by the introduction of an additional syllable. But in the lines

> Stream, as the eyes of those that love us close,
> We think on what they were with many fears,

lines to which the preceding observations will equally apply, this additional syllable is wanting. Did the rhyme admit of the alteration, everything necessary could be accomplished by writing

> We think on what they were with *many a* fear,
> Lest goodness die with them and leave the coming year.

These remarks may be considered hypercritical — yet it is undeniable that upon a rigid attention to minutiæ such as we have pointed out, any great degree of metrical success must altogether depend. We are more disposed, too, to dwell upon the particular point mentioned above, since, with regard to it, the American Monthly, in a late critique upon the poems of Mr. Willis, has evidently done that gentleman injustice. The reviewer has fallen into what we conceive the error of citing, *by themselves*, (that is to say insulated from the context) such verses as

> The night-wind with a *desolate* moan swept by.

> With *difficult* energy and when the rod.

> Fell through, and with the *tremulous* hand of age.

> With super*natural* whiteness loosely fell.

for the purpose of animadversion. "The license" he says "of turning such words as 'passionate' and 'desolate' into two syllables could only have been taken by a pupil of the Fantastic School." We are quite sure that Mr. Willis had no purpose of turning them into words of two syllables — nor

even, as may be supposed upon a careless examination, *of pronouncing them in the same time* which would be required for two ordinary, syllables. The excesses of measure are here employed (perhaps without any definite design on the part of the writer, who may have been guided solely by ear) with reference to the proper equalization, of *balancing*, if we may so term it, of time, *throughout* an entire sentence. This, we confess, is a novel idea, but, we think, perfectly tenable. Any musician will understand us. Efforts for the relief of monotone will necessarily produce fluctuations in the time of any metre, which fluctuations, if not subsequently counterbalanced, affect the ear like unresolved discords in music. The deviations then of which we have been speaking, from the strict rules of prosodial art, are but improvements upon the rigor of those rules, and are a merit, not a fault. It is the nicety of this species of equalization more than any other metrical merit, which elevates Pope as a versifier above the mere couplet-maker of his day; and, on the other hand, it is the extension of the principle to *sentences of greater length* which elevates Milton above Pope. Knowing this, it was, of course, with some surprise that we found the American Monthly (for whose opinions we still have the highest respect,) citing Pope in opposition to Mr. Willis upon the very point to which we allude. A few examples will be sufficient to show that Pope not only made free use of the license referred to, but that he used it for the reasons, and under the circumstances which we have suggested.

> Oh thou! whatever title please thine ear,
> Dean, Drapier, Bickerstaff, or Gulliver!
> Whether thou choose Cervantes' serious air,
> Or laugh and shake in *Rabelais'* easy chair.

Any person will here readily perceive that the third line

> Whether thou choose Cervantes' serious air,

differs in time from the usual course of the rhythm, and requires some counterbalance in the line which succeeds. It is indeed precisely such a verse as that of Mr. Bryant's upon which we have commented,

> Stream, as the eyes of those that love us close,

and commences in the same manner with a Trochee. But again, from Pope we have —

> Hence hymning Tyburn's elegiac lines
> Hence Journals, Medleys, *Mercuries*, Magazines.

> Else all my prose and verse were much the same,
> This prose on stilts, that *poetry* fallen lame.

> And thrice he lifted high the birth-day brand
> And thrice he dropped it from his *quivering* hand.

> Here stood her opium, here she nursed her owls,
> And here she planned the *imperial* seat of fools.

> Here to her chosen all her works she shows;
> Prose swell'd to verse, verse *loitering* into prose.

> Rome in her Capitol saw Querno sit
> Throned on *seven* hills, the Antichrist of wit.

> And his this drum whose hoarse heroic bass
> Drowns the loud *clarion* of the braying ass.

> But such a bulk as no twelve bards could raise,
> Twelve *starveling* bards of these *degenerate* days.

These are all taken at random from the first book of the *Dunciad*. In the last example it will be seen that the *two* additional syllables are employed with a view of equalizing the time with that of the verse,

> But such a bulk as no twelve bards could raise,

a verse which will be perceived to labor in its progress — and which Pope, in accordance with his favorite theory of making sound accord with sense, evidently intended so to labor. It is useless to say that the words should be written with elision — *starv'ling* and *degen'rate*. Their *pronunciation* is not thereby materially affected — and, besides, granting it to be so, it may be as well to make the elision also in the case of Mr. Willis. But Pope had no such intention, nor, we presume, had Mr. W. It is somewhat singular, we may remark, en passant, that the American Monthly, in a subsequent portion of the critique alluded to, quotes from Pope as a line of "sonorous grandeur" and one beyond the ability of our American poet, the well known

> Luke's iron crown and Damien's bed of steel.

Now this is indeed a line of "sonorous grandeur" — but it is rendered so principally if not altogether by that very excess of metre (in the word Damien) which the reviewer has condemned in Mr. Willis. The lines which we quote below from Mr. Bryant's poem of *The Ages* will suffice to show that the author we are now reviewing fully appreciates the force of such occasional excess, and that he has only neglected it through oversight in the verse which suggested these observations.

Peace to the just man's *memory* — let it grow
Greener with years, and blossom through the flight
Of ages — let the mimic canvass show
His calm *benevolent* features.

Does *prodigal* Autumn to our age deny
The plenty that once swelled beneath his sober eye?

Look on this beautiful world and read the truth
In her fair page.

Will then the *merciful* One who stamped our race
With his own image, and who gave them sway
O'er Earth and the glad dwellers on her face,
Now that our *flourishing* nations far away
Are spread, where'er the moist earth drinks the day,
Forget the ancient care that taught and nursed
His latest offspring?

He who has tamed the *elements* shall not live
The slave of his own passions.

When liberty awoke
New-born, amid those *beautiful* vales.

Oh Greece, thy *flourishing* cities were a spoil
Unto each other.

And thou didst drive from thy *unnatural* breast .
Thy just and brave.

Yet her *degenerate* children sold the crown.

Instead of the pure heart and *innocent* hands —

Among thy gallant sons that guard thee well
Thou laugh'st at *enemies*. Who shall then declare —

Far like the comet's way thro' *infinite* space.

The full region leads
New *colonies* forth.

Full many a horrible worship that, of old,
Held o'er the *shuddering* realms unquestioned sway.

All these instances, and some others, occur in a poem of but thirty-five stanzas — yet, in only a very few cases is the license improperly used. Before quitting this subject it may be as well to cite a striking example from Wordsworth —

> There was a youth whom I had loved so long,
> That when I loved him not I cannot say.
> Mid the green moun*tains many and many* a song
> We two had sung like gladsome birds in May.

Another specimen, and one still more to the purpose may be given from Milton whose accurate ear (although he cannot justly be called the best of versifiers) included and balanced without difficulty the rhythm of the longest passages.

> But say, if our *Deliverer* up to heaven
> Must re-ascend, what will betide the few
> His faithful, left among the unfaithful herd,
> The enemies of truth? who then shall guide
> His people, who defend? Will they not deal
> More with his *followers* than with him they dealt?
> Be sure they will, *said the Angel.*

The other metrical faults in *The Ages* are few. Mr. Bryant is not always successful in his Alexandrines. Too great care cannot be taken, we think, in so regulating this species of verse as to admit of the necessary pause at the end of the third foot — or at least as not to render a pause necessary elsewhere. We object, therefore, to such lines as

> A palm like his, and catch from him the hallowed flame.

>

> The truth of heaven, and kneel to Gods that heard them not.

That which concludes Stanza X, although correctly cadenced in the above respect, requires an accent on the monosyllable *the,* which is too unimportant to sustain it. The defect is rendered the more perceptible by the introduction of a Trochee in the first foot.

> The sick untended then
> Languished in *the* damp shade, and died afar from men.

We are not sure that such lines as

> A boundless sea of blood and *the* wild air.

>

> The smile of heaven, till *a* new age expands.

are in any case justifiable, and they can be easily avoided. As in the Alexandrine mentioned above, the course of the rhythm demands an accent on monosyllables too unimportant to sustain it. For this prevalent heresy in metre we are mainly indebted to Byron, who introduced it freely, with the view of imparting an abrupt energy to his verse. There are, however, many better ways of relieving a monotone.

Stanza VI is, throughout, an exquisite specimen of versification, besides embracing many beauties both of thought and expression.

> Look on this beautiful world and read the truth
> In her fair page; see every season brings
> New change, to her, of everlasting youth;
> Still the green soil with joyous living things
> Swarms; the wide air is full of joyous wings;
> And myriads, still, are happy in the sleep
> Of ocean's azure gulfs, and where he flings
> The restless surge. Eternal love doth keep
> In his complacent arms the earth, the air, the deep.

The cadences, here, at the words *page, swarms,* and *surge* respectively, cannot be surpassed. We shall find, upon examination, comparatively few consonants in the stanza, and by their arrangement no impediment is offered to the flow of the verse. Liquids and the most melodious vowels abound. *World, eternal, season, wide, change, full, air, everlasting, wings, flings, complacent, surge, gulfs, myriads, azure, ocean, sail,* and *joyous,* are among the softest and most sonorous sounds in the language, and the partial line after the pause at *surge,* together with the stately march of the Alexandrine which succeeds, is one of the finest imaginable of finales —

> Eternal love doth keep
> In his complacent arms, the earth, the air, the deep.

The higher beauties of the poem are not, we think, of the highest. It has unity, completeness, — a beginning, middle and end. The tone, too, of calm, hopeful, and elevated reflection, is well sustained throughout. There is an occasional quaint grace of expression, as in

> Nurse of full streams, and lifter up of proud
> Sky-mingling mountains that o'erlook the cloud —

or of antithetical and rhythmical force combined, as in

> The shock that hurled
> To dust in many fragments dashed and strewn
> The throne whose roots were in another world
> And whose far-stretching shadow awed our own.

But we look in vain for something more worthy commendation. At the same time the piece is especially free from errors. Once only we meet with an unjust metonymy, where a sheet of water is said to

> *Cradle*, in his soft *embrace*, a gay
> Young group of grassy islands.

We find little originality of thought, and less imagination. But in a poem essentially didactic, of course we cannot hope for the loftiest breathings of the Muse.

To the Past is a poem of fourteen quatrains — three feet and four alternately. In the second quatrain, the lines

> And glorious ages gone
> Lie deep within the shadow of thy womb.

are, to us, disagreeable. Such things are common, but at best, repulsive. In the present case there is not even the merit of illustration. The womb, in any just imagery, should be spoken of with a view to things future; here it is employed, in the sense of the tomb, and with a view to things past. In Stanza XI the idea is even worse. The allegorical meaning throughout the poem, although generally well sustained, is not always so. In the quatrain

> Thine for a space are they —
> Yet shalt thou yield thy treasures up at last;
> Thy gates shall yet give way
> Thy bolts shall fall, inexorable Past!

it seems that *The Past*, as an allegorical personification, is confounded with *Death*.

The Old Man's Funeral is of seven stanzas, each of six lines — four Pentameters and Alexandrine rhyming. At the funeral of an old man who has lived out his full quota of years, another, as aged, reproves the company for weeping. The poem is nearly perfect in its way — the thoughts striking and natural — the versification singularly sweet. The third stanza embodies a fine idea, beautifully expressed.

> Ye sigh not when the sun, his course fulfilled,
> His glorious course rejoicing earth and sky,
> In the soft evening when the winds are stilled,
> *Sings where his islands of refreshment lie,*
> And leaves the smile of his departure spread
> O'er the warm-colored heaven, and ruddy mountain head.

The technical word *chronic* should have been avoided in the fifth line of Stanza VI —

> No chronic tortures racked his aged limb.

The Rivulet has about ninety octo-syllabic verses. They contrast the changing and perishable nature of our human frame, with the greater durability of the Rivulet. The chief merit is simplicity. We should imagine the poem to be one of the earliest pieces of Mr. Bryant, and to have undergone much correction. In the first paragraph are, however, some awkward constructions. In the verses, for example

> This little rill that from the springs
> Of yonder grove its current brings,
> Plays on the slope awhile, and then
> Goes prattling into groves again.

the reader is apt to suppose that *rill* is the nominative to *plays*, whereas it is the nominative only to *drew* in the subsequent lines,

> Oft to its warbling waters drew
> My little feet when life was new.

The proper verb is, of course, immediately seen upon reading these latter lines — but the ambiguity has occurred.

The Prairies. This is a poem, in blank Pentameter, of about one hundred and twenty-five lines, and possesses features which do not appear in any of the pieces above mentioned. Its descriptive beauty is of a high order. The peculiar points of interest in the Prairie are vividly shown forth, and as a local painting, the work is, altogether, excellent. Here are moreover, evidences of fine imagination. For example —

> The great heavens
> Seem to *stoop down upon the scene* in love —
> A nearer vault and of a tenderer blue
> Than that which bends above the eastern hills.

> ———————

> Till twilight blushed, and lovers walked and wooed
> In a forgotten language, and old tunes
> From instruments of unremembered form
> *Gave the soft winds a voice.*

> ———————

> The bee
> Within the hollow oak. *I listen long*
> *To his domestic hum, and think I hear*
> *The sound of the advancing multitude*
> *Which soon shall fill these deserts.*

> ———————

> Breezes of the south!
> *Who toss the golden and the flame-like flowers,*
> And pass the prairie-hawk that poised on high,
> Flaps his broad wings yet moves not!

There is an objectionable ellipsis in the expression "I behold them from the first," meaning "first time;" and either a grammatical or typographical error of moment in the fine sentence commencing

> Fitting floor
> For this magnificent temple of the sky —
> With flowers whose glory and whose multitude
> Rival the constellations!

Earth, a poem of similar length and construction to *The Prairies,* embodies a noble conception. The poet represents himself as lying on the earth in a "midnight black with clouds," and giving ideal voices to the varied sounds of the coming tempest. The following passages remind us of some of the more beautiful portions of Young.

> On the breast of Earth
> I lie and listen to her mighty voice;
> *A voice of many tones — sent up from streams*
> *That wander through the gloom, from woods unseen,*
> *Swayed by the sweeping of the tides of air,*
> *From rocky chasms where darkness dwells all day,*
> *And hollows of the great invisible hills,*
> *And sands that edge the ocean stretching far*
> *Into the night — a melancholy sound!*

> Ha! how the murmur deepens! I perceive
> And tremble at its dreadful import. *Earth*
> *Uplifts a general cry for guilt and wrong*
> *And Heaven is listening. The forgotten graves*
> *Of the heart broken utter forth their plaint.*
> The dust of her who loved and was betrayed,
> And him who died neglected in his age,
> The sepulchres of those who for mankind
> Labored, and earned the recompense of scorn,
> Ashes of martyrs for the truth, and bones
> Of those who in the strife for liberty
> Were beaten down, their corses given to dogs,
> Their names to infamy, all find a voice!

In this poem and elsewhere occasionally throughout the volume, we meet with a species of grammatical construction, which, although it is to be found in writing of high merit, is a mere affectation, and, of course, objectionable. We mean the abrupt employment of a direct pronoun in place of the customary *relative.* For example —

> Or haply dost thou grieve for those that die —
> For living things *that* trod awhile thy face,

> The love of thee and heaven, and how *they* sleep,
> Mixed with the shapeless dust on which thy herds
> Trample and graze?

The note of interrogation here, renders the affectation more perceptible.

The poem *To the Apenines* resembles, in meter, that entitled *The Old Man's Funeral*, except that the former has a Pentameter in place of the Alexandrine. This piece is chiefly remarkable for the force, metrical and moral, of its concluding stanza.

> In you the heart that sighs for Freedom seeks
> Her image; there the winds no barrier know;
> Clouds come and rest, and leave your fairy peaks;
> While even the immaterial Mind, below,
> And Thought, her winged offspring, chained by power,
> Pine silently for the redeeming hour.

The Knight's Epitaph consists of about fifty lines of blank Pentameter. This poem is well conceived and executed. Entering the Church of St. Catherine at Pisa, the poet is arrested by the image of an armed knight graven upon the lid of a sepulchre. The epitaph consists of an imaginative portraiture of the knight, in which he is made the impersonation of the ancient Italian chivalry.

Seventy-six has seven stanzas of a common, but musical versification, of which these lines will afford an excellent specimen.

> That death-stain on the vernal sword,
> Hallowed to freedom all the shore —
> In fragments fell the yoke abhorred —
> The footsteps of a foreign lord
> Profaned the soil no more.

The Living Lost has four stanzas of somewhat peculiar construction, but admirably adapted to the tone of contemplative melancholy which pervades the poem. We can call to mind few things more singularly impressive than the eight concluding verses. They combine ease with severity, and have antithetical force without effort or flippancy. The final thought has also a high ideal beauty.

> But ye who for the living lost
> That agony in secret bear
> Who shall with soothing words accost
> The strength of your despair?
> Grief for your sake is scorn for them
> Whom ye lament, and all condemn,
> And o'er the world of spirit lies
> A gloom from which ye turn your eyes.

The first stanza commences with one of those affectations which we noticed in the poem "Earth."

> Matron, the children of whose love,
> Each to his grave in youth have passed,
> And now the mould is heaped above
> The dearest and the last.

The Strange Lady is of the fourteen syllable metre, answering to two lines, one of eight syllables, the other six. This rhythm is unmanageable, and requires great care in the rejection of harsh consonants. Little, however, has been taken, apparently, in the construction of the verses

> As if they loved to breast the breeze that sweeps the cool
> clear sky.
>
>
>
> And thou shoudst chase the nobler game, and I bring
> down the bird.
>
>

Or that strange dame so gay and fair were some mysterious foe, which are not to be pronounced without labor. The story is old — of a young gentleman who going out to hunt, is inveigled into the woods and destroyed by a fiend in the guise of a fair lady. The ballad character is nevertheless well preserved, and this, we presume, is nearly every thing intended.

The Hunter's Vision is skilfully and sweetly told. It is a tale of a young hunter who, overcome with toil, dozes on the brink of a precipice. In this state between waking and sleeping, he fancies a spirit-land in the fogs of the valley beneath him, and sees approaching him the deceased lady of his love. Arising to meet her, he falls, with the effort, from the crag, and perishes. The state of reverie is admirably pictured in the following stanzas. The poem consists of nine such.

> All dim in haze the mountains lay
> With dimmer vales between;
> And rivers glimmered on their way
> By forests faintly seen;
> While ever rose a murmuring sound
> From brooks below and bees around.
>
> He listened till he seemed to hear
> A strain so soft and low
> That whether in the mind or ear
> The listener scarce might know.
> With such a tone, so sweet and mild
> The watching mother lulls her child.

Catterskill Falls is a narrative somewhat similar. Here the hero is also a hunter — but of delicate frame. He is overcome with the cold at the foot of the falls, sleeps, and is near perishing — but, being found by some woodmen, is taken care of, and recovers. As in the *Hunter's Vision*, the dream of the youth is the main subject of the poem. He fancies a goblin palace in the icy network of the cascade, and peoples it in his vision with ghosts. His entry into this palace is, with rich imagination on the part of the poet, made to correspond with the time of the transition from the state of reverie to that of nearly total insensibility.

> They eye him not as they pass along,
> But his hair stands up with dread,
> When he feels that he moves with that phantom throng
> Till those icy turrets are over his head,
> And the torrent's roar as they enter seems
> Like a drowsy murmur heard in dreams.
>
> The glittering threshold is scarcely passed
> When there gathers and wraps him round
> A thick white twilight sullen and vast
> In which there is neither form nor sound;
> The phantoms, the glory, vanish all
> Within the dying voice of the waterfall.

There are nineteen similar stanzas. The metre is formed of Iambuses and Anapests.

———

The Hunter of the Prairies (fifty-six octosyllabic verses with alternate rhymes) is a vivid picture of the life of a hunter in the desert. The poet, however, is here greatly indebted to his subject.

———

The Damsel of Peru is in the fourteen syllable metre, and has a most spirited, imaginative and musical commencement —

> Where olive leaves were twinkling in every wind that blew,
> There sat beneath the pleasant shade a damsel of Peru.

This is also a ballad, and a very fine one — full of action, chivalry, energy and rhythm. Some passages have even a loftier merit — that of a glowing ideality. For example —

> For the noon is coming on, and the sunbeams fiercely beat,
> And the silent hills and forest-tops seem reeling in the heat.

———

The Song of Pitcairn's Island is a sweet, quiet and simple poem, of a versification differing from that of any preceding piece. We subjoin a specimen. The Tahetian maiden addresses her lover.

Come talk of Europe's maids with me
　　Whose necks and cheeks they tell
Outshine the beauty of the sea,
　　White foam and crimson shell.
I'll shape like theirs my simple dress
And bind like them each jetty tress,
　　A sight to please thee well,
And for my dusky brow will braid
A bonnet like an English maid.

There are seven similar stanzas.

Rispah is a scriptural theme from 2 Samuel, and we like it less than any poem yet mentioned. The subject, we think, derives no additional interest from its poetical dress. The metre resembling, except in the matter of rhyme, that of "Catterskill Falls," and consisting of mingled Iambuses and Anapaests, is the most positively disagreeable of any which our language admits, and, having a frisky or fidgetty rhythm, is singularly ill-adapted to the lamentations of the bereaved mother. We cannot conceive how the fine ear of Mr. Bryant could admit such verses as,

And Rispah once the loveliest of all
That bloomed and smiled in the court of Saul, &c.

The Indian Girl's Lament and *The Arctic Lover* have nearly all the peculiarities of the "*Song of Pitcairn's Island.*"

The Massacre at Scio is only remarkable for inaccuracy of expression in the two concluding lines —

Till the last link of slavery's chain
Is shivered to be worn no more.

What shall be worn no more? The chain — but the link is implied.

Monument Mountain is a poem of about a hundred and forty blank Pentameters and relates the tale of an Indian maiden who loved her cousin. Such a love being deemed incestuous by the morality of her tribe, she threw herself from a precipice and perished. There is little peculiar in the story or its narration. We quote a rough verse —

The mighty columns with which earth props heaven.

The use of the epithet *old* preceded by some other adjective, is found so frequently in this poem and elsewhere in the writings of Mr. Bryant, as to excite a smile upon each recurrence of the expression.

In all that *proud old* world beyond the deep —
There is a tale about these *gray old* rocks —

The *wide old* woods resounded with her song —
And the *gray old* men that passed —
And from the *gray old* trunks that high in heaven.

We dislike too the antique use of the word *affect* in such sentences as

They deemed
Like worshippers of the elder time that God
Doth walk in the high places and *affect*
The earth-o'erlooking mountains.

Milton, it is true, uses it — we remember it especially in Comus —

'T is most true
That musing meditation most *affects*
The pensive secrecy of desert cell —

but then Milton would not use it were he writing Comus *today*.
In the *Summer Wind*, our author has several successful attempts at
making "the sound an echo to the sense." For example —

For me, I lie
Languidly in the shade, where the thick turf
Yet virgin from the kisses of the sun
Retains some freshness.

All is silent, save the faint
And interrupted murmur of the bee
Settling on the sick flowers, and then again
Instantly on the wing.

All the green herbs
Are stirring in his breath; a thousand flowers
By the road side, and the borders of the brook
Nod gaily to each other.

Autumn Woods. This is a poem of much sweetness and simplicity
of expression, and including one or two fine thoughts, viz:

the sweet South-west *at play*
Flies, rustling, where the painted leaves are strown
Along the winding way.

But 'neath yon crimson tree
Lover to listening maid might breathe his flame,
Nor mark within its roseate canopy
Her flush of maiden shame.

> The mountains that unfold
> In their wide sweep the colored landscape round,
> Seem *groups of giant kings in purple and gold*
> *That guard the enchanted ground.*

All this is beautiful — the sentences italicized especially so. Happily to endow inanimate nature with sentience and a capability of moral action is one of the severest tests of the poet. Even the most unmusical ear will not fail to appreciate the rare beauty and strength of the extra syllable in the line

> Seem groups of giant kings in *purple* and gold.

The Distinterred Warrior has a passage we do not clearly understand. Speaking of the Indian our author says —

> For he was fresher from the hand
> That formed of earth the human face,
> And to the elements did stand
> In nearer kindred than our race.

There are ten similar quatrains in the poem.

The Greek Boy consists of four spirited stanzas, nearly resembling, in metre, *The Living Lost*. The two concluding lines are highly ideal.

> A shoot of that old vine that made
> The nations silent in its shade.

When the Firmament Quivers with Daylight's Young Beam, belongs to a species of poetry which we cannot be brought to admire. Some natural phenomenon is observed, and the poet taxes his ingenuity to find a parallel in the moral world. In general, we may assume, that the more successful he is in sustaining a parallel, the farther he departs from the true province of the Muse. The title, here, is a specimen of the metre. This is a kind which we have before designated as exceedingly difficult to manage.

To a Musquito, is droll, and has at least the merit of making, at the same time, no efforts at being sentimental. We are not inclined, however, to rank *as poems*, either this production or the article on *New England Coal*.

The Conjunction of Jupiter and Venus has ninety Pentameters. One of them

> Kind influence. Lo! their orbs burn more bright,

can only be read, metrically, by drawing out *influence* into three marked syllables, shortening the long monosyllable, *Lo!* and lengthening the short one, *their*.

June is sweet and soft in its rhythm, and inexpressibly pathetic. There is an illy subdued sorrow and intense awe coming up, per force as it were to the surface of the poet's gay sayings about his grave, which we find thrilling us to the soul.

> And what if cheerful shouts, at noon,
> Come, from the village sent,
> Or songs of maids, beneath the moon
> With fairy laughter blent?
> And what if, in the evening light,
> Betrothed lovers walk in sight
> Of my low monument?
> I would the lovely scene around
> Might know no sadder sight nor sound.
> I know, I know I should not see
> The season's glorious show,
> Nor would its brightness shine for me
> Nor its wild music flow;
> But if, around my place of sleep,
> The friends I love should come to weep,
> They might not haste to go
> Soft airs, and song, and light, and bloom
> Should keep them lingering by my tomb.

Innocent Child and Snow-White Flower, is remarkable only for the deficiency of a foot in one of its verses.

> White as those leaves just blown apart
> *Are the folds of thy own young heart.*

and for the graceful repetition in its concluding quatrain

> Throw it aside in thy weary hour,
> Throw to the ground the fair white flower,
> Yet as thy tender years depart
> Keep that white and innocent heart.

Of the seven original sonnets in the volume before us, it is somewhat difficult to speak. The sonnet demands, in a great degree, point, strength, unity, compression, and a species of completeness. Generally, Mr. Bryant has evinced more of the first and the last, than of the three mediate qualities. *William Tell* is feeble. No forcible line ever ended with *liberty*, and the best of the rhymes — *thee, he, free,* and the like, are destitute of the necessary vigor. But for this rhythmical defect the thought in the concluding couplet —

> The bitter cup they mingled strengthened thee
> For the great work to set thy country free

would have well ended the sonnet. *Midsummer* is objectionable for the variety of its objects of allusion. Its final lines embrace a fine thought —

> As if the day of fire had dawned and sent
> Its deadly breath into the firmament —

but the vigor of the whole is impaired by the necessity of placing an unwonted accent on the last syllable of *firmament*. *October* has little to recommend it, but the slight epigrammatism of its conclusion —

> And when my last sand twinkled in the glass,
> Pass silently from men — *as thou dost pass.*

The Sonnet *To Cole*, is feeble in its final lines. and is worthy of praise only in the verses —

> Paths, homes, graves, ruins, from the lowest glen
> To where life shrinks from the fierce Alpine air.

Mutation, a didactic sonnet, has few either of faults or beauties. *November* is far better. The lines

> And the blue Gentian flower that, in the breeze,
> Nods lonely, of her beauteous race the last,

are very happy. A single thought pervades and gives unity to the piece. We are glad, too, to see an Alexandrine in the close. In the whole metrical construction of his sonnets, however, Mr. Bryant has very wisely declined confining himself to the laws of the Italian poem, or even to the dicta of Capel Lofft. The Alexandrine is beyond comparison the most effective finale, and we are astonished that the common Pentameter should ever be employed. The best sonnet of the seven is, we think, that *To* ——. With the exception of a harshness in the last line but one it is perfect. The finale is inimitable.

> Ay, thou art for the grave; thy glances shine
> Too brightly to shine long; another Spring
> Shall deck her for men's eyes, but not for thine —
> Sealed in a sleep which knows no wakening.
> The fields for thee have no medicinal leaf,
> And the vexed ore no mineral of power;
> And they who love thee wait in anxious grief
> Till the slow plague shall bring the fatal hour.
> Glide softly to thy rest, then; Death should come
> Gently to one of gentle mould like thee,
> As light winds wandering through groves of bloom
> Detach the delicate blossom from the tree.
> Close thy sweet eyes, calmly, and without pain,
> And we will trust in God to see thee yet again.

To a Cloud, has another instance of the affectation to which we alluded in our notice of *Earth*, and *The Living Lost*.

> Whose sons at length have heard the call that comes
> From the old battle fields and tombs,
> And risen, and drawn the sword, and on the foe
> Have dealt the swift and desperate blow,
> And the Othman power is cloven, and the stroke
> Has touched its chains, and they are broke.

Of the *Translations* in the volume it is not our intention to speak in detail. *Mary Magdalen*, from the Spanish of Bartolemé Leonardo De Argensola, is the finest specimen of versification in the book. *Alexis*, from the Spanish of Iglesias, is delightful in its exceeding delicacy, and general beauty. We cannot refrain from quoting it entire.

> Alexis calls me cruel —
> The rifted crags that hold
> The gathered ice of winter,
> He says, are not more cold.
>
> When even the very blossoms
> Around the fountain's brim,
> And forest walks, can witness
> The love I bear to him.
>
> I would that I could utter
> My feelings without shame
> And tell him how I love him
> Nor wrong my virgin fame.
>
> Alas! to seize the moment
> When heart inclines to heart,
> And press a suit with passion
> Is not a woman's part.
>
> If man come not to gather
> The roses where they stand,
> They fade among their foliage,
> They cannot seek his hand.

The *Waterfowl* is very beautiful, but still not entitled to the admiration which it has occasionally elicited. There is a fidelity and force in the picture of the fowl as brought before the eye of the mind, and a fine sense of *effect* in throwing its figure on the background of the "crimson sky," amid "falling dew," "while glow the heavens with the last steps of

day." But the merits which possibly have had most weight in the public estimation of the poem, are the melody and strength of its versification, (which is indeed excellent) and more particularly its *completeness*. Its rounded and didactic termination has done wonders:

> on my heart,
> Deeply hath sunk the lesson thou hast given
> And shall not soon depart.

> He, who, from zone to zone,
> Guides through the boundless sky thy certain flight
> In the long way that I must tread alone
> Will lead my steps aright.

There are, however, points of more sterling merit. We fully recognize the poet in

> Thou 'rt gone — the abyss of heaven
> Hath swallowed up thy form.

> There is a power whose care
> Teaches thy way along that pathless coast —
> *The desert, and illimitable air* —
> Lone, wandering, but not lost.

The Forest Hymn consists of about a hundred and twenty blank Pentameters of whose great rhythmical beauty it is scarcely possible to speak too highly. With the exception of the line

> The solitude. Thou art in the soft winds,

no fault, in this respect, can be found, while excellencies are frequent of a rare order, and evincing the greatest delicacy of ear. We might, perhaps, suggest, that the two concluding verses, beautiful as they stand, would be slightly improved by transferring to the last the metrical excess of the one immediately preceding. For the appreciation of this, it is necessary to quote six or seven lines in succession

> Oh, from these sterner aspects of thy face
> Spare me and mine, nor let us need the wrath
> Of the mad unchained elements, to teach
> Who rules them. Be it ours to meditate
> In these calm shades thy milder majesty,
> *And to the beautiful order of thy works*
> *Learn to conform the order of our lives.*

There is an excess of one syllable in the first of the lines italicized. If we discard this syllable here, and adopt it in the final line, the close will acquire strength, we think, in acquiring a fuller volume.

> Be it ours to meditate
> In these calm shades thy milder majesty,
> And to the perfect order of thy works
> Conform, if we can, the order of our lives.

Directness, boldness, and simplicity of expression, are main features in the poem.

> Oh God! when thou
> Dost *scare* the world with tempests, set on fire
> The heavens with falling thunderbolts, or fill
> With all the waters of the firmament
> The swift dark whirlwind that uproots *the* woods,
> And drowns *the* villages.

Here an ordinary writer would have preferred the word *fright* to *scare*, and omitted the definite article before *woods* and *villages*.

To the Evening Wind has been justly admired. It is the best specimen of that *completeness* which we have before spoken of as a characteristic feature in the poems of Mr. Bryant. It has a beginning, middle, and end, each depending upon the other, and each beautiful. Here are three lines breathing all the spirit of Shelley.

> Pleasant shall be thy way, *where meekly bows*
> *The shutting flower, and darkling waters pass,*
> *And 'twixt the o'ershadowing branches and the grass.*

The conclusion is admirable —

> Go — but the circle of eternal change,
> Which is the life of Nature, shall restore,
> With sounds and scents from all thy mighty range,
> Thee to thy birth-place of the deep once more;
> *Sweet odors in the sea air, sweet and strange,*
> *Shall tell the home-sick mariner of the shore,*
> *And, listening to thy murmur, he shall deem*
> *He hears the rustling leaf and running stream.*

Thanatopsis is somewhat more than half the length of *The Forest Hymn*, and of a character precisely similar. It is, however, the finer poem. Like *The Waterfowl*, it owes much to the point, force, and general beauty of its didactic conclusion. In the commencement, the lines

> To him who, *in the love of nature,* holds
> Communion with her visible forms, &c.

belong to a class of vague phrases, which, since the days of Byron, have obtained too universal a currency. The verse

> Go forth under the open sky and list —

is sadly out of place amid the forcible and even Miltonic rhythm of such lines as

> Take the wings
> Of morning, and the Barcan desert pierce,
> Or lose thyself in the continuous woods
> Where rolls the Oregon.

But these are trivial faults indeed and the poem embodies a great degree of the most elevated beauty. Two of its passages, passages of the purest ideality, would alone render it worthy of the general commendation it has received.

> So live, that when thy summons comes to join
> *The innumerable caravan that moves*
> *To that mysterious realm where each shall take*
> *His chamber in the silent halls of death,*
> Thou go not, like the quarry slave at night,
> Scourged to his dungeon; but, sustained and soothed
> By an unfaltering trust, approach thy grave
> *Like one who wraps the drapery of his couch*
> *About him, and lies down to pleasant dreams.*

> ———

> *The hills*
> *Rock-ribbed and ancient as the sun — the vales*
> *Stretching in pensive quietude between —*
> *The venerable woods — rivers that move*
> *In majesty, and the complaining brooks*
> *That make the meadows green — and, poured round all,*
> *Old Ocean's gray and melancholy waste —*
> *Are but the solemn decorations all*
> *Of the great tomb of man.*

> ———

Oh, *fairest of the Rural Maids!* is a gem, of which we cannot sufficiently express our admiration. We quote in full.

> *Oh, fairest of the rural maids!*
> *Thy birth was in the forest shades;*
> *Green boughs and glimpses of the sky*
> *Were all that met thine infant eye.*

> *Thy sports, thy wanderings when a child*
> *Were ever in the sylvan wild;*
> *And all the beauty of the place*
> *Is in thy heart and on thy face.*

The twilight of the trees and rocks
Is in the light shade of thy locks,
Thy step is as the wind that weaves
Its playful way among the leaves.

Thine eyes are springs, in whose serene
And silent waters Heaven is seen;
Their lashes are the herbs that look
On their young figures in the brook.

The forest depths by foot impressed
Are not more sinless than thy breast;
The holy peace that fills the air
Of those calm solitudes, is there.

A rich simplicity is a main feature in this poem — simplicity of design and execution. This is strikingly perceptible in the opening and conclud- ing lines, and in *expression* throughout. But there is a far higher and more strictly *ideal* beauty, which it is less easy to analyze. The original conception is of the very loftiest order of true Poesy. A maiden is born in the forest —

Green boughs and glimpses of the sky
Are all which meet her infant eye —

She is not merely *modelled in character* by the associations of her child- hood — this were the thought of an ordinary poet — an idea that we meet with every day in rhyme — but she imbibes, in her physical as well as moral being, the traits, the very features of the delicious scenery around her — *its loveliness becomes a portion of her own —*

The twilight of the trees and rocks
Is in the light shade of her locks,
And all the beauty of the place
Is in her heart and on her face.

It would have been a highly poetical idea to imagine the tints in the locks of the maiden deducing *a resemblance* to the "twilight of the trees and rocks," from the constancy of her associations — but the spirit of Ideality is immeasurably more apparent when the "twilight" is repre- sented as becoming *identified* with the shadows of her hair.

The twilight of the trees and rocks
Is in the light shade of her locks,
And all the beauty of the place
Is in her heart and on her face.

Feeling thus, we did not, in copying the poem, italicize the lines, al- though beautiful,

Thy step is *as* the wind that weaves
Its playful way among the leaves,

nor those which immediately follow. The two concluding verses, how-
ever, are again of the most elevated species of poetical merit.

> The forest depths by foot impressed
> Are not more sinless than thy breast —
> The holy peace that fills the air
> Of those calm solitudes, *is there*.

The image contained in the lines

> Thine eyes are springs in whose serene
> And silent waters Heaven is seen —

is one which, we think, for appropriateness, completeness, and every
perfect beauty of which imagery is susceptible, has never been surpassed
— but *imagery* is susceptible of *no* beauty like that we have designated
in the sentences above. The latter idea, moreover, is not original with
our poet.

In all the rhapsodies of Mr. Bryant, which have reference to the
beauty or the majesty of nature, is a most audible and thrilling tone of
love and exultation. As far as he appreciates her loveliness or her august-
ness, no appreciation can be more ardent, more full of heart, more
replete with the glowing soul of adoration. Nor, either in the moral or
physical universe coming within the periphery of his vision, does he at
any time fail to perceive and designate, at once, the legitimate items of
the beautiful. Therefore, could we consider (as some have considered)
the mere enjoyment of the beautiful when perceived, or even this enjoy-
ment when combined with the readiest and truest perception and dis-
crimination in regard to beauty presented, as a sufficient test of the
poetical sentiment, we could have no hesitation in according to Mr. Bry-
ant the very highest poetical rank. But something more, we have else-
where presumed to say, is demanded. Just above, we spoke of "objects
in the moral or physical universe coming within the periphery of his
vision." We now mean to say, that the relative extent of these periph-
eries of poetical vision must ever be a primary consideration in our
classification of poets. Judging Mr. B. in this manner, and by a *general*
estimate of the volume before us, we should, of course, pause long before
assigning him a place with the spiritual Shelleys, or Coleridges, or Words-
worths, or with Keats, or even Tennyson, or Wilson, or with some other
burning lights of our own day, to be valued in a day to come. Yet if his
poems, as a whole, will not warrant us in assigning him this grade, one
such poem as the last upon which we have commented, is enough to
assure us that he may attain it.

The writings of our author, as we find them *here*, are characterized
by an air of calm and elevated contemplation more than by any other
individual feature. In their mere didactics, however, they err essentially

and primitively, inasmuch as such things are the province rather of Minerva than of the Camenæ. Of imagination, we discover much — but more of its rich and certain evidences, than of its ripened fruit. In all the minor merits Mr. Bryant is pre-eminent. His *ars celare artem* is most efficient. Of his "completeness," unity, and finish of style we have already spoken. As a versifier, we know of no writer, living or dead, who can be said greatly to surpass him. A Frenchman would assuredly call him *"un poëte des plus correctes."*

Between Cowper and Young, perhaps, (with both of whom he has many points of analogy,) would be the post assigned him by an examination at once general and superficial. Even in this view, however, he has a juster appreciation of the beautiful than the one, of the sublime than the other — a finer taste than Cowper — an equally vigorous, and far more delicate imagination than Young. In regard to his proper rank among American poets there should be no question whatever. Few — at least few who are fairly before the public, have more than very shallow claims to a rivalry with the author of *Thanatopsis*.

The Old Curiosity Shop, and Other Tales

By Charles Dickens. With Numerous Illustrations by Cattermole and Browne. Philadelphia: Lea & Blanchard.

Master Humphrey's Clock

By Charles Dickens. (Boz.) With Ninety-one Illustrations by George Cattermole and Hablot Browne. Philadelphia: Lea & Blanchard.

What we here give in Italics is the duplicate title, on two separate title-pages, of an octavo volume of three hundred and sixty-two pages. Why this method of nomenclature should have been adopted is more than we can understand — although it arises, perhaps, from a certain confusion and hesitation observable in the whole structure of the book itself. Publishers have an idea, however, (and no doubt they are the best judges in such matters) that a complete work obtains a readier sale than one "to be continued;" and we see plainly that it is with the design of intimating the *entireness* of the volume now before us, that "*The Old Curiosity Shop and other Tales*," has been made not only the primary and main title, but the name of the whole publication as indicated by the back. This may be quite fair in trade, but is morally wrong not the less. The volume is only one of a series — only part of a whole; and the title has no right to *insinuate otherwise*. So obvious is this intention to misguide, that it has led to the absurdity of putting the inclusive, or general, title of the series, as a secondary instead of a primary one. Anybody may see that if the wish had been fairly to represent the plan and extent of the volume, something like this would have been given on a single page —

Master Humphrey's Clock

By Charles Dickens. Part I. Containing The Old Curiosity Shop, and other Tales, with Numerous Illustrations, &c. &c.

This would have been better for all parties, a good deal more honest, and a vast deal more easily understood. In fact, there is sufficient uncertainty of purpose in the book itself, without resort to mystification in the matter of title. We do not think it altogether impossible that the rumors in respect to the sanity of Mr. Dickens which were so prevalent during the publication of the first numbers of the work, had some slight — some very slight foundation in truth. By this, we mean merely to say that the mind of the author, at the time, might possibly have been struggling with some of those manifold and multiform *aberrations* by which the nobler order of genius is so frequently beset — but which are still so very far removed from disease.

There are some facts in the physical world which have a really wonderful analogy with others in the world of thought, and seem thus to give some color of truth to the (false) rhetorical dogma, that metaphor or simile may be made to strengthen an argument, as well as to embellish a description. The principle of the *vis inertiae*, for example, with the amount of *momentum* proportionate with it and consequent upon it, seems to be identical in physics and metaphysics. It is not more true, in the former, that a large body is with more difficulty set in motion than a smaller one, and that its subsequent impetus is commensurate with this difficulty, than it is, in the latter, that intellects of the vaster capacity, while more forcible, more constant, and more extensive in their movements than those of inferior grade, are yet the less readily moved, and are more embarrassed and more full of hesitation in the first few steps of their progress. While, therefore, it is not impossible, as we have just said, that some slight mental aberration might have given rise to the hesitancy and indefinitiveness of purpose which are so very perceptible in the first pages of the volume before us, we are still the more willing to believe these defects the result of the moral fact just stated, since we find the work itself of an unusual order of excellence, even when regarded as the production of the author of "Nicholas Nickleby." That the evils we complain of are not, and were not, fully perceived by Mr. Dickens himself, cannot be supposed for a moment. Had his book been published in the old way, we should have seen no traces of them whatever.

The design of the general work, "Humphrey's Clock," is simply the common-place one of putting various tales into the mouths of a social party. The meetings are held at the house of Master Humphrey — an antique building in London, where an old-fashioned clock case is the place of deposit for the M.S.S. Why such designs have become common is obvious. One half the pleasure experienced at a theatre arises from the

spectator's sympathy with the rest of the audience, and, especially, from his belief in their sympathy with him. The eccentric gentleman who not long ago, at the Park, found himself the solitary occupant of box, pit, and gallery, would have derived but little enjoyment from his visit, had he been suffered to remain. It was an act of mercy to turn him out. The present absurd rage for lecturing is founded in the feeling in question. Essays which we would not be hired to read — so trite is their subject — so feeble is their execution — so much easier is it to get better information on similar themes out of any Encyclopaedia in Christendom — we are brought to tolerate, and alas, even to applaud in their tenth and twentieth repetition, through the sole force of our sympathy with the throng. In the same way we listen to a story with greater zest when there are others present at its narration besides ourselves. Aware of this, authors without due reflection have repeatedly attempted, by supposing a circle of listeners, to imbue their narratives with the interest of sympathy. At a cursory glance the idea seems plausible enough. But, in the one case, there is an actual, personal, and palpable sympathy, conveyed in looks, gestures and brief comments — a sympathy of real individuals, all with the matters discussed to be sure, but then especially, *each with each*. In the other instance, we, alone in our closet, are required to sympathise *with* the sympathy of fictitious listeners, who, so far from being present in body, are often studiously kept out of sight and out of mind for two or three hundred pages at a time. This is sympathy double-diluted — the shadow of a shade. It is unnecesary to say that the design invariably fails of its effect.

In his preface to the present volume, Mr. Dickens seems to feel the necessity for an apology in regard to certain portions of his commencement, without seeing clearly what apology he should make, or for what precise thing he should apologize. He makes an effort to get over the difficulty, by saying something about its never being "his intention to have the members of 'Master Humphrey's Clock' active agents in the stories they relate," and about his "picturing to himself the various sensations of his hearers — thinking how Jack Redburn might incline to poor Kit — how the deaf gentleman would have his favorite and Mr. Miles his," &c. &c. — but we are quite sure that all this is as pure a fiction as "The Curiosity Shop" itself. Our author is deceived. Occupied with little Nell and her grandfather, he had forgotten the very existence of his interlocutors until he found himself, at the end of his book, under the disagreeable necessity of saying a word or two concerning them, by way of winding them up. The simple truth is that, either for one of the two reasons at which we have already hinted, or else because the work was begun in a hurry, Mr. Dickens did not precisely know his own plans when he penned the five or six first chapters of the "Clock."

The wish to preserve a certain degree of unity between various narratives naturally unconnected, is a more obvious and a better reason for

employing interlocutors. But such unity as may be thus had is scarcely worth having. It may, in some feeble measure, satisfy the judgment by a sense of completeness; but it seldom produces a pleasant effect; and if the speakers are made to take part in their own stories (as has been the case here) they become injurious by creating confusion. Thus, in "The Curiosity Shop," we feel displeased to find Master Humphrey commencing the tale in the first person, dropping this for the third, and concluding by introducing himself as the "single gentleman" who figures in the story. In spite of all the subsequent explanation we are forced to look upon him as two. All is confusion, and what makes it worse, is that Master Humphrey is painted as a lean and sober personage, while his second self is a fat, bluff and boisterous old bachelor.

Yet the species of connexion in question, besides preserving the unity desired, *may* be made, if well managed, a source of consistent and agreeable interest. It has been so made by Thomas Moore — the most skilful literary artist of his day — perhaps of any day — a man who stands in the singular and really wonderful predicament of being undervalued on account of the profusion with which he has scattered about him his good things. The brilliancies on any one page of Lalla Roohk would have sufficed to establish that very reputation which has been in a great measure self-dimmed by the galazied lustre of the entire book. It seems that the horrid laws of political economy cannot be evaded even by the inspired, and that a perfect versification, a vigorous style, and a never-tiring fancy, may, like the water we drink and die without, yet despise, be so plentifully set forth as to be absolutely of no value at all.

By far the greater portion of the volume now published, is occupied with the tale of "The Old Curiosity Shop," narrated by Master Humphrey himself. The other stories are brief. The "Giant Chronicles" is the title of what appears to be meant for a series within a series, and we think this design doubly objectionable. The narrative of "The Bowyer," as well as of "John Podgers," is not altogether worthy of Mr. Dickens. They were probably sent to press to supply a demand for copy, while he was occupied with the "Curiosity Shop." But the "Confession Found in a Prison in the Time of Charles the Second" is a paper of remarkable power, truly original in conception, and worked out with great ability.

The story of "The Curiosity Shop" is very simple. Two brothers of England, warmly attached to each other, love the same lady, without each other's knowledge. The younger at length discovers the elder's secret, and, sacrificing himself to fraternal affection, quits the country and resides for many years in a foreign land, where he amasses great wealth. Meantime his brother marries the lady, who soon dies, leaving an infant daughter — her perfect resemblance. In the widower's heart the mother lives again through the child. This latter grows up, marries unhappily, has a son and a daughter, loses her husband, and dies herself shortly afterward. The grandfather takes the orphans to his home. The boy spurns his protection,

falls into bad courses, and becomes an outcast. The girl — in whom a third time lives the object of the old man's early choice — dwells with him alone, and is loved by him with a most doting affection. He has now become poor, and at length is reduced to keeping a shop for antiquities and curiosities. Finally, through his dread of involving the child in want, his mind becomes weakened. He thinks to redeem his fortune by gambling, borrows money for this purpose of a dwarf, who, at length, discovering the true state of the old man's affairs, seizes his furniture and turns him out of doors. The girl and himself set out, without farther object than to relieve themselves of the sight of the hated city, upon a weary pilgrimage, whose events form the basis or body of the tale. In fine, just as a peaceful retirement is secured for them, the child, wasted with fatigue and anxiety, dies. The grandfather, through grief, immediately follows her to the tomb. The younger brother, meantime, has received information of the old man's poverty, hastens to England, and arrives only in time to be at the closing scene of the tragedy.

This plot is the best which could have been constructed for the main object of the narrative. This object is the depicting of a fervent and dreamy love for the child on the part of the grandfather — such a love as would induce devotion to himself on the part of the orphan. We have thus the conception of a childhood, educated in utter ignorance of the world, filled with an affection which has been, through its brief existence, the sole source of its pleasures, and which has no part in the passion of a more mature youth for an object of its own age — we have the idea of this childhood, full of ardent hopes, leading by the hand, forth from the heated and wearying city, into the green fields, to seek for bread, the decrepid imbecillity of a doting and confiding old age, whose stern knowledge of man, and of the world it leaves behind, is now merged in the sole consciousness of receiving love and protection from that weakness it has loved and protected.

This conception is indeed most beautiful. It is simply and severely grand. The more fully we survey it, the more thoroughly we are convinced of the lofty character of that genius which gave it birth. That in its present simplicity of form, however, it was first entertained by Mr. Dickens, may well be doubted. That it was *not*, we are assured by the title which the tale bears. When in its commencement he called it "The Old Curiosity Shop," his design was far different from what we see it in its completion. It is evident that had he now to name the story he would not so term it; for the shop itself is a thing of an altogether collateral interest, and is spoken of merely in the beginning. This is only one among a hundred instances of the disadvantage under which the periodical novelist labors. When his work is done, he never fails to observe a thousand defects which he might have remedied, and a thousand alterations, in regard to the book as a whole, which might be made to its manifest improvement.

But if the conception of this story deserves praise, its execution is beyond all — and here the subject naturally leads us from the generalization which is the proper province of the critic, into details among which it is scarcely fitting that he should venture.

The Art of Mr. Dickens, although elaborate and great, seems only a happy modification of Nature. In this respect he differs remarkably from the author of "Night and Morning." The latter, by excessive care and by patient reflection, aided by much rhetorical knowledge, and general information, has arrived at the cabability of producing books which be mistaken by ninety-nine readers out of a hundred for the genuine inspirations of genius. The former, by the promptings of the truest genius itself, has been brought to compose, and evidently without effort, works which have effected a long-sought consummation — which have rendered him the idol of the people, while defying and enchanting the critics. Mr. Bulwer, through art, has almost created a genius. Mr. Dickens, through genius, has perfected a standard from which Art itself will derive its essence, in rules.

When we speak in this manner of the "Old Curiosity Shop," we speak with entire deliberation, and know quite well what it is we assert. We do not mean to say that it is perfect, as a whole — this could not well have been the case under the circumstances of its composition. But we know that, in all the higher elements which go to make up literary greatness, it is supremely excellent. We think, for instance, that the introduction of Nelly's brother (and here we address those who have read the work) is supererogatory — that the character of Quilp would have been more in keeping had he been confined to petty and grotesque acts of malice — that his death should have been made the *immediate* consequence of his attempt at revenge upon Kit; and that after matters had been put fairly in train for this poetical justice, he should not have perished by an accident inconsequential upon his villany. We think, too, that there is an air of *ultra*-accident in the finally discovered relationship between Kit's master and the bachelor of the old church — that the sneering politeness put into the mouth of Quilp, with his manner of commencing a question which he wishes answered in the affirmative, with an affirmative interrogatory, instead of the ordinary negative one — are fashions borrowed from the author's own Fagin — that he has repeated himself in many other instances — that the practical tricks and love of mischief of the dwarf's boy are too nearly consonant with the traits of the master — that so much of the propensities of Swiveller as relate to his inapposite appropriation of odds and ends of verse, is stolen from the generic loafer of our fellow-townsman, Neal — and that the writer has suffered the overflowing kindness of his own bosom to mislead him in a very important point of art, when he endows so many of his *dramatis personae* with a warmth of feeling so very rare in reality. Above all, we acknowledge that the death of Nelly is excessively painful — that it leaves a most distress-

ing oppression of spirit upon the reader — and should, therefore, have been avoided.

But when we come to speak of the excellences of the tale these defects appear really insignificant. It embodies more *originality* in every point, but in character especially, than any single work within our knowledge. There is the grandfather — a truly profound conception; the gentle and lovely Nelly — we have discoursed of her before; Quilp, with mouth like that of the panting dog — (a bold idea which the engraver has neglected to embody) with his hilarious antics, his cowardice, and his very petty and spoilt-child-like malevolence; Dick Swiveller, that prince of good-hearted, good-for-nothing, lazy, luxurious, poetical, brave, romantically generous, gallant, affectionate, and not over-and-above honest, "glorious Apollos;" the marchioness, his bride; Tom Codlin and his partner; Miss Sally Brass, that "fine fellow;" the pony that had an opinion of its own; the boy that stood upon his head; the sexton; the man at the forge; not forgetting the dancing dogs and baby Nubbles. There are other admirably drawn characters — but we note these for their remarkable originality, as well as for their wonderful keeping, and the glowing colors in which they are painted. We have heard some of them called caricatures — but the charge is grossly ill-founded. No critical principle is more firmly based in reason than that a certain amount of exaggeration is essential to the proper depicting of truth itself. We do not paint an object to be true, but to appear true to the beholder. Were we to copy nature with accuracy the object copied would seem unnatural. The columns of the Greek temples, which convey the idea of absolute proportion, are very considerably thicker just beneath the capital than at the base. We regret that we have not left ourselves space in which to examine this whole question as it deserves. We must content ourselves with saying that caricature seldom exists (unless in so gross a form as to disgust at once) where the component parts are in *keeping;* and that the laugh excited by it, in any case, is radically distinct from that induced by a properly artistical *incongruity* — the source of all mirth. Were these creations of Mr. Dickens' really caricatures they would not live in public estimation beyond the hour of their first survey. We regard them as *creations* — (that is to say as original combinations of character) only not all of the highest order, because the elements employed are not always of the highest. In the instances of Nelly, the grandfather, the Sexton, and the man of the furnace, the force of the creative intellect could scarcely have been engaged with nobler material, and the result is that these personages belong to the most august regions of the *Ideal*.

In truth, the great feature of the "Curiosity Shop" is its chaste, vigorous, and glorious *imagination*. This is the one charm, all potent, which alone would suffice to compensate for a world more of error than Mr. Dickens ever committed. It is not only seen in the conception, and general handling of the story, or in the invention of character; but it per-

vades every sentence of the book. We recognise its prodigious influence in every inspired word. It is this which induces the reader who is at all ideal, to pause frequently, to reread the occasionally quaint phrases, to muse in uncontrollable delight over thoughts which, while he wonders he has never hit upon them before, he yet admits that he never has encountered. In fact it is the wand of the enchanter.

Had we room to particularize, we would mention as points evincing most distinctly the ideality of the "Curiosity Shop" — the picture of the shop itself — the newly-born desire of the worldly old man for the peace of green fields — his whole character and conduct, in short — the schoolmaster, with his desolate fortunes, seeking affection in little children — the haunts of Quilp among the wharf-rats — the tinkering of the Punchmen among the tombs — the glorious scene where the man of the forge sits poring, at deep midnight, into that dread fire — again the whole conception of this character; and, last and greatest, the stealthy approach of Nell to her death — her gradual sinking away on the journey to the village, so skilfully indicated rather than described — her pensive and prescient meditation — the fit of strange musing which came over her when the house *in which she was to die* first broke upon her sight — the description of this house, of the old church, and of the churchyard — everything in rigid consonance with the one impression to be conveyed — that deep meaningless well — the comments of the Sexton upon death, and upon his own secure life — this whole world of mournful yet peaceful idea merging, at length, into the decease of the child Nelly, and the uncomprehending despair of the grandfather. These concluding scenes are so drawn that human language, urged by human thought, could go no farther in the excitement of human feelings. And the pathos is of that best order which is relieved, in great measure, by ideality. Here the book has never been equalled, — never approached except in one instance, and that is in the case of the "Undine" of De La Motte Fouqué. The imagination is perhaps as great in this latter work, but the pathos, although truly beautiful and deep, fails of much of its effect through the material from which it is wrought. The chief character, being endowed with purely fanciful attributes, cannot command our full sympathies, as can a simple denizen of earth. In saying, a page or so above, that the death of the child left too painful an impression, and should therefore have been avoided, we must, of course, be understood as referring to the work as a whole, and in respect to its general appreciation and popularity. The death, as recorded, is, we repeat, of the highest order of literary excellence — yet while none can deny this fact, there are few who will be willing to read the concluding passages a second time.

Upon the whole we think the "Curiosity Shop" very much the best of the works of Mr. Dickens. It is scarcely possible to speak of it too well. It is in all respects a tale which will secure for its author the enthusiastic admiration of every man of genius.

The edition before us is handsomely printed, on excellent paper. The designs by Cattermole and Browne are many of them excellent — some of them outrageously bad. Of course, it is difficult for us to say how far the American engraver is in fault. In conclusion, we must enter our solemn protest against the final page full of little angels in smock frocks, or dimity chemises.

The Quacks Of Helicon

A *Satire*. By L. A. WILMER

A SATIRE, professedly such, at the present day, and especially by an American writer, is a welcome novelty indeed. We have really done very little in the line upon this side of the Atlantic — nothing certainly of importance — Trumbull's clumsy poem and Halleck's "Croakers" to the contrary notwithstanding. Some things we have produced, to be sure, which were excellent in the way of burlesque, without intending a syllable that was not utterly solemn and serious. Odes, ballads, songs, sonnets, epics, and epigrams, possessed of this unintentional excellence, we could have no difficulty in designating by the dozen; but in the matter of directly meant and genuine satire, it cannot be denied that we are sadly deficient. Although, as a literary people, however, we are not exactly Archilochuses — although we have no pretensions to the ηχεηντες ιαμβοι — although in short, we are no satirists ourselves, there can be no question that we answer sufficiently well as subjects for satire.

We repeat that we are glad to see this book of Mr. Wilmer's; first, because it is something new under the sun; secondly, because, in many respects, it is well executed; and thirdly, because, in the universal corruption and rigmarole, amid which we gasp for breath, it is really a pleasant thing to get even one accidental whiff of the unadulterated air of *truth*.

"The Quacks of Helicon," as a poem and otherwise, has many defects, and these we shall have no scruple in pointing out — although Mr. Wilmer is a personal friend of our own, and we are happy and proud to say so — but it has also many remarkable merits — merits which it will be quite useless for those aggrieved by the satire — quite useless for any *clique,* or set of *cliques,* to attempt to frown down, or to affect not to see, or to feel, or to understand.

Its prevalent blemishes are referable chiefly to the leading sin of *imitation.* Had the work been composed professedly in paraphrase of the whole manner of the sarcastic epistles of the times of Dryden and Pope, we should have pronounced it the most ingenious and truthful thing of the kind upon record. So close is the copy that it extends to the most trivial points — for example, to the old forms of punctuation. The turns

of phraseology, the tricks of rhythm, the arrangement of the paragraphs, the general conduct of the satire — everything — all — are Dryden's. We cannot deny, it is true, that the satiric model of the days in question is insusceptible of improvement, and that the modern author who deviates therefrom must necessarily sacrifice something of merit at the shrine of originality. Neither can we shut our eyes to the fact that the imitation in the present case has conveyed, in full spirit, the high qualities, as well as in rigid letter, the minor elegancies and general peculiarities of the author of "Absalom and Achitophel." We have here the bold, vigorous, and sonorous verse, the biting sarcasm, the pungent epigrammatism, the unscrupulous directness, as of old. Yet it will not do to forget that Mr. Wilmer has been *shown how* to accomplish these things. He is thus only entitled to the praise of a close observer, and of a thoughtful and skilful copyist. The images are, to be sure, his own. They are neither Pope's, nor Dryden's, nor Rochester's, nor Churchill's — but they are moulded in the identical mould used by these satirists.

This servility of imitation has seduced our author into errors, which his better sense should have avoided. He sometimes mistakes intentions; at other times, he copies faults, confounding them with beauties. In the opening of the poem, for example, we find the lines —

> Against usurpers, Olney, I declare
> A righteous, just, and patriotic war.

The rhymes *war* and *declare* are here adopted from Pope, who employs them frequently; but it should have been remembered that the modern relative pronunciation of the two words differs materially from the relative pronunciation of the era of the "Dunciad."

We are also sure that the gross obscenity, the filth — we can use no gentler name — which disgraces "The Quacks of Helicon," cannot be the result of innate impurity in the mind of the writer. It is but a part of the slavish and indiscriminating imitation of the Swift and Rochester school. It has done the book an irreparable injury, both in a moral and pecuniary view, without affecting anything whatever on the score of sarcasm, vigour or wit. "Let what is to be said, be said plainly." True; but let nothing vulgar be *ever* said or conceived.

In asserting that this satire, even in its mannerism, has imbued itself with the full spirit of the polish and of the pungency of Dryden, we have already awarded it high praise. But there remains to be mentioned the far loftier merit of speaking fearlessly the truth, at an epoch when truth is out of fashion, and under circumstances of social position which would have deterred almost any man in our community from a similar Quixotism. For the publication of "The Quacks of Helicon" — a poem which brings under review, by name, most of our prominent *literati*, and treats them, generally, as they deserve (what treatment could be more bitter?)

— for the publication of this attack, Mr. Wilmer, whose subsistence lies in his pen, has little to look for — apart from the silent respect of those at once honest and timid — but the most malignant open or covert persecution. For this reason, and because it is the truth which he has spoken, do we say to him, from the bottom of our hearts, "God speed!"

We repeat it: *it is* the truth which he has spoken; and who shall contradict us? He has said unscrupulously what every reasonable man among us has long known to be "as true as the Pentateuch" — that, as a literary people, we are one vast perambulating humbug. He has asserted that we are *clique*-ridden; and who does not smile at the obvious truism of that assertion? He maintains that chicanery is, with us, a far surer road than talent to distinction in letters. Who gainsays this? The corrupt nature of our ordinary criticism has become notorious. Its powers have been prostrated by its own arm. The intercourse between critic and publisher, as it now almost universally stands, is comprised either in the paying and pocketing of blackmail, as the price of a simple forebearance, or in a direct system of petty and contemptible bribery, properly so-called — a system even more injurious than the former to the true interests of the public, and more degrading to the buyers and sellers of good opinion, on account of the more positive character of the service here rendered for the consideration received. We laugh at the idea of any denial of our assertions upon this topic; they are infamously true. In the charge of general corruption, there are undoubtedly many noble exceptions to be made. There are, indeed, some very few editors, who, maintaining an entire independence, will receive no books from publishers at all, or who receive them with a perfect understanding, on the part of these latter, that an unbiassed *critique* will be given. But these cases are insufficient to have much effect on the popular mistrust; a mistrust heightened by late exposure of the machinations of *coteries* in New York — *coteries* which, at the bidding of leading booksellers, manufacture, as required from time to time, a pseudo-public opinion by wholesale, for the benefit of any little hanger-on of the party, or pettifogging protector of the firm.

We speak of these things in the bitterness of scorn. It is unnecessary to cite instances, where one is found in almost every issue of a book. It is needless to call to mind the desperate case of Fay — a case where the pertinacity of the effort to gull — where the obviousness of the attempt at forestalling a judgment — where the wofully overdone bemirrorment of that man-of-straw, together with the pitiable platitude of his production, proved a dose somewhat too potent for even the well-prepared stomach of the mob. We say it is supererogatory to dwell upon "Norman Leslie," or other by-gone follies, when we have before our eyes hourly instances of the machinations in question. To so great an extent of methodical assurance has the *system* of puffery arrived, that publishers, of late, have made no scruple of keeping on hand an assortment of commendatory notices, prepared by their men of all work, and of sending

these notices around to the multitudinous papers within their influence, done up within the fly leaves of the book. The grossness of these base attempts, however, has not escaped indignant rebuke from the more honourable portion of the press; and we hail these symptoms of restiveness under the yoke of unprincipled ignorance and quackery (strong only in combination) as the harbinger of a better era for the interests of real merit, and of the national literature as a whole.

It has become, indeed, the plain duty of each individual connected with our periodicals heartily to give whatever influence he possesses to the good cause of integrity and the truth. The results thus attainable will be found worthy his closest attention and best efforts. We shall thus frown down all conspiracies to foist inanity upon the public consideration at the obvious expense of every man of talent who is not a member of a *clique* in power. We may even arrive in time at that desirable point from which a distinct view of our men of letters may be obtained, and their respective pretensions adjusted by the standard of a rigorous and self-sustaining criticism alone. That their several positions are as yet properly settled; that the posts which a vast number of them now hold are maintained by any better tenure than that of the chicanery upon which we have commented, will be asserted by none but the ignorant, or the parties who have best right to feel an interest in the "good old condition of things." No two matters can be more radically different than the reputation of some of our prominent *litterateurs* as gathered from the mouths of the people (who glean it from the paragraphs of the papers), and the same reputation as deduced from the private estimate of intelligent and educated men. We do not advance this fact as a new discovery. Its truth, on the contrary, is the subject, and has long been so, of every-day witticism and mirth.

Why not? Surely there can be few things more ridiculous than the general character and assumptions of the ordinary critical notices of new books! An editor, sometimes without the shadow of the commonest attainment — often without brains, always without time — does not scruple to give the world to understand that he is in the *daily* habit of critically reading and deciding upon a flood of publications, one-tenth of whose title pages he may possibly have turned over, three-fourths of whose contents would be Hebrew to his most desperate efforts at comprehension, and whose entire mass and amount, as might be mathematically demonstrated, would be sufficient to occupy, in the most cursory perusal, the attention of some ten or twenty readers for a month! What he wants in plausibility, however, he makes up in obsequiousness; what he lacks in time he supplies in temper. He is the most easily pleased man in the world. He admires everything, from the big Dictionary of Noah Webster to the last diamond edition of Tom Thumb. Indeed, his sole difficulty is in finding tongue to express his delight. Every pamphlet is a miracle — every book in boards is an epoch in letters. His phrases,

therefore, get bigger and bigger every day, and, if it were not for talking Cockney, we might call him a "regular swell."

Yet, in the attempt at getting definite information in regard to any one portion of our literature, the merely general reader, or the foreigner, will turn in vain from the lighter to the heavier journals. But it is not our intention here to dwell upon the radical, antique, and systematized rigmarole of our Quarterlies. The articles here are anonymous. Who writes? — who causes to be written? Who but an ass will put faith in tirades which *may* be the result of personal hostility, or in panegyrics which nine times out of ten may be laid, directly or indirectly, to the charge of the author himself? It is in the favour of these saturnine pamphlets that they contain, now and then, a good essay *de omnibus rebus et quibusdam aliis*, which may be looked into, without decided somnolent consequences, at any period, not immediately subsequent to dinner. But it is useless to expect criticism from periodicals called "Reviews" from never reviewing. Besides, all men know, or should know, that these books are sadly given to verbiage. It is a part of their nature, a condition of their being, a point of their faith. A veteran reviewer loves the safety of generalities and is therefore rarely particular. "Words, words, words," are the secret of his strength. He has one or two ideas of his own and is both wary and fussy in giving them out. His wit lies, with his truth, in a well, and there is always a world of trouble in getting it up. He is a sworn enemy to all things simple and direct. He gives no ear to the advice of the giant Moulineau — "*Belier, mon ami, commencez au commencement.*" He either jumps at once into the middle of his subject, or breaks in at a back door, or sidles up to it with the gait of a crab. No other mode of approach has an air of sufficient profundity. When fairly into it, however, he becomes dazzled with the scintillations of his own wisdom, and is seldom able to see his way out. Tired of laughing at his antics, or frightened at seeing him flounder, the reader, at length, shuts him up, with the book. "What song the Syrens sang," says Sir Thomas Browne, "or what name Achilles assumed when he hid himself among women, though puzzling questions, are not beyond *all* conjecture"; — but it would puzzle Sir Thomas, backed by Achilles and all the Syrens in Heathendom, to say, in nine cases out of ten, *what is the object* of a thoroughgoing Quarterly Reviewer.

Should the opinions promulgated by our press at large be taken, in their wonderful aggregate, as an evidence of what American literature absolutely is (and it may be said that, in general, they are really so taken), we shall find ourselves the most enviable set of people upon the face of the earth. Our fine writers are legion. Our very atmosphere is redolent of genius; and we, the nation, are a huge, well-contented chameleon, grown pursy by inhaling it. We are *teretes et rotundi* — enwrapped in excellence. All our poets are Miltons, neither mute nor inglorious; all our poetesses are "American Hemanses"; nor will it do to deny that all

our novelists are Great Knowns or Great Unknowns, and that everybody who writes, in every possible and impossible department, is the Admirable Crichton, or, at least, the Admirable Crichton's ghost. We are thus in a glorious condition, and will remain so until forced to disgorge our ethereal honours. In truth there is some danger that the jealousy of the Old World will interfere. It cannot long submit to that outrageous monopoly of "all the decency and all the talent," of which the gentlemen of the press give such undoubted assurance of our being the possessors.

But we feel angry with ourselves for the jesting tone of our observations upon this topic. The prevalence of the spirit of puffery is a subject far less for merriment than for disgust. Its truckling, yet dogmatical character — its bold, unsustained, yet self-sufficient and wholesale laudation — is becoming, more and more, an insult to the common sense of the community. Trivial as it essentially is, it has yet been made the instrument of the grossest abuse in the elevation of imbecility, to the manifest injury, to the utter ruin, of true merit. Is there any man of good feeling and of ordinary understanding — is there one single individual among all our readers — who does not feel a thrill of bitter indignation, apart from any sentiment of mirth, as he calls to mind instance after instance of the purest, of the most unadulterated quackery in letters, which has risen to a high post in the apparent popular estimation, and which still maintains it, by the sole means of a blustering arrogance, or of a busy wriggling conceit, or of the most barefaced plagiarism, or even through the simple immensity of its assumptions — assumptions not only unopposed by the press at large, but absolutely supported in proportion to the vociferous clamour with which they are made — in exact accordance with their utter baselessness and untenability? We should have no trouble in pointing out to-day some twenty or thirty so-called literary personages, who, if not idiots, as we half think them, or if not hardened to all sense of shame by a long course of disingenuousness, will now blush in the perusal of these words, through consciousness of the shadowy nature of that purchased pedestal upon which they stand — will now tremble in thinking of the feebleness of the breath which will be adequate to the blowing it from beneath their feet. With the help of a hearty good will, even *we* may yet tumble them down.

So firm, through a long endurance, has been the hold taken upon the popular mind (at least so far as we may consider the popular mind reflected in ephemeral letters) by the laudatory system which we have deprecated, that what is, in its own essence, a vice, has become endowed with the appearance, and met with the reception of a virtue. Antiquity, as usual, has lent a certain degree of speciousness even to the absurd. So continuously have we puffed, that we have, at length, come to think puffing the duty, and plain speaking the dereliction. What we began in gross error, we persist in through habit. Having adopted, in the earlier days of our literature, the untenable idea that this literature, as a whole,

could be advanced by an indiscriminate approbation bestowed on its every effort — having adopted this idea, we say, without attention to the obvious fact that praise of all was bitter although negative censure to the few alone deserving, and that the only result of the system, in the fostering way, would be the fostering of folly — we now continue our vile practice through the supineness of custom, even while, in our national self-conceit, we repudiate that necessity for patronage and protection in which originated our conduct. In a word, the press throughout the country has not been ashamed to make head against the very few bold attempts at independence which have from time to time been made in the face of the reigning order of things. And if in one, or perhaps two, insulated cases, the spirit of severe truth, sustained by an unconquerable will, was not to be so put down, then, forthwith, were private chicaneries set in motion; then was had resort, on the part of those who considered themselves injured by the severity of criticism (and who were so, if the just contempt of every ingenuous man is injury), resort to arts of the most virulent indignity, to untraceable slanders, to ruthless assassination in the dark. We say these things were done while the press in general looked on, and, with a full understanding of the wrong perpetrated, spoke not against the wrong. The idea had absolutely gone abroad — had grown up little by little into toleration — that attacks, however just, upon a literary reputation, however obtained, however untenable, were well retaliated by the basest and most unfounded traduction of personal fame. But is this an age — is this a day — in which it can be necessary even to advert to such considerations as that the book of the author is the property of the public, and that the issue of the book is the throwing down of the gauntlet to the reviewer — to the reviewer whose duty is the plainest; the duty not even of approbation, or of censure, or of silence, at his own will, but at the sway of those sentiments and of those opinions which are derived from the author himself, through the medium of his written and published words? True criticism is the reflection of the thing criticized upon the spirit of the critic.

But à *nos moutons* — to "The Quacks of Helicon." This satire has many faults besides those upon which we have commented. The title, for example, is not sufficiently distinctive, although otherwise good. It does not confine the subject to *American* quacks, while the work does. The two concluding lines enfeeble instead of strengthening the *finale*, which would have been exceedingly pungent without them. The individual portions of the thesis are strung together too much at random — a natural sequence is not always preserved — so that, although the lights of the picture are often forcible, the whole has what, in artistical parlance, is termed an accidental and spotty appearance. In truth, the parts of the poem have evidently been composed each by each, as separate themes, and afterwards fitted into the general satire in the best manner possible.

But a more reprehensible sin than any or than all of these is yet to

be mentioned — the sin of indiscriminate censure. Even here Mr. Wilmer has erred through imitation. He has held in view the sweeping denunciations of the Dunciad, and of the later (abortive) satire of Byron. No one in his senses can deny the justice of the general charges of corruption in regard to which we have just spoken from the text of our author. But are there *no* exceptions? We should, indeed, blush if there were not. And is there *no* hope? Time will show. We cannot do everything in a day — *Non se gano Zamora en un ora.* Again, it cannot be gainsaid that the greater number of those who hold high places in our poetical literature are absolute nincompoops — fellows alike innocent of reason and of rhyme. But neither are we *all* brainless, nor is the devil himself so black as he is painted. Mr. Wilmer must read the chapter in Rabelais's "*Gargantua,*" "*de ce qu'est signifié par les couleurs blanc et bleu,*" — for there is *some* difference after all. It will not do in a civilized land to run a-muck like a Malay. Mr. Morris *has* written good songs. Mr. Bryant is not *all* a fool. Mr. Willis is not *quite* an ass. Mr. Longfellow *will* steal, but, perhaps, he cannot help it (for we have heard of such things), and then it must not be denied that *nil tetigit quod non ornavit.*

The fact is that our author, in the rank exuberance of his zeal, seems to think as little of discrimination as the Bishop of Autun * did of the Bible. Poetical "things in general" are the windmills at which he spurs his Rozinante. He as often tilts at what is true as at what is false; and thus his lines are like the mirrors of the temples of Smyrna, which represent the fairest images as deformed. But the talent, the fearlessness, and especially the *design* of this book, will suffice to preserve it from that dreadful damnation of "silent contempt," to which editors throughout the country, if we are not much mistaken, will endeavour, one and all, to consign it.

Exordium

[*Graham's Magazine, January, 1842*]

In commencing, with the New Year, a New Volume, we shall be permitted to say a very few words by way of *exordium* to our usual chapter of Reviews, or, as we should prefer calling them, of Critical Notices. Yet we speak *not* for the sake of the *exordium*, but because we have really something to say, and know not when or where better to say it.

That the public attention, in America, has, of late days, been more than usually directed to the matter of literary criticism, is plainly apparent. Our periodicals are beginning to acknowledge the importance of the science (shall we so term it?) and to disdain the flippant *opinion* which so long has been made its substitute.

* Talleyrand.

Time was when we imported our critical decisions from the mother country. For many years we enacted a perfect farce of subserviency to the *dicta* of Great Britain. At last a revulsion of feeling, with self-disgust, necessarily ensued. Urged by these, we plunged into the opposite extreme. In throwing *totally* off that "authority," whose voice had so long been so sacred, we even surpassed, and by much, our original folly. But the watchword now was, "a national literature!" — as if any true literature *could be* "national" — as if the world at large were not the only proper stage for the literary *histrio*. We became, suddenly, the merest and maddest *partizans* in letters. Our papers spoke of "tariffs" and "protection." Our Magazines had habitual passages about that "truly native novelist, Mr. Cooper," or that "staunch American genius, Mr. Paulding." Unmindful of the spirit of the axioms that "a prophet has no honor in his own land" and that "a hero is never a hero to his *valet-de-chambre*" — axioms founded in reason and in truth — our reviews urged the propriety — our booksellers the necessity, of strictly "American" themes. A foreign subject, at this epoch, was a weight more than enough to drag down into the very depths of critical damnation the finest writer owning nativity in the States; while, on the reverse, we found ourselves daily in the paradoxical dilemma of liking, or pretending to like, a stupid book the better because (sure enough) its stupidity was of our own growth, and discussed our own affairs.

It is, in fact, but very lately that this anomalous state of feeling has shown any signs of subsidence. Still it *is* subsiding. Our views of literature in general having expanded, we begin to demand the use — to inquire into the offices and provinces of criticism — to regard it more as an art based immovably in nature, less as a mere system of fluctuating and conventional dogmas. And, with the prevalence of these ideas, has arrived a distaste even to the home-dictation of the bookseller-*coteries*. If our editors are not as yet *all* independent of the will of a publisher, a majority of them scruple, at least, *to confess* a subservience, and enter into no positive combinations against the minority who despise and discard it. And this is a *very* great improvement of exceedingly late date.

Escaping these quicksands, our criticism is nevertheless in some danger — some very little danger — of falling into the pit of a most detestable species of cant — the cant of *generality*. This tendency has been given it, in the first instance, by the onward and tumultuous spirit of the age. With the increase of the thinking-material comes the desire, if not the necessity, of abandoning particulars for masses. Yet in our individual case, as a nation, we seem merely to have adopted this bias from the British Quarterly Reviews, upon which our own Quarterlies have been slavishly and pertinaciously modelled. In the foreign journal, the review or criticism properly so termed, has gradually yet steadily degenerated into what we see it at present — that is to say, into anything but criticism. Originally a "review" was not so called as *lucus a non lucendo*. Its name

conveyed a just idea of its design. It reviewed, or surveyed the book whose title formed its text, and, giving an analysis of its contents, passed judgment upon its merits or defects. But, through the system of anonymous contribution, this natural process lost ground from day to day. The name of a writer being known only to a few, it became to him an object not so much to write well, as to write fluently, at so many guineas per sheet. The analysis of a book is a matter of time and of mental exertion. For many classes of composition there is required a deliberate perusal, with notes, and subsequent generalization. An easy substitute for this labor was found in a digest or compendium of the work noticed, with copious extracts — or a still easier, in random comments upon such passages as accidentally met the eye of the critic, with the passages themselves copied at full length. The mode of reviewing most in favor, however, because carrying with it the greatest *semblance* of care, was that of diffuse essay upon the subject matter of the publication, the reviewer(?) using the facts alone which the publication supplied, and using them as material for some theory, the sole concern, bearing, and intention of which, was mere difference of opinion with the author. These came at length to be understood and habitually practised as the customary or conventional *fashions* of review; and although the nobler order of intellects did not fall into the full heresy of these fashions — we may still assert that even Macaulay's nearest approach to criticism in its legitimate sense, is to be found in his article upon Ranke's "History of the Popes" — an article in which the whole strength of the reviewer is put forth *to account* for a single fact — the progress of Romanism — which the book under discussion has established.

Now, while we do not mean to deny that a good essay is a good thing, we yet assert that these papers on general topics have nothing whatever to do with that *criticism* which their evil example has nevertheless infected *in se*. Because these dogmatizing pamphlets, which *were once* "Reviews," have lapsed from their original faith, it does not follow that the faith itself is extinct — that "there shall be no more cakes and ale" — that criticism, in its old acceptation, does not exist. But we complain of a growing inclination on the part of our lighter journals to believe, on such grounds, that such is the fact — that because the British Quarterlies, through supineness, and our own, through a degrading imitation, have come to merge all varieties of vague generalization in the one title of "Review," it therefore results that criticism, being everything in the universe, is, consequently, nothing whatever in fact. For to this end, and to none other conceivable, is the tendency of such propositions, for example, as we find in a late number of that very clever monthly magazine, Arcturus.

"But *now*" (the emphasis on the *now* is our own) — "but now," says Mr. Mathews, in the preface to the first volume of his journal, "criticism has a wider scope and a universal interest. It dismisses errors of gram-

mar, and hands over an imperfect rhyme or a false quantity to the proof-reader; it looks *now* to the heart of the subject and the author's design. It is a test of opinion. Its acuteness is not pedantic, but philosophical; it unravels the web of the author's mystery to interpret his meaning to others; it detects his sophistry, because sophistry is injurious to the heart and life; it promulgates his beauties with liberal, generous praise, because this is his true duty as the servant of truth. Good criticism may be well asked for, since it is the type of the literature of the day. It gives method to the universal inquisitiveness on every topic relating to life or action. A criticism, *now*, includes every form of literature, except perhaps the imaginative and the strictly dramatic. It is an essay, a sermon, an oration, a chapter in history, a philosophical speculation, a prose-poem, an art-novel, a dialogue; it admits of humor, pathos, the personal feelings of autobiography, the broadest views of statesmanship. As the ballad and the epic were the productions of the days of Homer, the review is the native characteristic growth of the nineteenth century."

We respect the talents of Mr. Mathews, but must dissent from nearly all that he here says. The species of "review" which he designates as the "characteristic growth of the nineteenth century" is only the growth of the last twenty or thirty years *in Great Britain*. The French Reviews, for example, which are *not* anonymous, are very different things, and preserve the *unique* spirit of true criticism. And what need we say of the Germans? — what of Winckelmann, of Novalis, of Schelling, of Goethe, of Augustus William, and of Frederick Schlegel? — that their magnificent *critiques raisonnées* differ from those of Kames, of Johnson, and of Blair, in principle not at all, (for the principles of these artists will not fail until Nature herself expires,) but solely in their more careful elaboration, their greater thoroughness, their more profound analysis and application of the principles themselves. That a criticism *"now"* should be different in spirit, as Mr. Mathews supposes, from a criticism at any previous period, is to insinuate a charge of variability in laws that cannot vary — the laws of man's heart and intellect — for these are the sole basis upon which the true critical art is established. And this art *"now"* no more than in the days of the "Dunciad," can, without neglect of its duty, "dismiss errors of grammar," or "hand over an imperfect rhyme or a false quantity to the proof-reader." What is meant by a "test of opinion" in the connection here given the words by Mr. M., we do not comprehend as clearly as we could desire. By this phrase we are as completely enveloped in doubt as was Mirabeau in the castle of *If*. To our imperfect appreciation it seems to form a portion of that general vagueness which is the *tone* of the whole philosophy at this point: — but all that which our journalist describes a criticism to be, is all that which we sturdily maintain it *is not*. Criticism is *not*, we think, an essay, nor a sermon, nor an oration, nor a chapter in history, nor a philosophical speculation, nor a prose-poem, nor an art-novel, nor a dialogue. In fact, it *can be* nothing

in the world but — a criticism. But if it were all that Arcturus imagines, it is not very clear why it might not be equally "imaginative" or "dramatic" — a romance or a melodrama, or both. That it would be a farce cannot be doubted.

It is against this frantic spirit of *generalization* that we protest. We have a word, "criticism," whose import is sufficiently distinct, through long usage, at least; and we have an art of high importance and clearly-ascertained limit, which this word is quite well enough understood to represent. Of that conglomerate science to which Mr. Mathews so eloquently alludes, and of which we are instructed that it is anything and everything at once — of this science we know nothing, and really wish to know less; but we object to our contemporary's appropriation in its behalf, of a term to which we, in common with a large majority of mankind, have been accustomed to attach a certain and very definitive idea. Is there no word but "criticism" which may be made to serve the purposes of "Arcturus"? Has it any objection to Orphicism, or Dialism, or Emersonism, or any other pregnant compound indicative of confusion worse confounded?

Still, we must not pretend a total misapprehension of the idea of Mr. Mathews, and we should be sorry that he misunderstood *us*. It may be granted that we differ only in terms — although the difference will yet be found not unimportant in effect. Following the highest authority, we would wish, in a word, to limit literary criticism to comment upon *Art*. A book is written — and it is only *as the book* that we subject it to review. With the opinions of the work, considered otherwise than in their relation to the work itself, the critic has really nothing to do. It is his part simply to decide upon *the mode* in which these opinions are brought to bear. Criticism is thus no "test of opinion." For this test, the work, divested of its pretensions as an *art-product*, is turned over for discussion to the world at large — and first, to that class which it especially addresses — if a history, to the historian — if a metaphysical treatise, to the moralist. In this, the only true and intelligible sense, it will be seen that criticism, the test or analysis of *Art*, (*not* of opinion,) is only properly employed upon productions which have their basis in art itself, and although the journalist (whose duties and objects are multiform) may turn aside, at pleasure, from the *mode* or vehicle of opinion to discussion of the opinion conveyed — it is still clear that he is "*critical*" only in so much as he deviates from his true province not at all.

And of the critic himself what shall we say? — for as yet we have spoken only the *proem* to the true *epopea*. What *can* we better say of him than, with Bulwer, that "he must have courage to blame boldly, magnanimity to eschew envy, genius to appreciate, learning to compare, an eye for beauty, an ear for music, and a heart for feeling." Let us add, a talent for analysis and a solemn indifference to abuse.

Ballads and Other Poems

By Henry Wadsworth Longfellow, author of "Voices of the Night,"
"Hyperion," &c. Second edition. John Owen, Cambridge.

"IL Y A À PARIER," says Chamfort, *"que toute idée publique, toute convention reçue, est une sottise, car elle a convenu au plus grand nombre."*
— One would be safe in wagering that any given public idea is erroneous, for it has been yielded to the clamor of the majority; — and this strictly philosophical, although somewhat French assertion has especial bearing upon the whole race of what are termed maxims and popular proverbs; nine-tenths of which are the quintessence of folly. One of the most deplorably false of them is the antique adage, *De gustibus non est disputandum* — there should be no disputing about taste. Here the idea designed to be conveyed is that any one person has as just right to consider his own taste *the true*, as has any one other — that taste itself, in short, is an arbitrary something, amenable to no law, and measurable by no definite rules. It must be confessed, however, that the exceedingly vague and impotent treatises which are alone extant, have much to answer for as regards confirming the general error. Not the least important service which, hereafter, mankind will owe to *Phrenology*, may, perhaps, be recognized in an analysis of the real principles, and a digest of the resulting laws of taste. These principles, in fact, are as clearly traceable, and these laws as really susceptible of system as are any whatever.

In the meantime, the inane adage above mentioned is in no respect more generally, more stupidly, and more pertinaciously quoted than by the admirers of what is termed the "good old Pope," or the "good old Goldsmith school" of poetry, in reference to the bolder, more natural, and *more ideal* compositions of such authors as Coëtlogon and Lamartine * in France; Herder, Körner, and Uhland, in Germany; Brun and Baggesen in Denmark; Bellman, Tegnér, Nyberg † in Sweden; Keats, Shelley, Coleridge, and Tennyson in England; Lowell and Longfellow in America. "*De gustibus non*," say these "good-old school" fellows; and we have no doubt that their mental translation of the phrase is — "We pity your taste — we pity every body's taste but our own."

It is our purpose hereafter, when occasion shall be afforded us, to controvert in an article of some length, the popular idea that the poets just mentioned owe to novelty, to trickeries of expression, and to other meretricious effects, their appreciation by certain readers: — to demonstrate (for the matter is susceptible of demonstration) that such poetry and such alone has fulfilled the legitimate office of the muse; has thoroughly satisfied an earnest and unquenchable desire existing in the heart of man.

* We allude here chiefly to the "David" of Coëtlogon and *only* to the "Chûte d'un Ange" of Lamartine.

† C. Julia Nyberg, author of the "Dikter von Euphrosyne."

In the present number of our Magazine we have left ourselves barely room to say a few random words of welcome to these "Ballads," by Longfellow, and to tender him, and all such as he, the homage of our most earnest love and admiration.

The volume before us (in whose outward appearance the keen "taste" of genius is evinced with nearly as much precision as in its internal soul) includes, with several brief original pieces, a translation from the Swedish of Tegnér. In attempting (what never should be attempted) a literal version of both the words and the metre of this poem, Professor Longfellow has failed to do justice either to his author or himself. He has striven to do what no man ever did well and what, from the nature of the language itself, never can be well done. Unless, for example, we shall come to have an influx of *spondees* in our English tongue, it will always be impossible to construct an English hexameter. Our spondees, or, we should say, our spondiac words, are rare. In the Swedish they are nearly as abundant as in the Latin and Greek. We have only "compound," "context," "footfall," and a few other similar ones. This is the difficulty; and that it *is* so will become evident upon reading "The Children of the Lord's Supper," where the sole *readable* verses are those in which we meet with the rare spondaic dissyllables. We mean to say *readable as Hexameters*; for many of them will read very well as mere English Dactylics, with certain irregularities.

But within the narrow compass now left us we must not indulge in anything like critical comment. Our readers will be better satisfied perhaps with a few brief extracts from the original poems of the volume — which we give for their rare excellence, without pausing now to say in what particulars this excellence exists.

> And, like the water's flow
> Under December's snow
> Came a dull voice of woe,
> From the heart's chamber.

> So the loud laugh of scorn,
> Out of those lips unshorn
> From the deep drinking-horn
> Blew the foam lightly.

> As with his wings aslant
> Sails the fierce cormorant
> Seeking some rocky haunt,
> With his prey laden,
> So toward the open main,
> Beating to sea again,
> Through the wild hurricane,
> Bore I the maiden.

Down came the storm and smote amain
 The vessel in its strength;
She shuddered and paused like a frighted steed
 Then leaped her cable's length.

She drifted a dreary wreck,
And a whooping billow swept the crew
 Like icicles from her deck.

He hears the parson pray and preach
 He hears his daughter's voice,
Singing in the village choir,
 And it makes his heart rejoice;
It sounds to him like her mother's voice
 Singing in Paradise!
He needs must think of her once more
 How in the grave she lies;
And with his hard rough hand he wipes
 A tear out of his eyes.

Thus at the flaming forge of life
 Our fortunes must be wrought;
Thus on its sounding anvil shaped
 Each burning deed and thought.

The rising moon has hid the stars
Her level rays like golden bars
 Lie on the landscape green
 With shadows brown between.

Love lifts the boughs whose shadows deep
Are life's oblivion, the soul's sleep,
 And kisses the closed eyes
 Of him who slumbering lies.

Friends my soul with joy remembers!
 How like quivering flames they start,
When I fan the living embers
 On the hearth-stone of my heart.

Hearest thou voices on the shore,
That our ears perceive no more
Deafened by the cataract's roar?

And from the sky, serene and far
A voice fell like a falling star.

Some of these passages cannot be fully appreciated apart from the context — but we address those who have read the book. Of the translations we have not spoken. It is but right to say, however, that "The Luck of Edenhall" is a far finer poem, in every respect, than any of the original pieces. Nor would we have our previous observations misunderstood. Much as we admire the genius of Mr. Longfellow, we are fully sensible of his many errors of affectation and imitation. His artistical skill is great, and his ideality high. But his conception of the *aims* of poesy *is all wrong;* and this we shall prove at some future day — to our own satisfaction, at least. His didactics are all *out of place.* He has written brilliant poems — by accident; that is to say when permitting his genius to get the better of his conventional habit of thinking — a habit deduced from German study. We do not mean to say that a didactic moral may not be well made the *under-current* of a poetical thesis; but that it can never be well put so obtrusively forth, as in the majority of his compositions. There is a young American who, with ideality not richer than that of Longfellow, and with less artistical knowledge, has yet composed far truer poems, merely through the greater propriety of his themes. We allude to James Russell Lowell; and in the number of this Magazine for last month, will be found a ballad entitled "Rosaline," affording an excellent exemplification of our meaning. This composition has unquestionably its defects, and the very defects which are not perceptible in Mr. Longfellow — but we sincerely think that *no American poem equals it* in the higher elements of song.

In our last number we had some hasty observations on these "Ballads" — observations which we propose, in some measure, to amplify and explain.

It may be remembered that, among other points, we demurred to Mr. Longfellow's *themes,* or rather to their general character. We found fault with the too obtrusive nature of their *didacticism.* Some years ago, we urged a similar objection to one or two of the longer pieces of Bryant; and neither time nor reflection has sufficed to modify, in the slightest particular, our conviction upon this topic.

We have said that Mr. Longfellow's conception of the *aims* of poesy is erroneous; and that thus, labouring at a disadvantage, he does violent wrong to his own high powers; and now the question is, What *are* his ideas of the aims of the Muse, as we gather these ideas from the *general* tendency of his poems? It will be at once evident that, imbued with the peculiar spirit of German song (a pure conventionality), he regards the inculcation of a *moral* as essential. Here we find it necessary to repeat that we have reference only to the *general* tendency of his compositions; for there are some magnificent exceptions, where, as if by accident, he has permitted his genius to get the better of his conventional prejudice. But didacticism is the prevalent *tone* of his song. His invention, his

imagery, his all, is made subservient to the elucidation of some one or more points (but rarely of more than one) which he looks upon as *truth*. And that this mode of procedure will find stern defenders should never excite surprise, so long as the world is full to overflowing with cant and conventicles. There are men who will scramble on all fours through the muddiest sloughs of vice to pick up a single apple of virtue. There are things called men who, so long as the sun rolls, will greet with snuffling huzzas every figure that takes upon itself the semblance of truth, even although the figure, in itself only a "stuffed Paddy," be as much out of place as a toga on the statue of Washington, or out of season as rabbits in the days of the dog-star.

Now, with as deep a reverence for "the true" as ever inspired the bosom of mortal man, we would limit, in many respects, its modes of inculcation. We would limit, to enforce them. We would not render them impotent by dissipation. The demands of truth are severe. She has no sympathy with the myrtles. All that is indispensable in song is all with which she has nothing to do. To deck her in gay robes is to render her a harlot. It is but making her a flaunting paradox to wreathe her in gems and flowers. Even in stating this our present proposition, we verify our own words — we feel the necessity, in enforcing this *truth*, of descending from metaphor. Let us then be simple and distinct. To convey "the true" we are required to dismiss from the attention all inessentials. We must be perspicuous, precise, terse. We need concentration rather than expansion of mind. We must be calm, unimpassioned, unexcited — in a word, we must be in that peculiar mood which, as nearly as possible, is the exact converse of the poetical. He must be blind indeed who cannot perceive the radical and chasmal difference between the truthful and the poetical modes of inculcation. He must be grossly wedded to conventionalisms who, in spite of this difference, shall still attempt to reconcile the obstinate oils and waters of Poetry and Truth.

Dividing the world of mind into its most obvious and immediately recognisable distinctions, we have the pure intellect, taste and the moral sense. We place *taste* between the intellect and the moral sense, because it is just this intermediate space which, in the mind, it occupies. It is the connecting link in the triple chain.

It serves to sustain a mutual intelligence between the extremes. It appertains, in strict appreciation, to the former, but is distinguished from the latter by so faint a difference that Aristotle has not hesitated to class some of its operations among the Virtues themselves. But the *offices* of the trio are broadly marked. Just as conscience, or the moral sense, recognises duty; just as the intellect deals with *truth*; so is it the part of taste alone to inform us of BEAUTY. And Poesy is the handmaiden but of Taste. Yet we would not be misunderstood. This handmaiden is not forbidden to moralise — in her own fashion. She is not forbidden to depict — but to reason and preach of virtue. As of this latter, conscience recognises

the obligation, so intellect teaches the expediency, while taste contents herself with displaying the beauty; waging war with vice merely on the ground of its inconsistency with fitness, harmony, proportion — in a word with τὸ καλόν.

An important condition of man's immortal nature is thus, plainly, the sense of the Beautiful. This it is which ministers to his delight in the manifold forms and colours and sounds and sentiments amid which he exists. And, just as the eyes of Amaryllis are repeated in the mirror, or the living lily in the lake, so is the mere *record* of these forms and colours and sounds and sentiments — so is their mere oral or written repetition a duplicate source of delight. But this repetition is not Poesy. He who shall merely sing with whatever rapture, in however harmonious strains, or with however vivid a truth of imitation, of the sights and sounds which greet him in common with all mankind — he, we say, has yet failed to prove his divine title. There is still a longing unsatisfied, which he has been impotent to fulfil. There is still a thirst unquenchable, which to allay he has shown us no crystal springs. This burning thirst belongs to the *immortal* essence of man's nature. It is equally a consequence and an indication of his perennial life. It is the desire of the moth for the star. It is not the mere appreciation of the beauty before us. It is a wild effort to reach the beauty above. It is a forethought of the loveliness to come. It is a passion to be satiated by no sublunary sights, or sounds, or sentiments, and the soul thus athirst strives to allay its fever in futile efforts at *creation*. Inspired with a prescient ecstasy of the beauty beyond the grave, it struggles by multiform novelty of combination among the things and thoughts of Time, to anticipate some portion of that loveliness whose very elements, perhaps, appertain solely to Eternity; and the result of such effort, on the part of souls fittingly constituted, is alone what mankind have agreed to denominate Poetry.

We say this with little fear of contradiction. Yet the spirit of our assertion must be more heeded than the letter. Mankind have *seemed* to define Poesy in a thousand, and in a thousand conflicting, definitions. But the war is one only of words. Induction is as well applicable to this subject as to the most palpable and utilitarian; and by its sober processes we find that, in respect to compositions which have been really received as poems, the *imaginative*, or, more popularly, the creative portions *alone* have ensured them to be so received. Yet these works, on account of these portions, having once been so received and so named, it has happened naturally and inevitably, that other portions totally unpoetic have not only come to be regarded by the popular voice as poetic, but have been made to serve as false standards of perfection in the adjustment of other poetical claims. Whatever has been found in whatever has been received as a poem, has been blindly regarded as *ex statu* poetic. And this is a species of gross error which scarcely could have made its way into any less intangible topic. In fact that license which appertains to the

Muse herself, it has been thought decorous, if not sagacious, to indulge in all examination of her character.

Poesy is thus seen to be a response — unsatisfactory it is true — but still in some measure a response, to a natural and irrepressible demand. Man being what he is, the time could never have been in which poesy was not. Its first element is the thirst for supernal BEAUTY — a beauty which is not afforded the soul by any existing collocation of earth's forms — a beauty which, perhaps, *no possible* combination of these forms would fully produce. Its second element is the attempt to satisfy this thirst by *novel* combinations among those forms of beauty which already exist — or by novel combinations of *those combinations which our predecessors, toiling in chase of the same phantom, have already set in order.* We thus clearly deduce the *novelty*, the *originality*, the *invention*, the *imagination*, or lastly the *creation* of BEAUTY (for the terms as here employed are synonymous), as the essence of all Poesy. Nor is this idea so much at variance with ordinary opinion as, at first sight, it may appear. A multitude of antique dogmas on this topic will be found when divested of extrinsic speculation, to be easily resoluble into the definition now proposed. We do nothing more than present tangibly the vague clouds of the world's idea. We recognize the idea itself floating, unsettled, indefinite, in every attempt which has yet been made to circumscribe the conception of "Poesy" in words. A striking instance of this is observable in the fact that no definition exists in which either the "beautiful," or some one of those qualities which we have mentioned above designated synonymously with "creation," has not been pointed out as the *chief* attribute of the Muse. "Invention," however, or "imagination," is by far more commonly insisted upon. The word ποίησις itself (creation) speaks volumes upon this point. Neither will it be amiss here to mention Count Bielfeld's definition of poetry as *"L'art d'exprimer les pensées par la fiction."* With this definition (of which the philosophy is profound to a certain extent) the German terms *Dichtkunst*, the art of fiction, and *Dichten*, to feign, which are used for *"poetry"* and *"to make verses,"* are in full and remarkable accordance. It is, nevertheless, in the *combination* of the two omniprevalent ideas that the novelty and, we believe, the force of our own proposition is to be found.

So far we have spoken of Poesy as of an abstraction alone. As such, it is obvious that it may be applicable in various moods. The sentiment may develop itself in Sculpture, in Painting, in Music, or otherwise. But our present business is with its development in words — that development to which, in practical acceptation, the world has agreed to limit the term. And at this point there is one consideration which induces us to pause. We cannot make up our minds to admit (as some have admitted) the inessentiality of rhythm. On the contrary, the universality of its use in the earliest poetical efforts of all mankind would be sufficient to assure us, not merely of its congeniality with the Muse, or of its adapta-

tion to her purposes, but of its elementary and indispensable importance. But here we must, perforce, content ourselves with mere suggestion; for this topic is of a character which would lead us too far. We have already spoken of Music as one of the moods of poetical development. It is in Music, perhaps, that the soul most nearly attains that end upon which we have commented — the creation of supernal beauty. It may be, indeed, that this august aim is here even partially or imperfectly attained, *in fact*. *The elements* of that beauty which is felt in sound, *may be* the mutual or common heritage of Earth and Heaven. In the soul's struggles at combination it is thus not impossible that a harp may strike notes not unfamiliar to the angels. And in this view the wonder may well be less that all attempts at defining the character or sentiment of the deeper musical impressions have been found absolutely futile. Contenting ourselves, therefore, with the firm conviction that music (in its modifications of rhythm and rhyme) is of so vast a moment in Poesy as *never* to be neglected by him who is truly poetical — is of so mighty a force in furthering the great aim intended that he is mad who rejects its assistance — content with this idea we shall not pause to maintain its absolute essentiality, for the mere sake of rounding a definition. We will but add, at this point, that the highest possible development of the Poetical Sentiment is to be found in the union of song with music, in its popular sense. The old Bards and Minnesingers possessed, in the fullest perfection, the finest and truest elements of Poesy; and Thomas Moore, singing his own ballads, is but putting the final touch to their completion as poems.

To recapitulate, then, we would define in brief the Poetry of words as the *Rhythmical Creation of Beauty*. Beyond the limits of Beauty its province does not extend. Its sole arbiter is Taste. With the Intellect or with the Conscience it has only collateral relations. It has no dependence, unless incidentally, upon either Duty or *Truth*. That our definition will necessarily exclude much of what, through a supine toleration, has been hitherto ranked as poetical, is a matter which affords us not even momentary concern. We address but the thoughtful, and heed only their approval — with our own. If our suggestions are truthful, then "after many days" shall they be understood as truth, even though found in contradiction of *all* that has been hitherto so understood. If false, shall we not be the first to bid them die?

We would reject, of course, all such matters as "Armstrong on Health," a revolting production; Pope's "Essay on Man," which may well be content with the title of an "Essay in Rhyme"; "Hudibras," and other merely humorous pieces. We do not gainsay the peculiar merits of either of these latter compositions — but deny them the position they have held. In a notice of Brainard's Poems, we took occasion to show that the common use of a certain instrument (rhythm) had tended, more than aught else, to confound humorous verse with poetry. The observation is now recalled to corroborate what we have just said in respect to the vast

effect or force of melody in itself — an effect which could elevate into even momentary confusion with the highest efforts of mind, compositions such as are the greater number of satires or burlesques.

Of the poets who have appeared most fully instinct with the principles now developed, we may mention *Keats* as the most remarkable. He is the sole British poet who has never erred in his themes. Beauty is always his aim.

We have thus shown our ground of objection to the general *themes* of Professor Longfellow. In common with all who claim the sacred title of poet, he should limit his endeavours to the creation of novel moods of beauty, in form, in colour, in sound, in sentiment; for over all this wide range has the poetry of words dominion. To what the world terms *prose* may be safely and properly left all else. The artist who doubts of his thesis, may always resolve his doubt by the single question — "might not this matter be as well or better handled in *prose?*" If it *may*, then is it no subject for the Muse. In the general acceptation of the term *Beauty* we are content to rest; being careful only to suggest that, in our peculiar views, it must be understood as inclusive of the *sublime*.

Of the pieces which constitute the present volume there are not more than one or two thoroughly fulfilling the idea above proposed; although the volume as a whole is by no means so chargeable with didacticism as Mr. Longfellow's previous book. We would mention as poems *nearly true*, "The Village Blacksmith," "The Wreck of the Hesperus," and especially "The Skeleton in Armor." In the first-mentioned we have the *beauty* of simple-mindedness as a genuine thesis; and this thesis is inimitably handled until the concluding stanza, where the spirit of legitimate poesy is aggrieved in the pointed antithetical deduction of a *moral* from what has gone before. In "The Wreck of the Hesperus" we have the *beauty* of child-like confidence and innocence, with that of the father's courage and affection. But, with slight exception, those particulars of the storm here detailed are not poetic subjects. Their thilling *horror* belongs to prose, in which it could be far more effectively discussed, as Professor Longfelow may assure himself at any moment by experiment. There *are* points of a tempest which afford the loftiest and truest poetical themes — points in which pure beauty is found, or, better still, beauty heightened into the sublime, by terror. But when we read, among other similar things, that

> The salt sea was frozen on her breast,
> The salt tears in her eyes.

we feel, if not positive disgust, at least a chilling sense of the inappropriate. In "The Skeleton in Armor" we find a pure and perfect thesis artistically treated. We find the beauty of bold courage and self-confidence, of love and maiden devotion, of reckless adventure, and finally the life-contemning grief. Combined with all this, we have numerous

points of beauty apparently insulated, but all aiding the main effect or impression. The heart is stirred, and the mind does not lament its mal-instruction. The metre is simple, sonorous, well-balanced, and fully adapted to the subject. Upon the whole, there are few truer poems than this. It has not one defect — an important one. The prose remarks prefac-ing the narrative are really *necessary*. But every work of art should con-tain within itself all that is requisite for its own comprehension. And this remark is especially true of the ballad. In poems of magnitude the mind of the reader is not, at all times, enabled to include, in one comprehen-sive survey, the proportions and proper adjustment of the whole. He is pleased, if at all, with particular passages; and the sum of his pleasure is compounded of the sums of the pleasurable sentiments inspired by these individual passages in the progress of perusal. But, in pieces of less extent, the pleasure is *unique*, in the proper acceptation of this term — the under-standing is employed, without difficulty, in the contemplation of the picture *as a whole*; and thus its effect will depend, in great measure, upon the perfection of its finish, upon the nice adaptation of its constituent parts, and especially, upon what is rightly termed by Schlegel *the unity* or totality of interest. But the practice of prefixing explanatory passages is utterly at variance with such unity. By the prefix, we are either put in possession of the subject of the poem, or some hint, historic fact, or sug-gestion, is thereby afforded, not included in the body of the piece, which, without the hint, is incomprehensible. In the latter case, while perusing the poem, the reader must revert, in mind at least, to the prefix, for the necessary explanation. In the former, the poem being a mere paraphrase of the prefix, the interest is divided between the prefix and the para-phrase. In either instance the totality of effect is destroyed.

Of the other original poems in the volume before us there is none in which the aim of instruction, or *truth*, has not been too obviously sub-stituted for the legitimate aim, *beauty*. We have heretofore taken occa-sion to say that a didactic moral might be happily made the *under-current* of a poetical theme, and we have treated this point at length in a review of Moore's "Alciphron"; but the moral thus conveyed is invariably an ill effect when obtruding beyond the upper-current of the thesis itself. Per-haps the worst specimen of this obtrusion is given us by our poet in "Blind Bartimeus" and the "Goblet of Life," where it will be observed that the *sole* interest of the upper-current of meaning depends upon its relation or reference to the under. What we read upon the surface would be *vox et præterea nihil* in default of the moral beneath. The Greek *finales* of "Blind Bartimeus" are an affectation altogether inexcusable. What the small, second-hand, Gibbonish pedantry of Byron introduced, is unworthy the imitation of Longfellow.

Of the translations we scarcely think it necessary to speak at all. We regret that our poet will persist in busying himself about such matters. *His* time might be better employed in original conception. Most of these

versions are marked with the error upon which we have commented. This error is, in fact, essentially Germanic. "The Luck of Edenhall," however, is a truly beautiful poem; and we say this with all that deference which the opinion of the "Democratic Review" demands. This composition appears to us *one of the very finest*. It has all the free, hearty, *obvious* movement of the true ballad-legend. The greatest force of language is combined in it with the richest imagination, acting in its most legitimate province. Upon the whole, we prefer it even to the "Sword-Song" of Körner. The pointed moral with which it terminates is so exceedingly natural — so perfectly fluent from the incidents — that we have hardly heart to pronounce it in ill-taste. We may observe of this ballad, in conclusion, that its subject is more *physical* than is usual in Germany. Its images are rich rather in physical than in moral beauty. And this tendency in Song is the true one. It is chiefly, if we are not mistaken — it is chiefly amid forms of physical loveliness (we use the word *forms* in its widest sense as embracing modifications of sound and colour) that the soul seeks the realisation of its dreams of BEAUTY. It is to her demand in this sense especially, that the poet, who is wise, will most frequently and most earnestly respond.

"The Children of the Lord's Supper" is, beyond doubt, a true and most beautiful poem in great part, while, in some particulars, it is too metaphysical to have any pretension to the name. We have already objected, briefly, to its metre — the ordinary Latin or Greek Hexameter — dactyls and spondees at random, with a spondee in conclusion. We maintain that the hexameter can never be introduced into our language, from the nature of that language itself. This rhythm demands, *for English ears*, a preponderance of natural spondees. Our tongue has few. Not only does the Latin and Greek, with the Swedish, and some others, abound in them; but the Greek and Roman ear had become reconciled (why or how is unknown) to the reception of artificial spondees — that is to say, spondaic words formed partly of one word and partly of another, or from an excised part of one word. In short, the ancients were content to read *as they scanned*, or nearly so. It may be safely prophesied that we shall never do this; and thus we shall never admit English hexameters. The attempt to introduce them, after the repeated failures of Sir Philip Sidney and others, is perhaps somewhat discreditable to the scholarship of Professor Longfellow. The "Democratic Review," in saying that he has triumphed over difficulties in this rhythm, has been deceived, it is evident, by the facility with which some of these verses may be read. In glancing over the poem, we do not observe a single verse which can be read, *to English ears, as a Greek hexameter*. There are many, however, which can be well read as mere English dactylic verses; such, for example, as the well-known lines of Byron, commencing

Know ye the | land where the | cypress and | myrtle.

These lines (although full of irregularities) are, in their perfection, formed of three dactyls and a cæsura — just as if we should cut short the initial verse of the Bucolics thus —

<div align="center">Tityre | tu patu | læ recu | bans —</div>

The "myrtle," at the close of Byron's line, is a double rhyme, and must be understood as one syllable.

Now a great number of Professor Longfellow's hexameters are merely these dactylic lines, *continued for two feet*. For example —

Whispered the | race of the | flowers and | merry on | balancing | branches.

In this example, also, "branches," which is a double ending, must be regarded as the cæsura, or one syllable, of which alone it has the force.

As we have already alluded, in one or two regards, to a notice of these poems which appeared in the "Democratic Review," we may as well here proceed with some few further comments upon the article in question — with whose general tenor we are happy to agree.

The Review speaks of "Maidenhood" as a poem, "not to be understood but at the expense of more time and trouble than a song can justly claim." We are scarcely less surprised at this opinion from Mr. Langtree than we were at the condemnation of "The Luck of Edenhall."

"Maidenhood" is faulty, it appears to us, only on the score of its theme, which is somewhat didactic. Its *meaning* seems simplicity itself. A maiden on the verge of womanhood, hesitating to enjoy life (for which she has a strong appetite) through a false idea of duty, is bidden to fear nothing, having purity of heart as her lion of Una.

What Mr. Langtree styles "an unfortunate peculiarity" in Mr. Longfellow, resulting from "adherence to a false system," has really been always regarded by us as one of his idiosyncratic merits. "In each poem," says the critic, "he has but *one* idea, which, in the progress of his song, is gradually unfolded, and at last reaches its full development in the concluding lines: this singleness of thought might lead a harsh critic to suspect intellectual barrenness." It leads *us*, individually, only to a full sense of the artistical power and knowledge of the poet. We confess that now, for the first time, we hear unity of conception objected to as a defect. But Mr. Langtree seems to have fallen into the singular error of supposing the poet to have absolutely *but one idea* in each of his ballads. Yet how "one idea" can be "gradually unfolded" without other ideas is, to us, a mystery of mysteries. Mr. Longfellow, very properly, has but one *leading* idea which forms the basis of his poem; but to the aid and development of this one there are innumerable others, of which the rare excellence is that all are in keeping, that none could be well omitted, that each tends to the one general effect. It is unnecessary to say another word upon this topic.

In speaking of "Excelsior," Mr. Langtree (are we wrong in attributing the notice to his very forcible pen?) seems to labour under some similar misconception. "It carries along with it," says he, "a false moral which

greatly diminishes its merit in our eyes. The great merit of a picture, whether made with the pencil or pen, is its *truth;* and this merit does not belong to Mr. Longfellow's sketch. Men of genius may, and probably do, meet with greater difficulties in their struggles with the world than their fellow men who are less highly gifted; but their power of overcoming obstacles is proportionately greater, and the result of their laborious suffering is not death but immortality."

That the chief merit of a picture is its *truth,* is an assertion deplorably erroneous. Even in Painting, which is, more essentially than Poetry, a mimetic art, the proposition cannot be sustained. Truth is not even *the aim.* Indeed it is curious to observe how very slight a degree of truth is sufficient to satisfy the mind, which acquiesces in the absence of numerous essentials in the thing depicted. An outline frequently stirs the spirit more pleasantly than the most elaborate picture. We need only refer to the compositions of Flaxman and of Retzsch. Here all details are omitted — nothing can be farther from *truth.* Without even colour the most thrilling effects are produced. In statues we are rather pleased than disgusted with *the want of the eyeball.* The hair of the Venus de Medicis *was gilded.* Truth indeed! The grapes of Zeuxis as well as the curtain of Parrhasius were received as indisputable evidence of the truthful ability of these artists — but they were not even *classed among their pictures.* If truth is the highest aim of either Painting or Poesy, then Jan Steen was a greater artist than Angelo, and Crabbe is a nobler poet than Milton.

But we have not quoted the observation of Mr. Langtree to deny its philosophy; our design was simply to show that he has misunderstood the poet. "Excelsior" has not even a remote tendency to the interpretation assigned it by the critic. It depicts the *earnest upward impulse of the soul* — an impulse not to be subdued even in Death. Despising danger, resisting pleasure, the youth, bearing the banner inscribed *"Excelsior!"* (higher still!) struggles through all difficulties to an Alpine summit. Warned to be content with the elevation attained, his cry is still *"Excelsior!"* and even in falling dead on the highest pinnacle, his cry is *still "Excelsior!"* There is yet an immortal height to be surmounted — an ascent in Eternity. The poet holds in view the idea of never-ending *progress.* That he is misunderstood is rather the misfortune of Mr. Langtree than the fault of Mr. Longfellow. There is an old adage about the difficulty of one's furnishing an auditor both with matter to be comprehended and brains for its comprehension.

Hawthorne's Twice-Told Tales

By NATHANIEL HAWTHORNE. *James Munroe & Co.: Boston*

WE HAVE always regarded the *Tale* (using this word in its popular acceptation) as affording the best prose opportunity for display of the

highest talent. It has peculiar advantages which the novel does not admit. It is, of course, a far finer field than the essay. It has even points of superiority over the poem. An accident has deprived us, this month, of our customary space for review; and thus nipped in the bud a design long cherished of treating this subject in detail; taking Mr. Hawthorne's volumes as a text. In May we shall endeavor to carry out our intention. At present we are forced to be brief.

With rare exception — in the case of Mr. Irving's "Tales of a Traveller" and a few other works of a like cast — we have had no American tales of high merit. We have had no skilful compositions — nothing which could bear examination as works of art. Of twaddle called tale-writing we have had, perhaps more than enough. We have had a superabundance of the Rosa-Matilda effusions — gilt-edged paper all *couleur de rose*: a full allowance of cut-and-thrust blue-blazing melodramaticisms; a nauseating surfeit of low miniature copying of low life, much in the manner, and with about half the merit, of the Dutch herrings and decayed cheeses of Van Tuyssel — of all this, *eheu jam satis!*

Mr. Hawthorne's volumes appear misnamed to us in two respects. In the first place they should not have been called "Twice-Told Tales" — for this is a title which will not bear repetition. If in the first collected edition they were twice-told, of course now they are thrice-told. — May we live to hear them told a hundred times. In the second place, these compositions are by no means *all* "Tales." The most of them are essays properly so called. It would have been wise in their author to have modified his title, so as to have had reference to all included. This point could have been easily arranged.

But under whatever titular blunders we receive this book, it is most cordially welcome. We have seen no prose composition by any American which can compare with *some* of these articles in the higher merits, or indeed in the lower; while there is not a single piece which would do dishonor to the best of the British essayists.

"The Rill from the Town Pump" which, through the *ad captandum* nature of its title, has attracted more of the public notice than any other of Mr. Hawthorne's compositions, is perhaps, the *least* meritorious. Among his best we may briefly mention "The Hollow of the Three Hills"; "The Minister's Black Veil"; "Wakefield"; "Mr. Higginbotham's Catastrophe"; "Fancy's Show-Box"; "Dr. Heidegger's Experiment"; "David Swan"; "The Wedding Knell"; and "The White Old Maid." It is remarkable that all of these, with one exception, are from the first volume.

The style of Mr. Hawthorne is purity itself. His *tone* is singularly effective — wild, plaintive, thoughtful, and in full accordance with his themes. We have only to object that there is insufficient diversity in these themes themselves, or rather in their character. His *originality* both of incident and reflection is very remarkable; and this trait alone would

insure him at least *our* warmest regard and commendation. We speak here chiefly of the tales; the essays are not so markedly novel. Upon the whole we look upon him as one of the few men of indisputable genius to whom our country has as yet given birth. As such, it will be our delight to do him honor; and lest, in these undigested and cursory remarks, without proof and without explanation, we should appear to do him *more* honor than is his due, we postpone all farther comment until a more favorable opportunity.

We said a few hurried words about Mr. Hawthorne in our last number, with the design of speaking more fully in the present. We are still, however, pressed for room, and must necessarily discuss his volumes more briefly and more at random than their high merits deserve.

The book professes to be a collection of *tales,* yet is, in two respects, misnamed. These pieces are now in their third republication, and, of course, are thrice-told. Moreover, they are by no means *all* tales, either in the ordinary or in the legitimate understanding of the term. Many of them are pure essays; for example, "Sights from a Steeple," "Sunday at Home," "Little Annie's Ramble," "A Rill from the Town Pump," "The Toll-Gatherer's Day," "The Haunted Mind," "The Sister Years," "Snow-Flakes," "Night Sketches," and "Foot-Prints on the Sea-Shore." We mention these matters chiefly on account of their discrepancy with that marked precision and finish by which the body of the work is distinguished.

Of the Essays just named, we must be content to speak in brief. They are each and all beautiful, without being characterized by the polish and adaptation so visible in the tales proper. A painter would at once note their leading or predominant feature, and style it *repose*. There is no attempt at effect. All is quiet, thoughtful, subdued. Yet this respose may exist simultaneously with high originality of thought; and Mr. Hawthorne has demonstrated the fact. At every turn we meet with novel combinations; yet these combinations never surpass the limits of the quiet. We are soothed as we read; and withal is a calm astonishment that ideas so apparently obvious have never occurred or been presented to us before. Herein our author differs materially from Lamb or Hunt or Hazlitt — who, with vivid originality of manner and expression, have less of the true novelty of thought than is generally supposed, and whose originality, at best, has an uneasy and meretricious quaintness, replete with startling effects unfounded in nature, and inducing trains of reflection which lead to no satisfactory result. The Essays of Hawthorne have much of the character of Irving, with more of originality, and less of finish; while, compared with the Spectator, they have a vast superiority at all points. The Spectator, Mr. Irving, and Mr. Hawthorne have in common that tranquil and subdued manner which we have chosen to denominate *repose*; but, in the case of the two former, this repose is attained rather by the

absence of novel combination, or of originality, than otherwise, and consists chiefly in the calm, quiet, unostentatious expression of common-place thoughts, in an unambitious unadulterated Saxon. In them, by strong effort, we are made to conceive the absence of all. In the essays before us the absence of effort is too obvious to be mistaken, and a strong under-current of *suggestion* runs continuously beneath the upper stream of the tranquil thesis. In short, these effusions of Mr. Hawthorne are the product of a truly imaginative intellect, restrained, and in some measure repressed, by fastidiousness of taste, by constitutional melancholy and by indolence.

But it is of his tales that we desire principally to speak. The tale proper, in our opinion, affords unquestionably the fairest field for the exercise of the loftiest talent, which can be afforded by the wide domains of mere prose. Were we bidden to say how the highest genius could be most advantageously employed for the best display of its own powers, we should answer, without hesitation — in the composition of a rhymed poem, not to exceed in length what might be perused in an hour. Within this limit alone can the highest order of true poetry exist. We need only here say, upon this topic, that, in almost all classes of composition, the unity of effect or impression is a point of the greatest importance. It is clear, more-over, that this unity cannot be thoroughly preserved in productions whose perusal cannot be completed at one sitting. We may continue the reading of a prose composition, from the very nature of prose itself, much longer than we can persevere, to any good purpose, in the perusal of a poem. This latter, if truly fulfilling the demands of the poetic sentiment, induces an exaltation of the soul which cannot be long sustained. All high excitements are necessarily transient. Thus a long poem is a paradox. And, without unity of impression, the deepest effects cannot be brought about. Epics were the offspring of an imperfect sense of Art, and their reign is no more. A poem *too* brief may produce a vivid, but never an intense or enduring impression. Without a certain continuity of effort — without a certain duration or repetition of purpose — the soul is never deeply moved. There must be the dropping of the water upon the rock. De Béranger has wrought brilliant things — pungent and spirit-stirring — but, like all im-massive bodies, they lack *momentum,* and thus fail to satisfy the Poetic Sentiment. They sparkle and excite, but, from want of continuity, fail deeply to impress. Extreme brevity will degenerate into epigrammatism; but the sin of extreme length is even more unpardonable. *In medio tutissimus ibis.*

Were we called upon, however, to designate that class of composition which, next to such a poem as we have suggested, should best fulfil the demands of high genius — should offer it the most advantageous field of exertion — we should unhesitatingly speak of the prose tale, as Mr. Hawthorne has here exemplified it. We allude to the short prose narra-tive, requiring from a half-hour to one or two hours in its perusal. The

ordinary novel is objectionable, from its length, for reasons already stated in substance. As it cannot be read at one sitting, it deprives itself, of course, of the immense force derivable from *totality*. Worldly interests intervening during the pauses of perusal, modify, annul, or counteract, in a greater or less degree, the impressions of the book. But simple cessation in reading, would, of itself, be sufficient to destroy the true unity. In the brief tale, however, the author is enabled to carry out the fulness of his intention, be it what it may. During the hour of perusal the soul of the reader is at the writer's control. There are no external or extrinsic influences — resulting from weariness or interruption.

A skilful literary artist has constructed a tale. If wise, he has not fashioned his thoughts to accommodate his incidents; but having conceived, with deliberate care, a certain unique or single *effect* to be wrought out, he then invents such incidents — he then combines such events as may best aid him in establishing this preconceived effect. If his very initial sentence tend not to the out-bringing of this effect, then he has failed in his first step. In the whole composition there should be no word written, of which the tendency, direct or indirect, is not to the one pre-established design. And by such means, with such care and skill, a picture is at length painted which leaves in the mind of him who contemplates it with a kindred art, a sense of the fullest satisfaction. The idea of the tale has been presented unblemished, because undisturbed; and this is an end unattainable by the novel. Undue brevity is just as exceptionable here as in the poem; but undue length is yet more to be avoided.

We have said that the tale has a point of superiority even over the poem. In fact, while the *rhythm* of this latter is an essential aid in the development of the poem's highest idea — the idea of the Beautiful — the artificialities of this rhythm are an inseparable bar to the development of all points of thought or expression which have their basis in *Truth*. But Truth is often, and in very great degree, the aim of the tale. Some of the finest tales are tales of ratiocination. Thus the field of this species of composition, if not in so elevated a region on the mountain of Mind, is a table-land of far vaster extent than the domain of the mere poem. Its products are never so rich, but infinitely more numerous, and more appreciable by the mass of mankind. The writer of the prose tale, in short, may bring to his theme a vast variety of modes or inflections of thought and expression — (the ratiocinative, for example, the sarcastic or the humorous) which are not only antagonistical to the nature of the poem, but absolutely forbidden by one of its most peculiar and indispensable adjuncts; we allude, of course, to rhythm. It may be added, here, *par parenthèse,* that the author who aims at the purely beautiful in a prose tale is laboring at great disadvantage. For Beauty can be better treated in the poem. Not so with terror, or passion, or horror, or a multitude of such other points. And here it will be seen how full of prejudice are the usual animadversions against those *tales of effect,* many fine examples of which were

found in the earlier numbers of Blackwood. The impressions produced were wrought in a legitimate sphere of action, and constituted a legitimate although sometimes an exaggerated interest. They were relished by every man of genius: although there were found many men of genius who condemned them without just ground. The true critic will but demand that that the design intended be accomplished, to the fullest extent, by the means most advantageously applicable.

We have very few American tales of real merit — we may say, indeed, none, with the exception of "The Tales of a Traveller" of Washington Irving, and these "Twice-Told Tales" of Mr. Hawthorne. Some of the pieces of Mr. John Neal abound in vigor and originality; but in general, his compositions of this class are excessively diffuse, extravagant, and indicative of an imperfect sentiment of Art. Articles at random are, now and then, met with in our periodicals which might be advantageously compared with the best effusions of the British Magazines; but, upon the whole, we are far behind our progenitors in this department of literature.

Of Mr. Hawthorne's Tales we would say, emphatically, that they belong to the highest region of Art — and Art subservient to genius of a very lofty order. We had supposed, with good reason for so supposing, that he had been thrust into his present position by one of the impudent *cliques* which beset our literature, and whose pretensions it is our full purpose to expose at the earliest opportunity; but we have been most agreeably mistaken. We know of few compositions which the critic can more honestly commend than these "Twice-Told Tales." As Americans, we feel proud of the book.

Mr. Hawthorne's distinctive trait is invention, creation, imagination, originality — a trait which, in the literature of fiction, is positively worth all the rest. But the nature of originality, so far as regards its manifestation in letters, is but imperfectly understood. The inventive or original mind as frequently displays itself in novelty of *tone* as in novelty of matter. Mr. Hawthorne is original at *all* points.

It would be a matter of some difficulty to designate the best of these tales; we repeat that, without exception, they are beautiful. "Wakefield" is remarkable for the skill with which an old idea — a well-known incident — is worked up or discussed. A man of whims conceives the purpose of quitting his wife and residing *incognito*, for twenty years, in her immediate neighborhood. Something of this kind actually happened in London. The force of Mr. Hawthorne's tale lies in the analysis of the motives which must or might have impelled the husband to such folly, in the first instance, with the possible causes of his perseverance. Upon this thesis a sketch of singular power has been constructed.

"The Wedding Knell" is full of the boldest imagination — an imagination fully controlled by taste. The most captious critic could find no flaw in this production.

"The Minister's Black Veil" is a masterly composition of which the

sole defect is that to the rabble its exquisite skill will be *caviare.* The *obvious* meaning of this article will be found to smother its insinuated one. The *moral* put into the mouth of the dying minister will be supposed to convey the *true* import of the narrative; and that a crime of dark dye, (having reference to the "young lady") has been committed, is a point which only minds congenial with that of the author will perceive.

"Mr. Higginbotham's Catastrophe" is vividly original and managed most dexterously.

"Dr. Heidegger's Experiment" is exceedingly well imagined, and executed with surpassing ability. The artist breathes in every line of it.

"The White Old Maid" is objectionable, even more than the "Minister's Black Veil," on the score of its mysticism. Even with the thoughtful and analytic, there will be much trouble in penetrating its entire import.

"The Hollow of the Three Hills" we would quote in full, had we space; — not as evincing higher talent than any of the other pieces, but as affording an excellent example of the author's peculiar ability. The subject is commonplace. A witch subjects the Distant and the Past to the view of a mourner. It has been the fashion to describe, in such cases, a mirror in which the images of the absent appear; or a cloud of smoke is made to arise, and thence the figures are gradually unfolded. Mr. Hawthorne has wonderfully heightened his effect by making the ear, in place of the eye, the medium by which the fantasy is conveyed. The head of the mourner is enveloped in the cloak of the witch, and within its magic folds there arise sounds which have an all-sufficient intelligence. Throughout this article also, the artist is conspicuous — not more in positive than in negative merits. Not only is all done that should be done, but (what perhaps is an end with more difficulty attained) there is nothing done which should not be. Every word *tells,* and there is not a word which does *not* tell.

In "Howe's Masquerade" we observe something which resembles a plagiarism — but which *may be* a very flattering coincidence of thought. We quote the passage in question.

"*With a dark flush of wrath* upon his brow they saw the general *draw his sword* and *advance to meet* the figure *in the cloak* before the latter had stepped one pace upon the floor.

" 'Villain, *unmuffle* yourself,' cried he, 'you pass no farther!'

"The figure, without blanching a hair's breadth from the sword which was pointed at his breast, made a solemn pause, and lowered the cape of the cloak from his face, yet not sufficiently for the spectators to catch a glimpse of it. But Sir William Howe had evidently seen enough. The sternness of his countenance gave place to a look of wild amazement, if not horror, while he recoiled several steps from the figure, *and let fall his sword* upon the floor."

The idea here is, that the figure in the cloak is the phantom or reduplication of Sir William Howe; but in an article called "William Wilson," one of the "Tales of the Grotesque and Arabesque," we have not only the same idea, but the same idea similarly presented in several respects. We quote two paragraphs, which our readers may compare with what has been already given. We have italicized, above, the immediate particulars of resemblance.

"The brief moment in which I averted my eyes had been sufficient to produce, apparently, a material change in the arrangement at the upper or farther end of the room. A large mirror, it appeared to me, now stood where none had been perceptible before: and as I stepped up to it in extremity of terror, mine own image, but with features all pale and dabbled in blood, *advanced* with a feeble and tottering gait to meet me.

"Thus it appeared I say, but was not. It was Wilson, who then stood before me in the agonies of dissolution. Not a line in all the marked and singular lineaments of that face which was not even identically mine own. *His mask and cloak lay where he had thrown them, upon the floor.*"

Here it will be observed, not only are the two general conceptions identical, but there are various *points* of similarity. In each case the figure seen is the wraith or duplication of the beholder. In each case the scene is a masquerade. In each case the figure is cloaked. In each, there is a quarrel — that is to say, angry words pass between the parties. In each the beholder is enraged. In each the cloak and sword fall upon the floor. The "villain, unmuffle yourself," of Mr. H. is precisely paralleled by a passage at page 56 of "William Wilson."

In the way of objection we have scarcely a word to say of these tales. There is, perhaps, a somewhat too general or prevalent *tone* — a tone of melancholy and mysticism. The subjects are insufficiently varied. There is not so much of *versatility* evinced as we might well be warranted in expecting from the high powers of Mr. Hawthorne. But beyond these trivial exceptions we have really none to make. The style is purity itself. Force abounds. High imagination gleams from every page. Mr. Hawthorne is a man of the truest genius. We only regret that the limits of our Magazine will not permit us to pay him that full tribute of commendation, which, under other circumstances, we should be so eager to pay.

The American Drama

A BIOGRAPHIST of Berryer calls him *"l'homme qui, dans ses description, demande le plus grande quantité possible d' antithèse,"* — but that ever-recurring topic, the decline of the drama, seems to have consumed of late more of the material in question than would have sufficed for a dozen prime ministers — even admitting them to be French. Every trick

of thought and every harlequinade of phrase have been put in operation for the purpose *"de nier ce qui est, et d'expliquer ce qui n'est pas."*

Ce qui n'est pas: — for the drama has *not declined.* The facts and the philosophy of the case seem to be these. The great opponent to Progress is Conservatism. In other words — the great adversary of Invention is Imitation: the propositions are in spirit identical. Just as an art is imitative, is it stationary. The most imitative arts are the most prone to repose — and the converse. Upon the utilitarian — upon the business arts, where Necessity impels, Invention, Necessity's well-understood offspring, is ever in attendance. And the less we see of the mother the less we behold of the child. No one complains of the decline of the art of Engineering. Here the Reason, which never retrogrades or reposes, is called into play. But let us glance at Sculpture. We are not *worse* here than the ancients, let pedantry say what it may (the Venus of Canova is worth, at any time, two of that of Cleomenes), but it is equally certain that we have made, in general, no advances; and Sculpture, properly considered, is perhaps the *most* imitative of all arts which have a right to the title of Art at all. Looking next at Painting, we find that we have to boast of progress only in the ratio of the inferior imitativeness of Painting, when compared with Sculpture. As far indeed as we have any means of judging, our improvement has been exceedingly little, and did we know anything of ancient Art in this department, we might be astonished at discovering that we had advanced even far less than we suppose. As regards Architecture, whatever progress we have made has been precisely in those particulars which have no reference to imitation: — that is to say, we have improved the utilitarian and not the ornamental provinces of the art. Where Reason predominated, we advanced; where mere Feeling or Taste was the guide, we remained as we were.

Coming to the Drama, we shall see that in its mechanisms we have made progress, while in its spirituality we have done little or nothing for centuries certainly — and, perhaps, little or nothing for thousands of years. And this is because what we term the spirituality of the drama is precisely its imitative portion — is exactly that portion which distinguishes it as one of the principal of the imitative arts.

Sculptors, painters, dramatists, are, from the very nature of their material, — their spiritual material — imitators — conservatists — prone to repose in old Feeling and in antique Taste. For this reason — and for this reason only — the arts of Sculpture, Painting, and the Drama have not advanced — or have advanced feebly, and inversely in the ratio of their imitativeness.

But it by no means follows that either has *declined.* All *seem* to have declined, because they have remained stationary while the multitudinous other arts (of reason) have flitted so rapidly by them. In the same manner the traveller by railroad can imagine that the trees by the wayside are retrograding. The trees in this case are absolutely stationary — but

the Drama has not been altogether so, although its progress has been so slight as not to interfere with the general effect — that of seeming retrogradation or decline.

This seeming retrogradation, however, is to all practical intents an absolute one. Whether the Drama has declined, or whether it has merely remained stationary, is a point of no importance, so far as concerns the public encouragement of the Drama. It is unsupported, in either case, because it does not deserve support.

But if this stagnation, or deterioration, grows out of the very idiosyncracy of the drama itself, as one of the principal of the imitative arts, how is it possible that a remedy shall be applied — since it is clearly impossible to alter the nature of the art, and yet leave it the art which it now is?

We have already spoken of the improvements effected in Architecture, in all its utilitarian departments, and in the Drama, at all the points of its mechanism. "Wherever Reason predominates, we advance; where mere Feeling or Taste is the guide, we remain as we are." We wish now to suggest that, by the engrafting of Reason upon Feeling and Taste, we shall be able, and thus alone shall be able, to force the modern drama into the production of any profitable fruit.

At present, what is it we do? We are content if, with Feeling and Taste, a dramatist does *as other dramatists have done*. The most successful of the more immediately modern playwrights has been Sheridan Knowles, and to play Sheridan Knowles seems to be the highest ambition of our writers for the stage. Now the author of "The Hunchback" possesses what we are weak enough to term the true "dramatic feeling," and this true dramatic feeling he has manifested in the most preposterous series of imitations of the Elizabethan drama by which ever mankind were insulted and begulled. Not only did he adhere to the old plots, the old characters, the old stage conventionalities throughout; but he went even so far as to persist in the obsolete phraseologies of the Elizabethan period — and, just in proportion to his obstinacy and absurdity at all points, did we pretend to like him the better, and pretend to consider him a great dramatist.

Pretend — for every particle of it was pretence. Never was enthusiasm more utterly false than that which so many "respectable audiences" endeavoured to get up for these plays — endeavoured to get up, first, because there was a general desire to see the drama revive, and secondly, because we had been all along entertaining the fancy that "the decline of the drama" meant little, if anything, else than its deviation from the Elizabethan routine — and that, consequently, the return to the Elizabethan routine was, and of necessity must be, the revival of the drama.

But if the principles we have been at some trouble in explaining are true — and most profoundly do we feel them to be so — if the spirit of imitation is, in fact, the real source of the drama's stagnation — and if

it is so because of the tendency in all imitation to render Reason sub-
servient to Feeling and to Taste — it is clear that only by deliberate
counteracting of the spirit, and of the tendency of the spirit, we can hope
to succeed in the drama's revival.

The first thing necessary is to burn or bury the "old models," and to
forget, as quickly as possible, that ever a play has been penned. The sec-
ond thing is to consider *de novo* what are the *capabilities* of the drama —
not merely what hitherto have been its conventional purposes. The third
and last point has reference to the composition of a play (showing to
the fullest extent these capabilities) conceived and constructed with
Feeling and with Taste, but with Feeling and Taste guided and con-
trolled in every particular by the details of Reason — of Common Sense
— in a word, of a Natural Art.

It is obvious, in the meantime, that towards the good end in view
much may be effected by discriminative criticism on what has already
been done. The field, thus stated, is, of course, practically illimitable —
and to Americans the American drama is the special point of interest.
We propose, therefore, in a series of papers, to take a somewhat delib-
erate survey of some few of the most noticeable American plays. We
shall do this without reference either to the date of the composition or
its adaptation for the closet or the stage. We shall speak with absolute
frankness both of merits and defects — our principal object being under-
stood not as that of mere commentary on the individual play — but on
the drama in general, and on the American drama in especial, of which
each individual play is a constituent part. We will commence at once
with

TORTESA, THE USURER

This is the third dramatic attempt of Mr. Willis, and may be regarded
as particularly successful, since it has received, both on the stage and in
the closet, no stinted measure of commendation. This success, as well as
the high reputation of the author, will justify us in a more extended notice
of the play than might, under other circumstances, be desirable.

The story runs thus: — Tortesa, a usurer of Florence, and whose char-
acter is a mingled web of good and evil feelings, gets into his possession
the palace and lands of a certain Count Falcone. The usurer would wed
the daughter (Isabella) of Falcone, not through love, but in his own
words,

"To please a devil that inhabits him — "

in fact, to mortify the pride of the nobility, and avenge himself of their
scorn. He therefore bargains with Falcone [a narrow-souled villain] for
the hand of Isabella. The deed of the Falcone property is restored to the
Count upon an agreement that the lady shall marry the usurer — this
contract being invalid should Falcone change his mind in regard to the

marriage, or should the maiden demur — but valid should the wedding be prevented through any fault of Tortesa, or through any accident not springing from the will of the father or child. The first Scene makes us aware of this bargain, and introduces us to Zippa, a glover's daughter, who resolves, with a view of befriending Isabella, to feign a love for Tortesa [which, in fact, she partially feels], hoping thus to break off the match.

The second Scene makes us acquainted with a young painter (Angelo), poor, but of high talents and ambition, and with his servant (Tomaso), an old bottle-loving rascal, entertaining no very exalted opinion of his master's abilities. Tomaso does some injury to a picture, and Angelo is about to run him through the body when he is interrupted by a sudden visit from the Duke of Florence, attended by Falcone. The Duke is enraged at the murderous attempt, but admires the paintings in the studio. Finding that the rage of the great man will prevent his patronage if he knows the aggressor as the artist, Angelo passes off Tomaso as himself (Angelo), making an exchange of names. This is a point of some importance, as it introduces the true Angelo to a job which he has long coveted — the painting of the portrait of Isabella, of whose beauty he had become enamoured through report. The Duke wishes the portrait painted. Falcone, however, on account of a promise to Tortesa, would have objected to admit to his daughter's presence the handsome Angelo, but in regard to Tomaso has no scruple. Supposing Tomaso to be Angelo and the artist, the Count writes a note to Isabella, requiring her "to admit the painter Angelo." The real Angelo is thus admitted. He and the lady love at first sight (much in the manner of Romeo and Juliet), each ignorant of the other's attachment.

The third Scene of the second Act is occupied with a conversation between Falcone and Tortesa, during which a letter arrives from the Duke, who, having heard of the intended sacrifice of Isabella, offers to redeem the Count's lands and palace, and desires him to preserve his daughter for a certain Count Julian. But Isabella, — who, before seeing Angelo, had been willing to sacrifice herself for her father's sake, and who, since seeing him, had entertained hopes of escaping the hateful match through means of a plot entered into by herself and Zippa — Isabella, we say, is now in despair. To gain time, she at once feigns a love for the usurer, and indignantly rejects the proposal of the Duke. The hour for the wedding draws near. The lady has prepared a sleeping potion, whose effects resemble those of death. (Romeo and Juliet.) She swallows it — knowing that her supposed corpse would lie at night, pursuant to an old custom, in the sanctuary of the cathedral; and believing that Angelo — whose love for herself she has elicited, by a stratagem, from his own lips — will watch by the body, in the strength of his devotion. Her ultimate design (we may suppose, for it is not told) is to confess all to her lover on her revival, and throw herself upon his protection

— their marriage being concealed, and herself regarded as dead by the world. Zippa, who *really* loves Angelo — (her love for Tortesa, it must be understood, is a very equivocal feeling, for the fact cannot be denied that Mr. Willis makes her love both at the same time) — Zippa, who really loves Angelo — who has discovered his passion for Isabella — and who, as well as that lady, believes that the painter will watch the corpse in the cathedral, — determines, through jealousy, to prevent his so doing, and with this view informs Tortesa that she has learned it to be Angelo's design to steal the body *for artistical purposes,* — in short, as a model to be used in his studio. The usurer, in consequence, sets a guard at the doors of the cathedral. This guard does, in fact, prevent the lover from watching the corpse, but, it appears, does *not* prevent the lady, on her revival and disappointment in not seeing the one she sought, from passing unperceived from the church. Weakened by her long sleep, she wanders aimlessly through the streets, and at length finds herself, when just sinking with exhaustion, at the door of her father. She has no resource but to knock. The Count, who here, we must say, acts very much as Thimble of old — the knight, we mean, of the "scolding wife" — maintains that she is dead, and shuts the door in her face. In other words, he supposes it to be the ghost of his daughter who speaks; and so the lady is left to perish on the steps. Meantime Angelo is absent from home, attempting to get access to the cathedral; and his servant Tomaso takes the opportunity of absenting himself also, and of indulging his bibulous propensities while perambulating the town. He finds Isabella as we left her; and through motives which we will leave Mr. Willis to explain, conducts her unresistingly to Angelo's residence, and — *deposits her in Angelo's bed.* The artist now returns — Tomaso is kicked out of doors — and we are not told, but left to presume, that a full explanation and perfect understanding are brought about between the lady and her lover.

We find them, next morning, in the studio, where stands, leaning against an easel, the portrait (a full length) of Isabella, with curtains adjusted before it. The stage-directions, moreover, inform us that "the black wall of the room is such as to form a natural ground for the picture." While Angelo is occupied in retouching it, he is interrupted by the arrival of Tortesa with a guard, and is accused of having stolen the corpse from the sanctuary — the lady, meanwhile, having stepped behind the curtain. The usurer insists upon seeing the painting, with a view of ascertaining whether any new touches had been put upon it, which would argue an examination, *post mortem,* of those charms of neck and bosom which the living Isabella would not have unveiled. Resistance in vain — the curtain is torn down; but, to the surprise of Angelo, the lady herself is discovered, "with her hands crossed on her breast, and her eyes fixed on the ground, standing motionless in the frame which had contained the picture." The *tableau,* we are to believe, deceives Tortesa,

who steps back to contemplate what he supposes to be the portrait of his betrothed. In the meantime, the guards, having searched the house, find the veil which had been thrown over the imagined corpse in the sanctuary, and upon this evidence the artist is carried before the Duke. Here he is accused, not only of sacrilege, but of the murder of Isabella, and is about to be condemned to death, when his mistress comes forward in person; thus resigning herself to the usurer to save the life of her lover. But the noble nature of Tortesa now breaks forth; and, smitten with admiration of the lady's conduct, as well as convinced that her love for himself was feigned, he resigns her to Angelo — although now feeling and acknowledging for the first time that a fervent love has, in his own bosom, assumed the place of the misanthropic ambition which, hitherto, had alone actuated him in seeking her hand. Moreover, he endows Isabella with the lands of her father Falcone. The lovers are thus made happy. The usurer weds Zippa; and the curtain drops upon the promise of the Duke to honour the double nuptials with his presence.

This story, as we have given it, hangs better together (Mr. Willis will pardon our modesty), and is altogether more easily comprehended, than in the words of the play itself. We have really put the best face upon the matter, and presented the whole in the simplest and clearest light in our power. We mean to say that "Tortesa" (partaking largely, in this respect, of the drama of Cervantes and Calderon) is over-clouded — rendered misty — by a world of unnecessary and impertinent *intrigue*. This folly was adopted by the Spanish comedy, and is imitated by us, with the idea of imparting "action," "business," "vivacity." But vivacity, however desirable, can be attained in many other ways, and is dearly purchased, indeed, when the price is intelligibility.

The truth is that *cant* has never attained a more owl-like dignity than in the discussion of dramatic principle. A modern stage critic is nothing, if not a lofty contemner of all things simple and direct. He delights in mystery — revels in mystification — has transcendental notions concerning P. S. and O. P., and talks about "stage business and stage effect" as if he were discussing the differential calculus. For much of all this we are indebted to the somewhat overprofound criticisms of Augustus William Schlegel.

But the *dicta* of common sense are of universal application, and, touching this matter of *intrigue*, if, from its superabundance, we are compelled, even in the quiet and critical *perusal* of a play, to pause frequently and reflect long — to re-read passages over and over again, for the purpose of gathering their bearing upon the whole — of maintaining in our mind a general connection — what but fatigue can result from the exertion? How, then, when we come to the representation? — when these passages — trifling, perhaps, in themselves, but important when considered in relation to the plot — are hurried and blurred over in the stuttering enunciation of some miserable rantipole, or omitted altogether

through the constitutional lapse of memory so peculiar to those lights of the age and stage, bedight (from being of no conceivable use) supernumeraries? For it must be borne in mind that these bits of *intrigue* (we use the term in the sense of the German critics) appertain generally, indeed altogether, to the after thoughts of the drama — to the underplots — are met with consequently, in the mouth of the lackeys and chambermaids — and are thus consigned to the tender mercies of the *stellæ minores*. Of course we get but an imperfect idea of what is going on before our eyes. Action after action ensues whose mystery we can not unlock without the little key which these barbarians have thrown away and lost. Our weariness increases in proportion to the number of these embarrassments, and if the play escape damnation at all, it escapes *in spite* of that intrigue to which, in nine cases out of ten, the author attributes his success, and which he *will* persist in valuing exactly in proportion to the misapplied labour it has cost him.

But dramas of this kind are said, in our customary parlance, to "abound in *plot*." We have never yet met any one, however, who could tell us what precise ideas he connected with the phrase. A mere succession of incidents, even the most spirited, will no more constitute a plot than a multiplication of zeros, even the most infinite, will result in the production of a unit. This all will admit — but few trouble themselves to think further. The common notion seems to be in favour of mere *complexity*; but a plot, properly understood, is perfect only inasmuch as we shall find ourselves unable to detach from it *or disarrange* any single incident involved, without *destruction* to the mass.

This we say is the point of perfection — a point never yet attained, but not on that account unattainable. Practically, we may consider a plot as of high excellence, when no one of its component parts shall be susceptible of *removal* without *detriment* to the whole. Here, indeed, is a vast lowering of the demand — and with less than this no writer of refined taste should content himself.

As this subject is not only in itself of great importance, but will have at all points a bearing upon what we shall say hereafter, in the examination of various plays, we shall be pardoned for quoting from the "Democratic Review" some passages (of our own which enter more particularly into the *rationale* of the subject: —

"All the Bridgewater treatises have failed in noticing the *great* idiosyncrasy in the Divine system of adaptation: — that idiosyncrasy which stamps the adaptation as divine, in distinction from that which is the work of merely human constructiveness. I speak of the complete *mutuality* of adaptation. For example: — in human constructions, a particular cause has a particular effect — a particular purpose brings about a particular object; but we see no reciprocity. The effect does not react upon the cause — the object does not change relations with the purpose. In Divine constructions, the object is either object or purpose as we choose

to regard it, while the purpose is either purpose or object; so that we can never (abstractly — without concretion — without reference to facts of the moment) decide which is which.

"For secondary example: — In polar climates, the human frame, to maintain its animal heat, requires, for combustion in the capillary system, an abundant supply of highly azotized food, such as train oil. Again: — in polar climates nearly the sole food afforded man is the oil of abundant seals and whales. Now whether is oil at hand because imperatively demanded? or whether is it the only thing demanded because the only thing to be obtained? It is impossible to say: — there is an absolute reciprocity of adaptation for which we seek in vain among the works of man.

"The Bridgewater tractists may have avoided this point, on account of its apparent tendency to overthrow the idea of *cause* in general — consequently of a First Cause — of God. But it is more probable that they have failed to perceive what no one preceding them has, to my knowledge, perceived.

"The pleasure which we derive from any exertion of human ingenuity, is in the direct ratio of the *approach* to this species of reciprocity between cause and effect. In the construction of *plot*, for example, in fictitious literature, we should aim at so arranging the points, or incidents, that we cannot distinctly see, in respect to any one of them, whether that one depends from any one other or upholds it. In this sense, of course, perfection of plot is unattainable *in fact* — because Man is the constructor. The plots of God are perfect. The Universe is a plot of God."

The pleasure derived from the contemplation of the unity resulting from plot is far more intense than is ordinarily supposed, and, as in Nature we meet with no such combination of *incident*, appertains to a very lofty region of the ideal. In speaking thus we have not said that plot is more than an adjunct to the drama — more than a perfectly distinct and separable source of pleasure. It is *not* an essential. In its intense artificiality it may even be conceived injurious in a certain degree (unless constructed with consummate skill) to that real *lifelikeness* which is the soul of the drama of character. Good dramas have been written with very little plot — capital dramas might be written with none at all. Some plays of high merit, having plot, abound in irrelevant incident — in incident, we mean, which could be displaced or removed altogether without effect upon the plot itself, and yet are by no means objectionable as dramas; and for this reason — that the incidents are *evidently* irrelevant — *obviously* episodical. Of their disgressive nature the spectator is so immediately aware that he views them, as they arise, in the simple light of interlude, and does not fatigue his attention by attempting to establish for them a connection, or more than an illustrative connection, with the great interests of the subject. Such are the plays of Shakespeare. But all this is very different from *that* irrelevancy of

intrigue which disfigures and very usually damns the work of the un-
skilful artist. With him the great error lies in *inconsequence*. Underplot
is piled upon underplot (the very word is a paradox), and all to no pur-
pose — *to no end*. The interposed incidents have no ultimate effect upon
the main ones. They may hang upon the mass — they may even coalesce
with it, or, as in some intricate cases, they may be so intimately blended
as to be lost amid the chaos which they have been instrumental in bring-
ing about — but still they have no portion in the plot, which exists, if
at all, independently of their influence. Yet the *attempt* is made by the
author to establish and demonstrate a dependence — an identity; and it
is the *obviousness of this attempt* which is the cause of weariness in the
spectator, who, of course, cannot at once see that his attention is chal-
lenged to no purpose — that intrigues so obtrusively forced upon it are
to be found, in the end, without effect upon the leading interests of
the day.

"Tortesa" will afford us plentiful examples of this irrelevancy of in-
trigue — of this misconception of the nature and of the capacities of
plot. We have said that our digest of the story is more easy of compre-
hension than the detail of Mr. Willis. If so, it is because we have for-
borne to give such portions as had no influence upon the whole. These
served but to embarrass the narrative and fatigue the attention. How
much was irrelevant is shown by the brevity of the space in which we
have recorded, somewhat at length, all the influential incidents of a
drama of five acts. There is scarcely a scene in which is not to be found
the germ of an underplot — a germ, however, which seldom proceeds
beyond the condition of a bud, or, if so fortunate as to swell into a
flower, arrives, in no single instance, at the dignity of fruit. Zippa, a lady
altogether without character (dramatic), is the most pertinacious of all
conceivable concoctors of plans never to be matured — of vast designs
that terminate in nothing — of *cul-de-sac* machinations. She plots in one
page and counter-plots in the next. She schemes her way from P. S. to
O. P., and intrigues perseveringly from the footlights to the slips. A very
singular instance of the inconsequence of her manœuvres is found to-
wards the conclusion of the play. The whole of the second scene (occu-
pying five pages), in the fifth act, is obviously introduced for the pur-
pose of giving her information, through Tomaso's means, of Angelo's
arrest for the murder of Isabella. Upon learning his danger she rushes
from the stage, to be present at the trial, exclaiming that her evidence
can save his life. We, the audience, of course applaud, and now look
with interest to her movements in the scene of the judgment-hall. She,
Zippa, we think, is somebody after all; she will be the means of Angelo's
salvation; she will thus be the chief unraveller of the plot. All eyes are
bent, therefore, upon Zippa — but, alas! upon the point at issue, Zippa
does not so much as open her mouth. It is scarcely too much to say that
not a single action of this impertinent little busybody has any real influ-

ence upon the play; — yet she appears upon every occasion — appearing only to perplex.

Similar things abound; we should not have space even to allude to them all. The whole conclusion of the play is supererogatory. The immensity of pure *fuss* with which it is overloaded forces us to the reflection that all of it might have been avoided by one word of explanation to the Duke — an amiable man who admires the talents of Angelo, and who, *to prevent Isabella's marrying against her will*, had *previously* offered to free Falcone of his bonds to the usurer. That he would free him *now*, and thus set all matters straight, the spectator cannot doubt for an instant, and he can conceive no better reason why explanations are *not* made than that Mr. Willis does not think proper they should be. In fact, the whole drama is exceedingly ill *motivirt*.

We have already mentioned an inadvertence, in the fourth Act, where Isabella is made to escape from the sanctuary through the midst of guards who prevented the ingress of Angelo. Another occurs where Falcone's conscience is made to reprove him, upon the appearance of his daughter's supposed ghost, for having occasioned her death by forcing her to marry against her will. The author had forgotten that Falcone submitted to the wedding, after the Duke's interposition, only upon Isabella's assurance *that she really loved the usurer*. In the third Scene, too, of the first Act, the imagination of the spectator is no doubt a little taxed when he finds Angelo, in the first moment of his introduction to the palace of Isabella, commencing her portrait by laying on colour after colour, before he has made any attempt at an outline. In the last Act, moreover, Tortesa gives to Isabella a deed

> "Of the Falcone palaces and lands,
> And all the money forfeit by Falcone."

This is a terrible blunder, and the more important as upon this act of the usurer depends the development of his newborn sentiments of honour and virtue — depends, in fact, the most salient *point* of the play. Tortesa, we say, gives to Isabella the lands forfeited by Falcone; but Tortesa was surely not very generous in giving what, clearly, was not his own to give. Falcone had *not forfeited* the deed, which had been restored to him by the usurer, and which was then in his (Falcone's) possession. Here Tortesa: —

> He put it in the bond,
> *That if, by any humour of my own,*
> Or accident that came not from himself,
> Or from his daughter's will, the match were marred,
> *His tenure stood intact.*"

Now Falcone is still resolute for the match; but this new generous "humour" of Tortesa induces him (Tortesa) to decline it. Falcone's tenure

is then intact; he retains the deed, the usurer is giving away property not his own.

As a drama of character, "Tortesa" is by no means open to so many objections as when we view it in the light of its plot; but it is still faulty. The merits are so exceedingly negative, that it is difficult to say anything about them. The Duke is nobody; Falcone, nothing; Zippa, less than nothing. Angelo may be regarded simply as the medium through which Mr. Willis conveys to the reader his own glowing feelings — his own refined and delicate fancy — (delicate, yet bold) — his own rich voluptuousness of sentiment — a voluptuousness which would offend in almost any other language than that in which it is so skilfully apparelled. Isabella is — the heroine of the Hunchback. The revolution in the character of Tortesa — or rather the final triumph of his innate virtue — is a dramatic point far older than the hills. It may be observed, too, that although the representation of no human character should be quarrelled with for its inconsistency, we yet require that the inconsistencies be not absolute antagonisms to the extent of neutralization: they may be permitted to be oils and waters, but they must not be alkalis and acids. When, in the course of the *dénouement*, the usurer bursts forth into an eloquence virtue-inspired, we cannot sympathize very heartily in his fine speeches, since they proceed from the mouth of the self-same egotist who, urged by a disgusting vanity, uttered so many sotticisms (about his fine legs, etc.) in the earlier passages of the play. Tomaso is, upon the whole, the best personage. We recognize some originality in his conception, and conception was seldom more admirably carried out.

One or two observations at random. In the third Scene of the fifth Act, Tomaso, the buffoon, is made to assume paternal authority over Isabella (as usual, without sufficient purpose), by virtue of a law which Tortesa thus expounds: —

> "My gracious liege, there is a law in Florence
> That if a father, for no guilt or shame,
> Disown and shut his door upon his daughter,
> She is the child of him who succours her,
> Who by the shelter of a single night,
> Becomes endowed with the authority
> Lost by the other."

No one, of course, can be made to believe that any such stupid law as this ever existed either in Florence or Timbuctoo; but, on the ground *que le vrai n'est pas toujours le vraisemblable*, we say that even its real existence would be no justification of Mr. Willis. It has an air of the far-fetched — of the desperate — which a fine taste will avoid as a pestilence. Very much of the same nature is the attempt of Tortesa to extort a second bond from Falcone. The evidence which convicts Angelo of murder is ridiculously frail. The idea of Isabella's assuming the place of

the portrait, and so deceiving the usurer, is not only glaringly improbable, but seems adopted from the "Winter's Tale." But in this latter-play, the deception is at least possible, for the human figure but imitates a statue. What, however, are we to make of Mr. W.'s stage direction about the back wall's being "so arranged as to form a natural ground for the picture"? Of course, the very slightest movement of Tortesa (and he makes many) would have annihilated the illusion by disarranging the perspective; and in no manner could this latter have been arranged at all for more than one particular point of view — in other words, for more than one particular person in the whole audience. The "asides," moreover, are unjustifiably frequent. The prevalence of this folly (of speaking aside) detracts as much from the acting merit of our drama generally as any other inartisticality. It utterly destroys verisimilitude. People are not in the habit of soliloquising aloud — at least, not to any positive extent; and why should an author have to be told, what the slightest reflection would teach him, that an audience, by dint of no imagination, can or will conceive that what is sonorous in their own ears at the distance of fifty feet cannot be heard by an actor at the distance of one or two?

Having spoken thus of "Tortesa" in terms of nearly unmitigated censure — our readers may be surprised to hear us say that we think highly of the drama as a whole — and have little hesitation in ranking it before most of the dramas of Sheridan Knowles. Its leading faults are those of the modern drama generally — they are not peculiar to itself — while its great merits *are*. If in support of our opinion we do not cite points of commendation, it is because those form the mass of the work. And were we to speak of fine passages, we should speak of the entire play. Nor by "fine passages" do we mean passages of merely fine language, embodying fine sentiment, but such as are replete with truthfulness, and teem with the loftiest qualities of the dramatic art. *Points* — capital points abound; and these have far more to do with the general excellence of a play than a too speculative criticism has been willing to admit. Upon the whole, we are proud of "Tortesa" — and her again, for the fiftieth time at least, record our warm admiration of the abilities of Mr. Willis.

We proceed now to Mr. Longfellow's

SPANISH STUDENT

The reputation of its author as a poet, and as a graceful writer of prose, is, of course, long and deservedly established — but as a dramatist he was unknown before the publication of this play. Upon its original appearance, in *Graham's Magazine*, the general opinion was greatly in favour — if not exactly of "The Spanish Student" — at all events of the writer of "Outre-Mer." But this general opinion is the most equivocal thing in the world. It is never self-formed. It has very seldom indeed an original development. In regard to the work of an already famous or infamous author it decides, to be sure, with a laudable promptitude;

making up all the mind that it has, by reference to the reception of the author's immediately previous publication — making up thus the ghost of a mind *pro tem.* — a species of critical shadow that fully answers, nevertheless, all the purposes of a substance itself until the substance itself shall be forthcoming. But beyond this point the general opinion can only be considered that of the public, as a man may call a book *his,* having bought it. When a *new* writer arises, the shop of the true, thoughtful, or critical opinion is not simultaneously thrown away — is not immediately set up. Some weeks elapse; and, during this interval, the public, at a loss where to procure an opinion of the *debutante,* have necessarily no opinion of him at all for the nonce.

The popular voice, then, which ran so much in favour of "The Spanish Student," upon its original issue, should be looked upon as merely the ghost *pro tem.* — as based upon critical decisions respecting the previous works of the author — as having reference in no manner to "The Spanish Student" itself — and thus as utterly meaningless and valueless *per se.*

The few, by which we mean those who think, in contradistinction from the many who think they think — the few who think at first hand, and thus twice before speaking at all — these received the play with a commendation somewhat less *pronounced* — somewhat more guardedly qualified — than Professor Longfellow might have desired, or may have been taught to expect. Still the composition was approved upon the whole. The few words of censure were very far indeed from amounting to condemnation. The chief defect insisted upon was the feebleness of the *dénouement,* and, generally, of the concluding scenes, as compared with the opening passages. We are not sure, however, that anything like detailed criticism has been attempted in the case — nor do we propose now to attempt it. Nevertheless, the work has interest, not only within itself, but as the first dramatic effort of an author who has remarkably succeeded in almost every other department of light literature than that of the drama. It may be as well, therefore, to speak of it, if not analytically, at least somewhat in detail; and we cannot, perhaps, more suitably commence than by a quotation, without comment, of some of the finer passages:

> "And, though she is a virgin outwardly,
> Within she is a sinner; like those panels
> Of doors and altar-pieces the old monks
> Painted in convents, with the Virgin Mary
> On the outside, and on the inside Venus."

> "I believe
> That woman, in her deepest degradation,
> Holds something sacred, something undefiled,

Some pledge and keepsake of her higher nature,
And, like the diamond in the dark, retains
Some quenchless gleam of the celestial light."

"And we shall sit together unmolested,
And words of true love pass from tongue to tongue
As singing birds from one bough to another."

 "Our feelings and our thoughts
Tend ever on and rest not in the Present,
As drops of rain fall into some dark well,
And from below comes a scarce audible sound,
So fall our thoughts into the dark Hereafter,
And their mysterious echo reaches us."

"Her tender limbs are still, and, on her breast,
The cross she prayed to, ere she fell asleep,
Rises or falls with the soft tide of dreams,
Like a light barge safe moored."

"Hark! how the large and ponderous mace of Time
Knocks at the golden portals of the day!"

"The lady Violante bathed in tears
Of love and anger, like the maid of Colchis,
Whom thou, another faithless Argonaut,
Having won that golden fleece, a woman's love,
Desertest for this Glaucé."

"I read, or sit in reverie and watch
The changing colour of the waves that break
Upon the idle sea-shore of the mind."

"I will forget her. All dear recollections
Pressed in my heart, like flowers within a book,
Shall be torn out and scattered to the winds."

 "Oh yes! I see it now —
Yet rather with my heart than with mine eyes,
So faint it is. And all my thoughts sail thither,
Freighted with prayers and hopes, and forward urged,
Against all stress of accident, as, in
The Eastern Tale, against the wind and tide
Great ships were drawn to the Magnetic Mountains."

"But there are brighter dreams than those of Fame,
Which are the dreams of Love! Out of the heart
Rises the bright ideal of these dreams,
As from some woodland fount a spirit rises
And sinks again into its silent deeps,
Ere the enamoured knight can touch her robe!
'Tis this ideal that the soul of Man,
Like the enamoured knight beside the fountain,
Waits for upon the margin of Life's stream;
Waits to behold her rise from the dark waters,
Clad in a mortal shape! Alas, how many
Must wait in vain! The stream flows evermore,
But from its silent deeps no spirit rises!
Yet I, born under a propitious star,
Have found the bright ideal of my dreams."

"Yes; by the Darro's side
My childhood passed. I can remember still
The river, and the mountains capped with snow;
The villages where, yet a little child,
I told the traveller's fortune in the street;
The smuggler's horse; the brigand and the shepherd;
The march across the moor; the halt at noon;
The red fire of the evening camp, that lighted
The forest where we slept; and, farther back,
As in a dream, or in some former life,
Gardens and palace walls."

"This path will lead us to it,
Over the wheatfields, where the shadows sail
Across the running sea, now green, now blue,
And, like an idle mariner on the ocean,
Whistles the quail."

These extracts will be universally admired. They are graceful, well expressed, imaginative, and altogether replete with the true poetic feeling. We quote them *now*, at the beginning of our review, by way of justice to the poet, and because, in what follows, we are not sure that we have more than a very few words of what may be termed commendation to bestow.

"The Spanish Student" has an unfortunate beginning, in a most unpardonable, and yet to render the matter worse, in a most indispensable "Preface": —

"The subject of the following play," says Mr. L., "is taken in part from the beautiful play of Cervantes, *La Gitanilla*. To this source, however, I am indebted for the main incident only, the love of a Spanish

student for a Gipsy girl, and the name of the heroine, Preciosa. I have not followed the story in any of its details. In Spain this subject has been twice handled dramatically; first by Juan Perez de Montalvan in *La Gitanilla,* and afterwards by Antonio de Solis y Rivadeneira in *La Gitanilla de Madrid.* The same subject has also been made use of by Thomas Middleton, an English dramatist of the seventeenth century. His play is called *The Spanish Gipsy.* The main plot is the same as in the Spanish pieces; but there runs through it a tragic underplot of the loves of Rodrigo and Dona Clara, which is taken from another tale of Cervantes, *La Fuerza de la Sangre.* The reader who is acquainted with *La Gitanilla* of Cervantes, and the plays of Montalvan, Solis, and Middleton, will perceive that my treatment of the subject differs entirely from theirs."

Now the autorial originality, properly considered, is threefold. There is, first, the originality of the general thesis; secondly, that of the several incidents or thoughts by which the thesis is developed; and thirdly, that of manner or *tone,* by which means alone an old subject, even when developed through hackneyed incidents or thoughts, may be made to produce a fully original *effect* — which, after all, is the end truly in view.

But originality, as it is one of the highest, is also one of the rarest of merits. In America it is especially and very remarkably rare: — this through causes sufficiently well understood. We are content perforce, therefore, as a general thing, with either of the lower branches of originality mentioned above, and would regard with high favour indeed any author who should supply the great *desideratum* in combining the three. Still the three *should* be combined; and from whom, if not from such men as Professor Longfellow — if not from those who occupy the chief niches in our Literary Temple — shall we expect the combination? But in the present instance, what has Professor Longfellow a complished? Is he original at any one point? Is he original in respect to the first and most important of our three divisions? "The *subject* of the following play," he says himself, "is taken *in part* from the beautiful play of Cervantes, 'La Gitanilla.' To this source, however, I am indebted for *the main incident only,* the love of the Spanish student for a Gipsy girl, and the name of the heroine, Preciosa."

The Italics are our own, and the words italicized involve an obvious contradiction. We cannot understand how "the love of the Spanish student for the Gipsy girl" can be called an "incident," or even a "main incident," at all. In fact, this love — this discordant and therefore eventful or incidental love — is the true *thesis* of the drama of Cervantes. It is this anomalous "love," which originates the incidents by means of which itself, this "love," the thesis, is developed. Having based his play, then, upon this "love," we cannot admit his claim to originality upon our first count; nor has he any right to say that he has adopted his "subject" "in part." It is clear that he has adopted it altogether. Nor would he have been entitled to claim originality of subject, even had he based his story

upon *any variety* of love arising between parties naturally separated by prejudices of *caste* — such, for example, as those which divide the Brahmin from the Pariah, the Ammonite from the African, or even the Christian from the Jew. For here in its ultimate analysis, is the real thesis of the Spaniard. But when the drama is founded, not merely upon this general thesis, but upon this general thesis in the identical application given it by Cervantes — that is to say, upon the prejudice of *caste* exemplified in the case of a Catholic, and this Catholic a Spaniard, and this Spaniard a student, and this student loving a Gipsy, and this Gipsy a dancing-girl, and this dancing-girl bearing the name Preciosa — we are not altogether prepared to be informed by Professor Longfellow that he is indebted for an "incident only" to the "beautiful 'Gitanilla' of Cervantes.'"

Whether our author is original upon our second and third points — in the true incidents of his story, or in the manner and *tone* of their handling — will be more distinctly seen as we proceed.

It is to be regretted that "The Spanish Student" was not sub-entitled "A Dramatic Poem," rather than "A Play." The former title would have more fully conveyed the intention of the poet; for, of course, we shall not do Mr. Longfellow the injustice to suppose that his design has been, in any respect, *a play*, in the ordinary acceptation of the term. Whatever may be its merits in a merely poetical view, "The Spanish Student" could not be endured upon the stage.

Its plot runs thus: — Preciosa, the daughter of a Spanish gentleman, is stolen, while an infant, by Gipsies; brought up as his own daughter, and as a dancing-girl, by a Gipsy leader, Cruzado; and by him betrothed to a young Gipsy, Bartolomé. At Madrid, Preciosa loves and is beloved by Victorian, a student of Alcalá, who resolves to marry her, notwithstanding her *caste*, rumours involving her purity, the dissuasions of his friends, and his betrothal to an heiress of Madrid. Preciosa is also sought by the Count of Lara, a *roué*. She rejects him. He forces his way into her chamber, and is there seen by Victorian, who, misinterpreting some words overheard, doubts the fidelity of his mistress, and leaves her in anger, after challenging the Count of Lara. In the duel, the Count receives his life at the hands of Victorian: declares his ignorance of the understanding between Victorian and Preciosa; boasts of favours received from the latter; and, to make good his words, produces a ring which she gave him, he asserts, as a pledge of her love. This ring is a duplicate of one previously given the girl by Victorian, and known to have been so given by the Count. Victorian mistakes it for his own, believes all that has been said, and abandons the field to his rival, who, immediately afterwards, while attempting to procure access to the Gipsy, is assassinated by Bartolomé. Meantime, Victorian, wandering through the country, reaches Guadarrama. Here he receives a letter from Madrid, disclosing the treachery practiced by Lara, and telling that Preciosa, rejecting his addresses,

had been through his instrumentality hissed from the stage, and now again roamed with the Gipsies. He goes in search of her; finds her in a wood near Guadarrama; approaches her, disguising his voice; she recognizes him, pretending she does not, and unaware that he knows her innocence; a conversation of *equivoque* ensues; he sees his ring upon her finger; offers to purchase it; she refuses to part with it; a full *éclaircissement* takes place; at this juncture a servant of Victorian's arrives with "news from court," giving the first intimation of the true parentage of Preciosa. The lovers set out, forthwith, for Madrid, to see the newly discovered father. On the route, Bartolomé dogs their steps; fires at Preciosa; misses her; the shot is returned; he falls; and "The Spanish Student" is concluded.

This plot, however, like that of "Tortesa," looks better in our naked digest than amidst the details which develop only to disfigure it. The reader of the play itself will be astonished, when he remembers the name of the author, at the inconsequence of the incidents — at the utter want of skill — of art — manifested in their conception and introduction. In dramatic writing, no principle is more clear than that nothing should be said or done which has not a tendency to develp the catastrophe, or the characters. But Mr. Longfellow's play abounds in events and conversations that have no ostensible purpose, and certainly answer no end. In what light, for example, since we cannot suppose this drama intended for the stage, are we to regard the second scene of the second act, where a long dialogue between an Archbishop and a Cardinal is wound up by a dance from Preciosa? The Pope thinks of abolishing public dances in Spain, and the priests in question have been delegated to examine, personally, the proprieties or improprieties of such exhibitions. With this view, Preciosa is summoned and required to give a specimen of her skill. Now this, in a mere spectacle, would do very well; for here all that is demanded is an occasion or an excuse for a dance; but what business has it in a pure drama? or in what regard does it further the end of a dramatic poem, intended only to be read? In the same manner, the whole of Scene the eighth, in the same act, is occupied with six lines of stage directions, as follows: —

The Theatre: the orchestra plays the Cachuca. Sound of castanets behind the scenes. The curtain rises and discovers Preciosa in the attitude of commencing the dance. The Cachuca. Tumult. Hisses. Cries of Brava! and Aguera! She falters and pauses. The music stops. General confusion. Preciosa faints.

But the *inconsequence* of which we complain will be best exemplified by an entire scene. We take Scene the Fourth, Act the First: —

"*An inn on the road to Alcalá.* BALTASAR *asleep on a bench. Enter* CHISPA."

CHISPA. And here we are, half way to Alcalá, between cocks and midnight. Body o' me! what an inn this is! The light out and the landlord asleep! Holá! ancient Baltasar!

BALTASAR [*waking*]. Here I am.

CHISPA. Yes, there you are, like a one-eyed alcalde in a town without inhabitants. Bring a light, and let me have supper.

BALTASAR. Where is your master?

CHISPA. Do not trouble yourself about him. We have stopped a moment to breathe our horses; and if he chooses to walk up and down in the open air, looking into the sky as one who hears it rain, that does not satisfy my hunger, you know. But be quick, for I am in a hurry, and every one stretches his legs according to the length of his coverlet. What have we here?

BALTASAR [*setting a light on the table*]. Stewed rabbit.

CHISPA [*eating*]. Conscience of Portalegre! stewed kitten, you mean!

BALTASAR. And a pitcher of Pedro Ximenes, with a roasted pear in it.

CHISPA [*drinking*]. Ancient Baltasar, amigo! You know how to cry wine and sell vinegar. I tell you this is nothing but Vino Tinto of La Mancha, with a tang of the swine-skin.

BALTASAR. I swear to you by Saint Simon and Judas, it is all as I say.

CHISPA. And I swear to you by Saint Peter and Saint Paul, that it is no such thing. Moreover, your supper is like the hidalgo's dinner — very little meat and a great deal of tablecloth.

BALTASAR. Ha! ha! ha!

CHISPA. And more noise than nuts.

BALTASAR. Ha! ha! ha! You must have your joke, Master Chispa. But shall I not ask Don Victorian in to take a draught of the Pedro Ximenes?

CHISPA. No; you might as well say, "Don't you want some?" to a dead man.

BALTASAR. Why does he go so often to Madrid?

CHISPA. For the same reason that he eats no supper. He is in love. Were you ever in love, Baltasar?

BALTASAR. I was never out of it, good Chispa. It has been the torment of my life.

CHISPA. What! are you on fire, too, old hay-stack? Why, we shall never be able to put you out.

VICTORIAN [*without*]. Chispa!

CHISPA. Go to bed, Pero Grullo, for the cocks are crowing.

VICTORIAN. Ea! Chispa! Chispa!

CHISPA. Ea! Señor. Come with me, ancient Baltasar, and bring water for the horses. I will pay for the supper tomorrow. [*Exeunt.*]

Now here the question occurs — what is accomplished? How has the subject been forwarded? We did not need to learn that Victorian was

in love — that was known before; and all that we glean is that a stupid imitation of Sancho Panza drinks in the course of two minutes (the time occupied in the perusal of the scene) a bottle of vino tinto, by way of Pedro Ximenes, and devours a stewed kitten in place of a rabbit.

In the beginning of the play this Chispa is the valet of Victorian; subsequently we find him the servant of another; and near the *dénouement* he returns to his original master. No cause is assigned, and not even the shadow of an object is attained; the whole tergiversation being but another instance of the gross inconsequence which abounds in the play.

The author's deficiency of skill is especially evinced in the scene of the *éclaircissement* between Victorian and Preciosa. The former having been enlightened respecting the true character of the latter by means *of a letter* received at Guadarrama, from a friend at Madrid (how wofully inartistical is this!), resolves to go in search of her forthwith, and forthwith, also, discovers her in a wood close at hand. Whereupon he approaches, disguising *his voice:* — yes, we are required to believe that a lover may so disguise his voice from his mistress as even to render his person in full view irrecognizable! He approaches, and each knowing the other, a conversation ensues under the hypothesis that each to the other is unknown — a very unoriginal, and, of course, a very silly source of *equivoque*, fit only for the gum-elastic imagination of an infant. But what we especially complain of here is that our poet should have taken so many and so obvious pains to bring about this position of *equivoque*, when it was impossible that it could have served any other purpose than that of injuring his intended effect! Read, for example, this passage: —

VICTORIAN. I never loved a maid;
For she I loved was then a maid no more.
 PRECIOSA. How know you that?
 VICTORIA. A little bird in the air
Whispered the secret.
 PRECIOSA. There, take back your gold!
Your hand is cold like a deceiver's hand!
There is no blessing in its charity!
Make her your wife, for you have been abused;
And you shall mend your fortunes mending hers.
 VICTORIAN. How like an angel's speaks the tongue of woman,
When pleading in another's cause her own!

Now here it is clear that if we understood Preciosa to be really ignorant of Victorian's identity, the "pleading in another's cause her own" would create a favourable impression upon the reader or spectator. But the advice — "Make her your wife, etc.," takes an interested and selfish turn when we remember that she knows to whom she speaks.

Again, when Victorian says:

> That is a pretty ring upon your finger,
> Pray give it me!

and when she replies:

> No, never from my hand
> Shall that be taken,

we are inclined to think her only an artful coquette, knowing, as we do, the extent of her knowledge; on the hand we should have applauded her constancy (as the author intended) had she been represented ignorant of Victorian's presence. The effect upon the audience, in a word, would be pleasant in place of disagreeable were the case altered as we suggest, while the effect upon Victorian would remain altogether untouched.

A still more remarkable instance of deficiency in the dramatic *tact* is to be found in the mode of bringing about the discovery of Preciosa's parentage. In the very moment of the *éclaircissement* between the lovers, Chispa arrives almost as a matter of course, and settles the point in a sentence: —

> Good news from Court; Good news! Beltran Cruzado,
> The Count of the Calés, is not your father,
> But your true father has returned to Spain
> Laden with wealth. You are no more a Gipsy.

Now here are three points: — first, the extreme baldness, platitude, and *independence* of the incident narrated by Chispa. The *opportune* return of the father (we are tempted to say the *excessively* opportune) stands by itself — has no relation to any other event in the play — does not appear to arise, in the way of *result*, from any incident or incidents that have arisen before. It has the air of a happy chance, of a God-send, of an ultra-accident, invented by the play-wright by way of compromise for his lack of invention. *Nec Deus intersit*, etc. — but here the God has interposed, and the knot is laughably unworthy of the God.

The second point concerns the return of the father "laden with wealth." The lover has abandoned his mistress in her poverty, and, while yet the words of his proffered reconciliation hang upon his lips, comes his own servant with the news that the mistress' father has returned "laden with wealth." Now, so far as regards the audience, who are behind the scenes and know the fidelity of the lover — so far as regards the audience, all is right; but the poet had no business to place his heroine in the sad predicament of being forced, provided she is not a fool, to suspect both the ignorance and the disinterestedness of the hero.

The third point has reference to the words — "You are now no more a Gipsy." The thesis of this drama, as we have already said, is love disregarding the prejudices of *caste*, and in the development of this thesis, the

powers of the dramatist have been engaged, or should have been engaged, during the whole of the three acts of the play. The interest excited lies in our admiration of the sacrifice, and of the love that could make it; but this interest immediately and disagreeably subsides when we find that the sacrifice has been made to no purpose. "You are no more a Gipsy" dissolves the charm, and obliterates the whole impression which the author has been at so much labour to convey. Our romantic sense of the hero's chivalry declines into a complacent satisfaction with his fate. We drop our enthusiasm, with the enthusiast, and jovially shake by the hand the mere man of good luck. But is not the latter feeling the more comfortable of the two? Perhaps so; but "comfortable" is not exactly the word Mr. Longfellow might wish applied to the end of his drama, and then why be at the trouble of building up an effect through a hundred and eighty pages, merely to knock it down at the end of the hundred and eighty-first?

We have already given, at some length, our conceptions of the nature of *plot* — and of that of "The Spanish Student" it seems almost superfluous to speak at all. It has nothing of construction about it. Indeed there is scarcely a single incident which has any necessary dependence upon any one other. Not only might we take away two-thirds of the whole without ruin — but without detriment — indeed with a positive benefit to the mass. And, even as regards the mere order of arrangement, we might with a very decided *chance* of improvement, put the scenes in a bag, give them a shake or two by way of shuffle, and tumble them out. The whole mode of collocation — not to speak of the feebleness of the incidents in themselves — evinces, on the part of the author, an utter and radical want of the adapting or constructive power which the drama so imperatively demands.

Of the unoriginality of the thesis we have already spoken; and now, to the unoriginality of the events by which the thesis is developed, we need do little more than allude. What, indeed, *could* we say of such incidents as the child stolen by Gipsies — as her education as a *danseuse* — as her betrothal to a Gipsy — as her preference for a gentleman — as the rumours against her purity — as her persecution by a *roué* — as the irruption of the *roué* into her chamber — as the consequent misunderstanding between her and her lover — as the duel — as the defeat of the *roué* — as the receipt of his life from the hero — as his boasts of success with the girl — as the *ruse* of the duplicate ring — as the field, in consequence, abandoned by the lover — as the assassination of Lara while scaling the girl's bed-chamber — as the disconsolate peregrination of Victorian — as the *equivoque* scene with Preciosa — as the offering to purchase the ring and the refusal to part with it — as the "news from court," telling of the Gipsy's true parentage — what *could* we say of all these ridiculous things, except that we have met them, each and all, some two or three hundred times before, and that they have formed, in a great or less degree, the

staple material of every Hop-O'My-Thumb tragedy since the flood? There is not an incident, from the first page of "The Spanish Student" to the last and most satisfactory, which we would not undertake to find bodily, at ten minutes' notice, in some one of the thousand and one comedies of intrigue attributed to Calderon and Lope de Vega.

But if our poet is grossly unoriginal in his subject, and in the events which evolve it, may he not be original in his handling or *tone?* We really grieve to say that he is not, unless, indeed, we grant him the need of originality for the peculiar manner in which he has jumbled together the quaint and stilted tone of the old English dramatists with the *dégagée* air of Cervantes. But this is a point upon which, through want of space, we must necessarily permit the reader to judge altogether for himself. We quote, however, a passage from the second scene of the first act, by way of showing how very easy a matter it is to make a man discourse Sancho Panza: —

Chispa. Abernuncio Satanas! and a plague upon all lovers who ramble about at night, drinking the elements, instead of sleeping quietly in their beds. Every dead man to his cemetery, say I; and every friar to his monastery. Now, here's my master Victorian, yesterday a cow-keeper and to-day a gentleman; yesterday a student and to-day a lover; and I must be up later than the nightingale, for as the abbot sings so must the sacristan respond. God grant he may soon be married, for then shall all this serenading cease. Ay, marry, marry, marry! Mother, what does marry mean? It means to spin, to bear children, and to weep, my daughter! and, of a truth, there is something more in matrimony than the wedding-ring. And now, gentlemen, *Pax vobiscum!* as the ass said to the cabbages!

And we might add, as an ass *only* should say.

In fact, throughout "The Spanish Student," as well as throughout other compositions of its author, there runs a very obvious vein of *imitation.* We are perpetually reminded of something we have seen before — some old acquaintance in manner or matter; and even where the similarity cannot be said to amount to plagiarism, it is still injurious to the poet in the good opinion of him who reads.

Among the minor defects of the play, we may mention the frequent allusion to book incidents not generally known, and requiring each a *Note* by way of explanation. The drama demands that everything be so instantaneously evident that he who runs may read; and the only impression effected by these *Notes* to a play is, that the author is desirous of showing his reading.

We may mention, also, occasional tautologies, such as: —

Never did I behold thee so *attired*
And *garmented* in beauty as to-night!

Or —

> What we need
> Is the celestial fire to change the fruit
> Into *transparent* crystal, *bright and clear!*

We may speak, too, of more than occasional errors of grammar. For example, page 23: —

> "Did no one see thee? None, my love, but *thou*."

Here "but" is not a conjunction, but a preposition, and governs *thee* in the objective. "None but *thee*" would be right; meaning none *except* thee, *saving* thee. At page 27, "mayst" is somewhat incorrectly written "may'st." At page 34, we have: —

> I have no other saint than *thou* to pray to.

Here authority and analogy are both against Mr. Longfellow. "Than" also is here a preposition governing the objective, and meaning *save* or *except*. "I have none other God than thee, etc." See Horne Tooke. The Latin *"quam te"* is exactly equivalent. At page 80 we read: —

> *Like thee* I am a captive, and, *like thee,*
> I have a gentle gaoler.

Here "like thee" (although grammatical of course) does not convey the idea. Mr. L. does not mean that the speaker is *like* the bird itself, but that his *condition* resembles it. The true reading would thus be: —

> *As thou* I am a captive, and, *as thou,*
> I have a gentle gaoler.

That is to say, *as thou art and as thou hast.*

Upon the whole, we regret that Professor Longfellow has written this work, and feel especially vexed that he has committed himself by its republication. Only when regarded as a mere poem can it be said to have merit of any kind. For in fact it is only when we separate the poem from the drama that the passages we have commended as beautiful can be understood to have beauty. We are not too sure, indeed, that a "dramatic poem" is not a flat contradiction in terms. At all events a man of true genius (and such Mr. L. unquestionably is) has no business with these hybrid and paradoxical compositions. Let a poem be a poem only; let a play be a play and nothing more. As for "The Spanish Student," its thesis is unoriginal; its incidents are antique; its plot is no plot; its characters have no character; in short, it is a little better than a play upon words to style it "A Play" at all.

Preface to The Raven and Other Poems

THESE trifles are collected and republished chiefly with a view to their redemption from the many improvements to which they have been sub-

jected while going "the rounds of the press". I am naturally anxious that if what I have written is to circulate at all, it should circulate as I wrote it. In defence of my own taste, nevertheless, it is incumbent on me to say that I think nothing in this volume of much value to the public, or very creditable to myself. Events not to be controlled have prevented me from making, at any time, any serious effort in what, under happier circumstances would have been the field of my choice. With me poetry has not been a purpose, but a passion; and the passions should be held in reverence; they must not — they cannot at will be excited, with an eye to the paltry compensations, or the more paltry commendations, of mankind

E. A. P.

The Philosophy of Composition

CHARLES DICKENS, in a note now lying before me, alluding to an examination I once made of the mechanism of "Barnaby Rudge," says — "By the way, are you aware that Godwin wrote his 'Caleb Williams' backwards? He first involved his hero in a web of difficulties, forming the second volume, and then, for the first, cast about him for some mode of accounting for what had been done."

I cannot think this the *precise* mode of procedure on the part of Godwin — and indeed what he himself acknowledges, is not altogether in accordance with Mr. Dickens' idea — but the author of "Caleb Williams" was too good an artist not to perceive the advantage derivable from at least a somewhat similar process. Nothing is more clear than that every plot, worth the name, must be elaborated to its *dénouement* before anything be attempted with the pen. It is only with the *dénouement* constantly in view that we can give a plot its indispensable air of consequence, or causation, by making the incidents, and especially the tone at all points, tend to the development of the intention.

There is a radical error, I think, in the usual mode of constructing a story. Either history affords a thesis — or one is suggested by an incident of the day — or, at best, the author sets himself to work in the combination of striking events to form merely the basis of his narrative — designing, generally, to fill in with description, dialogue, or autorial comment, whatever crevices of fact, or action, may, from page to page, render themselves apparent.

I prefer commencing with the consideration of an *effect*. Keeping originality *always* in view — for he is false to himself who ventures to dispense with so obvious and so easily attainable a source of interest — I say to myself, in the first place, "Of the innumerable effects, or impressions, of which the heart, the intellect, or (more generally) the soul is susceptible, what one shall I, on the present occasion, select?" Having chosen a novel, first, and secondly a vivid effect, I consider whether it can be best wrought

by incident or tone — whether by ordinary incidents and peculiar tone, or the converse, or by peculiarity both of incident and tone — afterward looking about me (or rather within) for such combinations of event, or tone, as shall best aid me in the construction of the effect.

I have often thought how interesting a magazine paper might be written by any author who would — that is to say, who could — detail, step by step, the processes by which any one of his compositions attained its ultimate point of completion. Why such a paper has never been given to the world, I am much at a loss to say — but, perhaps, the autorial vanity has had more to do with the omission than any one other cause. Most writers — poets in especial — prefer having it understood that they compose by a species of fine frenzy — an ecstatic intuition — and would positively shudder at letting the public take a peep behind the scenes, at the elaborate and vacillating crudities of thought — at the true purposes seized only at the last moment — at the innumerable glimpses of idea that arrived not at the maturity of full view — at the fully-matured fancies discarded in despair as unmanageable — at the cautious selections and rejections — at the painful erasures and interpolations — in a word, at the wheels and pinions — the tackle for scene-shifting — the step-ladders, and demon-traps — the cock's feathers, the red paint and the black patches, which, in ninety-nine cases out of a hundred, constitute the properties of the literary *histrio*.

I am aware, on the other hand, that the case is by no means common, in which an author is at all in condition to retrace the steps by which his conclusions have been attained. In general, suggestions, having arisen pell-mell, are pursued and forgotten in a similar manner.

For my own part, I have neither sympathy with the repugnance alluded to, nor, at any time, the least difficulty in recalling to mind the progressive steps of any of my compositions, and, since the interest of an analysis or reconstruction, such as I have considered a *desideratum*, is quite independent of any real or fancied interest in the thing analysed, it will not be regarded as a breach of decorum on my part to show the *modus operandi* by which some one of my own works was put together. I select 'The Raven' as most generally known. It is my design to render it manifest that no one point in its composition is referable either to accident or intuition — that the work proceeded step by step, to its completion, with the precision and rigid consequence of a mathematical problem.

Let us dismiss, as irrelevant to the poem, *per se*, the circumstance — or say the necessity — which, in the first place, gave rise to the intention of composing *a* poem that should suit at once the popular and the critical taste.

We commence, then, with this intention.

The initial consideration was that of extent. If any literary work is too long to be read at one sitting, we must be content to dispense with the immensely important effect derivable from unity of impression — for,

if two sittings be required, the affairs of the world interfere, and every-
thing like totality is at once destroyed. But since, *ceteris paribus*, no poet
can afford to dispense with *anything* that may advance his design, it
but remains to be seen whether there is, in extent, any advantage to
counterbalance the loss of unity which attends it. Here I say no, at once.
What we term a long poem is, in fact, merely a succession of brief ones —
that is to say, of brief poetical effects. It is needless to demonstrate that
a poem is such only inasmuch as it intensely excites, by elevating the
soul; and all intense excitements are, through a psychal necessity, brief.
For this reason, at least, one-half of the "Paradise Lost" is essentially
prose — a succession of poetical excitements interspersed, *inevitably*, with
corresponding depressions — the whole being deprived, through the ex-
tremeness of its length, of the vastly important artistic element, totality,
or unity of effect.

It appears evident, then, that there is a distinct limit, as regards length,
to all works of literary art — the limit of a single sitting — and that, al-
though in certain classes of prose composition, such as "Robinson Crusoe"
(demanding no unity), this limit may be advantageously overpassed, it
can never properly be overpassed in a poem. Within this limit, the extent
of a poem may be made to bear mathematical relation to its merit — in
other words, to the excitement or elevation — again, in other words, to
the degree of the true poetical effect which it is capable of inducing; for
it is clear that the brevity must be in direct ratio of the intensity of the
intended effect — this, with one proviso — that a certain degree of dura-
tion is absolutely requisite for the production of any effect at all.

Holding in view these considerations, as well as that degree of excite-
ment which I deemed not above the popular, while not below the critical
taste, I reached at once what I conceived the proper *length* for my in-
tended poem — a length of about one hundred lines. It is, in fact, a hun-
dred and eight.

My next thought concerned the choice of an impression, or effect, to
be conveyed: and here I may as well observe that, throughout the con-
struction, I kept steadily in view the design of rendering the work *uni-
versally* appreciable. I should be carried too far out of my immediate topic
were I to demonstrate a point upon which I have repeatedly insisted, and
which, with the poetical, stands not in the slightest need of demonstra-
tion — the point, I mean, that Beauty is the sole legitimate province of
the poem. A few words, however, in elucidation of my real meaning,
which some of my friends have evinced a disposition to misrepresent. That
pleasure which is at once the most intense, the most elevating, and the
most pure is, I believe, found in the contemplation of the beautiful.
When, indeed, men speak of Beauty, they mean, precisely, not a quality,
as is supposed, but an effect — they refer, in short, just to that intense and
pure elevation of *soul* — *not* of intellect, or of heart — upon which I have
commented, and which is experienced in consequence of contemplating

the "beautiful." Now I designate Beauty as the province of the poem, merely because it is an obvious rule of Art that effects should be made to spring from direct causes — that objects should be attained through means best adapted for their attainment — no one as yet having been weak enough to deny that the peculiar elevation alluded to is *most readily* attained in the poem. Now the object Truth, or the satisfaction of the intellect, and the object Passion, or the excitement of the heart, are, although attainable to a certain extent in poetry, far more readily attainable in prose. Truth, in fact, demands a precision, and Passion, a *homeliness* (the truly passionate will comprehend me), which are absolutely antagonistic to that Beauty which, I maintain, is the excitement, or pleasurable elevation of the soul. It by no means follows, from anything here said, that passion, or even truth, may not be introduced, and even profitably introduced, into a poem for they may serve in elucidation, or aid the general effect, as do discords in music, by contrast — but the true artist will always contrive, first, to tone them into proper subservience to the predominant aim, and, secondly, to enveil them, as far as possible, in that Beauty which is the atmosphere and the essence of the poem.

Regarding, then, Beauty as my province, my next question referred to the *tone* of its highest manifestation — and all experience has shown that this tone is one of *sadness*. Beauty of whatever kind, in its supreme development, invariably excites the sensitive soul to tears. Melancholy is thus the most legitimate of all the poetical tones.

The length, the province, and the tone, being thus determined, I betook myself to ordinary induction, with the view of obtaining some artistic piquancy which might serve me as a key-note in the construction of the poem — some pivot upon which the whole structure might turn. In carefully thinking over all the usual artistic effects — or more properly *points*, in the theatrical sense — I did not fail to perceive immediately that no one had been so universally employed as that of the *refrain*. The universality of its employment sufficed to assure me of its intrinsic value, and spared me the necessity of submitting it to analysis. I considered it, however, with regard to its susceptibility of improvement, and soon saw it to be in a primitive condition. As commonly used, the *refrain*, or burden, not only is limited to lyric verse, but depends for its impression upon the force of monotone — both in sound and thought. The pleasure is deduced solely from the sense of identity — of repetition. I resolved to diversify, and so heighten the effect, by adhering in general to the monotone of sound, while I continually varied that of thought: that is to say, I determined to produce continuously novel effects, by the variation *of the application* of the *refrain* — the *refrain* itself remaining, for the most part, unvaried.

These points being settled, I next bethought me of the *nature* of my refrain. Since its application was to be repeatedly varied it was clear that the *refrain* itself must be brief, for there would have been an insur-

mountable difficulty in frequent variations of application in any sentence of length. In proportion to the brevity of the sentence would, of course, be the facility of the variation. This led me at once to a single word as the best *refrain*.

The question now arose as to the character of the word. Having made up my mind to a *refrain*, the division of the poem into stanzas was of course a corollary, the *refrain* forming the close to each stanza. That such a close, to have force, must be sonorous and susceptible of protracted emphasis, admitted no doubt, and these considerations inevitably led me to the long *o* as the most sonorous vowel in connection with *r* as the most producible consonant.

The sound of the *refrain* being thus determined, it became necessary to select a word embodying this sound, and at the same time in the fullest possible keeping with that melancholy which I had pre-determined as the tone of the poem. In such a search it would have been absolutely impossible to overlook the word "Nevermore." In fact it was the very first which presented itself.

The next *desideratum* was a pretext for the continuous use of the one word "nevermore." In observing the difficulty which I had at once found in inventing a sufficiently plausible reason for its continuous repetition, I did not fail to perceive that this difficulty arose solely from the preassumption that the word was to be so continuously or monotonously spoken by a *human* being — I did not fail to perceive, in short, that the difficulty lay in the reconciliation of this monotony with the exercise of reason on the part of the creature repeating the word. Here, then, immediately arose the idea of a *non*-reasoning creature capable of speech, and very naturally, a parrot, in the first instance, suggested itself, but was superseded forthwith by a Raven as equally capable of speech, and infinitely more in keeping with the intended tone.

I had now gone so far as the conception of a Raven, the bird of ill-omen, monotonously repeating the one word "Nevermore" at the conclusion of each stanza in a poem of melancholy tone, and in length about one hundred lines. Now, never losing sight of the object — *supremeness* or perfection at all points, I asked myself — "Of all melancholy topics what, according to the *universal* understanding of mankind, is the *most* melancholy?" Death, was the obvious reply. "And when," I said, "is this most melancholy of topics most poetical?" From what I have already explained at some length the answer here also is obvious — "When it most closely allies itself to *Beauty*: the death then of a beautiful woman is unquestionably the most poetical topic in the world, and equally is it beyond doubt that the lips best suited for such topic are those of a bereaved lover."

I had now to combine the two ideas of a lover lamenting his deceased mistress and a Raven continuously repeating the word "Nevermore." I had to combine these, bearing in mind my design of varying at every

turn the *application* of the word repeated, but the only intelligible mode of such combination is that of imagining the Raven employing the word in answer to the queries of the lover. And here it was that I saw at once the opportunity afforded for the effect on which I had been depending, that is to say, the effect of the *variation of application*. I saw that I could make the first query propounded by the lover — the first query to which the Raven should reply "Nevermore" — that I could make this first query a commonplace one, the second less so, the third still less, and so on, until at length the lover, startled from his original *nonchalance* by the melancholy character of the word itself, by its frequent repetition, and by a consideration of the ominous reputation of the fowl that uttered it, is at length excited to superstition, and wildly propounds queries of a far different character — queries whose solution he has passionately at heart — propounds them half in superstition and half in that species of despair which delights in self-torture — propounds them not altogether because he believes in the prophetic or demoniac character of the bird (which reason assures him is merely repeating a lesson learned by rote), but because he experiences a frenzied pleasure in so modelling his questions as to receive from the *expected* "Nevermore" the most delicious because the most intolerable of sorrows. Perceiving the opportunity thus afforded me, or, more strictly, thus forced upon me in the progress of the construction, I first established in my mind the climax or concluding query — that query to which "Nevermore" should be in the last place an answer — that query in reply to which this word "Nevermore" should involve the utmost conceivable amount of sorrow and despair.

Here then the poem may be said to have had its beginning — at the end where all works of art should begin — for it was here at this point of my preconsiderations that I first put pen to paper in the composition of the stanza:

> "Prophet!" said I, "thing of evil! prophet still if bird or devil!
> By that Heaven that bends above us — by that God we both adore,
> Tell this soul with sorrow laden, if, within the distant Aidenn,
> It shall clasp a sainted maiden whom the angels name Lenore —
> Clasp a rare and radiant maiden whom the angels name Lenore."
> Quoth the Raven — "Nevermore."

I composed this stanza, at this point, first that, by establishing the climax, I might the better vary and graduate, as regards seriousness and importance, the preceding queries of the lover, and secondly, that I might definitely settle the rhythm, the metre, and the length and general arrangement of the stanza, as well as graduate the stanzas which were to precede, so that none of them might surpass this in rhythmical effect. Had I been able in the subsequent composition to construct more vigorous stanzas I should without scruple have purposely enfeebled them so as not to interfere with the climacteric effect

And here I may as well say a few words of the versification. My first object (as usual) was originality. The extent to which this has been neglected in versification is one of the most unaccountable things in the world. Admitting that there is little possibility of variety in mere *rhythm*, it is still clear that the possible varieties of metre and stanza are absolutely infinite, and yet, *for centuries, no man, in verse, has ever done, or ever seemed to think of doing, an original thing*. The fact is that originality (unless in minds of very unusual force) is by no means a matter, as some suppose, of impulse or intuition. In general, to be found, it must be elaborately sought, and although a positive merit of the highest class, demands in its attainment less of invention than negation.

Of course I pretend to no originality in either the rhythm or metre of the "Raven." The former is trochaic — the latter is octametre acatalectic, alternating with heptametre catalectic repeated in the *refrain* of the fifth verse, and terminating with tetrametre catalectic. Less pedantically — the feet employed throughout (trochees) consist of a long syllable followed by a short; the first line of the stanza consists of eight of these feet, the second of seven and a half (in effect two-thirds), the third of eight, the fourth of seven and a half, the fifth the same, the sixth three and a half. Now, each of these lines taken individually has been employed before, and what originality the "Raven" has, is in their *combination into stanza*; nothing even remotely approaching this combination has ever been attempted. The effect of this originality of combination is aided by other unusual and some altogether novel effects, arising from an extension of the application of the principles of rhyme and alliteration.

The next point to be considered was the mode of bringing together the lover and the Raven — and the first branch of this consideration was the *locale*. For this the most natural suggestion might seem to be a forest, or the fields — but it has always appeared to me that a close *circumscription of space* is absolutely necessary to the effect of insulated incident — it has the force of a frame to a picture. It has an indisputable moral power in keeping concentrated the attention, and, of course, must not be confounded with mere unity of place.

I determined, then, to place the lover in his chamber — in a chamber rendered sacred to him by memories of her who had frequented it. The room is represented as richly furnished — this in mere pursuance of the ideas I have already explained on the subject of Beauty, as the sole true poetical thesis.

The *locale* being thus determined, I had now to introduce the bird — and the thought of introducing him through the window was inevitable. The idea of making the lover suppose, in the first instance, that the flapping of the wings of the bird against the shutter, is a "tapping" at the door, originated in a wish to increase, by prolonging, the reader's curiosity, and in a desire to admit the incidental effect arising from the

lover's throwing open the door, finding all dark, and thence adopting the half-fancy that it was the spirit of his mistress that knocked.

I made the night tempestuous, first to account for the Raven's seeking admission, and secondly, for the effect of contrast with the (physical) serenity within the chamber.

I made the bird alight on the bust of Pallas, also for the effect of contrast between the marble and the plumage — it being understood that the bust was absolutely *suggested* by the bird — the bust of *Pallas* being chosen, first, as most in keeping with the scholarship of the lover, and secondly, for the sonorousness of the word, Pallas, itself.

About the middle of the poem, also, I have availed myself of the force of contrast, with a view of deepening the ultimate impression. For example, an air of the fantastic — approaching as nearly to the ludicrous as was admissible — is given to the Raven's entrance. He comes in "with many a flirt and flutter."

Not the *least obeisance made he* — not a moment stopped or stayed he,
But with mien of lord or lady, perched above my chamber door.

In the two stanzas which follow, the design is more obviously carried out: —

Then this ebony bird, beguiling my sad fancy into smiling
By the *grave and stern decorum of the countenance it wore*,
"Though thy *crest be shorn and shaven*, thou," I said, "art sure no craven,
Ghastly grim and ancient Raven wandering from the Nightly shore —
Tell me what thy lordly name is on the Night's Plutonian shore?"
 Quoth the Raven — "Nevermore."

Much I marvelled *this ungainly fowl* to hear discourse so plainly,
Though its answer little meaning — little relevancy bore;
For we cannot help agreeing that no living human being
Ever yet was blessed with seeing bird above his chamber door —
Bird or beast upon the sculptured bust above his chamber door,
 With such name as "Nevermore."

The effect of the *dénouement* being thus provided for, I immediately drop the fantastic for a tone of the most profound seriousness — this tone commencing in the stanza directly following the one last quoted, with the line,

But the Raven, sitting lonely on that placid bust, spoke only, etc.

From this epoch the lover no longer jests — no longer sees anything even of the fantastic in the Raven's demeanour. He speaks of him as a "grim, ungainly, ghastly, gaunt, and ominous bird of yore," and feels

the "fiery eyes" burning into his "bosom's core." This revolution of thought, or fancy, on the lover's part, is intended to induce a similar one on the part of the reader — to bring the mind into a proper frame for the *dénouement* — which is now brought about as rapidly and as *directly* as possible.

With the *dénouement* proper — with the Raven's reply, "Nevermore," to the lover's final demand if he shall meet his mistress in another world — the poem, in its obvious phase, that of a simple narrative, may be said to have its completion. So far, everything is within the limits of the accountable — of the real. A raven, having learned by rote the single word "Nevermore," and having escaped from the custody of its owner, is driven at midnight, through the violence of a storm, to seek admission at a window from which a light still gleams — the chamber-window of a student, occupied half in poring over a volume, half in dreaming of a beloved mistress deceased. The casement being thrown open at the fluttering of the bird's wings, the bird itself perches on the most convenient seat out of the immediate reach of the student, who amused by the incident and the oddity of the visitor's demeanour, demands of it, in jest and without looking for a reply, its name. The raven addressed, answers with its customary word, "Nevermore" — a word which finds immediate echo in the melancholy heart of the student, who, giving utterance aloud to certain thoughts suggested by the occasion, is again startled by the fowl's repetition of "Nevermore." The student now guesses the state of the case, but is impelled, as I have before explained, by the human thirst for self-torture, and in part by superstition, to propound such queries to the bird as will bring him, the lover, the most of the luxury of sorrow, through the anticipated answer, "Nevermore." With the indulgence, to the extreme, of this self-torture, the narration, in what I have termed its first or obvious phase, has a natural termination, and so far there has been no overstepping of the limits of the real.

But in subjects so handled, however skillfully, or with however vivid an array of incident, there is always a certain hardness or nakedness which repels the artistical eye. Two things are invariably required — first, some amount of complexity, or more properly, adaptation; and, secondly, some amount of suggestiveness — some under-current, however indefinite, of meaning. It is this latter, in especial, which imparts to a work of art so much of that *richness* (to borrow from colloquy a forcible term), which we are too fond of confounding with *the ideal*. It is the *excess* of the suggested meaning — it is the rendering this the upper instead of the under-current of the theme — which turns into prose (and that of the very flattest kind), the so-called poetry of the so-called transcendentalists.

Holding these opinions, I added the two concluding stanzas of the poem — their suggestiveness being thus made to pervade all the narrative which has preceded them. The under-current of meaning is rendered first apparent in the line —

"Take thy beak from out *my heart*, and take thy form from off my door!"
 Quoth the Raven "Nevermore!"

It will be observed that the words, "from out my heart," involve the first metaphorical expression in the poem. They, with the answer, "Nevermore," dispose the mind to seek a moral in all that has been previously narrated. The reader begins now to regard the Raven as emblematical — but it is not until the very last line of the very last stanza that the intention of making him emblematical of *Mournful and never ending Remembrance* is permitted distinctly to be seen:

And the Raven, never flitting, still is sitting, still is sitting,
On the pallid bust of Pallas just above my chamber door;
And his eyes have all the seeming of a demon that is dreaming,
And the lamplight o'er him streaming throws his shadow on the floor;
And my soul *from out that shadow* that lies floating on the floor
 Shall be lifted — nevermore.

The Rationale of Verse

THE WORD "Verse" is here used not in its strict or primitive sense, but as the term most convenient for expressing generally and without pedantry all that is involved in the consideration of rhythm, rhyme, metre, and versification.

There is, perhaps, no topic in polite literature which has been more pertinaciously discussed, and there is certainly not one about which so much inaccuracy, confusion, misconception, misrepresentation, mystification, and downright ignorance on all sides, can be fairly said to exist. Were the topic really difficult, or did it lie, even, in the cloudland of metaphysics, where the doubt-vapors may be made to assume any and every shape at the will or at the fancy of the gazer, we should have less reason to wonder at all this contradiction and perplexity; but in fact the subject is exceedingly simple; one-tenth of it, possibly, may be called ethical; nine-tenths, however, appertain to mathematics; and the whole is included within the limits of the commonest common sense.

"But, if this is the case, how," it will be asked, "can so much misunderstanding have arisen? Is it conceivable that a thousand profound scholars, investigating so very simple a matter for centuries, have not been able to place it in the fullest light, at least, of which it is susceptible?" These queries, I confess, are not easily answered: at all events, a satisfactory reply to them might cost more trouble than would, if properly considered, the whole *vexata quæstio* to which they have reference. Nevertheless, there is little difficulty or danger in suggesting that the "thousand profound scholars" *may* have failed first, because they were scholars; secondly, because they were profound; and thirdly, because they were a thousand — the impotency of the scholarship and profundity hav-

ing been thus multiplied a thousand fold. I am serious in these suggestions; for, first again, there is something in "scholarship" which seduces us into blind worship of Bacon's Idol of the Theatre — into irrational deference to antiquity; secondly, the proper "profundity" is rarely profound — it is the nature of Truth in general, as of some ores in particular, to be richest when most superficial; thirdly, the clearest subject may be over-clouded by mere superabundance of talk. In chemistry, the best way of separating two bodies is to add a third; in speculation, fact often agrees with fact and argument with argument, until an additional well-meaning fact or argument sets everything by the ears. In one case out of a hundred a point is excessively discussed because it is obscure; in the ninety-nine remaining it is obscure because excessively discussed. When a topic is thus circumstanced, the readiest mode of investigating it is to forget that any previous investigation has been attempted.

But, in fact, while much has been written on the Greek and Latin rhythms, and even on the Hebrew, little effort has been made at examining that of any of the modern tongues. As regards the English, comparatively nothing has been done. It may be said, indeed, that we are without a treatise on our own verse. In our ordinary grammars and in our works on rhetoric or prosody in general, may be found occasional chapters, it is true, which have the heading, "Versification," but these are, in all instances, exceedingly meagre. They pretend to no analysis; they propose nothing like system; they make no attempts at even rule; everything depends upon "authority." They are confined, in fact, to mere exemplification of the supposed varieties of English feet and English lines — although in no work with which I am acquainted are these feet correctly given or these lines detailed in anything like their full extent. Yet what has been mentioned is all — if we except the occasional introduction of some pedagogue-ism, such as this borrowed from the Greek Prosodies: "When a syllable is wanting the verse is said to be catalectic; when the measure is exact, the line is acatalectic; when there is a redundant syllable, it forms hypermeter." Now, whether a line be termed catalectic or acatalectic is, perhaps, a point of no vital importance — it is even possible that the student may be able to decide, promptly, when the *a* should be employed and when omitted, yet be incognizant, at the same time, of *all* that is worth knowing in regard to the structure of verse.

A leading defect in each of our treatises (if treatises they can be called) is the confining the subject to mere *Versification*, while *Verse* in general, with the understanding given to the term in the heading of this paper, is the real question at issue. Nor am I aware of even one of our Grammars which so much as properly defines the word versification itself. "Versification," says a work now before me, of which the accuracy is far more than usual — the "English Grammar" of Goold Brown — "Versification is the art of arranging words into lines of correspondent length, so as to produce harmony by the regular alternation of syllables

differing in quantity." The commencement of this definition might apply, indeed, to the *art* of versification, but not to versification itself. Versification is not the art of arranging, etc., but the actual arranging — a distinction too obvious to need comment. The error here is identical with one which has been too long permitted to disgrace the initial page of every one of our school grammars. I allude to the definitions of English Grammar itself. "English Grammar," it is said, "is the art of speaking and writing the English language correctly." This phraseology, or something essentially similar, is employed, I believe, by Bacon, Miller, Fisk, Greenleaf, Ingersoll, Kirkland, Cooper, Flint, Pue, Comly, and many others. These gentlemen, it is presumed, adopted it without examination from Murray, who derived it from Lily (whose work was *"quam solam Regia Majestas in omnibus scholis docendam præcipit"*), and who appropriated it without acknowledgment, but with some unimportant modification, from the Latin Grammar of Leonicenus. It may be shown, however, that this definition, so complacently received, is not, and cannot be, a proper definition of English Grammar. A definition is that which so describes its object as to distinguish it from all others — it is no definition of any one thing if its terms are applicable to any one other. But if it be asked — "What is the design — the end — the aim of English Grammar?" our obvious answer is, "The art of speaking and writing the English language correctly" — that is to say, we must use the precise words employed as the definition of English Grammar itself. But the object to be obtained by any means is, assuredly, not the means. English Grammar and the end contemplated by English Grammar are two matters sufficiently distinct; nor can the one be more reasonably regarded as the other than a fishing-hook as a fish. The definition, therefore, which is applicable in the latter instance, *cannot*, in the former, be true. Grammar in general is the analysis of language; English Grammar of the English.

But to return to Versification as defined in our extract above. "It is the art," says the extract, "of arranging words into lines *of correspondent length*." Not so: — a correspondence in the length of lines is by no means essential. Pindaric odes are, surely, instances of versification, yet these compositions are noted for extreme diversity in the length of their lines.

The arrangement is moreover said to be for the purpose of producing *"harmony* by the regular alternation," etc. But *harmony* is not the sole aim — not even the principal one. In the construction of verse, *melody* should never be left out of view; yet this is a point which all our Prosodies have most unaccountably forborne to touch. Reasoned rules on this topic should form a portion of all systems of rhythm.

"So as to produce harmony," says the definition, "by the *regular alternation*," etc. A *regular* alternation, as described, forms no part of any principle of versification. The arrangement of spondees and dactyls, for example, in the Greek hexameter, is an arrangement which may be

termed *at random*. At least it is arbitrary. Without interference with the line as a whole, a dactyl may be substituted for a spondee, or the converse, at any point other than the ultimate and penultimate feet, of which the former is always a spondee, the latter nearly always a dactyl. Here, it is clear, we have no "*regular* alternation of syllables differing in quantity."

"So as to produce harmony," proceeds the definition, "by the regular alternation of *syllables differing in quantity*," — in other words by the alternation of long and short syllables; for in rhythm all syllables are necessarily either short or long. But not only do I deny the necessity of any *regularity* in the succession of feet and, by consequence, of syllables, but dispute the essentiality of any *alternation*, regular or irregular, of syllables long and short. Our author, observe, is now engaged in a definition of versification in general, not of English versification in particular. But the Greek and Latin metres abound in the spondee and pyrrhic — the former consisting of two long syllables, the latter of two short; and there are innumerable instances of the immediate succession of many spondees and many pyrrhics.

Here is a passage from Silius Italicus:

> Fallit te mensas inter quod credis inermem
> Tot bellis quæsita viro, tot cædibus armat
> Majestas aeterna ducem: si admoveris ora
> Cannas et Trebium ante oculos Trasymenaque busta
> Et Pauli stare ingentem miraberis umbram.

Making the elisions demanded by the classic Prosodies, we should scan these Hexameters thus:

> Fāllīt | tē mēn | sās ĭn | tēr qŭod | crēdĭs ĭn | ērmēm |
> Tŏt bēl | līs qūæ | sītă vĭ | rō tŏt | caedĭbŭs | ārmāt |
> Mājēs | tās æ | tērnă dŭ | cēm s' ād | mōvĕrĭs | ōrā |
> Cānnās | ēt Trĕbī' | ānt' ŏcŭ | lōs Trăsў | mēnăquĕ | būstā
> Et Pāu | lĭ stā | r' ĭngēn | tēm mī | rābĕrĭs | ūmbrām |

It will be seen that, in the first and last of these lines, we have only two short syllables in thirteen, with an uninterrupted succession of no less than *nine* long syllables. But how are we to reconcile all this with a definition of versification which describes it as "the art of arranging words into lines of correspondent length so as to produce harmony by the *regular alternation of syllables differing in quantity*"?

It may be urged, however, that our prosodist's *intention* was to speak of the English metres alone, and that, by omitting all mention of the spondee and pyrrhic, he has virtually avowed their exclusion from our rhythms. A grammarian is never excusable on the ground of good intentions. We demand from him, if from any one, rigorous precision of style. But grant the design. Let us admit that our author, following the ex-

ample of all authors on English Prosody, has, in defining versification at large, intended a definition merely of the English. All these prosodists, we will say, reject the spondee and pyrrhic. Still all admit the iambus, which consists of a short syllable followed by a long; the trochee, which is the converse of the iambus; the dactyl, formed of one long syllable followed by two short; and the anapæst — two short succeeded by a long. The spondee is improperly rejected, as I shall presently show. The pyrrhic is rightfully dismissed. Its existence in either ancient or modern rhythm is purely chimerical, and the insisting on so perplexing a nonentity as a foot of *two short* syllables, affords, perhaps, the best evidence of the gross irrationality and subservience to authority which characterise our Prosody. In the meantime the acknowledged dactyl and anapæst are enough to sustain my proposition about the "alternation," etc., without reference to feet which are assumed to exist in the Greek and Latin metres alone — for an anapæst and a dactyl may meet in the same line, when, of course, we shall have an uninterrupted succession of four short syllables. The meeting of these two feet, to be sure, is an accident not contemplated in the definition now discussed; for this definition, in demanding a "regular alternation of syllables differing in quantity," insists on a regular succession of similar *feet*. But here is an example:

Sīng tŏ mĕ | Isăbĕlle.

This is the opening line of a little ballad now before me which proceeds in the same rhythm — a peculiarly beautiful one. More than all this: — English lines are often well composed, entirely, of a regular succession of syllables *all of the same quantity*: — the first line, for instance, of the following quatrain by Arthur C. Coxe:

March! march! march!
Making sounds as they tread,
Ho! ho! how they step,
Going down to the dead!

The line italicised is formed of three cæsuras. The cæsura, of which I have much to say hereafter, is rejected by the English Prosodies, and grossly misrepresented in the classic. It is a perfect foot — the most important in all verse — and consists of a single *long syllable; but the length of this syllable varies.*

It has thus been made evident that there is *not one* point of the definition in question which does not involve an error; and for anything more satisfactory or more intelligible we shall look in vain to any published treatise on the topic.

So general and so total a failure can be referred only to radical misconception. In fact the English Prosodists have blindly followed the pedants. These latter, like *les moutons de Panurge*, have been occupied in incessant tumbling into ditches, for the excellent reason that their

leaders have so tumbled before. The Iliad, being taken as a starting point, was made to stand instead of Nature and common sense. Upon this poem, in place of facts and deduction from fact, or from natural law, were built systems of feet, metres, rhythms, rules, — rules that contradict each other every five minutes, and for nearly all of which there may be found twice as many exceptions as examples. If any one has a fancy to be thoroughly confounded — to see how far the infatuation of what is termed "classical scholarship," can lead a bookworm in the manufacture of darkness out of sunshine, let him turn over for a few moments any of the German Greek Prosodies. The only thing clearly made out in them is a very magnificent contempt for Leibnitz's principle of "a sufficient reason."

To divert attention from the real matter in hand by any further reference to these works is unnecessary, and would be weak. I cannot call to mind at this moment one essential particular of information that is to be gleaned from them, and I will drop them here with merely this one observation, — that, employing from among the numerous *"ancient"* feet the spondee, the trochee, the iambus, the anapæst, the dactyl, and the cæsura alone, I will engage to scan *correctly* any of the Horatian rhythms, or any true rhythm that human ingenuity can conceive. And this excess of chimerical feet is perhaps the very least of the scholastic supererogations. *Ex uno disce omnia*. The fact is that *quantity* is a point in whose investigation the lumber of mere learning may be dispensed with, if ever in any. Its appreciation is universal. It appertains to no region, nor race, nor era in special. To melody and to harmony the Greeks hearkened with ears precisely similar to those which we employ for similar purposes at present, and I should not be condemned for heresy in asserting that a pendulum at Athens would have vibrated much after the same fashion as does a pendulum in the city of Penn.

Verse originates in the human enjoyment of equality, fitness. To this enjoyment, also, all the moods of verse, rhythm, metre, stanza, rhyme, alliteration, the *refrain*, and other analagous effects, are to be referred. As there are some readers who habitually confound rhythm and metre, it may be as well here to say that the former concerns the *character* of feet (that is arrangements of syllables) while the latter has to do with the *number* of these feet. Thus by "a dactylic *rhythm*" we express a sequence of dactyls. By "a dactylic hexa*meter*" we imply a line or measure consisting of six of these dactyls.

To return to *equality*. Its idea embraces those of similarity, proportion, identity, repetition, and adaptation or fitness. It might not be very difficult to go even behind the idea of equality, and show both how and why it is that the human nature takes pleasure in it, but such an investigation would, for any purpose now in view, be supererogatory. It is sufficient that the *fact* is undeniable — the fact that man derives enjoyment from his perception of equality. Let us examine a crystal. We are at once

interested by the equality between the sides and between the angles of one of its faces; the equality of the sides pleases us, that of the angles doubles the pleasure. On bringing to view a second face in all respects similar to the first, this pleasure seems to be squared; on bringing to view a third it appears to be cubed, and so on. I have no doubt, indeed, that the delight experienced, if measurable, would be found to have exact mathematical relation such as I suggest, that is to say, as far as a certain point, beyond which there would be a decrease in similar relations.

The perception of pleasure in the equality of *sounds* is the principle of *Music.* Unpractised ears can appreciate only simple equalities, such as are found in ballad airs. While comparing one simple sound with another they are too much occupied to be capable of comparing the equality subsisting between these two simple sounds taken conjointly, and two other similar simple sounds taken conjointly. Practised ears, on the other hand, appreciate both equalities at the same instant, although it is absurd to suppose that both are *heard* at the same instant. One is heard and appreciated from itself, the other is heard by the memory, and the instant glides into and is confounded with the secondary appreciation. Highly cultivated musical taste in this manner enjoys not only these double equalities, all appreciated at once, but takes pleasurable cognizance, through memory, of equalities the members of which occur at intervals so great that the uncultivated taste loses them altogether. That this latter can properly estimate or decide on the merits of what is called scientific music is of course impossible. But scientific music has no claim to intrinsic excellence; it is fit for scientific ears alone. In its excess it is the triumph of the *physique* over the *morale* of music. The sentiment is overwhelmed by the sense. On the whole, the advocates of the simpler melody and harmony have infinitely the best of the argument, although there has been very little of real argument on the subject.

In *verse*, which cannot be better designated than as an inferior or less capable Music, there is, happily, little chance for complexity. Its rigidly simple character not even Science — not even Pedantry can greatly pervert.

The rudiment of verse may possibly be found in the *spondee.* The very germ of a thought seeking satisfaction in equality of sound would result in the construction of words of two syllables, equally accented. In corroboration of this idea we find that spondees most abound in the most ancient tongues. The second step we can easily suppose to be the comparison, that is to say, the collocation of two spondees — or two words composed each of a spondee. The third step would be the juxtaposition of three of these words. By this time the perception of monotone would induce further consideration; and thus arises what Leigh Hunt so flounders in discussing under the title of "The *Principle* of Variety in Uniformity." Of course there is no principle in the case — nor in maintaining it. The "Uniformity" is the principle — the "Variety" is but

the principle's natural safeguard from self-destruction by excess of self. "Uniformity," besides, is the very worst word that could have been chosen for the expression of the *general* idea at which it aims.

The perception of monotone having given rise to an attempt at its relief, the first thought in this new direction would be that of collating two or more words formed each of two syllables differently accented (that is to say, short and long) but having the same order in each word — in other terms, of collating two or more iambuses, or two or more trochees. And here let me pause to assert that more pitiable nonsense has been written on the topic of *long* and *short* syllables than on any other subject under the sun. In general, a syllable is long or short, just as it is difficult or easy of enunciation. The *natural* long syllables are those encumbered — the *natural* short syllables are those *un*encumbered with consonants; all the rest is mere artificiality and jargon. The Latin Prosodies have a rule that a "vowel before two consonants is long." This rule is deduced from "authority" — that is, from the observation that vowels so circumstanced, in the ancient poems, are always in syllables long by the laws of scansion. The philosophy of the rule is untouched, and lies simply in the physical difficulty of giving voice to such syllables — of performing the lingual evolutions necessary for their utterance. Of course, it is not the *vowel* that is long (although the rule says so), but the syllable of which the vowel is a part. It will be seen that the length of a syllable, depending on the facility or difficulty of its enunciation, must have great variation in various syllables; but for the purposes of verse we suppose a long syllable equal to two short ones, and the natural deviation from this relativeness we correct in perusal. The more closely our long syllables approach this relation with our short ones, the better, *ceteris paribus*, will be our verse: but if the relation does not exist of itself we force it by emphasis, which can, of course, make any syllable as long as desired; — or, by an effort we can pronounce with unnatural brevity a syllable that is naturally too long. *Accented* syllables are, of course, always long, but where *un*encumbered with consonants, must be classed among the *unnaturally* long. Mere custom has declared that we shall accent them — that is to say, dwell upon them; but no inevitable lingual difficulty forces us to do so. In fine, every long syllable must of its own accord occupy in its utterance, or must be *made* to occupy, precisely the time demanded for two short ones. The only exception to this rule is found in the cæsura — of which more anon.

The success of the experiment with the trochees or iambuses (the one would have suggested the other) must have led to a trial of dactyls or anapæsts — natural dactyls or anapæsts — dactylic or anapæstic *words*. And now some degree of complexity has been attained. There is an appreciation, first, of the equality between the several dactyls or anapæsts, and secondly, of that between the long syllable and the two short conjointly. But here it may be said, that step after step would have been

taken, in continuation of this routine, until all the feet of the Greek Prosodies became exhausted. Not so; these remaining feet have no existence except in the brains of the scholiasts. It is needless to imagine men inventing these things, and folly to explain how and why they invented them, until it shall be first shown that they are actually invented. All other "feet" than those which I have specified are, if not impossible at first view, merely combinations of the specified; and, although this assertion is rigidly true, I will, to avoid misunderstanding, put it in a somewhat different shape. I will say, then, that at present I am aware of no *rhythm* — nor do I believe that any one can be constructed — which, in its last analysis, will not be found to consist altogether of the feet I have mentioned, either existing in their individual and obvious condition, or interwoven with each other in accordance with simple natural laws which I will endeavour to point out hereafter.

We have now gone so far as to suppose men constructing indefinite sequences of spondaic, iambic, trochaic, dactylic, or anapæstic words. In *extending* these sequences, they would be again arrested by the sense of monotone. A succession of spondees would *immediately* have displeased; one of iambuses or of trochees, on account of the variety included within the foot itself, would have taken longer to displease; one of dactyls or anapæsts, still longer; but even the last, if extended very far, must have become wearisome. The idea first of curtailing, and secondly of defining, the length of a sequence would thus at once have arisen. Here then is the *line* of verse proper.* The principle of equality being constantly at the bottom of the whole process, lines would naturally be made, in the first instance, equal in the number of their feet; in the second instance, there would be variation in the mere number; one line would be twice as long as another; then one would be some less obvious multiple of another; then still less obvious proportions would be adopted — nevertheless there would be *proportion*, that is to say, a phase of equality, still.

Lines being once introduced, the necessity of distinctly defining these lines *to the ear* (as yet written verse does not exist), would lead to a scrutiny of their capabilities *at their terminations* — and now would spring up the idea of equality in sound between the final syllables — in other words, of *rhyme*. First, it would be used only in the iambic, anapæstic, and spondaic rhythms (granting that the latter had not been thrown aside long since, on account of its tameness), because in these rhythms the concluding syllable being long, could best sustain the necessary protraction of the voice. No great while could elapse, however, before the effect, found pleasant as well as useful, would be applied to the two remaining rhythms. But as the chief force of rhyme must lie in the

* Verse, from the Latin *vertere*, to turn, is so called on account of the turning or re-commencement of the series of feet. Thus a verse strictly speaking is a line. In this sense, however, I have preferred using the latter word alone; employing the former in the general acceptation given it in the heading of this paper.

accented syllable, the attempt to create rhyme at all in these two remaining rhythms, the trochaic and dactylic, would necessarily result in double and triple rhymes, such as *beauty* with *duty* (trochaic), and *beautiful* with *dutiful* (dactylic).

It must be observed that in suggesting these processes I assign them no date; nor do I even insist upon their order. Rhyme is supposed to be of modern origin, and were this proved my positions remain untouched. I may say, however, in passing, that several instances of rhyme occur in the "Clouds" of Aristophanes, and that the Roman poets occasionally employed it. There is an effective species of ancient rhyming which has never descended to the moderns: that in which the ultimate and penultimate syllables rhyme with each other. For example:

Parturiunt montes; nascetur ridicu*lus mus.*

And again:

Litoreis ingens inventa sub ilici*bus sus.*

The terminations of Hebrew verse (as far as understood) show no signs of rhyme; but what thinking person can doubt that it did actually exist? That men have so obstinately and blindly insisted, *in general,* even up to the present day, in confining rhyme to the *ends* of lines, when its effect is even better applicable elsewhere, intimates in my opinion the sense of some *necessity* in the connection of the ends with the rhyme — hints that the origin of rhyme lay in a necessity which connected it with the end — shows that neither mere accident nor mere fancy gave rise to the connection — points, in a word, at the very necessity which I have suggested (that of some mode of defining lines *to the ear*), as the true origin of rhyme. Admit this and we throw the origin far back in the night of Time — beyond the origin of written verse.

But to resume. The amount of complexity I have now supposed to be attained is very considerable. Various systems of equalization are appreciated at once (or nearly so) in their respective values and in the value of each system with reference to all the others. As our present *ultimatum* of complexity, we have arrived at triple-rhymed, natural-dactylic lines, existing proportionally as well as equally with regard to other triple-rhymed, natural-dactylic lines. For example:

Virginal Lilian, rigidly, humblily dutiful;
Saintlily, lowlily,
Thrillingly, holily
Beautiful!

Here we appreciate, first, the absolute equality between the long syllable of each dactyl and the two short conjointly; secondly, the absolute equality between each dactyl and any other dactyl, in other words, among all the dactyls; thirdly, the absolute equality between the two mid-

dle lines; fourthly, the absolute equality between the first line and the three others taken conjointly; fifthly, the absolute equality between the last two syllables of the respective words "dutiful" and "beautiful"; sixthly, the absolute equality between the two last syllables of the respective words "lowlily" and "holily"; seventhly, the proximate equality between the first syllable of "dutiful" and the first syllable of "beautiful"; eighthly, the proximate equality between the first syllable of "lowlily" and that of "holily"; ninthly, the proportional equality (that of five to one) between the first line and each of its members, the dactyls; tenthly, the proportional equality (that of two to one) between each of the middle lines and its members, the dactyls; eleventhly, the proportional equality between the first line and each of the two middle, that of five to two; twelfthly, the proportional equality between the first line and the last, that of five to one; thirteenthly, the proportional equality between each of the middle lines and the last, that of two to one; lastly, the proportional equality, as concerns number, beween all the lines taken collectively, and any individual line, that of four to one.

The consideration of this last equality would give birth immediately to the idea of *stanza*,* that is to say, the insulation of lines into equal or obviously proportional masses. In its primitive (which was also its best) form the stanza would most probably have had absolute unity. In other words, the removal of any one of its lines would have rendered it imperfect, as in the case above, where if the last line, for example, be taken away there is left no rhyme to the "dutiful" of the first. Modern stanza is excessively loose, and where so, ineffective as a matter of course.

Now, although in the deliberate written statement which I have here given of these various systems of equalities, there seems to be an infinity of complexity so much that it is hard to conceive the mind taking cognisance of them all in the brief period occupied by the perusal or recital of the stanza, yet the difficulty is in fact apparent only when we will it to become so. Any one fond of mental experiment may satisfy himself, by trial, that in listening to the lines he does actually (although with a seeming unconsciousness, on account of the rapid evolutions of sensation) recognise and instantaneously appreciate (more or less intensely as his ear is cultivated) each and all of the equalizations detailed. The pleasure received or receivable has very much such progressive increase, and in very nearly such mathematical relations as those which I have suggested in the case of the crystal.

It will be observed that I speak of merely a proximate equality between the first syllable of "dutiful" and that of "beautiful," and it may be asked why we cannot imagine the earliest rhymes to have had absolute instead of proximate equality of sound. But absolute equality would have involved the use of identical words, and it is the duplicate same-

* A stanza is often vulgarly, and with gross impropriety, called a *verse*.

ness or monotony, that of sense as well as that of sound, which would have caused these rhymes to be rejected in the very first instance.

The narrowness of the limits within which verse composed of natural feet alone must necessarily have been confined would have led, after a *very* brief interval, to the trial and immediate adoption of artificial feet, that is to say, of feet *not* constituted each of a single word but two, or even three words, or of parts of words. These feet would be intermingled with natural ones. For example:

ă brēath | căn māke | thĕm ās | ă brēath | hăs māde.

This is an iambic line in which each iambus is formed of two words. Again:

Thĕ ūn | ĭmā | gĭnā | blĕ mīght | ŏf Jōve.

This is an iambic line in which the first foot is formed of a word and a part of a word; the second and third of parts taken from the body or interior of a word; the fourth of a part and a whole; the fifth of two complete words. There are no *natural* feet in either line. Again:

Cān ĭt bĕ | fāncĭĕd thăt | Dēĭtў | ēvĕr vĭn | dīctĭvelў
Māde ĭn hĭs | imăge ă | mānnĭkĭn | mērelў tŏ | māddĕn ĭt?

These are two dactylic lines in which we find natural feet ("Deity," "mannikin"); feet composed of two words ("fancied that," "image a," "merely to," "madden it"); feet composed of three words, ("can it be," "made in his"); a foot composed of a part of a word ("dictively"); and a foot composed of a word and a part of a word ("ever vin").

And now, in our suppositional progress, we have gone so far as to exhaust all the *essentialities* of verse. What follows may, strictly speaking, be regarded as embellishment merely, but even in this embellishment the rudimental sense of *equality* would have been the never-ceasing impulse. It would, for example, be simply in seeking further administration to this sense that men would come in time to think of the *refrain* or burden, where, at the closes of the several stanzas of a poem, one word or phrase is *repeated;* and of alliteration, in whose simplest form a consonant is *repeated* in the commencements of various words. This effect would be extended so as to embrace repetitions both of vowels and of consonants in the bodies as well as in the beginnings of words, and at a later period would be made to infringe on the province of rhyme by the introduction of general similarity of sound between whole feet occurring in the body of a line — all of which modifications I have exemplified in the line above.

Made in his image *a mannikin* merely *to madden it.*

Further cultivation would improve also the *refrain* by relieving its monotone in slightly varying the phrase at each repetition, or (as I have at-

tempted to do in "The Raven") in retaining the phrase and varying its application, although this latter point is not strictly a rhythmical effect *alone*. Finally, poets when fairly wearied with following precedent, following it the more closely the less they perceived it in company with Reason, would adventure so far as to indulge in positive rhyme at other points than the ends of lines. First, they would put it in the middle of the line, then at some point where the multiple would be less obvious, then, alarmed at their own audacity, they would undo all their work by cutting these lines in two. And here is the fruitful source of the infinity of "short metre" by which modern poetry, if not distinguished, is at least disgraced. It would require a high degree, indeed, both of cultivation and of courage on the part of any versifier to enable him to place his rhymes, and let them remain at unquestionably their best position, that of unusual and *unanticipated* intervals.

On account of the stupidity of some people, or (if talent be a more respectable word), on account of their talent for misconception — I think it necessary to add here, first, that I believe the "processes" above detailed to be nearly, if not accurately, those which *did* occur in the gradual creation of what we now call verse; secondly, that, although I so believe, I yet urge neither the assumed fact nor my belief in it as a part of the true propositions of this paper; thirdly, that in regard to the aim of this paper, it is of no consequence whether these processes did occur either in the order I have assigned them, or at all; my design being simply, in presenting a general type of what such processes *might* have been and *must* have resembled, to help *them*, the "some people," to an easy understanding of what I have further to say on the topic of Verse.

There is one point, which, in my summary of the processes, I have purposely forborne to touch; because this point, being the most important of all, on account of the immensity of error usually involved in its consideration, would have led me into a series of detail inconsistent with the object of a summary.

Every reader of verse must have observed how seldom it happens that even any one line proceeds uniformly with a succession, such as I have supposed, of absolutely equal feet; that is to say, with a succession of iambuses only, or of trochees only, or of dactyls only, or of anapæsts only, or of spondees only. Even in the most musical lines we find the succession interrupted. The iambic pentameters of Pope, for example, will be found on examination, frequently varied by trochees in the beginning, or by (what seem to be) anapæsts in the body of the line.

 ŏh thōu | whătē | vĕr tī | tlĕ pleāse | thīne eār |
 Dĕan Drā | pĭer Bĭck | ĕrstāff | ŏr Gūll | ĭvēr |
 Whēthēr | thŏu choōse | Cĕrvān | tĕs' | sē | rĭoŭs āir |
 ŏr laūgh | ănd shāke | ĭn Rāb | ĕlaĭs' eā | sŷ chaīr |

Were any one weak enough to refer to the Prosodies for the solution of the difficulty here, he would find it *solved* as usual by a *rule*, stating the fact (or what it, the rule, supposes to be the fact), but without the slightest attempt at the *rationale*. "By a *synæresis* of the two short syllables," say the books, "an anapæst may sometimes be employed for an iambus, or dactyl for a trochee. . . . In the beginning of a line a trochee is often used for an iambus."

Blending is the plain English for *synæresis* — but there should be *no* blending; neither is an anapæst *ever* employed for an iambus, or a dactyl for a trochee. These feet differ in time; and *no* feet so differing can ever be legitimately used in the same line. An anapæst is equal to four short syllables — an iambus only to three. Dactyls and trochees hold the same relation. The principle of *equality*, in verse, admits, it is true, of variation at certain points, for the relief of monotone, as I have already shown, but the point of *time* is that point which, being the rudimental one, must never be tampered with at all.

To explain: — In further efforts for the relief of monotone than those to which I have alluded in the summary, men soon came to see that there was no absolute necessity for adhering to the precise number of syllables, provided the time required for the whole foot was preserved inviolate. They saw, for instance, that in such a line as

ŏr lāugh | ănd shāke | ĭn Rāb | ĕlaĭs' ĕa | sў̆ chāir, |

the equalisation of the three syllables *elais ea* with the two syllables composing any of the other feet, could be readily effected by pronouncing the two syllables *elais* in double quick time. By pronouncing each of the syllables *e* and *lais* twice as rapidly as the syllable *sy*, or the syllable *in*, or any other short syllable, they could bring the two of them, taken together, to the length, that is to say to the time, of any one short syllable. This consideration enabled them to effect the agreeable variation of three syllables in place of the uniform two. And variation was the object — variation to the ear. What sense is there, then, in supposing this object rendered null by the *blending* of the two syllables so as to render them, in absolute effect, one? Of course, there must be *no* blending. Each syllable must be pronounced as distinctly as possible (or the variation is lost), but with twice the rapidity in which the ordinary short syllable is enunciated. That the syllables *elais ea* do not compose an *anapæst* is evident, and the signs (ᾰ ᾰ ā) of their accentuation are erroneous. The foot might be written thus (a a a) the inverted crescents expressing double quick time; and might be called a bastard iambus.

Here is a trochaic line:

Sēe thĕ | dĕlĭcăte — fōotĕd | rēin-deĕr.

The prosodies — that is to say the most considerate of them — would here decide that "*delicate*" is a dactyl used in place of a trochee, and

would refer to what they call their "rule" for justification. Others, vary-
ing the stupidity, would insist upon a Procrustean adjustment thus
(del'cate) an adjustment recommended to all such words as *silvery, mur-
muring,* etc., which, it is said, should be not only pronounced but writ-
ten *silv'ry, murm'ring,* and so on, whenever they find themselves in
trochaic predicament. I have only to say that "delicate," when circum-
stanced as above, is neither a dactyl nor a dactyl's equivalent; that I
would suggest for it this (a̱ a̯ a̱) accentuation; that I think it as well to
call it a bastard trochee; and that all words, at all events, should be
written and pronounced *in full,* and as nearly as possible as nature in-
tended them.

About eleven years ago, there appeared in "The American Monthly
Magazine" (then edited, I believe, by Messrs Hoffman and Benjamin,)
a review of Mr. Willis's Poems; the critic putting forth his strength, or
his weakness, in an endeavor to show that the poet was either absurdly
affected, or grossly ignorant of the laws of verse; the accusation being
based altogether on the fact that Mr. W. made occasional use of this
very word "delicate," and other similar words, in "the Heroic measure,
which every one knew consisted of feet of two syllables." Mr. W. has
often, for example, such lines as

> That binds him to a woman's *delicate* love —
> In the gay sunshine, *reverent* in the storm
> With its *invisible* fingers my loose hair.

Here of course, the feet *licate love, verent in* and *sible fin,* are bastard
iambuses; are *not anapaests* and are *not* improperly used. Their em-
ployment, on the contrary, by Mr. Willis, is but one of the innumer-
able instances he has given of keen sensibility in all those matters
of taste which may be classed under the general head of *fanciful
embellishment.*

It is also about eleven years ago, if I am not mistaken, since Mr. Horne
(of England,) the author of "Orion," one of the noblest epics in any
language, thought it necessary to preface his "Chaucer Modernized" by
a very long and evidently a very elaborate essay, of which the greater
portion was occupied in a discussion of the seemingly anomalous foot
of which we have been speaking. Mr. Horne upholds Chaucer in its fre-
quent use; maintains his superiority, *on account of* his so frequently using
it, over all English versifiers; and indignantly repelling the common idea
of those who make verse on their fingers — that the superfluous syllable
is a roughness and an error — very chivalrously makes battle for it as a
"grace." That a grace it *is,* there can be no doubt; and what I complain
of is, that the author of the most happily versified long poem in existence,
should have been under the necessity of discussing this grace merely *as*
a grace, through forty or fifty vague pages, solely because of his inability

to show *how* and *why* it is a grace — by which showing the question would have been settled in an instant.

About the trochee used for an iambus, as we see in the beginning of the line,

> Whēthĕr thou choose Cervantes' serious air,

there is little that need be said. It brings me to the general proposition that, in all rhythms, the prevalent or distinctive feet may be varied at will, and nearly at random, by the *occasional* introduction of equivalent feet — that is to say, feet the sum of whose syllabic times is equal to the sum of the syllabic times of the distinctive feet. Thus, the trochee, *whēthĕr* is equal, in the sum of the times of its syllables, to the iambus, *thŏu choōse*, in the sum of the times of *its* syllables; each foot being in time equal to three short syllables. Good versifiers who happen to be also good poets, contrive to relieve the monotony of a series of feet by the use of equivalent feet only at rare intervals, and at such points of their subject as seem in accordance with the *startling* character of the variation. Nothing of this care is seen in the line quoted above — although Pope has some fine instances of the duplicate effect. Where vehemence is to be strongly expressed, I am not sure that we should be wrong in venturing on *two consecutive* equivalent feet — although I cannot say that I have ever known the adventure made, except in the following passage, which occurs in "Al Aaraaf," a boyish poem written by myself when a boy. I am referring to the sudden and rapid advent of a star:

> Dim was its little disk, and angel eyes
> Alone could see the phantom in the skies,
> Whĕn first thĕ phāntŏm's cōurse wăs fōund tŏ bē
> Hĕadlŏng hīthĕrward o'er the starry sea.

In the "general proposition" above, I speak of the *occasional* introduction of equivalent feet. It sometimes happens that unskilful versifiers, without knowing what they do, or why they do it, introduce so many "variations" as to exceed in number the "distinctive" feet, when the ear becomes at once balked by the *bouleversement* of the rhythm. Too many trochees, for example, inserted in an iambic rhythm would convert the latter to a trochaic. I may note here that in all cases the rhythm designed should be commenced and continued, *without* variation, until the ear has had full time to comprehend what *is* the rhythm. In violation of a rule so obviously founded in common sense, many even of our best poets do not scruple to begin an iambic rhythm with a trochee, or the converse; or a dactylic with an anapæst, or the converse; and so on.

A somewhat less objectionable error, although still a decided one, is that of commencing a rhythm not with a different equivalent foot, but with a "bastard" foot of the rhythm intended. For example:

Mãnȳ ă | thoūght wĭll | cōme tŏ | mĕmŏrȳ. |

Here *many a* is what I have explained to be a bastard trochee, and to be understood should be accented with inverted crescents. It is objectionable solely on account of its position as the *opening* foot of a trochaic rhythm. *Memory*, similarly accented is also a bastard trochee, but *un-objectionable*, although by no means demanded.

The further illustration of this point will enable me to take an important step.

One of our finest poets, Mr. Christopher Pearse Cranch, begins a very beautiful poem thus:

> Many are the thoughts that come to me
> In my lonely musing;
> And they drift so strange and swift
> There's no time for choosing
> Which to follow; for to leave
> Any, seems a losing.

"A losing" to Mr. Cranch, of course — but this *en passant*. It will be seen here that the intention is trochaic; — although we do *not* see this intention by the opening foot as we should do, or even by the opening line. Reading the whole stanza, however, we perceive the trochaic rhythm as the general design, and so after some reflection, we divide the first line thus:

Many are the | thōughts thăt | cōme tŏ | mē.

Thus scanned, the line will seem musical. It *is* — highly so. And it is because there is no end to instances of just such lines of apparently incomprehensible music, that Coleridge thought proper to invent his nonsensical *system* of what he calls "scanning by accents" — as if "scanning by accents" were anything more than a phrase. Whenever "Christabel" is really *not rough*, it can be as readily scanned by the true *laws* (not the supposititious *rules*) of verse, as can the simplest pentameter of Pope; and where it *is* rough (*passim*) these same laws will enable any one of common sense to show *why* it is rough and to point out, instantaneously the remedy for the roughness.

A reads and re-reads a certain line, and pronounces it false in rhythm — unmusical. B, however, reads it *to* A, and A is at once struck with the perfection of the rhythm, and wonders at his dulness in not "catching" it before. Henceforward he admits the line to be musical. B, triumphant, asserts that, to be sure the line is musical — for it is the work of Coleridge — and that it is A who is *not*; the fault being in A's false reading. Now here A is right and B wrong. *That* rhythm is erroneous (at some point or other more or less obvious), which *any* ordinary reader *can*, without design, read improperly. It is the business of the poet so to construct

his line that the intention *must* be caught *at once*. Even when these men have precisely the same understanding of a sentence, they differ, and often widely, in their modes of enunciating it. Any one who has taken the trouble to examine the topic of emphasis (by which I here mean not *accent* of particular syllables, but the dwelling on entire words), must have seen that men emphasize in the most singularly arbitrary manner. There are certain large classes of people, for example, who persist in emphasizing their monosyllables. Little uniformity of emphasis prevails; because the thing itself — the idea, emphasis — is referable to no natural — at least to no well comprehended and therefore uniform — law. Beyond a very narrow and vague limit, the whole matter is conventionality. And if we differ in emphasis even when we agree in comprehension, how much more so in the former when in the latter too! Apart, however, from the consideration of natural disagreement, is it not clear that, by tripping here and mouthing there, any sequence of words may be twisted into any species of rhythm? But are we thence to deduce that all sequences of words are rhythmical in a rational understanding of the term? — for this is the deduction precisely to which the *reductio ad absurdum* will, in the end, bring all the propositions of Coleridge. Out of a hundred readers of "Christabel," fifty will be able to make nothing of its rhythm, while forty-nine of the remaining fifty will, with some ado, fancy they comprehend it, after the fourth or fifth perusal. The one out of the whole hundred who shall both comprehend and admire it at first sight — must be an unaccountably clever person — and I am by far too modest to assume, for a moment, that that very clever person is myself.

In illustration of what is here advanced I cannot do better than quote a poem:

> Pease porridge hot pease porridge cold
> Pease porridge in the pot — nine days old.

Now those of my readers who have never *heard* this poem pronounced according to the nursery conventionality, will find its rhythm as obscure as an explanatory note; while those who *have* heard it, will divide it thus, declare it musical, and wonder how there can be any doubt about it.

> Pease | porridge | hot | pease | porridge | cold |
> Pease | porridge | in the | pot | nine | days | old. |

The chief thing in the way of this species of rhythm, is the necessity which it imposes upon the poet of travelling in constant company with his compositions, so as to be ready at a moment's notice, to avail himself of a well-understood poetical license — that of reading aloud one's own doggerel.

In Mr. Cranch's line,

> Many are the | thoughts that | come to | me, |

the general error of which I speak is, of course, very partially exemplified, and the purpose for which, chiefly, I cite it, lies yet further on in our topic.

The two divisions (*thoughts that*) and (*come to*) are ordinary trochees. The first division (many are the) would be thus accented by the Greek Prosodies (mānў ăre thĕ), and would be called by them ἀστρόλογος. The Latin books would style the foot *Pæon Primus*, and both Greek and Latin would swear that it was composed of a trochee and what they term a pyrrhic — that is to say, a foot of two *short* syllables — a thing that *cannot be*, as I shall presently show.

But now, there is an obvious difficulty. The *astrologos*, according to the Prosodies' own showing, is equal to *five* short syllables, and the trochee to *three* — yet, in the line quoted, these two feet are equal. They occupy, *precisely*, the same time. In fact, the whole music of the line depends upon their being *made* to occupy the same time. The Prosodies then, have demonstrated what all mathematicians have stupidly failed in demonstrating — that three and five are one and the same thing. After what I have already said, however, about the bastard trochee and the bastard iambus, no one can have any trouble in understanding that *many are the* is of similar character. It is merely a bolder variation than usual from the routine of trochees, and introduces to the bastard trochee one additional syllable. But this syllable is not short. That is, it is not short in the sense of "*short*" as applied to the final syllable of the ordinary trochee, where the word means merely *the half of long*.

In this case (that of the additional syllable) "short," if used at all, must be used in the sense of *the sixth of long*. And all the three final syllables can be called *short* only with the same understanding of the term. The three together are equal only to the one short syllable (whose place they supply) of the ordinary trochee. It follows that there is no sense in thus (˘) accenting these syllables. We must devise for them some new character which shall denote the sixth of long. Let it be (ͨ) — the crescent placed with the curve to the left. The whole foot (many are the) might be called a *quick trochee*.

We now come to the final division (*me*) of Mr. Cranch's line. It is clear that this foot, short as it appears, is fully equal in time to each of the preceding. It is, in fact, the cæsura — the foot which, in the beginning of this paper, I called the most important in all verse. Its chief office is that of pause or termination; and here — at the end of a line — its use is easy, because there is no danger of misapprehending its value. We pause on it, by a seeming necessity, just so long as it has taken us to pronounce the preceding feet, whether iambuses, trochees, dactyls, or anapæsts. It is thus a *variable foot*, and, with some care, may be well introduced into the body of a line, as in a little poem of great beauty by Mrs. Welby:

I have | a lĭt | tle step | sŏn | of on | ly three | years old. |

Here we dwell on the cæsura, *son*, just as long as it requires us to pronounce either of the preceding or succeeding iambuses. Its value, therefore, in this line, is that of three short syllables. In the following dactylic line its value is that of four short syllables.

<div align="center">Pale as a | lily was | Emily | $\overset{\frown\frown\frown}{\text{Gray.}}$</div>

I have accented the cæsura with a ($\frown\frown$) by way of expressing this variability of value.

I observed just now that there could be no such foot as one of two short syllables. What we start from in the very beginning of all idea on the topic of verse, is quantity, *length*. Thus when we enunciate an independent syllable it is long, as a matter of course. If we enunciate two, dwelling on both equally, we express equality in the enunciation, or length, and have a right to call them two long syllables. If we dwell on one more than the other, we have also a right to call one short, because it is short in relation to the other. But if we dwell on both equally, and with a tripping voice, saying to ourselves here are two short syllables, the query might well be asked of us —"in relation to what are they short?" Shortness is but the negation of length. To say, then, that two syllables, placed independently of any other syllable, are short, is merely to say that they have no positive length, or enunciation — in other words, that they are no syllables — that they do not exist at all. And if, persisting, we add anything about their equality, we are merely floundering in the idea of an identical equation, where, x being equal to x, nothing is shown to be equal to zero. In a word, we can form no conception of a pyrrhic as of an independent foot. It is a mere chimera bred in the mad fancy of a pedant.

From what I have said about the equalization of the several feet of a *line*, it must not be deduced that any *necessity* for equality in time exists between the rhythm of *several* lines. A poem, or even a stanza, may begin with iambuses in the first line, and proceed with anapæsts in the second, or even with the less accordant dactyls, as in the opening of quite a pretty specimen of verse by Miss Mary A. S. Aldrich:

<div align="center">The wa | ter li | ly sleeps | in pride |</div>

<div align="center">Dŏwn ĭn thĕ | dēpths ŏf thĕ | āzūre | $\overset{\frown\frown\frown}{\text{lake.}}$ |</div>

Here *azure* is a spondee, equivalent to a dactyl; *lake* a cæsura.

I shall now best proceed in quoting the initial lines of Byron's "Bride of Abydos":

<div align="center">Know ye the land where the cypress and myrtle

Are emblems of deeds that are done in their clime,

Where the rage of the vulture, the love of the turtle

Now melt into softness, now madden to crime?</div>

Know ye the land of the cedar and vine,
Where the flowers ever blossom, the beams ever shine,
And the light wings of Zephyr, oppressed with perfume,
Wax faint o'er the gardens of Gul in their bloom?
Where the citron and olive are fairest of fruit
And the voice of the nightingale never is mute —

.

Where the virgins are soft as the roses they twine,
And all save the spirit of man is divine?
'Tis the land of the East — 'tis the clime of the Sun —
Can he smile on such deeds as his children have done?
Oh, wild as the accents of lovers' farewell
Are the hearts that they bear and the tales that they tell.

Now the flow of these lines (as times go) is very sweet and musical. They have been often admired, and justly — as times go — that is to say, it is a rare thing to find better versification of its kind. And where verse is pleasant to the ear, it is silly to find fault with it because it refuses to be scanned. Yet I have heard men, professing to be scholars, who made no scruple of abusing these lines of Byron's on the ground that they were musical in spite of *all law*. Other gentlemen, *not* scholars, abused "all law" for the same reason — and it occurred neither to the one party nor to the other that the law about which they were disputing might possibly be no law at all — an ass of a law in the skin of a lion.

The Grammars said nothing about dactylic lines, and it was easily seen that *these* lines were at least meant for dactylic. The first one was, therefore, thus divided:

Knōw yĕ thĕ | lānd whĕre thĕ | cyprĕss ănd | my̆rtlĕ. |

The concluding foot was a mystery; but the Prosodies said something about the dactylic "measure" calling now and then for a double rhyme; and the court of inquiry were content to rest in the double rhyme, without exactly perceiving what a double rhyme had to do with the question of an irregular foot. Quitting the first line, the second was thus scanned:

āre ĕmblĕms | ŏf deĕds thăt | āre dŏne ĭn | theīr clĭme. |

It was immediately seen, however, that *this* would not do — it was at war with the whole emphasis of the reading. It could not be supposed that Byron, or any one in his senses, intended to place stress upon such mono-syllables as "are," "of," and "their," nor could "their clime," collated with "to crime," in the corresponding line below, be fairly twisted into anything like a "double rhyme," so as to bring everything within the category of the Grammars. But farther these Grammars spoke not. The inquirers, therefore, in spite of their sense of harmony in the lines, when considered without reference to scansion, fell upon the idea that the

"Are" was a blunder — an excess for which the poet should be sent to Coventry — and, striking it out, they scanned the remainder of the line as follows:

— ēmblĕms ŏf | deĕds thăt ăre | dŏne ĭn thĕir | clīme. |

This answered pretty well; but the Grammars admitted no such foot as a foot of one syllable; and besides the rhythm was dactylic. In despair, the books are well searcl.ed, however, and at last the investigators are gratified by a full solution of the riddle in the profound "Observation" quoted in the beginning of this article: — "When a syllable is wanting, the verse is said to be catalectic; when the measure is exact, the line is acatalectic; when there is a redundant syllable it forms hypermeter." This is enough. The anomalous line is pronounced to be catalectic at the head and to form hypermeter at the tail — and so on, and so on; it being soon discovered that nearly all the remaining lines are in a similar predicament, and that what flows so smoothly to the ear, although so roughly to the eye, is, after all, a mere jumble of catalecticism, acatalecticism, and hypermeter — not to say worse.

Now, had this court of inquiry been in possession of even the shadow of the *philosophy* of Verse, they would have had no trouble in reconciling this oil and water of the eye and ear, by merely scanning the passage without reference to lines, and, continuously, thus:

Know ye the | land where the | cypress and | myrtle Are | emblems of | deeds that are | done in their | clime Where the | rage of the | vulture the | love of the | turtle Now | melt into | softness now | madden to | *crime* | Know ye the | land of the | cedar and | vine Where the | flowers ever | blossom the | beams ever | shine And the | light wings of | Zephyr op | pressed by per | *fume Wax* | faint o'er the | gardens of | Gul in their | bloom Where the | citron and | olive are | fairest of | fruit And the | voice of the | nightingale | never is | mute Where the | virgins are | soft as the | roses they | *twine And* | all save the | spirit of | man is di | vine. 'Tis the | land of the | East 'tis the | clime of the | Sun Can he | smile on such | deeds as his | children have | *done Oh* | wild as the | accents of | lovers' fare | well Are the | hearts that they | bear and the | tales that they | *tell*.

Here "crime" and "tell" (italicised) are cæsuras, each having the value of a dactyl, four short syllables, while "fume Wax," "twine And," and "done Oh," are spondees which, of course, being composed of two long syllables are also equal to four short, and are the dactyl's natural equivalent. The nicety of Byron's ear has led him into a succession of feet which, with two trivial exceptions as regards melody, are absolutely accurate, a very rare occurrence this in dactylic or anapæstic rhythms. The exceptions are found in the spondee "*twine And*," and the dactyl "*smile on such*." Both feet are false in point of melody. In "*twine And*" to make out the rhyme we must force "*And*" into a length which it will not naturally bear.

We are called on to sacrifice either the proper length of the syllable as demanded by its position as a member of a spondee, or the customary accentuation of the word in conversation. There is no hesitation, and should be none. We at once give up the sound for the sense, and the rhythm is imperfect. In this instance it is *very* slightly so, not one person in ten thousand could by ear detect the inaccuracy. But the *perfection* of verse as regards melody, consists in its *never* demanding any such sacrifice as is here demanded. The rhythmical must agree *thoroughly* with the reading flow. This perfection has in no instance been attained, but is unquestionably attainable. *"Smile on such,"* a dactyl, is incorrect, because *"such,"* from the character of the two consonants *ch* cannot *easily* be enunciated in the ordinary time of a short syllable, which its position declares that it is. Almost every reader will be able to appreciate the slight difficulty here, and yet the error is by no means so important as that of the *"And"* in the spondee. By dexterity we *may* pronounce *"such"* in the true time, but the attempt to remedy the rhythmical deficiency of the *And* by drawing it out, merely aggrevates the offence against natural enunciation by directing attention to the offence.

My main object, however, in quoting these lines is to show that in spite of the Prosodies, the length of a line is entirely an arbitrary matter. We might divide the commencement of Byron's poem thus: —

Know ye the | land where the |

or thus:

Know ye the | land where the | cypress and |

or thus:

Know ye the | land where the | cypress and | myrtle are |

or thus:

Know ye the | land where the | cypress and | myrtle are | emblems of |

In short, we may give it any division we please, and the lines will be good, provided we have at least *two* feet in a line. As in mathematics two units are required to form number, so rhythm (from the Greek ἀριθμος, number) demands for its formation at least two feet. Beyond doubt, we often see such lines as

Know ye the —
Land where the —

lines of one foot, and our Prosodies admit such, but with impropriety, for common sense would dictate that every so obvious division of a poem as is made by a line, should include within itself all that is necessary for its own comprehension, but in a line of one foot we can have no appreciation of *rhythm*, which depends upon the equality between *two* or more

pulsations. The false lines, consisting sometimes of a single cæsura, which are seen in mock Pindaric odes, are, of course, "rhythmical" only in connection with some other line, and it is this want of independent rhythm which adapts them to the purposes of burlesque alone. Their effect is that of incongruity (the principle of mirth), for they include the blankness of prose amid the harmony of verse.

My second object in quoting Byron's lines was that of showing how absurd it often is to cite a single line from amid the body of a poem for the purpose of instancing the perfection or imperfection of the line's rhythm. Were we to see by itself

Know ye the land where the cypress and myrtle,

we might justly condemn it as defective in the final foot, which is equal to only three, instead of being equal to four short syllables.

In the foot "*flowers ever*" we shall find a further exemplification of the principle of the bastard iambus, bastard trochee, and quick trochee, as I have been at some pains in describing these feet above. All the Prosodies on English verse would insist upon making an elision in "flowers," thus (flow'rs), but this is nonsense. In the quick trochee (mānў ăre thĕ) occurring in Mr. Cranch's *trochaic* line, we had to equalize the time of the three syllables (*ny, are, the*) to that of the one *short* syllable whose position they usurp. Accordingly each of these syllables is equal to the third of a short syllable, that is to say, the *sixth of a long*. But in Byron's *dactylic* rhythm, we have to equalize the time of the three syllables (*ers, ev, er*) to that of the one *long* syllable whose position they usurp, or (which is the same thing) of the *two short*. Therefore the value of each of the syllables (*ers, ev*, and *er*) is the *third of a long*. We enunciate them with only half the rapidity we employ in enunciating the three final syllables of the quick trochee — which latter is a rare foot. The "*flowers ever*," on the contrary, is as common in the dactylic rhythm as is the *bastard* trochee in the trochaic, or the bastard iambus in the iambic. We may as well accent it with the curve of the crescent to the right and call it a *bastard dactyl*. A *bastard anapæst*, whose nature I now need be at no trouble in explaining, will of course occur now and then in an anapæstic rhythm.

In order to avoid any chance of that confusion which is apt to be introduced in an essay of this kind by too sudden and radical an alteration of the conventionalities to which the reader has been accustomed, I have thought it right to suggest for the accent marks of the bastard trochee, bastard iambus, etc. etc., certain characters which, in merely varying the direction of the ordinary short accent (˘) should imply, what is the fact, that the feet themselves are not *new* feet, in any proper sense, but simply modifications of the feet, respectively, from which they derive their names. Thus a bastard iambus is, in its essentiality, that is to say, in its time an iambus. The variation lies only in the *distribution* of this

time. The time, for example, occupied by the one short (*or half of long*) syllable in the ordinary iambus is in the bastard spread equally over two syllables, which are accordingly the *fourth of long*.

But this fact — the fact of the essentiality, or whole time, of the foot being unchanged, is now so fully before the reader, that I may venture to propose, finally, an accentuation which shall answer the real purpose — that is to say, what should be the real purpose, of all accentuation — the purpose of expressing to the eye the exact relative value of every syllable employed in Verse.

I have already shown that enunciation, or *length*, is the point from which we start. In other words, we begin with a *long syllable*. This then is our unit; and there will be no need of accenting it at all. An unaccented syllable, in a system of accentuation, is to be regarded always as a long syllable. Thus a spondee would be without accent. In an iambus, the first syllable being "short," or the *half* of long, should be accented with a small 2, placed *beneath* the syllable; the last syllable, being long, should be unaccented; the whole would be thus (control). In a trochee, these

₂

accents would be merely converse, thus (manly). In a dactyl, each of the

₂

two final syllables, being the half of long, should also be accented with a small 2 beneath the syllable; and the first syllable left unaccented, the whole would be thus (happiness). In an anapæst we should converse the

_{2 2}

dactyl thus (in the land). In the bastard dactyl, each of the three con-

_{2 2}

cluding syllables being the *third* of long, should be accented with a small 3 beneath the syllable, and the whole foot would stand thus (flowers

₃

ever). In the bastard anapæst we should converse the bastard dactyl thus

_{3 3}

(in the rebound). In the bastard iambus, each of the two initial syllables

_{3 3 3}

being the fourth of long, should be accented below with a small 4; the whole foot would be thus, (in the rain). In the bastard trochee, we should

_{4 4}

converse the bastard iambus thus (many a). In the quick trochee, each

_{4 4}

of the three concluding syllables, being the *sixth* of long, should be accented below with a small 6; the whole foot would be thus (many are

_{6 6}

the). The quick iambus is not yet created, and most probably never will

₆

be; for it will be excessively useless, awkward, and liable to misconception — as I have already shown that even the quick trochee is; — but, should

it appear, we must accent it by conversing the quick trochee. The cæsura, being variable in length, but always *longer than "long,"* should be accented *above*, with a number expressing the length or value of the distinctive foot of the rhythm in which it occurs. Thus a cæsura, occurring in a spondaic rhythm, would be accented with a small 2 above the syllable, or rather foot. Occurring in a dactylic or anapæstic rhythm, we also accent it with the 2 above the foot. Occurring in an iambic rhythm, however, it must be accented above with 1½; for this is the relative value of the iambus. Occurring in the trochaic rhythm, we give it of course the same accentuation. For the complex 1½, however, it would be advisable to substitute the simpler expression 3/2, which amounts to the same thing.

In this system of accentuation Mr. Cranch's lines quoted above, would thus be written:

$$\frac{3}{2}$$
Many are the | thoughts that | come to | me
 6 6 6 2 2

In my | lonely | musing |
 2 2 2

$$\frac{3}{2}$$
And they | drift so | strange and | swift
 2 2 2

There's no | time for | choosing |
 2 2 2

$$\frac{3}{2}$$
Which to | follow | for to | leave
 2 2 2

Any, | seems a | losing. |
 2 2 2

In the ordinary system the accentuation would be thus:

Mān&ymacr; arĕ thĕ | thōughts thăt | cōme tŏ | mē
īn m&ymacr; | lōnel&ymacr; | mūsĭng, |
ānd thĕy | drīft sŏ | strānge ănd | swīft |
Thēre's nŏ | tīme fŏr | choōsĭng |
Whīch tŏ | fōllŏw, | fōr tŏ | lēave
ān&ymacr;, | seēms ă | lōsĭng. |

It must be observed here that I do not grant this to be the "ordinary" *scansion.* On the contrary, I never yet met the man who had the faintest comprehension of the true scanning of these lines, or of such as these. But granting this to be the mode in which our Prosodies would divide the feet they would accentuate the syllables as just above.

Now let any reasonable person compare the two models. The first advantage seen in my mode is that of simplicity, or time, labour, and ink saved. Counting the fractions as *two* accents even there will be found only *twenty-six* accents to the stanza. In the common accentuation there

are *forty-one*. But admit that all this is a trifle, which it is *not*, and let us proceed to points of importance. Does the common accentuation express the truth in particular, in general, or in any regard? Is it consistent with itself? Does it convey either to the ignorant or to the scholar a just conception of the rhythm of the lines? Each of these questions must be answered in the negative. The crescents being precisely similar must be understood as expressing, all of them, one and the same thing, and so all prosodies have always understood them and wished them to be understood. They express indeed "short," but this word has all kinds of meanings. It serves to represent (the reader is left to guess *when*) sometimes the half, sometimes the third, sometimes the fourth, sometimes the sixth, of "long," while "long" itself in the books is left undefined and undescribed. On the other hand, the horizontal accent, it may be said, expresses sufficiently well and unvaryingly the syllables which are meant to be long. It does nothing of the kind. This horizontal accent is placed over the cæsura (wherever, as in the Latin Prosodies, the cæsura is recognised) as well as over the ordinary long syllable, and implies anything and everything, just as the crescent. But grant that it does express the ordinary long syllables (leaving the cæsura out of question) have I not given the identical expression by not employing any expression at all? In a word, while the Prosodies, with a certain number of accents, express *precisely nothing whatever*, I with scarcely half the number, have expressed everything which in a system of accentuation demands expression. In glancing at my mode in the lines of Mr. Cranch, it will be seen that it conveys not only the exact relation of the syllables and feet, among themselves, in those particular lines, but their precise value in relation to any other existing or conceivable feet or syllables in any existing or conceivable system of rhythm.

The object of what we call *scansion* is the distinct marking of the rhythmical flow. Scansion with accents or perpendicular lines between the feet, that is to say scansion *by* the voice only, is scansion *to* the ear only, and all very good in its way. The written scansion addresses the ear through the eye. In either case the object is the distinct marking of the rhythmical, musical, or reading flow. There *can* be no other object, and there is none. Of course, then, the scansion and the reading flow should go hand in hand. The former must agree with the latter. The former represents and expresses the latter, and is good or bad as it truly or falsely represents and expresses it. If by the written scansion of a line we are not enabled to perceive any rhythm or music in the line, then either the line is unrhythmical or the scansion false. Apply all this to the English lines which we have quoted at various points in the course of this article. It will be found that the scansion exactly conveys the rhythm, and thus thoroughly fulfils the only purpose for which scansion is required.

But let the scansion *of the schools* be applied to the Greek and Latin verse, and what result do we find? — that the verse is one thing and the

scansion quite another. The ancient verse *read* aloud is in general musical, and occasionally *very* musical. *Scanned* by the Prosodial rules we can, for the most part, make nothing of it whatever. In the case of the English verse the more emphatically we dwell on the divisions between the feet the more distinct is our perception of the kind of rhythm intended. In the case of the Greek and Latin the more we dwell the *less* distinct is this perception. To make this clear by an example:

> Mæcenas, atavis edite regibus,
> O, et præsidium et dulce decus meum,
> Sunt quos curriculo pulverem Olympicum
> Collegisse juvat, metaque fervidis
> Evitata rotis, palmaque nobilis
> Terrarum dominos evehit ad Deos.

Now in *reading* these lines there is scarcely one person in a thousand who, if even ignorant of Latin, will not immediately feel and appreciate their flow, their music. A prosodist, however, informs the public that the *scansion* runs thus:

> Mæce | nas ata | vis | edite | regibus |
> O, et | præsidi' | et | dulce de | cus meum |
> Sunt quos | curricu | lo | pulver' O | lympicum |
> Colle | gisse ju | vat | metaque | fervidis |
> Evi | tata ro | tis | palmaque | nobilis |
> Terra | rum domi | nos | evehit | ad Deos. |

Now I do not deny that we get a *certain sort* of music from the lines if we read them according to this scansion, but I wish to call attention to the fact that this scansion and the certain sort of music which grows out of it are entirely at war, not only with the reading flow which any ordinary person would naturally give the lines, but with the reading flow universally given them, and never denied them by even the most obstinate and stolid of scholars.

And now these questions are forced upon us — "Why exists this discrepancy between the modern verse with its scansion and the ancient verse with its scansion?" — "Why in the former case are there agreement and representation, while in the latter there is neither the one or the other?" or, to come to the point, "How are we to reconcile the ancient verse with the scholastic scansion of it?" This absolutely necessary conciliation — shall we bring it about by supposing the scholastic scansion wrong because the ancient verse is right, or by maintaining that the ancient verse is wrong because the scholastic scansion is not to be gainsaid?

Were we to adopt the latter mode of arranging the difficulty, we might, in some measure at least, simplify the expression of the arrangement by putting it thus — Because the pedants have no eyes therefore the old poets had no ears.

"But," say the gentlemen without the eyes, "the scholastic scansion, although certainly not handed down to us in form from the old poets themselves (the gentlemen without the ears), is nevertheless deduced from certain facts which are supplied us by careful observation of the old poems."

And let us illustrate this strong position by an example from an American poet, who must be a poet of some eminence or he will not answer the purpose. Let us take Mr. Alfred B. Street. I remember these two lines of his:

> His sinuous path, by blazes, wound
> Among trunks grouped in myriads round.

With the *sense* of these lines I have nothing to do. When a poet is in a "fine frenzy," he may as well imagine a large forest as a small one — and "by blazes!" is *not* intended for an oath. My concern is with the rhythm, which is iambic.

Now let us suppose that, a thousand years hence, when the "American language" is dead, a learned prosodist should be deducing from "careful observation" of our best poets, a system of scansion for our poetry. And let us suppose that this prosodist had so little dependence in the generality and immutability of the laws of Nature as to assume in the outset that, because we lived a thousand years before his time, and made use of steam engines instead of mesmeric balloons, we must therefore have had a *very* singular fashion of mounting our vowels, and altogether of *Hudsonising* our verse. And let us suppose that with these and other fundamental propositions carefully put away in his brain, he should arrive at the line —

> Among | trunks grouped ¦ in my | riads round.

Finding it an obviously iambic rhythm, he would divide it as above; and observing that "trunks" made the first member of an iambus, he would call it short, as Mr. Street intended it to be. Now further: — if instead of admitting the possibility that Mr. Street (who by that time would be called Street simply, just as we say Homer) — that Mr. Street might have been in the habit of writing carelessly, as the poet of the prosodist's own era did, and as all poets will do (on account of being geniuses) — instead of admitting this, suppose the learned scholar should make a "rule" and put it in a book, to the effect that, in the American verse, the vowel *u, when found imbedded among nine consonants,* was *short*: what, under such circumstances, would the sensible people of the scholar's day have a right not only to think, but to say of that scholar? — why, that he was a "fool — by blazes!"

I have put an extreme case, but it strikes at the root of the error. The "rules" are grounded in "authority" — and this "authority" — can any one tell us what it means? or can any one suggest anything that it may *not*

mean? Is it not clear that the "scholar" above referred to, might as readily
have deduced from authority a totally false system as a partially true one?
To deduce from authority a consistent prosody of the ancient metres
would indeed have been within the limits of the barest possibility; and
the task has *not* been accomplished, for the reason that it demands a
species of ratiocination altogether out of keeping with the brain of a
bookworm. A rigid scrutiny will show that the very few "rules" which
have not as many exceptions as examples, are those which have, by acci-
dent, their true bases not in authority, but in the omniprevalent laws of
syllabification; such, for example, as the rule which declares a vowel be-
fore two consonants to be long.

In a word, the gross confusion and antagonism of the scholastic pros-
ody, as its marked inapplicability to the reading flow of the rhythms it
pretends to illustrate, are attributable, first, to the utter absence of natural
principle as a guide in the investigations which have been undertaken by
inadequate men; and secondly, to the neglect of the obvious considera-
tion that the ancient poems, which have been the *criteria* throughout,
were the work of men who must have written as loosely, and with as
little definitive system as ourselves.

Were Horace alive to-day, he would divide for us his first Ode thus,
and "make great eyes" when assured by the prosodists that he had no
business to make any such division!

> Mæcenas | atavis | edite | regibus |
> 2 2 2 2 2 2 2 2
>
> O et præ | sidium et | dulce de | cus meum |
> 2 2 3 3 3 2 2 2 2
>
> Sunt quos cur | riculo | pulverem O | lympicum |
> 2 2 2 2 3 3 3 2 2
>
> Collegisse | juvat | metaque | fervidis |
> 3 3 3 2 2 2 2
>
> Evitata | rotis | palmaque | nobilis |
> 3 3 3 2 2 2 2
>
> Terrarum | dominos | evehit | ad Deos. |
> 2 2 2 2 2 2 2 2

Read by this scansion, the flow is preserved; and the more we dwell on
the divisions, the more the intended rhythm becomes apparent. More-
over, the feet have all the same time; while in the scholastic scansions,
trochees — admitted trochees — are absurdly employed as equivalents
to spondees and dactyls. The books declare, for instance, that the first
foot of this species of verse may be a trochee, and seem to be gloriously
unconscious that to put a trochee in apposition with a longer foot, is to
violate the inviolable principle of all music, *time*.

It will be said, however, by some people, that I have no business to
make a dactyl out of such obviously long syllables as *sunt, quos, cur*.
Certainly I have no business to do so. I *never* do so. And Horace should

not have done so. But he did. Mr. Bryant and Mr. Longfellow do the same thing every day. And merely because these gentlemen now and then forget themselves in this way, it would be hard if some future prosodist should insist upon twisting the "Thanatopsis," or the "Spanish Student," into a jumble of trochees, spondees, and dactyls.

It may be said also by some other people that, in the word *decus*, I have succeeded no better than the books, in making the scansional agree with the reading flow; and that *decus* was not pronounced de*cus*. I reply, that there can be no doubt of the word having been pronounced, in this case, de*cus*. It must be observed that the Latin inflection, or variation of a word in its terminating syllables, caused the Romans — *must* have caused them — to pay greater attention to the termination of a word than to its commencement, or than we do to the termination of our words. The end of the Latin word established that relation of the word with other words which we establish by preposition or auxiliary verbs. Therefore it would seem infinitely less odd to them, than it does to us, to dwell at any time, for any slight purpose, abnormally, on a terminating syllable. In verse, this license — scarcely a license — would be frequently admitted. These ideas unlock the secret of such lines as the

> Litoreis ingens inventa sub illici*bus sus*,

and the

> Parturiunt montes; nascetur ridicu*lus mus*.

which I quoted some time ago while speaking of rhyme.

As regards the prosodial elisions, such as that of *rem* before O, in *pulverem Olympicum*, it is really difficult to understand how so dismally silly a notion could have entered the brain even of a pedant. Were it demanded of me why the books cut off one *vowel* before another, I might say — It is perhaps because the books think that, since a bad reader is so apt to slide the one vowel into the other at any rate, it is just as well to print them *ready-slided*. But in the case of the terminating *m*, which is the most readily pronounced of all consonants (as the infantile *mamma* will testify), and the most impossible to cheat the ear of by any system of sliding — in the case of the *m*, I should be driven to reply that, to the best of my belief, the prosodists did the thing, because they had a fancy for doing it, and wished to see how funny it would look after it was done. The thinking reader will perceive that, from the great facility with which *em* may be enunciated, it is admirably suited to form one of the rapid short syllables in the bastard dactyl (pulverem O); but because

$$\overset{3}{}\quad\overset{3}{}\quad\overset{3}{}$$

the books had no conception of a bastard dactyl, they knocked it on the head at once — by cutting off its tail!

Let me now give a specimen of the true scansion of another Horatian measure — embodying an instance of proper elision.

Integer | vitæ | scelerisque | purus |
 2 2 3 3 3

Non eget | Mauri | jaculis ne | que arcu |
 2 2 3 3 3

Nec vene | natis | gravida sa | gittis,
 2 2 3 3 3

Fusce, pha | retrâ.
 2 2

Here the regular recurrence of the bastard dactyl gives great animation to the rhythm. The *e* before the *a* in *que arcu*, is, almost of sheer necessity, cut off — that is to say, run into the *a* so as to preserve the spondee. But even this license it would have been better not to take.

Had I space, nothing would afford me greater pleasure than to proceed with the scansion of *all* the ancient rhythms, and to show how easily, by the help of common sense, the intended music of each and all can be rendered instantaneously apparent. But I have already overstepped my limits, and must bring this paper to an end.

It will never do, however, to omit all mention of the heroic hexameter.

I began the "processes" by a suggestion of the spondee as the first step towards verse. But the innate monotony of the spondee has caused its disappearance as the basis of rhythm from all modern poetry. We *may* say, indeed, that the French heroic — the most wretchedly monotonous verse in existence — is to all intents and purposes spondaic. But it is not designedly spondaic, and if the French were ever to examine it at all, they would no doubt pronounce it iambic. It must be observed that the French language is strangely peculiar in this point — *that it is without accentuation and consequently without verse.* The genius of the people, rather than the structure of the tongue, declares that their words are for the most part enunciated with a uniform dwelling on each syllable. For example *we* say "syll*a*bific*a*tion." A Frenchman would say syl-la-bi-fi-ca-ti-on, dwelling on no one of the syllables with any noticeable particularity. Here again I put an extreme case in order to be well understood, but the general fact is as I give it — that, comparatively, the French have *no* accentuation; and there can be nothing worth the name of verse without. Therefore, the French have no verse worth the name — which is the fact put in sufficiently plain terms. Their iambic rhythm so superabounds in absolute spondees as to warrant me in calling its basis spondaic; but French is the *only* modern tongue which has any rhythm with such basis, and even in the French it is, as I have said, unintentional.

Admitting, however, the validity of my suggestion, that the spondee was the first approach to verse, we should expect to find, first, natural spondees (words each forming just a spondee) most abundant in the most ancient languages; and, secondly, we should expect to find spondees

forming the basis of the most ancient rhythms. These expectations are in both cases confirmed.

Of the Greek hexameter the intentional basis is spondaic. The dactyls are the *variation* of the theme. It will be observed that there is no absolute certainty about *their* points of interposition. The penultimate foot, it is true, is usually a dactyl, but not uniformly so, while the ultimate, on which the ear *lingers*, is always a spondee. Even that the penultimate is usually a dactyl may be clearly referred to the necessity of winding up with the *distinctive* spondee. In corroboration of this idea, again, we should look to find the penultimate spondee most usual in the most ancient verse, and, accordingly, we find it more frequent in the Greek than in the Latin hexameter.

But besides all this, spondees are not only more prevalent in the heroic hexameter than dactyls, but occur to such an extent as is even unpleasant to modern ears, on account of monotony. What the modern chiefly appreciates and admires in the Greek hexameter is the *melody of the abundant vowel sounds*. The Latin hexameters *really* please very few moderns — although so many pretend to fall into ecstasies about them. In the hexameters quoted several pages ago, from Silius Italicus, the preponderance of the spondee is strikingly manifest. Besides the natural spondees of the Greek and Latin, numerous artificial ones arise in the verse of these tongues, on account of the tendency which inflection has to throw full accentuation on terminal syllables, and the preponderance of the spondee is further ensured by the comparative infrequency of the small prepositions which *we* have to serve us *instead* of case, and also the absence of the diminutive auxiliary verbs with which *we* have to eke out the expression of our primary ones. These are the monosyllables whose abundance serves to stamp the poetic genius of a language as tripping or dactylic.

Now paying no attention to these facts, Sir Philip Sidney, Professor Longfellow, and innumerable other persons, more or less modern, have busied themselves in constructing what they supposed to be "English hexameters on the model of the Greek." The only difficulty was that (even leaving out of question the melodious masses of vowel) these gentlemen never could get their English hexameters to *sound* Greek. Did they *look* Greek? — that should have been the query, and the reply might have led to a solution of the riddle. In placing a copy of ancient hexameters side by side with a copy (in similar type) of such hexameters as Professor Longfellow, or Professor Felton, or the Frogpondian Professors collectively, are in the shameful practice of composing "on the model of the Greek," it will be seen that the latter (hexameters, not professors) are about one-third longer *to the eye*, on an average, than the former. The more abundant dactyls make the difference. And it is the greater number of spondees in the Greek than in the English, in the ancient

than in the modern tongue, which has caused it to fall out that while these eminent scholars were groping about in the dark for a Greek hexameter, which is a spondaic rhythm varied now and then by dactyls, they merely stumbled, to the lasting scandal of scholarship, over something which, on account of its long-leggedness, we may as well term a Feltonian hexameter, and which is a dactylic rhythm interrupted rarely by artificial spondees which are no spondees at all, and which are curiously thrown in by the heels at all kinds of improper and impertinent points.

Here is a specimen of the Longfellow hexameter:

Also the | church with | in was a | dorned for | this was the | season |
In which the | young their | parents' | hope and the | loved ones of |
 Heaven |
Should at the | foot of the | altar re | new the | vows of their | baptism |
Therefore each | nook and | corner was | swept and | cleaned and the |
 dust was |
Blown from the | walls and | ceiling and | from the | oil-painted |
 benches. |

Mr. Longfellow is a man of imagination, but *can* he imagine that any individual, with a proper understanding of the danger of lockjaw, would make the attempt of twisting his mouth into the shape necessary for the emission of such spondees as "par*ents*," and "from the," or such dactyls as "cleaned and the," and "loved ones of"? "Baptism" is by no means a bad spondee — perhaps because it happens to be a dactyl, — of all the rest, however, I am dreadfully ashamed.

But these feet, dactyls and spondees, all together, should thus be put at once into their proper position:

"Also the church within was adorned; for this was the season in which the young, their parents' hope, and the loved ones of Heaven, should, at the foot of the altar, renew the vows of their baptism. Therefore, each nook and corner was swept and cleaned; and the dust was blown from the walls and ceiling, and from the oil-painted benches."

There! — That is respectable prose, and it will incur no danger of ever getting its character ruined by anybody's mistaking it for verse.

But even when we let these modern hexameters go as Greek, and merely hold them fast in their proper character of Longfellowine, or Feltonian, or Frogpondian, we must still condemn them as having been committed in a radical misconception of the philosophy of verse. The spondee, as I observed, is the *theme* of the Greek line. Most of the ancient hexameters *begin* with spondees, for the reason that the spondee *is* the theme, and the ear is filled with it as with a burden. Now the Feltonian dactylics have, in the same way, dactyls for the theme, and most of them begin with dactyls — which is all very proper if not very Greek

— but unhappily, the one point at which they *are* very Greek is that point, precisely, at which they should be nothing but Feltonian. They always *close* with what is meant for a spondee. To be consistently silly they should die off in a dactyl.

That a truly Greek hexameter *cannot*, however, be readily composed in English, is a proposition which I am by no means inclined to admit. I think I could manage the point myself. For example:

Do tell! | when may we | hope to make | men of sense | out of the |
 Pundits
Born and brought | up with their | snouts deep | down in the | mud of
 the | Frog-pond?
Why ask? | who ever | yet saw | money made | out of a | fat old
Jew, or | downright | upright | nutmegs | out of a | pine-knot?

The proper spondee predominance is here preserved. Some of the dactyls are not so good as I could wish, but, upon the whole the rhythm is very decent — to say nothing of its excellent sense.

The Poetic Principle

In speaking of the Poetic Principle, I have no design to be either thorough or profound. While discussing, very much at random, the essentiality of what we call Poetry, my principal purpose will be to cite for consideration, some few of those minor English or American poems which best suit my own taste, or which, upon my own fancy, have left the most definite impression. By "minor poems" I mean, of course, poems of little length. And here, in the beginning, permit me to say a few words in regard to a somewhat peculiar principle, which, whether rightfully or wrongfully, has always had its influence in my own critical estimate of the poem. I hold that a long poem does not exist. I maintain that the phrase, "a long poem," is simply a flat contradiction in terms.

I need scarcely observe that a poem deserves its title only inasmuch as it excites, by elevating the soul. The value of the poem is in the ratio of this elevating excitement. But all excitements are, through a psychal necessity, transient. That degree of excitement which would entitle a poem to be so called at all, cannot be sustained throughout a composition of any great length. After the lapse of half an hour, at the very utmost, it flags — fails — a revulsion ensues — and then the poem is, in effect, and in fact, no longer such.

There are, no doubt, many who have found difficulty in reconciling the critical dictum that the "Paradise Lost" is to be devoutly admired throughout, with the absolute impossibility of maintaining for it, during perusal, the amount of enthusiasm which that critical dictum would demand. This great work, in fact, is to be regarded as poetical, only

when, losing sight of that vital requisite in all works of Art, Unity, we view it merely as a series of minor poems. If, to preserve its Unity — its totality of effect or impression — we read it (as would be necessary) at a single sitting, the result is but a constant alternation of excitement and depression. After a passage of what we feel to be true poetry, there follows, inevitably, a passage of platitude which no critical prejudgment can force us to admire; but if, upon completing the work, we read it again, omitting the first book — that is to say, commencing with the second — we shall be surprised at now finding that admirable which we before condemned — that damnable which we had previously so much admired. It follows from all this that the ultimate, aggregate, or absolute effect of even the best epic under the sun, is a nullity: — and this is precisely the fact.

In regard to the Iliad, we have, if not positive proof, at least very good reason for believing it intended as a series of lyrics; but, granting the epic intention, I can say only that the work is based in an imperfect sense of art. The modern epic is, of the supposititious ancient model, but an inconsiderate and blindfold imitation. But the day of these artistic anomalies is over. If, at any time, any very long poem *were* popular in reality, which I doubt, it is at least clear that no very long poem will ever be popular again.

That the extent of a poetical work is, *ceteris paribus*, the measure of its merit, seems undoubtedly, when we thus state it, a proposition sufficiently absurd — yet we are indebted for it to the Quarterly Reviews. Surely there can be nothing in mere *size*, abstractly considered — there can be nothing in mere *bulk*, so far as a volume is concerned, which has so continuously elicited admiration from these saturnine pamphlets! A mountain, to be sure, by the mere sentiment of physical magnitude which it conveys, *does* impress us with a sense of the sublime — but no man is impressed after *this* fashion by the material grandeur of even "The Columbiad." Even the Quarterlies have not instructed us to be so impressed by it. *As yet*, they have not *insisted* on our estimating Lamartine by the cubic foot, or Pollock by the pound — but what else are we to *infer* from their continual prating about "sustained effort"? If, by "sustained effort," any little gentleman has accomplished an epic, let us frankly commend him for the effort — if this indeed be a thing commendable — but let us forbear praising the epic on the effort's account. It is to be hoped that common sense, in the time to come, will prefer deciding upon a work of Art rather by the impression it makes — by the effect it produces — than by the time it took to impress the effect, or by the amount of "sustained effort" which had been found necessary in effecting the impression. The fact is, that perseverance is one thing and genius quite another — nor can all the Quarterlies in Christendom confound them. By and by, this proposition, with many which I have been just urging, will be received as self-evident. In the meantime, by being

generally condemned as falsities, they will not be essentially damaged as truths.

On the other hand, it is clear that a poem may be improperly brief. Undue brevity degenerates into mere epigrammatism. A *very* short poem, while now and then producing a brilliant or vivid, never produces a profound or enduring effect. There must be the steady pressing down of the stamp upon the wax. De Beranger has wrought innumerable things, pungent and spirit-stirring, but in general they have been too imponderous to stamp themselves deeply into the public attention, and thus, as so many feathers of fancy, have been blown aloft only to be whistled down the wind.

A remarkable instance of the effect of undue brevity in depressing a poem, in keeping it out of the popular view, is afforded by the following exquisite little Serenade —

> I arise from dreams of thee
> > In the first sweet sleep of night,
> When the winds are breathing low,
> > And the stars are shining bright.
> I arise from dreams of thee,
> > And a spirit in my feet
> Has led me — who knows how? —
> > To thy chamber-window, sweet!
>
> The wandering airs they faint
> > On the dark the silent stream —
> The champak odors fail
> > Like sweet thoughts in a dream;
> The nightingale's complaint,
> > It dies upon her heart,
> As I must die on thine,
> > O, beloved as thou art!
>
> O, lift me from the grass!
> > I die, I faint, I fail!
> Let thy love in kisses rain
> > On my lips and eyelids pale.
> My cheek is cold and white, alas!
> > My heart beats loud and fast:
> O, press it close to thine again,
> > Where it will break at last.

Very few perhaps are familiar with these lines — yet no less a poet than Shelley is their author. Their warm, yet delicate and ethereal imagination will be appreciated by all, but by none so thoroughly as by him

who has himself arisen from sweet dreams of one beloved to bathe in the
aromatic air of a southern midsummer night.

One of the finest poems by Willis — the very best in my opinion
which he has ever written — has no doubt, through this same defect of
undue brevity, been kept back from its proper position, not less in the
critical than in the popular view: —

> The shadows lay along Broadway,
> 'Twas near the twilight-tide —
> And slowly there a lady fair
> Was walking in her pride.
> Alone walk'd she; but, viewlessly,
> Walk'd spirits at her side.
>
> Peace charm'd the street beneath her feet,
> And Honour charm'd the air;
> And all astir looked kind on her,
> And called her good as fair —
> For all God ever gave to her
> She kept with chary care.
>
> She kept with care her beauties rare
> From lovers warm and true —
> For heart was cold to all but gold,
> And the rich came not to woo —
> But honour'd well her charms to sell,
> If priests the selling do.
>
> Now walking there was one more fair —
> A slight girl, lily-pale;
> And she had unseen company
> To make the spirit quail —
> 'Twixt Want and Scorn she walk'd forlorn,
> And nothing could avail.
>
> No mercy now can clear her brow
> From this world's peace to pray,
> For as love's wild prayer dissolved in air,
> Her woman's heart gave way! —
> But the sin forgiven by Christ in Heaven,
> By man is cursed alway!

In this composition we find it difficult to recognise the Willis who
has written so many mere "verses of society." The lines are not only
richly ideal, but full of energy, while they breathe an earnestness, an

evident sincerity of sentiment, for which we look in vain throughout all the other works of this author.

While the epic mania, while the idea that to merit in poetry prolixity is indispensable, has for some years past been gradually dying out of the public mind, by mere dint of its own absurdity, we find it succeeded by a heresy too palpably false to be long tolerated, but one which, in the brief period it has already endured, may be said to have accomplished more in the corruption of our Poetical Literature than all its other enemies combined. I allude to the heresy of *The Didactic*. It has been assumed, tacitly and avowedly, directly and indirectly, that the ultimate object of all Poetry is Truth. Every poem, it is said, should inculcate a moral, and by this moral is the poetical merit of the work to be adjudged. We Americans especially have patronized this happy idea, and we Bostonians very especially have developed it in full. We have taken it into our heads that to write a poem simply for the poem's sake, and to acknowledge such to have been our design, would be to confess ourselves radically wanting in the true poetic dignity and force: — but the simple fact is that would we but permit ourselves to look into our own souls we should immediately there discover that under the sun there neither exists nor *can* exist any work more thoroughly dignified, more supremely noble, than this very poem, this poem *per se*, this poem which is a poem and nothing more, this poem written solely for the poem's sake.

With as deep a reverence for the True as ever inspired the bosom of man, I would nevertheless limit, in some measure, its modes of inculcation. I would limit to enforce them. I would not enfeeble them by dissipation. The demands of Truth are severe. She has no sympathy with the myrtles. All *that* which is so indispensable in Song is precisely all *that* with which *she* has nothing whatever to do. It is but making her a flaunting paradox to wreathe her in gems and flowers. In enforcing a truth we need severity rather than efflorescence of language. We must be simple, precise, terse. We must be cool, calm, unimpassioned. In a word, we must be in that mood which, as nearly as possible, is the exact converse of the poetical. *He* must be blind indeed who does not perceive the radical and chasmal difference between the truthful and the poetical modes of inculcation. He must be theory-mad beyond redemption who, in spite of these differences, shall still persist in attempting to reconcile the obstinate oils and waters of Poetry and Truth.

Dividing the world of mind into its three most immediately obvious distinctions, we have the Pure Intellect, Taste, and the Moral Sense. I place Taste in the middle, because it is just this position which in the mind it occupies. It holds intimate relations with either extreme; but from the Moral Sense is separated by so faint a difference that Aristotle has not hesitated to place some of its operations among the virtues them-

selves. Nevertheless we find the *offices* of the trio marked with a suffi-
cient distinction. Just as the Intellect concerns itself with Truth, so
Taste informs us of the Beautiful, while the Moral Sense is regardful of
Duty. Of this latter, while Conscience teaches the obligation, and Rea-
son the expediency, Taste contents herself with displaying the charms:
— waging war upon Vice solely on the ground of her deformity — her
disproportion — her animosity to the fitting, to the appropriate, to the
harmonious — in a word, to Beauty.

An immortal instinct deep within the spirit of man is thus plainly a
sense of the Beautiful. This it is which administers to his delight in the
manifold forms, and sounds, and odors and sentiments amid which he
exists. And just as the lily is repeated in the lake, or the eyes of Amaryllis
in the mirror, so is the mere oral or written repetition of these forms, and
sounds, and colors, and odors, and sentiments a duplicate source of de-
light. But this mere repetition is not poetry. He who shall simply sing,
with however glowing enthusiasm, or with however vivid a truth of de-
scription, of the sights, and sounds, and odors, and colors, and sentiments
which greet *him* in common with all mankind — he, I say, has yet failed
to prove his divine title. There is still a something in the distance which
he has been unable to attain. We have still a thirst unquenchable, to
allay which he has not shown us the crystal springs. This thirst belongs
to the immortality of Man. It is at once a consequence and an indica-
tion of his perennial existence. It is the desire of the moth for the star.
It is no mere appreciation of the Beauty before us, but a wild effort to
reach the Beauty above. Inspired by an ecstatic prescience of the glories
beyond the grave, we struggle by multiform combinations among the
things and thoughts of Time to attain a portion of that Loveliness whose
very elements perhaps appertain to eternity alone. And thus when by
Poetry, or when by Music, the most entrancing of the poetic moods, we
find ourselves melted into tears, we weep then, not as the Abbaté Gravina
supposes, through excess of pleasure, but through a certain petulant,
impatient sorrow at our inability to grasp *now*, wholly, here on earth,
at once and for ever, those divine and rapturous joys of which *through*
the poem, or *through* the music, we attain to but brief and indeter-
minate glimpses.

The struggle to apprehend the supernal Loveliness — this struggle, on
the part of souls fittingly constituted — has given to the world all *that*
which it (the world) has ever been enabled at once to understand and
to *feel* as poetic.

The Poetic Sentiment, of course, may develop itself in various modes
— in Painting, in Sculpture, in Architecture, in the Dance — very espe-
cially in Music — and very peculiarly, and with a wide field, in the com-
position of the Landscape Garden. Our present theme, however, has
regard only to its manifestation in words. And here let me speak briefly
on the topic of rhythm. Contenting myself with the certainty that Music,

in its various modes of metre, rhythm, and rhyme, is of so vast a moment in Poetry as never to be wisely rejected — is so vitally important an adjunct, that he is simply silly who declines its assistance, I will not now pause to maintain its absolute essentiality. It is in Music perhaps that the soul most nearly attains the great end for which, when inspired by the Poetic Sentiment, it struggles — the creation of supernal Beauty. It *may* be, indeed, that here this sublime end is, now and then, attained in *fact*. We are often made to feel, with a shivering delight, that from an earthly harp are stricken notes which *cannot* have been unfamiliar to the angels. And thus there can be little doubt that in the union of Poetry with Music in its popular sense, we shall find the widest field for the Poetic development. The old Bards and Minnesingers had advantages which we do not possess — and Thomas Moore, singing his own songs, was, in the most legitimate manner, perfecting them as poems.

To recapitulate then: — I would define, in brief, the Poetry of words as *The Rhythmical Creation of Beauty*. Its sole arbiter is Taste. With the Intellect or with the Conscience it has only collateral relations. Unless incidentally, it has no concern whatever either with Duty or with Truth.

A few words, however, in explanation. *That* pleasure which is at once the most pure, the most elevating, and the most intense, is derived, I maintain, from the contemplation of the Beautiful. In the contemplation of Beauty we alone find it possible to attain that pleasurable elevation, or excitement *of the soul*, which we recognise as the Poetic Sentiment, and which is so easily distinguished from Truth, which is the satisfaction of the Reason, or from Passion, which is the excitement of the heart. I make Beauty, therefore — using the word as inclusive of the sublime — I make Beauty the province of the poem, simply because it is an obvious rule of Art that effects should be made to spring as directly as possible from their causes: — no one as yet having been weak enough to deny that the peculiar elevation in question is at least *most readily* attainable in the poem. It by no means follows, however, that the incitements of Passion, or the precepts of Duty, or even the lessons of Truth, may not be introduced into a poem, and with advantage; for they may subserve incidentally, in various ways, the general purposes of the work: but the true artist will always contrive to tone them down in proper subjection to that *Beauty* which is the atmosphere and the real essence of the poem.

I cannot better introduce the few poems which I shall present for your consideration, than by the citation of the Proem to Longfellow's "Waif": —

> The day is done, and the darkness
> Falls from the wings of Night,
> As a feather is wafted downward
> From an Eagle in his flight.

I see the lights of the village
 Gleam through the rain and the mist,
And a feeling of sadness comes o'er me,
 That my soul cannot resist;

A feeling of sadness and longing,
 That is not akin to pain,
And resembles sorrow only
 As the mist resembles the rain.

Come, read to me some poem,
 Some simple and heartfelt lay,
That shall soothe this restless feeling,
 And banish the thoughts of day.

Not from the grand old masters,
 Not from the bards sublime,
Whose distant footsteps echo
 Through the corridors of Time.

For, like strains of martial music,
 Their mighty thoughts suggest
Life's endless toil and endeavour;
 And to-night I long for rest.

Read from some humbler poet,
 Whose songs gushed from his heart,
As showers from the clouds of summer,
 Or tears from the eyelids start;

Who through long days of labor,
 And nights devoid of ease,
Still heard in his soul the music
 Of wonderful melodies.

Such songs have power to quiet
 The restless pulse of care,
And come like the benediction
 That follows after prayer.

Then read from the treasured volume
 The poem of thy choice,
And lend to the rhyme of the poet
 The beauty of thy voice.

> And the night shall be filled with music,
> And the cares that infest the day
> Shall fold their tents like the Arabs,
> And as silently steal away.

With no great range of imagination, these lines have been justly admired for their delicacy of expression. Some of the images are very effective. Nothing can be better than —

> ——————— the bards sublime,
> Whose distant footsteps echo
> Down the corridors of Time.

The idea of the last quatrain is also very effective. The poem on the whole, however, is chiefly to be admired for the graceful *insouciance* of its metre, so well in accordance with the character of the sentiments, and especially for the *ease* of the general manner. This "ease" or naturalness, in a literary style, it has long been the fashion to regard as ease in appearance alone — as a point of really difficult attainment. But not so: — a natural manner is difficult only to him who should never meddle with it — to the unnatural. It is but the result of writing with the understanding, or with the instinct, that *the tone*, in composition, should always be that which the mass of mankind would adopt — and must perpetually vary, of course, with the occasion. The author who, after the fashion of "The North American Review," should be upon *all* occasions merely "quiet," must necessarily upon *many* occasions be simply silly, or stupid; and has no more right to be considered "easy" or "natural" than a Cockney exquisite, or than the sleeping Beauty in the waxworks.

Among the minor poems of Bryant, none has so much impressed me as the one which he entitles "June." I quote only a portion of it: —

> There, through the long, long summer hours,
> The golden light should lie,
> And thick young herbs and groups of flowers
> Stand in their beauty by.
> The oriole should build and tell
> His love-tale, close beside my cell;
> The idle butterfly
> Should rest him there, and there be heard
> The housewife-bee and humming bird.
>
> And what, if cheerful shouts at noon,
> Come, from the village sent,
> Or songs of maids, beneath the moon,
> With fairy laughter blent?

And what if, in the evening light,
Betrothed lovers walk in sight
 Of my low monument?
I would the lovely scene around
Might know no sadder sight nor sound.

I know, I know I should not see
 The season's glorious show,
Nor would its brightness shine for me;
 Nor its wild music flow;
But if, around my place of sleep,
The friends I love should come to weep,
 They might not haste to go.
Soft airs and song, and the light and bloom,
Should keep them lingering by my tomb.

These to their soften'd hearts should bear
 The thoughts of what has been,
And speak of one who cannot share
 The gladness of the scene;
Whose part in all the pomp that fills
The circuit of the summer hills,
 Is — that his grave is green;
And deeply would their hearts rejoice
To hear again his living voice.

 The rhythmical flow here is even voluptuous — nothing could be more melodious. The poem has always affected me in a remarkable manner. The intense melancholy which seems to well up, perforce, to the surface of all the poet's cheerful sayings about his grave, we find thrilling us to the soul — while there is the truest poetic elevation in the thrill. The impression left is one of a pleasurable sadness. And if, in the remaining compositions which I shall introduce to you, there be more or less of a similar tone always apparent, let me remind you that (how or why we know not) this certain taint of sadness is inseparably connected with all the higher manifestations of true Beauty. It is, nevertheless,

 A feeling of sadness and longing
 That is not akin to pain,
 And resembles sorrow only
 As the mist resembles the rain.

 The taint of which I speak is clearly perceptible even in a poem so full of brilliancy and spirit as "The Health" of Edward Coate Pinckney: —

I fill this cup to one made up
 Of loveliness alone,
A woman, of her gentle sex
 The seeming paragon;
To whom the better elements
 And kindly stars have given
A form so fair that, like the air,
 'Tis less of earth than heaven.

Her every tone is music's own,
 Like those of morning birds,
And something more than melody
 Dwells ever in her words;
The coinage of her heart are they,
 And from her lips each flows
As one may see the burden'd bee
 Forth issue from the rose.

Affections are as thoughts to her,
 The measures of her hours;
Her feelings have the fragrancy,
 The freshness of young flowers;
And lovely passions, changing oft,
 So fill her, she appears
The image of themselves by turns, —
 The idol of past years!

Of her bright face one glance will trace
 A picture on the brain,
And of her voice in echoing hearts
 A sound must long remain;
But memory, such as mine of her,
 So very much endears,
When death is nigh my latest sigh
 Will not be life's, but hers.

I fill'd this cup to one made up
 Of loveliness alone,
A woman, of her gentle sex
 The seeming paragon —
Her health! and would on earth there stood,
 Some more of such a frame,
That life might be all poetry,
 And weariness a name.

It was the misfortune of Mr. Pinckney to have been born too far south. Had he been a New Englander, it is probable that he would have been ranked as the first of American lyrists by that magnanimous cabal which has so long controlled the destinies of American Letters, in conducting the thing called "The North American Review." The poem just cited is especially beautiful; but the poetic elevation which it induces we must refer chiefly to our sympathy in the poet's enthusiasm. We pardon his hyperboles for the evident earnestness with which they are uttered.

It was by no means my design, however, to expatiate upon the *merits* of what I should read you. These will necessarily speak for themselves. Boccalini, in his "Advertisements from Parnassus," tells us that Zoilus once presented Apollo a very caustic criticism upon a very admirable book: — whereupon the god asked him for the beauties of the work. He replied that he only busied himself about the errors. On hearing this, Apollo, handing him a sack of unwinnowed wheat, bade him pick out *all the chaff* for his reward.

Now this fable answers very well as a hit at the critics — but I am by no means sure that the god was in the right. I am by no means certain that the true limits of the critical duty are not grossly misunderstood. Excellence, in a poem especially, may be considered in the light of an axiom, which need only be properly *put*, to become self-evident. It is *not* excellence if it require to be demonstrated as such: — and thus to point out too particularly the merits of a work of Art, is to admit that they are *not* merits altogether.

Among the "Melodies" of Thomas Moore is one whose distinguished character as a poem proper seems to have been singularly left out of view. I allude to his lines beginning — "Come, rest in this bosom." The intense energy of their expression is not surpassed by anything in Byron. There are two of the lines in which a sentiment is conveyed that embodies the *all in all* of the divine passion of Love — a sentiment which, perhaps, has found its echo in more, and in more passionate, human hearts than any other single sentiment ever embodied in words: —

> Come, rest in this bosom, my own stricken deer
> Though the herd have fled from thee, thy home is still here;
> Here still is the smile, that no cloud can o'ercast,
> And a heart and a hand all thy own to the last.
>
> Oh! what was love made for, if 'tis not the same
> Through joy and through torment, through glory and shame?
> I know not, I ask not, if guilt's in that heart,
> I but know that I love thee, whatever thou art.

Thou hast call'd me thy Angel in moments of bliss,
And thy Angel I'll be, 'mid the horrors of this, —
Through the furnace, unshrinking, thy steps to pursue,
And shield thee, and save thee, — or perish there too!

It has been the fashion of late days to deny Moore Imagination, while
granting him Fancy — a distinction originating with Coleridge — than
whom no man more fully comprehended the great powers of Moore. The
fact is, that the fancy of this poet so far predominates over all his other
faculties, and over the fancy of all other men, as to have induced, very
naturally, the idea that he is fanciful *only*. But never was there a greater
mistake. Never was a grosser wrong done the fame of a true poet. In the
compass of the English language I can call to mind no poem more pro-
foundly — more weirdly *imaginative*, in the best sense, than the lines
commencing — "I would I were by that dim lake" — which are the com-
position of Thomas Moore. I regret that I am unable to remember them.

One of the noblest — and, speaking of Fancy — one of the most singu-
larly fanciful of modern poets, was Thomas Hood. His "Fair Ines" had
always for me an inexpressible charm: —

O saw ye not fair Ines?
 She's gone into the West,
To dazzle when the sun is down,
 And rob the world of rest;
She took our daylight with her,
 The smiles that we love best,
With morning blushes on her cheek,
 And pearls upon her breast.

O turn again, fair Ines,
 Before the fall of night,
For fear the moon should shine alone,
 And stars unrivall'd bright;
And blessed will the lover be
 That walks beneath their light,
And breathes the love against thy cheek
 I dare not even write!

Would I had been, fair Ines,
 That gallant cavalier,
Who rode so gaily by thy side,
 And whisper'd thee so near!
Were there no bonny dames at home
 Or no true lovers here,
That he should cross the seas to win
 The dearest of the dear?

I saw thee, lovely Ines,
 Descend along the shore,
With bands of noble gentlemen,
 And banners waved before;
And gentle youth and maidens gay,
 And snowy plumes they wore;
It would have been a beauteous dream,
 If it had been no more!

Alas, alas, fair Ines,
 She went away with song,
With music waiting on her steps,
 And shoutings of the throng;
But some were sad and felt no mirth,
 But only Music's wrong,
In sounds that sang Farewell, Farewell,
 To her you've loved so long.

Farewell, farewell, fair Ines,
 That vessel never bore
So fair a lady on its deck,
 Nor danced so light before, —
Alas for pleasure on the sea,
 And sorrow on the shore!
The smile that blest one lover's heart
 Has broken many more!

"The Haunted House," by the same author, is one of the truest poems ever written, — one of the *truest*, one of the most unexceptionable, one of the most thoroughly artistic, both in its theme and in its execution. It is, moreover, powerfully ideal — imaginative. I regret that its length renders it unsuitable for the purposes of this lecture. In place of it permit me to offer the universally appreciated "Bridge of Sighs": —

One more Unfortunate,
Weary of breath,
Rashly importunate
Gone to her death!

Take her up tenderly,
Lift her with care; —
Fashion'd so slenderly,
Young and so fair!

Look at her garments
Clinging like cerements;
Whilst the wave constantly

Drips from her clothing;
Take her up instantly,
Loving, not loathing.

Touch her not scornfully;
Think of her mournfully,
Gently and humanly;
Not of the stains of her,
All that remains of her
Now is pure womanly.

Make no deep scrutiny
Into her mutiny
Rash and undutiful;
Past all dishonor,
Death has left on her
Only the beautiful.

Where the lamps quiver
So far in the river,
With many a light
From window and casement
From garret to basement,
She stood, with amazement,
Houseless by night.

The bleak wind of March
Made her tremble and shiver;
But not the dark arch,
Or the black flowing river:
Mad from life's history,
Glad to death's mystery,
Swift to be hurl'd —
Anywhere, anywhere
Out of the world!

In she plunged boldly,
No matter how coldly
The rough river ran, —
Over the brink of it,
Picture it, — think of it,
Dissolute Man!
Lave in it, drink of it
Then, if you can!

Still, for all slips of hers,
One of Eve's family —
Wipe those poor lips of hers
Oozing so clammily,
Loop up her tresses
Escaped from the comb,
Her fair auburn tresses;
Whilst wonderment guesses
Where was her home?

Who was her father?
Who was her mother?
Had she a sister?
Had she a brother?
Or was there a dearer one
Still, and a nearer one
Yet, than all other?

Alas! for the rarity
Of Christian charity
Under the sun!
Oh! it was pitiful!
Near a whole city full,
Home she had none.

Sisterly, brotherly,
Fatherly, motherly,
Feelings had changed:
Love, by harsh evidence,
Thrown from its eminence;
Even God's providence
Seeming estranged.

Take her up tenderly;
Lift her with care;
Fashion'd so slenderly,
Young, and so fair!
Ere her limbs frigidly
Stiffen too rigidly,
Decently, — kindly, —
Smooth and compose them;
And her eyes, close them,
Staring so blindly!

Dreadfully staring
Through muddy impurity,
As when with the daring
Last look of despairing
Fixed on futurity.

Perishing gloomily,
Spurred by contumely,
Cold inhumanity,
Burning insanity,
Into her rest, —
Cross her hands humbly,
As if praying dumbly,
Over her breast!
Owning her weakness,
Her evil behaviour,
And leaving, with meekness,
Her sins to her Saviour!

The vigour of this poem is no less remarkable than its pathos. The versification although carrying the fanciful to the very verge of the fantastic, is nevertheless admirably adapted to the wild insanity which is the thesis of the poem.

Among the minor poems of Lord Byron is one which has never received from the critics the praise which it undoubtedly deserves: —

Though the day of my destiny's over,
 And the star of my fate hath declined
Thy soft heart refused to discover
 The faults which so many could find;
Though thy soul with my grief was acquainted,
 It shrunk not to share it with me,
And the love which my spirit hath painted
 It never hath found but in *thee*.

Then when nature around me is smiling,
 The last smile which answers to mine,
I do not believe it beguiling,
 Because it reminds me of thine;
And when winds are at war with the ocean,
 As the breasts I believed in with me,
If their billows excite an emotion,
 It is that they bear me from *thee*.

Though the rock of my last hope is shivered,
 And its fragments are sunk in the wave,
Though I feel that my soul is delivered
 To pain — it shall not be its slave.
There is many a pang to pursue me:
 They may crush, but they shall not contemn —
They may torture, but shall not subdue me —
 'Tis of *thee* that I think — not of them.

Though human, thou didst not deceive me,
 Though woman, thou didst not forsake,
Though loved, thou forborest to grieve me,
 Though slandered, thou never couldst shake, —
Though trusted, thou didst not disclaim me,
 Though parted, it was not to fly,
Though watchful, 'twas not to defame me,
 Nor mute, that the world might belie.

Yet I blame not the world, nor despise it,
 Nor the war of the many with one —
If my soul was not fitted to prize it,
 'Twas folly not sooner to shun:
And if dearly that error hath cost me,
 And more than I once could foresee,
I have found that whatever it lost me,
 It could not deprive me of *thee*.

From the wreck of the past, which hath perished,
 Thus much I at least may recall,
It hath taught me that which I most cherished
 Deserved to be dearest of all:
In the desert a fountain is springing,
 In the wide waste there still is a tree,
And a bird in the solitude singing,
 Which speaks to my spirit of *thee*.

Although the rhythm here is one of the most difficult, the versification could scarcely be improved. No nobler *theme* ever engaged the pen of poet. It is the soul-elevating idea that no man can consider himself entitled to complain of Fate while in his adversity he still retains the unwavering love of woman.

From Alfred Tennyson, although in perfect sincerity I regard him as the noblest poet that ever lived, I have left myself time to cite only a very brief specimen. I call him, and *think* him the noblest of poets, *not* because the impressions he produces are at *all* times the most profound — *not* because the poetical excitement which he induces is at *all* times the most intense — but because it is at all times the most ethereal — in other

words, the most elevating and most pure. No poet is so little of the earth, earthy. What I am about to read is from his last long poem, "The Princess": —

> Tears, idle tears, I know not what they mean,
> Tears from the depth of some divine despair
> Rise in the heart, and gather to the eyes,
> In looking on the happy Autumn fields,
> And thinking of the days that are no more.
>
> Fresh as the first beam glittering on a sail,
> That brings our friends up from the underworld,
> Sad as the last which reddens over one
> That sinks with all we love below the verge;
> So sad, so fresh, the days that are no more.
>
> Ah, sad and strange as in dark summer dawns
> The earliest pipe of half-awaken'd birds
> To dying ears, when unto dying eyes
> The casement slowly grows a glimmering square;
> So sad, so strange, the days that are no more.
>
> Dear as remember'd kisses after death,
> And sweet as those by hopeless fancy feign'd
> On lips that are for others; deep as love,
> Deep as first love, and wild with all regret;
> O Death in Life, the days that are no more.

Thus, although in a very cursory and imperfect manner, I have endeavoured to convey to you my conception of the Poetic Principle. It has been my purpose to suggest that, while this principle itself is strictly and simply the Human Aspiration for Supernal Beauty, the manifestation of the Principle is always found in *an elevating excitement of the soul*, quite independent of that passion which is the intoxication of the Heart, or of that truth which is the satisfaction of the Reason. For in regard to passion, alas! its tendency is to degrade rather than to elevate the Soul. Love, on the contrary — Love — the true, the divine Eros — the Uranian as distinguished from the Dionæan Venus — is unquestionably the purest and truest of all poetical themes. And in regard to Truth, if, to be sure, through the attainment of a truth we are led to perceive a harmony where none was apparent before, we experience at once the true poetical effect; but this effect is referable to the harmony alone, and not in the least degree to the truth which merely served to render the harmony manifest.

We shall reach, however, more immediately a distinct conception of what the true Poetry is, by mere reference to a few of the simple elements

which induce in the Poet himself the true poetical effect. He recognises the ambrosia which nourishes his soul in the bright orbs that shine in Heaven — in the volutes of the flower — in the clustering of low shrub- beries — in the waving of the grain-fields — in the slanting of tall eastern trees — in the blue distance of mountains — in the grouping of clouds — in the twinkling of half-hidden brooks — in the gleaming of silver rivers — in the repose of sequestered lakes — in the star-mirroring depths of lonely wells. He perceives it in the songs of birds — in the harp of Æolus — in the sighing of the night-wind — in the repining voice of the forest — in the surf that complains to the shore — in the fresh breath of the woods — in the scent of the violet — in the voluptuous perfume of the hya- cinth — in the suggestive odour that comes to him at eventide from far- distant undiscovered islands, over dim oceans, illimitable and unexplored. He owns it in all noble thoughts — in all unworldly motives — in all holy impulses — in all chivalrous, generous, and self-sacrificing deeds. He feels it in the beauty of woman — in the grace of her step — in the lustre of her eye — in the melody of her voice — in her soft laughter, in her sigh — in the harmony of the rustling of her robes. He deeply feels it in her winning endearments — in her burning enthusiasms — in her gentle charities — in her meek and devotional endurances — but above all — ah, far above all, he kneels to it — he worships it in the faith, in the purity, in the strength, in the altogether divine majesty — of her *love*.

Let me conclude by — the recitation of yet another brief poem — one very different in character from any that I have before quoted. It is by Motherwell, and is called "The Song of the Cavalier." With our modern and altogether rational ideas of the absurdity and impiety of warfare, we are not precisely in that frame of mind best adapted to sympathize with the sentiments, and thus to appreciate the real excellence of the poem. To do this fully we must identify ourselves in fancy with the soul of the old cavalier: —

> Then mounte! then mounte, brave gallants all,
> And don your helmes amaine:
> Deathe's couriers, Fame and Honour call
> Us to the field againe.
> No shrewish teares shall fill your eye
> When the sword-hilt's in our hand, —
> Heart-whole we'll part, and no whit sighe
> For the fayrest of the land;
> Let piping swaine, and craven wight,
> Thus weepe and puling crye,
> Our business is like men to fight,
> And hero-like to die!

VI

MARGINALIA

1

*D*EMOCRATIC *REVIEW*, November, 1844

In getting my books, I have been always solicitous of an ample margin; this not so much through any love of the thing in itself, however agreeable, as for the facility it affords me of pencilling suggested thoughts, agreements, and differences of opinion, or brief critical comments in general. Where what I have to note is too much to be included within the narrow limits of a margin, I commit it to a slip of paper, and deposit it between the leaves; taking care to secure it by an imperceptible portion of gum tragacanth paste.

All this may be whim; it may be not only a very hackneyed, but a very idle practice; — yet I persist in it still; and it affords me pleasure; which is profit, in despite of Mr. Bentham, with Mr. Mill on his back.

This making of notes, however, is by no means the making of mere

memoranda — a custom which has its disadvantages, beyond doubt. *"Ce que je mets sur papier,"* says Bernadine de St. Pierre, *"je remets de ma mémoire et par conséquence je l'oublie;"* — and, in fact, if you wish to forget anything upon the spot, make a note that this thing is to be remembered.

But the purely marginal jottings, done with no eye to the Memorandum Book, have a distinct complexion, and not only a distinct purpose, but none at all; this it is which imparts to them a value. They have a rank somewhat above the chance and desultory comments of literary chit-chat — for these latter are not unfrequently "talk for talk's sake," hurried out of the mouth; while the *marginalia* are deliberately pencilled, because the mind of the reader wishes to unburthen itself of a *thought*; — however flippant — however silly — however trivial — still a thought indeed, not merely a thing that might have been a thought in time, and under more favorable circumstances. In the *marginalia*, too, we talk only to ourselves; we therefore talk freshly — boldly — originally — with *abandonnement* — without conceit — much after the fashion of Jeremy Taylor, and Sir Thomas Browne, and Sir William Temple, and the anatomical Burton, and that most logical analogist, Butler, and some other people of the old day, who were too full of their matter to have any room for their manner, which, being thus left out of question, was a capital manner, indeed, — a model of manners, with a richly marginalic air.

The circumscription of space, too, in these pencillings, has in it something more of advantage than of inconvenience. It compels us (whatever diffuseness of idea we may clandestinely entertain), into Montesquieu-ism, into Tacitus-ism (here I leave out of view the concluding portion of the "Annals") — or even into Carlyle-ism — a thing which, I have been told, is not to be confounded with your ordinary affectation and bad grammar. I say "bad grammar," through sheer obstinacy, because the grammarians (who should know better) insist upon it that I should not. But then grammar is not what these grammarians will have it; and, being merely the analysis of language, with the result of this analysis, must be good or bad just as the analyst is sage or silly — just as he is Horne Tooke ·or a Cobbett.

But to our sheep. During a rainy afternoon, not long ago, being in a mood too listless for continuous study, I sought relief from *ennui* in dipping here and there, at random, among the volumes of my library — no very large one, certainly, but sufficiently miscellaneous; and, I flatter myself, not a little *recherché*.

Perhaps it was what the Germans call the "brain-scattering" humor of the moment; but, while the picturesqueness of the numerous pencil-scratches arrested my attention, their helter-skelter-iness of commentary amused me. I found myself at length forming a wish that it had been some other hand than my own which had so bedevilled the books, and fancying that, in such case, I might have derived no inconsiderable pleas-

ure from turning them over. From this the transition-thought (as Mr. Lyell, or Mr. Murchison, or Mr. Featherstonhaugh would have it) was natural enough: — there might be something even in *my* scribblings which, for the mere sake of scribbling, would have interest for others.

The main difficulty respected the mode of transferring the notes from the volumes — the context from the text — without detriment to that exceedingly frail fabric of intelligibility in which the context was imbedded. With all appliances to boot, with the printed pages at their back, the commentaries were too often like Dodona's oracles — or those of Lycophron Tenebrosus — or the essays of the pedant's pupils, in Quintilian, which were "necessarily excellent, since even he (the pedant) found it impossible to comprehend them": — what, then, would become of it — this context — if transferred? — if translated? Would it not rather be *traduit* (traduced) which is the French synonym, or *overzezet* (turned topsy-turvy) which is the Dutch one?

I concluded, at length, to put extensive faith in the acumen and imagination of the reader: — this as a general rule. But, in some instances, where even faith would not remove mountains, there seemed no safer plan than so to re-model the note as to convey at least the ghost of a conception as to what it was all about. Where, for such conception, the text itself was absolutely necessary, I could quote it; where the title of the book commented upon was indispensable, I could name it. In short, like a novel-hero dilemma'd, I made up my mind "to be guided by circumstances," in default of more satisfactory rules of conduct.

As for the multitudinous opinion expressed in the subjoined *farrago* — as for my present assent to all, or dissent from any portion of it — as to the possibility of my having, in some instances, altered my mind — or as to the impossibility of my not having altered it often — these are points upon which I say nothing, because upon these there can be nothing cleverly said. It may be as well to observe, however, that just as the goodness of your true pun is in the direct ratio of its intolerability, so is nonsense the essential sense of the Marginal Note.

I have seen many computations respecting the greatest amount of erudition attainable by an individual in his life-time; but these computations are falsely based, and fall infinitely beneath the truth. It is true that, *in general*, we retain, we remember to available purpose, scarcely one-hundredth part of what we read; yet there *are* minds which not only retain *all* receipts, but keep them at compound interest forever. Again: — were every man supposed to read *out*, he could read, of course, very little, even in half a century; for, in such case, each individual word must be dwelt upon in some degree. But, in reading to ourselves, at the ordinary rate of what is called 'light reading,' we scarcely *touch* one word in ten. And, even physically considered, knowledge breeds knowledge, as gold gold; for he who reads really much, finds his capacity to read in-

crease in geometrical ratio. The *helluo librorum* will but glance at the page which detains the ordinary reader some minutes; and the difference in the absolute *reading* (its uses considered), will be in favor of the *helluo*, who will have winnowed the matter of which the *tyro* mumbled both the seeds and the chaff. A deep-rooted and strictly continuous habit of reading will, with certain classes of intellect, result in an instinctive and seemingly magnetic appreciation of a thing written; and now the student reads by pages just as other men by words. Long years to come, with a careful analysis of the mental process, may even render this species of appreciation a common thing. It may be taught in the schools of our descendants of the tenth or twentieth generation. It may become the method of the mob of the eleventh or twenty-first. And should these matters come to pass — as they will — there will be in them no more legitimate cause for wonder than there is, to-day, in the marvel that, syllable by syllable, men comprehend what, letter by letter, I now trace upon this page.

Is it not a law that need has a tendency to engender the thing needed?

Moore has been noted for the number of appositeness, as well as novelty of his similes; and the renown thus acquired is indicial of his deficiency in that noble merit — the noblest of all. No poet thus distinguished was ever richly ideal. Pope and Cowper are instances. Direct similes are of too palpably artificial a character to be artistical. An artist will always contrive to weave his illustrations into the metaphorical form.

Moore has a peculiar facility in prosaically telling a poetical story. By this I mean that he preserves the tone and method of arrangement of a prose relation, and thus obtains great advantage, in important points, over his more stilted compeers. His is no poetical *style* (such as the French have — a distinct style for a distinct purpose) but an easy and ordinary prose manner, which rejects the licenses because it does not require them, and is merely *ornamented into poetry*. By means of this manner he is enabled to encounter, effectually, details which would baffle any other versifier of the day; and at which Lamartine would stand aghast. In "Alciphron" we see this exemplified. Here the minute and perplexed incidents of the descent into the pyramid, are detailed, in verse, with quite as much precision and intelligibility as could be attained even by the coolest prose of Mr. Jeremy Bentham.

Moore has vivacity; verbal and constructive dexterity; a musical ear not sufficiently cultivated; a vivid fancy; an epigrammatic spirit; and a fine taste — *as far as it goes*.

Democratic Review, December, 1844

I am not sure that Tennyson is not the greatest of poets. The uncertainty attending the public conception of the term "poet" alone prevents me from demonstrating that he *is*. Other bards produce effects which are, now and then, otherwise produced than by what we call

poems; but Tennyson an effect which only a poem does. His alone are idiosyncratic poems. By the enjoyment or non-enjoyment of the "Morte D'Arthur" or of the "Œnone," I would test any one's ideal sense.

There are passages in his works which rivet a conviction I had long entertained, that the indefinite is an element in the true ποίησις. Why do some persons fatigue themselves in attempts to unravel such fantasy-pieces as the "Lady of Shalott"? As well unweave the *"ventum textilem."* If the author did not deliberately propose to himself a suggestive indefinitiveness of meaning with the view of bringing about a definitiveness of vague and therefore of spiritual *effect* — this, at least, arose from the silent analytical promptings of that poetic genius which, in its supreme development, embodies all orders of intellectual capacity.

I *know* that indefinitiveness is an element of the true music — I mean of the true musical expression. Give to it any undue decision — imbue it with any very determinate tone — and you deprive it at once of its ethereal, its ideal, its intrinsic and essential character. You dispel its luxury of dream. You dissolve the atmosphere of the mystic upon which it floats. You exhaust it of its breath of fäery. It now becomes a tangible and easily appreciable idea — a thing of the earth, earthy. It has not, indeed, lost its power to please, but all which I consider the distinctiveness of that power. And to the uncultivated talent, or to the unimaginative apprehension, this deprivation of its most delicate air will be, not unfrequently, a recommendation. A determinateness of expression is sought — and often by composers who should know better — is sought as a beauty rather than rejected as a blemish. Thus we have, even from high authorities, attempts at absolute *imitation* in music. Who can forget the silliness of the "Battle of Prague"? What man of taste but must laugh at the interminable drums, trumpets, blunderbusses, and thunder? "Vocal music," says L'Abbate Gravina, who would have said the same thing of instrumental, "ought to imitate the natural language of the human feelings and passions, rather than the warblings of canary birds, which our singers, now-a-days, affect so vastly to mimic with their quaverings and boasted cadences." This is true only so far as the "rather" is concerned. If any music must imitate anything, it were assuredly better to limit the imitation as Gravina suggests.

Tennyson's shorter pieces abound in minute rhythmical lapses sufficient to asure me that — in common with all poets living or dead — he has neglected to make precise investigation of the principles of metre; but, on the other hand, so perfect is his rhythmical instinct in general that, like the present Viscount Canterbury, he seems *to see with his ear.*

Godey's Lady's Book, September, 1845

The increase, within a few years, of the magazine literature, is by no means to be regarded as indicating what some critics would suppose it to indicate — a downward tendency in American taste or in Ameri-

can letters. It is but a sign of the times, an indication of an era in which men are forced upon the curt, the condensed, the well-digested in place of the voluminous — in a word, upon journalism in lieu of dissertation. We need now the light artillery rather than the peace-makers of the intellect. I will not be sure that men at present think more profoundly than half a century ago, but beyond question they think with more rapidity, with more skill, with more tact, with more of method and less of excrescence in the thought. Besides all this, they have a vast increase in the thinking material; they have more facts, more to think about. For this reason, they are disposed to put the greatest amount of thought in the smallest compass and disperse it with the utmost attainable rapidity. Hence the journalism of the age; hence, in especial, magazines. Too many we cannot have, as a general proposition; but we demand that they have sufficient merit to render them noticeable in the beginning, and that they continue in existence sufficiently long to permit us a fair estimation of their value.

Broadway Journal, Oct. 4, 1845

Much has been said, of late, about the necessity of maintaining a proper *nationality* in American Letters; but what this nationality *is*, or what is to be gained by it, has never been distinctly understood. That an American should confine himself to American themes, or even prefer them, is rather a political than a literary idea — and at best is a questionable point. We would do well to bear in mind that "distance lends enchantment to the view." *Ceteris paribus*, a foreign theme is, in a strictly literary sense, to be preferred. After all, the world at large is the only legitimate stage for the autorial *histrio*.

But of the need of *that* nationality which defends our own literature, sustains our own men of letters, upholds our own dignity, and depends upon our own resources, there can not be the shadow of a doubt. Yet here is the very point at which we are most supine. We complain of our want of International Copyright, on the ground that this want justifies our publishers in inundating us with British opinion in British books; and yet when these very publishers, at their own obvious risk, and even obvious loss, do publish an American book, we turn up our noses at it with supreme contempt (this is a general thing) until it (the American book) has been dubbed "readable" by some literate Cockney critic. Is it too much to say that, with us, the opinion of Washington Irving — of Prescott — of Bryant — is a mere nullity in comparison with that of any anonymous sub-sub-editor of the *Spectator*, the *Athenaeum*, or the London *Punch*? It is *not* saying too much to say this. It is a solemn — an absolutely awful fact. Every publisher in the country will admit it to be a fact. There is not a more disgusting spectacle under the sun than our subserviency to British criticism. It is disgusting, first because it is truckling, servile, pusillanimous — secondly, because of its gross irrationality.

We *know* the British to bear us little but ill will — we know that, in no case, do they utter unbiased opinions of American books — we know that in the few instances in which our writers have been treated with common decency in England, these writers have either openly paid homage to English institutions, or have had lurking at the bottom of their hearts a secret principle at war with Democracy: — we *know* all this, and yet, day after day, submit our necks to the degrading yoke of the crudest opinion that emanates from the fatherland. Now if we *must* have nationality, let it be a nationality that will throw off this yoke.

The chief of the rhapsodists who have ridden us to death like the Old Man of the Mountain, is the ignorant and egotistical Wilson. We use the term rhapsodists with perfect deliberation; for, Macaulay, and Dilke, and one or two others, excepted, there is not in Great Britain a critic who can be fairly considered worthy the name. The Germans and even the French, are infinitely superior. As regards Wilson, no man ever penned worse criticism or better rhodomontade. That he is "egotistical" his works show to all men, running as they read. That he is "ignorant" let his absurd and continuous school-boy blunders about Homer bear witness. Not long ago we ourselves pointed out a series of similar inanities in his review of Miss Barret's [*sic*] poems — a series, we say, of gross blunders, arising from sheer ignorance — and we defy him or any one to answer a single syllable of what we then advanced.

And yet this is the man whose simple *dictum* (to our shame be it spoken) has the power to make or to mar any American reputation! In the last number of *Blackwood,* he has a continuation of the dull "Specimens of the British Critics," and makes occasion wantonly to insult one of the noblest of our poets, Mr. Lowell. The point of the whole attack consists in the use of slang epithets and phrases of the most ineffably vulgar description. "Squabashes" is a pet term. "Faugh!" is another. "We are Scotsmen to *the spine!*" says Sawney — as if the thing were not more than self-evident. Mr. Lowell is called a "magpie," an "ape," a "Yankee cockney," and his name is intentionally mis-written *John* Russell Lowell. Now were these indecencies perpetrated by an American critic, that critic would be sent to Coventry by the whole press of the country, but since it is Wilson who insults, we, as in duty bound, not only submit to the insult, but echo it, as an excellent jest, throughout the length and breadth of the land. "*Quamdiu Catilina?*" We do indeed demand the nationality of self-respect. In Letters as in Government we require a Declaration of Independence. A better thing still would be a Declaration of War — and that war should be carried forthwith "into Africa."

Graham's Magazine, March, 1846

Some Frenchman — possibly Montaigne — says: "People talk about thinking, but for my part I never think except when I sit down to write." It is this never thinking, unless when we sit down to write, which

is the cause of so much indifferent composition. But perhaps there is something more involved in the Frenchman's observation than meets the eye. It is certain that the mere act of inditing tends, in a great degree, to the logicalisation of thought. Whenever, on account of its vagueness, I am dissatisfied with a conception of the brain, I resort forthwith to the pen, for the purpose of obtaining, through its aid, the necessary form, consequence, and precision.

How very commonly we hear it remarked that such and such thoughts are beyond the compass of words! I do not believe that any thought, properly so called, is out of the reach of language. I fancy, rather, that where difficulty in expression is experienced, there is, in the intellect which experiences it, a want either of deliberateness or of method. For my own part, I have never had a thought which I could not set down in words, with even more distinctness than that with which I conceived it: — as I have before observed, the thought is logicalised by the effort at (written) expression.

There is, however, a class of fancies, of exquisite delicacy, which are *not* thoughts, and to which, *as yet*, I have found it absolutely impossible to adapt language. I use the word *fancies* at random, and merely because I must use *some* word; but the idea commonly attached to the term is not even remotely applicable to the shadows of shadows in question. They seem to me rather psychal than intellectual. They arise in the soul (alas, how rarely!) only at its epochs of most intense tranquillity — when the bodily and mental health are in perfection — and at those mere points of time where the confines of the waking world blend with those of the world of dreams. I am aware of these "fancies" only when I am upon the very brink of sleep, with the consciousness that I am so. I have satisfied myself that this condition exists but for an inappreciable *point* of time — yet it is crowded with these "shadows of shadows"; and for absolute *thought* there is demanded time's *endurance*.

These "fancies" have in them a pleasurable ecstasy, as far beyond the most pleasurable of the world of wakefulness, or of dreams, as the Heaven of the Northman theology is beyond its Hell. I regard the visions, even as they arise, with an awe which, in some measure moderates or tranquillises the ecstasy — I so regard them, through a conviction (which seems a portion of the ecstasy itself) that this ecstasy, in itself, is of a character supernal to the Human Nature — is a glimpse of the spirit's outer world; and I arrive at this conclusion — if this term is at all applicable to instantaneous intuition — by a perception that the delight experienced has, as its element, but *the absoluteness of novelty*. I say the absoluteness — for in the fancies — let me now term them psychal impressions — there is really nothing even approximate in character to impressions ordinarily received. It is as if the five senses were supplanted by five myriad others alien to mortality.

Now, so entire is my faith in the *power of words*, that at times I have

believed it possible to embody even the evanescence of fancies such as I have attempted to describe. In experiments with this end in view, I have proceeded so far as, first, to control (when the bodily and mental health are good), the existence of the condition: — that is to say, I can now (unless when ill), be sure that the condition will supervene, if I so wish it, at the point of time already described: of its supervention until lately I could never be certain even under the most favorable circumstances. I mean to say, merely, that now I can be sure, when all circumstances are favorable, of the supervention of the condition, and feel even the capacity of inducing or compelling it: — the favorable circumstances, however, are not the less rare — else had I compelled already the Heaven into the Earth.

I have proceeded so far, secondly, as to prevent the lapse from *the point* of which I speak — the point of blending between wakefulness and sleep — as to prevent at will, I say, the lapse from this border-ground into the dominion of sleep. Not that I can *continue* the condition — not that I can render the point more than a point — but that I can startle myself from the point into wakefulness; *and thus transfer the point itself into the realm of Memory* — convey its impressions, or more properly their recollections, to a situation where (although still for a very brief period) I can survey them with the eye of analysis.

For these reasons — that is to say, because I have been enabled to accomplish thus much — I do not altogether despair of embodying in words at least enough of the fancies in question to convey to certain classes of intellect, a shadowy conception of their character.

In saying this I am not to be understood as supposing that the fancies or psychal impressions to which I allude are confined to my individual self — are not, in a word, common to all mankind — for on this point it is quite impossible that I should form an opinion — but nothing can be more certain than that even a partial record of the impressions would startle the universal intellect of mankind, by the *supremeness of the novelty* of the material employed, and of its consequent suggestions. In a word — should I ever write a paper on this topic, the world will be compelled to acknowledge that, at last, I have done an original thing.

Democratic Review, April, 1846

In general, our first impressions are true ones — the chief difficulty is in making sure which *are* the first. In early youth we read a poem, for instance, and are enraptured with it. At manhood we are assured by our reason that we had no reason to be enraptured. But some years elapse, and we return to our primitive admiration, just as a matured judgment enables us precisely to see what and why we admired.

Thus, as individuals, we think in cycles, and may, from the frequency or infrequency of our revolutions about the various thought-centres, form

an accurate estimate of the advance of our thought toward maturity. It is really wonderful to observe how closely, in all the essentials of truth, the child-opinion coincides with that of the man proper — of the man at his best.

And as with individuals so, perhaps, with mankind. When the world begins to return, frequently, to its first impressions, we shall then be warranted in looking for the millennium — or whatever it is: — we may safely take it for granted that we are attaining our maximum of wit, and of the happiness which is thence to ensue. The indications of such a return are, at present, like the visits of angels — but we have them now and then — in the case, for example, of *credulity*. The philosophic, of late days, are distinguished by that very facility in belief which was the characteristic of the illiterate half a century ago. Skepticism in regard to apparent miracles, is not, as formerly, an evidence either of superior wisdom or knowledge. In a word, the wise now believe — yesterday they would not believe — and day before yesterday (in the time of Strabo, for example) they believed, exclusively, anything and everything: — here, then, is one of the indicative cycles of discretion. I mention Strabo merely as an exception to the rule of his epoch — (just as one in a hurry for an illustration, might describe Mr. So and So to be as witty or as amiable as Mr. This and That is *not* — for so rarely did men reject in Strabo's time, and so much more rarely did they *err* by rejection, that the skepticism of this philosopher must be regarded as one of the most remarkable anomalies on record.

I have not the slightest faith in Carlyle. In ten years — possibly in five — he will be remembered only as a butt for sarcasm. His linguistic Euphuisms might very well have been taken as prima facie evidence of his philosophic ones; they were the froth which indicated, first, the shallowness, and secondly, the confusion of the waters. I would blame no man of sense for leaving the works of Carlyle unread merely on account of these Euphuisms; for it might be shown *a priori* that no man capable of producing a definite impression upon his age or race, could or would commit himself to such inanities and insanities. The book about 'Hero-Worship' — is it possible that it ever excited a feeling beyond contempt? No hero-worshipper can possess anything within himself. That man is no man who stands in awe of his fellow-man. Genius regards genius with respect — with even enthusiastic admiration — but there is nothing of worship in the admiration, for it springs from a thorough cognizance of the one admired — from a perfect *sympathy*, the result of the cognizance; and it is needless to say, that sympathy and worship are antagonistic. Your hero-worshippers, for example — what do they know about Shakespeare? They worship him — rant about him — lecture about him — about *him, him* and nothing else — for no other reason than that he is utterly beyond their comprehension. They have arrived at an idea of

his greatness from the pertinacity with which men have called him great. As for their own opinion about him — they really have none at all. In general the very smallest of mankind are the class of men-worshippers. Not one out of this class have ever accomplished anything beyond a very contemptible mediocrity.

Carlyle, however, has rendered an important service (to posterity, at least) in pushing rant and cant to that degree of excess which inevitably induces reaction. Had he not appeared we might have gone on for yet another century, Emerson-izing in prose, Wordsworth-izing in poetry, and Fourier-izing in philosophy, Wilson-izing in criticism — Hudson-izing and Tom O'Bedlam-izing in everything. The author of the 'Sartor Resartus,' however, has overthrown the various arguments of his own order, by a personal *reductio ad absurdum*. Yet an Olympiad, perhaps, and the whole horde will be swept bodily from the memory of man — or be remembered only when we have occasion to talk of such fantastic tricks as, erewhile, were performed by the Abderites.

Graham's Magazine, January, 1848

If any ambitious man have a fancy a revolutionize, at one effort, the universal world of human thought, human opinion, and human sentiment, the opportunity is his own — the road to immortal renown lies straight, open, and unencumbered before him. All that he has to do is to write and publish a very little book. Its title should be simple — a few plain words — "My Heart Laid Bare." But — this little book must be *true to its title*.

Now, is it not very singular that, with the rabid thirst for notoriety which distinguishes so many of mankind — so many, too, who care not a fig what is thought of them after death, there should not be found one man having sufficient hardihood to write this little book? To *write*, I say. There are ten thousand men who, if the book were once written, would laugh at the notion of being disturbed by its publication during their life, and who could not even conceive *why* they should object to its being published after their death. But to write it — *there* is the rub. No man dare write it. No man ever will dare write it. No man *could* write it, even if he dared. The paper would shrivel and blaze at every touch of the fiery pen.

Southern Literary Messenger, April, 1849

I blush to see, in the ————, an invidious notice of Bayard Taylor's "Rhimes of Travel." What makes the matter *worse*, the critique is from the pen of one who, although undeservedly, holds, himself, some position as a poet: — and what makes the matter *worst*, the attack is anonymous, and (while ostensibly commending) most zealously endeavors to damn the young writer "with faint praise." In his whole life. the author of the criticism never published a poem, long or short, which

could compare, either in the higher merits, or in the minor morals of the Muse, with the *worst* of Mr. Taylor's compositions.

Observe the generalizing, disingenuous, patronizing tone: —

"It is the empty charlatan, to whom all things are alike impossible, who attempts everything. He can do one thing as well as another; for he can really do nothing. . . . Mr. Taylor's volume, as we have intimated, is an advance upon his previous publication. We could have wished, indeed, something more of restraint in the rhetoric, *but*," &c., &c., &c.

The concluding sentence, here, is an excellent example of one of the most ingeniously malignant of critical *ruses* — that of condemning an author, in especial, for what the world, in general, *feel* to be his principal merit. In fact, the "rhetoric" of Mr. Taylor, in the sense intended by the critic, is Mr. Taylor's *distinguishing excellence.* He is, unquestionably, the most terse, glowing, and vigorous of all our poets, young or old — in point, I mean, of *expression.* His sonorous, well-balanced rhythm puts me often in mind of Campbell (in spite of our anonymous friend's *implied* sneer at "mere jingling of rhymes, brilliant and successful for the moment,") and his rhetoric in general is of the highest order: — By "rhetoric" I intend the *mode generally* in which thought is presented. Where shall we find more magnificent passages than these?

> First queenly Asia, from the fallen thrones
> Of twice three thousand years
> Came *with the woe a grieving Goddess owns*
> *Who longs for mortal tears.*
> The dust of ruin to her mantle clung
> And dimmed her crown of gold,
> While *the majestic sorrows of her tongue*
> *From Tyre to Indus rolled.*
>
> Mourn with me, sisters, in my realm of woe
> *Whose only glory streams*
> *From its lost childhood like the Arctic glow*
> *Which sunless winter dreams.*
> *In the red desert moulders Babylon*
> *And the wild serpent's hiss*
> *Echoes in Petra's palaces of stone*
> *And waste Persepolis.*
>
> Then from her seat, *amid the palms embowered*
> *That shade the Lion-land,*
> Swart Africa in dusky aspect towered,
> The fetters on her hand.
> Backward she saw, from out the drear eclipse,
> The mighty Theban years,
> *And the deep anguish of her mournful lips*
> *Interpreted her tears.*

I copy these passages first, because the critic in question has copied them, without the slightest appreciation of their grandeur — for they *are* grand; and secondly, to put the question of "rhetoric" at rest. No artist who reads them will deny that they are the perfection of *skill* in their way. But thirdly, I wish to call attention to the glowing *imagination* evinced in the lines italicized. My very soul revolts at *such* efforts, (as the one I refer to,) to depreciate *such* poems as Mr. Taylor's. *Is* there *no* honor — no chivalry left in the land? Are our most deserving writers to be *forever* sneered down, or hooted down, or damned down with faint praise, by a set of men who possess little other ability than that which assures temporary success to *them*, in common with Swaim's Panaces or Morrison's Pills? The fact is, some person should write, at once, a Magazine paper exposing — *ruthlessly* exposing, the *dessous de cartes* of our literary affairs. He should show how and why it is that ubiquitous quack in letters can always "succeed," while *genius*, (which implies self-respect, with a scorn of creeping and crawling,) must inevitably succumb. He should point out the "easy arts" by which any one, base enough to do it, can get himself placed at the very head of American Letters by an article in that magnanimous journal, "The Review." He should explain, too, how readily the same work can be induced (in the case of Simms,) to vilify *personally*, any one not a Northerner, for a trifling "consideration." In fact, our criticism needs a thorough regeneration, *and must have it*.

Southern Literary Messenger, June, 1849

I have sometimes amused myself by endeavoring to fancy what would be the fate of any individual gifted, or rather accursed, with an intellect *very* far superior to that of his race. Of course, he would be conscious of his superiority; nor could he (if otherwise constituted as man is) help manifesting his consciousness. Thus he would make himself enemies at all points. And since his opinions and speculations would widely differ from those of *all* mankind — that he would be considered a madman, is evident. How horribly painful such a condition! Hell could invent no greater torture than that of being charged with abnormal weakness on account of being abnormally strong.

In like manner, nothing can be clearer than that a *very* generous spirit — *truly* feeling what all merely profess — must inevitably find itself misconceived in every direction — its motives misinterpreted. Just as extremeness of intelligence would be thought fatuity, so excess of chivalry could not fail of being looked upon as meanness in its last degree — and so on with other virtues. This subject is a painful one indeed. That individuals *have* so soared above the plane of their race, is scarcely to be questioned; but, in looking back through history for traces of their existence, we should pass over all biographies of "the good and the great," while we search carefully the slight records of wretches who died in prison, in Bedlam, or upon the gallows.

VII

BIBLIOGRAPHICAL AND TEXTUAL NOTES

NOTE: *An asterisk indicates the source of each poem and tale. When there was only one printing, no asterisk has been used. The Lorimer Graham copy of the* Raven and Other Poems *was used as the text of the poems.*

TAMERLANE

First printing: *Tamerlane and Other Poems.* Boston, 1827.
Reprinted: *Al Aaraaf, Tamerlane and Minor Poems.* Baltimore, 1829.
 Poems. New York, 1831.
 **The Raven and Other Poems.* New York, 1845.
With the exception of one line (57), the text of the 1845 edition is identical with that of 1829. There is a version in manuscript which lies between the versions of 1827 and 1829. The text in Poems (1831) shows many changes.

The real Timur-Lang, (1333–1405) was the son of Teragai, head of his tribe and was descended from the chief minister of the son of Jenghis Khan. Poe did not follow the career of his hero, but chose him to represent an ambitious conqueror who leaves his love and returns to find his conquests futile. Poe's "Notes" to the 1827 version of *Tamerlane* have a certain interest. They are reprinted here exactly as they appeared, including printer's errors. Lines starred are not included in present text.

1. *I have sent for thee holy friar.**

Of the history of Tamerlane little is known; and with that little, I have taken the full liberty of a poet. — That he was descended from the family of Zinghis Khan is more than probable — but he is vulgarly supposed to have been the son of a shepherd, and to have raised himself to the throne by his own address. He died in the year 1405 in the time of Pope Innocent VII.

How I shall account for giving him "a friar," as a death-bed confessor — I cannot exactly determine. He wanted some one to listen to his tale — and why not a friar? It does not pass the bounds of possibility — quite sufficient for my purpose — and I have at least good authority on my side for such innovations.

2. PAGE 16 *The mists of the* Taglay *have shed, &c.*

The mountains of Belur Taglay are a branch of the Immaus, in the southern part of Independent Tartary. — They are celebrated for the singular wildness, and beauty of their vallies.

3. *No purer thought **
 Dwelt in a seraph's breast than thine.

I must beg the reader's pardon for making Tamerlane, a Tartar of the fourteenth century, speak in the same language as a Boston gentleman of the nineteenth: but of the Tartar mythology we have little information.

4. *Which blazes upon Edis' shrine **

A deity presiding over virtuous love, upon whose imaginary altar, a sacred fire was continually blazing.

5. ———*who hardly will conceive **
 That any should become "great," born
 Born in their own sphere.

Although Tamerlane speaks this, it is not the less true. It is a matter of the greatest difficulty to make the generality of mankind believe that one, with whom they are upon terms of intimacy, shall be called, in the world, a "great man". The reason is evident. There are few great men. Their actions are consequently viewed by the mass of the

people thro' the medium of distance. — The prominent parts of their character are alone noted; and those properties, which are minute and common to every one, not being observed, seem to have no connection with a great character.

Who ever read the private memorials, correspondence, &c. which have become so common in our time, without wondering that "great men" should act and think "so abominably?"

6.　　　　　　*Her own Alexis who should plight,* &c.*
That Tamerlane acquir'd his renown under a feigned name is not entirely a fiction.

7.　PAGE 19　*Look 'round thee now on Samarcand*
I believe it was after the battle of Angoria that Tamerlane made Samarcand his residence. It became for a time the seat of learning and the arts.

8.　PAGE 19　*And who her sov'reign? Timur, &c.*
He was called Timur Bek as well as Tamerlane.

9.　　　　　　*The Zinghis' yet re-echoing fame.**
The conquests of Tamerlane far exceeded those of Zinghis Khan. He boasted to have two thirds of the world at his command.

10.　PAGE 20　*To the sound of the coming darkness (known*
　　　　　　To those whose spirits hark'n.)
I have often fancied that I could distinctly hear the sound of the darkness, as it steals over the horizon — a foolish fancy perhaps, but not more unintelligible than to see music —
"The mind the music breathing from her face."

11.　PAGE 20　*Let life then, as the day-flow'r fall.*
There is a flow'r, (I have never known its botanic name,) vulgarly called the day flower. It blooms beautifully in the day-light, but withers towards evening, and by night its leaves appear totally shrivelled and dead. I have forgotten, however, to mention in the text, that it lives again in the morning. If it will not flourish in Tartary, I must be forgiven for carrying it thither.

SONG

First printing: *Tamerlane* (1827), as "To ——— ———".
Reprinted: *Al Aaraaf* (1829), with same title.
　　　　Broadway Journal, 2 (September 20, 1845) 166, as "Song".
　　　　**The Raven* (1845), as "Song".
May be based on the early engagement with Elmira Royster.

DREAMS

First printing: *Tamerlane* (1827).

Though this poem was never reprinted by Poe, there is a later manuscript, dated 1828, in the Morgan Library. This text is based on the Morgan manuscript.

It did appear in the *North American* (Baltimore) 1 (October 20, 1827) 184, over the name of Poe's brother, William Henry Poe.

SPIRITS OF THE DEAD

First printing: *Tamerlane* (1827), as "Visit of the Dead".

Reprinted: *Burton's Gentleman's Magazine*, 5 (July, 1839) 51, as ["Spirits of the Dead".

EVENING STAR

First printing: *Tamerlane* (1827).

A DREAM WITHIN A DREAM

First printing: *Tamerlane* (1827), as "Imitation".

Reprinted: *Al Aaraaf* (1829), as "To —— —— ——".

Flag of Our Union, 4 (March 31, 1849) 2, as "A Dream [within a Dream".

The text here given is entirely different from those of 1827 and 1829, which, in turn, differ from each other. In *Poems* (1831), these verses were added to "Tamerlane".

Poe was constantly concerned with the dream-state. Here he refers to that middle stratum between sleeping and waking. Note the striking figure in the second stanza, similar to Tennyson's later use of the same figure of speech in *Locksley Hall*.

STANZAS

First printing: *Tamerlane* (1827).

These lines had no title in *Tamerlane*, the present title having been given to them by Stedman and Woodberry in their edition of Poe's works, vol. 10, p. 122.

Note the self revelation in the last two lines.

A DREAM

First printing: *Tamerlane* (1827), without a title.

Reprinted: *Al Aaraaf* (1829), without a title.

Broadway Journal, 2 (August 16, 1845) 85, as "A Dream".

The Raven (1845) as "A Dream".

In *Tamerlane* and *Al Aaraaf*, the poem was printed without a title and with a first stanza that was dropped in the *Broadway Journal* and *The Raven*.

"THE HAPPIEST DAY, THE HAPPIEST HOUR"

First printing: *Tamerlane* (1827), without a title.
Poe never reprinted this poem but it appeared in the *North American* (Baltimore), 1 (September 15, 1827) 144, over the name of Poe's brother, William Henry Poe.

THE LAKE: TO ———

First printing: *Tamerlane* (1827), as "The Lake".
Reprinted: *Al Aaraaf* (1829) as "The Lake: To ———". This title
[was used in all subsequent separate printings.
 Poems (1831), as part of *Tamerlane*.
 The Raven (1845).
 Missionary Memorial, N. Y., 1846, pp. 324–325.

SONNET — TO SCIENCE

First printing: *Al Aaraaf* (1829), as prelude to "Al Aaraaf".
Reprinted: *Poems* (1831), as prelude to "Al Aaraaf".
 Graham's Lady's and Gentleman's Magazine, 18 (June,
 [1841) 253–255, as a prefix to "The Island of the Fay".
 Saturday Evening Post, 9 (September 11, 1830) 1, as "Son-
 [net".
 Philadelphia Casket, No. 10 (October, 1830) 480; No. 5
 [(May, 1831) 240, as "Sonnet".
 Southern Literary Messenger, 2 (May, 1836) 366.
 Broadway Journal, 2 (August 2, 1845) 54.
 The Raven (1845).
Like many other writers of the nineteenth century, Poe resented the dogmatism of science.

AL AARAAF

First printing: *Al Aaraaf* (1829).
Reprinted: *Poems* (1831).
 The Raven (1845).
This poem was revised for *Poems*, but the original text was used in *The Raven*.
 According to Poe, Al Aaraaf is a star, discovered by Tycho Brahe, which appeared and disappeared suddenly.
 "It is a medium between Heaven and Hell where men suffer no punishment but yet do not attain that tranquil or even happiness which they suppose to be characteristic of heavenly enjoyment." (Poe's letter to Isaac Lea, May 27, 1829)

POE'S NOTES ON "AL AARAAF"

1. PAGE 30 *On the fair Capo Deucato, and sprang*
 On Santa Maura — olim Deucadia

2. **PAGE 30** *Of her who lov'd a mortal — and so died —*
 Sappho

3. **PAGE 30** *And gemmy flower, of Trebizond misnam'd —*
 This flower is much noticed by Lewenboeck and Tournefort.
The bee, feeding upon its blossom, becomes intoxicated.

4. **PAGE 30** *And Clytia pondering between many a sun,*
 Clytia — The Chrysanthemum Peruvianum, or, to employ a bet-
ter-known term — the turnsol which turns continually towards the sun,
covers itself, like Peru, the country from which it comes, with dewy
clouds which cool and refresh its flowers during the most violent heat of
the day. — *B. de St. Pierre*

5. **PAGE 30** *And that aspiring flower that sprang on Earth —*
 There is cultivated in the king's garden at Paris, a species of ser-
pentine aloes without prickles, whose large and beautiful flower exhales
a strong odour of the vanilla, during the time of its expansion, which is
very short — It does not bloom till towards the month of July — you then
perceive it gradually open its petals — expand them — fade and die. *St.
Pierre.*

6. **PAGE 30** *And Valisnerian lotus thither flown*
 There is found, in the Rhone, a beautiful lily of the Valisnerian
kind. Its stem will stretch to the length of three or four feet — thus pre-
serving its head above water in the swellings of the river.

7. **PAGE 30** *And thy most lovely purple perfume, Zante!*
 The Hyacinth.

8. **PAGE 30** *And the Nelumbo bud that floats for ever*
 It is a fiction of the Indians, that Cupid was first seen floating
in one of these, down the river Ganges — and that he still loves the
cradle of his childhood.

9. **PAGE 30** *To bear the Goddess' song, in odours, up to Heaven —*
 And golden vials full of odours which are the prayers of the
saints. — *Rev. St. John.*

10. **PAGE 31** *A model of their own —*
 The Humanitarians held that God was to be understood as hav-
ing really a human form — *vide Clarke's Sermons,* Vol. 1, page 26, folio
edit.
 The drift of Milton's argument, leads him to employ language which
would appear, at first sight, to verge upon their doctrine; but it will be

seen immediately, that he guards himself against the charge of having adopted one of the most ignorant errors of the dark ages of the church — *Dr. Sumner's Notes on Milton's Christian Doctrine.*

This opinion, in spite of many testimonies to the contrary, could never have been very general. Andeus, a Syrian of Messopotamia, was condemned for the opinion, as heretical. He lived in the beginning of the 4th century. His disciples were called Anthropomorphites. — *Vide Du Pin.*

Among Milton's minor poems are these lines;

> Dicite Sacrorum praesides nemorum Deae, &c.
> Quis ille primus cuius ex imagine
> Natura solers finxit humanum genus?
> Eternus, incorruptuus, aequaevus polo
> Unusque et universus exemplar Dei. — And afterwards
> Non cui profundum Caecitus lumen dedit
> Dircaeus augur vidit hunc alto sinu, &c.

11. PAGE 31 *By winged Fantasy,*
Seltsamen Tochter Jovis
Seinem Schosskinde
Der Phantasie. — *Goethe.*

12. PAGE 32 *What tho' in worlds which sightless Cycles run*
Sightless — too small to be seen. — *Legge*

13. PAGE 32 *Apart — like fire-flies in Sicilian night,*
I have often noticed a peculiar movement of the firefly — They will collect in a body and fly off, from a common center into innumerable radii.

14. PAGE 32 *Her way — but left not yet her Therasaean reign.*
Therasaea, or Therasea, the island mentioned by Seneca, which, in a moment, arose from the sea to the eyes of astonished mariners.

PART II

15. PAGE 32 *Of molten stars their pavement, such as fall*
Some star, which, from the ruin'd roof
Of shak'd Olympus, by mischance, did fall. — *Milton.*

16. PAGE 33 *Friezes from Tadmor and Persepolis —*
Voltaire, in speaking of Persepolis, says, "Je connois bien l'admiration qu' inspirent ces ruines — mais un palais érigé au pied du'ne chaine des rochers stérils, peut il etre un chef d'oeuvre des arts." — *Voila des arguments de M. Voltaire.*

17. PAGE 33 *Of beautiful Gomorrah! O! the wave*
 "Oh! the wave" Ula Deguisi is the Turkish appellation; but, on its own shores, it is called Bahar Loth, or Almotanah. There were undoubtedly more than two cities engulphed in the "dead sea". In the valley of Siddim were five — Adrah, Zeboin, Zoar, Sodom and Gomorrah. Stephen of Byzantium mentions eight, and Strabo thirteen, (engulphed) — but the last is out of all reason.
 It is said [Tacitus, Strabo, Josephus, Daniel of St. Saba, Nau, Maundrell, Troilo, D'Arvieux] that, after an excessive drought the vestiges of columns, walls, &c. are seen above the surface. At *any* season, such remains may be discovered by looking down into the transparent lake, and at such distances as would argue the existence of many settlements in the space now usurped by the "Asphaltites".

18. PAGE 33 *That stole upon the ear, in Eyraco,*
 Eyraco — Chaldea

19. PAGE 33 *Is not its form — its voice — most palpable and loud?*
 I have often thought I could distinctly hear the sound of the darkness as it stole over the horizon.

20. PAGE 34 *Young flowers were whispering in melody*
 Fairies use flowers for their charactery. — *Merry Wives of Windsor.*

21. PAGE 34 *The moonbeam away —*
 In Scripture is this passage — "The sun shall not harm thee by day, nor the moon by night." It is, perhaps, not generally known that the moon, in Egypt, has the effect of producing blindness to those who sleep with the face exposed to its rays, to which circumstance the passage evidently alludes.

22. PAGE 35 *Like the lone Albatross,*
 The Albatross is said to sleep on the wing.

23. PAGE 35 *The murmur that springs*
 I met with this idea in an old English Tale, which I am now unable to obtain, and quote from memory: — "The verie essence and, as it were, spring-heade, and origine of all musiche is the verie pleasannte sounde which the trees of the forest do make when they growe."

24. PAGE 36 *Have slept with the bee —*
 The wild bee will not sleep in the shade if there be moonlight. The rhyme in this verse, as in one about 60 lines before, has an ap-

pearance of affectation. It is, however, imitated from Sir W. Scott, or rather from Claud Halero — in whose mouth I admired its effect.

> O! were there an island,
> Tho' ever so wild
> Where a woman might smile, and
> No man be beguil'd, &c.

25. PAGE 36 *Apart from Heaven's Eternity — and yet how far from Hell!*

With the Arabians there is a medium between Heaven and Hell, where men suffer no punishment, but yet do not attain that tranquil and even happiness which they suppose to be characteristic of heavenly enjoyment.

> Un no rompido sueño —
> Un dia puro — allegre — libre
> Quiera
> Libre de amor — de zelo —
> De odio — de esperanzae — de rezelo
> *Luis Ponce de León*

Sorrow is not excluded from "Al Aaraaf" but it is that sorrow which the living love to cherish for the dead, and which, in some minds, resembles the delirium of opium. The passionate excitement of Love and the buoyancy of spirit attendant upon intoxication are its less holy pleasures — the price of which, to those souls who make choice of "Al Aaraaf" as their residence after life, is final death and annihilation.

26. PAGE 37 *Unguided Love hath fallen — 'mid "tears of perfect moan:"*

> There be tears of perfect moan
> Wept for thee in Helicon. — *Milton*

27. PAGE 37 *Was a proud temple call'd the Parthenon —*

> It was entire in 1687 — the most elevated spot in Athens.

28. PAGE 37 *Than ev'n thy glowing bosom beats withal,*

> Shadowing more beauty in their airy brows
> Than have the white breasts of the Queen of Love. — *Marlowe.*

29. PAGE 38 *Fail'd, as my pennon'd spirit leapt aloft,*

> Pennon — for pinion — Milton

ROMANCE

First printing: *Al Aaraaf* (1829), as "Preface".
Reprinted: *Poems* (1831) as "Introduction".

Saturday Museum, (March 4, 1843), as "Romance".
Broadway Journal, 2 (August 30, 1845) 119, as "Romance".
*The Raven (1845), as "Romance".
The version in Poems is almost three times as long as the earlier and later versions.

TO ———

First printing: Al Aaraaf (1829) as "To ——— ———".
Reprinted: Broadway Journal, 2 (September 20, 1845) 164.
 *The Raven (1845).

TO THE RIVER ———

First printing: Al Aaraaf (1829).
Reprinted: Burton's Gentleman's Magazine, 5 (August, 1839) 99.
 Saturday Museum (March 4, 1843).
 Broadway Journal, 2 (September 6, 1845) 131.
 *The Raven (1845).

TO ———

First printing: Al Aaraaf (1829), as "To M———".
The present text is based on a facsimile (see Woodberry's Life of Poe, II, 328), which shows the source of Griswold's text of 1850 and indicates Poe's preference for the shorter version.

FAIRY–LAND

First printing: Al Aaraaf (1829).
Reprinted: Poems (1831).
 Burton's Gentleman's Magazine, 5 (August, 1839) 70.
 Broadway Journal, 2 (October 4, 1845) 193–194.
 *The Raven (1845).
The expanded version printed in Poems was not used in the Broadway Journal and The Raven.

TO HELEN

First Printing: Poems (1831).
Reprinted: Southern Literary Messenger, 2 (March, 1836) 268.
 Graham's Lady's and Gentleman's Magazine, 19 (Septem-
 [ber 1841) 123.
 Saturday Museum (March 4, 1843).
 Graham's Lady's and Gentleman's Magazine, 26 (Febru-
 *The Raven (1845). [ary, 1845) 51.
Probably written in memory of Mrs. Jane Stith Craig Stanard, a young matron of Richmond, who was kind to Edgar Poe as a boy. The poem celebrates his love of beauty, symbolized by "Helen", the name synony-

mous with the classic ideal of beauty. It may also celebrate his return to classical study. The famous lines;

> "To the glory that was Greece,
> And the grandeur that was Rome"

are probably the most discriminating distinction, at least in verse form, between the civilizations of Greece and Rome. Among the various meanings suggested for "Nicean barks", the best is probably that the reference is to Nicaea, a city founded by Alexander the Great on the banks of the Jelum or Hydaspes River, where a fleet was built to convey a portion of the army homeward through the Red Sea (the "perfumed sea").

ISRAFEL

First printing: *Poems* (1831).
Reprinted: *Southern Literary Messenger*, 2 (August, 1836) 539.
 Graham's Lady's and Gentleman's Magazine, 19 (October,
 Saturday Museum (March 4, 1843). [1841) 183.
 Broadway Journal, 2 (July 26, 1845) 41.
 The Raven (1845).
 New York *Tribune* (Nov. 26, 1845)
 New York *Weekly Tribune* (Nov. 29, 1845)

The central idea, that of a poet's song being compared to the lute of Israfel, comes from Thomas Moore's "The Light of the Haram". The line quoted from the Koran, although Poe evidently knew it, is not in that book but probably came from Moore's "Fire-Worshippers", where a footnote reads, "The Angel Israfil, who has the most melodious voice of all God's creatures".

THE CITY IN THE SEA

First printing: *Poems* (1831), as "The Doomed City".
Reprinted: *Southern Literary Messenger*, 2 (August, 1836) 552, as "The
 [City of Sin".
 American Review, a Whig Journal, 1 (April, 1845) 393, as
 ["The City in the Sea — a Prophecy".
 Broadway Journal, 2 (August 30, 1845) 123, as "The City in
 [the Sea".
 The Raven (1845), as "The City in the Sea".

THE SLEEPER

First printing: *Poems* (1831), as "Irene".
Reprinted: *Southern Literary Messenger*, 2 (May, 1836) 387–388, as
 ["Irene".
 Poets and Poetry of America. Ed. by R. W. Griswold, N. Y.,
 [1842. Title changed to "The Sleeper".
 Saturday Museum (March 4, 1843), as "The Sleeper".

Broadway Journal, 1 (May 3, 1845) 278, as "The Sleeper".
**The Raven* (1845) as "The Sleeper".
The text of "The Sleeper" differs considerably from that of "Irene".

LENORE

First printing: *Poems* (1831), as "A Paean".
Reprinted: *Southern Literary Messenger*, 2 (January, 1836) 71, as "A
[Paean".

Pioneer, 1 (February, 1843) 60–61, as "Lenore".
Saturday Museum (March 4, 1843), as "Lenore".
Graham's Lady's and Gentleman's Magazine, 26 (February,
[1845) 53, as "Lenore".
Broadway Journal, 2 (August 16, 1845) 81, as "Lenore".
**The Raven* (1845) as "Lenore".
Poets and Poetry of America (1849), as "Lenore".
Richmond *Whig* (September 14, 1849), as "Lenore".
"Lenore" is a completely revised version of "A Paean".

THE VALLEY OF UNREST

First printing: *Poems* (1831), as "The Valley Nis".
Reprinted: *Southern Literary Messenger*, 2 (February, 1836) 154, as
["The Valley Nis".
American Review, 1 (April, 1845) 392, as "The Valley of
[Unrest".
Broadway Journal, 2 (September 6, 1845) 135, as "The Val-
[ley of Unrest".
**The Raven* (1845), as "The Valley of Unrest".
"The Valley Nis" meant "The Valley of Sin".

THE COLISEUM

First printing: *Baltimore Saturday Visiter*, n.s. 3 (October 26, 1833) 1,
[as "The Coliseum".
Reprinted: *Southern Literary Messenger*, 1 (August, 1835) 706, as "The
[Coliseum. A Prize Poem".
Saturday Evening Post, 21 (June 12, 1841) 1, as "The Coli-
[seum. A Prize Poem".
Poets and Poetry of America (1847) as "Coliseum".
Saturday Museum (March 4, 1843) as "The Coliseum".
Broadway Journal, 2 (July 12, 1845) 14, as "The Coliseum".
**The Raven* (1845) as "The Coliseum".

TO ONE IN PARADISE

First printing: *Godey's Lady's Book*, 8 (January, 1834) 40–43, as part
[of the tale "The Visionary".

Reprinted: *Southern Literary Messenger*, 1 (July, 1835) 637–640, as
[part of "The Visionary".

Tales of the Grotesque and Arabesque (1840), vol. 2, as
[part of "The Visionary".

Burton's Gentleman's Magazine, 5 (July, 1839) 49, as "To
[Ianthe in Heaven".

Saturday Museum (March 4, 1843), as "To One in Para-
[dise".

Broadway Journal, 1 (May 10, 1845) 295, as "To One in
[Paradise".

Broadway Journal, 1 (June 10, 1845) 357, as part of "The
[Assignation", the final title of "The Visionary".

**The Raven* (1845) as "To One in Paradise".

HYMN

First printing: *Southern Literary Messenger*, 1 (April, 1835) 448–450, as
[part of "Morella — A Tale".

Reprinted: *Burton's Gentleman's Magazine*, 5 (November, 1839) 264–
[266, as part of "Morella — A Tale".

Tales of the Grotesque and Arabesque (1840), vol. 1, as part
[of "Morella — A Tale".

Broadway Journal, 2 (August 16, 1845) 88, as "Catholic
[Hymn".

**The Raven* (1845) as "Catholic Hymn".

In the Lorimer Graham copy of *The Raven*, Poe crossed out the word
"Catholic".

TO F——

First printing: *Southern Literary Messenger*, 1 (July, 1835) 636, as "To
[Mary".

Reprinted: *Graham's Lady's and Gentleman's Magazine*, 20 (March,
[1842) 137, as "To One Departed".

Saturday Museum (March 4, 1843) as "To One Departed".

Broadway Journal, 1 (April 26, 1845) 260, as "To F——".

**The Raven* (1845) as "To F——".

Transferred to Mrs. Frances Sargent Osgood from "Mary" who may
have been Mary White, daughter of the proprietor of the *Southern Lit-
erary Messenger*. Since Poe constantly changed the names of the women
to whom he dedicated his poems (as many other young poets have
done), it is not very important to decide who was the original. Mrs.
Osgood was a good friend of both Poe and Virginia.

TO F——s S. O——d

First printing: *Southern Literary Messenger*, 1 (September, 1835) 748,
[as "Lines Written in an Album".

Reprinted: *Burton's Gentleman's Magazine*, 5 (August, 1839) 75, as
["To ———".
Broadway Journal, 2 (September 13, 1845) 48, as "To
[F———".
The Raven (1845), as "To F——s S. O——d".
To Mrs. Osgood, who was herself a writer of verse and prose stories,
with some degree of merit.

SCENES FROM "POLITIAN" AN UNPUBLISHED DRAMA

First printing: *Southern Literary Messenger*, 2 (December, 1835–Janu-
ary, 1836) 13–16, 106–108, as "Scenes from an Unpub-
[lished Drama".
Reprinted: Poe used parts of the work in his review of Anna Cora Mow-
att's *Fashion: Broadway Journal*, 1 (March 29, 1845) 203–
205.
The Raven (1845), as "Scenes from 'Politian' an Unpub-
[lished Drama".
The play, as left by Poe in manuscript, has been edited, with notes, by
Dr. Thomas Ollive Mabbott: *Politian, an Unfinished Tragedy, by Edgar
A. Poe, edited from the Original Sources, including the Autograph Ms.
in the Pierpont Morgan Library*. Richmond, 1923.
"Politian" was based on a tragedy which took place in Frankfort,
Kentucky, in 1825. Solomon P. Sharp was killed by Jereboam Beau-
champ, whose wife, Anne Cooke, had been seduced by Sharp a few years
before the marriage. Poe placed the tragedy in Rome in the seventeenth
century, following the literary fashion of that time in choosing a ro-
mantic setting.
The "Kentucky Tragedy", as it was called, was treated in drama by
T. H. Chivers in *Conrad and Eudora* (1834); by Charlotte Barnes in
Octavia Bragaldi, produced successfully in New York (1837); and by
John Savage in *Sybil* (1858). William Gilmore Simms based his novel
of *Beauchampe* (1842) on the same story.

BRIDAL BALLAD

First printing: *Southern Literary Messenger*, 3 (January, 1837) 5, as
["Ballad".
Reprinted: *Saturday Evening Post*, 31 (July 3, 1841) 1, as "Ballad".
Saturday Museum (March 4, 1843) as "Song of the Newly
[Wedded".
Broadway Journal, 2 (August 2, 1845) 58, as "Bridal Ballad".
The Raven (1845) as "Bridal Ballad".

SONNET — TO ZANTE

First printing: *Southern Literary Messenger*, 3 (January, 1837) 32.
Reprinted: *Saturday Museum* (March 4, 1843).

Broadway Journal, 2 (July 19, 1845) 21.
**The Raven* (1845).

THE HAUNTED PALACE

First printing: *American Museum of Science, Literature and the Arts,* 2
[(April, 1839) 320.
Reprinted: *Burton's Gentleman's Magazine,* 5 (September, 1839) 145–
[152, as part of "The Fall of the House of Usher".
Tales of the Grotesque and Arabesque (1840), vol. 1, and
[*Tales* (1845), as part of "The Fall of the House of Usher".
Prose Writers of America: Edited by R. W. Griswold. Phila.,
[1847. As part of "The Fall of the House of Usher".
Poets and Poetry of America (1842) as "The Haunted
[Palace".
Saturday's Museum (March 4, 1843) as "The Haunted
[Palace".
Graham's Lady's and Gentleman's Magazine, 26 (Febru-
[ary, 1845) 52–53, as "The Haunted Palace".
Broadway Journal, 1 (May 24, 1845) (In Part).
**The Raven* (1845) as "The Haunted Palace".
Poe's allegorical picture of the decline of a human soul. He seems to
have coined the word "Porphyrogene" — from Porphyrogenitus," born
in the purple, therefore more truly royal than a ruler who had been born
when his father was not on the throne.

SONNET — SILENCE

First printing: *Saturday Courier,* 9 (January 4, 1840) 1, as "Silence — A
[Sonnet".
Reprinted: *Burton's Gentleman's Magazine,* 6 (April, 1840) 166, as
["Silence — A Sonnet".
Saturday Museum, (March 4, 1843) as "Sonnet — Silence".
Broadway Journal, 2 (July 26, 1845) 45, as "Sonnet —
[Silence".

**The Raven* (1845), as "Sonnet — Silence".

THE CONQUEROR WORM

First printing: *Graham's Lady's and Gentleman's Magazine,* 22 (Janu-
[ary, 1843) 32.
Reprinted: *Saturday Museum* (March 4, 1843).
Broadway Journal, 1 (May 24, 1845) 331.
New World (February 15, 1845), as part of the tale "Ligeia".
Broadway Journal, 2 (September 27, 1845) 171, as part of the
**The Raven* (1845). [tale "Ligeia".
Poets and Poetry of America (1847).

DREAM-LAND

First printing: *Graham's Lady's and Gentleman's Magazine*, 24 (June, [1844) 256.

Reprinted: *Broadway Journal*, 1 (June 28, 1845) 407.
The Raven (1845).
Richmond *Examiner* (October 2, 1849).

THE RAVEN

First printing: *American Review*, 1 (February, 1845) 143–145; New York [*Evening Mirror* (January 29, 1845).

Reprinted: *New York Tribune* (February 4, 1845).
Broadway Journal, 1 (February 8, 1845) 90.
Southern Literary Messenger, 11 (March, 1845) 186–188.
London *Critic* (June 14, 1845).
Literary Emporium, 2 (December, 1845) 376.
The Raven (1845).
Saturday Courier, 16 (July 25, 1846) [1].
Poets and Poetry of America (1847).
Richmond *Examiner* (September 25, 1849).

See "Introduction" for comment.

EULALIE — A SONG

First printing: *American Review*, 2 (July, 1845) 79.
Reprinted: *Broadway Journal*, 2 (August 9, 1845) 65.
The Raven (1845).

The poem was written early in 1843 and sent to Lowell's Magazine, *The Pioneer*, but the journal expired before it could be published. It is a celebration of married love; a tribute to Virginia.

A VALENTINE

First printing: New York *Evening Mirror* (February 21, 1846), as "To [Her Whose Name is Written Below".

Reprinted: *Sartain's Union Magazine of Literature and Art*, 4 (March, [1849) 173, as "A Valentine. To —— —— ——".
Flag of Our Union, 4 (March 3, 1849) 2, as "A Valentine".

Addressed to Frances Osgood and read at the home of Miss Anne Lynch in New York, February 14, 1846.

TO M. L. S——

First printing: *Home Journal*, No. 11 (March 13, 1847) 4.
To Mrs. Marie Louise Shew, a friend of Poe and Virginia, who helped them both in the dark days of Virginia's last illness.

ULALUME — A BALLAD

First printing: *American Review*, 6 (December, 1847) 599, as "To
[—— —— —— Ulalume: A Ballad".
Reprinted: *Home Journal*, No. 1 (January 1, 1848) 4, as "Ulalume — A
[Ballad".
Saturday Courier, 17 (January 22, 1848) [4], as "Ulalume —
[a Ballad".
Providence *Journal* (November 22, 1848) as "Ulalume — a
[Ballad".
Literary World, 4 (March 3, 1849) 202 as "Ulalume — A
Poets and Poetry of America (1849). [Ballad".
*Ms. in Morgan Library.

"Ulalume" represents the conflict in the poet's soul between his passion-
ate love for someone who is symbolized by Astarté or Venus, the goddess
of fertility, and his spiritual passion, probably for Virginia, symbolized
by Psyche. According to Mrs. Whitman, the poem was written after
Virginia's death.

AN ENIGMA

First printing: *Union Magazine of Literature and Art*, 2 (March 1848),
[as "Sonnet".
This poem was not reprinted in Poe's lifetime, the present title having
been adopted by Griswold in 1850.
It was written for Mrs. Estelle Anna Lewis, whose pen name, Sarah
Anna Lewis, is to be found in the verses. She was a poetess whose atten-
tions were somewhat annoying to Poe.

TO —— —— ——

First printing: *The Columbian Lady's and Gentleman's Magazine*, 8
[(March, 1848) 138.
To Mrs. Shew. See To M. L. S—— (above).

TO HELEN

First printing: *Union Magazine of Literature and Art*, 3 (November,
[1848) 200, as "To —— —— ——".
The present title was given to the poem by Griswold in 1850. See Intro-
duction.

ELDORADO

First printing: *Flag of Our Union*, 4 (April 21, 1849) 2.

FOR ANNIE

First printing: *Flag of Our Union*, 4 (April 28, 1849) 2.
A revised version appeared, on the same date, in the *Home Journal*, No.
18 (April 28, 1849) 2.
See Introduction.

SONNET — TO MY MOTHER

First printing: *Flag of Our Union*, 4 (July 7, 1849) 2, as "Sonnet — To
[My Mother".
Reprinted: *Leaflets of Memory . . . for 1850*, Phila. [1849], p. 48, as
["Sonnet — To My Mother".
Poe's sincere tribute to Mrs. Clemm, his aunt and mother-in-law, and
through her to his wife.

ANNABEL LEE

First printing: *New York Tribune* (October 9, 1849).
Reprinted: **Southern Literary Messenger* (November, 1849)
Sartain's Union Magazine of Literature and Art, 6 (Janu-
[ary, 1850) 99–100, as "Annabel Lee: A Ballad".
Written in memory of Virginia.

THE BELLS

First printing: *Sartain's Union Magazine of Literature and Art*, 5 (No-
[vember, 1849) 304.
The original version of the poem, seventeen lines — the accepted text has
one hundred twelve lines — was published in *Sartain's Union Magazine*,
5 (December, 1849) 386, as "The Bells — A Song".

Of the poems not printed by Poe in any collected edition, the only
two worth preserving follow: "Elizabeth" exists in Poe's autograph in the
Collection of Mr. Bradley Martin. "Serenade" was first discovered by
Professor John C. French. See his article "Poe and the Saturday Visiter",
Modern Language Notes, 33 (May, 1918) 258–267.

ELIZABETH

This poem was written by Poe in an album belonging to his cousin,
Elizabeth Rebecca Herring.

SERENADE

First printing: *Baltimore Saturday Visiter*, n.s. 3 (April 20, 1833) 1.

METZENGERSTEIN

First printing: *Saturday Courier*, 2 (January 14, 1832) 1, as "Metzenger-
[stein"
Reprinted: *Southern Literary Messenger*, 2 (January, 1836) 97–100, as
["Metzengerstein, a Tale in Imitation of the German"
**Tales of the Grotesque and Arabesque* (1840); Vol. 2, pp.
[151–165, as "Metzengerstein".

THE DUC DE L'OMELETTE

First printing: *Saturday Courier*, 2 (March 3, 1832) 1, as "The Duke de
[L'Omelette".

Reprinted: *Southern Literary Messenger*, 2 (February, 1836) 150–151,
[as "The Duc de L'Omelette"
Tales of the Grotesque and Arabesque (1840); Vol. 1, pp.
[105–110, as "The Duc de L'Omelette".
Broadway Journal, 2 (October 11, 1845) 206–208, as "The
[Duc de L'Omelette". [Signed: Littleton Barry].

A TALE OF JERUSALEM

First printing: *Saturday Courier*, 2 (June 9, 1832) 1.
Reprinted: *Southern Literary Messenger*, 2 (April, 1836) 313–314.
Tales of the Grotesque and Arabesque (1840); Vol. 1, pp.
[97–103.
Broadway Journal, 2 (September 20, 1845) 166–167.

LOSS OF BREATH. A TALE NEITHER IN NOR OUT OF BLACKWOOD

First printing: *Saturday Courier*, 2 (November 10, 1832) 1, as "A De-
[cided Loss".
Reprinted: *Southern Literary Messenger*, 1 (September, 1835) 735–740,
[as "Loss of Breath. A Tale à la Blackwood".
Tales of the Grotesque and Arabesque (1840); Vol. 2, pp.
[123–149, as "Loss of Breath. A Tale à la Blackwood".
Broadway Journal, 2 (January 3, 1846) 397–401, as "Loss of
Breath. A Tale Neither In nor Out of Blackwood". [Signed:
[Littleton Barry].

BON–BON

First printing: *Saturday Courier*, 2 (December 1, 1832) 1, as "The Bar-
[gain Lost".
Reprinted: *Southern Literary Messenger*, 1 (August, 1835) 693–698, as
["Bon-Bon".
Tales of the Grotesque and Arabesque (1840); Vol. 1, pp.
[127–151, as "Bon-Bon".
Broadway Journal, 1 (April 19, 1845) 243–247, as "Bon-
[Bon".
Spirit of the Times, 15 (July 22, 23, 1845) 1, 1, as "Bon-Bon".

MS. FOUND IN A BOTTLE

First printing: *Baltimore Saturday Visiter*, 3 (October 19, 1833) 1.
Reprinted: *The People's Advocate* (Newburyport, Mass.) (October 26,
[1833).
The Gift: A Christmas and New Year's Present for 1836.
[Phila. [1835] pp. 67–87.

Southern Literary Messenger, 2 (December, 1835) 33–37.
Tales of the Grotesque and Arabesque (1840); Vol. 1, pp.
[111–126.
**Broadway Journal*, 2 (October 11, 1845) 203–206.

THE ASSIGNATION

First printing: *Godey's Lady's Book*, 8 (January, 1834) 40–43, as "The
[Visionary".
Reprinted: *Southern Literary Messenger*, 1 (July, 1835) 637–640, as
["The Visionary".
Tales of the Grotesque and Arabesque (1840); Vol. 2, pp.
[193–211, as "The Visionary".
**Broadway Journal*, 1 (June 7, 1845) 357–360, as "The As-
[signation".

BERENICE

First printing: *Southern Literary Messenger*, 1 (March, 1835) 333–336.
Reprinted: *Tales of the Grotesque and Arabesque* (1840); Vol. 2, pp.
**Broadway Journal*, 1 (April 5, 1845) 217–219. [167–181.

MORELLA

First printing: *Southern Literary Messenger*, 1 (April, 1835) 448–450,
[as "Morella — A Tale".
Reprinted: *Burton's Gentleman's Magazine*, 5 (November, 1839) 264–
[266, as "Morella — A Tale".
Tales of the Grotesque and Arabesque (1840); Vol. 1, pp.
[9–18, as "Morella — A Tale".
**Broadway Journal*, 1 (June 21, 1845) 388–389, as "Morella".

LIONIZING

First printing: *Southern Literary Messenger*, 1 (May, 1835) 515–516, as
["Lionizing".
Reprinted: *Tales of the Grotesque and Arabesque* (1840); Vol. 1, pp.
[19–25, as "Lionizing".
Broadway Journal, 1 (March 15, 1845) 164–166, as "Some
[Passages from the Life of a Lion".
**Tales* (1845); pp. 58–63, as "Lionizing".

HANS PHAALL

First printing: *Southern Literary Messenger*, 1 (June, 1835) 565–580, as
["Hans Phaall — A Tale".

Reprinted: New York *Transcript*, (September 2–5, 1835), as "Lunar Discoveries, Extraordinary Aerial Voyage by Baron Hans Phaall".

Tales of the Grotesque and Arabesque (1840); Vol 2, pp. [25–92, 223–228, as "Hans Phaall".

KING PEST: A TALE CONTAINING AN ALLEGORY

First printing: *Southern Literary Messenger*, 1 (September, 1835) 757–761, as "King Pest the First. A Tale Containing an Allegory".

Reprinted: *Tales of the Grotesque and Arabesque* (1840); Vol. 1, pp. [193–212, as "King Pest: A Tale Containing an Allegory".

Broadway Journal, 2 (October 18, 1845) 219–223, as "King Pest: A Tale Containing an Allegory". [Signed: Littleton Barry].

SHADOW — A PARABLE

First printing: *Southern Literary Messenger*, 1 (September, 1835) 762–[763, as "Shadow. A Fable".

Reprinted: *Tales of the Grotesque and Arabesque* (1840); Vol 1, pp. [153–156, as "Shadow. A Fable".

Broadway Journal, 1 (May 31, 1845) 341–342, as "Shadow [— a Parable".

Some of the observations concerning the pestilence may be due to Poe's own experience with a cholera epidemic in Baltimore in 1831.

FOUR BEASTS IN ONE — THE HOMO–CAMELEOPARD

First printing: *Southern Literary Messenger*, 2 (March, 1836) 235–238, [as "Epimanes".

Reprinted: *Tales of the Grotesque and Arabesque* (1840); Vol. 2, pp. [5–17, as "Epimanes".

Broadway Journal, 2 (December 6, 1845) 333–335, as "Four [Beasts in One — the Homo-Cameleopard".

MYSTIFICATION

First printing: *American Monthly Magazine*, n.s. 3 (June, 1837) 562–[571, as "Von Jung, the Mystic".

Reprinted: *Tales of the Grotesque and Arabesque* (1840); Vol. 2, pp. [105–122, as "Von Jung, the Mystic".

Broadway Journal, 2 (December 27, 1845) 382–384, as "Mys-[tification". [Signed: Littleton Barry].

SILENCE — A FABLE

First printing: *The Baltimore Book, a Christmas and New Year's Present*, Baltimore, 1837, pp. 79–85, as "Siope — A Fable".

Reprinted: *Tales of the Grotesque and Arabesque* (1840); Vol. 2, pp.
[19–24, as "Siope — a Fable".
Broadway Journal, 2 (September 6, 1845) 135–136, as "Si-
[lence — A Fable".

LIGEIA

First printing: *American Museum of Science, Literature and the Arts*,
[1 (September, 1838) 25–37.
Reprinted: *Tales of the Grotesque and Arabesque* (1840); Vol. 1, pp.
New World (February 15, 1845) [171–192.
Broadway Journal, 2 (September 27, 1845) 171–176.
In some respects the finest of Poe's stories. The triumph of the will to
live, which brings Ligeia back to take possession of the body of her rival,
is developed through a supernatural atmosphere which permits such a
transfer.

HOW TO WRITE A BLACKWOOD ARTICLE

First printing: *American Museum of Science, Litarature and the Arts*, 1
[(November, 1838) 301–310, as "Psyche Zenobia".
Reprinted: *Tales of the Grotesque and Arabesque* (1840); Vol. 1, pp.
[213–227, as "Signora Zenobia".
Broadway Journal, 2 (July 12, 1845) 1–4, as "How to Write
[a Blackwood Article".

A PREDICAMENT

First printing: *American Museum of Science, Literature and the Arts*, 1
[(November, 1838) 310–317, as "The Scythe of Time".
Reprinted: *Tales of the Grotesque and Arabesque* (1840); Vol. 1, pp.
[229–243, as "The Scythe of Time".
Broadway Journal, 2 (July 12, 1845) 4–7, as "A Predica-
[ment".

THE DEVIL IN THE BELFRY

First printing: *Saturday Chronicle and Mirror of the Times*, 4 (May 18,
[1839) 1.
Reprinted: *Tales of the Grotesque and Arabesque* (1840); Vol. 1, pp.
[157–169.
Broadway Journal, 2 (November 8, 1845) 271–273.

THE MAN THAT WAS USED UP. A TALE OF THE LATE BUGABOO AND KICKAPOO CAMPAIGN

First printing: *Burton's Gentleman's Magazine*, 5 (August, 1839) 66–70.
Reprinted: *Tales of the Grotesque and Arabesque* (1840); Vol. 1, pp.
New Mirror, 1 (September 9, 1843) 362–365. [59–74.
The Prose Romances of Edgar A. Poe (1843).
Broadway Journal, 2 (August 9, 1845) 68–71.

THE FALL OF THE HOUSE OF USHER

First printing: *Burton's Gentleman's Magazine,* 5 (September, 1839)
[145–152.

Reprinted: *Tales of the Grotesque and Arabesque* (1840); Vol. 1, pp.
 Bentley's Miscellany (August, 1840) [75–103.
 Tales (1845); pp. 64–82.
 Prose Writers of America. Ed. by R. W. Griswold. Phila.
 [1847, pp. 524–530.

Poe's own fear of mental decay, which came upon him at times, due to his family history, is probably reflected here.

WILLIAM WILSON

First printing: *The Gift: A Christmas and New Year's Present for 1840,*
 [Phila., 1839, pp. 229–253, as "William Wilson, a Tale".

Reprinted: *Burton's Gentleman's Magazine,* 5 (October, 1839) 205–212,
 [as "William Wilson. A Tale".
 Tales of the Grotesque and Arabesque (1840); Vol. 1, pp.
 [27–57, as "William Wilson. A Tale".
 Broadway Journal, 2 (August 30, 1845) 113–119, as "Wil-
 [liam Wilson".
 Spirit of the Times, 15 (September 5, 6, 8, 1845) 204, 205,
 [206, as "William Wilson".

The second William Wilson is the personification of the conscience of the first. The continued effort of William Wilson to separate his own identity from his moral life brings on the tragedy. The description of the school follows closely that of the real Manor House School which Poe attended in England. It was located in Stoke Newington, at that time a suburb, but now incorporated in the City of London. Poe included some details from a house across the way, which has led to a confusion in most of the biographies, in which a picture of the wrong house is given.

THE CONVERSATION OF EIROS AND CHARMION

First printing: *Burton's Gentleman's Magazine,* 5 (December, 1839)
[321–323.

Reprinted: *Tales of the Grotesque and Arabesque* (1840); Vol. 2, pp.
 [213–221.
 Saturday Museum, 1 (April 1, 1843) 1, as "The Destruction
 Tales (1845); 110–115. [of the World".

Poe had seen a rain of meteors in Baltimore in 1833.

WHY THE LITTLE FRENCHMAN WEARS HIS HAND IN A SLING

First printing: *Tales of the Grotesque and Arabesque* (1840); Vol. 2, pp.
[183–191.

Reprinted: *Broadway Journal*, 2 (September 6, 1845) 129–131. [Signed:
[Littleton Barry].

THE BUSINESS MAN

First printing: *Burton's Gentleman's Magazine*, 6 (February, 1840) 87–
[99, as "Peter Pendulum, the Business Man".
Reprinted: *Broadway Journal*, 2 (August 2, 1845) 49–52, as "The Busi-
[ness Man".

THE MAN OF THE CROWD

First printing: *Burton's Gentleman's Magazine*, 7 (December, 1840)
Reprinted: *Tales* (1845); pp. 219–228. [267–270.

THE MURDERS IN THE RUE MORGUE

First printing: *Graham's Lady's and Gentleman's Magazine*, 18 (April,
[1841) 166–179
Reprinted: *The Prose Romances of Edgar A. Poe* (1843).
Tales (1845); pp. 116–150.
While this is not the first story of detection, it is quite different from
those preceding it or from the work of Poe's followers. These are usually
stories of situation. Poe created in C. Auguste Dupin a character who
solves his problems by analysis. He proceeds to find the *unusual* elements
in the testimony of the witnesses to the murder and eliminates any
human being as a suspect. The name "Dupin", Poe took from the hero-
ine of a story in *Burton's Gentleman's Magazine*, dealing with the life
of Vidocq, the French Minister of Police.

A DESCENT INTO THE MAELSTRÖM

First printing: *Graham's Lady's and Gentleman's Magazine*, 18 (May,
Reprinted: *Tales* (1845); pp. 83–99. [1841) 235–241
Boston Museum, 1 (May 26, 1849) 399.

THE ISLAND OF THE FAY

First printing: *Graham's Lady's and Gentleman's Magazine*, 18 (June,
[1841) 253–255.
Reprinted: *Broadway Journal*, 2 (October 4, 1845) 188–190.

THE COLLOQUY OF MONOS AND UNA

First printing: *Graham's Lady's and Gentleman's Magazine*, 19 (Au-
Reprinted: *Tales* (1845); pp. 100–109. [gust, 1841) 52–55.

NEVER BET THE DEVIL YOUR HEAD. A TALE
WITH A MORAL

First printing: *Graham's Lady's and Gentleman's Magazine*, 19 (Septem-
ber, 1841) 124–127, as "Never Bet Your Head. A Moral
Tale".

Reprinted: *Jonathan's Miscellany*, 1 (September 7, 1841) 67, as "Never
[Bet Your Head. A Moral Tale".
**Broadway Journal*, 2 (August 16, 1845) 85–88, as "Never Bet
[the Devil Your Head. A Tale with a Moral".

ELEONORA

First printing: *The Gift: A Christmas and New Year's Present for 1842*,
[Phila., 1841, pp. 154–162.
Reprinted: *Boston Notion*, 2 (September 4, 1841) 1.
Roberts' Semi-Monthly Magazine for Town and Country, 2
[(September 15, 1841) 701–703.
New York Weekly Tribune, 1 (September 18, 1841).
New York Daily Tribune (September 20, 1841).
Literary Souvenir, 4–5 (November 13, 1841; July 9, 1842)
[147–148, 214–215.
**Broadway Journal*, 1 (May 24, 1845) 322–324.
While "Lygeia" is more powerful, "Eleonora" is the most exquisite of
Poe's prose treatments of the theme of the loss of a beautiful woman.
His relations with Virginia are obviously the basis of the story.

THREE SUNDAYS IN A WEEK

First printing: *Saturday Evening Post*, 22 (November 27, 1841) 1, as "A
[Succession of Sundays".
Reprinted: **Broadway Journal*, 1 (May 10, 1845) 293–295, as "Three
[Sundays in a Week".
Spirit of the Times, 15 (May 14, 1845) 1–2, as "Three
[Sundays in a Week".
Star of Bethlehem, 5 (June 7, 1845) 20, as "Three Sundays
[in a Week".

THE OVAL PORTRAIT

First printing: *Graham's Lady's and Gentleman's Magazine*, 20 (April,
[1842) 200–201, as "Life in Death".
Reprinted: **Broadway Journal*, 1 (April 26, 1845) 264–265, as "The
[Oval Portrait".

THE MASQUE OF THE RED DEATH

First printing: *Graham's Lady's and Gentleman's Magazine*, 20 (May,
1842) 257–259, as "The Mask of the Red Death. A
Fantasy".
Reprinted: *Literary Souvenir*, 5 (June, 1842) 172–173, as "The Mask
[of the Red Death. A Fantasy".
**Broadway Journal*, 2 (July 19, 1845) 17–19, as "The Masque
[of the Red Death".

THE LANDSCAPE GARDEN

First printing: *Ladies' Companion*, 17 (October, 1842) 324–327.
Reprinted: **Broadway Journal*, 2 (September 20, 1845) 161–164.

THE MYSTERY OF MARIE ROGÊT

First printing: *Ladies' Companion*, 18 (November–December, 1842; [February, 1843) 15–20, 93–99, 162–167.
Reprinted: **Tales* (1845); pp. 151–199.
Based on the murder of Mary Cecilia Rogers, a clerk in the tobacconist's store of John Anderson, in Liberty Street, New York City in August, 1841. Poe laid the scene in Paris to give Dupin more freedom in establishing the fact that the murder was the work of one man, not of a gang.

THE PIT AND THE PENDULUM

First printing: *The Gift: A Christmas and New Year's Present for 1843,* [Phila., 1842, pp. 133–151.
Reprinted: **Broadway Journal*, 1 (May 10 [17] 1845) 307–311.

THE TELL–TALE HEART

First printing: *Pioneer*, 1 (January, 1843) 29–31.
Reprinted: **Broadway Journal*, 2 (August 23, 1845) 97–99.
Spirit of the Times, 15 (August 27, 1845).

THE GOLD BUG

First printing: *Dollar Newspaper*, 1 (June 21, 1843) 1. [First half of [story].
Dollar Newspaper, 1 (June 28, 1843) 1–4. [Complete].
Reprinted: *Saturday Courier*, 13 (June 24, July 1–8, 1843) 1, 1, 1.
Dollar Newspaper, 1 (July 12, 1843) 1–2. [Broadside Sup-
Volunteer (August 3, 10, 17, 1843). [plement].
**Tales* (1845); 2–36.
Boston Museum, 1 (July 22, 1848) 46–47.
Poe sold this story to Graham for $52.00. Hearing that a prize of $100.00 for a short story had been offered by the *Dollar Newspaper* of Philadelphia, he secured its exchange from Graham for some critical reviews and won the prize. It was dramatized by Silas A. Steele and produced at the Walnut Street Theatre, Philadelphia, on August 8. Legrand, who solves the cipher, is a real character. His interest in shells comes from Poe's own knowledge gained while he was in the United States Army, stationed on Sullivan's Island. Poe made up his "Gold Bug" out of the physical characterists of two different beetles.

In *Alexander's Weekly Messenger*, December 18, 1839, Poe offered to solve any cryptogram sent in to the journal. Poe received one hun-

dred cryptograms in consequence, all of which he solved, except one, which he proved was impossible of solution.

THE BLACK CAT

First printing: *United States Saturday Post* [Saturday Evening Post] 23
Reprinted: *Tales* (1845); 37–46. [(August 19, 1843) 1.
 Pictorial National Library, 1 (November, 1848) 255–259.

DIDDLING CONSIDERED AS ONE OF THE EXACT SCIENCES

First printing: *Saturday Courier*, 13 (October 14, 1843) 1, as "Raising the Wind; or, Diddling Considered as One of the Exact Sciences".
Reprinted: *Lloyd's Entertaining Journal*, 2 (January 14, 1845) 721–723, [as "Diddling Considered as One of the Exact Sciences".
 Broadway Journal, 2 (September 13, 1845) 145–148, as "Did-[dling Considered As One of the Exact Sciences".

MORNING ON THE WISSAHICCON

First printing: *The Opal: A Pure Gift for the Holy Days*, N. Y., 1844, This piece was later named "The Elk". [pp. 249–256.
 Poe's fondness for natural beauty is reflected in this description of the Wissahickon, one of the loveliest of streams. He really did see an elk, which belonged in the Sanatarium known as "Spring Bank" where a number of pets were kept to amuse the patients. The "villa" still exists.

THE SPECTACLES

First printing: *Dollar Newspaper*, 2 (March 27, 1844) 1–2.
Reprinted: *Broadway Journal*, 2 (November 22, 1845) 299–307.

A TALE OF THE RAGGED MOUNTAINS

First printing: *Godey's Lady's Book*, 28 (April, 1844) 177–181.
Reprinted: *Columbia Spy* (April 27, 1844).
 Broadway Journal, 2 (November 29, 1845) 315–318.

THE BALLOON HOAX

First printing: *New York Sun* (April 13, 1844) [A broadside printed on [one side only]
This fictitious account created such excitement that the *New York Sun* office was surrounded by a great crowd and copies of the paper sold for fifty cents apiece.

THE PREMATURE BURIAL

First printing: *Dollar Newspaper*, 2 (July 31, 1844) 1.
Reprinted: *The Rover* (August 17, 1844).
 **Broadway Journal*, 1 (June 14, 1845) 369–373.

MESMERIC REVELATION

First printing: *Columbian Lady's and Gentleman's Magazine*, 2 (Au-
 [gust, 1844) 67–70.
Reprinted: *New World*, 9 (August 3, 1844) 132–134.
 Saturday Museum, 2 (August 31, 1844) 1.
 **Tales* (1845); pp. 47–57.
 Universalist Watchman, 17 (August 30, September 6, 1845)
 Star of Bethlehem, 5 (October 4, 1845) 88. [56, 64.
 Popular Record of Modern Science, No. 35 (November 29,
 1845) 126–129, as "The Last Conversation of a Somnam-
 bule".

THE OBLONG BOX

First printing: *Godey's Lady's Book*, 29 (September, 1844) 132–136.
Reprinted: **Broadway Journal*, 2 (December 13, 1845) 349–352.

THE ANGEL OF THE ODD — AN EXTRAVAGANZA

First printing: *Columbian Lady's and Gentleman's Magazine*, 2 (Octo-
 [ber, 1844) 158–161.

"THOU ART THE MAN"

First printing: *Godey's Lady's Book*, 29 (November, 1844) 219–224.

THE LITERARY LIFE OF THINGUM BOB, ESQ., LATE EDITOR OF THE "GOOSETHERUMFOODLE"

First printing: *Southern Literary Messenger*, 10 (December, 1844) 719–
Reprinted: **Broadway Journal*, 2 (July 26, 1845) 33–39. [727.
The references to editors are, of course, burlesque. But the insertion of
"Lewis G[aylord] Clarke", in the revised version of the story, is a re-
flection of Poe's fight with the New York *Knickerbocker Magazine*, of
which Clark was editor. This was the organ of one of the most powerful
cliques in New York City.

THE PURLOINED LETTER

First printing: *The Gift: A Christmas, New Year's and Birthday Present.*
 [MDCCCXLV, N. Y., 1845, pp. 41–46.
Reprinted: *Chambers Edinburgh Journal*, No. 48 n.s. (November 30,
 [1844) 343–347. [Abridged].
 **Tales* (1845); pp. 200–218.

The influence of this story has been almost universal. The principle of Dupin that the best way to hide an object is to place it in the most conspicuous place has been the basis for many detective stories and has recently been alluded to in a radio version of a story of "Sherlock Holmes", who is of course based on Dupin.

THE THOUSAND–AND–SECOND TALE OF
SCHEHERAZADE

First printing: *Godey's Lady's Book*, 30 (February, 1845) 61–67.
Reprinted: **Broadway Journal*, 2 (October 25, 1845) 235–240.

SOME WORDS WITH A MUMMY

First printing: *American Review*, 1 (April, 1845) 363–370.
Reprinted: **Broadway Journal*, 2 (November 1, 1845) 251–256.

THE POWER OF WORDS

First printing: *United States Magazine and Democratic Review*, 16
[(June, 1845) 602–604.
Reprinted: **Broadway Journal*, 2 (October 25, 1845) 243–244.
Poe here extended the principle of the conservation of energy to the power of a word once spoken. The story is, in a sense, a forecast of the radio waves.

THE IMP OF THE PERVERSE

First printing: *Graham's Lady's and Gentleman's Magazine*, 27 (July,
[1845) 1–3.
Reprinted: **The Mayflower, for MDCCCXLVI*, Boston, 1846, pp.
[11–12.
The revelation of one phase of Poe's own nature and the criticism of pseudo-science.

THE SYSTEM OF DR. TARR AND PROF. FETHER

First printing: *Graham's Lady's and Gentleman's Magazine*, 27 (Novem-
[ber, 1845) 193–200.

THE FACTS IN THE CASE OF M. VALDEMAR

First printing: *American Review*, 2 (December, 1845) 561–565, as "The
[Facts of M. Valdemar's Case".
Reprinted: **Broadway Journal*, 2 (December 20, 1845) 365–368, as
["The Facts in the Case of M. Valdemar".
Mesmerism "In Articulo Mortis", London, 1846.
Morning Post (London) (January 3, 1846), as "Mesmer-
[ism in America".

Popular Record of Modern Science (January 10, 1846) as
"Mesmerism in America. Death of M. Valdemar of New
York".

Boston Museum, 2 (August 18, 1849) 79, as "Facts of M.
[Valdemar's Case".

This story was taken seriously in England, where it was reprinted as a
pamphlet entitled *Mesmerism "in Articulo Mortis". An Astounding and
Horrifying Narrative Showing the Extraordinary Power of Mesmerism
in Arresting the Progress of Death*. London, 1846. Price three pence.

THE SPHINX

First printing: *Arthur's Ladies' Magazine*, 5 (January, 1846) 15–16.

THE CASK OF AMONTILLADO

First printing: *Godey's Lady's Book*, 33 (November, 1846) 216–218.

THE DOMAIN OF ARNHEIM

First printing: *Columbian Lady's and Gentleman's Magazine*, 7 (March,
1847) 123–129. [A completely rewritten version of "The
Landscape Garden".]

MELLONTA TAUTA

First printing: *Godey's Lady's Book*, 38 (February, 1849) 133–138.

HOP–FROG, OR THE EIGHT CHAINED
ORANG–OUTANGS

First printing: *The Flag of Our Union*, 4 (March 17, 1849) 2.
This story is usually said to have been derived from an incident given
in the Chronicles of Froissart. But Poe need not have read these in the
original, for an excerpt in the *Broadway Journal* for February 1, 1845,
contains all the details he used. No jester and no revenge are in the
Chronicles. A story, "Frogère and the Emperor Paul", of the revenge of
a jester upon the Emperor of Russia, in the *New Monthly Magazine*,
XXVIII (1830) 387–392, signed "P", probably suggested the motive of
"Hop-Frog". The point is that Poe created the character of Hop-Frog
out of incidents in the two narratives, and thus contributed the impor-
tant portion of the story.

VON KEMPELEN AND HIS DISCOVERY

First printing: *The Flag of Our Union*, 4 (April 14, 1849) 2.

X–ING A PARAGRAB

First printing: **The Flag of Our Union* 4 (May 12, 1849) 2.
Reprinted: *The Spanish Galleon*. Joseph Holt Ingraham. Boston, 1849,
[PP. 92–95.

LANDOR'S COTTAGE. A Pendant to "The Domain of Arnheim"
First printing: *The Flag of Our Union*, 4 (June 9, 1849) 2.
"Annie" was Mrs. Richmond (See Introduction). The cottage was based on the Fordham house.

THE NARRATIVE OF ARTHUR GORDON PYM
OF NANTUCKET

First printing: *Southern Literary Messenger*, 3 (January–February, 1837)
[13–16, 109–116. [In Part].
*The Narrative of Arthur Gordon Pym of Nantucket . . .
[Phila., 1838. [Complete].
Reprinted: *Novel Newspaper*, part 43, London, 1841. [Complete].
For background, Poe drew mainly upon Benjamin Morrell's *Narrative of Four Voyages to the South Seas and the Pacific*, 1822–1831, (1832) and an address by Jeremiah N. Reynolds, given in the House of Representatives in 1836. Poe mentions these in his text.

LETTER TO B——

First printing: *Poems* (1831), pp. 2–29, as "Letter to Mr. —— ——".
Reprinted: *Southern Literary Messenger*, 2 (July, 1836) 501–503, as
["Letter to B——".
Mr. B—— may have been Elam Bliss, the publisher of the *Poems* of 1831. Poe followed Coleridge in defining a poem as being opposed to a work of science by having for its immediate object pleasure, not truth.

THE CULPRIT FAY, AND OTHER POEMS
Joseph Rodman Drake

ALNWICK CASTLE, WITH OTHER POEMS
Fitz-Greene Halleck

First printing: *Southern Literary Messenger*, 2 (April, 1836) 326–336.
This criticism owes something to Coleridge's *Biographia Literaria*, Chapter XIV, and possibly to A. W. Schlegel — though it is always dangerous to allot a specific source to Poe's work, owing to his assimilative power. Here are his distinctions between Imagination and Fancy, and his definition of Ideality as an essential quality of a poem.

POEMS
William Cullen Bryant

First printing: *Southern Literary Messenger*, 3 (January, 1837) 41–49.

THE OLD CURIOSITY SHOP AND OTHER TALES
MASTER HUMPHREY'S CLOCK
Charles Dickens

First printing: *Graham's Lady's and Gentleman's Magazine*, 18 (May,
[1841) 248–251.

Note Poe's defense of the characterization by Dickens of exceptional men and women, and his understanding of the methods of an artist whose material was so different from that of Poe.

THE QUACKS OF HELICON: A SATIRE
L. A. Wilmer

First printing: *Graham's Lady's and Gentleman's Magazine*, 19 (Au-
[gust, 1841) 90–93.
This essay is important because it represents Poe in his indictment of the conditions under which reviewing was conducted in his day. He is not altogether fair in his charges, but he was evidently smarting under the treatment he received from the "*Knickerbocker* Clique", of which Theodore S. Fay was a member and which had revenged themselves upon him for his criticism of Fay's novel, *Norman Leslie*. The review contains one of his definitions — "True criticism is the reflection of the thing criticized upon the spirit of the critic".

[EXORDIUM TO CRITICAL NOTES]

First printing: *Graham's Lady's and Gentleman's Magazine*, 20 (Janu-
[ary, 1842) 68–69.

BALLADS AND OTHER POEMS
Henry Wadsworth Longfellow

First printing: *Graham's Lady's and Gentleman's Magazine*, 20 (March–
[April, 1842) 189–190; 248–251.
Poe's criticism of Longfellow's *Ballads* is significant because it was writ-
ten before his unfortunate belief in Longfellow's plagiarisms became an obsession with him. In this essay he showed his ability to select the best of the ballads, and his discussion of the nature of poetry in general is a landmark in our criticism.

TWICE-TOLD TALES
Nathaniel Hawthorne

First printing: *Graham's Lady's and Gentleman's Magazine*, 20 (April–
[May, 1842) 254; 298–300.
This criticism is preferable to the later revision published in *Godey's* in 1847, which included a reference to the *Mosses from an Old Manse*. The latter has a long and somewhat tiresome discussion of originality.

AMERICAN DRAMA

First printing: *American Review*, 2 (August, 1845) 117–131.
Poe criticizes N. P. Willis for inventing a law which would give Tomaso paternal authority over Isabella in *Tortesa the Usurer*, because of her father's refusal to admit her to her home. There was such a law in

Florence, however, as Poe might have seen by consulting Thomas Roscoe's *Italian Novelists*, (1825) Vol. 4, in which it is made the basis of "La Sepolta Viva" by Domenico Manni.

PREFACE

First printing: *The Raven and Other Poems*, N. Y., 1845. (Unpaged)

PHILOSOPHY OF COMPOSITION

First printing: *Graham's Lady's and Gentleman's Magazine*, 28 (April, [1846) 163–167.

THE RATIONALE OF VERSE

First printing: *Pioneer*, 1 (March, 1843) 102–112, as "Notes on English [Verse".

Reprinted: *Southern Literary Messenger*, (October–November, 1848) [577–585; 673–682.

This essay is a revelation of the manner in which one of the most skilful artists in verse could go astray when he discussed the nature and laws of English versification. He was unaware of the history of English versification, made clear fifty years later by Eduard Sievers, and he discourses upon "long" and "short" syllables, which do not occur in English, and fails to recognize the accentual basis of English verse.

THE POETIC PRINCIPLE

First printing: *Home Journal*, No. 36 (August 31, 1850) 1.

Reprinted: *Sartain's Union Magazine*, 7 (October, 1850) 231–239.

Poe modifies somewhat, in this, the best of his essays upon poetry, his earlier objections to the introduction of "Truth" into a poem, but he still insisted on its subservience to "Beauty".

Bibliography

BIBLIOGRAPHIES

BRIGHAM, Clarence S. "Edgar Allan Poe's Contributions to Alexander's Weekly Messenger." *Proceedings of the American Antiquarian Society*, 52 (April, 1942) 45–125. (Also published as a separate pamphlet: Worcester, Mass., 1943.)

CAMPBELL, Killis "Edgar Allan Poe." Cambridge History of American Literature. Vol. 2, pp. 452–468.

CAMPBELL, Killis *The Mind of Poe and Other Studies.* Cambridge, Mass., 1933.

EVANS, May Garrettson. *Music and Edgar Allan Poe; a Bibliographical Study.* Baltimore, 1939.

HARRISON, James A. "Bibliography." *The Complete Works of Edgar Allan Poe.* N. Y., 1902. 17 vols. Vol. 16, pp. 355–379.

HEARTMAN, Charles F. and CANNY, James R. *A Bibliography of the First Printings of the Writings of Edgar Allan Poe.* Hattiesburg, 1940. Rev. Ed., 1943.

JACKSON, David K. *The Contributors and Contributions to the Southern Literary Messenger.* Charlottesville, Va., 1936.

——. *Poe and the Southern Literary Messenger.* Richmond, Va., 1934.

O'NEILL, Edward H. "Poe-Griswold-Harrison Text of the 'Marginalia.'" *American Literature*, 15 (November, 1943) 238–250.

OSTROM, John H. *Check List of Letters to and from Poe.* Charlottesville, Va., 1941.

QUINN, Arthur H. "Bibliography." *Edgar Allan Poe. A Critical Biography.* N. Y., 1941. pp. 763–770.

ROBERTSON, John W. *A Bibliography of the Writings of Edgar A. Poe.* San Francisco, 1934. 2 vols.

STEDMAN, E. C. and WOODBERRY, G. E. "Bibliography." *The Works of Edgar Allan Poe.* Chicago, 1894–1895. Vol. 10, pp. 267–281.

WHITTY, J. H. "Bibliography." *Complete Poems of Edgar Allan Poe.* Boston, 1917 (Rev. Ed.). pp. 331–339.

WYLLIE, John C. "A List of the Texts of Poe's Tales." *Humanistic Studies in Honor of John Calvin Metcalf.* Charlottesville, Va., 1941. pp. 322–338.

COLLECTED WORKS

The Works of the Late Edgar Allan Poe, with a Memoir by Rufus Wilmot Griswold and Notices of His Life and Genius by Nathaniel Parker Willis and James Russell Lowell. N. Y., 1850–1856. 4 vols.

The Works of Edgar Allan Poe. Newly Collected and Edited with a Memoir, Critical Introduction and Notes by Edmund Clarence Stedman and George Edward Woodberry. Chicago, 1894–1895. 10 vols.

The Complete Works of Edgar Allan Poe. Edited by James A. Harrison. N. Y., 1902. 17 vols.

The Poems of Edgar Allan Poe. Edited by Killis Campbell. Boston, 1917.

Poe's Short Stories. Edited by Killis Campbell. N. Y., 1927.

Tales of Edgar Allan Poe. Edited by James Southall Wilson. N. Y., 1927.

Selected Poems of Edgar Allan Poe. Edited by Thomas Ollive Mabbott. N. Y., 1928.

SEPARATE WORKS

Tamerlane and Other Poems. By a Bostonian. Boston, 1827.

Tamerlane and Other Poems. Reproduced in Facsimile from the Edition of 1827, with an Introduction by Thomas O. Mabbott. N. Y., 1941.

Al Aaraaf, Tamerlane, and Minor Poems. Baltimore, 1829.

Al Aaraaf, Tamerlane, and Minor Poems. Reproduced from the Edition of 1829, with a Bibliographical Note by Thomas O. Mabbott, N. Y., 1933.

Poems. Second Edition. N. Y., 1831.

Poems. Second Edition. Reproduced from the Edition of 1831, with a Bibliographical Note by Killis Campbell. N. Y., 1936.

The Narrative of Arthur Gordon Pym, of Nantucket, Comprising the Details of a Mutiny and Atrocious Butchery on Board the American Brig Grampus, on her Way to the South Seas in the Month of June, 1827. N. Y., 1838.

The Conchologist's First Book; Or, A System of Testaceous Malacology. Phila., 1839.

Tales of the Grotesque and Arabesque. Phila., 1840. 2 vols.

The Prose Romances of Edgar A. Poe. Uniform Serial Edition No. 1. The Murders in the Rue Morgue and The Man That Was Used Up. Phila., 1843.

The Raven and Other Poems. N. Y., 1845.

The Raven and Other Poems by Edgar Allan Poe. Reproduced in Facsimile from the Lorimer Graham Copy of the Edition of 1845 with Author's Corrections. With an Introduction by Thomas O. Mabbott. N. Y., 1942.

Tales. N. Y., 1845.

Eureka: A Prose Poem. N. Y., 1848.

LETTERS

The Letters of Edgar A. Poe to George W. Eveleth. Edited by James
Southall Wilson. Charlottesville, Va., 1924. [Originally published
in the Alumni Bulletin of the University of Virginia, 17 (January,
1924) 34–59.]
"The Letters from George W. Eveleth to Edgar Allan Poe," edited by
Thomas O. Mabbott in *Bulletin of the New York Public Library.*
New York, 1922. Reprinted separately, 1922.
*Edgar Allan Poe Letters Till Now Unpublished, in the Valentine Mu-
seum, Richmond, Virginia.* Introductory Essay and Commentary
by Mary Newton Stanard. Phila., 1925.
Edgar Allan Poe Letters and Documents in the Enoch Pratt Library.
Edited by Arthur Hobson Quinn and Richard H. Hart. N. Y., 1941.

BIOGRAPHICAL AND CRITICAL

ALLEN, Hervey, *Israfel. The Life and Times of Edgar Allan Poe,* 2 vols.
N. Y., 1926. Revised Edition, 2 vols. in one (1934).
BAUDELAIRE, Charles, "Edgar Poe, sa vie et ses oeuvres" in *Histories
Extraordinaires, traduit D'Edgar Poe,* Paris, 1856. Vol. VI of
Oeuvres Complètes de Ch. Baudelaire, Paris, 1891.
——, "Notes Nouvelles sur Edgar Poe" in *Nouvelles Histories Extraordi-
naires, traduit D'Edgar Poe,"* Paris, 1857. Vol. VII of *Oeuvres
Complètes de Ch. Baudelaire,* Paris, 1892.
CAMPBELL, Killis, "Poe," in *Cambridge History of American Litera-
ture* (N. Y., 1918), II, 55–69.
——, *The Mind of Poe, and Other Studies.* Cambridge, 1932.
Facts About Poe. Portraits and Daguerreotypes of Edgar Allan Poe. By
Amanda P. Schulte, *with a sketch of the Life of Poe, by James S.
Wilson,* University of Virginia Record Extension Series, X, No. 8,
April, 1926.
FRENCH, John C., "Poe and the Baltimore Saturday Visiter," *Modern
Language Notes,* 33 (May, 1918) 257–267.
HARRISON, James A., *Life and Letters of Edgar Allan Poe,* 2 vols.
N. Y., 1903. Revision of Vols. I and XVII in Virginia Edition.
INGRAM, John H. *Edgar Allan Poe, His Life, Letters, and Opinions,*
2 vols. London, 1880; revised editions, 1 vol., 1884, 1891.
LAUVRIÈRE, Émile, *Edgar Poe. Sa vie et son oeuvre.* 2 vols. Paris,
1904.
——, *Le Gènie Morbide D'Edgar Poe. Poésies et Contes.* Paris, n.d.
[1935].
LEMONNIER, Léon, *Edgar Poe et la Critique Française de 1845 à 1875.*
Paris, 1928.

LEMONNIER, Léon, *Les Traducteurs d'Edgar Poe en France de 1845 à 1875: Charles Baudelaire*. Paris, 1928.

LOWELL, James Russell, "Our Contributors, No. XVII, Edgar Allan Poe," *Graham's Magazine*, 27 (February, 1845) 49–53.

MABBOTT, Thomas Ollive, Editor, *Merlin, Baltimore, 1827, Together with Recollections of Edgar A. Poe by Lambert A. Wilmer*. N. Y., 1941.

PHILLIPS, Mary E., *Edgar Allan Poe, the Man*, 2 vols. Phila., 1926.

QUINN, Arthur H., *Edgar Allan Poe: A Critical Biography*. N. Y., 1941.

WHITMAN, Sarah Helen, *Edgar Poe and his Critics*. N. Y., 1907.

WOODBERRY, George, *Edgar Allan Poe*. Boston, 1885. (American Men of Letters.)

——, *The Life of Edgar Allan Poe, Personal and Literary, with His Chief Correspondence with Men of Letters*, 2 vols. Boston, 1909.

PRINTER'S NOTE

This book is set in Linotype ELECTRA, *designed by W. A. Dwiggins. This face cannot be classified as either "modern" or "old-style." It is not based on any historical model, nor does it echo any particular period or style. It avoids the extreme contrast between "thick" and "thin" elements that mark most "modern" faces, and attempts to give a feeling of fluidity, power, and speed.*